The Criminal Justice
System and Women

The Criminal Justice System and Women

Offenders, Prisoners, Victims, and Workers

THIRD EDITION

Edited by
Barbara Raffel Price and Natalie J. Sokoloff

John Jay College of Criminal Justice

City University of New York

Mc
Graw
Hill

Boston   Burr Ridge, IL   Dubuque, IA   Madison, WI   New York   San Francisco   St. Louis
Bangkok   Bogotá   Caracas   Kuala Lumpur   Lisbon   London   Madrid   Mexico City
Milan   Montreal   New Delhi   Santiago   Seoul   Singapore   Sydney   Taipei   Toronto

Higher Education

THE CRIMINAL JUSTICE SYSTEM AND WOMEN: OFFENDERS, PRISONERS, VICTIMS, AND WORKERS

Published by McGraw-Hill, a business unit of The McGraw-Hill Companies, Inc., 1221 Avenue of the Americas, New York, NY, 10020. Copyright © 2004, 1995, by The McGraw-Hill Companies, Inc.
Some ancillaries, including electronic and print components, may not be available to customers outside the United States.

1982 edition published by Clark Boardman, Ltd.

This book is printed on acid-free paper.

1 2 3 4 5 6 7 8 9 0 DOC/DOC 0 9 8 7 6 5 4 3

ISBN 0-07-246399-6

Publisher: *Phillip A. Butcher*
Senior sponsoring editor: *Carolyn Henderson Meier*
Senior marketing manager: *Dan Loch*
Media producer: *Shannon Gattens*
Senior project manager: *Christina Thornton-Villagomez*
Manager, new book production: *Janean A. Utley*
Associate designer: *George J. Kokkonas*
Lead supplement producer: *Marc Mattson*
Cover and Interior design: *Kiera Pohl*
Cover photo: *©Corbis*
Typeface: *10/12 Bembo*
Compositor: *GAC Indianapolis*
Printer: *R.R. Donnelley and Sons, Inc.*

Library of Congress Cataloging-in-Publication Data

The criminal justice system and women: offenders, prisoners, victims, and workers/
  Barbara Raffel Price and Natalie J. Sokoloff, editors.—3rd ed.
    p. cm.
  Includes bibliographical references and index.
  ISBN 0-07-246399-6 (softcover: alk. paper)
  1. Sex discrimination in criminal justice administration—United States. 2. Female offenders—United States. 3. Women—Crimes against—United States. I. Price, Barbara R. II. Sokoloff, Natalie J.

HV9950.C743234 2004
364'.082'0973—dc21

                                                            2003042094

www.mhhe.com

In loving memory of Robert G. Price

In honor of Charlotte Sokoloff for her courage, strength, and inspiration

For Ben, Clara, Dakota, Josh, and their generation as they lead us into the future

About the Editors

BARBARA RAFFEL PRICE is a graduate of Smith College and holds an M.A. and Ph.D. from The Pennsylvania State University. She served as Dean of Graduate Studies and Professor of Criminal Justice at John Jay College of Criminal Justice, City University of New York, until her retirement. A former Vice President of the American Society of Criminology, she is a Fellow of both the American Society of Criminology and the Western Society of Criminology. She is on the board of the National Institute of Development and Research and the Graduate School Alumni Society at The Pennsylvania State University. She is author of several books, including *Police Professionalism: Rhetoric and Action* (Lexington, 1978) and numerous articles on women, law enforcement, and corrections.

NATALIE J. SOKOLOFF is Professor of Sociology at John Jay College of Criminal Justice and a member of the doctoral faculties in Sociology, Criminology, and Women's Studies at The Graduate School, City University of New York. Since 1994 she has been a Scholar of the Institute for Teaching and Research on Women at Towson University, part of the University of Maryland system. Formerly associated with the New York State Division for Youth in its research and evaluation program and the Mount Sinai School of Medicine in its Department of Community Medicine (New York City), she holds a B.A. from the University of Michigan (magna cum laude), an M.A. from Brown University (as an N.I.M.H scholar), and a Ph.D. from the City University of New York's Graduate School. Professor Sokoloff is the author of *Between Money and Love: The Dialectics of Women's Home and Market Work* (Praeger, 1980), *The Hidden Aspects of Women's Work* (co-editor, Praeger, 1987), and *Black Women and White Women in the Professions: Occupational Segregation by Race and Gender, 1960–1980* (Routledge, 1992). Currently she is working on an anthology titled *Domestic Violence: At the Intersection of Race, Class, Gender, Sexual Orientation, and Immigrant Status in the United States* (Routledge), forthcoming.

List of Contributors

Joanne Belknap
Kum-Kum Bhavnani
Angela Browne
Gray Cavender
Meda Chesney-Lind
Shamita Das Dasgupta
Angela Y. Davis
Karlene Faith
Kathryn Ann Farr
Kathryn M. Feltey
Jeanne Flavin
Kay B. Forest
Emily Gaarder
Carolyn Renae Griggs
Penny Harrington
Nancy Jurik
Andrew Karmen
Kamala Kempadoo
Kimberly A. Lonsway
Lisa Maher
Susan E. Martin
Jody Miller

Susan L. Miller
Imogene L. Moyer
Barbara Owen
Lynn M. Paltrow
Lois Presser
Diane F. Reed
Edward L. Reed
Luana Ross
Georganne Rundblad
Lynn Hecht Schafran
Dorothy Moses Schulz
Jennifer Schwartz
Nina Siegal
Darrell Steffensmeier
Julia Sudbury
Jeffrey Toobin
Neil Websdale
Carolyn M. West
Marjan Wijers
Nanci Koser Wilson
Jennifer Wriggins

Contents

PART 3

WOMEN VICTIMS AND SURVIVORS OF CRIME

Preface

In the years since the last edition of this book was published, much has changed in the criminal justice system and in the world. Although many women have made remarkable strides both in the United States and in countries around the world, other women still endure significant hardships. One of the harsh lessons learned by the entire world post–September 11, 2001, is that in many areas of the world women are severely repressed; they are denied the most essential human rights of medical care, education, and basic social, economic, political, and personal freedom. In a world with so much inequality in the bare necessities of life—both within and between countries—violence and corruption are capable of becoming widespread and humanity is endangered.

In many criminal justice systems around the world, women play a greater role today than in the past. Still, reforms continue to be needed at all levels. It is the case that many more women from diverse backgrounds are now lawyers, judges, and police, or corrections officers. And feminist political activism, including lobbying efforts, has strengthened laws that deal with some of the crimes against women, such as rape, battering, sexual harassment, and stalking. Yet other laws and the attitudes of those empowered to carry out the laws continue to harm women. Recent years have been marked by increased female drug addiction, poverty, racism, and incarceration—especially for the most marginalized in society. In spite of the undisputed fact that men are most often the perpetrators of violent crime, the rate of women's incarceration has been increasing dramatically in recent years, significantly more so than that of men.

Several factors are responsible for the growth of incarceration of women: increased poverty of women exacerbated by globalization, structural shifts in capitalism, and the world economy; an increase in income inequality in the United States not seen since the 1920s; selective enforcement of drug law violations targeted toward the poor and people of color; a more punitive set of societal attitudes that has produced a criminal justice system more inclined to incarceration of first-time offenders and less willing to use alternatives; the perpetuation of sentencing guidelines and a concomitant decline in judicial discretion; an increase in drug use and addiction among women; a political swing to the right in which criminality is often judged to be amoral, evil self-will; and forces largely ignored by mainstream politicians and leaders such as racism and sexism, homophobia, and a crushing class bias.

As we write this preface, the revelations of false financial statements, the theft of funds from U.S. corporations by corporate executives, the misuse of corporate funds—but not necessarily illegal acts, which, of course, is part of the problem—by these executives, the connections between these executives and the highest government leaders including the president and vice president, and the accompanying spiraling down of the stock market are just beginning to emerge in full force. Despite these events and despite talk about much-needed changes to prevent future corporate crime being debated by lawmakers, the punishments come down much more severely on the poor, the minority, and the marginalized than the rich and powerful. Thus, poor women of color, not white male executives and high-level politicians end up in prison despite the disproportional crime and harm caused by the elite.

We intend to give the reader a broad perspective on women in the criminal justice system—as offenders, as prisoners, as victims and survivors of crime, and as working members of the system. In the pages that follow, we hope to show how women affect and are affected by crime and the criminal justice system and how this treatment is related to issues of social justice and injustice.

THE THIRD EDITION

Since the last edition of this book was published, there has been an enormous growth in research on and activism around women offenders and prisoners. In addition, the research on victimization of women and women practitioners who work in the criminal justice system has been growing both in quantity and in quality. Hence, most of the chapters in this book are new. Only six chapters from the second edition have been retained because of their relevance today (chapters 1, 21, 31, 34, 35, and 36) and these have been updated by the authors of these chapters.

The original format of the previous two editions has been improved by the addition of a new section on women in prison, prompted by the significant growth of this population and the outpouring of research and activism in this area. The original format (separate parts for offenders, victims, and workers) has proven to be quite popular with our readers. In addition to the new section on women in prison, we have also changed the title of the section on women as victims to include women as survivors. All too often, women's victimization has been used to paint women as "passive" victims—disparagingly meant to imply that they do not stand up for themselves. As feminist scholars and activists have pointed out, society tends to understand victimization and agency as existing only in the *absence* of one another. As a result, it is very difficult to simultaneously draw attention to and evoke sympathy for women's victimization while underscoring the strengths and resilience of battered women. Thus, the feminist community has tried to educate itself and the public about women's agency, resistance, and resilience and in doing so has begun to describe women as both victims and survivors.

Additionally, readers will find more original chapters written specifically for this edition than in past editions (chapters 5, 6, 12, 17, 24, 29, 32, and 33, and an addendum to 36). We are indebted to those authors. New developments continue to emerge in criminological, feminist, multicultural, and international scholarship. We are pleased to be able to showcase some of these original thinkers from a wide range of disciplines. Not only those who labor in the criminological fields but also feminist sociologists, psychologists, political scientists, philosophers, lawyers, journalists and police officers are represented in the pages that follow. The flourishing of criminological research and of undergraduate and graduate programs as well as the increasing influence of multicultural feminist scholarship has enabled students to better understand the biases against women and racial and ethnic minorities and the ways in which those biases are embedded in the criminal justice system.

RECURRING THEMES

In the preceding editions of this book, we focused on race, class, and gender as the conceptual framework for understanding and examining the issues pertaining to women and crime. These themes remained paramount in the planning of this third edition; our objective is that students be able not only to explore the roles of women offenders, prisoners, victims and survivors, and workers but also to understand and question socially structured systems through which women from diverse backgrounds of society participate in the criminal justice system. Thus, this theme has been expanded and additional themes added:

- The *feminist perspective* produces an analysis embedded within the social forces of sexism, racism, heterosexism, and classism, and takes into account how the intersections of those forces impact on the lives of both individuals and communities.
- The impact of *globalization* on women and crime is new to this edition. Today, all students of women, crime, and justice must have a grasp of the impact that the processes of globalization have had on national economies and must understand the relationship of this phenomenon to women's crimes and their victimization and, indeed, their imprisonment.
- Globalization means that women are part of much larger systems of interaction; therefore, readers must be exposed to an *international* perspective. As part of that perspective, we have included several chapters that cover specific countries: Colombia, South America (chap. 12); the Netherlands and Cuba (chap. 11); Canada (chaps. 12 and 17); Europe and third-world countries (chap. 27); and three chapters with a general international focus (chaps. 8, 22, and 28). Two chapters (chaps. 8 and 12) address globalization specifically.
- A final theme, new to this edition, is understanding *heterosexism* and *homophobia* and how these are connected to the issues of women, crime, and justice.

Although this area is rarely recognized as germane to the study of criminology, the text contains three important chapters that cover the experiences of lesbians: as convicted felons, in this case on death row (chap. 14); as victims of domestic violence (chap. 23); and as police officers (chap. 33). The intersections of sexual orientation and homophobia with race and ethnicity, class, gender, and immigrant status are important issues that call for better research, theory, and practice. Only then can society understand more fully the impact of homophobia and sexuality on the lives of women offenders, prisoners, victims and survivors, and workers in the criminal justice system.

In addition to these themes a number of terms are used throughout the book:

- *Sexism* is defined as the socially organized cultural beliefs, practices, and institutions that result in systematic structures of male domination and attitudes of male superiority over women. Sexism means that women are treated on the basis of their socially defined "female nature."
- *Racism* refers to the socially organized attitudes, practices, policies, and institutions that result in systematic domination of one racial and ethnic group over another.
- *Capitalism* is defined as the economic and political ways in which private ownership of productive property and the production of services and goods are organized in the interests of profit making for the relatively few.
- *Homophobia* and *heterosexism* refer to socially structured systems of domination and subordination that disadvantage and promote fear of homosexuals (recently understood to include lesbians, gay men, bisexuals, and transgendered and transexual people).

Each of these terms describe conditions in which specific groups—women, racial and ethnic minorities, poor and working-class people, and lesbians and gay men—are severely disadvantaged in the daily course of life. *Intersectionality* refers to the phenomenon of various social forces, such as class, race and ethnicity, gender, and sexual orientation, impacting *simultaneously* on people's lives. This concept has great import for those women who are controlled by the criminal justice system.

As with the last two editions of this book, the chapters continue to draw on current feminist scholarship. This scholarship continues to evolve and remains eclectic. There has been no closure on epistemological, theoretical, or methodological issues at this point in the development of feminist scholarship, and as a result, feminist researchers do not necessarily share a paradigm or explanatory framework. However, feminist scholarship has become increasingly multicultural and intersectional as well as grounded in basic social structural conditions within society—and this set of assumptions is clearly expressed in the work of many contributors to the book.

ORGANIZATION

The book consists of 36 chapters presented in four parts:

- Part 1: Theories and Facts about Women Offenders
- Part 2: Women and Prison
- Part 3: Women Victims and Survivors of Crime
- Part 4: Women Workers in the Criminal Justice System

Part 1 presents the topic of women offenders by first examining theories about female criminality. To determine why women commit crimes, it is necessary to first consider some basic notions about criminal law. *Law* is defined in this book as a set of rules that control behavior through negative sanctions, and *crime* is understood as socially constructed behavior. With these definitions in mind, Sokoloff, Price, and Flavin in chapter 1 explore how law is created and changed as well as how law has affected and been affected by women from diverse racial, ethnic, and class backgrounds in the United States. Several other authors in parts 1 and 2 discuss issues of crime causation as it pertains to women and girls (chapters 2, 3, 4, 6, 8, 9, 10, and 12). In chapter 5, Steffensmeier and Schwartz provide statistics on crime by American women over a 35-year period; this chapter compares women's arrest rates with those of men's and identifies the women's share of specific crimes, for example, the percentage of all murders in a given year that are committed by women. Chapter 6, also by Steffensmeier and Schwartz, provides a set of possible explanations for women's crime today and does so within its historical context. Chapter 3 describes a small sample of women street robbers in one city; their ways of operating and their motivations are compared with those of men who rob. The author, J. Miller, employs a feminist perspective to discuss the intersectionality of race, class, and gender in her analysis. Chapter 7 by Maher and chapter 9 by Paltrow deal with the topic of women and drugs but from different perspectives. Chapter 7 describes street-level trade in drugs and women's roles in drug markets. Chapter 9, as it discusses the connection between the war on drugs as waged in the United States and the war on abortion, finds remarkable similarities between the two in terms of government strategies used to control and punish women, particularly the most vulnerable women from poor and minority groups.

Part 2, the new section, discusses women in prison. The eight chapters in this section examine different aspects of this issue, beginning with chapter 10 by Owen, which describes how women are impacted by the accelerated rate of growth in the imprisonment of Americans. Chapter 11 by Bhavnani and Davis examines the role of racism and sexism in women's imprisonment in three different countries. Chapter 12 by Sudbury returns to the issue raised in chapter 10 of the surge in women's imprisonment, especially that of Black women, but does so from a different point of view; Sudbury claims that globalization of national economies, the prison industry, and the war on drugs each contribute to the high incarceration rates. Chapter 13 by Ross describes the resistance to dehumanization waged by Native American women who are incarcerated.

Chapter 14 by Farr continues the theme of dehumanization by offering an explanation as to why lesbians are overrepresented on death row. Chapter 15 by Reed and Reed describes the severe consequences suffered by children whose mothers are prisoners. Chapter 16 by Siegal focuses on various government and advocacy group reports on violence perpetrated against women in prison in the United States. Finally, chapter 17 by Faith closes this section with a description of the failed Canadian experience in reforming prisons for women.

Part 3 examines women victims and survivors, primarily of male crime. The introduction to this section is written by Andrew Karmen (who also wrote the introduction in the last two editions). Karmen, who specializes in victimology, constructs three different paradigms for victimization and gives examples from the crimes of rape and battering. This introduction provides a foundation for the chapters that follow on specific forms of victimization. Chapter 18 by Websdale and Chesney-Lind contains an overview of research that has been done in recent years on many different types of violence perpetrated against women. This chapter is followed by two chapters on rape (chap. 19 by Feltey and chap. 20 by Wriggins). Next, we include several chapters on domestic violence because of its pervasiveness in society and its importance to our students. The first of these chapters (chap. 21) on woman battering by Browne, appeared in the last edition of the book. It has been updated for this volume by the author so that it provides the very latest information on this pervasive form of victimization. Chapter 22 by Dasgupta continues the discussion of battering by focusing on immigrant women as part of the international theme of the book. In chapter 23 by West, the topic is same-sex violence, a problem that receives inadequate attention from social services in the community and in the literature. Another rarely discussed problem—domestic violence in police families—is covered in chapter 24 by Griggs. Still focusing on battering, chapter 25 by Presser and Gaarder reports on efforts to provide social justice and healing between victims and batterers—all the while holding batterers responsible for their behavior and providing much-needed material and emotional support for battered women and their children as they are kept safe from the batterer. Sexual harassment, a sometimes less violent but pervasive and destructive form of abuse, is the topic in chapter 26 by Rundblad. The last two chapters in this section provide more material on the international theme. Chapter 27 by Wijers discusses the issue of trafficking, the coercion of women into prostitution (or sex work) through their transport across national boundaries. Chapter 28, a *Newsday* article, continues the discussion of smuggled women and their widespread victimization in the United States, which has accelerated in recent years.

Part 4 presents many aspects of women workers in the criminal justice system. The eight chapters in this section cover courts, police, corrections, and academia. In chapter 29 Schafran describes a widespread form of discrimination in the United States court system—gender and race bias against women who work in the courts as prosecutors and defense lawyers as well as those who serve as witnesses or defendants. Chapter 30 looks at the courts from a different perspective; by describing the conservative philosophy of two women judges in Texas,

Toobin adds to a growing understanding of what influences judges. Compassion and a liberal orientation are not inherent traits necessarily found in women judges nor lacking in men judges. Rather, a judge's philosophy, it appears, depends as much on early legal socialization and the local political climate as it does on gender. Chapters 31 through 34 deal with different aspects of women police—the history of women police, the barriers faced by women police today, the special problems encountered by lesbian officers, and the importance of the combined effects of race, gender, and sexual orientation on women in policing. We chose to give this extra attention to various issues on women and policing because of the quality of research here and the importance of this topic to our students. Chapter 31 by Schulz, a former police officer, has been updated from the second edition of the book. Schulz provides a detailed history of women's early days in policing up through today. This chapter provides an excellent foundation for the chapters on policing that follow. Chapter 32 written by Harrington, a former police chief, and Lonsway, a psychologist, covers the real barriers in police departments (institutional, attitudinal, and informal) that limit women officers' success on the job. Chapter 33 by S. Miller, Forest, and Jurik takes on a topic rarely discussed publicly or in the literature—the issues faced by lesbian police seeking to be accepted as the professionals that they are. The final police chapter, chapter 34 by Martin, was first published in the second edition of this book and has been updated here with an addendum. The chapter describes the interactive discriminatory effects of race and sex on women police officers. Chapter 35, significantly expanded from the second edition, was written by Belknap, who looks at the many issues that women corrections officers encounter in this traditionally male occupation. Belknap provides an excellent distinction between *sexual harassment* and *gender harassment;* and she does so in terms of how race and sexual orientation figure in this arena. The book closes with a chapter (chap. 36) by Wilson and Moyer that covers the academic preparation of criminal justice workers. It discusses the faculty and curriculum that students experience prior to becoming practitioners. Wilson and Moyer are concerned about the conservative nature of current academic preparation and discuss the importance of a diverse faculty who shape the body of knowledge in criminal justice and influence the thinking of students. An addendum by Jurik and Cavender at the end of this chapter provides the reader with additional material on how feminism and multiculturalism have impacted the new discipline of justice studies in academia.

Three of the chapters in part 4 (chaps. 29, 32, and 33) were written specifically for this edition, and four chapters (chaps. 31, 34, 35, and 36) were in the second edition and have been revised to bring them up to date. We think that these chapters—together with chapter 30, which was reprinted from the *New Yorker Magazine,* and chapter 24, on domestic violence in police families—provide a fresh look at the issues that face women criminal justice practitioners today. We look forward to a time when all women will be fully accepted in their chosen field of work. We hope further that the students who read these chapters will participate in that changed future. We urge readers to take the steps needed to transform the criminal justice system in ways that will eliminate all discrimination against offenders, prisoners, victims and survivors, and workers in the criminal justice system and will create a more socially just and humane society. And finally, we hope that the inclusion of chapters that discuss several different countries will enable us to better educate our students in the United States as well as readers in many different parts of the world and will make a small contribution to the goal of global justice for all women, men, and children.

PEDAGOGICAL AIDS

In this edition, the authors have sought to enhance the student's ability to master the material presented, to identify the interaction and connections between topics, and to pursue new research projects. To meet these objectives, this edition includes the following learning aids:

- At the beginning of each of the four parts of the book a listing of Internet websites has been added that provide additional statistical and other empirical information plus current activism information.
- Discussion questions have been added at the end of each chapter; these can contribute to classroom discussion and stimulate further student research and investigations.
- As in past editions, an abstract that highlights key ideas is presented at the beginning of each chapter.

IN APPRECIATION

As in our earlier editions, we want to especially acknowledge those women who have been important to us personally and important to the movement in transforming the sexist, racist, class-biased, and homophobic nature of our criminal justice system. This book is for Inez Garcia, Joan Little, Yvonne Wainrow, and Desi Woods and for all women imprisoned for protecting themselves against male attackers; for Kitty Genovese, Greta Rideout, Diane Williams, Carmita Wood, Anita Hill, Susan McDougal, and all victims and survivors of male assaults and intimidations; for Rhonda Copelon, Eleanor Holmes Norton, Vanita Gupta, Constance Baker Motley, Kris Glen, Patricia Williams, Sonia Sotomayor, Felicia Spritzer, Penny Harrington, Fannie Lou Hamer, Barbara Jordon, Angela Y. Davis, Beth Richie, Meda Chesney-Lind, Luz Santana, Susan Rosenberg, and Kemba Smith and for all women working for change in the criminal justice system. This book is also for our mothers, sisters, daughters, fathers, brothers, husbands, sons, and grandchildren; and especially for our students over the years who have been invaluable in teaching us about women, crime, and justice.

We want to thank the John Jay College of Criminal Justice of the City University of New York, President Gerald W. Lynch of the college, Provost Basil Wilson, and our colleagues for nurturing our scholarship over the years and for providing the kind of environment that promotes interdisciplinary analysis and a continuing quest for knowledge. It was in such a setting that 25 years ago the two editors of this book originally came together over our concerns around the issues of women, crime, and justice.

A project like this is impossible without the work of many people. Thus, we would also like to thank the marvelous authors, each a significant expert in her or his field, who wrote original material for this edition. New chapters were prepared by Darrell Steffensmeier and Jennifer Schwartz, Julia Sudbury, Karlene Faith, Carolyn Renae Griggs, Lynn Hecht Schafran, Penny Harrington and Kim Lonsway, Susan Miller, Kay Forest and Nancy Jurik, and Nanci Koser Wilson and Imogene Moyer. Partial chapters or updates or addenda were written by Jeanne Flavin (chap. 1), whose fine contributions to the rewrite lifted a major burden from the editors; Angela Browne; Dorothy Moses Schulz; Susan E. Martin; Joanne Belknap; and Nancy Jurik and Gray Cavender. With great regret, we could not include three chapters originally planned for this book. We wish to acknowledge these authors and their important material: "Contextualizing One Young Woman's Resort to Violence: Transcending the Divide between Individual and Collective Realities" by Cindy Ness; "Disparity in the Discipline of Male and Female Prisoners" by Dorothy Spektorov McCllellan; and "Gender, Race, and Habitual Offender Sentencing in Florida: Are African American Women Unfairly Sentenced?" by Charles Crawford.

A number of brave, strong, and spirited people inspired us and helped keep the momentum up for us to finish this work when personal considerations seemed to put completion out of reach. Like many of our colleagues, we are "sandwiched" between younger and older generations; because of that situation, we were confronted with finishing this book at the same time that Natalie's 88-year-old mother, Charlotte, experienced a serious fall from which she has now completely recovered. It is to her and Barbara's husband, Bob, who died in March 2002, that this book is especially dedicated. The support of Sarah and John and their partners, Susie and Liz, has been essential to Barbara during the completion of the book.

We are particularly indebted to Jeanne Flavin, a sociologist at Fordham University, who graciously, and despite her other heavy commitments helped us rewrite the first chapter of the book. It was only because of her generosity and scholarship that the chapter was appropriately updated and the book was able to proceed as quickly as it did. Additional inspiration came from Natalie's students in both undergraduate and graduate classes at John Jay College of Criminal Justice, from which Barbara retired as Dean of the Graduate Program in 1997. Further, one of those students worked as an assistant and diligently tracked down materials in the library and photocopied unending numbers of pages for us. For that effort we thank Erin Schultz.

Release time for one course was provided to Natalie by McGraw-Hill at a crucial time, further facilitating the completion of this book. In addition, we would like to thank the following reviewers: Mary Atwell of Radford University, Deborah Laufersweiler of the University of Arkansas, J. Robert Lilly of Northern Kentucky University, and Nancy Jurik of Arizona State University. Their careful reading of the manuscript identified gaps in our material and noted areas that required greater coverage. We thank them for their insightful and constructive reviews. The book is stronger as a result of their contributions. Of course, any errors, omissions, or other shortcomings in the book are the sole responsibility of the two of us.

No book comes to fruition without the guidance that only an editor can provide. For her years of work with us, for her understanding and forbearance when both of us faced personal difficulties, and for her counsel throughout this long journey we wish to extend our gratitude to Carolyn Henderson Meier, senior sponsoring editor. We also wish to express appreciation to Julie Abodeely, editorial coordinator for her prompt efficiency in responding to our numerous queries over a period of many months. We appreciate the final burst of work orchestrated by our senior project manager, Christina Thornton-Villagomez, and the excellence of our copyeditor, Karen Dorman who smoothed out many a rough spot in the manuscript.

As always, we wish to thank our husbands—Bob Price, who died before the book was finished, and Fred Pincus—for their loving support of us and this project. The month that this book came out in its first edition (September 1982), Natalie's son, Josh Pincus-Sokoloff, was born. He is now a young man. It has been a joy for Natalie to see him and the book grow and mature alongside each other.

Barbara Raffel Price and Natalie J. Sokoloff

The Criminal Justice System and Women

Part 1

Theories and Facts about Women Offenders

This section of the book provides the reader with recent feminist criminological theory on women offenders. Feminist scholarship encompasses a number of common themes including: (1) a focus on the social construction of knowledge and how, most typically, it is male-defined; (2) a recognition that research (an important source of theory) is strongly influenced by the power relations of gender, race, class, and more recently, sexual orientation, and their intersectionalities; (3) a rejection of deterministic thinking that holds that who we are (i.e., our gender) is determined primarily by our biology; (4) studying gender relations in such a way that questions are raised about its taken-for-granted nature in society; and (5) engaging participants in research as respected partners in the process.

WHAT IS FEMINIST SCHOLARSHIP?

Feminist scholarship today is best characterized as a *set of perspectives* representing a continuum of feminist thought. Each perspective has a theoretical framework that is linked to different assumptions about the causes of gender inequality and women's oppression. These perspectives also result in important differences in strategies for social change. Historically, the most common frameworks have included those of liberal, radical, Marxist, and socialist feminists, and more recently, diverse groups of feminists of color. (For a review of this literature, see Sokoloff 1980; Baca Zinn and Dill 1994; Andersen and Collins 2001; Sokoloff and Dupont 2004. For a

WEBSITES

New websites are continuously being developed while at the same time others disappear. This list gives some samples of the abundance of sites available. Also, check with a search engine, such as Google at **www.google.com**, to locate additional information. Insert a key word or phrase (e.g., women offenders) or organization in order to locate additional references.

Women Offenders

Lawrence Greenfeld and Tracy Snell. *Women Offenders.* Bureau of Justice Statistics Special Report. December 1999. NCJ175688. Can be found at **www.ojp.usdoj.gov/bjs/pub/pdf/wo.pdf**

Research on Women and Girls in the Justice System. September 2000. NCJ180973. Can be found at **www.ncjrs.org/pdffiles1/nij/189973.pdf**

Rand Organization for information on drug use and women at **www.rand.org/multi/dprc/projects/use.html**

Network of Sex Work Projects at **www.nswp.org**

The National Consortium on Violence Research for research reports on violence by women and minorities at **www.heinz.cmu.edu/researchers/centers.html**

Girls in the Juvenile Justice System

Critical issues related to girls, such as defining the population, providing recommendations, and so on. *Juvenile Justice* (6, #1). October 1999. OJJDP special issue on girls. Can be found at **www.ncjrs.org/html/ojjdp/jjjournal1099/contents.html**

Justice by Gender: The Lack of Appropriate Prevention Diversion and Treatment Alternatives for Girls in the Justice System. American Bar Association and National Bar Association. 2001. Available at **www.abanet.org/crimjust/juvjus/justicebygenderweb.pdf**

Girls in the Juvenile Justice System. Lists and summarizes several important articles on girls in the justice system. Available at **www.buildingblocksforyouth.org/issues/girls/ studies.html**

General References Useful in Studying Women Offenders and Girls

General reference for women's studies and issues related to women can be found at the home page for the Women's Studies Program at the City University of New York Graduate School at **www.web.gc.cuny.edu/womenstudies/index.html**

The *Sourcebook of Criminal Justice Statistics* contains data from 100 sources on all aspects of the criminal justice system in the United States—see Section 4 on persons arrested and Section 6 on persons under correctional supervision and look for "women" or "gender" at **www.albany.edu/sourcebook/**

The John Jay College of Criminal Justice Library provides an extensive number of links to criminal justice statistics and international criminal justice at **www.lib.jjay.cuny.edu**

Australian Institute of Criminology at **www.aic.gov.au/cgi-bin/htsearch**

National Council on Crime and Delinquency for information on juvenile delinquency at **www.nccd-crc.org**

Office of Juvenile Justice and Delinquency Prevention at **www.ojjdp.ncjrs.org**

discussion of this literature and its relationship to women and crime, see Daly and Chesney-Lind 1988; Daly and Stephens 1995; Daly 1997.)

It will help the reader to be aware of the basic thesis of each of these major feminist perspectives. *Liberal feminism,* the most mainstream of the perspectives, stresses the importance of equality of women with men within the *existing* political and social structures in society. From this perspective, the most common cause of gender inequality is identified as cultural attitudes with regard to gender role socialization. For example, liberal feminists (Adler 1975; Adler and Simon 1979) argued, in relation to crime, that more women were turning to crime as attitudes toward gender equality changed in society and as greater employment opportunities in the legal and illegal worlds emerged. In contrast, *radical feminism* identifies male dominance and control as the cause of gender inequality and argues that these must be eliminated from all social institutions. Men's control of women's sexuality and the norm of heterosexuality are identified as at the core of women's oppression. For example, it was the radical feminists who transformed our understanding of the crime of rape from that of sexuality and uncontrollable male sexual needs to one of systemic violence against women.

Marxist feminism views women's oppression as a function of class relations in a capitalist society. This approach sees the elimination of class oppression as a necessary (although no longer sufficient) prerequisite to the reduction of women's subordination. Women are twice burdened in this analysis: they are oppressed economically in low-wage jobs in the labor market and they are oppressed by their unpaid family responsibilities centered around reproductive labor (childbearing, child care, and housework). A Marxist feminist would argue that the persistently lower crime rates of women are due to their marginalization in relation to the means of production. With limited opportunities, petty theft and shoplifting are, therefore, among the typical female crimes.

Socialist feminists combine the Marxist and radical feminist perspectives and identify as the causes of gender inequality and women's oppression both patriarchy and capitalism in public as well as private spheres of life. (Other forms of socially structured inequality such as racism and heterosexism are equally important to but less developed in the socialist feminist analysis.) The obvious example here is the crime of prostitution, in which a woman is understood to have limited control over both her sexual life and her economic life; moreover, in a patriarchal capitalist society a poor young woman turns to prostitution not only because of prior sexual, physical, and economic abuse in her private life but also because of the limited opportunities and ongoing abuse in her public life.

Third-wave feminists (also called *women of color feminists, critical race feminists,* and *womanists*)[1] object to both (1) white, western feminists who early in the development of feminist thinking defined "women's issues" from their own standpoint without including concerns of women of color and third-world women specifically and (2) antiracist theory that presumes that racial and ethnic minority women's experiences are the same as their male counterparts. The third-wave approach focuses on the significant role that racism, sexism, class bias, heterosexism, and other forms of socially structured inequality have in the lives of women. Third-wave feminists introduce the concept of "intersectionalities" to understand the interlocking *sites* of oppression; they examine how the categories of race, class, gender, and sexuality in intersecting systems of domination rely on each other to function. The antiracist feminist analysis found in this book helps readers understand not only those behaviors of women that are defined as criminal but also the many crimes against women. This approach also makes clear the need to understand issues of social justice as well as criminal justice in evaluations of the criminalization of women.

Thus, feminist theory is made up of many different threads, and it remains on the cutting edge of analysis of women's lives and their relationship to crime and criminality. Moreover, feminist thinking assists criminologists in better understanding male crime. It has led to the introduction of a new concept of masculinities, which proposes that crime is a way for different groups of men to construct gender when conventional avenues for establishing their own masculinity have been blocked (Messerschmidt 1993). Clearly, race, ethnicity, and class are as important as gender in understanding men's as well as women's relationships to the criminal justice system. Unfortunately, in criminology as in the larger society, when people think of gender, they usually think only of women (not men and women), and when they talk about race, they tend to focus only on racial and ethnic minorities and not on white and European people too. Feminist scholarship helps change such thinking. It challenges these uncritically

---

[1]There are three waves of feminist theory historically: the first wave of the women's movement occurred in the mid to late 1800s; the second wave refers to the mainstream feminist perspective growing out of and largely sustained by the women's and civil rights movements of the 1960s and 1970s; the third wave of the women's movement emerged in the 1980s and 1990s and challenges the idea that poor women, lesbians, and women of color share the same problems as white middle-class women or similarly located poor men, gay men, or men of color.

accepted assumptions and in so doing has produced new perspectives and a powerful body of knowledge for the development of feminist criminology.

FEMINIST CRIMINOLOGY

Two questions persistently asked by feminist criminologists have been (1) do theories of men's crimes apply to women—and if not, how and why not; and (2) how can we explain the fact that women are far less likely than men to be involved in criminal activity (see J. Miller, chap. 3)? (For a review of this literature, see Daly and Chesney-Lind 1988.) What implications do these questions have for the study of crime—for both men and women? Further, women scholars of color have challenged how myths of gender expectations and socially structured inequality impact differently on white women and various groups of women of color in the study of female offenders. (In this anthology see J. Miller, chap. 3; Maher, chap. 7; Sudbury, chap. 12; and Ross, chap. 13; in addition, see Diaz-Cotto 1996 and Crawford 2000.)

Three defining features of feminist criminology have been described by Dorie Klein (2000). These features are (1) an interest in the well-being of women offenders, prisoners, victims and survivors, and workers in the criminal justice system; (2) a focus on gender in explaining individual and institutional behaviors related to crime and crime control; and (3) an understanding that in virtually every society on the globe today gender relations are socially constructed (not simply a natural fact) and place women in a subordinate status to that of men.

Since the publication of the first edition of this book in 1982, the contributions of various feminist perspectives to the study of criminology and specifically to the study of female offenders have grown steadily. Two areas are of particular significance. The first contribution is in theory and research. Work is in progress, for example, on building a firm theoretical foundation for explaining crime causation that directly addresses female criminality. This effort, which has accelerated during the past decade, is described by several authors in part 1, especially Flavin (chap. 2), Gaarder and Belknap (chap. 4), and Steffensmeier and Schwartz (chap. 6), and in part 2, especially Sudbury (chap. 12).

Feminist scholars have made the case and incorporated into their research the principle that *not all women are the same* (e.g., in part 1 see Sokoloff et al., chap. 1; Flavin, chap. 2; and Kempadoo, chap. 8; in part 2 see Bhavnani and Davis, chap. 11, and Ross, chap. 13; in part 3 see Wriggins, chap. 20, and Dasgupta, chap. 22). Because the social conditions and experiences of women's lives vary according to where they are located at the points of intersectionalities in societal systems of race, class, gender, nationality, and sexual orientation, the lives of women must be understood and examined within these contexts. Although sexual orientation is of great importance, literature on crimes by and against lesbians, as well as the treatment of lesbians by the criminal justice system, is abysmally lacking. Nevertheless, this edition of the book contains the findings from the limited research in this area in chapters by Farr (chap. 14), West (chap. 23), and S. Miller et al. (chap. 33). Further, feminist research does not limit inquiry to an analysis of aggregate data (Steffensmeier and Schwartz, chap. 5), but also engages in dialogue with research participants so that women's realities are used to create new theories as well as to provide the context for better understanding of cold statistics (e.g., J. Miller, chap. 3; Gaarder and Belknap, chap. 4; and Maher, chap. 7).

The second area of contribution is a different approach to studying criminality and women's offending by putting the behavior into a larger context. Maher (chap. 7) and Kempadoo (chap. 8) provide two examples of this methodology. In both cases economic pressures and the marginality of women in the economy play an important role in understanding women's offending. Moreover, Kempadoo (and Sudbury, chap. 12 in part 2) locates these economic pressures in the context of a global capitalist system that puts great hardship on poor people, disproportionately minority, whose opportunity to work is dependent on market forces far beyond their control.

In the United States today there continues to be a backlash to the women's movement that first emerged in the 1960s. Resistance to its objectives and a particularly harsh reaction to its successes is a fact of life (Faludi 1992). The backlash can be seen among the fervent antiabortionists for whom religion merges with politics. It can be seen as well in the sharply increased rate of incarceration of women—particularly poor and minority—throughout the 1990s despite a significant decrease in female violent offenses (see Steffensmeier and Schwartz, chap. 5). The backlash is seen also in the passing of laws periodically by various jurisdictions around the country that define pregnant women on drugs as criminals because they are alleged to be "delivering controlled substances to their unborn child" (see Paltrow, chap. 9, and Sokoloff, Price, and Flavin, chap. 1). Finally, the ongoing backlash is reflected in the periodic reemergence of the myth that a new and more dangerous type of female criminal has arrived on the scene as a result of the women's movement (see Sokoloff 2001 for a review and critique of this literature).

THE ORGANIZATION OF PART 1

In the chapters that follow, we examine many of these issues as we focus on women offenders. In particular, we place the issues surrounding female criminality in the context of a society in which true equality for women, racial and ethnic minorities, and the poor has yet to become a reality. Part 1 consists of nine chapters that cover the law; theoretical analyses of crime causation; feminism and its relation to crime theory; arrest data; transfer of girls to adult female custody; the effects of race, class, and gender; and specific offenses for which women are arrested or otherwise controlled by social service agencies or the state: selling illegal drugs, sex work or prostitution, robbery, using drugs while pregnant, and reproductive choices.

Because the field of women and crime has evolved so rapidly in the past decade and because so much new research has emerged, only one of the original chapters (Sokoloff, Price, and Flavin, chap. 1) from the second edition was retained in part 1 and it has been fully updated; a third author, Jeanne Flavin, contributed substantially to the changes. Chapters 5 and 6 are two new chapters written by Darrell Steffensmeier (who authored a chapter in the last edition) and a second, new author, Jennifer Schwartz. Chapters 2, 3, 4, 7, 8 and 9 are reprints of important, recent articles.

Chapter 1 ("The Criminal Law and Women") provides the context for part 1 by discussing the historical, political, and social processes that influence the development of law and the underlying class, race, and gender biases within those processes. It has been substantially revised. (See also Barak, Flavin, and Leighton 2001 for detailed support of this approach.) It further shows the reader how the early sexism that governed law, while constantly being challenged and changing, still is found in society today. Finally, the chapter raises serious questions about the ability of the law to deliver fairness and justice to women, minorities, and the poor—particularly poor minority women.

In chapter 2 ("Feminism for the Mainstream Criminologist: An Invitation"), Jeanne Flavin describes the contributions that feminist thinking has made to criminological theory, research methodology, and criminal justice policy. Although feminist researchers share similar concerns about the welfare of women involved with the criminal justice system and the equity of treatment of offenders, victims, and workers, Flavin points out that there also exists diversity in their scholarship.

Chapter 3 ("Feminist Theories of Women's Crime: Robbery as a Case Study" by Jody Miller) demonstrates how gender really matters when it comes to certain crimes, in this case robbery. Men and women commit robbery in very different ways. For women it is important to avoid physically violent encounters in which they might be disadvantaged, whereas men generally do use violence. In this small-scale study, women and men have similar motivations for committing robbery, which include gaining money to buy things as well as enjoying the excitement that robbery brings them. These motives show the importance of class in understanding specific crimes. Miller also warns us that just because this sample is predominantly African American women and men does not mean this crime is committed only by blacks. The relative deprivation of offenders in poor communities is an important component of the decision to engage in street robberies.

Chapter 4 ("Tenuous Borders: Girls Transferred to Adult Court" by Emily Gaarder and Joanne Belknap) reviews traditional theories of crime causation and then examines the new directions of feminist theory in exploring pathways to offending. Gaarder and Belknap use one feminist method, that of interviewing and reporting girls' stories directly as they give them. This article describes a growing problem in the Unites States: the criminal justice system's handling of juveniles as adults. As of 2001, there were 3,147 young people under the age of 18 confined in adult state and federal prisons (Bureau of Justice Statistics 2000). One of the authors' important findings is that the girls who were tried in adult court and sentenced as adults did not exhibit offending patterns different from those girls kept in the juvenile justice system. This raises the question of what basis is used to make the decision to take this serious step?

Chapter 5 ("Trends in Female Crime: Is Crime Still a Man's World?") and chapter 6 ("Contemporary Explanations of Women's Crime") are written by

Darrell Steffensmeier and Jennifer Schwartz. In the first of their two chapters, they discuss trends in female crime by examining arrest rates and self-report studies. They are especially interested in the female percentage of arrests as they analyze the extent to which women's crime, in comparison to men's crime, is increasing or changing in nature. The chapter provides a detailed look at female arrest trends and concludes that the profile of the female offender, relative to males, has not changed and, most importantly, that the typical female offender has not become either more like men or more violent. In chapter 6 Steffensmeier and Schwartz discuss various explanations of female criminality. They evaluate a number of plausible explanations of the female arrest trends and patterns laid out in their previous chapter. They argue that women's crime is more a function of increasing poverty and racial segregation of marginalized communities than of women's liberation. They conclude, somewhat controversially, that future changes in female criminal activity will be governed more by opportunities in the criminal world than by changes in motivation of women.

Part 1 next turns its attention—in chapter 7, "A Reserve Army: Women and the Drug Market" by Lisa Maher—to the illegal drug market. This issue is significant for women because the large increase in female incarceration rates largely stems from drug arrests. The chapter supports Steffensmeier and Schwartz's argument in chapter 6 as it discusses how and why women's access for working in the drug trade at the street level is very limited. Using an ethnographic approach to field observation, Maher is able to trace the neighborhood patterns in the drug business over a period of time. She reports that women, as economic actors in the illegal drug business, are underrepresented among drug dealers and are restricted from full participation by men in the trade because they are perceived to lack two important characteristics: ability to exercise violence and terror and a strong racial or ethnic kinship. The first characteristic is needed to enforce payment and secure market locations, and the second is needed to be considered trustworthy. Thus, ironically, sexism operates to exclude women from an ability to gain a significant foothold in this criminal activity. Yet, a review of offenses of women over the last decade indicates that for women in state prisons or federal prisons, a drug offense is the most frequently reported crime (Greenfeld and Snell 1999, p. 6). Maher's work adds additional factual evidence that refutes the liberation theory, which holds that as women are emancipated and enter the work world in larger numbers, they will also participate as equal partners with men in the criminal world. No sign of the liberated female criminal is found in Maher's study of urban neighborhoods.

Chapter 8 ("Prostitution and the Globalization of Sex Workers' Rights" by Kamala Kempadoo) has an international focus. Kempadoo discusses third-world sex workers—primarily prostitutes—and describes how racism is used to paint a picture to potential customers of migrant women as desirable and exotic on the one hand and as ignorant and dependent on the other hand. In recent years the global economy has had a negative impact on women's economic condition, and the sex industry has been one of the few available sources of income for women. Therefore, it has attracted a growing number of women. Kempadoo describes how and why workers are moved into other countries. The income gap for women, growing in recent years with global restructuring of capitalist production and investment, has resulted in an influx of new sex workers who are moved increasingly in large numbers across national boundaries.

In the final chapter in part 1 ("The War on Drugs and the War on Abortion"), Lynn Paltrow explains the connections between the drug laws and abortion laws in the United States. Both criminalize women's bodies and behavior, and both have a disproportionate impact on poor black women. Paltrow's main point is that both drug use and pregnancy are used by conservatives to highlight individual deviance while they ignore the underlying social problems of unemployment, poverty, racism, and sexism.

Taken together, these nine chapters provide both a theoretically challenging and empirically powerful picture of women offenders in the United States and, to some extent, in other countries. Although we would encourage the reader to proceed through the selections in the order presented, other orders may well be appropriate. We are confident that each chapter stands on its own and makes a valuable contribution to the body of knowledge on women and crime.

The reader should be aware that part 1 does not cover all the topics related to women, crime, and justice. For example, other issues of significance to consider are gender and white-collar crime (e.g., Coleman 1998; Daly 1989), gender and violence (e.g., Kruttschnitt 2001; Mann 1990; Simpson 1991; Ness 2002), women partners of male prisoners (e.g., Fishman 1990; Padilla and Santiago 1993; Girshick, 1996), delinquency and girls (e.g., Acoca 1999; Chesney-Lind 2001; Holsinger 2000), and diverse cultural standpoints of women caught up in the criminal justice system from different classes and racial and ethnic communities such as Latina (Diaz-Cotto 1996), Native American (Ross 1998), and Asian (Diaz-Cotto 1996; Mann 1995), and sexual orientations (Robson 1992). It is important to note the dearth of systematic studies in the literature on racial and ethnic minority women (other than African Americans) and lesbian offenders. Although this paucity applies to literature on women in prison as well (see part 2), we were especially struck by the small amount of feminist criminology literature (both theoretical and empirical work) on female offenders from the standpoint of race, class, ethnicity, and sexual orientation. As a useful reference on a range of women and criminal justice topics, the reader might want to consult Rafter's *Encyclopedia of Women and Crime* 2001). We invite our readers to investigate the growing but still small body of multiracial and multiethnic feminist literature on female offenders, to participate in the research process so as to increase both the body of knowledge and the resources necessary for change, and to engage as activists in reforming the criminal justice system as we all move toward transforming society to be more humane and socially just.

REFERENCES

Acoca, Leslie. 1999. Investing in Girls: A Twenty-First Century Strategy. *Juvenile Justice* 6(1):3–13.

Adler, Freda. 1975. *Sisters in Crime: The Rise of the New Female Criminal*. New York: McGraw-Hill.

Adler, Freda and Rita James Simon. 1979. *The Criminology of Deviant Women*. Boston: Houghton Mifflin.

Andersen, Margaret, and Patricia Hill Collins. 2001. Shifting the Center and Reconstructing Knowledge: Introduction to Part 1. In *Race, Class, and Gender*, 4th ed., ed. Margaret Andersen and Patricia Hill Collins, 1–11. Belmont, CA: Wadsworth/Thomson Learning.

Baca Zinn, Maxine, and Bonnie Thornton Dill. 1994. Difference and Domination. In *Women of Color in U.S. Society*, ed. Maxine Baca Zinn and Bonnie Thornton Dill, 3–12. Philadelphia, PA: Temple University.

Barak, Gregg, Jeanne Flavin, and Paul Leighton. 2001. *Class, Race, Gender, and Crime*. Los Angeles: Roxbury.

Barry, Kathleen. 1979. *Female Sexual Slavery*. Englewood Cliffs, NJ: Prentice Hall.

Bell, Laurie, ed. 1987. *Good Girls/Bad Girls: Feminists and Sex Trade Workers Face to Face*. Seattle, WA: Seal.

Bureau of Justice Statistics. 1992. *National Update*, 1(4). NCJ135722. Washington, DC: U.S. Department of Justice.

Bureau of Justice Statistics. 2000. *Profile of State Prisoners under Age 18, 1985–97*. NCJ176989. Washington, DC: U.S. Department of Justice.

Butterfield, Fox. 1992. Are American Jails Becoming Shelters from the Storm? *The New York Times,* July 19, E4.

Canedy, Dana. 2002. Boys Case Is Used in Bid to Limit Trials of Minors as Adults. *The New York Times,* September 6:18.

Chancer, Lynn. 1993. Prostitution, Feminist Theory, and Ambivalence: Notes from the Sociological Underground. Paper given at the American Sociological Association meeting, Miami.

Chesney-Lind, Meda. 2001. What About Girls? Delinquency Programming as if Gendered Mattered. *Corrections Today*. February, 38–43.

Clark, Judy, and Kathy Boudin. 1990. Community of Women Organize Themselves to Cope with the AIDS Crisis: A Case Study from the Bedford Hills Correctional Facility. *Social Justice* 17(2):90–109.

Clines, Francis X. 1993. Tough Matriarch, Easy Touch, and Good Listener. *The New York Times,* April 24:25, 28.

Coleman, J. W. 1998. *The Criminal Elite: Understanding White Collar Crime*, 4th ed. New York: St. Martin's.

Collins, Patricia Hill. 1990. *Black Feminist Thought*. New York: Routledge, Chapman, Hall.

Crawford, Charles. 2000. Gender, Race, and Habitual Offender Sentencing in Florida. *Criminology* 38(1): 263–280.

Daly, Kathleen. 1997. Different Ways of Conceptualizing Sex/Gender in Feminist Theory and Their Implications for Criminology. *Theoretical Criminology* 1(1):25–52.

Daly, Kathleen. 1989. Gender and Varieties of White-Collar Crime. *Criminology* 24(4): 769–793.

Daly, Kathleen, and Meda Chesney-Lind. 1988. Feminism and Criminology. *Justice Quarterly* 5(December): 497–538.

Daly, Kathleen, and Deborah J. Stephens. 1995. The Dark Figure of Criminology: Towards a Black and Multi-Ethnic Feminist Agenda for Theory and Research. In *International Feminist Perspectives in Criminology: Engendering a Discipline,* ed. Nicole Hahn Rafter and Frances Heidensohn, 189–215. Philadelphia, PA: Open University.

Diaz-Cotto, Juanita. 1996. *Gender, Ethnicity, and the State: Latina and Latino Prison Politics*. Albany: State University of New York.

Diaz-Cotto, Juanita. 2002. Race, ethnicity, and gender in studies of incarceration. In *States of Confinement: Policing, Detention, and Prisons,* ed. Joy James. New York: Palgrave.

Faludi, Susan. 1992. *Backlash: The Undeclared War against American Women*. New York: Crown.

Fishman, Laura T. 1990. *Women at the Wall: A Study of Prisoner's Wives Doing Time on the Outside*. Albany: State University of New York.

Fortune, Edith P., Manuel Vega, and Ira J. Silverman. 1980. Study of Female Robbers in Southern Correctional Institutions. *Journal of Criminal Justice* (8): 317–325.

Greenfeld, Lawrence A., and Stephanie Minor-Harper. 1991. *Women in Prison*. Washington, DC: U.S. Department of Justice, Bureau of Justice Statistics.

Greenfeld, Lawrence A., and Tracy L. Snell. 1999. *Women Offenders*. Washington, DC: U.S. Department of Justice, Bureau of Justice Statistics.

Girschick, Lori. 1996. *Wives of Prisoners Speak Out*. Westport, CT: Praeger.

Holsinger, Kristi. 2000. Feminist Perspectives on Female Offending: Examining Real Girl's Lives. *Women and Criminal Justice* 12(1): 23–52.

hooks, bell. 1984. *Feminist Theory: From Margin to Center*. Boston: South End.

Jaggar, Allison. 1983. *Feminist Politics and Human Nature.* Totowa, NJ: Ballanheld Harvester.

Jankowski, Lewis W. 1992. *Correctional Populations in the United States, 1990.* NCJ-134946. Washington, DC: Bureau of Justice Statistics.

Jenness, Valerie. 1990. From Sex as Sin to Sex as Work: COYOTE and the Reorganization of Prostitution as a Social Problem. *Social Problems* 37(August):

Klein, Dorie. 2000. Feminist Criminology, USA. In *Encyclopedia of Women and Crime,* ed. Nicole Hahn Rafter, 80–81. Phoenix, Arizona: Oryx.

Kruttschnitt, Candace. 2001. Gender and Violence. In *Women, Crime and Criminal Justice,* ed. Claire Renzeti and Lynne Goodstein 77–92, Los Angeles: Roxbury.

Maher, Lisa, and Elin J. Waring. 1990. Beyond Simple Differences: White-Collar Crime, Gender and Workforce Position. *Phoebe* 2(1):44–54.

Mann, Coramae Richey. 1995. Women of Color and the Criminal Justice System. In *The Criminal Justice System and Women,* 2d ed., ed. Barbara Raffel Price and Natalie J. Sokoloff, 136–145. New York: McGraw-Hill.

Mann, Coramae Richey. 1990. Black Female Homicide in the United States. *Journal of Interpersonal Violence* 5(June):176–201.

Messerschmidt, J. W. 1993. *Masculinities and Crime.* Lanham, MD: Rowman and Littlefield.

Murphy, Sheila, and Marsha Rosenbaum. 1999. *Pregnant Women on Drugs: Combating Stereotypes and Stigma.* New Brunswick, NJ: Rutgers University.

Ness, Cindy. 2002. Contextualizing One Young Womans Resort to Violence: Transcending the Divide Between Individual and Collective Realities. Unpublished manuscript, New York.

Padilla, Felix M., and Lourdes Santiago. 1993. *Outside the Wall: A Puerto Rican Woman's Struggle.* New Brunswick, NJ: Rutgers University.

Paltrow, Lynn M. 1990. When Becoming Pregnant Is a Crime. *Criminal Justice Ethics* 9: (winter/spring):41–47.

Rafter, Nicole Hahn. 2000. *Encyclopedia of Women and Crime.* Phoenix: Oryx.

Ristock, Janice. 2002. *No More Secrets: Violence in Lesbian Relationships.* New York: Routledge.

Robson, Ruthann. 1992. *Lesbian (Out)law: Survival under the Rule of Law.* Ithaca, NY: Firebrand.

Ross, Luana. 1998. *Inventing the Savage: The Social Construction of Native American Criminality.* Austin: University of Texas.

Simpson, Sally. 1991. Caste, Class, and Violent Crime: Explaining Difference in Female Offending. *Criminology* 29(1):115–135.

Sokoloff, Natalie J. 1980. *Between Money and Love: The Dialectics of Women's Home and Market Work.* New York: Praeger.

Sokoloff, Natalie J. 2001. The Violent Female Offender in New York City: Myths and Facts. In *Crime and Justice in New York City,* Vol. 1, ed. Andrew Karmen, 132–146. Cincinnati, OH: Thomson Learning.

Sokoloff, Natalie J., and Ida Dupont. 2004. Feminist Multicultural Perspectives on Domestic Violence in the U.S.: An Overview. In *Domestic Violence: At the Intersections of Race, Class and Gender in the United States,* ed. Natalie J. Sokoloff, forthcoming. New York: Routledge.

Waring, Nancy, and Betsy Smith. 1991. The AIDS epidemic: Impact on Women Prisoners in Massachusetts—An Assessment with Recommendations. *Women and Criminal Justice* 2(2):117–143.

Young, Vernetta. 1986. Gender Expectations and Their Impact on Black Female Offenders and Victims. *Justice Quarterly* 3(September):305–327.

Chapter 1

The Criminal Law and Women

Natalie J. Sokoloff, Barbara Raffel Price, and Jeanne Flavin

ABSTRACT

Literature dealing with offenders—including that which focuses on women—frequently fails to take into account the historical, political, economic, and social events that influence the development of laws. These laws determine who will be defined as criminal and which forms of behavior are labeled as criminal offenses. Many changes in the law have occurred since the first and second editions of this book were published in 1982 and 1995. One far-reaching change has been mandatory sentencing, especially for drug offenses (laws that emerged during a politically conservative era). This sentencing change in the law helped quadruple the U.S. prison population in the last two decades of the twentieth century, leading to almost two million men and women in prison—a historic rise in the prison population and larger than any other industrial country in the world. Another change was the trend, until recently, of a downturn in crime rates in cities, suburbs, and rural areas. However, with state and national economies now in trouble, crime rates again appear to be going up. Still another change is the reduction in mandatory sentencing laws in some jurisdictions beginning in the late 1990s, especially for drug offenses. Tough-on-crime sentencing laws and the so-called war on drugs helped bring about a sevenfold increase of women in state and federal prisons between 1980 and 2000 (from 13,400 to 91,000), with an additional 70,000 women currently in jail. Today, many jurisdictions are eliminating some mandatory sentences because the costs of imprisonment have overburdened state budgets.

Laws are enacted norms. This textbook definition, while technically accurate, leaves much unsaid about the ways in which our laws produce both opportunity and oppression. The definition also downplays the ways in which the legal system is ever-changing, sometimes dramatically—as in landmark decisions such as *Brown v. Board of Education* (1954), which declared that "separate but equal" education is unconstitutional—and sometimes incrementally, as with the growing willingness to consider nonincarcerative sentences for drug offenders today. But although the political climate in which laws are made and enforced is never static, the key issues surrounding the law remain as important today as they were more than

20 years ago when this chapter was first written, namely: What is the law? Whose interests do the laws best reflect? How does the law impact women? And how does this impact differ by racial, ethnic, and class backgrounds and by sexual orientation?

The pursuit of criminal justice cannot be separated from the quest for social justice. Many of the problems that victims and survivors, offenders, and criminal justice workers face are neither unique nor intrinsic features of the criminal justice system; instead, they stem from broader realities of sexism, racism, homophobia, and capitalism in American life that are reflected in the organization and administration of the system itself. The future integrity of the criminal justice system depends as much on broad-based and systemic social change as on conscientious reform efforts within the criminal justice system. Feminist criminologists aim to build a more rational and equitable world through the development of feminist theory and research that is conscious of gender, race, and class. To do so requires not only that they scrutinize the theories, policies, and practices of the existing criminal justice system, but also that they identify and undertake strategies for social change.

Since the 1970s, people have debated whether, in the interests of fairness, the criminal justice system should treat women the same as men (in the name of gender neutrality or equality) or differently (given the real and "special" differences that exist in men's and women's social locations). Either approach, however, is limited in its ability to achieve justice. For one, both approaches assume a male norm. "Gender neutrality is thus simply the male standard, and the special protection rule is simply the female standard, but do not be deceived: masculinity, or maleness, is the referent for both" (MacKinnon 1991, 83). Further, both approaches reflect a preoccupation with sex differences while ignoring the role of power and domination. Whatever their similarities and differences, men and women are not equally powerful. Most of men's and women's differences can be traced to a society structured such that women tend to be subordinate and men dominant. Instead of trying to create a single standard (the sameness approach) or a double standard (the difference approach), we must address the inequality in power existing between—and within—the sexes.

The legal system seems a natural place to redress women's and men's unequal footing. The courts and the law, however, do not exist in a society that is neutral with regard to gender, race, nationality, class, age, sexual orientation, or physical ability. Consequently, the legal system frequently fails to acknowledge that "legal rights are sometimes overshadowed by social realities" (Chesney-Lind and Pollock 1995, 157). For instance, women have the legal right to be treated like any other assault victim and to have their battering partner arrested and punished. Yet many women may be prevented from taking full advantage of their legal rights by social, economic, and cultural barriers such as a distrust of the police, fear of reprisal or deportation, or lack of means to hire an attorney (see part 3, "Women Victims and Survivors of Crime").

One of the hardest challenges for scholars and students, practitioners and policymakers alike to overcome is "essentialism," that is, a tendency to assume a homogenous "women's experience" that can be described independent of other characteristics such as race, class, age, and sexual orientation. Essentialism occurs when a voice—typically a white, heterosexual, and socioeconomically privileged voice—claims to speak for everyone. As the chapters in this book illustrate, racial and ethnic minority women victims and survivors, offenders, and workers are not simply subjected to "more" disadvantage than white women; their oppression may be of a qualitatively different kind.

Source: This article was written expressly for inclusion in this text.

To effect realistic reforms that address the system's most serious weaknesses, people must understand *why* injustices occur throughout an institution premised on "justice for all," *how* the system itself perpetuates these injustices, and *what* needs to be done to maximize the system's strengths without sacrificing its ideals. This understanding requires an examination of the criminal law. Thus, we begin by providing a brief overview of offenders and victims. Next, we address basic questions such as: What is the law? What differences exist between criminal law and civil law in terms of their purpose and how they are applied? Third, we consider who makes the law and whose interests are reflected in and best served by those laws. Fourth, we ask: What assumptions about why crime exists are inherent in the criminal law? How might an understanding of the law benefit from consideration of critical and feminist perspectives? Fifth, how does the law impact women, both directly and indirectly? How is the impact of the law differentially felt among women in different social locations? Finally, we focus on the past and present efforts to effect social change via changing the criminal laws.

WHO ARE THE VICTIMS? WHO ARE THE CRIMINALS?

As illustrated by the growing amount of evidence that many men and women offenders have histories of victimization, *victim* and *criminal* are not mutually exclusive categories (Shavelson 2001). Women and men arrested for drugs, theft, prostitution, and assault frequently have had childhoods dominated by abuse and neglect. For many women, victimization continues into adolescence and adulthood in the form of battering and other violence (Richie 1996). Moreover, "many of the women in most need of services are ineligible for or unwelcome at treatment or shelter programs because they themselves break the law and 'misbehave' through drug use, streetwalking, or public order transgressions" (Klein 1997, 83).

Bearing in mind the blurry line separating so-called victims and offenders, it is nonetheless possible to provide a brief and broad overview of victims

and offenders. The likelihood of becoming a victim or an offender is not evenly distributed across race, gender, class, or combinations thereof. Although, overall, men are still more likely than women to be victims of violence, their victimization rates are getting closer, with some groups of men being less likely to be victimized than some groups of women. Simply asserting that men are more likely to be victimized masks the fact that for many crimes, black women's victimization rate is similar to or higher than that of white men's. Black men's and black women's personal victimization rates are 42.7 and 43.0 per 1,000 persons age 12 and older, respectively. By contrast, white men's estimated victimization rate is 38.1 and white women's victimization rate is 27.6 (Bureau of Justice Statistics 2001a). Regardless of race, two-thirds or more of women's violent victimizations are committed by someone they know (e.g., a friend or acquaintance, an intimate partner, or other relative), whereas most of men's violent victimizations are committed by strangers (Bureau of Justice Statistics 2001b).

Socioeconomic status also contributes to one's vulnerability to becoming a crime victim, with persons in poor households (i.e., incomes less than $7,500) experiencing higher rates of violence than those in all other income categories. Among whites, members of poor households were victims of violent crime and aggravated assaults at rates about three times that of persons in households earning more than $75,000 per year. Among black households, this pattern is less pronounced, with poor black households having victimization rates 20 percent higher than wealthy households (Bureau of Justice Statistics 2001a). Several studies have documented that the gender gap in wage earnings persists in spite of the fact that wages generally have been increasing. In fact, that gap in earnings has actually increased and is found at every level of education (Gender Gap in Earnings Persists 2002).

Poor men and women of color are particularly vulnerable not only to becoming victims of violence but also to being labeled a criminal and becoming involved in the criminal justice system as offenders. As this chapter later points out, the law, created in large part by and for the dominant class in society, defines which behavior is punishable and thereby determines which groups of people are most likely to be punished. In this society, people are commonly arrested for driving under the influence, drug use violations, assault, larceny theft, and a host of other, lesser offenses (Federal Bureau of Investigation, 2000). Those most likely to be arrested and convicted of these crimes are overwhelmingly male and disproportionately black. Men—who comprise around 48 percent of all adults—make up 83 percent of all persons convicted of felonies in state courts, and 90 percent of those convicted of violent offenses and weapons offenses. Blacks are overrepresented in all categories of felony convictions, making up 12 percent of the population but 44 percent of all state felony convictions, half of those convicted of weapons offenses, and 53 percent of all drug convictions (Durose and Levin 2001). Differential patterns of offending may account for some differences in arrests, conviction, or incarceration rates across gender, race, and class but do not explain why some offenses are ignored or defined as less serious; nor do they negate the existence of institutionalized or situational discrimination.

WHAT IS THE LAW?

The law defines which behavior will be punished, how it will be punished, and who will be punished. Law, in the broadest sense, is a set of formalized and codified rules that govern people's behavior and carry negative sanctions for violation. Laws are enacted norms; they are explicitly brought into being by legislation written by elected public officials and frequently generated by various interest groups. In part, laws are considered formal norms because they are written down. They are also considered formal norms because public agencies (police, courts, and corrections) have been created to enforce the laws (Coleman 1998).

Although the law defines what behavior is considered a crime, the definition of what is considered a crime is neither static nor value free but varies across space and time. Admittedly some morals—such as the value placed on human life—are generally held

to be so important that they warrant being backed up by the law. But, as the following discussion illustrates, laws also exist to serve the interests of the ruling class.

Criminal and Civil Law

Laws can be distinguished by the relationship between the wrongs they address and the remedies they provide. The two broadest categories of the law are *criminal law* and *civil law*. Both categories of law seek to control behavior and impose sanctions (Senna and Siegel 1998). In the U.S. legal system, criminal and civil proceedings are completely separate from one another, though some similar areas of legal action exist.

Civil law refers primarily to the body of law concerned with resolving private conflicts, particularly those involving private property, such as contracts, divorce, child support, and so on. Criminal law, on the other hand, responds to crimes perceived as being against the state rather than against an individual person or corporation—even though the act may have been committed against an individual. This differentiation exists because criminal law applies to acts that are considered so serious and important to the general welfare that the state has determined that it must take action in order to preserve and restore public order. Thus the state initiates the prosecution. In some cases the victim may bring a civil action against the defendant as well. For example, the crime of rape is a felony under criminal law in every jurisdiction, and the state prosecutes the accused in criminal court. A victim also can initiate an action in civil court, demanding compensation for injury suffered.

In *criminal law,* if someone harms someone else, the wrong is interpreted as a "social wrong," as a crime against society. As such, the state musters all its force and brings suit against the violator; that is, the force and legal machinery is deployed in the interest of the "victim." In civil law, however, the state interprets a violation as a private wrong against an individual, and therefore it is the individual's duty to seek redress. Because the violation is not regarded by the state as a social wrong, it is up to the individual to take his or her case to the courts. Typically, the remedy sought is compensation to the complainant for the harm done and possibly some punitive damages. In criminal law, the remedy sought is punishment for the harm done. Penalties range all the way from a monetary fine (which goes to the state or federal treasury instead of an individual) to probation, to a jail or prison sentence, and in some states, to death. Criminal law assumes that by announcing certain standards of conduct and attaching negative consequences to those who violate these standards, people will be motivated to conform.

In practical terms, criminal law means that if a person threatens someone on the street for money, or holds up a bank, or shoplifts, that person will be punished as a criminal if caught and convicted. On the other hand, if an automobile company makes a car with faulty parts and people are injured or killed, typically the company may be sued for civil but not criminal damages; that is, the company may be fined or reprimanded, but rarely is someone in the corporation seen as criminally responsible and incarcerated or otherwise punished.

The possibility of punishment does not overly intimidate corporations or white-collar offenders (Potter and Miller 2002). This lack of intimidation is due in part because corporations are never certain if they will be accused of any wrongdoing; in part because the stigmatization of being taken to court is absent or minimal compared to the loss of face that a person can experience if accused of a crime; and in part because the punishments, when applied, are weak.

For example, in 2000, Firestone was forced to recall 6.5 million tires after their Wilderness and ATX tires were linked to accidents that resulted in more than 100 deaths and 400 injuries in the United States. This incident is not the first time, however, that Firestone was called on the carpet for manufacturing unsafe tires. In 1978, Firestone executives sat before a House subcommittee defending themselves against hundreds of complaints that a radial tire, the Firestone 500, disintegrated on the rim and was linked to 41 deaths. Then (as in 2000), the senior officers did not admit to a defect in their conduct but instead cited user problems (like underinflation and poor maintenance practices) and weak federal tire testing laws. In the 1978 case, Firestone ended up paying a $500,000 civil penalty and was required to

recall 14.5 million tires, a punishment that did not deter them from continuing to manufacture unsafe tires (Skrzycki 2000).

The criminal law is most often used against individuals rather than corporations. What accounts for this difference? First, the criminal law was developed to apply to individual human behavior and motivation. This emphasis on individual accountability is embedded in U.S. culture. Another issue is that the requirement of *mens rea* (i.e., that for some crimes the state must demonstrate that an actor *intended* to behave in a manner defined as illegal) makes prosecuting a large corporation difficult if not impossible. Typically, intent must be found in an identifiable high officer of the corporation—hardly an easy charge to prove.[1]

Another reason criminal law is so rarely leveled against corporate or white-collar offenders is that these groups are able to exert considerable influence over the law to ensure that the law protects their own interests. The institution or corporation responsible for a violation may, at most, be ordered to compensate the victim, lose federal funds, or be subject to court orders directed toward compliance. Even when penalties might be imposed, the offender frequently risks incurring the penalty rather than change and conform to the law, given the limited burdens imposed by the law and its limited enforcement.

Some might argue that the criminal law is rarely applied to white-collar and corporate criminals because white-collar crime is less damaging than street crime. This assumption, however, is incorrect (see Potter and Miller 2002). White-collar crime is far more costly than street crime, and many of these crimes are very violent, killing and crippling far more people than all street crimes put together. In *The Rich Get Richer and the Poor Get Prison* (2001), author Jeffrey Reiman compiles a rough estimate of the cost of white-collar crime based on a variety of forms of individual and corporate white-collar crime, including Internet fraud, credit card fraud, insurance fraud and security thefts and frauds, consumer fraud, illegal competition, deceptive practices, bankruptcy fraud, bribery, kickbacks, and payoffs. He concludes that in 1997, white-collar crime cost $338 billion, more than 10,000 times the total amount stolen in all bank robberies and more than 20 times the amount taken in all thefts reported in the FBI's *Uniform Crime Reports* for that year (Reiman 2001, 121). In a separate analysis, Reiman concludes that three times as many deaths and seven times as many other harms are caused by occupational diseases and accidents as by crime (80–82). His figures include 6,218 fatal work injuries reported in 1997 alone.

A review of the distinction between criminal law and civil law makes it clear that the criminal law works against specific groups (typically the less powerful) whereas the civil law operates to the advantage of powerful individuals, interest groups, and corporations. The law works far less well to protect people from the harmful impact of corporations' often admittedly unintended acts (Coleman 1998; Reiman 2001).

In terms of the law's impact on women, a tendency exists to focus on acts done by individual women and defined in criminal codes, such as prostitution and shoplifting. There is little discussion, on the other hand, about systemic harms done *to* women but that are not defined as criminal. For example, in 1999, New York City obstetrician Dr. Allen Zarkin carved his initials into a woman's abdomen after delivering a baby by emergency cesarean section. The public was understandably outraged, and to some degree, this outrage was reflected in the punishment. Zarkin pleaded guilty to first-degree assault and was sentenced to probation in a deal that required him to give up the practice of medicine. The victim received a $1.75 million settlement. But the actions of the hospital are also blameworthy, though they received significantly less media attention.

After the victim reported the incident, Zarkin's privileges at the hospital were immediately suspended. But it took three weeks for the hospital to report Zarkin's suspension to the state, in an account that depicted Zarkin's actions toward a patient as "grossly inappropriate" without providing additional details or filing proper reports. Also, even though Zarkin was barred from the hospital, the chair of the hospital's obstetrics department met with him to talk about a possible alliance between the hospital and the clinic where Zarkin had been hired as med-

ical director. Because of the hospital's delay in reporting the full details of the incident, Zarkin's medical license was not suspended until four months after the incident. The hospital was eventually fined $14,000, and the court ordered it to improve its oversight of doctors.

For the record, this incident was the second time in two years that the supervision and disciplinary practices of the obstetrics department in that hospital had been the subject of a state health department investigation. In 1997, a young woman underwent a fairly common gynecological surgery at the hospital and then became comatose because an anesthesiologist failed to monitor her condition after the surgery. Apparently, her two surgeons used a new piece of equipment that neither of them was authorized or trained to operate; the device was run by the manufacturer's sales representative, who was trying to sell it to the hospital. When the device malfunctioned or was mishandled, the patient's uterus burst and she drowned. One of the surgeons was already on state probation for 20 complaints (Bazzi 2000; Grossman 1999; MacDonald 2000; Steinhauer 2000).

These cases illustrate not only individual-level or institutional-level problems in gynecological and obstetric care but also the ways in which medical economics influence medical care. Many other systemic harms to women receive similarly scant attention. Such harms include questionable medical procedures (e.g., unwarranted hysterectomies or cesarean sections), brown lung disease among female textile workers, and other workplace-related hazards. In the United States, the national rate of cesarean delivery has risen to nearly 25 percent, even though the World Health Organization reports that, globally, cesarean sections are warranted in only 5 percent and 15 percent of all births. Women working in male-dominated fields such as construction face hazards from personal protective equipment and clothing designed for average-sized men. Homicide is the leading cause of workplace injury and death for women, accounting for 40 percent of all workplace deaths among women workers.[2] Approximately 80 percent of the health care industry is comprised of women facing hazards that include musculoskeletal disorders and exposure to hazardous substances (NIOSH 2001). These serious, sometimes life-threatening abuses against women are not considered crimes against women by the law. In short, criminal law tends to be most often used as an enforcement strategy against street crime or organized crime; it does not focus on pervasive corporate crime or other actions that are harmful to large numbers of people, including women.

Statutory Law, Case Law, and Regulatory Law

Laws can be distinguished not only by the relationships between the wrongs they address and the remedies they offer but also by their sources, whether legislatures, courts, or administrative agencies. When legislative action is taken, typically at the state or federal level, the result is *statutory law*. The criminal codes are statutory law. There are 51 separate limited jurisdiction criminal codes in this country, one for each state and the District of Columbia, as well as a federal criminal code, which has national applicability and is the responsibility of Congress.

When court decisions and opinions are handed down, a body of precedents is developed that influences subsequent interpretations of the law; this body of law is known as *case law*. Case law, also known as constitutional law when decided at the highest level of the state or federal court system, is potentially useful in seeking remedies where women are concerned, including cases criminalizing women's bodies. For example, in March 2001, the Supreme Court ruled in *Ferguson v. City of Charleston* (186 F. 3d 469) that a public hospital cannot test pregnant women for drug use without their consent and turn the results over to police (Firestone 2001; Roth 2001).

The U.S. Constitution also provides for due process and equal protection of the law under the Fourteenth Amendment. The Supreme Court has used this equal protection clause to respond to women in prison who had challenged the conditions of their confinement, which included unequal

opportunities (for work, schooling, etc.) in comparison to their male counterparts in prison. Elsewhere, however, appellate courts have ruled that the differing sizes of the men's and women's inmate population can be taken into account in decisions about whether women and men inmates are "similarly situated," which may end the use of equal protection arguments to improve conditions in women's facilities (Collins and Collins 1996).

When government agencies are empowered by legislatures to write rules and regulations binding on specific persons and organizations, the result is *regulatory* and *administrative law*. The latter category includes the regulations that govern employment discrimination including sexual harassment and the activities of parole boards as well as the Internal Revenue Service; some of these regulations define crimes. For example, women are protected from sex discrimination (including sexual harassment) in the workplace under Title VII of the 1964 Civil Rights Act and in educational settings that receive federal funds under Title IX of the Education Amendments Act of 1972. Title VII and Title IX have improved women's and girls' opportunities by increasing women's acceptance into criminal justice occupations and participation in athletic programs. But both the Equal Employment Opportunity Commission and the Department of Education have been criticized for not assertively enforcing the regulations. In 1992, a Supreme Court ruling that victims could be awarded monetary compensatory and punitive damages in sex discrimination cases briefly gave Title IX some teeth. As a result, women successfully pursued cases against educational institutions for refusing to comply with Title IX. Unfortunately, in a 1998 decision, the Supreme Court eliminated this strategy (Dowling-Sendor 1998).

WHO MAKES THE LAW?

Proportionate representation of women (and other minority groups) among lawmakers is of concern for two reasons. One is the issue of fairness. "Descriptive" or "symbolic" representation of women and minority men creates at least the appearance of a system that reflects the will of "We the People." Second, it is important to achieve not only *symbolic* representation but also *substantive* representation because a diverse group of people bring different experiences and insights to the table that a homogenous group of people do not have (see, for example, Williams 1991). Ideas about the proper role of women in society are not static: women have fought hard throughout the course of history to better their conditions. Representation by white women and minority women and men in public offices helps call attention to problems that white male politicians may not be aware of or interested in addressing, including racial profiling, stalking, or hate crimes.[3]

How lawmakers consider and treat women is reflected in the legal system's consideration and treatment of women. In reality, however, much of the criminal law is written by state legislatures and the U.S. Congress, whose members are overwhelmingly wealthy, white, heterosexual men. The U.S. population is approximately 70 percent white and 49 percent male. Yet in the 107th Congress, the Senate (with 100 seats) was 97 percent white and 87 percent male. There were no openly gay, lesbian, or bisexual senators. The House (with 435 seats) was 86 percent white and 86 percent male, and only three representatives were openly gay or lesbian.[4] In 2002, California Democrat Nancy Pelosi became the most powerful woman ever in the House when she was elected the first woman minority whip (and next in line to be Speaker of the House). Yet six states have never sent a woman to Congress. The state legislatures have slightly more women, 22.4 percent nationally, but there is great variation in the percentages of women from state to state (National Foundation for Women Legislators 2001). Out of a half million elected officials in America in 2001, only around 200 were openly gay, lesbian, or bisexual (Phelps 2001).

The wealthy are overrepresented in the House, the Senate, and the presidential cabinet. When Jimmy Carter was president, the majority of senators owned at least a quarter million dollars in stocks and assets, and at least 22 of the 100 senators were millionaires (The Millionaire Contingent in Congress 1980). Under President Ronald Reagan's more open, "big business–favored" administration, four out of five of influential cabinet-level officials were at least half-millionaires, and more than half (ten of seventeen) were millionaires (Financial Reports Show 1981). When the first George Bush became president in 1989, his initial cabinet had six millionaires (*St. Louis Post Dispatch* 1993). President Bill Clinton's cabinet consisted of nine millionaires (Keil 1993). Not surprisingly, most members of George W. Bush's cabinet are also wealthy, and many hold stock in companies affected by federal actions. At least 12 of the group of people comprised of President Bush, Vice President Cheney, and the 14 members of the White House cabinet are millionaires. The wealthiest seven officials have combined assets of between $188 million and $632 million, quite possibly the wealthiest cabinet in history (Scherer 2001; see also Ivins 2001). Equally important, these public servants have very direct connections to corporate America. (For a brief listing of the ties of President George W. Bush's cabinet, as of this writing, see Ivins 2001.)

The impact of this economic domination is demonstrated in myriad ways. As this chapter is written, the Enron scandal continues to unfold. It appears that for years, Enron hid debts of $1 billion off the corporate books to keep Enron's stock price inflated. More than 4,000 Enron workers lost their jobs, and most lost their pensions when Enron declared bankruptcy on December 2, 2001—the biggest corporate collapse in U.S. history. Meanwhile, executives cashed in $600 million in stock equity and awarded the company's 500 highest paid employees $55 million just before declaring bankruptcy. How could this situation happen? Evidence strongly suggests that Enron's political payoffs contributed to federal regulators' and politicians' overlooking Enron's criminal activity and may even have resulted in politicians' actively looking after Enron's interests. For example, Wendy Gramm is an Enron board member as well as a member of Enron's audit committee. She is also married to Sen. Phil Gramm (R–Texas), who was chair of the powerful Senate Banking Committee before the Democrats regained control of the Senate. Consider too that Enron donated over $1.7 million to Republicans in the 2000 elections and was the largest contributor to George W. Bush's political career. Another $677,000 went to Democrats. Overall, Enron made contributions to 71 of 100 senators.[5] In 2000, Congress passed a law permitting Enron's energy derivative business to avoid government regulation.

Clearly, the concentration of corporate and banking power, with concomitant political power in relatively few hands, is a critical consideration in a realistic analysis of the criminal law. In short,

the law became the ultimate means by which the state secures the interests of the governing class. Laws institutionalize and legitimize property relations. It is through the legal system, then, that the state explicitly and forcefully protects the interests of the capitalist class. Crime control becomes the coercive means of checking threats to its economic arrangements . . . The state did not appear as a third party in the conflict between classes [as pluralists have argued], but arose to protect and promote the interests of the dominant economic class, which owns and controls the means of production. (Quinney 1975, 290)

In sum, although some individuals who participate in making the laws have come from the poor and working classes and are racial and ethnic minority men and women or white women, the system of lawmaking is controlled by those with vested interests in private property and directed toward the protection of individual and corporate wealth or those who represent those interests. In the legal system in particular, women have long sought changes that would improve their lives. Nonetheless, members of the legal system are for the most part men. Thus, even if many laws were not sexist, the fact that those who make the laws (federal and state legislators, government administrators, and judges) and those who enforce the laws (police, lawyers, probation and parole officers) are disproportionately men affects in major ways how women are thought of and treated by the legal system. Increasing the number of women from a variety of racial, ethnic, and class backgrounds in positions of recognition and power is of crucial importance but does not guarantee the needed changes in the underlying structures of power in society. As Kopkind (1992, 123) has argued, although since the 1990s we have seen increasing numbers of women political candidates, "real feminization has hardly begun. Properly understood, that entails radical changes in the patriarchal relations, affecting class, race, the military establishment and the corporate economy [itself]." Yet despite the alliance between the wealthy business class and the legal system, the law is not static. As we discuss at the end of this chapter, many individuals who believe the ruling elite to be indifferent to or in conflict with their interests have organized to challenge the system.

WHAT ASSUMPTIONS UNDERLIE THE CRIMINAL LAW?

The law reflects not only the biases and interests of the lawmakers but also larger assumptions about why crime exists. The law and the penalties prescribed for violations of the criminal law reflect particular assumptions of crime causation. This section summarizes two of the dominant criminological paradigms, the classical and positivist schools. We then contrast these perspectives with critical and feminist approaches to crime and the criminal law.

Classical and Positivist Criminology

The two major bodies of early criminological theory were classicism and positivism: a debate between individual free will or social determinism, between punishment that fits the crime or punishment that fits the criminal, in fact, between punishment and rehabilitation of the criminal. Contemporary criminology is largely one of triumph of positivism over classicism; even neoclassical criminology—which emerged as a compromise solution to the extremes—has developed in positivist terms (Beirne and Messerschmidt 1991). Although criminological theoretical work tends to give positivism more weight, many crime policies continue to be based on the individual rational calculus of classical criminology.

The classical approach holds that people have free will, are responsible for their acts, and generally will be rational in their behavior, thus avoiding punishment where foreseeable by abiding by the law.

Accordingly, law clearly states both penalties and crimes (supposedly making punishment severe enough to encourage right behavior), anticipating the general compliance of the public. The classical school, therefore, fits penalties to crimes and considers punishment a way to deter or prevent certain behavior. Law must be certain and punishment must be swift, according to the classical school, so that people will be clear about the relationship between their acts and punishment. The trend to incarcerate women for nonviolent drug offenses, often with lengthy sentences, is an example of classical theory in action. The emphasis on deterrence, however, discounts the role that addiction, mental illness, or desperation may play in one's ability to "choose" lawful behavior.

The positivist perspective on crime causation shapes much of modern criminal law. Positivists view criminal behavior as determined by measurable biological factors (e.g., brain characteristics, body structure, specific physical features) and social factors (e.g., the social environment, social forces such as poverty and racism, and institutions such as family, religion, and school). An early positivist explanation of women who come into conflict with the law would state that these women are victims of their own unique biology, which made them either irrational or irresponsible or both (see Klein 1995). A contemporary positivist perspective views the purpose of punishment to be rehabilitation; in theory, medical models do not distinguish between punishment and treatment. Positivists would have the law focus on the offender's resocialization—psychological help or job training—whatever is needed to turn the offender into a law-abiding citizen. Although the members of the early positivist school downplayed the role of free will, contemporary positivists nonetheless consider criminals legally and socially responsible for their acts (Cohn 1976).

Critical and Feminist Criminology

Critical Criminology   Most contemporary criminologists recognize that the classical perspective—because it assumes that all people are deterred by similar consequences and that deterrence figures prominently in people's decision to commit a crime while denying that social forces play a role in people's behavior—is deeply flawed. Although the positivist model may hold more appeal, with its emphasis on individual rehabilitation and treatment, it shares with classical criminology the shortcoming of failing to recognize the ways in which definitions of crime are socially constructed. Furthermore, what good does it do to provide a person with job skills if high unemployment rates or discrimination prevent that person from getting a job using those skills? Who decides into what role a person should be "resocialized"? For example, does teaching women to cut hair, sew, or cook really help them, or does it reinforce notions of "appropriate" roles for women and prepare them for low-wage, undervalued work?

In contrast to classical and positivist criminological perspectives, which accept the confines of the existing social system, critical perspectives (including radical, Marxist, and many feminist perspectives) strive to present a new vision of equality and social justice (Rafter and Heidensohn 1995). Critical theorists focus on ruling-class control of all major institutions (e.g., business, legislatures, courts) and the social relations between the rich and powerful and the working class and poor. Critical perspectives attribute much crime to injustices in the organization and production of criminal law. Those in power create the legal code—in their own interest—and thereby define some acts as serious crimes while ignoring or reducing others to violations of administrative regulations.

Although critical criminology recognizes that street crime is a serious matter to be handled by the law, critical criminologists are concerned with how the political economic system itself promotes the conditions (poverty, unemployment, etc.) that cause typical street criminal behavior (Platt 1974; Beirne and Messerschmidt 1991). At the same time, critical criminology emphasizes that the system largely ignores the economic and social exploitation of workers, minorities, and poor people by factory owners, big business, government officials, and others in power. Critical criminology calls for a transformation of the entire political economic system. This approach argues for changing the criminal justice and legal systems by changing the underlying social relations between dominant and subordinate groups in society, particularly between the capitalist class and the working class.

The critical perspective, which emerged in the late 1960s and 1970s, basically reduced the issues of race and gender to the issues of economics and class. Economic and political power is correlated with race and gender. A combination of the factors of gender, race, and class location leads to a situation in which wealthy white men will be relatively most advantaged within the social structure (including the criminal justice system) whereas poor minority women will be most disadvantaged. Over time, however, the almost exclusive focus on class broadened to give greater importance to race and gender. More criminologists recognize that gender and race are not just correlates of class but also are structuring forces that affect how people act and how others respond to a person's actions, that determine who has the power to define and label certain actions as "criminal" or "deviant," and that influence how law and law enforcement are organized to control behavior (Lynch 1996, 4–5).

Feminist Criminology Feminist thought embraces a variety of perspectives, including Marxist, socialist, critical, women of color, and postmodern.[6] Much, but not all, of feminist theorizing could also be categorized as "critical." All feminist theories encompass a common view of the importance of understanding women's oppression, and each argues for a different set of strategies for social change based on its analysis of the causes of that oppression. *Liberal feminists* focus on discrimination and consider legal and customary restraints to be the main barriers to women getting their piece of the pie. Thus, the goal is to ensure that men and women have equal civil rights and economic opportunities. *Critical feminists* differ in the emphasis they place on economic, biological, racial, and sexual sources of oppression (or some combination thereof). Unlike liberal feminists, critical feminists do not seek to reform the existing system but rather aim to fundamentally restructure private and public life and to recast relations be-

tween women and men in political terms. Critical feminists object to liberal approaches not only for failing to question the existing system but also for wanting equality in it. As Colette Price framed the issue 25 years ago, " 'Do we really want equality with men in this nasty competitive capitalist system?' 'Do we want to be equally exploited with men?' 'Do we want a piece of the pie or a whole different pie?' " (Redstockings 1978, 94).

Critical race theory developed in the late 1970s through the efforts of scholars such as Derrick Bell and Alan Freeman who were discontent with the slow pace of achieving racial justice (see, for example, Delgado 1995). Building on critical sociology, neo-Marxism, and postmodern approaches, critical race theorists assume that racism is an ordinary, ingrained aspect of American society that cannot be readily remedied by law. The racism that permeates society is part of a socially constructed reality that exists to promote the interests of elite groups. Critical race theorists, then, aim not only to expose the ways in which existing arrangements support racism but also to construct alternative social realities. Relatedly, *critical white studies* prompt whites and nonwhites alike to consider the legacy of whiteness and to ask questions such as: How do whites benefit from membership in the dominant race? How does our culture construct whiteness, blackness, brownness, and so on such that they are not neutral descriptors but laden with meaning, value, and status? (see, for example, Delgado and Stefancic 1997). *Critical race feminism* emerged from critical race theory (see, for example, Wing 1997). Specifically, critical race feminists have objected both to feminist approaches that presume that white middle-class women's experiences are representative of all women's experiences and to critical race scholarship that presumes that minority women's experiences are the same as their minority male counterparts (Crenshaw 1991; Hill Collins 1998; Williams 1991).

What a person perceives as the source of the problem naturally influences that person's ideas about what ought to be done. The case of pregnant women who use cocaine illustrates how theory influences practice in the criminal justice system. The classical approach employed in several jurisdictions in the late 1980s and early 1990s resulted in many women being incarcerated in an attempt to deter other women from using drugs during pregnancy. Persons from a more positivist-oriented perspective advocate that women be forced to enter drug treatment and attend courses on prenatal nutrition and parenting. Both orientations erroneously assume women who use drugs are unwilling (at worst) or incapable (at best) of exerting a positive effect over their pregnancy or their children (Flavin 2002). By contrast, feminists have highlighted the fact that punitive measures overwhelmingly and disproportionately have been leveled against poor women, especially women of color. Many feminists have called for responding to maternal drug use as a public health issue rather than a criminal justice concern. Instead of resorting to punishment, advocates call for the increased availability of treatment on demand that addresses the diverse factors contributing to women's substance use and abuse (e.g., histories of violent victimization, poverty, mental illness), for adequate health care for *all* women, and for a view of pregnant women who use drugs as partners in the promotion of a healthy pregnancy rather than as adversaries.

HOW DOES THE LAW IMPACT WOMEN?

Historically, all property of a marriage belonged to the husband. Until the middle of the nineteenth century, married women had no separate legal identity; rather, their identity was merged with their husband's. In practical terms women were often considered as property under the law, first of their fathers and then of their husbands. The concept of *mens rea* mentioned earlier is applicable here because the law often required the state to prove that a person intended to do an act before it could prosecute. Women were once viewed legally as not being mentally capable of *intending* to do something; they were thought to be too childlike. On this basis, they were exempted from the penalties that many laws imposed. This "chivalrous" attitude meant that some women—most notably white, middle-class and upper-class

women—received special treatment, but only when it suited men and always at the expense of women's independence. Women from poor, working-class, slave, and immigrant origins were never afforded such "chivalrous protections" (Klein and Kress 1976).

It was not until the twentieth century that women acquired independent legal rights in western societies. In the United States this effectively occurred in 1971 when the Supreme Court ruled in *Reed v. Reed* (404 U.S. 71; 92 S. Ct. 251; 30 L. Ed. 2d 225) that women were to be interpreted as persons with equal protection under the Fourteenth Amendment of the Constitution. Until 1971, courts considered a woman's rights and responsibilities to be determined by her status as wife and mother (Freeman 1989).

For centuries, men were not held accountable for their crimes against women. The failure to recognize domestic violence as criminal behavior both sprang from and was reinforced by the patriarchal idea that "a man's home is his castle." Only since the 1970s has society begun to consider this behavior criminal. As a result, "private matters" such as acquaintance rape, marital rape, and stalking are increasingly likely to be recognized as crimes.

Women in the United States have always been defined in the law primarily by their patriarchal relation to the home, and this definition continues to influence how women victims are treated in the larger society. For example, historically, because women were considered their husbands' common-law property, men could not be prosecuted for raping their spouses. In 1976, Nebraska became the first state to enact a law criminalizing marital rape. Over a quarter of a century later, it is now against the law in all 50 states for a woman's husband to rape her. But such figures paint an overly positive picture of the situation. Thirty-two states continue to exempt spouses accused of rape from prosecution under certain circumstances, for example, if the couple lives together or if the victim is "only" threatened but not physically harmed (Rein 2002).

Law enforcement often reflects a preoccupation with women's reproductive capacities. Since the 1980s, more than 200 women (mainly poor women of color) in more than 30 states have been arrested and charged for their alleged drug use or other actions during pregnancy (Swift 2000; CRLP 1996, 2000). In some of these cases, charges were dropped before trial, but in many others, women were pressured into pleading guilty or accepting plea bargains. Many—though not all—of these convictions eventually were overturned. The aforementioned *Ferguson* decision by the Supreme Court, which prevented public hospitals from performing drug tests on pregnant women without their consent, was largely informed by amicus briefs submitted by dozens of organizations (including the American Medical Association and the American Public Health Association) who pointed out that the harms associated with maternal cocaine use were not nearly as severe or inevitable as early medical and media reports had indicated (see Frank et al. 2001). Furthermore, not only does prosecution typically occur late in the pregnancy or after delivery (making it of dubious value in promoting a healthy pregnancy over the course of nine months), but it may also deter women from seeking prenatal care and drug treatment for fear of being prosecuted, and it overlooks the shortage of drug treatment for pregnant women or women who need child care.

Two more recent measures appear to be backdoor efforts to establish fetal personhood under the law (Chavkin 2001; Roth 2001). The Unborn Victims of Violence Act, passed by the House on April 26, 2000, makes it a federal crime to injure or kill the fetus of a pregnant woman (exempting abortion). Similarly, in 2001, the Bush administration proposed to extend Child Health Plus Program (CHIP) coverage for prenatal care on behalf of the fetus. It is impossible to hurt a fetus without somehow inflicting damage on the woman who carries it, and so too is it impossible for a fetus to transport itself to a doctor's visit. These measures thus beg the question of why such legislation focuses on the fetus rather than extending prenatal care coverage to pregnant woman or increasing the penalties for assaulting pregnant women.

Women are also impacted indirectly by laws and practices that disproportionately affect men. For example, men's ability to offer emotional and practical support to their families is severely curtailed when they are incarcerated, resulting in more women bearing sole responsibility for the well-being of their households. As corrections and enforcement budgets increase, fewer government funds are available to support low-income women and their children. Women relatives frequently assume responsibility for the children of incarcerated men and women at considerable emotional, financial, and physical expense to themselves (Zucchino 1997). Social service jobs that are disproportionately staffed by women may be cut (Danner 1998).

In sum, although today women increasingly are seen as equal before the law, socially entrenched biases continue to pose barriers to full recognition of women's rights as human beings. As later chapters illustrate, incarcerated women continue to be dehumanized and devalued in ways that reflect the multiple and overlapping dimensions of sexism and racism (see part 2, "Women and Prison"). Women who are immigrants, racial or ethnic minorities, in same-sex relationships, or dating or married to police officers may face additional obstacles in their attempts to access the justice system as a means to escape violence or exploitation (see part 3, "Women Victims and Survivors of Crime").

CAN THE CRIMINAL JUSTICE SYSTEM BE REFORMED?

Criminal laws that are explicitly sexually discriminatory have gradually been modified or eliminated at the state and federal levels, largely because of the legacy of the U.S. civil rights and women's movements in the mid-twentieth century. The civil rights movement grew out of the struggle by blacks to overcome the laws and customs that segregated blacks from whites, thereby preventing blacks from gaining economic and political equality. The dominant force in the black liberation movement between the mid-1950s and mid-1960s was the civil rights struggle. Through marches, demonstrations, sit-ins, boycotts, speeches, political lobbying, community organizing, and oftentimes massive arrests and beatings, two major pieces of legislation—the Civil Rights Act of 1964 and the Voting Rights Act of 1965—gave black women and men the legal tools to fight for their civil rights. Although blacks have made some important strides in access to schools and employment, the underlying economic and political structure of U.S. society continues to be organized on the basis of race, class, and gender inequality. Black women have made considerable gains in education and the workplace, but they continue to be disproportionately overrepresented in the criminal justice system and among the poor. Currently, too, more young black men are under the control of the criminal justice system than are enrolled in four-year colleges (Haney and Zimbardo 1998).

The women's movement of the 1960s modeled many of its tactics on those developed by the civil rights movement of the 1950s. Ironically, the wording that outlawed discrimination against women was inserted by conservative members of Congress at the last minute in an attempt to defeat Title VII of the Civil Rights Act of 1964. Although the attempt ultimately backfired, women had so little political power at that time that the Equal Employment Opportunity Commission established to enforce Title VII ignored the provision on gender (Freeman 1989). Soon after, the women's movement became highly visible and active through several national organizations, the National Organization for Women being the largest and most influential. The subsequent successes of the women's movement include decreasing discriminatory laws and practices in the public and private sectors, and educating the public about the harmful effects of gender discrimination. Pressure on Congress has resulted in federal legislation prohibiting gender discrimination in employment, education, credit, insurance, taxes, pensions, and even in some areas of the military. However, the enforcement of these laws is seriously jeopardized in cities and regions across the country because of restricted public budgets and, despite more liberal trends in the 1990s, the persistence into the twenty-first century of powerful conservative decision makers. Their political strength has resulted in reduced federal protection in civil rights laws generally and a movement toward severely weakening affirmative ac-

tion. Despite uneven progress, the struggle to make the criminal justice system consistent with social justice ideals continues. The remainder of this section briefly discusses activism in three areas: prison reform, drug policy reform, and reproductive rights.

Prison Reform and Alternatives to Incarceration

The prisoners' rights movement of the 1960s began to splinter in the 1970s when some of the individual leaders of the movement ran afoul of the law. As people became disillusioned, they left the movement. In the absence of strong, vocal resistance, the prison system expanded dramatically. Concerned with this development, many women activists organized to protest this expansion and to advocate for alternatives to incarceration. In 1998, Angela Y. Davis (a contributor to this volume) and 30 others organized a conference that was attended by an unanticipated 3,500 participants. Since then, prison activists, many if not most of whom are women, have reached out to diverse groups committed to new ways of thinking about prisons, prisoners, and community (Chevigny 2000).

Organizations large and small, such as the American Civil Liberties Union, Amnesty International, Critical Resistance, Families Against Mandatory Minimums, Legal Services for Prisoners with Children, and state "prison moratorium" projects, have undertaken reform efforts to address problems that include the prison industrial complex (in which private business and government intertwine to emphasize profit and social control rather than public safety and crime prevention); prisoner health care and medical neglect (including obstetrical and gynecological care for women); control units and permanent lockdowns (which frequently feature long-term solitary confinement and sensory deprivation); and the death penalty. Many efforts are also undertaken to expand alternatives to incarceration (including models based on restorative justice principles, mediation, and other nonincarcerative sanctions). Perhaps this society eventually will see a day when alternatives to incarceration are not alternatives at all, when incarceration returns to being a punishment of last resort rather than a first response.

Drug Policy Reform

The rising incarceration rates of the 1990s can be attributed in large part to the so-called war on drugs. Drug law enforcement does not seem to correlate with patterns of offending, because blacks are arrested and confined in numbers way out of line with their use or sale of drugs (Tonry 1995, 49). The devastating impact of the war on drugs and the attendant incarceration binge on the social, political, and economic well-being of women and minority men has been well documented (see Barak, Flavin, and Leighton 2001).

In the 1980s and 1990s, many organizations formed to reverse this destructive trend. Organizations such as the Drug Policy Alliance, the National Organization for the Reform of Marijuana Laws, and Common Sense for Drug Policy have joined forces with prison reform advocates and feminist organizations. Together they seek to decriminalize drug use (including reducing or eliminating prison terms for drug possession); expand and improve drug treatment; legalize medical marijuana; liberalize sterile syringe access and other forms of harm reduction; increase funding for drug prevention; refocus federal resources onto large-scale drug smugglers, suppliers, and distributors rather than street-level dealers; and eliminate sentencing disparities indicative of institutionalized racism.

Reproductive Rights

The war on drugs has also been a war against women, particularly poor women who are racial or ethnic minorities. Although prosecution of pregnant women for drug use has slowed since the 1990s, other threats to women's reproductive rights remain. Black women have been particularly vulnerable to being defined as deviant in part because their largely unmarried status animates fears about the dysfunctionality of the black family (Flavin 2001; Fineman 1995; Humphries 1999). Similarly, the shifting welfare policy emphasis on work requirements instead of

suitable home environments suggests that, increasingly, in order for poor women to be considered "good mothers" they must be employed (Mullins 2000). Other examples of increasing control over women's ability to reproduce or rear children include welfare reform's family caps or child exclusion policies, the campaign to prescribe contraceptive implants to poor women, the persistent erosion of public assistance recipients' privacy rights, the expedition of parental termination rights (as when a mother's incarceration is deemed "abandonment"), and the Temporary Assistance to Needy Families (TANF) ban preventing persons convicted of nonviolent drug felonies from receiving TANF or food stamps for the rest of their lives (Roberts 1996).

Organizations like the Center for Reproductive Law and Policy, EMILY's List, the Feminist Majority, National Abortion and Reproductive Rights Action League, National Advocates for Pregnant Women, National Organization for Women, and Planned Parenthood, along with civil rights organizations such as the American Civil Liberties Union, are concerned about such legislation and other efforts to erode a woman's reproductive rights while reducing her value as a human being (Chavkin 2001). Since the 1970s, such organizations have mobilized not only to ensure that all women have access to safe and legal abortion but also to secure women's human and civil rights (including the right to privacy) and to ensure women's access to quality reproductive health care and information, effective contraceptive options, and safe and legal abortion.

CONCLUSION

"Laws are enacted norms." Consistent with this textbook definition, this chapter has introduced readers to much "standard" information about the law, for example, the difference between civil and criminal law, and positivist and classical approaches to crime. But to this standard definition, we add that "laws are also social constructs" and thus are prone to the same biases and assumptions that are found throughout society. Yes, laws are enacted norms, but not everyone's norms are given the same consideration.

Many people cling to a view of the law as neutral, objective, or value free, preferring to attribute different experiences "under the law" to the differences of individuals. Many mainstream criminologists continue to focus on developing different coping mechanisms for women to better function in the existing social structures of society rather than challenging the structures themselves. Clearly, not all women share the same interests, problems, goals, or life experiences, but the relationship between gender and the law cannot be understood apart from the systems of domination and subordination of race, ethnicity, class, and homophobia. Do all victims have their victimization acknowledged by the law? Do all offenders face the same odds of being identified and treated as such by the criminal justice system? Are all harmful actions likely to be defined as criminal and punished? Does everyone have the opportunity to engage the system successfully on their own behalf? Ample evidence suggests that the answer to each of these questions is a resounding "No."

"Justice for all" is unquestionably a worthy and rewarding pursuit, as numerous social movements and reform efforts have demonstrated. One should not, however, confuse the ideal with the current reality. We hope that the chapters in this book will compel all readers to consider how to achieve a more equitable system of opportunities and rewards for all people. We encourage readers to examine and challenge the social structures that not only undergird every aspect of society but also undermine the well-being of millions of society's members. It is only through an understanding of the large-scale social forces that real change will occur for all women, men, and children in this society.

DISCUSSION QUESTIONS

1. According to Sokoloff, Price, and Flavin, who (i.e., which groups in society) makes laws? In whose interest? Who is more likely to be victimized? Who is more likely to become a criminal? Why?

2. According to Sokoloff, Price, and Flavin, law is not static; rather, it is constantly in the making and is influenced greatly by those in power. Discuss the implications of this premise for women in the United States. How does this process vary across race and ethnicity, class, and sexual orientation?

3. What assumptions about crime are inherent in the law? How do these assumptions advantage and disadvantage women? Give an example in each case.

4. Define criminal and civil law. According to Sokoloff, Price, and Flavin, why is this distinction important? Give an example of how each type of law impacts specifically on women.

5. What reforms are needed from a feminist, antiracist perspective to bring about meaningful social change for men and women defined as criminal in the United States?

NOTES

1. The criminal law, however, does recognize that harms committed with other states of mind are also criminal. For example, the modern penal code's definition of murder includes any death caused by "extreme indifference to human life." Such language potentially could cover situations in which employers intentionally violated health and safety regulations (Frank 1988, 18).

2. Women are also the victims in almost two-thirds of the nonfatal workplace assaults. Seventy percent of these assaults are directed at women employed in service occupations, such as health care, while 20 percent occur in retail locations (NIOSH 2001).

3. Of course, a woman or a minority man who holds public office is not guaranteed to possess a more inclusive or sensitive orientation to the law any more than a wealthy, heterosexual,

white man is precluded from demonstrating such inclusiveness.

4. Of the 435 seats in the House, 36 were held by blacks, 19 by Hispanics, and 4 by Asians. Of the 100 seats in the Senate, 2 were held by Asians, and none were held by blacks or Hispanics.

5. This information can be found in mainstream and radical publications alike. See Duffy and Dickerson (2002), Pizzo (2002), and Sustar (2002).

6. The discussion of feminist criminology presented here relies heavily on material in *Class, Race, Gender, and Crime: The Social Realities of Justice in America* (Barak, Flavin, and Leighton 2001).

REFERENCES

Barak, Gregg, Jeanne M. Flavin, and Paul S. Leighton. 2001. *Class, Race, Gender, and Crime: Social Realities of Justice in America.* Los Angeles, CA: Roxbury.

Bazzi, Mohamad. 2000. Medical Oversight? Clinic's Hiring of "Dr. Zorro" Raises Monitoring Concerns. *Newsday,* May 14, A6.

Beirne, Piers, and James Messerschmidt. 1991. *Criminology.* San Diego: Harcourt Brace Jovanovich.

Bureau of Justice Statistics. 2001a. *Criminal Victimization in the United States: 1999 Statistical Tables.* NCJ-184938. Available at www.ojp.usdoj.gov/bjs/abstract/cvusst.htm.

———. 2001b. *Violent Victimization and Race, 1993–98.* Special Report. NCJ-176354, p. 10, table 13. Washington DC: U.S. Department of Justice.

CRLP (Center for Reproductive Law and Policy). 1996. *In the Courts: Decisions Involving Penalties Imposed Against Women for Their Conduct during Pregnancy.* New York: CRLP. February.

———. 2000. *Punishing Women for their Behavior during Pregnancy.* New York: CRLP. September.

Chavkin, Wendy. 2001. Sex, Lies, and Silence: Reproductive Health in a Hostile Environment. *American Journal of Public Health* 91(11):1739–41.

Chesney-Lind, Meda, and Joycelyn M. Pollock. 1995. Women's Prisons: Equality with a Vengeance. In *Women, Law, and Social Control,* eds. Alida V. Merlo and Joycelyn M. Pollack, 155–75. Needham Heights, MA: Allyn and Bacon.

Chevigny, Bell Gale. 2000. Prison Activists Come of Age. *The Nation* 271(4):27–30.

Cohn, Alvin. 1976. *Crime and Justice Administration.* Philadelphia: J. B. Lippincott.

Coleman, James William. 1998. *The Criminal Elite: The Sociology of White Collar Crime.* New York: St. Martin's.

Collins, William C., and Andrew W. Collins. 1996. *Women in Jail: Legal Issues.* Washington, DC: National Institute of Corrections.

Crenshaw, Kimberle. 1991. Mapping the Margins: Intersectionality, Identity Politics, and Violence against Women of Color. *Stanford Law Review* 43:1258–99.

Danner, Mona J. E. 1998. Three Strikes and It's Women Who Are Out: The Hidden Consequences for Women of Criminal Justice Policy Reforms. In *Crime Control and Women,* ed. Susan L. Miller, 1–14. Thousand Oaks, CA: Sage.

Delgado, Richard, ed. 1995. *Critical Race Theory: The Cutting Edge.* Philadelphia: Temple University.

Delgado, Richard, and Jean Stefancic. 1997. *Critical White Studies: Looking Behind the Mirror.* Philadelphia: Temple University.

Dowling-Sendor, Benjamin. 1998. When Teachers Harass Students. *The American School Board Journal,* October.

Duffy, Michael, and John F. Dickerson. 2002. Enron Spoils the Party. *Time.* 159(5):18–25.

Durose, Matthew R., and David J. Levin. 2001. *Felony Sentences in State Courts, 1998.* Washington, DC: Bureau of Justice Statistics.

Federal Bureau of Investigation. 2000. *Crime in the United States, 1999.* Washington, DC: GPO.

Financial Reports Show That Ten Members of Cabinet Are Worth $1 Million or More. 1981. *The New York Times,* January 26; 24.

Fineman, Martha Albertson. 1995. *The Neutered Mother, the Sexual Family and other Twentieth Century Tragedies.* New York: Routledge.

Firestone, David. 2001. Woman is Convicted of Killing Her Fetus by Smoking Cocaine. *The New York Times,* May 18, A12.

Flavin, Jeanne. 2002. A Glass Half Full?: Harm Reduction among Pregnant Women Who Use Cocaine. *Journal of Drug Issues,* 32(3):973–98.

Flavin, Jeanne. 2001. Of Punishment and Parenthood: Family Based Social Control and the Sentencing of Black Drug Offenders. *Gender and Society* 15(4): 611–33.

Frank, Nancy. 1988. Unintended Murder and Corporate Risk-Taking: Defining the Concept of Justifiability. *Journal of Criminal Justice* 16:17–24.

Frank, Deborah A., Marilyn Augustyn, Wanda Grant Knight, Tripler Pell, and Barry Zuckerman. 2001. Growth, Development, and Behavior in Early Childhood Following Prenatal Cocaine Exposure. *Journal of the American Medical Association* 285(12):1613–25.

Freeman, Jo. 1989. *The Politics of Women's Liberation: A Case Study of an Emerging Social Movement and its Relation to the Policy Process.* New York: David McKay.

Gender Gap in Earnings Persists Despite Wage Increases with Education. 2002. Women and Policing Newswire. Available at www.womenandpolicing.org.

Grossman, Edward. 1999. God's Work. *The American Spectator* 32(2):42–45.

Haney, Craig, and Philip Zimbardo. 1998. The Past and Future of U.S. Prison Policy: Twenty Five Years after the Stanford Prison Experiment. *American Psychologist* 53(7):709–27.

Hill Collins, Patricia. 1998. Fighting Words: Black Women and the Search for Justice. Minneapolis: University of Minnesota.

Humphries, Drew. 1999. *Crack Mothers: Pregnancy, Drugs, and the Media.* Columbus: Ohio State University.

Ivins, Molly. 2001. This Cabinet is Full of Corporate America. February 10. Available from portside@yahoogroups.net.

Keil, Richard. 1993. Clinton Has More Millionaire Aides than Reagan or Bush. Associated Press, January 27.

Klein, Dorie. 1997. An Agenda for Reading and Writing about Women, Crime, and Justice. *Social Pathology* 3(2):81–91.

———. 1995. The Etiology of Female Crime: A Review of the Literature. In *The Criminal Justice System and Women,* 2d ed., ed. Barbara Raffel Price and Natalie J. Sokoloff, 30–53. New York: McGraw-Hill.

Klein, Dorie, and June Kress. 1976. Any Woman's Blues: A Critical Overview of Women, Crime, and the Criminal Justice System, *Crime and Social Justice* 5(spring/summer): 34–49.

Kopkind, Andrew. 1992. Sisters Start Doing It for Themselves. *The Nation* August 3–10, 121, 123, 124.

Lynch, Michael J. 1996. Class, Race, Gender, and Criminology: Structured Choices and the Life Course. In *Race, Gender, and Class in Criminology,* ed. Martin D. Schwartz and Dragan Milovanovic, 3–28. New York: Garland.

MacDonald, John A. 2000. Should Data on Troubled Doctors Be Available to Public? *Hartford Courant,* March 2, A10.

MacKinnon, Catharine A. 1991. Difference and Dominance: On Sex Discrimination [1984]. In *Feminist Legal Theory,* ed. Katharine T. Bartlett and Rosanne Kennedy, 81–94. Boulder, CO: Westview.

The Millionaire Contingent in Congress. 1980. *U.S. News and World Report* March 17, 4.

Mullins, Kerry. 2000. Celibacy, Matrimony, or Unchastity? Race and Gender and the Welfare System. Ph.D. diss. American University, Washington, DC.

National Foundation for Women Legislators. 2001. Available at www.womenlegislators.org.

NIOSH (National Institute for Occupational Safety and Health). 2001. *Women's Safety and Health Issues at Work.* Washington, DC: U.S. Department of Health and Human Services, Public Health Service, Centers for Disease Control and Prevention, National Institute for Occupational Safety and Health. Publication No. 2001-123.

Phelps, David. 2001. Out to Win. Available at www.advocate.com.

Pizzo, Stephen. 2002. George and Dick's Amazing Corporate Misadventures. Available at www.corpwatch.org/issues/PRT.jsp?articleid=2988.

Platt, Tony. 1974. Prospects for a Radical Criminology in the United States. *Crime and Social Justice* 1(spring/summer).

Potter, Gary, and Karen Miller. 2002. Thinking about White Collar Crime. In *Controversies in White Collar Crime,* ed. Gary W. Potter, 1–36. Cincinnati, OH: Anderson.

Quinney, Richard. 1975. *Class, State, and Crime: On the Theory and Practice of Criminal Justice.* New York: Longman.

Rafter, Nicole Hahn, and Frances Heidensohn, eds. 1995. *International Feminist Perspectives in Criminology: Engendering a Discipline. Buckingham.* U.K.: Open University.

Redstockings, Inc. 1978. *Feminist Revolution.* New York: Random House.

Reiman, Jeffrey. 2001. *The Rich Get Richer and the Poor Get Prison: Ideology, Class, and Criminal Justice,* 6th ed. Boston: Allyn and Bacon.

Rein, Lisa. 2002. Virginia House Votes against Wife Rape. *The Washington Post,* February 8, B9.

Richie, Beth E. 1996. *Compelled to Crime: The Gender Entrapment of Battered Black Women.* New York: Routledge.

Roberts, Dorothy E. 1996. Race and the New Reproduction. *Hastings Law Journal* 47:935–49.

Roth, Rachel. 2001. The Way We Live Now: A Chronicle of Assaults on Women's Rights. *Sojourner: The Women's Forum* 27(4).

Scherer, Michael. 2001. Bush's Tax Savings: Unreal! *The Nation* 272(25):18–19.

Senna, Joseph J., and Larry J. Siegel. 1998. *Essentials of Criminal Justice,* 2d ed. Belmont, CA: West/Wadsworth.

Shavelson, Lonny. 2001. *Hooked: Five Addicts Challenge our Misguided Drug Rehab System.* New York: New Press.

Skrzycki, Cindy. 2000. The Regulators: "Firestonewalling" Again? Two Decades Later, Echoes of Earlier Testimony. *The Washington Post,* September 12, E1.

St. Louis Post Dispatch. 1993. Clinton Has More Millionaires Among Advisers than Bush—Republicans Find Cabinet Members' Wealth Ironic. St. Louis, MO: Feb. 7, 1993. 10C.

Steinhauer, Jennifer. 2000. At Beth Israel, Lapses in Care Mar Gains in Technology. *The New York Times,* February 15, B1.

Sustar, Lee. 2002. The Fall of the House of Enron. *International Socialist Review* 21:7–8.

Swift, Pat. 2000. Author Argues that Fetal Rights are Fundamental Attack on Women. *Buffalo News,* November 4, D1.

Tonry, Michael. 1995. *Malign Neglect: Race, Crime, and Punishment in America.* New York: Oxford University.

Williams, Patricia J. 1991. *The Alchemy of Race and Rights.* Cambridge, MA: Harvard University.

Wing, Adrien Katherine, ed. 1997. *Critical Race Feminism: A Reader.* New York: New York University.

Zucchino, David. 1997. *Myth of the Welfare Queen.* New York: Scribner.

Chapter 2

Feminism for the Mainstream Criminologist:
An Invitation ...

Jeanne Flavin

ABSTRACT

In this chapter, Flavin invites mainstream criminologists to consider the benefits of feminist analyses of crime. In so doing, she explains the basic aspects of feminist criminology as well as the need for a diversity of feminist scholarship. Flavin describes the contributions that feminist thinking has made to the three main components of criminology: criminological theory, research methodology, and criminal justice policy.

Feminists have pointed out that the concept of gender is important to a fuller understanding of every aspect of criminology. This importance is apparent in the basic observation that gender is by far the strongest predictor of criminal activity (men are four out of five people arrested and more than 9 out of 10 people incarcerated). Moreover, on the topic of female crime, Flavin warns that not all women are alike. Rather, female offenders differ in background, motive, and crime depending on their social locations in the intersecting systems of race, class, and gender as well as sexual orientation in this society, where the most marginalized women are the most likely to be caught in the criminal justice system (see Sokoloff, Price, and Flavin, chap. 1).

Feminist theories, she argues, challenge the ways that people gain knowledge. Such theories contend that gender neutral theory and research has little value when it denies sexual and other victimization, the gendered character of violence, and the exercise of discretion within the criminal justice system. Feminist thinking also rejects male-centered (androcentric) thinking as reflective of only one part of humanity at best and as bad social science at worst.

In research methodology, feminist scholars faulted quantitative studies that too often failed to bring out the realities of women's lived experiences. Instead, many feminists turned to narrative research (e.g., interviews, ethnographies, life histories) to identify important themes and realities that help provide a human face to their findings; and numerous feminist criminologists used a combination of quantitative as well as qualitative methods. They also raised the issue of reflexivity, which refers to the effort of the researcher to identify underlying assumptions of a particular research project and thus locate sources of bias. Perhaps feminism's greatest contribution to methodology was in seeking to eliminate the hierarchical nature of the research process by working toward a collaborative and reciprocal relationship with study participants and by increasing participants' involvement in the research process. The objective of all these efforts was to utilize good research practices that can lead to quality research and knowledge.

In the policy area, feminists focus on action, advocacy, and ways to bring about social change and gain fair and woman-conscious treatment for women offenders, victims, and workers. To a degree, this focus was a bold new direction for social science researchers who in the past were content to do their research and leave the findings to someone else to identify practical implications. Finally, all feminist research has as its underlying goal the elimination of domination of men over women, whereas more recent multicultural feminist scholarship emphasizes the need to eliminate all forms of domination, including that of men over women.

INTRODUCTION

It seems pro forma to begin an article on feminism deploring the fact that mainstream criminologists do not "get it." This work, however, is authored by someone who herself did not always "get" feminism and only in recent years has come to recognize feminist insights as not just helpful to understanding the relationship between gender and crime, but essential. This article assumes that many criminologists' dismissal of feminism stems as much from ignorance and misinformation as deliberate, ideological resistance. The purpose here is neither to attack mainstream approaches nor to unequivocally defend feminist ones. Rather, this article represents an invitation to academicians and practitioners from all intellectual and professional backgrounds to consider the contributions of feminist thought in theory, methods, policy, and practice.[1]

The rapidly expanding body of literature on women and gender suggests that the days when a criminologist could pass off a study of men as being a general and generalizable study of crime are numbered.[2] Accompanying the increased attention to gender has been increased opportunities for funding for research on women, gender, and crime. For instance, the 1994 Violence Against Women Act not only provided additional rights to victims of stalking, domestic violence, and sexual assault, but also marked US$1.6 billion for programs providing services to women victims of domestic violence. To take full advantage of the opportunities available to integrate gender into this research, teaching, and practice, however, requires an understanding of the myriad ways in which gender shapes both men's and women's experiences in the criminal justice system.

Feminist criminologists have been at the forefront in pointing out that when women and other marginalized groups are ignored, devalued, or misrepresented, society in general and the understanding of crime and justice in particular suffer as a result. "Feminism" and "feminist criminology" refer not to one perspective but a diverse set of perspectives that, generally speaking, focus on women's interests, are overtly political, and strive to present a new vision of equality and social justice (Rafter & Heidensohn, 1995). Feminists generally share a view that gender inequalities exist in society and that these inequalities should be addressed, though they may differ in their location of the source of the problem and the measures to be pursued.[3] As will be described in greater detail below, feminist contributions to the understanding of crime and justice cannot be underestimated: Arguably "no other perspective has done as much to raise societal consciousness about the oppression of women and gender inequality" (Wonders, 1999, p. 113).

Source: Jeanne Flavin. 2001. Feminism for the Mainstream Criminologist: An Invitation. *Journal of Criminal Justice* 29:271–85.

Despite feminism's impact on the study and practice of criminal justice, many scholars and practitioners lack an understanding of even the most rudimentary aspects of feminist criminological thought, much less feminism's relevance to criminal justice. Part of the problem is that much feminist scholarship is still published in specialized journals (e.g., *Women and Criminal Justice, Gender and Society, Violence Against Women, Feminist Theory*), included in "special issues" focusing on some aspect of women and crime [cf., *Journal of Contemporary Criminal Justice, 14* (2) (1998); *American Psychologist, 54* (1) (1999); *Homicide Studies, 2* (4) (1998); *Corrections Today, 60* (7) (1998); *International Journal of Comparative and Applied Criminal Justice, 21* (2) (1997); *Crime and Delinquency, 41* (4) (1995); *Journal of Criminal Justice Education, 3* (2) (1992); *Southern California Review of Law and Women's Studies, 2* (1) (1992); *Social Pathology, 3* (2) (1997); *Law and Social Inquiry, 19* (4) (1995); *Justice Quarterly, 12* (1) (1995); *Crime and Delinquency, 35* (1) (1989)] or receives book-length treatments that require more of a commitment than many nonfeminist criminologists are willing to invest.[4] This literature frequently assumes a baseline level of knowledge that nonfeminists or scholars new to the study of gender and crime may not possess. As with other approaches, feminist scholarship often relies on terminology (e.g., "androcentricism," "intersectionality," "standpoint epistemology," "gender essentialism," "reflexivity," "doing gender," "hegemonic masculinity") that—while widely recognized by many feminist-oriented criminologists—alienates rather than informs practitioners or scholars from more mainstream orientations.[5]

Feminism and mainstream criminology seem trapped in, if not a vicious cycle, at least an unproductive one. Historically, feminism has had a peripheral relationship to the discipline on the whole and mainstream criminologists have not been widely exposed to feminist perspectives. Many men and women continue to assume (falsely) that "feminism is about women, while criminology is about men" (Naffine, 1996, pp. 1–2), which, in turn, keeps feminist perspectives marginal to the discipline.[6] The result is that many academicians, practitioners, and policymakers have yet to understand, much less appreciate, the importance of gender and feminism's contribution to criminology.

To address this problem, the present work dedicates itself to explaining some of the major feminist insights in the interrelated areas of theory (including theories of knowledge), methodology, and policy to criminologists unfamiliar with feminism. Following an overview of how gender was addressed in the study and practice of criminal justice, examples are presented that illustrate feminist concerns as well as the diversity of feminist scholarship.[7]

WOMEN AND GENDER IN CRIMINOLOGY

When the question arises as to why many standard criminal justice texts dedicate relatively little attention to women, one of the most oft-cited responses is that women comprise a small percentage of those involved in the criminal justice system. For example, according to official crime statistics, women comprise only around 7 percent of prison inmates and 11 percent of jail inmates, 21 percent of those arrested, and 14 percent of all sworn officers in large police departments (Federal Bureau of Investigations [FBI], 1998; Gilliard, 1999; National Center for Women and Policing, 1999).

As a justification for neglect, many people recognize that this explanation falls short on a number of fronts. First, while women are underrepresented as victims, offenders, and workers, the *number* of women involved in the criminal processing system is large and growing. Currently, women account for nearly 2.3 million of those arrested, including half a million arrests for index crimes and 83,000 arrests for violent crimes (FBI, 1998). Nearly 64,000 adult women were being held in local jails at midyear 1998 and almost 83,000 women were imprisoned under the jurisdiction of state and federal authorities (Gilliard, 1999). Over 32,000 women are employed in large law enforcement agencies and another 42,000 are custody/security staff employed in state and federal correctional facilities (Bureau of Justice

Statistics [BJS], 1997; National Center for Women and Policing, 1999).

Secondly, policies and practices that disproportionately affect men have an impact on women as well. For instance, it is women who shoulder the economic and emotional responsibility for child-care when a male parent is incarcerated. Also, as corrections budgets have been increased, state funds to support low-income women and their children have been cut along with social service jobs that are disproportionately staffed by women (Danner, 1998).

Moreover, while the criminal justice system *is* overwhelmingly male, gender is relevant when we are discussing men's involvement in the system as well as women's. Gender is the strongest predictor of criminal involvement: boys and men perpetrate more, and more serious crimes than do girls and women. There is a benefit from asking, "Why are women so underrepresented in crime?" as well as examining why men are overrepresented. Also, both men and women "do gender," that is, handle situations in such a way that the outcome is considered gender-appropriate. Studying how men and women accomplish masculinity and femininity prompts one to consider how social structures constrain and channel behavior that, in turn, may influence a person's criminal or law-abiding behavior or their actions in the workplace (Martin & Jurik, 1996; Messerschmidt, 1997; West & Zimmerman, 1987).

Discussing gender and crime is definitely an easier exercise now than it would have been thirty years ago. Since the 1970s, hundreds of books and articles have appeared that reflect the in-roads feminism has made into criminology and related fields. Feminism's influence, though, has been far from uniform. Most criminal justice scholarship, practice, and policymaking that consider women and gender adopt one of three general approaches (Daly, 1995; Goodstein, 1992).

In the main, most criminological scholarship focuses on men or extends theorizing based on men's experiences to women without offering any reconceptualization (Daly, 1995). In contrast, some scholars recognize that women's criminal justice experiences are often ignored or distorted when one simply "adds women and stirs." A second approach, then, includes feminist research that focuses attention on crimes that adversely affect women more than they affect men, such as domestic violence. This approach also pays attention to the ways in which women's experiences differ not just from men's, but from each other based on characteristics such as race, ethnicity, class, age, and sexual orientation. While addressing women's "invisibility" is an improvement over simply adding women and stirring, scholarship in this category still evinces a tendency to treat men as the norm and women as the anomalies. Such an approach precludes efforts to achieve fairer treatment of men and women throughout the criminal justice system. If an entire field has been shaped by a male norm, then one must seriously question whether the issues deemed important to the understanding of victims, offenders, and workers include those that are important for women.

Recognizing the importance of studying women on their own terms, some scholars have adopted a more advanced feminist approach. For example, Beth E. Richie's (1996) interviews with women inmates led her to develop the idea of "gender entrapment" as a means of understanding the criminal behavior of battered African American women. For many of these women, Richie (p. 4) concluded criminal behavior is a logical extension of "their racialized gender identities, their culturally expected gender roles, and the violence in their intimate relationships." Richie found that nearly all of the battered Black women in her study occupied a privileged status in their families growing up, receiving extra attention, opportunities, and material possessions. These women, however, also felt burdened by a responsibility to "make good" on their families' investments in their futures. As a result, their identities were closely aligned with meeting the needs of others, an identity that made them vulnerable to abuse as adults (Richie, 1996).

Feminist criminologists hope that, in the future, approaches such as Richie's, which recognize a multiplicity of factors and offer a richer contextual analysis, will be the rule rather than the exception. Theories and research will "reach beyond the current stereotypes of women, and beyond the current real lives of women, to think of women differently" (Naffine, 1996, p. 143). The knowledge base will be transformed to include a theoretical and analytical focus on the interacting relations of class, race, and gender, as well as sexual orientation, age, and ethnicity. Admittedly, to date, feminist approaches have worked better to criticize than to construct core theoretical frameworks as Richie did. Although critiques are valuable in that they call attention to women's invisibility or misrepresentation in criminology, feminists and nonfeminists alike generally recognize that feminist perspectives must move beyond criticizing from the sidelines if the criminal justice system's approach to gender is to be reconstructed. This poses a major challenge given that one's inherited ways of thinking obstruct one's ability to imagine or comprehend new ways of viewing crime and criminal justice (Collins, 1998; Daly, 1995; Eichler, 1988). By acknowledging some of the limitations of mainstream approaches and considering feminist perspectives as one possible means of advancing the understanding of gender and crime, feminist and nonfeminist scholars hopefully can work together to address the criminal justice ground remaining not only to be covered, but plowed and replanted.

Feminist Epistemologies

Epistemology refers to "theories of what knowledge is, what makes it possible, and how to get it" (Harding, 1991, p. 308). Feminist perspectives have made more progress in fields that have stronger traditions of interpretive understanding such as literature and history. By contrast, the criminological tradition continues to be deeply embedded in the scientific method (Naffine, 1996). Much of mainstream criminology is rooted in claims that "science is value neutral" and "scientific methods protect against our scholarship being contaminated by subjectivity." Studies can be replicated, positivism assumes, because researchers produce knowledge in similar ways, rendering individual criminologists interchangeable with others.

Are some beliefs better supported by empirical evidence than others? Yes. Are there advantages to using traditional (e.g., quantitative) research methods? Absolutely. Does the use of certain research procedural safeguards mitigate against biased results? Of course. These points are not disputed here. What *is* challenged is the assumption that one can and should strive to achieve "absolute objectivity" and universally valid knowledge.

Recently, in a special issue of *The New York Times Magazine,* Richard Powers heralded the "vesting of authority in experiment" as the best idea of the millennium. Powers (1999, p. 83) acknowledged, however, that thinkers "from Ludwig Wittgenstein to Thomas Kuhn and beyond" have expressed concern

> that fact and artifact may be closer than most empiricists are comfortable accepting . . . That great empiricists have rejected initial data on hunches, until their observations produced more acceptable numbers. That scientists need pre-existing theory and supposition even to ask the questions that will lead to data. That the shape of a question produces the data that answer it.

These concerns and others lie at the heart of feminist epistemology.[8] The most conservative feminist epistemological program, feminist empiricism, basically accepts the value of the scientific method, but points out that ignoring women or misrepresenting their experiences is methodologically unsound. Feminist empiricism tries to correct "bad science" through stricter adherence to existing norms of scientific inquiry. This approach has filled in gaps in the knowledge of women victims of crime (particularly violence in the home and between inmates), the judicial treatment of offending women and girls, and the experiences of women criminal justice workers (Martin & Jurik, 1996; Naffine, 1996; Smart, 1995).

By contrast, other feminist epistemologies—feminist standpoint theories, for example—go beyond critiquing empirical practice to challenging mainstream criminology's empirical assumptions. Many feminists consider science and knowledge (as well as our definitions of crimes, masculinity, and femininity) to be socially situated and question how disinterested knowledge or "objectivity" is possible in a society that is deeply stratified by gender, race, and class. As philosopher Sandra Harding (1991, p. 59) observes, . . . [T]he subject of belief and of knowledge is never simply an individual, let alone an abstract one capable of transcending its own historical location. It is always an individual in a particular social situation."

Feminist standpoint theories assume that the perspective of the researcher influences what is known. Standpoint feminists try to construct knowledge from the perspective of the persons being studied on the grounds that the perspective of the oppressed or marginalized tends to be less distorted. The powerful have more interest in obscuring the conditions that produce their privileges and authority than the dominated groups have in hiding the conditions that produce their situation (Harding, 1991).

A third feminist epistemological approach, feminist postmodernism, criticizes standpoint feminists for assuming that women are a "clearly defined and uncontroversially given interest group" (Smart, 1995, p. 10). While positivists and other "modernists" (including many feminists) claim that the truth can be determined provided all agree on responsible ways of going about it, postmodern critics argue for multiple truths that take context into account (Collins, 1998, pp. 196–197; Wonders, 1999). Many criminologists recognize that "knowledge" or "truth" often reflects the perspective of those with more power (e.g., definitions of what actions are considered illegal, what constitutes a fair punishment). Postmodernists take this further, questioning whether *any* knowledge is knowable and rejecting the ideas that there is a universal definition of justice, i.e., one that would be true for all people, all of the time (DeKeseredy & Schwartz, 1996; Wonders, 1999). Toward this end, postmodernism emphasizes the importance of alternative discourses and accounts and frequently takes the form of examining the effects of language and symbolic representation, e.g., how legal discourse constructs different "types of women" such as "prostitute" or "bad mother" (Smart, 1998, pp. 28–30).

Some charge that postmodernism basically amounts to a "call for inaction" (Tong, 1989, p. 232). If justice is different for everyone depending on one's perspective, then what is the point of trying to pursue it? If one cannot be certain that the good quality knowledge produced will provide useful insight (or a fair outcome) then, as one student asked, "Why not just sit by the pool?" (Smart, 1995, p. 212). Such criticism, however, paints an overly dismal view of the postmodern perspective. Postmodern and feminist scholars recognize a responsibility to build bridges across diverse groups in order to work collectively—not to arrive at a universal understanding of justice, but "to do our best to make judgments that make the world a good place to be" for everyone (Wonders, 1999, p. 122).

Regardless of where one falls on the "knowledge is scientifically derived" to "knowledge is socially produced" to "knowledge is power/power is knowledge" continuum, it is hard to imagine a criminal justice enterprise where epistemology is irrelevant. Yet rarely does it receive even passing mention. Given that one routinely encounters "totalitarianism," "bureaucratization," "psychopharmacology," and "heteroskedasticity" in academic publications, it is more than a matter of "epistemology" being a word that does not roll easily off the tongue.

The nature of the concept itself may contribute to the reluctance to address it. It is far easier to open a discussion by stating "The following are some of the major theories of crime causation . . . " than challenging whether one can ever claim to "know" why people commit crimes or any other class of "truths." Questioning how knowledge has been or ought to be produced can be unsettling, and the process of inquiry—almost by definition—does not lead to straightforward, universally accepted answers. Even among feminists, this process has been described as painful, if inevitable and productive (Smart, 1995, p. 11). At the root of the problem, no doubt, is that most people were not intellectually reared to appreciate the importance of epistemology, much less articulate it. Yet recognition of the importance of epistemology and the biases of the scientific method lies at the core of transforming the discipline. Gaining a better understanding of gender and crime requires not only filling in gaps in knowledge but also challenging the assumptions upon which existing "knowledge" is based.

THEORETICAL CONTRIBUTIONS

Charges that criminology is "male-centered" (or "androcentric") raise hackles among students, practitioners, and scholars alike who incorrectly reduce the criticism to an attack on the sex of the researchers. The reality is that women are vulnerable to androcentric bias just as men are capable of overcoming it. Male dominance of the discipline contributes to androcentricity, but is by no means the only source.

Ideally, theoretical development is grounded in a larger literature, building upon the insights and strengths of past scholarship. Past theorizing regarding the relationship between gender and crime has been seriously hampered by the fact that historically, most of it has focused on explaining men's experiences of crime and justice and assuming these explanations also apply to women. By contrast, feminist scholarship has strengthened criminological theory in two major ways: by pointing out the limitations of applying theories of male criminality to women and by developing theories of men's and women's criminality.

Scholars such as Dorie Klein (1973/1995) and Eileen Leonard (1973/1995) have made systematic attempts to apply traditional theories of crime (i.e., anomie theory, labeling theory, differential association, subcultural theory, and Marxism) to women, and concluded that these theories are unsuited for explaining female patterns of crime. For example, Robert Merton (1938) also neglected to apply his anomie theory to women. His theory holds that when people lack legitimate means (e.g., a job, a savings account) to achieve socially accepted goals (e.g., material and monetary success), they innovate (e.g., steal, write bad checks). His theory also assumes that financial success is as important a goal for women as it is for men and fails to address why women—who are overrepresented among the poor and thus arguably subjected to more strain than men—are less likely to deviate.

Feminists have also taken issue with more recent theorizing that, while showing signs of trying to be more sensitive to issues of women and gender, also has shortcomings. One pitfall occurs when scholars strive to create a "gender-neutral" theory that makes no differentiation regarding the theory's applicability to men and women. For example, Michael R. Gottfredson and Travis Hirschi's (1990) *A General Theory of Crime* attempts to be linguistically gender-neutral in discussing victimization and parenting. In doing so, Gottfredson and Hirschi overlook the reality that violent victimization is *not* gender-neutral (nor race- or class-neutral, for that matter); nearly two-thirds of men's nonfatal violent victimizations are committed by a stranger, while nearly two-thirds of women's nonfatal violent victimizations are committed by someone she knows (Craven, 1997). Elsewhere, Gottfredson and Hirschi assert that mothers and fathers are interchangeable in their influence in the socialization process, apparently denying the gendered character of parenting. Gottfredson and Hirschi's inattention to gendered inequalities is illustrated by "both their gender-neutral stance when inappropriate and by lack of gender specificity when appropriate" (Miller & Burack, 1993, p. 116).

Feminist scholarship has been invaluable in calling attention to the "generalizability problem" of many traditional theoretical approaches (Daly & Chesney-Lind, 1988) but feminist contributions to theory have not been confined to the level of critique. Increasingly, feminist perspectives are serving as the basis for theories of crime and crime control. For example, Julia and Herman Schwendinger's (1983) Marxist feminist analysis, *Rape and Inequality,* links the nature and extent of rape to the unequal gender relations and class struggles that capitalism produces. James Messerschmidt's (1986) socialist feminist work, *Capitalism, Patriarchy, and Crime,* sees both class and patriarchy as contributing to the type and seriousness of crime. Radical feminist approaches, which emphasize the role of patriarchy and masculine control of women's labor and sexuality, arguably have had more impact on woman abuse research than any other theoretical perspective (Simpson, 1989).

Another feminist theoretical contribution has been to point out the absence of research on masculinity. Men have been treated as the norm in the criminal justice system to such a degree that their gender has been ignored. The failure of criminological theories to address gender has led not only to the neglect of women in theory and research, but also to the delay in recognizing that gender shapes men's experiences as well as women's. Naffine (1996, p. 6) observes that "crime, men and masculinity have an intimate relationship, so intimate that we often fail to see it, and so intimate that it can seem natural."

In recent years, the attention to women and gender prompted the reconsideration of what is "known" about men's experiences and led to studies of masculinities and crime. Much of this research relies on Robert W. Connell's (1987, 1995) conceptualizations of "hegemonic masculinity" and "emphasized femininity" that is, the "dominant forms of gender to which other types of masculinity and femininity are subordinated or opposed" (Messerschmidt, 1997, p. 10.)* In the United States, the dominant, culturally supported form of masculinity is based on White, middle-class, heterosexual men and emphasizes characteristics such as paid employment, subordination of women and girls, authority, control, and rationality (Pyke, 1996).

This scholarship emphasizes that race, gender, and class are not only social constructs, but also processes involving creative human actors, rather than static, categorical variables. As such, gender, race, and class are not equally significant in every social setting, but vary in importance depending upon the context (Messerschmidt, 1997; West & Zimmerman, 1987). Crime provides one structurally permitted means of establishing a man's masculinity when other channels for doing so are blocked due to one's race, ethnicity, class, or age.

For example, Jana Bufkin (1999) relies on James Messerschmidt's structured action theory to illustrate how bias crimes are a means of "doing" gender.

These overwhelmingly male bias crime offenders situationally achieve masculinity by attacking members of groups (i.e., women, homeless people, people with disabilities, religious, racial, and ethnic minorities, and homosexuals/bisexuals) who undermine the hegemonic masculine ideal. Several characteristics of known bias crimes (i.e., age, sex, number, and alcohol consumption of the perpetrators, the language used during and after the attacks, the seriousness of the injuries) suggest that the prime motivation for bias crimes is to accomplish masculinity.

Similarly, Jody Miller [see chap. 3] reports that while the women and men in her study reported similar motivations to commit robbery, the ways in which they commit robbery highlight the clear gender hierarchy that exists on the streets. Men tend to use physical violence and/or a gun to confront the victim, and typically target other men. Miller (1998, pp. 50–51) concludes that "male robbers . . . clearly view the act of robbery as a masculine accomplishment in which men compete with other men for money and status . . . The routine use of guns, physical contact, and violence in male-on-male robberies is a reflection of the masculine ideologies shaping men's robberies." By contrast, women robbers take into account the gendered nature of their environment by robbing other females who are less likely than males to be armed and are perceived as weak and easily intimidated. When women do rob men, they use perceptions of women as weak and sexually available to their advantage to manipulate men into situations where they become vulnerable to being robbed.

The growing body of scholarship that considers the situational constructions of gender, race, and class also helps to address concerns that much feminist criminology (as with mainstream criminology) tends to be gender essentialist; implying that there is a universal "women's experience" or "men's experience" that can be described independently of other facets of experience such as race, ethnicity, and class (Rice, 1990). The effect of essentialist perspectives has been to "reduce the lives of people who experience multiple forms of oppression to addition problems: 'racism + sexism = straight Black women's experi-

---

*Editors' note: An ideology is hegemonic when the social arrangements that are in the best interests of the dominant groups are presented and perceived as being in everyone's best interests. In the United States, images of masculinity and femininity are associated with white, middle-class heterosexuals. Hegemonic masculinity is the culturally idealized form of masculinity in a given historical society emphasizing, for example, paid employment, heterosexism, uncontrollable sexuality, authority, emotional flatness, success orientation, control, aggressiveness, rationality, subordination of women and girls. A corresponding emphasized femininity may idealize, for example, sociability, fragility, sexual receptivity, marriage, nurturing, child care.

ence' " (Harris, 1997, p. 11). Racial and ethnic minority women victims, offenders, and workers are not simply subjected to "more" disadvantage than White women; their oppression is often of a qualitatively different kind. Theories of crime and justice need to acknowledge, for example, that "Black women experience sexual and patriarchal oppression by Black men but at the same time struggle alongside them against racial oppression" (Rice, 1990, p. 63).

In sum, overcoming androcentric theorizing involves more than simply extending theories designed to explain male criminality to women or presenting theories in gender-neutral terms. It requires recognizing gender as a social process relevant to the actions of men as well as women. It demands that we overcome essentialist tendencies to consider the complex ways in which gender interacts with other social characteristics. Compared to thirty years ago, more research and policymaking efforts consider feminist theoretical contributions. By and large, however, feminist theories have not been fully integrated into the study and practice of criminal justice and consequently have not received the same attention as varieties of strain theories, social control theories, or individualist theories. As a result, the richness and insights of feminist perspectives have yet to be widely appreciated.[9] At minimum, evaluations of a theory's merits should be broadened to include feminist critiques and to consider how a given theory might be revised to recognize gender as a central organizing factor in social life (Renzetti, 1993). Ideally, to ensure that successive generations of practitioners and scholars will not replicate existing androcentric and essentialist biases, efforts to fully integrate feminist theoretical critiques and feminist theorizing into undergraduate and graduate curricula should be expanded (see Goodstein, 1992; Wilson, 1991; Wonders & Caulfield, 1993, for specific strategies for doing so).

RESEARCH METHODOLOGY AND METHODS

Just as feminists vary in their theoretical orientation and their views of how knowledge should be

acquired, "there is not a distinctive feminist methodology but rather a feminist perspective on the research process" (Taylor & Rupp, 1991, p. 127). With this in mind, the following sections discuss major feminist methodological themes as they are manifested in criminological research. These themes relate to the choice of topic, choice of research methods, the subjective experiences of doing research (or "reflexivity"), and the relationship between the researcher and the research subjects (Gelsthorpe, 1990). Another area of feminist concern—the relationship between policy/action and research—is discussed in the next section. Admittedly, many of the methodological issues presented below are not unique to feminism but are shared by scholars of other orientations, particularly other critical ones, but their close identification with feminism warrants their inclusion here.

Choice of Research Topic

As the work cited throughout this article illustrates, feminist criminological scholarship comprises a substantial and mature body of literature that poses "some of the more difficult and interesting questions about the nature of (criminological) knowledge" (Naffine, 1996, p. 4). For example,

> [t]here are feminists who have carried out the more conventional (but necessary) empirical work of documenting sex bias within the criminal justice system. Feminists have questioned the scientific methods deployed by criminologists, as well as their highly orthodox approach to the nature of knowledge. Feminists have engaged with criminological theory, across the range, questioning its ability to provide general explanations of human behaviour. Feminists have provided an abundance of data about crime from the viewpoint of women (to counter the more usual viewpoint of men), and feminists have also helped to develop new epistemologies that question the very sense of writing from the perspective of a woman (or, for that matter, from the perspective of a man) (Naffine, 1996, p. 4).

While sharing a view that gender is central to the understanding of crime and justice, feminist criminological scholarship reflects considerable diversity and originality in the choice of topic. As the above quotation suggests, feminists have addressed time-honored criminological questions. More recently, feminists have applied themselves to newer lines of criminological inquiry such as the impact of sentencing policies on women (cf., Raeder, 1993), the blurred boundaries between victimization and criminalization (cf. Daly & Maher, 1998), and the media's role in shaping perceptions of crime and justice (cf. Chancer, 1998; Danner & Carmody, 1999), to name but a few.

M. Joan McDermott (1992) observes that feminist research has evolved such that it is no longer just scholarship that is "on, by, and for women" but encompasses a larger sphere of inquiry. Feminist scholarship includes research "on" gender that includes men and masculinity; it recognizes that research conducted "by" a woman is not representative of all women's experiences nor does being biologically male disqualify one from working from a feminist perspective. And, though remaining committed to positions "for" women, feminism ultimately aims to benefit both men and women.

Choice of Research Methods and Methodologies

One of the thorniest points of contention is the discussion surrounding the use of qualitative and quantitative research methodologies; a debate that has been described as "sterile and based on false polarization" (Jayartne & Stewart, 1991, p. 85). Despite a perception that feminist scholarship is primarily qualitative, "feminist researchers use just about any and all of the methods . . . that traditional androcentric researchers have used. Of course, precisely how they carry out these methods of evidence gathering is often strikingly different . . . it is not by looking at research methods that one will be able to identify the distinctive features of the best of feminist research" (Harding, 1987, pp. 2–3). Not all feminist research is qualitative and not all studies that rely on qualitative methods are conducted from a feminist orientation.

Quantitative approaches obviously offer a number of advantages to the study of gender and crime,

e.g., findings from representative samples may be more generalizable, statistical techniques can handle more contextual variables and permit simultaneous evaluation of complex theoretical models and interaction terms. Quantitative methods have come under fire, though, for obscuring the experience of women. Surveys frequently require coding individuals' responses into categories predefined by researchers, but the reality is that "experiences don't come in little boxes that are ready to be labeled and counted" (McDermott, 1992, p. 247). Also, when using existing data, it is hard to avoid adopting a "dataset mentality" and limit research questions to those that can be answered by available variables. These problems present a Catch-22 of sorts: one only collects and records information thought to be important, but characteristics cannot be established as important until the data are possessed. For example, because most large databases were originally designed to capture information salient to the processing and treatment of men offenders, characteristics that were particularly salient to women might not be recorded (e.g., extent of caretaking responsibilities for children and the elderly, childhood victimization experiences, obstetric/gynecological history).[10]

By contrast, qualitative approaches such as interviews, ethnographies, and life histories permit women and men to articulate or conceptualize their experiences more completely and in their own terms, potentially providing more accurate and valid information. This is particularly important given many feminists' interest in examining the situation-at-hand, "taking real life as the starting point, its subjective concreteness as well as its societal entanglements" (Mies, 1991, p. 66). This view that subjective experience is part of science should not be misconstrued as a belief that simply describing an individual's experiences or feelings in itself comprises a scientific treatment of a problem. Feminists in the main recognize the problem of viewing "the personal as inherently paradigmatic, the individual life story as coherent, unified, morally inspiring" (Kauffman, 1992/1993, pp. 262–263). Instead, many feminist scholars use narrative statements to identify important themes while at the same time giving their findings a human face. For example, one can report that many incarcerated girls are concerned about leaving the institutional setting, but the point is better illustrated by quoting girls' statements such as, "I've been here so long, I don't want to just be thrown out. I'm anxious" and "I was scared to help an old lady cross the street when I was on [a day] leave once. I felt like I had institution written all over me" (Belknap, Holsinger, & Dunn, 1997, p. 396).

Despite their advantages and roots in the Chicago School in the work of scholars such as W. I. Thomas and Robert Park, qualitative research methods have had to fight off a reputation as an oxymoron in mainstream criminal justice circles.[11] Qualitative methods are sometimes stereotyped as unsystematic and politically motivated and therefore unscientific and overtly biased (Jayartne & Stewart, 1991, p. 93). Also, because qualitative research may be very time-consuming since it tends to involve more and more intensive contact with the research subjects, the samples in a qualitative study tend to be relatively small and homogenous (Cannon, Higginbotham, & Leung, 1988/1991). In view of the limitations of both methodologies, many feminists join mainstream methodologists in employing a combination of quantitative and qualitative methods in order to compensate for the weaknesses in one method by incorporating the strengths of another. For example, Barbara Owen's (1998) study of women prisoners, *In the Mix,* includes a quasi-ethnographic study of a women's prison as well as a systematic survey of female prisoners and parolees. Kathleen Daly's (1994) *Gender, Crime and Punishment* uses both a statistical analysis of sentencing disparity for a wide sample of cases, as well as qualitative analysis of a "deep sample" of forty matched pairs of women and men convicted of similar offenses.

Reflexivity

While most scholars support acknowledging the limitations of a particular methodological technique employed (be it quantitative or qualitative), feminist scholarship also emphasizes the importance of critically examining the nature of the research process itself. "Reflexivity" refers to identifying the assumptions underlying the research endeavor and often includes the investigator's reaction to doing the research.

> For the most part, criminology is unreflective. While conscious that researchers should not bring their prejudices to the research table, many criminologists, in their search for neutrality, fail to consider their own identity in their investigative enterprises. Perhaps this is the aftershock of attempting to impose the strictures and methods of the physical sciences on criminology in our effort to make it more "scientific" (Pettiway, 1997, pp. xv–xvi).

Reflecting on the research process calls attention to possible sources of bias introduced as well as provides guidance to future researchers. Reflexivity also prompts examination of whether research can ever truly be said to be "objective." The identity of a researcher shapes even a deliberately noninterpretive research endeavor such as presenting transcripts of taped interviews with women involved in drugs and crime given that the researcher frames the questions, focuses the interviews, and edits the transcripts for publication (Pettiway, 1997). Not only do many feminists consider subjectivity as unavoidable, but some argue it may be a strength of a study. Barbara Owen (1998) reported that the relationships she formed with several prisoners led her to better appreciate the women's experiences from their own point of view. The result, she suggested, is a study that not only contributed to a "scientific" understanding of women prisoners, but to a political awareness of their marginalized status.

In other words, it cannot simply be assumed that one's choice of methods guarantees objective research. Reflexivity strengthens the research process by promoting greater honesty and awareness of the limitations and biases inherent in the research. It also provides a valuable guide to other researchers who may be considering undertaking similar research projects. Further, as will be discussed next, reflexivity encourages one to think about the relationship between themselves as researchers and the people who comprise the research subjects.

Relationship between Researcher and Subjects

Feminists have criticized researchers' objectification and exploitation of their subjects, particularly when information is gained through interviews or surveys. Objectification occurs when it is assumed that a radical difference exists between the roles of scientist and subject. In the most extreme positivist forms, studying human beings is treated, in principle, as no different from studying things (Gorelick, 1996, p. 24). While conventional criminology assumes that scientific detachment requires emotional detachment, the quest for neutrality and objectivity can be a disadvantage when so much emphasis is placed on "maintaining distance" that context and recognition of the individual humanity of the subjects are stripped away.

Part of the problem is that traditional guidelines for interviewing (i.e., advise interviewers to adopt an objective, noninvolved stance; view interviews as noninteractive) assumes the situation is a one-way hierarchical process. When one assumes that the interviewer's role is to collect but never to provide information, the interviewee is reduced to mere data (Carty, 1996). By contrast, many feminists propose treating interviewees as informants or experts, and using an open-ended format in order to permit new questions to emerge during the course of the interview (Taylor & Rupp, 1991). A feminist methodological approach tries to minimize hierarchical relationships within the research process. Ideally, the research enterprise will strive for a collaborative and reciprocal association between the researcher and the subject consistent with Ann Oakley's maxim: "No intimacy without reciprocity" (quoted in May, 1993, p. 90).

Admittedly, there are difficulties and some drawbacks in minimizing the distance between interviewer and subject. Researchers responsible to funding agencies may not have total control of how their studies are conducted. The subjects themselves may not embrace the idea of collaboration. Particularly in criminal justice, it seems unlikely that offenders, victims, and even many criminal justice workers will see themselves on equal footing with the academic researchers. Language, dress, age, and other cues may serve as constant reminders of the differences in roles and status between the researcher and the subjects. For instance, Belknap et al. (1997) noticed that while juvenile justice professionals seemed to forget the presence of researcher–onlookers while participating in a focus group, many of the incarcerated girls in the same study tended to check how the researchers responded to their own and their peers' comments (Belknap et al., 1997).

Confidentiality and privacy issues—always a concern when a study involves human subjects—become even more important when researchers form rapport, ties, even friendships with the study participants. Women respondents may find it easier to reveal intimate details of their victimization or offending experiences when the interviewer is a woman. All researchers "must take extra precautions not to betray the trust so freely given" (Fonow & Cook, 1991, p. 8) given that researchers may not have complete control of how information will be used once it is gathered from respondents. In spite of these obstacles, a number of specific actions may be undertaken to reduce the distance between researchers and subjects, e.g., sharing drafts of the report with the subjects and soliciting their feedback, encouraging subjects to ask questions and responding with reasonable answers, and reciprocating subjects for the help they provide.

As noted earlier, "feminist research methods" is something of a misnomer. Many of the measures championed by feminist criminologists can be and have been adopted by researchers from mainstream orientations. There remains a need, though, for criminologists to give more thought to the approach to research. This not only means giving qualitative methods their due but also considering reflexivity and the relationship between researcher and subject. For example, research proposals routinely justify their choice of a mail survey versus face-to-face interviews on the grounds of time and money. It should also be considered how the subject's race, gender, and class might influence the choice of research methods. Proposals should be critiqued not only on the basis of sample selection and measurements, but also whether subjects were reciprocated for their participation in the study and what steps were taken to reduce the distance between researcher and subject. Attending to these aspects of the research process does not constitute subscribing to a "feminist methodology" per se. Rather, it indicates a commitment to good research practices designed to give greater visibility to the experiences of women (and other historically marginalized groups) and to increase the subject's involvement in the research process.

POLICY AND ACTION

In reviewing the presidential addresses to the American Society of Criminology, Ngaire Naffine (1996) observes that increasingly, mainstream criminologists are encouraged to be applied and practical, to inform policymakers, and contribute to the public debate about crime. Here again is an area where feminist criminology has proven valuable to the larger criminal justice arena. Feminists have always placed a premium on policy and action; one of feminism's defining components is a standing and overt commitment to identifying "a set of strategies for change" (Daly & Chesney-Lind, 1988, p. 502).

Feminists are perhaps best known for raising awareness of violence against women and the need for laws and policies regarding marital rape, acquaintance rape, stalking, and other crimes that disproportionately involve women victims. Feminists have also called for responses to women victims of crime that reflect an appreciation for the differences that exist among women. For example, a shortage of bilingual and bicultural criminal justice workers creates a system ill-prepared to address many battered Latinas' claims. Latinas and other racial and ethnic minority women must decide whether to seek assistance from an outsider who "may not look like her, sound like her, speak her language, or share any of her cultural values" (Rivera, 1994/1997, p. 261). Minority women may fear that the police will not do enough (ignoring their complaints) and/or that the police will do too much (being overly zealous toward the minority men they arrest). Some women also may encounter a failure on the part of their racial, ethnic, religious, and

community leaders to recognize "a sexist problem within the community . . . as important as a racist problem outside of it" (Rasche, 1988/1995, p. 257).

Feminism's impact in the arena of domestic violence and other forms of violence against women has been substantial, but to confine feminism's contribution to these issues is to sell feminism short. Feminists also engage in policy evaluation, asking "What is this policy supposed to accomplish?," "How will it actually be implemented?," "Who wins and who loses if this policy is adopted?," "What can we do to improve on this?" (Miller 1998a, 1998b; Renzetti, 1998).

Women's stake in the "war on crime" is important, though often unrecognized. While the public construction of the criminal is male, "the hidden victims of many of the get-tough policies have been women, particularly women of color" (Chesney-Lind, 1998, p. xi). Feminists have played an important role in calling attention to the unintended or unforeseen consequences of purportedly "gender-neutral" policies. New sentencing policies have been implemented with the goal of treating women and men the same. With regard to the Federal Sentencing Guidelines, Myrna Raeder (1993) suggests considering sentencing fewer men to prison on the grounds that it would be more humane for men, women, and their children. Instead, women have been increasingly incarcerated; a shift that has been described as "equality with a vengeance." There are other, less well-known examples to consider too, such as Massey, Miller, and Wilhelmi's (1998) finding that in civil forfeiture cases (involving the confiscation of assets from suspected drug offenders), judges falsely assume that social and economic power are equally distributed in a marriage or intimate relationship. Moreover, judges blame wives for their failure or inability to control their husband. Judicial interpretations thus "often ignore not only the gendered power dynamics within intimate relationships but also the structural limits to women's efficacy in disentangling themselves from such relationships that are present in these situations" (p. 29).[12]

In addition to women being harmed by purportedly "gender-neutral" policies or policies aimed primarily at men, some policies have been targeted specifically at women and therefore are cause for concern. For instance, according to a 1996 report prepared by the Center for Reproductive Law and Policy, at least 200 women in more than thirty states have been arrested for their alleged drug use or other actions during pregnancy. Feminist perspectives encourage us to recognize the harmful consequences of criminalizing pregnant women's behavior rather than expanding the availability of treatment for pregnant women (including those who have small children, are infected with HIV, and/or are on Medicaid). One major concern is that criminalizing maternal conduct discourages drug-using women from seeking prenatal care and drug treatment out of fear that they will be subjected to prosecution (Humphries, 1999).

Feminists have not limited their interests to policies aimed at or affecting women, but have also challenged the masculine basis of many programs and policies. Feminists have been critical of correctional officer and police training programs for their overemphasis on physical strength, intimidation, and aggressiveness as a means for resolving disputes while devaluing interpersonal skills. Similarly, feminist criminologists are among those critical of boot camps for being unnecessarily demeaning and abusive to inmates. The boot camp model embodies a distorted image of masculinity, one that emphasizes aggressiveness, unquestioned authority, and insensitivity to others' pain while deemphasizing "feminine" characteristics such as group cooperation and empathy. "Why," Merry Morash and Lila Rucker (1990/1998, pp. 35 and 38) ask, "would a method that has been developed to prepare people to go into war, and as a tool to manage legal violence, be considered as having such potential in deterring or rehabilitating offenders? . . . [T]he program elements of militarism, hard labor, and fear engendered by severe conditions do not hold much promise, and they appear to set the stage for abuse of authority."

The aforementioned examples are just a few of the myriad ways in which feminists have contributed to criminal justice policymaking and evaluation. Feminist scholarship has called attention to previously ignored policy issues, evaluated the impact of

purportedly "gender-neutral" policies on women, examined the effects of policies targeted specifically at women, and challenged the value of criminal justice policies and practices based on stereotypical ideas of masculinity and femininity. By definition, feminism gives great weight to identifying strategies for social change and ending domination in all its forms. Feminist perspectives remind one—not only of one's professional responsibilities—but also one's social responsibility to consider the implications of our research and policy for women.

CONCLUSIONS

"If I can't dance, it's not my revolution." Emma Goldman's statement may make a great T-shirt, but her view is hardly universal among feminists. While feminist criminologists generally agree that a transformation of criminal justice discipline is desirable, there is less consensus regarding how to go about actually carrying it out. Do feminists wait for mainstream criminology to invite them to the dance? If invited, do feminists attend even if it means being reduced to standing against the walls waiting to be asked to dance, or dancing by themselves as a token feminist or woman on the faculty or editorial board? Do feminists hold their own dance, that is, continue to publish articles in specialized journals and books, teach specialized classes on "gender and crime," and sit on panels comprised almost entirely of like-minded scholars? While this approach offers the benefit of facilitating the exchange of ideas and support, it also risks making feminism even more peripheral to the discipline. As the scholarship cited throughout this article illustrates, feminists engage in a variety of strategies, working as both insiders and outsiders to the criminal justice enterprise. By attempting to meet mainstream criminologists midway by explaining the strength and diversity of feminist perspectives, this article presents another strategy.

Regardless of one's political or theoretical orientation, feminism challenges criminology to reject androcentric thinking. More generally, it challenges all people working in the discipline to be thoughtful and relevant: Thoughtful in the theoretical assumptions upon which the research is based, the methods used, the conclusions drawn, and the policies recommended. Thoughtful in developing the content of the classes taught. Thoughtful in acknowledging the limitations of criminological scholarship, in considering the complexities and diversity of the people's lives and experiences upon which scholarship is based, and in communicating with research participants, students, and colleagues.

Given the overt emphasis placed upon policy and action, feminism also challenges one to be relevant. A colleague once observed that best-selling detective fiction writer Walter Mosley had more of an impact on what the public thought of crime and justice than academics did if for no other reason than millions of people read Mosley's novels while most criminological research was not considered outside of academic circles. Part of being relevant means making scholarship accessible in how and where it is presented. Prioritizing relevance also encourages collaboration—not only among academics at other universities, and of other ranks and disciplinary backgrounds—but also with people outside the university setting, including policymakers, practitioners, lawmakers, journalists, victims, offenders, and advocates. It means treating the implications of research for policy and practice as being at least as important as individual careers and egos.

Although feminist perspectives pose a demanding set of standards, the pursuit of these standards can be very rewarding. Feminism presents an invitation to criminologists, practitioners, and policymakers to recognize the existence of sexism, to try to understand its causes, and to work toward identifying and overcoming all forms of discrimination that operate throughout the justice system. Criminology colleagues consider yourselves invited.

DISCUSSION QUESTIONS

1. According to Flavin, what constitutes feminist research methods and how do they differ from mainstream research methods?

2. Can feminist research methods be used to study male crime? Give an example.

3. Describe some of the changes that feminist scholarship and activism have brought about in the area of crime and justice. Consider victimization of women in at least two of these categories: access to law enforcement work, access to law schools, and treatment of women offenders.

4. In what areas are crimes against women still in need of significant action and change? Answer this question in terms of such issues as work opportunities within criminal justice, women's incarceration, or violence against women.

5. Discuss the need for changes in current criminal justice policies that negatively impact different groups of women and men. Pay particular attention to the ways in which intersectionalities of race, class, gender, and sexual orientation might influence your answer.

ACKNOWLEDGMENTS

This article has benefited greatly from the thoughtful suggestions offered by Lynn Chancer of Fordham University, Mona Danner of Old Dominion University, and Helen Eigenberg of the University of Tennessee at Chattanooga.

NOTES

1. As used here, the terms "mainstream criminology" and "conventional criminology" do not refer to a theory but to an amalgam of dominant sociological approaches to crime, such as strain, social control, interactionist, and ecological theories (DeKeseredy & Schwartz, 1996; Thomas & O'Maolchatha, 1989).

2. While in the 1970s, the typical article published in one of four major criminology journals used an all-male sample, by the 1990s, most articles

published in these same journals included a sample of both men and women (Hannon & Dufour, 1998).

3. Readers interested in a discussion of the various feminist theories are urged to consult Daly and Chesney-Lind (1988), Martin and Jurik (1996), and Tong (1989).

4. Readers interested in learning more about feminist approaches to criminology are urged to consult any number of the excellent texts on the subject (cf. Belknap, 1996; Daly & Maher, 1998; Gelsthorpe & Morris, 1990; Heidensohn, 1995; Naffine, 1996; Price & Sokoloff, 1995; Smart, 1976, 1995).

5. Obviously, other factors serve to marginalize feminism from criminology. For instance, Comack (1999, p. 165) posits that "the essentialist and dualistic thinking that has pervaded our approaches to understanding issues like violence against women [i.e., 'women as victims/men as offenders'] . . . has had significant implications for the placement of feminism within the criminological enterprise. So long as women are recognized only as victims and not as active agents, there is little need to embrace or integrate feminist analyses into the criminological agenda." Others (including one of the reviewers of this article) point to "a refusal to engage in the ideas . . . [It is] too hard and ultimately scary for those scholars or practitioners who have devoted their lives to either ignoring gender or to developing 'gender-neutral' theories to change."

6. The peripheral position of feminism is not unique to criminology but is a problem of larger sociology as well. In the classic essay, *The Missing Feminist Revolution in Sociology,* Judith Stacey and Barrie Thorne (1985/1993, p. 177) observe that feminist perspectives have made more progress in fields which have stronger traditions of interpretive understanding. Scholars in anthropology, literature, and history are more open to questions such as "What are the effects of the social and political circumstances in which knowledge is created and received? . . . What are the effects of the gender of the researcher, the audience, or those studied or written about?"

7. Before proceeding, three caveats are in order. First, this article is a primer rather than a comprehensive treatment of feminist criminology. In the interests of clarity and conciseness, some concepts have been omitted from discussion and some important distinctions have been glossed over. While feminists tend to share a general notion of what is meant by a particular concept, the reality is that a given term encompasses a range of perspectives and understandings. In some respects, the concepts presented in this article and any categories discussed in connection with them are "ideal types." Relatedly, issues of epistemology, theory, methods and methodology, and policy are presented in separate sections here, even though they are intertwined. Every attempt has been made to make the overlap and interconnections apparent without being overly repetitious. Lastly, the near-exclusive focus on feminist perspectives is not meant to suggest that only feminism has "the answers" or asks the right questions. Many concerns presented in this article are shared by other criminological approaches, particularly critical ones. For example, feminism generally shares a view with other critical approaches that the major sources of crime are the class, ethnic, and patriarchal relations that control society, and regards structural and cultural change as essential to reducing criminality (DeKeseredy & Schwartz, 1996; Thomas & O'Maolchatha, 1989).

8. The present discussion of epistemology is grossly simplified in the interest of clarity and brevity. For excellent treatments of epistemology, empiricism, and criminology, readers are encouraged to consult Carol Smart's (1995) *Law, Crime and Sexuality: Essays in Feminism* or Ngaire Naffine's (1996) *Feminism and Criminology.*

9. This deficiency is also found in standard textbooks. Earlier studies of introductory criminal justice and criminology textbooks conclude that women are typically ignored or depicted in stereotypical ways (Baro & Eigenberg, 1993; Wright, 1992). A nonrandom sampling of the texts on my shelves suggests the problem persists and the short shrift extends to feminist perspec-

tives as well. For example, in discussing "other branches of conflict theory," Senna and Siegel (1998) cite only one feminist perspective—radical feminism—ignoring other major critical feminist perspectives such as Marxist feminism, socialist feminism, and postmodern feminism.

10. As Jayartne and Stewart (1991) point out, quantitative procedures that are inconsistent with feminist values can be adapted without abandoning those strategies that can be beneficial to the research enterprise.

11. Thomas's own work on female crime showed an appreciation for the interaction between society and the individual. He, however, saw women's physiology and biology as being at the root of their inferior position in society (see Klein 1973/1995).

12. For example, in one case a woman claimed she lived in fear of bodily harm from her husband—a man who had threatened her in the past and had beaten to death his previous wife. The appellate court, however, rejected her claim of lack of consent under duress because the threat was not "immediate."

REFERENCES

Baro, A., and H. Eigenberg, 1993. Images of Gender: A Content Analysis of Photographs in Introductory Criminology and Criminal Justice Textbooks. *Women and Criminal Justice,* 5: 3–36.

Belknap, J. 1996. *The Invisible Woman: Gender, Crime, and Justice.* Belmont, CA: Wadsworth Publishing.

Belknap, J., K. Holsinger, & M. Dunn, 1997. Understanding Incarcerated Girls: The Results of a Focus Group Study. *Prison Journal,* 77: 381–404.

Bufkin, J. L. 1999. Bias Crime as Gendered Behavior. *Social Justice,* 26: 155–176.

Bureau of Justice Statistics. 1997. *Correctional Populations in the United States, 1995.* Washington, DC: U.S. Department of Justice.

Cannon, L. W. W., E. Higginbotham, and M. L. A. Leung, 1991. Race and Class Bias in Qualitative Research on Women. In *Beyond Methodology: Feminist Scholarship as Lived Research,* ed. M. M. Fonow and J. A. Cook, 107–118. Bloomington, IN: Indiana Univ. Press.

Carty, L. 1996. Seeing Through the Eye of Difference: A Reflection on Three Research Journeys. In *Feminism and Social Change: Bridging Theory and Practice,* ed. H. Gottfried, 123–142. Urbana, IL: University of Chicago Press.

Chancer, L. S. 1998. Playing Gender Against Race Through High-Profile Crime Cases. *Violence Against Women,* 4:100–113.

Chesney-Lind, M. 1998. Foreward. In *Crime Control and Women,* ed. S. L. Miller, ix–xiii. Thousand Oaks, CA: Sage Publications.

Collins, P. H. 1998. *Fighting Words: Black Women and the Search for Justice.* Minneapolis: University of Minnesota Press.

Comack, E. 1999. New Possibilities for a Feminism in Criminology? From Dualism to Diversity. *Canadian Journal of Criminology,* 41:161–170.

Connell, R. W. 1987. *Gender and Power: Society, the Person, and Sexual Politics.* Stanford, CA: Stanford Univ. Press.

Connell, R. W. 1995. *Masculinities.* Los Angeles: University of California Press.

Craven, D. 1997. *Sex Differences in Violent Victimization, 1994.* Washington, DC: U.S. Department of Justice.

Daly, K. 1994. *Gender, Crime and Punishment.* New Haven: Yale Univ. Press.

Daly, K. 1995. Looking Back, Looking Forward: The Promise of Feminist Transformation. In *The Criminal Justice System and Women,* 2d ed., ed. B. R. Price and N. J. Sokoloff, 443–457. New York: McGraw-Hill.

Daly, K., and M. Chesney-Lind, 1988. Feminism and Criminology. *Justice Quarterly,* 5:497–538.

Daly, K., and L. Maher, 1998. *Criminology at the Crossroads: Feminist Readings in Crime and Justice.* Oxford: Oxford Univ. Press.

Danner, M. J. E. 1998. Three Strikes and It's Women Who Are Out: The Hidden Consequences for Women of Criminal Justice Police Reforms. In *Crime Control and Women,* ed. S. L. Miller, 1–14. Thousand Oaks, CA: Sage Publications.

Danner, M. J. E., and D. C. Carmody, 1999. *Missing Gender in Cases of Infamous School Violence: Investigating Research and Media Explanations.* Unpublished manuscript.

DeKeseredy, W. S., and M. D. Schwartz, 1996. *Contemporary Criminology.* Belmont, CA: Wadsworth Publishing.

Eichler, M. 1988. *Nonsexist Research Methods: A Practical Guide.* Winchester, MA: Allen and Unwin.

Federal Bureau of Investigations. 1998. *Crime in the United States, 1997.* Washington, DC: United States Government Printing Office.

Fonow, M. M., and J. A. Cook, 1991. Back to the Future: A Look at the Second Wave of Feminist Epistemology and Methodology. In *Beyond Methodology,* ed. M. M.

Fonow and J. A. Cook, 1–15. Bloomington, IN: Indiana Univ. Press.

Gelsthorpe, L. 1990. Feminist Methodologies in Criminology: A New Approach or Old Wine in New Bottles. In *Feminist Perspectives in Criminology,* ed. L. Gelsthorpe, and A. Morris, 89–106. Buckingham, UK: Open Univ. Press.

Gelsthorpe, L., and Morris, A. 1990. *Feminist Perspectives in Criminology.* Buckingham, UK: Open Univ. Press.

Gilliard, D. K. 1999. *Prison and Jail Inmates at Midyear 1998.* Washington, DC: U.S. Department of Justice.

Goodstein, L. 1992. Feminist Perspectives and the Criminal Justice Curriculum. *Journal of Criminal Justice Education,* 3: 165–181.

Gorelick, S. 1996. Contradictions of Feminist Methodology. In *Feminism and Social Change: Bridging Theory and Practice,* ed. H. Gottfried, 23–45. Urbana, IL: University of Chicago Press.

Gottfredson, M. R., and T. Hirschi, 1990. *A General Theory of Crime.* Stanford, CA: Stanford Univ. Press.

Hannon, L., and L. R. Dufour, 1998. Still Just the Study of Men and Crime? A Content Analysis. *Sex Roles,* 38: 63–71.

Harding, S. (Ed.) 1987. *Feminism and Methodology: Social Science Issues.* Bloomington, IN: Indiana Univ. Press.

Harding, S. 1991. *Whose Science? Whose Knowledge?.* Ithaca, NY: Cornell Univ. Press.

Harris, A. P. 1997. Race and Essentialism in Feminist Legal Theory. In *Critical Race Feminism: A Reader,* ed. A. K. Wing, 11–18. New York: New York Univ. Press.

Heidensohn, F. M. 1995. *Women and Crime,* 2d ed. New York: New York Univ. Press.

Humphries, D. 1999. *Crack Mothers: Pregnancy, Drugs, and the Media.* Columbus, OH: Ohio State Univ. Press.

Jayartne, T. E., and A. J. Stewart, 1991. Quantitative and Qualitative Methods in the Social Sciences: Current Feminist Issues and Practical Strategies. In *Beyond Methodology: Feminist Scholarship as Lived Research,* ed. M. M. Fonow and J. A. Cook, 85–106. Bloomington, IN: Indiana Univ. Press.

Kauffman, L. S. 1993. The Long Goodbye: Against Personal Testimony, or An Infant Grifter Grows Up. In *American Feminist Thought at Century's End: A Reader,* ed. L. S. Kauffman, 258–280. Cambridge, MA: Blackwell.

Klein, D. 1995. The Etiology of Female Crime: A Review of the Literature. In *The Criminal Justice System and Women,* 2d ed., ed. B. R. Price and N. J. Sokoloff, 30–53. New York: McGraw-Hill.

Leonard, E. 1995. Theoretical Criminology and Gender. In *The Criminal Justice System and Women,* 2d ed., ed. B. R. Price and N. J. Sokoloff, 54–70. New York: McGraw-Hill.

Martin, S. E., and N. C. Jurik, 1996. *Doing Justice, Doing Gender: Women in Law and Criminal Justice Occupations.* Thousand Oaks, CA: Sage Publications.

Massey, J., S. L. Miller, A. Wilhelmi, 1998. Civil Forfeiture of Property: The Victimization of Women as Innocent Owners and Third Parties. In *Crime Control and Women,* ed. S. L. Miller, 15–31. Thousand Oaks, CA: Sage Publications.

May, T. 1993. Feelings Matter: Inverting the Hidden Equation. In *Interpreting the Field: Accounts of Ethnography,* ed. D. Hobbs and T. May, 69–97. Oxford: Oxford Univ. Press.

McDermott, M. J. 1992. The Personal is Empirical: Feminism, Research Methods, and Criminal Justice Education. *Journal of Criminal Justice Education,* 3: 237–249.

Merton, R. K. 1938. Social Structure and Anomie. *American Sociological Review,* 3:672–683.

Messerschmidt, J. W. 1986. *Capitalism, Patriarchy, and Crime.* Totowa, NJ: Rowman and Littlefield.

Messerschmidt, J. W. 1997. *Crime as Structured Action: Gender, Race, Class, and Crime in the Making.* Thousand Oaks, CA: Sage Publications.

Mies, M. 1991. Women's Research or Feminist Research? The Debate Surrounding Feminist Science and Methodology. In *Beyond Methodology,* ed. M. M. Fonow and J. A. Cook, 60–84. Bloomington, IN: Indiana Univ. Press.

Miller, J. 1998. Up It Up: Gender and the Accomplishment of Street Robbery. *Criminology,* 36:37–65.

Miller, S., and C. Burack, 1993. A Critique of Gottfredson and Hirschi's General Theory of Crime: Selective (In)attention to Gender and Power Positions. *Women and Criminal Justice,* 4:115–134.

Miller, S. L. 1998. Introduction. In *Crime Control and Women,* ed. S. L. Miller, xv–xxiv. Thousand Oaks, CA: Sage Publications.

Morash, M., and L. Rucker, 1998. A Critical Look at the Idea of Boot Camp as a Correctional Reform. In *Crime Control and Women,* ed. S. L. Miller, 32–51. Thousand Oaks CA: Sage Publications.

Naffine, N. 1996. *Feminism and Criminology.* Philadelphia: Temple Univ. Press.

National Center for Women and Policing. 1999. *Equality Denied, the Status of Women and Policing: 1998.* Los Angeles: National Center for Women and Policing.

Owen, B. 1998. *In the Mix: Struggle and Survival in a Woman's Prison.* Albany, NY: State University of New York Press.

Pettiway, L. E. 1997. *Workin' It: Women Living Through Drugs and Crime.* Philadelphia: Temple Univ. Press.

Powers, R. 1999. Eyes Wide Open. *New York Times Magazine* (April 18, special issue), 6:80–83.

Price, B. R., and N. J. Sokoloff, 1995. *The Criminal Justice System and Women: Offenders, Victims, and Workers,* 2d ed.). New York: McGraw-Hill.

Pyke, K. D. 1996. Class-Based Masculinities: The Interdependence of Gender, Class, and Interpersonal Power. *Gender and Society,* 10:527–549.

Raeder, M. S. 1993. Gender and Sentencing: Single Moms, Battered Women, and Other Sex-Based Anomalies in the Gender-Free World of the Federal Sentencing Guidelines. *Pepperdine Law Review,* 20:905–920.

Rafter, N. H., and F. Heidensohn, 1995. *International Feminist Perspectives in Criminology: Engendering a Discipline.* Buckingham, UK: Open Univ. Press.

Rasche, C. E. 1995. Minority Women and Domestic Violence. In *The Criminal Justice System and Women,* 2d ed., ed. B. R. Price and N. J. Sokoloff, 246–261. New York: McGraw-Hill.

Renzetti, C. M. 1993. On the Margins of the Malestream (or, They *Still* Don't Get It, Do They?): Feminist Analyses in Criminal Justice Education. *Journal of Criminal Justice Education,* 4:219–234.

Renzetti, C. M. 1998. Connecting the Dots: Women, Public Policy, and Social Control. In *Crime Control and Women,* ed. S. L. Miller, 181–189. Thousand Oaks, CA: Sage Publications.

Rice, M. 1990. Challenging Orthodoxies in Feminist Theory: A Black Feminist Critique. In *Feminist Perspectives in Criminology,* ed. L. Gelsthorpe and A. Morris, 57–69. Buckingham, UK: Open Univ. Press.

Richie, B. E. 1996. *Compelled to Crime: The Gender Entrapment of Battered Black Women.* New York: Routledge.

Rivera, J. 1997. Domestic Violence Against Latinas by Latino Males: An Analysis of Race, National Origin, and Gender Differentials. In *Critical Race Feminism: A Reader,* ed. A. K. Wing, 259–266. New York: New York Univ. Press.

Schwendinger, J. R., and H. Schwendinger, 1983. *Rape and Inequality.* Newbury Park, CA: Sage Publications.

Senna, J. J., and Siegel, L. J. 1998. *Essentials of Criminal Justice,* 2d ed. Belmont, CA: Wadsworth Publishing.

Simpson, S. S. 1989. Feminist Theory, Crime, and Justice. *Criminology,* 27, 605–631.

Smart, C. 1976. *Women, Crime and Criminology: A Feminist Critique.* Boston: Routledge and Kegan Paul.

Smart, C. 1995. *Law, Crime and Sexuality: Essays in Feminism.* London: Sage Publications.

Smart, C. 1998. The Woman of Legal Discourse. In *Criminology at the Crossroads,* ed. K. Daly and L. Maher, 21–36. New York: Oxford Univ. Press.

Stacey, J., and B. Thorne, 1993. The Missing Feminist Revolution in Sociology. In *American Feminist Thought at Century's End: A Reader,* ed. L. S. Kauffman, 167–188. Cambridge, MA: Blackwell.

Taylor, V., and L. J. Rupp, 1991. Researching the Women's Movement: We Make Our Own History, But Not Just as We Please. In *Beyond Methodology: Feminist Scholarship as Lived Research,* ed. M. M. Fonow and J. A. Cook, 119–132. Bloomington, IN: Indiana Univ. Press.

Thomas, J., and A. O'Maolchatha, 1989. Reassessing the Critical Metaphor: An Optimistic Revisionist View. *Justice Quarterly,* 6:143–172.

Tong, R. 1989. *Feminist Thought: A Comprehensive Introduction.* Boulder, CO: Westview Press.

West, C., and D. H. Zimmerman, 1987. Doing Gender. *Gender and Society,* 1:125–151.

Wilson, N. K. 1991. Feminist Pedagogy in Criminology. *Journal of Criminal Justice Education,* 2:81–93.

Wonders, N. 1999. Postmodern Feminist Criminology and Social Justice. In *Social Justice/Criminal Justice,* ed. B. A. Arrigo, 111–128. Belmont, CA: West/Wadsworth.

Wonders, N. A., and S. L. Caufield, 1993. Women's Work?: The Contradictory Implications of Courses on Women and the Criminal Justice System. *Journal of Criminal Justice Education,* 4:79–100.

Wright, R. 1992. From Vamps and Tramps to Teases and Flirts: Stereotypes of Women in Criminology Textbooks, 1956 to 1965 and 1981 to 1990. *Journal of Criminal Justice Education,* 3:223–236.

Chapter 3

Feminist Theories of Women's Crime:
Robbery as a Case Study

Jody Miller

ABSTRACT

This article is a good example of the type of feminist research that Flavin talks about in chapter 2: women-centered theory and research that simultaneously appreciates the need for understanding the intersectionalities of race and class with gender, in-depth qualitative interviews with women (and men) involved in crime, and a deep respect for the study participants. Past studies designed to understand women's participation in violence have had a tendency to either overemphasize gender differences or to downplay the significance of gender. This chapter tries to reconcile these approaches through an examination of the lived experiences of female and male street robbers in an urban setting. Miller provides two theoretical approaches to explain women's criminal behavior, using a case study of street robbery. On the one hand, she describes women's criminal networks by showing how *gender stratification* shapes the nature of women's involvement in crime. On the other hand, she uses *gender as situational accomplishment* to understand how men and women use crime in different ways to establish their senses of masculinity and femininity and points out how gender varies across race and class inequalities.

Miller conducted in-depth interviews with 37 active offenders and compared women's and men's accounts of why they commit robbery, examining how gender influences robbery. Miller reports that a clear gender hierarchy exists on the street, where many robberies occur. Men use physical violence when committing robbery whereas women do not; men target other men whereas women do not. Men, in short, view robbery as one means to accomplish their masculinity—a situation in which men compete with each other for money and status through the use of guns, physical contact, and violence. Women, in contrast, take into account the gendered nature of their environment by robbing other women, who are less likely to be armed and are considered to be weak and easily intimidated. When women do rob men, they often use their sexuality to manipulate men into being easy targets.

Motivation for robbery is the one aspect of the crime that women and men appear to share in this study. They both rob to obtain money to buy things and for the excitement it brings. These motives remind the reader that class and race as well as gender are critical to understanding crime, because the relative deprivation of offenders in urban poor communities provides a powerful pathway to street crime. In fact, Miller warns, one must distinguish between motives and etiology (causes) of crime. Thus, she outlines the underlying structural conditions (deindustrialization, unemployment, poverty, and existence of an underground drug economy as well as racism in the economy and racial segregation in residences) that provide the context within which robbery occurs in this urban St. Louis neighborhood.

Finally, it is important to understand the role of race in any research such as this. At the same time, Miller alerts us to the fact that the reason that all but two of the women robbers were African American is because of the way the sample was derived: from a key informant who was a black man. That robbing tends to be racially segregated should come as no surprise. What should not be lost from this picture, though, is that whites are a much greater proportion of robbery arrestees in St. Louis than is reflected in this small (N = 37; 14 women and 23 men), nearly all-black sample. Each study should be appreciated for what it tells us about the specific population's experiences. Other studies are needed to learn more about robbery in different communities.

Feminist scholarship emerges from rich and diverse theoretical traditions. Nowhere is this more apparent than in the field of criminology. Feminist criminologists draw from a number of schools of feminist thought that often begin with very different premises about the nature and root causes of female oppression (for overviews, see Daly and Chesney-Lind, 1988; Simpson 1989, and Flavin, chapter 2). Nonetheless, there are a number of central beliefs that guide feminist inquiries. Daly and Chesney-Lind (1988:504) list five aspects of feminist thought that distinguish it from traditional forms of inquiry:

- Gender is not a natural fact but rather a complex social, historical, and cultural product; it is related to, but not simply derived from, biological sex differences and reproductive capacities.

- Gender and gender relations order social life and social institutions in fundamental ways.
- Gender relations and constructs of masculinity and femininity are not symmetrical but rather are based on an organizing principle of men's superiority and social and political-economic dominance over women.
- Systems of knowledge reflect men's views of the natural and social world; the production of knowledge is gendered.
- Women should be at the center of intellectual inquiry, not peripheral, invisible, or appendages to men.

In addition, contemporary feminist scholars strive to be attentive to the interlocking nature of race, class, and gender oppression, recognizing that women's experiences of gender vary according to their position in racial and class hierarchies (Daly and Stephens 1995; Maher 1997; Schwartz and Milovanovic 1996; Simpson 1991; Simpson and Elis 1995).

Source: Adapted from Sally Simpson, ed. 2000. *Of Crime and Criminality: The Use of Theory in Everyday Life.* Thousand Oaks: Pine Forge, pp. 25–46.

Several key issues have guided feminist inquiries of gender and offending.[1] First is the issue of generalizability. For nearly a century, theories developed to explain why people commit crime have actually been theories of why *men* commit crime. Feminist scholars have been keen on the question of whether (or the extent that) these theories can explain *women's* participation in crime. If not, then what alternative explanations can account for women's offending? Second is what is called the "gender ratio" problem: what are the reasons behind men's much greater participation in crime as compared to women? Traditional approaches explained these differences drawing on stereotypical images of women's supposed inferiority (Smart 1976:chaps. 2–3) and viewed gender as an individual trait. By contrast, feminist scholars offer theoretical accounts that draw on the recognition that gender is a key element of social organization (Kruttschnitt 1996:136).

A third issue, which has received less attention, is how gender inequality and stratification within criminal networks shape women's patterns of offending. For example, how do perceptions of women shape the criminal opportunities available to them? Are they excluded from particular types of crime? How do they overcome or resist the blocked opportunities they face in primarily masculine criminal enterprises? These are the issues I explore in this chapter. Using street robbery as a case study, I compare female and male robbers' accounts of their crimes to examine how gender shapes the accomplishment of robbery. First, let me provide more background on each of the feminist themes I have just described.

THE ISSUE OF GENERALIZABILITY

Theories about the etiology of crime have been quite diverse. One thing they have routinely shared, however, is a primary orientation toward explaining men's (or boys') crime. Thus, feminist scholars have posed the following questions: "Do theories of men's crime apply to women? Can the logic of such theories be modified to include women?" (Daly and Chesney-Lind 1988:514). Scholars who have attempted to test whether these theories can be generalized to women have focused on things such as the family, social learning, delinquent peer relationships, and (to a lesser extent) strain and deterrence. For the most part, these studies have found mixed results (for an overview, see Smith and Paternoster 1987). As Kruttschnitt (1996) summarizes, "It appears that the factors that influence delinquent development differ for males and females in some contexts but not others" (p. 141).

Feminist scholars have posed two critiques of the generalizability approach. First, racial and economic inequalities often are overlooked in this work. Given that women (and men) live in diverse structural conditions—conditions that are shaped especially by racial inequality—approaches that seek to find general causal patterns in women's and men's offending beg the question of how these factors differentially shape offending across race, class, *and* gender (Simpson 1991). For example, research suggests that urban African American females are somewhat more likely to engage in serious crime than are their female counterparts in other racial groups or settings (Ageton 1983; Hill and Crawford 1990; Laub and McDermott 1985; Mann 1993). Specifically, there is evidence of a link between "underclass" conditions (Wilson 1996) and urban African American women's offending. Hill and Crawford (1990) report that structural indicators appear to be most significant in predicting the criminal involvement of African American women, whereas social-psychological indicators are more predictive for white women. They conclude, "The unique position of black women in the structure of power relations in society has profound effects not shared by their white counterparts" (p. 621; see also Baskin and Sommers 1998; Richie 1996). Thus, theories that attempt to generalize across gender often miss the importance of racial and class inequalities in the causes of crime.

A second critique raised against the generalizability approach is that whereas theorists in this tradition look to find out whether the same processes are at work in explaining women's and men's crime, they cannot account for the gender ratio of offending, that is, men's disproportionate involvement in most crime.

Moreover, as I noted earlier, feminist scholars recognize gender as an important feature of the social organization of society and, consequently, of women's and men's experiences. Theories that attempt to be gender neutral are unable to address this pivotal issue (Daly and Chesney-Lind 1988). For example, in much of the generalizability research, it often is taken for granted that variables or constructs (e.g., "family attachment," "supervision") have the same meanings for males and females, but in fact this is an empirical question (Heimer and De Coster 1999).

THE GENDER RATIO PROBLEM

This brings us to the gender ratio problem. Scholars who address this issue raise the following questions: "Why are women less likely than men to be involved in crime? Conversely, why are men more crime prone than women? What explains [these] gender differences?" (Daly and Chesney-Lind 1988:515). These questions have led scholars to pay attention to gender differences and to develop theories that can account for variations in women's and men's offending (Hagan, Gillis, and Simpson 1985; Heimer and De Coster 1999). Moreover, attention to gender inequality has led feminist theorists to examine the impact of women's victimization as an explanatory factor for their crime (Arnold 1990; Chesney-Lind 1997; Daly 1992; Gilfus 1992; Richie 1996). As such, these works have allowed feminist scholars to move beyond a gender ratio approach to an understanding of "gendered lives" (Daly and Maher 1998).

One such theoretical perspective has been to focus on gender as situated accomplishment (West and Fenstermaker 1995; West and Zimmerman 1987). Here, gender is recognized as "much more than a role or [an] individual characteristic; it is a mechanism whereby situated social action contributes to the reproduction of social structure" (West and Fenstermaker 1995:21). Women and men "do gender," or behave in gendered ways, in response to normative beliefs about femininity and masculinity. The performance of gender is both an indication of and a reproduction of gendered social hierarchies. This approach has been incorporated into feminist ac-

counts of crime as a means of explaining differences in women's and men's offending (Messerschmidt 1993, 1995; Newburn and Stanko 1994; Simpson and Elis 1995). Here, crime is described as "a 'resource' for accomplishing gender—for demonstrating masculinity within a given context or situation" (Simpson and Elis 1995:50).

This approach can help to account for men's greater involvement in particular types of crime (e.g., violence) and also for women's involvement in crime in ways scripted by femininity (e.g., prostitution). In addition, this approach can help to account for differences resulting from racial and class inequalities, with the recognition that constructions of femininity and masculinity vary across these important contexts (Simpson 1991; Simpson and Elis 1995). For example, Simpson (1989) notes that some of women's participation in violent street crime might stem from "the frustration, alienation, and anger that are associated with racial and class oppression" (p. 618). When violence is an extensive part of their lives and communities, urban women might be more likely to view violence as an appropriate or a useful means of dealing with their environment (Simpson 1991).

GENDER STRATIFICATION IN CRIMINAL NETWORKS

Regardless of women's position vis-à-vis racial and class inequalities, they also remain in a society that is inextricably shaped by gender inequality. Consequently, feminist scholars recently have focused on how gender stratification within criminal networks mirrors gender stratification elsewhere in society, shaping women's experiences. This work has provided overwhelming evidence that gender inequality is a salient feature of urban street scenes—something with which women involved in these networks must constantly contend (Campbell 1984; Jacobs and Miller 1998; Maher 1997; Maher and Daly 1996; Miller 1986; Miller 1998a; Steffensmeier 1983). Thus, this scholarship is concerned with examining both the nature of gender stratification and women's responses to it.

Steffensmeier (1983) was the first scholar to detail the institutional nature of gender inequality on the streets, examining how homosocial reproduction, gender segregation, and "sex typing" limited women's participation in street networks. Male street offenders often view women as unreliable, untrustworthy, and weak, shunning them as would-be criminal associates (Steffensmeier and Terry 1986). Consequently, women "continue to find themselves with a deficit of 'criminal capital' [Hagan and McCarthy 1997]—the connections, ties, and pull that come with extensive and enduring involvement in street networks" (Jacobs and Miller 1998:554). As a result, they face limited options, restricted participation, and victimization in these settings.

Perhaps the most sophisticated analysis of gender stratification on the streets is Maher's (1997) ethnography of a drug market in Brooklyn, New York. She documents a rigid gender division of labor in the drug economy, shaped as well along racial lines, in which women are "clearly disadvantaged compared to their male counterparts" (p. 54). Describing the three spheres of income generation on the streets—drug business hustles, non-drug hustles, and "sexwork"—Maher details the ways in which women are excluded from more lucrative opportunities and found sexwork to be one of their few viable options for making money. [See Maher, chap. 7.]

The current study is housed in this tradition of examining how gender stratification shapes women's involvement in crime. In this chapter, I examine a crime for which the gender ratio problem I described earlier is striking. Robbery is one of the most gender-differentiated serious crimes in the United States; that is, the proportion of men who commit robbery as compared to women is greater than that for nearly every other serious crime. According to the Federal Bureau of Investigation's (1996) Uniform Crime Reports for 1995, women accounted for only 9.3 percent of all robbery arrestees, whereas men accounted for 90.7 percent of those arrested for this crime. As you read my discussion of women's participation in robbery, therefore, it is very important to keep two things in mind. First, women are only a small percentage of street robbers.

As such, I am studying a very unusual behavior among women. Second, my discussion of the crime is not meant to suggest that women's participation in robbery is increasing. Instead, I am interested in comparing women's and men's accounts of why they commit street robbery and how gender organizes their commissions of the crime.

WOMEN'S VIOLENCE AS RESISTANCE TO MALE OPPRESSION

Feminist scholars who address the use of street violence by women often suggest that women's violence differs from that of men's—women use violence in response to their vulnerability to or actual victimization in the family and/or at the hands of men (Campbell 1993; Joe and Chesney-Lind 1995; Maher 1997; Maher and Curtis 1992; Maher and Daly 1996). In her ethnography of a Brooklyn drug market, Maher notes that women adopt violent presentations of self as a strategy of protection. She explains, "'Acting bad' and 'being bad' are not the same. Although many of the women presented themselves as 'bad' or 'crazy,' this projection was a street persona and a necessary survival strategy" (1997:95; see also Maher and Daly 1996). These women were infrequently involved in violent crime and most often resorted to violence in response to threats or harms against them. She concludes that "unlike their male counterparts, for women, reputation was about 'preventing victimization'" (Maher 1997:95–96; see also Campbell 1993). In this account, even when women's aggression is offensive, it can still be understood as a defensive act, because it emerges as resistance to victimization.

Maher's research uncovered a particular form of robbery—"viccing"—in which women involved in the sex trade rob their clients. Although the phenomenon of prostitutes robbing tricks is not new, Maher's work documents the proliferation of viccing as a form of resistance against their greater vulnerability to victimization and against cheapened sex markets within the drug economy. Comparing viccing with traditional forms of robbery, Maher and Curtis conclude, "The fact that the act [of viccing] itself is little different to any other instrumental robbery belies the reality that the motivations undergirding it are more complex and, indeed, are intimately linked with women's collective sense of the devaluation of their bodies and their work" (1992:246). However, it is likely that not all of women's street violence can be viewed as resistance to male oppression; instead, some women may be motivated to commit violent crimes for many of the same reasons some men are. In certain contexts, norms favorable to women's use of violence may exist, and they are not simply about avoiding victimization, but also result in status and recognition.

GENDER AND STREET ROBBERY

The Study

One way in which to find out how gender shapes patterns of offending is to talk to female and male offenders and to compare what they have to say about their crime.[2] As Daly and Chesney-Lind (1988) point out, feminist scholarship often involves interviews because this approach provides "texture [and] social context" (p. 518) that allow us to present more nuanced accounts of women's involvement in crime. Using this method, I draw from in-depth interviews with active male and female robbers. The findings I discuss come from a larger study of urban street robbers in St. Louis, Missouri (Wright and Decker 1997).[3] Respondents were recruited from impoverished urban neighborhoods in the city. St. Louis is typical of a number of midwestern cities devastated by structural changes brought about by deindustrialization. The city is characterized by tremendous economic and racial segregation. Deindustrialization has exacerbated these conditions, also resulting in population loss, the social isolation of many urban dwellers, losses in community resources, and a deepened concentration of urban poverty among African Americans in the city. The neighborhoods from which respondents were drawn are characteristic of what some scholars have called "underclass" conditions (Sampson and Wilson 1995; Wilson 1996). Although I do not discuss these structural conditions

further, they are important contexts to keep in mind as I discuss the activities of urban street robbers.

The sample consists of 37 active robbers, a matched sample of 14 women and 23 men who were approximately the same age and who reported committing their first robberies at the same age. Respondents ranged in age from 16 to 46 years, although the majority were in their late teens or early 20s. Criteria for inclusion in the sample included the following: the individual had committed a robbery in the recent past, defined him- or herself as currently active, and was regarded as active by other offenders. Though it is not possible to determine the representativeness of this sample of active offenders (see Glassner and Carpenter 1985), the approach nonetheless overcomes many of the shortcomings associated with interviewing ex-offenders or offenders who are incarcerated (see Agar 1977). In fact, in the current study snowball sampling allowed for the purposive oversampling of both female and juvenile robbers. The vast majority of participants were African American—all of the men and all but 2 of the women. This is one of the greatest limitations of the sample. Whites were a much greater proportion of robbery arrestees in St. Louis than is reflected in the nearly all-black sample. This bias in the data was the result of the snowball sampling techniques used. One individual, an African American ex-offender, was hired and given the charge of locating his former criminal associates to get them to participate in the study. These respondents then referred their friends and associates to participate, and the process continued until the sample was built. Nearly all of these contacts yielded African American robbers. Despite the fact that there were a number of white robbers in St. Louis, "successfully making contact with active black armed robbers proved to be of almost no help . . . in locating white offenders" (Wright and Decker 1997:11).

Data were gathered by using semistructured in-depth interviews. Interviews lasted one to two hours and included a range of questions about the respondents' involvement in robbery. Respondents were asked to describe why they committed robbery, their typical approach when committing robbery, and the details of their most recent offenses. The goal was to gain a thorough understanding of the contexts of these events from the respondents' perspectives. Now, I turn my attention to the two questions that guide my inquiry: situational motives for committing robbery and the accomplishment of the crime.

Motivations to Commit Robbery

Because many of the respondents in the sample were young and had begun committing robberies as teenagers, their descriptions of the reasons why they committed the crime resonate with the typical desires of adolescents and young adults. Most of the participants, both female and male, said that they committed robberies to get things such as jewelry and spending money and also because they found the crime exciting. My study cannot address etiological factors, that is, those factors in individuals' lives that led them to commit crime. Instead, my discussion is of motivations that are situational or that emerge in the context of their decisions to commit robbery.

Perhaps what is most striking in their discussions, as I have noted, is that women and men give very similar descriptions of their motives. For example, T-Bone[4] said that he decides to commit robberies when he is "tired of not having money." When the idea comes about, he typically is with friends from the neighborhood and, he explained, "we all bored, broke, mad." Likewise, CMW said that she commits robberies "out of the blue, just something to do. Bored at the time and just want to find some action." She explained, "I be sitting on the porch and we'll get to talking and stuff. See people going around, and they be flashing in they fancy cars, walking down the street with that jewelry on, thinking they all bad, and we just go get'em." For both males and females, robbery typically was a means of achieving conspicuous consumption.

If anything, imperatives to gain money and material goods through robbery appear to be stronger for males than females, so that young men explain that they sometimes commit robberies because they feel some economic pressure, whereas young women typically do not. Masculine street identity is tied to the ability to have and spend money, and included in this is the appearance of economic self-sufficiency. Research has documented women's support networks in urban communities, including among criminally involved women (see Maher 1997; Stack 1974). This may help explain why the imperative for young men is stronger than for young women: Community norms may give women wider latitude for obtaining material goods and economic support from a variety of sources, including other females, family members, and boyfriends; whereas the pressure of society's view of men as breadwinners differentially affects men's emotional experience of relying on others economically. This may explain why several young men specifically describe that they do not like relying on their parents in order to meet their consumer needs.

Asked to explain why they commit robberies instead of other crimes with similar economic rewards, both women and men said that they chose robberies, as Cooper explained, because "it's the easiest." Libbie Jones reported that robbery provides her with the things she wants in one quick and easy step:

> I like robbery. I like robbery 'cause I don't have to buy nothing. You have a herringbone. I'm gonna take your herringbone, and then I have me a herringbone. I don't have to worry about going to the store, getting me some money. If you got some little earrings on, I'm gonna get 'em.

Often they targeted individuals whom they believed were "safe" victims, usually other street-involved individuals who were less likely to go to the police. Most robberies, whether committed by females or males, occurred in the larger contexts of street life, and their victims reflected this. Most also were involved in street contexts, either as adolescents or young adults who hang out on the streets and go to clubs or as individuals involved (as dealers and/or users) in the street-level drug economy (for more on target selection, see Wright and Decker 1997: chap. 3).

In addition to the economic incentives that draw the respondents toward robbery, many also derived an emotional thrill from committing robbery. Little Bills said, "When my first robbery started, my second, the third one, it got more fun. . . . If I keep on doing it, I think that I will really get addicted to it." Likewise, Buby noted, "You get, like, a rush. It be fun at the time." In particular, when they perceived individuals as "high-catting" or showing off, both female and male robbers viewed these individuals as deserving targets. For example, Treason Taylor described a woman he robbed at a gas station: "Really, I didn't like the way she came out. She was, like pulling out all her money like she think she hot shit." A few respondents even specifically targeted people they did not like or people who had insulted or hurt them in the past.

For both women and men, then, motivations to commit robbery were primarily economic—to get money, jewelry, and other status-conferring goods—but also included elements of thrill seeking, attempting to overcome boredom, and revenge. Most striking is the continuity across women's and men's accounts of their motives for committing robbery. As the following subsections show, there are clear differences in the accomplishment of robbery by gender. However, these differences apparently are not driven by differences in motivation.

Men's Commission of Street Robbery
The men in my study committed street robberies in a strikingly uniform way. Their descriptions of robberies were variations around one theme: using physical violence and/or a gun placed close to (or touching) the victim in a confrontational manner. This is reflected in Looney's description of being taught how to commit his first robbery at the age of 13 years by his stepbrother:

We was up at [a fast-food restaurant] one day, and a dude was up there tripping. My stepbrother had gave me a .22 automatic. He told me to walk over behind him and put the gun to his head and tell him to give me all his stuff. That's what I did. I walked up to him and said, "Man, this is a jack, man. Take off all your jewelry and take your money out of your pockets, throw it on the ground, and walk off." So that's what he did. I picked up the money and the jewelry and walked away.

The most common form of robbery described by male respondents was to target other men involved in street life*—drug dealers, drug users, gang members, or other men who looked "flashy" because of their clothes, cars, or jewelry. Only seven men (30 percent) said they robbed women as well as men. All of the men in the sample used guns when they robbed, although not everyone used a gun every time. The key was to make sure, as Syco said, that the victims know "that we ain't playing." They conveyed this message by positioning the guns close to the victims' bodies or by physically assaulting the victims. For example, Bob Jones confronted his victims by placing his gun at the backs of their heads, where "they feel it," and saying to them, "Give it up motherfucker. Don't move or I'll blow your brains out!" Explaining the positioning of the gun, he said, "When you feel that steel against your head . . . [it] carries a lot of weight."

Without guns, and sometimes even when they used guns, some men reported using physical violence to ensure the victims' cooperation and the robbers' getaways. Cooper said, "You always got to either hit 'em, slap 'em, or do something to let them know you for real." Likewise, Mike J. said, "You might shake them a little bit. If there is more than one of you, you can really do that kind of stuff like shake them up a little bit to show them you're not messing around." When male robbers did not have guns, they typically used more physical violence to make sure that the victims did not resist. Taz explained,

If it's a strong-arm [a robbery without a weapon], like, I'll just get up on them and I'll just hit 'em, and [my partner] will grab them or, like, he will hit them and I'll grab 'em, and we keep on hitting them until they fall or something. . . . [Then,] we just go in his pockets, leave him there, we gone.

As I already noted, seven men said that they robbed women as well as men. However, male respondents, including those who did not rob women, said that they believed that robbing women was different from robbing men. They felt that robbing women was less dangerous because women were less

*Editors' note: 96 percent of the men robbed other men.

likely to resist. Looney explained, "Men gonna act like they the tough guy, . . . but a lady, I just tell them to give it up and they give me they whole purse or whatever they got." Whereas physical violence often was used routinely when men robbed other men, these men said that they rarely used physical violence against women and did so only when the women resisted. Although violence often was deemed necessary to establish a credible threat with male victims, it was not seen as necessary with women victims. Perhaps what is most ironic is that although male robbers were in agreement that women were "easy" victims, as a rule, these men did not target women. Perhaps this was because they did not believe that women would have the kind of money on them that men would (particularly criminally involved men), but it also was because they viewed robbery as a prototypically masculine endeavor, best carried out in male-on-male encounters (see also Katz 1988; Messerschmidt 1993).

> Male robbers, then, clearly view the act of robbery as a masculine accomplishment in which men compete with other men for money and status. While some rob women, those robberies are deviations from the norm of "badass" against "badass" that dominates much of men's discussions of street robbery (see Katz, 1988).

In sum, males' robberies were characterized by the routine use of guns, physical contact with the victim, and (in some cases) physical violence. Men's descriptions of their robberies were strikingly similar to each other. By contrast, women's descriptions of their robberies revealed much more varied techniques and provided a telling contrast about the nature of gender on the streets.

Women's Commission of Street Robbery

Women in the sample described three predominant ways in which they committed robberies: targeting female victims in physically confrontational robberies, targeting male victims by appearing sexually available, and participating with males during street robberies of men. It is noteworthy that most women described participating in two or more types of these robberies. Thus, as we will see, they committed

robberies differently depending on the circumstances and on who their victims were. In all, 10 women (71 percent) described targeting female victims, usually on the streets but occasionally at dance clubs or in cars. In addition, 7 women (50 percent) described setting up men through promises of sexual favors including 2 women who did so in the context of prostitution. Among the women, 7 (50 percent) described working with male friends, relatives, or boyfriends in street robberies, with 3 (21 percent) reporting this as their exclusive form of robbery.

Robbing Females   The most common form of robbery reported by women in the study was to rob other females in a physically confrontational manner. Of the 14 female respondents, 10 reported committing these types of offenses. Typically, women's robberies of other females occurred on the streets, although a few young women also reported robbing females in the bathrooms or parking lots of clubs, and 1 robbed women in cars. These robberies sometimes were committed alone and other times were committed with another woman or several additional women. But they were not committed with male robbers. In fact, Ne-Ne said that even when she is out with male friends and sees a female target, the men do not get involved: "They'll say, 'Well, you go on and do her.'"

Most robberies of females either involved no weapons or involved knives. Women rarely described using guns to rob other women. Female respondents said that when they chose women victims, it was because they believed that the other women were not likely to be armed and also were not likely to resist or fight back. DMW explained, "See, women, they won't really do nothing. They say, 'Oh, oh, okay, here take this.' A dude, he might try to put up a fight." Likewise, Libbie Jones said, "I wouldn't do no men by myself," but she added that women victims "ain't gonna do nothing because they be so scared." Typically, women felt that it was not necessary to use weapons in these robberies. Quick explained that she sometimes used a knife, "but sometimes I don't need anything. Most of the time it be girls, you know, just snatching they chains or jewelry. You don't need nothing for that."

On occasion, female victims belied the stereotype of them and fought back. When that occurred, several women described stabbing their victims. Janet Outlaw described one such encounter:

> I walked up to her, and I pulled out the knife. I said, "Up that purse." And she looked at me. I said, "Shit, do you think I'm playing? Up that purse." She was like, "Shit, you ain't getting my purse. Do what you got to do." I was like, "Shit, you must be thinking I'm playing." So I took the knife, stabbed her a couple of times on the shoulder, stabbed her on the arm, and snatched the purse. Cut her arm and snatched the purse. She just ran, "Help, help." We were gone.

However, stabbing female victims was a rare occurrence. Instead, women's robberies of other women routinely involved physical confrontation such as hitting, shoving, or beating up the victim. Describing a recent robbery, Nicole Simpson said, "I have bricks in my purse, and I went up to her and hit her in the head and took her money." Kim Brown said that she will "just whop you and take a purse but not really put a gun to anybody's face." Libbie Jones said that she has her victims throw their possessions on the ground, "then you push 'em, kick 'em, or whatever. You pick it up, and you just burn out." Describing why this type of physical force was necessary, Janet Outlaw explained, "It's just a woman-to-woman thing, and we just, like, just don't, just letting them know like it is, we let them know we ain't playing." As will be seen below, this approach is vastly different from women's approaches when they rob men or when they commit robberies with males.

To summarize, notable elements of women's robberies of other women are that they most frequently occurred within street-oriented settings; did not include male accomplices; and typically involved physical force such as hitting, shoving, and kicking rather than the use of weapons. When weapons were used, they were most likely to be knives. In these contexts, women chose to rob other females rather than males because they believed that females were less likely to fight back. They typically did not use weapons such as guns because they believed that female targets were unlikely to be armed.

Robbing Males by Appearing Sexually Available   Women's robberies of men almost always involved guns and rarely involved physical contact. Janet Outlaw, who described using a great deal of physical violence in her robberies of other women (see previous subsection), described her robberies of men in much different terms. She explained, "If we waste time touching men, there is a possibility that they can get the gun off of us. While we wasting time touching them, they could do anything. So we just keep the gun straight on them. No touching, no moving, just straight gun at you." The circumstances of these robberies were different as well. When women robbed men, the key was to pretend to be sexually interested in the male victims, who then would drop their guard, providing safe opportunities for the crime to occur. Two women, Jayzo and Nicole Simpson, robbed men in the context of prostitution. The other five typically chose victims at clubs or on the streets, flirted and appeared sexually interested, and then suggested that they go to a hotel, where the robberies took place.

Nicole Simpson prostituted to support her drug habit, but sometimes she "just don't be feeling like doing it" and will rob her trick rather than complete the sexual transaction. She chose tricks whom she felt would make safe victims and would be unlikely to resist. Typically, she waited until the man was in a vulnerable position before pulling out her knife. As she explained, "If you are sucking a man's dick and you pull a knife on them, they not gonna too much argue with you." Jayzo's techniques paralleled those of Nicole Simpson, although she used a gun instead of a knife.

Young women who targeted men outside of the context of prostitution played on the men's beliefs about women to accomplish these robberies, including the assumptions that women would not be armed, would not attempt to rob them, and could be taken advantage of sexually. Quick explained, "They don't suspect that a girl gonna try to get 'em. You know what I'm saying? So it's kind of easier 'cause they, like, 'She looks innocent, she ain't gonna do this,' but that's how I get 'em. They put they guard down to a woman." She said that when she sets up men, she parties with them first but makes sure that she does not consume as much as them. "Most of the time when girls get high, they think they can take advantage of us, so they always, 'Let's go to a hotel or my crib or something.'" Janet Outlaw said, "They easy to get. We know what they after—sex." Likewise, CMW said, "They thinking we little freaks . . . whores or something." Men's assumptions that they could take advantage of women led them to place themselves at risk for robbery, on which these women acted.

Except for the two women who robbed tricks when they were prostituting, women typically held their guns at a safe distance from the victims rather than pressing the guns up against them as the male robbers did when they robbed men. Doing so decreased the risk that a victim could resist, grab the gun, and use it on the woman. This was necessary precisely because the women chose male victims who thought that they could take advantage of the women. Janet Outlaw encountered one such man. She picked him up in a nightclub, they went to a hotel together, and then his resistance led her to fire her weapon. She explained,

> We got to smoking a little bud, he got to taking off his little shit, laying it on a little table. He was like, "Shit, what's up, ain't you gonna get undressed?" I was like, "Shit, yeah, hold up," and I went in my purse and I pulled out the gun. He was like, "Damn, what's up with you, gal?" I was like, "Shit, I want your jewelry and all the money you got." He was like, "Shit, bitch, you crazy. I ain't giving you my snit." I said, "Do you think I'm playing, nigger? You don't think I'll shoot your motherfucking ass?" He was like, "Shit, you crazy, fuck that, you ain't gonna shoot me." So then I had fired the thing, but I didn't fire it at him, shot the gun. He was like, "Fuck no." I snatched his shit. He didn't have on no clothes. I snatched the shit and ran out the door. Hopped in my car.

Women often committed these robberies alone, but sometimes they did so in pairs or even had male accomplices follow them to the hotels for backup. In each case, however, the woman always used a weapon and avoided physical contact as much as she could. Thus, the women's robberies of men were strikingly different from their robberies of women.

Street Robberies with Male Robbers   As the previous two subsections illustrated, women commit robberies in very different ways depending on whether their victims are female or male. As a rule, women described that they did not rob females with male accomplices but did sometimes work with male accomplices to set up and rob men. In addition, half of the women in the sample described committing street robberies of males with male accomplices. The difference between these robberies of men and those I described previously is that, with street robberies, women did not act sexually available so as to rob men. Instead, in conjunction with their male partners, they conducted these robberies in much the same way as the male respondents described robbing men on the streets. Three women in the sample—Buby, Tish, and Lisa Jones—described working with males on the streets as their only form of robbery. Each of these women described her participation as secondary. By contrast, other women who engaged in street robberies with males engaged in other forms of robbery and did not distinguish their roles from roles of their male accomplices in these robberies.

Lisa Jones and Tish both assisted their boyfriends in the commission of robberies. Buby went along with her brother and cousins. Lisa Jones said, "Most of the time, we'll just be driving around and he'll say, 'Let's go to this neighborhood and rob somebody.'" Usually, she stayed in the car while he approached the victim, but she was armed and would get out and assist when necessary. Describing one such incident, she said, "One time, there was two guys, and one guy was in the car and the other guy was out of the car, and I seen that one guy getting out of the car, I guess to help his friend. That's when I got out, and I held the gun and I told him to stay where he was." Tish and Lisa Jones were the only white respondents in the study, and each robbed with an African American boyfriend. Both described their boyfriends as the decision makers in the robberies—deciding when, where, and whom to rob.

It is striking that all of these young women routinely committed armed robberies wielding guns on victims yet rejected the view of themselves as criminals. In fact, during her interview, Lisa Jones was adamant, telling the interviewer, "I'm not a criminal." Lisa Jones and Tish were the only respondents who downplayed their involvement in armed robbery. It probably is not coincidental that they were young white women who used their beliefs about race and gender to minimize the implications of the serious nature of their crimes.

These respondents were at the far end of the continuum of women's involvement in robbery, clearly taking subordinate roles in the crime and defining themselves as less culpable as a result. For the most part, other women who participated in street robberies with male accomplices describe themselves as equal participants. Robberies with male accomplices typically involved guns and came about when a group of people were driving around and spotted a potential victim. They committed the crime using the same techniques as male respondents described, that is, using physical contact and, when necessary, violence. In fact, Ne-Ne said that she preferred committing street robberies with males rather than with females because she viewed her male accomplices as more reliable. She explained,

> I can't be bothered with too many girls. That's why I try to be with dudes or whatever. They gonna be down. If you get out of the car and if you rob a dude or jack somebody and you with some dudes, then you know if they see he tryin' to resist, they gonna give me some help. Whereas a girl, you might get somebody that's scared and might drive off. That's the way it is.

In fact, Ne-Ne was the only woman interviewed to report having committed this type of street robbery of a male victim on her own. Her actions paralleled those of male-on-male robbers described earlier. She explained, "I just turned around the corner, came back down the street. He was out by himself, and I got out of the car, had the cap pulled down over my face, and I just went to the back and upped him. Put the gun up to his head." Importantly, Ne-Ne told the interviewer that this robbery was successful because the man she robbed did not realize that she was a woman. Describing herself physically, she said, "I'm big, you know." In addition, her dress and manner masked that she was a woman.

Being large, wearing a ball cap, and committing the robbery in a masculine style (e.g., putting a gun to his head) allowed her to disguise the fact that she was a woman and thus decrease the victim's likelihood of resisting. She said, "He don't know right now to this day if it was a girl or a dude."

DISCUSSION

Feminist scholars have been hesitant to grapple with the issue of women's violence, both because a focus on women's violence draws attention away from the fact that violence is a predominantly male phenomenon and because studying women's violence can play into sensationalized accounts of female offenders. Nonetheless, as this and other studies have shown, "gender alone does not account for variation in criminal violence" (Simpson 1991:118). A small number of women are involved in violent street crime in ways that go beyond "preventing victimization," and appear to find support among their male and female peers for these activities. To draw this conclusion is not to suggest that women's use of violence is increasing, that women are "equals" on the streets, or that gender does not matter. It does suggest that researchers should continue developing feminist perspectives to address the issue.

Perhaps what is most notable about this study is the incongruity between women's and men's motives for committing robbery and the ways in which they go about conducting the crime. Although the comparison of women's and men's motivations revealed gender similarities, when women and men actually committed robbery, the ways in which they went about doing the crime were strikingly different. These differences highlight the clear gender hierarchy that exists on the streets. Although some women are able to carve out a niche for themselves in this setting and even establish partnerships with males, they are participating in a male-dominated environment, and their actions reflect an understanding of this.

To successfully commit robbery, women must take into account the gendered nature of their environment. One way in which they do so is by targeting other females. Both male and female robbers held the view that females were easy to rob because they were less likely than males to be armed and because they were perceived as weak and easily intimidated. Janet Outlaw described women's robbery of other women as "just a woman-to-woman thing." This is supported by Ne-Ne's description that her male friends did not participate with her in robberies of females, and it is supported by men's accounts of robbing women. Whereas women routinely robbed other women, men were less likely to do so, perhaps because these robberies did not result in the demonstration of masculinity (West and Zimmerman 1987).

At the same time as women articulated the belief that other women were easy targets, they also drew on these perceptions of women to rob men. Two of the women described committing robberies much in keeping with Maher's (1997) descriptions of "viccing." In addition, a number of women used men's perceptions of women as weak, sexually available, and easily manipulated to turn the tables and manipulate men into circumstances in which they became vulnerable to robbery by flirting and appearing sexually interested in the men. Unlike women's robberies of other women, these robberies tended not to involve physical contact but did involve the use of guns. Because they recognized men's perceptions of women, the women also recognized that men were more likely to resist being robbed by females, and thus they committed these robberies in ways that minimized their risk of losing control and maximized their ability to show that they were "for real."

West and Zimmerman (1987) note that there are circumstances in which "parties reach an accommodation that allow[s] a woman to engage in presumptively masculine behavior" (p. 139). In this study, it is notable that both women and men recognized the urban street world as a male-dominated one. Nonetheless, a few of the women gained access to male privilege by adopting male attitudes about females, constructing their own identities as more masculine, and following through by behaving in masculine ways. Ne-Ne and Janet Outlaw both come to mind in this regard as women who completed robberies in equal partnerships with men and identi-

fied with men's attitudes about other women. Other women, such as Lisa Jones and Tish, accepted not only women's position as secondary but also their own positions as secondary. Whereas Ne-Ne and Janet Outlaw appeared to draw status and identity from their criminality in ways that went beyond their gender identity, Lisa Jones and Tish used their gender identity to construct themselves as noncriminal.

In sum, the women in this sample did not appear to commit robbery differently from men so as to meet different needs or to accomplish different goals. Instead, the differences that emerge reflected practical choices made in the context of a gender-stratified environment in which, on the whole, males are perceived as strong and women are perceived as weak. Motivationally, then, it appears that women's participation in street violence can result from the same structural and cultural underpinnings that shape some of men's participation in this type of crime. Yet, gender remains a salient factor shaping their actions as well as the actions of men.

Though urban African American women have higher rates of violence than other women, their participation in violent crime is nonetheless significantly lower than that of their male counterparts in the same communities (Simpson 1991). An important line of inquiry for future research is to assess what protective factors keep the majority of women living in underclass settings from adopting violence as a culturally legitimate response. While research shows that racial and economic oppression contribute to African American women's greater participation in violent crime, they do not ensure its occurrence. Daly and Stephens (1995:208) note: "Racism in criminological theories occurs when racial or cultural differences are overemphasized or mischaracterized *and* when such differences are denied." Future research should strive to strike this balance and attend to the complex issues surrounding women's participation in violence within the urban street world.

There are a number of additional questions about gender and robbery that this study cannot address. Although I have noted the striking gender ratio with regard to the commission of robbery, the data I have presented cannot allow me to address the question of why so many more men than women choose to commit robbery. Moreover, as I noted earlier, my discussion of motivation is not the same as discussing the causes of women's and men's crime. Although the women and men in this study gave similar accounts of why they committed robbery, this does not mean that they became criminally involved for the same reasons. However, it does provide an additional layer to our attempts to understand the gendered lives of female offenders by focusing on the ways in which women participate in the urban street world. I opened this chapter by suggesting that gender is a "complex social, historical, and cultural product" and that "gender and gender relations order social life and social institutions in fundamental ways" (Daly and Chesney-Lind 1988:504). Hopefully, seeing how women and men talked about their commission of robbery has helped to bring to life these important insights of feminist theory.

POLICY IMPLICATIONS

Feminist research, including this study, raises a number of important issues that should be considered in the development of policies for dealing with female offenders. First among these is the recognition that both women and men really do lead gendered lives. That is, in very complex ways, gender has an impact on our experiences at all levels of interactions with others as well as within the social structures of society. The unique features of women's lives need to be taken into account in developing and implementing policies in gender-specific ways. For example, women often are the primary caregivers in their children's lives, and policies for dealing with female offenders should assess the impact of various strategies not just on women but also on their children. Gender inequality and the victimization of women are important causal factors for crime that need to be considered in understanding female offenders. In addition, it is important to recognize that gender inequality constrains the types of opportunities women have available to them. This is especially true in poor communities and even is true when it comes to the commission of crime.

However, as this chapter has highlighted, it is important to strike a balance between recognizing the significance of gender and gender inequality but not to reduce everything to gender. This is important for at least two reasons. First, we have a long history within both our criminal and juvenile justice systems of treating women offenders differently from men offenders, often to the detriment of the women (for an overview, see Chesney-Lind 1997). This often plays itself out through an overemphasis on controlling young women's independence and sexuality (Alder 1998) and through treating women in particularly harsh ways when they do not conform to traditional notions of appropriate femininity (Visher 1983). In fact, Baines and Alder (1996) suggest that notions of girls' "difference," particularly tied to an overemphasis on girls' victimization, negatively affects the treatment that girls receive within juvenile justice.

As important is the second reason for not paying exclusive attention to gender, that is, the need to consider the importance of racial and class inequalities for understanding women's, as well as men's, offending. As this study has documented, many of the motivations both women and men described for why they committed robberies were responses to the relative deprivation they face as marginalized members of an urban underclass community. Paying attention to the broad spectrum of factors that lead to women's offending—both gendered and those they share with their male counterparts—is necessary to create effective solutions for female offenders and society. The important insights of feminist scholarship have led to the recognition of the need to strike this important balance in developing policies to both empower women and create a more equitable society.

DISCUSSION QUESTIONS

1. What does Miller mean when she describes gender as "situated accomplishment"?
2. How do women and men "accomplish" robbery differently? What role does race and gender play in this analysis? How

does Miller explain these differences? Do you agree or disagree with her analysis? Why?

3. What does Miller mean when she says that there is "gender stratification" in criminal networks? How does it play out in this study of male and female robbers?
4. Why is it important to separate *motivation* from *causation* in a study of crime?
5. Discuss the implications of gender-based differential behavior during the commission of robbery: What are the implications for the victim? What are the implications for the sanctioning process?

NOTES

1. I limit my discussion in this chapter to feminist work on the question of female offending. However, it is important to note that feminist scholars have focused on several additional important issues in criminology. These include (1) violence against women (e.g., rape, domestic violence, sexual abuse), (2) the impact of gender on women's processing and experiences in the criminal and juvenile justice systems, and (3) how gender shapes women's experiences in law enforcement and criminal justice careers. These topics are beyond the scope of this chapter, but there are a number of sources available for further information. See Belknap (1997), Chesney-Lind and Shelden (1998), Daly and Maher (1998), Dobash and Dobash (1992), Merlo and Pollock (1995), and Price and Sokoloff (1995).
2. This discussion is a condensed version of Miller (1998b).
3. Wright and Decker's (1997) study was funded by the Harry Frank Guggenheim Foundation and the National Institute of Justice (NIJ Grant 94-IJ-CX-0030).
4. The names I use are pseudonyms provided by the respondents to disguise their identities.

REFERENCES

Agar, Michael. 1977. In Ethnography in the Streets and in the Joint: A Comparison. *Street Ethnography: Selected Studies of Crime and Drug Use in Natural Settings,* ed. Robert Weppner, 143–156. Beverly Hills, CA: Sage.

Ageton, Suzanne S. 1983. The Dynamics of Female Delinquency 1976–1980. *Criminology* 21:555–84.

Alder, Christine. 1998. Passionate and Willful Girls: Confronting Practices. *Women & Criminal Justice* 9:81–101.

Arnold, Regina. 1990. Processes of Victimization and Criminalization of Black Women. *Social Justice* 17:153–66.

Baines, M., and Christine Alder. 1996. Are Girls More Difficult to Work With? Youth Workers' Perspectives in Juvenile Justice and Related Areas. *Crime and Delinquency* 42:467–85.

Baskin, Deborah, and Ira Sommers. 1998. *Casualties of Community Disorder: Women's Careers in Violent Crime.* Boulder, CO: Westview.

Belknap, Joanne. 1997. *The Invisible Woman: Gender, Crime, and Justice.* Belmont, CA: Wadsworth.

Campbell, Anne. 1984. *The Girls in the Gang.* London: Basil Blackwell.

Campbell, Anne. 1993. *Men, Women and Aggression.* New York: Basic Books.

Chesney-Lind, Meda. 1997. *The Female Offender: Girls, Women, and Crime.* Thousand Oaks, CA: Sage.

Chesney-Lind, Meda, and Randall G. Shelden. 1998. *Girls, Delinquency, and Juvenile Justice.* 2d ed. Belmont, CA: Wadsworth.

Daly, Kathleen. 1992. Women's Pathways to Felony Court: Feminist Theories of Lawbreaking and Problems of Representation. *Review of Law and Women's Studies* 2:11–52.

Daly, Kathleen, and Meda Chesney-Lind. 1988. Feminism and Criminology. *Justice Quarterly* 5:497–538.

Daly, Kathleen, and Lisa Maher. 1998. *Criminology at the Crossroads: Feminist Readings in Crime and Justice.* Oxford, UK: Oxford University Press.

Daly, Kathleen, and Deborah J. Stephens. 1995. The "Dark Figure" of Criminology: Towards a Black and Multiethnic Feminist Agenda for Theory and Research. In *International Feminist Perspectives in Criminology: Engendering a Discipline,* ed. Nicole Hahn Rafter and Frances Heidensohn. 189–215. Philadelphia: Open University Press.

Dobash, R. Emerson, and Russell P. Dobash. 1992. *Women, Violence, and Social Change.* New York: Routledge.

Federal Bureau of Investigation. 1996. *Crime in the United States 1995.* Washington, DC: Government Printing Office.

Gilfus, Mary E. 1992. From Victims to Survivors to Offenders: Women's Routes of Entry and Immersion Into Street Crime. *Women and Criminal Justice* 4:63–89.

Glassner, Barry, and Cheryl Carpenter. 1985. The Feasibility of an Ethnographic Study of Adult Property Offenders. Unpublished report prepared for the National Institute of Justice, Washington, DC.

Hagan, John, A. R. Gillis, and John Simpson. 1985. The Class Structure of Gender and Delinquency: Toward a Power-Control Theory of Common Delinquent Behavior. *American Journal of Sociology* 90:1151–78.

Hagan, John, and Bill McCarthy. 1997. *Mean Streets: Youth Crime and Homelessness.* Cambridge, UK: Cambridge University Press.

Heimer, Karen, and Stacy De Coster. 1999. The Gendering of Violent Delinquency. *Criminology* 37:277–317.

Hill, Gary D., and Elizabeth M. Crawford. 1990. Women, Race, and Crime. *Criminology* 28:601–23.

Jacobs, Bruce, and Jody Miller. 1998. Crack Dealing, Gender, and Arrest Avoidance. *Social Problems* 45:550–69.

Joe, Karen, and Meda Chesney-Lind. 1995. Just Every Mother's Angel: An Analysis of Gender and Ethnic Variations in Youth Gang Membership. *Gender and Society* 9(4):408–430.

Katz, Jack. 1988. *Seductions of Crime.* New York: Basic Books.

Kruttschnitt, Candace. 1996. Contributions of Quantitative Methods to the Study of Gender and Crime, or Bootstrapping Our Way Into the Theoretical Thicket. *Journal of Quantitative Criminology* 12:135–61.

Laub, John H., and M. Joan McDermott. 1985. An Analysis of Serious Crime by Young Black Women. *Criminology* 23:81-98.

Maher, Lisa. 1997. *Sexed Work: Gender, Race, and Resistance in a Brooklyn Drug Economy.* Oxford, UK: Clarendon.

Maher, Lisa, and Kathleen Daly. 1996. Women in the Street-Level Drug Economy: Continuity or Change? *Criminology* 34:465–92.

Maher, Lisa, and Richard Curtis. 1992. Women on the Edge of Crime: Crack Cocaine and the Changing Contexts of Street-Level Sex Work in New York City. *Crime, Law and Social Change* 18:221–58.

Mann, Coramae Richey. 1993. Sister Against Sister: Female Intrasexual Homicide. In *Female Criminality: The State of the Art,* ed. C. C. Culliver, 195–223. New York: Garland.

Merlo, Alida V., and Joycelyn M. Pollock. 1995. *Women, Law, and Social Control.* Boston: Allyn & Bacon.

Messerschmidt, James W. 1993. *Masculinities and Crime.* Lanham, MD: Rowman & Littlefield.

———. 1995. From Patriarchy to Gender: Feminist Theory, Criminology, and the Challenge of Diversity. In *International Feminist Perspectives in Criminology: Engendering a Discipline,* ed. Nicole Hahn Rafter and Frances Heidensohn, 167–88. Philadelphia: Open University Press.

Miller, Eleanor M. 1986. *Street Woman.* Philadelphia: Temple University Press.

Miller, Jody. 1998a. Gender and Victimization Risk Among Young Women in Gangs. *Journal of Research in Crime and Delinquency* 35:429–53.

———. 1998b. "Up It Up"; Gender and the Accomplishment of Street Robbery. *Criminology* 36:37–66.

Newburn, Tim, and Elizabeth A. Stanko, eds. 1994. *Just Boys Doing Business?* New York: Routledge.

Price, Barbara Raffel, and Natalie J. Sokoloff. 1995. *The Criminal Justice System and Women: Offenders, Victims, and Workers.* 2d ed. New York: McGraw-Hill.

Richie, Beth E. 1996. *Compelled to Crime: The Gender Entrapment of Battered Black Women.* New York: Routledge.

Sampson, Robert J., and William Julius Wilson. 1995. Toward a Theory of Race, Crime, and Urban Inequality. In *Crime and Inequality,* ed. John Hagan and Ruth D. Peterson, 37–54. Stanford, CA: Stanford University Press.

Schwartz, Martin D., and Dragan Milovanovic. 1996. *Race, Gender, and Class in Criminology: The Intersection.* New York: Garland.

Simpson, Sally. 1989. Feminist Theory, Crime, and Justice. *Criminology* 27:605–31.

———. 1991. Caste, Class, and Violent Crime: Explaining Differences in Female Offending. *Criminology* 29:115–35.

Simpson, Sally, and Lori Elis. 1995. Doing Gender: Sorting Out the Caste and Crime Conundrum. *Criminology* 33:47–81.

Smart, Carol. 1976. *Women, Crime, and Criminology: A Feminist Critique.* London: Routledge and Kegan Paul.

Smith, Douglas A., and Raymond Paternoster. 1987. The Gender Gap in Theories of Deviance: Issues and Evidence. *Journal of Research in Crime and Delinquency* 24:140–72.

Stack, Carol. 1974. *All Our Kin: Strategies for Survival in a Black Community.* New York: Harper and Row.

Steffensmeier, Darrell J. 1983. Organizational Properties and Sex Segregation in the Underworld: Building a Sociological Theory of Sex Differences in Crime. *Social Forces* 61:1010–32.

Steffensmeier, Darrell J., and Robert Terry. 1986. Institutional Sexism in the Underworld: A View From the Inside. *Sociological Inquiry* 56:304–23.

Visher, Christy. 1983. Gender, Police Arrest Decisions, and Notions of Chivalry. *Criminology* 21:5–28.

West, Candace, and Sarah Fenstermaker. 1995. Doing Difference. *Gender & Society* 9:8–37.

West, Candace, and Don H. Zimmerman. 1987. Doing Gender. *Gender & Society* 1:125–51.

Wilson, William Julius. 1996. *When Work Disappears: The World of the New Urban Poor.* New York: Knopf.

Wright, Richard T., and Scott Decker. 1997. *Armed Robbers in Action: Stickups and Street Culture.* Boston: Northeastern University Press.

Chapter 4

Tenuous Borders:
Girls Transferred to Adult Court[1]

Emily Gaarder and Joanne Belknap

ABSTRACT

In this chapter Gaarder and Belknap point out the large gaps that exist in theories and knowledge about girls who commit crimes that are considered so serious by the authorities that sentencing as an adult is deemed warranted. First, in a section that reviews existing literature, the reader learns what is known about theories on pathways (causes) of girls' crime. Then Gaardner and Belknap turn to the girls themselves for an understanding of their lives. The authors employ a feminist research tool similar to that used by J. Miller in chapter 3: twenty-two girls adjudicated and sentenced as adults in a large Midwestern state tell their stories. Through in-depth interviews, two topics are covered in the girls' own words: their lives before they were imprisoned and their perceptions of being tried in a court and convicted as adults.

The girls describe lives filled with violence and victimization, sexism, racism, and economic marginalization. These reported conditions are consistent with other research on girls and women who have been labeled as offenders. Moreover, the offending pattern of girls tried as adults was found to be similar to that of girls who remained in the juvenile system. Status offenses play a major role in the group of girls tried as adults, which has also been found in prior studies of girls in the juvenile system. The title of the chapter, "Tenuous Borders," implies that there is a thin distinction between being treated by the criminal justice system as a girl or as a woman. It also suggests that the transfer decision may be lacking a sound basis. This view is reinforced by the findings on pathways to crime, which have demonstrated that there is a fine line between being a victim and an offender. The authors call for a more complex model of the relationship between agency, victimization, and responsibility and a simultaneous understanding of the social structural limitations and constraints placed on individual female offenders. This greater complexity is particularly important when trying to understand pathways to crime for those girls proclaimed "adults" by the legal system.

In the past decade, there has been a nationwide effort to process and confine delinquent youth as adults in the United States. The "get tough on crime" attitudes promoted by politicians and the media portray youthful offenders as increasingly dangerous, out of control, and in need of punishment rather than rehabilitation or care. The result is an unprecedented number of delinquent girls and boys housed in adult prisons. Between 1992 and 1995, 41 states passed laws that facilitated trying juveniles as adults. Indeed, the number of juvenile cases waived to adult court increased by 71% between 1985 and 1994 (Glick and Sturgeon, 1998). A Pennsylvania study reported the increase in juveniles waived to adult court between 1986 and 1994 was likely due to changes in the waiver criteria, with more drug offenders and less serious prior record youth waived in the latter year (Snyder, et al., 2000). Although boys constitute about 95% of youth transferred and remanded to adult facilities in the United States, well over 400 girls were sent to adult women's prisons in 1994 and 1996, and they were disproportionately African-American (Glick and Sturgeon, 1998; Puzzanchera, 2000).

Girls who have been adjudicated as adults and are currently serving time in adult women's prisons are still considered an anomaly—a minor constituency among the thousands of cases that are processed every day in courts of law. There are tremendous gaps in our theories and knowledge about girls and crime, particularly for this group of offenders deemed so serious as to justify adult criminal sentencing. To date, there have been no studies focusing exclusively on the lives, past or present, of girls in adult prisons. Several quantitative studies have been conducted to determine which factors affect the likelihood of judicial transfer (see Bortner, 1986; Fagan et al., 1987; Houghtalin and Mays, 1991; Ohio Department of Youth Services, 1993; Peterson, 1988;

Virginia Commission on Youth, 1994). A small body of knowledge exists on juvenile boys' experiences in men's prisons (Fagan et al., 1987; Forst et al., 1989; McShane and Williams, 1989), but this research is far from complete and cannot be generalized to girls.

This article reports on the life histories and prior records of 22 girls adjudicated and sentenced as adults in a large Midwestern women's prison. We explored specific factors, such as the nature and severity of the crime, the age at the offense that resulted in their incarceration in an adult prison, prior record, class/race factors, and family, community, and systemic experiences.[2] The purpose of this article, then, is to answer two questions. First, what are the histories and profiles of girls who end up in prison? We examine their life stories and trajectories into criminal behavior. Second, we take up the question of identity, agency, and responsibility in the lives of girls whose actions have been proclaimed "adult" by the legal system. We consider such factors as gender, race/ethnicity, class, and sexual orientation, and how these identities shape the girls' reported experiences. Moreover, we report on these girls' sense of their own agency and their perceptions of having been bound over to adult court and committed to adult prisons.

This study examines girls in what we might call the "deepest end of the system" (adult prison), and applies their stories both to existing theories about delinquent girls and to the scholarship on agency. Our guiding framework expands the question of "blurred boundaries" to include not just the fluidity of victimization/offending experiences, but also the developmental continuum of child-to-adult in these girls' lives. Legalistic categories of "victim" and "offender" cannot adequately describe the meaning or interconnections of such experiences in young women's lives. Similarly, "youths do not graduate from irresponsible childhood one day to responsible adulthood the next except as a matter of law" (Feld, 1999:9). Thus, how might we change our legal and cultural sensibilities to better understand and explore their experiences and the choices they have made?

Source: Emily Gaarder and Joanne Belknap. 2002. Tenuous Borders: Girls Transferred to Adult Court. *Criminology* 40(3):481–517.

A REVIEW OF THE LITERATURE

Pathways to Crime

The traditional theories of crime causation, which tend to be based on male models of crime and behavior, cannot adequately explain the experiences of delinquent girls (see Arnold, 1990; Belknap, 2001; Campbell, 1999; Chesney-Lind, 1997; Chesney-Lind and Shelden, 1998; Gilfus, 1992), and too little research even bothers to try. For example, a recent book, *Deadly Consequences,* describes the marginalization of inner city, poor boys combined with violent media portrayals, as culminating in violent behavior committed by boys: "Boys and men who are poor, who are urban, and who have witnessed or been victimized by violence in their families are more at risk for the dangerous lessons television teaches" (Prothrow-Stith, 1991:47). Unfortunately, the author has little to say about similarly placed girls. However, Campbell's (1999:255) analysis of the serious aggression sometimes used by girls in gangs is consistent in many ways with this assessment of similarly marginalized boys:

> If we are willing to allow young women to be exploited by poverty and crime—if we can offer them no way out of victimization—then we can hardly be surprised if they respond by nurturing a self-protective reputation for craziness. If women like men are forced to see trust as weakness and vulnerability, the attraction of being a "hardwoman" is easy to see.

Indeed, some recent studies suggest that female gang members come from even more seriously harmful families than do male gang members (Joe and Chesney-Lind, 1999; Moore, 1999), and Sommers and Baskin (1994) report that the most seriously violent women with the earliest ages of offending describe their neighborhoods and families as fraught with poverty and violence.

The "Life Course Development Model" theorizes that offending behavior is related to various developmental stages and is thus "age-associated" (see Elder, 1985; Laub and Lauritsen, 1993; Sampson and Laub, 1990). Significant life events or transitions are a central aspect of the life-course perspective, particularly in terms of changes in status, relationships, and social roles (Caspi et al., 1989; Elliott and Williams, 1995). Adolescence is perceived as an acute time of risk for offending behavior because of the stress of peer pressure, puberty, and so on. Two hypotheses resulted from this developmental approach, identified by Sampson and Laub (1990). First, problems in adult development are a result of childhood antisocial behaviors. Second, changes in offending behavior and development over the life span can be explained by social bonds to work and family in adulthood. Unfortunately, not only do most of the existing applications of the life-course perspective focus exclusively on male samples (Laub and Sampson, 1993; Moffitt, 1990, 1993; Nagin et al., 1995; Sampson and Laub, 1990; Stattin and Magnusson, 1991), but also little effort is made to suggest how this theory might pertain to females. Kruttschnitt (1996:141) notes that, "[f]ailing to address how family and peer influences on delinquency change for males and females over the course of adolescence limits our ability to predict and explain the gender-crime relationship." A rare study including girls and boys in a developmental pathway model indicates gender differences in the development of antisocial youth behaviors. In particular, the onset of girls' severe and overt antisocial behavior (including that caused by a dysfunctional family environment) appears to be more likely than boys' to be delayed (from childhood) until adolescence (Silverthorn and Frick, 1999).

An appealing aspect of the life-course perspective is that it attempts to address the complexities of life and how various life events and circumstances interact in safeguarding against or predicting offending behavior. However, although the life-course studies often operationalize concepts such as "poor family functioning," they do not adequately address childhood victimizations such as neglect, physical abuse, and sexual abuse, including those perpetrated by participants' parents. Additionally, the life-course perspective in its current state, even if females were included, does not adequately address how discrimination and oppression, such as those based on one's race or sex, can shape a person's experiences, options, and identity.

A feminist approach to understanding the etiology of females' (and sometimes males') offending is termed by some as "pathways to crime." Similar to the life-course perspective, this approach attempts to determine life experiences, particularly childhood ones, that place one at risk of offending. The pathways research indicates that traumas such as physical and sexual abuse and child neglect are not only defining features in the lives of many female offenders, but also these traumas are often related to one's likelihood of committing crimes (e.g., Arnold, 1990; Belknap and Holsinger, 1998; Chesney-Lind and Rodriguez, 1983; Daly, 1992; Gilfus, 1992; Richie, 1996; Silbert and Pines, 1981).[3]

The connection between victimization and delinquency has been examined in multiple ways. For instance, some posit that girls' survival strategies are criminalized by the "justice" system (e.g., Arnold, 1990; Belknap and Holsinger, 1998; Chesney-Lind, 1995a). Behaviors such as running away from home, chemical use, prostitution, theft, and gang involvement may serve as resistance strategies and coping mechanisms in girls' lives. Additionally, dimensions of victimization often included in the pathways approach (and ignored or rarely addressed in the life-course perspective) frequently include patriarchy, family violence, economic marginality, racism, and negative educational experiences (see Arnold, 1990; Owen, 1998; Richie, 1996; Sommers and Baskin, 1994). The criminalization of girls, in turn, may reinforce the alienation they experience in their homes, communities, and schools (which is consistent with the life-course perspective).

A major contribution of the pathways perspective, then, is recognition that girls' crimes are usually grounded heavily in the social conditions of their lives and their roles as females within a patriarchal society (Chesney-Lind, 1995a). For example, the fact that young girls are characterized as sexually desirable means that their place in the family, their lives on the street, and their survival strategies take on particular forms that are shaped by patriarchal values (Chesney-Lind, 2001). The sacrifice of daughters and the sexualization and commodification of the young, female body are historical features of patriarchy that continue today. For example, girls may be "lent out" to drug dealers so their parents or partners can get high. Girls on the streets are encouraged to sell their bodies because they have little else of value to trade (Campagna and Poffenberger, 1988).

In a society that limits the options and choices of girls, the multiple marginality of many delinquent girls is intrinsically tied to how the criminal processing system responds to their offending. Thus, the "blurred boundaries" theory of victimization and criminalization is an overriding theme in many recent models of women's crime. Gilfus (1992:86) writes, "criminalization is connected to women's subordinate position in society where victimization by violence coupled with economic marginality related to race, class, and gender all too often blur the boundaries between victims and offenders."

Some feminist scholars argue that although the concept of "blurred boundaries" is an important feminist contribution to the field of criminology, describing women's acts only in the context of their economic survival or sexual/physical abuse histories may not capture the complexities and meanings of agency and responsibility involved in women's law-breaking (Daly, 1992; Maher, 1997). For example, "How should feminist scholars represent women who abuse, harm or hurt others? Or women who steal from others? How should the idea of 'responsibility' relate to these acts, or would feminist legal or criminological scholars propose a different definition of 'responsibility'?" (Daly, 1992:48). We will consider these questions later in our discussion and explore their particular relevance for girls who have been transferred and are serving time in the adult system.

The Processing of Delinquent Girls

Early theories and assumptions about the role of gender in criminal processing typically viewed women's and girls' treatment as "chivalrous," relative to their male counterparts, because they were considered more innocent, weaker, and less responsible for their crimes than were men and boys (Belknap, 2001). The "women" being referred to in these theories, however, were generally white heterosexual women, particularly from middle or upper classes. More recent research assessing gender differences in the processing of offenders suggests that this relationship is infinitely more complex (for a review, see Belknap, 2001; Chesney-Lind, 1997). Females, in comparison with males, are usually treated more harshly in the earlier stages of the criminal processing system, and chivalry is more likely for less serious offenses. The glaring exception to the last point is that girls are processed far more harshly than are boys for status offenses and are more likely to be picked up by police for such offenses (Alder, 1998; Chesney-Lind, 1987; Kempf-Leonard and Sample, 2000).

Not surprisingly, some research documents how women and girls of color are processed more harshly than are their white counterparts (Agozino, 1997; Chesney-Lind, 1997; Chigwada-Bailey, 1997; Crawford, 2000; Gilbert, 1999; Mauer and Huling, 1995; Miller, 1996; Spohn et al., 1987). In terms of the juvenile justice system, Chesney-Lind argues that the deinstitutionalization of status offenders in the United States "may have actually signaled the development of a two-track juvenile system—one track for girls of color and another for white girls" (1997:75).

Although statistical evidence of harsher treatment in the sentencing stage is mixed (see Daly and Bordt, 1995), women and girls of color are overrepresented in all stages of the criminal processing system and are more likely to be targeted for arrest (see Mann, 1995). Indeed, Gilbert (1999:234) attributes African-American women's sentencing to prison as related more to "their racial status, sex role, and life circumstances rather than their law violations." Thus, quantitative studies may "miss" the impact of race given the complexity of measuring concepts such as "racial profiling" and "life circumstances."[4]

Over the past two decades, a growing body of black feminist scholarship has examined the derogatory images and commonly held stereotypes of black women (Collins, 1990; Gilkes, 1992; hooks, 1981; Young, 1986). These images have proved persistent over time, and they are fundamental in maintaining interlocking systems of race, class, and gender oppression.[5] Vernetta Young examines these images within the context of criminal justice processes and systems, providing a critical evaluation of the impact they have on black female offenders and victims: "Before we attempt to provide theoretical explanations of the criminality and victimization of black females, we must assess the possible effects of false imagery on criminology as a discipline" (Young, 1986:324). In other words, the labeling of African-American girls and women as "deviant" is a process that begins long before any crime is actually committed. As Chesney-Lind writes, "This racist legacy, the exclusion of black women from the chivalry accorded white women, should be kept in mind when the current explosion of women's prison populations is considered" (1995b:113).

It is not difficult to imagine that discrimination is also likely against lesbian girls and women, who are rendered deviant by their sexual orientation. For example, lesbians have been stereotyped as hypermasculine, aggressive, and delinquent (see Robson, 1992). Although very little research exists on how negative images and stereotypes might affect lesbian girls and women who have committed crimes, one study found that lesbians received longer sentences, were arrested at an earlier age, and had served more time than heterosexual women (Leger, 1987).

In sum, a number of common risk factors indicate an increased likelihood of girls' involvement with the criminal processing system, particularly childhood victimization. Research also suggests that gender, race, socioeconomic status, and sexual orientation play a role in how girls are processed at many stages of the juvenile system. Building on previous research concerning girls' pathways to crime and delinquent processing, this study examines the life histories of a particular (and one might assume, most serious) group of delinquent girls—those transferred to adult court and sentenced to an adult prison.

METHOD

Between July 1998 and August 1999, we conducted interviews with 22 young women[6] incarcerated in a medium-security women's prison in the Midwest. The prison administration provided us with a list of prisoners we were allowed to interview. We were able to interview 22 of the 24 girls who fit the research criteria (two girls declined to be interviewed). Twenty-one of the girls were juveniles upon confinement to the prison, and the remaining girl was bound over as an adult when she was 17, but not sentenced until nearly a year later when she had already turned 18. The young women ranged from 16 to 19 years of age at the time of the interviews. Regarding race/ethnicity, half ($N = 11$) of the participants identified themselves as white, more than one-quarter ($N = 6$) as black, about 15% ($N = 3$) as white and Native American, one as Hispanic, and one as Mexican-American and black. Half of the sample characterized their families as middle-class, and the other half described their families as poor or working-class. From the way they defined their lives and communities, many of the self-identified "middle-class" girls were likely lower class or poor, but within their neighborhoods, they saw themselves as "average" or "in the middle."

Notably, during the first day of data collection in the prison, the staff informed the first author that most of the girls in the unit were reluctant to participate. In fact, the first girl who was interviewed confirmed the general caution they shared about being part of the research project. She noted, "Some of the girls in here don't want to be interviewed. . . . they say they don't want to be used as guinea pigs, or be exploited. Trust is a big thing." During the interviews, a number of girls echoed this concern and anger, directed specifically at television and newspaper journalists who interviewed them and then presented them in a sensationalized manner.

The interviews were conducted in administrative offices located in the "under-21" housing unit. Each office had a small window cut into the door for security reasons, but staff could not hear the conversations taking place within the room. Interviews lasted from 1 to $3\frac{1}{2}$ hours, with most averaging around 2 hours. The prison did not allow us to use a tape recording device,[7] so the first author took extensive handwritten notes during each interview. These were transcribed onto a computer within 48 hours of the interview to provide the most accuracy and

detail. The second author used a laptop computer to collect data during the interviews. Both interviewers also took time to write personal responses about the individual interviews, including concerns we had about the interview, awkwardness, interruptions, and so on.

The interview format was designed to build on prior research with girls incarcerated in juvenile facilities (Belknap et al., 1997). Questions focused primarily on childhood experiences, histories of law-breaking, encounters with legal (i.e., police and courts) and social service agencies, and experiences in prison (e.g., programming, health care, and schooling). We also borrowed from Taylor et al.'s (1995) interview format to address our own position as interviewers. For instance, one of the questions we asked was, "Were there any times where you felt I might not have understood something due to our different backgrounds (whether that be age, race, class, legal status, etc.) . . . something that another person might have understood?" Girls were given an opportunity to discuss their feelings about interviewers and researchers, and how it felt to share their stories with us.

Limitations of the Study

Despite the unique and important aspects of this study, there were some limitations. First, we were not allowed to conduct formal interviews with the unit officers working in the prison. The prison administration told us that pulling officers off the unit would disrupt the staffing pattern and officers would not be compensated for any time they spent being interviewed after their shift ended. However, the first author was able to engage in spontaneous conversations with some of the officers working in the unit. Within the course of these exchanges, the project goals were sometimes described to them. Their casual remarks about what it was like to work in the juvenile unit, as well as their perceptions of the young women housed there, were noted by this author.

Another limitation of this study was that we were not allowed access to any of the information in the girls' files beyond verifying their conviction offense and sentence. Although most of the girls' histories were obtained directly from the girls, the administrative staff verified the girls' self-reported offenses, and sometimes offered more detailed insight. This method is a limitation of the research; however, it seems appropriate that an explanatory project such as this should begin with the words and experiences of girls, rather than solely relying on an outsider's interpretation of their world. Similarly, "standpoint feminist theorists" suggest that research on women requires that the women studied speak for themselves, acknowledging that "women are direct eyewitnesses to their own lives" (Naffine, 1996:47). Other research also emphasizes this need to let incarcerated women speak for themselves (e.g., Carlen et al., 1985; Richie, 1996).

This is not to say that girls' accounts of themselves exemplify the only representation of their lives. Daly (1992), for instance, cautions against privileging any one account of a biography and suggests using multiple methods to gather information and generate theories about women involved in crime. On the other hand, most of the existing theories on the etiology of crime fail to take into account the lived experiences of girls. Therefore, this project attempts to follow the goals of feminist ethnography (Reinharz, 1992) by documenting the lives and activities of girls, understanding girls' experiences from their own point of view, and placing these experiences within their particular historical, political, and social contexts.

Another limitation of this research project is that both interviewers were white. The only potential participants who declined to be in the study were African-American. Related to this, we believe that the African-American girls who did participate may have been more open with an African-American researcher, particularly regarding racism in the systems both in and outside of the prison. We also noted that the two potential participants who declined to be in the study, declined when the older of the two researchers was interviewing, and that the participants generally talked "more" to (i.e., had longer interviews with) the younger researcher. Thus, research of this type might be ideally suited where

the interviewer and participant are matched more closely on race/ethnicity and age.

Finally, this research project had no comparison group of boys who had been bound over as adults and sentenced to a men's prison. Although we suspect that boys incarcerated in adult male prisons encounter similar difficulties in many respects, this project's intention is to focus specifically on the experiences of juvenile girls. Considering that much written about delinquent girls has been grounded in male-centered theories and explanations, we take the position that delinquent girls need to be understood on their own terms, rather than always through a gender-comparative model.

THE FINDINGS

This section presents the findings from the interviews conducted with both the girls and staff at the prison. The findings are divided into two sections: life histories and the girls' reflections on their crimes and punishment. First, we discuss the life histories of the girls interviewed, including their childhood experiences, family background, sexual and physical victimization, racism, economic issues, school experiences, chemical use, and structural dislocation from primary social institutions. Second, we report on the girls' reflections on both their crimes and their punishments. Using their comments as foundation, we discuss the dilemma of representation—how we might begin to characterize these girls and their crimes.

Life Histories

One of the goals behind examining the life histories of the girls was to gain an understanding of their general life experiences, particularly their histories of victimization and offending. Although there is a growing body of knowledge concerning delinquent girls, their histories, and their pathways to offending, it was unclear whether these girls, whose actions had been labeled "adult," fit similar profiles. Did their lives and delinquent behaviors differ significantly from those of girls involved in the juvenile justice system?

We also believe it is necessary to examine the lives of girls before their entry into prison in order to understand how the problems they face in the outside world follow them inside the prison walls. Their problems do not disappear or become solved as they enter prison; rather, they become exacerbated within the confines of an institution that provides little for the individual needs of prisoners. Patterns of abusive relationships, self-medication, violence, and limited familial contact continue to plague these girls' progress and development toward adulthood. Building on previous scholarship on girls and crime, we discuss in this section how the young women in this sample became involved in crime, resulting in their eventual processing as adult criminals.

Violence and Victimization   The presence of violence in the family was a powerful memory for Angela,[8] an 18-year-old African-American girl whose case was transferred to the adult court when she was 17. When asked what her childhood was like, Angela replied, "Mostly what I think of is the nights—the screaming and fighting. I would be lying in my bed at night and my stomach would be hurting. There were good times too, like going to the park and family reunions. But I remember the bad stuff more." Angela's father would routinely get drunk and hit other family members, including her mother, older siblings, and herself. Angela became more resistant to her father's violence as she became older. She wanted to protect her mother and became less willing to be passive about the violence in her household. She recalled, "When I really started to have problems is when I was a teenager. I wasn't as submissive as I used to be. I didn't want to stand around and get hit, or watch it happen."

When she was 16, her mother filed a restraining order against her father in response to a recent incident in which he had strangled Angela, leaving bruises and scratches on her neck. Although the order was supposed to stay in effect until she was 18, her mother let him back in the house shortly after:

> I told her I'd leave if he came back, but she let him anyway. I was thinking, you know, she should be worrying about me. I left and went to my cousin's house.

Nobody even called me, Mom didn't talk to me for two weeks, and Dad said to me, "Don't call." It was like they didn't care. I started smoking weed a lot then, drinking, skipping school, and shoplifting. . . . I had no [delinquency] record before this happened.

When Angela was 17, she began robbing houses with a pellet gun. The night of her second robbery, she got drunk, went to her parents' house, and slit her wrists. "I was crying, I was telling my mom, 'I need you-all.' I just wanted them to pay attention to me, and I was miserable." Her mother took her to the hospital, where she was eventually questioned by police detectives about the robberies, although she was not charged at that time. Angela was diagnosed with depression and put on medication, and then allowed to go home with her parents. One month later, Angela committed another robbery:

> I didn't care if I got caught. But after a few days, I was just real tired of it all. I didn't want to go to school, because I knew they would question me again, but I wanted to take my school exams so I would pass for the year. I was so tired. Finally I went to school and told them if they let me take my exams, I would just turn myself in to the police afterwards. They let me take my exams, and then they arrested me.

Angela was convicted of three charges of aggravated burglary and three charges of aggravated robbery. She is serving a three-year sentence for the crimes.

Sandy, a white 19-year-old, suffered abuse by multiple family members. Sandy's mother beat her on a frequent basis. Several other siblings had already been removed from the home or left to live with relatives and friends. Sandy stayed behind to care for her younger, 11-year-old brother. In addition to the physical abuse Sandy endured at the hands of her mother, she was also sexually molested by one of her older brothers. When Sandy was 16 years old, she beat her mother to death with a baseball bat. At the time of the incident, Sandy was covered with both old and new bruises from her mother. She was sentenced to 5 to 25 years for involuntary manslaughter.

Jamie, a white 16-year-old convicted of involuntary manslaughter, reported moving to the Midwest with her mother and younger sister at a very young age when her parents separated:

My dad came and kidnapped me and my sister from my mom when I was 4 and my sister was 2. And we was down there living with my dad for 5 years. My dad had my mom's phone number, but my mom didn't know where we were. My mom called this children thing and found us 5 years later. I was 9 and my sister was 7. We came back and my mom had had two more kids since then and was living with my stepdad. And everything was all right, until when I was 12, my stepdad started molesting me. I told my mom and she didn't believe me. I just kept telling her and she didn't want to believe me. So I started running away. I don't remember how many times I ran away because I ran away so much. Because my mom wouldn't listen to me, so I kept running away to let him know. When she finally believed me, she said it was my fault. . . . They'd take me to juvenile jail, and they'd let me go the next day. They'd keep me overnight. I've been in and out of so many foster homes because I didn't like living with people I don't know.

Tammy, a white 19-year-old serving 4 to 15 years for attempted murder, had a long history of sexual and physical abuse. Tammy's parents divorced when she was 2, and she shuffled back and forth between their homes as she got older. Her mother was a drug addict, and her father was an alcoholic who hit her frequently. Between the ages of 8 and 13, she was sexually molested by different men who hung around her mother's house. She said, "My mom knew, but she let it happen. Then she wouldn't have to have sex with them herself, for the drugs and stuff." At age 13, Tammy moved back to her father's house. It was there that she was sexually abused by one of her father's friends. Although she told her father what had happened, "he chose not to believe it, not to believe me. He'd call me names, saying that if it did happen, it was my fault, that I was a slut." Tammy was sent to a foster home, while the man who had abused her remained in her home. She ran from the foster home a week later and conducted a drive-by shooting with a boy she knew. While Tammy drove the car, he shot at her house and ended up paralyzing her father's friend, the man who had raped her. She was 15 at the time.

Consistent with some other research (e.g., Levy, 1991; Rennison and Welchans, 2000; Schwartz and DeKeseredy, 1997), approximately one-fourth the girls in this study reported being battered in an intimate relationship. Jackie, a young white woman serving time for aiding and abetting in an aggravated murder, described her relationship with an abusive boyfriend who stalked her:

One day in school the principal saw him shove me into the lockers. They called my mom and he ended up getting house arrest for two weeks. He still kept coming over, even on house arrest. He got a key to my house somehow. I would call the police when he showed up, but they couldn't do anything. By the time they got there, he was gone. I didn't really want to press charges. I figured he'd come back and do it [beat me] worse next time.

Tracy, a white 19-year-old, was beaten by her older brother frequently while growing up. When she was just 13, she began an intimate relationship with a 21-year-old woman who also beat her:

When my mom or I would report the abuse, they [the police] would just tell my mom she should do something about it. Once, after my girlfriend hurt my face pretty bad, I told my mom and went to the police. They told me to try and press charges downtown . . . we went down there and had pictures taken of my face, but they wouldn't do anything else because I was in the wrong precinct. They told me I had to go back to my precinct. Mom got pissed off, and we didn't go back to the police in our town. Mom told me I should just stay home. So I moved back home for a while, but then my brother came back there to live and was beating on me. Then I went back to live with my girlfriend.

Racism and Economic Marginality   The struggles of economic hardship or the experiences of being "the wrong color" (an expression used in some of the interviews) play an important and early role in the lives of many delinquent girls. The experience of growing up female differs greatly along these intersections. Although race and class terms should not be used interchangeably (the girls of color of this sample did not all grow up poor, and the white girls were not all middle-class), it is also true that racism and poverty often go hand and hand. Richelle described the difficulties of growing up as a young black girl in an impoverished neighborhood. She commented, "It was rough . . . all the shootings, all the negativity, all the discriminations . . . Blacks can't do this, whites can't do that. Blacks can't come to this store if our skin is a certain color. Being watched on videotapes. Stuff like that." Richelle also spoke of negative encounters with police officers in her neighborhood. She described her interactions with police:

> When I wasn't being arrested they were always nit-picking with us. When I was being arrested they didn't try to talk to me; they didn't read me my rights. Everything they wasn't supposed to be doing, they was doing. They'd walk past and say, "Richelle, you got any drugs on you today?" or "Richelle, let me buy a dime off ya." Just stuff like that

When asked about her childhood experiences, Shanda, an 18-year-old African-American girl, remembered feeling like an outsider in her school and her community. She lived with both her grandmother and mother in her early childhood. Shanda's mother gave birth to her at the age of 12 and was not awarded custody until Shanda was 4. She said, "My mom lived in an all-white neighborhood. I was always hanging out in the ghetto. I didn't like my neighborhood. The next-door neighbors didn't like the friends I would bring around." Like Richelle, Shanda believed her race marked her as a target for harassment. Consequently, she expressed distrust of the police, social workers, and other "officials" she came into contact with. "I hate the police. I wouldn't call them for nothing in the world . . . Some officers are very prejudiced—none of them care about you." Amanda, a white and Native-American girl, reported that her being bound over was related to racism:

> It was him [the detective] tried to get me . . . I feel like I was forced to say what I said. He made me believe that if I cooperated with him I'd go home that night. When he made the charges he also made racial slurs because I was with two black guys who committed the charge. So I think he pushed more because I was with two black guys. [What were the racial slurs?] Two innocent white girls like us shouldn't be hanging around

with two black guys from the ghetto. He started calling one of them nigger, but stopped mid-sentence. He said that me and my co-defendant's problem was that we acted black. That since we lived in a black neighborhood it had rubbed off on us.

Maria, a 19-year-old who described herself as Mexican-American and black, talked about how racism affected how others saw her. She said, "People point fingers at you for being colored. I'd go to the store, and my white friend would go in with me. I don't steal, okay, but she did all the time. And while she's stealing, they're looking at me!" Maria also reflected on how her family was deeply affected by economic concerns. Although her father owned a bar, he also sold drugs to make extra money. After he was sent to prison, her mother had to assume complete responsibility for the household. Maria said, "[My mother] had to work extra hard to make sure we had enough money . . . she tried to kill herself when I was younger and had to go to the hospital. She started drinking a lot after my dad went to prison. I didn't understand my mom's situation at that time, but I do now."

Rosenbaum's (1993) study of girls in the California Youth System found considerable financial strain and disorder in the families of delinquent girls. The mother's psychological and financial resources were severely limited, and the added burden of children only increased this strain. Many of the girls' mothers were unable to provide emotional support for their daughters, because their energy was focused on "just trying to survive" (1993:408). This was also the case for Maria. Growing up, she recalled feeling very angry with her mother. She wanted more attention from her mother and didn't feel she could burden her with additional problems. "When I was sad, my mom took me to the store and bought me something—[but] what I needed was love. I never really talked to my mom about personal things. When I started my menstrual period, I never told her. I went to my cousins and aunt instead."

In addition to the strain on parenting caused by poverty, many girls who grew up in poor neighborhoods described their communities as dangerous places. Lisa remarked, "I grew up in a pretty bad neighborhood—lots of gang activity, drugs, and fighting." Tammy described her neighborhood as "a bad place . . . we lived in the rough part of town . . . the lower-class part." Amanda believed that the environment she grew up in was a strong contributor to her problems with crime. She said, "I grew up in an apartment complex that was real low class. My parents did what they could and were there when they could be there. I lived basically a hop from the ghetto. Projects are all around . . . that type of environment."

School Experiences Along with the turmoil within their families and negative attention from other institutional forces, school formed yet another atmosphere of oppression and alienation for most of the girls. Many felt bored by the material they were supposed to be learning and believed that it did not relate to their interests or their lives. Rather than providing a support system, schools seemed unequipped to deal with the multiple problems these girls faced.

Tracy was stigmatized in both her home and school because of her sexual orientation. She said, "My parents didn't like that I was gay; my mom thought it was a phase. My sisters wanted to beat my girlfriend up." Tracy hated attending school, where other kids called her a "dyke" and a "lesbian," and teachers and other staff members did nothing to stop it. Sandy remarked that teachers at school ignored the obvious signs of physical abuse and neglect. She recalled many times when she had come to school covered in bruises or had fallen asleep in class:

> One time I came to school with sunglasses on. This teacher told me to take them off, so I did and you could see the two black eyes I had from mom. I just sat there the rest of class and stared at him the whole time. After class, he told me I could wear the sunglasses. Another time I went to the guidance counselor and told him about some stuff . . . that I was taking care of my brother, my mom was gone a lot . . . he gave me a pamphlet called, "Raising Children in the 90's." No one at school ever asked me directly about abuse.

Both Maria and Shanda seemed to pass through school virtually unnoticed, unless they were in

trouble. Shanda remarked, "I never liked school . . . I always skipped. I think they passed me just to pass me." None of the girls could name a school figure (e.g., teacher, principal, or counselor) who had provided mentoring or assistance. Although an assistant principal at Angela's school took her aside to ask what was wrong, she felt unable to speak about anything that was happening at home. She said, "I guess I didn't know him that well. It was kind of private, family stuff . . . I didn't really feel I should talk about it." Angela's general uneasiness and cautious attitude toward school officials is reasonable, and even logical, considering that schools, social service agencies, and other public institutions have often been intrusive and adversarial toward black families, or have ignored their problems altogether (Arnold, 1990; Richie and Kanuha, 1997). Research indicates that girls from low-income families or families of color are particularly isolated by the school curriculum and policies, and ignored or mistreated by teachers and other school staff (Fine, 1986; Fine and Zane, 1989). Black, Asian-American, Latina, and Native-American girls experiencing abuse or other problems at home may feel embarrassed or guilty about "airing the family's dirty laundry" to school officials or social service agencies who may already stereotype families of color as generally dysfunctional.

Structural Dislocation When young girls experience problems in their homes and schools (two of the primary socializing institutions for young people), others in similar situations may become their socializing agents. A substitute for the family may be created with criminal others on the streets. Prostitution, drug dealing, gang involvement, and theft may be used to fulfill economic needs. The labeling process increases the probability of further involvement in crime as conventional community and familial ties become strained (Arnold, 1990). Examining Shanda's story within this context provides some insight into her path toward crime. She began "running the streets" at an early age, staying out all night or not coming home for days at a time:

When I was 13, I was kidnapped by a pimp. I was hanging out in the street one night fighting with this other guy about something. This Cadillac pulled up, and the guy in it asked me if I needed a ride. Once I got in the car, he handcuffed me. He ended up taking me to California for a while. I was out whoring on the streets, and he got me addicted to crack. I was on drugs all the time. He had 6 other girls, but I was the youngest one. I never made any money, he took it all. he gave us money for clothes, makeup, the stuff we needed, but he had all the money.

At first Shanda's family was not even aware of what had transpired, because she had run away from home many times before. Her pimp would not allow her to contact her mother, and by the time they came back from California, she was hooked on crack. She said, "My family saw me as a druggie . . . my Mom was mad at me a lot and we fought a lot." During the next four years, Shanda was in and out of detention centers and drug treatment programs. She worked as a prostitute and stole to support her habit. She also gave birth to two children (one at age 14, one at age 16) whom her mother raised. Shanda was eventually transferred to the adult court for a crime in which she kidnapped and robbed a woman for drug money.

Lisa, a young white woman serving time for attempted murder, sought refuge in drugs, alcohol, and gangs to escape the pain and troubles of her home life. Her mother was an alcoholic, and her father was serving time in prison for two counts of rape. Her stepfather sexually and physically abused her from the ages of 9 to 11. Lisa began skipping school around this time, although she "had always liked school until then." She also started using alcohol, acid, and marijuana ("I smoked joints with embalming fluid at the tips") and joined a gang when she was 12 years old. "They were like a family to me," Lisa remarked. "But I became involved in a lot of stuff . . . I got high a lot, I robbed people, burglarized homes, stabbed people, and was involved in drive-bys." At age 15, she stabbed a woman in a fight. She is serving 7 to 15 years for the crime.

I had just gotten out of this group home. The lady I stabbed had been messing with my sister's fiancé.

This woman [had] a bunch of my sister's stuff, like her stereo and VCR, so me, my sister, her fiancé, and my boyfriend went over to pick up the stuff. We were all getting high beforehand. When we got [to] the house, my sister and I went in . . . they [her sister and the victim] started fighting over him, and I started stabbing her with a knife. I always carried a knife with me because I was in a gang.

Drug/Alcohol Use   A recurring theme in the interviews was the use of drugs and alcohol as self-medication. The abuse of drugs and alcohol factor heavily into the lives of girls and women before imprisonment (see Chesney-Lind, 1997; Chesney-Lind and Shelden, 1998; Daly, 1994). Nearly all of the girls in the sample had one, if not two, chemically dependent parents or stepparents. Half reported that they were addicted to either alcohol or drugs, or both. Many of the girls interviewed reported being high or intoxicated when they committed their crimes. Their patterns of chemical use served to isolate them from their families and schools, and led them to form associations with other drug/alcohol users and sellers.

Carrie, a white 18-year-old serving time for possession of drugs, came from a family where drugs and alcohol use was the norm. She said, "All I knew was drugs . . . Dad was a drug addict. Mom was an alcoholic and a drug user." Carrie was shuffled back and forth among various relatives' homes, changing school every six months. "I started into drugs myself at 14½. I tried alcohol, pot, acid, and didn't like any of them. Then I tried crystal meth, and I loved it. Soon I was using it every day." Her mother (who has ceased her chemical use and remarried) kicked her out when she discovered her drug use, and Carrie moved back to her father's house. She said, "My dad knew I was using, but he was using too. When he found my drugs, he threw them out—or took them himself—I don't know. That's really all he could do. I mean, he was on drugs too, what could he say?" Although Carrie had a record as a status offender (running away, shoplifting), she had only been placed in a juvenile detention center twice (once for two weeks, once for an overnight stay), and had never been recommended for a drug treatment program. She was transferred to the adult court for possession of crystal methamphetamine and is serving a two-year sentence.

Are These Histories Unique?

Although we cannot provide a direct comparison between the histories of the girls in this study and the histories of delinquent girls who remain in the juvenile justice system, it is possible to note some broad similarities. The life histories and criminal activities of delinquent girls and incarcerated women documented in other studies (e.g., Arnold, 1990; Bottcher, 1986; Belknap et al., 1997; Browne et al., 1999; Chesney-Lind and Shelden, 1998; Gilfus, 1992; Rosenbaum, 1993) did not appear to differ significantly from the girls in this study. Economic marginality, sexism, and racism formed multiple layers of oppression for many of the girls. Nearly all experienced multiple incidents of sexual or physical abuse and neglect. Some girls committed crimes directly related to the abuse they had experienced. Most were raised in disordered households, many with one or both parents or stepparents chemically dependent.

The offending patterns of those girls tried as adults also appeared, for the most part, to be similar to those of delinquent girls who remain in the juvenile justice system. Table 1 provides a brief summary of each girl's case, including her age at the time of arrest, race/ethnicity, offense, arrest record/prior incarcerations, and the length of the adult sentence being served. Status offenses played a major part in the delinquency of the girls in this study, a pattern well documented in prior studies of girls in the juvenile justice system (Chesney-Lind, 1997; Chesney-Lind and Shelden, 1998; Kempf-Leonard and Sample, 2000; Poe-Yamagata and Butts, 1996). In the current study, 5 of the 22 girls had no contact with the juvenile justice system prior to their adult criminal court case.

How, then, did these particular girls feel about being processed and sentenced in the adult court system? In each of the interviews, we asked girls to reflect on their crimes and punishments, including

their experiences in court and their assessment of whether the punishment they received was "fair" or just. The next section reports on the girls' responses to these questions and explores the questions of identity, agency, and criminal responsibility.

Reflections on Their Crimes and Punishments

Angela, an African-American girl convicted of aggravated robbery, had vivid memories of her experience in juvenile court. The white judge presiding over the case ruled that Angela was not amenable to a juvenile placement, even though she had no prior record (not even a status offense). In addition, a psychologist testified on behalf of Angela at the proceeding, stating that she believed Angela was appropriate for a juvenile placement. Angela recalled, "She [the judge] said I didn't show any facial expressions, that I didn't care or seem sorry for what I had done. . . . But I was scared, you know, being in court. I guess I didn't look right. I told her that I did care and I was sorry for what I had done." The final strike against her was the appearance of one of the victims she had robbed. The victim was an older woman, who testified that Angela made her feel like her life was worthless, and that she had feared Angela was going to kill her. After that point in the proceeding, Angela said, "I knew I was going to be bound over. I expected it."

Tracy had only been arrested twice and had never been in a placement, yet her crime was a serious and violent one—she and her partner had robbed and murdered a woman. Tracy's long-term partner and codefendant in the case was a woman nearly 10 years older than she was. Although her partner routinely battered her, it appears that both Tracy and the court were reluctant to recognize the dynamics of power, control, and abuse present in the relationship.[9] Tracy had an enormous amount of loyalty toward her partner and was unwilling to place the majority of the blame on her. It is not surprising that her public defender, who had spent little time with her, was unable to persuade her to testify against her partner. When Tracy refused ("I

TABLE 1
Selected Characteristics of the Sample

Name	Age*	Race	Crime	Sentence	Prior record/placements
Sandy	16	White/ Native American	Involuntary manslaughter	5–25 years	Never arrested; no prior placements.
Tracy	17	White	Aggravated murder, Aggravated robbery, Aggravated burglary	30–life	Arrested once for assault and once for driving without a license. No prior placements.
Jana	17	White	Burglary	2 years	Arrested 27 times, offenses ranging from felonious assault to stealing to drug possession. Multiple placements.
Carrie	17	White	Possession of drugs	2 years	Arrested several times for running away and once for shoplifting. Locked in county detention twice, no prior placements.
Tammy	15	White	Felonious assault; Gunspect,** Discharging a firearm into a residential dwelling***	7–15 years	Arrested several times for running away and once for breaking and entering. Prior placements include foster homes and juvenile detention.
Maria	17	Mexican-American/ African-American	Felonious assault, Theft	3–10 years	Arrested multiple times for running away. Spent 8 months in a juvenile correctional facility for felonious assault on a peer.
Deidre	16	White	Attempted murder, Aggravated burglary, Kidnapping	16–50 years	Arrested multiple times for status offenses (mainly running away), once for driving w/o license. Spent time in shelters, children's homes, detention.
Angela	17	African-American	3 counts of Aggravated robbery, 3 counts of Aggravated burglary	3 years	Never arrested; no prior placements.
Jackie	16	White	Aiding and abetting (for aggravated murder)	23–life	Never arrested; no prior placements.
Crystal	17	White	Aggravated murder, Gunspect	26–life	Arrested twice, for disorderly conduct and shoplifting. No prior placements.
Shanda	17	African-American	Kidnapping, robbery	4 years	Arrested multiple times for runaway, shoplifting, and assault. Spent 6 months in a juvenile correctional facility for receiving stolen property, drug treatment multiple times.
Lisa	15	White	Felonious assault	7–15 years	Arrested multiple times for runaway and assault. Sent to a detention center several times, spent 9 months in a group home for Aggravated Robbery.

Name	Age[*]	Race	Crime	Sentence	Prior record/placements
Amanda	17	White/Native-American	2 counts robbery	2 years	Arrested for runaway (1x), and driving without a license (1x). No prior placements.
Corinne	17	African-American	Involuntary manslaughter, Aggravated robbery	7 years	Never arrested; no prior placements.
Richelle	15	African-American	Felonious assault, Aggravated riot, Sexual battery	8 years	Arrested many times, offenses ranging from felonious assault to theft to running away. Multiple placements.
Jamie	16	White	Involuntary manslaughter, Resisting arrest, Aggravated vehicular homicide	5 years	Arrested several times for running away. Spent overnights in juvenile detention, many foster home placements.
Toni	16	African-American	Aggravated robbery	4 years	Arrested for assault.
Kendra	17	White	Voluntary manslaughter	9 years	Arrested for runaway and put on house arrest/probation. Had been in mental institutions for depression.
Rebecca	17	White/Native-American	Theft, Failure to appear	2 years	Arrested multiple times for runaway, curfew violations. Multiple placements.
Elizabeth	16	Hispanic	Burglary, 2 counts Theft, Aggravated robbery, Tampering w/evidence	1 year	Never arrested; no prior placements.
Erin	17	White	Receiving stolen property (misuse of a credit card)	3 months	Arrested for check forgery, car theft, runaway, escape charges (cut off house arrest monitoring tag). Multiple placements.
Alice	17	African-American	2 counts of Receiving stolen property	1 year	Arrested for runaway, aiding and abetting (assault). Spent 20 days in a detention center, no other placements.

[*]Indicates age at time of arrest.
[**]A gunspect charge indicates that a firearm was used in the commission of a felony.
[***]Additional charges included receiving stolen property and failure to comply with an officer.

wasn't going to bail on her"), there appeared to be little by way of an alternative defense offered to her. She said, "The domestic violence stuff was used against me in court, because I had fought back. So my fighting was used against me to show that I was violent or something."

Corinne, an 18-year-old African-American serving time for involuntary manslaughter and aggra-

vated robbery, felt that her past experiences of victimization were not adequately considered in court. Corinne grew up the youngest of 15 siblings. Child welfare reported that Corinne lived in a house where there was no food in the cupboards, children ran around with no diapers, and feces covered the floor. Corinne described her childhood as, "Bad, very bad. Umm . . . I was molested by my brothers. I was beat. I was always in a foster home. I was mentally abused. Very bad, very bad." Although Corinne felt she had committed an "adult" crime, she also believed the court judged her too harshly. She remarked, "They don't judge you of who you are but what you did. They don't go into your history or anything. They don't care why you did it, what brought you to do something like that."

Significantly, most of the girls in this study did not minimize responsibility for their behavior and crimes. Although many of the girls made connections between the victimization they experienced and their subsequent offending, they generally did not blame their parents, their abusers, or "the system" for the choices they made. For instance, Sandy, who had been beaten by her mother for her entire life, said, "I chose . . . I'm not blaming my parents. But . . . no one did anything. All these people in the community knew [about the beatings] but didn't really do anything."

Tammy echoed similar sentiments. When she was eight years old, her mother began putting her in a motel to prostitute for drug money. Her father physically abused her throughout her life, and placed her in a foster home when she accused his friend of sexually assaulting her. When asked if there was anything in her life that might have contributed to her being an offender, she replied, "The violence in my house. It made me violent and angry inside. I'm not using it as an excuse, but the violence made it hard." Carrie, who was convicted of drug possession, said, "Those repressed memories of what happened as a child, when they come it's like boom, boom, boom. . . . I'm not blaming, or justifying anything. But my surroundings . . . that's all I knew was drugs."

It should not be surprising that some of the girls sought to maximize responsibility for their crimes, or that they did not always articulate the connections between their criminal activities and their own victimization. After all, it appears that few adults in their lives made these connections either. Institutions that might have offered support, such as school, social services, or the juvenile justice system, often ignored their signs of distress, or criminalized their coping mechanisms. Also, when asked about

what they thought about having been tried and sentenced as adults, many of the girls seemed to spout a sort of prison "party line"; something to the effect of "since I did an adult crime, I have to be here." When asked whether it made sense to them that they had been tried and convicted as adults, their responses included:

- "Yes. Well, it does, but then again it don't. It's my first time getting in trouble—all I did was take the money. I didn't kill nobody so it wasn't right. But then again, I did an adult crime, so I should be tried as an adult."

- "Now it does. At first it didn't, I had no understanding. Now it does. You do adult things, you get adult things."

- "In a way I do, in a way I don't. I've never been in trouble before. I've never done anything, so I don't think I should be here. But I did do an adult crime. I ran from the police and hit somebody [with a car] and killed them. [So you have mixed feelings?] Yeah."

Many girls also expressed mixed feelings about their time in prison. In her 1998 book, *"In the Mix": Struggle and Survival in a Women's Prison,* Barbara Owen writes, "For many women, prison is a better and safer place than their disrupted and disruptive lives on the streets" (p. 40). Several girls alluded to this somber reality. However, they also believed there were alternatives besides incarceration in an adult prison that might have helped them. One girl remarked, "It's made me grow up. I wouldn't have gotten my GED and be going to college at 18 if I wasn't here. I would have ended up dead, probably. It saved my life. I just don't think I should have so much time here. It would have been better if I had gone to [name of a delinquent girls' institution] until I was 21 instead." Other girls made similar comments:

- "One thing I want to say is that being in prison saved my life. God sent me here to get schooling and get off drugs."

- "I think I deserve to be here. I needed to dissect my life . . . to step back and take a look at it. [Otherwise] I'd probably be dead. Somebody would have took it [my life] or I would have. I should be here, but I should also have a chance at rehabilitation, to leave here."

- "I'm a scared little girl growing up in a penitentiary. I don't think people should be bound over. I'm not asking to get off, I just think . . . they had other options than sending me here."

- "I'm glad I came; it got my life together, but I wish I'd have gone to [name of a delinquent girls' institution] . . . I think that could have changed me too."

For many girls, the hardest part of prison was being separated from their families, particularly their mothers. When asked to describe her experiences in prison, 16-year-old Toni responded:

> It's hard. I just wanna have my momma here, and now I've got to take care of myself. . . . They [staff] tell me I'm an adult, and I'm not. I know I did an adult crime, but in, you know, my mind, I'm not an adult. They're always telling me I'm a grown up now. One day I told a CO I need my momma, and she said, "You're a grown-up now."

Discussion of the Findings

The comments made by the girls about their crimes and punishments strike at the dilemma of representation. A recent discussion of desert theory suggests that punishments for juveniles should be scaled far below those of adults due to juveniles' lesser culpability, a principle of greater tolerance, and the tremendous impact of punishment on young people's lives (von Hirsch, 2001). It is generally recognized that the reasoning and decision-making capacities of adolescents differ from those of adults (Scott and Grisso, 1997:157).[10] In addition, youth do not have the same access to options or decisions about their lives that adults hold. Our contemporary legal system includes an abundance of laws that govern and regulate children, including child labor laws, compulsory school attendance, and the right to choose an abortion. These laws reinforce the dependent status of children. Many aspects of their lives are in some way controlled by adults—schooling, living situations—yet we see fit to hold youth completely responsible for the choices they make when they commit a crime. As Bortner and Williams (1997:xiii) contend, "Imprisoned youth are childlike but also excluded from being children. Their situations can be explained, in part, by this disjuncture." Ironically, delinquent girls are granted sovereignty at only one point: as they stand before the court waiting to be judged.

Inadvertently, "levels" of victimization (and therefore, responsibility) are assigned to girls being considered for transfer. Effectively, we are deciding which girls are still "salvageable," or deserving of our compassion. As Ferraro (1996:89) has pointed out with regard to battered women, "victimization carries cultural notions of deservedness." Victims are subject to interrogation of their conduct, motives, and efforts to protect themselves. The public and legal image of who constitutes a victim is further influenced by race, class, and sexual orientation. How do we as researchers deal with this problem when asked to quantify violence, crime, abuse, and responsibility in the lives of girls? For instance, if we establish who has been abused, do we unwittingly categorize other girls in the "not (as) abused" box of responsibility?

These questions of responsibility and agency hold unique relevance for girls who have been transferred to adult court. The concept of blurred boundaries can help describe the pathways of victimization and offending; it might also be used to illustrate the indefinite demarcation between child and adulthood. For girls facing conviction in adult court, another element of blurred boundaries is the point at which a girl becomes an adult. Bortner and Williams's (1997:68–69) book on youth in prison addresses this contradiction:

> Larger social forces have stripped most of these young people of any meaningful childhood. The precarious nature of their existence is exacerbated by current political strategies that essentially deny their youthfulness. In fundamental ways, they have never gotten to be children and now they are being cast as nonchildren. *Yet they are still children.* It is a tremendous irony. These

youth have not been afforded the protection presumed to be part of childhood, and yet the harshness of their lives frequently is disregarded or minimized, even while their presumed responsibility and guilt worthiness are used to justify punitive responses to them.

Judgments of responsibility and agency must consider how blurred boundaries affect children in ways that are different from adults—legally, economically, and emotionally. Children are deeply affected by the choices of the adults around them to an extent that adults are not. For instance, Sanchez's (2001) study of prostitution reported it as "a social practice characterized by both active participation in illicit sexual exchanges and routine subjection to violence," indicating the blurred boundaries of agency for the young women involved. She found that womens'/girls' likelihood of prostituting was heavily influenced by their marginalization status in terms of age (most start while teenagers), socioeconomic position, strained interpersonal and family relationships, drug addiction, exposure to sex trade networks, and basic needs such as food, housing, and clothing.

In essence, how do we construct a coherent model of these girls' agency with the understanding of the limitations and constraints placed on individuals? We must also be wary of constructing girls' narratives in a way that portrays them solely as victims of circumstance. As Daly (1992:48–49) cautions, "A seamless web of victimization and criminalization tends to produce accounts which focus on victimization and leave little agency, responsibility, or meaning to women's lawbreaking."

Consequently, we should take care that the pendulum not swing too heavily to the side of victimization in our discussions of blurred boundaries. Sweeping proclamations of innocence ("It's not her fault because of factor x or y . . .") are not statements that most girls would make about their lives. Some girls have committed acts that have caused terrible harm to others. To deny them the chance to sort through their own conflicted emotions of sadness, guilt, and anger is to deny them the chance to repair harms and the relationships that have been damaged in the process. Nancy Scheper-Hughes's (1992)

ethnographic work deals with this classic "double bind" of agency. If we attribute great explanatory power to past or present oppressions, we risk reducing subjectivity to a discourse on victimization. On the other hand, it is also possible to exaggerate the weapons and strategies of the less powerful, to romanticize human suffering as "resistance," and to ignore the crippling effects oppression has on the human spirit. She writes, "Moreover, in granting power, agency, choice, and efficacy to the oppressed subject, one must begin to hold the oppressed accountable for their collusions, collaborations, rationalizations, 'false consciousness,' and more than occasional paralyses of will. With agency begin responsibility and accountability" (p. 533).

The notion of agency—that people can act collectively, in light of history and the structures in which they exist, is a complicated concept that is oversimplified by our legal system and decision makers. Furthermore, Maher (1997:200) argues that much nonfeminist research "continues to interpret the agency of women lawbreakers within the confines of a western cultural logic anchored in individualism and free choice." Too often, she points out, female lawbreakers are either characterized primarily as the victims of social structures and oppressive relationships, or alternatively, as individual agents who choose freely. If we endeavor to negate the binary terms of either passive victims or aggressive criminals, perhaps these girls emerge as resistant and complex actors struggling to manage the environment in which they move and make choices. This means that "moral" judgments about their crimes, responsibility, and agency will not be so definite or straightforward. The decision about "what to do" with these girls will not be as simple as a prison sentence or a sudden proclamation of adulthood.

The girls interviewed in this study often expressed a mixed sense of relief at being removed from their turbulent lives at home or on the streets. Although the majority wanted help for their problems and felt responsible for their crimes, they also felt they should have been sent to a juvenile program or institution. The results of this research support their view. Although juvenile courts can be as punitive as adult courts and programming for girls in the juvenile justice system is far from ideal, processing these girls in the adult system may prove more deeply harmful, in both an ideological and material sense. Beyond the mere fact of a permanent record, the ideological message sent by placing girls in adult courts and institutions is problematic in terms of a more complex understanding of agency and blurred boundaries. Along with these ideological concerns, the actual conditions in the prison we studied are at issue here.

To our knowledge, there is no existing research that addresses the differences between delinquent girls' institutions and women's prisons. However, in data beyond the scope of this paper to present, the girls and workers at the prison site in this study reported severely limited access to education, health professionals, vocational jobs, social activities, areas of the prison, and so on, even relative to the adult women in the prison. In essence, the prison was having an enormously difficult time simply caring for their youthful population, much less providing them with meaningful opportunities for rehabilitation.

Creating space to speak of both victimization and offending might have allowed the girls in this study to explore the illusory "contradictions" in their lives and make connections between them instead. As Herman (1977:69) writes, "From those who bear witness, the survivor seeks not absolution but fairness, compassion, and the willingness to share the guilty knowledge of what happens to people in extremity." Avery Gordon's (1997) work on the "ghostly" impact of history and social forces echoes this call. She argues, ". . . Even those who live in the most dire circumstances possess a complex and oftentimes contradictory humanity and subjectivity that is never adequately glimpsed by viewing them as victims, or, on the other hand, as superhuman agents" (p. 4).

We can move beyond the simplistic rendering of these girls as either complete victims of circumstance or blameworthy perpetrators of crimes if we are willing to embrace fluid interpretations and meanings of their life histories. It might be said that we are denying these girls "complex personhood" to do otherwise. As Gordon writes, "Complex personhood means that all people . . . remember and forget, are beset by contradiction, and recognize and misrecognize themselves and others . . . Complex personhood means that people suffer graciously and selfishly too, get stuck in the symptoms of their troubles, and also transform themselves" (1997:4).

Recognizing that a girl has had a set of experiences (even very violent and devastating ones) is not to reduce her to a simple pawn of that personal history, but rather to illuminate her physical, mental, and spiritual state of being. To do otherwise is to rob marginalized girls of the opportunity to name their experiences, explore their responsibilities, and begin to repair the damage done to themselves and others.

CONCLUSIONS

The life histories of the girls in this study provide important insights into girls' pathways to crime. Some of the most significant experiences in the lives of the young women interviewed were the interlocking oppressions of gender, race, class, and sexuality that brought them to this blurred domain of victimization and offending. Incidents of sexual and physical abuse, neglect and disorder in the family, school problems, and chemical dependency were persistent themes in their lives. The life histories documented in this study also suggest that although these girls were selected for transfer to the adult court, many of their life experiences were similar to those of girls who remain in the juvenile justice system. In fact, although 16 of the 22 girls were arrested for a serious crime, 5 had no prior record, and 10 had never been placed in foster care, residential treatment, or a long-term correctional program before being sentenced to adult prison. Essentially, many of these girls had never been given a chance to succeed in the juvenile justice system before being subject to adult sanctioning. In addition, the courts appeared to disregard the blurred boundaries between girls' victimization and offending. In many of these girls' narratives, the same system that often took their serious victimizations lightly, took their offenses extremely seriously. Even within this small sample, there were many transfer cases that appeared to be questionable decisions.

The limitations of this particular study indicate the need for further research in this area. A larger sample size, particularly one that reflects a cross section of the United States, would give us a better idea of who is being transferred and why. A larger, more diverse study might also yield results that could be generalized to most women's prisons. In addition, a comparison study of girls and boys should be undertaken to determine gender similarities and differences in histories, transfer processes, and experiences in prison. Comparing girls (and boys) transferred to or convicted in adult court with delinquent girls (and boys) who were not, would also increase knowledge about this process and make it possible to understand which variables are related to the transfer decision. Lastly, better access to case information (e.g., files and court records) and to officers working with girls in prison could significantly improve our understanding.

In conclusion, this research raises serious questions about the discretion and politics involved in transferring the cases of juvenile girls to adult criminal court. This being said, where do we go from here and how shall we go about making useful changes? Where should efforts be focused? In this article, we have argued that girls need the opportunity to engage in complex and lengthy discussions to sort out issues of responsibility and blame for themselves. In order to ensure more compassionate and restorative responses to delinquent girls, we must also learn ways to create space for these discussions among justice system workers, policymakers, and the general public.

The public remains grossly uninformed about the lives of girls who reside in the "deep end" of the justice system. Their main source of information, the media, fuels the flames of fear, anxiety, and racism with their portrayal of these youth, and their sensationalist stories of increasing crime rates. It is not difficult to imagine why "hard-line" approaches are so widely supported and why simplistic moral judgments are made about these youth. As Bauman (1993:56) suggests, "Given the torments of moral uncertainty, guarantees of righteousness are temptations difficult to resist."

This research does not pretend to provide easy answers or moral certainty. It does, however, call for a more careful look at the life histories of the girls transferred and the circumstances surrounding their crimes. The findings also prompt consideration regarding the appropriateness of placing girls in adult women's prisons. The challenge at hand is to expand the existing paradigm for delinquent girls—to move from a system that simply "deals" with them to one that attempts to grapple with questions of agency, responsibility, cognitive development, and rehabilitation. The research presented here asks that we consider the contradictions and complexities present in the lives of delinquent girls, the transfer process, and the incarceration of young persons in adult prisons. Perhaps then we can begin to make sense of the complicated and seemingly contradictory stories that girls tell about their lives. Perhaps then we can begin to formulate more informed and compassionate policies with regard to the transfer of girls to adult court, and direct our cultural sensibilities along a more holistic and restorative path.

DISCUSSION QUESTIONS

1. According to Gaarder and Belknap, a multicultural feminist theoretical perspective on "pathways to crime" is a useful framework within which to couch the experiences of young women who end up in the criminal justice system. Describe this theory and explain the importance of having a gender-specific theory of girls' "criminal" behavior that incorporates a race/class/gender (or intersectionalities) framework as discussed in chapter 1 by Sokoloff et al.

2. What criteria should govern the serious step of transferring young people to adult court?

3. What are the drawbacks of girls' serving a sentence in an adult prison?

4. Why are life histories important in studying issues surrounding crime causation?

> **5.** What role does the media have in supporting hard-line responses to delinquency?

NOTES

1. This research was funded in part by a research fellowship from the University of Cincinnati's Research Council. An earlier version of this paper was presented at the 2000 annual meetings of the American Society of Criminology in San Francisco, California. The authors wish to thank Patricia Van Voorhis, Peg Bortner, Lois Presser, and Courtney Sears for their critical feedback on earlier drafts of this article. Any shortcomings, however, are entirely due to the authors. We are also grateful to the staff at the prison studied who agreed to take part in this research. We are in the greatest debt to the young women who told us their stories, which were often painful, sometimes humorous, and always powerful and insightful.

2. We also asked girls about their evaluations of and experiences in an adult prison, but it is beyond the scope of this article to adequately report these findings.

3. Although the pathways research here is almost exclusively conducted by feminist scholars and on female populations, applications of a similar research approach to male populations, such as Widom's "cycle of violence" research, suggests that abuse and neglect histories in males place them at increased risk of subsequent offending as well (Dembo et al., 1992; McClellan et al., 1997; Rivera and Widom, 1990; Widom, 1989a, 1989b).

4. For a more expanded explanation on why the "evidence on disparate processing of women of color is not clear," see Gilbert (2001).

5. See Daly (1998) for a more complete examination of black women's relationship to white justice—both how white justice categorizes and defines black women, and how black women position themselves and negotiate within white justice.

6. We refer to the subjects interviewed as either "young women" or "girls" for several reasons. Although most of the subjects were not "girls" in the legal sense of the term (some were 18 or 19), they generally referred to themselves and others in the unit as girls. It is also a way to differentiate this group from what is considered to be the "adult" population within the prison—those women outside the under-21 unit. In addition, it reminds the reader that the young women being interviewed were under 18 when their cases were processed and have spent at least a portion of their time in prison as juveniles.

7. We remain unclear about the reason this request was denied. Our administrative contact at the prison told us this was for the protection of the girls. The administration "... Did not want these tapes to show up on the Geraldo show."

8. All of the names of the girls who were interviewed have been changed for reasons of confidentiality.

9. Although Tracy's crime was not against her batterer (it was committed with her batterer), the context of power and control in which the crime took place warrants careful consideration of whether battered woman syndrome might apply. The battered woman syndrome has been successfully argued in court to explain the crimes of battered women, particularly in cases of self-defense involving a batterer. However, it has been argued that battered woman syndrome fails as a defense mechanism for all battered women, because it relies on a traditional view of women as passive and helpless (Allard, 1997, 1988). Lesbians may be less likely to be perceived by police, judges, or juries as victims of battering because they are stereotyped as domineering, assertive, and masculine. In addition, the relationships between lesbian partners are not legally recognized, and lesbian battering has rarely been addressed in the courtroom (Mahoney, 1997). It is possible that these factors played a role in Tracy's experiences in court.

10. For a review of the research comparing the reasoning and decision-making capacities of adolescents and adults, see Mann et al., 1989.

REFERENCES

Agozino, Biko. 1997. Black Women and the Criminal Justice System. Aldershot, U.K.: Ashgate.

Alder, Christine. 1998. "Passionate and Willful" Girls: Confronting Practices. *Women and Criminal Justice* 9:81–101.

Allard, Sharon Angella. 1997. Rethinking Battered Women's Syndrome: A Black Feminist Perspective. In *The Legal Response to Violence Against Women,* ed. Karen J. Maschke, New York: Garland.

Arnold, Regina A. 1990. Women of Color: Processes of Victimization and Criminalization of Black Women. *Social Justice* 17:153–166.

Bauman, Zygmunt. 1993. *Postmodern Ethics.* Cambridge, MA: Blackwell.

Belknap, Joanne. 2001. The Invisible Woman: *Gender, Crime and Justice.* 2d ed. Belmont, CA: Wadsworth.

Belknap, Joanne, and Kristi Holsinger. 1998. An Overview of Delinquent Girls: How Theory and Practice Have Failed and the Need for Innovative Changes. In *Female Crime and Delinquency: Critical Perspectives and Effective Interventions.* ed. Ruth T. Zaplin, Gaithersburg, MD: Aspen Publishing.

Belknap, Joanne, Kristi Holsinger, and Melissa Dunn. 1997. Understanding Incarcerated Girls: The Results of a Focus Group Study. *Prison Journal* 77:381–404.

Bortner, M. A. 1986. Traditional Rhetoric, Organizational Realities: Remand of Juveniles to Adult Court. *Crime and Delinquency* 32:53–73.

Bortner, M. A., and Linda M. Williams. 1997. Youth in Prison: We the People of Unit Four. New York: Routledge.

Bottcher, Jean. 1986. Risky Lives: Female Versions of the Common Delinquent Life Pattern. Program Research and Review Division, California Youth Authority. Sacramento: State of California.

Browne, Angela, Brenda Miller, and Eugene Maguin. 1999. Prevalence and Severity of Lifetime Physical and Sexual Victimization Among Incarcerated Women. *International Journal of Law and Psychiatry* 22:301–322.

Campagna, Daniel S., and Donald L. Poffenberger. 1988. The Sexual Trafficking in Children. Dover: Auburn House.

Campbell, Anne. 1999. Female Gang Members' Social Representations of Aggression. In *Female Gangs in America,* ed. Meda Chesney-Lind and John M. Hagedorn, Chicago, IL: Lakeview Press.

Carlen, Pat, Diana Christine, Jenny Hicks, Josie O'Dwyer, and Chris Tchaikovsky. 1985. *Criminal Women.* Cambridge: Polity Press.

Caspi, Avshalom, Daryl J. Bem, and Glen Elder. 1989. Continuities and Consequences of Interactional Styles Across the Life Course. *Journal of Personality* 57:375–406.

Chesney-Lind, Meda. 1995a. Girls, Delinquency, and Juvenile Justice; Toward a Feminist Theory of Young Women's Crime. In *The Criminal Justice System and Women: Offenders, Victims, and Workers.* 2d ed., ed. Barbara Raffel Price and Natalie J. Sokoloff, New York: McGraw-Hill.

———. 1995b. Rethinking Women's Imprisonment: A Critical Examination of Trends in Female Incarceration. In *The Criminal Justice System and Women: Offenders, Victims, and Workers.* 2d ed., ed. Barbara Raffel Price and Natalie J. Sokoloff, New York: McGraw-Hill.

———. 1997. *The Female Offender: Girls, Women, and Crime.* Thousand Oaks, CA: Sage.

———. 2001. Out of Sight, Out of Mind: Girls in the Juvenile Justice System. In *Women, Crime and Criminal Justice: Original Feminist Readings.,* ed. Claire Renzetti and Lynne Goodstein. Los Angeles: Roxbury.

Chesney-Lind, Meda, and Noelie Rodriguez. 1983. Women Under Lock and Key. *Prison Journal* 63:47–65.

Chesney-Lind, Meda, and Randall G. Shelden. 1998. Girls, Delinquency, and Juvenile Justice. 2d ed. Belmont, CA: Wadsworth.

Chigwada-Bailey, Ruth. 1997. *Black Women's Experiences of Criminal Justice.* Winchester, U.K.: Waterside Press.

Collins, Patricia Hill. 1990. *Black Feminist Thought: Knowledge, Consciousness, and the Politics of Empowerment.* New York: Routledge.

Daly, Kathleen. 1992. Women's Pathways to Felony Court: Feminist Theories of Lawbreaking and Problems of Representation. *Southern California Review of Law and Women's Studies* 2:11–52.

———. 1994. *Gender, Crime, and Punishment.* New Haven, CT: Yale University Press.

———. 1998. Black Women, White Justice. In *Crossing Boundaries: Traditions and Transformation in Law and Society Research.* ed. Austin Sarat, Marianne Constable, David Engel, Valerie Hans, and Susan Lawrence, Evanston, IL: Northwestern University Press.

Daly, Kathleen, and Rebecca L. Bordt. 1995. Sex Effects and Sentencing: An Analysis of the Statistical Literature. *Justice Quarterly* 12:141–175.

Dembo, Richard, Linda Williams, Werner Wothke, James Schmeidler, and C. Hendricks Brown. 1992. The Role of Family Factors, Physical Abuse, and Sexual Victimization Experiences in High-Risk Youths' Alcohol and Other Drug Use and Delinquency: A Longitudinal Model. *Violence and Victims* 7:245–266.

Elder, Glen H. 1985. Perspectives in the Life Course. In *Life Course Dynamics.* ed. Glen H. Elder, Ithaca, NY: Cornell University Press.

Elliott, Delbert S., and Kirk R. Williams. 1995. A Life Course Developmental Perspective. Boulder, CO: Center for the Study and Prevention of Violence.

Fagan, Jeffrey, Martin Forst, and T. Scott Vivona. 1987. Racial Determinants of the Judicial Transfer Decision: Prosecuting Violent Juvenile Offenders. *Crime and Delinquency* 33:259–286.

Feld, Barry C. 1999. *Bad Kids: Race and the Transformation of the Juvenile Court.* New York: Oxford Press.

Ferraro, Kathleen J. 1996. The Dance of Dependency: A Genealogy of Domestic Violence Discourse. *Hypatia* 11:77–91.

Fine, Michelle. 1986. Why Urban Adolescents Drop Into and Out of Public High School. *Teacher's College Record* 87:393–409.

Fine, Michelle, and Nolan Zane. 1989. Bein' Wrapped Too Tight: When Low-Income Women Drop Out of High School. In *Dropouts from Schools: Issues, Dilemmas and Solutions,* ed. Lois Weis, Eleanor Farrar, and Hugh G. Petrie, Albany: State University of New York.

Forst, Martin, Jeffrey Fagan, and T. Scott Vivona. 1989. Youth in Prisons and Training Schools: Perceptions and Consequences of the Treatment–Custody Dichotomy. *Juvenile and Family Court Journal* 40:1–14.

Gilbert, Evelyn. 1999. Crime, Sex, and Justice: African American Women in U.S. Prisons. In *Harsh Punishment: International Experiences of Women's Imprisonment,* ed. Sandy Cook and Susanne Davies, Boston, MA: Northeastern University Press.

———. 2001. Women, Race, and Criminal Justice Processing. In *Women, Crime, and Criminal Justice,* eds. Claire M. Renzetti and Lynne Goodstein, Los Angeles, CA: Roxbury.

Gilfus, Mary E. 1992. From Victims to Survivors to Offenders: Women's Routes of Entry and Immersion into Street Crime. *Women and Criminal Justice* 4:63–90.

Gilkes, Cheryl T. 1983. From Slavery to Social Welfare: Racism and the Control of Black Women. In *Class, Race, and Sex: The Dynamics of Control,* ed. Amy Swerdlow and Hanna Lessinger, Boston, MA: G. K. Hall.

Glick, Barry, and William Sturgeon. 1998. *No Time to Play: Youthful Offenders in Adult Correctional Systems.* Lanham, MD: American Correctional Association.

Gordon, Avery F. 1997. *Ghostly Matters: Haunting and the Sociological Imagination.* Minneapolis: University of Minnesota Press.

Herman, Judith. 1997. *Trauma and Recovery.* New York: Basic Books.

Houghtalin, Marilyn, and G. Larry Mays. 1991. Criminal Dispositions of New Mexico Juveniles Transferred to Adult Court. *Crime and Delinquency* 37:393–407.

hooks, bell. 1981. *Ain't I a Woman: Black Women and Feminism.* Boston, MA: South End Press.

Joe, Karen, and Meda Chesney-Lind. 1999. Just Every Mother's Angel: An Analysis of Gender and Ethnic Variations in Youth Gang Membership. In *Female Gangs in America.* ed. Meda Chesney-Lind and John M. Hagedorn, Chicago, IL: Lakeview Press.

Kempf-Leonard, Kimberly, and Lisa Sample. 2000. Disparity Based on Sex: Is Gender-Specific Treatment Warranted? *Justice Quarterly* 17:89–128.

Kruttschnitt, Candace. 1996. Contributions of Quantitative Methods to the Study of Gender and Crime, or Bootstrapping Our Way into the Theoretical Thicket. *Journal of Quantitative Criminology* 12:135–161.

Laub, John H., and Janet L. Lauritsen. 1993. Violent Criminal Behavior Over the Life Course: A Review of the Longitudinal and Comparative Research. *Violence and Victims* 8:235–252.

Laub, John H., and Robert J. Sampson. 1993. Turning Points in the Life Course: Why Change Matters to the Study of Crime. *Criminology* 31:301–325.

Leger, Robert. 1987. Lesbianism Among Women Prisoners: Participants and Nonparticipants. *Criminal Justice and Behavior* 14:448–467.

Levy, Barrie. 1991. *Dating Violence: Young Women and Danger.* Seattle, WA: Seal.

Maher, Lisa. 1997. *Sexed Work: Gender, Race, and Resistance in a Brooklyn Drug Market.* New York: Oxford University Press.

Mahoney, Martha R. 1997. Legal Images of Battered Women: Redefining the Issue of Separation. In *The Legal Response to Violence Against Women,* ed. Karen J. Maschke, New York: Garland.

Mann, Coramae Richey. 1995. Women of Color and the Criminal Justice System. In *The Criminal Justice System and Women: Offenders, Victims, and Workers,* 2d ed., ed. Barbara Raffel Price and Natalie J. Sokoloff, New York: McGraw-Hill.

Mann, Leon, Rob Harmoni, and Colin Power. 1989. Adolescent Decision-Making: The Development of Competence. *Journal of Adolescence* 12:265–278.

Mauer, Marc, and Tracy Huling. 1995. *Young Black Americans and the Criminal Justice System.* Washington, DC: The Sentencing Project.

McClellan, Dorothy S., David Farabee, and Ben M. Crouch. 1997. Early Victimization, Drug Use, and Criminality: A Comparison of Male and Female Prisoners. *Criminal Justice and Behavior* 24:455–476.

McShane, Marilyn D., and Frank P. Williams III. 1989. The Prison Adjustment of Juvenile Offenders. *Crime and Delinquency* 35:254–269.

Miller, Jody. 1996. Race, Gender and Juvenile Justice: An Examination of Disposition Decision-making for Delinquent Girls. In *Race, Gender and Class in Criminology: The Intersection,* ed. Martin D. Schwartz and Dragan Milovanovic, New York: Garland.

Moffitt, Terrie E. 1990. Juvenile Delinquency and Attention Deficit Disorder: Boys' Development Trajectories from Age 3 to Age 15. *Child Development* 61: 893–910.

———. 1993. Adolescence-Limited and Life-Course-Persistent Antisocial Behavior: A Developmental Taxonomy. *Psychological Review* 100:674–701.

Moore, Joan W. 1999. Gang Members' Families. In *Female Gangs in America: Essays on Girls, Gangs and Gender,* ed. Meda Chesney-Lind and John M. Hagedorn, Chicago, IL: Lakeview Press.

Naffine, Ngaire. 1996. *Feminism and Criminology.* Philadelphia: Temple University Press.

Nagin, Daniel S., David P. Farrington, and Terrie E. Moffitt. 1995. Life-Course Trajectories of Different Types of Offenders. *Criminology* 33:111–138.

Ohio Department of Youth Services. 1993. Juveniles Transferred to Adult Court in Ohio: Fiscal Year 1992. Columbus: Ohio Department of Youth Services.

Owen, Barbara. 1998. *In the Mix: Struggle and Survival in a Women's Prison.* Albany: State University of New York Press.

Peterson, Ruth D. 1988. Youthful Offender Designations and Sentencing in the New York Criminal Courts. *Social Problems* 35:111–130.

Poe-Yamagata, Eileen, and Jeffrey A. Butts. 1996. Female Offenders in the Juvenile Justice System: A Statistics Summary. Washington, DC: Office of Juvenile Justice and Delinquency Prevention.

Prothrow-Stith, Deborah. 1991. *Deadly Consequences.* New York: HarperCollins.

Puzzanchera, Charles M. 2000. Delinquency Cases Waived to Criminal Court, 1988–1997. OJJDP Fact Sheet, U.S. Department of Justice.

Reinharz, Shulamit. 1992. *Feminist Methods in Social Research.* New York: Oxford University.

Rennison, Callie Marie, and Sarah Welchans. 2000. Intimate Partner Violence. Bureau of Justice Statistics. Department of Justice. Special Report.

Richie, Beth E. 1996. Compelled to Crime: The Gender Entrapment of Black Battered Women. New York: Routledge.

Richie, Beth E., and Valli Kanuha. 1997. Battered Women of Color in Public Health Care Systems: Racism, Sexism, and Violence. In *Through the Prism of Difference: Readings on Sex and Gender,* ed. Maxine Baca Zinn, Pierrette Hondagneu-Sotelo, and Michael A. Messner, Boston, MA: Allyn and Bacon.

Rivera, Beverly, and Cathy S. Widom. 1990. Childhood Victimization and Violent Offending. *Violence and Victims* 5:19–35.

Robson, Ruthann. 1992. *Lesbian (out)Law: Survival Under the Rule of Law.* Ithaca, NY: Firebrand.

Rosenbaum, Jill Leslie. 1993. The Female Delinquent: Another Look at the Family's Influence on Female Offending. In *It's a Crime: Women and Justice,* 2d ed., ed. Rosalyn Muraskin, New York: Prentice Hall.

Sampson, Robert J., and John H. Laub. 1990. Crime and Deviance Over the Life Course: The Salience of Adult Social Bonds. *American Sociological Review* 55:609–627.

Sanchez, Lisa. 2001. Gender Troubles: The Entanglement of Agency, Violence, and Law in the Lives of Women in Prostitution. In *Women, Crime, and Criminal Justice,* ed. Claire M. Renzetti and Lynne Goodstein, Los Angeles CA: Roxbury.

Scheper-Hughes, Nancy. 1992. *Death Without Weeping: The Violence of Everyday Life in Brazil.* Berkeley: University of California Press.

Scott, Elizabeth S., and Thomas Grisso. 1997. The Evolution of Adolescence: A Developmental Perspective on Juvenile Justice Reform. *The Journal of Criminal Law and Criminology* 88:139–195.

Schwartz, Martin D., and Walter S. DeKeseredy. 1997. Sexual Assault on the College Campus. Thousand Oaks, CA: Sage.

Snyder, Howard N., Melissa Sickmund, and Eileen Poe-Yamagata. 2000. Juvenile Transfers to Criminal Court in the 1990's: Lessons Learned From Four Studies. Washington, DC: Department of Justice, Office of Justice Programs, Office of Juvenile Justice and Delinquency Prevention.

Silbert, Mimi H., and Ayala M. Pines. 1981. Sexual Child Abuse as an Antecedent to Prostitution. *Child Abuse and Neglect* 5:407–411.

Silverthorn, Persaphanie, and Paul J. Frick. 1999. Developmental Pathways to Antisocial Behavior: The Delayed-Onset Pathway in Girls. *Development and Psychopathology* 11:101–126.

Sommers, Ira, and Deborah R. Baskin. 1994. Factors Related to Female Adolescent Initiation into Violent Street Crime. *Youth and Society* 25:468–489.

Spohn, Cassia, John Gruhl, and Susan Welch. 1987. The Impact of the Ethnicity and Gender of Defendants on the Decision to Reject or Dismiss Felony Charges. *Criminology* 25:175–191.

Stattin, Hakan, and David Magnusson. 1991. Stability and Change in Criminal Behaviour Up to Age 30. *The British Journal of Criminology* 31:327–346.

Taylor, Jill McLean, Carol Gilligan, and Amy M. Sullivan. 1995. *Between Voice and Silence: Women and Girls, Race and Relationship.* Cambridge, MA: Harvard University.

Virginia Commission on Youth. 1994. The Study of Serious Juvenile Offenders (General Assembly of Virginia, House Document No. 81). Richmond: General Assembly of Virginia.

von Hirsch, Andrew. 2001. Proportionate Sentences for Juveniles: How Different Than for Adults? *Punishment and Society* 3:221–236.

Widom, Cathy S. 1998a. The Cycle of Violence, *Science* 244:160–166.

———. 1998b. Child Abuse, Neglect, and Adult Behavior: Research Design and Findings on Criminality, Violence, and Child Abuse. *American Journal of Orthopsychiatry* 59:355–367.

Young, Vernetta D. 1986. Gender Expectations and Their Impact on Black Female Offenders and Victims. *Justice Quarterly* 3:305–326.

Chapter 5

Trends in Female Criminality:
Is Crime Still a Man's World?

Darrell Steffensmeier and Jennifer Schwartz

ABSTRACT

Although this chapter title appeared in the two earlier editions of this book, the chapter here is completely new and is coauthored with Jennifer Schwartz. Steffensmeier and Schwartz give a statistical portrait and assessment of female crime trends in the United States between 1965 and 2000. Data have been drawn from the FBI's *Uniformed Crime Report* and supplemented by additional sources of information, including the *National Crime Victimization Survey*. The result is a report on both quantitative and qualitative evidence of female criminality and changes in crime statistics and criminal opportunities.

The analysis reveals an increased number of offenses by females within crimes traditionally committed by women, such as fraud and larceny. The data also show increases in arrests for misdemeanor and felony assaults. But on close analysis, it appears that the increase does not involve a change in the female share of arrests for assault, suggesting that the increase is largely a reflection of more aggressive enforcement practices toward both men and women or, as the authors say, a "widening of the net" by law enforcement. Also of interest is Steffensmeier and Schwartz's finding that the pattern of change during this period is similar for both men and women, suggesting that social and legal forces underlie much of the arrest rates for both sexes. In addition to the analysis of the female percentage of arrests compared to all arrests (for both men and women), the authors analyze the offender-profile percentage, which is the percentage of all arrests within the male and the female group. In this analysis, gender differences emerge clearly: greater involvement of females in minor property crimes and greater involvement of males in crimes against persons and major property. It is worth noting that the percentage of female arrests for homicide has *decreased* steadily over the period of study, from 17 percent in 1965 to 11 percent in 2000.

The authors end by answering the question they posed in the title of the chapter. Their answer is yes, crime is primarily still a man's world—especially lucrative, serious, and violent crime. As you read the upcoming chapters in this section of the book, keep this analysis in mind. How do other authors handle the issue of increasing or decreasing female criminality? Do they compare the crime under discussion to male offending? If not, why not?

For generations, men were the primary perpetrators of most criminal activities. Now, according to some commentators, this male dominance is changing. Building on earlier arguments made by Freda Adler (1975) and Rita Simon (1975), one popular view is that changing gender roles and the women's movement have had a significant impact on female crime. The contention is that as women have gained self-esteem, confidence, and self-sufficiency (i.e., mainly via paid employment), female crime rates have increased and the type of female crime has shifted toward more "masculine" kinds of lawbreaking. Whereas Adler stressed the growth in violent crimes by women, Simon stressed the rise in women's white-collar and occupational crimes.

Over the years, however, a number of criminologists (e.g., Box and Hale 1984; Chesney-Lind 1986; Steffensmeier 1993) have questioned whether in recent decades female criminality has changed substantially in the United States and whether, if some changes have occurred, they are best explained in terms of women taking on new work roles and a new consciousness concerning themselves and their place in society. Instead, these criminologists contend (1) that the female share of criminal offending has increased for some offenses like larceny and fraud, but that the female share has not changed much for other offenses like homicide and drug law violations, and (2) that factors other than women's liberation explain as well or better those changes that have occurred.

The debate has drawn evidence primarily from nationwide arrest statistics from the FBI's *Uniform Crime Reports* (UCR), the only long-term, continuous national data available that indicate whether the arrestee is female or male. This chapter will provide a statistical portrait and assessment of female crime trends over the past several decades in the United States, focusing in particular on female offending patterns as revealed by the UCR. However, as we note, considerable caution should be exercised when generalizing about trends in crime using "official" criminal justice sources of data. Therefore, this primary source of evidence is supplemented with additional sources of information, including the *National Crime Victimization Survey* (NCVS), that provide both quantitative and qualitative evidence on female criminality, on the status of women in American society, and on changes in crime statistics and criminal opportunities.

The conclusions derived from analysis of the UCR, NCVS, and other data provide a mixed picture of female offending trends. Female-offending gains have been considerable in areas of crime where female involvement has traditionally been high, like fraud and larceny. In recent years, moreover, females also have made large gains in UCR arrests for misdemeanor assault and felony assault—which some observers have interpreted as due to changing gender roles that have swayed women to behave more like men (Fox and Levin 2001). However, evidence from self-report and survey studies shows little change in the female-to-male share of assaultive crime and thus suggests that the female arrest gains for assault are due mainly to changing enforcement patterns (e.g., domestic violence statutes have elevated female more than male arrest levels, even though the statutes were established to protect females). In general, the data taken as a whole do not support the view often depicted in the mass media and embraced by some social scientists of robust changes in female criminality or of females approaching similarity with males in type or degree of criminal involvement. Notably, whereas the female share of criminal offending apparently has been increasing for driving while intoxicated and for minor property crimes like forgery (e.g., bad checks) and larceny-theft (e.g., shoplifting), American women are not catching up with males in the commission of violent, masculine, serious, organized-racketeering, gang-related, or corporate white-collar crimes.

TRENDS IN CRIME: UCR ARREST STATISTICS

In this chapter, we review female arrest trends from 1965 to 2000 using mainly the UCR but also other

Source: This article was written expressly for inclusion in this text.

data sources such as the NCVS. The UCR is the only long-term continuous source of annual data on sex- and age-specific arrests categorized by offense that researchers can use to reliably gauge changes in female offending patterns.[1] Two principal methods of measuring change in female offending patterns are used. One is the *female percentage of arrests* (FP/A), which indicates the share of arrests that are female after adjusting for the sex composition of the population at large. Examining this statistic over time yields some evidence as to whether sex differences in crime are narrowing or widening. The other is the *offender-profile percentage,* which is defined as the percentage of all arrests within each sex that are arrests for that particular offense. This part of the analysis examines the distribution of offenses committed by females to determine if the profile of the female offender has changed (e.g., toward more violence)—that is, if the types of crime females commit have changed. Table 1 summarizes this information on female and male offending for all FBI offense categories except rape (a male crime) and runaways and curfew violations (juvenile offenses). Table 1 portrays arrest rates per 100,000 (col. 1–8), the female percentage of arrests (col. 9–12), and the profiles of female and male offenders (col. 13–20).

Some Cautions in Using UCR Arrest Statistics for Trend Comparisons

Despite the utility of the UCR for examining longitudinal patterns in crime, three major problems are associated with using UCR data to assess trends in female crime. First, the rate of arrests, like any other official measure of crime, is a function of behavior defined as criminal and the control measures established to deal with it. Because of changes in reporting practices and policing, the ability of law enforcement agencies to gather and record arrest statistics has improved greatly over time—especially since the 1960s. However, gauging the effect of these changes in reporting practices on female crime is difficult. Several factors have artificially increased the arrest probabilities of females relative to males over the past few decades (e.g., widening of the pool of potential arrestees by focusing on less serious

crimes), as will be discussed later. However, it is generally recognized that comparing sex differences in arrest rates over a given period of time (i.e., the between-sex comparison as measured by the FP/A) is safer than using the rates to assess changes in the level of female crime over time (i.e., within-sex comparison) or as an absolute measure of the incidence of female crime in any given year.

For example, table 1, which compares adult female arrest rates across four decades, demonstrates the considerable reliability problem that exists in within-sex comparisons. Note that adult female arrest rates have dropped precipitously for some offenses, like public drunkenness (female rate per 100,000 dropped from 259 in 1965 to 81 in 2000). Also note the marked increase in DUI arrests, especially since the 1980s (female rate per 100,000 increased from 35 in 1965 to 221 by the early 1990s). But it would be foolhardy to conclude from these rates that substantially less drinking (but considerably more driving under the influence) is occurring among women today.

The changes from category to category may reflect shifts over time in public attitudes and police practices more than actual behavior of arrested persons, either male or female. For example, the concern over public drunkenness in the 1960s has given way, beginning in the 1980s, to increased public concern over alcohol- or drug-impaired operation of motor vehicles (DUI) for both males and females. Similarly, public concern over the use of drugs is also reflected in the sizable increase in arrests for drug abuse, making it second in arrests among all UCR offenses for males and for females. These observed arrest patterns highlight why we (and most researchers) focus on sex differences in arrest rates. Nonetheless, using the UCR arrest data to make between-sex comparisons over time also carries some risks, as we specify next.

A second problem with the UCR data is that the offense categories are broad and are derived from a heterogeneous collection of criminal acts, meaning that between-sex comparisons of a given crime are complicated by the differing character and context of male and female crime. For example, the offense category of larceny-theft includes shoplifting a $10 item (typically a female crime),

TABLE 1

Male and Female Adult Arrests, per 100,000, Female Percentage of Arrests, and Profile Percentages, 1965, 1980, 1990, 2000

Offenses	Male rates[a]				Female rates[a]				Female percentage of arrests[b]				Profile percentage, males[c]				Profile percentage, females[c]			
	(1) 1965	(2) 1980	(3) 1990	(4) 2000	(5) 1965	(6) 1980	(7) 1990	(8) 2000	(9) 1965	(10) 1980	(11) 1990	(12) 2000	(13) 1965	(14) 1980	(15) 1990	(16) 2000	(17) 1965	(18) 1980	(19) 1990	(20) 2000
Against Persons																				
Homicide	13.5	20.1	20.2	12.7	2.8	2.8	2.4	1.5	17	12	11	11	0.2	0.2	0.2	0.1	0.3	0.2	0.1	0.1
Felony Assault	158	262	397	359	23	33	55	80	13	11	12	18	1.8	3.0	3.6	3.7	2.5	2.4	2.5	3.4
Weapons	98	168	193	131	7	13	15	10	7	7	7	7	1.1	1.9	1.8	1.3	0.8	0.9	0.7	0.4
Misd. Assault	383	434	825	898	38	56	130	219	9	11	14	20	4.4	4.9	7.5	9.2	4.0	4.1	6.0	9.3
Major Property																				
Robbery	75	122	137	81	4	9	11	9	5	7	8	10	0.9	1.4	1.3	0.8	0.4	0.6	0.5	0.4
Burglary	221	329	303	183	8	20	28	27	4	6	8	13	2.6	3.7	2.8	1.1	0.9	1.4	1.3	1.9
Stolen Property	28	97	126	85	3	11	17	16	9	11	12	16	0.3	1.1	1.2	0.7	0.3	0.8	0.8	0.9
Minor Property																				
Larceny-theft	321	650	843	583	100	270	377	292	24	29	31	33	3.7	7.4	7.7	6.0	10.6	19.5	17.4	12.4
Fraud	95	196	222	196	23	127	163	150	20	40	42	43	1.1	2.2	2.0	2.0	2.4	9.2	7.6	6.3
Forgery	54	60	67	66	12	25	32	39	18	30	33	37	0.6	0.7	0.6	0.7	1.2	1.8	1.5	1.7
Embezzlement	15	7	10	9	3	2	6	8	17	26	37	48	0.2	0.1	0.1	0.1	0.3	0.2	0.3	0.3
Malicious Mischief																				
Auto Theft	91	90	128	86	3	7	12	14	9	7	9	14	1.1	1.0	1.2	0.9	0.4	0.5	0.6	0.6
Vandalism	46	140	189	146	4	12	25	29	8	9	12	17	0.3	1.6	1.7	1.5	0.3	1.0	1.1	1.2
Arson	4	12	10	7	0.6	2	2	1	12	12	15	17	0.1	0.1	0.1	0.1	0.1	0.1	0.1	0.1
Drinking/Drugs																				
Public Drunkenness	3,404	1,263	864	604	259	92	86	81	7	7	9	12	39.5	14.3	7.9	6.2	27.4	6.7	4.0	3.4
DUI	553	1,557	1,670	1,216	35	147	221	214	6	9	12	15	6.4	17.6	15.2	9.0	3.7	10.7	10.2	12.5
Liquor Laws	277	336	470	418	32	39	83	93	10	10	15	18	3.2	3.8	4.3	4.3	3.4	2.8	3.8	3.9
Drug Abuse	92	520	1,005	1,175	14	68	186	240	13	12	16	17	1.1	5.9	9.2	12.1	1.5	5.0	8.6	10.1
Sex-Related																				
Prostitution	21	35	42	40	59	75	75	56	74	68	64	58	0.2	0.4	0.4	0.4	6.3	5.4	3.5	2.3
Sex Offenses	96	66	93	74	11	5	7	6	10	7	7	7	1.1	0.8	0.9	0.8	1.2	0.4	0.3	0.2
Disorderly Conduct	965	689	586	407	130	112	124	102	12	14	18	20	11.1	7.8	5.3	4.2	13.8	8.1	5.8	4.3
Vagrancy	246	31	36	24	23	6	5	6	9	17	11	19	2.9	0.4	0.3	0.3	2.4	0.5	0.2	0.2
Suspicion	144	14	16	4	19	2	2	1	12	12	14	18	1.7	0.2	0.1	.04	2.0	0.1	0.1	.04
Miscellaneous																				
Against Family	131	60	76	109	12	5	14	27	8	8	16	20	1.5	0.7	0.7	1.1	1.3	0.4	0.7	1.1
Gambling	238	55	18	9	20	6	3	1	8	9	13	12	2.8	0.6	0.2	0.1	2.1	0.4	0.1	0.1
Other except Traffic	815	1,603	2,739	2,778	99	236	481	646	11	13	15	19	9.5	18.1	25.0	28.6	10.5	17.0	22.2	27.3
Total[d]	8,612	8,848	10,975	9,725	942	1,383	2,162	2,366	10	14	16	20	—	—	—	—	—	—	—	—

[a]Rates represent three-year averages: 1965 (1964, 1965, 1966); 1980 (1979, 1980, 1981); 1990 (1989, 1990, 1991); 2000 (1998, 1999, 2000). Rates are adjusted for the sex composition of the country and for changes in UCR coverage over time. The population base includes ages 18 and over.

[b]FP/A = Female Rate/(Female Rate + Male Rate) ★ 100%.

[c]Profile Percentage = (Offense Count/Total Count of All Offenses) ★ 100%. Note: May not sum to 100% due to rounding.

[d]Total excludes juvenile offenses (Runaways and Curfew Violations).

theft of a radio from a parked auto, theft of merchandise by an employee, and cargo theft amounting to thousands of dollars (typically a male crime). The broad offense category of fraud includes passing bad checks of small amounts and stock frauds involving large sums of money. The category of burglary includes both unlawful entry into an ex-spouse's apartment to retrieve merchandise and safecracking. Further, arrests are not distinguished in terms of whether the suspect is the sole or major perpetrator. Many females arrested for robbery or burglary act as accomplices to male offenders (Covington 1985; Steffensmeier and Terry 1986),[2] and many females arrested for homicide or assault act in response to considerable provocation from male associates (Browne 1992). These characteristics of UCR data are aggravated by the tendency of researchers to ignore secondary data sources and localized studies of arrests, court referrals, and so forth, as supplemental evidence to interpret the UCR statistics. As a result, inaccurate conclusions are easily drawn, such as the mistaken claim that female arrests for larceny and fraud typically involve occupational crimes or that increases in assault represent an increase in violent, predatory female offenders. This crucial point is reiterated throughout the chapter. In sum, offenses representing dissimilar events and covering a range of seriousness are included in the same UCR category, muddying the comparison of female-to-male crime.

A third problem concerns the label "serious crime" that is used in the UCR to refer to the Index (or Type I) offenses—homicide, forcible rape, aggravated assault, robbery, burglary, larceny-theft, auto theft, and arson. It is sometimes claimed that the proportion of women arrested for serious crimes has been increasing dramatically even when compared to male increases. On closer inspection, however, we find that the increase in arrests of women for serious, or index, crimes are disproportionately due to more women being arrested for larceny, especially shoplifting and other minor thefts. However, neither law enforcement nor the citizenry view larceny as a comparably serious crime (especially when compared with murder, robbery, and the like). So, more women are engaging in larceny—typically shoplifting inexpensive items—which is not considered a serious crime but is nevertheless included in the UCR serious crime category.

Trends in Arrest Rates

The first eight columns of table 1 show male and female arrest rates per 100,000 population for 1965, 1980, 1990, and 2000. For both males and females, arrest rates are higher for less serious offenses. Over the entire period examined, female rates are highest for the minor property crimes like larceny and fraud, for substance abuse (DUI, drugs, and liquor law violations), and for misdemeanor assault. Current arrest rates for prostitution-type offenses are comparatively smaller than rates from earlier periods, a pattern that largely reflects nonenforcement police practices. Other data sources indicate that prostitution continues to be a chief form of female offending, especially on the part of drug-dependent women and women facing adverse economic circumstances.

In general, the pattern of change over the period from 1965 to 2000 was similar for both sexes, with large increases occurring mainly for larceny, fraud, forgery, driving under the influence, drug violations, and assault; decreases in arrest rates for males and females occurred for public drunkenness, vagrancy, suspicion, and gambling. These findings suggest that similar social and legal forces underlie the arrest rates for both sexes, independent of any condition unique to women.

Trends in the Female Percentage of Arrests

The next four columns (col. 9–12) in table 1 show the female percentage of arrests (FP/A)[3] for various offenses. In 2000 (col. 12), the female share of arrests for most categories is 20 percent or less and is typically smallest for the most serious offenses, such as robbery and homicide. The female share of arrests is the largest for prostitution (including disorderly conduct and vagrancy statutes that are used in arresting females for prostitution) and for minor property crimes (larceny, fraud, forgery, and embezzlement).

Several important trends in female-to-male offending patterns are revealed in table 1.[4] First, when total arrests across all offenses are considered, the female percentage *rose substantially*—doubling between 1965 (10 percent) and 2000 (20 percent). However, as discussed in the following paragraphs, the bulk of that rise is due to sharp increases in the numbers of women arrested for minor property crimes like larceny and fraud, traditional female crimes.

Second, in the categories in which the female share of offending has increased, the FP/A has, for the majority of offenses, *inched* upward (about 1 percent to 2 percent per year); examples include arrests for misdemeanor assault and burglary. The female share of misdemeanor assaults has increased from 9 percent in 1965 to 20 percent in 2000; however, an examination of the FP/A across single years reveals incremental increases, with the most notable changes occurring between 1990 and 2000. Rates of arrest for misdemeanor assault have increased significantly over the past 40 years for both males and females, but somewhat more for females than males. A similar pattern of incremental increases also holds for aggravated assault. The increase in the FP/A for burglary that began in the mid-1970s (not shown) is due to sharply declining burglary rates among males as opposed to stable burglary rates among females. Such is also the case for auto theft. A caveat is that the base rate for females arrested for burglary (and auto theft) is small, so that even a doubling of the FP/A does not represent a large absolute increase in female offending.

Third, for a number of offenses, the female percentage held steady or declined slightly, including arrests for homicide and drug law violations. The female share of homicide arrests is now about 11 percent, compared to 17 percent in 1965. The female share of drug law violations has held steady around 15 percent for the past four decades. (This finding should not obscure the fact, however, that drug abuse arrests of both men and women have increased at a markedly higher rate than any other crime.)

Fourth, the female sex difference in arrests has narrowed considerably for the minor property crimes of larceny-theft, fraud, and forgery. Since 1960, females have made sizable gains in arrests for larceny, fraud, forgery, and embezzlement. The FP/A for larceny has continued to rise, from about 24 percent in 1965 to 29 percent in 1980, to 33 percent in 2000. Similarly, increases in the female share of fraud rose from about 20 percent in 1965 to 40 percent by 1980; since then, the female share of fraud has increased only slightly, to 43 percent by 2000. Most arrests of women in these offense categories are for shoplifting, passing bad checks, credit card fraud, theft of services, welfare fraud, and small con games (Giordano et al. 1981; Klemke 1992; Steffensmeier 1980; Watson 1993). The female share of forgery and embezzlement has also been rising, but very few females or males are arrested for embezzling. In fact, fewer men are arrested for embezzlement than for homicide. Thus, arrest rates for embezzlement are of little consequence in terms of overall male and female arrest trends. Moreover, most female arrests for embezzlement involve women who occupy low-level financial positions in banks, restaurants, hotels, government offices, and so forth. Typical occupational crimes include a female arrested for domestic theft while self-employed as a cleaning lady; a female arrested for pilfering clothes from a department store in which she worked; a male arrested for stealing carpentry tools from his employers; and a male and female arrested for misappropriation of funds by a local government official (Steffensmeier 1993; Watson 1993). Also, note that the FP/As for larceny, fraud, and forgery have held fairly stable since 1980, partly because continued gains are harder to come by once the female rate is at near parity with male rates (i.e., female gains were more possible in earlier years when the female rate was much smaller than the male rate). At the same time, the reclassification of theft from a motor vehicle to larceny (rather than burglary) has increased male larceny arrests.[5]

Finally, the most notable trend in recent years has been the rise in the female share of persons arrested for several violent crimes—most notably, misdemeanor assault and aggravated assault. Like other crimes, females tend to commit the less serious types of violence (e.g., scratching versus hitting), which are increasingly being included in the more serious violent crime categories. However, we later present evidence suggesting that these trends largely reflect changes in citizen reporting and law enforcement; that is, no real increase in the female share of assaultive or violent behavior has occurred, but instead there has been a "widening of the net," whereby females arrested under the current law-enforcement system might not have been arrested formerly.

Trends in Offender Profiles

The last four columns of table 1 compare the 1965 to 2000 arrest profiles of male and female offenders. The profile represents the percentage of all arrests within each sex that are arrests for that particular offense. For example, the homicide figures for 2000— .1 percent for men and for women—indicate that only one-tenth of 1 percent of all male and female arrests were for homicide. In comparison, a whopping 29 percent of all male arrests and 27 percent of all female arrests are in the category of other except traffic—a residual category that includes mostly criminal mischief, harassment, public disorder, local ordinance violations, and assorted minor crimes.

The similarities between the male and the female profiles (in this section) and their arrest trends (in the prior section) are considerable. For both males and females, among the five most common arrest categories in 2000 are other except traffic, larceny-theft, misdemeanor assault, drug abuse, and DUI; in total, these offenses account for about two-thirds of all male and female arrests. All these offenses involve relatively minor violations. For example, the offense category of misdemeanor assaults (also called other assaults or simple assaults) includes mostly minor, even trivial, incidents of threat or physical attack against another person, such as scratching, biting, throwing objects, shoving, hitting, or kicking. Arrests for murder, arson, and embezzlement are relatively rare for males and females alike, while arrests for offenses such as liquor law violations (mostly underage drinking), aggravated assault, and disorderly conduct represent "middling ranks" for both sexes.

The distribution of offenses for which both men and women are arrested has shifted a fair amount over the past 30 years, but the patterns of shifts for males and females are comparable. Of all persons arrested in 2000 versus 1965, a larger share of *both* male and female arrests are for DUI, larceny, fraud or forgery, drug law violations, and assault, whereas a smaller share are for public drunkenness and disorderly conduct. Relative to men, therefore, the profile of the female offender has not changed.

The most important gender difference in arrest profiles is the relatively greater involvement of females in minor property crimes such as larceny and fraud and in prostitution, and the relatively greater involvement of males in crimes against persons and major property crimes. These patterns are similar to those found in other comparisons of gender differences in crime (see the review by Steffensmeier and Allan 1996).

Juvenile versus Adult Trends in Female Percentage of Arrests

Thus far, the evidence does not show female crime rates to have increased markedly more than male crime rates for the majority of offenses, nor has the type of female crime shifted toward more masculine offenses (with the partial exception for assaultive crimes, which we examine more closely in the section titled "Female Involvement in Violence: Widening the Arrest Net"). It is plausible that shifting gender-role ideologies and other structural changes have had more of an effect on younger women than older women, so that the rise in offending by young women may be especially acute (see the review in Steffensmeier and Streifel 1991). In general, however, trends in the female share of offending across the four decades are quite similar for youths (ages 0–17) (table 2) and adults (18 and over) (table 1). (For example, note especially the similarities in the female share of offending for larceny, fraud, forgery, and embezzlement.)

Summary of Findings from the UCR

A number of overall conclusions can be drawn from UCR data. Females have relatively higher rates of arrest for the same types of crime for which males have higher arrest rates. Changes in the most common types of crime among females have paralleled those for males. However, women have lower rates of arrest for virtually all crime categories. The most striking gender difference is the proportionately greater involvement of females in minor property crimes and the relatively greater involvement of males in more serious person and serious property crimes. Although the sex difference for some crimes like homicide and robbery has remained fairly consistent over the past 40 years, females have made considerable gains (1) in the minor property crimes of larceny, fraud, and forgery; and (2) in recent years for assaultive crimes and drinking-related offenses like DUI and liquor-law violations (essentially a status offense, i.e., underaged drinking); but females, in comparison to males, have not made gains in arrests for drug-law violations. Overall, relative to men, both the female percentage of arrests and the profile of the typical offender have not changed.

TRENDS IN CRIME: OTHER SOURCES OF EVIDENCE

National Crime Victimization Survey

Evidence from other sources corroborates the relatively low female involvement in serious offending and also shows more stability than change in female crime relative to male crime over the past several decades. Data from the *National Crime Victimization Survey* (NCVS)—in which victims of personal crimes like robbery and assault are asked the sex of the offender(s)—reveal female-to-male totals that turn out to be quite close to those found in UCR data. In 2000, for example, women are reported to be responsible for about 10 percent of robberies, 14 percent of aggravated assaults, and 20 percent of misdemeanor assaults, as reported by victims. The comparable UCR figures are 10 percent, 18 percent, and 20 percent, respectively. The female share of violent offenders as reported by victims has remained much the same since the NCVS began in the mid-1970s (i.e., once crucial changes in methodology and questionnaire format are taken into account).

These findings are paralleled in numerous national self-report studies in which respondents (generally juveniles) have been asked to report their own offenses. See for example, the *National Youth Survey*, recognized as the best of the self-report delinquency studies providing male and female delinquency trends between the late 1960s and into the mid-1980s, and *Monitoring the Future,* an ongoing national survey of male and female high school seniors since 1975. Both surveys find stable gender differences in delinquency, including incidents of violence. In addition, the pattern of a higher female share of offending for mild forms of lawbreaking and a much lower share for serious offenses holds both for prevalence of offending (the percent of the male and female samples that report any offending) and especially for the frequency of offending (the number of crimes an active offender commits in a given period). Gender differences are smallest for offenses such as shoplifting and minor drug use (Steffensmeier and Allan 1996).

Incarceration Data

Statistics on males and females incarcerated in state and federal prisons reveal that from roughly the mid-1920s to the present, the female percentage of the total prison population varied between 3 percent and 7 percent (Beck and Karberg 2001; Greenfeld 1991). As with male incarceration rates, female rates have risen very sharply—more than tripling—over the past two decades. Most women in prison today were convicted for drug offenses or for property crimes that are drug-related; a smaller percentage were convicted for homicide and assault (usually against a spouse, lover, or child). A much larger percentage of female new court commitments than of male new court commitments today are entering prison for a drug offense. Also, a higher percentage of female prison inmates than male inmates were under the influence of drugs or alcohol at the time of the offense (Steffensmeier and Allan 1996).

National statistics on males and females convicted of felony offenses in state courts are available for 1988 through 1996 and also include a breakdown by

TABLE 2

Male and Female Juvenile Arrest Rates per 100,000 and Female Percentage of Arrests, 1965, 1980, 1990, 2000

	Male rates[a]				Female rates[a]				Female % (of arrests)			
	(1)	(2)	(3)	(4)	(5)	(6)	(7)	(8)	(9)	(10)	(11)	(12)
Offenses	1965	1980	1990	2000	1965	1980	1990	2000	1965	1980	1990	2000
Against Persons												
Homicide	2.5	5.1	9.2	4.1	0.2	0.5	0.5	0.4	8	9	6	9
Felony Assault	50	105	169	153	8	20	31	47	13	16	16	24
Weapons	44	76	125	108	2	5	9	12	4	6	7	10
Misd. Assault	107	207	358	465	20	57	112	216	16	22	24	32
Major Property												
Robbery	55	128	120	78	3	10	12	8	5	7	9	9
Burglary	407	652	406	262	16	47	38	35	4	7	8	12
Stolen Property	27	102	125	75	2	10	14	13	7	9	10	14
Minor Property												
Larceny-theft	708	1,006	1,045	720	172	377	419	420	20	27	29	37
Fraud	7	24	28	22	2	9	12	10	21	27	30	32
Forgery	10	21	18	13	3	9	9	7	20	31	33	36
Embezzlement	1	2	2	3	0.1	1	1.5	2	15	26	42	47
Malicious Mischief												
Auto Theft	257	172	257	124	12	21	32	26	4	11	11	17
Vandalism	264	347	372	299	15	31	36	44	6	8	9	13
Arson	16	24	24	22	1	3	3	3	6	10	10	12
Drinking/Drugs												
Public Drunkenness	96	113	59	53	11	19	12	13	11	14	16	20
DUI	8	84	51	48	0.4	10	8	11	4	11	14	18
Liquor Laws	170	343	326	310	28	104	131	145	14	23	29	32
Drug Abuse	21	279	252	496	4	57	33	86	14	17	12	15
Sex-Related												
Prostitution	1	3	2	2	2	7	3	2	71	68	57	54
Sex Offenses	42	34	51	44	16	3	4	4	28	8	7	8
Disorderly Conduct	316	320	309	361	56	69	82	148	15	18	21	29
Vagrancy	31	11	8	7	4	2	2	2	12	18	15	21
Suspicion	73	10	9	3	10	2	2	1	12	19	21	24
Miscellaneous												
Against Family	2	4	7	17	1	3	4	11	30	39	36	39
Gambling	10	6	3	4	0.3	0.3	0.2	0.1	3	5	5	4
Other except Traffic	511	785	780	914	138	201	215	323	21	20	22	26
Juvenile Offenses												
Curfew/Loitering	247	195	195	349	59	58	74	162	19	23	28	32
Runaway	196	201	232	179	180	275	311	267	48	58	57	60
Total	3,689	5,272	5,358	5,146	764	1,411	1,608	2,018	17	21	23	28

[a]Rates represent three-year averages: 1965 (1964, 1965, 1966); 1980 (1979, 1980, 1981); 1990 (1989, 1990, 1991); 2000 (1998, 1999, 2000); rates are adjusted for the sex and age composition of the population and for changes in UCR coverage over time; the population base includes ages 0–17.

type of offense (Brown and Langan 1998). The conviction data are consistent with arrest and self-report data in documenting the much greater involvement of males in violent and serious property crimes as well as the much smaller gender gap for minor property offenses and drug offenses. However, the female share of imprisonment for violent and serious property crime is less than their share as reported in UCR arrest data. This difference reflects the tendency of the police to cast a wider net and overcharge suspects when making arrests, whereas court practices operate to ferret out weak cases and better align the conviction offense with actual criminal behavior. This finding provides strong inferential support for the notion that increases in arrests for assaultive crimes by women represent changes in police behavior toward making arrests for more minor forms of violence rather than changes in female behavior toward greater aggression or violence. Moreover, although both sexes are more likely to be convicted for drug offenses in 1996 than 1988, the shift in offender profile toward drug offenses is somewhat greater among females.

Female Involvement in Gangs and Organized Crime

Studies of gang participation indicate that girls have long been members of gangs (Thrasher 1927), and some girls today continue to solve problems associated with gender, race, and class through gang participation. At issue is not their presence but the extent and form of their participation.

Ganging is still a predominantly male phenomenon. The most widely used and probably the best source of gang trend data comes from national surveys of law enforcement agencies conducted over the past several decades. The most recent survey, conducted in 1996, concluded that females accounted for about 10 percent of gang members (OJJDP 2000), essentially the same 10 percent figure that was found in national law enforcement surveys conducted in the 1960s and again in the early 1980s (Miller 1982).

Early studies, based largely on male gang informants, depicted female gang members as playing secondary roles as cheerleaders or camp followers. However, recent studies, which rely more on female gang informants, indicate that girls' roles in gangs have been considerably more varied than early stereotypes would have it.

The gang context may be an important source of initiating females into patterns of violent offending. Relative to the past, girls in gangs appear to be fighting in more arenas and even using many of the same weapons as males. The aggressive rhetoric of some female gang members notwithstanding, their actual behavior continues to display considerable deference to male gang members,[6] avoidance of excessive violence, and adherence to traditional gender-scripted behaviors (Campbell 1990; Chesney-Lind and Shelden 1998; Swart 1991). Females also tend to be excluded from most of the economic criminal activity of gangs (Bowker 1978; Maxson and Klein 1995).

Finally, female involvement in professional and organized crime has not increased and continues to lag far behind male involvement. Women continue to be hugely underrepresented in traditionally male-dominated associations that engage in safecracking, fencing operations, gambling operations, and racketeering. The *1990 Report* on organized crime and racketeering activities in the state of Pennsylvania (Pennsylvania Crime Commission 1991) identified only a handful of women who were major players in large-scale gambling and racketeering, and their involvement was a direct spin-off of association with a male figure (i.e., the woman was a daughter, spouse, or sister). The *1990 Report* also noted that the extent and character of women's involvement in the 1980s was comparable to their involvement during the 1970s.

Female Involvement in Violence: Widening the Arrest Net

The most controversial issue today concerns the growing perception in the media and among some criminologists that female violence is on the rise and that the gender gap in violent offending is narrowing, apparently because of changing gender roles (Fox and Levin 2001). Indeed, official UCR statistics indicate that the female share of arrests has increased for several violent offenses, most notably for misdemeanor assault but also for felony assault (see table 1). However, other sources of crime data cause us to call into question the conclusion that females are trending toward more violence. The evidence suggests that increases in the share of female violent offending are largely artifactual rather than the result of increased capacities for aggression among women.

All sources agree that females tend to commit the less serious forms of criminal behavior within the broad, widely heterogeneous offense categories of the UCR. Rather than any real changes in female violent behavior, the evidence suggests that police may be casting a "wider net" in arrest decisions such that more minor violent offenses, largely committed by women, are being picked up—disproportionately increasing the female share of violent offending. Thus, it may be that the UCR trends in the female share of violent offending are misleading because they largely reflect changing attitudes and enforcement practices.

Before turning to alternative sources of evidence to evaluate these claims, it is worthy to note that UCR data show no increase in the female share of homicide arrests. In fact, the female percentage of homicide arrests decreased steadily over the past four decades, from 17 percent in 1965 to 11 percent in 2000. The decline in homicide, the most serious form of violence, indicates that females have not disproportionately begun to commit more serious forms of violence. Since homicide is generally considered to be the most reliably measured crime, it is considered by many to be the best barometer of violent offending, whereas less serious crimes such as misdemeanor assault are generally deemed less accurate measures of offending. As such, a decline in female homicide offers strong evidence that females are not becoming more violent offenders. In addition, the female share of weapons violations, another indicator of violent crime, has not increased over the past 40 years.

Alternate sources of evidence, including self-report, victimization data, and imprisonment records, offer support for the notion that changes in law enforcement practices may account for the majority of the changes in UCR arrests for assault. As already discussed, self-report data (e.g., *Monitoring the Future, National Youth Survey*) indicate no shift toward females committing violent acts.

Victimization data, instituted to balance some of the inadequacies of official data (e.g., unreported or unrecorded crime), may offer some insights into trends in female violence.[7] The UCR shows a larger jump in female involvement in misdemeanor assault from 1993 to the present than does the NCVS (3 percent in the UCR versus 1 percent in the NCVS), suggesting that females are arrested more often now than in the past, even if behavior patterns remain largely the same. Prior to the redesign of the NCVS in 1992, the female share of misdemeanor assault remained markedly stable, as reported by both official and unofficial sources (hovering around 14 percent).[8]

Using UCR data, one is led to believe that the female share of aggravated assault increased over the past 10 years (from 13 percent in 1990 to 18 percent in 2000). However, no such increase is revealed in the NCVS. Since 1980, female involvement in felony assault, as reported by victims, has held steady between 11 percent and 14 percent. This finding is perhaps the strongest evidence that UCR reports of increased female violence are largely attributable to changes in law enforcement practices and societal definitions of acceptable thresholds of violence rather than any changes in gender roles and actual female violence.

Another way to examine this possibility is to determine whether female proportions of those incarcerated for violent offenses are increasing. An increase in the female share of prisoners offers evidence that females are increasingly committing more (serious) violent crimes. On the other hand, no increase in female representation in correctional facilities suggests that police may be arresting more female minor offenders who, in the past would have been overlooked. The latter seems to be the case. Table 3 presents the profile percentages (col. 1–6) and the

TABLE 3

Profile Percentages and Female Percentage of Prisoners for Violent Offenses, 1986, 1991, and 1999

Offenses	Profile %, males			Profile %, females			Female % imprisoned		
	(1)	(2)	(3)	(4)	(5)	(6)	(7)	(8)	(9)
	1986	1991	1999	1986	1991	1999	1986	1991	1999
Total Violent[a]	55	47	49	41	32	29	3.3	3.8	3.8
Murder	11.2	10.5	12.0	13.0	11.7	8.9	5.1	6.1	4.7
Assault	8.1	8.3	9.8	7.1	6.2	7.0	3.9	4.2	4.7
Other Violent[b]	0.8	0.5	2.1	1.2	1.1	2.0	3.2	11.0	6.0
Weapons[c]	1.5	1.9	—	0.9	0.5	—	2.7	1.5	—
Robbery	21.3	15.2	14.0	7.1	7.8	7.0	2.2	2.9	3.2

[a]Total Violent also includes negligent manslaughter, kidnapping, rape, and other sexual assault, so the profile percentages for individual offenses do not sum to the total violent index.
[b]Includes blackmail, extortion, hit-and-run driving with bodily injury, child abuse, and criminal endangerment.
[c]Not available in 1999. Included in public-order offenses.
Source: Survey of Inmates in State Correctional Facilities.

female share of imprisonment (col. 7–9) for state prison inmates serving time (at least one year) for a violent offense from 1986 to the present. According to the *Survey of Inmates in State Correctional Facilities,* the profile of the female prisoner has actually shifted *away* from violence (similar to the trend for males), with less than 30 percent of all female inmates imprisoned for a violent offense compared to 41 percent over a decade ago. In addition, the female percentage imprisoned has not increased since the mid-1980s for murder, assault, weapons, or robbery offenses.[9] Of greatest pertinence here is the fact that the female share of imprisonment for assault has remained stable at around 4 percent since the mid-1980s.

Taken as a whole, this body of evidence suggests that increases in the female share of assault, as reported in official statistics, is largely due to a "widening of the net" effect whereby police make arrests for less serious types of violence now than in the past. This practice disproportionately ensnares women, who, for the most part, commit these lesser types of violence. Self-report data and victimization data are consistent with this interpretation, because they show little to no increase in violence among women. In addition, although more women are arrested for violence (i.e., assault) now than in the past, the fact that female representation in prison for vio-

lence has not increased suggests that police are casting a wider net and capturing, largely, nonserious female offenders (e.g., the woman who slaps her boyfriend, the daughter who shoves her mother, the two girls who pull each other's hair on school grounds).

CONCLUSION

In summary, all these sources strongly document that crime—especially in its more serious and lucrative forms—largely remains a man's world. All sources confirm that the biggest gender difference in crime remains males' greater participation in violent and more serious property crime whereas female criminality is largely confined to minor property crime (and prostitution).

FUTURE PROSPECTS

The study of female crime has improved dramatically over the past several decades. Researchers have better and more diverse data sets, more appropriate analytical techniques, and therefore more conclusive empirical findings. Future inquiry into female-to-male trends in criminal behavior should focus on the following six areas.

First, localized studies of police and court records are needed to provide both a contextual understanding of the organizational management of crime (including changes in the law and in enforcement practices) and a detailed breakdown of the kinds of crime committed by women (and men). At present, researchers have too little systematic, qualitative data on the nature of contemporary female offending, especially as it compares to contemporary male offending or to female offending in the past. Such studies not only would help overcome a lack of knowledge about which sorts of crimes might be subsumed under which FBI categories but also would provide a baseline for evaluating future trends in female crime.

Second, background profiles, interviews, and case studies of female arrestees are needed. Eleanor Miller (1986, 5) has noted that those who interpret the UCR data as demonstrating the crime-producing effects of female emancipation did so because "they were out of touch with who the typical female criminal in this country is on both a demographic and a personal level." Demographic profiles and case studies of female arrestees are needed to develop a portrait of female offenders and to describe the nature of their criminal roles and the circumstances leading to criminal involvement. In particular, researchers need to examine whether women and men commit the same types of offenses for similar reasons and whether those reasons have changed over time. Both historical and contemporary research suggests that women differ somewhat in their motivations to commit crime and the vocabularies they use to justify their crimes. More than for men, the law violations of women are often tied to an emotional relationship to others and the fulfillment of role expectations within that relationship. Women may use the money gained for personal excesses, but more often the money is used to fulfill a caretaking role or to maintain a love relationship (Zeitz 1981; Simon and Landis 1991; Steffensmeier and Allan 1996).

Third, perhaps the most important research need is to examine how changes in productive activity in American society have affected the nature of crime opportunities that its citizens encounter. Females made large arrest gains over the past three decades in the kinds of nonviolent economic crimes that are likely to continue to grow in significance. Many of these crimes are within the reach of virtually every American citizen and are conducive to female involvement. Female-to-male arrest trends are likely to be influenced more by the nature of crime opportunities characterizing American society than by changes in female motivations or in the social and economic position of women. Research on this neglected area of criminology would benefit the study not only of female criminality but also of male criminality.

Fourth, also of paramount importance is the need to examine and develop alternative sources of data that allow an assessment of how shifts in the tolerance quotient for particular types of crime (or for crime as a whole) affect female criminality as officially measured in sources like the *Uniform Crime Reports*. Many commentators conclude that U.S. society as a whole is less tolerant of crime today than three or four decades ago and that a greatly expanded enforcement machinery coincides with this trend toward greater punitiveness (see the review in Steffensmeier and Harer 1999). At issue, in particular, are whether stricter laws and policing generate gender-specific effects on the production of crime statistics. For example, does "widening the net" to prosecute less serious forms of violence ipso facto translate into a higher female-to-male share of all persons arrested for violent crimes, as some evidence suggests?

Fifth, future inquiry needs to take into account the effects on female offending of both change and stability in gender roles, depending on which aspect of women's status is considered. It may be that informal social control structures that normally govern female behavior have been weakened by recent societal changes. In reverse fashion, Boritch and Hagan (1990) have argued that an ever-increasing enforcement of informal middle-class norms of femininity helped to reduce deviance and crime among working-class women in Toronto in the early part of the twentieth century. (Incidentally, Boritch and

Hagan also report that female crime levels declined at the same time that female employment levels were rising.) Importantly, the argument that the economic and occupational roles of women are rapidly changing and that the changes have substantially affected gender differences in criminality ignores other structures of male domination and the ways in which gender and gender relations structure social life (Ridgeway 1997). An understanding of the relationship between crime and gender roles will yield different interpretations depending on how gender is conceptualized.

Finally, the need is great for research that examines the joint effects of gender and of race and ethnicity on trends in criminal offending. Are there racial and ethnic differences, for example, in gendered patterns of violent crime and changes in those patterns over the past two to three decades? Do changes in community social and economic conditions predict changes (trends) in gender-specific offending over time, and are the effects of these conditions uniform over time and across racial and ethnic groups? In view of an increasingly multiracial society (especially the growth of Hispanic and Asian populations), the need is urgent for the development of data sources on crime that allow gender to be further disaggregated in order to examine both within-sex and between-sex differences in criminal offending across racial and ethnic groups.

Our goal has been to place female crime trends in the United States within a broad multivariate framework. By all accounts, however, crime—particularly its more lucrative, organized, and violent forms—primarily remains a man's world.

DISCUSSION QUESTIONS

1. In your own words, describe the basic patterns of female offending between 1965 and 2000 that emerge from the data in this chapter. Spell out your own reactions to these findings.

2. How have arrest patterns of women and men changed over time? How have they remained the same?

3. There is a lot of discussion these days about the "new violent female offender." Based on the findings in this study, how would you respond to such a statement? Do you agree or disagree with the authors?

4. What role does larceny-theft play in current beliefs that women engage in more serious crime today? According to Steffensmeier and Schwartz, why is this issue important?

5. Compare and contrast the methods used by Steffensmeier and Schwarz in this chapter to the studies of female offenders reported in the two previous chapters. What are the strengths and weaknesses of their different methods?

NOTES

1. A major limitation of the UCS is that a breakdown of arrests by gender *and* race is not available. Rather, arrest data are only available by gender (i.e., women versus men) *or* by race (i.e., black versus white).

2. Note this headline and story in *The Kansas City Star:* "Woman charged in robbery attack, three tourists accosted . . . A man and woman jumped out of the car and the man accosted one of the tourists, a 69-year-old woman. He punched the woman in the face, knocking her to the ground. He then ripped her purse from her hands. After handing the purse to his [female] accomplice, he turned to another tourist, a 59-year-old woman, and punched her in the face and tried to take her purse . . . The robbers then returned to their car and drove away. Witnesses recorded the license plate of the getaway car and detectives later arrested the woman. Police were still looking for the man involved in the robbery." (Byline by Christine Vendel, October 20, 2001, B2)

3. The formula to calculate the FP/A is as follows: Female Rate/(Female Rate + Male Rate) × 100. Therefore, a figure of 50 percent indicates an equal share of arrests for females and males. For example, the female rate for drug law violations in 2000 was 243/100,000 and the male rate was 1,189/100,000; so 243/(243 + 1,189) × 100 = 17% female share of all drug arrests.

4. Note that an increase in the female percentage of arrests (FP/A) will occur if female rates increase more than male rates, if female rates are constant but male rates decline, or if female rates decline less than male rates. Increases in the FP/A represent a narrowing of the gender gap in crime.

5. A paper decrease in burglary rates has occurred because, contrary to instructions from the Uniform Crime Reporting Program, many police departments had categorized "theft from a motor vehicle" (e.g., breaking into a parked auto to steal a radio) as a burglary rather than a larceny-theft. In response to UCR pressures, the trend today is for police departments to classify a theft from a motor vehicle as a larceny-theft. This change has depressed male burglary rates and pushed up male arrest rates for larceny-theft since the mid-1970s.

6. Although some independent female gangs have been identified, they have less continuity over time than the typical male gang, and the most common form of female gang involvement has remained as auxiliaries or branches of male gangs (Curry 1998; Swart 1991).

7. However, the victimization data have some problems as well. Specifically, there were major changes in the NCVS methodology and questionnaire format in 1992 designed to elicit a greater response by all interviewees, but especially those who are victims of crime at the hand of intimates and acquaintances. These changes will disproportionately impact the offending rates of females, who disproportionately offend against intimates and acquaintances rather than strangers. In addition, broadening the definition of violence to include less serious forms of violence will enumerate more females because they commit the less serious forms of violence. Despite problems with NCVS comparability over time, useful comparisons between the UCR and NCVS (pre- and post-redesign) may be drawn.

8. Because changes in the survey design of the NCVS coincide with observed increases in the female share of arrests for assault, it is difficult to disentangle effects of the survey redesign, effects of changes in police behavior, and actual changes in offending behavior. Unfortunately, misdemeanor assault is identified by the Bureau of Justice Statistics as one of the crimes that showed significant reporting differences due to the survey redesign, particularly for females. Even with changes that would tend to inflate the reported number of females committing a violent offense, the NCVS shows a smaller increase for misdemeanor assault than does the UCR.

9. Although the category of other violent female prisoners has increased somewhat, this category is made up of a heterogeneous mix of offenses that are not comparable to UCR or NCVS crime categories, nor are they necessarily violent—for example, blackmail. In addition, like embezzlement, these offenses represent a very small proportion of prisoners—less than 5 percent of all prisoners in 1999.

REFERENCES

Adler, F. 1975. *Sisters in Crime.* New York: McGraw-Hill.

Anglin, D., Y. Hser, and W. McGlothin. 1987. Sex Differences in Addict Careers. *American Journal of Drug and Alcohol Abuse* 13:59–71.

Baumer, Eric, J. L. Lauritsen, R. Rosenfeld, and R. Wright. 1998. The Influence of Crack Cocaine on Robbery, Burglary, and Homicide Rates: A Cross-City, Longitudinal Analysis. *Journal of Research in Crime and Delinquency* 35(3):316–40.

Beck, A., and J. Karberg. 2001. Prison and Jail Inmates at Midyear 2000. *Bureau of Justice Statistics Bulletin,* March. NCJ 185989.

Boritch, H., and J. Hagan. 1990. A Century of Crime in Toronto: Gender, Class, and Patterns of Social Control, 1859 to 1955. *Criminology* 28:567–99.

Bowker, L. 1978. *Women, Crime, and the Criminal Justice System*. Lexington, MA: Lexington.

Box, S., and C. Hale. 1984. Liberation/Emancipation, Economic Marginalization, or Less Chivalry: The Relevance of Three Theoretical Arguments to Female Crime Patterns in England and Wales, 1951–1980. *Criminology* 22:473–98.

Brown, J., and P. Langan. 1998. *State Court Sentencing of Convicted Felons, 1994*. Washington, DC: Bureau of Justice Statistics.

Browne, A. 1992. Violence against Women. *Journal of the American Medical Association*. 267:3184–95.

Campbell, A. 1990. Female Participation in Gangs. In *Gangs in America,* ed. C. Huff. Newbury Park, CA: Sage.

Canter, R. 1982. Sex Differences in Self-Report Delinquency. *Criminology* 20:373–93.

Chesney-Lind, M. 1986. Women and Crime: The Female Offender. *Signs* 12:78–96.

Chesney-Lind, M. 1995. Rethinking Women's Imprisonment: A Critical Examination of Trends in Female Incarceration. In *The Criminal Justice System and Women: Offenders, Victims, and Workers,* 2d ed., ed. Barbara Raffel Price and Natalie J. Sokoloff, 105–17. New York: McGraw-Hill.

Chesney-Lind, M., and R. Shelden. 1998. *Girls, Delinquency, and Juvenile Justice*. Belmont, CA: Wadsworth.

Covington, J. 1985. Gender Differences in Criminality among Heroin Users. *Journal of Research in Crime and Delinquency* 22:329–53.

Curry, G. D. 1998. Female Gang Involvement. *Journal of Research in Crime and Delinquency* 35(1):100–118.

Fox, J., and J. Levin. 2001. *The Will to Kill: Making Sense of Senseless Murder*. Boston: Allyn and Bacon.

Giordano, P., S. Kerbel, and S. Dudley. 1981. The Economics of Female Criminality: An Analysis of Police Blotters, 1890–1976. *Women and Crime in America,* ed. Lee H. Bowker, 65–81. New York: Macmillan.

Greenfeld, L. 1991. *Prisons and Prisoners in the United States, 1925–90*. Washington, DC: U.S. Department of Justice, Bureau of Justice Statistics.

Klemke, L. 1992. *The Sociology of Shoplifting: Boosters and Snitches Today*. Westport, CT: Praeger.

Maher, L., and K. Daly. 1996. Women in the Street-Level Economy: Continuity or Change? *Criminology* 34(4):465–91.

Maxson, C., and M. Klein. 1995. Investigating Gang Structures. *Journal of Gang Research* 3(1):33–40.

Miller, E. 1986. *Street Woman*. Philadelphia: Temple University.

Miller, W. 1973. The Molls. *Society* 11:32–35.

Miller, W. 1982. *Crime by Youth Gangs and Groups in the United States*. Washington, DC: U.S. Department of Justice, Office of Juvenile Justice and Delinquency Prevention.

OJJDP (Office of Juvenile Justice and Delinquency Prevention). 2000. *1998 National Youth Gang Survey*. Washington, DC: U.S. Department of Justice, Office of Juvenile Justice and Delinquency Prevention.

Pennsylvania Crime Commission. 1991. *1990 Report—Organized Crime in Pennsylvania: A Decade of Change*. Commonwealth of Pennsylvania.

Ridgeway, C. 1997. Interaction and the Conservation of Gender Inequality: Considering Employment. *American Sociological Review* 62:218–35.

Simon, R. 1975. *The Contemporary Woman and Crime*. Washington, DC: National Institute of Mental Health.

Simon, R., and J. Landis. 1991. *The Crimes Women Commit, the Punishments They Receive*. Lexington, MA: Lexington.

Sommers, I., and D. Baskin. 1992. Sex, Race, Age, and Violent Offending. *Violence and Victimology* 7:191–201.

Spain, D. 1997. Societal Trends: The Aging Baby Boom and Women's Increased Independence. Final report prepared for the Federal Highway Administration, U.S. Dept. of Transportation, Order no. DTFH61-97-P-00314.

Steffensmeier, D. 1980. Sex Differences in Patterns of Adult Crime, 1965–77: A Review and Assessment. *Social Forces* 58:1080–1108.

Steffensmeier, D. 1993. National Trends in Female Arrests, 1960–1990: Assessment and Recommendations for Research. *Journal of Quantitative Criminology* 9:413–41.

Steffensmeier, D., and E. Allan. 1996. Gender and Crime: Toward a Gendered Theory of Female Offending. *Annual Review of Sociology* 22:459–87.

Steffensmeier, D., and M. Harer. 1999. Making Sense of Recent U.S. Crime Trends, 1980–1998: Age-Composition Effects and Other Explanations. *Journal of Research in Crime and Delinquency* 36(3):235–74.

Steffensmeier, D., and D. Haynie. 2000. Gender, Structural Disadvantage, and Urban Crime: Do Macrosocial Variables also Explain Female Offending Rates? *Criminology* 38(2): 403–38.

Steffensmeier, D., and C. Streifel. 1991. Age, Gender, and Crime across Three Historical Periods: 1935, 1960, and 1985. *Social Forces* 69(3):869–94.

Steffensmeier, D., and C. Streifel. 1992. Time-Series Analysis of the Female Percentage of Arrests for Property Crimes, 1960–85: A Test of Alternative Explanations. *Justice Quarterly* 9:77–103.

Steffensmeier, D., and R. Terry. 1986. Institutional Sexism in the Underworld: A View from the Inside. *Sociological Inquiry* 56:304–23.

Streifel, C. 1990. *Cross-Sectional Analysis of Gender Differences in Rates of Offending.* Ph.D. diss., Pennsylvania State University, University Park.

Swart, W. 1991. Female Gang Delinquency: A Search for "Acceptably Deviant Behavior." *Mid-American Review of Sociology* 15(1):43–52.

Tannen, D. 1991. *You Just Don't Understand: Women and Men in Conversations.* New York: Morrow.

Thrasher, F. 1927. *The Gang: A Study of 1,313 Gangs in Chicago.* Chicago: University of Chicago.

U.S. Department of Justice. 1960-2000. *Uniform Crime Reports.* Washington, DC: U.S. Government Printing Office.

Watson, J. 1993. Gender Differences in Crime and Disposition in Pennsylvania Lower-Courts. Undergraduate honors thesis, Sociology Department, Pennsylvania State University.

Weisburd, D., S. Wheeler, E. Waring, and N. Bode. (1991). *Crimes of the Middle Classes: White-Collar Offenders in the Federal Courts.* New Haven, CT: Yale University.

Zeitz, D. 1981. *Women Who Embezzle or Defraud: A Study of Convicted Felons.* New York: Praeger.

Chapter 6

Contemporary Explanations of Women's Crime

Darrell Steffensmeier and Jennifer Schwartz

ABSTRACT

This chapter begins by reviewing the sparse history of theories of women's criminality. Although little attention was given to the subject historically, those writers who did examine criminality viewed women's involvement as a curiosity but not worthy of much attention. Women who engaged in crime were seen as exceptionally masculine, deranged, or amoral. Over time, studies became more objective, and both societal factors and cultural considerations were brought into explanations of female crime; however, this was done within the context of employing male-derived theories of offending.

In more recent years, the issue of gender and its strong influence in explaining behavior has been added to research protocols on female crime. Moreover, the subject has attracted a growing number of researchers and theorists, often with little agreement among them. In this chapter, Steffensmeier and Schwartz pull together many of the theories and factors that writers have identified to explain female criminality. The authors present a number of reasons for the increase in the ratio of female-to-male arrests and offending that was described in chapter 5. Two commonly accepted explanations of women's crime today include the war on drugs theory and the equality with a vengeance theory. These two theories are elaborated more fully in Owen (chap. 10) and Sudbury (chap. 12). Clearly, women's crime has increased as the drug laws have changed, so the war on drugs has been described as a "war on women"—especially black and Latina women. Moreover, a societal move to become tough on crime merged with a backlash against women's equality. These two movements have led to hostile "equality with a vengeance" treatment of women on the margins caught in the web of the criminal justice system.[1] An interpretation of the broader contextual issues surrounding globalization and the prison industrial complex and their impact on women's increased rates of offending are described by Sudbury.

---

[1]See Chapter 7, "Sentencing Women to Prison: Equality Without Justice," in *The Female Offender*, by Meda Chesney-Lind, Thousand Oaks, CA: Sage, 1997.

Steffensmeier and Schwartz identify here nine clusters of explanations for women's crime: (1) law and the organizational management of crime, (2) net widening and more punitive laws, (3) gender equality and female emancipation, (4) increased economic marginalization of women, (5) increased inner-city community disorganization, (6) expanded opportunities for female-type crimes, (7) changes in the criminal underworld, (8) trends in drug dependency, and (9) crime prevention programs for males. The authors end by warning the reader that all these forces impact more harshly on certain groups of women, particularly poor women of color.

This chapter offers a comprehensive examination of theoretical explanations of female crime currently found in the scholarly and popular literature. After reading this chapter, the reader will have sufficient information to begin to evaluate the various perspectives and, importantly, to consider ways to demonstrate the efficacy of the various explanations.

The gender difference in crime is universal: Throughout history, for all societies, for all groups, and for nearly every crime category, females offend less than males. Because the typical offender is a young male, many efforts to understand crime have been oriented toward male criminality. However, the examination of causes of female criminality and sources of gender differences in offending has not been entirely absent from criminology. This chapter outlines possible explanations of contemporary trends in female crime. First, however, we trace the development of theoretical perspectives on female criminality in order to demonstrate how theorizing on the female criminal has evolved and to place current explanations within a broader perspective.

EARLY EXPLANATIONS OF WOMEN'S CRIME

Prior to the 1950s, explanations of female (and male) crime tended to reflect prevailing views regarding human behavior more generally (see reviews in Pollock-Byrne 1990 and Steffensmeier and Clark 1980); social scientists primarily emphasized the role of biological and psychological factors in explaining

female crime. While psychological theories of crime maintained dominance in the 1930s, major sociological explanations of crime (differential association, anomie and social disorganization) were emerging that emphasized the importance of social and cultural factors in accounting for criminality.

Although early explanations of crime focused heavily on male criminality and treated female crime as somewhat of an anomaly, some attempts were made to explain female crime. As was the case in criminology more generally, these two competing viewpoints informed the writings on female offending in the late nineteenth and early twentieth centuries. One viewpoint emphasized the role of biological factors and psychological factors in women's and girls' crime, typically postulating that criminal women exhibited masculine biological or psychological orientations (e.g., Lombroso, Freud). The second view stressed the role of social or economic forces and assumed that the social and cultural influences affecting male criminality similarly influenced female criminality.

Current interpretations of the history of thought on female crime identify a strong biological (and psychological) bias in early treatments of female crime. Of course, biological and psychological explanations were also provided for male criminality. Lombroso, for example, linked both female and male

Source: This article was written expressly for inclusion in this text.

crime to biological predisposition. However, Lombroso (Lombroso and Ferraro 1895) also viewed female criminals as having an excess of male characteristics. He argued that biologically, criminal females were more similar to normal or criminal males than to normal females. The notion that female offending was an anomaly and attributable to "maleness" among female offenders was also emphasized by some psychologists. According to Freud (1933), female crime resulted from a masculinity complex, stemming from penis envy. He argued that although all females suffer from penis envy, those who cannot make a healthy adjustment to the realization that they do not have a penis overidentify with maleness and are likely to act out in criminal ways. Both Lombroso and Freud, then, viewed the female criminal as biologically or psychologically male in orientation.[1]

Early sociological explanations, manifest in textbooks published between 1920 and 1960, generally rejected this biological determinism and offered sociocultural interpretations (differential association, anomie, social disorganization) of both male and female crime as well as of gender differences in crime. Steffensmeier and Clark's (1980) review of early criminology texts does indicate a strong tendency to avoid biological explanations of sex differences in crime, emphasizing instead structural and cultural variables. Note, though, that textbook treatments of female crime or of gender differences in offending tended to be brief and were often patterned on prevailing explanations of male offending. Few textbooks contextualized female offending or offered a nuanced picture of gender differences in the nature of offending.

Otto Pollak's *The Criminality of Women,* published in 1950, represents a most important work on female crime prior to the modern period. The book summarized previous work on women and crime, and it challenged basic assumptions concerning the extent and quality of women's involvement in criminal behavior. Pollak himself explained female crime and the gender gap with reference to a mix of biological, psychological, and sociological factors.

According to Pollock, the extent of female crime probably approximated that of males, but due to its masked character, female crime was more likely to go undetected. In addition, the types of crimes women commit—shoplifting, domestic thefts, thefts by prostitutes, abortions, perjury—are underrepresented in crime statistics. These crimes are easily concealed and seldom reported; even when these crimes are detected and reported, women are less likely than men to be arrested or prosecuted, he argues, because of a double standard favorable to women and because women usually play accomplice or less overt roles when co-offending with men. He claimed that male victims are often too embarrassed to report female offenders, and law enforcement officials are too chivalrous to arrest or prosecute them. Also, when a man and a woman team up to commit crimes, the man is usually the more active partner and thus more likely to be caught and punished. Thus, as is often argued today, Pollak highlighted differences in citizen and law enforcement responses to female as compared to male offending.

A fundamental theme of Pollak's work is the attribution of a biological and psychological basis to female criminality. This theme is reflected in two important elements of his treatment. First, Pollak stressed an inherently deceitful nature in the female sex. He saw this deceitfulness as socially induced to some extent because physical weakness can force a woman to resort to deception and because of other basic facts in a woman's life—including societal pressures to conceal her period of menstruation and expectations that women attract a husband indirectly through wily charm. However, Pollak saw the primary source of women's deceitfulness as lying in the female physiology, in particular in the passive role assumed by women during sexual intercourse. Pollak considered this inactive role to be biologically rather than culturally determined. Second, Pollak reinforced the longstanding idea that the causative influence of biological factors and individual pathology is greater for explaining female than male criminality.[2] In his view, the influence of hormonal and generative phases (e.g., menstruation, pregnancy, and menopause) was particularly significant for female criminality due to the psychological disturbances they produced. These disturbances might create "needs" that act as an impetus to crime, or they may weaken the moral inhibitions of women that serve to prevent criminal behavior (p. 157).

Yet, Pollak also consistently emphasized the importance of social and environmental factors as causally related to female crime. He placed particular emphasis on social factors traditionally (and currently) highlighted in criminology, including poverty, crowded living conditions, broken homes, delinquent companions, and the adverse effects of doing time in reform schools or penitentiaries. Pollak also noted considerable overlap in causative factors for delinquency among girls and boys, women and men:

> It is either the criminal association in the home or that resulting from the attempts of girls to compensate for the failure of their home or school, which seems to have a decisive influence upon the causation of juvenile delinquency and professional crime. *This picture is basically the same for girls and boys.* The differential lies only in the role which illicit sex conduct for monetary gain plays in the shaping of the female criminal career, and in the observation that female professional criminals do not specialize in one line as do men (p. 139, emphasis ours).

Pollak also noted that other social factors—the double standard of sexual morality, the disadvantaged economic and occupational position of women, and the influence of modern advertising—contribute to female crime. These factors, he argues, foster frustration, resentment, and criminal desires that may lead to perjury or false accusations against men, aggressive behavior toward partners or others, and the temptation to steal (especially in women's roles as shoppers and domestics).

In sum, early theories of criminality tended to include or emphasize biological and psychological factors to a greater extent when explaining female offending than when explaining male offending. Nevertheless, despite recent critiques that characterize all early explanations of female crime as biologically or psychologically deterministic, early sociological explanations of female crime stressing sociocultural factors were also commonplace. Criminology textbooks and some other writings offered

an interpretation of female offending and the gender gap that took into account gender differences in role expectations, socialization patterns and application of social control, opportunities to commit particular offenses, and access to criminally oriented subcultures—all themes that have been further developed in more recent accounts (see a review in Steffensmeier and Clark 1980).

A rich and complex literature on female criminality has emerged over the past few decades. Embedded in this literature is the ongoing debate on how best to explain female criminality and the gender gap in offending. One side of the debate views female crime as a function of the same theoretical processes that explain male crime. From this perspective, the gender gap in crime reflects the criminogenic forces identified in mainstream criminological theory. Some feminist critics counter this view, arguing that male and female offending are qualitatively distinct (see Gelsthorpe and Morris 1990). More recent explanations have attempted to merge these two camps by recognizing both similarities and differences in the etiology of male and female offending.

CONTEMPORARY EXPLANATIONS OF WOMEN'S CRIME

Recall a number of conclusions from chapter 5 on trends in female crime. Although changes in female crime have largely paralleled those for male crime, the sex difference for some crimes has narrowed. The gender gap in homicide, robbery, and drug law violations has remained fairly consistent over the past 40 years. However, females have made considerable gains (a) in the minor property crimes of larceny, fraud, and forgery and (b) in more recent years for assaultive crimes and drinking-related offenses like DUI and liquor-law violations (essentially a status offense—underaged drinking).

How might these trends in female arrest be explained? There are at least nine plausible explanations of these trends and patterns in female arrests. Each should be viewed as a series of hypotheses in need of further empirical testing. We review these hypotheses and evaluate them based on the findings of empirical data (e.g., see Steffensmeier and Schwartz, chap. 5).

1. *Law and the organizational management of crime:* Changes in female arrest trends are due to "less biased" or more efficient official responses to criminality rather than to actual changes in criminal behavior among females.

2. *Net widening and changes in law:* Changes in law enforcement and in statutory law toward targeting less serious forms of lawbreaking (especially for violence) has increased the pool of female offenders at risk for arrest, since females are disproportionately involved in the less serious forms of lawbreaking. A more punitive political environment has been an important factor in the net widening process.

3. *Gender equality and female emancipation:* The improved status of women, particularly their advances in the paid workforce, offers females more desire and opportunity to commit crime.

4. *Increased economic marginalization of women:* Higher levels of economic insecurity faced by large subgroups of women in American society increases the pressure to commit (especially) consumer-based crimes.

5. *Increased inner-city community disorganization:* A growing detachment of many inner-city minorities from mainstream institutions, like education and employment, leads to weakened social controls and to adaptive strategies that include crime. The effects of weakened social controls are especially detrimental to female conformity.

6. *Expanded opportunities for female-type crimes:* Shifts in patterns of productive activity, including increased consumerism and the availability of consumer goods and greater reliance on a credit-based system, have expanded opportunities for "female-type" crimes more rapidly than "male-type" crimes.

7. *Changes in the underworld:* Recent changes in the criminal underworld, such as the reduced supply of male crime partners due to increased incarceration rates and the emerging dominance of drug trafficking, have augmented the prospects for female involvement.

8. *Trends in drug dependency:* Drug addiction amplifies income-generating crime for both sexes, but more so for females than males. Also, the likely incapacitation effects of locking up chronic, high-risk male offenders has opened up slots for females in drug and other crime networks while also tending to diminish overall levels of male offending.

9. *Crime prevention programs targeting male offenders:* Implementation of crime prevention programs aimed at male offenders has reduced male offending for some crimes, thereby narrowing the gender gap.

Law and the Organizational Management of Crime: Greater Visibility of Female Offending

The arrest rate, like any official measure of crime, is a function of the crime control measures that are established to deal with behaviors that are defined as criminal. Some of the increase in the female percentage of arrests may reflect changes in record keeping, policing, and citizen reporting that have raised female arrest rates relative to male rates in recent decades.

Computerization and improved record keeping in police departments that improves the accuracy of recording a suspect's sex, for example, has reduced the level of hidden female crime, because an "unknown" is often tabulated as a male arrest in published tables. In addition, policing has become more bureaucratized over time, introducing more universalistic standards of decision making and thus reducing the effects of gender on the probability of arrest (Steffensmeier 1980, 1993). The fact that bureaucratization and more formal policing tend to increase official ratios of female-to-male criminality is consistent with alternative sources of data on female crime that show less marked changes in the share of female offending than do official sources. Moreover, citizens appear more willing to report female offenders, especially if the citizen or "victim" benefits personally (e.g., estranged spouse reporting his partner for "terroristic threats" or "assault" in the context of disputes over child custody or visitation privileges). Thus, the female offender is more visible than in the past to agents of social control.

Net Widening and Changes in the Law

Changes in policing and law enforcement practices toward targeting less serious forms of lawbreaking have increased the risk of arrest for female offenders (e.g., filing assault charges for harassment or minor physical attacks). The ability of the authorities to dig more deeply into the pool of offenders will increase the female share of arrests because females are disproportionately involved in the less serious forms of lawbreaking, even within a specific offense category. The lesser tolerance and increased criminalization of deviant behavior has, to an extent, caused a rise in some types of crime—DUI, assault, drug violations—among both males and females,[3] but the overall impact has been greater on females. This statement from a county probation officer (widely shared by other law enforcement officials) points to the increased criminalization of female violent offending:

> The statistics say it's up [female violence] but I don't buy it. We've jacked up the charges. Girls fighting with their moms, stepdads or another girl, we used to look the other way. Same with domestic violence, has led to more women being arrested for harassment and assault, even aggravated assault. We've opened up a can of worms 'cause the police will just arrest both, the woman and her partner, then sort out later who was the main aggressor. Resisting arrest or just being rowdy is another area—the police won't put up with the lady like they used to. Bang, bang, charge her with assault.

Changes in laws that target less serious forms of lawbreaking will also have a disproportionate impact on female arrest rates. For example, the female share

of DUI arrests has increased, from 6 percent in 1965 to 15 percent in 2000 (see table 1 in chap. 5). A combination of factors helps explain this pattern. DUI statutes now have a less demanding criterion of intoxication that requires a smaller amount of alcohol consumption or blood alcohol content. Lowering the blood alcohol content (BAC) for making DUI arrests has increased the risk of arrest for females. Because females typically have a smaller body composition than males do, the effect of a few drinks on a female's BAC will be greater than on a male's BAC. Thus, lowering the acceptable BAC effectively broadens the pool of potential female offenders but probably has little effect on the pool of potential male offenders. In addition, the proportion of drivers who are female has increased (Spain 1997), and DUI enforcement practices have toughened. These factors have contributed to arrests of less intoxicated violators, particularly women drivers.

Net widening is a consequence, in part, of the harsher, more punitive laws that have been enacted over the past four decades within the context of a more law-and-order political environment (see Chesney-Lind 1995). Thus, for example, a move to broaden the scope of incidents defined as assaultive as well as truth-in-sentencing laws and mandatory minimum arrest and incarceration laws have significantly increased the pool of people who are arrested and incarcerated. Both men and women have been affected by the enhanced punishments for drug violations across the United States since the inception of the Rockefeller drug laws in New York State in 1973, but poor African American and, increasingly, Latina women appear to be the hardest hit by these mandatory minimum drug laws (Mauer and Huling 1995, Bush-Baskette 1998; see Sudbury, chap. 12).

Gender Equality and Female Emancipation

Both the popular press and some social scientists have linked recent trends in arrests to female emancipation and the improved status of women (Simon and Landis 1991). Less traditional gender-role attitudes and greater opportunities in the economic sphere, especially female advances in the paid workforce, are believed to have resulted in higher levels of female crime. Most notably, the increase in arrests of women for larceny and fraud is attributed to more women in the workforce and is interpreted as evidence that women are catching up with men in involvement in white-collar and corporate crimes.[4] However, many writers argue that it is theoretically unwarranted to assume that the effect of equalization of gender roles is necessarily criminogenic, because greater female social participation may reduce stress, increase self-esteem, and in other ways positively affect what are often described in the criminological literature as the causes of crime (see a review in Steffensmeier and Allan 1996).

The major predicament with the liberation thesis, however, is that it is inconsistent with much of what is known about both female crime and contemporary gender roles. Four types of evidence support this claim:

1. The changes in the female percentage of arrests for minor property crimes were as great or greater prior to the women's movement (the effect of which was beginning to be experienced by 1970; Steffensmeier, 1978) than in subsequent years when female labor force participation and other status-of-women indicators accelerated (Costello, Miles, and Stone 1998).

2. The female percentage of arrests is comparable across age groups both for the last 40 years (1960–2000) and for individual decades (e.g., 1960–1970), as evidenced by UCR data (see Steffensmeier and Schwartz, chap. 5). This finding contradicts the expectation that trends in female employment and women's status should have a greater impact on the criminality of young adult and middle-aged women than on adolescent and elderly women (Steffensmeier and Streifel 1991). For example, increases in the female percentage of embezzlement arrests are as large among juveniles as among working-age adults, which conflicts with the emancipation

thesis linking paid employment with increasing white-collar criminality among women.

3. Female offenders (especially those who commit street crimes and are incarcerated) typically bear little resemblance to the "liberated female crook" described by some commentators. Instead, these offenders typically are unemployed women or women working at low-paying jobs, or are minority women drawn from backgrounds of profound poverty (Chesney-Lind 1995; Steffensmeier and Allan 1996).

4. Finally, recent time-series and cross-sectional analyses indicate that higher female-to-male arrest levels are linked to structural conditions in which women face adverse rather than favorable economic circumstances (Steffensmeier and Haynie 2000).

Increased Economic Marginalization of Women

One of the better predictors of involvement in criminal activity is economic hardship (Steffensmeier and Haynie 2000). A larger segment of the female population faces greater economic insecurity today than 40 years ago, even though some women have become more emancipated and have moved into formerly male professions. Rising rates of divorce, illegitimacy, and female-headed households, coupled with continued segregation of women in low-paying occupations, have aggravated the economic pressures on women and have left them more responsible for child care than they were two or three decades ago. Growing economic adversity increases the pressures to commit consumer-based crimes such as shoplifting, check fraud, theft of services, and welfare fraud.[5]

The economic adversity thesis is consistent with studies of the characteristics of female offenders and with recent cross-sectional and time-series research on structural correlates of the female percentage of arrests (Steffensmeier and Streifel 1992). These studies show that the higher female-to-male arrest levels are linked to social conditions in which women face adverse rather than favorable economic circumstances, such as greater occupational segregation, more female-headed households, higher rates of illegitimacy, and higher rates of female unemployment. The adversity thesis also predicts female arrest gains in *all* the property crimes, which in fact has occurred.

Increased Inner-City Community Disorganization

Research on the urban underclass suggests a growing detachment on the part of many inner-city minorities (particularly blacks) from mainstream social institutions such as marriage, education, and employment. The complex set of disarticulation processes leading to this detachment include the lack of employment opportunities caused by industrial restructuring, the exodus of the black middle class from inner-city neighborhoods, and racial discrimination. Industrial restructuring in particular has contributed to a reduction in demand for workers with low levels of skill and education in those geographic areas where low-income blacks are most likely to live.

The same disarticulation processes (e.g., labor market disadvantage) facing black men also affect black women. Inner-city black women increasingly are concentrated in geographic areas with less favorable employment opportunities, higher levels of poverty, and higher prevalence of female-headed households. Some evidence suggests that the lesser supervision and weakened social controls characterizing these areas impacts as much or more on female than on male crime and delinquency. Truancy, street-corner hanging by teenage gangs, drug involvement, and violence may be seen as adaptive strategies by female (and male) inner-city residents to a social context that includes poor schools, unemployment, crime, family disruption, and weak community organizations (Steffensmeier and Haynie 2000). It appears that the social and institutional transformation of the inner city has created opportunities and facilitated entry of minority women into crime in ways that has escalated their

criminal offending perhaps as much as that of minority males.

Expanded Opportunities for Female-Type Crimes

Because female offenders (similar to male offenders) gravitate toward activities that are easily available and within their skills, the level and character of female crime in a given society will be strongly affected by the availability of crime opportunities that are suited to female interests and abilities. Changes in American society since World War II have created more opportunities for fraud and dishonesty and related offenses that "everywoman" (or "everyman") can commit (Steffensmeier 1980, 1993). These offenses do not require the physical prowess and dexterity of many forms of street crime, nor the learned skills of professional con artists. Instead, these crimes typically require "the ability to read, write, and fill out forms, along with some minimum level of presentation of a respectable self" (Weisburd et al. 1991, 182). Moreover, although collusion may often be present, many of these crimes can be committed on one's own—the modus operandi more typical of women.

Changing patterns of productive activity in at least four areas have created opportunities for the commission of new forms of crime, such as minor thefts and frauds, that favor female involvement: (1) production, merchandising, and marketing of goods; (2) the credit economy; (3) a welfare state and its programs; and (4) consumerism and the message of consumption.

Important conditions leading to more opportunities for larceny-theft and fraud are the increase in shopping malls, self-service marketing, and small, portable products and the expansion of the credit economy. Lines of credit and credit cards produce paper frauds such as credit fraud, bad checks, coupon fraud, and fraudulent theft of services. The latter typically involve the failure to make payment for rental property (e.g., videocassettes) or for contracted services like rent, water, heat, cable television, and telephone (see the section on the increased economic marginalization of women, especially in regard to female-headed households, for a motivational component as well). The growth in shopping malls and portable products enhances the opportunities (and incentives) for shoplifting, theft from parked automobiles, and the like.

Various programs of the welfare state also create the conditions for the commission of fraud and theft. Student loans, Social Security, Medicaid, and other welfare programs depend on written materials, and all involve the potential for fraudulent applications. There is also much potential for theft of government checks from mailboxes, delivery trucks, and the like. These changes are reinforced by the media's message of consumption that encourages excessive spending and buying on credit. The message to "consume" goods encourages theft (including shoplifting) and chiseling to stretch the paycheck or upgrade one's car, home, appearance, or lifestyle.

The rise in female property crime in particular can be seen as a by-product of opportunities created by the evolution of productive activity (e.g., transportation, merchandising, currency) rather than a result of changes in female motivation or in females' social and economic position. Although these changes have expanded the opportunities for both sexes, on balance the opportunities for traditional types of female crime (e.g., shoplifting, welfare fraud) have been expanding at a faster pace than have those for typically male crimes. In fact, opportunities for traditional types of male crimes, such as robbery and burglary, may have contracted. The growth of the credit-based system and the increased utilization of credit and debit cards might decrease the opportunities for robbery because people carry less cash on their person.

Changes in the Criminal Underworld

The criminal underworld has undergone important changes in recent decades that on balance appear to have contributed to increased opportunities for female offending. The changes include (1) a reduced supply of male crime partners due to increased incarceration rates; (2) transformation of illegal markets

and crime opportunities, particularly the emergence of drug trafficking as the dominant criminal market; and (3) shifts in ethnic composition.

Subtle shifts in the underworld may augment or dampen the prospects of female involvement. Given the male dominance of the underworld and the sexism characterizing it, female crime opportunities are partly dependent on whether male criminals find females to be useful (Maher and Daly 1996; Steffensmeier and Terry 1986). For example, in recent years women have become useful for successful drug trafficking because they are more likely to have clean records, create less suspicion, and can conceal drugs more easily. Also, rising incarceration rates have reduced the supply of males for recruitment into drug or other crime networks, thus enhancing or necessitating the recruitment of women into such networks. Further, it can be assumed that rising levels of incarceration have removed crime-prone males from the general population in ways that have dampened male rates for other crimes like robbery and burglary, thereby contributing to a narrowing of the gender gap for these offenses. In addition, due to shifts in the underworld away from burglary toward drug dealing and other theft offenses as more attractive money-making options for males (Steffensmeier and Harer 1999), the female percentage of burglary arrests has inched upward such that females are 12 percent of arrested burglars in 2000 as compared to only 4 percent in 1965. The major force pushing the female percentage has been a fairly steep drop in the male burglary rate since the mid-1970s, whereas female rates have remained fairly steady.

Major developments in crime opportunities (in drug dealing) on the one hand and crime-control measures on the other hand have contributed to a decline in burglaries committed by males. For example, the emergence of drug trafficking as the dominant criminal market offers a more open and easier (e.g., less skilled) crime route than burglary. Simultaneously, in neighborhoods characterized by heavy drug dependency, the money to be made through burglary has dwindled because addicts have flooded the stolen goods market with jewelry, guns, and consumer electronic goods (Baumer et al. 1998;

Steffensmeier and Harer 1999). Enhanced opportunities for replacement crimes, such as fraud offenses (e.g., bad checks, credit card fraud) and theft from a motor vehicle, dampen burglary involvement as well. Also, major improvements in domestic and commercial security systems (e.g., better lighting, better safes, alarm systems) may have deterred would-be burglars, just as enforcement programs targeted at career offenders (e.g., three strikes) may have reduced the number of active, or professional, burglars who commit many burglaries and who also recruit younger thieves for burglary involvement.

These types of changes in illegal markets and crime opportunities over the past couple of decades have lessened the attractiveness of burglary as a crime option and have eroded the subcultural elements and recruitment processes for the establishment of burglary networks and careers (Steffensmeier and Harer 1999). But these changes have mainly affected would-be male burglars. Other factors have produced slightly rising or stable female burglary rates. These factors include growth in burglary targets that are more suitable for novice female involvement (e.g., unoccupied houses and apartments during the day); increases in drug-related burglaries (and robberies) that involve women as solo perpetrators or women as accomplices of male offenders (see J. Miller, chap. 3); the expanding role of the informant system within law enforcement that leads to arrests of females for testimony against male offenders; a trend toward younger, more reckless criminals who appear more willing than their older and more professional counterparts to admit women into their groups or to exploit them for criminal purposes (Steffensmeier and Terry 1986); and a greater willingness of police to file burglary charges against females who, for example, illegally enter a former boyfriend or partner's premises to retrieve property or negotiate disputes such as child care.

Meanwhile, demographic shifts in the large urban areas of the United States where the bulk of reported crime occurs have affected both underworld crime and female lawbreaking. The increase in urban Hispanic and black populations that tend to have comparatively high levels of female-to-male offending,

especially in drug trafficking, may increase overall female rates of arrest (*1990 Report;* Anglin et al. 1987).

Trends in Drug Dependency and Its Amplifying Effect on Female Crime

Rising levels of illicit drug use by females over the past several decades may also help account for female crime trends. Drug addiction amplifies income-generating crimes of both sexes but more so for females than males (Anglin et al. 1987; Inciardi et al. 1993). Because females face greater constraints against crime (e.g., it is more stigmatizing), they may need greater motivational pressures before they will commit a crime. Female involvement in burglary and robbery, in particular, typically occurs after addiction and is likely to be abandoned when drug use ceases (Anglin et al. 1987). Drug use is also more likely to initiate females into the underworld and criminal subcultures and to connect them to drug-dependent males who use them as crime accomplices or exploit them as "old ladies" to support their addiction (Covington 1985; Miller 1986; Steffensmeier and Terry 1986). In these and other ways, the rise in drug dependency would have a greater impact on female criminality, even though female arrests for drug abuse have not outpaced male arrests over the past two to three decades.

Crime Prevention Programs Targeting Male Offenders

Crime prevention programs, along with the incapacitation effects of incarcerating high-risk offenders, have targeted primarily male offenders and presumably have contributed to a leveling off or reduction in male crime—thereby narrowing the female-to-male gap for some kinds of offending (e.g., burglary).

SUMMARY

In chapter 5 we evaluated recent trends in female arrests. The two main conclusions of that chapter were, first, females have made arrest gains (mostly small gains) in many UCR categories, but the most significant change in the female share of arrests involves the overall rise in minor property crime, especially minor thefts and fraud. Female-to-male involvement in serious or violent crimes has held fairly steady since 1960. Second, the distribution of offenses for which both males and females are arrested has changed but, relative to males, the profile of the female offender has not changed. Both sexes are arrested largely for minor crimes (i.e., theft, fraud, drinking, drugs), but the female profile is more slanted toward minor theft and fraud and prostitution, and the male profile is more slanted toward violent and serious property offending. The typical female offender has not become more violent over time. This conclusion is particularly evident if sources other than UCR arrest data are consulted.

Our aim in this chapter was to offer possible explanations for the identified trends in female crime. Historically, explanations of women's crime focused primarily on their biology and psychology, often likening criminal females to males; however, sociological explanations that highlighted the importance of sociocultural factors for female offending were also offered. More current accounts of gender differences in the extent and nature of crime tend to place a heavier emphasis on gender roles; the changing social, economic, and political conditions of society; and the structural position of women.

We find that gender differences in the quantity and quality of crime continue to be consistent with gender-role expectations, behaviors, and opportunities. Indeed, substantial changes in the illegitimate activities of women would be surprising. Attitudes have shifted toward greater acceptance of women in the workforce, combining career and family, and the gender role system favors more individual latitude. But there has been little change in many aspects of gender roles. For example, a female's status continues to be defined in terms of relationships with men, and the traditional gender roles centering around the focal concerns of relational issues (e.g., wife-mother) and virtue and beauty issues (e.g., morality, sexual attractiveness) have remained remarkably stable. Also, male roles have changed even less, and so it

is arguable that the overall organization of gender has undergone little change (see Steffensmeier and Streifel 1992; Tannen 1991).

Most important, perhaps, relative to women in the past, women today are just as limited by male constrictions on their roles and male leadership in the illegal marketplaces as they are in the legal one. Autobiographical and case history studies of professional and street criminals indicate that women continue to have limited access to criminal subcultures and the criminal underworld. In fact, traditional gender-role attitudes and the structure of sexism appear to be more pervasive within the arena of crime than "aboveground" (Maher and Daly 1996; Steffensmeier and Terry 1986).

Female economic participation per se does not necessarily lead to greater female criminality, just as improved economic opportunities and higher educational achievement do not lead to greater male criminality. This point does not mean that changes in the family and economy have not had an impact on female patterns of offending. Recent changes in the household economy and family have resulted in greater participation of women in economic production and the public sphere. This greater participation provides more opportunities for certain kinds of crime. At the same time, it leads to fewer familial or private social controls in some aspects of women's lives and to more legal controls, including arrest and official sanctioning. Increases in female arrests in, for example, minor property crime, assault, and DUI reflect those trends.

It is also possible that greater numbers of working women increase female crimes by contributing to a sense of relative deprivation among women who are being paid less than their male colleagues or even among women who are not working outside the home. Viewed this way, the female employment thesis may converge in some ways with the economic adversity hypothesis. There might be other, less obvious links between female employment and crime, such as the circuitous path by which female employment gains may contribute to female arrests for fraud and forgery. Employment enhances the prospects for acquiring credit and securing loans, so that working women may have greater opportunities to commit credit-based frauds like nonpayment of services and fraudulent unemployment claims (see Steffensmeier and Streifel 1992). This direction obviously is a very different causal path than that suggested by advocates of female liberation and emancipation arguments.

CONCLUSIONS

In chapter 5 we found that both stability and change characterize female-to-male arrest trends over the past several decades. Females have significant increased participation in the area of minor property crimes like larceny-theft and fraud, with the bulk of those gains taking place during the mid-1960s to 1980. Also, females have made incremental gains since the 1960s in several minor crimes like DUI, disorderly conduct, and misdemeanor assault. And, due largely to declining or steady male rates, females have made small gains in burglary and robbery. At the same time, the female percentage of offenses has remained the same for such offenses as illegal drug use and has declined for such offenses as murder. Importantly, in view of claims by certain commentators of rising levels of violence by female perpetrators, survey data from self-report and victimization studies indicate that the female share of violent offending has not been increasing. The female share of persons arrested for homicide and weapons possession is essentially the same as it was 10, 20, or even 40 years ago; and the somewhat higher percentage of females arrested for assaultive crimes reflects changes in citizen attitudes and stricter enforcement policies that have widened the net of violent offenders in ways that snare female suspects.

In this chapter we sought to understand the reasons for the changes in patterns of female offending in the recent past and today. We began by reviewing historical explanations of female crime. We then moved on to discussing contemporary ways of understanding female criminality. Here we find that combinations of the following factors try to explain the increase in female-to-male offending over the past five decades: changes in gender roles and in mainstream institutions that allowed females greater independence from traditional constraints; the forced need for greater self-reliance and difficulty in the ability of large numbers of women to earn a living or purchase popular consumer goods due to desertion by or the absence of the men in their lives as well as the irregularity of work and the low wages they can command; urban decay and the rise in drug dependency that appear to have affected the lives of girls and women as much as or more than the lives of boys and men; changes in the nature of crime and the underworld toward increased opportunities for crime that females traditionally commit; and changes in the law and the responses of law enforcement officials that have encouraged victims to complain and the authorities to take more vigorous action against female offenders. Finally, some evidence suggests that all these forces impact more harshly on certain groups of women, especially poor women of color. This topic is taken up in much greater detail in chapters 1, 8, and 9 in part 1 and chapters 10, 11, 12, and 13 in part 2.

DISCUSSION QUESTIONS

1. Find a newspaper, magazine, or web article about female offenders. Summarize the findings. Then describe how the authors explain their findings based on the different theories provided by Steffensmeier and Schwartz in this chapter.
2. Discuss how you would design a research study to test two competing explanations suggested by the authors of this chapter.
3. Steffensmeier and Schwartz suggest nine different explanations for female offending. Which explanations do you agree with? Why?

NOTES

1. While some theorists linked female crime to masculinity, others saw it as distinctly feminine. Eleanor and Sheldon Glueck (1934), based on

their studies of adult and juvenile delinquents, concluded that female crime reflected the inability of certain women—especially those from disadvantaged neighborhood and family contexts—to control their sexual impulses. The Gluecks also subscribed to the theme of the woman offender as a pathetic creature, a view that characterized much criminological writing in the 1930s.

2. Similarly, contemporaries of Pollak argued that environmental factors are much more predictive of male than female criminality and that females are not affected, or are affected differently, by the macrosocial variables that affect men. Female lawbreakers, again, were viewed as abnormal, whereas male lawbreaking was seen as a normal response to adverse economic conditions (for reviews, see Belknap 2001). Recent empirical work calls into question this assumption (e.g., see Steffensmeier and Haynie 2000).

3. Similarly, the decriminalization of other behaviors—gambling, vagrancy, public drunkenness—has caused a decrease in arrest rates among both males and females.

4. Consistent with this perspective are changes in arrests for some offenses that appear to have clear connections to changes in women's roles and activities. For example, the rise in the female percentage of arrests for DUI can be attributed, in part, both to women's greater participation in the public sphere (e.g., going to college, working, traveling) and to more women driving automobiles. However, it is debatable whether the expanding use of the automobile by women is better explained as a fundamental role change or as a societal-wide diffusion of a technological necessity (i.e., a required mode of transportation). The latter interpretation suggests a different type of explanation than the female emancipation account.

5. Economic adversity may also increase the pressure to commit more serious property crimes such as burglary and robbery, but these types of crimes are less consistent with traditional female roles; therefore, we would not expect female gains to be as large as the growth in minor property crimes, which are more consistent with the skills, interests, and opportunities of a typical woman.

REFERENCES

Adler, F. 1975. *Sisters in Crime.* New York: McGraw-Hill.

Anglin, D., Y. Hser, and W. McGlothin. 1987. Sex Differences in Addict Careers. *American Journal of Drug and Alcohol Abuse* 13:59–71.

Baumer, Eric, J. L. Lauritsen, R. Rosenfeld, and R. Wright. 1998. The Influence of Crack Cocaine on Robbery, Burglary, and Homicide Rates: A Cross-City, Longitudinal Analysis. *Journal of Research in Crime and Delinquency* 35(3):316–40.

Belknap, J. 2001. *The Invisible Woman: Gender, Crime, and Justice,* 2d ed. Belmont, CA: Wadsworth.

Bush-Baskette, S. 1998. The War on Drugs as a War against Black Women. In *Crime Control and Women,* ed. S. Miller, 113–29. Thousand Oaks, CA: Sage.

Chesney-Lind, M. 1995. Rethinking Women's Imprisonment: A Critical Examination of Trends in Female Incarceration. In *The Criminal Justice System and Women: Offenders, Victims, and Workers,* 2d ed., ed. Barbara Raffel Price and Natalie J. Sokoloff, 105–17. New York: McGraw-Hill.

Costello, Cynthia, Shari Miles, and Anne Stone, eds. 1998. *The American Woman, 1999–2000: A Century of Change—What's Next?* New York: Norton.

Covington, J. 1985. Gender Differences in Criminality among Heroin Users. *Journal of Research in Crime and Delinquency* 22:329–53.

Freud, S. 1933. *New Introductory Lectures.* New York: Norton.

Gelsthorpe, L., and A. Morris, eds. 1990. *Feminist Perspectives in Criminology.* Philadelphia: Open University.

Glueck, S., and E. Glueck. 1934. *Five Hundred Delinquent Women.* New York: Knopf.

Inciardi, James A., Frank Tims, and Bennett W. Fletcher. 1993. *Innovative Approaches in the Treatment of Drug Abuse.* Westport, CT: Greenwood.

Lombroso, C., and W. Ferraro. 1895. *The Female Offender.* London: Fisher Unwin.

Maher, L., and K. Daly. 1996. Women in the Street-Level Economy: Continuity or Change? *Criminology* 34(4):465–91.

Mauer, M., and T. Huling. 1995. *Young Black Americans and the Criminal Justice System: Five Years Later.* Washington, DC: The Sentencing Project.

Miller, E. 1986. *Street Woman*. Philadelphia: Temple University.

Pollack. O. 1950. *The Criminality of Women*. Philadelphia: University of Pennsylvania.

Pollock-Byrne, J. 1990. *Women, Prison, and Crime*. Pacific Grove, CA: Brooks/Cole.

Simon, R. 1975. *The Contemporary Woman and Crime*. Washington, DC: National Institutes of Mental Health.

Simon, R., and J. Landis. 1991. *The Crimes Women Commit, the Punishments They Receive*. Lexington, MA: Lexington.

Spain, D. 1997. Societal Trends: The Aging Baby Boom and Women's Increased Independence. Final report prepared for the Federal Highway Administration, U.S. Dept. of Transportation. Order no. DTFH61-97-P-00314.

Steffensmeier, D. 1980. Sex Differences in Patterns of Adult Crime, 1965–77: A Review and Assessment. *Social Forces* 58:1080–1108.

Steffensmeier, D. 1993. National Trends in Female Arrests, 1960–1990: Assessment and Recommendations for Research. *Journal of Quantitative Criminology* 9:413–41.

Steffensmeier, D., and E. Allan. 1996. Gender and Crime: Toward a Gendered Theory of Female Offending. *Annual Review of Sociology* 22:459–87.

Steffensmeier, D., and R. Clark. 1980. Sociocultural versus Biological/Sexist Explanations of Sex Differences in Crime: A Survey of American Criminology Textbooks, 1919–1965. *American Sociologist* 12:246–55.

Steffensmeier, D., and M. Harer. 1999. Making Sense of Recent U.S. Crime Trends, 1980–1998: Age-Composition Effects and Other Explanations. *Journal of Research in Crime and Delinquency* 35(3):235–74.

Steffensmeier, D., and D. Haynie. 2000. Gender, Structural Disadvantage, and Urban Crime: Do Macrosocial Variables Also Explain Female Offending Rates? *Criminology* 35(2):403–38.

Steffensmeier, D., and C. Streifel. 1991. Age, Gender, and Crime across Three Historical Periods: 1935, 1960, and 1985. *Social Forces* 69(3):869–94.

Steffensmeier, D., and C. Streifel. 1992. Time-Series Analysis of the Female Percentage of Arrests for Property Crimes, 1960–85: A Test of Alternative Explanations. *Justice Quarterly* 9:77–103.

Steffensmeier, D., and R. Terry. 1986. Institutional Sexism in the Underworld: A View from the Inside. *Sociological Inquiry* 56:304–23.

Tannen, D. 1991. *You Just Don't Understand: Women and Men in Conversations*. New York: Morrow.

Weisburd, D., S. Wheeler, E. Waring, and N. Bode. 1991. *Crimes of the Middle Classes: White-Collar Offenders in the Federal Courts*. New Haven, CT: Yale University.

Chapter 7

A Reserve Army:
Women and the Drug Market

Lisa Maher

ABSTRACT

As was demonstrated by Steffensmeier and Schwartz in chapter 6, one reason for the increase in women's crimes since the 1970s has been the emergence of more punitive drug laws. In this chapter, Maher provides the reader with a window into the street-level trade in drugs—primarily crack. Although there has reportedly been some increase in the last decade or two in the ability of women to generate income from the illegal drug trade, they have not been able to gain a serious foothold at any level of the drug world. Maher conducted an ethnographic study of the political economy and women's roles in drug markets in the Bushwick section of Brooklyn, New York. Drug business hustles are one of three areas of nonlegal work here, the other two being nondrug hustles and sex work. She found women operating only at the lowest levels of drug work—hustlers, steerers, and paraphernalia sellers—and at copping (purchasing drugs for others). They were neither managers nor in charge of other sellers.

In contrast to other studies, Maher's study found that women had neither increased participation in the drug economy nor attained substantial representation in sales positions on the streets. Maher attributes her findings, in part, to differences in methodological approaches. Past researchers conducted one-time interviews, whereas Maher employed an ethnographic approach; she remained in the field observing and talking to participants for several months at a time. This method allows the researcher to observe trends and patterns and to contextualize the drug workers' experiences. Maher also attributes her findings to a changing organizational context in the drug market in which violence and terror are prized and racial and ethnic kinship is strong. Maher focused on women as economic actors in an illegal drug market governed by organizational constraints, organizational norms, and workplace cultures. Here she finds that women are excluded because of underworld sexism that considers women not sufficiently violence-prone as well as unreliable and untrustworthy. This study adds one more refutation to the women's liberation thesis of women's criminality.

Maher connects women's increased involvement in drugs with prostitution. Elsewhere she elaborates on this process.[1] As the drug trade flounders, so too does the value of women's sex work. The advent of crack in the 1980s intensified larger social processes already in operation that facilitated violence: in particular the collapse of structures of formal and informal social control in communities already in decline. This collapse includes, most importantly, the depletion of capital and human resources necessary to sustain a formal economy. When jobs were lost, educational systems were sacrificed and housing was abandoned in the community, resulting in increased participation in the informal drug economy in the community. Because street-level prostitution is highly dependent on changes in the economic and drug markets, the women experience greater violence as drug markets dry up and become more concentrated. Competition increases, the conditions of street-level sex work deteriorate, and prostitution becomes less profitable and more dangerous for the women. Maher's claim is that what the public sees as "more violent women" is actually women's sometimes violent responses at the end of a long line of egregious violations against women who sell their sex work in a degraded labor market. Connections between women's work in two specific illegal markets—drugs and prostitution—and the relationship between victimization, violence, and incarceration are spelled out further in several chapters in part 2 (e.g., Sudbury, chap. 12) and part 3 (e.g., Websdale and Chesney-Lind, chap. 18). Whereas this current chapter focuses on drug work, the next chapter, by Kempadoo, looks at prostitution or sex work—albeit from an international globalization perspective.

My heart pumps no Kool Aid—I don't even drink the shit. (Latisha)

Within the street-level drug economy in Bushwick, options for income generation can be located within three distinct, yet overlapping and interdependent spheres: drug-business hustles, non-drug hustles, and sexwork. Drug-business hustles (Johnson et al., 1985) form the "core" or primary labour market, and non-drug hustles and sexwork constitute a "periphery" or secondary labour market. Women are virtually absent from the drug business, underrepresented in non-drug hustles and grossly over-represented in sexwork. In this chapter I focus on opportunities for income generation arising out of drug-business hustles. . . .

Drug-business hustles refer to the transfer of goods and/or services directly related to the distribution and consumption of illicit drugs.[1] In Bushwick, drug-business hustles are further distinguished by their location within a structural framework or organization: in theory at least, they offer the prospect of advancement and a potential "career" path. Non-drug hustles are defined as acts of income generation which, while they may provide revenue for the drug economy, are not directly related to distributing and selling drugs. They include crimes such as robbery, burglary, larceny, and shoplifting, as well as unlawful or quasi-legal activities involving the unregulated production of goods and services (e.g., manual and domestic labour,

Source: Lisa Maher. 1997. A Reserve Army: Women and the Drug Market. In *Sexed Work: Gender, Race, and Resistance in a Brooklyn Drug Market,* Oxford and New York: Clarendon/Oxford University, chapter 7, pp. 83–107.

begging and "scrapping"). In Bushwick, non-drug hustles did not usually involve structured criminal organizations; most were unplanned, opportunistic, and committed by individuals or small groups. As such, they are better characterized as secondary-sector activities. The secondary labour-market identified here also consists of street-level sexwork, the primary source of income for women drug users.

STREET-LEVEL DRUG MARKETS

Crack cocaine has had a profound impact on patterns of income generation among drug users in North America. Research during the late 1980s and early 1990s attests to the salience of crack distribution and sales activity as a source of income generation among drug users in the inner-city (e.g., Bourgois, 1989, 1995; Hamid, 1990, 1991a, 1991b; Mieczkowski, 1990; Johnson et al., 1994). In New York City in the early 1990s, it was estimated that 150,000 people were involved in selling or helping to sell crack cocaine on any given day (Williams, 1992:10). Utilizing a large sample of users of different types of drugs in New York, Johnson et al. (1994) found that crack sales were the most frequent crime and generated the largest cash income. A full third of crack abusers obtained most of their income from crack sales, with one-fifth engaging in four or more crack sales per day. Crack was clearly the most lucrative and frequently sold drug in street-level markets and even drug users active in other forms of lawbreaking were unable to generate income from these activities which rivalled that received from crack sales (Johnson et al., 1994).

The advent of crack cocaine has also had a dramatic impact on the distribution and consumption of illicit drugs (Bourgois, 1989, 1995; Hamid, 1990, 1991c, 1991d, 1992a, forthcoming; Johnson et al. 1990, 1991, 1994; Mieczkowski, 1990; Kleiman, 1992; Curtis et al., 1995; Curtis, 1996). During the late 1980s, crack markets in New York City experienced a profound shift in structure. This was characterized by a shift from the old "dope-den" style of operation known as the "crack house" to curbside or street-level selling operations. Crack houses had

been particularly vulnerable to police raids and it soon became apparent that such operations were not the most efficient way of "taking care of business" in terms of evading detection and pursuing illegal profits (Johnson et al., 1992). Their successors, street-level crack markets, have been characterized as unregulated markets of freelancers engaged in individual entrepreneurial activity (Reuter et al., 1990; Hunt, 1990) and described as a form of "capitalism gone mad" (*New York Times,* 12 March 1989).

According to Johnson and his colleagues (1987, 1992), the "freelance" model of street-level crack distribution is usually an incipient distribution system within a loosely-organized group of buyers and sellers. Identifying features include voluntary cooperation, flexible agreements between the parties, and the absence of clear employer-employee relationships (Hamid, 1993). Some evidence suggests, however, that once demand has been formally established, competition between retailers may influence the system of distribution and the freelance model may be superseded by a more structured system known as the "business" model (Johnson et al., 1992). This model, which has come to dominate drug markets in New York City, is characterized by pooled interdependence, vertical differentiation, and a formal, multi-tiered system of organization and control with well defined employer-employee relationships (Johnson et al., 1992; see also Mieczkowski, 1990; Curtis and Maher, 1993; Waterston, 1993). Those at the lowest level (generally street-level sales and associated roles) receive minimum compensation with maximum vulnerability (Scharff, 1987). The modus operandi is similar to what Mieczkowski, in the context of heroin distribution, has identified as the "runner system." This system

> is an organized, co-operative strategy . . . designed to market heroin in public places, most typically at the curbside of public roads or other open locales such as areas in front of shops and stores, playgrounds, parks and schoolyards . . . [It] uses individual participants who are organized into a rational division of labor. Interacting cooperatively in accordance with accepted rules, they direct their attention to the successful exchange of heroin for money (Mieczkowski, 1986:648).

In selling crack cocaine, drug business "owners" usually employ several "crew bosses," "lieutenants" or "managers" who work in shifts to ensure the efficient organization of street-level distribution. These "managers" (as they were known in Bushwick) act as conduits between owners and lower-level employees. They are responsible for organizing and delivering supplies and collecting revenues. Managers exercise considerable autonomy in relation to the hiring, firing, and payment of workers and are typically responsible for workplace discipline and the resolution of workplace grievances and disputes. Next down the hierarchy are the street-level sellers who perform retailing tasks involving little discretion. Sellers are usually located in a fixed space or "spot" and are often assisted by those below them in the hierarchy: lower level operatives acting as "lookouts," "steerers," "touts," "holders," and "enforcers."[2]

Sellers may be assisted in establishing the bona fides of potential customers through a street referral system known as "steering." Steerers are usually known users who negotiate an arrangement with the owner or manager, usually in return for a "PC" or payment in crack. Some sellers attempt to minimize risks by only selling to regular or established customers. In some markets, the volume of new or unknown customers has given rise to an occupational category known as "zoomers" who sell vials of fake crack: usually soap or peanuts. In neighbourhoods such as Bushwick, which host large drug markets attracting a considerable "drive-through" trade, it is almost impossible to resist selling to known customers. Here the function of steerers at the street level is to provide a conduit for the sharing of information. This function assumes particular importance in periods of intensive police intervention.

Prior to the advent of crack cocaine, research on women's participation in the drug economy used one or more of the following to explain women's roles in selling and distributing drugs: (1) intimate relationships with men; (2) restrictions on discretionary time as a result of household and childcare responsibilities; (3) the availability of alternative options for income generation (especially prostitution); and (4) institutionalized sexism in the underworld.

Female heroin users were often characterized as needing a man to support their consumption (e.g. Sutter, 1966; Fiddle, 1976; File, 1976; File et al., 1976). They were also described as being "led" into crime by individual men (Covington, 1985) although this may apply more to white than minority group women (Anglin and Hser, 1987; Pettiway, 1987). The typical pattern was of low-status roles where participation was short-lived, sporadic, and mediated by intimate relationships with men (Rosenbaum, 1981c; Adler, 1985). The availability of alternative sources of income generation for women drug users, such as prostitution and shoplifting, has also been suggested as a factor which may explain their relative under-representation in the drug economy (File, 1976; James, 1976; Rosenbaum, 1981c; Goldstein, 1979; Inciardi and Pottieger, 1986; Hunt, 1990). Some suggest, in addition, that women drug users have less discretionary time than their male counterparts because of household and childcare responsibilities (e.g., Rosenbaum, 1981c; A. Taylor, 1993; Wilson, 1993) which work to preclude full female participation in the drug economy.

Women's peripheral roles in male-dominated drug selling networks (Auld et al., 1986) can also be explained by "institutionalized sexism in the underworld" (Steffensmeier, 1983; Steffensmeier and Terry, 1986; see also Box, 1983). Steffensmeier (1983: 1013–15) argues that male lawbreakers prefer to "work, associate and do business with other men" (homosocial reproduction); they view women as lacking the physical and mental attributes considered essential to working in an uncertain and violent context (sex-typing and task environment of crime). In the drug economy, in particular, women are thought to be unsuitable for higher-level distribution roles because of an inability to manage male workers with threatened violence (Waterston, 1993:114).

SELLING AND DISTRIBUTING DRUGS

Since 1989, the displacement of users and sellers from surrounding neighbourhoods has prompted a steady increase in the amount of street-level drug dealing in Bushwick (Curtis and Maher, 1993; Curtis et al., 1995). Although some research suggests that there has been an increase in female participation in drug dealing in recent years (e.g., Baskin, Sommers and Fagan, 1993; Wilson, 1993; C. Taylor, 1993; Fagan, 1994, 1995), the entry of women into this male-dominated field has seldom penetrated up to the managerial level. In three years of ethnographic fieldwork spanning three Brooklyn neighbourhoods, I failed to encounter a single woman who was a business "owner" and discovered only one woman who worked as a manager. The dearth of women managers suggests that one outcome of more general perceptions of women's unsuitability for drug distribution roles is the belief that they are unable to effectively manage male workers: "[women's] difficulties in managing male workers may be attributed to the limits of female authority . . . [and control techniques such as] employing the ascribed female attribute of 'being nice,' as opposed to the more aggressive male technique of threatened violence" (Waterston, 1993:114).

Given the dominance of men at all levels of drug dealing, it has been suggested that, to the extent that women do participate, such participation will be mediated by involvement with husbands and boyfriends. Research conducted in Denver found that only four out of 24 women, interviewed as part of a study of users and street-level dealers, had sold crack. Only two had management roles and all four women had secured their positions through their boyfriends who were crack house managers or distributors. All subsequently lost their jobs when their boyfriends were arrested, the relationship ended, or when they were unable to control their drug use (Koester and Schwartz, 1993:192). For the women in the current study, past experience, rather than present practice, was more likely to conform to this model. For example, Sissy, a 35-year-old African American woman spoke about her short-lived and tangential involvement with the heroin business.

I moved up to Harlem, and um, I hooked up with this guy that was selling heroin. We used to get the quarter bags, and we used to cut it, and the shit used to be good. So I used to tap the bags, the quarter bags . . . I

didn't know I had a chippy (mild habit) till like about three years later, when he finally found out that I was messing with it—and all that time he trusted me. And I was handling the money and everything; everything was right there with me. But as soon as he found out that I was messing with it, it was like I was cut off.

Similarly, the experiences of Cindy, a 26-year-old European American woman, in selling powder cocaine, were also mediated by her boyfriend.

He had me workin' with him after a while, you know, to have some extra money for myself. I used to help him sell the coke. I was always with him you know. I would go run upstairs and get the package for him and re-up (replenish the supply).

In the neighbourhoods I studied, the highly-structured nature of the drug markets, coupled with their kin-based organization, militated against personal or intimate sexual relationships between female drug users and higher-level male operatives. To the limited extent that they participated in drug selling, women were overwhelmingly concentrated at the lowest levels of street-level sales. They were almost always used as temporary workers when men were arrested or refused to work or when it was "hot" because of the police presence.

The most common low-level distribution role for women in this study was as informal or unofficial steerers or touts. This typically involved recommending a particular brand of heroin to newcomers to the neighbourhood in return for "change," usually a dollar or so. Neighbourhood newcomers were usually white men who may have felt more comfortable about approaching women with requests for such information. Although they only used crack, both Yolanda and Boy engaged in this practice of "tipping" heroin consumers.

They come up to me. Before they come and buy dope and anything, they ask me what dope is good. I ain't done no dope, but I'm a professional player . . . They would come to me, they would pay me, they would come "What's good out here?" I would tell them, "Where's a dollar?", and that's how I use to make my money. Everyday somebody would come, "Here's a dollar, here's two dollars." (Yolanda)

[What other kinds of things?] Bummin' up change. [There ain't many people down here with change.] Jus' the white guys. They give you more faster than your own kind. [You go cop for them?] No, jus' change. You tell them was' good on the dope side. Tell them anything. I don' do dope, but I'll tell them any-thin': "Yeah, it's kickin' live man." They buy it. Boom! I got my dollar, bye. (Boy)

Women's perceptions of "white boys" allowed them to use this situation to their advantage with some women deliberately seeking out these newcomers in order to "bum up change" for which they provided little in the way of useful information.

Within the street-level drug economy, the avail-ability of labour is a strong determinant of women's participation in street-level distribution roles. Labour supply fluctuates in accordance with extra-market forces such as product availability, police interven-tion, and seasonal variations. One consequence of the police activity in Bushwick during the study period was a recurrent, if temporary, shortage of male work-ers.[3] These "gaps" in the labour market, produced by attrition as a result of police intervention, promoted instability in the marketplace: the replacement of "trusted" (i.e., Latino) sellers with "untrustworthy" drug users (i.e., women and non-Latinos) eroded the social and kinship ties that had previously served to reduce violence in drug-related disputes (Curtis and Sviridoff, 1994; Curtis et al. 1995).[4]

Early in the fieldwork period, both men and women perceived that more women were being given opportunities to work as street-level sellers than in the past. Such opportunities, as it turned out, were part of a calculated risk-minimization strategy on the part of drug-business owners and managers. As Princess observed, some owners thought that women were less likely to be noticed, searched or arrested by police.

Nine times out of ten when the po-leece roll up it's gonna (be) men. And they're not allowed to search a woman, but they have some that will. But if they don' do it, they'll call for a female officer. By the time she gets there [laughs], if you know how to move around you better get it off you—unless you jus' want to go to jail. [So you think it works out better for the owners to have women working for them?] Yeah, to use women all the time.

As the fieldwork progressed, and the neighbourhood became the site of intensive and sustained policing interventions, this view became less tenable. Latisha, a 32-year-old African American woman, reported that the police became more aggressive in searching women.

[You see some women dealing a little bit you know.] Yeah, but they starting to go. Now these cop around here starting to unzip girls' pants and go in their panties. It was, it's not like it was before. You could stick the drugs in your panties caus' you're a female. Now that's garbage.

Thus, when initially confronted by a shortage of regular male labour and large numbers of women seeking entry-level selling positions, some managers appear to have adopted the opportunistic use of women in order to avoid detection and disruption of their businesses. How frequent this practice was is uncertain; I do know that it was short-lived (see also Curtis and Sviridoff, 1994). While the sustained po-lice presence necessitated shifts in the operations of street-level drug markets in response to specific in-terventions, most organizations proved highly able to accommodate rapidly changing conditions and to modify their operations accordingly. Indeed, the im-pact of the sustained police presence in the neigh-bourhood was arguably felt more strongly by users than distributors (e.g., see Curtis et al., 1995).

While, in the past, most women's experience of the drug business was as the "girlfriend" of a distrib-utor, this was no longer the case. During the three-year study period, only 12 women (27 per cent) were involved in selling roles. Connie, a 25-year-old Latina, was typical of this small group of women who from time to time managed to secure low-level selling positions. In the following quotation, she de-scribes her unstable position within the organization for which she worked.

I'm currently working for White Top (crack). They have a five bundle limit. It might take me a hour or two to sell that, or sometimes as quick as half an hour. I got to ask if I can work. They say yes or no.

Typically, the managers said "no" to women's requests to work. Unlike many of the male street-level sellers who worked on a regular basis for this organization and were given "shifts" (generally lasting eight hours), Connie was forced to work off-hours (during daylight hours) which were often riskier and less financially rewarding. Temporary workers were usually given a "bundle limit" (one bundle contained 24 vials), which ensured that they worked for shorter periods of time. As Cherrie, a 22-year-old Latina told me,

> [t]he las' time I sold it was Blue Tops (crack). That was a week ago. [What they asked you or you asked them to work?] Oh, they ask me, I say "I want to work!" [How come they asked you?] I don't know. They didn't have nobody to work because it was too hot out there. There was too full of cops.

Similarly, although Princess was well-known to the owners and managers of "White Top" crack, had worked for them many times in the past year, and had "proven" herself by having never once "stepped off" with either drugs or money, she was only given sporadic employment. She reported that,

> [s]ometime you can't. Sometime you can (sell for them). That's why it's good to save money also. So when you don't get work. [How come they wouldn't give you work on some days?] Because of some favour that someone might of done or y'know, jus' . . . [It's not like they're trying to punish you?] No, but they will do that y'know. Somebody go and tell them something, "Oh, this one's doin' this to the bags or this one's doin' this to the bottles." OK, well hey check the bags and they don' see nothin' wrong, but they came to look at it so they're pissed off so they'll take it away from you, y'know.

In addition to their vulnerability to arrest and street robbery, street-level sellers who also use drugs constantly grapple with the urge to consume the product and to abscond with the drugs and/or the money. Retaliation by employers toward users who "mess up the money" (Johnson et al., 1985:174) was widely perceived as swift and certain. As Rachel, a 35-year-old European American woman told me, "[t]hose Dominicans, if you step off with one piece

of it, you're gonna get hurt. They don't play. They are sick people." In some instances, the prospect of violent retaliation may serve to deter women from selling drugs. As Boy put it.

> I don' like dere (the managers') attitude, like if you come up short, dey take it out on you. I . . . don' sell no crack or dope for dese niggers. Because dey is crazy. Say for instance you short ten dollars, niggers come across you wit bats and shit. It's not worth it, you could lose your life. If dey say you are short, you could lose your life. Even if you were not short and dey say you is short, whatever dey say is gonna go, so you are fucked all the way around.

However, considerable uncertainty surrounds the likelihood that physical punishment will be meted out (see also Waterston, 1993:113). This uncertainty can be seen in the following quotation from Princess, who had a long but sporadic history of street-level sales before and after the advent of crack.

> It's not worth it. Number one, it's not enough. Come on, run away and then *maybe* then these people want to heavily beat the shit out of you. And then they *may* hit you in the wrong place with the bat and *maybe* kill you.

Such disciplinary practices resemble what has been described elsewhere as the product of a complex interplay between "patronage" and "mercy" characterized by relations of dependence (Hay, 1975). Within the drug economy, the unpredictability and uncertainty of punishment may work as a more effective form of control than actual punishment. In Bushwick, the actuality of violent retaliation for sellers who "messed up" was further mediated by gender and race/ethnicity. In this Latino- and mainly Dominican-controlled market, the common perception was that men, and Black men especially, were more likely than Latino/as to be punished for "stepping off." Rachel described what happened after an African American man we both knew had been badly beaten.

> [What happened to him? I mean he stepped off with a package, right?] Yeah, but everybody has at one time or another. But it's also because he's a Black and not a Puerto Rican, and he can't, you know, smooze his way back in like, you know, Mildred steps off with every

other package, and so does, you know, Yolanda, they all do. But they're Spanish. And they're girls. So, you know, they can smooze their way back in. You know, a guy who's Black and ugly, you know, they don't want to hear about it . . . [B]ecause a girl, if she steps off, they're not gonna kick her ass like they would a guy. And you know, they're very serious about that shit . . . There was about eight of them. They had Joe up against the car. They were beating him up with like a motorcycle chain. I can't imagine the pain he was feeling. They had him pinned up against the car. And they were hitting him across the gut and like in the knees. The screams that were coming . . . They think nothing of really hurting a guy.

Relationships in the drug economy are fuelled by contradictory expectations.[5] On the one hand, attributes such as trust and reliability are frequently espoused as important to drug-selling organizations. To outsiders such as competitor organizations and the police, drug-selling organizations often present as intact social units.[6] For the most part, members are recruited from pre-existing social and kinship networks, which helps to ensure reliability by exploiting obligations that arise out of personal relations (Curtis and Maher, 1993). Ethnic and kinship ties are seen as the best way of ensuring trust among people who cannot rely on the law to protect their rights and obligations (Waterston, 1993). On the other hand, ethnographic informants often refer to the lack of trust and solidarity among organization members. This lack of trust is evident in the constant "scams" sellers and managers pull on each other and the ever-present threat of violence in owner-manager-seller relations.[7]

The image of crack-using street-networks as a "cruel world," perpetuated by users and exemplified by the oft-repeated refrain of "no friends, only associates," is reflected in, and shaped by, the crack marketplace. Characterized as a "culture of terror," the crack trade is dominated by violent and ruthless individuals with little regard for loyalty or relations of trust (Bourgois, 1989). Such a view contrasts sharply with the relations of trust and reliability that have historically been regarded as essential prerequisites to successful drug distribution by both employers and

employees. Among ethnographic informants, the comparison of drug markets pre- and post-crack almost inevitably renders the conditions of labour post-crack as much worse than in the "good old (heroin) days." As Ouellet and his colleagues (1993:88) have pointed out in relation to prostitution, a healthy scepticism of any "rose-colored glasses" rendition of the past is necessary. Almost without exception however, those informants with a history of street drug use pre-crack believed that crack had prompted a shift in employer-employee relations and the responsibilities or obligations that they believed rightfully attached to owner-seller relations. As Candy noted, these days "when you popped (get arrested), you popped."

Nowadays, it don't pay to sell drugs caus' they can get busted. The guy ain't going to get you out of jail. He don't care who the hell you are. If you go (to jail), the older times he would work it out. That would be the agreement—that I would work with him if he is goin' to bail my ass out of jail. If I get popped an' get me (dope) sick, come get me. And I'll be illing caus' I got a habit and you better get your ass down here real quick and get me out. The way they workin' nowadays they don't. When you popped, you popped. You on your own.

Violence, or the threat of violence, is endemic to the operation of crack markets by virtue of the nature of the organizations involved and their greater propensity toward its use, both in the pursuit of organizational stability and as a strategic weapon in turf battles (Fagan and Chin, 1989).[8] During the late 1980s and early 1990s, law enforcement strategies altered the equation between drug markets and violence and the "war on drugs" had profound effects on levels of violence, in low-income minority neighbourhoods (Curtis and Hamid, 1997). In Bushwick, an intensive police presence and large-scale arrests between 1988 and 1992 produced attrition in the ranks of street-level functionaries. The evolution of Bushwick as a drug supermarket was coterminous with the emergence of large corporate-style Dominican-controlled organizations which heightened the traditional rivalry between

Dominicans and Puerto Ricans. Puerto Ricans became an increasingly disaffected labour force who strongly resented their Dominican owners. As the gulf between management and labour widened, law enforcement pressures intensified. Mass arrests in the early 1990s depleted the supply of Latinos, prompting further instability in the market and the replacement of Latinos with non-Latinos and heavy drug users.

In the drug economy, violence can also be seen as "a judicious case of public relations, advertising, rapport building, and long-term investment in one's 'human capital development'" (Bourgois, 1989:632). In the context of a "culture of terror" characterized by male-dominated street networks which claim drug distribution and sales as boys' own turf, women who use the streets to sell or buy drugs are subject to constant harassment and are regularly victimized. In response, the women in this study employed several strategies to protect themselves. One of the most important was the adoption of a "badass" (Katz, 1988), "crazy" or "gangsta bitch" stance or attitude, of which having a "bad mouth" was an integral component. As Latisha was fond of telling me, "[m]y heart pumps no Kool Aid. I don't even drink the shit." Or, as Boy put it,

> [a]c' petite, dey treat you petite. I mean you ac' soft, like when you dress dainty and shit ta come over here an' sit onna fuckin' corner. Onna corner an' smoke an you dressed to da teeth, you know, you soft. Right then and there you the center of the crowd, y'know what I'm sayin'? Now put a dainty one and put me, she looks soft. Dey look at me like "Don't fuck wid dat bitch, she looks hard." Don' mess wid me caus I look hard y'know . . . Dey don't fuck wid me out here. Dey think I'm crazy.

"Acting bad" and "being bad" are not the same. Although many of the women presented themselves as "bad" or "crazy," this projection was a street persona and a necessary survival strategy.[9] Their instrumental rhetoric stands in sharp contrast to the middle-class feminine concept of expressive aggression. Their use of protective strategies, expressed in the cultivation of a "self-protective reputation or craziness" (Campbell, 1992:13), resembles that of their male counterparts: "to survive, force must be met with more than unspoken anger or frustrated

tears . . . the best line of defence is not attack, but the threat of attack" (Campbell, 1993:133).[10] But, unlike their male counterparts, for women, reputation was about "preventing victimization" (Campbell, 1993:140). Despite the external manifestation of aggression and toughness in terms of posture and rhetoric, and the pre-emptive use of aggression, women were widely perceived (by men and women alike) as less likely to possess the attributes associated with successful managers and street-level sellers. These included the prerequisite "street cred" and a "rep" for having "heart" or "juice": in general, masculine qualities associated with toughness and the capacity for violence (Waterston, 1993). As Bourgois has pointed out, "[r]egular displays of violence are necessary for success in the underground economy—especially the street-level drug-dealing world . . . [which] requires a systematic and effective use of violence" (1989:632–2).

The desirability of these characteristics appears to work against the employment of women in street-level drug distribution insofar as they are perceived as deficient in them.[11] While on face value, many women appear to manifest these traits, the reality remains that men and women are "far from equal in their power to make their own representations stick" (Campbell, 1993:143). Women's abilities to "talk tough" and "act bad" were apparently not enough to inspire employer confidence. Prospective drug business employers may need to feel that someone is capable of actually "being bad": "[e]mployers . . . are looking for people who can *demonstrate* their capacity for effective violence and terror" (Bourgois, 1989:632; emphasis added). Perceptions of women drug users as unreliable, untrustworthy, and unable to effectively deploy violence and terror are integral components of the sex/gender regime within the street-level drug economy which place would-be female sellers at a distinct disadvantage.

SALE AND HIRE OF DRUG PARAPHERNALIA

Although both crack stems/pipes and injecting equipment or "works" were illegal commodities in

Bushwick, the sale of crack paraphernalia was controlled by the bodegas, or corner stores, whereas needles and syringes were the province of the street. Men dominated both markets although women were sometimes employed as part-time works sellers. Men who regularly sold "sealed" (i.e. new) works generally had established suppliers (typically men who worked in local hospitals) from whom they purchased units called "ten packs" (ten syringes). The wholesale rate for ten packs varied. Sometimes it was as low as two or three dollars but more often it was $5 per pack, or a unit cost of 50 cents each. Retail prices for works also varied, with sealed works generally selling for $2 each, although sometimes they fetched as much as $3 depending on general availability, and the need of individual consumers. As a male informant told me,

> [f]ive dollars a pack bring you twenty. You giving five dollars a pack and you got fifteen dollars more (profit), you know. Sometime you got more 'caus you got people that come down there, "two-for-five" you know, buy two sets for five dollars, you understand what I'm sayin'?

The benefits of selling needles and syringes were twofold: the penalties were less severe than those for selling drugs and the rate of return was higher compared to the street-level sale of either heroin or crack. Street-level drug sellers typically received a ten percent cut on each unit of drugs sold. Drug sellers made $1 on each $10 bag of heroin they sold and 50 cents on a $5 vial of crack, compared to works sellers who usually made at least $1.50 per unit, depending on the purchase and sale prices.

Women who sold works were less likely than their male counterparts to have procured them "commercially." More often they "happened across" a supply of works through a family member or social contact who was diabetic. Women were also more likely to sell works for others or to sell "used works." Rosa, a 31-year-old Latina, described in detail the dangerous practice of collecting used works strewn around the neighbourhood. While she often stored them and later exchanged them for new works from the volunteer needle exchange (which was illegal at the time), Rosa would sometimes se-

lect the works she deemed in good condition, "clean" them with bleach and water, and re-sell them. Injecting equipment, including cookers and cottons, as well as needles and syringes, could also be hired from local "shooting galleries." Prices varied according to the establishment but typically ranged between $1 and $3 or a "taste" of the drug to be injected. Given the scarcity of female gallery owners, women had few opportunities to generate income through the hire of injecting equipment (see the next section).

Although crack stems and pipes, in addition to the ubiquitous Bic lighters, were available from neighbourhood bodegas at minimal cost, many smokers chose not to carry stems on their person. These users, almost exclusively men, were from outside the neighbourhood. Their reluctance to carry drug paraphernalia provided the women with an additional source of income in the form of a "hit" in exchange for the use of their stem. Sometimes these men were "dates" but more often they were "men on a mission" in the neighbourhood or "working men" who came to the area on Friday and Saturday nights with the express purpose of getting high. As Boy told me,

> I be there on the block an' I got my stem and my lighter. I see them cop and I be aksin' "Yo, you need a stem, you need a light?" People say "Yeah man," so they give me a piece.

Initially, it struck me as strange that these men did not purchase their own stems given their low unit cost of a dollar or two, even if they discarded them immediately after use. However, the demand for stem rental was seen to increase over the study period as the police presence in the neighbourhood intensified. An additional benefit for those women who rented their stems was the build up of crack residues in the stems. Many users savoured this resin, which they allowed to accumulate before periodically digging it out with "scrappers" fashioned from the metal ribs of discarded umbrellas. Stem renters, then, not only benefited directly in terms of a "hit" and/or a dollar or two, but accrued additional indirect benefits in the form of accumulated crack residues in their stems.

Some women also sold condoms, an ancillary form of drug-related paraphernalia in Bushwick. Although condoms were sold at local bodegas, usually for $1 each, many of the women obtained free condoms from health outreach workers. Sometimes they sold them at a reduced price (usually 25 cents) to other sexworkers, "white boys" and young men from the neighbourhood. Ironically, these same women would then have to pay the considerable mark-up charged by the bodegas when they had "smoked up" all their condoms.

OPERATING "SHOOTING GALLERIES"

A wide range of physical locations were used for the purposes of drug consumption in Bushwick. Although these sites were referred to generically as "galleries" by drug users and others in the neighbourhood, they differed from the traditional heroin "shooting gallery" in several respects.[12] Bushwick's "galleries" were dominated by men because they had the economic resources or physical prowess to establish and maintain control. Control was often achieved by exploiting women drug users with housing leases. Such women were particularly vulnerable, as the following quotation from Carol, a 41-year-old African American woman, illustrates.

> I had my own apartment, myself and my daughter. I started selling crack. From my house. [For who?] Some Jamaican. [Yeah, how did you get hooked up with that?] Through my boyfriend. They wanted to sell from my apartment. They were supposed to pay me something like $150 a week rent, and then something off the profits. They used to, you know, fuck up the money, like not give me the money. Eventually I went through a whole lot of different dealers. Eventually I stopped payin' my rent because I wanted to get a transfer out of there to get away from everything cause soon as one group of crack dealers would get out, another group would come along. [So how long did that go on for?] About four years. Then I lost my apartment, and I sat out in the street.

The few women who appeared to maintain "successful" galleries operated with, or under the control

of, a man or group of men. Cherrie's short-lived attempt to set up a gallery in an abandoned, burnt-out building on Crack Row is illustrative. Within two weeks of establishing the gallery (the principal patrons of which were other women), Cherrie was forced out of business by the police. The two weeks were marked by constant harassment, confiscation of drugs and property, damage to an already fragile physical plant, physical assaults, and the repeated forced dispersal of gallery occupants. Within a month, two men had established a new gallery on the same site which, more than a year later, was thriving.

This particular instance of differential policing is explicable in terms of a set of practices that have their roots not only in "individual" police discretion, but in light of the larger picture of policing low-income urban communities.[13] Here the primary function of policing is not so much to enforce the law but, rather, to regulate illegal activities (Whyte, 1943:138). As such the beat police officer must, to some degree at least, "conform to the social organization within which he [sic] is in direct contact" (1943:138). Within the highly gendered context of the street-level drug economy, police officers exercise considerable discretion in deciding which activities to ignore, which to police, and to what extent. Field observations suggest that the reason the police did not interfere as much in relation to galleries controlled by men was that they assumed that men were better able than women to "control" galleries and thus minimize problems of violence and disorder. An alternative view would suggest that in this instance, as in many others, police harass women drug users simply because they can.

Other factors contributed to women's disadvantage in operating galleries, crack houses, and other consumption sites. Male drug users were generally better placed economically than the women in this sample, most of whom were homeless and without a means of legitimate economic support. When women did have an apartment or physical site, rather than open up opportunities for their entrepreneurial activities, this made them a vulnerable target either for exploitation by male users or dealers (as in Carol's account) or to harassment by the police (as in Cherrie's). Even where women claimed to be in control of particular locations, field observations confirmed they were not. One woman, Kizzy, continued to maintain that she was the "boss" of the gallery which operated from her apartment, even as she complained to me about yet another unwelcome house guest imposed on her by her (male) cousin.

> She's stayin' ere 'cos a ma cousin. Cos she, she sucks his thing—he demands ma money from them . . . [How come you let her stay?] I changed my mind. You know why, caus' I told the bitch, and then she gonna go ask my cousin. Who the fuck is he, this is *my crib*. She want to be a stinky little dumb bitch, and gonna try to get permission from them too. I'm the boss.

In this situation, the attribution of ownership and control were confounded by the conflicting accounts that emerged in relation to economic transactions, rule setting, and rule enforcement in Kizzy's apartment. However, according to most of those who were familiar with the establishment, Kizzy's cousin Pops had the upper hand.

> [Let me just ask you, in your opinion who runs Kizzy's place, her cousin Pops or Kizzy?] You said it, the first one. You don't go in there honey because you think you're getting a break, shit. Not there. Pops doesn't give breaks. (Tameka)

Thus in Bushwick the presence of a man was a prerequisite to the successful operation of drug consumption sites. The only real choice for those women in a position to operate galleries or crack houses was between the "devils they knew" and those they did not.

COPPING DRUGS

Many women supplemented their incomes by "copping" or purchasing drugs for others. These others were usually white and almost always men. At times they were dates, but often they were users who feared being caught and were prepared to pay for someone else to take that risk. As Rachel explained,

> I charge them just what they want to buy they have to pay me. If they want twenty dollars they have to give me twenty dollars worth on the top, because I'm risking my free time. I could get busted copping. They have to pay me the same way, if not, they can go cop. Most of them can't because they don't know the people.

Those who cop drugs for others perform an important service which is integral to the functioning of the drug market. As Biernacki suggests in relation to heroin, "they help to minimize the possibility of infiltration by undercover agents and decrease the chance of a dealer's arrest" (1979:539). In Bushwick, the copping role attracted few men and was generally regarded by both men and women as a low-status, peripheral hustle: those who copped drugs for others were looked down on and "viewed as failures, as persons who are not competent enough to manage their addiction or who do so with little style and no character" (1979:539).[14] Nonetheless, it was difficult to ascertain whether the low status ascribed "copping agents" was a product of the feminization of this particular hustle or whether, following Biernacki, the fact that it yielded low returns for high risks and was universally regarded as low status, meant that it was "left to the girls." Most women viewed the female-dominated nature of the job as a product of their differential positioning in the marketplace in relation to contact with outsiders. Within the context of a parallel sex market, outsiders could readily approach women to buy drugs under the guise of buying sex and thereby minimize the risk of dealing with undercover police. As Rosa recounted,

> [y]ou would (be) surprise. They'd be ahm, be people very important, white people like lawyer, doctors that comes and get off, you'd be surprised. Iss like I got two lawyer, they come saying you know they give me money to go, to go and cop. And they stay down over there parking . . . [How do you meet them?] Well down the stroll one time they stop and say you know, "You look like a nice girl though, you know, you wanna make some money fast?" I say, "How?" So they say, you know, "Look out for me." First time they give me like you know, twenty dollars. They see I came

back, next time they give me thirty. Like that, you know. I have been copping for them like over six months already.

Sometimes this function was performed in conjunction with sexwork, as Latisha's account demonstrates.

> He's a cop. He's takin' a chance. He is petrified. Will not get out his car . . . But he never gets less than nine bags (of powder cocaine). [And he sends you to get it?] And he wants a blow job, right, OK. You know what he's givin' you, a half a bag of blue (blue bag cocaine). That's for you goin' to cop, an' for the blow job. That's two dollars fifty (worth). I can go to jail (for him) caus' I'm a piece of shit.

Women also felt that given the reputation of the neighbourhood as very "thirsty" (i.e. as having a thirst or craving for crack), male outsiders were more likely to trust women, especially white women, to purchase drugs on their behalf. Often this trust was misplaced. The combination of naive, inexperienced "white boys" and experienced, "street smart" women produced opportunities for additional income by, for example, absconding with the "cop money." This was a calculated risk and sometimes things went wrong. When they did, women sometimes received severe beatings from the angry "client." More often it meant "laying low" for a few hours while the angry client drove around the neighbourhood in search of the woman and his cash and, usually, a more trustworthy woman to fulfill the original mission. A safer practice was to inflate the actual purchase price of the drugs and pocket the difference. Rosa explained this particular scam.

> He think is a ten dollar bag, but issa five dollar. But at least I don't be rippin' him off there completely. [But you're taking the risk for him.] Exactly. Sometime he give me a hunert (hundred) dollars, so I making fifty, right? But sometime he don't get paid, he got no second money, eh. I cop then when I come back the car, he say, "Dear, I cannot give you nothin' today," you know. But I still like I say, I gettin' someting from him, because he think is a ten dollar bag.

Similar scams involve the woman returning to the client with neither drugs nor money, and claim-

ing that she had been "ripped off" or, less often, short-changing the client by tapping the vials (removing some crack) or adulterating the heroin or powder cocaine (cutting it with other substances). These scams attest to the diversity of women's experiences as copping agents and indicate that, while marginalized with respect to most drug-business hustles, many women were astute in making the most of the limited opportunities that came their way.

STREET DOCS

The practice of injecting those who are unable or unwilling to inject themselves, either because they are inexperienced or have deep or collapsed veins, has been documented by others (e.g. Johnson et al., 1985; Murphy and Waldorf, 1991). Those performing this role are referred to as street "docs" (Murphy and Waldorf, 1991:16–17). In Bushwick, men typically specialized in the provision of this service which was often extended as part of an established shooting gallery or consumption site. For example, Sam, a Latino injector in his late thirties, lived in one of the makeshift condos located adjacent to the principal heroin copping area. Those who were in a hurry to consume or who had nowhere else to go would use Sam's place to "get off." In addition to a supply of works (both used and unused, the latter obtained from the underground needle exchange), Sam provided water and a range of "cookers" and "cottons." Sam had a reputation as a good "hitter" and injected several of the women in the sample on a regular basis. He provided this service in exchange for a few dollars or, more often, a "taste" of the substance to be injected.

Only one woman in the sample, Latisha, capitalized on her reputation as a good "hitter" by playing the street-doc role. At one stage, Latisha had a regular arrangement with a young street thug named Crime, who had only recently commenced intravenous heroin use and was unable to "hit" himself. While experienced women injectors were as likely to have the requisite level of skill, they were less likely than men to be able to capitalize on it because they did not control established consumption settings.

CONCLUSION

Cat got busted. Yeah, the other night. And she was set up. She was in the train (station) and we were all smoking. And Crime and these other people were selling (on the corner). She finished smoking everything. She had no money left. She walked around the corner to speak to them. Like six cops rolled at once. The kid threw the package on the floor. It ended up in front of Cat. I don't know where the money ended up. They took Cat. It was no product on anybody, but they (the police) put it on her.

Cat was convicted and subsequently imprisoned. She was not the only woman in this study arrested for selling drugs who happened merely to be in the wrong place at the wrong time. Some women, like Jenny, were arrested as a result of their cohabitation with male sellers. Jenny was arrested when her pimp/boyfriend's hotel room was raided by the police and a large quantity of crack was found. Although the case against her was "constructive" possession with intent to sell, Jenny pleaded guilty, was subsequently convicted, and served one-and-a-half years in prison.

The findings presented here serve both to challenge and to contextualize the conditions of female participation in the drug business. They stand in sharp contrast both to analyses of official data, and to studies which highlight increased female participation in the drug economy. For example, in a study of women crack users in Miami, Inciardi and his colleagues found that drug-business offences (mainly street-level sales) represented a much greater proportion of crimes committed by women (94 per cent) than that found among two earlier cohorts of female heroin users (28 and 34 per cent respectively). The women in this sample were also significantly less likely to engage in prostitution (Inciardi et al., 1993).[15] However, such accounts provide little insight into the positioning of women in street-level drug markets.[16]

While disparate images of women's participation in drug distribution and sales may be the product of differences in study samples (including racial–ethnic variation in drug market organization, neighbourhood-level variation, variation in the kinds of drugs

sold, and when the study was conducted), they also reflect differences in the methodological approaches utilized by researchers. Virtually all North American studies of women drug users have employed one-time interviews. The ethnographic approach used in this study reveals that in the absence of a temporal frame and observational data, interviews may provide an incomplete and inaccurate picture. The one-time interview also misses the changing and fluid nature of relations in the informal economy. For example, for a short period there was a perception in Bushwick that "new opportunities" existed for women to sell crack. That perception faded as it became clear that owners and managers were "using" women to evade the constraints imposed on them by law enforcement and police search practices. Ethnographic approaches, then, can offer a more dynamic and contextualized picture of women's law-breaking. While such approaches are relatively numerous in the study of adolescent and adult men in the United States (e.g. Sullivan, 1989; Anderson, 1990; Padilla, 1992; Bourgois, 1995), they have rarely been utilized in the study of women and girls.

This chapter suggests not only that considerations of the status and positioning of women in the drug economy need to differentiate between the respective market sectors in which men and women typically generate illegal income, but also that generalizations about the nature and extent of women's participation in drug distribution typically fail to distinguish between the different types of "models" which characterize drug-distribution networks and the particular organizational forms they take at the neighbourhood level. Indeed, the fact that the women in this study were markedly under-represented in street-level sales positions reflects a number of features identified here, including fluctuations in the availability of labour in accordance with extra-market forces and the "business" model which characterized drug distribution in Bushwick. While, in theory, the built-in supervision and task differentiation of the business model should have provided opportunities for both men and women (Johnson et al., 1992), my findings suggest that sellers were overwhelmingly men whose involvement was further mediated by ethnic/kinship ties.

The theoretical tools used by researchers to examine women's participation in the drug economy have also been inadequate. Women drug users have rarely been studied as members of social networks or as participants in collective or group-based activity. Nor have they been viewed as economic actors in illegal markets governed by organizational constraints, occupational norms, and workplace cultures. Those making a general claim about "women's emancipation" in the drug economy ignore the obdurateness of a gender-stratified labour market and the beliefs and practices that maintain it. Those making the more restricted claim that male-dominated street networks and market processes have weakened, thus allowing entry points for women, need to offer proof for that claim. Assertions of women's changing and improved position in the drug economy have not been well proved. Nor are they grounded in theories of how work, including illegal work, is conditioned by relations of gender, race/ethnicity and sexuality (e.g. Kanter, 1977; Game and Pringle, 984; Messerschmidt, 1993).

Of the four elements that have been used to explain women's restricted involvement in drug economies of the past, I found evidence of change in two: a diminishing of women's access to drug selling roles via boyfriends and husbands, especially where drug markets are highly structured and kin-based; and decreased economic returns for street-level sexwork. Because few of the women had stable households or cared for children, I cannot comment on changes (if any) in discretionary time. Institutionalized sexism in the underworld was the most powerful element shaping women's experiences in the drug economy: it inhibited their access to drug-business work roles and effectively foreclosed their participation as higher-level distributors. All the elements of underworld sexism identified by Steffensmeier (1983)—homosocial reproduction, sex-typing, and the qualities required in a violent task environment—featured prominently in Bushwick's street-level drug economy.

The "new opportunities" said to have emerged with the crack-propelled expansion of drug markets from the mid-1980s onwards were not "empty slots" waiting to be filled by those with the requisite skill. Rather, they were slots requiring certain masculine qualities and capacities. These qualities, while presented as "human" are both gendered and raced. Their significance and the symbolism used to convey them was evident in the women's use of instrumental aggression. While fluctuations in the availability of labour appear to produce temporary ruptures or gaps which precipitate sporadic and short-lived opportunities for female participation in low-level distribution roles, highly gendered understandings continue to be reflected in, and shaped by, perceptions of women as unreliable, untrustworthy and incapable of demonstrating an effective capacity for violence. Ultimately these perceptions serve to reinforce the marginal status of women as a reserve army of labour within the drug business.

The formal organizational characteristics of highly-structured drug markets, the distribution networks which sustain them, and the cultural practices and beliefs of the social actors who inhabit them, work together to foster both sex/gender and race/ethnic segmentation in the (illegal) workplace. It not only remains the case that, as Klein and Kress observed almost twenty years ago, "[w]omen are no more big-time drug dealers than they are finance capitalists" (1976:4), but moreover, that this division of labour appears to permeate the street-level distribution hierarchy. With few exceptions, opportunities for income generation within this hierarchy—ranging from higher-level managerial and distribution roles to minimum-wage positions as street-level operatives—continue to be monopolized by males.

DISCUSSION QUESTIONS

1. Using information from this chapter, discuss the general belief that crime by women is on the increase in terms of the drug business.

2. Does this chapter support the general perception that women are becoming increasingly violent? Support your position using research from this chapter.
3. Up to this point several theoretical perspectives have been presented by different authors. Describe two of the theories that are used by Maher to explain women's position in the drug industry.
4. If, as this chapter maintains, women are discriminated against by underworld male decision makers, can a case be made that this form of discrimination actually "protects" women from committing felonies and facing long-term incarceration sentences? Discuss your own reactions to such an argument.
5. What similarities and differences do you find in the gender-related *attitudes* of drug offenders in this chapter and those who engage in robbery in chapter 3 by J. Miller? What similarities and differences in social *structural* conditions leading to their crimes do you find as well?

NOTES

1. Johnson et al. define drug-business crimes as including drug sales and a variety of associated distribution roles including steering, touting, copping, running, holding, guarding, acting as a lookout, testing, lending or renting works, picking-up, running a shooting gallery and injecting others (1985:61–5).
2. Runners "continuously supply the sellers," lookouts "warn of impending dangers," steerers and touts "advertise and solicit customers," holders "handle drugs or money but not both," and enforcers "maintain order and intervene in case of trouble" (Johnson et al., 1992:61–4).
3. These "gaps" (which result from short term fluctuations in the labour supply) must be distinguished from what some commentators view as structurally induced "gaps" of a more permanent nature reportedly utilized by women to gain access to the market (Baskin, Sommers and Fagan, 1993).
4. A recent study which examined a large core network of injecting drug users in Bushwick (n = 40) found that only 11 people (28 per cent) claimed to have sold drugs and that none of these was a full-time distributor (Curtis et al., 1995).
5. Mieczkowski has commented on the similar nature of relationships between members of heroin syndicates in Detroit. Contradictory expectations complicate these relationships. On the one hand, the crew boss expects and demands loyalty and obedience. On the other hand, the nature of the work demands considerable assertiveness and "street smarts." Often the very characteristics identified with the latter militate against the presence of the former (1986:658–9).
6. This view may be something of an urban myth with some evidence to suggest that, especially at higher levels, "informing or 'snitching' has become an integral part of the drug-trafficking and enforcement world, with both small and large operators willing to implicate or testify against rivals or friends in exchange for shorter sentences" (Woodiwiss, 1988:193).
7. Indeed Bourgois' informants in Spanish Harlem claimed that they did not need to rely on relations based on trust because they were tough enough to command respect and to enforce the contracts they entered into (1989:634).
8. According to Mieczkowski, "[t]he inability to have normal recourse to third-party resolution may contribute to the tension in such a system and exert a sort of 'Hobbesian effect' upon social relationships" (1986:658).
9. A study of street vending in Washington, DC by Spalter-Roth found that women street vendors adopt a number of strategies to protect themselves from harassment from male customers, vendors, and police. As one informant reported:

"You learn very fast to be as quick and as vulgar as they are, because if you do the standard female thing of being coy and shy and try to back off gently, they will take it as encouragement and it gets worse" (1988:174). To outsiders, the distinction between offensive and defensive aggression in such situations is not always apparent.

10. Campbell's research suggests that, among young female gang members, the containment of anger in the face of victimization results in a shift of allegiance from an expressive to an instrumental representation of aggression: "Aggression in their lives is a means of survival . . . the indisputable law on the street is fight or get beaten. The reasoning that leads women to this instrumental use of aggression is *not confined to the gang*. Wherever women face lives of brutal exploitation that destroys their faith in the value of trust and intimacy, they will be driven to it" (1993:140; emphasis added).

11. According to Miller, "the ability to maipulate [sic] people or 'con' people into giving you their money *without resorting to violence*" (1986:164; emphasis added) is an essential prerequisite of a "successful" street woman.

12. While consumption settings in Bushwick more closely resembled heroin shooting galleries (see, e.g. Des Jarlais et al., 1986; Murphy and Waldorf, 1991) than crack houses (see, e.g. Williams, 1992; Inciardi et al., 1993), many sites combined elements of both and most provided for polydrug (heroin and crack) consumption (see also Geter, 1994). For further details see Maher (1995b).

13. Historical research indicates that the policing strategy adopted in relation to working class gambling in the inter-war period in Britain was "one of differentiated rather than universal enforcement. The place and time of the behaviour, and the age, sex, status, and class of the actors determined in practice what was, and what was not, permissible . . . What was treated as deviant in practice did not match the formal definitions of illegality" (Dixon, 1991:267).

14. Biernacki was concerned with the attribution of social status among heroin addicts based on the hustles they employed. He found that heroin addicts who participated in dangerous hustles with low rewards had low self-esteem: "[those] who, for example provide street services for other users—appear to be attributed one of the lowliest statuses in the heroin world and correspondingly most often think of themselves in similar deprecating terms" (1979:540).

15. Seventy-six per cent of this Miami-based sample of 197 women crack users (a combination treatment/street sample) reported drug business crimes in the 90 days prior to interview (Inciardi et al., 1993:120–2).

16. Inciardi et al. (1993) claim that while the women in their research reportedly preferred drug sales to prostitution, drug shortages, rather than a segmented labour market, were what served to prevent them from exercising their employment preferences (see also Inciardi and Pottieger, 1986).

REFERENCES

Adler, P. A. 1985. *Wheeling and Dealing: An Ethnography of an Upper-Level Drug Dealing and Smuggling Community,* New York: Columbia University Press.

Anderson, E. 1990. *Streetwise: Race, Class and Change in an Urban Community,* Chicago: University of Chicago Press.

Anglin, M. D., and Y. Hser. 1987. Addicted Women and Crime, *Criminology* 25(2):359–97.

Auld, J., N. Dorn, and N. South. 1986. Irregular Work, Irregular Pleasures: Heroin in the 1980s. In *Confronting Crime,* ed. R. Matthews and J. Young, London: Sage, pp. 166–87.

Baskin, D., I. Sommers, and J. A. Fagan. 1993. The Political Economy of Violent Female Street Crime, *Fordham Urban Law Journal* 20:401–7.

Biernacki, P. 1979. Junkie Work, "Hustles" and Social Status Among Heroin Addicts, *Journal of Drug Issues* 9: 535–49.

Bourgois, P. 1995. *In Search of Respect: Selling Crack in El Barrio,* New York: Cambridge University Press.

Bourgois, P. 1996. In Search of Masculinity: Violence, Respect and Sexuality among Puerto Rican Crack

Dealers in East Harlem, *British Journal of Criminology* 36(3): 412–27.

Box, S., and C. Hale. 1983. Liberation and Female Criminality in England and Wales, *British Journal of Criminology* 23(1):35–49.

Campbell, A. 1992. Untitled Panel Presentation on Girls, Gangs and Violence, paper presented at the Annual Meeting of the American Society of Criminology, New Orleans, November.

Campbell, A. 1993. *Out of Control: Men, Women and Aggression,* London: Pandora.

Covington, J. 1985. Gender Differences in Criminality Among Heroin Users, *Journal of Research in Crime and Delinquency* 22(4):329–54.

Curtis, R. 1996. *An Ethnographic Study of the Effects of the Tactical Narcotics Team on Street-Level Drug Markets in Three Police Precincts in Brooklyn* (Doctoral dissertation, Columbia University), MI: University Microfilms International.

Curtis, R., and A. Hamid. 1997. State-sponsored Violence in New York City and Indigenous Attempts to Contain it: The Mediating Role of the Third Crown (Sgt. at Arms) of the Latin Kings, manuscript submitted for publication.

Curtis, R., and L. Maher. 1993. Highly Structured Crack Markets in the Southside of Williamsburg, Brooklyn, In *The Ecology of Crime and Drug Use in Inner Cities,* ed. J. Fagan, New York: Social Science Research Council.

Curtis, R., and M. Sviridoff. 1994. The Social Organization of Street-level Drug Markets and its Impact on the Displacement Effect. In *Crime Displacement: The Other Side of Prevention,* ed. R. P. McNamara, New York: Cummings and Hathaway, 155–71.

Curtis, R., S. R. Friedman, A. Neaigus, B. Jose, M. Goldstein, and G. Ildefonso. 1995. Street-level Drug Markets: Network Structure and HIV Risk, *Social Networks* 17:229–49.

Des Jarlais, D. C., S. Friedman, and D. Strug. 1986. AIDS and Needle Sharing Within the IV Drug Use Subculture. In *The Social Dimensions of AIDS: Methods and Theory,* ed. D. Feldman and T. Johnson, New York: Praeger, 141–60.

Dixon, D. 1991. *From Prohibition to Regulation: Bookmaking, Anti-Gambling and the Law.* Oxford: Clarendon Press.

Fagan, J. A. 1994. Women and Drugs Revisited: Female Participation in the Cocaine Economy, *Journal of Drug Issues* 24(2):179–225.

Fagan, J. A. 1995. Women's Careers in Drug Use and Drug Selling, *Current Perspectives on Aging and the Life Cycle* 4: 155–90.

Fagan, J. A., and K. Chin, 1989. Initiation into Crack and Cocaine: A Tale of Two Epidemics, *Journal of Contemporary Drug Problems* 16(4):579–617.

Fiddle, S. 1976. Sequences in Addiction, *Addictive Diseases: An International Journal* 2(4):553–68.

File, K. N. 1976. Sex Role and Street Roles, *International Journal of the Addictions* 11(2):263–8.

File, K. N., T. W. McCahill, and L. D. Savitz. 1974. Narcotics Involvement and Female Criminality, *Addictive Diseases: An International Journal* 1(2):177–88.

Game, A., and R. Pringle. 1983. *Gender At Work,* Sydney: George Allen and Unwin.

Geter, R. S. 1994. Drug User Settings: A Crack House Typology, *The International Journal of the Addictions* 29(8):1015–27.

Goldstein, P. J. 1979. *Prostitution and Drugs,* Lexington, MA: Lexington Books.

Hamid, A. 1990. The Political Economy of Crack-Related Violence, *Contemporary Drug Problems* 17(1):31–78.

Hamid, A. 1991a. From Ganja to Crack: Caribbean Participation in the Underground Economy in Brooklyn, 1976–1986, Part 1, Establishment of the Marijuana Economy, *International Journal of the Addictions* 26(6):615–28.

Hamid, A. 1991b. From Ganja to Crack: Caribbean Participation in the Underground Economy in Brooklyn, 1976–1986, Part 2, Establishment of the Cocaine (and Crack) Economy, *International Journal of the Addictions* 26(7):729–38.

Hamid, A. 1991c. Crack: New Directions in Drug Research, Part 1, Differences Between the Marijuana Economy and the Cocaine/Crack Economy, *International Journal of the Addictions* 26(8): 825–36.

Hamid, A. 1991d. Crack: New Directions in Drug Research, Part 2, Factors Determining the Current Functioning of the Crack Economy—A Program for Ethnographic Research, *International Journal of the Addictions* 26(9):913–22.

Hamid, A. 1992a. The Developmental Cycle of a Drug Epidemic: The Cocaine Smoking Epidemic of 1981–1991, *Journal of Psychoactive Drugs* 24(4):337–48.

Hamid, A. 1993. Nickels Markets in Flatbush. In *The Ecology of Crime and Drug Use in Inner Cities,* ed. J. Fagan New York: Social Science Research Council.

Hamid, A. (forthcoming). *The Political Economy of Drugs,* New York: Guilford Press.

Hay, D. 1975. Property, Authority and the Criminal Law. In *Albion's Fatal Tree,* ed. D. Hay, P. Linebaugh, J. G. Rule, E. P. Thompson and C. Winslow, London: Allen Lane, 17–63.

Hunt, D. 1990. Drugs and Consensual Crimes: Drug Dealing and Prostitution, In *Drugs and Crime,* (Crime and Justice, Volume 13), ed. J. Q. Wilson and M. Tonrey, Chicago: University of Chicago Press.

Inciardi, J. A., and A. E. Pottieger, 1986. Drug Use and Crime Among Two Cohorts of Women Narcotics Users: An Empirical Assessment, *Journal of Drug Issues* 16:91–106.

Inciardi, J. A., D. Lockwood, and A. E. Pottieger. 1993. *Women and Crack Cocaine,* New York: Macmillan.

James, J. 1976. Prostitution and Addiction: An Interdisciplinary Approach. *Addictive Diseases: An International Journal* 2(4):601–18.

Johnson, B. D., P. J. Goldstein, E. Preble, J. Schmeidler, D. S. Lipton, B. Spunt, and T. Miller. 1985. *Taking Care of Business: The Economics of Crime by Heroin Abusers,* Lexington, MA: Lexington Books.

Johnson, B. D., A. Hamid, and E. Morales. 1987. Critical Dimensions of Crack Distribution, paper presented at the Annual Meeting of the American Society of Criminology, Montreal, November.

Johnson, B. D., A. Hamid, and H. Sanabria. 1992. Emerging Models of Crack Distribution. In *Drugs and Crime: A Reader,* ed. T. M. Mieczkowski, Boston: Allyn and Bacon, 56–78.

Kanter, R. M. 1977. *Men and Women of the Corporation,* New York: Basic Books.

Katz, J. 1988. *Seductions of Crime,* New York: Basic Books.

Kleiman, M. R. 1992. *Against Excess: Drug Policy for Results,* New York: Basic Books.

Koester, S. and J. Schwartz, 1993. Crack, Gangs, Sex and Powerlessness: A View from Denver, In *Crack Pipe as Pimp: An Ethnographic Investigation of Sex-for-Crack Exchanges,* ed. M. S. Ratner, New York: Lexington Books, 187–203.

Maher, L. 1995b. Dope Girls: Gender, Race and Class in the Drug Economy, (Doctoral dissertation, Rutgers University), Ann Arbor, MI: University Microfilms International.

Messerschmidt, J. W. 1993. *Masculinities and Crime,* Lanham, MD: Rowan and Littlefield.

Mieczkowski, T. 1986. Geeking Up and Throwing Down: Heroin Street Life in Detroit, *Criminology* 24(4):645–66.

Mieczkowski, T. 1990. Crack Dealing on the Street: An Exploration of the YBI Hypothesis and the Detroit Crack Trade, paper presented at the Annual Meeting of the American Society of Criminology, Baltimore, November.

Miller, E. 1986. *Street Woman,* Philadelphia: Temple University Press.

Morris, A. 1987. *Women, Crime and Criminal Justice,* Oxford: Basil Blackwell.

Murphy, S., and D. Waldorf, 1991. Kickin' Down to the Street Doc: Shooting Galleries in the San Francisco Bay Area, *Contemporary Drug Problems* 18(1):9–29.

Ouellet, L. J., W. W. Wiebel, A. D. Jiminez, and W. A. Johnson. 1993. Crack Cocaine and the Transformation of Prostitution in Three Chicago Neighborhoods, In *Crack Pipe as Pimp: An Ethnographic Investigation of Sex-For-Crack Exchanges,* ed. M. S. Ratner, New York: Lexington Books, 69–96.

Padilla, F. 1992. *The Gang as an American Enterprise.* New Brunswick, NJ: Rutgers University Press.

Pettiway, L. E. 1987. Participation in Crime Partnerships by Female Drug Users: The Effects of Domestic Arrangements, Drug Use, and Criminal Involvement, *Criminology* 25(3):741–66.

Reuter, P., R. MacCoun, and P. Murphy. 1990. *Money from Crime: A Study of the Economics of Drug Dealing in Washington, DC.* Santa Monica, CA: The Rand Corporation Drug Policy Research Center.

Rosenbaum, M. 1981c. *Women on Heroin,* New Brunswick, NJ: Rutgers University Press.

Sharff, J. W. 1987. The Underground Economy of a Poor Neighborhood. In *Cities of the United States: Studies in Urban Anthropology,* ed. L. Mullings, New York: Columbia University Press, 19–50.

Spalter-Roth, R. M. 1988. The Sexual Political Economy of Street Vending in Washington, DC. In *Traders Versus the State: Anthropological Approaches to Unofficial Economies,* ed. G. Clark, Boulder, CO: Westview Press, 165–87.

Steffensmeier, D. 1983. Organization Properties and Sex-Segregation in the Underworld: Building a Sociological Theory of Sex Differences in Crime, *Social Forces* 61(4): 1010–32.

Sullivan, M. L. 1989. *Getting Paid: Youth Crime and Work in the Inner City,* Ithaca, NY: Cornell University Press.

Sutter, A. G. 1966. The World of the Righteous Dope Fiend, *Issues in Criminology* 2(2):177–222.

Taylor, A. 1993. *Women Drug Users: An Ethnography of a Female Injecting Community,* Oxford: Clarendon Press.

Taylor, C. S. 1993. *Girls, Gangs, Women and Drugs,* East Lansing: Michigan State University Press.

Waterston, A. 1993. *Street Addicts in the Political Economy*, Philadelphia: Temple University Press.

Whyte, W. F. 1943. *Street Corner Society*, Chicago: University of Chicago Press.

Williams, T. 1992. *Crackhouse: Notes From the End of the Line*, New York: Addison-Wesley.

Wilson, N. K. 1993. Stealing and Dealing: The Drug War and Gendered Criminal Opportunit. In *Female Criminality: The State of the Art*. ed. C. C. Culliver. New York: Garland Publishing, 169–94.

Woodiwiss, M. 1988. *Crime, Crusades and Corruption: Prohibitions in the United States 1900–1987*, London: Pinter Publishers.

Chapter 8

Prostitution and the Globalization of Sex Workers' Rights

Kamala Kempadoo

ABSTRACT

This chapter focuses on third–world sex workers. *Sex workers* is a term that came about as a result of the prostitutes' rights movement, which argues that prostitutes—as sex workers—should have employment rights and public protections from harm and exploitation just like any other workers. Kempadoo notes that the concept is not limited to prostitutes and women although it includes both these categories and they are a substantial, if not the largest, component. The chapter covers three main topics: racism, transnational sex work, and globalization. Sex work and racism combine to label and degrade third-world women as "exotic," "primitive," "dependent," and "ignorant." Sex work across national boundaries has existed in its current form for over 100 years but has, in recent times, intensified as a result of the global restructuring of capitalist production and investment, particularly since the 1970s. This restructuring has led to upheavals in labor markets in third-world countries, where prostitution must be understood within the context of the global exploitation of women's and children's labor. Sex trafficking is the third most lucrative criminal activity in the world (after smuggling arms and narcotics), according to the officials at the Second World Congress against Commercial Sexual Exploitation of Children held in 2001.[1]

One new development has been the emergence of sex tourism, which serves the interests of men who are business tourist promoters, pimps, and military and police officials. Many women find it necessary to supplement their inadequate wages as the global economy deflates wages and creates seasonal unemployment. (For a discussion of the impact of the global economy, economic restructuring, and the racialized feminization of poverty on women's work, involvement with drugs, and incarceration, see Sudbury, chap. 12.) Women's income gap—

---

[1]See Feminist Majority Foundation. Washington Post Urges Increased Effort to Combat Sex Slavery. May 29, 2002. Feminist Daily News Wire. Available at www.feminist.org/news/newsbyte/uswirestory.asp?id=6566.

especially for poor women around the world—is increasingly being filled, the author notes, by the growing sex industry. Migration is another result of globalization, as women seek opportunities elsewhere. Frequently, the dislocation and the concomitant criminalization of sex work as well as hostile immigration laws lead not to a better job and life but to sex work, often in its most degraded forms.

Although this chapter is not an easy one for Westerners to read, it is important that we begin to understand how the lives of so many poor women around the world are affected by the globalization of capital emanating from developed countries, and its impact on the criminalization of marginalized women in the United States and around the world.

When I first heard about prostitutes organizing for their rights in Suriname in 1993, I was both excited and puzzled by the news. Was it a singular incident spurred by an outsider, or did it reflect a local movement? I wanted to know. Also, in this part of the world, were women serious about staying in the sex industry or anxious to have prostitution abolished? What were the aims of such an organization, and who were the activists? Was this an isolated group, and what was the response to this initiative from the rest of the women's movement in this corner of South America? Questions outweighed any answer I could find in libraries or books—I decided to travel to Suriname to find out more.

Curiosity opened my world to a movement not just in Suriname, but in other parts of the "Third World."[1] I realized that sex workers' movements were no longer exclusive to the United States or Western Europe. Prostitutes and other sex workers were fighting to keep brothels open, challenging the various stigmas about prostitution, and exposing corruption within sex industries in many different countries—yet very few people had heard about these courageous steps. The voices and activities of sex workers outside the industrialized North went unheard, nearly invisible to all but those in the immediate surroundings. As someone trained to think that a documentation of social history is absolutely

vital for the construction of knowledge, I believed the one thing I could do was to facilitate the recording of this new international movement. . . .

SEX WORKER, PROSTITUTE OR WHORE?

Identity, rights, working conditions, decriminalization, and legitimacy have been central issues collectively addressed by prostitutes for many years. Through these struggles the notion of the sex worker has emerged as a counterpoint to traditionally derogatory names, under the broad banner of a prostitutes' rights movement, with some parts recovering and valorizing the name and identity of "whore." . . . We have chosen the term "sex worker" to reflect the current use throughout the world, although in many . . . essays "sex worker" and "prostitute" are used interchangeably. It is a term that suggests we view prostitution not as an identity—a social or a psychological characteristic of women, often indicated by "whore"—but as an income-generating activity or form of labor for women and men. The definition stresses the social location of those engaged in sex industries as working people.

The idea of the sex worker is inextricably related to struggles for the recognition of women's work, for basic human rights and for decent working conditions. The definition emphasizes flexibility and variability of sexual labor as well as its similarities with other dimensions of working people's lives. In particular, . . . sex work is experienced as an integral part of many women's and men's lives around the

Source: Kamala Kempadoo. 1998. Introduction: Globalizing Sex Workers' Rights. In Global Sex Workers: Rights, Resistance, and Redefinition, ed. Kamala Kempadoo and Jo Doezema, New York and London: Routledge, pp. 1–28.

world, and not necessarily as the sole defining activity around which their sense of self or identity is shaped. Moreover, commercial sex work in these accounts is not always a steady activity, but may occur simultaneously with other forms of income-generating work such as domestic service, informal commercial trading, market-vending, shoeshining or office work. Sex work can also be quite short-lived or be a part of an annual cycle of work—in few cases are women and men engaged full-time or as professionals. Consequently, in one person's lifetime, sex work is commonly just one of the multiple activities employed for generating income, and very few stay in prostitution for their entire adulthood. In most cases, sex work is not for individual wealth but for family well-being or survival; for working class women to clothe, feed and educate their children; and for young women and men to sustain themselves when the family income is inadequate. For many, sex work means migration away from their hometown or country. For others, it is associated with drug use, indentureship or debt-bondage. For the majority, participation in sex work entails a life in the margins.

The concept of sex work emerged in the 1970s through the prostitutes' rights movement in the United States and Western Europe and has been discussed in various publications.[2] Than-Dam Troung's study of prostitution and tourism in Southeast Asia produced one of the first extensive theoretical elaborations on the subject (1990). Defining human activity or work as the way in which basic needs are met and human life produced and reproduced, she argues that activities involving purely sexual elements of the body and sexual energy should also be considered vital to the fulfillment of basic human needs: for both procreation and bodily pleasure. Troung thus introduces the concept of sexual labor to capture the notion of the utilization of sexual elements of the body and as a way of understanding a productive life force that is employed by women and men. In this respect she proposes that sexual labor be considered similar to other forms of labor that humankind performs to sustain itself—such as mental and manual labor, all of which involve specific parts

of the body and particular types of energy and skills. Furthermore, she points out, the social organization of sexual labor has taken a variety of forms in different historical contexts and political economies, whereby there is no universal form or appearance of either prostitution or sex work. Instead, she proposes, analyses of prostitution need to address and take into account the specific ways in which sexual subjectivity, sexual needs and desires are constructed in specific contexts. Wet-nursing, temple prostitution, "breeding" under slavery, surrogate child-bearing, donor sex, commercial sex and biological reproduction can thus be seen as illustrations of historical and contemporary ways in which sexual labor has been organized for the re-creation and replenishment of human and social life.

Perhaps one of the most confounding dimensions in the conceptualization of prostitution as labor concerns the relation that exists in many people's minds between sexual acts and "love," and with prevailing ideas that without love, sexual acts are harmful and abusive. After all, isn't sex supposed to be about consensual sharing of our "most personal, private, erotic, sensitive parts of our physical and psychic being," as some would argue?[3] And aren't women in particular harmed or violated by sexual acts that are not intimate? In such perspectives, the sale of one's sexual energies is confused with a particular morality about sexual relations and essentialist cultural interpretations are imposed upon the subject. This conflation of sex with the highest form of intimacy presupposes a universal meaning of sex, and ignores changing perceptions and values as well as the variety of meanings that women and men hold about their sexual lives. In *Live Sex Acts,* Wendy Chapkis proposes that if we are able to understand how women experience and define their sexual acts in commercial transactions, then it is possible to move beyond a universalistic moralizing position and to develop some knowledge of the complex realities of women's experiences of sexual labor. Through extensive interviews with sex workers in the Netherlands and the United States, Chapkis concludes that prostitution can be likened to the sociological category of "emotional labor," activities and jobs for which care and feeling are required, commodified and commercialized, such as airline service work, acting, psychotherapy, massage work, or child-care (1997). The objectification of emotion that occurs in the process of this kind of work, including sex work, is not inherently destructive or harmful, she points out, rather the worker is able to "summon and contain emotion within the commercial transaction," to erect and maintain boundaries that protect the worker from abuse, and to develop a professionalism toward the job (76). Sex workers are thus able to distinguish intimacy and love from the sexual act itself, much in the same way that an actor or therapist is able to separate their work from private life, preserving a sense of integrity and distance from emotionally demanding work. Similarly, Heather Montgomery describes perceptions and experiences for children in the Thai sex industry.* She explains that the children are able to form a distinct ethical system that allows them to sell sex while preserving a sense of humanity and virtue.

While our approach suggests that social relations involving sexual labor are not inherently tied to specific gendered roles or bodies, there is a persistent pattern through much of history that positions the social gendered category "women" as the sellers or providers of sexual labor and "men" as the group deriving profits and power from the interactions. The subordination of the female and the feminine is the overriding factor for this arrangement in a variety of cultural, national and economic contexts, producing stigmas and social condemnation of persons who defy the socially defined boundaries of womanhood. Categories of "good" and "bad" women (virgin/whore, madonna/prostitute, chaste/licentious women) exist in most patriarchal societies, where the "bad" girl becomes the trope for female sexuality that threatens male control and domination. Female sexual acts that serve women's sexual or economic interests are, within the context of masculinist hegemony, dangerous, immoral, per-

verted, irresponsible and indecent. Construed in this fashion, the image of the whore disciplines and divides women, forcing some to conform to virginity, domesticity and monogamy and demonizing those who transgress these boundaries. Sex work positions women in dominant discourse as social deviants and outcasts. Today the majority of the world's sex workers are women, working within male-dominated businesses and industries, yet while the social definition of the provider of sexual labor is often closely associated with specific cultural constructions of femininity, and "the prostitute" rendered virtually synonymous with "woman," these gendered relations are clearly also being contested and redefined in different ways throughout the world. Various trends acutely challenge the tendency to essentialize the sex worker with biological notions of gender. In the Caribbean for example, so-called romance tourism is based on the sale by men of "love" to North American and European women, and "rent-a-dreads" and beach boys dominate the sex trade in the tourism industry in some islands (Press 1978, Pruit and Lafont, 1995). . . . Thai sex workers in Japan report to sometimes buy sex for their own pleasure from male strippers, Brazilian "miches"—young male hustlers—get by through selling sex to other men, and in Europe and Malaysia male-to-female transgender sex workers also service men.* Across the globe, "genetic" men and boys engage in sex work, selling sex to both men and women in homosexual and heterosexual relations, as feminine and masculine subjects.

Nevertheless, even with the increasing visibility of genetic men and boys in sex work, gender inequality and discrimination remain evident. Julian Marlowe argues that if we compare beliefs about male and female sex workers, two prominent yet very different sets of assumptions emerge with men commanding a more liberated and independent position in the discourse than their female counterparts (1997). . . . Dawn Passar and Johanna Breyer

---

*Editors note: See Kamala Kempadoo and Jo Doezema, eds. *Global Sex Workers: Rights, Resistance, and Redefinition.* New York and London: Routledge, 1998.

*Editor's note: See Kempadoo and Doezema. Mention of studies not listed in the notes at the end of the chapter can be found in their book.

discuss a setting in the U.S. where even though men are entering stripping and exotic dancing in greater numbers than before, they are paid different—and better—kinds of wages than women in clubs under the same management. In an attempt to address such gender inequalities, the women filed a case of sexual harassment and discrimination with the California Equal Employment Opportunity Commission.* For Brazil, . . . Paulo Longo describes a situation where young men and boys resist inferiorization that is associated with being defined and viewed as "feminine" by asserting a "macho" identity, and for Malaysia,* Khartini Slamah contends that transgendered persons are female, either through self-definition, medical operations or definition by others.* As Gail Pheterson notes, "male homosexuals and transvestites also provide sexual service in a minority of cases, but this does not change the gender pattern because like women, they service men and their role is often feminine" (1996:27). Within the sex industry, a gendered hierarchy and systematic privileging of the male and the masculine continues to be prevalent.

Children, both boys and girls, are also increasingly evident in prostitution, particularly in Third World settings, making the picture of gendered relations even more complex. However, child participation in sex industries invariably raises other questions and problems than those to do with gender, and it is within the international debates on "child prostitution" that a discourse of sexual labor and sex work is also apparent. While some attribute the rise of adolescents and pre-pubescent children in prostitution to the insatiable sexual appetites of depraved western men, or to cultural preferences in Third World countries for sex with virgins, a highly compelling explanation involves an analysis of the global political economy and processes of development and underdevelopment. Studies by the International Labor Organization (ILO) show that the proliferation of earning activity by children is asso-

ciated with the development process "with its intrinsic features of population and social mobility, urbanization, and progressive monetization of all forms of human activity," and the growth of the modern tourist industry based on the accumulation of wealth and disposable incomes in the industrialized world (Black 1995). The disruption that such development brings to the organization of production in developing countries, draws children into marginal and servile occupations sometimes requiring parents to deploy the income-generating capacity of their children in order to ensure that the household survives. The research suggests we include child prostitution in the context of the global exploitation of child labor in order to effectively address the problem. Such understandings of child labor undergirds various child worker movements around the world, some of which were represented at the 1997 Amsterdam Conference on Child Labor.[4] The organization of young male hustlers in Brazil . . . is also premised on the articulation of child prostitution as work.*

Sex work, as we understand it here, is not a universal or ahistorical category, but is subject to change and redefinition. It is clearly not limited to prostitution or to women, but certainly encompasses what is generally understood to fall into these two categories. However, even though human sexual and emotional resources have been organized and managed in different ways and acquired different meanings, capital accumulation, liberal free market politics and the commodification of waged labor has transformed various social arrangements in a consistent fashion. Louise White notes in her study of prostitution in colonial Nairobi, Kenya, "prostitution is a capitalist social relationship not because capitalism causes prostitution by commoditizing sexual relations but because wage labor is a unique feature of capitalism, capitalism commoditized labor" (1990:II). White's study proposes that capitalism shapes sex work into commoditized forms of labor rather than

---

*Editor's note: See Kempadoo and Doezema.

*Editor's note: See Kempadoo and Doezema.

causing sex work as a category of social activity. She understands prostitution as another form of domestic labor. Both White and Troung point out that the exploitation of sexual labor is intensified under systemic capitalism, leaving it open to similar kinds of pressures and manipulations that any other waged labor faces. Sexual labor today forms a primary source for profit and wealth, and it is a constituent part of national economies and transnational industries within the global capitalist economy.

If sexual labor is seen to be subject to exploitation, as with any other labor, it can also be considered as a basis for mobilization in struggles for working conditions, rights and benefits and for broader resistances against the oppression of working peoples, paralleling situations in other informal and unregulated sectors. And by recognizing sexual labor in this fashion, it is possible to identify broader strategies for change. Jo Bindman, from Anti-Slavery International, explains that "we first need to identify prostitution as work, as an occupation susceptible like the others to exploitation. Then sex workers can be included and protected under the existing instruments which aim to protect all workers from exploitation, and women from discrimination."[5] Anne McClintock observes that "historically the international labor movement has argued for the radical *transformation* of labor, not its abolition" (1993:8). She thus marks the difference between a movement that advocates the eradication of prostitution and that which is premised on understandings of prostitution as a form of sexual labor, highlighting the need to address issues of social transformations that are linked to the political economy. Situating prostitution as *work* allows then, for a recognition of what Chanda Talpade Mohanty sees as concrete "common interests" based on a shared understanding of location and needs, creating "potential bases of cross-national solidarity" between women (1997:7). The conceptualization of prostitutes, whores, strippers, lap dancers, escorts, exotic dancers, etc., as "sex workers" insists that working women's common interests can be articulated within the context of broader (feminist) struggles against the devaluation of "women's" work and gender exploitation within

capitalism. Indeed, sex worker Carol Leigh, inventor of the term "sex worker," recalls that she coined it out of a feminist priority to end divisions between women (1997).

Despite the marginality and vulnerability of sex workers internationally, the notion of sex workers as exclusively "victims" is rejected by [many] authors . . . Even in cases where women, men, boys and girls are clearly harmed within the sex industry or are caught in debt-bondage and indentureship situations, it is the respectful recognition of subjectivity and personal agency that [is important]. Explorations of agency encountered in *Global Sex Workers** identify sites of transformative practices within the context of both structural constraints and dominant relations of power in the global sex industry. By underlining agency, resistances to, and contestations of, oppressive and exploitative structures are uncovered, and the visions and ideologies inscribed in women's practices made visible. Such analyses position sex workers as actors in the global arena, as persons capable of making choices and decisions that lead to transformations of consciousness and changes in everyday life.

The approach taken here, regarding agency, is embedded in social theory that is informed by a notion of *praxis* (human activity) as central to the construction and reconstruction of society and social knowledge.[6] According to Judith Kegan Gardiner the recognition of agency is integral to feminist theories of social transformation, in " . . . that any theory that denies women 'agency' retards the changes in patriarchal social structure for which feminism strives, because it denies the existance of an entity to attach those structures" (1995:9). Feminism, from this understanding, is grounded in a notion of the social category "women"—the dominated, oppressed social collectivity within patriarchal relations—as the primary and necessary agents in processes of change. Chapkis (1997) confirms this approach in relationship to sex workers. "Practices of prostitution" she writes, "like other forms of com-

---

*Editor's note: See Kempadoo and Doezema.

modification and consumption can be read in more complex ways than simply as a confirmation of male domination. They may also be seen as sites of ingenious resistance and cultural subversion . . . the prostitute cannot be reduced to one of a passive object used in male sexual practice, but instead it can be understood as a place of agency where the sex worker makes active use of the existing sexual order" (29–30). However, even with such general acknowledgement that agency is an integral part of feminism, the idea of women's agency in prostitution is often vehemently rejected by feminists. Indeed, few are able to extend the theoretical position summarized by Gardiner and Chapkis to women's praxis in the sex trade. Sex workers who fight for changes within sex industries, and not for its abolition, are often charged by feminists, as Cheryl Overs remarks in her interview . . . with acting with a "false consciousness," or as handmaidens to patriarchal capitalism.* Clearly the "good girls" are privileged in much feminist theorizing, while sex workers remain relegated to the status of objects, seen to be violently manipulated and wrought into passivity and acquiescence. Prostitution appears to be one of the last sites of gender relations to be interrogated through a critical feminist lens that assumes that women are both active subjects and subjects of domination.

SEX WORK AND RACISM

Besides the location of women in the sex trade as workers, migrants and agents we address the specificity of racism in positioning Third World sex workers in international relations. Two distinct dimensions are [of importance here]: racisms embedded in structures and desires within specific local industries, and cultural imperialism refracted through international discourses on prostitution.

The first is analyzed in the studies of prostitution in Australia, Curaçao and Cuba where various ideologies and stereotypes of particular racial-ethnic categories of sex workers are evident.* In each place,

images of "the exotic" are entwined with ideologies of racial and ethnic difference: the "prostitute" is defined as "other" in comparison to the racial or ethnic origin of the client. Such boundaries, between which women are defined as "good" and "bad," or woman and whore, reinforce sexual relations intended for marriage and family and sets limits on national and ethnic membership. The brown or black woman is regarded as a desirable, tantalizing, erotic subject, suitable for temporary or non-marital sexual intercourse—the ideal "outside" woman— and rarely seen as a candidate for a long-term commitment, an equal partner, or as a future mother. She thus represents the unknown or forbidden yet is positioned in dominant discourse as the subordinated "other." Trends . . . [described in Kempadoo and Doezema's book] echo those identified in other studies, where it is argued that the exoticization of the Third World "other" is as equally important as economic factors in positioning women in sex work.[7] In other words, it is not simply grinding poverty that underpins a woman's involvement in prostitution. Race and ethnicity are equally important factors for any understanding of contemporary sex industries. To some scholars, racial/ethnic structuring visible in the global sex industry highly resembles the exoticist movement of the eighteenth and nineteenth centuries in which "labelling the anthropological Other as exotic legitimated treating the peoples of the "third world" as fit to be despised—destroyed even . . . while concurrently also constituting them as projections of western fantasies" (Rousseau and Porter 1990:7). The movement valorized peoples and cultures that were different and remote while simultaneously imposing a status of inferiority upon them. The eroticization of women of Third World cultures was an integral part of the approach whereby female sexuality was defined as highly attractive and fascinating, yet related to the natural primitiveness and lower order of the other cultural group. According to Porter, it was the exotic lands and peoples which provided Europeans in past centuries with "paradigms of the erotic." Away from the repressive mores of Western Europe, these strange cultures and particularly the

---

*Editor's note: See Kempadoo and Doezema.

women in them became sites where sex "was neither penalized, not pathologized nor exclusively procreative" (Porter 1990:118). Enslaved, indentured and colonized womanhood thus came to represent uninhibited and unrestricted sexual intercourse, a situation that in many ways is today reflected in the global sex industry. As the *New York Times* reports "Exotic Imports Have Captured Italy's Sex Market," referring to the increased importance of African women in sex work in Rome, and simultaneously illuminating the connection that is still made between Third World women and the exotic (July 9, 1997). However, . . . prostitution is a realm of contradictions. Thus, even with the heightened exoticization of the sexuality of Third World women and men, they are positioned within the global sex industry second to white women. White sex workers invariably work in safer, higher paid and more comfortable environments; brown women—Mulatas, Asians, Latinas—form a middle class; and Black women are still conspicuously overrepresented in the poorest and most dangerous sectors of the trade, particularly street work. Whiteness continues to represent the hegemonic ideal of physical and sexual attractiveness and desirability, and white sexual labor is most valued within the global sex industry.

The second dimension of racism is somewhat less obvious, yet concerns the neo-colonialism that is evinced in much recent feminist and pro-sex worker writings that have come out of the United States and Western Europe. Kathleen Barry's work on the trafficking of women best illustrates this tendency (1984). Her definition has captured many a feminist imagination regarding Third World women and has produced an emphasis and fascination with the subject of sex slaves in developing countries. While Barry argues that "trafficking" could involve any woman in the world, and that any woman could become a sex slave, on closer reading of her work another meaning emerges. She constructs a hierarchy of stages of patriarchal and economic development, situating the trafficking of women in the first stage that "prevails in pre-industrial and feudal societies that are primarily agricultural and where women are excluded from the public sphere" and where women, she states, are the exclusive property of men

(1995:51). At the other end of the scale she places the "post-industrial, developed societies" where "women achieve the potential for economic independence" and where prostitution is normalized (1995:53). Quite simply and without shame, she evokes an image of non-western women, that various Third World feminists have identified as common to much western feminist theorizing. The Third World/non-western woman is positioned in this discourse as "ignorant, poor, uneducated, tradition bound, domestic, family-oriented, victimized etc." and is conceptualized as leading a "truncated" sexual life (Mohanty 1991:56). She is not yet a "whole or developed" person, but instead resembles a minor needing guidance, assistance and help. The construct stands in opposition to that of the western woman who is believed to have (or at least has the potential to have) control over her income, body and sexuality: the emancipated, independent, postmodern woman.

In true colonial fashion, Barry's mission is to rescue those whom she considers to be incapable of self-determination. And along with this mission, goes a particular cultural definition of sex itself. Subaltern understandings and lived realities of sexuality and sexual-economic relations, such as found in various African or Caribbean countries for example, where one can speak of a continuum of sexual relations from monogamy to multiple sexual partners and where sex may be considered as a valuable asset for a woman to trade with, are ignored in favor of specific western ideologies and moralities regarding sexual relations.[8] Likewise the meanings young women and men have about their own sexuality, such as . . . in two essays . . . on Brazil and Thailand, are denied legitimacy and validity.* Barry's work has informed a plethora of activities and inquiries by women's organizations into the subject of prostitution and has helped form an international consciousness and discourse about the sex trade that is solely informed by western, non-sex working women's definitions of sexual relations and prostitution.

---

*Editor's note: See Kempadoo and Doezema.

The neo-colonialism that surfaces in such representations of the lives and situations of Third World women across the globe does not, however, end with radical feminists or the anti-trafficking lobby. Some prostitute's rights advocates assume that western development, capitalist modernization and industrialization will enable women in developing countries to exercise choice and attain "freedom."[9] Seen to be trapped in underdeveloped states, Third World prostitutes continue to be positioned in this discourse as incapable of making decisions about their own lives, forced by overwhelming external powers completely beyond their control into submission and slavery. Western women's experience is thus made synonymous with assumptions about the inherent superiority of industrialized capitalist development and Third World women placed in categories of pre-technological "backwardness," inferiority, dependency and ignorance. Jo Doezema demonstrates . . . that this distortion has crept into even some of the more progressive prostitutes' rights debates concerning "forced" and "voluntary" prostitution, resulting in a negation of Third World sex workers' rights to self-determination.*

The surge of writing about the position and identity of prostitutes, the redefinitions that have occurred, the various subject positions that are evident in the present discourse, and the struggles for recognition and rights have also contributed, albeit indirectly, to the creation of an hegemonic western script about prostitution. Shannon Bell's *Rewriting the Prostitute Body* presents an example. In her reading, the categorization and othering of the prostitute is located unequivocally in dichotomies that lie "at the heart of Western thought"—in short, a western concern (1994:40). Bell recovers and celebrates prostitute knowledge through a re-reading of western philosophy and U.S. prostitute performance art, validating distinctly culture-bound practices and knowledges. In so doing, she produces notions of a "new prostitute identity" that trace back to the sacred prostitute in Ancient Greece. Thus, while she

argues for a feminist postmodern reading of the subject position that allows for a recognition of differences within the category women represented by class, race, language, national boundaries, sexual orientation and age, and for a theorizing that creates space for new marginal, political subjects, her work results in an essentialist definition of the prostitute. Through an homogenization of the origins of prostitution and an erasure of contextual differences, she not only fails to validate histories and subjectivities that lie beyond her purview but subtly infers that the West defines the rest.[10]

The "canon" in prostitution studies reinforces this script.[11] For the most part, contemporary writers on sex work construct the prostitute/sex worker from testimonies and analyses that are derived from struggles of "First World" women in the United States and Western Europe. While all these writings are important in uncovering prostitute politics and identities in some parts of the world, and certainly contribute to a fuller apprehension of sex work, without historicization and geo-political contextualization, they run the risk of universalizing the subject from bounded locations and experiences. Lacking an analysis of international relations and notions of differing cultural constructions and meaning of sexuality and gender, this body of literature appropriates the "non-western" woman's experience without any investigation into the matter. Little research or theorizing to date is, for example, grounded in the lives, experiences, definitions and perspectives of Third World people in sex work, allowing western categories and subjects to be privileged in the international discourse on sex work. The distortion of relations between the First and Third Worlds, and privileging of the western prostitute subject thus places some prostitutes' rights activists and allies in danger of a political alignment with movements that consolidate western hegemony.

Third World and anti-racist feminisms have over the past two decades intensely critiqued the universalism and totalizing effect of unnuanced western (feminist) theorizing—modernist and postmodernist—arguing that many of the concepts and theories produced about women's oppression are, and have been for many years, grounded in struggles of

---

*Editor's note: See Kempadoo and Doezema.

middle-class white women and may be quite antithetical to other women's experiences, if not representative of imperialist feminist thought.[12] Nevertheless the need for feminist theory to engage with racialized sexual subjectivities in tandem with the historical weight of imperialism, colonialism and racist constructions of power has only been raised recently in the context of this feminist theorizing on prostitution.[13] In view of histories of the oversexualization of non-western women in western cultures and the colonial legacies of the rape and sexual abuse of indigenous, and other Third World women, a hesitancy to explore topics of Third World women's sexual agency and subjectivity in prostitution is quite understandable. Yet in an era when women can no longer be defined exclusively as victims, where Third World women speak for themselves in various forums, where increasingly analyses have shifted focus from simple hierarchies and dichotomies to the problematization of multiple spaces, seemingly contradictory social locations and plural sites of power, it would seem that experiences, identities and struggles of women in the global sex industry cannot be neglected. This [discussion] has taken shape in direct counterpoint to a North American–Western European hegemony within contemporary feminist and prostitute writings about the sex trade.

TRANSNATIONAL SEX WORK AND THE GLOBAL ECONOMY

Sex work across national boundaries is not new to the world. Donna Guy observes that "foreign prostitutes and pimps were already ensconced in Buenos Aires (Argentina) by 1860" and that between 1889 and 1901, seventy-five percent of the registered working women hailed from Europe and Russia (1990:14–16). Between 1865 and 1885, around one quarter of the registered prostitutes in Bologna, Italy, were migrants, and during the 1880s young British women worked in Belgium and other parts of Europe (Gibson 1986, Walkowitz 1980). In India, a number of European women worked as prostitutes in the latter part of the nineteenth century, the majority of whom originated from Central and Eastern

Europe, but also among them were English women (Levine 1994). In Russia, in the late 1880s, "non-Russian and foreign prostitutes" comprised around one-sixth of the registered prostitute population (Bernstein 1995:97). During World War II, "haole" (white) women were the majority in brothels in Hawaii. Korean and Thai women were forced to "comfort" the Japanese military, and Cuban and Venezuelan women serviced the Dutch and American navies on Curaçao (Bailey and Farber 1992, Hicks 1994, Kempadoo 1994). Specific political, economic and social events shaped the women's involvement in the sex trade at different times, in different places, within the context of a globalizing capitalist system, colonialism and masculinist hegemony.

In the late 1980s, Licia Brusa estimated that between thirty and sixty percent of the prostitutes in the Netherlands were from Third World countries, particularly Latin America and Asia (1989). Today, the migrant sex working population has been joined by women from Eastern Europe and West Africa. In 1991, around seventy percent of the sex workers in Japan were reported to be Filipino, and young Afghan and Bangladeshi women worked in prostitution in Pakistan (Korvinus 1992). In the same period, the red-light district in Bombay, India, relied predominantly upon migrant female labor, much of which originated in Nepal. By the mid-1990s, Eastern European, Russian and Vietnamese prostitutes were reported to be working in China while Russian women appeared in the Egyptian sex industry, and Mexican women moved into sex work in Japan (*BBC World Service*, April 28, 1994, *New York Times*, June 9, 1995, Azize et al. 1996). Besides these trends, [we can also look to the work on] Thai sex workers in Australia and Japan, Brazilians and Guyanese in Suriname, Dominicans and Colombians in Curaçao, Ghanaians in the Cote d'Ivoire and Austria, Nigerians in Senegal and Italy, Polish, Bulgarian, Czech and Ukranian women in Germany and Austria and so forth.[*]

Indeed, transnational sex work has continued over the past hundred years, but the question arises

---

[*]Editor's note: See Kempadoo and Doezema.

about whether it has intensified, as many will argue, during the twentieth century and particularly over the last two decades. Given the lack of figures and documentation of what in most countries is an outlawed and underground activity, and the multiplicity of activities worldwide that constitute "sex work," it is virtually impossible to state with certainty that numbers have increased. Also, as with any activity in the informal sector, information on populations involved, income, types of activities, and international migration or trafficking routes is imprecise. A glaringly obvious example of the inaccuracies that exist is related to the number of prostitutes in Asia. Figures for the city of Bombay in India range from 100,000 (*Asia Watch* 1993) to 600,000 (Barry 1995)—a difference of half a million. In the case of Thailand, figures for "child prostitutes" range between 2,500 and 800,000, with the age range being equally as imprecise (Black 1995). To any conscientious social scientist, such discrepancies should be cause for extreme suspicion of the reliability of the research, yet when it comes to sex work and prostitution, few eyebrows are raised and the figures are easily bandied about without question.[14]

Nonetheless, since the 1970s a global restructuring of capitalist production and investment has taken place and this can be seen to have wide-scale gendered implications and, by association, an impact on sex industries and sex work internationally. [See Maher, chap. 7 in this volume.] New corporate strategies to increase profit have developed, involving the movement of capital from industrial centers to countries with cheap labor, the circumvention of unionized labor, and so-called flexible employment policies. Unemployment and temporary work plagues the industrialized centers as well as "developing" countries. The ILO estimated that in January 1994, around thirty percent of the world's labor force was unemployed and unable to sustain a minimum standard of living (Chomsky 1994:188). The power and influence of transnational institutions such as the World Trade Organization, the World Bank and various corporations has superseded that of national governments and national businesses.[15] Measures imposed by the International Monetary

Fund (IMF) for national debt-repayment, such as Structural Adjustment programs, and international trade agreements, such as the North American Free Trade Agreement (NAFTA) and the General Agreement on Tariffs and Trade (GATT) squeeze national economies, creating displacement from rural agricultural communities, rising unemployment in urban centers, drops in real wages, and increasing poverty. Free Trade and Special Economic Zones for export-oriented production, cuts by governments in national expenditures in the social sector and the removal of trade restrictions, local food subsidies and price controls accompany these measures and agreements and impose even further hardships on working people.[16] The corporate drive to increase consumption, and hence profit margins, has also led to a proliferation of new products, goods and services and the cultivation of new desires and needs. Alongside apparel, automobile, electronic, computer and luxury good industries, sex industries have grown since the mid-1970s to fully encompass live sex shows, sex shops, massage parlors, escort services, phone sex, sex tours, image clubs, and exotic dancing, and to creating, as Edward Herman states, "one of the booming markets in the New World Order— a multi-billion dollar industry with finders, brokers, syndicate operations and pimp 'managers' at the scene of action" (1995:5). Sex tourism has become a new industry. Recruitment agencies and impresarios link the local sites and sex industries in various parts of the world, indicating a parallel with transnational corporations in the formal global economy. "The 'success' of the sex industry," write James Petras and Tienchai Wongchaisuwan about Thailand, "is based on a 'special relation' of shared interests among a complex network of military leaders, police officials, business tourist promoters, godfathers and pimps. At the international level, airline and hotel chains have worked closely with the local business–military elite to promote the sex tourist industry. The World Bank's support for the open economy and export oriented development strategy results in financial support of tourism" (1993:36). In Thailand, the authors estimate, direct and indirect earnings from sex enterprises is about $5 billion a year. Elsewhere, as in

Cuba and the Dominican Republic, the specter of sex tourism has become embedded in the economy. The sexual labor of young brown women in these playgrounds of the West has become increasingly important to the national economies, while prostitution remains condemned as degrading and destructive. In Cuba's case, it is viewed as a counter-revolutionary engagement. Nevertheless, State support or tolerance of this form of tourism is evident. Sex work fills the coffers of countries whose economic survival is increasingly dependent on global corporate capitalist interests.

The emerging global economic order has already wreaked havoc on women's lives. Recent studies document an increasing need of women to contribute to the household economy through waged labor, yet having to deal with declining real wages, lower wage structures than men and longer working hours.[17] Seasonal or flexible employment is the norm for women all over the world. Skilled and unskilled female workers constitute the main labor force in the new export-oriented industries—for shoe, toy, textile and garment production, in agribusinesses and electronic factories—where they are faced with poor working conditions, are continually threatened with unemployment due to automation and experience mass dismissals due to relocations of whole sectors of the industry. In many instances, minimum wage, health and safety laws are overridden by the transnational corporations in these new production zones, leaving women workers in particularly hazardous situations. Furthermore, with disruptions to traditional household and family structures, women are increasingly becoming heads of households, providing and nurturing the family. With dwindling family resources and the western emphasis on the independent nuclear family, women must also increasingly rely on the state for provisions such as maternity leave and child-care, yet fewer funds are allocated by governments for social welfare and programs.[18] Informal sector work and "moonlighting" is growing and engagement in the booming sex industries fills a gap created by globalization.

Migration is a road many take to seek other opportunities and to break away from oppressive local conditions caused by globalization. A 1996 ILO report describes the "feminization" of international labor migration as "one of the most striking economic and social phenomena of recent times" (I). This "phenomenon" according to the authors of the report, is most pronounced in Asian countries where women are migrating as "autonomous, economic agents" in their own right, "trying to seize economic opportunities overseas" (I). The Philippines has put more women onto the overseas labor market than any other country in the world (Rosca 1995). Within all this dislocation and movement, some migrant women become involved in sex work. However, laws prohibiting or regulating prostitution and migration, particularly from the South, combine to create highly complex and oppressive situations for women if they become involved in sex work once abroad. The illegal movement of persons for work elsewhere, commonly known as "trafficking" also becomes a very real issue for those who are being squeezed on all sides and have few options other than work in underground and informal sectors. Traffickers take advantage of the illegality of commercial sex work and migration, and are able to exert an undue amount of power and control over those seeking political or economic refuge or security. In such cases, it is the laws that prevent legal commercial sex work and immigration that form the major obstacles.

A related dimension to globalization with the expansion of sex industries, a heightened necessity for transnational migration for work, and increasing immiseration of women worldwide, is the spread of AIDS. Paul Farmer links the pandemic in sub-Saharan Africa to the social realities of the migrant labor system, rapid urbanization, high levels of war with military mobilization, landlessness and poverty that have been exacerbated by an economic crisis caused by "poor terms of trade, the contradictions of post-colonial economies which generate class disparities and burdensome debt service" since the mid 1970s (1996:71). These factors, he contends, are intricately intertwined with pervasive gender inequality and specific socially constructed meanings of gender and sex, creating a very complex situation regarding the epidemiology and, consequently, the prevention of AIDS. Around eighty-two percent of AIDS cases worldwide in 1996, he points out, were found in Africa, with women and children bearing the brunt of the epidemic. A similarly complex interrelationship between changing agriculture systems to meet New World Order demands, fueled by gendered traditions and inequalities, inadequate subsistence, a felt lack of desired consumption, goods, tourism and the drug trade enables the spread of AIDS in Asia (Farmer 1996:82–88). For the Americas, Bond et al. note that labor migration between the Caribbean and the United States has been an important factor in the spread of HIV and AIDS, and that "the development of tourist industries, frequently based on U.S. capital as a replacement for the decline in profits from older colonially established sources such as sugar cane, has also traced the routes for HIV to follow" (1997:7). With only an estimated four percent of the world's AIDS cases being registered in North America and Western Europe, it is particularly evident that it is the rest of the world that is at greatest risk (Farmer 1997).

This relatively new sexually transmitted disease and identification by world health authorities of a concentration of the epidemic in developing countries has led to government interventions. The attention has produced contradictions for sex workers around the world. As in the past, with state concern for public health matters, prostitutes are placed under scrutiny, subject to intense campaigning and roped into projects that define them as the vectors and transmitters of disease (Zalduondo 1991, Murray and Robinson 1996). Sex workers are continually blamed for the spread of the disease, with Eurocentric racist notions of cultural difference compounding the effect for Third World populations. Consequently, inappropriate methods of intervention have been introduced and sex workers burdened with having to take responsibility for the prevention and control of the disease. Farmer points out that " . . . while public health campaigns target sex workers, many African women take a different view of AIDS epidemiology and prevention. In their view, the epidemiology of HIV and Africa's eco-

nomic crises suggest that HIV spreads not because of the "exotic sexual practices" of Africans but because of the daily life within which women struggle to survive" (1996:74). Bond et al. in their studies of AIDS in Africa and the Caribbean apply a similar analysis. Arguing that there is "more to AIDS than 'truck drivers' and 'prostitutes'" the authors consider it of vital importance to examine relations of political and economic power in relationship to the spread of AIDS, with specific attention to the disempowered such as women and children (1997:xi). Placing the focus and blame on sex workers does not necessarily address the root of the problem but serves to push them further into marginality and social isolation. On the other hand, some AIDS-prevention work has contributed to the formation of new sex worker organizations, inadvertently empowering sex workers in other areas than just in health matters.

DISCUSSION QUESTIONS

1. Kempadoo suggests that "sex work" must be recognized as women's work deserving of basic human rights, decent work conditions, and limited exploitation. In this framework, prostitution is an occupation susceptible (like any other work in countries feeling the impact of capitalist globalization) to exploitation and thus able to be organized like any working group for better conditions. Discuss the pros and cons of such a position.

2. Sex workers both are victims and have agency to act on their own behalf.
   - First, explain both sides of this coin.
   - Next, explain what Kempadoo means when she says it is a "bad idea" to see sex workers exclusively as victims.

3. Globalization leads to upheavals in employment in third-world countries. Describe how sex industries in these

countries fill some of the income-generating gap created by globalization.

4. Discuss parallels and differences between this chapter's description of sex workers and Maher's (chap. 7) description of women working in the illegal drug trade
   - in terms of the racialized and gendered implications.
   - in terms of the impact of income generation from the sex industry and from the illegal drug trade in Brooklyn, New York.

NOTES

1. "Third World Women" is used here in keeping with the definition proposed by various "Third-World feminists," which captures the notion of a collectivity whose lives are conditioned and shaped by the struggles against neo-colonialism and imperialism, capitalism and gender subordination. See for example, the writings by Chandra Talpade, "Under Western Eyes: Feminist Scholarship and Colonial Discourses," in C. T. Mohanty, Ann Russo and Lourdes Torres, eds., *Third World Women and the Politics of Feminism* (Bloomington: Indiana University Press, 1991) and "Women Workers and Capitalist Scripts: Ideologies of Domination, Common Interest and the Politics of Solidarity," in M. Jaqui Alexander and C. T. Mohanty, eds., *Feminist Geneologies, Colonial Legacies, Democratic Futures* (New York: Routledge, 1997) 3–29; Chela Sandoval, "U.S. Third World Feminism: The Theory and Method of Oppositional Consciousness in the Postmodern World," *Genders,* vol. 10 (Spring 1994) 1–24; Uma Narayan, "Contesting Cultures:'Westernization,' Respect for Cultures and Third-World Feminists," in Linda Nicholson, ed., *The Second Wave: A Reader in Feminist Theory* (New York and London: Routledge, 1996) 396–414; Geraldine Heng, "'A Great Way to Fly': Nationalism, the State and Varieties of Third-World Feminism," in M. Jaqui Alexander

and C. T. Mohanty, eds., *Feminist Geneologies, Colonial Legacies, Democratic Futures* (New York: Routledge, 1997) 30–45.

2. See Frederique Delacoste and Priscilla Alexander, *Sex Work: Writings by Women in the Sex Industry* (Pittsburgh: Cleis Press, 1987); Laurie Bell, ed., *Good Girls: Feminists and Sex Trade Workers Face to Face* (Toronto: The Women's Press, 1987); Gail Pheterson, ed., *A Vindication of the Rights of Whores* (Washington: Seal Press, 1989); Nickie Roberts, *Whores in History: Prostitution in Western Society* (London: Harper Collins 1992); Valerie Jenness, *Making It Work: The Prostitutes' Rights Movement in Perspective* (Hawthorne, NY: Aldine de Gruyter, 1993); Anne McClintock, "Sex Workers and Sex Work: Introduction," *Social Text,* vol. 37 (Winter 1993) 1–10; Shannon Bell, *Reading, Writing and Rewriting the Prostitute Body* (Bloomington: Indiana University Press, 1994); Wendy Chapkis, *Live Sex Acts: Women Performing Erotic Labor* (New York: Routledge, 1997); Jill Nagle, ed., *Whores and Other Feminists* (New York: Routledge, 1997).

3. A position argued by Kathleen Barry, *The Prostitution of Sexuality: The Global Exploitation of Women* (New York: New York University Press, 1995).

4. Antony Swift reporting on the conference for the *New Internationalist,* describes perspectives and demands of child worker organizations from South and Central America, West Africa, and Asia. The entire issue of the magazine documents the emergence of vocal and articulate organized struggles for the rights of working children.

5. This perspective also underpins the Anti-Slavery International examination of existing international human rights and labor standards and instruments in relation to prostitution. See Jo Bindman and Jo Doezema, *Redefining Prostitution as Sex Work on the International Agenda* (London: Anti-Slavery International, 1997) and NSWP: The Network of Sex Work Projects.

6. Antony Gidden's *The Constitution of Society: Outline of the Theory of Structuration* (Cambridge:

Polity Press, 1984) and Pierre Bourdieu's *Outline of a Theory of Practice* (Cambridge University Press, 1977) are of particular interest here. Both stress the interwovenness of human agency and social structure whenever, according to the Marxian idea, humans "make their own history, but not in circumstances of their own choosing" stressing the ways in which humans produce and reproduce social, economic and political life. Sherry Ortner notes in her elaboration of practice theory, in *Making Gender: The Politics and Erotics of Culture:* "The challenge is to picture indissoluble formations of structurally embedded agency and intention-filled structures, to recognize the way in which the subject is part of larger social and cultural webs, and in which social and cultural 'systems' are predicated upon human desires and projects" (Boston: Beacon Press, 1996:12).

7. See Luise White, *The Comforts of Home: Prostitution in Colonial Nigeria* (Chicago: University of Chicago Press 1990); Than-Dam Troung, *Sex, Money and Morality: The Political Economy of Prostitution and Tourism in South East Asia* (London: Zed Books, 1990), James A. Tyner "Constructions of Filipina Migrant Entertainers," *Gender, Place and Culture,* vol. 3:1 (1996), 77–93; Anne McClintock, "Screwing the System: Sexwork, Race and the Law," *Boundary* 2 vol. 19, (Summer 1992), 70–95.

8. See Paola Tabet, "'I'm the Meat, I'm the Knife': Sexual Service, Migration and Repression in Some African Societies," in Gail Pheterson, ed., *Vindication of the Rights of Whores* (Washington: Seal Press, 1989) 204–226; Gloria Wekker, "'I Am Gold Money' (I Pass Through All Hands, But I Do Not Lose My Value): The Construction of Selves, Gender and Sexualities in a Female Working-Class, Afro-Surinamese Setting." Dissertation, University of California, 1992: Luise White, *The Comforts of Home: Prostitution in Colonial Nigeria* (Chicago: University of Chicago Press, 1990); Barbara de Zalduonda and Jean Maxius Bernard, "Meanings and Consequences of Sexual-Economic Exchange: Gender, Poverty and Sexual Risk Behavior in Urban Haiti," in *Conceiving Sexuality: Approaches to Sex Research in a Postmodern World,* ed. Richard G. Parker and John M. Gagnon (New York: Routledge, 1995) 157–80. These are studies of culturally specific "sexual-economic" relationships, in which women's bodies are not regarded as sacred sites, but rather sexuality is experienced as a resource that is strategically employed. See Lyn Sharon Chancer, "Prostitution, Feminist Theory and Ambivalance: Notes from the Sociological Underground," *Social Text,* vol. 37 (Winter 1993) 143–181. Chancer suggests that we can speak of "bodily" or "sexual capital" to distinguish the type of human resource that women and men draw upon for sex work.

9. See Hazel Carby, "White Women Listen! Black Feminism and the Boundaries of Sisterhood," in Centre for Contemporary Cultural Studies' *The Empire Strikes Back: Race and Racism in 70s Britain* (London: Hutchinson, 1982). Carby writing about this general trend in 1982, notes that "too often concepts of historical progress are invoked by the left and feminists alike, to create a sliding scale of 'civilized liberties.' " When barbarous sexual practices are to be described, the "Third World" is on display and compared to the "First World" which is seen to be more "enlightened" and "progressive" (216). In a similar vein, Marchand argues that "the implicit assumption is, of course, that when non-Western women have reached our level of modernization, they will subscribe to western feminist ideals. As a result the western feminist agenda can be presented (and defended) as embodying universal feminist values . . . " See Marianne H. Marchand, "Latin American Women Speak on Development: Are We Listening Yet?", in M. H. Marchand and Jane L. Parpart, eds., *Feminism, Postmodernism, Development* (London: Routledge, 1995) 59.

10. Similarly, McClintock, while stating that "sex workers do not speak with a univocal voice: there is not a single, authoritative narrative of prostitution . . . " nevertheless manage successfully

to make generalizations about "the prostitute" that are drawn exclusively from Western European and North American contexts (1993). See also Floya Anthias and Nira Yuval-Davis, *Racialized Boundaries: Race, Nation, Gender, Colour, Class and the Anti-Racist Struggle* (London: Routledge, 1992). Anthias and Yuval-Davis urge caution about such theorizing under the name of postmodernism, concluding that "there is a danger that 'the specificity of a particular experience' may itself become an expression of essentialism. To posit diversity therefore does not necessarily imply the abandonment of static and a-historical categories but may merely proliferate them" (99).

11. Apart from McClintock see also Jenness (1993), Gail Pheterson (1989), and Delacoste and Alexander (1987) as examples where the assumed reference point for developing generalized claims about "the" prostitutes' rights movement derive primarily from Western European and Euro-American contexts and experiences. In contrast, analyses of the sex industries and sex work in non-western and Third World countries are highly contextualized in terms of history, culture, gender relations, and location in the global economy. See for example, Troung, *Sex, Money and Morality* (London: Zed Books, 1990); Saundra Pollock Sturdevant and Brenda Stoltzfus, *Let the Good Times Roll: Prostitution and the U.S. Military in Asia* (New York: The New Press, 1992); Anne Allison, *Nightwork: Sexuality, Pleasure, and Corporate Masculinity in a Tokyo Hostess Club* (Chicago: University of Chicago Press, 1994); Cleo Odzer, *Patpong Sisters: An American Woman's View of the Bangkok Sex World* (New York: Arcade Publishing, 1994); and Carolyn Sleightholme and Indrani Sinha, *Guilty Without Trial: Women in the Sex Trade in Calcutta* (New Brunswick: Rutgers University Press, 1996).

12. Within this argument is also the notion that what may be defined for one race/ethnic, class or gendered group as oppressive could under conditions of racial domination or colonialism, be a site of resistance and potential liberation or at least a site of multiple meanings and contradictions. The construct of the family as singularly oppressive for women has thus been challenged. Likewise concepts of "the erotic," "patriarchy" and "womanhood" have been rescued from white feminist theory and redefined from Third-World/Black/anti-imperialist feminist perspectives to reflect the history and experiences of "the other."

13. See Patricia Hill Collins, *Black Feminist Thought: Knowledge, Consciousness and the Politics of Empowerment* (New York: Routledge, 1990); and Laurie Shrage, *Moral Dilemmas of Feminism: Prostitution, Adultery, and Abortion* (New York: Routledge, 1994). In the U.S., Collins notes "Perhaps the most curious omission has been the virtual silence of the Black feminist community concerning the participation of far too many Black women in prostitution. Ironically, while the image of African-American women as prostitutes has been aggressively challenged, the reality of African-American women who work as prostitutes remain unexplored" (164). Taking her cue from Collins, Shrage insists that "few researchers have explored how race and gender together condition one's participation in prostitution" (142). Sadly, even with these sharp observations neither author is able to get any further. In Collin's brief coverage of the subject, Black women in prostitution are situated as "victim and pet," with the force of her analysis attacking the relations of dominance that historically constructed this position. She gives no consideration to notions of Black female sexual agency but rather positions Black women as objects that have been formed by purely external forces and conditions. Shrage on the other hand, remains safely within an examination of representations and images. Both, in the end, manage to leave the void they signalled unfilled.

14. As an example of this careless use, see Robert I. Friedman, "India's Shame," *The Nation* April 8, 1996) 11–20.

15. See Sarah Anderson and John Cavanagh, *The Top 200: The Rise of Global Corporate Power* (Washington, DC: Institute for Policy Studies, 1996).

In this survey of the world's largest corporations, Anderson and Cavanagh, found that "of the top 100 largest economies in the world, 51 are now global corporations, only 49 are countries" with Wal-Mart, bigger than 161 countries, Mitsubishi "larger than the fourth most populous nation on earth: Indonesia" and Ford's economy larger than that of South Africa.

16. See Noam Chomsky, *World Orders Old and New* (New York: Columbia University, 1994); Jeremy Brecher and Tim Costello, *Global Village or Global Pillage: Economic Reconstruction, From the Bottom Up* (Boston: South End, 1994); see also, Kevin Danaher, ed., *Fifty Years Is Enough: The Case Against the World Bank and the International Monetary Fund* (Boston: South End, 1994).

17. For details on gender inequalities worldwide see the United Nation publications: *Human Development Report 1995* and *The World's Women 1995: Trends and Statistics.*

18. Among the many who have written specifically on women in the New World Order, see Carmen Diana Deere, et al., *In the Shadows of the Sun: Caribbean Development Alternatives and U.S. Policy* (Boulder: Westview, 1990); Sheila Rowbotham and Swasti Mitter, eds., *Dignity and Daily Bread: New Forms of Economic Organizing Among Poor Women in the Third World and The First* (London: Routledge, 1994); M. Jaqui Alexander and Chandra Talpade Mohanty, eds., *Feminist Geneologies, Colonial Legacies, Democratic Futures* (New York: Routledge, 1997); Edna Bonacich, et al., eds., *Global Production: The Apparel Industry in the Pacific Rim* (Philadelphia: Temple University, 1994); and Annie Phizacklea and Carol Wolkowitz, *Homeworking Women: Gender, Racism and Class at Work* (London: Sage, 1995).

Chapter 9

The War on Drugs and the War on Abortion

Lynn M. Paltrow

ABSTRACT

In this chapter, Paltrow, a lawyer who works on behalf of women's right to control their own bodies, makes the argument that government efforts in the United States to control reproduction and to control drug use are closely related. Both, she says, are grounded in the same sexist and racist systems of prejudice and oppression. Paltrow points out that historically drug laws have been based on appeals to racist fears. And reproductive health care, access to abortion, and the availability of contraception information are deliberately blocked by the U.S. government. In fact, given the conservative political climate under President George W. Bush the United States is moving in the direction of either overturning *Roe v. Wade* or severely restricting women's right to abortion. Ironically, while the government refuses to fund abortion services for poor women, it does fund permanent sterilization services. Sadly, the reader learns that the medical profession has been accepting of government intrusions into medical practices related to both abortion and drug use.

Paltrow concludes that both pregnancy and drug "epidemics" are issues that the government uses to stress individual deviance while it ignores the more fundamental social problems of unemployment, poverty, racism, and sexism. In recent years, one of the most publicized government actions in the name of protecting fetal rights has been the effort in many states to enact criminal penalties directed at women who use drugs while pregnant. Although many of these laws have been overturned, they are based on many myths surrounding "choice" as it pertains to reproduction and drug use. These myths are described in this chapter. The final section discusses the disproportionate impact of misguided government intrusion on African American women, who, Paltrow points out, are caught at the intersection of the war on reproductive rights and the war on drugs, including crack.

Paltrow also helps us understand in very concrete terms the importance of an analysis based on race, class, and gender. Thus, she shows that whether addressing drugs or abortion, efforts to criminalize and punish have historically "relied on the pretense that it was necessary to protect middle class white women and to reinforce their traditional place in society." Today, however, those systems of control and punishment have shifted, so they impact most harshly on poor minority, especially black, women who are pregnant and who use drugs.

This chapter echoes themes found in other chapters of this book. One of these themes is that when government focuses on the "immorality" of individuals—scapegoating drug users, for example—it diverts attention away from the structural problems that lead to individual troubles and it fails to further social justice. In short, discussions in this chapter anticipate a number of topics covered in part 2 of this book ("Women and Prison"), including the key issues of (1) overincarceration of women; (2) governmental investment of money in building and maintaining prisons rather than community programs such as job training, day care, and health maintenance; and (3) the plight of children of incarcerated women.

While many people view the war on abortion and the war on drugs as distinct, there are in fact many connections and overlaps between the two. Their history, the strategies used to control and punish some reproductive choices and those to control the use of certain drugs, the limitations that exist to access to reproductive health care and drug treatment, and the populations most harmed by those limitations are remarkably similar. These similarities are particularly apparent where the issues coalesce in the regulation and punishment of pregnant, drug-using women.[1]

Those who are concerned about fundamental issues of social justice may be losing ground, missing opportunities to build coalitions and strengthen arguments by failing to recognize the similarities among and relationships between the issues.

A comparison of the efforts to control reproduction and some (but significantly, not all) drug use reveals much about those who seek to control both and about their true agendas. If efforts to control reproduction and drugs are rooted in forms of bigotry and prejudice that are essentially the same, neither drug addiction nor pregnancy should be a basis for

scapegoating some individuals or for dividing progressive coalitions. If efforts to control both reflect a common political agenda, and are used to draw attention away from real underlying issues like poverty, race discrimination, and lack of a coherent national health-care policy, then those who fight against each must recognize that they have a common cause and develop a more comprehensive strategy that addresses both as fundamental issues of social justice rather than as single, separate and special interest issues. Finally, if some people—African American women—are particularly harmed by these efforts to control reproduction and some drug use,[2] there is both an opportunity and a need to develop interventions that respond effectively and specifically to these harms and to the barriers they face.

Only by recognizing those shared aspects of measures to control reproduction and drug use can we have the opportunity to develop more effective responses to each. While some of the parallels that are drawn in this examination may be inapt, and more cogent ones might be added by people better versed than this author in drug control policy and the history of reproductive rights, the similarities discussed here are intended to stimulate further exploration and discussion.

CONTROLLING REPRODUCTION, CONTROLLING DRUGS

Throughout history, women have sought to control their reproduction regardless of cultural, religious or family proscriptions against contraception, abortion

Editor's note: Footnote numbers refer to the original footnotes. These and the bibliography to this chapter are available at http://advocatesforpregnantwomen.org/articles/wod_abort.htm. For the reader's convenience, a brief list of selected sources is included at the end of the chapter.

Source: Linda Paltrow "The War on Drugs and The War on Abortion *Southern Law Review* (2001), 28:201.

and child bearing.[3] Similarly, people have always sought to alter their state of consciousness through a wide range of mind altering experiences and drugs, some of them associated with religious rites.[4] Thus, one obvious connection between the two subjects is that both relate to what people do and have always done, with or to their own bodies, even in the face of severe restrictions.

Both also reflect the extremes of the human experience. On the one hand, sex and drugs can give people mind expanding, life affirming, ecstatic experiences.[5] Each, however, can be associated with violence, abuse, and despair. A woman's relationship to her sexuality and her ability to reproduce may be affected deeply and permanently by experiences of incest, molestation and rape, all far too common in the lives of American women.[6] Similarly, for those who turn to drugs to numb the pain of such experiences,[7] drug use frequently becomes chaotic, dangerous and out of control.[8] Thus, efforts to address sexuality, reproduction and drug use all require responses that take into account an extremely broad range of experience and the disparate needs that emerge from that experience.

To state the obvious, both issues are marked by controversy, passion and politics. The temperament of that controversy however is surprisingly similar. What has been written about drug issues applies with equal descriptive accuracy to reproductive health issues: They are both "hopelessly intertwined with deeply ingrained notions of morality and sin, religious-style certitude, and righteous indignation."[9]

PROHIBITION

Both abortion and certain drugs have been outlawed at various times in American history. Another similarity: Even when outlawed and enforced through draconian measures, the effect of efforts to prohibit both abortion and drug use have been notoriously and consistently unsuccessful.[10] Not only do women continue to have abortions and people continue to use those drugs that have been outlawed, the criminalization of these activities results in flourishing illegal markets,[11] and a deeply ingrained cynicism

toward the government authority that attempts to enforce the law.[12]

JUSTIFYING CONTROL AND PUNISHMENT

Reproduction and drug use share many commonalities when it comes to justifications for prohibition and regulation. In both cases, various forms of stigma and prejudice, including but not limited to those based on race, ethnicity, and gender, have been employed to justify such control. For example, abortion became illegal in the United States, in part based on appeals to xenophobia and nativism.[13] As Carole Joffe summarizes: "The drive to criminalize abortion, which started in mid-century and peaked by the early 1880's, when all the states had enacted antiabortion statutes, stemmed from a variety of motivations, including societal anxiety about the declining birth rates of Anglo-Saxon women in comparison to those of newly arriving immigrants."[14] Similarly, efforts to sterilize certain populations have been justified by various forms of stigma and prejudice, including but not limited to those based on class and race.[15]

With respect to laws aimed at drug use, they too have been based on appeals to racist fears, in many instances unambiguously so:

> Racism was called into play early on. Popular literature of the time shows that racist propaganda, which played on white men's insecurities about their own power, flourished at the end of the 19th century. Among other things, the notion that using cocaine would heighten the desire of black men to rape white women was widely proclaimed. The same was held to be true with regard to the use of opium by Chinese men. Fears of "hopped up Negroes" and "opium smoking Chinamen" fueled anti-drug sentiment, especially in the South and West. Despite the fact that, at the time, the majority of addicts were actually those white housewives hooked on patent medicines, the alleged threat to "our women," viewed as poor innocents, was used to heighten moral outrage over intoxication.[16]

More recently, enforcement and increased penalties for using certain drugs were seen during the

Nixon administration as a way of controlling particular populations, specifically youth and black people.[17]

Today, the expansion of the war on drugs has been justified, at least in part by images of crack-using women, particularly pregnant African American women. By associating crack and its alleged harms with low-income African American women,[18] people have been willing both to believe vast amounts of misinformation about cocaine's effects[19] and to respond with a variety of proposals for punishing pregnant women and new mothers[20] rather than with calls for medical investigation, improved treatment and services including financial support for the women whose problems are significantly related to poverty.[21]

Whether addressing abortion or drugs, efforts to criminalize and punish also relied on the pretense that it was necessary to protect middle class white women and to reinforce their traditional place in society. The original efforts to outlaw abortion were led by physicians of the newly formed American Medical Association who wanted to establish their professional status by taking "control of the terms under which 'approved' abortions were performed."[22] By taking abortion out of the control of women and away from the physicians' business competitors—healers, homeopaths and midwives—doctors could monopolize this area of medical practice. Among the arguments the doctors used to justify this campaign was that abortion represented a threat to male authority over women. As the authors of an 1871 AMA report asserted about women who had abortions:

> She becomes unmindful of the course marked out for her by Providence, she overlooks the duties imposed on her by the marriage contract. She yields to the pleasures—but shrinks from the pains and responsibilities of maternity; and, destitute of all delicacy and refinement, resigns herself, body and soul, into the hands of unscrupulous and wicked men. Let not the husband of such a wife flatter himself that he possesses her affection. Nor can she in turn ever merit even the respect of a virtuous husband. She sinks into old age like a withered tree, stripped of its foliage; and with the stain of blood upon her soul, she dies without the hand of affection to smooth her pillow.[23]

Carrying these views forward, doctors in the 1930's claimed that "if women know they can destroy the fetus very easily, they become lax in their sexual morals."[24]

Similarly, "drug policy was constructed by dominant groups" as a mechanism for preserving "white women's innocence."[25] Assertions that white women would be raped by men of color on drugs perpetuated racist views of men of color, mythologized the effect that certain drugs have, and simultaneously portrayed white women as vulnerable and in need of protection, thus ignoring their status as moral agents, and distracting attention from victimization they might be encountering at the hands of white men.

In addition, drug policy itself has been used to reinforce stereotypes about different groups of women. Nancy Campbell elucidates how at various times, "white women are represented as using drugs to remain functional, orderly, and clean, while women of color who use drugs are depicted as the nonproductive inhabitants of chaos, decay and squalor."[26] Similarly Campbell notes that during the 1950's, "addicted white women were diagnosed with personality disorders; addicted women of color were 'sociopathically disturbed' and hence more 'deviant.'"[27]

The control of both drug use and reproduction have thus been justified by resort to popular prejudices and particular fears about certain populations and in turn used to reinforce deeply embedded stereotypes about the particular populations.

CONTROLLING SPEECH ABOUT DRUGS AND REPRODUCTION

Indirect methods of control, including restrictions on free speech concerning the beneficial uses of contraception, abortion, and those drugs deemed illegal are also remarkably similar. In 1961, Justice William O. Douglas observed that "the right of the doctor to advise his patients according to his best lights seems so obviously within First Amendment rights as to need no extended discussion."[28] This, however, has been anything but obvious when it comes to state regulation of information about both reproductive health care and drugs. To the contrary: government leaders have sought vigorously to suppress the dissemination of information about drugs and devices known unequivocally to save lives and to improve health and well-being.

In 1873, the Comstock law labeled advise on contraception and abortion "obscene, lewd, lascivious, and filthy."[29] This law, among other things, made it a crime to transport by the public mail system material including:

> Every obscene, lewd, or lascivious, and every filthy book, pamphlet, picture, paper, letter, writing, print, or other publication of an indecent character, and every article or thing designed, adapted, or intended for preventing conception or producing abortion, or for any indecent or immoral use; and every article, instrument, substance, drug, medicine, or thing which is advertised or described in a manner calculated to lead another to use or apply it for preventing conception or producing abortion, or for any indecent or immoral purpose.[30]

Until 1965 it was still illegal for Connecticut doctors, in the privacy of their offices, to advise married couples that contraception could prevent unwanted pregnancy and the health risks associated with it.[31] Until 1977 restriction on the sale and advertisement of contraception were still on the books in New York State and elsewhere.[32] Even today, US Supreme Court doctrine permits speech restrictions on the provision of reproductive health information—abortion—by doctors in certain government programs. As recently as 1991, the United States Supreme Court upheld "the gag rule" which prohibits a project funded under Title X—the federal program that funds family planning programs across the country—from engaging in activities that encourage, promote or advocate abortion as a method of family planning.[33]

Using a very similar strategy, the federal government, in response to passage of California's Proposition 215, "the Compassionate Use of Marijuana Act," threatened doctors with criminal prosecution, loss of Medicaid and Medicare payments and revocation of their federal prescription drug licenses if they advised their patients about medical benefits of marijuana.[34] This 1996 law provides, in part, that:

> Seriously ill Californians have the right to obtain and use marijuana for medical purposes where that medical use is deemed appropriate and has been recommended by a physician who has determined that the person's health would benefit from the use of marijuana in the treatment of cancer, anorexia, AIDS, chronic pain, spasticity, glaucoma, arthritis, migraine, or any other illness for which marijuana provides relief.[35]

Despite extensive evidence of the beneficial effects of marijuana,[36] it remains classified as an illegal drug whose distribution, sale and medical prescription are all illegal under federal law.[37] In May 2001, the United States Supreme Court rejected the argument that medical marijuana distributors could use a medical-necessity defense to the federal law criminalizing marijuana. While the court did not strike down California's compassionate use act, or address the availability of a medical necessity defense for the patients who somehow manage to get medical marijuana, the Court based its decision, in part, on the 1970 congressional finding that marijuana has "no currently accepted medical use."[38]

Thus even when it is clear that certain drugs or contraceptive devices could improve people's health, the government has used control over medical practice as a mechanism for preventing dissemination of that knowledge and information.

ACCESS TO REPRODUCTIVE HEALTH CARE AND DRUG TREATMENT

In both arenas, the state not only restricts information about medically safe and useful procedures, it also restricts access to them. In the case of reproduction, access to abortion, contraception and other reproductive health care is deliberately blocked or limited. In the case of drug use, access to treatment and other approaches that can reduce the harmful effects of drug use are deliberately blocked or limited.

For example, even though abortion is now legal, and has long been recognized as safe,[39] access is extremely limited as the result of a wide variety of restrictive laws. As Joffe explains:

Some 84 percent of all U.S. counties are without abortion facilities. The number of U.S. hospitals where abortions are performed decreased by 18 percent between 1988 and 1992, and less than one third of the nation's hospitals with the capability to perform abortions (defined as hospitals that offer obstetrical services) do so.[40] The majority of ob/gyns presently in practice do not perform abortions, and most residents in this specialty are not routinely being trained in abortion procedures.[41]

All sorts of restrictions exist in the abortion context for procedures that are safe and medically approved—from mandated counseling unrelated to the patient's needs, to unnecessary waiting periods, to notification requirements designed to delay and intimidate.[42] Until September 28, 2000, RU486, a medication known to be both safe and effective in inducing early abortion was banned in America, despite years of favorable research results in the U.S. and experience in other countries.[43]

Similarly, access to safe and effective treatment for drug addiction is deliberately limited in America today.[44] "Methadone is the most effective treatment for heroin addiction, yet government regulations largely block its prescription by primary-care physicians and its sale by pharmacies, instead limiting methadone distribution to special clinics (which tend to be poorly staffed and inconveniently located)."[45] Methadone's benefits "have been established by hundreds of scientific studies,"[46] and yet:

> . . . Methadone can be prescribed exclusively by "comprehensive treatment programmes," and not by physicians in their private offices, in hospital clinics, in community health centres, etc. Collectively, these programmes can accommodate less than 15% of those whom methadone treatment might help.[47]

Likewise, abortion services are now largely limited to free standing clinics. Although this was not the result of specific federal legislation as in the case of methadone treatment,[48] the isolation of abortion services from mainstream medical care similarly leaves patients and staff without adequate access to abortion services and, in addition, permits patients and staff to be easily targeted for violence and harassment.[49] Particular harms of these systems are startlingly similar, including harrowing stories of both methadone patients and abortion patients having to travel hundreds of miles to the "nearest clinic."[50]

While communities across the country have been using zoning laws to keep abortion clinics from opening, similar laws have long been used to prevent the establishment of methadone programs.[51] Moreover, efforts in both arenas, to give people greater access to health care through private physicians face serious hurdles. For example, although it was hoped that the availability of RU486 would enable significant numbers of women to get procedures from private physicians, abortion restrictions on the books may make the delivery of such services illegal,[52] just as private physicians still cannot prescribe methadone.[53]

Access has also been blocked to many "harm reduction" techniques that have proved effective both in terms of public health and cost savings.[54] Proponents of harm reduction recognize:

> Overcoming drug addiction is usually a difficult and gradual process. [Harm reductionists] seek to turn public policy away from punitive criminal justice approaches and toward providing drug abusers with information and assistance that can help them reduce consumption and minimize the risks associated with their continuing drug use. Harm reductionists favor drug treatment over imprisonment and favor broadening drug treatment to include non-abstinence-based models.[55]

As Ethan Nadelmann explains, "harm-reduction innovations include efforts to stem the spread of HIV by making sterile syringes readily available and collecting used syringes."[56] Making clean needles available to injection drug users through needle exchange programs[57] and permitting their sale at pharmacies[58] have proven highly effective in curtailing the transmission of HIV/AIDS and hepatitis.[59] This has also been shown to be an important first step in helping drug users obtain drug information, treatment, detoxification, social services and primary health care.[60] Moreover, numerous public health groups including the American Medical Association, the National Institutes of Health, the Centers for Disease Control and Prevention, and the Institute of Medicine, have endorsed needle exchange programs.[61] Despite the fact that government sponsored research has shown that such programs do not lead to increased drug use and does have numerous positive health effects, the federal policy prohibits use of its funds for such life- and cost-saving measures.[62]

The common governmental orientation toward control and punishment in both drug policy and reproductive health care policy is reflected in the funding priorities of each. The $16 billion dollar budget for drug law enforcement, interdiction and supply reduction represents two thirds of the total federal budget addressing drug use in this country.[63] And while the government ignores the need for treatment, the lack of treatment for women is even more acute.[64]

Similarly, the government refuses to fund abortion services for poor women[65] while ensuring that funding is available for permanent sterilization services for the same population of women.[66] The government has failed to increase adequately funding for the Title X family planning program, and fails to require private insurers to provide adequate coverage of contraceptive services and supplies.[67]

In stark contrast to the situation in other developed nations, where contraceptives are easily affordable under universal health insurance systems, contraceptive supplies and services are expensive in this country and American women must rely on a variety of fragmented systems and programs to help them cover these costs.[68]

The federal government has also permitted the states to deny increased "welfare" payments to a woman who conceives and bears another child while she is on welfare,[69] and state funding for a range of women's reproductive health care including screening and treatment for cervical cancer, sexually transmitted diseases, HIV prevention for women and obstetrical and gynecological care for low-income women—reflect a policy of extreme neglect.[70]

INTERFERING WITH MEDICAL PRACTICE AND THE MEDICAL PROFESSION'S RESPONSE

According to AMA ethical guidelines, a fundamental element of the Patient-Physician relationship includes the patient's "right to receive information from physicians and to discuss the benefits, risks, and costs of appropriate treatment alternatives."[71] These guidelines also state that, "patients should receive guidance from their physicians as to the optimal course of action" and that patients have a right to confidentiality.[72]

Many restrictions on both reproductive health care and certain drugs interfere with the physician's ability to follow these guidelines as well as their ability to prescribe treatment that may be most beneficial to the patient. For example, the "gag rule" on Title X providers would prevent doctors in these programs from mentioning abortion even if that was deemed to be the optimal medical course of action for a patient. Similarly, mandatory and scripted abortion consent laws force doctors to act as government spokespersons, in effect expressing the State's "preference for childbirth over abortion."[73] A doctor, for example, might have to inform a woman about state published materials describing the availability of child support from the father,[74] even if the pregnancy resulted from a rape or the woman had already spent years unsuccessfully attempting to collect child support for the children she already had.

Numerous states have passed what have been labeled "TRAP" regulations: Targeted Regulation of Abortion Providers.[75] "TRAP" laws regulate the medical practices or facilities of doctors who provide abortions by imposing burdensome and unnecessary requirements that are not mandated for comparable medical services.[76] Examples of these regulations are rules permitting state agencies to copy and remove patient records, jeopardizing patient confidentiality, or mandating unique structural or administrative specifications that are not medically warranted and that increase costs so significantly that doctors are dissuaded from providing abortion services.[77]

Attempts by the federal government to silence California doctors and prevent them from recommending medical marijuana would also prevent doctors from discussing with their patients the "optimal course of action." Drug laws in the United States also interfere with doctors' ability to provide the care deemed most appropriate for a patient. In England, doctors have at times had "broad discretion to prescribe whatever drugs help addicted patients manage their lives and stay away from illegal drugs and their dealers."[78] This is not the case in the United States. And, according to Mike Gray, as a result of drug law enforcement, doctors are extremely limited in their ability to prescribe narcotic pain medication to patients who need it and have largely "abandoned" patients with chronic pain who need ongoing narcotic painkillers "just to get out of bed."[79]

Despite these and other intrusions on medical practice in the name of abortion regulation and the war on drugs, the medical community has been relatively accepting of these measures. As discussed earlier, it was in fact the medical community that initially sought criminalization of abortion. And while leading medical groups did, nearly a century later, take positions supporting reform of such laws,[80] Carol Joffe argues, that today, "it is the medical community itself, and not [radical antiabortion groups like] Operation Rescue, that bears chief responsibility for the present marginalization of abortion provision."[81]

Similarly, Mike Gray argues that the medical profession made it easy for laws criminalizing certain drugs, originally disguised as tax regulations, to replace professional medical judgment:

> It may seem strange that a guild as powerful as the American Medical Association would allow a bunch of Treasury men to wade into their profession and start telling them how to write prescriptions, but the fact is most doctors found the narcotics issue disgusting. Addiction wasn't studied in medical school, nobody seemed to know much about it, and the only experience for most physicians these days was the occasional junkie who showed up wild-eyed, unwashed, and desperate, terrorizing everybody in the waiting room. Every word from his mouth was likely to be a lie and if you turned your back he'd clean the place out. (The average physician would probably have been astounded to know that only a decade before, many of the wretched desperados had held down jobs, owned homes, and raised families.) The medical profession was more than happy to turn this ugly problem over to the Treasury Department.[82]

Today, education in medical school about both abortion and addiction remains extremely limited. Only 12 percent of United States residency programs in obstetrics and gynecology require routine training in first trimester abortions.[83] Less than one percent of the curriculum in U.S. medical schools is devoted to drug abuse and addiction.[84]

"EPIDEMICS" OF DRUGS AND PREGNANCY

Very often, identical language is used to describe and define the terms of the public discussion about both drugs and reproduction. In the recent past, both the use of cocaine and pregnancy by teenagers have been reported and decried as "epidemics." Virtually everyone has heard about the crack "epidemic" of the 1980's. This term was used by policy-makers and media moguls to suggest that crack use was rampant across all strata of the U.S. population and as a justification for more punitive law enforcement measures. Government data and research into actual use patterns, however reveal that overall cocaine use was in fact down during this period and that "if the word 'epidemic' is used to mean a disease or disease-like condition that is 'widespread' or 'prevalent' then there has never been an epidemic of crack addiction (or even crack use) among the vast majority of Americans."[85] As authors Reinarman and Levine explain, a more proper use of the word epidemic would be to describe the extensive use of alcohol and tobacco.[86]

Significantly, during almost exactly the same period, the press and activists coined the term—an "epidemic of teen pregnancy." As Kristin Luker explains, "by the early 1980's Americans had come to believe that teenagers were becoming pregnant in epidemic numbers."[87] "Ironically (in view of all the media attention), births to teenagers actually declined in the 1970s and 1980s."[88] In fact in the 1980's "contrary to prevailing stereotypes—older women and white women were slowly replacing African Americans and teens as the largest groups within the population of unwed mothers."[89] Correctly applying the terminology required the conclusion that the "real 'epidemic' occurred when Dwight Eisenhower was in the White House and poodle skirts were the height of fashion."[90]

While there actually was no epidemic of cocaine use or teenage pregnancy, the use of that language did serve political purposes. As Reinarman and Levine argue:

> Crack was a godsend to the Right. They used it and the drug issue as an ideological fig leaf to place over the unsightly urban ills that had increased markedly under Reagan administration social and economic policies. "The drug problem" served conservative politicians as an all-purpose scapegoat. They could blame an array of problems on the deviant individuals and then expand the nets of social control to imprison people for causing the problems.[91]

Similarly, Kristin Luker observed that "pregnant teenagers made a convenient lightning rod for the anxieties and tensions in American's lives. Economic fortunes were unstable, a postindustrial economic order was evolving, and sexual and reproductive patterns were mutating. Representing such teenagers as the epitome of society's ills seemed one quick way of making sense of these enormous changes."[92] More specifically, poverty could be blamed on the "sexual and reproductive decisions that poor teenaged women make."[93]

Luker's research demonstrates that early childbearing was not a widespread phenomenon and that it would not impoverish women who were not already poor.[94] As she concluded: "Childbearing among teenagers has relatively little effect on the levels of poverty in the United States. But income disparities have become a pervasive fact of American life, and it is scarcely surprising that when ex-

perts . . . labeled 'teenage pregnancy' a fundamental cause of poverty, Americans were willing to listen.[95]

Both drug and pregnancy epidemics are used to redirect attention to "individual deviance, immorality, or weakness"[96] and away from fundamental, pervasive problems like unemployment, poverty, racism and sexism that drastically reduce individuals' ability to exercise choice and maintain control over their lives.[97]

JUST SAYING NO TO COMPREHENSIVE SEX AND DRUG EDUCATION PROGRAMS

Similarities also exist in government endorsement of and funding for prevention programs. Candid and comprehensive education programs that distinguish between the use and abuse of drugs, and that accept the inevitability that some young people will experiment with drugs and engage in sexual activity, can help prevent unwanted pregnancies and harmful drug use.[98] Nevertheless, our government has chosen, in both arenas, to limit support exclusively to programs based on abstinence only, fear based models that have proven to be at best ineffective—and possibly counterproductive.[99]

In the late 1970's and early 1980's, the federal government began funding abstinence only drug education programs, instituting as official policy, former First Lady, Nancy Reagan's "just say no" slogan.[100] The DARE program is a prototype of this approach.[101]

Since 1990, DARE has received over $8 million in direct federal funding plus millions more in state and local funds. Approximately 20,000 police officers have delivered drug education to an estimated 25 million youth as part of the DARE program. Evaluation after evaluation has shown "no long term effects resulting from DARE exposure."[102]

Negative assessments of the program are by no means limited to particular interest groups. A recent report from the United States Surgeon General concluded that:

> DARE is the most widely implemented youth drug prevention program in the United States. It receives

substantial support from parents, teachers, police, and government funding agencies, and its popularity persists despite numerous well-designed evaluations and meta-analyses that consistently show little or no deterrent effects on substance use. Overall, evidence on the effects of the traditional DARE curriculum, which is implemented in grades 5 and 6, shows that children who participate are as likely to use drugs as those who do not participate.[103]

Indeed, in light of the overwhelming evidence of lack of success, DARE program directors have finally acknowledged that their strategy "has not had sufficient impact and say they are developing a new approach to spreading their message."[104]

Despite evidence that abstinence only models did not work in the drug arena, the federal government chose to support comparable abstinence only models in sex education.[105] The welfare laws of the 1990's committed:

> nearly $850 million in public funds over five years . . . to promote abstinence for anyone who is not married and to reward states that reduce out-of-wedlock births and abortions among all women in the state. Moreover, the law guarantees these large expenditures of public funds without any evidence that the strategies it embraces will have their intended effects and without any specific plans to evaluate their impact to determine whether any of the funded programs are worthy of continuation and replication.[106]

Similarities between drug abstinence and sex abstinence programs are not accidental. As a leading proponent of sexual abstinence programs, Janet Parshall, of the Family Research Council, explicitly stated that: sex education programs should resemble the "Just Say No" anti-drug programs.[107] This is so despite the fact that:

> The scant research conducted on abstinence-only education (all aimed at teenagers) suggests that such programs have little or no effect on initiation of sexual intercourse, but researchers say too few data exists to make a definitive judgment. What is clear from the research is that more comprehensive sexuality education programs that provide information about both abstinence and contraception, teach communications skills and provide access to family planning services do have

some effect: They are more likely both to persuade adolescents to delay the initiation of sexual intercourse and to lead to greater contraceptive use among teenagers when they become sexually active.[108]

The extent to which the same abstinence only philosophy underlies both drug and sex education programs is demonstrated in the government's Girl Power! Campaign. Originally conceived as an anti drug program, it was simply "repackaged" as a teen pregnancy prevention program in response to welfare reform laws that directed the secretary of DHHS to implement an abstinence based "strategy for preventing out-of-wedlock teenage pregnancies."[109]

THE MYTHOLOGY OF CHOICE: REPRODUCTION AND DRUG ADDICTION

The term "choice" is often applied to both reproductive decisionmaking and to drug use. Women have a right to "choose" to have an abortion and drug addicts make a "choice" to use drugs. In both areas, however, it is a term that obscures the lack of choice that many people have and the larger economic and institutional barriers that deny people, and disproportionately deny people of color, particularly low-income women of color, the ability to make consumer-like choices.

This particular similarity is best exemplified in cases in which efforts to control both reproduction and drugs coalesce through the punishment and prosecution of pregnant drug-using women. Since the late 1970's, approximately 200 women have been arrested based on their status as pregnant, drug-using women, thousands of others—and their families—are being affected by state laws that equate a pregnant woman's drug use with evidence of civil child neglect, and new calls for sterilization of drug using women are receiving significant media attention and private financial support.[110] These laws, policies and practices combine the seemingly unrelated arguments that fetal rights should be recognized under the law[111] and the argument that the war on drugs should be expanded to women's wombs.

In one of these cases, a young African American woman who used cocaine while pregnant was charged under a statute that made it a crime to "deliver" drugs to a minor.[112] The state argued successfully at trial that the statute could be applied to the delivery of drugs through the umbilical cord. Although this conviction was ultimately reversed, the woman, Jennifer Johnson, was initially sentenced to 15 years of probation.

At sentencing the judge justified the verdict on two separate but interdependent grounds: she deserved punishment both because "the defendant . . . made a choice to become pregnant and to allow those pregnancies to come to term" and because the "choice to use or not to use cocaine is just that—a choice."[113]

"Choice" is a popular term that is equally inappropriate whether used in discussions about illicit drugs or reproductive rights.

In the context of reproduction, the word choice as used by the judge contained numerous assumptions and judgments about Ms. Johnson. In making these pronouncements, the judge assumed that the intercourse that resulted in the pregnancy was voluntary. He assumed that she had "chosen" not to use contraceptives, assumed that despite their imperfections she would not have become pregnant if she had used them, and assumed that contraceptive services were easily accessible to her. The judge also assumed that she made a choice not to have an abortion and clearly believed that was the wrong decision. He undoubtedly ignored the fact that Florida, where Ms. Johnson lived does not fund abortion services—thus making an abortion inaccessible even if her moral and ethical beliefs had allowed her to seek termination of the pregnancy. Hiding behind the language of "choice" the judge felt justified in punishing a low income African-American woman for having a child.[114]

The judge also felt that her drug use was merely a matter of "choice" and self control and thus should be punished as well. The United States Supreme Court[115] and the health community,[116] however, have long recognized that drug addiction is an illness that generally cannot be overcome with-out treatment. The American Medical Association has unequivocally stated: "it is clear that addiction is not simply the product of a failure of individual willpower. Instead, dependency is the product of complex hereditary and environmental factors. It is properly viewed as a disease, and one that physicians can help many individuals control and overcome."[117]

In the context of reproductive rights, the term "choice" has increasingly come under attack for the very reasons suggested by the lower court's statements in the Johnson case. The term simply does not reflect the reality of many women's lives. As Ricki Solinger argues in her new book, devoted to critiquing the language of "choice":

> When Americans began to refer to reproductive liberty by the simple name "choice," they obscured the fact that millions of women in the United States—and abroad—lived in conditions of poverty and oppression that precluded many of the kinds of choices that middle-class American women thought of as a matter of personal decisionmaking. Then and now, many Americans have glossed over this: poor and/or culturally oppressed women in the United States and abroad may lack the money to "choose" abortion. They may live where abortion is inaccessible, illegal, or lifethreatening. They may lack the resources to feed the children they have, much less a new baby. They may want to be mothers but lack the resources to escape stigma, punishment, or death for having a baby under the wrong conditions. They may lack the resources to avoid pregnancy from sexual violence. Can women in any of these circumstances be described as in a position to make a choice, a private, personal choice in the way that middleclass Americans generally use that term?[118]

Similarly, the language of choice when applied to drug use allows the government to evade responsibility for the lack of drug treatment and the social and economic circumstances that contribute to addictive and dangerous drug use. As Nancy Campbell argues:

> . . . policy-makers disclaim their own responsibility by attributing policy failure to human nature, immorality, or bad behavior choices on the part of the governed. . . . Holding individuals responsible for addiction reproduces deeply held American notions of personal

responsibility, risk, vulnerability, and productive citizenship. But not all individuals have the means or the capacities to discharge the responsibilities of citizenship and social reproduction. The uneven distribution of the means to realize autonomy, reduce vulnerability and violence, and carry out responsibilities is simply disregarded in drug policy.[119]

CHILD PROTECTION

In both arenas, reproductive rights and drugs, calls for prohibition and punishment are often justified by the claim that such punitive approaches are necessary to save the children.

In the drug arena, ongoing criminalization of certain drugs and the refusal to fund many harm reduction approaches is justified by the claim that such measures are necessary to keep young people from obtaining drugs or viewing them as tolerable in any way. For example, a primary reason given by the Clinton administration's drug Czar for not funding needle exchange programs was the claim that such programs would send a message to children that drugs are acceptable.[120] Similarly, arguments for continuing the war on drugs are frequently based on the claim that harsh and total criminalization is necessary to protect children. As the Altoona police chief argued in a letter to the editor:

> . . . when young people get the message that drugs are helpful and should be legalized, their drug usage increases. Legalization tells our children that adults believe that drugs can be used responsibly and even for fun. With such an atmosphere it becomes difficult, if not impossible, to reach children and convince them that "doing drugs" is dangerous.[121]

And, recently, President Bush, when asking for the largest budget in history for drug control, seeking "approximately $19 billion in total federal drug control funding," the Acting Director of the Office of National Drug Control Policy (ONDCP) justified this predominantly law enforcement budget explaining, "the President's budget will allow us to better protect our youth and our safety."[122]

In the case of reproductive rights—the children are embryos and fetuses who must be saved from death that results from abortion and even contraception. Claims that abortion is child murder are simply too numerous to cite, but there is a recent notable example of applying child abuse rhetoric to contraceptive services. In May of 2001, Representative Chris Smith called Planned Parenthood Federation "Child Abuse Incorporated."[123] By its own self description, Planned Parenthood is "the world's largest and oldest voluntary family planning organization."

The claim of child protection is particularly apparent where the issues coalesce, in the case of pregnant drug using women. Numerous approaches including arrest, sterilization and other violation of fundamental constitutional rights have been justified in the name of children's rights.

In Whitner v. South Carolina,[124] the Supreme Court of South Carolina declared that viable fetuses are "persons," and as a result, the state's criminal child endangerment statute applied to a pregnant woman who used an illicit drug or engaged in any other behavior that might endanger the fetus.[125] In Ferguson v. City of Charleston, the defendants argued that a hospital policy of secretly searching pregnant women for evidence of drug use and then turning that information over to the police did not violate the Fourth Amendment's prohibition on unreasonable searches because the search served the special need of protecting children.[126] Although the US Supreme Court recently rejected this argument, finding that the policy was in fact about criminal punishment, not treatment, a draconian program of dragging pregnant and newly delivered mothers out of their hospital beds in chains and shackles had nevertheless been in effect for five years based on claims of children's rights.[127]

Child protection is also a claimed rationale for the C.R.A.C.K. program. In 1994, Barbara Harris founded C.R.A.C.K. ("Children Require A Caring Kommunity") after unsuccessful efforts to convince the California state legislature to pass a law that would punish women who give birth to drug exposed infants.[128] When a bill to make it a crime to give birth to a "drug baby" died in committee,[129] Ms. Harris created a nonprofit organization that offers $200 to any drug-addicted or alcoholic woman who agrees to be sterilized or to use a long acting contraceptive such as Norplant or Depo–Provera. Her rationale is that the children suffer and would be better off having never been born.

The group's literature and statements until recently, portrayed all drug exposed children as severely damaged. The organization's web site provides examples only of stillbirths, or children born with "severe disabilities (deaf, feeding tubes, one in a wheelchair)."[130]

The C.R.A.C.K. program targets one group of women,[131] women who use drugs, and launched a significant public relations campaign[132] that focuses not on those barriers that prevent them from making reproductive choices or on the barriers to drug treatment—but rather on the harm they do to their children, the cost to society of their supposed irresponsibility, and on the value of controlling certain women's reproduction as a solution to complex public health and economic problems.

C.R.A.C.K. supporters suggest that alternative approaches, such as drug treatment, increasing access to contraception and abortion services, and responding to the social conditions of poverty that many of the women face are simply too costly or time consuming compared with their child protection "solution."[133]

Although, as of early 2001, the program had reached a relatively small number of women, fewer than 400,[134] C.R.A.C.K. has received significant media attention and appears to be a powerful force in promoting the principle that underlies both the war on drugs and efforts to control reproduction: that complex social problems including child health and welfare, poverty and ill-health can be blamed on individual "choices" and solved through quick fix solutions like sterilization or prohibition.[135]

Similarly, child protection has been the rationale for an increasing number of states to pass laws that treat a pregnant woman's drug use as evidence of parental neglect and unfitness.[136] "While bills proposing criminal penalties have failed, eighteen states have amended their civil child welfare laws to address the subject of a woman's drug use during pregnancy."[137] Some of these statutes treat a single positive drug test as the basis for presuming parental unfitness.[138] Re-

cent court decisions, relying on medical misinformation, have also expanded the scope of their civil child welfare laws to reach the conduct of pregnant women.[139] In fact, research has found no significant difference between addicted and non-addicted mothers in childrearing practices and addicted and drug using mothers have been found to look after and care adequately for their children.[140] Thus these cases and statutes permit significant state intrusion on certain women's lives and families without protecting children from actual harm.[141]

These state laws and policies have resulted in removal of custody from women who on occasion smoked marijuana and from those women who tested positive for legal drugs prescribed by doctors during labor and delivery.[142]

In both the drug and reproductive arenas punitive policies do not benefit real children. To the contrary: they increase public costs related to incarceration and foster care, and do so at the expense of drug treatment and other forms of health care. Indeed, South Carolina's punitive approach to pregnancy and drug use coincides with a new and significant increase in statewide infant mortality figures.[143]

Moreover, as Jean Schroedel documents, states most protective of fetal rights are the ones least likely to support health, education and welfare programs that actually benefit children.[144] Similarly, drug prohibition has, by and large, failed to reduce drug use by young people.[145]

EFFORTS TO CONTROL BOTH HURT EVERYONE, BUT ESPECIALLY AFRICAN AMERICAN WOMEN

Laws criminalizing and unnecessarily controlling illicit drug use and reproduction hurt a wide expanse of the population. As many commentators have noted, the war on drugs in particular has "shattered" numerous lives, placing hundreds of thousands of non-violent drug offenders into a criminal justice system that destroys families and fails to reduce drug use.[146]

The drug war's effects extend far beyond those who use illegal drugs. For example "one of the saddest by-products of the drug war—people who legitimately need narcotic painkillers and find it almost impossible to get them."[147] "Victims of accidents, botched surgery, degenerative diseases—sometimes require massive doses of drugs like morphine just to get out of bed" but too often find that the "medical profession, terrorized by federal drug agents," has abandoned them.[148] Other examples include people who have died in various police sponsored drug raids on private homes using excessive force and no-knock laws,[149] people who did not use illegal drugs but who have lost personal property under civil forfeiture laws that permit the government to seize property based on suspicion, rather than proof of involvement with illegal drugs,[150] people who are kicked out of public housing because one person in the household was identified as possessing drugs,[151] the thousands of people subjected to suspicionless searches while driving on the nation's highways,[152] and countless employees[153] and students subject to urine drug screens.[154] And, increasingly, people who do use drugs are not only at risk of arrest, but also subject to loss of a wide array of government support including welfare,[155] housing,[156] and federal college loans.[157]

Perhaps most obvious is the unprecedented rate of incarceration in the United States. Today, more than 2 million people are behind bars[158] and the U.S. nonviolent prisoner population is larger than the combined populations of Wyoming and Alaska.[159] By the end of 1998, there were 5.9 million adults in the "correctional population"; a rubric that encompasses people who are incarcerated, on probation or on parole.[160]

The increase in prison population is directly linked to the war on drugs.[161] The decision to address drug issues through a predominately criminal justice approach has profound effects on virtually everyone in our society. As Angela Davis explains:

As prisons take up more and more space on the social landscape, other government programs that have previously sought to respond to social needs—such as Temporary Assistance to Needy Families—are being squeezed out of existence. The deterioration of public education, including prioritizing discipline and security over learning in public schools located in poor communities, is directly related to the prison "solution." ... [The prison industrial complex] devours the social wealth that could be used to subsidize housing for the homeless, to ameliorate public education for poor and racially marginalized communities.[162]

Expenditures on a wide range of drug interdiction programs including but not limited to incarceration "cost American taxpayers billions of dollars that otherwise might be devoted to improving housing, education, employment opportunities and access to health care (one of every six residents in the world's wealthiest nation has no health insurance!)"[163] While the war on drugs and the closely related war on reproductive freedom both have far reaching impact on all people in the United States, these effects fall disproportionately on certain populations.

While black, Hispanic, and white Americans use illegal drugs at comparable rates, there are dramatic differences in the application of criminal penalties for drug offenses. African Americans are more than 20 times as likely as whites to be incarcerated for drug offenses, and drug-related emergency department visits, overdose deaths, and new HIV infections related to injecting drugs are many times higher for blacks than whites.[164]

The drug war has increasingly been recognized as a mechanism for controlling and punishing certain populations—particularly African Americans. Joseph McNamara, former San Jose police chief, put it succinctly: "The drug war has become a race war."[165] More than 70 percent of the imprisoned populations are people of color. Moreover, the war on drugs has provided justification for an extensive system of profiling, surveillance, and harassment of African Americans in the United States today.[166]

And while women continue to represent a minority of those behind bars, in recent years their numbers have increased at nearly double the rate for men.[167] This dramatic and disproportionate increase has a great deal to do with the war on drugs.[168] Drug offenses accounted for half (49%) of the rise in the number of women incarcerated in state prisons from 1986–1996 and Black and Hispanic women represent a disproportionate share of those sentenced for drug offenses.[169] "From 1986 to 1991, the number of black female drug offenders in state prison rose by 828%, Hispanic women by 328%, and white nonHispanic women by 241%."[170]

At the end of 1999, the number of women held in state or federal prisons had risen to 90,668, an incarceration rate of almost 60 per 100,000 or 1 out of every 1,695 U.S. females. More than 10% of the female prison population has been sentenced to federal institutions, and most women incarcerated in the federal system were there for drug offenses. The majority of these women had little or no prior criminal record and were directly involved in dealing or possessing only a relatively small amount of drugs. More than 80% were sentenced under mandatory minimum sentencing laws . . . Approximately 70% of these women were mothers of one or more children under the age of 18.[171]

Imprisonment has profound effects both on the women and the children for whom they are responsible. Two-thirds of the women in prison are mothers to children under the age of 18.[172] A 1991 survey found that 10% of the women prison inmates reported that their children were living in a foster home or children's agency.[173] Unnecessary separation of children from these mothers is not only enormously expensive in fiscal terms but is traumatic and harmful for all involved; it bodes ill for the next generation.[174]

Separation of children from their primary caretaker-parents can cause harm to children's psychological well-being and hinder their growth and development; many infants who are born shortly before or while their mothers are incarcerated are quickly separated from their mothers, preventing the parent-child bonding that is crucial to developing a sense of security and trust in children.[175]

The harm that results from refusing to fund public health measures such as needle exchange also falls most heavily on African American women and children, who are now the fastest growing population of people becoming infected with HIV.[176]

Again, there is a direct parallel with restrictions on reproductive health care, which also disproportion-ately affect African American women. As Dorothy Roberts explains:

> This connection between denying reproductive choice and oppression will necessarily be the hardest for poor women and women of color. Because of poverty, these women have fewer real options and are dependent on government funds to realize the decisions they make. Because the government is more involved in their lives through their use of public facilities and bureaucracies, they are more susceptible to government monitoring and supervision. Because it is harder for them to meet the ideal middleclass standard of what a woman or mother should be, society is more likely to approve of, or overlook, punishing them for making reproductive decisions. Because they have less access to lawyers, the media and advocacy organizations, and because society has convinced many that they are powerless, they are less likely to challenge government restrictions of their rights. Reproductive freedom is a right that belongs to all women; but its denial is felt the hardest by poor and minority women.[177]

Similarly, African American women leaders in the 1980's wrote an open letter to African Americans explaining:

> More than other Americans, we know what it is to be without reproductive options—to be forced to reproduce, as our forebears were in slavery; to be sterilized against our will or knowledge; and to be victims of crude abortion practices when the procedure was illegal . . . African-American women and other women of color have the most to lose if access to legal abortion is denied in any way.[178]

African American women in particular are caught at the intersection where the war on reproductive rights and the war on drugs meet. Despite the fact that substance abuse crosses all race and class lines,[179] African American women have been targeted for harsh and punitive prosecutorial responses and account for the vast majority of those arrested.[180]

While this disproportionality has been true nationwide, nowhere is it more apparent than in South Carolina. In Charleston, the Medical University Hospital ("MUSC") instituted a policy of reporting and facilitating the arrest of pregnant women who tested positive for cocaine.[181] Although the hospital claimed that their policy was required by state law, their hospital, a public teaching institution with a patient population base that is 70 percent African American, was the only one to systematically adopt and carry out such searches. Women were selectively searched, through urine drug screening, for evidence of cocaine use. If they tested positive, they were taken out of the hospital in chains and shackles, evoking sharp modern images of black women in slavery. All but one of the thirty women arrested at the hospital was African American.[182] The white nurse, Shirley Brown, who implemented the program admitted that she believed mixing of the races to be against "god's way,"[183] and noted in the medical records of the one white woman arrested pursuant to the policy that she lived "with her boyfriend who is a Negro."[184] Thus every woman arrested was either African American or gave birth to a mixed-race baby.

Medical staff at MUSC, working in collaboration with the prosecutor and police, in effect conducted an experiment to see if threats of arrest and actual arrest would be effective tools in deterring pregnant women's drug use.[185] The subjects of this Tuskegee-like experiment: poor black women.[186] As one local journalist observed: "The women were part of an unprecedented experiment between medical and law enforcement entities suffering the noble delusion that pregnant women would stop using drugs if they were sufficiently punished. The manner by which these dubious social cures were administered reads like something out of a C-grade Nazi movie."[187] This policy was challenged in a federal civil rights action, Ferguson et al. v. City of Charleston, filed in 1994.

One of the few people to speak up against the policy when it was first instituted was the Medical Director of the hospital's Neonatal Intensive Care Unit, Celeste Patrick. Dr. Patrick wrote a letter to the president of MUSC, Dr. Edwards, raising numerous concerns about the fairness and efficacy of the policy, which she described as "thinly veiled discrimination against a class of poor, black women who do not have the resources to defend themselves."[188]

The racial bias at the heart of many of these cases is also apparent in the statement a South Carolina state court judge made while reviewing the prosecution of a woman who had used cocaine while pregnant. He said:

> You know, we've got enough trouble with normal children. Now this little baby's born with crack. When he is seven years old, they have an attention span that long [holding his thumb and index finger an inch apart]. They can't run. They just run around in class like a little rat. Not just black ones. White ones too.[189]

Not only are the children viewed as animals, the mothers are as well. Throughout the Ferguson case, the policy of testing and arresting was justified as a "carrot and stick approach."[190] As explained by defendant Charles M. Condon, the carrot was treatment and the stick was the threat of arrest.[191] This metaphor derives from an approach used to motivate donkeys and mules to carry their loads.[192] The women subject to this policy—whether stigmatized as African American—as most in fact were, or as drug users, or simply as mothers—were to be handled as obstinate beasts of burden.[193]

Disturbing animal metaphors also pervade the C.R.A.C.K. program. Its founder insists on comparing drug using pregnant women to dogs: "I'm not saying these women are dogs, but they're not acting any more responsible than a dog in heat."[194] She has also stated "we don't allow dogs to breed. We spay them. We neuter them. We try to keep them from having unwanted puppies, and yet these women are literally having litters of children."[195]

The C.R.A.C.K. program leadership vehemently denies that it is racist.[196] Whether intentional or not, however, the choice of the name, C.R.A.C.K., a form of cocaine widely associated with African Americans, clearly suggests an emphasis on black women. Moreover the program's own data reflect a focus on African Americans. Although they make up approximately 12% of the population, and use drugs at about the same rate as people of other races, fully 40% (157 of a total of 392) of the women paid by the C.R.A.C.K. program to date, are African American. Adding other non-white people who have been paid, more than half are people of color.

African American women are also far more likely to be tested for the presence of drugs under civil child abuse reporting statutes even though white women have been shown to use illegal drugs at a higher rate.[197] This is one reason why African American women and their children are greatly over represented in the child welfare system:

> In January 1999, Black children made up forty-five percent of the foster care population although they were only fifteen percent of the general population under age eighteen. The disparity is even more alarming in the nation's big cities. Removal of children because of maternal substance abuse has contributed significantly to the increase in numbers of poor Black children pouring into foster care.[198]

Thus, while punitive restrictions on certain drugs and reproductive options have consequences on all people, both have particularly harsh and disproportionate effect on African American women and families.

CONCLUSION

Those who are concerned about fundamental issues of social justice may be losing ground, missing opportunities to build coalitions and strengthen their respective arguments by refusing to recognize the relationship between the drug policy and reproductive rights issues. Single issue organizations are understandably concerned that their legitimacy or respectability even among their own constituencies will be tainted if they stretch too far and take a position on what appears to be a drug case, or an abortion-rights case, or both.

The "Right" however, seems to understand the fundamental similarities all too well and is willing to exploit a range of intesectional issues[199] to promote its broad agenda. As Nancy Campbell argues "Neoconservative groups such as the Heritage Foundation or the American Enterprise Institute (AEI) use such policy debates as welfare reform, crime control, immigration, and illicit drug policy to gain an advantage in reproductive rights debates and cultural conversations about family formation."[200]

Samuel Friedman suggests that drug policies that ignore medical recommendations and maximize harm serve useful political purposes for those in power. Drug war policies use "'divide and rule' politics in which 'scapegoating' divides and distracts potential opposition."[201] He believes that:

> Politically, scapegoating drug users distracts attention from policies that aggravate the problems people face. Blaming unsafe streets, AIDS, poor services in hospitals, and the existence of children who act out in school on drug user's immorality points to certain solutions that are in tune with a belt-tightening, competition-oriented, fundamentalist world-view. More police, longer prison sentences, and family values, and also points to an analysis that says that problems are the result of guilty individuals. This distracts attention from the structural problems that cause problems for people and communities, such as the economic situation . . . governments that accept the need for profitability as a "given"; cutbacks in education, health, and welfare; racism and sexism.[202]

Nancy Campbell, likewise observes that "while evidence mounts that U.S. drug policy is seriously flawed, it has proven immune to charges of failure. This immunity stems from the utility of illicit drug policy in reinforcing class-and-race-based social divisions."[203]

The issue of drug using women is similarly seen by some commentators as an effective tool in a larger conservative political agenda. As Sheigla Murphy and colleagues argue:

> . . . pregnant drug users served as ideological offensives in the United States war on drugs. Pernicious images of drug using mothers having babies for the sole purpose of qualifying for government handouts in order to buy drugs and then neglecting and abusing these children were promulgated by the media and politicians. This contributed to the passage of legislation and funding allocations that resulted in the wholesale reduction of social welfare services to all poor women and children. The war on drugs has always been a war on the poor, particularly people of color. In 2001 it is very clear that drug use and drug users have played a very important role in defining women and children's poverty as an individual behavioral problem rather than the result of structural economic inequities.[204]

Dorothy Roberts argues that this issue advances both anti-abortion politics and the kind of government withdrawal of social supports articulated by Friedman and Murphy.

> In addition to legitimizing fetal rights enforcement, prosecuting crack-addicted mothers shifts public attention from poverty, racism, and a deficient health care system, implying instead that poor infant health results from the depraved behavior of individual mothers. Poverty—not maternal drug use—is the major threat to the health of Black Children in America.[205]

Focusing again on both issues simultaneously, through pregnant drug users, it is clear that combining both political hot-button topics has been a highly successful strategy for advancing specific goals of the right regarding drugs and reproduction. The South Carolina Whitner v. State, decision for example, reflects enormous gains for both those who oppose abortion, as well as those who support the war on drugs. The holding in Whitner goes to the heart of today's abortion debate, lending support to the anti-abortion position that fetuses have rights and that pregnant women's health and freedom may be subordinated to those rights. Indeed, conservative pundits, like Rush Limbaugh and opportunistic politicians seized on Whitner as the long-awaited chance to undermine and potentially overturn Roe v. Wade. The opinion has provided grounds for the South Carolina State Attorney General's office to assert that it now has legal authority to make all postviability abortions murder and to put to death women who have them, as well as the doctors who perform them.[206]

By focusing on pregnant women and harm to fetuses, the Whitner decision also creates a basis for prosecuting people solely because they suffer from the disease of addiction—opening new terrain in the war on drugs. In 1964, the Supreme Court held that people couldn't be arrested simply for having the status of being addicts.[207] While subsequent cases have made clear that people can be arrested for possession of even the smallest quantity of an illegal substance, the Supreme Court's 1964 decision recognized that it would be cruel and unusual punishment to lock people up simply because they have a problem with drugs. But Cornelia Whitner was imprisoned for precisely this reason—not because she was found with drugs in her possession—but because medical tests performed at the time of delivery suggested that she was an addict.

The need to address the policies and practices at this intersection is clear. Drug policy reform efforts to de-stigmatize drug users and to shift emphasis from punishment to treatment cannot succeed if myths regarding "crack babies" and "crack mothers" destroying a generation of children are left unchallenged. Similarly, efforts to protect reproductive freedom cannot succeed as long as the rhetoric of the drug war is able to pit fetal rights against women's legal status as autonomous persons. Without a comprehensive strategy to undo decades of misinformation and political posturing about both pregnancy and drug use, an ever-widening circle of women will be caught in increasingly punitive, intrusive, and coercive government controls that hurt rather than help women and their families.

Looking more broadly, the effectiveness of scapegoating drug users and certain pregnant women is clear. For example, if attention can be focused on selfish drug users, women who want abortions, or women who have too many children, it is unlikely that an effective coalition for a meaningful national health care system will ever get organized. If child welfare problems can be blamed on drug-using parents, or welfare mothers, or teens and drug users having too many children, then meaningful reform of the child welfare system, that will require addressing poverty and educational opportunity and pervasive violence in the lives of women, is unlikely ever to occur.[208]

Taking on these issues in a coherent manner affords a unique opportunity to develop the support of a broad coalition of organizations and communities in the struggle for reproductive freedom, drug policy reform, and a more just society. We also have the opportunity to develop programs and institutions that recognize the ways in which intersecting issues and identities create barriers to treatment, recovery and well-being.

Following Mari Matsuda's advice, it is by listening to the actual experiences of those people who "experience life on the bottom" that we can have a basis for "defining the elements of justice."[209] Many drug-using pregnant women experience that life, and by listening to their experiences, we have the opportunity to develop an agenda and programs that are more effective and responsive.[210] Few people fall into any one category. Drug treatment programs and shelters for women are often less effective than they should be, not because they can't work—but rather because they do not address comprehensively people who have more than one identity[211]—and in this case more than one problem.[212] A person can be a woman, of color and both addicted and pregnant, or battered and addicted,[213] or all of these and also lack the income that makes it possible to have housing, transportation and child care necessary to take advantage of any treatment that might be available.[214] Comprehensive programs that acknowledge and respond to the multiple and overlapping identities and issues have far greater evidence of success than those that do not.[215] In order to be fully effective, these programs must necessarily consider and respond to the particular circumstances, prejudices and stigmas African American and other women of color face.

By recognizing the similarity in the issues concerning reproductive rights and the drug war there is an opportunity not only for a deeper understanding of each issue, but also a basis for developing analysis and action that can counteract the dominating forces of punishment and prohibition and begin to build coalitions and movements toward preserving and expanding those social programs that can in fact empower women, preserve families, and create a more just society.

DISCUSSION QUESTIONS

1. Describe four ways in which the war on drugs and the war on abortion are in fact connected or similar in their history and control of certain populations. Where do women fit into this picture? Who benefits from these "wars"?
2. In discussing laws about drugs and abortion, Paltrow argues that the government adopts policies to control behavior rather than address the larger social conditions underlying that behavior. Discuss the pros and cons of this approach for the well-off and for the poor.
3. In what ways do poor people suffer disproportionately when the government intervenes in controlling abortion? How does such control hurt African American women in particular?
4. What role does racism play in these "wars"? Give at least two examples from this chapter.
5. Discuss alternative ways in which government efforts, programs, and money could reduce drug use and abortions. What special considerations must be taken into account for reducing drug use and abortions in the most marginalized parts of the U.S. population?

SELECTED REFERENCES

Baum, Dan. 1996. *Smoke and Mirrors; The War on Drugs and the Politics of Failure,* 8.

Bush-Baskette, Stephanie. 2000. The War on Drugs and the Incarceration of Mothers. *J. Drug Issues* 30:919, 924.

Campbell, Nancy D. 2000. *Using Women: Gender, Drug Policy, and Social Justice.*

Chavkin, Wendy. 2001. Cocaine and Pregnancy: Time to Look at the Evidence. *JAMA* 285 (March 28):1626.

Davis, Angela Y. 1998. Masked Racism: Reflection on the Prison Industrial Complex. *Colorlines* (fall).

Drucker, Ernest. 1999. Drug Prohibition and Public Health: 25 Years of Evidence. *Pub. Health Rep.* 114 (January–February):14.

Friedman, Samuel R. 1998. The Political Economy of Drug-User Scapegoating—and the Philosophy of Resistance. *Drugs: Education, Prevention, and Policy* 5(1):15.

Gordon, Linda. 1976. *Woman's Body, Woman's Right: Birth Control in America.*

Gray, Mike. 2000. *Drug Crazy: How We Got into This Mess and How We Can Get Out,* 188, 189.

Horowitz, Craig. 1996. Drugs Are Bad, Drugs Are Bad, Drugs Are Bad, Drugs Are Bad: The Drug War Is Worse. *New York Magazine,* February 5, 22–25.

Joffe, Carol. 1995. *Doctors of Conscience: The Struggle to Provide Abortion before and after Roe v. Wade,* viii.

Murphy, Sheigla, Paloma Sales, and Moira O'Neill. 2002. Pregnant Drug Users: Scapegoats of the Reagan/Bush and Clinton Era Economics. *International Journal of Social Justice,* 2.

Murphy, Sheigla, and Marsha Rosenbaum. 1999. *Pregnant Women on Drugs: Combating Stereotype and Stigma,* 100.

Paltrow, Lynn. 1999. Pregnant Drug Users: Fetal Persons, and the Threat to Roe v. Wade. *Alb. L. Rev.* 62:999.

Reinarman, Craig, and Harry G. Levine, eds. 1997. *Crack in America: Demon Drugs and Social Justice.*

Roberts, Dorothy. 1997. *Killing the Black Body,* 76.

Roth, Rachel. 2000. *Making Women Pay: The Hidden Costs of Fetal Rights,* 163–83.

Solinger, Rickie. 2001. *Beggars and Choosers: How the Politics of Choice Shapes Adoption, Abortion, and Welfare in the United States,* 47.

Vanderkloot, Peter. 2001. Methadone: Medicine, Harm Reduction, or Social Control. *Harm Reduction Communication* (spring):1, 4.

Part 2:

Women and Prison

HISTORY OF UNEQUAL TREATMENT OF WOMEN PRISONERS

A brief review of the history of women in prison in the United States provides insight into some of the inequities that incarcerated women encounter today not only in the United States but also in many countries around the world.* From the time of the first penitentiaries in the nineteenth century, women were treated much worse than men. Considered more depraved than men, women prisoners (who had been totally forgotten in the planning, building, and policy development of penitentiaries) were placed in makeshift spaces such as attics or spare cells in men's institutions. The women received no training in work skills, often were sexually abused by inmates and guards, and were supervised only by male guards. That legacy of inequitable treatment remains today.

The early abuses and inequities eventually led women reformers in the community to exert efforts on behalf of women prisoners. The reformers were successful in the late nineteenth and early twentieth centuries in having women, primarily white women, moved out of men's prisons and into women-only institutions called reformatories. The reformatories were physically very different from the old penitentiaries; they resembled a campus setting in which prisoners lived in cottages. Another departure from the past was the appearance of women matrons as guards and educators in the

---

*A good, brief summary of the history of women's prisons that focuses on gender disparities can be found in Fisher-Giorlando 2000.

WEBSITES

The following websites contain material on women prisoners. New websites are continuously being developed while at the same time others disappear. Check with a search engine, such as Google at **www.google.com,** to locate additional information. Insert a key word or phrase (women inmates, prisoners, offenders) or organization in order to locate additional references.

Women in Prison

Paige Harrison and Allen Beck. *Prisoners in 2001.* Bureau of Justice Statistics Bulletin. July 2002. NCJ195189. Can be found at
www.ojp.usdog.gov/bjs/pub/pdf/p01.pdf

Lawrence Greenfeld and Tracy Snell. *Women Offenders.* Bureau of Justice Statistics Special Report. December 1999. NCJ175688. Can be found at
www.ojp.usdoj.gov/bjs/pub/pdf/wo.pdf

Tracy Snell and Danielle Morton. *Women in Prison.* Bureau of Justice Statistics Special Report. March 1994. NCJ145321. Can be found at
www.ojp.usdoj.gov/bjs/pub/pdf/wopris.pdf

Research on Women and Girls in the Justice System. September 2000. NCJ180973. Can be found at
www.ncjrs.org/pdffiles1/nij/189973.pdf

Lawrence Greenfeld and Stephen Smith. *American Indians and Crime.* Bureau of Justice Statistics. February 1999. NCJ173386. Can be found at
www.ojp.usdoj.gov/bjs/pub/pdf/aic.pdf

Marc Mauer and Tracy Huling. *Young Black Americans and the Criminal Justice System: Five Years Later.* Report summary can be found at
www.sentencingproject.org/policy/9070smy.pdf

Marc Mauer, Cathy Potler, and Richard Wolf. *Gender and Justice: Women, Drugs, and Sentencing Policy.* Executive summary at
www.sentencingproject.org/policy/9042smy.pdf

WEBSITES—*Cont.*

Women in Prison: Eleven Things You Should Know about Women in Prison in the US. Can be found at **http://prisonactivist.org/women/ women-in-prison.html**

Patricia Allard. *Life Sentences: Denying Welfare Benefits to Women Convicted of Drug Offenses.* February 2002. Can be found at **www.sentencingproject.org/news/ lifesentences.pdf**

For a listing of references on women in prison by the National Criminal Justice Reference Service, go to **http://virlib.ncjrs.org/corr.asp?category= 44&subcategory=11**

Changing: The Impact of College in a (Women's) Maximum Security Prison (Bedford Hills, NY). 2001. Available at **www.changingminds.ws**

Christopher Mumola. *Incarcerated Parents and Their Children.* Bureau of Justice Statistics Special Report. 2000. NCJ18235. Can be found at **www.ojp.usdoj.gov/bjs/abstract/iptc.htm**

Pam Aquyres. *The Parent Trap: Caught between the War on Drugs and Federal Adoption Law.* 2001. Available at **www.motherjones.com/webexclusives/features/ news/prison_kids.html**

Neil Bernstein. *Left Behind: Tens of Thousands of Children Have a Parent Behind Bars.* 2001. Available at **www.motherjones.com/prisons/ print_left_behind.html**

Women's section from Prison Activist Resource Center. Can be found at **www.prisonactivists.org/women**

Prison Moratorium Project material on women. Can be found at **www.nomoreprisons.org**

Prisons, some of which covers women and prison. Can be found at **www.MotherJones.com**

National Clearinghouse for the Defense of Battered Women (in prison). Can be found at **http://dpa.state.ky.us/library/advocate/mar98/ battered.html**

reformatories. Life in reformatories centered on programs designed to turn incarcerated women into middle-class "ladies"—a frequently self-serving and futile effort. Many of the inmates, once released, were employed as servants in the homes of the reformers and their friends, while other former inmates who could not find work had little opportunity to practice the middle-class domestic skills that they were urged to emulate while incarcerated. At the same time, African American women were not deemed capable of being reformed into ladies and were discriminated against by being left behind in penitentiaries.

In the late 1950s most of the women's reformatories were closed. Women again were housed in traditional prisons, but this time in those built just for women. With the emergence in the 1960s of the women's movement and its objectives of creating equity for women in the workplace, in education, and in the law, women prisoners turned to the courts to seek more equitable treatment inside jails and prisons. Women prisoners sued jurisdictions on the basis of sex discrimination, claiming that all aspects of prison and jail life provided fewer or no services compared to men's prisons: for example, medical services, meaningful vocational and educational training, work assignments, and access to their children. The court settlements, however, even when favorable to women, often did not translate into improved conditions, and women found that they had to return to court again and again and continue to litigate the same issues for years. In other cases, the response of government jurisdictions found by courts to be discriminating against women prisoners was to remove some privileges from male institutions, thereby conforming to the court's order that equity in service prevail. In still other instances, jurisdictions made harsh punishments available in women's prisons (such as chain gangs and boot camps) in a cynical response to court-ordered equality.

CONTEMPORARY ISSUES ON WOMEN IN PRISON

The contemporary experience of women in prison in the last three decades of the twentieth century has been dubbed by Meda Chesney-Lind as one of "equality with a vengeance." (See, for example, Chesney-Lind 1998; for a more in-depth analysis, see Chesney-Lind 1997.)[*] Women, so to speak, have had "the book thrown at them" for demanding equality in the courts, at school and work, and in the home. Thus, despite the fact that prisons and punishments were designed for the violent male offender, women would get the same harsh sentences applied to them in a conservative punishment era that intensified under the burden of "mandatory minimums," "three-strikes" laws, and "truth-in-sentencing" laws.[†] All such laws had the effect of incarcerating more people, for longer periods of time, with less options for diversion from prison or opportunities for parole or rehabilitation. Women were swept into the penal dragnet without regard for the fact that they were primarily nonviolent drug and economic (theft, forgery, petty larceny) offenders (see Steffensmeier and Schwartz, chaps. 5 and 6). As women's incarceration for violent crime convictions fell (from almost half of all women prisoners—49 percent—in 1979 to a little over one-quarter—28 percent—in 1996), women's overall incarceration rate skyrocketed. Whereas in 1980 there were only 13,420 women in prison in the United States, by 2000 (the latest date for which information is available) more than 91,000 women were in prison. This figure by itself represents a sevenfold increase over 20 years. Further, an additional 70,000 women were in jail; a total of 161,000 women were incarcerated in 2000. This figure means that more and more women are being incarcerated for drugs, not violent crime, especially in the federal system (for a historical review of these statistics, see Sokoloff 2001).

California Coalition for Battered Women in Prison. Can be found at **http://freebatteredwomen.org/resource.htm**

Amnesty International's report on violence against women in U.S. prisons: *Not Part of My Sentence: Violations of the Human Rights of Women in Custody.* Can be found at **www.amnesty.orgailib/intca/women/index.html**

Human Rights Watch (HRW) publications on abuse of women in prison: Items listed include *Nowhere to Hide: Retaliation against Women in Michigan State Prisons* and *All Too Familiar: Sexual Abuse of Women in U.S. State Prisons.* Can be found at **www.hrw.org/women/custody.php?country= United%20States,%20Domestic.**

General References

General reference for crime statistics and statistics about prisoners in the criminal justice system is found in Section 6 of *The Sourcebook on Criminal Justice Statistics.* Available at **www.albany.edu/sourcebook**

The John Jay College of Criminal Justice Library provides an extensive number of links to criminal justice statistics and international criminal justice, including women. Available at **www.lib.jjay.cuny.edu**

General reference for E News on women, which often has information on women, crime, and justice information including women prisoners. Available at **www.womenenewstoday.org**

[*]Unless otherwise indicated, the comments in this section come from Chesney-Lind 2000.
[†]Clearly, both the law and the criminal justice system were historically created based on male gender norms, which reflect the position of white, propertied, heterosexual men. But women, who are located at different intersections of the race, class, gender, and sexual orientation systems, for the most part do not behave like men and should not be subjected to a system of punishment designed for (violent) men. But providing a female-centered prison may be a contradiction in terms. (See Faith, chap. 17, for further discussion.)

Overall, women's incarceration for drug offenses has increased from 1 in 10 women prisoners to almost 2 out of 5 (38 percent). In the federal prison system, 2 out of 3 women are in prison for drug offenses. And as Julia Sudbury shows in chapter 12 ("Women of Color, Globalization, and the Politics of Incarceration"), it is not all women, but mostly women of color (primarily black and secondarily Latina), who are incarcerated on drug charges. Because these women are mostly "low down on the totem pole" of the drug organizations, they have little to bargain with in terms of information on the operation or identification of drug ring leaders when faced by zealous prosecutors. Women are much more likely to be given mandatory minimum sentences—and for a much smaller amount of drugs, for example, crack, which carries a punishment 10 times longer in prison than does powder cocaine, more typically the drug of choice among the white population.[‡] Thus, the war on drugs has become a "war on poor black women," who make up more than 50 percent of the women's prison population despite the fact that they represent only 12 percent of the general female population in the United States (Bush-Baskette 1998). The explanation for much of the increase in women's incarceration is not a change in women's criminality but a change in criminal justice policies and practices. This is true even when it comes to violent crime.

When women are incarcerated for violent offenses, the offenses tend to be of a much less serious nature than those of men, and often too the behavior has only recently been defined as "offenses." For example, nearly three in four violent victimizations committed by women offenders were simple assaults (compared to about one-half of men's assaults).[§] Moreover, what previously might have been considered a shove between a mother and daughter can translate now into a violent criminal offense. Laws put into effect to protect battered women have led to three times as many women and girls being arrested now than a decade earlier. These arrests are happening because mandatory arrests for domestic violence all too often result in the battered woman herself being arrested along with the batterer.

Many researchers have found that women's (and men's) crime tends to reflect the role that "economic disadvantage" plays in their criminal careers. (For a review of this and other theories explaining women's crime, refer back to Steffensmeier and Schwartz, chap. 6.) However, gender likewise plays a role in shaping men's and women's responses to poverty. English (1993) found that women's criminal careers reflect "gender differences in legitimate and illegitimate opportunity structures, in personal networks, and in family obligations."

As Owen (chap. 10) points out, gender matters in the forces that propel women into criminal behavior. It took a feminist perspective to understand the

[‡]Although only 5 grams of crack leads to a mandatory minimum of five years in prison, it takes 500 grams of powder cocaine for this same punishment to occur.
[§]Even here, however, black women are much more likely to be incarcerated for violent offenses—even though "Black and white offenders accounted for nearly equal proportions of women committing robbery and aggravated assault; however, simple assault offenders were more likely to be describe as white" (Greenfeld and Snell 1999, p. 2).

nature of abuse against women and its importance in comprehending women's pathways to crime (Gilfus 1992; Richie 1996). Although it is true that both incarcerated men and incarcerated women have histories of sexual and physical violence against them in a family setting, this situation seems to be more prevalent and longer lasting in the lives of women than men who end up in prison. Thus, for example, 43 percent of women but only 12 percent of men report abuse at least once prior to their current imprisonment; women's prior physical abuse (33.5 percent) and sexual abuse (34 percent) is much greater than men's (10 percent and 5 percent, respectively); and although about a third (32 percent) of the women started being abused as girls and continued to be abused as adults, only 11 percent of the men report abuse as boys, and most importantly, this abuse did not continue into adulthood. Even when women commit violent offenses, gender and abuse play an important role in their crimes. Thus, many women convicted of murder or manslaughter had killed husbands or boyfriends who repeatedly and violently abused them. For example, one New York study showed that in 1986, 49 percent of the women committed to prison for homicide had been victims of abuse by that person at some point in their lives and 59 percent who killed someone close to them were being abused at the time of the offense (*Correctional Association Reporter* 1991).

Once again, it is inadequate to talk about women in prison without taking into account the racialized nature of women's incarceration. Sudbury (chap. 12, "Women of Color, Globalization, and the Politics of Incarceration") writes that a broader perspective must be taken to deal with the issues confronting women in prison, one that examines the impact of capitalist globalization forces as well as the demise of minority inner-city "ghettos" and rural white communities as a result of factories and other businesses moving overseas for cheaper labor. The result is unemployment of large numbers of poor, inner-city people of color and poor whites in rural areas, which leads to increased crime rates. At the same time, this process exploits, through very low wages, women and men in other countries throughout the third world. Simultaneously, Sudbury argues, a "profitable relationship between politicians, corporations, the media and state correctional institutions . . . generates the racialized use of incarceration as a response to social problems rooted in the globalization of capital." This situation has come to be known as the "prison-industrial complex." This complex process, combined with the globalization of the war on drugs, according to Sudbury, has led to the incarceration of poor women of color from around the globe: in the United States, Canada, and many European countries.

Black women, incarcerated in the United States at a rate eight times greater than white women and four times greater than Latinas, become "human sacrifices when education, job creation and welfare receive short shrift and profitable technologies of imprisonment garner more and more support." They should be seen—but rarely are, according to Davis (2000)—as "victims of racist and sexist discrimination."

The chapters in part 2 cover these issues in detail. The chapters focus on excessive incarceration of women, the types of discriminatory treatment and abuse that women prisoners encounter, the impact of globalization on women, and the plight of women in prison and their children.

THE ORGANIZATION OF PART 2

The chapters selected for part 2 follow directly from the early history in that they document the many challenges to equitable, decent, and constructive treatment facing incarcerated women today. In this section the reader will observe from chapter to chapter a consistency in terms of continuing *gender inequity*. Moreover, each chapter explains that race, class, and sexual orientation make clearer the ways in which gender matters in the lives of women caught within the prison system. Finally, although women have often fought for "equal treatment" to men in prison (for education, training, and so on), male prisoners not infrequently have received overly harsh and sometimes inhumane treatment in institutions with substandard or nonexistent services.

In the first chapter of this part, entitled "Women and Imprisonment in the United States: The Gendered Consequences of the U.S. Imprisonment Binge," Barbara Owen focuses on government policy that led to women becoming the fastest growing segment of the inmate population in the 1990s. That policy—using imprisonment as a way to discourage the use and sale of illegal drugs—resulted in the categorization of many women as criminals. Not only were these women labeled as deviant but once imprisoned, because of a lack of useful prison training and of transition programs out of prison, they had few ways to prepare for a law-abiding life after their release back into the community. The chapter describes many of the abuses to which women prisoners are subjected and depicts most prison services as inadequate. Moreover, Owen takes to task those who expect the criminal justice system to solve the larger social problems that lead to the imprisonment of large numbers of poor and minority women and men. We need to work for change within prisons but also within the larger society.

In chapter 11, "Women in Prison: Researching Race in Three National Contexts" the reader learns of the role that race plays in Cuba, the Netherlands, and the United States in women's imprisonment. Kum-Kum Bhavnani and Angela Y. Davis find in all three countries a disproportionate impact on women of color as well as a higher rate of incarceration for women than men.[1] This chapter provides an opportunity for readers to hear the women speak out about their own incarceration and their ideas on alternatives to incarceration. The authors also discuss a dilemma they encountered while conducting the research for this chapter: They are passionately against the use of prisons altogether and yet, as they talked with the imprisoned women, found themselves working to better conditions for those women who are currently incarcerated.

Chapter 12 returns to the concept of globalization first presented in part 1 (see Kempadoo, chap. 8). In "Women of Color, Globalization, and the Politics of

---

[1] As early as the 1970s, it was clear that there were no countries in which more women than men are in prison. Rather, the *rate* of incarceration increases *faster* for women than for men in all countries for which we have data. This situation is, in part, due to the much lower base numbers for women than for men (see Adler 1979).

Incarceration," Sudbury argues that the explosion in women's incarceration is the "hidden face of globalization" and cannot be understood without reference to three overlapping phenomena. First is the restructuring of national economies and social welfare provisions that has occurred as a result of the globalization of capital, which creates immense social and economic divisions between a mobile corporate elite and disenfranchised rural and urban working classes within and beyond the United States. The second is the emergence and international expansion of the "prison-industrial complex" that is made up of relations between criminal justice institutions, politicians, and profit-driven prison corporations. The third is the U.S.-led war on drugs, which also has been exported globally. These three factors combine to lead to the massive criminalization of women of color, who are turned into "raw material for the correctional industry." Sudbury provides us with a clear analysis of the ways in which intersectionalities work to the detriment of poor women of color. She, like Bhavnani and Davis (chap. 11), brings up the issue of decarceration and abolition of prisons for women caught in the criminal justice system.

Discussions of racism in the criminal justice system rarely include the experiences of Native Americans in the United States, just as the literature on women in prison usually fails to include Native American women prisoners. This paucity is despite the fact that Native Americans and women have been the fastest growing members of the prison population in recent history. Chapter 13 is written by Luana Ross, a Native American scholar, who explains how the survival efforts of Native American women in prison are misinterpreted by the prison authorities as "uncooperative" and hostile behavior. She, like other scholars, finds racism deeply embedded in the social structure of the prison system as well as in the practices and attitudes of the prison staff. The harsh treatment experienced by prisoners is seen again in this description of the reprisals these women prisoners face on a daily basis as a result of their determined and forceful acts of resistance.

Another area almost completely neglected in the literature is the topic of lesbians caught in the criminal justice system. Chapter 14 shows us that we do this at our peril. "Defeminizing and Dehumanizing Female Murderers: Depictions of Lesbians on Death Row" relates the experiences of 35 women who are on death row, in part *because* they are lesbians. Kathryn Ann Farr claims that homophobic attitudes have led to an overrepresentation of lesbians in atypical death sentence cases. She suggests that the courts' sentencing of these violent offenders to death may have been influenced by the women's defiance of appropriate gender roles.

In chapter 15, Diane Reed and Edward Reed's review of "Mothers in Prison and Their Children" introduces the reader to another facet of women's incarceration: the children of women in prison. Because mothers are more often the primary caregivers than fathers are, children are more harmed when a mother must serve a prison sentence. Likewise, incarcerated women risk termination of parental rights more than incarcerated men do. The short-term consequences to children are most obvious—loss of a sense of security, inadequate care, poverty, confusion, and their own inability to understand the situation. However, the long-term consequences, while less obvious, have significant social implications.

Studies have found that these children are more likely to be caught up in the justice system themselves as they grow older. This finding is especially true for poor families of color. The end result, whether intentional or not, is that 7 percent of all black children and almost 3 percent of Latino and Latina children have at least one parent in prison. When society fails to solve its larger social problems and incarcerates mothers (and fathers) instead, it is not just meting out punishment to a single individual, it is also creating one of the conditions leading to the next generation of prisoners (Mumola 2000).

In chapter 16, "Stopping Abuse in Prison," Nina Siegal presents the reader with another example of egregious gender discrimination. The focus here is on violence against women in prison in the United States, which, the author reports, has been investigated by a number of governmental and advocacy groups. Siegal recalls that the contemporary women's movement—which, beginning in the 1960s, advocated equal access to job opportunities—has had the unintended consequence of men having the right to work as correctional officers in women's prisons. With the advent of women's reformatories at the turn of the twentieth century, women guards were employed in order to give women prisoners some protection from abuses by male guards. Today, with male corrections officers having access to women inmates, sexual and physical abuse by males in authority positions is once again occurring. Many observers, including international human rights organizations, believe that the answer lies in removing male corrections officers from women's institutions. However, some feminists assert that federal legislation, which also protects the rights of women to work in men's prisons, would have to be changed and that women workers would probably be harmed. This dilemma captures the idea, mentioned earlier, that equality and fairness may not always be the most appropriate objective for women prisoners because standards of treatment are based on male norms that may cause further harm to women prisoners.

Part 2 ends with a warning issued by the Canadian feminist scholar and prison activist Karlene Faith. "Progressive Rhetoric, Regressive Policies: Canadian Prisons for Women" (chap. 17) describes the efforts of progressive and feminist reformers in Canada to change abusive practices directed against women prisoners. The story is one of hope and then despair as, first, the Correctional Services of Canada altered its language and adopted a progressive rhetoric that focused on establishing women-centered prisons, but soon found that the old philosophy (punishment and social control) and the new philosophy (empowerment, reasonable choices, and shared responsibility) were incompatible. Conservative correctional practices reemerged, and today women continue to experience abuses that include illegal strip searches, lack of legal counsel, segregation, and transfer to men's prisons. Progressive feminist rhetoric notwithstanding, Faith documents the failure of Canadian prisons for women to apply a truly feminist set of principles and practices. She, like Sudbury (chap. 12), asks us to question the whole concept of incarceration if we ever hope to provide the structures and resources needed by women (and men) who get caught in the criminal justice system so that they may become more productive members of society.

REFERENCES

Adler, Freda. 1979. The Interaction between Women's Emancipation and Female Criminality: A Cross-Cultural Perspective. In *The Criminology of Deviant Women,* ed. Freda Adler and Rita Simon, 407–18. Boston: Houghton Mifflin.

Bush-Baskette, Stephanie. 1998. The War on Drugs as a War against Black Women. In *Crime Control and Women,* ed. Susan L. Miller, 113–29. Thousand Oaks, CA: Sage.

Chesney-Lind, Meda. 1997. *The Female Offender: Girls, Women, and Crime.* Thousand Oaks, CA: Sage.

Chesney-Lind, Meda. 1998. Women in Prison: From Partial Justice to Vengeful Equity. *Corrections Today,* December, 67–73.

Chesney-Lind, Meda. 2000. Women and the Criminal Justice System: Gender Matters. *Topics in Community Corrections: Annual Issue,* 7–10. U.S. Department of Justice, National Institute of Corrections.

Correctional Association Reporter. 1991. New York: Correctional Association of New York.

Davis. Angela Y. 2000. Women in Prison: African-American Women have Fastest-Rising Incarceration Rate in U.S. *Essence.* Retrieved on January 26, 2002, from www.findarticles.com/cf_dls/ml264/5_31/65278158/print.html.

English, Kim. 1993. Self-Reported Crime Rates of Women Prisoners. *Journal of Quantitative Criminology* 9:357–82.

Fisher-Giorlando, Marianne. 2000. Gender Disparity in Prisons. In *The Encyclopedia of Women and Crime,* ed. Nicole Hahn Rafter, 99–102. Phoenix, AZ: Oryx.

Gilfus, Mary. 1991. From Victims to Survivors to Offenders: Women's Routes to Entry and Immersion into Street Crime. *Women and Criminal Justice* 4:63–89.

Greenfeld, Lawrence, and Tracy Snell. 1999. *Women Offenders: Bureau of Justice Statistics Special Report.* Washington, DC: Bureau of Justice Statistics. NCJ175688.

Mumola, Christopher. 2000. *Incarcerated Parents and Their Children: Bureau of Justice Statistics Special Report.* Washington, DC: Bureau of Justice Statistics. NCJ182335.

Richie, Beth. 1996. *Compelled to Crime: The Gender Entrapment of Battered Black Women.* New York: Routledge.

Sokoloff, Natalie J. 2001. Violent Female Offenders in New York City: Myths and Facts. In *Crime and Justice in New York City. Vol 1: New York City's Crime Problem,* ed. Andrew Karmen. Cincinnati, OH: Thompson Learning.

Chapter 10

Women and Imprisonment in the United States:
The Gendered Consequences
of the U.S. Imprisonment Binge

Barbara Owen

ABSTRACT

This chapter introduces part 2, Women and Prison, by providing an overview of the consequences of U.S. criminal justice policy for women. Specifically, Owen explains that misguided state and federal policy has resulted in women becoming the fastest growing segment of the prison population. She uses the term *gendered consequences* to underscore the point that the results of current policy have had a different—and very serious—impact on women than on men.

The focus on prison as the answer to the drug problem has led to women being treated as serious criminals. Echoing Paltrow's concerns (chap. 9), Owen faults the so-called war on drugs for producing this policy, which uses prison as the sole solution for very complicated social problems, that precede women's involvement in the world of drugs. Thus, a costly criminalization policy has supplanted other resources that could address the problems of women who typically get caught up in the criminal justice system. These problems include being economically marginal, being victims and survivors of prior abuse, and more generally, being victims of deeply embedded socially structured inequality. Building and running prisons consumes much needed resources that are then not available for educational programs, job training and viable jobs, and child care as well as an array of social services.

The *pains of imprisonment,* a term originally coined to describe the lives of incarcerated men, is discussed as it pertains to women. Owen states that numerous studies have shown that most women are unemployed and drug addicted when sent to prison. Once incarcerated, they face sexual and physical abuse, ineffective grievance procedures, separation from children, inadequate health care, and lack of substance abuse treatment. In short, women prisoners' lives become incomparably more painful, and at the same time, there is virtually no opportunity for them to receive the help necessary to deal with the complex problems that led to their incarceration in the first place.

As you read the chapters that follow in this part, keep in mind Owen's claim that women are being disproportionately harmed by the "prison solution" policy of the U.S. criminal justice system. Other countries' experiences will be discussed in several chapters. You may find it useful to consider whether and in what ways U.S. policy has influenced how other countries respond to the criminalization trend.

In the last twenty-five years the number of women imprisoned in the United States has increased rapidly and the rate of growth of women's imprisonment has far outpaced that of men's imprisonment.[1] As the United States continues its imprisonment binge,[2] the remarkable gender-based difference in the rate of this increase demands explanation. The "so-called 'war on drugs' and related changes in legislation, law enforcement practices and judicial decision making" has fueled this dramatic increase in the punishment and incarceration of women.[3] As the United States continues to increase criminal penalties through mandatory sentencing and longer sentence lengths, the gendered consequence of the imprisonment binge must be explained.

The "war on drugs" and analysis of actual crimes and arrests do not entirely explain the extraordinary increases in the numbers of women in prison or give a comprehensive picture of the women being imprisoned. Other factors that need to be examined to understand this include the patriarchal structure of the social control system and the decreasing economic opportunities available to women, including changes in the public welfare system. The following sections look at these factors, current research on the profile of imprisoned women, and the pain and the deprivation women prisoners experience.

PATRIARCHY AND WOMEN'S IMPRISONMENT

The unwillingness of U.S. society to address the real needs of women and girls on the margins of society and the adoption of the "Three Strikes and You're

Source: From *Harsh Punishment: The International Experiences of Women's Imprisonment* edited by Sandy Cook and Susanne Davies. Copyright 1999 by Sandy Cook and Susanne Davies. Reprinted with permission of Northeastern University Press.

Out" law-and-order philosophy inevitably create an increase in the number of women in prison. As Nancy Kurshan argues, the imprisonment of women, "as well as all other aspects of our lives, takes place against a backdrop of patriarchal relationships."[4] Kurshan defines patriarchy as "the manifestation and institutionalization of male dominance over women and children in the family and the extension of male dominance over women in society in general." She suggests that:

> the imprisonment of women in the US has always been a different phenomenon than that for men: women have traditionally been sent to prison for different reasons, and once in prison, they endure different conditions of incarceration. Women's "crimes" have often had a sexual definition and have been rooted in the patriarchal double standard. Therefore the nature of women's imprisonment reflects the position of women in society.[5]

The study of women in prison must be framed through the lens of patriarchy and its implications for the everyday lives of women. When women's imprisonment itself is examined separately, the rising numbers of women in prison can be seen as a measure of society's failure to care for the needs of women and children who live outside the middle-class protection afforded by patriarchy. The increased numbers of women in prison reflect the cost of allowing the systematic abuse of women and children, the problem of increased drug use, and a continuing spiral of marginalization from conventional institutions.[6]

THE GENDERED IMPLICATIONS OF "THREE STRIKES AND YOU'RE OUT"

Current U.S. prison policy is grounded in law-and-order legislative efforts to control crime, such as mandatory minimum prison sentences and increased sentence lengths.[7] Mona Danner describes the ways in which these trends in correctional policy have affected the lives of women, particularly the increasing penalties for drug offenses. She suggests that the consequences for women in this era of expanded punishments have been largely unexplored. In her view, public debate over "Three Strikes" and law-and-order policy ignores the reality of women's lives and the fact that often women are forced to bear the emotional and physical brunt of these misguided policies.[8] She argues that women bear these costs in three ways. First, the enormous cost of the correctional institutions needed to accommodate an increasing number of prisoners has direct implications for other social services. Danner cites a study by the RAND Corporation that predicts that California's "three strikes" law will require cuts in other government services totaling 40 percent over eight years.[9] She predicts that social services for the poor, especially for women and children, will be hardest hit.

Second, Danner argues that the reduction in these services will result in increased unemployment for women working as social service providers; for example, those employed as social workers, case workers, counselors, and support staff within social service agencies. Third, Danner feels that the "three strikes" laws disproportionately affect women as caregivers, both through the imprisonment of men and women's own imprisonment. Because almost 1.5 million children in the United States are children of prisoners, a significant number of children are growing up with at least one parent incarcerated. The financial and social implications for the community as well as for the individual life chances of these children are yet another cost of the "three strikes" bandwagon.[10]

CRIME RATES, THE ECONOMIC CONTEXT, AND SOCIAL WELFARE CHANGES

In analyzing data from the 1970–1995 Uniform Crime Reports, Darrell Steffensmeir and Emilie Allan found that current arrest trends for women are based, in part, on "the sharp increase in the numbers of women arrested for minor property crimes, like larceny, fraud and forgery."[11] Drug offenses, they state, nevertheless have the most significant impact on female arrest rates. Steffensmeir and Allan argue that "it is female inequality and economic vulnerability that shape most female offending patterns."[12] Elliot Currie has examined the connections between crime, work, and welfare, and asserts that unemployment is a steady predictor of criminality and subsequent imprisonment.[13] Currie sees the lack of adequate economic and social supports for women and children in U.S. society as a key feature in the rising crime rates. The poverty of their lives and the lack of educational and economic opportunity makes crime a reasonable choice for some women; subsequent imprisonment is a predictable outcome. Currie argues that material disadvantage and quality of family life are intimately related and may in fact combine to create conditions that foster crime. Currie also presents evidence that unemployment is also tied directly to substance abuse.[14] As mentioned in the previous section, Danner suggests that social services that benefit women and children are likely to be sacrificed in order to expand the criminal justice system.[15] One specific example of social service cuts is in the Welfare Reform Bill of 1996 that imposed a limit on the period poor women may receive Aid to Families with Dependent Children. She ties the costs of the expansion of the prison system directly to the reduction in these benefits.

These findings have direct relevance for explaining the problems of female imprisonment. Most imprisoned women in the United States struggle with both unemployment and substance abuse. The majority of imprisoned women were unemployed prior to their arrest and have experienced problems with chronic substance abuse. Over half the women surveyed by the Bureau of Justice Statistics (BJS) did not work at the time of their arrest.[16] A study of California's women prisoners I co-authored with Barbara Bloom found that over 60 percent of the women interviewed in 1994 reported that they were unemployed prior to imprisonment.[17] Many of these women prisoners indicated that drug and alcohol problems contributed to their inability to work. "Making more money from crime and hustling," child care responsibilities, and lack of training and education were also reported as reasons for unemployment.[18]

Drug problems and violation of the increasingly stringent drug laws bring women into contact with the justice system at ever increasing rates and aggravate existing personal and social problems. The war on drugs and corresponding punitive incarceration policies have resulted in a disproportionate sanction against women[19] and have contributed to their economic marginalization. As I have argued previously, three central issues shape the lives of women prior to imprisonment: multiplicity of abuse in their pre-prison lives; family and personal relationships, particularly those relating to male partners and children; and spiraling economic marginality leading to criminality.[20] To further explain the connection between America's current imprisonment binge and the effect of economic hardship and changes in public welfare systems on women's lives prior to incarceration, the following section describes the changing profile of women in U.S. prisons.

CHANGING PROFILE OF WOMEN IN U.S. PRISONS

The national surveys conducted by the BJS, the American Correctional Association (ACA), and the Federal Bureau of Prisons provide profiles of women in prison in the United States.[21] These profiles describe a population that is poor, that is disproportionately African American and Hispanic, and that has little education and few job skills. This population is primarily composed of young women who are single heads of households; the majority of those who are imprisoned (80 percent) have at least two children. Most women enter prison with a complex set of health and personal problems that are not addressed by the U.S. prison system. The most current BJS survey, based on 1991 data, found that women in prison were most likely to be Black, un-

employed at the time of arrest, and never married. With a median age of thirty-one years in 1991, the female prison population was somewhat older than those imprisoned in 1986.[22] In the federal system, women were more likely to be somewhat older, with an average age of thirty-six years, and more likely to be White than women in state prisons.[23]

Research on the racial makeup of U.S. prison populations and incarceration patterns clearly shows the disproportionate use of imprisonment in the United States. Bloom uses the term "triple jeopardy" to describe the complex interaction of class, race, and gender that contributes to the ever increasing rates of imprisonment.[24] Stephanie Bush-Baskette examines the impact of the war on drugs on Black women prisoners, offering a strong analysis of the relationship between race, gender, and arrests for drug-related offenses.[25] She notes that Black women have been imprisoned for drug offenses at rates of about twice that of Black males and more than three times the rate of White females.[26] Coramae Mann makes a similar argument in her study of arrest categories in three states (California, Florida, and New York).[27] Although demographic profiles describe the problem of racial/ethnic overrepresentation in the female prison population, few studies have examined this issue empirically. Sharon McQuaide and John Ehrenreich suggest that "virtually nothing is known about the characteristics of women prisoners across the racial and ethnic groupings."[28] They further state:

> If knowledge of female prisoners as a group is thin, knowledge of the strengths and differences of female prisoners of different racial and ethnic backgrounds, the unique needs of particular groups of female offenders or the interactions between racial or ethnic identity and the prison experience is all but non-existent.[29]

The issue of social and economic class also needs to be taken into account. Most criminologists see that poor people are much more likely to become imprisoned than individuals from the middle, upper, and propertied classes.[30] In one of our California studies, we found that less than one-half of the women were employed at the time of their arrest and only about one-half had completed high school. About one-fifth of the California prisoners said they were on some form of public assistance in the year prior to their arrest.[31] Clearly poor women, particularly those of color, suffer disproportionately under the punitive sentencing structures of the war on drugs and mandatory sentencing policies.

THE PAINS OF IMPRISONMENT

Women in U.S. prisons, like prisoners throughout the world, face specific pains and deprivations arising from their imprisonment. The Women's Institute for Leadership Development for Human Rights (WILDHR) has indeed argued that U.S. prisons violate three basic human rights:

1. The right to bodily integrity, including freedom from physical and sexual abuse
2. The right to health, including adequate and responsive medical care
3. The right to economic security, including the ability to work and to have an adequate standard of living.[32]

Joy Pollock has described the range of pains and deprivations experienced by women prisoners and their consequences. She found that stress shapes the daily life of women inmates and has three primary sources: arbitrary rule enforcement, assaults on self-respect that are endemic to prison life, and the loss of children. Additionally, she states, lack of autonomy and control over decision making and the impact of monotony and routine create problems for women in U.S. prisons.[33] Detailed below are several specific issues that contribute to the pain and deprivation of women prisoners.

Disparate Disciplinary Practices

Although male prisons typically hold a much greater percentage of violent offenders, women tend to receive disciplinary infractions at a greater rate than men. In her comparative study of Texas prisons,

Dorothy McClelland found that women prisoners were cited more frequently and punished more severely than males. The infractions committed by the women in McClelland's Texas sample were overwhelmingly petty and, she suggests, perhaps a result of a philosophy that expects rigid and formalistic rule compliance on the part of women but not on the part of the men.[34] The most common infractions among the women were "violation of a written or posted rule" and "refusing to obey an order." McClelland found that women were more likely to be strictly supervised than men and cited for behavior that would be overlooked in an institution for men.[35] The patriarchal patterns of social control that propel women into prison may also be responsible for the differences in rule enforcement between male and female institutions.

Sexual Abuse

In *All Too Familiar: Sexual Abuse of Women in U.S. Prisons,* Human Rights Watch examines the serious problem of sexual abuse.[36] [Editors' note: See also Siegal, chap. 16.] In their careful review of sexual abuse in selected U.S. prisons, the Human Rights Watch investigators identified four specific issues:

1. The inability to escape one's abuser
2. Ineffectual or nonexistent investigative and grievance procedures
3. Lack of employee accountability (either criminally or administratively)
4. Little or no public concern.

They state bluntly that: "our findings indicate that being a woman in U.S. state prisons can be a terrifying experience."[37] As Barbara Bloom and Meda Chesney-Lind note, the sexual victimization of women prisoners is difficult to uncover due to inadequate protection afforded women who file complaints and an occupational subculture among the staff that discourages complete investigation of these allegations. Additionally, they suggest, the public stereotype of women as "bad girls" compromises the legitimacy of the women's claims.[38]

Separation from Children and Significant Others

Most research on women in prison describes the importance of family, particularly children, in the lives of imprisoned women.[39] National surveys of women prisoners found that three-quarters of women prisoners were mothers; two-thirds had children who were under the age of eighteen years.[40] Bloom and Chesney-Lind discuss the implications of motherhood among U.S. women prisoners. They argue that mothers in prison face multiple problems in maintaining relationships with their children and encounter obstacles created by both the correctional system and child welfare agencies.[41] Bloom and Chesney-Lind state that the distance between the prison and the children's homes, lack of transportation, and limited economic resources compromise a woman prisoner's ability to maintain these relationships. Slightly over one-half of the women responding to Barbara Bloom and David Steinhart's 1993 survey of imprisoned mothers reported never receiving visits from their children.[42] (See also Reed and Reed, chap. 15.)

The limited economic resources of caregivers, too, is an added difficulty for women prisoners who wish to maintain relationships with their children. Susan Phillips and Barbara Bloom analyze the impact of the changing welfare system on relatives caring for children of incarcerated parents.[43] They argue that lack of financial support for these children is grounded in the inflexibility of public assistance programs that were not designed to meet the needs of care-giving relatives.

Inadequate Health Care

As WILDHR notes, the physical and mental health needs of women prisoners are often neglected, if not ignored. Leslie Acoca argues that the enormity of health care issues may in fact eclipse other correctional concerns as the female inmate population continues to grow.[44] The majority of imprisoned women have significant health care problems and few of these needs are met in the nation's prisons.

Acoca suggests that the lack of women-specific drug treatment is one of the factors linked to the high incidence of HIV infection among imprisoned women.[45] Nationwide, about 3.3 percent of women prisoners are thought to be HIV-positive, compared to about 2 percent of male prisoners.[46] Women in prison are also at greater risk of contracting other infectious diseases, such as tuberculosis, sexually transmitted diseases, and hepatitis B and C infections. Acoca asserts that inadequate prison health care as well as risky behavior prior to arrest contributes to this problem.[47]

Pregnancy and reproductive health needs are another neglected area of health care. Estimates of the percentage of pregnant women in prisons and jails range from 4 percent to 9 percent. Acoca states that pregnancy during incarceration must be understood as a high-risk situation, both medically and psychologically, for inmate mothers and their children. She notes that deficiencies in the response of prisons to the needs of pregnant inmates include lack of prenatal and postnatal care, including nutrition; inadequate education regarding childbirth and parenting; and inadequate preparation for the mother's separation from the infant after delivery. An opportunity to provide reproductive health care and education to this group of women through basic education and family planning is also being missed.[48]

Lack of Recognition of Prior Victimization

Closely related to these mental health needs is the need to recognize the impact of the physical, sexual, and emotional abuse experienced by women who are in prison. Studies of women in prison establish that many women have been violently victimized both as children and adults. Joycelyn Pollock-Byrne has summarized this research by saying:

> Some researchers suggest female inmates come from families marked by alcoholism, drug addiction, mental illness, desertion and child abuse. Several studies show that in a sample of incarcerated women, a majority had been physically and sexually abused as children, had greater difficulties in their interpersonal relationships

with family and peers than others and had been treated for mental problems.[49]

Studies consistently report a high incidence of physical, sexual, and emotional victimization in the personal histories of women prisoners; 30 to 80 percent of the women in these studies have a background of abuse.[50] In our studies, we found that physical, sexual, and emotional abuse is a defining experience for the majority of women in California prisons. In our sample, which included the category of emotional abuse, 80 percent of the women interviewed reported experiencing some kind of abuse. With the exception of sexual assault, most women indicated that they were harmed by family members and other intimates.[51] Most prisons lack programs to deal with this fundamental problem.[52]

Lack of Substance Abuse Treatment

The vast majority of imprisoned women have a need for substance abuse services. National and statewide surveys consistently demonstrate that women in prison are quite likely to have an extensive history of drug and alcohol use. This research concludes that drug use acts as a multiplier in interaction with criminality.[53] Even in the face of this significant problem, providing prison-based services for women has only recently been considered throughout the nation.[54] A national survey of drug programs for female prisoners found that a relatively small percentage of women prisoners in prisons and jails receive any treatment while incarcerated. In a review of treatment strategies for drug-abusing female offenders, Jean Wellisch and colleagues argue that in-prison treatment must be designed specifically to address the needs of women offenders and that current substance abuse services are not sufficiently tailored to meet the needs of women prisoners. These researchers found that programs were hampered by insufficient individual assessment; limited treatment for pregnant, mentally ill, and violent women prisoners; a lack of appropriate treatment; and insufficient vocational training of program providers.[55] These findings are supported by a recent study released by the National Center on Addiction and Substance Abuse (CASA). CASA found that women substance abusers are more prone to intense emotional distress, psychosomatic symptoms, depression, and low self-esteem than male inmates. The CASA report examines the cost and consequence of the war on drugs and concludes that, nationwide, women substance abusers are not receiving an adequate level of treatment.[56]

Insufficient Mental Health Services

Mental health disorders are equally neglected in U.S. prisons. Although few studies accurately assess the prevalence and incidence of these needs, estimates suggest that 25 percent to over 60 percent of the female prison population requires mental health services.[57] Many inmates are often diagnosed as experiencing both substance abuse and mental health problems.[58] Singer and others report that many incarcerated women have had experience with both the criminal justice system and the mental health system.[59] Teplin, Abraham, and McClelland found that over 60 percent of female jail inmates had symptoms of drug abuse, over 30 percent had signs of alcohol dependence, and one-third had post-traumatic stress disorder.[60] These problems and other problems associated with imprisoned women are best managed outside the punitive environment of U.S. prisons.[61]

Lack of Educational and Vocational Programs

In addition to inadequate substance abuse programs and mental health services, educational and vocational programs are also in short supply. In 1990, Joycelyn Pollock-Byrne found that female prisons offered fewer vocational and educational program opportunities than did prisons for men.[62] The situation today is not much better. Morash, Haarr, and Rucker reviewed prison programs for men and women and found that, in general, women across the country lack programming adequate to their needs.[63] One aspect of this inadequacy is that many vocational programs for female inmates emphasize the traditional roles of women and women's work.[64]

CONCLUSION

In 1994, Bloom, Chesney-Lind, and Owen offered this explanation for the incredible increases in the female prison population:

> The increasing incarceration rate for women in the State of California, then, is a direct result of short-sighted legislative responses to the problems of drugs and crime—responses shaped by the assumption that the criminals they were sending to prison were brutal males. Instead of a policy of last resort, imprisonment has become the first order response for a wide range of women offenders that have been disproportionately swept up in this trend. This politically motivated legislative response often ignores the fiscal or social costs of imprisonment. Thus, the legislature has missed opportunities to prevent women's crime by cutting vitally needed social service and educational programs to fund ever-increasing correctional budgets.[65]

Today I continue to argue that the problems and issues women who have been sent to prison have experienced—abuse and battering, economic disadvantage, substance abuse, and unsupported parenting responsibilities—are best addressed outside the punitive custodial environment.[66] Under current policy, these complex problems are laid at the feet of the prison by a society unwilling or unable to confront the problems of women on the margin. As a whole, the prison system is designed to deal with the criminality of men and their behavior while incarcerated. The women confined in U.S. prisons are enmeshed in a criminal justice system that is ill-equipped and confused about handling the problems of women—the problems that brought them to prison and the problems they confront during their incarceration. The prison, with its emphasis on security and population management and lack of emphasis on gender-specific treatment and programs, is nevertheless left to deal with the failings of society's institutions. In the United States we expect too much from prisons. Prisons are called upon to deal with deep and com-

plicated problems that society ignores. The number of imprisoned women will continue to rise until the reality of their lives on the streets, and inside the prisons, forces a reexamination of prison policy and its gendered consequences.

DISCUSSION QUESTIONS

1. Spell out the "gendered" implications of the U.S. imprisonment binge for women. Give a few concrete examples in your answer.
2. Describe the women who end up in prison. How does this description help us evaluate stereotypes about women in prison?
3. Discuss strategies for ending the current "prison-as-solution" response using as reference points, first, the United States and, second, your own locality.

NOTES

1. Russ Immarigeon and Meda Chesney-Lind, *Women's Prisons: Overcrowded and Overused* (San Francisco: National Council on Crime and Delinquency, 1992).
2. John Irwin and James Austin, *It's About Time: America's Imprisonment Binge* (Belmont, Calif.: Brooks Cole, 1997).
3. Human Rights Watch, *All Too Familiar: Sexual Abuse of Women in U.S. Prisons* (New York: Human Rights Watch, 1996), 23.
4. Nancy Kurshan, "Women and Imprisonment in the U.S.," in *Cages of Steel,* eds. W. Churchill and J. J. Vander Wall (Washington, DC: Maisonneuve Press, 1992), 331–58.
5. Ibid., 331.
6. Barbara Owen, *In the Mix: Struggle and Survival in a Women's Prison* (Albany: State University of New York Press, 1998), 13–14.
7. Mona J. E. Danner, "Three Strikes and It's Women Who Are Out," in *Crime Control and Women,* ed. S. Miller (Thousand Oaks, Calif.: Sage Publications, 1998), 1–11.

8. Ibid., 5.
9. Peter W. Greenwood, C. Peter Rydell, Allan F. Abrahamse, Jonathan P. Caulkins, James Chiesa, Karyn E. Model, and Stephen P. Klein, *Three Strikes and You're Out: Estimated Benefits and Costs of California's New Mandatory Sentencing Laws* (Santa Monica, Calif.: The RAND Corporation, 1994).
10. Danner, "Three Strikes," 8.
11. Darrell Steffensmeir and Emilie Allan, "The Nature of Female Offending: Patterns and Explanations," in *Female Offenders: Critical Perspectives and Interventions,* ed. R. Zupan (Gaithersburg, Md.: Aspen Publishing, 1998), 10.
12. Ibid., 11.
13. Elliot Currie, *Confronting Crime: An American Challenge* (New York: Pantheon, 1985).
14. Ibid., 107–108.
15. Danner, "Three Strikes," 6.
16. Bureau of Justice Statistics, *Women in Prison* (Washington, DC: U.S. Department of Justice, 1994).
17. Barbara Owen and Barbara Bloom, *Profiling the Needs of California's Female Prisoners: A Needs Assessment* (Washington, DC: National Institute of Corrections, 1995).
18. Ibid., 22.
19. Barbara Bloom, Meda Chesney-Lind, and Barbara Owen, *Women in California Prisons: Hidden Victims of the War on Drugs* (San Francisco: The Center on Juvenile and Criminal Justice, 1994); Human Rights Watch, *All Too Familiar;* Mark Mauer and Tracey Huling, *Young Black Americans and the Criminal Justice System: Five Years Later* (Washington, DC: The Sentencing Project, 1995); Stephanie Bush-Baskette, "The War on Drugs as a War on Black Women," in *Crime Control and Women,* ed. S. Miller (Thousand Oaks, Calif: Sage Publications, 1998), 113–29.
20. Barbara Owen, *In the Mix.*
21. Bureau of Justice Statistics, *Women in Prison,* 1994; Bureau of Justice Statistics, *Prisoners in 1989* (Washington, DC: U.S. Department of Justice, 1990); Bureau of Justice Statistics, *Prisoners in 1990* (Washington, DC: U.S. Department of Justice, 1991); Bureau of Justice Statistics, *Special Report: Women in Prison* (Washington, DC: U.S. Department of Justice, 1991); Bureau of Justice Statistics, *Women in Jail in 1989* (Washington, DC: U.S. Department of Justice, 1992); American Correctional Association (ACA), *The Female Offender: What Does the Future Hold?* (Washington, DC: St. Mary's Press, 1990); Sue Klien, "A Profile of Female Offenders in State and Federal Prisons," in *Female Offenders: Meeting the Needs of a Neglected Population,* ed. American Correctional Association (Laurel, Md.: American Correctional Association, 1993), 1–6.
22. Bureau of Justice Statistics, *Women in Prison,* 1994.
23. Klien, "Profile of Female Offenders," 1–6.
24. Barbara Bloom, "Triple Jeopardy: Race, Class, and Gender as Factors in Women's Imprisonment" (Ph.D. diss., University of California-Riverside, 1996).
25. Bush-Baskette, "War on Drugs," 119.
26. Ibid., 113.
27. Coramae Richey Mann, "Women of Color in the Criminal Justice System," in *The Criminal Justice System and Women,* ed. B. Price and N. Sokoloff (New York: McGraw-Hill, 1995), 118–35.
28. Sharon McQuaide and John Ehrenreich, "Women in Prison: Approaches to Studying the Lives of a Forgotten Population," *Affilia: Journal of Women and Social Work* 13, no. 2 (1998): 233–47.
29. Ibid., 236.
30. Jeffery Reiman, *The Rich Get Richer and the Poor Get Prison* (Needham Heights, Mass.: Allyn and Bacon, 1990).
31. Owen and Bloom, *Profiling Women Prisoners.*
32. The Women's Institute for Leadership Development for Human Rights (WILDHR), *Human Rights for Women in U.S. Custody* (San Francisco, Calif.: WILDHR, n.d.).
33. Joycelyn Pollock, *Counseling Women in Prison* (Thousand Oaks, Calif.: Sage Publications, 1998), 32–33.
34. Dorothy McClelland, "Disparity in the Discipline of Male and Female Inmates in Texas Pris-

ons," *Women and Criminal Justice 5*, no. 2 (1994): 71–97.

35. Pollack, *Counseling Women in Prison*, 35.
36. Human Rights Watch, *All Too Familiar*.
37. Ibid., 1.
38. Barbara Bloom and Meda Chesney-Lind, "Women in Prison: Vengeful Equity," in *It's a Crime: Women and Criminal Justice*, ed. R. Muraskin Upper Saddle River, NJ: Prentice Hall, 2003.
39. Owen, *In the Mix*, 119–20.
40. Bureau of Justice Statistics, *Special Report: Women in Prison*, 1991.
41. Bloom and Chesney-Lind, "Women in Prison."
42. Barbara Bloom and David Steinhart, *Why Punish the Children? A Reappraisal of the Children of Incarcerated Parents* (San Francisco, Calif.: National Council on Crime and Delinquency, 1993).
43. Susan Phillips and Barbara Bloom "In Whose Best Interest? The Impact of Changing Public Policy on Relatives Caring for Children of Incarcerated Parents," *Child Welfare: Special Issue—Children with Parents in Prison* 77 (1998): 531–41.
44. Leslie Acoca, "Defusing the Time Bomb: Understanding and Meeting the Growing Health Care Needs of Incarcerated Women in America," *Crime and Delinquency* 44, no. 1 (1998): 49–70.
45. Ibid., 51.
46. Bureau of Justice Statistics, *Surveys of Inmates in State Correctional Facilities, 1995.* (Washington, DC: U.S. Department of Justice, 1997).
47. Acoca, "Defusing the Time Bomb," 54.
48. Acoca, "Defusing the Time Bomb."
49. Joycelyn Pollock-Byrne, *Women, Prison and Crime* (Pacific Grove, Calif.: Brooks/Cole, 1990), 70.
50. Bureau of Justice Statistics, *Women in Prison;* Bureau of Justice Statistics, *Special Report: Women in Prison;* American Correctional Association, *The Female Offender;* Klein, "Profile of Female Offenders," 1–6; Owen and Bloom, *Profiling the Needs of California's Female Prisoners;* Pollock-Byrne, *Women, Prison and Crime.*

51. Owen and Bloom, *Profiling the Needs of California's Female Prisoners,* 30–31.
52. Pollock, *Counseling Women in Prison;* Beverley Fletcher, Lynda Dixon Shaver, and Dreama Moon, *Women Prisoners: A Forgotten Population* (Westport, Conn.: Praeger, 1993); Owen and Bloom, *Profiling the Needs of California's Female Prisoners.*
53. Owen, "In the Mix," 44–45; National Center on Addiction and Substance Abuse, *Behind Bars: Substance Abuse and America's Prison Population* (New York: Columbia University, 1998).
54. Jean Wellisch, M. Douglas Anglin, and Michael Prendergast, "Treatment Strategies for Drug-Abusing Women Offenders," in *Drug Treatment and the Criminal Justice System,* ed. J. Inciardi (Thousand Oaks, Calif.: Sage Publications, 1994), 5–25.
55. Ibid., 20–22.
56. National Center on Addiction and Substance Abuse, *Behind Bars.*
57. Acoca, "Defusing the Time Bomb," 54.
58. Acoca, "Defusing the Time Bomb."
59. Mark Singer, Janet Bussey, Li Yu Song, and Lisa Lunghofer, "The Psychosocial Issues of Women Serving Time in Jail," *Social Work* 40, no. 1 (1995); 103–14.
60. Linda Teplin, Karen Abraham and Gary McClelland, "Prevalence of Psychiatric Disorders among Incarcerated Women," *Archives of General Psychiatry* 53 (1996): 505–12.
61. Owen, *In the Mix*, 16–17.
62. Pollock-Byrne, *Women, Prison and Crime.*
63. Merry Morasch, Robin Haarr, and L. Rucker, "A Comparison of Programming for Women and Men in U.S. Prisons in the 1980s," *Crime and Delinquency* 40, no. 2 (1994): 197–221.
64. Pamela Schram, "Stereotypes about Vocational Programming for Female Inmates," *Prison Journal* 78, no. 3 (1998): 244–67.
65. Bloom, Chesney-Lind, and Owen, *Women in California Prisons,* 2.
66. Owen, *In the Mix,* 17.

REFERENCES

Acoca, Leslie. 1998. Defusing the Time Bomb: Understanding and Meeting the Growing Health Care Needs of Incarcerated Women in America. *Crime and Delinquency* 44(1).

American Correctional Association. 1990. *The Female Offender: What Does the Future Hold?* Washington, DC: St. Mary's Press.

Bloom, Barbara. 1996. Triple Jeopardy: Race, Class and Gender as Factors in Women's Imprisonment. Ph.D. diss., University of California-Riverside, 1996.

Bloom, Barbara, and Meda Chesney-Lind. 2003. Women in Prison: Vengeful Equity. In *It's a Crime: Women and Criminal Justice,* ed. by R. Muraskin. Upper Saddle River, NJ: Prentice Hall.

Bloom, Barbara, Meda Chesney-Lind, and Barbara Owen, 1994. *Women in California Prisons: Hidden Victims of the War on Drugs.* San Francisco: The Center on Juvenile and Criminal Justice, 1994.

Bloom, Barbara, and David Steinhart. 1993. *Why Punish the Children? A Reappraisal of the Children of Incarcerated Parents.* San Francisco, CA.: National Council on Crime and Delinquency.

Bureau of Justice Statistics, *Prisoners in 1989.* Washington, DC: U.S. Department of Justice, 1990.

———. 1991. *Prisoners in 1990.* Washington, DC: U.S. Department of Justice.

———. 1991. *Special Report: Women in Prison.* Washington, DC: U.S. Department of Justice.

———. 1992. *Women in Jail in 1989.* Washington, DC: U.S. Department of Justice.

———. 1994. *Women in Prison.* Washington, DC: U.S. Department of Justice.

———. 1997. *Survey of Inmates in State Correctional Facilities, 1995.* Washington, DC: U.S. Department of Justice.

Bush-Baskette, Stephanie. 1998. The War on Drugs as a War on Black Women. In *Crime Control and Women,* ed. S. Miller. Thousand Oaks, CA: Sage Publications.

Chesney-Lind, Meda. 1997. *The Female Offender: Girls, Women and Crime.* Thousand Oaks, CA: Sage Publications.

———. 1991. Patriarchy, Prisons and Jails: A Critical Look at Trends in Women's Incarceration. *The Prison Journal* 71 (1).

Currie, Elliot. 1985. *Confronting Crime: An American Challenge.* New York: Pantheon.

Danner, Mona J. E. 1998. Three Strikes and Its Women Who Are Out. In *Crime Control and Women,* ed. by S. Miller. Thousand Oaks, CA: Sage Publications.

Fletcher, Beverly, Lynda Dixon Shaver, and Dreama Moon, eds. 1993. *Women Prisoners: A Forgotten Population.* Westport, CT: Praeger.

Greenwood, Peter W., C. Peter Rydell, Allan F. Abrahamse, Jonathan P. Caulkins, James Chiesa, Karyn E. Model, and Stephen P. Klein. 1994. *Three Strikes and You're Out: Estimated Benefits and Costs of California's New Mandatory Sentencing Laws.* Santa Monica, CA: The RAND Corporation.

Human Rights Watch. 1996. *All Too Familiar: Sexual Abuse of Women in U.S. Prisons.* New York: Human Rights Watch.

Immarigeon, Russ, and Meda Chesney-Lind. 1992. *Women's Prisons: Overcrowded and Overused.* San Francisco: National Council on Crime and Delinquency.

Irwin, John, and James Austin, 1997. *It's About Time: America's Imprisonment Binge.* Belmont, CA: Brooks Cole.

Klein, Sue. 1993. A Profile of Female Offenders in State and Federal Prisons. In *Female Offenders: Meeting the Needs of a Neglected Population,* ed. American Correctional Association. Laurel, MD: American Correctional Association, 1993.

Kurshan, Nancy. 1992. Women and Imprisonment in the U.S. In *Cages of Steel,* ed. W. Churchill and J. J. Vander Wall. Washington, DC: Maisonneuve Press.

Mann, Coramae Richey. 1995. Women of Color in the Criminal Justice System. In *The Criminal Justice System and Women,* ed. by B. Price and N. Sokoloff. New York: McGraw-Hill, 1995.

Mauer, Marc, and Tracey Huling. 1995. *Young Black Americans and the Criminal Justice System: Five Year Later.* Washington, DC: The Sentencing Project.

McClelland, Dorothy. 1994. Disparity in the Discipline of Male and Female Inmates in Texas Prisons. *Women and Criminal Justice* 5(2).

McQuaide, Sharon, and John Ehrenreich. 1998. Women in Prison: Approaches to Studying the Lives of a Forgotten Population. *Affilia: Journal of Women and Social Work* 13(2).

Morash, Merry, Robin Haarr, and L. Rucker. 1994. A Comparison of Programming for Women and Men in U.S. Prisons in the 1980s, *Crime and Delinquency* 40(2).

National Center on Addiction and Substance Abuse (CASA). 1998. *Behind Bars: Substance Abuse and America's Prison Population.* New York: Columbia University.

Owen, Barbara. 1998. *In the Mix: Struggle and Survival in a Women's Prison*. Albany: State University of New York Press.

Owen, Barbara, and Barbara Bloom. 1995. *Profiling the Needs of California's Female Prisoners: A Needs Assessment*. Washington, DC: National Institute of Corrections.

Phillips, Susan, and Barbara Bloom. 1998. In Whose Best Interest? The Impact of Changing Public Policy on Relatives Caring for Children of Incarcerated Parents. *Child Welfare: Special Issue—Children with Parents in Prison* 77.

Pollock, Joycelyn. 1998. *Counseling Women in Prison*. Thousand Oaks, CA: Sage Publications.

Pollock-Byrne, Joycelyn. 1990. *Women, Prison and Crime*. Pacific Grove, CA: Brooks/Cole.

Reiman, Jeffery. 1990. *The Rich Get Richer and the Poor Get Prison*. Needham Heights, MA: Allyn and Bacon.

Schram, Pamela. 1998. Stereotypes about Vocational Programming for Female Inmates." *Prison Journal* 78(3).

Singer, Mark, Janet Bussey, Li Yu Song, and Lisa Lunghofer. The Psychosocial Issues of Women Serving Time in Jail. *Social Work* 40, no. 1 (1995).

Steffensmeier, Darrell, and Emilie Allan. 1998. The Nature of Female Offending: Patterns and Explanations. In *Female Offenders: Critical Perspectives and Interventions*, ed. R. Zupan. Gaithersburg, MD: Aspen Publishing.

Teplin, Linda, Karen Abraham, and Gary McClelland. 1996. Prevalence of Psychiatric Disorders among Incarcerated Women. *Archives of General Psychiatry* 53.

Wellisch, Jean, M. Douglas Anglin, and Michael Prendergast. 1994. Treatment Strategies for Drug-Abusing Women Offenders. *In Drug Treatment and the Criminal Justice System*, ed. J. Inciardi. Thousand Oaks, CA: Sage Publications.

Women's Institute for Leadership Development for Human Rights (WILDHR). *Human Rights for Women in U.S. Custody*. San Francisco, CA: WILDHR, n.d.

Chapter 11

Women in Prison:
Researching Race in Three National Contexts (the Netherlands, Cuba, and the United States)

Kum-Kum Bhavnani and Angela Y. Davis

ABSTRACT

In this chapter two researchers, themselves women of color, interview over 100 women prisoners in three countries—the Netherlands, Cuba, the United States—in order to learn from imprisoned women how they explain the increased incarceration of women and the role of racism as well as sexism in women's imprisonment. Instead of learning "about" subjugated women in prison, Bhavnani and Davis want to bring the women's voices into a public discourse of "resistance" to imprisonment as well as to learn about their thoughts on alternatives to incarceration. The authors discuss several themes similar to Owen's in chapter 10: the greater rate of incarceration of women than men and its disproportionate impact on women of color as well as the inappropriate overutilization of prison to address a range of larger social problems.

Bhavnani and Davis note that because race plays a key role in decisions as to who goes to prison and for how long in the United States, they were anxious to discover what significance race has in imprisonment in the Netherlands and Cuba. Not surprisingly, the whole meaning of race is differently understood in those two countries and thus impacts on the lives of incarcerated women in Cuba and the Netherlands in different ways. For example, in the Dutch prison, racism was synonymous with xenophobia (the fear and hatred of "foreigners," i.e., immigrants). Thus, immigrants, often darker-skinned, frequently are the ones who end up in prison.

As sometimes happens in research, accidental discoveries are made. In the United States, Bhavnani and Davis did not originally plan to go into the San Francisco County Jail but, rather, to a California state prison, which, when the time came, denied them access. Once in the San Francisco jail, the authors learned that the jail had an antiracist, antisexist and antihomophobic contract that each inmate was required to sign. Violations of the contract could lead to punishment, yet the authors were told by the inmates that it did not eliminate racism among the jail staff.

One of the major contributions of this chapter is its collaborative methodology with the women in prison. Rather than treating the women as subjects, Bhavnani and Davis listen to the insights of the prisoners to inform their work and take it in new directions. The authors also make clear the activist, antiracist, and feminist nature of their research. This approach is in contrast with mainstream social science in which research and policy are treated as independent from one another and advocacy is considered antithetical to research.

This article is important for its description of the authors' experiences in trying to study a difficult topic and in learning of their findings. But it is equally important because the reader learns of the authors' own struggles to keep their commitment to work toward abolishing prisons while still seeking to improve prison life for those women (and men) already incarcerated.

Women in prison comprise an enormous, invisible, and silenced population. This chapter draws on research based on interviews with over one hundred imprisoned women in the United States, the Netherlands, and Cuba. Our collaborative research contests their multiple marginalizations, not the least of which is racism, that render them invisible and silent. We also question the ubiquitous status of prisoners (particularly women prisoners of color) as objects of research. In our study, women prisoners' insights about the conditions of their imprisonment have been used to raise new questions, which in turn have informed the ultimate direction of our work.[1]

We are interested in the ways in which presently and formerly incarcerated women can help explain the increasing reliance on public forms of punishment for women who historically have been punished largely within private spheres. We are also interested in the extent to which counterdiscourses forged by antiracist social movements inform imprisoned women's ability to explicitly theorize the role of racism in imprisonment practices. As women researchers of color—one South Asian and the other African-American—who have been involved in antiracist movements in Britain and the United States for many years, our own perspectives are informed both by our experiences as activists in different na-

tional contexts and by our commitment to link our academic research to strategies for radical social change. Our study thus begins with the assumption that the overutilization of imprisonment to address a range of social problems—which would more appropriately be dealt with by nonpunitive institutions—constitutes a major contemporary crisis. This means that our work is linked to efforts to transform public policy and to activist strategies that emphasize the importance of including imprisoned women in a new public discourse of resistance to imprisonment rather than to more conventional research agendas to generate knowledge *about* a subjugated group.

In conceptualizing this study of women's imprisonment and our role as researchers, we considered our own racialized backgrounds within the political contexts defining our activist histories. We were—and continue to be—concerned with the possibility of forging feminist alliances across racial boundaries. Where Kum-Kum Bhavnani was involved during the seventies and eighties in labor, feminist, and prison activism in Britain at a time when the category "black" was politically defined as embracing people of African, Asian, and Middle Eastern descent, Angela Davis was active during the same era in a number of campaigns informed by the category "women of color," which addressed political issues affecting Native American, Latina, African-American, and Asian American women. The issues addressed were thus not racially exclusive. In imagining the groups of imprisoned women we would interview,

Source: Kum-Kum Bhavnani and Angela Davis. Women in Prison: Researching Race in Three National Contexts. In *Racing Research, Researching Race*, eds. F. W. Twine and J. W. Warren 2000. New York: New York University, pp. 227–245.

we did not establish goals for specific racial *groups* but rather considered the general racialization of imprisonment *practices,* which have a disproportionate impact on women of color and poor white women. We were much more interested in the women's critical perspectives about racialized and gendered prison systems and the way they might help demystify the role of the state than in learning about *individuals* and their relationship to the racial groups with which they identified. The democratic framework in which we attempted to formulate this project is a reflection of our own attempt to render the boundaries between research and activism more permeable.

We chose the three countries where we conducted our interviews for specific reasons. We are most familiar with the penal system in the United States and are concerned with the gendered character of the emergent prison industrial complex, which has resulted in the proliferation of women's prisons and an attendant intensification of penal repression. Within the United States, the number of prisoners per capita far exceeds that of any other capitalist country.[2] The Netherlands, which is experiencing a significant increase in the number of prisoners for the first time in its history, has one of the lowest per capita rates of incarceration, as well as a history of progressive penal reform.[3] As far as Western capitalist countries go, it is at the other end of the spectrum. Finally, we chose Cuba so that we might ascertain the differences, if any, between penal regimes for women in capitalist countries and penal regimes under socialism. While our study of imprisoned women in the United States began with the premise that race played a pivotal role in determining who goes to prison and how long a convicted woman remains behind bars, we set out to discover the significance of race in the other two national settings as well.

It is worth noting that Angela Davis's history as a political prisoner during the early seventies and as an internationally known political activist both obstructed and facilitated our research. We attribute the fact that we were unable to gain access to the California Institution for Women (CIW) to her reputa-

tion as a former prisoner and prison activist. As we indicate below, we changed the venue of our U.S. interviews to the San Francisco County Jail because the warden at CIW never granted us permission to enter the prison. On the other hand, the director of the women's prison in the Netherlands was herself a prison activist and was aware of Angela's history as a former political prisoner and of her work on prisoners' rights. This clearly facilitated our ability to conduct research in the prison she supervised. Our access to women's prisons in Cuba was directly related to Angela's historical connections with the Association of Cuban Women, an organization that had played a major role in organizing the Cuban campaign for her freedom.

While Angela's experiences and history as a former political prisoner facilitated our access to prisons in the Netherlands and in Cuba, it also sometimes led to a tendency on the part of the prison staffs to treat Angela as the primary researcher, which contradicted the egalitarian way we had structured our research relationship. We made it clear that in our collaborative project, we both claimed equal status as coinvestigators. But in spite of tactful reminders, Kum-Kum's name was frequently misspelled and in official documents was listed after Angela's, even though our own practice was to list our names in alphabetical order. On the other hand, the prisoners we interviewed seemed far more sophisticated than their keepers. Even though many of them knew of Angela—one even had a child named after her—they always treated us as equals and never indicated a preference for being interviewed by one of us over the other. Collaborative research relationships rarely unfold without complications. In our case, the assumption of a hierarchal relationship by the prison administrations could have negatively affected our research relationship. However, we talked openly about the impact this behavior might have on our work, thus struggling to preserve our own collaborative spirit.

Explanations for the sparsity of literature on imprisoned women usually point to the relatively small percentage of women in prison compared to their male counterparts. It is true that in most countries

women constitute between 5 and 10 percent of imprisoned populations.

> On average only one out of every twenty prisoners is
> a woman. Women constitute roughly 50 percent of the
> population of any country, yet provide only 5 percent
> of its prisoners. . . . This is not specific to any one coun-
> try or region, but is reflected all over the world. There
> are variations. In Spain, the proportion of women in
> prison is 10 percent, in the United States over 6 per-
> cent, in France 4 percent, in Russia 3 percent and in
> Morocco it is 2 percent. But nowhere in the world do
> women make up more than one in ten of the whole
> [prison] population.[4]

What is rarely taken into consideration, however, is
the fact that modes of punishment are both racialized
and gendered in ways that indicate a historical continuum linking women's imprisonment with incarceration in mental institutions and with modes of
private punishment such as domestic violence.[5] In
the context of a developing global prison industrial
complex, the relatively small percentages of imprisoned women are now rising. In the United States,
the rate of increase in women's incarceration has sur-
passed the rate of increase in men's.[6] As international
women's movements contest patriarchal structures
and ideologies, a new consciousness of women's
rights in "private" settings has begun to subvert old
attitudes of acquiescence toward misogynist violence.
However, even as the private punishment of women
becomes less hidden from view and less taken for
granted, the state-inflicted punishment of women
still remains relatively invisible. In the United States
and Europe, as well as in countries in which people
of European descent are most dominant, women of
color are disproportionately targeted by contemporary modes of public punishment. Thus the hyper-
invisibility of women's prisons reflects a larger
contemporary tendency to incarcerate structures of
racism within those institutions that function in public discourse as sites where expendable populations
and problems are deposited and hidden away.

According to Mary Helen Washington, "the class,
gender, and racial politics of prisons in this country
conspire to make most of us feel, not only separate
from the world of prison but indifferent to it, un-

touched and unconcerned."[7] Racialized socioeconomic patterns are camouflaged by representational
practices that criminalize poor women and men of
color, thereby justifying their imprisonment and allowing the racist structures that affect access to employment, health care, education, and housing to go
unrecognized. It may not be entirely fortuitous that
California, the first state to abolish affirmative action, also has the largest prison population in the
country. It is therefore important to view prisons as
productive sites for research on racism and an important opportunity to challenge conservative claims
regarding the "end of racism."

In the United States, the current shift from a social welfare state to one prioritizing social control[8]
has helped to generate the conditions for an emergent prison industrial complex and has caused the
numbers of imprisoned women to rise even more
strikingly than those of their male counterparts.[9] As
government policies in Canada, in many parts of
Europe, and in some African and Latin American
countries reveal a similar shift toward larger penal
systems, the practice of imprisonment disproportionately affects people of color—not only in the
United States but on an international level.[10] In the
Netherlands, for example, the imprisoned population has begun to increase significantly for the first
time in that country's history, due largely to the influx of black and immigrant men and women who
can be found disproportionately in the prisons.
While our research on and with imprisoned women
in the United States, the Netherlands, and Cuba is
largely concerned with the ways women prisoners
think about alternatives to incarceration, our study
also tries to highlight the gendering of racism in imprisonment practices and in general attempts to address the intersections of class, race, gender, and
sexuality as they are perceived and theorized by the
women with whom we spoke and as we ourselves
attempt to theorize these intersections. In this sense,
our project attempts to address issues that exceed
both conventional research agendas and activist
strategies that treat prisoners—and especially
women prisoners—as objects of knowledge or as
simply the beneficiaries of liberatory movements.

COLLABORATION AND ACCESS

Having previously met each other through political and intellectual work, in the early 1990s we began to explore the possibility of long-term collaborative research that would allow us to productively draw from our respective training in the humanities and social sciences. In 1993, we were awarded resident research fellowships at the University of California Humanities Research Institute (UCHRI) in connection with its Minority Discourse Initiative which that year called upon fellows to think critically about the normalization of certain social science discourses in relation to public policy. It was in this context that we decided to conduct a series of interviews with women prisoners in California. Since the UCHRI is housed on the Irvine campus in Southern California, we planned to interview prisoners at the California Institute for Women (CIW), located in Frontera, a relatively short distance from Irvine.

As activists, we were not unaware of the general difficulties of access to prisons. Nevertheless, we assumed that a legitimate and compelling scholarly project would be accepted by the California Department of Corrections (CDC). However, our instincts as scholars did not adequately reflect our sophistication as political activists, for, despite prompt submission of our application, the CDC never granted us permission to enter the prison. After submitting all the necessary documents to the CDC authorities in charge of approving research proposals, we were led to believe that the approval of our project by the warden at CIW was simply a formality. As we made final preparations for our move to Irvine and for our visits to CIW, we waited to hear from the warden. In further communications with the research department of CDC, we were advised to be patient with the department's slow-moving bureaucracy. However, once we arrived in Irvine and still had not received word from CIW, it became obvious to us that more might be at issue than bureaucratic sluggishness. After numerous messages left at the warden's office went unanswered, the director of the Humanities Research Institute intervened for

us, under the assumption that his messages would not be so easily disregarded. While he was never allowed to speak with the warden, he was told by an unidentified official in an off-the-record communication that "Angela Davis would never be allowed inside the California Institute for Women." The warden, the official indicated, felt that she had things under control in the prison and would not allow Angela Davis to come in and "rock the boat." We received the official denial of our request after the proposed research period would already have begun.

Because we were determined to pursue our project with imprisoned women, we decided to investigate the possibility of another interview site. Since Angela had previously taught at the San Francisco County Jail, we decided to submit our project proposal to Michael Morcum, the director of the County Jail system's program facility, who had previously served a sentence in San Quentin and was active during the 1970s in the formation of the California Prisoners' Union. The fact that an access permit came through in a matter of days caused us to think in more complex terms about the ways in which individual administrators are interpolated within the correctional system. Ironically, we had applied for the UCHRI fellowship in Irvine because CIW was in the vicinity and had both moved to Irvine to conduct the interviews. Now we would be required to make numerous research trips to the San Francisco Bay Area during the course of our residence in Southern California. Despite these initial difficulties, we soon recognized that given the San Francisco Program Facility's pioneering efforts to minimize racism within the jail, which we discuss later in this essay, the interviews would be extremely productive.

We interviewed thirty-five of the approximately one hundred women at the San Francisco County Jail's Program Facility. In this section of the County Jail, located in San Bruno, California, male and female inmates were required to participate in "programs"—that is, in educational classes, cultural programs, Alcoholic or Narcotic Anonymous sessions, and organic gardening classes. Men were housed in four dormitories and women in the remaining two. Our interview pool was comprised of women who volunteered to participate after attending a session during which we described our project. In our introductory statements, we described our activist and academic histories, our desire to use a "grounded theory" approach and generally democratic research methods, as well as our hopes that this work would ultimately help to transform public discourses and policies around women in prison. We explained that we were not interested in the women's legal cases and therefore would not ask them to explain to us why they were in jail. Rather, we wanted them to offer their own perspectives about women's imprisonment and about alternatives to incarceration.

As with the other two sites of our study, we first asked for volunteers to participate in focus groups, to help us think about the kinds of questions that would be most productive. That far more women volunteered than we expected may have been a result of our decision not to construct them as research subjects whose criminal histories we wanted to probe. As at the other two sites, women who had not initially volunteered later attempted to join the project as news about the interviews traveled. While we were able to accommodate some of them, we never succeeded in talking to all the women who volunteered. In San Francisco, our interview pool, like the overall jail population, was comprised of an African-American majority, but also Latinas, white women, and one Asian American. However, in the individual interviews, we did not ask different questions based on the assumed racial identities of these women.

While the U.S. component of the research presented huge access problems, we gained entrance to the prison in the Netherlands—Amerswiel Prison for Women—with relative ease. The director, Bernadette van Dam, was herself a well-known advocate of the rights of imprisoned women and, unlike the warden at CIW, welcomed scholarly work designed to make a difference in the lives of women in prison. Angela had visited this prison the previous year and had interviewed the director, as well as several prisoners. When we formally submitted a re-

quest to the Dutch Ministry of Justice to conduct interviews at Amerswiel, both the prison director and the Ministry of Justice immediately approved our proposal. While we spent most of our 1996 visit to the Netherlands in Amerswiel, we did have the opportunity to visit two other women's prisons—in Breda and Sevenum—as well as the men's prison in Breda.

Amerswiel Prison is located in the town of Heerhugowaard, thirty miles outside Amsterdam. At the time of our interviews, the prison consisted of four residential units—the Short Term, Long Term, Individual Guidance, and Drug Rehabilitation Units—housing seventy-nine women altogether. With one exception, our interviewees were women in the Short and Long Term Units, which housed twenty-seven and twenty-six women respectively. Approximately half of the women imprisoned in Amerswiel were women of color—of Surinamese, South American, and Asian descent. Our interview pool, consisting of volunteers, comprised approximately the same percentage of women of color.

While our own racial and national backgrounds were sometimes noted by the women we interviewed, it was our status as researchers and prison activists that most interested the women who raised questions about our research project. Virtually all the women we interviewed were aware of the prison director's international advocacy on behalf of women in prison, especially with respect to the rights of imprisoned mothers. In fact, some of the women criticized Bernadette van Dam for devoting more time to public campaigns around imprisoned women than to the women under her direct supervision. They pointed out that they saw more of her on television than in person. In general, however, most of the women expressed their appreciation for her public advocacy. Because of their awareness of the director's work as a prison activist, the prisoners tended to locate our work within a similar political framework. However, when we presented our work to the two groups from which the volunteer pool was selected, we did not attempt to conceal our own leanings toward prison abolitionism. While we were explicit about our interest in the racialization of the prison regime in general and in the awareness of racism exhibited by the prisoners, we raised no specific questions about particular racial groups. In our own discussions about interview strategies, "racial matching" was never really an issue. Therefore both of us conducted interviews with black, Asian, South American, and white Dutch prisoners. Since almost all the prisoners were fluent in English, all our interviews, except those with women from Colombia, were conducted in English. We talked with the Colombian women with the aid of a Spanish-English translator.

The organization of the Cuban component of our research was much more complicated, not only because of the general communication difficulties related to the U.S. embargo on Cuba, but also because we were required to obtain a research license from the U.S. State Department in order to legitimately travel to Cuba. Our Cuban sponsor, the Association of Cuban Women, acted as the intermediary to allow us to gain clearance to visit women's prisons there.

Initially, both of us had planned to make the trip to Cuba. However, just as we had scheduled the trip, Kum-Kum, who had been attempting for some time to adopt, was informed that a baby was available for adoption. Consequently, she faced the dilemma, encountered by many women (and some men), of negotiating a balance between her domestic desires and her research passions. Ultimately she decided that she did not want to be separated from her small baby at such a critical stage in the baby's development and decided to forgo the trip. We decided that Angela should go on with the project, accompanied by one of her students, Isabel Velez, whose bilingual skills would allow her to serve as translator. Since we had previously used a translator in the Dutch prison for interviews with women from South America, we felt a translator would be able to help us again.

Angela and Isabel conducted forty-five interviews at women's prisons in three Cuban provinces—Pinar del Río, Havana, and Camagüey. At the time of the interviews, there were seventy women in the prison in Pinar del Río, six hundred in Havana, and one hundred and sixty-three in Camagüey. In accordance with the overall conceptualization of our project, our concerns focused less on the racial identities of our interviewees than on the way in which they perceived and characterized the racial dynamics of the prison regimes. However, it was inevitable that questions about racial identification should arise, especially since racial categories in Cuba are far more fluid than in the United States. Some people with whom we talked indicated that their official identity cards listed them as "white," although they would describe themselves as *mulatta* or *jabao* (the color of a fruit). In fact, many of the women who counted as "white" by Cuban standards, would be characterized as "women of color" by U.S. standards. Therefore, our questions regarding the proportion of women of color in the prison and differential treatment based on race could never be simply answered. As a result, the Cuban component of our project raised by far the most complicated questions regarding race.

ETHICAL DILEMMAS

In the three sets of interviews we conducted, many of the women expressed their appreciation for what they considered to be better conditions of imprisonment than they imagined to exist elsewhere. At the same time they were emphatic that although they had abundant educational and vocational opportunities, they were still in prison and they had been deprived of their most precious possession, their liberty. That a significant number of the women we interviewed made positive comments about the conditions of their confinement, along with the critiques they proposed, was in part related to the way we chose the sites of our research. In each instance, we had developed relationships either with the authorities directly in charge of the prison or, as in Cuba, had previous relationships with organizations that intervened for us. These relationships were based on our own respect for the comparatively progressive penal methods employed in each of the sites. However, our own prison politics are best described as abolitionist,[11] and at no time did we attempt to conceal our political leanings from the authorities. As a result, the space we negotiated for our research was fraught with contradictions. Like the women prisoners who constantly pointed out—in the Netherlands, for example—that despite the creature comforts they enjoyed, they were still in prison, or—in California—that regardless of the prison's antiracist and antihomophobic policies, they were still in prison, or—in Cuba—that regardless of their prospects of reintegrating themselves into society, they were still in prison, we too continually reminded ourselves that the purpose of our research was to point to the possibility of handling much behavior legally constructed as "crime" without resorting to imprisonment.

As we have reflected on our research, our one overarching dilemma with its methodological and ethical dimensions has been precisely this: how do we balance our abolitionist perspective with our role as scholars and as human beings who clearly recognize that the prisons in which we worked did indeed provide relatively liveable conditions for the women who inhabited them? As we conducted our field research, we talked at length about how we might best draw on the progressive aspects of the penal settings and regimes we were studying and simultaneously negotiate a relationship between our ultimate political aims and the need to affirm the importance of humane conditions of confinement for women and men in prison. A constant theme of our discussions was how we might be able to forge a productive research and activist agenda out of the tension between our ultimate goal of prison abolition and our recognition that penal reform is also essential, if only to improve the daily lives of the millions who have been removed from the free world. Given the historical tendency of reform movements to strengthen prison institutions and discourses,[11] we were especially concerned about how to locate our work within a larger long-term political project of opposing the prison industrial complex and of arresting the proliferation of prisons.

Even as we recognized the power circuits that flowed through the research process and through the prison systems we were studying, we tried to forge collaborative relationships in our conversations with the prisoners. By not withholding information about our political motives and goals and by not treating the women as individuals whom we expected to generate knowledge about themselves to be later collectivized by the researchers, we hoped to demonstrate the possibility of more democratic approaches to research. Just as we did not want to address them as representatives of their respective racial groups, nor did we want to treat them as somehow representing a class of prisoners who could benefit from but not act as agents in an emancipatory political project. When it proved difficult for our interviewees to imagine social landscapes in which prisons were not prominent features, we did not assume that it was any easier for us, despite our adherence to abolitionism. As researchers and as prisoners, we struggled with the same overwhelming ideological constraints.

A related dilemma was whether to interview the administrative and custodial staff in the prisons we studied. Because we did not want to convey the impression to our primary interviewees that we were approaching them with preconceptions and biases acquired from the administrators and guards, we initially decided against interviewing prison personnel. Although we did not naively assume that it was possible to obtain ideas from the prisoners that were "pure" and unmediated, we did feel that this was the best way to achieve our goal of involving imprisoned women in a larger conversation about the radical transformation of punishment systems. However, early on in the actual interview process, we realized that we needed certain information that could only be provided by the administrators and guards. As a result, we decided that while we would talk with prison officials, these interviews would take place only after we had completed our interviews with the prisoners.

We did not treat this methodological decision as a satisfactory solution to our quandary, but rather recognized that practical decisions sometimes highlight the artificiality and abstractness of theoretical research frameworks. Seemingly contradictory on-the-ground decisions can open up new paths of inquiry. Moreover, this decision led us to acknowledge that just as we had tried to avoid essentializing the women we interviewed in relation to their racial backgrounds and their status as prisoners, civilian and uniformed prison personnel were also more than representatives of the state. Ironically, this particular decision to interview prison personnel yielded some interesting results, especially with respect to the official contract that prisoners at the San Francisco County Jail Program Facility were required to sign, agreeing to adhere to the announced antiracist, antisexist, and antihomophobic policies of the jail.

RESEARCHING RACISM

Throughout the world, prisons are predictably the most consistently multiracial and multicultural locations,[12] making them not only important sites for negative inquiry but also productive sites for positive multicultural, multiracial alliance building. Of course, race is understood differently in different national contexts. Based on the long history of antiracist social movements in the United States, racism in this country is often understood to refer to institutional and individual discrimination against black, Latino, Native American, and Asian-American people. In Europe, *racism* is viewed as synonymous with *xenophobia*. Thus in the Netherlands, which often prides itself—though not always justifiably—as being the least racist country in Europe, responses to our questions about racism tended to focus on attitudes toward foreigners, rather than on racism by white Dutch people against nonwhite Dutch citizens.

In the Program Facility at the San Francisco County Jail, specific efforts were undertaken to minimize racism, sexism, and homophobia in the operation of the jail. In fact, according to the director, each prisoner was required to sign the following contract upon being booked into the Program Facility in which she or he agreed not to engage in racist, sexist, or homophobic behavior:

> I understand that I am required to treat others and myself with respect and dignity. I understand that racism, sexism, anti-gay/lesbian remarks, glorification of sub-

stance abuse or criminal behavior and any other form of anti-social behavior will result in loss of privileges, extra work duty or removal from the program facility.[13]

This clause in the contract provided jail personnel with the leverage to avoid a more complicated discussion of racism, as jail rules barred prisoners from exhibiting perceptibly racist behavior. Because antiracism was constructed as a jail rule implemented by guards and administrators, it was linked to the regimes of power and surveillance and attributed to the prisoners as subjects of prison authority. Discussions with the jail personnel who thought of themselves as progressive revealed that they were proud of their pioneering roles as overseers charged with identifying potential violations of the antiracist, antisexist, and antihomophobic rule. In a sense, this pattern was a microcosmic reflection of the larger contemporary proclivity to relegate the process of minimizing racism to the U.S. legal sphere—which constitutes the subject as a rational, free *individual*—and to use legal prohibitions as evidence of the decline of racism in civil society.[14]

However, many of the prisoners we interviewed—both women of color and white—noticed a disparity between the official policy and the treatment they received, thus proposing astute political analyses regarding the persistence of racism within a putatively antiracist framework. One woman said that some guards treated prisoners differently based on their racial backgrounds. Her observations regarding the racism of deputies contested the relegation of racist behavior to the prisoners.[15] She described incidents in which she and other black women were severely limited in the amount of time they were allowed to use the telephone, whereas the deputies allowed a white prisoner to stay on the pay phone for several hours. She said that she and a group of her black friends had consciously monitored certain deputies' practices of allowing white prisoners to spend much more time on the telephone than prisoners of color. This was an obvious example of everyday strategies of resistance to racism within the jail.

Given the shifting definitions of racism referred to above, we were not entirely surprised that the questions we asked women prisoners about the impact of racism within the prison setting did not always travel well from one research site to another. Since our questions were informed by popular and scholarly discourses on race in the United States, they were most easily understood by and most directly answered by prisoners, guards, and administrators alike at the jail in San Francisco. One interviewee in the Netherlands indicated that there was little overt discussion of racism in the prison, but that she was planning to raise this issue with the prison authorities in the near future.[16] Responses by a substantial number of our interviewees in the Netherlands helped us understand the implicit xenophobia that informed attitudes and behavior toward prisoners from South America. A Colombian woman said: "There's a lot of racism here. If you're Colombian, black or from another country they don't give you anything. . . . There's nothing for [Dutch] people . . . in jail, and less if they are Colombian."[17] Another South American woman also criticized the xenophobic attitudes of the custodial personnel when she told us about her skin rash that had gone untreated: "It's not normal that my skin is like this and I've got a rash. It's already twenty days [that I have been] asking for the doctor. If I'd been Dutch, the doctor would have shown up immediately."[18]

A white Dutch woman was critical of the general tendency on the part of the Dutch to represent themselves as egalitarian:

> I always feel attracted to other cultures. But I didn't catch it by birth, because my mother and father are totally white, and they were very . . . yeah, I think my father was a racist, in a way that he doesn't speak it aloud, but in his thinking, like I've seen with many Dutch, they say, "I am not a racist," but if you see their behavior, you can see that their behavior has racist elements.[19]

She also pointed to the pattern among prison guards and administrators of infantilizing prisoners from South America: "So if they deal with the Spanish women, they deal with them like they're not grown-up people. Like they're dealing with children, you know? And I am very much irritated by that type of approach. I hate it. I really hate it."[20] She also indicated that there was a pattern of belittling non-Dutch-speaking prisoners, and particularly women whose cultural and language practices involved gesticulating with their hands. Our interviews in the Dutch prison thus revealed that women of color were not the only prisoners who had thought about the workings of racism. In fact, one white Dutch woman, expressing her solidarity with the women from South America, indicated that she was attempting to learn Spanish in order to communicate with her coprisoners.[21]

In Cuba, the prisoners' reluctance to engage in discussions about race seemed to be linked to the way in which popular discourses on race and racism are overdetermined by the particular history of racism in the United States and by Cuban solidarity with antiracist activists in black, Puerto Rican, and Native American movements. They talked with ease about such figures as Martin Luther King and Malcolm X, and although most of the prisoners were too young to have experienced the Cuban solidarity campaign which developed around Angela's case during the early seventies, many of them had learned about her history as well. Because our questions about race and racism were generally understood within a U.S. context, all the interviewees insisted that racism was neither an issue in the prison nor in society at large. When we asked one woman whether she felt there was a way to talk about race that was enlightening and not indicative of discrimination, she answered, "Yes, you can talk about it in order to unify instead of separate or discriminate. The more unity there is between people, white and black, there would be a better world, more unified."[22] She also felt that people in the United States might learn important lessons from Cuba in the quest for racial equality.

The administrators' observations about the role of race in the prison context both reflected and diverged from prisoners' comments. In Cuba, for example, the prison directors and guards, like the prisoners themselves, tended to interpret questions referring to race as questions about racial discrimination. In San Francisco, questions about race and racism led administrators to refer us to the contract each prisoner was required to sign upon entering the program facility. However, the Sheriff of San Francisco, who is in charge of the county jail system, initiated discussion about the disproportionately high numbers of black and brown prisoners in his jails. He indicated that his responsibility as sheriff required a special sensitivity toward prisoners of color as he instituted social programs for inmates.

Just as administrators of the Program Facility in San Francisco tended to interpret questions about racism as synonymous with race relations among the prisoners, so in the Netherlands, the director of Amerswiel Prison responded to our questions about racism by focusing on relations between prisoners, especially between white Dutch women and women from South America. Further, her comments suggested to us that the enforced equality of prison—where each one is equally deprived of certain rights and liberties, regardless of race—makes it an interesting test of the limits of liberal thinking around racism.

CONCLUSION

Many of the contradictions we confronted—our knowledge that prisoners were ubiquitous subjects of research, the discrepancies between official policy and everyday practice, the fact that denials of entry arrived too late to matter, that assurances of equality could proliferate, and that equality was imagined as the morally correct action of each free individual toward the other backed up by the force of a state that would never be analyzed as a subject—were about the nature of a liberal system and the limits of a research methodology that would fail to address its own hegemonic context first and last. The prisoner from the Netherlands told us she was learning Spanish in order to communicate with her fellow prisoners is a far better example of how to create a just society than a state like California that abolishes affirmative action and bilingual education, while building more prisons to hold those populations who cannot fail to be endlessly misapprehended by the system. Thus, the "results" of our research exceed the scope of most research agendas that can be imagined around prisoners, including even those that might be significant, like gathering information

about health care in prison, family relations and social welfare, and even racism.

The prison was our best research site not because conditions are so bad there but because the segmentation of the prison system away from our consciousness allows the liberal state to manage its population. To attempt to solve the problem of racism without considering the most degraded of its subjects would be contrary to any analytic agenda. Still, the information garnered in this process would also outstrip its intended uses, since learning the language of those with whom you seek to build community is not only a means toward bettering conditions in prison but toward their betterment in the free world outside.

DISCUSSION QUESTIONS

1. Discuss the collaborative methodology used by Bhavnani and Davis as they interviewed women prisoners in three countries. How does it differ from traditional or more mainstream social science methodology?
2. The authors, two researchers who are women of color—one South Asian and one African American—are antiracist, feminist activists. Discuss how their backgrounds and activism affect their research and findings.
3. According to the women prisoners interviewed for this project, how does racism operate in the different countries?
4. What do the authors mean when they write: "we did not establish goals for specific racial *groups* but rather considered the general racialization of imprisonment *practices*, which have a disproportionate impact on women of color and poor white women"?
5. What is your reaction to the San Francisco jail and its antiracist, antisexist, antihomophobic policies?
6. How can reformers reconcile two seemingly incompatible objectives:

abolishing all prisons and improving
existing prison conditions?

NOTES

1. See Kum-Kum Bhavnani, *Talking Politics: A Psychological Framing for Views from Youth in Britain* (Cambridge: Cambridge University Press, 1991). See especially chapter 3.

2. Elliot Currie, *Crime and Punishment in America* (New York: Henry Holt, 1998), p. 16.

3. Willen de Haan, *The Politics of Redress, Crime, Punishment and Penal Abolition* (London: Unwin, Hyman, 1990), p. 37. See also Willen de Haan, "Abolitionism and the Politics of 'Bad Conscience,'" in *Abolitionism: Toward a Non-Repressive Approach to Crime,* edited by Herman Bianchi and Rene van Swaaningen (Amsterdam: Free University Press, 1986), p. 158.

4. Vivien Stern, *A Sin against the Future: Imprisonment in the World* (London: Penguin Books, 1998), p. 138.

5. See Angela Y. Davis, "Public Imprisonment, Private Violence: Reflections on the Hidden Punishment of Women," *New England Journal on Criminal and Civil Confinement* 24, no. 2 (summer 1998): 339–49.

6. Since 1980, the U.S. imprisoned female population has increased by 275 percent, while the male population has increased by 160 percent. Marc Mauer and Tracy Huling, *Young Black Men and the Criminal Justice System: Five Years Later* (Washington, D.C.: The Sentencing Project, 1995).

7. Mary Helen Washington, "Prison Studies as Part of American Studies," *American Studies Newsletter* 22, no. 1 (March 1999): 1.

8. See Katherine Beckett, *Making Crime Pay: Law and Order in Contemporary American Politics* (New York: Oxford University Press, 1997).

9. Mauer and Huling, *Young Black Men and the Criminal Justice System.*

10. All around the world the same pattern can be seen. Prisons contain higher proportions than would be expected of people from groups that suffer from racism and discrimination. How does this disproportion happen? There are many reasons, often related to blatant discrimination in the wider society, and crude racism by the law enforcement agencies. Sometimes the disproportion arises from policies which concentrate minorities in poor areas and restrict their opportunities. Often the criminal justice processes tend to discriminate against minorities, sometimes in very subtle ways. . . . The cumulative effect of all this discrimination is the disproportionate number of minorities in the prisons of the world. (Stern, *A Sin against the Future,* p. 117)

11. Ruth Wilson Gilmore, "Globalization and U.S. Prison Growth: From Military Keynesianism to Post-Keynesian Militarism," *Race and Class* 40, nos. 2/3 (1998–99): 171–88. See also Michel Foucault, *Discipline and Punish: The Birth of the Prison,* translated by Alan Sheridan (New York: Vintage, 1979). Originally published in English in 1977.

12. In Australia, for example, although aboriginal people constitute only 1 to 2 percent of the general population, they comprise 30 percent of the imprisoned population. Stern, *A Sin against the Future.*

13. From the contract drawn up by the San Francisco Sheriff's Department.

14. See Kimberlé Crenshaw, Neil Gotanda, Gary Peller, and Kendall Thomas, eds. *Critical Race Theory: The Key Writings That Formed the Movement* (New York: New Press, 1995).

15. Interview at San Francisco County Jail, Program Facility, November 1993.

16. Interview at Amerswiel Prison for Women, April 1996.

17. Interview at Amerswiel Prison for Women, April 1996.

18. Interview at Amerswiel Prison for Women, April 1996.

19. Interview at Sevenum Prison, April 1996.

20. Ibid.

21. Interview at Amerswiel Prison for Women, April 1996.

22. Interview at the Prison for Women in Havana, June 1997.

Chapter 12

Women of Color, Globalization, and the Politics of Incarceration

Julia Sudbury

ABSTRACT

This chapter continues the theme of globalization, an important concept in understanding the issues relating to women, crime, and incarceration. Sudbury's purpose is to explain the surge in women's imprisonment over the last decade by looking at three seemingly unrelated phenomena: (1) the globalization of national economies; (2) the worldwide expansion of the prison industry as a private profit-making business; and (3) the war on drugs that began in the United States and has been exported worldwide.

Sudbury uses examples from many areas of the world—Europe, West Africa, Australia, Latin America, North America, and the Caribbean—to make her case. Much of her argument centers on poverty and its disproportionate impact on women of color. That poverty, she observes, is a result of global events, the integration of national economies, and the information technology revolution that has facilitated globalization. In her analysis she takes feminist criminology to task for linking punishment to crime—as if there is a direct connection—and for failing to give sufficient weight to the importance of contemporary capitalism, actions by the state, and racism in understanding women's incarceration. In fact, she argues that an intersectionalities approach (using a race, class, and gender analysis, as was discussed in chapter 1) "requires us to examine the racialized feminization of poverty, the impoverishment and surveillance of communities of color, and global inequalities between the third- and first-world nations as causal factors behind the growing criminalization of women."

The second half of the chapter focuses on case studies of three women—one from Canada, one from Colombia, South America, and one from the United States—who have been caught up in these worldwide processes. Each story helps clarify the concepts and analyses presented earlier in the chapter.

Sudbury offers a well thought out and carefully argued analysis of the surge in women's imprisonment, especially of young black women and other women of color, in countries around the world. However, many criminologists will be critical of her approach. They might argue that the author discounts other factors commonly said to lead to imprisonment by overemphasizing macrostructural conditions. As you read this chapter, see for yourself in what ways you agree with her arguments and in what ways you would challenge her analysis.

In November 1999, 40,000 people came together in an explosion of street activism to protest the policies of the World Trade Organization and to highlight the impact of neoliberal globalization on the global south and poor communities in the global north.[1] While the mainstream media represented the mass action in Seattle, Washington, as lacking a coherent political agenda, social commentators have heralded the emergence of a new social movement against global capitalism and corporate trade dominance. Labor, environmental, human rights, housing, antiracist, and feminist activists came to Seattle out of a common understanding that problems such as sweatshop working conditions, toxic dumping in black neighborhoods, and cutbacks in welfare, housing, and health care are all rooted in a global capitalist system that values corporate interests and freedoms over human needs for decent wages, shelter, food, and health care. At the Seattle protests, as well as at subsequent antiglobalization events at the Republican Convention in Philadelphia and Democratic Convention in Los Angeles, activists used puppets, banners, and flyers to link the struggle against global capital with opposition to the current criminal justice system.[2] Activists challenged police brutality, racial profiling, the death penalty, and the prison industrial complex, arguing that dramatic increases in prison populations have occurred as a result of globalization.

While these connections are being made at the street level, feminist criminologists have had little to say about what connections, if any, may be made between women's imprisonment and the rise of global corporate capital that has occurred in the past two decades. Such an analysis would need to stray beyond the boundaries of what has traditionally been

considered within the scope of criminology to examine the broader socioeconomic context of women's criminalization and incarceration. This chapter will argue that the explosion in women's incarceration is the hidden face of globalization and cannot be understood without reference to three overlapping phenomena. The first is the restructuring of national economies and social welfare provision that has occurred as a result of the globalization of capital. The second and related phenomenon is the emergence and subsequent global expansion of what has been labeled a "prison industrial complex" made up of an intricate web of relations between criminal justice institutions, politicians, and profit-driven prison corporations. The third is the emergence of a U.S.-led war on drugs that has crossed national borders to become a global phenomenon.

THE BOOM IN WOMEN'S IMPRISONMENT

The past 25 years have witnessed dramatic increases in the use of incarceration in the United States, leading to a prison building boom as federal and state governments rush to keep up with demand for prison beds. Although there are more men in prison than women, the rate of women's imprisonment is spiraling upward at a greater rate than that of men. Between 1985 and 1995, the number of men in U.S. prisons and jails doubled.[3] In the same 10-year period, women's imprisonment tripled. Whereas in 1970, there were 5,600 women in federal and state prisons, by 1996, there were 75,000.[4] The prison boom has not been limited to the United States. Similar patterns have occurred in Canada, Europe, and Australasia. In Britain, for example, the number of women in prison doubled between 1985 and 1998, causing feminist activists to call for drastic measures to counter "the crisis in women's prisons."[5] Here, too, the rate of increase is greater for women

Source: This article was written expressly for inclusion in this text.

than for men, growing by 9 percent in the year to April 2001 compared to 2 percent for men.[6]

Statistics that look at gender but not race underrepresent the impact of the prison boom on women of color and indigenous women. In all the countries just mentioned, oppressed racialized groups are disproportionately targeted by the criminal justice system. For example, in the United States, Latinas and African American women make up 60 percent of the prison population. And despite their small numbers in the population, Native Americans are 10 times more likely than whites to be imprisoned.[7] In New South Wales, Australia, where all women's imprisonment increased by 40 percent in five years, aboriginal women's incarceration increased by 70 percent in only two years.[8] In Canada, aboriginal people comprise 3 percent of the general population and 12 percent of federal prisoners, a figure that increases to over 60 percent in provinces like Saskatchewan and Alberta.[9] African Canadians are also disproportionately policed, prosecuted, and incarcerated.[10] Finally, 12 percent of women prisoners in England and Wales are British citizens of African Caribbean descent compared to 1 percent of the general population.[11] In addition, British prisons hold numerous women from West Africa, the Caribbean, and Latin America, either as immigration detainees or serving sentences for drug importation. The crisis of women's prisons can therefore be read as a crisis for women of color and indigenous women worldwide.

EXPLAINING THE PRISON BOOM

How can we explain this explosion in the population of women prisoners? In the 1970s, "emancipation theorists" put forward a possible explanation for an upward trend in women's incarceration. In her influential study, Freda Adler suggested that the women's liberation movement had opened up new opportunities for women, both in the legitimate and in the criminal worlds.[12] Thus women who were now working in white-collar jobs could commit crimes such as fraud and embezzlement, which previously would have been inaccessible to

them. Women's liberation was also credited with giving women a more assertive stance and enabling them to engage in violence, burglary, and organized crime, acts that were previously the domain of men.

Subsequent studies challenged Adler's findings; they contested her claim that there had been a rise in women's offending and suggested that any increase could in fact be explained by social factors such as an increase in women's poverty (see Steffensmeier and Schwartz, chap. 6).[13] Despite vigorous challenges to Adler's claims, subsequent work by feminist criminologists has failed to shift the debate around women and crime in two important ways. First, it perpetuates the commonsense equation between crime and punishment that is at the core of both Adler's work and mainstream criminology. This equation leads us to look to women's behavior for explanations of increases in women's incarceration. If more women are being arrested, prosecuted, and punished, this argument goes, it must be because they are committing more crimes. Sociologists working within a radical framework make a different argument. Rather than looking to women's behavior, we should look at the shifting actions of the state as it seeks to control poor communities and populations of color. Rather than women's criminality, the focus of study should be the role of the state in labeling, prosecuting, and punishing women—that is, women's criminalization. Our search for an explanation for the prison boom must therefore ask: Who benefits when more women are imprisoned? What are the processes by which certain actions are labeled criminal and others are not, and how are women channeled into these actions and thus into conflict with the criminal justice system?

The second limitation of feminist criminology is its unwillingness to engage meaningfully with the significance of race in the criminal justice system, choosing to view women first as gendered beings and only secondly as having a social class, national, or racialized identity. The past three decades have witnessed an important shift in feminist theory as women of color have challenged the belief that patriarchy is the primary system of dominance shaping women's lives. Black feminists, womanists, Xicanistas (i.e., Chicana feminists), and third-world feminists argue instead that there is a need to theorize women's experiences as structured by the intersection of white supremacy, patriarchy, and capitalism.[14] Rather than talking about "woman" as a unitary category, as if all women's experiences were fundamentally the same, feminists of color argue that we must always be explicit about the ways that racism and racial privilege intersect with class location and gender to create unique experiences for diverse women. Intersectionality may produce unexpected outcomes. In some instances, for example, women of color may have as much in common with men of color as they do with middle-class white women. Deploying an intersectional approach to explain women's criminalization therefore requires us to pay as much attention to racial profiling and racialized discrepancies within the criminal justice system as we do to gender disparities. It also requires us to examine the feminization of poverty, the impoverishment and surveillance of communities of color, and global inequalities between third- and first-world nations as causal factors behind the growing criminalization of women.

1. Globalization and the Racialized Feminization of Poverty

Globalization refers to a process by which national economies as well as political and social systems have become increasingly integrated, enabling the movement of goods, capital, people, culture, and knowledge across national borders. At the root of these shifts is the information technology revolution that has enabled international communication to occur at the touch of a keyboard and money to be transferred instantaneously across the globe. This revolution fueled a dramatic shift in the way in which corporations operate. Corporate executives based in the Silicon Valley in California can now manage assembly lines in Taiwan, Haiti, or the Philippines, thus cutting their overheads and increasing profits by employing exploitable third-world women. As corporations relocate their manufacturing operations to the third world, working-class

communities in the United States, Canada, and Europe have faced layoffs in industries that have traditionally provided unionized jobs with significant worker protections. The jobs that remain—in service industries such as restaurants and hotels, and in agriculture and construction—are largely nonunionized and casual (irregular and part-time), paying minimum wage or less and offering few protections.

Both urban "ghettos" and small rural towns have been hard hit by the downsizing of manufacturing since the 1970s, suffering high unemployment and a decline in tax revenues. For inner-city residents, especially African Americans and Latinos, these declines have meant underfunded schools, dirty streets, insufficient public housing, and poor health care facilities. Neighborhoods have been taken over by liquor stores, crack houses, and prostitution as supermarkets and department stores relocate to more profitable locations. Women bear the brunt of this social dislocation, because they tend to be the primary caretakers of children and elderly relatives and are responsible for providing adequate food, shelter, medicine, and clothing. For working-class women of color in the inner cities, the globalization of capital translates into few opportunities for a living wage, food and clothing that is expensive and of poor quality, and inadequate day care and schooling for their children.

Rural areas have also been affected by the radical restructuring signaled by globalization. Faced with global commodities markets that set the price for meat, milk, or grain according to the lowest price that can be obtained internationally, small farmers have been unable to compete and have been forced to sell their land or contract to sell their produce to large farming corporations.[15] The emergence of agribusiness as the primary supplier of the nation's food has led to a rise in rural poverty as farm workers, particularly immigrant workers, are forced to work for low wages in insecure, seasonal jobs. Small rural towns that relied on car, munitions, and other industries have also been hit as factories have relocated abroad or closed as a result of a decline in cold war–era military investment. When a factory pulls out, not only the jobs directly provided by that company are lost, but the local bars, shops, and motels are also devastated. Finally, as wages drop and unemployment increases, the town's tax revenues are drastically depleted, thus leading to a cycle of economic depression.

This newfound mobility has given corporations the ability to pack up and move to a new location if they find that policies and legislation governing workers' rights, wages, and environmental protections are not to their liking. Thus, national governments within the global capitalist economy have seen their policy options narrowed if they wish to remain attractive to corporate capital. The 1990s, therefore, witnessed a shift toward neoliberal policies being pursued by conservative and liberal governments alike. These policies aim to create a liberal environment for corporate profit making and financial speculation. This environment occurs in multiple arenas. In the environmental arena, neoliberal reforms tend to limit environmental protections and sanctions for toxic dumping and open up natural resources for mineral and oil extraction. In the arena of workers' rights, access to collective bargaining, sick leave, maternity leave, compensation for injury, and a living wage have been reduced. In the public sector, services from water to public transportation have been privatized, raising the cost for the consumer and creating a new arena for corporate profit making. In the financial arena, national markets have been opened up to financial investment by international traders, introducing international trade agreements such as the North American Free Trade Agreement (NAFTA) and the European Union, and providing free trade zones, so that corporate capital is unrestricted by national borders.

The global spread of neoliberal social and economic policies is underpinned by two international institutions. The World Trade Organization (WTO) was established as the global headquarters for the drafting and policing of international trading rules. In the past decade, the WTO has come under criticism by activists who claim that by enforcing rules that benefit corporate profit while ignoring the exploitation of child laborers, the use of sweatshops, and environmental destruction by those same cor-

porations, it is complicit in these exploitative practices.[16] The International Monetary Fund (IMF) is an organization with 183 member countries that promotes international monetary exchange and trade and provides loans and economic guidance to impoverished countries. The IMF has been criticized for imposing economic policies on formerly colonized countries that generate immense poverty and suffering. Governments have been forced to cut back public expenditure. In Jamaica, for example, policies introduced since the mid-1980s by the Jamaican Labour Party working closely with the IMF have led to cuts in public-sector employment; the scaling back of local government services in health, and education; increases in the cost of public utilities as state-owned companies are sold to the private sector; and a dramatic decline in real wages. Such cuts hit working-class Jamaican women particularly hard because they carry the burden of caring for children and sick or elderly relatives. This disproportionate impoverishment of third-world women is referred to as the racialized feminization of poverty.

At the same time that the Jamaican state has cut back its role in social welfare, it has stepped up its role in subsidizing foreign and domestic capital. Free trade zones established in Kingston, Montego Bay, and elsewhere offer foreign garment, electronic, and communications companies factory space and equipment, tax exemptions, a cheap female workforce, and for the busy foreign executive, weekends of sun, sea, and sand.[17] Foreign-owned agribusiness and mining companies have also been encouraged, displacing traditional subsistence farming and causing migration from rural areas to the cities, which now account for 50 percent of the Jamaican population. As the economy has shifted, women working in the informal economy as farmers and higglers[18] find themselves unable to keep up with the rising costs of survival. Whereas younger women may find employment in the tourist industry as maids, entertainers, or prostitutes, or within the free trade zones assembling clothes or computers for Western markets, working-class women in their 30s and older have fewer options. Even where these women do find employment, low wages—driven down by multinational corporations in search of ever greater profit margins and kept low by governments unwilling to set a living minimum wage for fear of losing foreign investment—mean that women cannot earn a sufficient income to support their families. The failure of the legal economy to provide adequate means for women's survival then becomes a key incentive for Jamaican women who enter the drug trade as couriers and are subsequently incarcerated in British, Canadian and U.S. prisons. The shift from social welfare to corporate welfare can be seen from Nigeria to Indonesia, as neoliberal policies are marketed by the IMF as the panacea to third-world underdevelopment and debt.

2. The Prison Industrial Complex

Why has the racialized feminization of poverty under neoliberal globalization led to an explosion in the imprisonment of women? In other words, how can we explain the current state response to the increase in poverty among working-class women and women of color, a response that deploys criminalization and punishment rather than poverty relief or empowerment? Scholars, activists, and former prisoners seeking to explain this problem have come up with the concept of the prison industrial complex.[19] Joel Dyer argues that three components make up the "perpetual prisoner machine" that transforms criminalized populations in the United States into fodder for the prison system.[20] The first are the large media corporations, like CNN and NBC, that rely on violent and crime-oriented content to grab ratings. The disproportionate airtime dedicated to crime-related news, dramas such as *NYPD Blue* and *Law and Order,* and real-life shows such as *America's Most Wanted* and *Cops* have created a dramatic rise in the fear of crime in the U.S. population at large.[21] These shows provide stereotypical representations of communities of color, from the black drug dealer to the Latino "gangbanger," that fuel a racialized fear of crime. The second is the use of market research by politicians to align their platforms with popular views about policy areas. Since the voting population tends to believe

that criminal penalties are too soft and that "criminals" are unlikely to serve adequate prison sentences, politicians can win votes by appearing to be "tough on crime." Although Republicans have traditionally positioned themselves as tougher on crime than Democrats, it is only by positioning themselves as equally punitive that liberals can achieve power. Thus the unfounded assumption that building more prisons and jails and incapacitating more people for longer periods will solve deep-rooted social problems, such as drug use, poverty and violence, remains unchallenged by both major parties. This argument is in turn translated into policies such as mandatory minimum sentences, truth-in-sentencing, and three strikes laws. These policies cause more people to serve prison sentences, cause longer terms, and lead to spiraling prison populations.

The third component is the intervention of private prison corporations such as Wackenhut Corporation and Corrections Corporation of America, which have generated millions for their shareholders by designing, constructing, financing, and managing prisons, jails, and detention centers. The mutually profitable relationship between private corporations and public criminal justice systems enables politicians to mask the enormous cost of their tough-on-crime policies. Instead of allocating millions for new prison construction in their annual budgets, politicians can simply reallocate revenue funds from welfare, health, or education into contracts with privately run for-profit prisons. Since the 1980s, the private sector has allowed prison building in the United States to continue, even where public coffers have been exhausted by the prison construction boom. Private prisons have been seen by some small rural towns as a solution to the socioeconomic decline caused by closed factories and failing farms.[22] They have wooed prison corporations with cheap or free land, tax breaks, and discounts in sewage and utilities charges, making prison corporations a major beneficiary of corporate welfare.

These three components constitute the "political and economic chain reaction" that we have come to know as the prison industrial complex: *a symbiotic and profitable relationship between politicians, corporations, the media and state correctional institutions that generates the racialized use of incarceration as a response to social problems rooted in the globalization of capital.* Although the prison industrial complex emerged in the United States, the past 15 years have witnessed its transformation into a transnational phenomenon. Multinational prison corporations have fueled this expansion through an aggressive strategy of pursuing foreign contracts through sophisticated marketing techniques. U.S.-based prison corporations and their subsidiaries now manage prisons in Britain, Canada, New Zealand, Puerto Rico, Australia, and South Africa; and in all these locations, prison populations are rising. The prison industrial complex incorporates diverse interest groups, all of which stand to profit from the global prison boom. State and national politicians, correctional officer unions, media and corporate executives, and shareholders all benefit in very direct ways from the growth in women's imprisonment.

3. The Global War on Drugs

The third factor implicated in the explosion in women's imprisonment is the global war on drugs. The contemporary war on drugs was announced by U.S. president Ronald Reagan in the early 1980s and formalized in the 1986 Anti Drug Abuse Act. The act made a critical break with the concept of drug users as a medical population in need of treatment and instead targeted them as a criminal population. It also utilized the erroneous assumption that users would be deterred from their habit and dealers and traffickers incapacitated by extensive use of penal sanctions. It was assumed that by removing those involved in the criminalized drug trade from the streets for long periods of time, syndicates would be severely damaged in their ability to get drugs to the streets.[23] Since "liberal" judges could not be trusted to hand down sufficiently severe sentences to deter and incapacitate those involved in the drug trade, the act removed judicial discretion and imposed mandatory minimum sentences.

Thus, treatment programs and community service were effectively barred in cases involving drugs,

and sentence length related not to the role of the defendant in the offense, but to the weight and purity of drugs involved. In the United States, African American women and Latinas are disproportionately affected by mandatory minimums for reasons that are both gendered and racialized. The only way a lesser sentence can be given is in cases in which the defendant provides "substantial assistance" in the prosecution of another person. However, women, who tend to be in subordinate positions within drug syndicates and thus have little access to information, are usually unable to make such a deal. The crack-cocaine disparity also feeds the disproportionate impact on women of color. The mandatory minimum sentence for cocaine is one hundred times harsher for crack than for powder cocaine. Thus, being caught with 500 grams of powder cocaine is equivalent to being caught with only 5 grams of crack, itself a derivative of powder cocaine. Since crack is cheaper and has flooded poor inner city neighborhoods, African Americans and Latinos and Latinas receive disproportionate sentences when compared with powder cocaine users and dealers, who are much more likely to be white.[24]

Although the war on drugs has had a dramatic impact on U.S. communities of color, it has reached far beyond U.S. borders. From the mid-1980s, the war on drugs increasingly played a key role in U.S. foreign policy decisions as the Reagan and Bush administrations pushed a U.S. drug agenda on the global community. Initial efforts focused on the G7 countries[25] as the Reagan administration used U.S. economic clout to push for international compliance with U.S. drug policy. In 1988 the Toronto Summit endorsed a U.S.-proposed task force, which in turn led to the 1988 United Nations Convention Against Illicit Traffic in Narcotic Drugs and Psychotropic Substances, also known as the Vienna Convention.[26] The convention contained a number of controversial conditions that ran counter to the policies of other member states. Member states were required to criminalize drug cultivation, possession, and purchase for personal use; maximize the use of criminal sanctions and deterrence; and limit early release and parole in drug-related cases. Thus, the

Vienna Convention represented the transnational spread of the U.S. punitive "law and order" agenda.[27] By signing the convention, member states pledged to use criminal justice sanctions in place of medical or social solutions as they turned decisively away from legalization.[28] Whereas the domestic war on drugs is fought primarily by the police beyond the borders of the United States, it has become a military war justifying U.S. military interventions throughout Latin America. By the mid-1990s, Canada, Australia, New Zealand, Taiwan, South and Central America, the Caribbean, and African countries including Nigeria and South Africa were full-fledged partners in the U.S.-driven global war on drugs.

INSIDE THE TRANSNATIONAL PRISON INDUSTRIAL COMPLEX: THREE WOMEN'S STORIES

Accounts of structural economic and political processes are important if we are to understand the reasons behind the boom in women's imprisonment. However, by putting these macrolevel processes in the foreground, we risk losing sight of women's agency. Indeed, in such accounts, women, especially women of color and third-world women, are often reduced to faceless victims while corporations, governments, and supranational bodies such as the IMF and World Bank take center stage. In order to move women of color from the margin to the center, I have chosen to highlight three women's stories. These stories reflect the lives of women incarcerated in three national locations: Britain, Canada, and the United States. Looking beyond the borders of the United States enables us to examine the ways in which globalization, the transnational prison industrial complex, and the global war on drugs lead to the criminalization and incarceration of women of color and third-world women.

Narrative One: Militarization, Displacement, and the War on Drugs

Teresa is a Colombian woman in her early 40s.[29] As a single mother, she struggled to support her three

children. Carrying Class A drugs (cocaine) between Colombia and England enabled her to supplement her meager income. She was arrested at Heathrow airport in England and was given a five-year sentence, which she is serving at HMP Winchester women's annex. She does not know what has become of her three children and has not been able to contact them since she was arrested. Her fear is that they will be homeless since she did not leave any emergency funds for them. Teresa's story challenges us to rethink commonsense ideas about dangerous Latin American "drug traffickers" flooding the United States and Europe with cocaine. In common with many drug "mules" from developing countries, Teresa was pushed into trafficking drugs by desperation. In her words:

> Cargamos drogas porque lo necesitamos; porque tenemos situaciones de financia. Somos de Colombia, de paises del tercer mundo, que son pobres. La situacion en lo que viven, por eso lo hicemos.
>
> We carry drugs because we need to, because we have financial difficulties. We come from Colombia, the third world, which are poor countries. The conditions we live in, that's what pushed us.

Colombia is a country shackled by foreign debt, political and social dislocation, violence, war, and kidnappings. As a leading harvester of the coca leaf, estimated to produce 80 percent of the world's cocaine, Colombia has been a key target of U.S. anti-drug interventions. Instead of alleviating horrendous social, political, and economic conditions for women in Latin America, U.S. financial assistance is targeted at building military forces that participate in the war on drugs. These forces have been used to carry out counterinsurgency wars against revolutionary groups like the FARC (Revolutionary Armed Forces of Colombia) and ELN (National Liberation Army) that have spearheaded the struggle for indigenous and poor people's rights. The U.S. military alleges that such groups have received millions of dollars per annum for protecting coca plantations, drug trafficking routes, and airstrips. By identifying these revolutionary groups as "narco-terrorists," the U.S. administration is able to justify providing military expertise and assistance to Colombia, despite its poor human rights record and evidence of collusion between the military and right-wing paramilitary death squads.[30] In the fall of 2000, President Clinton announced a $1.3 billion contribution toward Plan Colombia, a strategy put forward by Colombian president Pastrana to end the internal war, eradicate the coca crop, and strengthen the rule of law in areas in which the state has been replaced by revolutionary groups and right-wing paramilitaries. U.S. funding for the plan provides 60 attack helicopters and weapons training. In addition, U.S. scientists have developed Agent Green, a modified fungus that the administration plans to release in coca-producing areas to attack and kill the coca plants.

In tying aid to military gains against the FARC, the United States finances a four-decade-old civil war in which at least 35,000 people have died and two million have been internally displaced or forced to emigrate. The displacement of peasants and indigenous people is further exacerbated by the use of herbicides and organic toxins that affect large areas of rain forest and groundwater and create health problems for local people in addition to destroying the coca.[31] Women bear the brunt of this atmosphere of violence and instability as displaced landless peasants, as primary caretakers seeking to feed their children, and as spouses of men killed in the fighting. Ironically, the very conditions that pushed Teresa to risk importing Class A drugs are caused in part by the war on drugs. She, like many other foreign nationals in U.S. and European prisons, will be deported after serving a long sentence to a homeland where she has no house, no income, and no social security. In the meantime, she will be replaced by any of the millions of impoverished and desperate women in Latin America, the Caribbean, and Africa who become drug mules each year.

Narrative Two: Racialization, Labeling, and Exclusion

Camille is a 21-year-old African Canadian woman. Camille's mother, an immigrant from Jamaica, brought her up in public housing in the declining West End of Toronto. As a young girl, Camille was in constant conflict with her mother's expectations. She experienced difficulties at school, was labeled as having attention deficit hyperactive disorder (ADHD), and was sent to a school for children with special needs:

> They always told me I was bad, but you know kids. They said I had attention deficit disorder. I went to a couple of behavior schools, after that my mum switched us to Catholic school. I was going there for a while, then grade 2, me and the teacher got into something. I think I hit the teacher. They sent me to another behavior school for a couple of years.

At age 11, Camille was sent by her mother to a group home; this move started a pattern of disruption as she was shuttled between group homes and her mother's apartment. Raising two girls in the racist and often dangerous environment of the inner city, Camille's mother attempted to impress rigid gender roles on her daughters, encouraging them to limit themselves to the domestic sphere. African Caribbean women in Canada are located within a racially gendered capitalist economy in which black femininity is constructed as simultaneously a sign of hard labor and sexual availability.[32] Fearing the racialized sexual subordination of their Canadian-born children, many immigrant women seek to enforce strict sexual mores and harsh discipline. Such attempts can lead to generational conflicts that are sometimes interpreted as a culture gap but in fact arise out of the survival strategies engendered by the experience of migration. Camille resisted her mother's attempts to "protect" her by curtailing her freedom:

> I was a tomboy. Me and my brother always used to do stuff. But then he got older, he didn't want to hang out with me no more. He always got to go outside, and she's always telling me I'm a girl and I can't do this and that. She was always beating me. But I always did my own thing.

On leaving school with few qualifications, Camille found herself unemployed and living with her mother with no source of income. When she was approached by a male friend who asked her if she was interested in earning $5,000 in a week by importing cocaine from Jamaica, she accepted. After being detained by customs at Toronto airport, she was sentenced to two years and four months, which she served at Grand Valley Institution for women in Kitchener, Ontario, and at the Elizabeth Fry halfway house in Toronto.

Unlike Teresa, Camille did not have children to support, and her mother paid for her basic needs. However, her situation is indicative of the problems facing young black Canadians who have been failed by an underfunded educational system that is unwilling to deal with the diverse needs of a multiracial population. Rather than places of education, inner-city schools have become locations where young black people are warehoused and, increasingly, policed. Unfamiliar with the Canadian school system, immigrant parents are ill equipped to challenge the labeling of their children as educationally subnormal or suffering from ADHD. Rather than dealing with working-class black children's needs, schools and child psychiatrists treat difficult behavior as medical problems, thus justifying notions of inherent (racialized) mental incapacity. Camille emerged from the school system with few skills and qualifications into a racially and gender stratified labor market that offers, at best, minimum-wage jobs to young women of color. In the context of a North American youth culture that defines personal value via consumerism, Camille's lack of legitimate access to money, or routes to better earning power, is a significant motivation for her involvement in drug importation.

For the past five years, Ontario has been governed by a conservative provincial government under Canadian premier Mike Harris that has pursued a "Common Sense Revolution." Under this neoliberal revolution, welfare, education, health, and social services have been dramatically cut back, the minimum wage frozen, and employment equity provisions repealed in order to increase Ontario's competitiveness within NAFTA and the global market.[33] Simultaneously, the province has engaged in the biggest prison-building project of the century, with the goal of constructing three "superjails," modeled on the United States.[34] The superjails will house all of the provincial prisoners currently scat-

tered throughout the large province in small jails and police cells. Although the provincial government argues that it will eventually recoup the estimated $325 million in construction costs through lower operating costs, these "savings" are predicated on bringing in private operators, reducing staff salaries, creating an austere environment, and denying contact visits to prisoners who refuse to work in the prison industries.[35] When funding for prisons and additional policing is squeezed from the budget of a government committed to making tax cuts, further cuts in social spending become inevitable. Youth programs, shelters for women and teens, schools, black community projects, and social workers are all affected. As social workers are forced to raise minimum intervention levels, families with problems that are not considered urgent are left without support. Underfunded social programs are limited to crisis intervention rather than prevention. As schools are forced to operate on limited budgets, the incentive to exclude children who behave in difficult ways is increased. The pattern of Camille's life, dotted with family conflict and violence, school exclusions, and unemployment, is evidence of an absence of appropriate social support. By redirecting tax monies from social programs into the prison industrial complex and by promoting a low-wage, "flexible"[36] labor market, the state exacerbates this trend and ensures that there will be a pool of young women from Ontario's inner-city projects willing to risk their lives by importing drugs.

Narrative Three: Gender Entrapment and the Crack Cocaine Disparity

Kemba Smith was a middle-class African American student at Hampton College, a traditionally black college in Virginia. She became involved with a young man, Khalif Hall, who, unknown to her, was a key figure in a large drug operation. When Hall began to abuse Kemba and threatened to kill her, she did not leave him because she was afraid for her family and herself and because she had become pregnant. Shortly before the drug ring was apprehended, Hall was shot and killed. Kemba pleaded guilty to conspiracy to distribute crack cocaine, but hoped Hall's intimidation would be taken into account. Instead, she was held responsible for the full 255 kilos involved in the offense—although she personally was not found to have handled the drugs—and was sentenced to 24.5 years in prison. Kemba's case has been adopted by activists who oppose the war on drugs, including Families Against Mandatory Minimums, the Kemba Smith Justice Project, and the Million Woman March.[37] Her case is important not because the long sentence she received is unusual, but because the case highlights the inequitable impact of the war on drugs. The 24.5-year sentence Kemba received is not indicative of a particularly unsympathetic judge but of a series of laws and policies introduced since the mid-1980s that have targeted users and street-level retail sales, highlighting crack cocaine as a particular threat. As Kemba argues:

> While laws should be designed to protect our communities from drug kingpins, instead, low level offenders with little or no involvement in the sale of drugs are being locked up for 15, 25, 30 [years], or 13 life sentences. In fact, I know a 30 year old Black woman, mother of two girls who was sentenced to 13 life sentences.[40]

Under the Anti Drug Abuse Act, Kemba's knowledge of her boyfriend's drug dealing was sufficient for her to receive a mandatory minimum sentence. However, her lack of involvement in the drug ring prevented her from providing information that might have reduced her sentence.

Kemba's case also illustrates what Beth Richie calls the "gender entrapment of battered black women": the high levels of male violence and abuse experienced by African American women entering the criminal justice system.[38] Many women are incarcerated as a direct result of a coercive and violent male figure. The woman's situation may have been caused by involvement in criminal activities, such as prostitution and drug dealing, in which the male is profiting from her; alternatively, her incarceration may be because of self-defense against a violent male partner. Feminist activists have organized around the cases of women incarcerated for killing their abusive partners, but there has been less awareness of the role

of male violence—from early childhood sexual abuse to domestic violence—in the lives of women incarcerated for other types of offenses.[39] In this sense, the psychological, physical, and sexual abuse that women are subjected to in prison is just one aspect of a continuum of violence in incarcerated women's lives. Women of color who live in emotionally and economically vulnerable positions in relation to men may be pressured by them to serve as free or cheap labor in the drug business. Although the women's movement has attempted to reduce women's dependence on men, welfare reforms and cutbacks in funding for women's shelters and day care under the Clinton and Bush administrations in the United States have further limited the choices of working-class women in particular. Kemba's case demonstrates that mandatory minimums and heightened police surveillance of communities of color, when combined with women's dependence on and coercion by male family members, create the conditions under which increasing numbers of women of color have been criminalized and turned into fodder for the prison industrial complex. As Kemba argues:

> With the entering of the New Year, I want to give you the gift of vision, to see this system of Modern Day Slavery for what it is. The government gets paid $25,000 a year by you (taxpayers) to house me (us). The more of us that they incarcerate, the more money they get from you to build more prisons. The building of more prisons create more jobs. The federal prison system is comprised of 61% drug offenders, so basically this war on drugs is the reason why the Prison Industrial Complex is a skyrocketing enterprise.[40]

CONCLUSIONS AND REFLECTIONS ON ABOLITIONISM

This chapter has described an exponential increase in women's imprisonment internationally and has suggested a new set of questions for feminist researchers and criminologists who wish to explain this phenomenon. The prison is typically examined from within the framework provided by mainstream criminologists and criminal justice officials, with their focus on offending behavior, rehabilitation, correction, and punishment. In contrast, radical scholars and activists are increasingly asking the question, Who benefits from the current prison boom? The concept of the prison industrial complex provides a way of answering this question. It highlights the roles of politicians seeking votes by pursuing "tough on crime" policies; of media corporations gaining ratings while fueling a racialized fear of crime in the general public; of prison corporations and their shareholders, generating massive profits in building and managing prisons; and of correctional officer associations and other law enforcement agencies gaining revenues and political power.

The prison industrial complex is the engine that has fueled the recent growth in prison populations; however, it does not provide us with a clear understanding of why women's incarceration should be growing faster than that of men. To understand this phenomenon, we need to look at two other factors: *globalization* and the global *war on drugs*. Neoliberal socioeconomic policies brought about by the globalization of capital and promoted by the IMF and World Bank have led to the racialized feminization of poverty. Women in the global south have been hit by the shift from social welfare to corporate welfare, whereby government resources for social services, health, and education have been cut back and instead are poured into wooing corporate investment. Women of color in the global north have been hit by cutbacks in welfare, shelters, day care, and social programs. Because women carry the primary burden of feeding, clothing, and caring for children and elderly relatives, they come under immense pressure when public services are cut back. This racialized feminization of poverty limits women's survival options and leads to involvement in criminalized activity.

Because drug use and involvement in drug trade are common responses to economic and emotional stresses, the war on drugs has also disproportionately impacted women of color and third-world women. In the United States and Canada, poor communities of color have been targeted for surveillance and policing, which lead to more arrests. The pursuit of

crack cocaine as a greater threat than powder cocaine (or other drugs commonly sought by middle-class users) and disproportionate sentencing of crack cocaine offenders has also led the war on drugs to become a war on poor communities, particularly poor women of color. Women's unequal relationships with men and their experiences of domestic violence may also serve to propel them into conflict with the law. In the global south, the war on drugs has led to massive military interventions, further exacerbating situations of war and conflict. Women have been particularly negatively affected by the displacement and breakdown of communities caused by military conflict. The lack of alternative ways of supporting their families leads poor women in Latin America into working as drug mules and thus risking incarceration in the global north.

At a time when increasing numbers of women are being incarcerated, families separated, and communities devastated, any discussion of women, crime, and punishment must end with proposals for change. There are three possible approaches for those wishing to challenge the status quo regarding women's imprisonment: reform, decarceration, and abolition. *Reformers* focus on producing suggestions for change that are practical within the existing system. Feminist reformers have proposed women-centered prison regimes, for example, that require female prison officers, introduce programs on domestic violence and rape, or provide therapists working within a framework of women's empowerment. Feminist reformers have also proposed reforms to the law, legalizing prostitution, for example, or removing status offenses from the criminal law.

There are three problems with reformism. First, as Foucault argues, reform tends to be incorporated into the prison and used as justification for its expansion.[41] For example, in Canada, demands for women-centered prison regimes led to the construction of five new federal prisons, thus increasing the number of women behind bars[42] (see Faith, chap. 17). In Britain, the provision of a mother and baby unit led judges to feel more comfortable with sentencing pregnant women to prison. Second, reformers tend to work with the system, thus enabling the stigmatization of those with more radical proposals as idealist and unrealistic. Finally, reformers frequently fail to question why and whether women should be imprisoned in the first place and instead focus on reducing the pains of imprisonment. They are therefore ill equipped to oppose the explosion in women's imprisonment.

The second possibility is *decarceration*. This strategy goes a step further than reform by pushing for laws that will lead to people being released from prison. For example, decarceration strategies emphasize alternative forms of punishment, including fines and community service, as well as rehabilitation and reeducation programs in the free world, such as sex offender training and anger management. Finally, proponents of decarceration support measures such as Proposition 36 in California, which redirects drug users away from prison and into drug rehabilitation programs. A first step toward decarceration is the establishment of a prison moratorium, whereby states are petitioned to pass a resolution preventing the construction of any new prisons. If no new prison beds are made available, the argument goes, officials will have to find other ways to deal with men and women in conflict with the law. Decarceration is an important political strategy that challenges the constant expansion of the prison industrial complex and seeks to reduce the profit motive in prison growth. However, decarceration policies are vulnerable to political swings, and a moratorium can swiftly be reversed.

The third possibility is *abolition*. Prison abolitionists use this term to identify the prison as a fundamentally unjust institution that, like slavery, cannot be reformed.[43] They argue that prisons do not work, fail to reduce crimes, and fail to make vulnerable populations—including women and people of color—safer. Abolitionists also argue that prisons are incapable of rehabilitating people; instead, they brutalize prisoners and return them to their communities ill equipped to survive by legitimate means. Abolitionists point out the huge economic costs of imprisonment, and they argue that public funds could more effectively be spent preventing social

problems by creating jobs with a living wage, providing women's shelters, creating youth programs, and developing high-quality education. They also point out the social costs of incarcerating two million people in the United States, with a devastating impact on their families and communities, particularly communities of color.

Abolitionism is the only strategy that requires a fundamental rethinking of the way in which justice is delivered. It requires that we look for the *root causes* of antisocial acts, such as assault, burglary, or domestic violence, and look for alternatives that address these root causes. Abolitionism has not been viewed with great enthusiasm by many feminists, however. After spending years campaigning for the criminal justice system to take rape, domestic violence, and child abuse seriously, many feminists have seen abolitionism as a mechanism that will remove valuable legal protections from women. Feminist abolitionists have dealt with this problem in two ways. First, some have called for the abolition of women's prisons only, arguing that women are imprisoned for very different reasons than men and therefore need different treatment.[44] This argument is, however, unsustainable in the light of calls for equal treatment of women under the law. Second, others have challenged the idea that "the nonsolution of imprisonment" makes women safe and have argued that, in fact, an overreliance on punitive strategies prevents a more fundamental challenge to the patriarchal gender roles —and the institutions that support them—that are at the root of male violence against women.[45]

Reform *in isolation of a broader strategy for social change* serves to legitimize and even expand the prison industrial complex, and decarceration is only a stopgap measure. In contrast, abolitionism promises a revolutionary and long-lasting solution. It offers a radical critique of the punitive approach to women's survival strategies. Abolitionism is the only strategy that removes the profit motive from the criminal justice system and the only approach that challenges the belief that prison works. Although it does not offer an immediate solution, it does provide a *critical framework* within which proposed legislation, campaigns, and activism can be assessed. By working together within an abolitionist framework, scholars, activists, prisoners, and their families are building a movement for lasting social change and for a safe and just global community.[46]

DISCUSSION QUESTIONS

1. Define each of the three major processes that lead to increased incarceration for women according to Sudbury:
   - globalization of the economy
   - the war on drugs
   - the prison industrial complex
2. Sudbury argues that these three social processes (globalization, war on drugs, and prison industrial complex) have led to a disproportionate incarceration of women of color in the United States and elsewhere. Explain what she means by this statement.
3. Sudbury's thesis focuses on macrostructural causes of women's increased incarceration. Consider competing criminological theories that might argue that by focusing on these larger structural conditions, Sudbury's analysis permits offenders to blame outside forces beyond their control for their own criminal behavior.
4. How might you reconcile the opposing theoretical and political approaches presented by Sudbury and her critics?
5. Explain the difference between prison reform, decarceration, and abolition. Which do you support and why?

NOTES

1. The concepts *global south* and *global north* have been adopted by antiglobalization activists and scholars in place of terms like *third world* and *the West*. These concepts indicate the causal relationship between poverty in Africa, Asia, Latin America and the Caribbean, and wealth in North America and Europe. Neoliberalism is a philosophy that views the unfettered market as the key to economic and social progress. Neoliberal policies include the reduction of trade barriers, in particular through international trade agreements such as NAFTA and FTAA; privatization of state assets and services; encouragement of foreign as well as domestic private investment through free trade zones and tax breaks; and lessening of regulations including environmental or worker's protections that impinge on corporate profit-making. See Noam Chomsky. 1998. *Profit over People: Neoliberalism and Global Order.* New York: Seven Stories.

2. Leslie Cagan, 2000. The Meaning of the Philadelphia Protests, *Dialogue and Initiative,* Fall, p. 3.

3. Department of Justice. 1998. *Women in Criminal Justice: A Twenty Year Update,* http://www.usdoj.gov/reports/98Guide/wcjc98/execsumm.htm, accessed July 3, 2001.

4. Elliott Currie. 1998. *Crime and Punishment in America.* New York: Henry Holt and Co.

5. Press release, Leeds Metropolitan University, April 7, 1999, http//www.lmu.ac.uk/news/press/archive/apr99/prisons.htm.

6. Prison Reform Trust. 2001. *Justice for Women: The Need for Reform.* London: Prison Reform Trust.

7. Patricia Macias Rojas. 1998. Complex Facts, *Colorlines,* Fall.

8. Parliament of New South Wales, Select Committee on the Increase in Prisoner Population, www.parliament.nsw.gov.au, accessed July 4, 2000.

9. Canadian Criminal Justice Association. 2000. *Aboriginal Peoples and the Criminal Justice System,* Ottawa.

10. Commission on System Racism in the Ontario Criminal Justice System. 1994. *Racism Behind Bars,* Toronto: Queens Printers.

11. Mike Elkins, Carly Gray, and Keith Rogers. 2001. *Prison Population Brief: England and Wales*

April 2001. London: Home Office Research Development Statistics.

12. Freda Adler, 1975. *Sisters in Crime: The Rise of the New Female Criminal.* New York: McGraw Hill.

13. Carol Smart. 1979. The New Female Offender: Reality or Myth, *British Journal of Criminology* 19(1): 50–59

14. Patricia Hill Collins. 1990. *Black Feminist Thought: Knowledge, Consciousness, and the Politics of Empowerment.* New York: Routledge; Cherrie Moraga and Gloria Anzaldua, eds. 1981. *This Bridge Called My Back: Writings by Radical Women of Color.* New York: Kitchen Table; Chandra Mohanty, Ann Russo, and Lourdes Torres, eds. 1991. *Third World Women and the Politics of Feminism.* Bloomington: Indiana University; Ana Castillo. 1995. *Massacre of the Dreamers: Essays on Xicanisma.* New York: Plume, 1995.

15. William Grieder. 2000. "The Last Farm Crisis," *The Nation,* November 20.

16. Manning Marable. 2000. Seattle and Beyond: Making the Connection in the 21st Century, *Dialogue and Initiative,* Fall.

17. "As Jamaica gets ready to go global and sticks to liberal policies, international investors need look no further than this Caribbean island to find opportunities which they won't regret." Quoted from *Jamaica: Island of Opportunity,* www.vegamedia.com/jamaica/jamaica.html, accessed January 20, 2002.

18. Higglers are traders, often women, who buy and resell cheap clothing, food, and other low-cost products in Jamaica's informal economy.

19. Angela Y. Davis. 1998. Race and Criminalization: Black Americans and the Punishment Industry. In *The Angela Y. Davis Reader,* ed. Joy James. Malden, MA: Blackwell.

20. Joel Dyer. 2000. *The Perpetual Prisoner Machine: How America Profits from Crime.* Boulder, CO: Westview.

21. Mark Fishman and Gray Cavender, eds. 1998. *Entertaining Crime: Television Reality Programs.* New York: Aldine DeGruyter.

22. Jennifer Gonnerman. 1997. Portrait of a Prison Town, *Village Voice,* March, pp. 44–47. Ruth Gilmore argues that prisons have not provided the economic benefits promised and in many instances lead to greater hardship for local residents. (Ruth Gilmore. 2001. Prisons and Local Economic Development. Unpublished paper for *Joining Forces: Environmental Justice and the Fight Against Prison Expansion,* Conference, February 10; see also Mike Lewis. 2000. Economic Lockdown," *The Fresno Bee,* January 9.)

23. This has not been the case; instead, criminalization and targeting by law enforcement artificially inflate the price of drugs, so that manufacturing, trafficking, and selling them become immensely profitable and increasingly associated with violence. This mutually profitable relationship between law enforcement and the drug trade has been labeled the "international drug complex" (Hans Van Der Veen. 2000. *The International Drug Complex.* Amsterdam: Center for Drug Research, University of Amsterdam).

24. Maxine Waters. 1998. Congressional Black Caucus Blasts President's Crack/Powder Cocaine Sentencing Recommendations. Press release, July 22.

25. The G7 is made up of the major industrial democracies, which since 1975 have met at annual summits to deal with major economic and political issues. In 1998, Russia became a full member, joining France, the United States, Britain, Germany, Japan, Italy, and Canada to form the G8.

26. H. Richard Friman. 1996. *Narcodiplomacy: Exporting the US War on Drugs.* Ithaca, New York, and London: Cornell University.

27. Hans-Jorg Albrecht. 2001. The International System of Drug Control: Developments and Trends. In *Drug War, American Style: The Internationalization of Failed Policy and Its Alternatives,* ed., Jurg Gerber and Eric Hensen. New York and London: Garland.

28. Although Dutch coffee shops selling cannabis and the British practice of prescribing to heroin addicts have gone largely unaffected by the 1988 convention, they are in opposition to and theoretically threatened by its provisions.

29. Pseudonyms have been used to protect the identities of the first two interviewees. The case of Kemba Smith has reached national prominence due to the clemency granted her by president Bill Clinton at the end of his term in office. I have therefore used her real name.

30. Human Rights Groups Criticize Clinton over Aid to Colombian Military. 2000. *San Francisco Chronicle*, August 29.

31. Agent Green, otherwise known as Fusarium, was rejected for spraying on marijuana crops in Florida because of its unpredictable mutagenic properties and the danger it posed to the environment (US Sprays Poison in Drug War. 2000. *Observer*, July 2).

32. Dionne Brand. 1999. Black Women and Work: The Impact of Racially Constructed Gender Roles on the Sexual Division of Labour. In *Scratching the Surface: Canadian Anti-Racist Feminist Thought*. ed. Enakshi Dua and Angela Robertson. 1999. Toronto: Women's Press.

33. Christina Gabriel. 1999. Restructuring at the Margins: Women of Colour and the Changing Economy. In *Scratching the Surface: Canadian Anti-Racist Feminist Thought*. ed. Enakshi Dua and Angela Robertson. Toronto: Women's Press.

34. Ministry of Correctional Services. 1999. Infrastructure Renewal Project: Ontario Adult Correctional Institutions. Ontario.

35. Tracey Tyler. 2000. Will 'Jumbo' Jails Cut Costs? *Toronto: The Sunday Star*, April 6.

36. Corporations prefer a workforce that can be hired and fired according to seasonal fluctuations in demand. This "flexible" workforce is thereby denied stable, permanent employment and adequate compensation for being laid off.

37. For information on the campaigns on behalf of Kemba Smith, see www.geocities.com/CapitolHill/Lobby/8899. These groups were largely responsible for bringing about the pardoning of Kemba Smith in the last days of the Clinton administration in 2000. Kemba has continued to campaign on behalf of the thousands of low-level, drug-involved prisoners who remain incarcerated for obscenely long terms of imprisonment.

38. Beth Richie. 1996. *Compelled to Crime: The Gender Entrapment of Battered Black Women*. London and New York: Routledge.

39. Luana Ross. 1998. *Inventing the Savage: The Social Construction of Native American Criminality*. Austin: University of Texas, pp. 92–107.

40. Kemba Smith, From the Desk of Kemba Smith, www.geocities.com/CapitolHill/Lobby/8899/pen.html, December 13, 1999.

41. Michel Foucault. 1979. *Discipline and Punish: The Birth of the Prison*. New York: Vintage, pp. 264–71.

42. Correctional Service of Canada, 1990. *Creating Choices: The Report of the Task Force on Federally Sentenced Women*, Ottawa.

43. A useful summary of the literature on abolitionism can be found in Jim Thomas and Sharon Boehlefeld. 1991. Rethinking Abolitionism: "What Do We Do with Henry?" *Social Justice* 18(3): 239–25.

44. Pat Carlen. 1998. *Sledgehammer: Women's Imprisonment at the Millennium*. Basingstoke and London: MacMillan.

45. Fay Honey Knopp. 1993. On Radical Feminism and Abolition. In *We Who Would Take No Prisoners: Selections from the Fifth International Conference on Penal Abolition*, ed. Brian D. MacLean and Harold E. Pepinsky, p.55. Vancouver: Collective Press.

46. Organizations working within this framework include Critical Resistance http://www.criticalresistance.org and the International Conference on Penal Abolition (ICOPA) http://www.interlog.com/~ritten/icopa.html

Chapter 13

Resistance and Survivance:
Cultural Genocide and Imprisoned Native Women

Luana Ross

ABSTRACT

Native Americans and women are the two fastest-growing groups of prisoners in the United States. In this chapter the reader has the opportunity to learn from a Native American scholar about some of the hardships facing Native American women in a Montana prison. Ross explains the resistance of these prisoners and describes the ways they attempt to cope. These incarcerated women resist in prison because they feel that the prison officials are not recognizing and honoring the cultural differences between Native American and Euro-American, or white, prisoners and that the prison is not offering the women access to native spiritual leaders and culturally relevant programs. When the prisoners engage in resistance, Ross says, prison officials take retaliatory action against them. Ross's main point is that the prison system is racially discriminatory, it lacks programs appropriate for Native American women, and its staff is either uninformed about, disinterested in, or hostile to the Native American culture. Native American women continue to resist the prison's assaults on their sense of integrity by creating and demanding their own supports as much as possible.

The reader may come to the realization that the prisoners and the prison staff seem to live on two different planets. The staff subjects the women to the dominant culture's ideas of rehabilitation, which consists of counseling and therapy to cure what are considered the "savages' mental derangements" or deviance. The prisoners say that they are being denied access to their culture and to the spiritual practices that they believe would aid in their survival in prison. Moreover, the prisoners see the staff as disrespectful of their culture, verbally abusive, and generally racist.

Ross concludes the chapter by citing her findings of specific discriminatory treatment of Native American women: their disproportionate numbers in the prison system; the generally harsh treatment of Native American women prisoners including their overrepresentation in maximum security; the denial in prison of their culture and their spiritual leaders; and more generally, the reprisals they face.

INTRODUCTION

*A society can be judged by what goes on
in its prisons*

—Dostoevsky

The belief that law (a Euro-American construct) itself, and the administration of law, is biased against certain categories of people is crucial to understanding Native American criminality and the experiences of imprisoned Natives. Native worlds have been devastated by the course of their relationship with Euro-Americans and their laws. The number of jailed Natives is a chilling indication: A reminder that, because deviance is socially constructed, crime statistics reveal discretion in defining and apprehending "criminals" (Quinney 1970; Sheley 1985). Native people are now locked up in great numbers. The disproportion of Native prisoners is more clearly seen at the state level where they comprised 32 percent of the total prisoner population in Alaska, 25 percent in South Dakota, 22 percent in North Dakota, and 18 percent in Montana (Camp and Camp 1992).

Race, gender, and class play critical roles in the responses of both informal and formal agents of control. The use of arrest statistics as evidence of the relative involvement of different social groups has been criticized by both labeling and Marxist theorists, who argue that individuals do not come to the attention of the criminal justice system solely on the basis of their behavior. The definition of behavior as criminal, in addition to the course of action taken in response to it, depends upon contextual features. Hence, factors independent of the behavior of supposed criminal individuals enter into official statistics. These differential reactions—depending upon one's race, gender, and class—are therefore assumed to systematically distort arrest statistics. Racism, sexism, and classism are systems of oppression and, accordingly discrimination can be direct by involving individual attitudes or indirect by comprising structural inequalities.

There is scant empirical research on incarcerated Native Americans, although they are disproportionately imprisoned. Moreover, while sociological studies of female criminality have disregarded women of color (Mann 1993), the subject of imprisoned Native American women is virtually an unexplored area. Imprisoned Native women have been rendered invisible and, as put forth by Patricia Hill Collins (1991), invisibility allows structural arrangements of inequality to exist.

The first study of imprisoned Native American women was conducted in 1991 (Ross 1992). That study gave voice to those women by describing and defining their experiences as prisoners. The lives of these women were complex; bound up in race, gender, and class oppression. The data suggested that experiences of imprisoned women varied according to race, culture, and location of confinement. Incarcerated Natives experienced prison differently than white prisoners; and prisoners housed in maximum-security, where Natives were disproportionately represented, experienced prison differently than prisoners in the general-population building. Generally, conditions faced by the prisoners were deficient in many ways, including the physical condition of the prison, medical care, counseling and treatment programs, and other rehabilitative programs. Moreover, the social environment of the prison represented one of control, not rehabilitation.

Conditions of oppression prompted resistance by the imprisoned Native women. Acts of resistance included: unity as Native women, maintenance of culture, letters to the American Civil Liberties Union and the Native American Prisoners Rehabilitation Research Project, letters to local newspapers and political figures, time in maximum security for disobeying prison rules, or escaping as two Native women did in 1994 and 1995. Some do not survive prisonization; the prison regime becomes intolerable. There is a "breaking" process which many prisoners experience. Partly this involves the overuse of mind-altering drugs, lengthy time in maximum security, and denial of visitation with children (see Ross 1993 and 1994). One Native woman interviewed attempted

Source: Luana Ross. 1996. Resistance and Survivance: Cultural Genocide and Imprisoned Native Women. *Race, Gender & Class* 3(2):125–141.

suicide multiple times. Although this was viewed by the treatment specialist as "attention-getting" behavior, it can be seen as a desperate cry for help.

This article focuses on resistance and survivance as a response to prisonization. Specifically, I examine racism, sexism, and rehabilitative programming. In addition, I briefly discuss reprisal on behalf of prison officials to prisoners' acts of resistance. I do so gingerly, because I fear for the Native women who are presently incarcerated in Montana.

METHODOLOGY

This study was designed to focus on women from two different races and cultures—Native American and white—who were incarcerated in Montana's women's prison, the Women's Correctional Center (WCC). A comparison allowed me to examine race and culture as critical variables. The findings were based on in-depth interviews (tape-recorded) with 27 imprisoned women, the prison warden, treatment specialist, parenting-class facilitator, and county social worker. The data were supplemented with nonparticipant observation, informal conversations with prisoners and staff, reports from the State Department of Institutions, and reports and letters from the American Civil Liberties Union (ACLU). Prisoners were questioned concerning the prison's social environment, their major concerns as imprisoned mothers, and institutional support offered to them as imprisoned mothers. Interviews with prison staff and the county social worker focused on programs offered to imprisoned mothers, and how mothers' relationships with their children were facilitated.

PRISONER PROFILE

The sample included 14 Native American and 13 white imprisoned women. In 1991, 70 percent of the total female population was white (n = 48), 25 percent Native American (n = 17), and 5 percent Hispanic (n = 3). In Montana in 1991, Native Americans were just under 6 percent of the total state population. This, coupled with Public Law 280—these figures are for male prisoners; it is not surprising the

data were not broken down by gender—revealed that Native women were significantly overrepresented in the state prison population. A factor that complicates the position of imprisoned Native Americans is the jurisdictional maze created by the Federal government. In Montana, all Indian reservations, except one, are subjected to federal control over criminal matters; the exception is under state control concerning criminal matters. This means that, on all reservations, excluding the one under state control, Natives sentenced to prison are incarcerated in out-of-state federal prisons; only those arrested on the state-controlled reservation and off the reservation are sent to the same prison. The age range of the interviewees was between 18 and 45 years old, with an average of 30.1 years old. Of the 27 interviewees, 7 reported they were single, 12 divorced, and 8 married. However, of the 8 who reported they were married, 4 had spouses who were also imprisoned. The sample population had between 1 to 5 children, with 3 children the most frequent number reported. The educational level ranged between the fifth grade and a college degree (one woman had a college degree). The most frequent educational level reported was 12 years. It is important to note Native American women had extremely low-levels of education with 5 women reporting only an eighth grade level and one reporting a fifth grade level. All interviewees were from lower-income levels.

The following is a typical profile of an incarcerated Native female drawn from the sample: She is thirty years old, most likely a Landless Native, single or divorced, with one to three children. The number of living children would be higher because several Native women have children who are deceased. Prior to incarceration she experienced much violence in her life, was not employed, and has a eighth grade education. Her crime is alcohol- or drug-related, and she was convicted of a "male-type" crime (murder, robbery, assault, escape, etc.). The sentence length for Native women ranged from 5–60 years; the average was 19.1 years.

The following is a typical profile of an incarcerated white female drawn from the sample: She is thirty years old, most likely divorced with two or three children. She either completed high school or received her GED. She experienced much violence in her life prior to incarceration and if she was employed she held a low-level, low-paying position. Her crime is alcohol- or drug-related, and she was convicted of a "female-type" crime (e.g., bad checks). The sentence length for white women ranged from 5–20 years; the average was 9 years.

Clearly, Native women in the sample population were given longer sentences than white women. However, they were convicted more for male-type crimes than white women, which could account for longer sentence lengths. There was, thus, a qualitative difference in crime-type which makes comparisons difficult. Despite this, sentence disparity warrants immediate investigation because when the crimes were the same, Native women received longer sentences than white women.

PRISON REHABILITATION

Punishment pains man, but does not make him better

—Nietzsche

"If prison really rehabilitated people, then a lot of Indians are saints." This remark was made by two tribal attorneys from the Confederated Salish and Kootenai Tribes as they commented on the high conviction rates of Natives from that particular reservation. What exactly is *rehabilitation?* The idea, theoretically, is to restore well-being via various therapeutic models and education. The assumption is that someone has been ill or deviant in some manner. In line with that opinion, is the premise that imprisoned individuals are guilty of a crime and are in need of rehabilitation.

Some women, Native and non-Native, were imprisoned at the Women's Correctional Center for killing abusive family members and others for writing "bad checks" to adequately care for their children. Furthermore, some women maintain their innocence. Several women were found guilty by judges, although their husbands or partners acknowledged their guilt. In all cases it was the husband who assaulted foster-children and apparently

the judges assumed the responsibility of the wives. Other women were imprisoned because they pled guilty to spare their spouses/partners prison time. And other women were named by their spouses/partners as the guilty ones, although the women insist it was their spouses/partners who actually committed the crimes. We are discovering more and more that because someone is in prison does not mean they are guilty. And, after years of unjust incarceration there is no compensation.

The WCC's rehabilitative programming is based conceptually on the notion of "therapy." The idea of therapy, as implemented in women's prisons, operates on the outdated assumption that imprisoned women are mentally deranged (Pollak 1950). Women are seen as neurotic and therefore in need of "treatment." Given this, it is no surprise that Montana's women's prison was located on the grounds of the state mental institution. This notion is embedded in the language of prison personnel. For instance, prison personnel refer to incarcerated women as "inmates" and the prison as a "center." In contrast, I name things as imprisoned women experience them. Words like inmate and center are too gentle and, subsequently, misleading in the description of the experiences of imprisoned women.

Dobash, Dobash, and Gutteridge (1986) explain that early prisons in the United States and Britain attempted to create an environment conducive to moral transformation. The authors inform us that from the onset imprisoned women and men were handled differently. Imprisoned women were deemed more "morally depraved and corrupt and in need of special, closer forms of control and confinement" than imprisoned men (Dobash et al. 1986, 1). Moreover, the authors argue this sentiment continues today. An examination of women's prisons in the U.S. in the 1970s, disclosed that rehabilitative programs were designed to aid prisoners in the development of "empathy, maturity, unselfishness, [and] warmth" (Velimesis 1975, 105). Important historical research by Nichole Hahn Rafter (1985, 1990) advises that women's prisons in the 1870s emerged as a bifurcated system: white women were sent to reformatories, while African American women were housed in prisons. Although women sent to reformatories were subjected to therapy—based on the ideals of *true* womanhood—women of color confined to prisons experienced dreadful conditions.

As in the past, contemporary prisons are powerful, dehumanizing institutions. Regardless of the rhetoric of rehabilitation, prisons create an environment that is not conducive to regeneration (Dobash et al. 1986; Ross 1994; Sugar and Fox 1990). Prisons are organized to discipline and punish, not to reintegrate the supposed transgressor back into their communities. The conditions in women's prisons many times result in women fending for themselves, in whatever way they see best (Carlen 1985; Dobash et al. 1986; Ross 1994). Indeed, it is no wonder that some prisoners rebel as a way to maintain their integrity as human beings. Correspondingly, it is understandable when others comply in order to do "easy time" as a way to survive.

An article written by Little Rock Reed (1990) is critical of existing prison programs which he perceives as Judeo-Christianity in the guise of rehabilitation. Reed suggests that Native Americans perceive rehabilitation differently than those from Euro-American culture. In Reed's view, culture should be a consideration when designing various rehabilitative programs for prisoners. In recognizing that, amid other ills, substance abuse is a serious problem among Native people, Reed advocates the cultural-specificity of all prison counseling programs. Especially important and central to rehabilitation for Natives is, according to Reed, the purification ceremony or sweat lodge. A sweat lodge is similar to a church. In the purification ceremony conducted within the sweat lodge, one is cleansed physically, emotionally, and spiritually. The idea is that one enters the sweat in ignorance, then exits enlightened and purified in all ways. In most Native cultures (if not all), the sweat lodge is of utmost importance and is seen as reintegrating the person into a whole human being. Reed, citing numerous studies (by Hanson, the Navajo Nation, Reed, Seven, Specktor, and Spotted Eagle) that document the positive, truly rehabilitative effects of the sweat lodge, argues that without Native American spirituality, imprisoned Natives cannot effectively be rehabilitated. Furthermore, Reed believes that prison programs which are modeled for Euro-American society are another way to control Native people. Rather than focusing on the societal structure as the primary problem, Native prisoners are diverted by rehabilitative programs that search for internal deficiencies as the true problem.

Reed (1989) submits that the United States has historically subjected Native people to colonial rule, and continues to exercise this rule by denying them the right to practice their religion. Crucial to understanding the experiences of imprisoned Natives are the disruptive events brought about by assimilationist policy and prohibitive legislation mandated by the Federal Government. At one time Native American religious practices were misunderstood and forbidden by the Federal Government. Those Natives who dared to openly carry out their religion were incarcerated, and subsequently Native spirituality was forced underground (Beck and Walters 1977). Indeed, Native American religion was banned by the U.S. Government from the late 1800s until 1934. Years later, the opposition continues and Native people cannot openly practice their religion. To remedy this, the *American Indian Religious Freedom Act* was passed by Congress in 1978. This Act specifically states that Native prisoners cannot be denied the right to practice their religion.

Today, many Native prisoners are forbidden religious autonomy despite a U.S. Supreme Court ruling in 1972 which specified that all prisoners have the right to religious freedom, as well as the passage of the *American Indian Religious Freedom Act*. Using the Southern Ohio Correctional Facility as an example, Reed argues that Native prisoners in this prison are denied the opportunity to practice their religion. For example, they cannot use the religious-service facility for worship, are segregated from one another so that they cannot meet for religious activities, and are denied access to sacred objects. I found the same denial of religious freedom at the WCC. This rejection of Native culture permeated the prison and was glaring in all rehabilitative programs.

COUNSELING AND TREATMENT PROGRAMS

Concurring with an early study (Glick and Neto 1977), counseling and treatment in this prison were often left to untrained staff. The prison employed, in addition to a psychologist and psychiatrist, one full-time alcohol/drug counselor, a counselor for Native prisoners who came to the prison once a week for one hour, a full-time treatment specialist who served as the primary counselor for a variety of group sessions, and the parenting-class facilitator. The warden said the prison planned on revising all treatment programs to concentrate on building self-esteem. The treatment specialist asserted that the "unique" staff at the prison aided in facilitating a positive self-esteem for prisoners. What she said directly contradicted what all prisoners told me. No prisoners, regardless of race, discussed the boosting of their self-esteem by prison staff. As a matter of fact, prisoners expressed the opposite—the continual lowering of self-esteem and disrespectful behavior shown to them by most prison personnel. In the words of one prisoner, "if you had any self-esteem when you walked in here, you can guarantee you ain't going to have any when you leave." Most prisoners, regardless of race, did not trust prison staff especially the guards, counselors, psychiatrist, and psychologist. Consequently, most prisoners did not engage in any real dialogue with staff, with the exception of the parenting-class facilitator and Native counselor. Moreover, the counseling model solely focused on individual deficiencies and the building of self-esteem, hence, overlooking the social structure or the effects of the prison regime on prisoners' mental health.

The prison contracted with one psychiatrist—whom the prisoners called "Dr. Feel Good" due to the amount of mind-altering drugs he prescribed to prisoners—and with one psychologist who conducted group-therapy sessions and in a few cases saw prisoners for individual counseling. Most prisoners, regardless of race, had major complaints about the psychologist and his approach to counseling. Prisoners complained that he frequently called them vile,

profane names. An example from a Native prisoner is revealing:

> [The psychologist] said, "We're going to talk about your mom." I said, "What?" And, he said, "I hear that you're your grandfather's child instead of your dad's child." I said, "So." He said, "How do you feel about that?" I said, "Well, I hate my grandfather." He said, "How do you feel about your mom?" I said, "I didn't know her long enough; she died when I was little, but I think I hate her too." And he said, "Do you think she went willingly?" And, I said, "No." And he says, "Well, what if your grandfather said the little slut just crawled into bed with him?" I said, "What? Are you calling my mom a slut?" And he said, "Yes." I jumped off the desk and he scooted the chair way back. I was going to hit him and I said, "You big-nosed son-of-a-bitch! You better shut-up!" It took me a whole year to even talk to him. He'd come into my cell and I'd say, "What the hell do you want; I don't have anything to say to you."

Slut evidently was a favored word for the psychologist. Many prisoners, Native and white, claimed he had called them that particular name.

Most white prisoners were not satisfied with the AA (Alcoholics Anonymous) counseling because others were only in it for the good-time credit, hence, the group was superficial. Native prisoners generally did not attend AA because they felt like outsiders and could not relate to the group. Instead, they attended AA counseling facilitated by a Native woman counselor. Native prisoners highly praised the Native counselor who facilitated AA sessions. They especially enjoyed this group because a variety of topics were covered including sexual abuse, codependency, substance abuse, cultural issues, and problems coping with prison life. All Native women said the group benefited them because the counselor was Native and everyone in the group was Native.

Women confined to maximum security, where Natives were overrepresented, did not receive any counseling with the exception of a group simply called the Behavior Group. Some Native women did not take pleasure from this counseling, facilitated by the treatment specialist, because they believed she purposely belittled them in front of other prisoners. White prisoners also were subjected to verbal abuse, although no one specifically referred to the treatment specialist. This is an example of the unconscious racism exercised by the treatment specialist. Native women alleged the Native counselor was not allowed to visit or counsel women in maximum security; subsequently, they did not attend any counseling sessions. Native prisoners in maximum security were forced to rely on the treatment specialist and psychologist for counseling.

Reed (1990) proposes that prison counseling and treatment programs are culture-bound and racist. All Native women were critical of the prison's programs, especially reservation women. In one Native woman's words:

They have nothing for the Indian women, and we've been trying to get people aware of that and to have programs for the Indian women. We need our own form of rehabilitation because there are so many cultural barriers. We can go through their recovery programs to a limit here and then we have to start dealing with Indian issues—we have none of that here. I've been one to bring up a lot of issues here and, of course, I'm not one of the favorites among the administration here—I've become assertive. And when people come in to speak with inmates they [the administrative personnel] make sure I'm not one of them.

When this woman tried to secure cultural-specific programming for Native prisoners, the prison branded her as a "troublemaker."

This is a traditional Native American: She was raised immersed in Native culture, has little knowledge of Euro-American culture, and speaks her native tongue. She commented on how "ashamed" white society made her feel and, consequently, she did not communicate well with most white people. She said feeling ashamed primarily stemmed from white people harassing her about the way she talked and, thus, making her feel "backward." She was definitely most at ease with Native people. She remarked, "they [white people] don't really understand what you're talking about." Moreover, she added that because Natives were surrounded by whites in prison, they must learn to "walk a little bit stronger."

Regarding Native prisoners, the treatment specialist said most were reluctant to work with white staff members and, thus, many did not participate in the counseling and treatment offered at the prison. She added that she tried to modify treatment programs for Native prisoners. When discussing culture specific programming, however, the treatment specialist gave an example which led me to believe that she knew little about Native culture:

I think you have to be careful when you work with a Native American woman. [You have to be careful not to] destroy her cultural ties because it's important that she keep it. You have to always keep in mind that she has those ties. I'd say to a white woman who is married to somebody who's abusing the hell outta her, "You need to make a choice—either be abused or move out." I might say to a Native American woman, "Why don't you attempt to move him towards treatment," because it's going to devastate her to break up that family. The white woman has accepted divorce as a way of life, but [the Native woman] is not going to feel that way about it.

This staff member exhibited a stereotypic perception of Native American families. In precontact Native societies this type of abuse within families was a rare occurrence (Allen 1985; Etienne and Leacock 1980). Today, although many forms of abuse are common in contemporary Native communities, it is neither appropriate nor a part of Native culture to abuse one's wife/partner. The staff member holds the notion that this type of violence is acceptable in Native culture. Undoubtedly this racialized perception, albeit unconscious, will interfere with her ability to adequately counsel Native women, particularly those caught in oppressive relationships.

SPIRITUALITY AS REHABILITATION AND SURVIVANCE

Early women's prisons focused on religion as part of the prisoner's rehabilitation (Dobash et al. 1986). Following that philosophy, rehabilitation in the WCC, in theory, emphasized the notion of spirituality. Prison staff believed spirituality was an integral part of rehabilitation for all prisoners. In the view of the treatment specialist and the warden, the issue was not religious preference but involvement of the prisoners in their religion. Although prisoners had full access to both Catholic and Protestant clergy and services, few prisoners attended any religious services. Native prisoners had minimum access, due to prison rules, to religious leaders from their communities.

Native women requested from the warden the opportunity to have Native spiritual leaders come into the prison to pray with them. The women viewed this as an important part of their survival and rehabilitation. They professed the warden related they could have leaders come into the prison, however, they must select the leaders from a list he had. They were denied access, when they asked to see the roster; thus, a catch-22 situation was created: They were told "yes," they could invite religious leaders, and then never given the list from which to select the leaders.

Native men incarcerated in Montana have fought long and hard to have Native American religion recognized as credible, and since 1983 a sweat lodge has existed in the men's prison. In the women's prison, however, the situation is much different. Imprisoned Native women contend that, although they submitted a formal proposal, the warden refused to provide them with a sweat lodge. On January 17, 1991 the Associate Director of the Native American Prisoners Rehabilitation Research Project sent a letter to the warden of the women's prison (personal communication). In the letter he expressed his concern regarding the lack of cultural-specific programming and offered solutions. The warden did not reply.

On February 20, 1991 imprisoned Native women, under the leadership of two Native women branded as troublemakers by prison personnel, presented a proposal to the warden. The intent was to establish a Native women's society within prison walls. The goals included cultural-specific counseling, instilling of cultural pride and improvement of self-image of Natives, availability of spiritual leaders, and the involvement of Native people in all aspects of the criminal justice system. There was no reply from the warden. On March 15, 1991 the prisoners

submitted another proposal. This action led to the establishment of a Native women's group. They were "allowed" by the prison to meet for one hour every Sunday. The women saw this group as part of their rehabilitation and survival, although the prison classified it as "recreation." This classification is telling in itself given that Native American spirituality is sacred, not recreation.

Some Native prisoners complained that many times one hour of group prayer was not long enough and prison staff would not extend the time, although various Christian groups were allowed longer time periods for their prayer meetings. Moreover, after much prodding on behalf of Native women, they were permitted by the prison to burn sweetgrass during prayer time, if they resided in the general-population building. (Initially, sweetgrass was not perceived in a positive way by prison staff because they thought it smelled too much like marijuana and feared it might be a drug.) Although white women confined to maximum security or isolation cells had full access to their religion, Native women housed in these units were not allowed to *smudge* (bless) themselves with sweetgrass.

In addition, when guards would investigate cells of Native prisoners, they would carelessly touch their sweetgrass and medicine bundles. One traditional Native woman was extremely upset over this kind of disrespect:

> I tell them [the guards], "These items are sacred to us. We have respect for them; that's all we ask from you—show a little respect. Is it any different from you going in there and jerking the Protestant's Bibles? And throwing them around? Is it any different from you running in there and telling the Catholics or jerking their rosaries away? Tell me," I said, "don't Protestants have their own sacred items? Do you dump the Catholic's holy water out just to check if they have chemicals in them?"

When I first met the warden, he apologetically told me that he did not understand Native American culture or religion. At that time, I offered to conduct a free cultural-awareness workshop for prison staff. After several months, I approached the warden again with the idea of a workshop and, although he appeared positive, he never contacted me. Furthermore, according to Native prisoners, various people sent videotapes on Native American culture and religion for prison staff to view, but the officers refused to watch them.

Cultural pluralism has not worked in Euro-American society and undoubtedly does not operate within prison. Prisoner relationships were definitely tense in this prison and ignorance of Native American culture spilled over into prisoner/prisoner interactions. For instance, one Native woman said she was the only Native in her cell with three white women. She said it was a particularly difficult situation because her white cellmates ridiculed her religion by calling it "voodoo." The term voodoo was also used by a guard in a write-up (reprimand) issued to a Native prisoner. The guard accused the prisoner of threatening her with voodoo when the prisoner jokingly told the guard she knew "Indian ways" to punish her. This is another illustration that both prisoners and prison staff were ignorant of Native American culture. Moreover, although voodoo is a credible religion, yet in this case it was used as a racial slur. Furthermore, several Native women declared that, when they finally won the right to burn sweetgrass at prayer meetings, white prisoners told the guards Native prisoners were mixing marijuana with sweetgrass. This resulted not only in several shakedowns of rooms occupied by Native women, but also increased existing racial tension between Natives and whites. Moreover, Native women were insulted when they were accused of using marijuana with sweetgrass because, in the Native American way, the mixing of prayers and drugs or alcohol is seen as sacrilegious.

The spiritual group formed by Native women was not perceived positively by most white prisoners. One white prisoner said many white prisoners did not appreciate that Native women had their own group. She insisted their ignorance about Native American spirituality and culture was the reason why many white women prisoners were prejudiced against the formation of the group. This prisoner acknowledged that many white women called Native American spirituality voodoo. Hence, ignorance about another culture was turned into ugly racism.

According to imprisoned Native women, it would be advantageous to both prisoners and the institution if a Native counselor were hired full-time and if treatment programs were modified to be culture-specific. At a meeting scheduled between the Governor of Montana and Native prisoners (both men and women), Native prisoners proposed that the prisons hire both Native religious leaders and Native counselors. Native prisoners argued they would be better served by their own people. In a statement on a local television news broadcast (April 21, 1992), the Governor stated he would implement this plan if the tribes in the state would aid in the financing of the positions. This is another example of unconscious racism. The Governor did not approach various white communities in the state and ask them to finance white counselors who work in the prison system. And, he was asking the poorest people in Montana to finance programs for which the state typically pays. Furthermore, the burden would fall most heavily on the one reservation that is forced to utilize the state prison system—the P.L. 280 reservation (Flathead). Why should other reservations contribute to the funding when they may have few or no tribal members in the state prison system?

Tired of discriminatory treatment and in a desperate action, Native women prisoners issued a position paper (1993). They requested from the warden Native spiritual advisors to guide them, access to a sweat lodge, and an end to racism in the prison system. Prompted by reports from prisoners, in April of 1993, the ACLU filed a class action law suit regarding the inhumane conditions for women imprisoned in Montana. An excerpt from the press release read: "Solely because of their gender, women prisoners are subjected to invidious discrimination with respect to education, employment, vocational training, visitation, recreation, religious and other programs" (Crichton 1993a). The lawsuit regarding Native women prisoners and religion read: "No Spiritual Leader is available for Native American women and they do not have a Sweat Lodge. Male prisoners have the opportunity to participate in weekly religious services and Montana State Prison has a Sweat Lodge" (Crichton 1993b, 18). The ACLU was assured by the State of Montana that conditions would be changed once the new prison was built. Primarily due to unsafe prison conditions and overcrowding, the legislature approved building a new women's prison. The new building was never constructed; however, in September 1994, the women's prison relocated from the "campus" of the State Mental Institution at Warm Springs to the former site of Rivendell Psychiatric Center in Billings. In March of 1995, I telephoned the director of Montana's ACLU regarding the status of the lawsuit. He said the lawsuit is in limbo because the prison recently moved. The rationale is that the prison needs time to adjust to its new location and a team of experts have one year to monitor the prison's progress regarding the conditions cited in the lawsuit. According to prisoners, and contrary to the media, nothing has changed. The cultural genocide continues; the blatant racism and sexism persist.

FEAR AND REPRISAL

There are many Indian prisoners around the country who would like to tell their stories, but who fear reprisal by vindictive prison officials.

Little Rock Reed

Reed (1993) advises that many imprisoned Native Americans would like to relay their experiences and would, indeed, file lawsuits because of the discriminatory treatment they face in prison. They are, however, intimidated by prison officials; hence, many stories go untold and Native prisoners continue to remain invisible. Currently, Little Rock Reed remains in hiding; he fears reprisal because of the book he wrote on the horror of imprisonment (Reed 1993). Reed tells us that prisoners who have fallen out of favor with prison officials suffer a range of retaliation by prison officials including: withholding of mail, food and visits, tear gas, beatings, more

time in prison and/or solitary confinement, falsified misconduct reports, and excessive cell searches where personal property is destroyed. Many Native prisoners in Montana experience the same kind of reprisal.

Native prisoners wrote letters to local newspapers criticizing the prison system and offering cost-effective alternatives to imprisonment and to existing prison conditions. As stated earlier, these women were subsequently perceived as troublemakers by staff, and treated harshly. For instance, according to one Native woman, prison staff told her to "either knock it off or you're going to be here or the rest of your life." Another Native woman had written multiple letters to Native American newspapers and organizations expressing the negative treatment imprisoned Native women were receiving. She described the prison's reaction to her:

> So, therefore, I was labeled a *radical;* like I discriminate against white people. And, of course, they don't even understand that term, yet they hear someone else say it so they say it. They say I'm prejudiced in some ways because I want to help the Native Americans.

This prisoner avers that, because she was labeled in a negative way by the warden and treatment specialist, other prison staff would not speak to her. The treatment specialist warned me about this prisoner, whom she described as "a manipulator—even the Indian women hate her" and as one who "hates white people." This Native prisoner, who was aware the staff called her a racist, thought it odd she was negatively labeled: "I mean, they call me a racist and here I am in a white prison, run by white people, based on white values."

These examples illustrate the threatening, risky environment produced by prison staff when Native prisoners were assertive and tried to support other Native prisoners. It should not bewilder anyone that Native women serve long stretches in maximum security for "behavioral" problems. Additionally, imprisoned Native women suffer sexual abuse at the hands of guards and jailers (Ross 1994).

CONCLUSION

Injustice anywhere is a threat to justice everywhere.

—Martin Luther King, Jr.

Prisons, as employed by the Euro-American system, operate to keep Native Americans in a colonial situation. Presently, indigenous people are confronted with overrepresentation in Euro-America's criminal justice system. Partially this is due to negative racialized images of Native people that have been portrayed (Berkhofer 1978) and endure today. This image is one of the "savage," backward Indian who needs to be assimilated, "rehabilitated," into the dominant society.

Rafter (1990) suggests one function of prisons is to control not only crime, but also gender and race. Domination was exerted in this prison over prisoners not only as women, but also as Native Americans. The effects of colonialism were reflected in the disproportionate number of imprisoned Native women, the general treatment of imprisoned Native women, denial of culture, and reprisal. The narratives suggested that, although all women were subjected to horrendous treatment, Native women were additionally discriminated against because of their race and culture. Natives' lack of social and economic power in conjunction with negative stereotypes about Natives were likely to be the reasons for more severe societal reactions in general and within the prison system. Concurring with Dobash et al. (1986), it is imperative to research the notion of criminality by examining the socio-economic conditions in which crimes have occurred. The personal experiences of imprisoned women, regardless of race, reflect the structure of Euro-American society in which certain subgroups are not only penalized because of their race, gender, and class but controlled as well.

Native American spirituality was not seen by prison staff or most white prisoners as credible. There are fundamental problems with the prohibition of religious freedom in prisons: One is that the denial of this right for imprisoned Native women is illegal. Imprisoned Native men in Montana are per-

mitted to practice the sweat lodge ceremony, and white women have access to their religion. Hence, there exists separate rules for men and women, and for Native Americans and Euro-Americans. Another issue is that Native American spirituality has helped Native people survive the brutal dynamics of colonization and experiences of incarceration. The sweat lodge ceremony, which operates on the concept of interdependence and the notion of helping others, is crucial in an environment that produces bitterness and hatred. This would not only promote unity among Native prisoners, but solidarity among all prisoners regardless of race. To many Native prisoners, spirituality is the answer to their well-being, not tranquilizers or "confrontive" counseling sessions with a psychologist who has a fancy for the word "slut." This is not to suggest all imprisoned Natives seek out their culture or religion as a way to resist and survive prisonization. For those who do seek solace in their culture, however, there should be no barriers.

Although some Native women maintained their innocence, those who transgressed believed they were incarcerated because they fell away from their culture; that they were living in a world that was unholy, unbalanced. Indigenous people suffer today from poverty, substance abuse, and high rates of incarceration which are direct indicators of the stresses connected with being a Native person in a racist society. These negative conditions in our communities are symptoms of colonialism and have been termed "ethnostress" (Antone, Miller, and Myers 1986). Feelings of despair and powerlessness have disrupted our lives as Native people. Since we are emerging from a dehumanizing experience, we need to immerse ourselves in what Antone, et al. (p. 24) phrase a "rehumanization process." To be a whole person is to be humanized.

Native American women in Montana's prison system are decolonizing and rehumanizing. They are resisting domination and the imposition of another culture—as Native people have for centuries. In this way, imprisoned Native women can be viewed as revolutionaries. By conserving a Native worldview within an oppressive, godless institution, these women are, indeed, activists. Although none of these women would define themselves as a "radical," they are engaged in a struggle to transform a racist, sexist, and classist institution and should be applauded, not punished, for their efforts.

DISCUSSION QUESTIONS

1. The title of Luana Ross's chapter is "Resistance and Survivance: Cultural Genocide and Imprisoned Native Women." First, give several examples of the cultural genocide experienced by imprisoned Native American women. Second, list the acts of resistance to the oppression these women engage in while in prison.

2. Typically, resistance is seen as a negative behavior when expressed by women in prison. Ross is arguing that these acts of defiance are positive acts of agency and survival by the women. How do you feel about Ross's position on this topic? Write a statement of your own reactions to the prisoner's acts of resistance.

3. Often, counseling and treatment programs in prison are the mainstay of a rehabilitative program. However, the Native American women resented these programs. Compare the dominant culture's idea of rehabilitation and the Native American women's idea of rehabilitation. How could this clash be resolved?

4. Compare the problems faced by Native American prisoners with those of imprisoned women of other races, ethnicities, and cultures. In what ways are the issues alike? In what ways are the issues unique to Native American women?

5. What are some of the important ways in which all women in prison are forced to deal with similar deprivations?

6. Now that you have read the first four chapters in this section (Owen, chap. 10; Bhavnani and Davis, chap. 11; Sudbury, chap. 12; and Ross, chap. 13), describe how the experiences of women in U.S. prisons compare with those of women in prison in other countries.

REFERENCES

Allen, P. G. 1985. *The Sacred Hoop: Recovering the Feminine in American Indian Traditions.* Boston: Beacon Press.

Antone, R. A., D. L. Miller, and B. A. Myers, 1986. *The Power within People: A Community Organizing Perspective.* Deseronto, Ontario: Peace Tree Technologies.

The American Indian Religious Freedom Act of 1978. P.L. 95–341, 42 U.S.C.§1996.

Native American Women Prisoners. 1993. Position paper. Warm Springs, MT, January 29.

Beck, P. V., and A. L. Walters, 1977. *The Sacred: Ways of Knowledge, Sources of Life.* Tsaile, AZ: Navajo Community College Press.

Berkhofer, R. F., Jr. 1978. *The White Man's Indian: Images of the American Indian from Columbus to the Present.* New York: Vintage.

Camp, G., and C. Camp, 1992. *The Corrections Yearbook.* South Salem, NY: Criminal Justice Institute.

Carlen, P. ed. 1985. *Criminal Women: Autobiographical Accounts.* Cambridge, Great Britain: Polity Press.

Collins, P. H. 1991. *Black Feminist Thought: Knowledge, Consciousness, and the Politics of Empowerment.* New York: Routledge.

Crichton, S. 1993a. ACLU Class Action Suit Filed on Behalf of Female Prisoners. Press release, April 21, 1993.

———. 1993b. Personal communication, April 28, 1993.

Dobash, R. P., R. E. Dobash, and S. Gutteridge, 1986. *The Imprisonment of Women.* New York: Blackwell.

Etienne, M., and E. Leacock, eds. 1980. *Women and Colonization: Anthropological Perspectives.* New York: Praeger.

Glick, R. M., and V. V. Neto, 1977. *A National Study of Women's Correctional Programs* (National Institute of Law Enforcement and Criminal Justice No. 74-N1-99-0052). Washington, DC: U.S. Government Printing Office.

Grobsmith, E. 1994. *Indians in Prison: Incarcerated Native Americans in Nebraska.* Lincoln: University of Nebraska Press.

Mann, C. R. 1993. *Unequal Justice: A Question of Color.* Bloomington: Indiana University Press.

Pollak, O. 1950. *The Criminality of Women.* Philadelphia: University of Pennsylvania Press.

Quinney, R. 1970. *The Social Reality of Crime.* Boston: Little, Brown.

Rafter, N. H. 1985. *Partial Justice: Women in State Prisons, 1800–1935.* Boston: Northeastern University Press.

———. 1990. *Partial Justice: Women, Prisons, and Social Control,* 2d ed. New Brunswick, NJ: Transaction Books.

Reed, L. R. 1989. The American Indian in the White Man's Prisons: A Story of Genocide. *Humanity and Society* 13:403–20.

———. 1990. Rehabilitation: Contrasting Cultural Perspectives and the Imposition of Church and State. *Journal of Prisoners on Prison* 2(2):3–28.

———. 1991. Personal communication, March 21, 1991.

———. 1993. The Fear of Reprisal. In *The American Indian in the White Man's Prisons: A Story of Genocide,* ed. L. R. Reed, 253–274. Taos, NM: Uncompromising Books.

Ross, L. 1992. *Mothers Behind Bars: A Comparative Study of the Experiences of American Indian and White Women.* Unpublished dissertation, University of Oregon, Eugene.

———. 1993. Major Concerns of Imprisoned American Indian and White Mothers. In *Gender: Multicultural Perspectives,* ed. J. T. Gonzalez-Calvo, 154–182. Dubuque, Kendall/Hunt.

———. 1994. Race, Gender, and Social Control: Voices of Imprisoned Native American and White Women. *Wicazo Sa Review* 10(2):17–39.

Sheley, J. F. 1985. *America's "Crime Problem": An Introduction to Criminology.* Belmont, CA: Wadsworth.

Spotted Eagle, C. (Producer/Director). 1983. *The Great Spirit within the Hole* [Film]. Minneapolis: Spotted Eagle Productions.

Sugar, F., and L. Fox, 1990. Nistum Peyako Seht'wawin Iskwewak (First Nations Women): Breaking Chains. *Canadian Journal of Women and Law* 3:465–483.

Velimesis, M. L. 1975. Criminal Justice for the Female Offender. *Crime and Delinquency Literature* 7:94–112.

Chapter 14

Defeminizing and Dehumanizing Female Murderers:
Depictions of Lesbians on Death Row
Kathryn Ann Farr

ABSTRACT

In Chapter 13, Ross illustrated not only how Native American women in prison are dehumanized but also how they resist this dehumanization. So, too, Farr describes not only how lesbians in prison are made to be seen as less than human but also how they are punished for their defiance of appropriate gender roles—and specifically how they are defeminized in this process.

Farr uses case studies of 35 women on death row to show that a heterosexually feminine image is important in engendering chivalry and presumably leniency toward female offenders. Farr argues that lesbians in particular were overrepresented in atypical death sentence cases. Her chapter features media and prosecutorial representations of the cases of five lesbians on death row. These offenders were depicted as "manly" and "man-hating" women who occupy additional marginalized statuses and who are said to have vented their rage and irrational desire for revenge through killing. Farr argues that this homosexualized portrayal of female evil may affect sentencing decisions as an additional "aggravating circumstance" in an already heinous crime.

This chapter is the first of three chapters (the other two are chaps. 23 and 33) in this book on lesbians. The chapter is important because of the dearth of information on lesbians and the criminal justice system. It is important to have more research, more understanding, and better treatment of those women who are lesbian, bisexual, and transgendered who are caught in the criminal justice system. Gender bias in the courts is discussed in part 4, "Women Workers in the Criminal Justice System." As you read the first chapter in that section by Lynn Hecht Schafran (chap. 29, "Overwhelming Evidence: Gender and Race Bias against Women in the Courts"), keep in mind this chapter's description of how lesbians are viewed and ask yourself if and how the recommendations for eliminating gender and race bias would have an impact on the treatment of lesbians, too.

INTRODUCTION

Public reactions to the recent executions of two women, Karla Faye Tucker in Texas and Judias Buenoano in Florida, reflect the importance of constructions of gender in the restoration of chivalry to previously dehumanized female murderers. Both Tucker, sentenced to die for the pickax murder of a woman and man, and Buenoano, death-sentenced for the poisoning murder of her husband, re-emerged during their years on death row as "born-again" Christians. The extensive media coverage surrounding Tucker's execution was feminized, with reports describing her as pretty, young and demure. One newspaper account (Graczyk, 1998), for example, notes "Tucker's soft, brown eyes, bashful smile and long dark curls" (p. A5). Indeed, she had married the prison chaplain while on death row; restricted by the "no-conjugal-contact" policy, the marriage was literally virginal. Tucker's sympathizers included men from the Christian right, such as preacher/politician Pat Robertson, who opined that Tucker deserved mercy because of her "authentic spiritual conversion" (Robertson, quoted in Pearson, 1998, p. A19).

Interestingly, the execution of Buenoano came and went with nary a word of sympathy and in fact very little media coverage of any sort. But then Buenoano, born-again as she may have been, did not strike a chivalrous chord. Pictures of her show a grim and masculine visage with pursed lips and short, slicked-back hair (see, for example, Word, 1998)—unlike Tucker's "thick tumble of hair" (Rust, 1992, p. G12). All along, Buenoano was portrayed as a man-hater, the "black widow" who fed upon the men in her life. These two cases support research (see Julian, 1993; Smart, 1992) showing that gender images affect beliefs about which female offenders are deserving (or not) of leniency. As Edwards (1984) puts it: "Women defendants are on trial both

for their legal infractions and for their defiance of appropriate femininity and gender roles" (p. 216).

Women who are sentenced to die have usually committed heinous murders. But is an (un)feminine image also a factor in the sentencing decision? In our (Farr & Farr, 1998) study of the total population of women on death row in the United States at a single point in 1993 (N = 35), we found depictions of many of these capital offenders as manly, man-hating, and/or lesbian. This article focuses primarily on media portrayals of the cases of five women within this population in which lesbianism was fused with other gender-deviant images to produce a representation that was "compatible" with a death sentence for an already heinous crime.

Although their numbers have increased in the five years since the data for this study were collected (by the end of 1997 there were 46 women on death row in the U.S.), women account for little more than 1% of persons on death row in the U.S. (Streib, 1993a). To begin with, women are much less likely than men to commit murders that qualify for the death penalty, i.e., premeditated murders of strangers, committed for or to cover up felonious instrumental gain, such as murder in the course of robbery (Rapaport, 1990). Women murderers are more likely than men to have killed an intimate other, most commonly a husband or boyfriend, and to have an affective or defensive rather than a material motive for killing (Campbell, 1993; Silverman, Vega & Danner, 1993). Additionally, women who kill tend to be less likely than their male counterparts to have prior felony convictions for violent crimes or to be heavily involved in a criminal subculture (Silverman et al., 1993). Capital murders committed by women are more similar to *non-capital* murders committed by women than to *capital* murders committed by men.

Findings from the present study indicate that lesbians are over-represented in death sentence cases that are atypical of either the male or female "norm." Reflected in the prosecutorial strategy and passed on through the media are character-focused accounts of the lesbian defendants in these capital cases. The implication is two-fold: First, that these

The author acknowledges Sharon M. Lee and Erin E. Farr for comments on earlier drafts of this article. The author also appreciates the comments from the anonymous reviewers.

*Source: Women & Criminal Justice,*11(1): 49–66, 2000. © 2000 by The Haworth Press, Inc. All rights reserved.

women repudiate and strike out against men, and second that they wish to be the patriarch, controlling men through violence. This chapter contends that the reconstructed identities of these women may serve as an extra-legal aggravating factor in the capital sentence decision.

METHODOLOGY

The study population consisted of the 35 women on death row in the U.S. when data collection began in 1993. Data describing "facts" of their cases came from trial transcripts, appeal documents, case summaries produced by legal offices, and scholarly works. Media reports were from newspapers, news magazines, and crime or criminal justice magazines, and included case "facts" as well as more subjective representations of the women and their cases.

Media reports were identified through searches, by name of defendant, of national and local sources. Eventually, accounts were yielding the same findings, providing evidence of "saturation" (in the Glaser & Strauss, 1967, tradition).

Not surprisingly, there were distinct differences between defense and prosecutorial descriptions of the defendants, with defense representations emphasizing the troubled backgrounds of their clients and prosecutorial portrayals featuring the women's patterns of deviance. More interesting was the consistency among media sources, and across media and prosecutorial accounts. That is, descriptions of the women and their cases were similar, whether found in an urban newspaper or a "true crime" magazine. Moreover, media accounts featured prosecutorial depictions of the women's gender and general deviance, along with the shocking nature of their crimes. That is, media reports primarily contained excerpts from the state's case.

(HETERO)SEXISM AND REPRESENTATIONS OF LESBIANS AS KILLERS

The focus in this analysis is on the five cases in which homosexual orientation had been validated,

i.e., acknowledged by the defendant and/or confirmed by others who knew her, and emphasized in prosecutorial and media accounts. At least three additional women on death row at the time of the study were described in some public reports as possibly lesbian or bisexual, and another five were regularly depicted as masculine in appearance, demeanor or behavior.

Other estimates of the proportion of women on death row who are lesbians are much higher—Anderson (1996), for example, sets it at close to one half. Brownworth (1992b), who claims that at least one third of the women on death row are lesbians, refers to concerns of many gay and lesbian activists that lesbians are being "targeted for capital punishment" (p. 62). She quotes Paula Ettelbrick, director of Lambda Legal Defense and Education Fund, a gay rights group, who states that "The criminal law absolutely does discriminate against women and even more so against lesbians . . . There is nothing more threatening than the thought of a woman who has already chosen not to have men in her life—a lesbian—unless it's a lesbian killer" (p. 62). The alleged links between gender, sexual orientation and violence are variously arranged. As Van Gelder (1992) points out: "Since women are primarily defined as lovers of men, lesbians are easily stereotyped as 'man-haters' " (p. 82). There is also the myth that lesbians kill because they are "male wannabes" (Van Gelder, 1992) or at least are violent like men (MacNamara, 1992), and, juxtaposed, that women who kill are masculine *and* (or, *and thus*) lesbians (Holmlund, 1994).

In his examination of cases of lesbians on death row, Streib (1993b) argues that there were sufficient, legitimate aggravating circumstances in each of the murders to warrant the death penalty. He notes, nevertheless, that when the defendant in a capital case is a woman, prosecutors must defeminize and dehumanize the defendant in order to convince juries that she is deserving of the death penalty. "The more 'manly' her sexuality, her dress, and her demeanor," Streib continues, "the more easily the jury may forget that she is a woman" (p. 10). Defeminization is followed by dehumanization through the description of the crime and her life leading up to it.

This discrediting task is facilitated by the ongoing reproduction of images of "lesbian evil" in U.S. culture. Representations via the movie screen have depicted lesbians as dangerous women-predators and killers (Freedman, 1996; Hart, 1994; Holmlund, 1994; Van Gender, 1992; Russo, 1981). Films have capitalized on the collective fascination with the "demonic lesbian." Holmlund (1994), for example, points to the cult-like status of Susan Sarandon based upon her role as a scientist (a woman out of her place?) transformed into a lesbian vampire in *The Hunger.*

Eerily similar to the fictional accounts of lesbian killer vampires was the infamous and heavily publicized Australian case of convicted murderer Tracey Wigginton (see Verhoeven, 1994). Wigginton, a prostitute, was convicted of the stabbing murder of a man whom she allegedly lured to his death with a promise of sex. Accompanying Wigginton were three women who were rumored to be her love slaves, and whom she was said to dominate with her Satanic powers. It was, Verhoeven argues, through this trial that the "lesbian vampire killer" legend was promulgated (p. 97).

According to Macdonald (1995), a general fear of female power is reflected in past and modern representations of women in the popular media. Although the precise images vary—vamp, black widow, femme fatale, she-devil, monstrous-feminine—the danger evoked is in women's challenge to male authority. As Macdonald points out, that authority is challenged in film in two ways: " . . . by men being duped by women, and by the latent [female] homosexuality [in a number of films]" (p. 119).

The lesbian is understood at some level as the enemy of patriarchal power, but she is more concretely vilified as a man-hater. As Pharr (1998, p. 18) notes, "To be lesbian is to be *perceived* as someone who has stepped out of line, who has moved out of sexual/economic dependence on a male, who is woman-identified." Although illogical, Pharr continues, the assumption has often been that women who live independently of men are anti-men. A contradictory theme is that lesbians want to *be* men, and thus the stereotype of the man-hater co-exists with

that of the "bull-dyke" (Eliason, Donelan & Randall, 1992; Pharr, 1988). Historically, condemnation of women's usurpation of "the male" was expressed in heterosexist repudiation of lesbian cross-dressing and sexual desire for women. In contrast, "romantic friendships" between women of the genteel class were quite acceptable (Blackwood, 1993; Duggan, 1993; Woodward, 1993). The "mannish" lesbian intensified the threat to heterosexual male dominance and buoyed the image of lesbian-as-invert (see Rule, 1975). Cultural and medical representations combined to engender the image of lesbians as abnormal women-aggressive, corrupt and violent.

The criminological literature also presumes links between female deviance and lesbianism (see Hart, 1994). In tracing the evolution of representations of the "prison lesbian" in the U.S., Freedman (1996) points out that after World War II, criminologists increasingly focused on lesbian prisoners as "menacing social types." Freedman also discusses the race and class contours of such representations, noting that prior to the mid-20th century, studies stereotypically presented African American female prisoners as lesbian sexual aggressors, and white women as their victims and/or temporary partners (i.e., not "true" lesbians). Later, lesbian prisoner stereotypes were applied to white working-class women, and by the 1960s clinical profiles linking lesbianism and female psychopathy featured white working-class women.

In her research, Robson (1992) found that justification for the killing of women who are lesbians has a lengthy history in Anglo-American life. Robson uncovered numerous cases of male violence against women in which the perpetrator accused his victim of lesbianism, and she speculates that lesbicide may be about eradicating not just lesbians but all possibility of lesbianism.

A number of studies have shown that women viewed by criminal courts as "manly" or as having committed "masculine" offenses, and as having violated norms of white, middle class femininity, are treated more harshly (Campbell, 1993; Julian, 1993; Visher, 1983; Smart, 1977; Nagel & Weitzman, 1971). In her Massachusetts study, Daly (1989) found that judges viewed mothers who took care of their children as "good" and treated them more leniently than female defendants who were less exemplary in their mothering. And, as quoted by Julian (1993), the words of one defense attorney are instructive: "I hate to say this, I really do, but a young, attractive, feminine, demure woman is a cinch to defend" (p. 345).

While gender, class and race have all been implicated in sentencing biases, sexuality has most commonly been addressed in regard to women's deviant *heterosexual* behavior. Prostitutes, for example, are not only victimized by violence (rape, assault, murder) on the job, but are also treated with disdain or open hostility in the criminal justice system (Miller & Schwartz, 1995; Fairstein, 1993; Andersen, 1988; E. Miller, 1986; Edwards, 1984; Silbert & Pines, 1982).

Interestingly, representations linking prostitution and lesbianism—both as deviant forms of female sexuality—also have a lengthy history (Hart, 1994; Nestle, 1987). In his analysis of 19th century iconography of female sexuality, Gilman (1985) implicates race as a critical part of this triumvirate. Using art and medical works as illustrations, Gilman points to the sameness of contrived images of the overdeveloped sexual physiognomy of the Black woman and the prostitute; these physical "excesses": have also been associated with the "excesses" of "lesbian love" (p. 237). Threats to patriarchal control then, include the abandonment of *both* virginal, hetero-feminine behavior and heterosexual commitment. Made explicit in Euro-American constructions is the greater likelihood of such abandonment among Black women.

VARIATIONS IN GENDER REPRESENTATIONS OF WOMEN ON DEATH ROW

Almost half of the women on death row (16 of 35) at the time of the study were sentenced to die for the murder of an intimate other, most commonly a husband or a lover. Many of these women were portrayed as "cold calculators"[1] who ruthlessly murdered an intimate other for financial gain, or as "black widows" who preyed upon and murdered several intimate others over a long period of time, without clear motive.

Another eight women were convicted, along with their intimate male partners, of multiple murders, typically of strangers. These women were described as ruthlessly evil, tenaciously loyal to "their man," and most commonly as (hetero)sexually wanton and depraved. In most of these cases, the women were themselves victims of abuse by their crime partner, a factor that was rarely mentioned in media reports. Karla Faye Tucker was in this category. Widely reported was her statement that she had achieved orgasm each time she struck her victims with the pickax (Cox, 1985). Following her conviction, however, Tucker's (hetero)sexuality was called into question, with media accounts of her alleged inability to achieve (hetero)sexual satisfaction (Cox, 1985), as well as the allegation that she had sexually molested a female inmate while in jail (Walker, 1984). Media depictions of Tucker immediately prior to her execution included her conversion not only to spiritual but also to (hetero)sexual piety.

In 21 of the 24 cases above, the female defendant was typically portrayed as representing the evil side of heterosexual female nature—ruthless, manipulative, seductive and often lustful. Sixteen of these 21 women were white. The victims were primarily white men.

In the remaining 14 cases, representations were masculinized. In four of these 14, the women were convicted of murder in the course of felony robbery, a male-dominated and more typical capital crime. These women all acted alone and committed "hands-on" murders (two stabbed their victims, and two beat and strangled their victims). All but one of them were women of color (see Farr, 1997, for an analysis of the role of race in the 35 cases).

And, in 10 of the 14 cases, the defendants were portrayed as "explosive avengers," aggressive, hotheaded, and motivated to kill by anger or revenge. They often acted alone or took the lead in the murder and, like the "robber-predators," were presented as heterosexually unattached (without husband or male partner). The majority of these women were also minorities, *and* four of the five acknowledged lesbians were in this category.

TABLE 1
Lesbians on Death Row, Selected Characteristics

	Offender Race	#	Victim Race	Sex	Characterization
Case #1	Black	1	Black	f	Explosive Avenger
Case #2	Latina	1	Latino	m	Explosive Avenger
Case #3	White	1	White	m	Cold Calculator
Case #4	Black	2	Black, Asian	m	Explosive Avenger
Case #5	White	7	White	m	Explosive Avenger

As shown in Table 1, two of these four lesbians had only one victim, and the two with more than one victim killed their "johns," victims whose own deviance precipitated the relationship which ended in their deaths. The victims of the three lesbians of color were also racial minorities. The one lesbian characterized as a "cold calculator" was white, and was given the death penalty for the murder-for-hire of her gay male roommate. None of these women had prior murder convictions, nor lengthy histories of serious violent crime. Following is an elaboration of representations of these women and their capital crimes.

PORTRAYALS OF LESBIANS ON DEATH ROW AND THEIR CAPITAL CASES

Case #1. In December of 1988, the perpetrator in this case shot her lesbian lover to death in front of a police department. As reported and not denied by the defense, the shooting occurred following an argument over a welfare check and the ensuing decision by the victim to move out of the home that she and the perpetrator shared. As stated in *Allen v. The State of Oklahoma* (1989), the victim and defendant "had been involved in a homosexual relation, and [the victim] did not wish to continue the relationship" (p. 1). Upon the advice of a police officer responding to a domestic dispute call, the victim drove to the police station, followed in another car by her lover. Outside the police station a confrontation between the two women occurred. The defendant then retreated to her car, got a gun and fatally shot her lover.

While this would appear to be a "heat of passion" killing, the Appeals Court turned down the perpetrator's claim of such, as well as her argument that the jury was not given instructions in regard to her claim of self-defense. Both the victim and the offender were lesbians, women of color, and welfare recipients. Thus, the portrayal of the defendant as particularly undeserving of sympathy could have been countered by a similar picture of the victim. This balance may have been tipped, however, by the "flaunting" of the authority of a male police officer and by the flagrancy of carrying out the crime in front of the police station.

Case #2. Sentenced to death in April of 1992 for the murder of her three-year-old son, the defendant in Case #2 was the only woman on death row in 1993 for having murdered her child by abuse. The identification of the child's mother, a Cuban immigrant, as his killer, and the news that she was a lesbian whose lover was also implicated in the crime, fueled the public fire. The defendant's lover testified against her in exchange for a plea agreement (a guilty plea to the charge of second-degree murder and child abuse) in regard to her own involvement in the murder. The prosecutor made routine references to the defendant's lesbianism, arguing at one point that it should be considered as an "aggravating circumstance" (Brownworth, 1992b), and, at another time, that the lovers hated the victim because he was male (Anderson, 1996). Additionally, the press provided the public with courtroom representations of the defendant's deviance, such as a prosecutor's description of her as "a cocaine-addicted mother who neglected and repeatedly abused [the victim] before killing him with a baseball bat" (*Sun Sentinel*, 1992, p. 3B). Her volatile courtroom behavior upon hearing her sentence was also widely reported. For example, the *Sacramento Bee* (1992) stated that "[the defendant] shouted hysterically in Spanish at [the judge] after he announced the sentence" (p. A10). And, reporter Yanez (1992) wrote that "[the defendant] shook visibly in her seat as [the judge] pronounced the death sentence. She then jumped to her feet in a fit of fury. 'They call this justice?' she yelled" (p. 1B).

Certainly, the facts of this case are horrific. However, similar cases in which mothers or fathers chronically abuse and eventually kill their children have rarely resulted in the death penalty.

Case #3. Accounts of this case also drew attention to particular sordid features of the crime and the marginalized statuses of those involved in it. In April of 1985, a woman called the police to report the murder of her male roommate. The woman, a 37-year-old medical center nurse with no prior criminal record, told police that she was confronted by three men who threatened to cut off her breasts and to rape her, after which, she said, she must have passed out (Lasseter, 1991). Upon awakening, she found her male roommate dead of multiple stab wounds; his penis had been cut off.

She was eventually charged with and convicted of the victim's murder (by hire). The actual killer was a gay Latino man with an extensive prior record, including lewd conduct and assault with a deadly weapon; his accomplices in the capital murder were two African American men. In exchange for a sentence of life in prison, the killer testified against the woman who had hired him. The two accomplices turned state's evidence for immunity from prosecution. The hired killers reported that the woman had asked them to genitally-mutilate her roommate so that it would look like a homosexual-related killing. Her motive was said to be financial gain from an insurance policy on the home the two owned (Corwin, 1992).

Again, this was a heinous crime, but was the court further "aggravated" by this woman's apparent duplicity in her public persona vs. her "real" self?

The state's presentation tarnished her straight, professional demeanor and reputation as a skilled and compassionate nurse. In court she was described as a "frequenter of gay bars." Two ex-roommates testified to her lesbian jealousy, including an attempt to put a "bug" in her girlfriend's room to catch her and another woman "going at it," for which she would "beat the hell out of both of them" (Lasseter, 1991, p. 24). The descriptor in the title of Lasseter's (1991) article, "Trail of the Gay Mutilator," could refer to either the victim or the defendant.

And, she had ordered the amputation of the male organ—a brutal affront to maleness regardless of the sexual orientation of the victim. Moreover, this white woman had hired men of color to mutilate and kill a white man. Through the lens of our culture's (hetero)sexist and racist camera, the master planner of such a deed deserves the ultimate punishment.

Cases #4 and #5. In both of these cases, lesbians who were prostitutes were given the death sentence for the murder of customers whom they claimed had cheated or abused them. The woman in Case #4, a young African American, was convicted in 1992 of the murder of two "johns" (an African American and an Asian American) in separate incidents. Following her sentencing, a headline in a local newspaper announced: "Sentenced to Die for Slayings, Prostitute Spits at Jury" (Mowatt, 1992, p. 6). An article in *The Philadelphia News* (Racher, 1992) quoted the prosecutor: "I've been a DA for 15 years and I've never seen anyone react that way . . . She had a certain look in her eyes before she spit at the jurors" (p. 26). This article, entitled, "Killer Prostitute Spits at Jury After Being Sentenced to Die," was next to another, both under a supra-headline, reading "It's Life and Death for Hooker Crimes." The second article (Racher, 1992, p. 26) was entitled "John Who Slew His Sex Mate to Live Out Existence in Jail," and reported that a man who had fatally stabbed one prostitute and severely beaten another was sentenced to life in prison.

The lesbian defendant in Case #4 was also publicly described as a drug-addicted mother of two young children, and as a man-hating killer (Brownworth, 1992b). The victims' heterosexuality was implied by their purchase of (but she claimed non-payment for) her services.

Probably the most notorious woman on death row is the lesbian and prostitute in *Case #5.* This white woman was convicted of the murder of seven white men. She had intermittently solicited business while hitchhiking on Florida's highways, and it was here that she was picked up by the victims she subsequently killed. She has been dubbed the "first female serial killer," in spite of the fact that many other women have killed multiple victims with "cooling off" periods in between (Geehr, 1992), and that she did not appear to kill randomly for thrill or from compulsion, or mutilate the victim (FBI-profile attributes) (Kelleher & Kelleher, 1998; Hart, 1994; Levin & Fox, 1993; Brownworth, 1992a). She claimed in her first and only trial (following her conviction she plead guilty to another six murders) that she had killed her victim in self-defense after he raped, sodomized and threatened to kill her (Chesler, 1992). The jury was not allowed to hear evidence that might have helped substantiate her self-defense claim. Among such evidence was the victim's prior record, including an attempted rape conviction and prison time for burglary (Carr, 1994; Hart, 1994; Chesler, 1992). Chesler (1992) points out that police interviewees stated that the man "suffered from mood swings, drank too much, was violent towards women, enjoyed the strip bars, was into pornography, was erratic in business and in trouble with the IRS . . ." (p. 30). None of this legitimizes his murder, but he was hardly the naive, rule-abiding "middle aged motorist" depicted in some accounts of the crime.

Described as perhaps her first stable relationship, the lover with whom she lived at the time of her capital crimes testified against her in exchange for immunity from prosecution. Wrote one journalist (Chambers, 1992): "She blamed her lesbian lover for turning against her, accused the prosecutor of lying, and said she had been 'framed by law enforcement . . .'" (p. 43). But, as quoted in another account (Geehr, 1992), she said: "I'm deeply hurt by reports that [the lover] will testify against me in court. . . . Of course, I still love her, but I realize I'll never be able to see her again, and that hurts inside" (p. 22).

The headline of an article in one crime magazine (Geehr, 1992, p. 6) read "————: Lethal Lesbian Hooker," and was followed by a subheading describing her victims as "six male motorists." Another headline announced its topic as "Rampage of the Bull-Dyke Man-Eater" (Roen, 1992, p. 51), with a sub-heading that read: "Now she would be the one dishing out violence and death—she would wear the pants and do the strapping" (p. 50). She was described by another journalist (Kahler, 1992) as a "hitchhiking hooker who worked Florida's highways, killing men who solicited her" (p. A2), and by yet another (Carr, 1994) as the "hooker-from-hell." Eschewing any possibility of victim precipitation, newspaper accounts stated that she "stalked highways in central and north Florida" (Buck, 1992), and that she lured men to isolated areas (Smothers, 1991). Reported in one newspaper account (Flores, 1992) was the prosecutor's statement that "She liked control. . . . She'd been controlling men for years and she took everything [the victim] had, including his life," and that she had "shot a businessman when her lust for power over men took 'a vengeful turn . . .'" (p. A13).

In the above two representations "lesbian" and "prostitute" are fused and become the modifier with which to describe a prototypical enemy of men, part of what Hart (1994) refers to as the "masculine imaginary," but this time the "fantasy has crossed a certain boundary" (p. 141). Hart adds that the lesbian defendant in this latter case generated further wrath by maintaining that the man had violently assaulted her and that it was she who was initially the victim. Like numerous other journalists, Geehr (1992) reported on the defendant's response to the guilty verdict: "'I am innocent,' she said calmly, as the jurors began to file out of the courtroom. Then, in a much louder voice, [she] shouted after them, 'I was raped!' As her defense attorneys tried to restrain her, she called out to the last of the jurors leaving the room, 'Scumbags of America!'" (p. 26). Carr (1994) described her during the sentencing as "in a rage, near tears and clenching her teeth." Then, the report continues, "she boiled over, snarling at the prosecutor" and shouting obscenities. Carr concludes that she had "blossomed into a full-blown she-devil" (p. 76).

TABLE 2

Possible Extra-Legal "Aggravating Circumstances" in the Capital Sentencing of Five Lesbians on Death Row

Case	Circumstances		
	Offender	**Victim**	**Crime**
Case #1	Black, lesbian welfare recipient, unrepentant, self-defense claim	Police protection at home shared with offender	Crime occurred at police station
Case #2	Latina, drug addict, lesbian, abusive mother, courtroom anger	Toddler with history of abuse by mother and lover, murdered by abuse	Accomplice was lesbian lover; putative motive: hatred of men
Case #3	Lesbian, unrepentant	White man, offender's roommate	Hired men of color to kill and genitally mutilate white man
Case #4	Black, drug addict, lesbian, prostitute, unrepentant, court-room anger, non-payment motive	Men, "tricks"	Putative motive: hatred of men
Case #5	Alcoholic, lesbian, prostitute, unrepentant, court-room anger, self-defense claim	White middle class men, "tricks"	Putative motive: hatred of men

It is through this last case, perhaps because the perpetrator's life and self have been so fully uncovered and reconstructed, that the defeminization and dehumanization of a death-sentenced lesbian is most clearly played out. However, representations in all five cases offer a masculinized and man-hating version of the unpredictably dangerous woman. As one of the police officers investigating Case #5 said (quoted in Brownworth, 1992a): "It was important that we warn people that these very dangerous women were out there. Hitchhikers, women who seemed to be stranded on the roadside—they could be killers" (p. 26).

SUMMARY

Summarized in Table 2 are extra-legal circumstances that were frequently cited in media portrayals of the five offenders, their courtroom behavior, their victim(s) and their capital crime(s).

Although differing clusters of circumstances provided the fodder for discrediting depictions in each case, several themes emerge. Lesbianism was named alongside other deviant or marginalized statuses, e.g., drug addict, prostitute, welfare recipient, as composite parts of a heinous whole. Reports of the women's aggressive and rage-filled courtroom behavior further testified to their out-of-(patriarchal) control volatility. And "they" (i.e., the "lesbian other") even betrayed one another—one killed her lover, another had her gay roommate killed, and the lovers of another two testified against them.

Race is implicated in more than one way in these cases—an over-representation of defendants of color, a white woman hiring men of color to kill a white man. Moreover, the threat to maleness is clear—all but one of the victims were men, and in that one case (#1) there was symbolic male victimization, i.e., in the disregard for the authority of the summoned police officer, and for the police station itself. Commonly, references were made to the women's hatred of men, and indeed one woman ordered the amputation of the male organ.

The ultimate penalty, the death sentence is typically given when a case meets a number of standards, including a list of legalistic, aggravating circumstances surrounding the murder. The crimes of these lesbians met some, but not all of those criteria. However, the cases are linked through portrayals of the perpetrators as embodiments of defeminized and dehumanized female evil for whom chivalry must be forfeited and the most severe punishment delivered.

DISCUSSION QUESTIONS

1. According to Farr, what is the relationship between defeminizing women who are charged with murder and dehumanizing them? Write a statement about your own reactions to this issue.

2. Explain how lesbians are discriminated against in the criminal justice system. How does feminist theory help you to evaluate this question?

3. There is a dearth of information on lesbians, gays, bisexuals, and transgendered (LGBT) people in relation to the criminal justice system. What steps would you propose to remedy the lack of research in this area? What steps would you propose to remedy the lack of adequate advocacy for LGBT people in the courts and in prison?

NOTE

1. See Farr and Farr (1998) for an elaboration of the five categories of gender representations, la-

beled by the authors as Cold Calculators, Black Widows, Depraved or Accommodating Partners, Explosive Avengers, and Robber-Predators.

REFERENCES

Allen v. The State of Oklahoma. 1989. Court of Criminal Appeals of the State of Oklahoma: Case # F-89-549.

Andersen, M. L. 1988. *Thinking about Women: Sociological Perspectives on Sex and Gender.* New York: Macmillan.

Anderson, D. 1996. Caged Women. *Girlfriends,* November/December, 24–27.

Blackwood, E. 1993. Breaking the Mirror: The Construction of Lesbianism and the Anthropological Discourse on Homosexuality. In *Psychological Perspectives on Lesbian and Gay Male Experiences,* ed. L. D. Garnets and D. C. Kimmel, 297–315. New York: Columbia University Press.

Brownworth, V. 1992a. Crime and Punishment. *QW,* October 25, 24–27.

———. 1992b. Dykes on Death Row. *The Advocate,* June 16, 62–64.

Buck, J. 1992. Smart Worries Role Will Spark Sympathy. *The Oregonian,* November 16, A16.

Campbell, A. 1993. *Men, Women and Aggression.* New York: Basic Books.

Carr, C. 1994, Making a Killing. *Mirabella,* March. 72–77.

Chambers, M. M. 1992. Three's a Crowd. *Crime Beat,* April, 43.

Chesler, P. 1992. Sex, Death and the Double Standard. *On the Issues,* Summer, 29–31.

Corwin, M. 1992. Death's Door: State's Only Condemned Woman Awaits Her Fate. *Los Angeles Times,* April 19, A3, A26.

Cox, N. 1985. The Nude Couple Was Bludgeoned with a Pick-ax! *True Detective,* July, 24–25, 61–66.

Daly, K. 1989. Rethinking Judicial Paternalism: Gender, Work-Family Relations, and Sentencing. *Gender and Society* 3:9–36.

Duggan, L. 1993. The Trials of Alice Mitchell: Sensationalism, Sexology, and the Lesbian Subject in Turn-of-the-Century America. *Signs: Journal of Women in Culture and Society* 18:791–814.

Edwards, S. M. 1984. *Women on Trial.* Manchester: Manchester University Press.

Eliason, M., C. Donelan, and C. Randall, 1993. Lesbian Stereotypes. In *Lesbian Health: What Are the Issues,* ed. P. Noerager, 41–54. Washington DC: Taylor & Francis.

Fairstein, L. A. 1993. *Sexual Violence: Our War Against Rape.* New York: William Morrow.

Farr, K. A. 1997. Aggravating and Differentiating Factors in the Cases of White and Minority Women on Death Row. *Crime and Delinquency,* 43:260–278.

Farr, K. A., and S. J. Farr, (in press). Representations of Female Evil: Cases and Characterizations of Women on Death Row. *Quarterly Journal of Ideology.*

Flores, I. 1992. Women's Trial Starts in Serial Killings. *The Oregonian,* January 16, A13.

Freedman, E. B. 1996. The Prison Lesbian: Race, Class, and the Construction of the Aggressive Female Homosexual, 1915–1965. *Feminist Studies,* 22:397–423.

Geehr, B. 1992. Aileen Wuoros: Lethal Lesbian Hooker. *True Detective,* October, 6–10, 12, 14, 16–18, 22, 24, 26.

Gilman, S. L. 1985. Black Bodies, White Bodies: Toward an Iconography of Female Sexuality in Late Nineteenth-century Art, Medicine, and Literature. In *"Race," Writing, and Difference* ed. H. L. Gates, Jr., 223–261. Chicago: The University of Chicago Press.

Glaser, B., and A. Strauss, 1967. *The Discovery of Grounded Theory.* Chicago: Aldine.

Graczyk, M. 1998. Texas Killer Finds Gender, Religion Gains Her Allies. *The Oregonian,* January 16, A5.

Hart, L. 1994. *Fatal Women: Lesbian Sexuality and the Mark of Aggression.* Princeton, NJ: Princeton University Press.

Holmlund, C. 1994. A Decade of Deadly Dolls: Hollywood and the Woman Killer. In *Moving Targets: Women, Murder and Representation,* ed. H. Birch, 127–151. Berkeley: University of California Press.

Julian, F. H. 1993. Gender and Crime: Different Sex, Different Treatment? In *Female Criminality: The State of the Art,* ed. C. C. Culliver, 343–361. New York: Garland.

Kahler, K. 1992, More Women Enter a Male-Dominated Career: Violent Crime. *The Oregonian,* May 3, A27.

Kelleher, D., and C. L. Kelleher. 1998. *Murder Most Rare: the Female Serial Killer.* Westport, CT: Praeger.

Lasseter, D. 1991, Trail of the Gay Mutilator. *Detective Cases,* January, 6–22.

Levin, J., and J. A. Fox, 1993. Female Serial Killers. In *Female Criminality: The State of the Art,* ed. C. C. Culliver, 249–261. New York: Garland.

Macdonald, M. 1995. *Representing Women: Myths of Femininity in Popular Media.* New York: St. Martin's Press.

MacNamara, M. 1992, Kiss and Tell. *Vanity Fair,* June, 90, 92, 96, 98, 100, 104, 106.

Miller, E. 1986. *Street Woman.* Philadelphia: Temple University Press.

Miller, J., and M. D. Schwartz, 1995. Rape Myths and Violence Against Street Prostitutes. *Deviant Behavior,* 16:1–23.

Mowatt, R. V. 1992, Sentenced to Die for Slayings, Prostitute Spits at Jury. *Philadelphia Inquirer,* April 9, B6.

Nagel, S. S., and L. J. Weitzman, 1971. Women as Litigants. *Hastings Law Journal,* 23:171–198.

Nestle, J. 1987. *A Restricted Country.* Ithaca, NY: Firebrand.

Pearson, P. 1998, Sex Discrimination on Death Row. *The New York Times,* January 15, A19.

Pharr, S. 1988. *Homophobia: A Weapon of Sexism.* Little Rock, AR: Chardon Press.

Racher, D. 1992, It's Life and Death for Hooker Crimes. *The Philadelphia Daily News,* April 9, 26.

Rapaport, E. 1990. Some Questions about the Death Penalty. *Golden Gate University Law Review* 20:501–565.

Robson, R. 1992. *Lesbian (Out)law.* Ithaca, NY: Firebrand.

Roen, S. 1992. Rampage of the Bull-Dyke Man-Eater. *True Police,* December, 50–56.

Rule, Jane. 1975. *Lesbian Images.* Trumansburg, NY: The Crossing Press.

Russo, V. 1981. *The Celluloid Closet: Homosexuality in the Movies.* New York: Harper & Row.

Rust, Carol. 1992, Amazing Grace. *Houston Chronicle,* June 14, G10–G13.

Sacramento Bee. 1992, Mother Sentenced to Die, April 2, A10.

Silbert, M. H., and A. M. Pines, 1982. Victimization of Street Prostitutes. *Victimology: An International Journal,* 7:122–133.

Silverman, I. J., M. Vega, and T. A. Danner, 1993. The Female Murderer. In *Homicide: The Victim-Offender Connection,* ed. A. V. Wilson, 175–190. Cincinnati, OH: Anderson.

Smart, C. 1992. The Woman of Legal Discourse. *Social and Legal Studies,* 1:29–44.

———. 1977. *Women, Crime and Criminology: A Feminist Critique.* London: Routledge & Kegan Paul.

Smothers, R. 1991. Woman Is Arrested in a Series of Killings in Florida. *The New York Times,* January 18, A16.

Streib, V. L. 1993a. Capital Punishment for Female Offenders: Present Female Death Row Inmates and Death Sentences and Executions of Female Offenders, January 1, 1973 to May 1, 1993. Report available from Victor L. Streib, Cleveland State U.

———. 1993b, Death Penalty for Lesbians: A Preliminary Inquiry into the Significance of a Capital Defendant's

Lesbianism in the Context of the Sentencing of Female Offenders to Death in the United States, 1972–1993. Paper presented at the annual meeting of the Law and Society Association, Chicago, May 28.

Sun Sentinel. 1992, Jury Calls for Death, March 27, 3B.

Van Gelder, L. 1992. Attack of the "Killer Lesbians." *Ms.,* January/February, 80–82.

Verhoeven, D. 1994. Biting the Hand That Breeds. In *Moving Targets: Women, Murder and Representation,* ed. H. Birch, 95–126. Berkeley: University of California Press.

Visher, C. A. 1983. Gender, Police Arrest Decisions and Notions of Chivalry. *Criminology,* 21:5–27.

Walker, C. 1984, Houston's Horny Pick-axe Murderess. *True Police,* December, 24–27, 41–45.

Woodward, C. 1993. "My Heart So Wrapt": Lesbian Disruptions in Eighteenth-Century British Fiction. *Signs: Journal of Women in Culture and Society,* 18:838–865.

Word, Ron. 1998. Florida Executes "Black Widow" for Fatally Poisoning Her Husband. *The Oregonian,* March 31, A8.

Yanez, L. 1992, Child's Killer Pleads for Mercy, "Baby Lollipops" Mom Could Get Electric Chair When Judge Sentences Her Today. *Sun Sentinel,* April 1, 3B.

Chapter 15

Mothers in Prison and Their Children

Diane F. Reed and Edward L. Reed

ABSTRACT

When parents become caught up in the criminal justice system, their children are hurt too. The children experience social, psychological and economic consequences—even more so when the sole parent is the mother. Reed and Reed offer an understanding into the plight of these children by describing the children's experiences in terms of likely substitute caregivers, short- and long-term consequences of their mothers' incarcerations, and public policy issues surrounding the children left behind. This social issue is a significant one: The best estimate is that more than 10 million children in the United States currently have or had a parent incarcerated.

Gender makes an enormous difference here. In 1999 (like in the early 1990s, as reported by Reed and Reed), when the father is imprisoned, nine out of ten times the mother carries on the responsibility of child care alone.[1] However, when the mother is incarcerated, only 28 percent of the fathers care for their children. Grandparents (53 percent, primarily grandmothers), and other relatives (26 percent) carry the burden of caring for imprisoned women's children today, but nonetheless 10 percent of the children end up in foster care or in an agency. Moreover, the brunt of having parents in prison is borne by children of color: A full 7 percent of black children and almost 3 percent of Latino and Latina children have an imprisoned parent. This situation applies to less than 1 percent of white children.

The children's suffering comes from several problems: separation from parent and difficulties with visitation, inadequate care, poverty, loss of sense of security, and lack of understanding of the situation. Because reunification laws became more punitive in the 1990s, both mother and children suffer greatly from the permanent termination of the woman's parental rights after 6 to 18 months of incarceration.[2] A long-term consequence highlighted by Reed and Reed is that

---

[1]Information in this paragraph comes from Christopher J. Mumola, "Incarcerated Parents and Their Children," Bureau of Justice Statistics Special Report, August 2000, NCJ 182335.
[2]Ellen Barry, a well-known lawyer for women in prison (personal communication, 2001).

the next generation (the children) often become involved subsequently in the juvenile justice or adult criminal justice systems, especially if the children are from low-income families or families of color. The reality is that one-half of all juveniles in custody have a parent or close relative behind bars.[3] This cycle of incarceration is the result of lack of opportunities for these children and lack of resources in their communities.

The chapter concludes with a section on public policy issues. The question underpinning this section requires serious attention: Is the increasing societal reliance on prison to address crime the best way to ensure that the next generation will not also end up in prison? Reed and Reed observe that policy makers and lawmakers actually know very little about the children of parents who are in the control of the criminal justice system. But a review of what is known about these children leaves little room for optimism about their chances for enjoying successful adult lives unless major changes are made in the socially structured systems of race, class, and gender in this society. In chapter 10, Owen argued that prison cannot solve society's larger social problems: poverty, racism, and inadequate educational and job opportunities. Here, Reed and Reed go one step further by suggesting that prison actually increases these problems for far too many of society's most disadvantaged and vulnerable children.

---

[3]Fox Butterfield, As Inmate Population Grows, So Does a Focus on Children, *New York Times,* May 7, 1999, pp. A1, A8.

INTRODUCTION

Most of the [almost two] million persons incarcerated in U.S. jails and prisons on any given day and the millions more on probation or parole are parents. Although a considerable body of information has been collected about individuals who have been or are under some form of criminal justice system control, very little is known about their children, particularly those under the age of 18. There are approximately 10 million children in the U.S. who have had one or both parents incarcerated. These children and youth have little or no voice about who, in the absence of the parent who is the primary caregiver, will take care of them, or if they will be allowed to visit or communicate with the incarcerated parent. The children of parents involved in the criminal justice system have no voice because they are invisible to the larger society.

The national trend to use incarceration to punish even minor offenses guarantees that children will continue to be adversely affected by policies enacted with no consideration of the harm done to family systems. There are many complex and interrelated contributing factors: the intensification of politically motivated "get tough on crime" rhetoric and the "War on Drugs," public discourse about crime designed to instill fear, the enactment of increasingly harsh sentencing laws such as "Three Strikes," and the ratings-driven media preoccupation with policing and arrests, leading to public support for a prison-building frenzy. The virtual disappearance of work, along with stores, transportation, and other components of a viable infrastructure, from many inner-city communities has resulted in a concentration of poverty that has devastated neighborhoods and marginalized residents, making them easy first to criminalize and then to dehumanize.

Source: Diane F. Reed and Edward L. Reed. *Children of Incarcerated Parents.* "Social Justice" 24(3) 1995: 152–169.

The original intent of this article was to examine what is presently known about the children of incarcerated parents. Its scope has been expanded to include the more realistic continuum of parental crime, arrest, incarceration, release, and recidivism that children experience and must contend with as their lives are disrupted, and sometimes shattered. . . . Available information about the children of incarcerated parents is provided, followed by a discussion of caregivers, custody, and visitation issues. The next sections describe what is known about the impact on children of parental involvement in the criminal justice system, as well as observable intergenerational trends, and then look at how law enforcement and social service agencies regard and respond to children of arrested and incarcerated parents. We conclude with interventions that address and alleviate the problems resulting from parental involvement in the criminal justice system.

. . .

CHILDREN OF PARENTS INVOLVED IN THE CRIMINAL JUSTICE SYSTEM

For the children of parents under some form of correctional supervision—whether arrest, incarceration, parole, or probation—the social, psychological, and economic consequences of present policies will exact profound harm for years and generations to come.

The minor children of parents under some form of criminal justice system control are among the most at-risk, yet least visible, populations of children. Though rising incarceration rates suggest an increasing number of children who have lost one or both parents to incarceration, very little is known about this highly vulnerable population. A 1992 study by the California State Assembly Office of Research (Lawhorn, 1992) reported:

No precise count exists of the number of children in California who have incarcerated parents. Data on the number, ages, gender, location, or needs of children of incarcerated parents are not collected by the Department of Corrections, the Department of Social Services, or the Department of Education. *These children*

are not recognized as a group by any state agency or department in California (emphasis added).

A study by the Virginia Commission on Youth (1992) yielded similar results. The Commission found no information about the number and conditions of children whose parents were incarcerated, or any statewide systems or service models in place to address the needs of children who are affected.

Most of the information known about children of people in the criminal justice system is obtained from surveys of incarcerated populations, the majority of whom—78% of women and 64% of men—are parents (USDJ, 1994).

- A 1991 study of state prison inmates found that 67% of the women and 56% of the men surveyed were parents of over 826,000 children under 18 years of age (USDJ, 1993).
- A 1989 survey of 5,675 women incarcerated in 424 local jails showed that 68% had a child or children under 18 (USDJ, 1992).
- Six to nine percent of incarcerated women are pregnant when they enter prison (USDJ, 1994; Bloom and Steinhart, 1993), and about 15% have had a baby within the previous year (McCall et al., 1985).
- A 1991 National Council on Crime and Delinquency survey of mothers in jails and prisons in eight states and the District of Columbia found that 439 respondents had an average of 2.6 children each (Bloom and Steinhart, 1993).

Denise Johnston, M.D., with the Center for Children of Incarcerated Parents in Pasadena, California, estimates that nationally about five million children under the age of 18 have one or both parents under some form of criminal justice system supervision (arrest, incarceration, parole, or probation), out of which about 1.5 million have at least one parent who is incarcerated. An additional five million children have parents who are not now under such supervision, but have been in the past. All told, *about 10 million children in the U.S. are affected by current or past parental involvement with the criminal justice system.*[1] Peter Breen, executive director of

Centerforce, a nonprofit agency dedicated to serving families of prison inmates, estimates that 350,000 children living in California have lost one or both parents to incarceration.[2]

CAREGIVERS OF CHILDREN OF INCARCERATED PARENTS

Children's lives are seriously disrupted when a parent is arrested and/or incarcerated. Families of incarcerated fathers are more likely to remain intact than those of incarcerated mothers. Of the approximately 1.5 million children of U.S. prisoners, about 1.2 million, or 87%, of children of male inmates are in the care of their biological mothers (USDJ, 1993), while only about 20%, or 29,000 children, of incarcerated mothers are in the care of their biological fathers (USDJ, 1993; American Correctional Association, 1990). This leaves over a quarter of a million children of incarcerated parents in the care of grandparents, other relatives, friends, or foster care.

The majority of incarcerated mothers of minor children were the primary caregivers for their children prior to confinement. Studies of prison and jail inmates have found that about 70% of female inmates with children under age 18 had lived with their children prior to incarceration, compared to about 50% of males (USDJ, 1993; 1992).

• A 1991 survey of mothers in jails and prisons in eight states and the District of Columbia found that 17% of children whose mothers were incarcerated were living with their fathers, nearly half (47%) with their grandparents, 22% with relatives or friends, and about 7% had been placed in foster care (Bloom and Steinhart, 1993).
• The 1989 national "Women in Jail" study reported that half the minor children of incarcerated women were living with their grandparents, 23.5% were in their father's care, and 27% were living with other relatives or friends. About eight percent were in foster or other institutional care (USDJ, 1992).

CUSTODY ISSUES

In 1991, 10% of women and two percent of men incarcerated in state prisons reported that their children were in a foster home, children's agency, or institution (USDJ, 1993). Unlike most children who enter the child protective services system due to parental neglect or abuse, children of arrested or incarcerated parents become dependents of the juvenile court and are subsequently placed in foster care if no relative is available to provide care for them.[3]

The 1980 federal Adoption Assistance and Child Welfare Reform Act (P.L. 96-272) mandates that children who are placed in foster care must either be returned to their parents or placed with long-term guardians within 12 to 18 months. If neither has occurred, parental rights can be terminated by the state. Although this legislation was meant to avoid multiple short-term placements that worsen the disruption for children, parents with sentences that exceed the allowable time may be unable to comply with reunification requirements before or after their release (Barry, 1995). Recognizing this circumstance, many states have held that positive actions on the part of incarcerated parents, such as maintaining contact with children and following reunification plans, can avert termination of parental rights.

However, incarcerated mothers whose children are in foster care must overcome numerous obstacles to maintain their parental rights (Barry, 1995). Children often go through multiple placements, making it difficult for mothers to keep up with their current whereabouts (Kampfner, 1995), a situation that is exacerbated when the social services caseworker does not maintain timely communication with the mother. Distance, lack of transportation, and limited economic resources on the part of the caregiver can become insurmountable barriers for regular or any visitation by children, and are further exacerbated when siblings are separated from each other. Inadequate family reunification services during incarceration, and inability to meet contact requirements and statutory schedules for reunification, put many incarcerated mothers at considerable risk of losing custody of their children (Johnston and Gabel, 1995).[4]

Incarcerated parents whose children are in foster care must rely on the caseworker appointed by social services to help them in the process of reunifying with their children. The caseworker needs to involve the parent in developing a reunification plan and help the parent meet the requirements of the plan. The caseworker also has a vital role in allowing visits by the children and notifying the incarcerated parent about child custody hearings. In practice, however, despite their mandated responsibility to provide assistance, in practice caseworkers may be opposed to the reunification of a parent and child (most often due to the mother's prior child welfare history and/or previous drug history) and thus not communicate with the parent or allow jail or prison visits for the children (Bloom, 1995).

In addition, the courts may be unwilling to permit parents to use incarceration as a reason for failure to provide necessary emotional and material support to their children. Several state appellate court cases have regarded a parent's incarceration to be an aspect of abandonment and, therefore, a reason to terminate parental rights (Muhar, 1991). At least 25 states, including California, have termination-of-parental-rights or adoption laws that specifically pertain to incarcerated parents (Bloom, 1995).[*] Although no studies have systematically examined the extent of this issue, the Center for Children of Incarcerated Parents has found that involuntary termination of parental rights occurs disproportionately among women. About 25% of women offenders whose children participate in the Center's therapeutic programs lost their parental rights (Johnston, 1992). The National Black Child Development Institute (1989) found that from 12 to 18% of terminations of parental rights in African American families occur among incarcerated parents.

Smith (1995) identified several key factors that lead to termination of parental rights:

- Parental incarceration in facilities at very long distances from where the children live, lack of transportation, and limited financial resources of caregivers;
- Overall lack of prison programs and services to assist parents in developing and following a reunification plan;

- Lack of communication and coordination between foster care workers and corrections staff;
- Lack of joint counseling for parents and children to deal with problems and reactions related to the separation;
- Lack of adequate screening, training, and support for caregivers to support the parent-child bond and eventual reunification;
- Lack of legal counseling for incarcerated parents; and
- Systematically excluding incarcerated parents in decisions concerning placement of children, planning for reunification, and case reviews.

VISITATION

Maintaining close family ties during incarceration has been shown to result in decreased recidivism rates, improved mental health of inmates and other family members, increased likelihood of family reunification following release, and greater potential for parole success (Hairston, 1991; Schaefer, 1991). Nevertheless, many incarcerated parents have infrequent or no contact with their children.

The most recent survey of state prison inmates revealed that while most parents of minor children had some form of contact, 28% of mothers and 40% of fathers reported never having called or received a telephone call from their children,[5] 21% of mothers and 32% of fathers never sent or received any mail from their children, and fully 52% of mothers and 55% of fathers were never once visited by their children (USDJ, 1994).

Bloom and Steinhart (1993) found similarly disturbing trends in the frequency of visits from children during the mother's incarceration. Over half (54%) of the 439 mothers in that study reported that their children had *never* visited them in jail or prison. Seventeen percent were visited by their children once a month, 12% every four to six months, and seven percent once a year or less. Only 10% saw their children once or more a week. The distance from the child's residence to the correctional facility accounted for 43% of the reasons cited by mothers for having infrequent or no visits from their children. Fully *61.5% of the children lived over 100 miles from the*

---

[*]Editors' note: The 1997 Adoption and Safe Family Act mandated loss of custody if parents have no contact with child for 6 months or if a child has been in foster care for 15 of the last 22 months.

mother's place of incarceration. Thirty percent lived 21 to 100 miles away and only nine percent lived within 20 miles of the correctional facility.

Hairston (1989) reported that nearly one-third of the incarcerated fathers she surveyed had not seen their children since entering prison and more than half had not seen their children in the six months prior to the survey. The main reasons given by inmates for the lack of visits were transportation, escort problems, and opposition by the child's mother—this last factor due to the large percentage of incarcerated fathers who report not having an active or ongoing relationship with the mothers of their children. One study of federal prisoners found that 87% of unvisited fathers chose to relinquish visits from their children out of shame, embarrassment, and feelings of overall powerlessness (Koban, 1983).

This trend is likely to continue, as has been seen in California, as new prisons are built in remote, rural areas, at long distances from the cities where children of incarcerated parents are most likely to live.

IMPACT ON CHILDREN

The cycle of parental crime, arrest, incarceration, releases and recidivism is particularly devastating for children, but no study has as yet directly observed a large sample of these children. Instead, most of what is known is obtained from information provided by the children's incarcerated parents or caregivers. The few studies that have directly examined the children of offenders yield troubling results. Johnston (1995a) found that of the 56 children identified by their teachers as having the most severe behavioral and disciplinary problems at school, 80 to 90% had experienced parental crime, arrest, and incarceration, and 25% had a parent who was incarceration at the time of the study.

Researchers have documented a variety of behavioral, psychological, and educational problems in children traumatized by the arrest, separation, incarceration, and absence of a parent. The process of forcibly separating children from their primary caregiver generally ignores the emotional needs of children, who feel vulnerable and frightened about losing their parent (Kampfner, 1995), and is further

exacerbated for siblings who may have been separated from each other. Caregivers may not allow children to talk about their feelings or tell others about their parent's incarceration. Sometimes, children are not told the truth about where their parent really is (Bloom and Steinhart, 1993). Most children receive little or no emotional support to process their feelings of grief, loss, anger, anxiety, and fear.

Children respond in various ways, including sadness, withdrawal, low self-esteem, excessive crying, depression, diminished school performance, truancy, disciplinary problems, alcohol and other drug use, running away, and aggressive behavior (Sack et al., 1976; Fritsch and Burkhead, 1981; Johnston, 1995b). Many children, including very young ones, blame themselves for the parent's absence (Kiser, 1991). Seventy percent of the children of imprisoned mothers studied by Baunach (1985) were reported to have psychological or emotional problems. The depression, feelings of anger and fear, flashbacks, and "survivor" guilt reported in one study by children of women prisoners have been associated with post-traumatic stress disorder (Kampfner, 1995).

Johnston (1992) identified three characteristics found in most of the children of offenders with whom she has worked: (1) multiple parent-child separations (lack of family support), (2) inadequate quality of care (associated with poverty, multiple placements, etc.), and (3) the stress associated with enduring childhood trauma (experiencing *repeated,* in contrast to single or occasional, traumatic events).

The cycle of parental crime, arrest, incarceration, release, and recidivism seems to have a cumulative effect that increases as children grow older. According to Johnston (1995a):

- Parental incarceration in the first year of a child's life may prevent the development of parent-child bonding.
- The development of autonomy and initiative in children aged two to six may be compromised by the trauma of witnessing parental arrest and the loss of a parent due to incarceration. "The long-term effects of these experiences may be worse at this stage of childhood . . . because young children have the ability to perceive and remember trau-

matic events, but they cannot process or adjust to trauma without assistance . . . " (p. 74).

- Children ages 7 to 10 may have a hard time achieving in school and getting along with others, precipitating aggressive behavior in reaction to experienced trauma.
- While some young adolescents aged 11 to 14 may overcome their parent's absence, poverty, stigma, and multiple placements, many children act out.
- The cumulative effects of parental involvement in the criminal justice system appear in 15 to 18 year olds. "Their experiences have left many with negative attitudes toward law enforcement and the criminal justice system. The parents of many have served multiple jail and/or prison sentences and will not reunify with them. A large but unknown proportion will engage in criminal activity . . . " (p. 82).

INTERGENERATIONAL TRENDS

As each successive generation of children becomes absorbed into a social process that involves the criminalization of a growing underclass, involvement in the criminal justice system is increasingly becoming part of the family system for many low-income families, particularly in communities of color.

- A U.S. Department of Justice jail study (1992) found that 44% of women and 34.5% of males reported having a close family member who served time in jail or prison.
- Bloom et al. (1994) found that nearly 75% of women incarcerated in California prisons had family members who had been arrested and 63% reported having close relatives who had been incarcerated.
- The American Correctional Association (1990) reported that up to 50% of incarcerated juveniles have a parent who has been incarcerated.

According to the model for intergenerational crime and incarceration developed by the Center for Children of Incarcerated Parents, children exposed to enduring trauma (such as parent–child separation, sexual or physical abuse, or witness to violence)

produce emotional responses (sadness, grief, anger) that lead, absent intervention, to reactive behavior (withdrawal, physical aggression, hyper-vigilance) and become fixed in patterns that help children to cope (fighting with peers, substance abuse, gang activity, promiscuity), ultimately leading to crime and incarceration (Johnston, 1995a).

The growing prison culture observed in many low-income, inner-city neighborhoods plays a big part in assimilating children into what is becoming an intergenerational norm. Anecdotal information provided by veteran prison guards[6] who recalled prisoners whose children and grandchildren have been—sometimes even simultaneously—incarcerated attests to the unraveling of already marginalized families. According to Schiraldi et al. (1996), "as one travels through many inner-city neighborhoods, the contemporary expressions and subculture are increasingly being borrowed from the prison yard, a tangible sign of the 'prisonization' of many communities of color." In other words, children whose parents or other close relatives have experienced criminal justice system involvement are environmentally socialized to follow in their footsteps, just as surely as their more affluent counterparts are prepared for higher education and professional careers.

INSTITUTIONAL RESPONSE TO CHILDREN OF ARRESTED/ INCARCERATED PARENTS

The complex problems resulting from increasing numbers of arrested and incarcerated parents who are the sole caregivers of young children suggest the need for coordinated, systemwide approaches. Yet, most law enforcement and child welfare agencies lack both awareness of the issues and the means to respond to children following the arrest and/or incarceration of their parents. This conclusion was reached by the American Bar Association (ABA) Center on Children and the Law (1994) from its national study examining how law enforcement and child welfare agencies address the needs of this group of children.

The ABA Children and the Law study found that overall, the agencies responsible for the emergency and long-term placement of children of arrestees lack specific policies, procedures, and interagency coordination:

- *Law enforcement.* The majority of jurisdictions interviewed have no specific policy that police officers follow for emergency child placement following parental arrest, and 43% rarely even ask an arrestee if they have minor children. Nearly half (49%) do not notify any other agency upon the arrest of a mother who is a sole caregiver and 54% are not required to coordinate efforts with notified agencies. Seventy-eight percent said the police are mandated to report the placement only if they suspect the child was abused or neglected.
- *Child protective services.* Only 20% of child protective services agencies interviewed had a specific policy on the placement of children of arrestees. Two-thirds reported having no formal team approach with local law enforcement with respect to children of arrestees, and 34% believed that the placement needs of children whose mothers were arrested are not being adequately met. Most child welfare agencies, already overwhelmed by increasing numbers of child abuse and neglect cases, lack the resources to meet the needs of children who are not in immediate danger of being abused. Many social worker respondents tended to regard the children of arrested parents as being less at risk than are children who are physically or sexually abused or neglected.
- *Foster care.* A stunning 97% of foster care system respondents reported not having a specific policy on foster care placement of children of arrestees.

Correctional facilities also lack critical information about inmates. According to the most recent Department of Justice inmate study, "*official records are often incomplete, are not easily compared across jurisdictions, and lack crucial personal data*" (USDJ, 1993: 11). This is clear from survey data collected from Departments of Corrections throughout the country, which reveal an enormous lack of information about the needs of female inmates. Out of 43 responding states, 15 had no records on the number of women who were mothers and/or who had dependent children, and 32 had no knowledge about how many children would be living with their mothers upon release (Clement, 1993).

INTERVENTIONS

The multiple or recurrent traumatic events that affect children of parents involved in the criminal justice system are rarely addressed. These children typically live in poverty before, during, and after their parents' incarceration, reside in low-quality housing, and lack the means to visit their parents. Johnston (1995c) describes some models designed to address and alleviate the problems that result from parental involvement in the criminal justice system:

- *Crisis nurseries* for very young children, 0 to 6 years of age, are temporary residential care settings, designed to prevent children's exposure to acute trauma such as parental arrest, sudden homelessness, or domestic violence. One such program, the Bay Area Crisis Nursery in Concord, California, provides services to 400 children annually.
- *Crisis intervention counseling* for children following the arrest of a parent can reduce the immediate and long-term negative effects of that experience, as well as provide reliable information about the process in which the parent is involved and referral to sources of ongoing support for family members. No program of this kind currently exists in the U.S.
- *Therapeutic interventions* to help traumatized children master the effects of current and previous traumas and overcome future trauma by improving individual coping skills. The Center for Children of Incarcerated Parents provides community-based therapeutic services for young children of prisoners through its Early Therapeutic Intervention Project.
- *Therapeutic visitation* designed to help reduce the incidence of post-release domestic violence among families of formerly incarcerated parents, and thus reduce exposure of children of those families to that particular source of trauma. Project

ImPACT (Importance of Parents and Children Together) has offered these services for the families of men imprisoned at New Mexico's Las Lunas Correctional Facility.

- *Community-based mother-infant correctional programs* to foster maternal bonding, provide a stable placement during infancy and early childhood, and increase the rate of family preservation. The model California Mother-Infant Care (MIC) Program is conducted by private agencies. MIC has seven sites throughout the state that allow pregnant and parenting women sentenced to relatively short terms of incarceration to live with their infants and/or young children up to six years old in community settings.
- *Parent-child visitation programs* held in child-oriented environments in the correctional facility to make visits with incarcerated parents a more positive experience for children. The Prison MATCH Program, started at the Federal Correctional Facility at Pleasanton in 1978 and later moved to the San Francisco County Jail, provides a child-friendly, enriched recreational setting for children to visit with their incarcerated parent for four hours once a week.
- *Children's support groups* that provide social support in a structured setting that is safe for children to express their concerns and to help dispel the sense of shame connected with parental incarceration. The Parents and Children Together (PACT) Program offers age-appropriate Support for Kids of Incarcerated Parents (SKIP) groups in the residential communities that surround Fort Worth Correctional Facility.

PUBLIC POLICY

Although reported crime rates have remained fairly stable over the past few decades, public misperception that crime is on the rise has contributed to the development of new mandatory minimum sentencing laws that have led to the increase in incarceration. The sentences now given to nonviolent offenders convicted of property and drug-related of-

fenses are at times harsher than those given to individuals convicted of violent crimes.

In addition, the prevailing focus on the isolated offender systematically disregards the needs and issues of families, making the profound impact children experience even more intense (Bloom, 1995). One result of these interrelated trends is the destruction of often fragile but viable family systems. Some researchers view these trends as an urgent wake-up call:

> . . . if compulsive behaviors and criminal activity represent relatively resilient responses to life in poor, violent, chaotic families and neighborhoods, then our society is condemned to incarcerating an ever-increasing number of the people who live in these circumstances, unless we can help them to reduce the poverty, violence, and chaos in their lives (Johnston, 1995d: 314).

As the trend increases to address crime by building new prisons and jails at the expense of preventing crime through the funding of education, vocational training programs, drug treatment, health care, and other services, the need grows to explore ways of developing public policy that will prevent the destruction of vulnerable family systems (Smith, 1995; Bloom, 1995; ABA, 1994) by:

- Using alternative or creative sentencing instead of imprisonment for primary caregiver parents who were convicted of nonviolent offenses. Options could include restitution, community service, substance abuse treatment, counseling, vocational or educational training, and community-based residential sentencing programs in which parents and children stay together.
- Appropriating funds for parent-child visits whenever an incarcerated parent lived with a child prior to incarceration.
- Screening foster parents for their willingness and ability to be supportive of the parent-child relationship. Training and support services should be available to teach foster parents and the birth parent how to cooperatively co-parent the child. Counseling and support groups should be available for the foster parent(s), child, and birth parent(s).

- Providing high-quality services in prisons, including classes on parenting, family and juvenile law, counseling for survivors of childhood sexual abuse and domestic violence, and vocational and educational programs.
- Making available legal services and representation for incarcerated parents.
- Passing open adoption statutes that allow parents and children to have ongoing contact in the event adoption is used to obtain permanency placement for children whose parents have very long sentences.
- Developing law enforcement and child welfare policies and procedures to meet the needs of children of arrestees.
- Coordinating efforts between law enforcement and child welfare agencies to develop a collaborative, coordinated systemwide approach to meeting the needs of children of arrestees and incarcerated parents.
- Developing correctional practices that allow increased communication or contact between incarcerated parents and their children, including specialized services offered through partnerships between correctional facilities and community agencies, such as mother-infant and mother-child community corrections programs and extended contact visitation programs.

CONCLUSION

U.S. policymakers, legislators, and children's advocates know virtually nothing about the approximately 10 million children under the age of 18 whose parents are or have been under some type of criminal justice system control. Although this growing population of children has not yet been formally recognized, many are well known to their teachers as disciplinary problems, to social service caseworkers as foster care placements, to counselors as behavioral problems, and to law enforcement authorities. The increasingly serious behaviors of many of these children tend to be regarded out of context. They are seen as withdrawn or acting out or violent rather than as children reacting to the aggravated stress of multiple separations due to parental arrest, incarceration, and recidivism.

The often cyclical nature of parental involvement in the criminal justice system results in serious and sometimes permanent destabilization of family systems and subjects children to ongoing trauma. Many of these children will themselves follow in their parent's footsteps and repeat the process with their own children. Meanwhile, legislation mandating ever harsher sentencing requirements continues to be passed in a heavily polarized political environment that rhetorically labels those who support creative alternatives for nonviolent offenders as being "soft" on crime. Unchecked, present trends suggest that the increasing criminalization of today's underclass holds an extremely daunting portent for the future of American society.

Like the canaries that served as an early warning about poisoned air, the children of incarcerated parents alert us to the grave consequences resulting from a polluted political environment that sustains these larger trends. It is possible to check the course of present policy development and its intergenerational consequences, but for this we need to learn the lessons these children's lives can teach us. As a first step, the millions of children affected by incarceration need to be identified and acknowledged. Much more direct work with these children and their parents is needed to fully understand their circumstances and to develop meaningful responses. The public must be educated about the families and children who are caught in the "tough on crime" net along with the individual offender, and policymakers must be supported to seek less punitive, more pro-family, community-based alternatives for victimless and nonviolent crimes. Law enforcement, correctional facilities, child welfare service systems, schools, and other community-based agencies need to collaborate in developing coordinated responses to affected children and their families.

ACKNOWLEDGMENTS

We especially acknowledge: The National Institute of Justice and National Criminal Justice Reference

Service (NCJRS), which provided the most recent national surveys of prison and jail inmates, including special reports prepared about incarcerated women, and the latest topical search on Inmates and Their Families (1996), which includes 30 of the most representative citations and abstracts on the subject; the 1992 Assembly Office of Research of the California Legislature for their report, *Children of Incarcerated Parents,* which provided promising research studies, including studies by the American Bar Association Center on Children and the Law and the Center for Children of Incarcerated Parents at Pacific Oaks College in Pasadena, California; the 1994 ABA Center on Children and the Law study for their report, *Children on Hold: Improving the Response to Children Whose Parents Are Arrested and Incarcerated,* which helped us understand how the law enforcement and child welfare service systems view and respond to children whose sole caregiver is arrested or incarcerated; Katherine Gabel and Denise Johnston, M.D., both of the Center for Children of Incarcerated Parents, for their report, *Children of Incarcerated Parents* (1995), and for state-of-the-art information on a broad range of issues related to children whose parents are or were under some form of criminal justice system control, including but not limited to incarceration; the National Center on Crime and Delinquency in San Francisco, for a copy of their much cited *Why Punish the Children? A Reappraisal of the Children of Incarcerated Mothers in America,* and for access to other relevant NCCD publications; Ellen Barry, J.D., director of Legal Services for Prisoners with Children in San Francisco, and some of her legal staff, whom we met and interviewed; and Peter Breen, executive director of Marin-based Centerforce, a nonprofit agency dedicated to providing services to families of prison inmates.

DISCUSSION QUESTIONS

1. List four or five ways in which children become vulnerable when a parent is incarcerated. What are the likely harms to a child when the father is in prison? How are these problems different from those the child faces when the mother is in prison?

2. Explain the concept of involuntary termination of parental rights. Why are incarcerated mothers especially at risk of losing their parental rights? What social policies are needed to remedy this situation?

3. Discuss the concept of intergenerational incarceration. What strategies can be used to prevent children of inmates from becoming the next generation of prisoners? When looking at strategies for change, analyze this issue from the perspectives of the individual family, the larger community, and the wider society.

4. Discuss the differential racial and class impact on black, white, and Latino children as a result of the incarceration of their mothers (and fathers) in the United States.

5. Reed and Reed end this chapter by saying: "Like the canaries that served as an early warning about poisoned air, the children of incarcerated parents alert us to the grave consequences resulting from a polluted political environment that sustains these larger trends [e.g., tough on crime laws]." In fact, Reed and Reed warn that crime policies in the United States actually *increase* harm to the most disadvantaged children in this society. Explain what the authors mean by this warning and your own reaction to it. What policies would you suggest to remedy this situation?

NOTES

1. [Based on] the April 16, 1996, telephone conversation with Denise Johnston, M.D., Center for Children of Incarcerated Parents, Pacific

Oaks College, Pasadena, California. Johnston (1995b) has also developed a formula to estimate the number of prisoners' children based on data collected from past studies, wherein 67% of incarcerated women have an average of 2.4 minor children each, and 56% of incarcerated men have an average of two children each.

2. [Based on a] telephone conversation with Peter Breen, Executive Director, Centerforce, headquartered at San Quentin, California (December 1995).

3. In California, about nine percent of reports investigated by county Child Protective Services involve "caretaker absence or incapacity," the category used for parents who are absent due to arrest, incarceration, hospitalization, or death (California Department of Social Services, 1994).

4. Pregnant women are also at risk for termination of parental rights when they give birth while incarcerated. Most correctional systems separate incarcerated mothers from their newborns within 24 to 48 hours after birth (Barry, 1995).

5. Communication with an incarcerated parent is limited by the ability of the child's caregiver to afford to pay for collect telephone calls from the parent.

6. Informal interviews conducted by Edward L. Reed with correctional officers at San Quentin State Prison since 1992.

REFERENCES

ABA Center on Children and the Law. 1994. Children on Hold: Improving the Response to Children Whose Parents Are Arrested and Incarcerated. Washington, DC: Center on Children and the Law.

Adalist-Estrin, A. 1986. Parenting from Behind Bars. *Family Resources Coalition Report* 5(1):12–13.

American Correctional Association. 1990. *The Female Offender: What Does the Future Hold?* Washington, DC: St. Mary's Press.

Barry, E. 1995. Legal Issues for Prisoners with Children. In *Children of Incarcerated Parents,* ed. K. Gabel and D Johnston, 147–166. New York: Lexington Books.

Baunach, P. J. 1985. *Mothers in Prison.* New Brunswick, NJ: Transaction Books.

Bloom, B. 1995. Public Policy and the Children of Incarcerated Parents. In *Children of Incarcerated Parents.* ed. K. Gabel and D. Johnston, 271–284. New York: Lexington Books.

Bloom, B., M. C. Lind, and B. Owen. 1994. *Women in California Prisons: Hidden Victims of the War on Drugs.* San Francisco: Center on Juvenile and Criminal Justice.

Bloom, B., and D. Steinhart. 1993. *Why Punish the Children? A Reappraisal of the Children of Incarcerated Mothers in America.* San Francisco: National Council on Crime and Delinquency.

California Department of Corrections (CDC). 1995a. *California Prisoners and Parolees 1992.* Sacramento, CA: State of California.

———. 1995b. *California Department of Corrections, Average Daily Prison Population, October 1994–September 1995.* Data Analysis Unit, Offender Information Services Branch (October).

———. 1994. *Inside Corrections: Public Safety, Public Services.* Sacramento, CA: State of California.

———. 1991. *California Prisoners and Parolees 1990.* Sacramento, CA: State of California.

California Department of Justice. 1993. *California Criminal Justice Profile 1993, Statewide.* Sacramento, CA.

California Department of Social Services. 1994. *Preplacement Preventive Services for Children in California.* Annual Statistical Report for Calendar Year 1994. Sacramento, CA.

Clement, M. J. 1993. Parenting in Prison: A National Survey of Programs for Incarcerated Women. *Journal of Offender Rehabilitation* 19(1–2):89–100.

Criminal Justice Institute, Inc. 1994. *1994 Corrections Yearbook: Probation and Parole,* as cited in Schiraldi et al. (1996) referenced below.

Foote, C. 1993. *The Prison Population Explosion: California's Rogue Elephant.* San Francisco: Center on Juvenile and Criminal Justice.

Fritsch, T. A., and J. D. Burkhead. 1981. Behavioral Reactions of Children to Parental Absence Due to Imprisonment. *Family Relations* 30(1).

Hairston, C. F. 1995. Fathers in Prison. In *Children of Incarcerated Parents.* ed. K. Gabel and D. Johnston, 31–40. New York: Lexington Books.

———. 1991. Family Ties During Imprisonment: Important to Whom and for What? *Journal of Sociology and Social Welfare* 18(1): 87–104.

———. 1989. Men in Prison: Family Characteristics and Family View. *Journal of Offender Counseling, Services, and Rehabilitation* 14(1): 23–30.

Johnston, D. 1995a. Effects of Parental Incarceration. In *Children of Incarcerated Parents*. ed. K. Gabel and D. Johnston, New York: Lexington Books.

———. 1995b. Parent-Child Visitation in the Jail or Prison. In *Children of Incarcerated Parents*. ed. K. Gabel and D. Johnston, 135–143. New York: Lexington Books.

———. 1995c. Intervention. In *Children of Incarcerated Parents*. ed. K. Gabel and D. Johnston, 199–236. New York: Lexington Books.

———. 1995d. Conclusion, In *Children of Incarcerated Parents*. ed. K. Gabel and D. Johnston, 311–314. New York: Lexington Books.

———. 1994. *Caregivers of Prisoners' Children*. Pasadena, CA: Pacific Oaks Center for Children of Incarcerated Parents.

———. 1992. *Children of Offenders*. Pasadena, CA: Pacific Oaks Center for Children of Incarcerated Parents.

Johnston, D. and K. Gabel. 1995. Incarcerated Parents. In *Children of Incarcerated Parents*. ed. K. Gabel and D. Johnston, 3–20. New York: Lexington Books.

Kampfner, C. J. 1995. Post-Traumatic Stress Reactions in Children of Imprisoned Mothers. In *Children of Incarcerated Parents*. ed. K. Gabel and D. Johnston, 89–100. New York: Lexington Books.

Kiser, G. C. 1991. Female Inmates and Their Families. *Federal Probation* 55(3).

Koban, L. 1983. Parents in Prison: A Comparative Analysis of the Effects of Incarceration on the Families of Men and Women. *Research in Law, Deviance, and Social Control* 5: 171–183.

Lawhorn, S. 1992. *Children of Incarcerated Parents*. A Report to the Legislature Pursuant to ACR 38 (Resolution Chapter 89, Statutes of 1991, Filante). Sacramento, CA: Assembly Office of Research.

McCall, C., J. Casteel, and N. C. Shaw. 1985. *Pregnancy in Prison: A Needs Assessment of Prenatal Outcome in Three California Penal Institutions* (Contract 84-84085). Sacramento: California Department of Health Services.

Muhar, G. 1991. Incarceration and Termination of Parental Rights. *Journal of Juvenile Law* 12:70–78.

National Black Child Development Institute. 1989. *Who Will Care When Parents Can't: A Study of Black Children in Foster Care*. Washington, DC.

Owen, B., and B. Bloom. 1994. Profiling the Needs of California's Female Prisoners. Paper presented at the Western Society of Criminology (February).

Sack, W. H., J. Seidler, and S. Thomas. 1976. The Children of Imprisoned Parents: A Psychosocial Exploration. *American Journal of Orthopsychiatry* 46(4).

Schaefer, N. E. 1991. Prison Visiting Policies and Practices. *International Journal of Offender Therapy and Comparative Criminology* 35(3): 263–275.

Schiraldi, V., S. Kuyper, and S. Hewitt. 1996. *Young African Americans and the Criminal Justice System in California: Five Years Later*. San Francisco: Center on Juvenile and Criminal Justice.

Schmitt, C. H. 1996. Plea Bargaining Favors Whites as Blacks, Hispanics Pay Price. *San Jose Mercury News* (December 8, 1991, cited in Schiraldi et al.).

Smith, G. 1995. Practical Considerations Regarding Termination of Incarcerated Parents' Rights. In *Children of Incarcerated Parents*. ed. K. Gabel and D. Johnston, 183–195. New York: Lexington Books.

U.S. Department of Health and Human Services. 1992. *National Household Survey on Drug Abuse*. Washington, DC.

U.S. Department of Justice (USDJ). 1994. *Special Report, Women in Prison* (Report No. NCJ-145321). Washington, DC: Bureau of Justice Statistics.

———. 1993. *Survey of State Prison Inmates* (Report No. NCJ-136949). Washington, D.C.: Bureau of Justice Statistics.

———. 1992. *Special Report, Women in Jail 1989*. Washington, DC: Office of Justice Programs, Bureau of Justice Statistics.

Virginia Commission for Children and Youth. 1992. *Study of the Needs of Children Whose Parents Are Incarcerated*. Richmond, VA: Commission for Children and Youth.

Chapter 16

Stopping Abuse in Prison

Nina Siegal

ABSTRACT

This chapter focuses on the sexual, physical, and emotional abuse of women prisoners. Efforts on several fronts to stop the abuse have included class action lawsuits against individual states, the U.S. federal government, and the District of Columbia. Siegal reports here on the investigations and resulting reports by various governmental organizations and advocacy groups on violence against women in prison.

Some changes have occurred, such as state laws criminalizing sexual conduct between correctional staff and prisoners as well as the initiation of training programs for staff and prisoners to explain the law, the prison's policies, and ways to report abuse. Still, most advocates point out that *the abuse continues.* And in some cases, there are backlashes to the reports and ensuing legislation. Michigan, for example, passed a law in 2000 that excluded prisoners from the protections provided under the state civil rights act prohibiting discrimination based on race and gender. "Through this legislation, Michigan effectively eliminated the possibility that women prisoners could seek redress for sexual abuse in prison through lawsuits against the corrections department."[*] Advocates for women prisoners argue that a major cultural change is necessary within institutions and that this change will not happen unless the unions, to which correctional staff belong, work toward an end to violence against women under their control.

One of the early twentieth-century reform efforts on behalf of women incarcerated in the United States was the creation of separate facilities so that women would not be subjected to abuse by male prisoners and guards. This reform came about, and women were for many years incarcerated in all-women facilities with staff predominantly comprised of women. But in the 1970s, with the emergence of federal equal rights legislation, women won the right to work in men's prisons. An additional result, however, was that the legislation further

---

[*]*All Too Familiar: Sexual Abuse of Women in U.S. State Prisons.* Human Rights Watch (1996).

legitimated men working in women's prisons. Today, faced with an extremely serious situation, some advocates of women prisoners think that, once again, it is necessary to remove all men from women's institutions in order to end the abuse.

LAWYERS FOR WOMEN BEHIND BARS AND HUMAN RIGHTS GROUPS ARE MAKING A DIFFERENCE

Widespread abuses of women behind bars barely received notice until [the early 1990s]. Across the country, there were incidents of prison or jail staff sexually molesting inmates with impunity. Slowly but surely, the nation's correctional facilities are responding to this abuse.

"Ten years ago, I think we knew it was going on, but we hadn't named it," says Brenda Smith, a Practitioner-in-Residence at Washington College of Law at American University. "Until you raise it as a problem, and until people start coming forward and talking about it, it is not perceived as a problem."

The changes are the result of several landmark legal cases, a shift in government policy, and the attention of human-rights groups. Still, problems remain. Guards continue to rape women inmates. But now there is a process to bring them to justice.

The stories were too consistent to be ignored. Numerous female inmates in three Washington, D.C., prison and jail facilities said they had been awakened at two or three in the morning for a "medical visit" or a "legal visit" only to be led into the kitchen, the clinic, the visiting hall, or a closet to have sex. Many inmates were becoming pregnant in a system that allowed no conjugal visits.

"There were a lot of places where people could have sex," says Smith. "A lot of it was in exchange for cigarettes." Prison employees offered other deals: " 'I will give you phone calls, I will make sure you

get a better job assignment, I'll give you drugs if you have sex with me.' The sex involved not just correctional officers. It involved chaplains, administration, deputy wardens, contractors, and food-service workers. It involved not just male staff but female staff as well," Smith says.

In 1993, the National Women's Law Center and a District of Columbia law firm filed a class-action suit, Women Prisoners vs. District of Columbia Department of Corrections, in U.S. District Court. The suit alleged a pattern of discrimination against women in the jail, the Correctional Treatment Facility, and the Lorton Minimum Security Annex, a D.C. facility in Lorton, Virginia. A large portion of the case focused on issues of sexual misconduct, based on evidence that the law firm had collected during an investigation. The following year, a judge found that there was a pattern and practice of misconduct so severe that it violated the Eighth Amendment protection against cruel and unusual punishment. The decision was appealed and is still in court.*

As extreme as the D.C. situation was, it was not unique.

Lawyers in Georgia had been preparing a class-action suit on behalf of men and women in the state's prisons for almost ten years when they began to come across striking charges of sexual misconduct in the Georgia Women's Correctional Facility in Milledgeville and the nearby camp, Colony Farm. The alleged activities included rape, criminal sexual contact, leering, and abusive catcalling of inmates. One lieutenant had sex with at least seven prisoners from 1987 to 1991, directing women to meet him in various locations in the prisons for sex.

In 1992, the lawyers for the suit, Cason v. Seckinger, amended their complaint to add allegations of sexual abuse that had taken place over a period of fourteen years. Seventeen staff members

Source: Reprinted by permission from *The Progressive,* 409 E. Main St., Madison, WI 53703. www.progressive.org. April 1999, 63(4): 31–33.

*Editors' note: The case was appealed to the U.S. Court of Appeals for the D.C. Circuit. The court upheld the findings of fact and liability on sexual misconduct.

were indicted. None were convicted, though several were dismissed from their jobs as a result of the lawsuit. The suit resulted in a number of federal court orders requiring the department to rectify many of its practices. It also influenced the department to close Milledgeville and move all the female inmates to a different facility.

These two suits—and the criminal prosecutions that ensued—were the first major legal attempts to address a problem that had been plaguing the criminal justice system for decades.

One of the biggest cases for the rights of women prisoners was settled [in 1998]. The case (Lucas vs. White) involved three inmates of a federal facility in Pleasanton, California, called FCI Dublin, who were sold as sex slaves to male inmates in an adjoining facility. Inmates paid guards to allow them into the cells of female inmates who were being held in the men's detention center, which is across the street from Dublin.

The plaintiffs settled their civil suit against the Federal Bureau of Prisons for $500,000 and forced the agency to make dramatic changes in the way it handles allegations of misconduct. According to the settlement, the Bureau of Prisons was to set up a confidential hotline, or some other reporting mechanism, so that inmates and staff can inform the authorities of problems inside. It was also supposed to provide medical and psychological treatment for inmates who have been victimized and establish new training programs for staff and inmates.

Geri Lynn Green, one of the two attorneys for the Lucas case, has been monitoring the changes at the prison since the case was settled. After the lawsuit and the subsequent training, she says, "it appears there was a tremendous impact."

Brett Dignam, clinical professor of law at Yale University, agrees that the Lucas case made a big difference: "More prison staff members are resigning over issues of sexual misconduct."

Human rights advocates, too, have taken up the cause. In 1996, the Women's Rights Project at Human Rights Watch issued "All Too Familiar: Sexual Abuse of Women in U.S. Prisons."

The 347-page report detailed problems in California, Washington, D.C., Michigan, Georgia, and New York. "We have found that male correctional employees have vaginally, anally, and orally raped female prisoners and sexually assaulted and abused them," says the report. "We found that in the course of committing such gross misconduct, male officers have not only used actual or threatened physical force, but have also used their near total authority to provide or deny goods and privileges to female prisoners to compel them to have sex or, in other cases, to reward them for having done so."

Last June, the United Nations sent a special rapporteur, Radhika Coomaraswamy, to the United States to investigate sexual misconduct in the nation's women's facilities. She argued that stronger monitoring was needed to control widespread abuses.

"We concluded that there has been widespread sexual misconduct in U.S. prisons, but there is a diversity—some are dealing with it better than others," Reuters reported her saying in December. "Georgia has sexual misconduct but has set up a very strong scheme to deal with it. In California and Michigan, nothing has been done and the issue is very prevalent." In April, Coomaraswamy will give a final report to the U.N. Commission on Human Rights.

[In 1990,] Amnesty International released its own report, "'Not Part of My Sentence': Violations of the Human Rights of Women in Custody," which includes a section on sexual abuse. "Many women inmates are subjected to sexual abuse by prison officials, including: sexually offensive language, observation by male officers while showering and dressing, groping during daily pat-down searches, and rape." In addition to the problems detailed in the Human Rights Watch report, Amnesty investigators found problems in Illinois, Massachusetts, New Hampshire, Texas, West Virginia, and Wyoming.

Lawyers and human rights groups have won some important reforms. In 1990, only seventeen states had a law on the books defining sexual misconduct in prisons as either a misdemeanor or a felony offense. Today, there are only twelve states left that do not criminalize sexual relations between staff and inmates—Alabama, Kentucky, Massachusetts, Minnesota, Missouri, Montana, Nebraska, Oregon, Utah, Vermont, West Virginia, and Wisconsin— according to Amnesty International, which is campaigning to get all these states to pass their own laws.

The U.S. Justice Department is also taking a more active role. It has filed two suits charging that the correctional systems in Michigan and Arizona were responsible for violations of prisoners' constitutional rights. The suits cite numerous allegations of abuse, including rape, lack of privacy, prurient viewing, and invasive pat searches. Both cases are still pending.

Meanwhile, state prison systems are training personnel. Andie Moss was a project director with the Georgia Department of Corrections in 1992 when the department was asked to help interview inmates for the class-action lawsuit. She ended up culling information from women who said they had been subjected to misconduct over a fourteen-year period. Today, Moss works with the National Institute of Corrections, part of the Bureau of Prisons. Her primary responsibility is to develop training programs to educate both staff and inmates about sexual misconduct, the new laws, and their rights.

Since her program, "Addressing Staff Sexual Misconduct," was initiated in early 1997, Moss and her team have provided training for more than thirty state correctional systems, and she expects to complete training for all fifty states by the end of 1999.

The training involves four basic elements: clarifying the departments' sexual misconduct policy, informing inmates and staff of the law in their state, telling inmates and staff how to report abuse that they witness, and giving examples of how people have intervened in the past.

"We know it's still an issue. We know corrections departments still need to work diligently on this," says Moss. "It's a constant effort because it is a cultural change. But if you could follow the change in the law, the change in policy and practice, there's been an amazing effort in the last three years."

Despite all the positive steps, however, women are being abused still in America's prisons and jails.

Investigators from a number of California-based law firms who recently visited the Valley State Prison for Women in Chowchilla, California, heard stories of at least a dozen assaults by specific guards. They also found "a climate of sexual terror that women are subjected to on a daily basis," says Ellen Barry, founding director of Legal Services for Prisoners with Children, based in San Francisco.

"The instances of both physical and sexual abuse are much higher than any other institution where I've interviewed women," she says. "The guards are really brutalizing women in a way that we really haven't seen before."

Valley State Prison inmate Denise Dalton told investigators that a doctor at the facility groped her and conducts inappropriate pelvic exams. "If I need Tylenol, all I need to do is ask him for a pelvic and he will give me whatever I want," she said.

But most of the abusive conduct was of the type that, Barry says, made for "a climate of sexual terror" in the prison. Coreen Sanchez, another inmate, said that in December, she entered the dayroom at the facility and asked a correctional officer if the sergeant had come in, and he responded by saying, "Yeah, he came in your mouth." She also reported seeing correctional officers flaunt their erections in front of inmates.

Advocates for prisoners say there still needs to be a dramatic cultural shift within the system before women are safe from the people who guard them behind bars.

"I think we have to keep in perspective the limitations of litigation and advocacy work for truly making a change in this arena," says Barry.

One problem that advocates cite is the recalcitrance of the unions that represent prison guards. "The people we really have to win over are not legislators, but the unions," says Christine Doyle, research coordinator for Amnesty International U.S.A. "Guards look at this as a workplace violation, as something fun to do on the job. They don't look at these women as human beings. The message that these are human beings they are exploiting isn't getting through."

For them to get that message, says Doyle, corrections officers will have to hear it from within the unions, and not from any set of codes, procedures, or laws. "We have states that have legislation, and some of them are just as bad, if not worse, than states without legislation," Doyle says. "So, obviously, that doesn't work. If it comes from within, and the unions themselves say, 'We can do this internally,' workers will respond better."

Human rights groups, for now, are focusing on legislative solutions. In 1996, Human Rights Watch recommended that Congress require all states, as a precondition of receiving federal funding for prisons, criminalize all sexual conduct between staff and inmates. It also urged the Department of Justice to establish secure toll-free telephone hotlines for reporting complaints.

Amnesty International's new report takes an additional step, arguing that the role of male staff be restricted in accordance with the United Nations' Standard Minimum Rules for the Treatment of Prisoners, which state that "women prisoners shall be attended and supervised only by women officers."

Debra LaBelle, a civil rights attorney who filed a class-action suit on behalf of abused women inmates in Michigan, says she would like to see men taken out of women's institutions altogether.

"I resisted going there for a long time, but I don't know another solution," she says. "When we started out, they didn't do any training, much supervision, investigation. In the last three years, they've changed countless policies and yet it is still happening. Get them out of there. It's not like they're losing employment opportunities. There are, unfortunately, many more facilities that men can work in."

Sheila Dauer, director of the Women's Human Rights Program for Amnesty International, says the group's report aims to persuade the final thirteen states without laws against sexual misconduct to initiate legislation, starting with eight state campaigns this year. She says the campaign will also lend support to a federal bill that would do the same thing.

Amnesty's report, she says, is designed to "wake up the American public to the horrible abuses that women inmates are suffering in prison and stop the suffering."

DISCUSSION QUESTIONS

1. Make a detailed list of as many abuses and violations of women prisoners by staff as you can find in this brief article.
2. Describe the policies and practices that are needed to protect women from custodial sexual, physical, and emotional violence and misconduct. Which do you think are the most important and why?
3. Explain what is meant by a cultural shift within women's prisons, and elaborate on the reasons why this cultural shift is a necessary component of reducing abuse.
4. International women's groups attempting to reduce abuse against women in prison in countries around the world have advocated removing all male correctional officers from women's facilities. Discuss the pros and cons of this approach for the United States.
5. Log onto the Internet and find the laws in your home state that relate to protection of women inmates from abuse by correctional staff. How do the laws in your state compare with the results presented in this chapter?

Chapter 17

Progressive Rhetoric, Regressive Policies:
Canadian Prisons for Women

Karlene Faith

ABSTRACT

Following a long period of Canadian government neglect and apathy toward women prisoners that culminated in a televised exposé of strip searches of women prisoners accused of hiding contraband, a government plan was drawn up for women-centered prisons. These were to be caring, empowering, and supportive facilities in which punishment would no longer be the guiding principle. In addition, the government agreed to open a healing lodge for First Nation women prisoners. Recall that this issue was an important one for Native American women incarcerated in Montana, as reported by Ross in chapter 13.

Thus, the Correctional Service of Canada (CSC), which operates the federal prisons for both men and women, adopted a progressive and indeed decarcerative rhetoric in response to public pressure from diverse venues, including feminists. Within a short time it became clear that the old and new perspectives were inherently incompatible, and the CSC today has regressed to its former ways. Abuses continue: illegal strip searches, lack of legal counsel, inappropriate classification, segregation, and the transfer of women to men's prisons. As in the United States and elsewhere, cell space for women in Canada has tripled during this "reform" period. Correctional practice remains conservative and punitive because the philosophy and politics of feminist advocates have been overridden by politics of a different sort and by the conservative mood of the times. Remember, this situation was predicted by Sudbury (chap. 12, "Women of Color, Globalization, and the Politics of Incarceration") in her discussion of the distinction between the three approaches to prison: reform, decarceration, and abolition of prisons.

My deep appreciation to Natalie J. Sokoloff for her practical assistance and her substantive contributions to this article. Also, my thanks to SISter-friends Liz Elliott, Gayle Horii, Kris Lyons, the late Jo-Ann Mayhew, and Kim Pate for their direct or unwitting assistance with this chapter. An earlier version of this article was published in "Transformative Justice versus Re-entrenched Correctionalism: The Canadian Experience," in S. Cook and S. Davies eds., *Harsh Punishment: International Experiences of Women's Imprisonment.* Boston: Northeastern University, 1999, pp. 99–122.

INTRODUCTION

Since the early 1990s, Canadian feminists have been advocating community-based "women-centered" approaches to justice for women who are incarcerated in prison. The promise of such a vision was usurped almost immediately by forces for correctionalism, punishment, and institutional control—not empowerment, reasonable choices, and shared responsibility as articulated by feminist principles. The first edited text to be published in Canada on the subject of women in prison was titled *Too Few to Count,* because women have been an afterthought in the correctional enterprise.[1] Because of their small numbers (2.5 percent of all prisoners)[2] and the inappropriateness for women of the rigid, militaristic, masculinist, hierarchical model of male prisons, activists call for transformative policies in addressing crimes by women.

BACKGROUND: SIGNIFICANT EVENTS IN CANADIAN WOMEN'S INCARCERATION IN THE 1990S

Feminist Principles for Women's Prisons

In 1990, a task force appointed by the solicitor general of Canada to evaluate federal corrections for women produced its report, *Creating Choices.*[3] This document represented the work of hundreds of people, primarily women—many feminists, First Nation women, and representatives of many national women's organizations, notably the Elizabeth Fry Society, which provides leadership for effective prisoner advocacy work and human rights monitoring. Prisoners were also directly involved in the research. Like the task forces that preceded them, this task force first recommended the closure of the federal Prison for Women (P4W) in Kingston, Ontario, an archaic structure situated far from most women's families. To replace it, they recommended regional minimum security facilities that would make room for children and that would draw on noncarceral community resources to assist women in rebuilding their lives.

Five of the "women-centered" principles by which the task force formulated their recommendations, as discussed by Margaret Shaw,[4] were based on the women's need for personal empowerment, meaningful choices, respect and dignity, a supportive environment, and shared responsibility. The success of the regional centers would depend on the implementation of those principles.

Creation of Correctional Facilities for Women

The solicitor general promised to close P4W by 1994 and to follow the task force recommendation for small, low-custody, regional, cottage-style homes for women in conflict with the law. Local communities submitted proposals for four of the new prisons and the sites were selected: Edmonton, Alberta; Joliette, Quebec; Truro, Nova Scotia; and Kitchener, Ontario. In addition, a healing lodge for First Nation women was to be constructed outside Maple Creek, Saskatchewan. Meanwhile, in 1993, the Burnaby Correctional Centre for Women opened in British Columbia (capacity of 120), with responsibility for both provincially sentenced women and federally sentenced women from British Columbia and the Yukon and Northwest Territories. In an exchange-of-services agreement, the federal government helped fund the new prison, which houses both women prisoners serving up to two years provincial time (including weekends) and federal prisoners serving up to life sentences. The provincial authorities govern the prison according to provincial regulations, which are often more punitive and restrictive than federal regulations and which often deny long-term prisoners their rights under federal law. The concern is that other regional prisons will be similarly abandoned by the federal government and put under the control of the host province, to the detriment of federally sentenced women.

By 1995, P4W was still crowded with women but the new regional prisons were under construction. The rhetoric of the five newly appointed wardens was generally in the direction of community involvement and allocation of attention and resources to the issues women face in and out of prison concerning

Source: This article was written expressly for inclusion in this text.

children, employability, housing and transportation, drug and alcohol dependencies, and unresolved issues such as rape, battering, or childhood sexual abuse. At the same time a videotape of the abuse at P4W had been televised nationally, which spurred the Correctional Service of Canada (CSC) to rush completion of the new prisons. It was announced that when the remaining prisoners were transferred, P4W would definitely close.

The Exposé

A videotape of abuses against eight women in segregation cells at P4W, committed in April 1994 by an emergency response team from a neighboring men's prison, was televised in February 1995. The clandestine video, obtained by the Canadian Broadcasting Corporation, was taped according to official policy of the CSC; restraint incidents that could produce personal injury are recorded for later evidence of "professionalism." When CSC learned that a popular news commentary television program, *The Fifth Estate,* was planning to air the tape, they filed an injunction. Months later the courts ruled in favor of public access.

The images televised across the nation included, first, a silent late-night platoon of six or seven men (the exact number was never reported), wearing identical Darth Vader–type outfits. They were unidentifiable behind helmets, heavily padded combat suits, masks, shields, gloves and enormous boots. Part of this platoon's function is to intimidate, and they are successful. On orders of the prison warden to conduct emergency strip searches and cell extractions in the segregation unit, they first burst into the cell of a woman who was asleep on her cot. They roused her by slamming her onto the cement floor, then cut and ripped off her night clothing and underwear. They confined her with leg irons and handcuffs. Two or three of the "team" held her naked body to the cement floor with their padded knees pressed into her back. Then they stood her against the cement wall and banged their batons right next to her ear. They repeated this procedure from one cell to the next. After the televised scene, the women were led away, one by one, for "body cavity" searches. Their cells were overturned; their meager belongings were taken away; and the cots, mattresses, and bedding were removed.

Following the strip searches in the cells and the body cavity searches, "the women were left in shackles and leg irons, wearing paper gowns, on the cement floors of empty cells."[5] Nothing at all was found. None of the eight women had been guilty of holding contraband of any kind. But their punishment continued because they had been judged to be threatening to the guards in the days preceding the assault. Coinciding with these events inside the prison, the guards' union was demonstrating with pickets outside the prison, expressing serious anger about management decisions and demanding policy changes. As detailed in an investigative report,[6] tensions and hostilities produced by the prison culture itself were pervasive prior to and following the assault on the eight women in segregation in April 1994. The women in segregation were denied bedding, mattresses, showers, telephone calls, reading or writing materials, hot water, radios, adequate feminine hygiene products, legal counsel, and clothing. Some of them were transferred to men's prisons, including men's mental hospital prisons and prisons housing sex offenders. Some were kept in segregation at P4W for as long as nine months, which posed a serious mental and physical health risk to these women. Despite this, John Edwards, the commissioner of corrections, publicly defended the actions of the emergency response team (ERT). However, he resigned soon thereafter.

The P4W assault event was a historical milestone in public education in Canada regarding women's prisons, and that event is bracketed by other significant events in the 1990s, most of which have promised changes in the way that "corrections" are done to women in this country.

The Arbour Commission

In 1995, spurred by the public outcry over the televised strip searches, the solicitor general commissioned an official "Inquiry into Certain Events at the Prison for Women." The commission was chaired by an appeals court judge, the Honorable Louise

Arbour, who later became the chief justice in the United Nations war tribunal court and who now sits on the Supreme Court of Canada. As commissioner, Judge Arbour was meticulous in her investigation, seeking perspectives and information from the prisoners, guards, and management on the inside and from researchers, activists, lawyers, and academics on the outside. In documenting the events before, during, and after the assaults, Judge Arbour and her two assistants, Dr. Tammy Landau and Dr. Kelly Hannah-Moffat,[7] presented abundant evidence of lawbreaking on the part of the correctional service.[8] The very act of the ERT entering the segregation unit was illegal, because, with women in bed in their cells, there was no emergency.

Although Judge Arbour's focus was primarily on the particular need of prison authorities to observe and strictly adhere to the law and to function under the direct eye of the judiciary, she also examined evidence of practices that were legal but nevertheless inhumane. For example, she was outraged at the abuses permitted through extended segregation practices, and she referred to corrections as a "deplorable defensive culture."[9]

CSC's defiance in responding to so few of the commission's recommendations was met with scorn by critics. The one potentially significant recommendation offered by Judge Arbour that has been implemented is the establishment of the position of deputy commissioner in charge of women's prisons, held by Nancy Stableforth. And although feminists opposed the action, the CSC did heed another recommendation from the Arbour report: They created all-female emergency response teams. This move is best understood as regressive because it wrongly assumes that women, as men's "equals," have need for these teams. Giving women the entitlement and skills to conduct forced strip searches of other women is not a step forward for women in either role.

The Arbour recommendations included numerous demands that the judicial system increase surveillance of prison wardens and staff. And yet, within several years, prison violence was again inflicted and blamed on women who were incarcerated—in men's prisons in Saskatchewan and Nova Scotia, and in two of the new women's prisons—again bringing in unwarranted "emergency" responses. Old habits die hard (that is, using force to address an "emergency"), and the standard for what constitutes an "emergency" (that is, justifying force) has not risen.

A Healing Lodge for Women

In late 1995, the Okimaw Ohci Healing Lodge was opened to 30 First Nation women. The brochure for the opening states: "Healing for Aboriginal women means the opportunity, through Aboriginal teachings, spirituality and culture, to recover from histories of abuse, regain a sense of self-worth, gain skills and rebuild families." Planned and designed by members of various First Nations, the buildings are arranged in the shape of an eagle seen from the sky, situated in a beautiful prairie setting near aspen woods and green hills; initially, the staff were mostly Native people who had no history with corrections. The Healing Lodge posed a significant challenge to punishment models. Yet CSC gave considerable latitude to the planning committee and did not object to the plans for healing circles; the steady availability of elders for personal counsel; or the absence of locks, fences, and walls.[10]

Healing and Empowerment: A Short-Lived Moment in Women's Imprisonment

After several suicide and escape attempts in the new prisons and one death, the CSC, rather than address the women's underlying reasons, immediately concluded that what was needed was tighter security. The Edmonton prison was virtually shut down for several months and opportunistically transformed into a maximum-security prison. The prison in Truro, Nova Scotia, likewise became a maximum-security prison after a woman walked away and others were in conflicts with staff and each other. All the other new "minimum-security facilities" followed suit; hiring more staff; constructing high, double chain-linked fences topped with coiled razor wire; and installing radar detection, cameras, tape recorders, and other security devices. Once a visitor has passed through a security check and is on the grounds, these prisons appear very attractive until that visitor recognizes the level of technology surveillance or hears cries from the segregation units.

Pastel walls and "living units" notwithstanding, the negative consequence of these new prisons has been to illustrate the impossibility of creating a "community" involving freedoms, responsibilities, and choices within a "correctional" penological enterprise. These new prisons serve as both empirical and symbolic evidence that punishment and healing practices are incompatible.[11] Some women do heal in prison, not through institutional regimens but with self-help such as peer counseling or through the Native Sisterhood groups organized by First Nation women in Canadian prisons.

In the new prisons, planned as alternatives to the penitentiary model, guards now unapologetically use pepper spray on women who are disruptive and exercise the control that is fundamental to a total institution. In 1996, a woman in the Truro prison became very agitated and cut herself. Jo-Ann Mayhew, a former prisoner, reported that "the staff responded by using pepper spray, locking her in an isolation unit, stripping her naked, repeated use of pepper spray, then left her in the shackles and handcuffs, naked on a steel frame without a mattress or blanket for several hours."[12] The Board of Investigation concluded that all this punishment, force, and restraint was "not seen as excessive and appears reasonable." They did say that leaving her naked on the cell floor was unjustified.[13]

PROGRESSIVE RHETORIC, REGRESSIVE PRACTICES

In 1998, Solicitor General Andy Scott spoke in various public venues, to the press, and in Parliament about the futility of prisons as a response to illegal behaviors. Scott came into office following the decision for the new prison construction. He acknowledged that prison "can be detrimental or counterproductive" for most people. He stated that offenders "could be more safely and effectively handled through community programs." And he spoke of the "need to develop effective alternatives to incarceration for offenders." Scott argued that public safety, his number one priority, would be better met with community programs that included education and job training and that interpersonal conflicts involving illegal behaviors should be resolved through restorative justice methods.[14]

Also in 1998, Commissioner of Corrections Ole Ingstrup, in charge of 56 prisons and camps, halfway houses, and other aspects of "corrections," stated unequivocally: "Prison is a costly and often destructive response to social ills. We must deal with the public perception, and fear, that crime is greater than it actually is."[15] Notions of various forms of restorative justice, either innovative or based on traditional First Nation practices, had officially entered the lexicon of criminal justice agencies.

In his report, evaluating the performance of CSC over the previous year, Scott concluded decisively,

> Keeping offenders in prison for long periods of time is costly. There does not, furthermore, appear to be any clear link between crime in society and levels of incarceration. In addition, community-based interventions appear to equal or outperform institutional measures in the safe reintegration of offenders. There is a growing acceptance of the principle that incarceration should be reserved for higher risk offenders who have committed violent crimes, and that non-violent offenders are best managed through community-based supervision and programs.[16]

Even the Canadian National Parole Board states in its manual, "The lowest recidivism rates occur when incarceration is used as a last resort and treatment is offered by programs outside the correctional system."[17]

Because relatively few women prisoners are a threat to public safety, the increased use of incarceration (for both men and women) suggests that courts are still operating on the basis of prison as the norm and that community-based alternatives are not yet sufficiently developed to provide the courts with new options. Because of cutbacks in social services, state funding for alternative justice services is very limited. Victims' rights groups, via the media, have aggressively persuaded the public of a need for more stringent incarceration practices. Law-and-order politicians respond to their constituents by putting pressure on parole boards to withhold releases.[18]

In late 1999, around 20 women were incarcerated at P4W with up to 90 men and women on the staff to guard them day and night. In that final year, P4W cost CSC and the taxpayers Can$300,000 per woman (approximately U.S.$187,500).[19] Many of these women had served virtual life sentences at P4W for incremental or steady failure to adapt to prison. They would act up, get write-ups, and be denied parole. The original plan was to send them to the notoriously "masculinist" Kingston Penitentiary across the street, which houses sex offenders. Construction of a segregated women's section in the psychiatric ward was already under way when four of these women developed a court case against CSC. With public support for the women, represented by Elizabeth Fry Societies across Canada,[20] CSC relented and permitted the women to stay at P4W until 2000. The maximum security classification had been assigned to these women because they had not learned how to be compliant prisoners, because, instead of "fighting the system," they had retreated into drugs, injuring themselves or attempting suicide. The women, almost half of whom were First Nation, did not represent a threat to public safety.

Even as the rhetoric of officials has shifted to a decarceration philosophy, the ratio of guards to prisoners has increased, and women's cell space in Canada has nearly tripled since 1992 with the new prisons near Truro, Edmonton, Kitchener, Joliette, Vancouver, and Maple Creek. Maximum-security technology had been installed in each of the new women's prisons, and on May 8, 2000, the last woman at P4W was transferred to a regional prison. However, at the first signs of trouble, CSC then transferred all the women with maximum-security classification to isolated segregation units and psychiatric wards in men's prisons. Over time, women have been sent to the Saskatchewan Penitentiary, the Regional Psychiatric Centre in Saskatchewan, Ste-Anne-des-Plaines in Quebec, and the Springhill Institution in Nova Scotia. At one point before P4W

closed, a total of 350 women were incarcerated in 11 different prisons.

Far from the vision of the *Creating Choices* Task Force and far from the stern judgment of the Honorable Louise Arbour that "corrections" lawlessness had to cease, some of the new women's prisons perpetuate many of the same old abuses: "illegal strip searches, no access to counsel, excessive use of force and segregation, illegal involuntary transfers."[21] The departure of women prisoners with maximum-security classification left primarily minimum- and medium-security women in the new regional maximum-security prisons. Even the healing lodge, contrary to its intended mission and despite the recommendations of the Arbour Commission and initial CSC agreement, was not permitted in the end to accept women with a maximum-security classification. Contradictorily, the healing lodge itself had added custody features characteristic of maximum-security prisons.

Although it continued to expound on a decarcerative philosophy to pacify its more liberal critics, CSC in practice traveled full circle in reentrenching correctionalism in the women's system. Despite its purported commitment to the principles of the *Creating Choices* recommendations, despite the findings of a federal commission of inquiry that CSC was breaking the law, despite the men at the top who profess a belief in community-based restorative justice, more women are being locked up—without an increase in their crime rate. Instead of giving women choices for turning their lives around, the punishment industry, which leads to a dead end, is thriving as never before.[22]

Clearly, having women-centered and feminist goals integrated into new prisons specifically for women is not possible within a decidedly punishment-and-control framework.[23] Much more than progressive rhetoric is needed to cut through harsh, punitive, masculinist correctionalist practices. For real change to happen, prisons must be abolished, with investment instead going to schools, occupational training, decent employment, social services, and the rights of the most marginalized of women (and men) in Canadian society.

DISCUSSION QUESTIONS

1. According to Faith, there is a difference between a correctionalism framework and a feminist, or woman-centered, framework for the prison environment. Define each of these terms.

2. Feminists, activists, and scholars were initially welcomed into the Canadian reform effort, but the effort failed. What was the role of feminist activists in trying to make change? State several reasons why they were unsuccessful in this reform effort and why the project failed.

3 What other strategies, as discussed by Siegal (chap. 16), might have been used in Canada to make positive changes for women in prison? Do these actions need to be country-specific?

4. Discuss the treatment of First Nation women inmates by the CSC. Does it seem that they were treated especially harshly in comparison to the other women inmates? If so, why? How does their treatment compare with the treatment of Native American women prisoners discussed by Ross (chap. 13)?

5. What role does the public have in influencing prison practices? How could the public be more effective?

REFERENCES

1. Ellen Adelberg and Claudia Currie, eds., 1987. *Too Few to Count: Canadian Women in Conflict with the Law.* (Vancouver: Press Gang.

2. Correctional Service of Canada. 1997. *Basic Facts about Corrections in Canada.* Ottawa: Solicitor General 14.

3. Task Force on Federally Sentenced Women. 1990. *Creating Choices.* Ottawa: Solicitor General.

4. Margaret Shaw. 1996. Is There a Feminist Future for Women's Prisons? In *Prisons 2000: An International Perspective on the Current State and Future of Imprisonment,* ed. R. Matthews and P. Francis, 183–184. London and New York: Macmillan.

5. Allan Manson. 1997. Security from the Outside: The Arbour Commission, the Prison for Women, and the Correctional Service of Canada. *Canadian Criminal Law Review,* 321–337.

6. Louise Arbour. 1996. *Commission of Inquiry into Certain Events at the Prison for Women in Kingston,* Ottawa: Solicitor General.

7. Kelly Hannah-Moffat. 2001. *Punishment in Disguise: Penal Governance and Federal Imprisonment of Women in Canada.* Toronto: University of Toronto.

8. Arbour, *Commission of Inquiry,* 174.

9. Prison Not Prepared for Violent Women. 1997. *Globe and Mail,* Toronto, September 20, A3.

10. Karlene Faith. 1995. Aboriginal Women's Healing Lodge: Challenge to Penal Correctionalism? *Journal of Human Justice* 6(2) (Spring/Autumn): 79–104.

11. See Kathleen Kendall. 1994. Therapy behind Prison Walls: A Contradiction in Terms? Paper prepared for Prisons 2000 Conference, University of Leicester, April.

12. Jo-Ann Mayhew. 1997. A Working Paper on the Status of Women Incarcerated at Nova and Springhill Institutions. Halifax: Nova Scotia Status of Women, April, 3.

13. John Alderson. 1997. Administrative Investigation on Minor Disturbance and Use of Force. Nova Institution, Ottawa: Correctional Service of Canada, 16 (January):14–15.

14. Solicitor General. 1998. Speaking Notes for the Honourable Andy Scott, Solicitor General of Canada, to the Beyond Prisons International Symposium. Kingston: Solicitor General, March 17.

15. Incarceration Rates Too High, Official Says. 1998. *Globe and Mail,* Toronto, March 17, B1.

16. Solicitor General. 1997. *Correctional Service Canada: Performance Report.* Ottawa: Solicitor General, March 31, 12.

17. National Parole Board. 1997. *Risk Assessment Manual* Ottawa: Solicitor General, 13.

18. Canadian Criminal Justice Association. 1998. Prison Overcrowding and the Reintegration of Offenders. Discussion paper. Ottawa: Canadian Criminal Justice Association, March, 2.

19. Kim Pate. 1997. *Executive Director's Report* Ottawa: Canadian Association of Elizabeth Fry Societies, 3.

20. Pate, *Executive Director's Report.*

21. Prison to Cost $5.1 Million. 1997. *Whig Standard.* Kingston, Ontario, December 20, A3.

22. Kelly Hannah-Moffat and Margaret Shaw eds. 2000. *An Ideal Prison? Critical Essays on Women's Imprisonment in Canada.* Halifax: Fernwood.

23. Gayle Horii. 1995. Twelve Proposals with Regard to Policy Which May Govern the Future of Incarcerated Women in Canada. Brief submitted to the Commission of Inquiry into Certain Events at the Prison for Women in Kingston, December 31.

Part 3

Women Victims and Survivors of Crime

THE VICTIMIZATION OF GIRLS AND WOMEN BY BOYS AND MEN: COMPETING ANALYTICAL FRAMEWORKS

Andrew Karmen

The articles in this section focus on acts of male-on-female aggression—especially forcible rapes and beatings, but also stalkings, sexual harassment and exploitation, and certain murders. For centuries, the plight of girls and women victimized in these ways was largely overlooked because of entrenched sexism within the male-dominated legal system. Now, how well or how poorly the criminal justice system routinely addresses the needs of female crime victims is finally being systematically examined.

However, bitter disagreements about the specific causes of and cures for the violence that men direct at women still divide academic researchers, government policy makers, practitioners in the helping professions, victim advocates, political activists, police administrators, prosecutors, defense attorneys, judges, jurors, students of criminal justice, and members of the public. Therefore, the primary contribution of this introduction is to provide a framework for classifying and understanding the clashing ideological interpretations of the nature of the problem (what is wrong) and its possible solutions (what must change).

WEBSITES

The following websites contain material on women victims and survivors of violence against them. New websites are continuously being developed while at the same time others disappear. Check with a search engine, such as Google at www.google.com, to locate additional information. Insert a key word (rape) or phrase (violence against women, domestic violence) or organization (Survivor Project) in order to locate additional references.

Domestic Violence

Callie Marie Rennison and Sarah Welchans. *Intimate Partner Violence*. Bureau of Justice Statistics Special Report. Can be found at
www.ojp.usdoj.gov/bjs/pub/pdf/ipv.pdf

Patricia Tjaden and Nancy Thoennes. *Full Report of the Prevalence, Incidence, and Consequences of Violence against Women: Findings of the National Violence against Women Survey*. November 2000 (NCJ-183781). National Institute of Justice/Centers for Disease Control and Prevention. Available at
www.rainn.org/fullnvawsurvey.pdf

"Violence against Women of Color. Incite! Women of Color against Violence." Available at
www.incite-national.org/issues/violence.html

"Family Violence: Basic Data." For access to Violence against Women; Child Abuse; Elder Abuse, go to
www.pcvp.org/pcvp/media/familyv.html

Centers for Disease Control and Prevention. "Intimate Partner Violence Fact Sheet." Can be found at
www.cdc.gov/ncipc/factsheets/ipvfacts.htm

Diana Courvant and Loree Cook-Daniels. "Trans and Intersex Survivors of Domestic Violence: Defining Terms, Barriers, and Responsibilities." Available at
www.survivorproject.org/defbarresp.html

Emi Koyama. "Toward a Harm Reduction Approach in Survivor Advocacy." Available at
http://eminism.org/readings/harmreduction.html

Human Rights Watch has reports on domestic violence at
www.hrw.org/women/domesticviolence.html

THREE COMPETING FRAMEWORKS: VICTIM-BLAMING VERSUS VICTIM-DEFENDING AND OFFENDER BLAMING VERSUS INSTITUTION FAULTING

Whenever offenders harm victims, whether through property crimes like burglary or auto theft or through interpersonal acts of violence such as assaults, the question inevitably arises, "Who—or what—is to blame?" Determining responsibility is an important matter in terms of social policy because isolating a "root cause" can lead to a "cure." Three distinct responses usually can be discerned (see Karmen 2001), and they lead to very different courses of action when applied to the gender-based crimes of forcible rape, partner battering, stalking, street harassment, and certain killings of girls and women (see Mechanic and Uhlmansiek 2000).

Victim-blaming faults the injured party and holds her accountable to a greater or lesser degree for what happened. *Victim-defending* (coupled with *offender-blaming*) rejects as unfounded and unfair the accusation that the injured party's downfall was partly of her own doing and insists that the offender alone is fully culpable for choosing to violate the law and inflicting pain and suffering. A more macroscopic *institution faulting* analysis tries to transcend the microscopic tendencies inherent in the first two perspectives to merely scrutinize the particular words and deeds of both parties in specific incidents—who said and did what—without taking the larger social context into account. This third approach does not overlook or deny that offenders bear responsibility for their crimes or that their targets have the potential for "agency" before, during, and after the attack. But it emphasizes a fundamental insight of sociology: that all people—assailants as well as their victims—are largely products of their social environments; their attitudes and behaviors are profoundly shaped by conditions not of their choosing and largely beyond their individual abilities to escape or control. In any social system, the culture (the mainstream way of life), structure (how society is organized), and institutions (established methods of accomplishing functions) serve as outside influences that pressure both males and females to play out their well-rehearsed roles as aggressors and sufferers in an all-too-familiar tragedy.

Blaming Victims for Their Plight

Victim-blaming proceeds from the assumption that those who suffer misfortunes are different from non-victims in terms of their outlooks and actions and that these self-defeating attitudes and behaviors are presumed to be the source of their miseries. To avoid any further trouble in the future, victims must change their ways (see Ryan 1971). By closely examining the injured party's actions right before and during the crime, it becomes "obvious"—in hindsight—what she should have said and ought to have done to avoid being sexually harassed, stalked, attacked, raped, even murdered.

Victim-blaming assumes that there are certain kinds of women who go around asking for trouble and eventually get themselves raped. Such harsh condemnations rest on two premises: that the offender was overwhelmed by sexual desire and lost his self-control and that the victim somehow facilitated the assault (perhaps through drugs or alcohol), thoughtlessly precipitated it (by setting up a temptation-opportunity situation in which she was isolated from sources of outside help), or even provoked his overpowering response (by suggestive and seductive words or deeds; see Gibbs 1991). Victim-blaming chastises women who suffer sexual assaults for acts of omission (not being cautious enough) as well as acts of commission, like hitchhiking (Amir 1971). The victim-blaming interpretation of date rape characterizes the incident as a terrible misunderstanding in "he said–she said" terms: he says she wanted to, whereas she says he forced her. This kind of miscommunication can result when a woman gives off mixed messages, fails to make her true intentions clear, and doesn't protest vehemently enough about unwanted sexual advances, a common problem during this period of rapid change in courtship rituals, sexual mores, and the rules of the dating game (see Warshaw 1988; Muelenhard et al. 1992). In extreme

Feminist Internet Gateway on Violence against Women (describes a variety of violence against women organizations and resources). Can be found at **www.feminist.org/gateway/vs_exec2.html**

California Coalition for Battered Women in Prison. Can be found at **http://freebatteredwomen.org/resource.htm**

Dating Violence, Rape, and Marital Rape

Jay Silverman, Anita Raj, Lorelei Mucci, and Jeanne Hathaway. Dating Violence Against Adolescent Girls and Associated Substance Use, Unhealthy Weight Control, Sexual Risk Behavior, Pregnancy, and Suicidality. *Journal of American Medical Association*, 286 (5), August 1, 2001. Available at **http://jama.ama.assn.org**

Bonnie Fisher, Francis Cullen, and Michael Turner. The Sexual Victimization of College Women. National Institute of Justice, December 2000 (NCJ-182369). Available at **www.ojp.usdoj.gov/bjs**

"Dating Violence." Centers for Disease Control and Prevention. Available at **www.cdc.gov/ncipc/factsheets/datviol.htm**

Cybergirls (domestic and dating violence information) at **www.cybergirl.com**

Men Can Stop Rape. Can be found at **www.mencanstoprape.org/**

National Clearinghouse on Marital and Date Rape/Women's History Library can be found at **http://members.aol.com/ncmdr/links.html**

Marital Rape at **www.vaw.umn.edu/Vawnet/mrape.htm**

Sexual Harassment

"Information on Sexual Harassment" has links to sexual harassment in schools, in the workplace, in the military, against lesbians and gay men both internationally and in the United States. Can be found at **www.de.psu.edu/harassment/webpages/**

Sexual Harassment in Schools can be found at **www.ed.gov/offices/OCR/index.html**

and relevant publications can be found at
www.ed.gov/offices/OCR/publications.html

National Organization for Women report on sexual
harassment in the workplace can be found at
www.now.org/issues/harass/issuerep.html

Trafficking in Women and Girls

For a series of articles including "Dreams Ending in
Nightmares: Many Immigrant Women, Girls Trapped in
Sex Industry," (New York) *Newsday,* March 11, 2001, go to
www.newsday.com

Global Alliance against Trafficking in Women can be
found at
www.inet.co.th/org/gaatw

Human Rights Watch has reports on trafficking in
women at
www.hrw.org/women/trafficking.html

Stop Traffic at
www.stop-traffic.org

Stalking

Patricia Tjaden and Nancy Thoennes. Stalking in
America: Findings from the National Violence against
Women Survey. NIJ/CDC. April 1998. Can be found at
www.ncjrs.org/pdffiles/169592.pdf

Stalking and Domestic Violence. NCJ-172204. July 1998.
Can be found at
www.ojp.usdoj.gov/vawo/grants/stalk98.pdf

Anti-stalking website has research studies and resources
for stalking victims at
www.antistalking.com

National Institute of Justice has stalking information at
the following website:
http://www.ojp.usdoj.gov/nij
Click on "programs" for a description of the agency's
violence against women and family violence programs.

NCJRS has a victims page on stalking with numerous
references. Can be found at
**http://virlib.ncjrs.org/more.asp?category=51&sub
category=150**

versions of victim-blaming, the woman's mental
health is questioned for setting up a situation that en-
acts her secretly harbored fantasies of being taken
against her will (see MacDonald 1971).

The victim-blaming approach places the burden
of rape prevention squarely on the backs of potential
victims (see Brownmiller 1975). They must take precautions to reduce the risks they face by imposing
strict limits on themselves in terms of the males they
interact with, what clothing styles they wear, what
they say, and where and when they travel. They are
told they must observe the old-fashioned restrictions
of respectable behavior and the traditions of defensive
dating.

Similarly, a battered woman must have done
something wrong to infuriate her partner and provoke his wrath, according to the victim-blaming
perspective. Often the battered woman is "damned if
she does and damned if she doesn't." She is condemned if she arouses his anger by her assertive
actions but she is also faulted if she invites abuse by
her submissiveness. She is denounced either for
masochistically enjoying the suffering inflicted by
his beatings or for starting fights simply because she
treasures the period of tenderness that follows when
they make up. She is criticized if she breaks up the
family by deserting him, or she is belittled for not
leaving him (see Walker 1984; Pagelow 1984; Frieze
and Browne 1989).

If the cycle of violence spirals upward and a battered woman kills her abusive mate, she is castigated
for turning the tables, reversing roles, and transforming into a vigilante, appointing herself as judge, jury,
and executioner. She is condemned for not exhausting all other options (having him arrested, getting an
order of protection from the courts, fleeing their
home to escape his clutches) before resorting to
deadly force. Her violence cannot be excused and
must be punished, victim-blaming prosecutors,
judges, and juries conclude (see Stevens 1999;
Leonard 2001).

Victim-blaming's appeal lies in its apparently re-
assuring message (to outside observers) that a just
world exists (Maes 1994). Tragedy and trouble don't
strike at random; victims must have done something

wrong and hence deserve to suffer (see Ford, Liwag, and Foley 1998; Lambert and Raichle 2000). Also, victim-blaming is in sync with the popular doctrine of "no excuses" that holds individuals fully responsible for their own fate (and disregards intensely influential unresolved social problems that afflict millions of people). Finally, this perspective seems to promote an empowering message that encourages a variety of "agency": Females are not necessarily the weaker sex, and they need not feel hopelessly vulnerable and accept their lot with passivity. Girls can profit from the misfortunes of others if they can avoid making the same foolish mistakes or rash decisions. They must use common sense and watch what they say, how they dress, and how they act. Women must learn how to defuse male anger and learn ways to limit their exposure to risky situations and potentially dangerous characters. Defensive tactics and risk-reduction measures incorporated into lifestyles and routine activities can enhance personal security, even if the world can't be remade into a more equitable and safe place to live.

Defending Victims from Charges That They Are Partly to Blame

Victim-defending, like victim-blaming, takes an up close and personal interactionist look at how the incident unfolded. But victim-defending regards victim-blaming as a validation of the offender's point of view because it shifts some of the burden of responsibility from the perpetrator to his target. Victim-defending seeks to expose the falseness and unfairness of accusations of victim facilitation, cooperation, precipitation, escalation, or provocation. Whatever happened was not her fault in any legal, moral, or even practical sense. Her attitudes and behaviors are not strikingly different from the thoughts and actions of nonvictims, and she does not have to change her ways. The risk-reduction strategies recommended by victim-blaming impose unreasonable restrictions on active lifestyles that undercut the struggle for women's equality. After defending the victim from what are considered to be false allegations, this perspective evolves either into mere offender-blaming

Violence against Women in the Military

Domestic Violence in the Military. "Facts and Statistics." Can be found at **http://userpages.aug.com/captbarb/violence.html**

A series of articles and resources on domestic violence in the armed services can be found at **www.defenselink.mil/specials/domesticviolence/**

Gregory Flannery. "Military Rape: The Ugly Secret in the American Armed Forces." *Cincinnati City Beat,* 8 (41), August 22–28, 2002. Can be found at **www.citybeat.com/2002-08-22/printable/news2.html**

Sexual harassment of women in the military can be found at **www.feminist.org/911/sexharnews_military.html**

Other Forms of Violence against Women

Human Rights Watch has reports on sexual violence against women in armed conflict at **www.hrw.org/women/sexualviolence.html**

Human Rights Watch has a report titled "Hidden in the Home: Abuse of Domestic Workers in the U.S." at **www.hrw.org/reports/2001/usadom/**

Human Rights Watch has a report titled "Hatred in the Hallways: Violence and Discrimination against Lesbian, Gay, Bisexual, and Transgendered Students in U.S. Schools" at **www.hrw.org/reports/2001/uslgbt**

or into a more complex understanding that centers on institution-faulting (which holds the criminal largely but not totally responsible for his behavior).

In the early 1970s, antirape activists developed victim-defending perspectives as they challenged the widely held traditional view that attributed sexual assaults to outpourings of uncontrollable lust stimulated knowingly or unwittingly by women's seductive behavior. Sexual assaults were reinterpreted as outbursts of aggression fueled by hatred and contempt and motivated by a desire to dominate, subjugate, and humiliate. Nothing suggestive or erotic that she said, wore, or did could trigger or justify such hostile and degrading reactions from a complete stranger, or an acquaintance, or even an intimate (see Clark and Lewis 1978 and Griffin 1979 for a comprehensive rejection of these "old-fashioned" views).

As for date rapes, victim-defending asserts that whenever forced intercourse occurs, a real rape has been committed and not a seduction as the culmination of a romantic courtship ritual nor a terrible misunderstanding stemming from miscommunication. The boy or man has used coercion to take from her what he wanted and planned to get all along, violating her personhood in the process. Furthermore, any silence, passivity, or lack of physical resistance on her part should not be taken as a sign of apparent acquiescence, because that kind of interpretation overlooks the paralyzing effects of the aggressor's overwhelming physical strength, his use of force at the outset, his tactics that caught the victim by surprise, or the implied threat posed by the presence of a weapon (see LaFree 1989).

As for woman-battering, victim-defending argues that a boyfriend's or husband's violence really is not triggered by his partner's shortcomings or instigations. His attempts to pin responsibility on her provocations are just rationalizations designed to justify and excuse his controlling behavior. Victim-defending provides a number of reasons why battered women stay with their abusive mates: they still love their partners and cling to the belief that their men can and will change, as the aggressors so often promise to do. Battered women often feel trapped (economically dependent and socially isolated); they worry about their children's welfare (emotional damage, loss of support or of custody); and they are burdened by guilt and shame because of cultural and religious exhortations against abandoning a husband in a failed marriage. Some women are intimidated by jealously possessive men who are obsessed by a mentality of "You belong to me" and "If I can't have you, no one else will," who threaten severe reprisals if their partners dare to try to escape. These victims often do not call the police during a beating because they have been raised to believe that their tribulations behind closed doors are a private matter that is not the law's business. When called to the scene, officers might side with the man, or arrest both parties, or pressure the woman to leave, or insist that she seek professional help and marital counseling, or proceed with the prosecution even if she wants to drop the charges (see Frieze and Browne 1989; Barnett and LaViolette 1993; Bennett, Goodman, and Dutton 1999).

When a battered woman kills her abusive mate, the victim-defending perspective identifies with the survivor and charges that the dead man is not the genuine victim but rather a chronic offender who provoked his own demise. She had turned to the criminal justice system but it was either unresponsive or its services (arrest, order of protection, prosecution, conviction, punishment, compulsory treatment) failed to stem the cycle of violence. She tried to escape but he tracked her down and became even angrier with her. She lived in constant fear, even when she was not under immediate attack, and eventually committed a justifiable homicide in self-defense (see Jones 1980; Browne 1987; Walker 1989; Bannister 1992).

Victim-defending's appeal arises from its embodiment of the most elemental principles of justice: don't add insult to injury by trying to find some reason to fault the behavior of individuals targeted by wrongdoers. Instead, condemn the lawbreaker and punish him. When coupled with offender-blaming in this dichotomous framework of totally innocent or completely guilty, victim-defending offers a simple and seemingly practical solution to immediate problems and future threats: try to improve the effectiveness of the criminal justice system as a public safety mechanism to weed out those males who pose a clear and present danger to females. Stalkers, batterers, lesbian-bashers, street harassers, child molesters, rapists, and other predators must be arrested, prosecuted, convicted, and incarcerated and then kept under tight control after they are released.

Exposing the Institutional Roots of Female Victimization

An institutional analysis attempts to go beyond either victim-blaming or victim-defending and offender-blaming. Both perspectives are considered to be inadequate, nearsighted frameworks that focus on the roles and scripts of the two leading actors in the drama and, in so doing, overlook the supporting cast and the background that impact on everyone's attitudes, judgments, and decisions. Although the facts surrounding each crime are important and although reconstructing the motives, actions, and responses of both parties is a worthwhile and necessary endeavor, such a limited interactionist approach fails to account for the influences of outside forces. Providing some context for specific incidents clarifies how these all-too-common forms of interpersonal conflicts are outgrowths of flawed social institutions, such as families, schooling, the job market, and the criminal justice system. A recognition of the role played by societal institutions does not relieve the offender of his criminal responsibility or excuse his wrongdoing, and it does not deny that the victim has "agency" or freedom of action to avoid, escape, or resist the attack or to transcend the ordeal and become a survivor. But instead of merely putting either the lawbreaker or his victim "on trial," institution-blaming indicts the system and refuses to let it off the hook for the violence it generates. Moreover, an analysis of the responsibility for the problem borne by basic social institutions leads to the conclusion that worthy efforts to rehabilitate offenders and to assist victims to recover do not eradicate the sources of violence and victimization.

The root causes of stalking, battering, molesting, and forcible rape are believed to be structural (built-in to the system): the irrationalities embedded in prevailing economic arrangements; inequities in the distribution of power and

wealth; intense competition over scarce resources and desirable jobs; the limitations of nuclear families; harmful child-rearing practices; discriminatory mechanisms based on social class, race and ethnicity, and gender; oppressive cultural
traditions; outmoded religious teachings; and the exploitive norms of patriarchy
that bolster male domination and female subordination.

A thorough and sound institutional analysis takes into account the difficulties
and special needs that victims face if they are subjected to the multiple burdens
of discriminatory practices because they are of the "wrong" social class, racial or
ethnic group, or sexual orientation. For example, an institutional analysis of
wife-beating addresses the shortcomings of merely instructing women about
how to cope with their husband's efforts to totally dominate them, or of count-
ing on the police to arrest the batterer. Victims of partner violence need shelters
for refuge during a crisis, staffed by advocates who can provide culturally sensitive emotional support and concrete services like counseling about legal matters
(concerning separation, divorce, and child custody). In order to make the transition from victim to survivor, battered women need training and meaningful
access to jobs that pay a living wage to permit financial independence; high-
quality affordable child care; low-cost higher education opportunities; decent
and reasonably priced permanent housing; and supportive public assistance policies (see Websdale and Johnson 1997; Fine and Weis 2000).

The most valuable contribution of an institutional analysis is that it provides
context by showing how the broader social environment and the specific social
background of the participants is relevant to a more complete understanding of
social problems and the exercise of what appears to be "free will" by individuals.
A study of the impact of institutions, structures, and cultures points to the intersection (see Sokoloff and Dupont 2002), or overlapping, of accumulated disadvantages that limit the freedom of action and options of victims who come from
poverty-stricken families in a money-based society; or who are members of dis-
favored racial or sexual minority groups (see Wyatt 1992); or whose native
tongues or cultures are not the predominant ones (see Dasgupta, chap. 22).

IDENTIFYING THE THREE PERSPECTIVES IN ACTION

It is not productive to try to categorize individuals as either victim-blamers,
victim-defenders, offender-blamers, or critics of existing institutional arrangements. Most people are not ideologically consistent but rather espouse a complex mixture of views and allegiances, depending on the nature of the crime, the
circumstances, and the particular man and woman involved in the incident. It is
more constructive to identify victim-blaming arguments, victim-defending re-
buttals, offender-blaming policies, and institution-faulting recommendations for
reform in discussions of specific incidents featured in the news, in debates over
the intended impact of new laws, in a candidate's campaign promises, or in studies concerning violence against women.

Does the research conclude that both partners in outbreaks of mutual combat between intimates share responsibility for their violent conflicts (see Moffitt,

Robins, and Caspi 2001)? Does the study emphasize the debilitating effects of drinking (Corbin, Bernat, and Calhoun 2001) or taking drugs (Flack, Wang, and Carlson 2001) as risk factors that heighten a potential target's vulnerability to a sexual assault? If so, then studies like these are establishing the basis for victim-blaming (see Winkel and Denkers 1995). Is the question framed as, Which groups are most prone to accept the traditional negative stereotypes and even the myths about women who get stalked and harassed (Cowan 2000), battered (Chornesky 2000), or raped (see Koss 2000; Lambert and Raichle 2000; Bondurant 2001; Carmody and Washington 2001; and Monto and Hotaling 2001)? If so, these research projects are advancing victim-defending arguments. However, an analysis on the institutional level has been carried out whenever a study exposes cultural supports for the victimization of females—as are found in some military units, college fraternities, and sports teams—in which young women are disparaged as mere pawns, trophies, or sex objects and behavior labeled as "feminine" is mocked and demeaned (see Martin and Hummer 1989; Buchwald, Fletcher, and Roth 1993; and Humphrey and Kahn 2000). Another level of institutional analysis, focusing on social structure, takes place when the goal is how to reform the legal system or economic system to counteract long-standing social disadvantages and facilitate the empowerment of battered women (see Schneider 2000 and Smith 2001).

The stakes are very high in this three-sided debate, because performing a diagnosis of the reasons why males victimize females is a prerequisite for developing effective crime control and prevention strategies. If key social institutions churn out one generation after another of exploitive and abusive males, then the offender-blaming strategy of relying on the machinery of criminal justice to effectively incapacitate and hopefully rehabilitate dangerous deviants one case at a time seems doomed as too little too late. Furthermore, to count on the good intentions of the largely male leadership of legislatures, law enforcement agencies, prosecutors' offices, the judiciary, prisons, probation departments, and parole divisions to protect girls and women from predatory boys and men is an unpromising strategy at best. Even less productive are the mere stop-gap "dos and don'ts" exhortations derived from victim-blaming that pressure girls and women to be more crime-conscious and to take greater precautions to thwart the desires of the sexually and physically aggressive males they are sure to encounter (see Lederer 1980). If the "social institutions are largely responsible" perspective makes sense, it follows that sweeping changes are necessary: Genuine equality that permits individual autonomy, self-actualization, and empowerment must replace traditional modes of control—for both women and men; subtle as well as blatant mechanisms of discrimination on the basis of social class or race or ethnicity must be overcome; and women and men must work in close collaboration to raise boys and girls to think about and act toward one another in entirely new ways. Social movements struggling on many fronts are needed to overhaul contemporary society's basic institutions—the root causes of female vulnerability to victimization—and to empower survivors of stalkings, beatings, and sexual assaults (see Smart 1995; Richie 1996; Chancer 1998; Robinson and Chandek

2000; Sokoloff 2003). Otherwise, the persistence of crimes by males against females as a widespread and acute problem is ensured.

The articles in part 3, for the most part, present an analysis that zeroes in on the institutions, structures, and cultural supports that are believed to be responsible for the victimization of girls and women by boys and men. Websdale and Chesney-Lind (chap. 18, "Doing Violence to Women: Research Synthesis on the Victimization of Women") recount the many forms that male aggression can take (from abuse to murder) and conclude that the common denominator is the prevalence of a structure of "hetero-patriarchical" control that imposes a constellation of disadvantages on females throughout history and across the globe. Feltey (chap. 19, "Gender Violence: Rape and Sexual Assault") classifies sexual assault as a form of gender violence that is encouraged by victim-blaming myths and pro-rape cultural themes. Wriggins (chap. 20, "Rape, Racism, and the Law") exposes the criminal justice system's double standard regarding victim-offender combinations, by chronicling how, from the time of slavery in the United States, the rape of black women by white men never provoked the level of outrage or vigorous prosecution (and certainly not the lynchings) that resulted from incidents in which black men raped white women. This dichotomy remains true today. Browne (chap. 21, "Fear and Perception of Alternatives: Asking 'Why Battered Women Don't Leave' Is the Wrong Question") examines in depth the reasons why a small number of battered women are driven to kill their tormentors. Her victim-defending analysis focuses on the seriousness of the threat posed by the men rather than on the mental states of the women. Dasgupta (chap. 22, "Women's Realities: Defining Violence against Women by Immigration, Race, and Class") dispels some misconceptions surrounding intimate partner violence among recent immigrants and diagrams how the problem is nested within supportive circles of the community's cultural values and its patriarchal institutions. Marriage and welfare laws and insensitive criminal justice policies also contribute to newcomers' problems of isolation, vulnerability, and subordination. West's review (chap. 23, "Leaving a Second Closet: 'Outing' Partner Violence in Same-Sex Couples") of the similarities and differences surrounding partner abuse in same-sex couples and opposite-sex couples identifies drug-taking and a legacy of family violence as offender-blaming (and even victim-blaming) factors. But the chapter also highlights the importance of focusing on two cultural factors, internalized homophobia and a tendency to divide up domestic labor inequitably—as potential sources of role conflict that create both offenders and victims. Griggs (chap. 24, "Domestic Violence in Police Families") calls attention to the difficulties of enforcing the law firmly and impartially in defense of all victims when the wrongdoers are members of a law enforcement agency. Presser and Gaarder (chap. 25, "Can Restorative Justice Reduce Battering?") question whether the traditional structure of retributive criminal justice should be supplanted by a nonpunitive paradigm, which is the goal of the rapidly growing restorative justice movement. Rundblad (chap. 26, "Gender, Power, and Sexual Harassment") shows how the sexual harassment of subordinates is a structural problem that results in lawsuits by victims but actually requires a redistribution of power to resolve. Wijers (chap. 27, "Women, Labor, and

Migration: The Position of Trafficked Women and Strategies for Support") and an article from *Newsday* (chap. 28, "Dreams Ending in Nightmares: Many Immigrant Women, Girls Trapped in Sex Industry") shine a light on organized crime's latest racket—smuggling desperate and vulnerable immigrants across borders in order to exploit them, particularly in the sex trade. An understanding of why teenage girls and women subject themselves to the debasement and dangers of prostitution must take into account their limited opportunities for economic subsistence in their home countries and must be compared to the seemingly more rewarding prospects of becoming a sex worker in the unregulated, all-cash underground economy that has become entrenched within relatively more prosperous societies, including the United States.

All the chapters in part 3 stress the importance of an analysis of traditional institutions, social structures, and cultural supports because their authors believe that these outside influences must be understood if injustices are to be corrected and social conflicts resolved. But the crucial question for readers that remains to be answered is, Do each of these three competing frameworks contribute toward helping victims recover and preventing future crimes? Read the following set of articles and then decide.

REFERENCES

Amir, M. 1971. *Patterns in Forcible Rape.* Chicago: University of Chicago.

Bannister, S. 1992. Battered Women Who Kill Their Abusers: Their Courtroom Battles. In *It's a Crime: Women and Justice,* ed. R. Muraskin and T. Alleman, 316–333. Englewood Cliffs, NJ: Regents/Prentice Hall.

Barnett, O., and A. LaViolette. 1993. *It Could Happen to Anyone: Why Battered Women Stay.* Newbury Park, CA: Sage.

Bennett, L., L. Goodman, and M. Dutton. 1999. Systematic Obstacles to the Criminal Prosecution of a Battering Partner: A Victim Perspective. *Journal of Interpersonal Violence* 14(7):761–772.

Bondurant, B. 2001. University Women's Acknowledgement of Rape: Individual, Situational, and Social Factors. *Violence against Women* 7(3):294–314.

Browne, A. 1987. *When Battered Women Kill.* New York: Free Press.

Brownmiller, S. 1975. *Against Our Will: Men, Women, and Rape.* New York: Simon and Schuster.

Buchwald, E., P. Fletcher, and M. Roth. 1993. *Transforming a Rape Culture.* Minneapolis, MN: Milkwood Editions.

Carmody, D., and L. Washington. 2001. Rape Myth Acceptance among College Women. *Journal of Interpersonal Violence* 16(5):424–436.

Chancer, L. 1998. Gender, Class, and Race in Three High Profile Crimes. In *Crime Control and Women: Feminist Implications of Criminal Justice Policy,* ed. S. Miller, 72–94. Thousand Oaks, CA: Sage.

Chornesky, A. 2000. The Dynamics of Battering Revisited. *Journal of Women and Social Work* 15(4):480–501.

Clark, L., and D. Lewis. 1978. *Rape: The Price of Coercive Sexuality.* Toronto: The Woman's Press.

Corbin, W., J. Bernat, and K. Calhoun. 2001. The Role of Alcohol Expectancies and Alcohol Consumption among Sexually Victimized and Non-Victimized College Women. *Journal of Interpersonal Violence* 16(4):297–311.

Cowan, G. 2000. Women's Hostility toward Women and Rape and Sexual Harassment Myths. *Violence Against Women* 6(3):238–246.

Elias, R. 1986. *The Politics of Victimization: Victims, Victimology, and Human Rights.* New York: Oxford University.

Estrich, S. 1986. *Real Rape.* Cambridge: Harvard University.

Flack, R., J. Wang, and R. Carlson. 2001. The Epidemiology of Physical Attack and Rape among Crack-Using Women. *Violence and Victim* 16(1):79–89.

Fine, M., and L. Weis. 2000. Disappearing Acts: The State and Violence against Women in the Twentieth Century. *Signs* 25(4):1139-1146.

Ford, T., M. Liwag, and L. Foley. 1998. Perceptions of Rape Based on Sex and Sexual Orientation of Victims. *Journal of Social Behavior and Personality* 13(2):253–263.

Frieze, I., and A. Browne. 1989. Violence in Marriage. In *Crime and Justice: An Annual Review of Research,* vol. 10, ed. L. Ohlin and M. Tonry, 163–218. Chicago: University of Chicago.

Gibbs, N. 1991. When Is It Rape? *Time* magazine, June 3, 48–55.

Gillespie, C. 1989. *Battered Women, Self-Defense, and the Law.* Columbus: Ohio State University.

Goldberg-Ambrose, C. 1992. Unfinished Business in Rape Law Reform. *Journal of Social Issues* 48(1):173–185.

Griffin, S. 1979. *Rape: The Power of Consciousness.* New York: Harper and Row.

Humphrey, S., and A. Kahn. 2000. Fraternities, Athletic Teams, and Rape. *Journal of Interpersonal Violence* 15(12):1313–1322.

Jones, A. 1980. *Women Who Kill.* New York: Holt, Rinehart, and Winston.

Karmen, A. 2001. *Crime Victims: An Introduction to Victimology,* 4th ed. Belmont, CA: Wadsworth.

Koss, M. 2000. Blame, Shame, and Community: Justice Responses to Violence against Women. *American Psychologist* 55(11):1332–1343.

LaFree, G. 1989. *Rape and Criminal Justice.* Santa Fe: University of New Mexico.

Lambert, A., and K. Raichle. 2000. The Role of Political Ideology in Mediating Judgments of Blame in Rape Victims and Their Assailants. *Personality and Social Psychology Bulletin* 26(7):853–863.

Largen, M. 1981. Grassroots Centers and National Task Forces: A Herstory of the Anti-Rape Movement. *Aegis* 32 (Autumn):46–52.

Largen, M. 1987. A Decade of Change in the Rape Reform Movement. *Response* 10(2):4–9.

Lederer, L. 1980. *Take Back the Night.* New York: Morrow.

LeGrande, C. 1973. Rape and Rape Laws: Sexism in Society and the Law. *California Law Review* 61:919–941.

Leonard, E. 2001. Convicted Survivors: Comparing and Describing California's Battered Women's Inmates. *Prison Journal* 81(1):73–86.

MacDonald, J. 1971. *Rape: Offenders and Victims.* Springfield, IL: Charles C. Thomas.

Maes, J. 1994. Blaming the Victim: Belief in Control or Belief in Justice. *Social Justice Research* 7(1):69–90.

Marsh, J., A. Geist, and N. Caplan. 1982. *Rape and the Limits of Law Reform.* Boston: Auburn House.

Martin, D. 1976. *Battered Wives.* San Francisco: Glide.

Martin, P., and R. Hummer. 1989. Fraternities and Rape on Campus. *Gender and Society* 3 (December):457–473.

Mechanic, M., and M. Uhlmansiek. 2000. The Impact of Severe Stalking Experienced by Acutely Battered Women. *Violence and Victims* 15(4):443–458.

Moffitt, T., R. Robins, and A. Caspi. 2001. A Couples Analysis of Partner Abuse with Implications for Abuse-Prevention Policy. *Criminology and Public Policy* 1(1):5–36.

Monto, M., and N. Hotaling. 2001. Predictors of Rape Myth Acceptance among the Male Clients of Female Street Prostitutes. *Violence against Women* 7(3):275–293.

Muelenhard, C., I. Powch, J. Phelps, and L. Giusti. 1992. Definitions of Rape: Scientific and Political Implications. *Journal of Social Issues* 48(1):23–44.

O'Neill, D. 1998. A Post-Structuralist Review of the Theoretical Literature Surrounding Wife Abuse. *Violence against Women* 4:457–490.

Pagelow, M. 1984. *Women-Battering: Victims and Their Experiences.* Beverly Hills, CA: Sage.

Rafter, N. 1990. The Social Construction of Crime and Crime Control. *Journal of Research in Crime and Delinquency* 27(4):376–389.

Richie, B. 1996. *Compelled to Crime: The Gender Entrapment of Battered Black Women.* New York: Routledge.

Robinson, A., and M. Chandek. 2000. Differential Police Response to Black Battered Women. *Women and Criminal Justice* 12(2):29–61.

Ryan, W. 1971. *Blaming the Victim.* New York: Vintage.

Schneider, E. M. 2000. *Battered Women and Feminist Lawmaking.* New Haven, CT: Yale University.

Schwendinger, H., and J. Schwendinger. 1983. *Rape and Inequality.* Beverly Hills, CA: Sage.

Smart, C. 1995. *Law, Crime, and Sexuality.* London: Sage.

Smith, A. 2001. Domestic Violence Laws: The Voices of Battered Women. *Violence and Victims* 16(1):91–111.

Sokoloff, N. J., and I. Dupont. 2004. Domestic Violence: Examining the Intersections of Race, Class, and Gender. In *Domestic Violence: At the Intersections of Race, Class, and Gender in the United States,* ed. N. J. Sokoloff. New York: Routledge (forthcoming).

Sokoloff, N. J. 2004. *At the Intersections of Race, Class, and Gender in the United States.* ed. N. J. Sokoloff. New York: Routledge (forthcoming).

Stevens, D. 1999. Interviews with Women Convicted of Murder: Battered Women's Syndrome Revisited. *International Review of Victimology* 6(2):117–135.

Straus, M., R. Gelles, and S. Steinmetz. 1980. *Behind Closed Doors: Violence in the American Family.* New York: Doubleday.

Walker, L. 1984. *The Battered Woman Syndrome.* New York: Springer.

Walker, L. 1989. *Terrifying Love: Why Battered Women Kill and How Society Responds.* New York: Harper and Row.

Warshaw, R. 1988. *I Never Called It Rape.* New York: Harper and Row.

Websdale, N., and B. Johnson. 1997. Structural Approaches to Reducing Woman-Battering. *Social Justice* 24:54–81.

Winkel, F., and A. Denkers. 1995. Crime Victims and Their Social Network: A Field Study on the Cognitive Effects of Victimization, Attributional Responses, and the Victim-Blaming Model. *International Review of Victimology* 3(4):309–322.

Wyatt, G. 1992. The Sociocultural Context of African American and White American Women's Rape. *Journal of Social Issues* 48(1):77–91.

Chapter 18

Doing Violence to Women:
Research Synthesis on the Victimization of Women

Neil Websdale and Meda Chesney-Lind

ABSTRACT

This chapter introduces part 3, by providing an overview of violence against women. Websdale and Chesney-Lind note that violence takes many forms: physical and sexual violence, economic violence, and institutional violence as well as emotional abuse and psychological torture. Based on the research of feminist scholars, the hard facts are that men commit much more violence against women (and other men) than women commit against men or other women.

From this basic understanding, Websdale and Chesney-Lind go on to describe the numerous types of both nonlethal and lethal violence. They devote a section to mass killings as a special form of male violence against women. Much of the violence against women is sexual, and the authors divide this type into violence by men known to their victims—for example, husbands, fathers, boyfriends, neighbors (which is the most common)*—and that which occurs by men who are not known to the victims. These latter abusers include street predators, soldiers, and religious and ethnic zealots. Websdale and Chesney-Lind explain these old concepts in new ways. For example, the authors discuss the gendered nature of war and argue that the mass rape of women must be understood in the wider context of violence in war and ethnic cleansing.

Two other sections of the chapter are devoted to victimization, first, of prostitutes and, second, of imprisoned women. For an alternate understanding of violence and prostitution than the one in this chapter, make sure to see Kempadoo (chap. 8). Kempadoo argues that prostitution must be recognized as sex work, one type of women's labor; once prostitution is recognized as legitimate work (even if considered socially undesirable by many), women working

---

*The National Violence against Women Survey sponsored by the National Institute of Justice and the Centers for Disease Control and Prevention confirmed past studies that have found that most violence against women is primarily intimate partner violence (see Patricia Tjaden and Nancy Thoennes. 2000. *Extent, Nature, and Consequences of Intimate Partner Violence: Findings from the National Violence against Women Survey*). Washington DC: National Institute of Justice. NCJ-181867

as prostitutes can be provided with safeguards that other unionized labor offers. Abuse of women prisoners is covered in depth by Siegal (chap. 16).

Websdale and Chesney-Lind end this chapter by expanding on the fact that despite the reality that "hetero-patriarchy" (heterosexually dominated patriarchy) does not take the same form in all societies, violence against women is not limited to certain political and economic systems; it seems to be present everywhere, although not always to the same harsh degree. The earlier, narrow view that women are at risk mostly from predatory male strangers is replaced here by an account of the pervasive, entrenched nature of violence against women at individual as well as societal levels, by both intimates and strangers, by both individuals and groups of men, and by the state. As the authors conclude: "To make sense of male violence against women, then, is to grasp the limited social, political, and economic opportunities available to women. Women do not enjoy or invite male violence. They are not responsible for that violence and they are not susceptible to it because of certain psychological frailties. Rather, the constellation of disadvantaged situations women live out expose them to violence at the hands of men." As you read through this chapter, try to locate the socially structured and culturally approved "constellation of disadvantaged situations" encountered by women from diverse backgrounds. What social policies would be needed to change those situations that are conducive to violence against women?

At the World Conference on Women, held in 1999 in Beijing and Huairou, China, women from across the world shared their political and cultural experiences. Many topics surfaced, including women's poverty, education, health, and access to decision making; the media and women; and women's role in shaping the environment. Amid all these issues and more, violence against women was of central and critical importance as an experience that transcended both national and cultural boundaries. . . .

The World Conference on Women served as yet one more vehicle for reemphasizing the international and epidemic proportions of violence against women. This violence cannot be explained away as a deviant phenomenon that lies outside of the otherwise "harmonious" relationships between men and women. Rather, violence against women is endemic

to the social condition of women, across both time and cultures. To write of the victimization of women, then, is to enter the lives of different women and expose their various social conditions. Therefore we cannot document the magnitude or locus of violence against women without simultaneously mapping women's social, economic, and political disadvantage vis-à-vis men.

Our conception of men's violence is broad and includes not only physical and sexual violence, its threat, or both, but also emotional abuse, economic violence, and institutional violence. As Jalna Hanmer (1996) observes, whether perpetrated by known or unknown men, this violence is "designed to control, dominate and express authority and power" (p. 8). Our comprehensive conception of violence against women recognizes that women themselves define violence much more broadly than men (see Hearn 1996, p. 27; Stanko, 1994). For example, women are more likely than men to identify emotional abuse and economic subordination as forms

Source: In *Masculinities and Violence.* Lee Bowker, ed. 1998. Sage Websdale and Chesney-Lind, Thousand Oaks: CA, pp. 55–81. Reprinted by permission of Sage Publications, Inc.

of violence. We identify the imprisonment of women in general, and more specifically of those who have killed their abusers, as forms of state violence. The incarceration of battered women resembles what Pierre Bourdieu (1993) refers to as "symbolic violence" insofar as their confinement utterly ignores the underlying power relations that women are subject to and that lead women to commit acts of resistive violence. At the same time, we note the harassment and degradation of women inmates by correctional personnel as yet another form of violence.

Our wide-ranging and fluid use of the word *violence* allows us to explore a number of forms of women's victimization. Often these forms of victimization are seen as discrete entities and are written and talked about widely in isolation from each other and the broader deployment of men's power. However, we highlight so-called social phenomena such as nonlethal and lethal battering, the mass killing of women, the sexual victimization of women by known and unknown men, the victimization of women prostitutes, sexual harassment, and the incarceration of women as continuities in the politics of gender relations.

During the past 20 years an enormous amount of multidisciplinary and interdisciplinary research has been published on violence against women. Much of this research has been stimulated by feminist concerns to publicize the hitherto marginalized personal experiences of women, particularly women's relationships with men. As Linda Gordon (1988) shows, violence such as woman battering has been elevated to the status of a "social problem" during periods when the feminist movement has been strong.

NONLETHAL VIOLENCE AGAINST WOMEN

Men are much more likely to commit acts of violence against women than women are against men. If women do use violence, it is often in self-defense or as a preemptive strategy to prevent further brutalization or death. Dawson and Langan (1994), using data from 1987 through 1991, found that females re-

ported more than 10 times as many incidents of male violence as males reported incidents of female violence (p. 2). Judging from available research, this gendered nature of interpersonal violence has a long history (see Fink, 1992; Gordon, 1988; Pleck, 1987; Taves, 1989; Tomes, 1978; Websdale, 1992). Both historical and contemporary research also shows that interpersonal male violence against women is as common in allegedly more tranquil, rural communities as it is in urban centers (see Bachman, 1994; Websdale, 1995).

A number of studies have linked the power relationships within families to the levels and severity of intimate violence. Kalmuss and Straus (1982) found that the greater the economic dependence of a woman on a man, the more likely she was to experience acts of severe violence. Dobash and Dobash (1979) found in their interviews with 109 battered women in Scottish shelters that men resorted to battering when they perceived that their wives were not living up to the patriarchally ordained role prescriptions of the "good wife." There were three main triggers that sparked male violence: his jealousy; his perception that she fails to perform her housework or other wifely services such as preparing him a hot meal; and her challenging him about economic matters within the family such as housekeeping money. For Dobash and Dobash (1979), male violence is a cultural phenomenon that is linked to the patriarchal domination of women by men. That most men do not batter their wives should not be understood to mean that patriarchy does not exist. Rather, men have many avenues of control available to them, some coercive and some more consensual.[1]

Work by Yllo and Straus (1984) finds that levels of wife beating are highest when the family norms are the most patriarchal. Levels of wife beating are highest in states where women's status is highest, prompting the researchers to suggest that perhaps the tension between the relatively high structural position of women and the intrafamilial descendancy of men is the trigger for more male violence.

Michael Smith (1990) employs the notion of "patriarchal ideology" to describe that system of beliefs, values, and ideas that supports men's domination of women and depicts that domination as natural. Although acknowledging that patriarchal relations vary by culture, Smith argues that most societies have some form of patriarchy. Quoting Kate Millett (1969), he notes how these different forms of patriarchy are sustained in part by ideologies that act as the "energy source" of patriarchal domination (Smith, 1990, p. 258). These ideologies cast men and women in different roles. Smith, using data from a telephone survey of 604 Toronto women, finds that men who adhere to an ideology of familial patriarchy (according to their female partners) are more likely to have assaulted their female partners at some point in their relationships. Husbands who are less well educated and in low-income or low-status jobs are more likely to subscribe to "an ideology of familial patriarchy" (Smith, 1990, p. 268). Smith's findings are consistent with others' that point to the existence of a "patriarchal subculture" of men who are socialized into keeping their women in line, through the use of violence if necessary (see Bowker, 1983, 1985).

LETHAL VIOLENCE AGAINST WOMEN

The fact that in the U.S. wives kill husbands nearly as often as husbands kill wives, has led some researchers to suggest that spousal murder is a similar process for men and women (see McNelly & Mann, 1990; McNelly & Robinson-Simpson, 1987; Steinmetz, 1977–1978; Straus & Gelles, 1990). These researchers focus on the fact that in the United States, for every 100 men who kill their wives, 75 women kill their husbands. This ratio is based on statistics from the period 1976 through 1985, during which time 10,529 wives were killed by husbands and 7,888 husbands were killed by wives (see Maxfield, 1989, p. 677; Mercy & Saltzman, 1989). More recent figures show that for U.S. interspousal killings, women constituted 41% of the killers (U.S. Department of Justice, 1994, p. 1).

However, these statistics do not tell us about the reasons for the homicides and especially whether there was any history of violence in the relationship. According to Stark and Flitcraft (1996), woman battering lies at the root of the majority of spousal,

intersexual, and child homicides (p. 124). Dobash and Dobash (1992) report the same, pointing out that,

> When the woman dies, it is usually the final and most extreme form of violence at the hands of her male partner. When the man dies, it is rarely the final act in a relationship in which she has repeatedly beaten him. (p. 6)

Most intrafamilial homicides are what Stark and Flitcraft (1996) call "gendered homicides," insofar as the central dynamic is a "female's subordination to a male partner" (p. 124). This dynamic is not widely appreciated in either the scholarly literature on lethal violence or in popular discourses on homicide. Stark and Flitcraft note: "In contrast to the prevailing opinion that homicide is generally impulsive and unpredictable, gendered homicides have a predictable etiology, usually rooted in woman battering" (p. 124).

From their research, Stark and Flitcraft argue that at least three themes are common to gendered homicides: rising entrapment, intense conflict around gender role behavior, and a history of interactions with helping agencies. Prior to the fatality, the partner abuse culminates in a degree of "entrapment," usually characterized by physical and sexual abuse in tandem with the rigid control of women's movements, sociability, money, food, working life, and sexual activities (p. 146). It is this rising level of entrapment that is the most significant risk factor for gendered homicide.

Another important antecedent to gendered homicide is the intense conflict between partners over the respective roles in the relationship. In discussing the case of "Dila," who endured 6 years of battering before finally killing her abusive husband, Stark and Flitcraft (1996) highlight aspects of the sexual politics that for them "frame every aspect of intersexual homicide" (p. 147). Dila's abuser "Mic" not only made Dila keep a log of all her daily activities, including her meal plans, but he also tried to regulate her contacts with other men, her control over the money she earned, her body weight, and her various housework activities.

Daly and Wilson (1988), using a theoretical model they call "evolutionary psychology," examine homicides across a wide range of cultural settings including industrial and aboriginal societies. They argue that marital violence arises out of men's attempts to control women, especially women's reproductive capacities. For these authors, spousal murder, whether committed by men or women, is rooted in "male sexual proprietariness" (p. 295).

Many domestic homicides in the United States are preceded by a trail of contacts with so-called helping agencies. Angela Browne (1987) points to the "cries for help" in domestic homicides prior to the fatal incident. Citing research in Detroit and Kansas City, Browne observes that in 85% to 90% of domestic homicides police had been called to the scene at least once (pp. 10–11). For Stark and Flitcraft (1996), the health, justice, and social service response to battering often ends up reinforcing women's entrapment, thereby increasing rather than decreasing the chances of a fatality (p. 148).

Homicide-suicide entails the killing of one or more persons followed soon after by the suicide of the perpetrator. There is no national data on the incidence of homicide-suicide. However, preliminary studies show that this form of killing constitutes a form of gendered homicide followed by suicide. It is nearly always men who kill their wives, ex-wives, lovers, and ex-lovers, sometimes in combination with the couple's children. Woman battering is a significant antecedent to the homicide-suicide episode. In tandem with Stark and Flitcraft's observations on gendered homicides, Marzuk, Tardiff, and Hirsch (1992) note, "While some murder-suicides occur shortly after the onset of 'malignant jealousy,' more often there has been a chronically chaotic relationship fraught with jealous suspicions, verbal abuse, and sub-lethal violence" (p. 3180).[2]

A Kentucky study also reveals that many homicide-suicides are preceded by a history of woman abuse. Currens (1991) notes that, "the typical perpetrator is a man married or living with a woman in a relationship marked by physical abuse" (p. 653).[3]

The murder of Glenda Greer, and the subsequent suicide of husband Shannon, in the state of Kentucky, epitomizes a number of characteristics of murder-suicides, and indeed the violent victimization of women in general. Glenda decided to end her relationship with her abusive husband Shannon by filing for divorce. These and other similar acts of resistance by women to terminate violent relationships often enrage abusers. It is during this period of attempted separation that roughly three quarters of battered women are killed. Glenda Greer was well known in the small community of Waynesburg, Kentucky, where she had worked as a secretary at the local elementary school for 11 years. When Shannon learned of the pending divorce he went to the elementary school and shot Glenda in the face and back with a 12-gauge shotgun, killing her. Shannon then drove to a remote forest where he killed himself. On the dashboard of Shannon's car police later found the divorce papers. Across the papers Shannon had written a note saying, "there was not a divorce" (Slain Secretary, 1990).

The Mass Killing of Women

So far we have explored women's experience of nonlethal and lethal violence at the hands of men they know. Our analysis would be incomplete without examining the profoundly gendered character of intersexual mass killing. We distinguish between two types of these albeit rare, but nevertheless often highly publicized, forms of murder. By *simultaneous mass killing* we refer to the killing of several people in one brief episode. By *serial killing* we mean the killing of a number of people in distinctive episodes, often separated by long periods of time. The intersexual variants of these forms of killing almost always involve men as perpetrators and women as corpses. The meaning of this gendered dynamic must not be underestimated, for these offenses are often underpinned by or tinged with an intense misogynism on the part of the perpetrator. Radford and Russell (1992) employ the specific term *femicide* to refer to the "misogynist killing of women by men." Many mass killings of women fall into this category.

During the early stages of deer hunting season in 1957 in rural Waushara County, Wisconsin, Edward

Gein killed a number of women. One victim, Bernice Worden, was found hanging in a barn. She had been "completely dressed out like a deer with her head cut off at the shoulders" (Levin & Fox, 1990, p. 66). Her body had been gutted, and investigators felt she had been butchered elsewhere. Gein later admitted to robbing the body parts of dead women from gravesites. Apparently Gein made a belt of nipples, and crafted a hanging human head as part of an ornament collection. In a shoe box, nine vulvas were found.

In what Joanne Stato (1993) has called the "Montreal Gynocide," Marc Lepine killed 14 women on December 6, 1989, in their classroom at the engineering school at the University of Montreal. Lepine later shot himself. In a three-page statement found by police, Lepine blamed feminists for his problems. As Stato notes, this incident could not be attributed to the ravings of an isolated maniac because Lepine stated that his intent was to kill feminists (p. 132). Stato therefore links these 14 killings to misogynism in general, thereby typing them into the systemic oppression of women in patriarchal societies. In a similar vein, Jane Caputi (1993) theorizes the still unknown number of women murdered and mutilated by Christopher Wilder as "sexually political murders" (p. 6). Wilder apparently bound, raped, and systematically tortured his victims before killing them. Likening this killing to lynching, Caputi observes, "His were sexually political murders, a form of murder rooted in a system of male supremacy in the same way that lynching is based in white supremacy. Such murder is, in short, a form of patriarchal terrorism" (p. 6).

Most serial killers are men. Jenkins argues that only 10% to 15% have been women (see Jenkins, 1994, chap. 7). Women murdered by serial killers are typically relatively powerless women who work in vulnerable occupations such as prostitution. Therefore, even with serial killers and their actions we see the social condition of women playing a crucial role in placing them at risk. Although all women are at risk from male violence, it seems that acutely disadvantaged women such as prostitutes, runaways, "street women, women of color, poor women,

single and elderly women, are at an elevated risk of being killed by serial killers" (see Egger, 1984, p. 348).[4] As in the case of rapists, these simultaneous mass murderers and serial killers appear, for the most part, to be ordinary men rather than deeply disturbed individuals. For a number of researchers, this normalcy is yet further evidence of the powerful connection between the structure of heteropatriarchal relations and the murder and mutilation of women. The small number of women serial killers tend to share life experiences with those battered women who have killed their abusers. As noted, when women kill it is usually after they have suffered at the hands of their abusers. Aileen Wournros, one of the few women serial killers, suffered tremendous abuse at the hands of men throughout her life. She was convicted of killing a number of johns she claimed abused her while she was providing sexual services to them in her role as a prostitute (see Kelly, 1996, p. 41). To comprehend fully the act of killing another human being it is always necessary to look at the sociopolitical context within which that killing occurs. The actions of Wournros cannot, we contend, be equated to the murderous actions of male serial killers, because male serial killers are backed by a social power, the likes of which the Aileen Wournros's of this world do not have access.

SEXUAL VICTIMIZATION

Known Men as Perpetrators

The traditional image of the rapist is that of the strange and mentally disturbed man who preys impulsively upon unknown women. However, a plethora of studies attest to the fact that rapists are more often known to their victims (Finkelhor & Yllo, 1985; Russell, 1990), are not psychiatrically disturbed (Smart & Smart, 1978), and more often than not plan their attacks (Amir, 1971). Indeed, it is within the confines of heterosexual relationships in general that the majority of rape and sexual assault occurs. Although Russell (1990) found that 5% of rapes reported to the police were committed by strangers, her random sample survey of 930 women in San Francisco revealed that only 6% of the total number of 2,588 rapes or attempted rapes were committed by strangers. Out of these 2,588 incidents, 38% were committed by husbands or ex-husbands and 13% by lovers or ex-lovers (see Russell, 1990, p. 67, table 5-3)[5] Other surveys also point to the high percentage of raped women who know their abusers. For example, surveys of college age students on 32 college campuses found that 84% of rape victims knew their attackers (see Warshaw, 1988).

If the rapist is known by the victim, then there is a greater likelihood of a repeat offense. In the Russell survey, between 70% and 80% of the victims of wife rape reported being raped more than once. This high figure is borne out by the research of Finkelhor and Yllo (1985) using a sample of 323 women in Boston. These authors found that half the victims of wife rape had experienced sexual assault on more than 20 occasions (p. 23). Although a number of authors have noted that roughly 30% to 60% of intimate violence against women involves sexual abuse (Walker, 1979, p. 112), and that battered women are twice as likely to experience multiple marital rapes (Finkelhor & Yllo, 1985, pp. 23–24), some authors stress that the rape of women by intimates is not always accompanied by battering (Russell, 1990, pp. 100–101). In their survey of Boston women, Finkelhor and Yllo (1985) found that marital rape "occurred in relationships in which there was little or no other violence; in relationships where there was little verbal or psychological abuse" (p. 37).

Finkelhor and Yllo (1985) distinguish between forced sex and rape. They argue that in cases where wives submit to husbands' sexual advances because they feel it is their duty as wives to submit, they experience forced sex but not rape. They comment:

> A woman whose husband tells her he is going to humiliate her publicly if she won't perform some sexual act, for instance, may be making a more fearsome and devastating threat than a man who threatens only to push himself on his wife. We would be prepared to call this kind of coercion forced sex, but not rape. (pp. 89–90)

Finkelhor and Yllo's concern about expanding the definition of rape to include nonconsensual sexual intercourse is that it will end up "diluting" the meaning of the word *rape* (p. 86).

The suggestion that rape sometimes occurs without violence, or the threat of violence, draws attention to those instances of coerced sexual intercourse that occur, for example, in workplaces where pressure is used by men that does not amount to threats of violence or outright violence (see Box, 1983, pp. 122–127). Similarly, when such "nonviolent" rape occurs between couples in heterosexual relationships, it alerts us to the fact that sexual relations do not have to be violent to be nonconsensual. For Box, and a number of feminist authors, the definition of rape warrants expansion to all those cases where a women's overt genuine consent is absent (see Box, 1983, p. 125). In a similar vein, Catherine MacKinnon (1987) reminds us that seeing rape only as a form of violence is limited:

> Calling rape, violence, not sex, thus evades . . . the issue of who controls women's sexuality and the dominance/submission dynamic that has defined it. When sex is violent, women may have lost control over what is done to us, but absence of force does not ensure the presence of that control. (p. 144)

Unknown Men as Perpetrators

The rape of women by strangers has been so enmeshed in the ideology of the individual "predator" who lurks and pounces, that it is easy to lose sight of the mass rape of women in much broader contexts of mass violence such as war and ethnic cleansing. The commission of sexual atrocities against women for the purposes of furthering genocidal regimes is well documented. Nenadic (1996) draws attention to a number of studies showing the use of sexual atrocities by the Nazis against Jewish women in the extermination camps (see Lengyel, 1947; Perl, 1948; and Rittner & Roth, 1993, all cited by Nenadic, 1996, p. 459). For example, Jewish women who were pregnant upon entering the extermination camps were targeted for immediate gassing (Nenadic, 1996, p. 459). In a similar vein, Susan Brownmiller (1976) observes that approximately 200,000 to 400,000 Bengali women were raped by Pakistani soldiers during the 9-month conflict between the Bengalis and Pakistanis in 1971 (pp. 78–86). Of these raped women, roughly 25,000 became pregnant and, as a consequence, became virtual outcasts in Bengali society. Some Bengalis speculated that this mass rape represented an official policy on the part of the Pakistani government to create a new race or to dilute Bengali nationalism.

As Brownmiller (1976) notes, the sexual victimization and related killing of women during war has a long history (chap. 3). During medieval times, when foot soldiers were poorly and irregularly paid by their leaders, the promise of women's bodies was often held up as one of the perks of successful conquest. In many instances, sexual conquest went hand in hand with military conquest, with the former being both an incentive for the latter and a badge of military success. Brownmiller (1976) puts is as follows:

> Down through the ages, triumph over women by rape became a way to measure victory, part of a soldier's proof of masculinity and success, a tangible reward for services rendered. . . . Booty and beauty General Andrew Jackson supposedly named it in New Orleans during the War of 1812. He was commenting, naturally, on the English attitude. (pp. 35–36)

Women in Serb-occupied Bosnia-Hercegovina and Croatia . . . endure[d] sexual atrocities and systematic extermination. As Nenadic (1996) reports, the use of sexual atrocities as a means of genocide [was] undertaken by Serbian fascists as a way of cleansing society of non-Serbs. Nenadic locates women and girls at the center of the ethnic cleansing and identifies rape and other sexual atrocities as central technologies in the purification process. She comments that, "Rape is an efficient and economical tool of genocide" (p. 457). According to Nenadic, the systematic sexual atrocities directed at Moslem women goes far beyond that experienced by Jewish women in Nazi extermination camps (p. 459). She observes,

> The sexual atrocities during the Shoah did not occur with the same breadth and frequency as in this geno-

cide, in which almost every survivor reports being a witness to, or a victim of, sexual atrocities and in which almost every woman who entered one of a variety of Serbian concentration camps or a rape/death camp was a victim of sexual atrocities whether or not she, herself, lived to tell about it. Moreover, Nazi policy against Jews did not conceptualize rape for forced impregnation and forced childbirth as a method of genocide as does Serbian genocidal policy. (p. 459)

The sexual mutilation and murder of Moslem women in Serb-occupied Bosnia-Hercegovina and Croatia include[d] the slicing off of women's breasts and the ripping out of their wombs. In Odzak, the bodies of 600 women were found butchered and laying on the street. According to Omerdic (1992), "The dead women were naked, propped up on fence spikes" (cited in Nenadic, 1996, p. 458, footnote 7). Ian Geoghegan (1996), reporting for the *Guardian Weekly* from the War Crimes Tribunal in the Hague, recalls how a drunken Serb soldier shot dead a young man after ordering him to rape his dead mother, who had been killed by the same soldier moments before (p. 5). The Serb soldier apparently forced the mother to strip off her upper clothing. He then shot her in the back of the head. One Moslem survivor of the Bosnian prison camp, Suljeman Besic, told the tribunal how he was taken to a complex that housed women and girls. There he was shown blood-spattered bodies of two girls in their early teens lying by an outside toilet. Other inmates of the Bosnian camp told Besic that groups of Serb soldiers had arrived during the night to select girls they liked. Elderly women who tried to prevent this selection were killed.

While the rape, mutilation, and killing of women during war serve to remind us of the utility of women to men in battle, the entire discourse on the victimization of women "during war" leaves us with a silence that is itself one of the great mantras of patriarchy. By this "silence" we refer to the "gender war" seemingly hidden by the glory of men fighting each other with all the destructive power their respective military regimes can muster. To talk and write of the brutalization and sexual mutilation of women during war risks understating that such wartime victimization is, in fact, part of one of the longest wars every fought, rather than an incidental, albeit horrendous, sideshow in the particular and localized war being fought by men against men. As Foucault (1981) so eloquently reminds us, the arena of sexuality is saturated with power and replete with its own weaponry, tactics, propaganda, victims, and resistive strategies. It has been our argument that everyday gender relations constitute a type of battlefield or war zone. In military conflicts between nations, not all of the citizenry have to be employed in the military to ensure the military and political might of one nation over another. Likewise in the gender war, which takes place at numerous levels, not all men have to use lethal and sublethal violence against women to enjoy the fruits of patriarchy.

THE VICTIMIZATION OF PROSTITUTES

Within the broader power relations of what Hester, Kelly, and Radford (1996) call "hetero-patriarchy," women occupy a range of subordinate positions. When women become wives, partners, and mothers, patriarchal discourse extends to them the role of decent/respectable womanhood. Patriarchal ideology deems that decent/respectable women who "choose" marriage and maternity live out their biological destiny as both the physical and emotional complements of their husbands, and the producers of children.

The maintenance of images of "ideal" womanhood depends in part upon the construction of "evil" women, or women who, for whatever reasons, eschew the "trappings" of marriage and family. Prostitutes constitute one such group of women who adopt a lifestyle where they sell their sexual skills for money. As we shall demonstrate, prostitutes experience tremendous levels of violence, rape, and sexual assault at the hands of men. However, few of these experiences have permeated the research literature on violence and rape. In documenting these levels of victimization, Miller and Schwartz (1995) argue that people often see prostitutes as unrapeable; incapable of being harmed, and

"deserving of" being raped. Nanette Davis (1990) cites studies that reveal high levels of victimization reported by prostitutes (Barry, 1981; Edwards, 1984; James & Meyerding, 1978; Hatty, 1989; Hunter, 1989; Millman, 1980). These prostitutes were raped, physically and sexually assaulted, and murdered. Erbe (1984) concluded that more than 70% of the prostitutes in her survey had been the victims of sexual assault. Davis (1990) argues that, "prostitution is an extension of a culture that devalues women and provides unconditional sexual access so that some women are available for purposes of sexual abuse and exploitation" (p. 3).

Violence is first and foremost a reason that many young women "decide" to engage in prostitution. Escaping from homes characterized by high levels of sexual and physical abuse, girls often engage in "survival sex" while on the streets as runaways. Research on teenage prostitutes consistently finds that they are more likely than their male counterparts to have been sexually abused, and they are more likely to use prostitution to survive on the streets (see Chesney-Lind & Shelden, 1992, for a summary of this research).

But why do young women stay in sex work? The answer is linked to the nature of women's work in patriarchal economies, where, contrary to what one might expect, prostitution might be seen as an "outgrowth" of certain types of women's jobs. James (1976), in her work on prostitution in Seattle, cites two studies that connect the employment in "occupations . . . that adhere most closely to the traditional female service role, often emphasizing physical appearance as well as service," to the entrance of women into prostitution (p. 188). Employers often require women employees in service jobs to "flirt with customers and 'be sexy,' " which frequently results in the women finding that the men they must serve at their jobs already consider them to be "no better than a prostitute" (James, 1976, p. 188).

In Hawaii, women were recruited directly out of what might be called bar-related female professions into prostitution. Interviews with women in prison who had a history of prostitution revealed that half were working off and on in these entertainment or bar-related jobs while they were involved in sex work—indicating that these occupations, in themselves, serve as "adjuncts rather than alternatives to female criminal activity" (Chesney-Lind & Rodriguez, 1983, p. 55).

Interviews with women prostitutes in both Milwaukee and Hawaii link their decision to prostitute to their survival needs. Women's comments indicated that the most common reason they started working as prostitutes was financial. Prostitution, it is often observed, does not provide women with "easy" money, but it is "fast" money. In the words of one former prostitute, however, "fast money doesn't last" (Kelly Hill, personal communication with Chesney-Lind, April 11, 1996).

Due to the degradation and violence that is so much a part of the street prostitute's life, drug use and addiction often becomes a problem for women involved in prostitution, even for those who were not involved in prostitution to support their drug habits. Chesney-Lind and Rodriguez (1983) found that the need to buy drugs was a factor in women's involvement in theft, burglary, and robbery, for which they were also more likely to be incarcerated than for prostitution. In the interviews with these women, it was obvious that, for most, their entry into prostitution predated their heavy drug use. However, drug dependency, perhaps developed as part of life "in the fast lane," quickly made their exit from the profession unlikely and quite probably encouraged them to seek even more money through burglary and theft (Chesney-Lind & Rodriguez, 1983, p. 57).

What is life like for women engaged in prostitution? Ethnographic fieldwork conducted in the neighborhoods of Chicago (Ouellet, Wiebel, Jimenez, & Johnson, 1993), Harlem (Bourgois & Dunlap, 1993), and New York (Maher & Curtis, 1992; Williams, 1992), as well as interviews with young women in Miami (Inciardi, Lockwood, & Pottieger, 1993), Harlem (Fullilove, Lown, & Fullilove, 1992), and San Francisco (Schwarcz et al., 1992), clearly document the links between a woman's "choice" to engage in prostitution and

poverty and racism that surround her as she grows up. The role played by drugs, particularly crack cocaine, in modern prostitution is also important to explore because it clearly facilitates continued sexual and physical violence against women in economically devastated neighborhoods. Finally, the link between the victimization of prostitutes and other forms of women's crime, particularly offenses that sound violent (like robbery), must be briefly explored to challenge racist and sexist notions that women, particularly women of color, are somehow more "violent" today (Baskin, Sommers, & Fagan, 1993).

Three studies of street girls and women conducted in Miami during the years 1985 through 1991 (Inciardi et al., 1993) document the dramatic expansion of the role of crack cocaine in these women's lives. About half (49%) of the women reported "current" use of cocaine in the late 1970s compared to 73% in the early 1980s (Inciardi et al., 1993, p. 113). Bourgois and Dunlap (1993) caution the reader against demonizing such increases, noting that crack cocaine is simply the "latest medium through which the already desperate are expressing publicly their suffering and hopelessness" (p. 98). Research on the impact of different drugs (alcohol, marijuana, and crystal methamphetamine) among Hawaii's women underscores the need to study the situation of people in poverty, not particular drugs (however horrific) (Joe, 1996).

The extensiveness of the violence in girls' and women's lives is dramatically underscored in interviews with women crack users in Harlem, most of whom were African American. This research focused on the lives of 14 women crack users and documented that "trauma was a common occurrence in their lives," which, in turn, propelled the women into drug use (Fullilove et al., 1992, p. 277). These women's lives are full of the chaos and abuse common in neighborhoods of extreme poverty. They are also distressed and depressed at their inability to "maintain culturally defined gender roles" (specifically, functioning as mothers) because of their drug use. Finally, these women are further victimized by the "male-oriented drug culture," which has developed a bizarre and exploitative form of prostitution around women's addiction to crack cocaine.

Specifically, these neighborhoods have seen the development of a "barter system in which sex—rather than money—can be exchanged for drugs." This system feeds on the particular nature of crack usage where the drug is consumed in periodic binges and where "pursuit and use of the drug outweigh other concerns" (Fullilove et al., 1992, p. 276). This pattern of drug use has created the "crack 'ho'"—a prostitute who will trade sex for extremely small amounts of money or drugs—often, but not always, in crack houses generally run by men. Crack addiction, in short, has facilitated the development of a form of prostitution that "may involve participation in bizarre sexual practices for very small amounts of money" and the subsequent "degradation of women within crack culture" (Fullilove et al., 1992, p. 276).

An example of the sort of desperation seen in these neighborhoods is supplied by another Harlem researcher (Bourgois), who reported being stopped by a "high school girl" who grabbed him by the arms in a housing project stairwell, "sobbing hysterically" and begging him, "Please! Please! Let me suck you off for two dollars—I'll swallow it. Please! Please! I promise!" (Bourgois & Dunlap, 1993, p. 1021). Likewise, Inciardi and his associates (1993) observe that women have become the special victims of crack cocaine, and they provide harrowing stories of sex-for-drug exchanges in crack houses. Here, according to the authors, vulnerable and victimized girls and young women trade sex for extremely small amounts of crack (sometimes as little as $3 worth) and, in the process, expose themselves to the risk of AIDS.

These ethnographies leave no doubt that the crack scene has affected street prostitution, long a mainstay in women's survival in marginalized communities. In a study of the impact of crack in three Chicago neighborhoods, it was noted that although "street-level prostitution has probably always had rate cutters" (Ouellet et al., 1993, p. 88), the arrival of crack and the construction of the "crack 'ho'" has created a desperate form of prostitution involving instances of extreme degradation that had previously been seen only in extremely impoverished countries like the Philippines and Thailand (Enloe, 1989; Studervant & Stoltzfus, 1992).

Most women involved in prostitution, even those involved in crack-related prostitution, view their activities as "work" and feel that this work is more ethical and safer than either stealing or drug dealing (Bourgois & Dunlap, 1993, p. 104). According to this perspective, because the crack epidemic has virtually destroyed the economic viability of street prostitution in some neighborhoods, some women might even prefer to go to these houses to get their drugs directly, rather than to risk the dangers of the streets and violence from johns who are even less well known to them than the men in the crack houses.

Not all women addicted to crack choose this path, particularly when times get hard. For this reason, crack has also changed the nature of street prostitution in neighborhoods where it is present. Maher and Curtis's (1992) work on women involved in street-level sex markets in New York, as an example, notes that the introduction of crack cocaine "increased the number of women working the strolls and had a significant impact on the kind of work they did, the remuneration they received and the interactions that occurred in and around street-level sex markets" (p. 21). Maher and Curtis found that women involved in prostitution were also involved in other forms of crime, like shoplifting, stealing from their families, and, occasionally, robbing johns, as a way of surviving on the streets—not because they were seeking some sort of "equality" with male offenders.

In essence, increased competition among women involved in prostitution, plus the deflation in the value of their work, has created a more hostile environment among New York streetwalkers, as well as an increased willingness to rip off johns (see also Ouellet et al., 1993). To understand this, it is important to convey the enormity of the violence that women in sex work are routinely exposed to at the hands of johns. Maher and Curtis (1992) provide many such examples. One woman they talked to told them,

> I got shot twice since I bin here . . . was a car pulled up, two guys in it, they was like "C'mon gon on a date." I wouldn't go with that so they came back arund and shot me . . . in the leg and up here. (p. 23)

Here's another:

> I got punched in the mouth not too long ago they [two dates] ripped me off—they wanted their money back after we finished—threw me off the van naked—then hit me with a blackjack 'caus I jumped back on to the van because I wanted to get my clothes. It was freezing outside so I jumped back onto the van to try and get my clothes and he smacked me with a black-jack on my eye. (p. 244)

In fact, some "robbery" becomes much more under-standable, when seen up close as it is in this work. Take Candy's story:

> I robbed a guy up here not too long ago—5 o'clock Sunday morning . . . a real cheek gonna tell me $5 for a blow job and that pisses me off—arguing wit them. I don't argue no more—jus get in the car sucker, he open his pants and do like this and I do like this, put my hand, money first. He give me the money I say, "See ya, hate to be ya, next time motherfucker it cost you $5 to get me to come to the window." (Maher & Curtis, 1992, p. 246)

Prostitution is often called the "oldest profes-sion," which is a sad but telling comment about the stability of girls' and women's work—legal and ille-gal. Many have argued that it is a "victimless" crime because the customers and the prostitute are know-ing and willing participants. This section, however, has certainly provided evidence that the phenome-non can set the stage for violence against women, and certainly the prostitute herself sees little of the true profits of her labor. Finally, in part because she sees so little of the money due her, she is tempted to use the role of prostitution to rip off violent and cal-lous johns (Kelly Hill, personal communication with Chesney-Lind, April 11, 1996).

Finally, discussing prostitution and women's vio-lence responsibly is impossible without recognizing the gendered nature of the lives and work of the prostitutes themselves. As we have seen, women in-volved in drug use, prostitution, and other forms of women's crime, have experienced victimization di-rectly related to their gender in the form of incest, sexual abuse, and rape. Finally, contrary to notions that their "nontraditional" violent offenses—like robbery—signal a change in their orientation to-ward women's place in male society, their lives demonstrate, if anything, the tragic ways in which gender in marginalized communities works to create and legitimate horrific violence against women la-beled as prostitutes.

THE VICTIMIZATION OF IMPRISONED WOMEN

The number of women imprisoned in the United States tripled during the 1980s, and the 1990s have seen the continued escalation in the number of women behind bars. . . .

So, as the number of people imprisoned in the United States climbs, our nation has achieved the dubious honor of having the second highest incar-ceration rate in the world—following the newly formed Russian nation (Mauer, 1994). Who are these women in prison and are they so profoundly dangerous that vast sums must be expended to in-carcerate them?

The most recent research on the characteristics of women doing time in state prisons across the coun-try underscores the salience of themes identified earlier in this chapter—particularly the role of sex-ual and physical violence in the lives of women who come into the criminal justice system. It also argues forcefully for a national discussion of the situation of women in our jails and prisons.

Snell and Morton (1994) surveyed a random sam-ple of women and men ($N = 13,986$) in prisons around the country during 1991 for the Bureau of Justice Statistics. For the first time, a government study asked questions about women's *and* men's ex-periences of sexual and physical violence as children.

They found, when they asked these questions, that women in prisons have far higher rates of phys-ical and sexual abuse than their male counterparts.

Forty-three percent of the women surveyed "reported they had been abused at least once" before their current admission to prison; the comparable figure for men was 12.2% (Snell & Morton, 1994, p. 5).

For about a third of all women in prison (31.7%), the abuse started when they were girls, but it continued as they became adults. A key gender difference emerges here. A number of young men who are in prison (10.7%) also report abuse as boys, but this does not continue to adulthood. One in four women reported that their abuse started as adults compared to only 3% of male offenders. Fully 33.5% of the women surveyed reported physical abuse, and a slightly higher number (33.9%) had been sexually abused either as girls or young women, compared to relatively small percentages of men (10% of boys and 5.3% of adult men in prison).

This research also queried women on their relationship with those who abused them. Predictably, both women and men report that parents and relatives contributed to the abuse they suffered as children, but women prisoners are far more likely than their male counterparts to say that domestic violence was a theme in their adult abuse; fully half of the women said they had been abused by a spouse/ex-spouse compared to only 3% of male inmates.

A look at the offenses for which women are incarcerated quickly puts to rest the notion of hyper-violent, nontraditional women criminals. . . .

Snell and Morton also probed the gendered nature of women's violence that resulted in their imprisonment. They noted that women prisoners were far more likely to kill an intimate or relative (50% compared to 16.3%), whereas men were more likely to kill strangers (50.5% compared to 35.1%). Two New York studies provide further information on the relationship between abuse and women's violence. Examining women committed to the state's prisons for homicide offenses in 1986, the researchers found that 49% of these women had been the victims of abuse at some point in their lives and 59% of the women who killed someone close to them were being abused at the time of the offense. For more than half the women committed for

homicide, this was their first and only offense (Huling, 1991, p. 3).

A more recent interview study of 215 women incarcerated in New York prisons for homicide revealed that of the women who killed sexual intimates (one fifth of the total number), two thirds reported that the victims struck them prior to the homicide (Hall, Brownstein, Crimmins, Spunt, & Langley, 1996). Of the women who killed their children (about another fifth of the total group), extremely high levels of physical and sexual abuse as children were noted; 65% of that group of women had suffered physical abuse (an average of 12 or more incidents) and well over half (57%) had suffered sexual abuse (an average of nine or more incidents). The women who killed their children "drew direct connections between their own upbringing and their lack of coping skills," one mother saying,

> I was so stressed out and depressed . . . everytime I picked up the baby and she started crying and I said she must hate me . . . I was convinced this child hated me. . . . It was my mother and me all over again. (Hall et al., 1996, p. 7)

. . .

Thus, with virtually no public discussion or debate, thousands of women offenders are being swept into a system that has a long history of alternatively ignoring and abusing women inmates (see Rafter, 1990). The sexual abuse of women is a particular problem. In 1996, the international organization Human Rights Watch noted that, "in women's prisons across the United States, ill-trained male officers guard female prisoners with little appropriate guidance or oversight regarding sexual misconduct" (Craig, 1996a, p. 1A).

Sexual abuse of women inmates at the hands of male guards is as old as women's imprisonment (Beddoe, 1979). Nonetheless, with the soaring increases in women under lock and key in the United States, the sexual victimization of women in U.S. prisons is a problem of growing seriousness. Women prisoners in California, Georgia, Hawaii, Ohio, Louisiana, Michigan, Tennessee, New York, and New Mexico have brought this matter to public attention despite considerable risk to themselves (Craig, 1996a; Curriden, 1993; Lopez, 1993; Meyer, 1992; Sewenely, 1993; Stein, 1996; Watson, 1992). The assumption is increasingly that prisons, here in the United States and elsewhere, are rife with this problem. [See Siegal, chap. 16.]

...

It also appears that women in prison are "overpoliced" and overcontrolled in other ways. As an example, McClellan (1994) examined disciplinary practices at male and female prisons in Texas. Utilizing Texas Department of Corrections records, McClellan constructed two samples of inmates (271 males and 245 females) and followed them for a 1-year period (1989). She documented that although most men in her sample (63.5%) had no citation or only one citation for a rule violation, only 17.1% of the women in her sample had such records. Women prisoners were much more likely to receive numerous citations, and for different sorts of offenses then men. Most commonly, women were cited for "violating posted rules" while males were cited most frequently for "refusing to work" (McClellan, 1994, p. 77). Finally, women were more likely than men to receive the most severe sanctions, including solitary confinement (McClellan, 1994, p. 82).

Her review of the details of women's infractions subsumed under the category "violation of posted rules" includes such offenses as "excessive artwork ('too many family photographs on display'), failing to eat all the food on their plates, and for talking while waiting in the pill line" (McClellan, 1994, p. 85). Possession of contraband could include such things as an extra bra or pillowcase, peppermint sticks, or a properly borrowed comb or hat. Finally, "trafficking" and "trading" included instances of sharing shampoo in a shower and lighting another inmate's cigarette (McClellan, 1994, p. 85).

The author concludes by observing that there exist "two distinct institutional forms of surveillance and control operating at the male and female facilities . . . this policy not only imposes extreme constraints on adult women but also costs the people of the State of Texas a great deal of money" (McClellan, 1994, p. 87). Research like this provides clear ev-

idence that women in prison are overpoliced and overcontrolled in institutional settings—a finding earlier researchers have noted as well (see Burkhart, 1973; Mann, 1984).

What is clear from all these accounts is that women in modern prisons may be subjected to what might be called the "worst of both worlds." If McClellan's findings can be extended to other states, women in modern prisons continue to be overpoliced and overcontrolled (a feature of the separate spheres legacy of women's imprisonment). At the same time, they are also the recipients of a form of equity with a vengeance that results in abuses that are likely unparalleled in male institutions (sexual exploitation at the hands of guards and degrading strip searches). Beyond this, correctional leaders are, in some cases, implementing grossly inappropriate and clearly male-modeled interventions such as chain gangs and even boot camps to deal with women's offending (Kim, 1996; MacKenzie, Elis, Simpson, & Skroban, 1994). Proclaiming his department "an equal opportunity incarcerator," an Arizona sheriff has started a chain gang for women "now locked up with three or four others in dank, cramped disciplinary cells" (Kim, 1996, p. 1A). To escape these conditions, the women can "volunteer" for the 15-woman chain gang. Defending his controversial move, the sheriff commented, "If women can fight for their country, and bless them for that, if they can walk a beat, if they can protect the people and arrest violators of the law, then they should have no problem with picking up trash in 120-degrees" (Kim, 1996, p. 1A). In the few TV and print media stories on women in chain gangs, women are reported as having mixed reasons for "participating." On balance, it seems that women's willingness to participate stems largely from the conditions of the disciplinary cells rather than any great desire to venture into the great outdoors.

The enormous and rapid increase in women's imprisonment has clearly exposed tens of thousands of women, many of whom have extensive histories of abuse, to further abuse at the hands of a system designed with male offenders in mind and staffed by poorly trained correctional officers. The silence about women's victimization, particularly the violence in the lives of economically marginalized women of color, means that they are forced to survive in ways that bring them into the criminal justice system. Once there, they are further punished by a system whose very structure facilitates further abuse.

TOWARD A DIVERSE AND INCLUSIVE UNDERSTANDING OF DOING VIOLENCE TO WOMEN

We began by highlighting the worldwide nature of violence against women and framing that violence as part of the structure of hetero-patriarchy. It is not our argument that hetero-patriarchy takes the same form in all cultures. Rather, we have tried to show how men use violence against women in different cultural settings and social situations. Nevertheless, male violence against women is both a reflection of their sociopolitical domination over women, and, at the same time, yet another way of establishing control, maintaining it, or both. To make sense of male violence against women, then, is to grasp the limited social, political, and economic opportunities available to women. Women do not enjoy or invite male violence. They are not responsible for that violence and they are not susceptible to it because of certain psychological frailties. Rather, the constellation of disadvantaged situations women live out expose them to violence at the hands of men.

The structure of hetero-patriarchy results in women being controlled in a number of ways. Not all men have to commit violence against women to enjoy the fruits of social superiority. Women's employment opportunities are more limited than those of men; they perform more hidden, undervalued, and unpaid labor; and they are culturally channeled by the ideology of pornography, being depicted as the objects of male desire, rather than human subjects in their own right.[6] Violence is but one mechanism in the arsenal of patriarchal control mechanisms. It is a powerful mechanism, however, and as we have shown in our discussion of lethal violence, it is a chilling mechanism of last resort.

We have argued for a diverse and inclusive understanding of men's violence against women. It is crucial to frame the lethal and nonlethal violence against women by men they know alongside the killing and brutalization of women by men who are strangers. The murder of Glenda Greer with a 12-gauge shotgun by her soon-to-be-divorced husband, Shannon, is part of a mosaic of murder that includes the loss of the 14 women in the Montreal Gynocide and the serial killing of prostitutes. Likewise, rape within marriage is conceptually continuous with the much less common rape by predatory strangers and the very common sexual harassment of women in the workplace. The fact that rape is most common between those in intimate relationships tells us something about "intimacy" under patriarchy. Various forms of violence against women coalesce in the mass murder and rape of women in Serb-occupied Bosnia-Hercegovina and Croatia. Rather than understanding this mass rape and murder as simply a "by-product" of war, we emphasize that these atrocities are part of a worldwide war against women. Though not all men are front-line soldiers in this war, all men do occupy a different political territory than women.

Due to the tendency to fragment the literature on violence against women, some victims of male violence have received more attention than others. Feminists and others successfully confronted the myth that women are only at threat from predatory men they do not know. As noted, we now have a much better sense of the interpersonal victimization of women. However, violence against certain groups of women has not received due attention. In our "inclusive" approach we report the victimization of sex workers and argue for the recognition of the continuities between their victimization and the brutalization of other women. Sex workers, like married women prior to the passage of marital rape laws, are indeed "rapeable." If we do not include women such as sex workers, we run the risk of ignoring violence against some of the most profoundly victimized women in the patriarchal regime.

Our fluid and diverse analysis of violence against women, and our framing of that violence as just one weapon in the patriarchal arsenal, might appear to present patriarchy, to borrow the Weberian phrase, as an "iron cage." This is not our intent. As we also pointed out, women sometimes resort to violence themselves. Our discussion of the incarceration of women and the abuse women inmates endure shows yet another face of violence against women. The patriarchal state has a long history of not taking violence against women seriously when passing laws on divorce, child custody, and marital rape. We argue strongly that the state, and often its individual male personnel, actively revictimize women in prison. If ever there was an "iron cage" of patriarchy, the women's prison is it. Incarcerating women for killing their spouses who abused them for years is to reproduce the oppressive patriarchal dynamic from whence these women came. The miserable condition of women in prison and the harassment and abuse they endure there, is, for us, in many ways the ultimate victimization because it punishes many women for their resistance and courage in the face of grave desperation.

DISCUSSION QUESTIONS

1. Explain the meaning of the gendered nature of interpersonal violence (whether the violence is rape, domestic homicide, the mass killing of women, or the victimization of sex workers and prostitutes).
2. How does an intersectionalities perspective (race, class, gender, sexual orientation) provide more in-depth questions about this protracted, complex social issue of violence against women? Give an example.
3. Websdale and Chesney-Lind argue that the pervasive nature of violence against women is a fact that can only be explained if everyone recognizes that women are socially, politically, and economically disadvantaged. Explain what the authors mean by this statement.

Give at least one concrete example of how this perspective translates into violence against women at home and also in public places. What social policies would be needed to change these social situations that are conducive to violence against women?
4. Compare and contrast the problems facing prostitutes in the United States, as described in this chapter, with those of sex workers in other countries affected by globalization, discussed in chapter 8 by Kempadoo.
5. Violence is but one mechanism in the arsenal of patriarchal control mechanisms. Discuss this statement and its implications for solving problems of violence against women in the home and in the broader society. What are some of the other mechanisms of patriarchal control?

NOTES

1. See, for example, Edgell (1980) for an analysis of decision making in middle-class families and the way in which husbands make most of the "important" decisions with only minor input from wives. No important decisions were made by wives alone.
2. Marzuk refers to the research of Allen (1983), Berman (1979), and Dorpat (1966) to support his argument.
3. Studies cited in support of a prior history of domestic violence include Rosenbaum (1990) and West (1967).
4. As Jane Caputi (1993) points out, there are a couple of notable exceptions to the argument that serial killers generally victimize the most disadvantaged women. Both Ted Bundy and David Berkowitz (Son of Sam) "chose victims on the basis of their correspondence to a pornographic, objectifying, and racist ideal" (p. 19).
5. Russell's analysis of "completed rape" yields a higher proportion of strangers among the ranks

of rapists. Twelve percent of all completed rapes were reportedly committed by strangers, 23% were committed by husbands and ex-husbands, 17% by acquaintances, and 15% by lovers or ex-lovers (see Russell, 1990, p. 65, table 5-1).

6. For a good discussion of the nature of patriarchy, see the work of realist feminist Sylvia Walby (1990, 1992).

REFERENCES

Allen, N. H. 1983. Homicide Followed by Suicide: Los Angeles, 1970–1979. *Suicide and Life Threatening Behavior,* 13:155–165.

Amir, M. 1971. *Patterns of Forcible Rape.* Chicago: University of Chicago.

Bachman, R. 1994. *Violence against Women: A National Crime Victimization Survey Report.* Washington, DC: Bureau of Justice Statistics.

Barry, K. 1981. *Female Sexual Slavery.* Englewood Cliffs, NJ: Prentice Hall.

Baskin, D., I. Sommers, and J. Fagan. 1993. The Political Economy of Female Violent Street Crime. *Fordham Urban Law Journal* 20(Spring): 401–417.

Beddoe, D. 1979. *Welsh Convict Women.* Barry, Wales: Stewart Williams.

Berman, A. L. 1979. Dyadic Death: Murder-Suicide. *Suicide and Life Threatening Behavior* 9(1): 15–23.

Bourdieu P. 1993. *The Field of Cultural Reproduction.* Cambridge, UK: Polity Press.

Bourgois, P., and E. Dunlap. 1993. Exorcising Sex—for Crack: An Ethnographic Perspective from Harlem. In *The Crack Pipe as Pimp,* ed. M. Ratner, 97–132. Lexington, MA: Lexington Books.

Bowker, L. H. 1983. *Beating Wife-Beating.* Lexington, MA: Lexington Books.

Bowker, L. H. 1985. The Effects of National Development on the Position of Married Women in the Third World: The Case of Wife Beating. *International Journal of Comparative and Applied Criminal Justice* 9:1–13.

Box, S. 1983. Power, Crime and Mystification. New York: Tavistock.

Browne, A. 1987. *When Battered Women Kill.* New York: Free Press.

Brownmiller, S. 1976. *Against Our Will: Men, Women, and Rape.* New York: Penguin.

Burkhart, K. 1973. *Women in Prison.* Garden City, NY: Doubleday.

Caputi, J. 1993. The Sexual Politics of Murder. In *Violence against Women: The Bloody Footprints,* eds. P. Bart and E. G. Moran, 5–25. Newbury Park, CA: Sage.

Chesney-Lind, M., and N. Rodriguez. 1983. Women under Lock and Key. *The Prison Journal* 63:47–65.

Chesney-Lind, M., and R. G. Shelden. 1992. *Girls, Delinquency, and the Juvenile Justice System.* Pacific Grove, CA: Brooks/Cole.

Craig, G. 1996a. Advocates Say Nude Filming Shows Need for New Laws. *Rochester Democrat and Chronicle,* March 23, pp. A1, A6.

Currens, S. 1991. Homicide Followed by Suicide—Kentucky, 1985–1990. *Journal of the American Medical Association* 266:2062–2063.

Curriden, M. 1993, September 20. Prison Scandal in Georgia: Guards Traded Favors for Sex. *National Law Journal,* p. 8.

Daly, M., and M. Wilson. 1988. *Homicide.* New York: Aldine de Gruyter.

A Damaging Remedy. 1992. *New York Times* [Editorial], April 13, p. 13.

Davis, N. 1990. *Alternatives to Prostitution.* Paper presented at meeting of the Pacific Sociological Association, Spokane, WA, April.

Dawson, J. M., and P. A. Langan. 1994. *Murder in Families.* U.S. Department of Justice, Bureau of Justice Statistics Special Report. Washington, DC: Government Printing Office.

Dobash, R. E., and R. Dobash. 1979. *Violence against Wives.* New York: Free Press.

Dobash, R. E., and R. Dobash. 1992. *Women, Violence and Social Change.* New York: Routledge.

Dorpat, T. L. 1966. Suicide in Murderers. *Psychiatry Digest* (7):51–55.

Edgell, S. 1980. *Middle-class Couples.* London: George Allen and Unwin.

Edwards, S. 1984. *Women on Trial.* Manchester, UK: Manchester University.

Egger, S. A. 1984. A Working Definition of Serial Murder and the Reduction of Linkage Blindness. *Journal of Police Science and Administration* 12:348–357.

Enloe, C. 1989. *Bananas, Beaches and Bases: Making Feminist Sense of International Politics.* Berkeley: University of California.

Erbe, S. 1984. Prostitutes: Victims of Men's Exploitation and Abuse. *Law and Inequality: Journal of Theory and Practice* 2:607–623.

Fink, D. 1992. *Agrarian Women: Wives and Mothers in Rural Nebraska 1880–1940.* Chapel Hill: University of North Carolina.

Finkelhor, D., and K. Yllo. 1984. *License to Rape: Sexual Abuse of Wives.* New York: Holt, Rinehart and Winston.

Foucault, M. 1981. *The History of Sexuality,* vol. 1. Harmondsworth, UK: Pelican.

Fullilove, M., A. Lown, and R. Fullilove. 1992. Crack Hos and Skeezers: Traumatic Experiences of Women Crack Users. *The Journal of Sex Research* 29(2):275–287.

Geoghegan, I. 1996. Boy "Forced to Rape His Dead Mother." *Guardian Weekly,* June 30, p. 5.

Gordon, L. 1988. *Heroes of Their Own Lives: The Politics and History of Family Violence.* New York: Penguin.

Hall, D., H. H. Brownstein, S. Crimmins, B. Spunt, and S. Langley. 1996. *Homicide by Women.* New York: New York State Division of Criminal Justice Services.

Hanmer, J. 1996. Women and Violence: Commonalities and Diversities. In *Violence and Gender Relations: Theories and Interventions,* ed. B. Fawcett, B. Featherstone, J. Hearn, and C. Toft, 7–21. Thousand Oaks, CA: Sage.

Hatty, S. 1989. Violence against Prostitute Women: Social and Legal Dilemmas. *Australian Journal of Social Issues* 24(4):235–248.

Hearn, J. 1996. Men's Violence to Known Women: Historical, Everyday, and Theoretical Constructions by Men. In *Violence and Gender Relations: Theories and Interventions,* eds. B. Fawcett, B. Featherstone, J. Hearn, and C. Toft, 22–37. Thousand Oaks, CA: Sage.

Hester, M., L. Kelly, and J. Radford, eds. 1996. *Women, Violence and Male Power: Feminist Activism, Research and Practice.* Philadelphia: Open University.

Huling, T. 1991. *New York Groups Call on State Lawmakers to Release Women in Prison.* New York: Correctional Association of New York.

Huling, T. 1996. Drug Mules. In *Drug Couriers: A New Perspective,* ed. P. Green. London: Quartet Books.

Hunter, S. K. 1989. *Alternatives to Prostitution.* Paper prepared for the Third National Workshop on Female Offenders, Pittsburgh, PA.

Inciardi, J., D. Lockwood, and A. E. Pottieger. 1993. *Women and Crack-cocaine.* New York: Macmillan.

James, J. 1976. Motivations for Entrance into Prostitution. In *The Female Offender,* ed. L. Crites. Lexington, MA: Lexington Books.

James, J., and J. Meyerding. 1978. Early Sexual Experience as a Factor in Prostitution. *Archives of Sexual Behavior* 7(1):31–42.

Jenkins, P. 1994. *Using Murder: The Social Construction of Serial Homicide.* New York: Aldine de Gruyter.

Joe, K. 1996. The Life and Times of Asian American Women Drug Users: An Ethnographic Study. *Journal of Drug Issues* 26(1):125–142.

Kalmuss, D., and M. Straus. 1982. Wife's marital dependency and wife abuse. *Journal of Marriage and Family* 44:277–286.

Kelly, L. 1996. When Does the Speaking Profit Us? In *Women, Violence and Male Power: Feminist Activism, Research and Practice,* eds. M. Hester, L. Kelly, and J. Radford, 34–49. Philadelphia: Open University.

Kim, E.-K. 1996, August 26. Sheriff Says He'll Have Chain Gangs for Women. *Tuscaloosa News,* p. 1A.

Lengyel, O. 1947. *Five Chimneys: The Story of Auschwitz.* Chicago: Ziff-Davis.

Levin, J., and J. A. Fox. 1990. Mass Murder: America's Growing Menace. In *Violence: Patterns, Causes, Public Policy,* eds. N. Weiner, M. A. Zahn, and R. Sagi, 65–69. San Diego, CA: Harcourt Brace Jovanovich.

Lopez, S. 1993. Fifth Guard Arrested on Sex Charge. *Albuquerque Journal,* July 8, pp. A1, A2.

Maxfield, M. G. 1989. Circumstances in Supplementary Homicide Reports: Variety and Validity. *Criminology* 27:671–695.

MacKenzie, D., L. A. Elis, S. S. Simpson, and S. B. Skroban. 1994. *Female Offenders in Boot Camp Prisons.* College Park, University of Maryland, Institute of Criminal Justice and Criminology.

MacKinnon, C. 1987. Feminism, Marxism, Method and the State: Toward a Feminist Jurisprudence. In *Feminism and Methodology,* ed. S. Harding, 135–156. Indianapolis: Indiana University.

Maguire, K., and A. L. Pastore, eds. 1994. *Sourcebook of Criminal Justice Statistics.* Washington, DC: U.S. Department of Justice.

Maher, L., and R. Curtis. 1992. Women on the Edge: Crack Cocaine and the Changing Contexts of Street-Level Sex Work in New York City. *Crime, Law and Social Change* 18:221–258.

Mann, C. 1984. *Female Crime and Delinquency.* University: University of Alabama.

Maran, R. 1996. After the Beijing Women's Conference: What Will Be Done? *Social Justice* 23(1–2):352–367.

Marzuk, P. M., K. Tardiff, and C. S. Hirsch. 1992. The Epidemiology of Murder-Suicide. *Journal of the American Medical Association* 267:3179–3183.

Mauer, M. 1994. *Americans Behind Bars: The International Use of Incarceration, 1992–1993.* Washington, DC: The Sentencing Project.

McClellan, D. S. 1994. Disparity in the Discipline of Male and Female Inmates in Texas Prisons. *Women and Criminal Justice* 5(2):71–97.

McNelly, R. L., and C. R. Mann. 1990. Domestic Violence Is a Human Issue. *Journal of Interpersonal Violence* 5:129–132.

McNelly, R. L., and G. Robinson-Simpson. 1987. The Truth about Domestic Violence: A Falsely Framed Issue. *Social Work* 32:485–490.

Mercy, J. A., and L. Saltzman. 1989. Fatal Violence among Spouses in the United States, 1976–1985. *American Journal of Public Health* 79:595–599.

Meyer, M. 1992. Coercing Sex Behind Bars: Hawaii's Prison Scandal. *Newsweek,* November 9, pp. 23–25.

Miller, J., and M. Schwartz. 1995. Rape Myths and Violence Against Street Prostitutes. *Deviant Behaviors* 16(1):1–23.

Millett, K. 1969. *Sexual Politics.* New York: Avon.

Millman, J. 1980. New Rules for the Oldest Profession: Should We Change Our Prostitution Laws? *Harvard Women's Law Journal* 3:1–35.

Nenadic, N. 1996. Femicide: A Framework for Understanding Genocide. In *Radically Speaking: Feminism Reclaimed,* eds. D. Bell and R. Klein, 456–464. North Melbourne, Australia: Spinifex.

Omerdic, M. 1992. Another Genocide against Muslims: Let It Be Known and Never Repeated. *Preporod* 3:11.

Ouellet, L. J., W. W. Wiebel, A. D. Jimenez, and W. A. Johnson. 1993. Crack Cocaine and the Transformation of Prostitution in Three Chicago Neighborhoods. In *The Crack Pipe as Pimp,* ed. M. Ratner, 69–96. Lexington, MA: Lexington.

Perl, G. 1948. *I Was a Doctor in Auschwitz.* New York: Arno.

Pleck, E. 1987. *Domestic Tyranny.* New York: Oxford University.

Radford, J., and D. E. H. Russell. 1992. *Femicide.* Milton Keynes, UK: Open University.

Rafter, N. H. 1990. *Partial Justice: Women, Prisons and Social Control.* New Brunswick, NJ: Transaction.

Rittner, C., and J. K. Roth, eds. 1993. *Different Voices: Women and the Holocaust.* New York: Paragon House.

Rosenbaum, M. 1990. *The Role of Depression in Couples Involved in Murder-Suicide and Homicide.* New York: Paragon House.

Russell, D. E. H. 1990. *Rape in Marriage.* Bloomington: Indiana University.

Schwarcz, S. K., G. A. Bolan, M. Fullilove, J. McCright, R. Fullilove, R. Kohn, and R. T. Rolfs. 1992. Crack Cocaine and the Exchange of Sex for Money or Drugs. *Sexually Transmitted Diseases* 19:7–13.

Sewenely, A. 1993. Sex Abuse Charges Rock Women's Prison. *Detroit News,* January 6, pp. B1, B7.

"Slain Secretary Feared Husband Would Be Violent." 1990. *The Advocate Messenger,* May 11, pp. A1–A7.

Smart, C., and B. Smart, eds. 1978. *Women, Sexuality and Social Control.* London: Routledge and Kegan Paul.

Smith, M. D. 1990. Patriarchal Ideology and Wife Beating: A Test of a Feminist Hypothesis. *Violence and Victims* 5:257–273.

Snell, T. L., and D. C. Morton. 1994. *Women in Prison* (Special report). Washington, DC: Bureau of Justice Statistics.

Stanko, E. A. 1994. Challenging the Problem of Men's Individual Violence. In *Men, Masculinities, and Crime: Just Boys Doing Business?* ed. T. Newburn and E. A. Stanko, 32–45. London: Routledge and Kegan Paul.

Stark, E., and A. Filtcraft. 1996. *Women at Risk: Domestic Violence and Women's Health.* London: Sage.

Stato, J. 1993. Montreal Gynocide. In *Violence against Women: The Bloody Footprints,* ed. P. Bart and E. G. Moran, 132–133. Newbury Park, CA: Sage.

Stein, B. 1996. Life in Prison: Sexual Abuse. *The Progressive,* July, pp. 23–24.

Steinmetz, S. 1977–1978. The Battered Husband Syndrome. *Victimology* 2:499–509.

Straus, M. A., and R. Gelles. 1990. Societal Change and Change in Family Violence from 1975 to 1985 as Revealed by Two National Surveys. In *Criminal Behavior,* 2d ed., ed. D. Kelly, 114–136. New York: St. Martin's.

Studervant, S. P., and B. Stoltzfus. 1992. *Let the Good Times Roll: Prostitution and the U.S. Military in Asia.* New York: New Press.

Taves, A., ed. 1989. *Religion and Domestic Violence in Early New England: The Memoirs of Abigail Abbott Bailey.* Bloomington: Indiana University.

Tomes, N. 1978. A Torrent of Abuse: Crimes of Violence Between Working-Class Men and Women in London, 1840–1875. *Journal of Social History* 11(Spring):328–345.

U.S. Department of Justice. 1994. Violence between Inmates (Rep. No. Ci-149259). Washington, DC: Bureau of Justice Statistics. November.

Walby, S. 1990. *Theorizing Patriarchy.* Oxford, UK: Basil Blackwell.

Walby, S. 1992. Post-Post-Modernism? Theorizing Social Complexity. In *Destabilizing Theory: Contemporary Feminist Debates,* ed. M. Barrett and A. Phillips, 31–52. Palo Alto, CA: Stanford University.

Walker, L. 1979. *The Battered Woman.* New York: Harper and Row.

Warshaw, R. 1988. *I Never Called It Rape.* New York: Harper & Row.

Watson, T. 1992, Ga. Indictments Charge Abuse of Female Inmates. *USA Today,* November 16, p. A3.

Websdale, N. 1992. Female Suffrage, Male Violence and Law Enforcement. *Social Justice* 19(3):82–106.

West, D. 1967. *Murder Followed by Suicide.* Cambridge, MA: Harvard University.

Williams, T. 1992. *Crackhouse: Notes from the End of the Line.* New York: Penguin.

Yllo, K., and M. Straus. 1984. Patriarchy and Violence Against Wives: The Impact of Structural and Normative Factors. *Journal of International and Comparative Social Welfare* 1:1–13.

Chapter 19

Gender Violence:
Rape and Sexual Assault

Kathryn Feltey

ABSTRACT

In this chapter, Feltey focuses on one of Websdale and Chesney-Lind's topics: rape. She describes the culture of rape and its social structural context in the United States, calling it "gender violence." Today's attitudes and norms related to gender violence have emerged from a historical period when rape laws were written to protect the sexual property rights of men. Those early laws had little to do with the well-being of the victim. Feltey points out that, today, women are much more likely to be raped or sexually assaulted by acquaintances and intimate partners than by strangers and that in cases of intimate and acquaintance rape, prosecution is less likely to be pursued and convictions less likely to be obtained. Feltey describes how both men and women often believe the rape myths (false beliefs) that hold the victim responsible, a view that makes defining an incident of rape problematic.

Feltey explains that rape tends to occur in societies in which women are devalued and exploited. As noted in chapter 18, rape has historically been used as a weapon of war; today the military throughout the world continues to give structure and form to violent masculinity. Rape of women officers in the U.S. military is also a major problem. According to Terri Spahr, the author of *For Love of Country: Confronting Rape and Sexual Harassment in the U.S. Military*, two-thirds of female service members experience unwanted, uninvited sexual behavior in the military. Between 4 percent and 8 percent of women in the Army, Navy, Air Force, and Coast Guard reported a rape or attempted rape in one year alone.[*]

Critical to the creation of a rape-free society is an increase in social awareness that the responsibility for rape and sexual assault rests not with the victims and survivors but with individual offenders. But responsibility also resides in any society that tolerates, even encourages, the rape of women. Such societies are not humane. Societal-wide changes in the social relations of gender, race, class, and

---

[*]See Gregory Flannery. 2002. Military Rape: The Ugly Secret in the American Armed Forces. *Cincinnati City Beat*, August 22–28.

sexuality must be the goal. As Feltey writes, "Although gender violence occurs within individual lives and is experienced as a very personal event (a woman jogging through the park is attacked and raped; a gay man is abducted, beaten, and left to die), it is culturally produced out of intersecting relations [throughout society's institutions of family, school, work, etc.] of gender, race, social class, and sexuality." Thus, if advocacy to reduce gender violence at the individual level is to be successful, the broader social structural and cultural levels of society must be addressed as well.

A white woman jogging through Central Park one early spring evening in 1989 is attacked by a group of six young black teenagers age 14 to 16. She is sexually assaulted, beaten into unconsciousness, and left to die. The assailants are identified, arrested, and tried within weeks of the attack. The city's mayor calls for the death penalty; half receive the maximum sentence. The media follow the case with headlines focused on the race and class of the assailants and their victim, coining the term "wilding" to describe the attack as a savage act of random violence. The vulnerability of (white) women to attack by (black) men in urban places becomes the key issue in public discussion and debate.

One month earlier, in the nearby affluent white suburb of Glen Ridge, New Jersey, a white 17-year-old mentally retarded girl is taken to the basement of a neighbor's house, where she is sexually assaulted by seven white high school male athletes she has known for most of her life. The response of the community is one of defensiveness for the males, who are defined as innocent victims of the girl's seductiveness and sexual availability. Four of the seven are convicted; three receive indeterminate sentences, one is put on probation, and all are sent home pending the appeals process. At issue is the promising future of these All-American athletes, potentially in jeopardy as a result of their arrest and conviction.

Rape, as illustrated in these two cases, is violence that involves gender, race, social class, sexuality, and community. In the case of the Central Park "wilding," race and social class were central in shaping public reaction to the event and prosecution of the offenders. The victim, a white, upper-class Wellesley- and Yale-educated investment banker, lived in a different social world from that of her [alleged] assailants, who were from the African-American working class. The immediate and widespread media coverage and the response of the judicial system in giving the maximum penalties are directly related to the race and class differences of the offenders and the victim. This case was different from most in that regard, because sexual assault usually occurs within communities of people who know one another and share the same social class and racial category.*

The second case was more typical in that the victim lived in the same neighborhood as her assailants and had known them most of her life. Also more common was the reaction of the community, which blamed the victim for the assault and its consequences and defended the young men by describing their circumstances as a tragedy. Unlike the Central Park case, the media, claiming the young men did not pose an ongoing threat to the community, did not report the arrest of the Glen Ridge offenders until a month after the fact. Both cases were unusual in that the victims were attacked not by a lone actor but by a group; less than 10 percent of sexual assault involves multiple offenders.

What do these commonalities and differences say about rape and sexual assault? Although rape occurs at the level of individual experience, it is a social phenomenon. For sociologists, the important question is how rape is institutionally situated and socially expressed within cultural practices. The fact of rape and the response to rape (including whether it

---

Source: Dana Vannoy, ed. 2001. *Gender Mosaics.* Los Angeles: Roxbury. pp. 363–373.

*Editors' note: The author omits a critical factor contributing to the public outcry and widespread media coverage in the case of the Central Park jogger: she was not only raped but brutally beaten losing 75 percent of her blood. While 5 of the 15 arrested teenagers were tried, convicted, and sentenced to 7 to 15 years, 10 years later a serial rapist confessed to the crime and the teens' convictions were overturned.

is defined as rape or not) occur in the context of *gender inequality* where men are in a dominant position, women have secondary status, and masculinity is valued over femininity. This sex-based system of stratification is produced and maintained by social-structural arrangements, including the family, economy, state, and religion, among others. From a sociological perspective, rape is a form of gender violence that both reflects and perpetuates the social inequality that exists between men and women.

The cases described reflect dimensions not only of gender inequality but of race and social class [inequalities] as well. For example, the differential treatment of the offenders reflects their race, social class, and community. In the New Jersey case the athletes were seen as having a future with potential for success (their victim was not, given her mentally retarded status); in the Central Park case the offenders were seen as a continued threat to the social order (which their victim's life and circumstances represented). In addition, these two assaults, like other cases of gender violence, perpetuate inequality by limiting the geographic and social mobility of women and supporting the autonomy and power of men.

Men do not have to use violence to benefit from the ways that violence maintains men's domination over women. The fact that women's lives are circumscribed by violence and the fear of violence, and sexual violence in particular, means that their sense of autonomy and independence is limited. In fact, fear of rape significantly restricts the daily activities of women, including leaving their home and traveling in their communities (Warr 1985). In a discussion with her college students, Carole Sheffield found that the fear of attack governed the choices that the female students made while "male students said they *never* feared being attacked simply because they were male. They *never* feared going to a movie or to a mall alone. Their daily activities were not characterized by a concern for their physical integrity" (1995, 4, italics in the original). Gender violence, even when it does not directly affect an individual's life, has ongoing consequences for women and men.

Gender violence can be defined as "any interpersonal, organizational, or politically oriented violation

perpetrated against people due to their gender identity, sexual orientation, or location in the hierarchy of male-dominated social systems such as families, military organizations, or the labor force" (O'Toole and Schiffman 1997, xii). Accordingly, gender violence serves as a power-preserving mechanism whereby systems of inequality are protected. Gender violence manifests itself in many forms: child sexual abuse, workplace and classroom sexual harassment, rape and sexual assault, wife battering, torture, and murder. Although gender violence occurs within individual lives and is experienced as a very personal event (a woman jogging through the park is attacked and raped; a gay man is abducted, beaten, and left to die), it is culturally produced out of intersecting relations of gender, race, social class, and sexuality. Rape and sexual assault, as forms of gender violence, are pervasive in the United States.

RAPE AND SEXUAL ASSAULT

Rape, according to the National Crime Victimization Survey (NCVS), is forced sexual intercourse including vaginal, anal, or oral penetration involving psychological coercion as well as physical force. *Sexual assault* is attacks or attempted attacks involving unwanted sexual contact or verbal threats of attack (Bachman and Saltzman 1995). As measured by both prevalence (number of rape victims) and incidence (number of separate victimizations), rape occurs in the United States in epidemic proportions. According to the Federal Bureau of Investigation (1997), one forcible rape is committed every six minutes in the United States. In 1995, 260,300 rapes and 95,000 sexual assaults were reported to law enforcement officials (Greenfeld 1997). The National Violence Against Women Survey revealed an annual rate of 500,000 rapes and sexual assaults for women, a rate 10 times higher than that for men (Bachman and Saltzman 1995). Rape and sexual assault are, however, the least likely crimes to be reported to the police, resulting in serious underreporting and low official statistics.

Research on rape in the general population reveals that 18 percent of women and 3 percent of men have experienced an attempted or completed rape at some time in their lives (Tjaden and Thoennes 1998). The majority of women who have been raped were not adults (22 percent were under the age of 12 at the time of the first rape, while 32 percent were between the ages of 12 and 17), making young women particularly vulnerable to this form of gender violence. Women who are raped as children and adolescents are at much greater risk for subsequent sexual assault as adults; 18 percent of the women who were raped as children were raped again once they became adults, twice the rate for women not raped as children (Tjaden and Thoennes 1998). This repetition is likely to be due to the families and social environments in which these particular women existed.

Other surveys indicate higher rates of sexual victimization for women than for men. In a random sample of 930 women in San Francisco, 24 percent had experienced forced or coercive intercourse; only 9.5 percent of these women reported their experience to the police (Russell 1984). In a smaller random sample of 481 college women, 25 percent reported being coerced sexually during their college years (Fenstermaker 1989). In a sample of over 3,000 college women, 54 percent had experienced some form of sexual victimization, with 27 percent reporting attempted or completed rape (Koss 1989).

Reported rates of rape in one's lifetime reveal similar rates for African American (19 percent) and white (18 percent) women, a slightly lower rate for Hispanic women (15 percent), and the highest rate for American Indian and Alaska Native women (34 percent) (Tjaden and Thoennes 1998). Despite the seeming racial neutrality of victimization (with the exception of Indian or Alaska Native women), Judith Howard (1988) cautions that pervasive racism results in severe underreporting of rape and other crimes by black victims. Opal Palmer Adisa (1997) provides a historical perspective on the rape of African American women and concludes that they are more likely to be raped but less likely to be believed, and that their assailants receive the lightest sentences. She draws on the work of black feminist writers to demonstrate that rape has been part of the system-

atic subjugation and disempowerment of black women since the days of slavery.

One of the most striking aspects of rape and sexual assault is that the majority of cases involve *acquaintance rape,* where the victim knows or is familiar with her assailant. . . . Women are most likely to be raped or sexually assaulted by friends or acquaintances (50 percent of all reported rapes) and intimate partners (26 percent) (Bachman and Saltzman 1995). Although most of the research has focused on single, young women as victims of rape, married women of all ages are not exempt from this form of victimization. *Marital rape* occurs in 9 to 14 percent of all U.S. marriages (Bergen 1996). More than one-third of battered women are also victims of wife rape (Russell 1982).

RAPE AND SEXUAL ASSAULT AND THE LAW

Historically and cross-culturally, women have not been legally protected from rape within the context of intimate relationships, particularly marriage. In fact, rape laws were based on the premise of unlawful extramarital sexual activity; rape laws were written to protect the sexual property rights of men over their wives (Russell 1982). Thus, sexual activity within marriage, by definition, was exempt from legal intervention. In the United States, early efforts to apply rape laws in the context of marital relationships were resisted. In one striking example, United States Senator Bob Wilson asked a group lobbying for marital rape laws, "If you can't rape your wife, who can you rape?" (Russell 1982). Since that time marital rape laws have been enacted in all of the states, but exemptions still exist depending upon the circumstances (e.g., in some states, rape laws apply only if the partners are legally separated or have filed for divorce).

Laws governing rape and sexual assault have served as a mechanism of institutionalized social control. Prior to the Civil War, laws were written to protect the sexual property rights of white men over white women and their ownership rights over black slave women. White men raped black women with impunity; the supremacy of white men was maintained, in part, by the sexual assault of minority women (Donat and D'Emilio 1992). Black men accused of sexually assaulting white women received the harshest sentences, often execution or castration; lynching served as a form of racial and sexual control outside of the legal system (Davis 1983). The myth of the black rapist still affects sentencing today, with the most severe sentences reserved for black men who sexually assault white women and the most lenient sentences applied in black intraracial cases (LaFree 1989). Interestingly, of the various possible configurations of race and gender, black men raping white women is the *smallest* percentage.

Present-day laws and legal intervention in cases of rape and sexual assault reflect normative expectations based on race and gender. For example, in one study researchers found that nontraditional gender behavior on the part of the victim (staying out late at night, engaging in sexual activity outside of marriage, drinking alcohol) was the most important predictor of the verdict in rape cases, above any evidence or severity of the crime (LaFree 1989). Prosecution is less likely to be pursued when the offender and victim are acquainted, and convictions are more successfully obtained when they are strangers. Overall, conviction rates for rape are low. Fewer than one-fourth of those arrested are convicted; two-thirds of those convicted receive a prison sentence, the majority serving less than five years in prison (Greenfeld 1997).

MEN AS VICTIMS AND PERPETRATORS

Little is known about males as victims of sexual assault and rape. Men commit the majority of rapes against women and children. When males are raped, it is most often by other males who are asserting their strength and manhood by dominating another man (Pelka 1997). In rapes of both women and men, sex is used as a source of power rather than as an expression of sexuality or sexual desire. Men who

are victimized lose the higher status of male and are "demoted" to female status. As Fred Pelka describes in his own account of being raped by another man:

> It was obvious to me at the police station that I was held in contempt because I was a victim—feminine, hence perceived as less masculine. Had I been an accused criminal, even a rapist, chances are I would have been treated with more respect, because I would have been seen as more of a man. To cross that line, to become victims of the violence which works to circumscribe the lives of women marks us somehow as traitors to our gender. Being a male rape survivor means I no longer fit our culture's neat but specious definition of masculinity, as one empowered, one always in control. (1997, 213–214)

The most consistent finding in research on sexual aggression is that females are the victims and males the perpetrators. This fact fits with the more general finding that violence is dominated by those who enact masculinity in all modern societies; 90 to 100 percent of all violence is perpetrated by men, while less than 10 percent is perpetrated by women (Bowker 1998). Males who participate in sexual aggression are not significantly different from nonaggressive males across most behaviors. Psychological tests do not consistently discriminate between rapists and nonrapists (Scully and Marolla 1985). Differences have been found in terms of level of sexual activity in some studies; in one sample admitted rapists differed from nonrapists in higher levels of sexual activity and the pressure for sex they exerted in the early stages of dating (62 percent of the rapists attempted to seduce first dates, compared to 19 percent of the controls) (Kanin 1985). Sexual exploitation of females permeates their approach to male-female interaction.

This approach is not, according to Edwin Schur (1988), unusual in the social construction of sexuality in American culture. Specifically, he criticizes the male-female system of domination where men approach women as a sexualized category, rather than as individuals, and sexual aggression in men is seen as normal and acceptable. An examination of the linking of sexuality and violence and the portrayal of women and men in the media provides an understanding of this relationship. In the documentary film *Dreamworlds,* Sut Jully explores the themes of violence, sexuality, male dominance, female submission, and rape in rock video. Interweaving the gang rape scene from the film *The Accused* with clips from popular music videos, Jully demonstrates that rape imagery is common and ordinary in this context. His conclusion is that men construct a view of women that gives them ultimate power derived from the secondary status of women that is primarily about sex and sexual availability vis-à-vis male desire.

A study of convicted incarcerated rapists conducted by Diana Scully and Joseph Marolla (1985) revealed this sexualized view of women and male power. The men they interviewed asserted their right to dominate women sexually. They talked about being in charge, in command, and women being powerless and submissive in the act of rape. Sex was seen as a "male entitlement," rape a method of conquering resistant partners. One man in the study explained:

> Rape is a man's right. If a woman doesn't want to give it, the man should take it. Women have no right to say no. Women are made to have sex. It's all they are good for. Some women would rather take a beating, but they always give in; it's what they are for. (1985, 261)

Men arrested and convicted on rape charges are in their early thirties on average, white (6 out of 10), and married (6 out of 10). Rape and sexual assault offenders make up less than 5 percent of the total correctional population in the United States (Greenfeld 1997).

However, a significant number of men who have never had contact with the criminal justice system claim to have perpetrated some form of sexual aggression against women. In studies based on the experiences of college men, rape and sexual assault are reported as common occurrences. In one study, one-quarter of the men admitted they had been sexually aggressive, with the actions of 7 percent fitting the legal definition of rape (Koss 1989). In another sample 57 percent of the men admitted to sexual aggression, and 7 percent admitted to rape (Muehlenhard and

Linton 1987). Nevertheless, the majority of college men (88 percent) who admitted to sexual assault that met the legal definition of rape did not feel that they had raped (Koss 1989). In this same study the majority of women whose experiences met the legal definition of rape (73 percent) also did not label their experiences as rape.

ATTITUDES AND BELIEFS ABOUT RAPE

Part of the problem in defining rape and identifying when a rape has actually occurred is that women and men view rape from the perspective of their socialization around issues of gender, power, and sexuality. *Rape myths,* false beliefs about rape that hold the victim responsible for the rape at the same time that the effects on the victim are denied, are the outcome. Sexually aggressive males are more likely to believe in rape myths, as well as to accept traditional gender roles, violence towards women, and adversarial sexual beliefs (Muehlenhard and Linton 1987). Both women and men, however, subscribe to elements of these belief systems, which makes it difficult to come to terms with the impact of rape and sexual assault in the lives of individuals and the communities where they live.

Common myths about rape include the following: women enjoy forced sex, victims provoke rape and sexual assault, seductive clothing and behavior precipitate rape ("she asked for it"), and rape victims do not suffer any real harm. In the Glen Ridge case, a number of rape myths were used to interpret and explain the assault: the victim was seductive in her behavior, she invited the attack by her willingness to enter the basement with the males, she was not physically harmed by the assault, she actually enjoyed the attention and sexual activity, and she did not physically fight back against the offenders.

Studies of attitudes toward rape and sexual coercion indicate that males are more likely than females to accept rape myths and to support sexually coercive behavior (Gilmartin-Zena 1988). Males who hold more traditional attitudes toward women and women's roles consider rape to be more justifiable than men who hold more egalitarian views (Muehlenhard, Friedman, and Thomas 1985). In addition, males are more likely to see rape as justifiable when victims engage in certain behaviors, such as going to a man's apartment alone with him, and interpret this behavior as implied consent to sexual activity.

The perception of rape and sexual coercion as acceptable under certain circumstances was explored in a study of high school students' attitudes and beliefs (Feltey, Ainslie, and Geib 1991). In the study, 378 high school students were presented with a wide array of forced sexual behaviors, from kissing to sexual intercourse within a variety of social situations and asked to indicate which behavior would be acceptable within each context. There were three major findings from the study: (1) gender was the strongest predictor of attitudes towards rape and sexual coercion, with males more likely to support sexually coercive behavior across situations; (2) when the situation involved couples in a relationship (from dating couples who had a sexual relationship to engagement to marriage), both males and females were more likely to rate sexually coercive behavior as acceptable; and (3) both males and females saw sexual coercion as unacceptable when a female used self-defense and physically fought back against a would-be assailant.

Although males were more likely to see sexual coercion as acceptable, both males and females felt that coercion was acceptable in the context of a sexual relationship, supporting the belief that rape can only occur between people who do not have a prior sexual relationship. Other studies substantiate that sexual coercion is more acceptable when it occurs between intimate partners. Further, men are seen as having increasing entitlement to sexual access the longer partners are together and the more formal their commitment becomes (moving from engagement to marriage, for example) (Margolin, Miller, and Moran 1989).

The only circumstance in which males and females agreed that sexual coercion was unacceptable was when a female said no and reinforced the verbal communication by using physical force. Actions, it would seem, speak louder than words, so that fighting back is interpreted to mean that a female does not want to engage in sexual activity and a male does not have the right to use force against her. Research indicates, in fact, that fighting back increases the likelihood that a woman will escape rape attempts (Bart and O'Brien 1985).

Women report that it is difficult to refuse sexual advances comfortably, leaving them vulnerable to victimization. In traditional gender-role socialization, women are taught to question and deny their perceptions about intimate encounters, resulting in the feeling that they have relinquished their right to withdraw consent (or resist) when the encounter advances beyond a preliminary stage (Berger and Searles 1985). Women who are less traditional in their gender-role orientations are more likely to use a variety of strategies to resist sexual assault and rape. However, women who reject even minor male advances (attempts to kiss a date early in the evening, for example) are labeled as "frigid, prudish, weird, and strange" by both women and men (Margolin, Miller, and Moran 1989, 241). Nontraditional women who assert sexual independence from men (e.g., lesbians and women who never marry) are especially likely to be stigmatized and to be perceived as a threat to the patriarchal status quo (Weitz 1995).

Adherence to prescribed gender roles and the promotion of gender-appropriate responses in male-female interaction (with males dominant and females submissive) are rooted in cultural practices. Cultures that socialize males and females with different meanings and beliefs about sexuality, legitimize and normalize coercive sexuality, and legally regulate sexual coercion when (rather than if) it occurs, will never eliminate rape.

RAPE AS CULTURAL PRACTICE

Peggy Reeves Sanday (1981), in a study of 156 tribal societies, identified cultural characteristics related to sexual violence and rape. She found that in *rape-prone* societies, people compete for diminishing resources, women are seen as objects to be controlled, men are accorded greater prestige and status, the sexes are separated, and men are required to prove their manhood through dominance. In *rape-free* societies women are accorded respect, their reproductive and productive roles are valued and they participate in community decision making. In addition, the environment in these societies is approached with reverence, rather than exploitation, and violence is rare. Maria Lepowsky's 1994 study of South Pacific island society, Vanatinai, provides evidence that violence, especially violence against women, is rare in egalitarian societies. In Vanatinai, both men and women are valued as life-giving and nurturing, and both are responsible for managing the expression of anger in interpersonal relationships.

Rape occurs in societies where women and the environment are devalued and exploited and where violence is commonly used. Men and women in this cultural context are unequal, and *power* is enacted as masculine supremacy and dominance. Rape as a cultural product is an expression of gender inequality and the practice of power as force and control. Accordingly, feminist theorists claim that rape results from institutionalized sexism, with rape and the threat of rape serving as "mechanisms by which men maintain women's subordination in an inequitable social system" (LaFree 1989, 23). In rape-prone societies, men prove their manhood and maintain their superior status through physical force and sexual violence.

The United States qualifies as a rape-prone society: gender inequality exists in all social institutions; the roles of women are devalued, as is femininity; and the use of force and violence for proving manhood is prevalent and common. Gender socialization prepares males and females for different social roles, competencies, and interpersonal styles. A critical outcome of gender socialization is that females and males have different attitudes about sex and different sexual behaviors. The double standard of sexuality for males and females is still alive and well at the start of the twenty-first century. Males are expected and encouraged to become sexually active and to give expression to sexual desire; females are given more ambivalent messages about cultivating sexual desirability in appearance and style, at the same time that

they are expected to limit sexual availability and control potential sexual encounters.

The Spur Posse case in Lakewood, California, a predominantly white suburban community, exemplifies this sexual double standard. Members of the Posse, a group of 20 to 30 high school athletes, were accused of raping and sexually molesting teenage and preteen girls. The Posse received national attention; invited as guests on nationally syndicated talk shows, they explained that they were "keeping score" in a masculinity contest where each act of sex "counted" in the competition. At the time of the arrests, the "winner" had accumulated more than 50 "points." The young women, by contrast, quietly transferred to other schools as they were identified and labeled. The parents of the boys blamed the young women for their sons' behavior and described them as seductive and promiscuous.

The social life of the male athletes involved in the Glen Ridge rape case serves as another example of the way some adolescent males are introduced to and participate in sexualized subcultures. Viewing pornography as a group was a common activity for these young men, as was voyeurism. According to Bernard Lefkowitz, who studied the Glen Ridge community in the aftermath of the gang rape, the "devotion to activities, such as circle-jerks, 'voyeuring' oral sex performed by one girl on a number of guys, humiliating girls, and watching pornography together . . . [was] an effort to prove heterosexual dominance and to establish masculine authority within the group" (1997, 243–244). The goal was sexual control and domination, which proves one's manhood in a rape-prone culture.

Females are socialized to be passive and submissive and to play the role of sexual object in relation to men (Schur 1988). The process of socialization begins early; girls are taught to emphasize physical attractiveness over other characteristics, while boys are taught dominance and control (Sobieraj 1998). As they move into adolescence, males and females find increased acceptance of sexual activity for both sexes, but women are expected to be sexual only in the context of a committed heterosexual relationship, while a broader range of heterosexual experiences are accepted (or at least overlooked) for men.

Over time, the status of women (and their ability to survive economically) has been dependent on their securing a relationship with a male "provider" in marriage. Further, it is through their relationships with men (primarily marriage) that women gain an identity and social status (for example, the linguistic practice of distinguishing between married and unmarried women with Mrs. and Miss, while the same practices does not hold for men). Some developmental theories posit that male identity develops prior to and separate from their intimate ties to women, while women are dependent upon those intimate ties to forge an identity (Gilligan 1979). Thus women are taught to focus on their appearance and to compete with one another for the attention (and commitment) of men.

As a result, women's sexuality is their commodity and women are valued primarily for their sexual desirability, as defined by men. This "compulsory heterosexuality" involves the institutional control of women's lives, where women (and their sexuality) is the property of men. According to Adrienne Rich, compulsory heterosexuality, along with other institutions of social control, are being strengthened in a backlash against the feminist movement that is based on the fear that "the autonomy and equality of women threaten family, religion, and state" (1993, 158).

RAPE AS INSTITUTIONAL CONTROL

Rape as an expression of aggressive masculinity is most apparent in male-dominated subcultures within social institutions such as the military, sports teams, and fraternities. . . . Rape has historically been used as a weapon of war, with soldiers "raping and pillaging" villages as part of their conquest of the enemy. This military, by forcing males to disown femininity within themselves and to control it in others, plays a significant role in giving structure and form to violent masculinity. The Tailhook incident of 1991 made public the ritualized mistreatment of women in the military and the widespread use of sexual co-

ercion by members of the military. Training in the military involves the systematic devaluing of women verbally and symbolically and the sexualization of male dominance over women (Michalowski 1994).

Sports teams are trained on militaristic principles, with control over pain as the key to winning. Further, sports are organized to shape developing masculine identity in terms of power and privilege, leading many male athletes to rape (Messner and Sabo 1994). Team cohesiveness is built, in part, through the sexual objectification of women (Messner 1992), with "locker room talk" that both dehumanizes women and promotes rape (Curry 1991). As a former professional football player told Lefkowitz,

> In my sophomore year of college . . . there were girls we treated like property. They were our "whores" and the jocks shared them. We could do whatever we wanted with them. Lots of people in the school knew about it, but nobody said a word. We were the jocks and we got what we wanted. (1997, 241)

In a similar vein, in the film *He Got Game,* Jesus is recruited to university basketball teams with a number of perks, including sex with women who are plentiful, willing, and seemingly have no purpose beyond sexually gratifying male athletes.

College athletes are implicated in a significant number of the rapes that occur on campuses; NCAA basketball and football players were reported to the police for sexual assault 38 percent more than males in the general college population (Lefkowitz 1997). Robin Warshaw (1988) found athletic teams to be "breeding grounds" for rape, priding themselves on the physical aggressiveness of their members and their group loyalty.

Rape serves as a bonding ritual for men in fraternities (Sanday 1990). The purpose of gang rape ("pulling train") is to solidify the brotherhood and affirm the shared masculinity of its members. The initiation rites of pledges involves demeaning them as "women and homosexuals" until they have proven themselves through the pledging process. Patricia Martin and Robert Hummer analyzed the practices and conditions in fraternities that create a climate hostile toward women. Their research indicated that fraternities are concerned above all else with masculinity. "Valued members display, or are willing to go along with, a narrow conception of masculinity that stresses competition, athleticism, dominance, winning, conflict, wealth, material possessions, willingness to drink alcohol, and sexual prowess vis-à-vis women" (1989, 460). The organizations of fraternities, including the expectation of group loyalty and the degradation and subordination of women, contributes to coercive and violent sex.

In all-male or male-dominated peer groups, sexual coercion and rape are about the relationships between the men involved. The rape becomes a proving ground for masculinity through "heterosexual dominance and exploitation of a woman" (O'Sullivan 1998, 105). Of course, not all men in these settings rape or endorse rape. Some men voluntarily withdraw from groups or teams; others find "alternative models of masculinity—regular guys who enjoy watching a tightly pitched baseball game but who also demonstrate compassion, fairness, and thoughtfulness . . . [who] take more pleasure in appreciating females than humiliating them" (Lefkowitz 1997, 242). The key seems to lie in creating alternative models of masculinity across social contexts and within social institutions.

CONCLUSION: CREATING A RAPE-FREE SOCIETY

Creating a society free of rape and sexual assault involves action on multiple levels. Rape occurs only in societies where systems of inequality divide people from one another and result in the differential valuing of categories of people based on gender, race, social class, and sexuality. Society needs to address the dynamics of gender socialization, the structured inequality between women and men, the interrelationship of sex and violence, and the intersecting dimensions of inequality that push too many to the margins of society. People's lived experiences of gender, as well as the institutionalization of gender inequality, should be explored, critiqued, and challenged. Attitudes and behaviors supportive of rape and violence (from pas-

sively ignoring woman-hating humor to actively objectifying women as sex prey or men as sexual predators) should be eliminated from personal interactions and social institutions.

Creating social awareness that the responsibility for rape and sexual assault ultimately rests with the offenders is a first and critical step. Annette Fuentes points out that rape-prevention policies and practices focusing on the victim miss the mark. She uses the social movement against drunk driving as a case in point: "Ad campaigns against drunk driving would never admonish people to avoid driving when or where drunks might be on the road" (1997, 22). We need a public-education campaign focused on the ways that gender shapes our perceptions and structures our experiences, emphasizing the high cost to both women and men of enacting gender in limited and limiting ways, and exploring the possibility of collectively and individually creating social change. Only when this change is defined and perceived as beneficial for both women and men will attitudes and behaviors about rape, sexuality, and inequality be transformed.

DISCUSSION QUESTIONS

1. Explain how rape and sexual assault are social phenomena as well as individual experiences.
2. Discuss the ways in which rape serves as an institutional control. What is it controlling? Whom is it controlling? Why?
3. According to Feltey, how do rape cases reflect an intersectional understanding of class, race, and gender systems of social relations?
4. After reading this chapter, what social policies might you suggest that would allow this society to attack rape at its structural and cultural as well as individual roots?

5. Describe four rape myths discussed in this chapter. How and why do you think such myths emerge?

6. What are some of the characteristics of rape-prone and rape-free societies? Why do you think the United States is among those that are rape-prone? What do you think would need to happen in the United States for it to become a rape-free society?

REFERENCES

Adisa, Opal Palmer. 1997. Undeclared War: African-American Women Writers Explicating Rape. In *Gender Violence: Interdisciplinary Perspectives,* ed. Laura O'Toole and Jessica R. Schiffman. New York: New York University Press.

Bachman, Ronet, and Linda E. Saltzman. 1995. *Violence Against Women: Estimates From the Redesigned Survey.* Washington, DC: U.S. Department of Justice, Office of Justice Programs.

Bart, Pauline, and Patricia O'Brien. 1985. *Stopping Rape: Successful Survival Strategies.* New York: Pergamon.

Bergen, Raquel Kennedy. 1996. *Wife Rape: Understanding the Response of Survivors and Service Providers.* Thousand Oaks, CA: Sage.

Berger, Ronald J., and Patricia Searles. 1985. Victim-Offender Interaction in Rape. *Women's Studies Quarterly* 13:9–15

Bowker, Lee H. 1998. *Masculinities and Violence.* Thousand Oaks, CA: Sage.

Curry, Timothy J. 1991. Fraternal Bonding in the Locker Room: A Profeminist Analysis of Talk about Competition and Women. *Sociology of Sport Journal* 8:119–135.

Davis, Angela Y. 1983. *Women, Race, and Class.* New York: Random House.

Donat, Patricia N., and John D'Emilio. 1992. A Feminist Redefinition of Rape and Sexual Assault: Historical Foundations and Change. *Journal of Social Issues* 48:9–22.

Federal Bureau of Investigation. 1997. *Crime in America.* Washington, DC: U.S. Government Printing Office.

Feltey, Kathryn M., Julie J. Ainslie, and Aleta Geib. 1991. Sexual Coercion Attitudes among High School Students: The Influence of Gender and Rape Education. *Youth and Society* 23:229–250.

Fenstermaker, Sarah. 1989. Acquaintance Rape on Campus: Responsibility and Attributions of Crime. In *Violence in Dating Relationships,* ed. Maureen A. Pirog-Good and Jan E. Stets. New York: Praeger.

Fuentes, Annette. 1997. Crime Rates are Down . . . But What About Rape? *MS* 8:19–22.

Gilmartin-Zena, Pat. 1988. Gender Differences in Students' Attitudes Toward Rape. *Sociological Focus* 21:279–292.

Gilligan, Carol. 1979. Women's Place in Man's Life Cycle. *Harvard Educational Review* 49:431–446.

Greenfeld, Lawrence A. 1997. *Sex Offenses and Offenders.* Washington, DC: U.S. Department of Justice, Bureau of Justice Statistics.

Howard, Judith. 1988. A Structural Approach to Sexual Attitudes. *Sociological Perspectives* 31:88–121.

Kanin, Eugene. 1985. Date Rapists: Differential Sexual Socialization and Relative Deprivation. *Archives of Sexual Behavior* 14:219–231.

Koss, Mary P. 1989. Hidden Rape: Sexual Aggression and Victimization in a National Sample of Studies in Higher Education. In *Violence in Dating Relationships,* ed. Maureen A. Pirog-Good and Jan E. Stets. New York: Praeger.

LaFree, Gary D. 1989. *Rape and Criminal Justice.* Belmont, CA: Wadsworth.

Lefkowitz, Bernard. 1997. *Our Guys: The Glen Ridge Rape and the Secret Life of the Perfect Suburb.* Berkeley: University of California Press.

Lepowsky, Maria. 1994. Women, Men, and Aggression. *Sex Roles* 30:199–211.

Margolin, Leslie, Melody Miller, and Patricia B. Moran. 1989. When a Kiss Is Not Just a Kiss: Relating Violations of Consent in Kissing to Rape Myth Acceptance. *Sex Roles* 20:231–243.

Martin, Patricia Yancey, and Robert A. Hummer. 1989. Fraternities and Rape on Campus. *Gender and Society* 3:457–473.

Messner, Michael. 1992. *Power at Play: Sports and the Problem of Masculinity.* Boston: Beacon.

Messner, Michael, and Donald Sabo. 1994. *Sex, Violence and Power in Sports.* Freedom, CA: Crossing.

Michalowski, Helen. 1980. The Army Will Make a "Man" Out of You. WIN Magazine.

Michalowski, Helen. 1994. The Army Will Make a "Man" Out of You. In *Living With Contradictions: Controversies in Feminist Social Ethics,* ed. Alison M. Jaggar. Boulder, CO: Westview.

Muelenhard, Charlene L., Debra E. Friedman, and Celeste M. Thomas. 1985. Is Date Rape Justifiable? *Psychology of Women Quarterly* 9: 297–310.

Muelenhard, Charlene L., and Melaney A. Linton. 1987. Date Rape and Sexual Aggression in Dating Situations: Incidence and Risk Factors. *Journal of Counseling Psychology* 34:186–196.

O'Sullivan, Chris. 1998. Ladykillers: Similarities and Divergences of Masculinities in Gang Rape and Wife Battery. In *Masculinities and Violence,* ed. Lee H. Bowker, Thousand Oaks, CA: Sage.

O'Toole, Laura L. 1997. Subcultural Theory of Rape Revisited. In *Gender Violence: Interdisciplinary Perspectives,* ed. Laura O'Toole and Jessica R. Schiffman. New York: New York University Press.

O'Toole, Laura L., and Jessica R. Schiffman eds. 1997. *Gender Violence: Interdisciplinary Perspectives.* New York: New York University Press.

Pelka, Fred. 1997. Raped: A Male Survivor Breaks His Silence. In *Gender Violence: Interdisciplinary Perspectives.* ed. Laura O'Toole and Jessica R. Schiffman. New York: New York University Press.

Rich, Adrienne. 1993. Compulsory Heterosexuality and Lesbian Existence. In *Feminist Frontier III,* ed. Laurel Richardson and Verta Taylor. New York: McGraw-Hill.

Russell, Diana E. H. 1982. *Rape in Marriage.* New York: MacMillan.

———. 1984. *Sexual Exploitation: Rape, Child Sexual Abuse, and Workplace Harassment.* Newbury Park, CA: Sage.

Sanday, Peggy Reeves. 1981. The Socio-Cultural Context of Rape: A Cross-Cultural Study. *Journal of Social Issues* 37:5–27.

———. 1990. *Fraternity Gang Rape.* New York: New York University Press.

Schur, Edwin L. 1988. *The Americanization of Sex.* Philadelphia: Temple University Press.

Scully, Diana, and Marolla, Joseph. 1985. Riding the Bull at Gilley's: Convicted Rapists Describe the Rewards of Rape. *Social Problems* 32:251–263.

Sheffield, Carole J. 1995. Sexual Terrorism. In *Women: A Feminist Perspective,* ed. Jo Freeman. Mountain View, CA: Mayfield.

Sobieraj, Sarah. 1998. Taking Control: Toy Commercials and the Social Construction of Patriarchy. *In Masculinities and Violence,* ed. Lee H. Bowker. Thousand Oaks, CA: Sage.

Tjaden, Patricia, and Nancy Thoennes. 1998. *Prevalence, Incidence and Consequences of Violence against Women: Findings from the National Violence against Women Survey.* Washington, DC: U. S. Department of Justice, Office of Justice Programs.

Warr, Mark. 1985. Fear of Rape Among Urban Women. *Social Problems* 32:238–250.

Warshaw, Robin. 1988. *I Never Called it Rape: The MS Report on Recognizing, Fighting, and Surviving Date and Acquaintance Rape.* New York: Harper and Row.

Weitz, Rose. 1995. What Price Independence? Social Reactions to Lesbians, Spinsters, Widows, and Nuns. In *Women: A Feminist Perspective,* ed. Jo Freeman. Mountain View, CA: Mayfield.

Chapter 20

Rape, Racism, and the Law

Jennifer Wriggins

ABSTRACT

In chapter 19, Feltey referred to the problem of racism and rape. This chapter examines in greater depth the historical attitudes and treatment of African American men accused of raping white women, beginning with the period of slavery in the United States. The strict rape laws of the time were enacted primarily to punish black men accused of raping white women. When it came to rape, Wriggins contends, race was the defining characteristic; little else was of significance. Both white and black men accused of raping black women were very likely to have the case dismissed because, during slavery, black women were legally white men's property and because women had no standing in court. In addition, black women were further unprotected by the law because they were deemed to be "promiscuous" and, hence, culpable for attacks against themselves. Accusations of rape of a white woman by a white man rarely made it into the courts, because the patriarchal culture allowed the white husband to seek revenge outside the law and, if the husband was the rapist, the culture precluded a white man from having to defend his behavior toward his wife (who was also considered his property).

The legacy of racial disparity, a claim echoed by many authors throughout this book, still influences the criminal justice system today, Wriggins clearly argues. For example, the legal system's denial of African American women's claims that they have been sexually abused and the frequent disparate sentencing in rape cases, depending on the race of the victim, still persists in many parts of the United States. Wriggins asserts that the legal system continues to treat the rape of white women more severely than the rape of any other groups of women (Latina, Asian, Muslim and especially African American women). Two themes dominate this chapter: the legacy of racism and the legacy of the subordination of women.

Wriggins claims that the public sensationalizes cases of African American men who commit crimes against white women and that in the past the public often turned to lynching in the resulting frenzy to punish. This view continues today, Wriggins suggests, with the legal system operating "as a functional equivalent of lynching." Consider the sensationalism still associated with black on white crime in the following two cases. National attention was given to the so-called wilding attack alleged to have been perpetrated by a group of teenage black and latino males on a white woman executive jogging in Central Park in New York City (see Feltey, chap. 19). Also, remember how the international media focused attention on the murder of Nicole Brown, the white ex-wife of the African American sports hero O. J. Simpson in Los Angeles in 1994. In what ways has this historical legacy impacted other minority groups today?

The history of rape in this country has focused on the rape of white women by Black men. From a feminist perspective, two of the most damaging consequences of this selective blindness are the denials that Black women are raped and that all women are subject to pervasive and harmful sexual coercion of all kinds.

. . .

THE NARROW FOCUS ON BLACK OFFENDER/WHITE VICTIM RAPE

There are many different kinds of rape. Its victims are of all races, and its perpetrators are of all races. Yet the kind of rape that has been treated most seriously throughout this nation's history has been the illegal forcible rape of a white woman by a Black man. The selective acknowledgement of Black accused/white victim rape was especially pronounced during slavery and through the first half of the twentieth century. Today a powerful legacy remains that permeates thought about rape and race.

During the slavery period, statutes in many jurisdictions provided the death penalty or castration for rape when the convicted man was Black or mulatto and the victim white. These extremely harsh penalties were frequently imposed. In addition, mobs occasionally broke into jails and courtrooms and

lynched slaves alleged to have raped white women, prefiguring Reconstruction mob behavior.

In contrast to the harsh penalties imposed on Black offenders, courts occasionally released a defendant accused of raping a white woman when the evidence was inconclusive as to whether he was Black or mulatto. The rape of Black women by white or Black men, on the other hand, was legal; indictments were sometimes dismissed for failing to allege that the victim was white. In those states where it was illegal for white men to rape white women, statutes provided less severe penalties for the convicted white rapist than for the convicted Black one. In addition, common-law rules both defined rape narrowly and made it a difficult crime to prove.

. . .

After the Civil War, state legislatures made their rape statutes race-neutral, but the legal system treated rape in much the same way as it had before the war. Black women raped by white or Black men had no hope of recourse through the legal system. White women raped by white men faced traditional common-law barriers that protected most rapists from prosecution.

Allegations of rape involving Black offenders and white victims were treated with heightened virulence. This was manifested in two ways. The first response was lynching, which peaked near the end of the nineteenth century. The second, from the early twentieth century on, was the use of the legal system as a functional equivalent of lynching, as illustrated by mob coercion of judicial proceedings, special doctrinal rules, the language of opinions, and the

Source: Patricia Searles and Ronald Berger, eds. 1995. *Rape and Society.* Boulder: Westview, pp. 215–222.

markedly disparate numbers of executions for rape between white and Black defendants.

Between 1882 and 1946 at least 4,715 persons were lynched, about three-quarters of whom were Black.[1] Although lynching tapered off after the early 1950s, occasional lynch-like killings persist to this day. The influence of lynching extended far beyond the numbers of Black people murdered because accounts of massive white crowds torturing, burning alive, and dismembering their victims created a widespread sense of terror in the Black community.

The most common justification for lynching was the claim that a Black man had raped a white woman. The thought of this particular crime aroused in many white people an extremely high level of mania and panic. One white woman, the wife of an ex-Congressman, stated in 1898, "If it needs lynching to protect woman's dearest possession from human beasts, then I say lynch a thousand times a week if necessary."[2] The quote resonates with common stereotypes that Black male sexuality is wanton and bestial, and that Black men are wild, criminal rapists of white women.

Many whites accepted lynching as an appropriate punishment for a Black man accused of raping a white woman. The following argument made to the jury by defense counsel in a 1907 Louisiana case illustrates this acceptance:

> Gentlemen of the jury, this man, a nigger, is charged with breaking into the house of a white man in the nighttime and assaulting his wife, with the intent to rape her. Now, don't you know that, if this nigger had committed such a crime, he never would have been brought here and tried; that he would have been lynched, and if I were there I would help pull on the rope.[3]

It is doubtful whether the legal system better protected the rights of a Black man accused of raping a white woman than did the mob. Contemporary legal literature used the term "legal lynching" to describe the legal system's treatment of Black men. Well past the first third of the twentieth century, courts were often coerced by violent mobs, which threatened to execute the defendant themselves

unless the court convicted him. Such mobs often did lynch the defendant if the judicial proceedings were not acceptable to them. A contemporary authority on lynching commented in 1934 that "the local sentiment which would make a lynching possible would insure a conviction in the court."[4] Even if the mob was not overtly pressuring for execution, a Black defendant accused of raping a white woman faced a hostile, racist legal system. State court submission to mob pressure is well illustrated by the most famous series of cases about interracial rape, the Scottsboro cases of the 1930s.[5] Eight young Black men were convicted of what the Alabama Supreme Court called "a most foul and revolting crime," which was the rape of "two defenseless white girls." The defendants were summarily sentenced to death based on minimal and dubious evidence, having been denied effective assistance of counsel. The Alabama Supreme Court upheld the convictions in opinions demonstrating relentless determination to hold the defendants guilty regardless of strong evidence that mob pressure had influenced the verdicts and the weak evidence presented against the defendants. In one decision, that court affirmed the trial court's denial of a change of venue on the grounds that the mobs' threats of harm were not imminent enough although the National Guard had been called out to protect the defendants from mob executions. The U.S. Supreme Court later recognized that the proceedings had in fact taken place in an atmosphere of "tense, hostile, and excited public sentiment." After a lengthy appellate process, including three favorable Supreme Court rulings, all of the Scottsboro defendants were released, having spent a total of 104 years in prison.

In addition, courts applied special doctrinal rules to Black defendants accused of the rape or attempted rape of white women. One such rule allowed juries to consider the race of the defendant and victim in drawing factual conclusions as to the defendant's intent in attempted rape cases. If the accused was Black and the victim white, the jury was entitled to draw the inference, based on race alone, that he intended to rape her. One court wrote, "In determining the question of intention, the jury may consider social conditions and customs founded upon racial differences, such as that the prosecutrix was a white woman and defendant was a Negro man.[6] The "social conditions and customs founded upon racial differences" which the jury was to consider included the assumption that Black men always and only want to rape white women, and that a white woman would never consent to sex with a Black man.

The Georgia Supreme Court of 1899 was even more explicit about the significance of race in the context of attempted rape, and particularly about the motivations of Black men. It held that race may properly be considered "to rebut any presumption that might otherwise arise in favor of the accused that his intention was to obtain the consent of the female, upon failure of which he would abandon his purpose to have sexual intercourse with her."[7] Such a rebuttal denied to Black defendants procedural protection that was accorded white defendants.

. . .

The outcome of this disparate treatment of Black men by the legal system was often the same as lynching—death. Between 1930 and 1967, thirty-six percent of the Black men who were convicted of raping a white woman were executed.[8] In stark contrast, only two percent of all defendants convicted of rape involving other racial combinations were executed. As a result of such disparate treatment, eighty-nine percent of the men executed for rape in this country were Black. While execution rates for all crimes were much higher for Black men than for white men, the differential was most dramatic when the crime was the rape of a white woman.

The patterns that began in slavery and continued long afterwards have left a powerful legacy that manifests itself today in several ways. Although the death penalty for rape has been declared unconstitutional, the severe statutory penalties for rape continue to be applied in a discriminatory manner. A recent study concluded that Black men convicted of raping white women receive more serious sanctions than all other sexual assault defendants.[9] A recent attitudinal study found that white potential jurors treated Black and white defendants similarly when the victim was Black. However, Black defendants received more severe punishment than white defendants when the victim was white.[10]

The rape of white women by Black men is also used to justify harsh rape penalties. One of the few law review articles written before 1970 that takes a firm position in favor of strong rape laws to secure convictions begins with a long quote from a newspaper article describing rapes by three Black men, who at 3 a.m. on Palm Sunday "broke into a West Philadelphia home occupied by an eighty-year-old widow, her forty-four-year-old daughter and fourteen-year-old granddaughter," brutally beat and raped the white women, and left the grandmother unconscious "lying in a pool of blood."[11] This introduction presents rape as a crime committed by violent Black men against helpless white women. It is an image of a highly atypical rape—the defendants are Black and the victims white, the defendants and victims are strangers to each other, extreme violence is used, and it is a group rape. Contemporaneous statistical data on forcible rapes reported to the Philadelphia Police Department reveals that this rape case was virtually unique.[12] Use of this highly unrepresentative image of rape to justify strict rape laws is consistent with recent research showing that it is a prevalent, although false, belief about rape that the most common racial combination is Black offender and white victim.[13]

Charges of rapes committed by Black men against white women are still surrounded by sensationalism and public pressure for prosecution. Black men seem to face a special threat of being unjustly prosecuted or convicted. One example is Willie Sanders.[14] Sanders is a Black Boston man who was arrested and charged with the rapes of four young white women after a sensational media campaign and intense pressure on the police to apprehend the rapist. Although the rapes continued after Sanders was incarcerated, and the evidence against him was extremely weak, the state subjected him to a vigorous twenty-month prosecution. After a lengthy and expensive trial, and an active public defense, he was eventually acquitted.

Although Sanders was clearly innocent, he could have been convicted; he and his family suffered incalculable damage despite his acquittal.

. . .

From slavery to the present day, the legal system has consistently treated the rape of white women by Black men with more harshness than any other kind of rape. . . .

This selective focus is significant in several ways. First, since tolerance of coerced sex has been the rule rather than the exception, it is clear that the rape of white women by Black men has been treated seriously not because it is coerced sex and thus damaging to women, but because it is threatening to white men's power over both "their" women and Black men. Second, in treating Black offender/white victim illegal rape much more harshly than all coerced sex experienced by Black women and most coerced sex experienced by white women, the legal system has implicitly condoned the latter forms of rape. Third, this treatment has contributed to a paradigmatic but false concept of rape as being primarily a violent crime between strangers where the perpetrator is Black and the victim white. Finally, this pattern is perverse and discriminatory because rape is painful and degrading to both Black and white victims regardless of the attacker's race.

THE DENIAL OF THE RAPE OF BLACK WOMEN

The selective acknowledgement of the existence and seriousness of the rape of white women by Black men has been accompanied by a denial of the rape of Black women that began in slavery and continues today. Because of racism and sexism, very little has been written about this denial. Mainstream American history has ignored the role of Black people to a large extent; systematic research into Black history has been published only recently. The experiences of Black women have yet to be fully recognized in those histories, although this is beginning to change. Indeed, very little has been written about

rape from the perspective of the victim, Black or white, until quite recently. Research about Black women rape victims encounters all these obstacles.

The rape of Black women by white men during slavery was commonplace and was used as a crucial weapon of white supremacy. White men had what one commentator called "institutionalized access" to Black women.[15] The rape of Black women by white men cannot be attributed to unique Southern pathology, however, for numerous accounts exist of northern armies raping Black women while they were "liberating" the South.

The legal system rendered the rape of Black women by any man, white or Black, invisible. The rape of a Black woman was not a crime. In 1859 the Mississippi Supreme Court dismissed the indictment of a male slave for the rape of a female slave less than 10 years old, saying:

> [T]his indictment can not be sustained, either at common law or under our statutes. It charges no offense known to either system. [Slavery] was unknown to the common law . . . and hence its provisions are inapplicable. . . . There is no act (of our legislature on this subject) which embraces either the attempted or actual commission of a rape by a slave on a female slave. . . . Masters and slaves can not be governed by the same system or laws; so different are their positions, rights and duties.[16]

This decision is illuminating in several respects. First, Black men are held to lesser standards of sexual restraint with Black women than are white men with white women. Second, white men are held to lesser standards of restraint with Black women than are Black men with white women. Neither white nor Black men were expected to show sexual restraint with Black women.

After the Civil War, the widespread rape of Black women by white men persisted. Black women were vulnerable to rape in several ways that white women were not. First, the rape of Black women was used as a weapon of group terror by white mobs and by the Ku Klux Klan during Reconstruction. Second, because Black women worked outside the home, they were exposed to employers' sexual aggression as white women who worked inside the home were not.

The legal system's denial that Black women experienced sexual abuse by both white and Black men also persisted, although statutes had been made race-neutral. Even if a Black victim's case went to trial—in itself highly unlikely—procedural barriers and prejudice against Black women protected any man accused of rape or attempted rape. The racist rule which facilitated prosecutions of Black offender/white victim attempted rapes by allowing the jury to consider the defendant's race as evidence of his intent, for instance, was not applied where both persons were "of color and there was no evidence of their social standing."[17] That is, the fact that a defendant was Black was considered relevant only to prove intent to rape a white woman; it was not relevant to prove intent to rape a Black woman. By using disparate procedures, the court implicitly makes two assertions. First, Black men do not want to rape Black women with the same intensity or regularity that Black men want to rape white women. Second, Black women do not experience coerced sex in the sense that white women experience it.

These attitudes reflect a set of myths about Black women's supposed promiscuity which were used to excuse white men's sexual abuse of Black women. An example of early twentieth century assumptions about Black women's purported promiscuity was provided by the Florida Supreme Court in 1918. In discussing whether the prior chastity of the victim in a statutory rape case should be presumed subject to defendant's rebuttal or should be an element of the crime which the state must prove, the court explained that:

> What has been said by some of our courts about an unchaste female being a comparatively rare exception is no doubt true where the population is composed largely of the Caucasian race, but we would blind ourselves to actual conditions if we adopted this rule where another race that is largely immoral constitutes an appreciable part of the population.[18]

Cloaking itself in the mantle of legal reasoning, the court states that most young white women are virgins, that most young Black women are not, and that unchaste women are immoral. The traditional law of statutory rape at issue in the above-quoted case provides that women who are not "chaste" cannot be raped. Because of the way the legal system considered chastity, the association of Black women with unchastity meant not only that Black women could not be victims of statutory rape, but also that they would not be recognized as victims of forcible rape.

The criminal justice system continues to take the rape of Black women less seriously than the rape of white women. Studies show that judges generally impose harsher sentences for rape when the victim is white than when the victim is Black.[19] The behavior of white jurors shows a similar bias. A recent study found that a sample of white jurors imposed significantly lighter sentences on defendants whose victims were Black than on defendants whose victims were white. Black jurors exhibited no such bias.[20]

Evidence concerning police behavior also documents the fact that the claims of Black rape victims are taken less seriously than those of whites. A 1968 study of Philadelphia police processing decisions concluded that the differential in police decisions to charge for rape "resulted primarily from a lack of confidence in the veracity of Black complainants and a belief in the myth of Black promiscuity."[21]

The thorough denial of Black women's experiences of rape by the legal system is especially shocking in light of the fact that Black women are much more likely to be victims of rape than are white women."[22] Based on data from national surveys of rape victims, "the profile of the most frequent rape victim is a young woman, divorced or separated, Black and poverty stricken."[23]

. . .

CONCLUSION

The legal system's treatment of rape both has furthered racism and has denied the reality of women's sexual subordination. It has disproportionately targeted Black men for punishment and made Black women both particularly vulnerable and particularly without redress. It has denied the reality of women's sexual subordination by creating a social meaning of rape which implies that the only type of sexual abuse is illegal rape and the only form of illegal rape is Black offender/white victim. Because of the interconnectedness of rape and racism, successful work against rape and other sexual coercion must deal with racism. Struggles against rape must acknowledge the differences among women and the different ways that groups other than women are disempowered. In addition, work against rape must go beyond the focus on illegal rape to include all forms of coerced sex, in order to avoid the racist historical legacy surrounding rape and to combat effectively the subordination of women.

DISCUSSION QUESTIONS

1. According to Wriggins, in what ways has the historical legacy in the United States surrounding slavery and rape impacted (1) how this society deals with rape victims today; (2) the tolerance of rape; and (3) the treatment of minority groups?
2. What has been the fallout from history in dealing with the rape of white women by black men?
3. Explain how black women are more vulnerable to rape than white women—even today—in the context of this nation's history. Discuss some of your own reactions to this issue.
4. Why is society so unwilling to accept that black women are subject to sexual coercion?

NOTES

1. Rose, 1948.
2. Reynolds, 1897–1898, p. 20
3. State v. Petit, 119 La., 44 So. (1907).
4. Chadbourn, 1931, p. 330.
5. Patterson v. State, 224 Ala., 141 So. (1932); Weems v. State, 224 Ala., 141 So. (1932); Powell v. State, 224 Ala., 141 So. (1932); Powell v. Alabama, 287 U.S. (1932).
6. McQuirter v. State, 36 Ala., 63 So. 2d (1953).
7. Dorsey v. State, 108 Ga., 34 S.E. (1899).
8. Wolfgang, 1974.
9. LaFree, 1980a, p. 842.
10. Feild and Bienen, 1980.
11. Schwartz, 1968, p. 509.
12. Amir, 1971. Out of 343 rapes reported to the Philadelphia police, 3.3% involved Black defendants accused of raping white women; 42% involved complaints of stranger rape; 20.5% involved brutal beatings; 43% involved group rapes.
13. In answer to the question, "Among which racial combination do most rapes occur?" 48% of respondents stated Black males and white females, 3% stated white males and Black females, 16% stated Black males and Black females, 33% stated white males and white females (Feild and Bienen, 1980, p. 80). Recent victim survey data contradict this prevalent belief; more than four-fifths of illegal rapes reported to researchers were between members of the same race, and white/Black rapes roughly equaled Black/white rapes (Bowker, 1981, p. 172).
14. Suffolk Superior Court indictment (1980).
15. L. Curtis, 1974, p. 22.
16. George v. State, 37 Miss. (1859).
17. Washington v. State, 38 Ga., 75 S.E. (1912).
18. Dallas v. State, 76 Fla., 79 So. (1918).
19. LaFree, 1980a.
20. Feild and Bienen, 1980.
21. *University of Pennsylvania Law Review*, 1968, p. 277.
22. Recent data from random citizen interviews suggest that Black women are much more likely to be victims of illegal rape than are white women (Bowker, 1981).
23. Karmen, 1982, p. 188.

REFERENCES

Amir, M. 1971. *Patterns in Forcible Rape.* Chicago: University of Chicago.
Bowker, L. 1981. *Women and Crime in America.* New York: Macmillan.

Chadbourn, J. 1931. Plan for Survey of Lynching and the Judicial Process. *North Carolina Law Review* 4:22–27.

Curtis, L. 1974. *Criminal Violence: National Patterns and Behavior.* Lexington, MA: Lexington.

Field, H., and L. Bienen. 1980. *Jurors and Rape: A Study in Psychology and Law.* Lexington, MA: Lexington.

Karmen, A. 1982. Women Victims of Crime: Introduction. In *The Criminal Justice System and Women: Women Offenders, Victims, Workers,* ed. B. R. Price and N. J. Sokoloff. New York: Clark Boardman.

LaFree, G. 1980. The Effect of Social Stratification by Race on Official Reactions to Rape. *American Sociological Review* 45:842–854.

Rose, A. 1948. *The Negro in America.* New York: Harper.

Reynolds, W. 1897–1988. The Remedy for Lynch Law. *Yale Law Journal* 7:20–25.

Schwartz, B. 1968. The Effect of Pennsylvania's Increased Penalties for Rape and Attempted Rape. *Journal of Criminal Law, Criminology, and Police Science* 59:509–515.

University of Pennsylvania Law Review. 1968. Police Discretion and the Judgment that a Crime has been Committed—Rape in Philadelphia, 117:277–322.

Wolfgang, M. 1974. Racial Discrimination in the Death Sentence for Rape. In *Executions in America,* ed. W. Bowers, 185–202. Lexington, MA: Lexington.

Chapter 21

Fear and the Perception of Alternatives:
Asking "Why Battered Women Don't Leave" Is the Wrong Question
Angela Browne

ABSTRACT

This chapter, which appeared in the second edition of this book, has been updated by Browne to reflect current changes in the law and recent research on this serious social problem. Browne, a national expert on wife abuse, provides the reader with one of the more comprehensive discussions of the complex issues that face women who are confronted with violence at home and who are trying to escape that violence. Despite all that has been learned about the social and psychological conditions underlying violence against women in the home since this chapter was originally published, women continue to be blamed for their own brutalization because it is assumed that if she did not "want" the battering, abuse, violence, and degradation, she would just leave.

Browne explains that asking battered women, "Why don't you just leave him?" is the *wrong question*. She points out that although many women *do* leave, leaving does not necessarily end the violence. For many women, it escalates it. More battered women are killed in the process of leaving or indicating that they will leave than at any other time. Equally disconcerting are the research findings, reported here, that children comprise 60 percent of the family members killed if someone in addition to the woman is killed. Clearly, leaving does not guarantee safety for women or their children.

The chapter contains a discussion of the psychological and practical barriers that women encounter in leaving a battering partner. The practical barriers include such issues as finding a place to live, fear of losing the children, an inability to receive public assistance because the woman is still married or does not have an address. The fear of retaliation is equally as powerful. Not only have many of the women been beaten during earlier attempts to leave, but almost all the women report death threats if they were to leave.

Browne likens women's victimization to the experiences of abuse suffered by prisoners of war. Some battered women eventually kill their abuser. She has studied the factors that lead battered women to kill.* The explanation, she found, lies not with the women but with the men—murdered batterers were different from batterers who were not murdered. The former had been more assaultive, raped more frequently, made more death threats, used alcohol and drugs more often, and had higher rates of child abuse than did batterers who were not killed. Browne's conclusion is that "the women's behavior seemed to be primarily in reaction to the level of threat and violence coming in."

*For a discussion of the battered woman's syndrome as a defense to killing an abuser see Elizabeth Schneider. 2000. *Battered Women and Feminist Lawmaking.* New Haven, CT: Yale University.

Probably the most frequently asked question about women who are being abused by their partners is, "Why don't they just leave?" Especially when the abuse is severe, it is hard to understand why a woman would stay around for the next attack. Actually, many women do leave; they are among our friends and neighbors and possibly our families. The majority of them, however, are never identified as abused women. Often they do not realize how many other women have shared similar experiences. Afraid that other people will not understand or will think less of them if they knew, many abused women do not discuss the abuse they suffered in the past. They may blame themselves for becoming involved with an abusive man in the first place, or for the failure of their interactions with him, and carry their memories and the lingering confusion alone. This chapter reports on a comparative study of women in violent relationships who killed their abusers (the "homicide group") and women in violent relationships who did not take lethal action (the "comparison" group). All the women in the homicide group were awaiting trial when interviewed. In the comparison group, over half the women (53 percent) had left their battering relationships by the time of the study; many had never talked about their experiences before. Even in the homicide group, many women left or attempted to leave their violent partners. Some had been separated or divorced for up to two years prior to the lethal incident.*

Editors' note: The subtitle of this chapter was added for this book.

Source: Reprinted with the permission of The Free Press, a Division of Simon & Schuster Adult Publishing Group, from *When Battered Women Kill* by Angela Browne. Copyright©1987 by the Free Press.

The problem with the question, "Why don't battered women leave?" is that it is based on the assumption that leaving will end the violence. This assumption may be true for some women who leave after the first or second incident (these women are rarely identified as battered, and still less often studied), but whether further violence occurs even after these separations depends on whether the abuser feels desperate or abandoned and on his willingness or tendency to do harm when faced with an outcome he does not want or cannot control. The longer the relationship continues and the more investment in it by both partners, the more difficult it becomes for a woman to leave a violent mate safely. Some estimates suggest that at least 50 percent of women who leave their abusers are followed and seriously harassed or further attacked by them (Cardarelli 1997; Koss et al. 1994; Mechanic, Weaver, and Resick 2000). To separate from an individual who has threatened to harm you if you go increases—at least in the short run—the very risk from which you are trying to escape (Mahoney 1991; Ptacek 1997).

*Editors' note: In this study Browne compares battered women who have killed their abusers (the homicide group) with battered women who have not killed their batterers (the comparison group). The *homicide group* consists of 42 women from 15 states charged with murder or attempted murder of their mates. Their average age was 36 years; 66 percent were white, 22 percent were black, and 12 percent were Spanish-American or Chicano. Half were from working-class backgrounds; one quarter each were from the middle and lower classes; 2 women (5 percent) were raised in upper-class homes. The *comparison group* of 205 women in abusive relationships were from six states. More than half (55 percent) were working-class, 41 percent were lower-class, and 4 percent were middle-class. Despite the self-identified class differences, there were no differences in educational levels between the homicide and comparison groups.

Additionally, getting away is not as simple as it sounds. After a crime such as a rape or robbery committed by a stranger, victims often change apartments or even houses to avoid another assault by the attacker. But it is difficult for an abused woman to just "disappear" from her partner or husband. Even if it were possible to sever an intimate relationship so cleanly, couples often hold property in common, have children in common, know one another's daily routines, families, and places of employment, and have mutual friends. It is extremely difficult for an abused woman to go into long-term hiding. A more appropriate question may be, "Why *should* the woman leave?" Why should the victim and, possibly, her children hit the road like fugitives, leaving the assailant safe in the home, when he is the one who broke the law?

Many women remain with abusive partners out of love and commitment—qualities that are considered virtues in other circumstances. They may hope for a favorable change and make attempts toward understanding and resolution, especially in the early days of a relationship when the violence is less frequent and less severe. Often they are ashamed to let others know the things that are occurring and lose time attributing the problems to themselves and attempting to make changes that will eliminate further assaults. For women who are married to their assailants, decisions about their relationships are complicated by legal and financial ties, overlapping family and support networks, and issues related to the care and custody of children. Women worry about the impact a separation might have on their children, and may stay for the sake of the children if the man is not abusive to them. Even when the severity and frequency of violence escalate, three factors affect a woman's decisions to stay with a violent partner: (1) practical problems in leaving, (2) fear of retaliation if they do leave, and (3) general shock reactions of victims to abuse.

PRACTICAL PROBLEMS IN LEAVING

The point at which many outsiders believe a woman *should* leave—immediately after an abusive incident—is precisely when she may be least able to plan such a move. Frightened, in shock, and often physically injured, all she wants to do is survive. Shelters that house abused women are established in many cities (although in rural areas, these facilities are often lacking or are located many miles from the woman's home). Yet they are often full. Shelters in many urban areas turn away thousands of women and children each year. Even when shelters have room for a woman, the maximum stay at most emergency shelters is only four to six weeks, so the woman still must find housing, provide for her children if she has any with her, obtain whatever legal help may be necessary, and plan for her continued safety from further assaults. Making these choices even more difficult, the majority of shelters will not accept boys over the age of 14, which forces women with teenage sons to leave them behind with the violent partner or to make other living arrangements for them during this time of crisis. During this period, women also must weigh whether to file for divorce and must find the money to pay, often in advance, for legal and other services—tasks most people find difficult even under the best of circumstances.

A move into hiding to escape a man's violence is particularly difficult to manage. If the woman is working, she must try to keep this move from interfering with her job, because that job will now be crucial to her survival. Yet if she has reason to fear retaliation by her partner, she must weigh the necessity of going to work against the danger that her partner will follow her there and inflict further harm. If she has school-age children, she must choose between keeping them out of school—a violation of the law—or facing the danger that their father may remove them from the school grounds if she lets them attend. She must also find a place to live where the man cannot find and harm her. In taking these steps, she must weigh the benefits of leaving town for her own safety against the disruptive impact it would have on her work situation and her children's lives as well as the complications such a move could produce in following through on litigation. Some forms of transportation also may not be available to her in an attempt to escape; since the year 2000, many airlines will not accept children as international passengers unless documentation is provided by both parents granting permission for the trip.

If a mother leaves her children behind, the man may refuse to let her have them and may charge her with desertion. If she takes her children with her, she disrupts their daily lives and runs the risk that any retaliatory violence may involve them as well. If she separates from or initiates divorce proceedings against the children's father, he will usually be granted some kind of visitation rights. (Butts Stahly 1999; Jaffe and Geffner 1998; Lemon 2000). The woman may be enjoined against moving out of state, even after the divorce is final. In many partner violence cases, the abuser fights the woman for custody of the children—a particularly effective strategy to maintain control over the woman, keep track of her whereabouts, and apply pressure for reconciliation. In 1990, the U.S. Congress passed a resolution declaring that, "for purposes of determining child custody, credible evidence of physical abuse of a spouse should create a statutory presumption that it is detrimental to the child to be placed in the custody of the abusive spouse" (Morella 1990). Since that time, there has been a strong statutory trend in the United States requiring courts to take partner violence into account when making custody and visitation decisions (Lemon 2000). By 1995, 44 states had enacted statutes with provisions related to partner violence in child custody disputes; by 1999, 14 states had adopted presumptions against custody being awarded to violent partners.

However, in real life, a man's violence against his wife is often not the primary issue before the court, especially if there is no evidence that he has physically abused the children. Women are often unable to afford adequate representation for cases before family court, and judges and guardian ad lidums often retain misperceptions about the seriousness of partner violence or believe that the violence will cease once the couple has separated permanently (Mahoney 1991; Lemon 2000). In addition, if the male partner seems established and has a good job whereas the woman appears in transition and unstable, he may be awarded custody of the children regardless of his wife's accusations of violence. Despite recent legal changes, men who perpetrate violence against their woman partners are being awarded custody in divorce cases as often as or more often than nonviolent men (Lemon 2000).

In one instance, the woman had been married to her husband for a year before the first incident of violence. After two more assaultive incidents during the next two years, the last one endangering the couple's infant son when her partner tipped her over backward in a rocking chair while she was breastfeeding, she decided to leave her mate and file for divorce. Although she loved him, she knew his verbal abuse was uncalled for and was unwilling to risk further physical assaults against herself or the baby. She wrote a letter explaining why she was leaving and, taking their child, went into hiding. She called a few nights later to let him know she and the baby were safe. She also consulted an attorney to file protection orders and obtain a divorce.

At the same time, the husband went to court to obtain custody of his son. He claimed that his wife had been depressed and emotionally unstable since the child's birth, and cited her "unexplained disappearance" from their home as evidence of her unpredictable mental state. He expressed strong concern for the safety of his child, and requested that she be found and the child removed from her care. Based on his allegations, when the woman appeared in court to obtain an order of protection, her son was taken from her and custody was awarded to the state until a temporary hearing could be arranged. The state placed the child with the abuser's family, since they were blood relatives and their place of residence was considered the most stable. The woman was allowed to have her baby one weekend every other week until temporary orders were established.

Even this visitation right was soon cancelled, after the husband and his family made further charges against her. While these new allegations were being investigated, the woman was allowed only brief supervised visits each week; this supervision was provided by her husband's parents at their home, and her husband was frequently present. Formally, the husband was now charging her with neglect, based on the advice of his attorney on how to win the custody of his child, although the charges were unfounded and she had performed all the child-care duties while they were together. Privately, he was pleading with her to come back and warning that she would lose her son forever if she did not return. Each court date was postponed by the husband's attorneys, as family members urged the woman to "come home" and reunite the family. The woman was separated from her infant for over a year and forced to remain in almost constant contact with her husband. Finally, custody was awarded to the husband's relatives, with whom the baby had been staying. As one state worker explained, the fact that the husband's and wife's stories remained so contradictory made both parents seem unstable.

This woman's story provides one answer to the question, "Why don't battered women just leave?" This woman acted independently and rationally: she left the situation when she began to realize that it would not improve and that others were in danger; she went into hiding but reassured her husband that she and their baby were safe; she immediately sought appropriate legal remedies. In taking these actions, she escaped her abuser before the violence became serious. She also lost her child.

FEAR OF REPRISAL

In the homicide group, many of the women stayed because they had tried to escape and been beaten for it or because they believed their partner would use further violence in retaliation against an attempt to leave him. Almost all the women in both the homicide and the comparison groups—98% percent and 90 percent, respectively—thought the abuser could or would kill them. Many, especially in the homicide group, were convinced that they could not escape this danger by leaving. Susan Jefferson's case is an example. (Although based on actual cases, all names have been changed to protect the women's privacy. Details of the violence are unchanged, however.) After Don's death, Susan said:

> We were separating, but I don't think that would have solved anything. Don always said he would come back around—that I belonged to him. Just that day he had gotten an apartment, but it was only right down the street. I knew he would come after me if he saw someone he didn't know come to the house. I was scared. It seemed like the more I tried to get away, the worse things got. He was never going to quit.

These women's fears of retaliation were supported by their past experiences with the men's violence as well as by threats of further violence if they at-

tempted to leave. Nearly all—83 percent—of the men in the homicide group had made threats to kill, and the women took these threats quite seriously. In the case of Karen and Hal Simon, Hal wrote in his journal:

> Every time, Karen would have ugly bruises on her face and neck. She would cry and beg me for a divorce, and I would tell her, "I am sorry. I won't do it again. But as for the divorce, absolutely not. If I can't have you for my wife, you will die. No one else will have you if you ever try to leave me."

Abused women's primary fear—that their abusers will find them and retaliate against their leaving—often is justified. Some women who have left an abusive partner have been followed and harassed for months or even years; some have been killed (Cardarelli 1997; Mahoney 1991; Browne and Williams 1993; Browne, Williams, and Dutton 1999; McFarlane et al. 1999). Many have called the police for help and still the assaults continue. As one woman in the homicide group, charged with the death of her husband, reported:

> I knew if I ran he would find me. He tracked down his first wife with only her social-security number. Can you imagine what it would be like to go through life knowing that a man who intends to kill you may be just around the corner?

Violent men do search desperately for their partner once the woman leaves (Mechanic, Weaver, and Resick 2000). Often, they spend their days and nights calling her family and mutual acquaintances; phoning her place of employment or showing up there; driving around the streets looking for her; haunting school grounds, playgrounds, and grocery stores. If they believe the woman has left town, they frequently attempt to follow her, traveling to all locations where they think she might be found. She is "theirs"—she cannot leave and refuse to talk to them! They may nearly *kill* their mates, but they do not want to *lose* them (Browne 1997). Some women in the homicide group had been separated or divorced for up to two years before the final incident, yet were still experiencing life-threatening harassment and abuse from men unwilling to relinquish their connection. Behaviors that outside observers may interpret as helplessness—such as staying with the abuser or refraining from legal actions against him—may simply be accurate evaluations of the assailant's potential for violent responses and others' inability to intervene in time to guarantee safety. Forcing a violent individual to stop aggressive behavior is virtually impossible, short of extreme medical or criminal justice measures. Orders restraining the assailant from the home or from proximity to the victim work only if the assailant respects those orders or at least does no harm during times of violation. Living in hiding is incompatible with maintaining gainful employment, raising and educating children, and other components of normal life (Browne 1993).

Homicide data for the 1980s and 1990s indicates that a woman who leaves a violent and threatening partner may also put children and other relatives at physical risk. If the woman moves out, she might not be able to go to her family, because the man would be likely to look for her there, an action that might endanger them as well. One study in Massachusetts found that nearly 60 percent of the people killed when someone besides the woman dies in a male-perpetrated partner homicide are children. About one-fifth are adult relatives present at the time of the homicide or those who tried to shelter the woman (Langford, Isaac, and Kabat 1999). If an abused woman is forced to relocate to a new city or state, away from her source of income and from family and friends—especially if she is moving children with her—the alternatives become more and more difficult to accomplish (Cardarelli 1997; Ferraro 1997).

For many battered women, leaving their mates and living in constant fear of reprisal or death seems more intolerable than remaining, despite their fears of further harm. Women in hiding relate how they are afraid to go into their apartment when they get home; to go to work in the morning or to leave at night; to approach their car in a parking lot; to visit friends or family. They know if their estranged partner finds them, he may simply retaliate and not wait to talk. And if he does begin a conversation and they do not agree to go home, they know it may trigger an attack. Every sound in the night, every

step in the hall, every pair of headlights pulling up behind them might be him. Accomplishing daily tasks against this wall of fear becomes exhausting. Added to the other stressors they are facing and the life-changing decisions that must be made, it is often too much and the women return home. Shelter personnel who work with battered women struggle against their frustration when women return to their abusers; yet in many cases, the women are simply overwhelmed.

ESCAPE ATTEMPTS

The point of, or even the discussion of, separation is one of the most dangerous times for partners in a violent relationship. Abusive men threatened with the loss of their mates may be severely depressed, angry, agitated, homicidal, or suicidal. Even attempts to *discuss* a separation can set off a violent attack.

> Susan couldn't take it anymore. She had been living with Don for six months, and the violence kept getting worse. Something happened nearly every week; Don would say he was sorry, but it never got any better. She decided that the only solution was to leave. When Don came home, Susan sat down to talk with him about it. She told him that she couldn't stand the fights, couldn't understand what was happening, couldn't take the things he said to her. She wanted him to understand. She wanted their parting to be amicable.
>
> Don began acting very strangely—running around and pulling furniture in front of the door; acting as though he was angry, but laughing and joking at the same time. Susan had never seen him behave like this and was suddenly very frightened. It seemed crazy to her. Don kept saying, "You're not going anywhere! You're my prisoner here. I'm going to put bars on the doors and windows, and keep you here. . . . You're my prisoner." He would laugh like he was kidding, then suddenly act furious and throw her across the room or onto the floor. He would smash things in the room with his fists or his foot and throw things against the wall. He made her sit in a corner like a child, saying, "Sit here. Face the wall. Hold still now. You just sit there and listen to me. Look at me now. . . . Don't look at me like that. . . . " He got a stick and hit her with it if she tried to move or speak to him. Susan was wearing a cotton shirt and he reached down and tore it off,

slapping her across the back and face with it. He'd laugh; then suddenly grab and choke her, shaking her by the neck, panting with anger and exertion. Susan started thinking, "I may never leave this house alive."

Finally, Don said, "OK. You go ahead and leave." Susan thought about not having anything on above the waist, but decided that was unimportant. She made it as far as the kitchen door when Don grabbed her and pulled her back inside laughing, then saying angrily, "No . . . you're not going anywhere like that. You're my prisoner here. I'll never let you go now. I'm going to keep you here forever." He resumed hitting her with the stick and his hands and made her sit facing the wall again. Finally, he said again that she could go and Susan ran outside and to the corner, but Don was right behind her. He started yelling at her on the street about "deserting" him. Then he suddenly became quiet and passive, took her hand, and walked her home. Susan remembers the feeling of the sun on her back and her hand in his. She knew any further move on her part would only endanger her. They cleaned up the house together and threw out the broken things. Then Don made her take a nap with him, although he left the heavy furniture stacked against the front door.

Irene Miller's experience also illustrates how dangerous it can be for a woman to talk with a violent mate about separation. The threat of abandonment is so devastating to some men that they would rather kill the woman than let her go (Browne, Williams, and Dutton 1999; McFarlane et al. 1999). Irene's case is typical of women in the homicide group in that repeated attempts at separation and escape always failed.

Irene gradually came to from a beating the night before, frightened, exhausted, and throwing up. Mark came into the bedroom to check on her, and Irene told him she thought they should get a divorce; she couldn't stand any more beatings, just please let her go. She reminded him of how much worse the violence was getting. This time, she wasn't sure if she'd been sleeping or unconscious. She confessed she was afraid he would kill her someday, and tried to persuade him that being apart for awhile would be the best thing for both of them.

Mark's mood changed suddenly. He denied that he beat her and held her down on the bed, shouting, "You'll *never* leave me. I'll fucking kill you if you ever

try to do that!" He grabbed her ankle and was bending her foot back, like he was going to break it, then came for her face. Irene turned on her stomach to protect herself and Mark grabbed a heavy vase from the dresser and hit her on the back of the head, splitting the skin open. Then he began hitting her repeatedly with the vase, yelling, "I'll kill you. I'll fucking kill you." Irene screamed to her son to get help, and Mark left the room to pursue him.

Irene was still struggling to get up when Mark came back. He tilted her head up toward him, she thought to see how badly she was hurt, but instead jammed his forefinger into her eye. Irene cried out and reached up reflexively, and Mark bit her hand so deeply that it required stitches. A neighbor pounded on the door, yelling at Mark to let him in, but Mark ignored him. He began to choke Irene, but then seemed to notice the blood running down her head for the first time. He seemed worried about that and quit being violent, saying to her, "Honey, what happened? What did you do here?" He was still trying to curtail the bleeding when the police arrived. Mark fought with them, and it took three men to subdue him. He was taken to jail, and an ambulance transported Irene to the hospital, where she had stitches and surgery on her eye.

After she was released from the hospital, Irene left Mark. She pressed assault charges against him and she and the children stayed with various relatives. But when Mark got out of jail he began calling everyone they knew, begging to talk to her, begging them to help him find her. She obtained a restraining order and filed for divorce, but after Mark was awarded weekly visitation rights to the children, she found it impossible to keep their whereabouts a secret. Irene got an apartment, and she and the kids moved in. Mark would come to visit the children while she was at work and then refused to leave. The children were too afraid not to let him in. If Irene locked the door, he broke in. Irene tried to have the restraining order enforced, but the police said it had already been violated when she let him visit the children at home. Arresting Mark always meant a physical fight; Irene thought they just didn't want to get involved.

In desperation, she took the children and left the state. It took Mark several months, but he quit his job and found them. Irene and the children moved again. Again he found them. After this, Irene just gave up. She thought, "What's the use? I can't get away from him.

All I'm doing is moving my kids around the country like gypsies." Both children were nearly a year behind in school, and both were doing poorly. Irene took them back to the schools they were used to and, as soon as she settled in, Mark moved in too. They were "reconciled" in March. Irene shot Mark in an attempt to hold him off until help could arrive during a last desperate escape in January of the next year.

Many times, women attempted escape when they could sense that an attack was imminent or during a break in an assaultive episode.

It was Saturday morning, and Karen and Hal Simon were sitting at the kitchen table. Hal was already drinking when Karen said they were spending too much money on beer. Hal always warned Karen not to tell him what to do. He reached over and, holding her wrist, put his cigarette out in the palm of her hand. Karen ran to the sink to run cold water over it and, to calm him down, said she was sorry. But Hal followed and slammed her into the counter, yelling at her about never leaving him alone. He hit her several times and then said he was going to get the gun. Karen knew what that meant and just stood there; they had been through this before. She never knew if someday he would really use it, but she knew she didn't have time to get away. She had terrible nightmares about him shooting her in the back as she ran across the yard, so she never tried.

Hal came back with the rifle. He pressed it against her temple and clicked the hammer, then began ramming it into her stomach, yelling, "I'll kill you, goddamn it! I'll kill you this time!" Finally, he laid the gun down and went outside. Karen could see him pacing around and knew he was still angry. He'd talk to himself about all the things she had done wrong and attack her later.

When Hal left to get more beer, Karen fled, taking her small dog with her. Hal had nearly killed the dog several times when he was angry. She couldn't bear to leave it at home, knowing what would happen to it. Hal never allowed her to have keys to the car, so Karen walked the back roads all the way to the nearest town and asked for directions to the police department, hoping they would help her. She told them she had to get away from Hal before he killed her. The police advised her to swear out a warrant for his arrest, but Karen was so afraid of what Hal would do that she hesitated. Finally, she called a friend for advice, but the friend called

Hal and he showed up at the police station a short while later. Hal was furious. He said she was not going to swear out a warrant against anyone; she was his wife, and he was taking her home. He took her elbow and walked her out the door, and nobody intervened.

All the way home, Hal was saying, "You goddamn bitch! You think you're going to leave me? When I get home we'll show you about leaving!" He snatched her over close to him, holding her clothes so she couldn't jump out. Karen was so terrified she couldn't focus on anything. She just sheltered the dog in her arms and prayed. When they got to the house, Hal came around and jerked her door open. He yanked her out of the seat and onto the ground, then began kicking her in the ribs. Each blow knocked Karen farther across the driveway. She knew she was sliding on her face, but there wasn't time to change positions. Finally, he stood over her, daring her to get up. Karen was afraid to move. The dog was still hiding in the truck; Hal carried it to the house and threw it against the concrete of the patio until he apparently thought he'd killed it. Then he pulled Karen inside.

Several days later, a friend helped Karen get to the emergency room of a local hospital. Karen had been in so much pain she could hardly breathe, and walking was difficult. They found that several ribs were broken, and there seemed to be damage to her spleen. The doctor was sympathetic and tried to get her to report it, but she told him, "That is how I got hurt so badly in the first place . . . trying to report it." She finally agreed to go to a local shelter and to receive outpatient care, but when they called to make arrangements they learned that the shelter wouldn't take dogs. Karen went home. The animal had survived, but it was badly hurt, and Karen felt responsible. She wanted to be there to take care of it; she knew Hal would kill it in retaliation if she left. After this, Karen was afraid to seek any more help. Instead, she began thinking about dying. She had always feared it, but now she thought it might not be so bad after all; like passing out, only you never got beaten again.

It is important to remember that even if these women had been able to leave their abuser, they had no guarantees of safety from further assault (Mechanic, Weaver, and Resick 2000). The case of Sharon and Roy Bikson provides an example of repeated attempts at self-protection and continuation of harassment and assault after separation and divorce.

Sharon had been separated from Roy for over two years and her divorce was almost final, yet he continued to harass her. He broke into her home, destroyed her furniture, poured acid in the motor of her car, and slit the seats with a knife. He cut power and phone lines to the house, set small fires, and bragged to others about how he was going to kill her. He attacked and severely injured her at work, and she finally took a leave of absence from her job. She had unlisted phone numbers, but he always got them. She repeatedly called the police for protection, but they came only after Roy had already broken in.

Sharon left home and moved to different apartments to try to escape Roy, and sent her two small children to live with a babysitter to protect them. Roy found the children, threatened to kill the babysitter, and kidnapped her infant son. When Sharon appealed for help to the judge involved in the divorce proceedings, she was advised that she couldn't leave the area with the children until the divorce action was complete and the court had issued a ruling on custody. She obtained a restraining order and several warrants, but they were never enforced. Most of her requests were simply not processed at all.

After Roy's death, the district attorney's office admitted that "her complaints were not taken seriously down here." The head deputy said that he didn't send some of the warrants on for evaluation because he "only sent those" he "thought were really important." And the hearing officer, who approves warrants for delivery, said he hadn't approved some of Sharon's because he "wasn't a marriage counselor"; they "sort of felt sorry for the guy, he seemed so upset"; and "some of these things just work themselves out, anyway." Sharon's desperate requests for help were being winnowed out at every step of the process.

Women are often blamed, or at least severely questioned, if they don't leave an abusive man, and they are too often ignored if they do. Occasionally—as demonstrated by the reaction of the hearing officer in Sharon's case—the situation gets completely turned around, and a woman's leaving for her own protection is used to excuse the actions of the partner.

In one case, the local newspaper in a state's capital city carried an article entitled, "Work term given in wife-killing: Judge says woman's departure provoked murder." It described the killing of an ele-

mentary school teacher who attempted to escape her husband of 15 years after a physically abusive incident. There was a documented history of prior abuse; she sought legal assistance immediately after leaving; she was reportedly terrified. An excerpt from the news article read as follows:

> A woman who was murdered by her estranged husband "provoked" her death by secretly leaving him without warning, according to [the judge] who sentenced the man Wednesday to two years of work-release in the . . . county jail.
>
> Partly because of [her] "highly provoking acts" . . . the District Judge ruled out a stiffer prison sentence for the husband, who shot his wife five times in the face at close range last Aug. 15. [The Judge] said that the wife had deceived her husband by being "extremely loving and caring" up to the morning that she left the family home to proceed with a divorce.

Such incidents lend credence to the fears of abused women that leaving their abusers could cost them their lives, and demonstrate a blatant lack of understanding for their plight. The prosecutor in the case commented, "I hope battered women hear about this. They're damned if they do, and damned if they don't."

BATTERED WOMEN AND OTHER VICTIMS

Even given the practical problems in leaving and the risks that may accompany separation from a violent man, battered women's apparent passivity in the face of danger is still a troubling factor in their reactions to the abuse they experience. Leaving the abuser in spite of the difficulties and risks seems the best option. The apparent helplessness of abused women who stay for years in a situation in which they are repeatedly brutalized—especially those who never attempt to escape—leads to a search for explanations for their apparent lack of ability to cope (Browne 1993; Ferraro 1997; Dutton 1993; Dutton and Goodman 1994; Dutton and Haring 1999; Walker 1984). Why didn't they just walk out one day when their abuser was away? Why don't they get in the car and drive in one direction, and figure it out when they get there? Anything seems better than living with repeated brutalization and threat.

Yet it is interesting to note that the reactions of abused women to the violence they experience correspond quite closely with the reactions of other types of victims—men and women—to catastrophe or threat (Browne 1993; Dutton 1993; Breslau 2001; Dutton 1992a). In 1979, Alexandra Symonds first proposed the "psychology of catastrophic events" as a model to view emotional and behavioral response of women to the violence directed against them. In contrast to theories that would interpret their behavior as indicative of a personality disorder, this theory suggests that women's response to the violence is what would be expected from any individual confronted with a life-threatening situation. These reactions may occur whether the victims are male or female and whether they are the victims of crime, war, natural disaster, or some other trauma (Breslau 2001; Herman 1992). (For purposes of comparing the literature on victims, the term *trauma* is used here to denote an event that inflicts pain or injury, whether this event is caused by accident, natural disaster, or deliberate action. The term *victim* applies to one who is threatened by, or suffers from, such an event.)

For instance, 50 years of research on both disaster and war victims indicates that during the "impact phase," when the threat of danger becomes a reality, an individual's primary focus is on self-protection and survival. Like battered women, other victims experience reactions of shock, denial, disbelief, and fear as well as withdrawal and confusion (Herman 1992; Dutton 1992b). They often deny the threat, which leads to a delay in defining the situation accurately, and respond with dazed or apathetic behavior (Bahnson 1964; Miller 1964; Powell 1954). After the initial impact, disaster victims may be extremely suggestible or dependent and—during the period that follows—may minimize the damage or personal loss. This response is often followed by a "euphoric" stage, marked by unrealistic expectations about recovery (Powell 1954; Martin et al. 2000; Mileti, Drabek, and Haas 1975). Victims convince them-

selves that they can "rebuild"; that somehow everything will be all right; that they will wake up and find it was all a horrible dream. For individuals in war situations, initial reactions also include responses of shock, disbelief, and apparent passivity. As the level of danger becomes overwhelming, individuals often respond by withdrawing and fail to employ appropriate escape behaviors, even when those seem possible (Grinker and Spiegel 1945; Spiegel 1955).

In a closer parallel to the victimization of battered women, emotional reactions of victims of assault by strangers include fear, anger, guilt, shame; a feeling of powerlessness or helplessness such as is experienced in early childhood; a sense of failure; and a sense of being contaminated or unworthy (Bard and Sangrey 1979). Experiences of personal attack and intrusion such as rape often lead to acute perceptions of vulnerability, loss of control, and self-blame (Herman 1992). During a personal assault, the victim may offer little or no resistance in an attempt to minimize the threat of injury or death. Again, the emphasis is on survival.

Long-term reactions of trauma victims are also quite similar to the responses of battered women. Victims report reactions of fear and confusion and acute sensations of powerlessness and helplessness. They may become dependent and suggestible and find themselves unable to make decisions or to function alone. Some victims remain relatively withdrawn and passive and exhibit long-term symptoms of depression and listlessness. Bard and Sangrey (1979), two of the early authorities on the responses of crime victims, noted that even "normal" recoveries can take months and are characterized by lapses into helplessness and fear. (Remember that the majority of these reactions are based on a *single* occurrence of a traumatic event, whereas most abused women are reacting to continuing threats and assaults.) Chronic fatigue and tension, intense startle reactions, disturbance of sleeping and eating patterns, and nightmares are often noted in assault victims (Koss et al. 1994; Browne 1993; Herman 1992; Goodman et al. 1993; Saunders 1994). With all types of trauma, whether related to a natural disaster or war or to a more personal offense, the fear is of a force that has been out of control. Victims become aware of their inability to manage their environment or to ensure their own safety and either attempt to adapt to a powerful aggressor or reassure themselves that the traumatic event will never occur again.

Captives and Captors

Probably the type of victimization that most closely approximates the experiences of battered women is abuse in captivity, such as that experienced by prisoners of war or in hostage situations. In these cases, the assailant or captor has a major influence on how the victim evaluates the situation and the alternatives available to him or her. Both old and new studies show that victims select coping strategies in light of their evaluation of the alternatives and their appraisal of whether a particular method of coping will further endanger them and to what degree (Cardarelli 1997; Arnold 1967; Lazarus 1967). A crucial factor in this decision is the perceived balance of power between the captor and the victim. The coping strategy selected is weighed against the aggressor's perceived ability to control or to harm.

For example, in situations of extreme helplessness, such as in concentration camps, surprisingly little anger is shown toward the captors; this may be a measure of the captors' power to retaliate. Fight or flight responses are inhibited by a perception of the aggressor's power to inflict damage or death, and depression often results, based on the perceived hopelessness of the situation. The victims' perceptions of their alternatives become increasingly limited the longer they remain in the situation, and those alternatives that do exist often seem to pose too great a threat to survival (Browne 1993). Because of the perceived power differential, victims in hostage situations may even come to view the captor as their protector and become ingratiating and appeasing in an effort to save themselves. In his foundational writing about the dynamics of captivity, Biderman (1967) discussed "antagonistic cooperation," a situation in which the dimension of conflict actually

dominates the relationship, but in which there also is a degree of mutual dependence. The relationship is then developed by a weaker partner in order to facilitate survival and obtain leniency. Biderman contended that a normal and healthy human being might be incapable of sustaining a totally hostile or antagonistic interaction over an extended period and that periods of acquiescence might be necessary for physiological and emotional survival.

Parallels also exist between traditional principles of brainwashing used on prisoners of war and the experiences of some women in battering relationships. Key ingredients of brainwashing include isolation of the victim from outside contacts and sources of help, and humiliation and degradation by the captor followed by acts of kindness coupled with the threat of a return to the degraded state if some type of compliance is not obtained (Symonds 1979). Over time, victims of such treatment may become apathetic, sometimes react with despair, and may finally totally submit (Meerlo 1961).

Survival versus Escape

Responses of women faced with assault and threat at home fit in well with this model of victim reactions. Physical menace plays a powerful role in the responses of women with violent mates. Recognition of the potential for severe bodily harm by even an unarmed partner deeply affects women's responses to actual or threatened physical assaults. The ability of most men to physically restrain the woman from leaving or from using the phone to summon help during assaultive incidents increases the woman's sense of powerlessness if an incident begins. Women in this study perceived themselves as being trapped in a dangerous situation and as having little or no control over their abusers' violent behavior. Their perception of their partners' ability to harm was strengthened by each successive assaultive incident and by threats to kill or to perpetrate further violence against them. Women in the homicide group often attempted to appease the aggressor by compliance and to work through the relationship to obtain leniency and safety. Their primary concern *during* assaultive incidents was to survive. Their main concern *after* abusive incidents was to avoid angering the partner again.

Women survivors of ongoing assaults by male partners evidence high rates of depression, suicide ideation, and suicide attempts (Cascardi, O'Leary, and Schlee 1999; Golding 1999; McCauley et al. 1995; Orava, McLeod, and Sharpe 1996). Some women also respond by abusing substances following the onset of severe or chronic assaults. Like other male and female victims, these women's affective, cognitive, and behavioral responses are likely to become distorted by their intense focus on survival (Browne 1993; Walker and Browne 1985). They may develop a whole range of responses—such as controlling their breathing or not crying out when in pain—in an effort to mitigate the severity of abuse during violent episodes, but not have developed any plans for escaping the abusive situation (Koss et al. 1994; Ferraro 1997; Dutton 1992a, 1992b). Women who are assaulted frequently sustain physical injuries, are sexually assaulted, or experience death threats evidence some of the most extreme effects, including an overwhelming sense of risk, intrusive memories or flashbacks, thoughts of suicide, and post-traumatic stress disorder (Browne 1993; Dutton 1992a, 1992b; Herman 1992; Saunders 1994; Cascardi, O'Leary, and Schlee 1999; Orava, McLeod, and Sharpe 1996; Austin, Lawrence, and Foy 1993; Campbell and Soeken 1999; Jones, Hughes, and Unterstaller 2001; Kemp et al. 1995; Sackett and Saunders 1999). Women who experience *both* physical and sexual aggression in a partner relationship tend to manifest even more serious aftereffects than women whose partners are physically but not sexually assaultive.

In this study, women in the homicide group showed a marked tendency to withdraw from outside contacts immediately after an abusive incident rather than attempt to escape or to take action against the abuser. They experienced feelings of helplessness and fear and found it extremely difficult to make decisions or plan ahead. They also tended to underestimate the "damage," as shown by their tendency to underreport the severity of abusive acts and resultant injuries. At least early in their relationship, they entertained unrealistic hopes for improvement of the abuser's behavior or of the relationship in the future. As the violence escalated in frequency and severity, the women's perceptions of alternatives for escape became increasingly limited, and taking action on any of those alternatives seemed too dangerous to try. Although frequently in terror, the women felt constrained by their partner's threats of harm or death if they left or attempted to leave. They were further persuaded of the danger of separation if they had tried to leave and been beaten for it or had sought outside intervention and found that the intervention was inadequate or that the violence only worsened after these attempts. Given the severity of the threats against leaving made by many abusers and the possibility of severe or even lethal reprisals, women often chose the known danger rather than risk the unthinkable.

Lack of adequate provision for safe shelter, relocation, or protection from further attack also contributed to the women's sense of entrapment (Carnigella-MacDonald 1997; Sullivan 1977). Most women in the homicide group concluded that their only alternative was to survive within the relationship. As Thibaut and Kelley (1959) noted in their theory of nonvoluntary interactions, when the probability of escape appears to be extremely low, "the least costly adjustment" for a victim may involve a "complex of adaptions," including a "drastic shortening of one's time perspective to a moment-by-moment or day-to-day focus" (p. 180). Trapped in an increasingly dangerous situation, women in the homicide group narrowed their focus to dealing with the immediate threat of violence and to gathering or maintaining their strength between attacks.

Still, the question remains: why did these women kill? Women in the comparison group had also experienced assaults from a violent partner; they also would have had the perception of the abuser's power to inflict harm; they would also have experienced some victim responses to assault. Yet they did not kill their abusers, and many managed to leave them. What was different about the women in the homicide group that they were unable to escape and eventually took lethal action against their partners?

DIFFERENCES BETWEEN WOMEN IN THE HOMICIDE AND COMPARISON GROUPS

Interestingly, there were very few differences in characteristics of the women in the homicide and comparison groups. The differences were primarily in the behaviors of the men they were with. Men in the homicide group used alcohol and drugs more often than did men in the comparison group and were generally more violent to others. The incidence of child abuse was much higher among men in the homicide group than among men in the comparison group. They also assaulted their partners more frequently, and the women's injuries were more severe. In addition, men in the homicide group more frequently raped or otherwise sexually assaulted their partners, and many more of them had made threats to kill. Over time, physical abuse tended to become more severe in both the homicide and the nonhomicide groups, but such increases were much more common in the homicide group while the decline in contrition was more precipitous.

In a test of which variables most clearly distinguished women who had killed their abusive mates from women who were abused but took no lethal action, seven key dynamics were identified: (1) the frequency with which abusive incidents occurred; (2) the severity of the women's injuries; (3) the frequency of forced or threatened sexual acts by the man; (4) the man's drug use; (5) the frequency of his intoxication; (6) the man's threats to kill; and (7) the woman's threats to commit suicide (Browne 1986). The women's behavior seemed to be primarily in reaction to the level of threat and violence coming in. Women in the homicide group reported that they had felt hopelessly trapped in a desperate situation, in which staying meant the possibility of being killed but attempting to leave also carried with it the threat of reprisal or death. Their sense of helplessness and desperation escalated along with the assaultive behavior of their partners.

The Turning Point

Given the extreme level of abuse and injury to which they were subjected, how then did women in the homicide group go from a seemingly passive response of helplessness and adaption to the highly active one of homicide? Although individuals have the legal right to defend themselves against the threat of imminent serious bodily harm or death, the process by which a woman makes the transition to this mode of reacting is still largely unknown.

One way to understand the shift from victim to perpetrator is suggested by the principles of social judgment theory. For example, Sherif and Hovland's (1961) model of social judgment involves the concept of a continuum on which incoming stimuli—or experiences—are ordered. The "latitude of acceptance" is that range of possibilities an individual is willing to agree with or adapt to; stimuli that fall outside that range are either in the latitude of rejection or the latitude of noncommitment (neither acceptable or unacceptable). These latitudes are defined by endpoints, or anchors, that determine the extremes of the scale. Internal anchors are those originating within the individual, while external anchors are provided by outside factors or social consensus. Past learning experiences also affect how acceptable or unacceptable a person will find a particular stimulus. In the absence of outside factors, a person's internal anchors play a major role in how he or she evaluates a situation. According to social judgment theory, if an event falls at the end of the continuum or even slightly above the endpoint, it will produce a shift of the range toward that anchor or assimilation. However, if the stimulus is too far beyond the others, a contrast effect will ensue, and the stimulus will be perceived as being even more extreme than it really is.

If the escalation of violent acts by the abuser is ordered along a continuum, then the latitude of acceptance for a battered woman would be that range of activities to which she can adapt (see also Ferraro 1997). This latitude would be affected by the degree to which she had been socialized to adjust to or accept a partner's behavior, by prior experiences with similar stimuli such as violence in her childhood home, and by the degree to which she perceives herself as trapped within the violent situation and as having to incorporate the abuse of her partner. Because society's actual responses to violence against partners sometimes are ambiguous and because women victims so rarely discuss their experiences with others, most women victims are quite dependent on such internal anchors to determine the latitude of behaviors they will accept.

If abusive acts continue to fall near the endpoints of the range, a battered woman's latitude of acceptance shifts in order to incorporate them. As demonstrated by the findings on victims of various kinds of trauma, human beings in extreme environments are able to alter their behavior quite dramatically if it seems necessary to survive. Thus, when the behaviors of the abuser are extreme, a woman may adapt far beyond normal limits in order just to coexist with him. A certain level of abuse and tension becomes the status quo: women progress from being horrified by each successive incident to being thankful they survived the last one. Survival becomes the criterion. The latitude of acceptance is what these women think they can live through. By the end of their relationships, women in the homicide group were experiencing attacks they would not have thought endurable at an earlier stage. They were involved in a constant process of assimilation and readjustment.

According to the principles of social judgment theory, however, a contrast phenomenon should come into effect when an act occurs that the woman perceives as significantly outside the "normal" range of violent behavior. In recounting the events that immediately preceded the lethal incident, women frequently said, "He had never done that before!" Often the women noticed a sudden change in the pattern of violence, which indicated to them that their death was imminent. One attack would be so much more brutal or degrading than all the rest that, even with their highly developed survival skills, the women believed it would be impossible to survive the next one. Or an act would suddenly be beyond the range of what the women were willing to assimilate. Frequently, this event involved the physical abuse of a child or the discovery that the man had forced sexual activity on a teenage daughter. The women would say, "He had never threatened the baby before" or "It was one thing when he beat me, but then he hurt my daughter."

Contrast theory would predict that once the woman had defined an act as significantly outside the latitude of what she could accept, she would then perceive that act as being more extreme than it actually was. However, given the amount of minimalization and assimilation engaged in by all types of victims and given the tendency of abused women to understate the levels of violence in their relationships, it is more probable that women in the homicide group were at last simply making a realistic appraisal of the danger. Their final hope had been removed. They did not believe they could escape the abusive situation and survive, and now they could no longer survive within it either.

This homicide study focused on the perceptions of women victims and their reactions to abuse by their partners. These perceptions are crucial, both from a legal and a psychological standpoint, for an understanding of the dynamics that lead an abused woman to take lethal action against her mate. Lack of effective response by the legal system to assaults in which the victim is a wife, along with a lack of adequate and established alternatives to ensure the woman's protection from further aggression, allows the violence in abusive relationships to escalate, leaving a battered woman in a potentially deadly situation from which she sees no practical avenue of escape. As is typical of victims, women who are being attacked by their partners often react with responses of fear and adaption, weighing their alternatives in accordance with their perceptions of the threat and attempting to choose options that will mitigate the danger and facilitate their survival.

In some cases, the violence escalates beyond the level a victim can assimilate. By the end of their relationships, women in the homicide group were subjected to frequent and injurious attacks from partners who were likely to be drinking heavily, using drugs, sexually assaulting them, endangering their children, and threatening murder. Most of these women had no history of violent behavior; yet, in these relationships, the women's attempts to adapt to an increasingly violent and unpredictable mate eventually resulted in an act of violence on their part as well.

DISCUSSION QUESTIONS

1. Explain why Browne says that asking "why battered women don't leave" is the wrong question.
2. What would be some of the right questions to ask a battered woman if the goal is the greatest degree of safety with the least amount of harm to women and their children?
3. Discuss the many barriers that keep women from leaving a violent partner. In this context, what changes would have to occur in the larger society for violence against women in the family to become less entrenched?
4. Stark has written that homicide is part of a larger pattern of interpersonal violence grounded in unequal gender relations in the family, which in turn is embedded in the broader systems of unequal economic, social, and sexual control (Evan Stark. 1990. Rethinking Homicide: Violence, Race, and the Politics of Gender. *International Journal of Health Services*, 20:1, 3–26.) How might you use Stark's position to expand on Browne's findings?
5. Describe the differences between those battered women who kill their abusive partners and those who do not.

REFERENCES

Arnold, J. D. 1967. Stress and Emotion. In *Psychological Stress*, ed. M. H. Appley and R. Trumbull, 123–150. New York: Appleton-Century-Crofts.

Astin, M. C., K. J. Lawrence, and D. W. Foy. 1993. Posttraumatic Stress Disorder among Battered Women: Risk and Resiliency Factors. *Violence and Victims* 8(1):17–28.

Bahnson, C. B. 1964. Emotional Reactions to Internally and Externally Derived Threats of Annihilation. In *The Threat of Impending Disaster*, ed. G. H. Grosser, H. Wechsler, and M. Greenblatt, 251–280. Cambridge, MA: MIT Press.

Bard, M., and D. Sangrey. 1979. *The Crime Victim's Book*. New York: Basic Books.

Biderman, A. D. 1967. Life and Death in Extreme Captivity Situations. In *Psychological Stress,* ed. M. H. Appley and R. Trumbull, 242–264. New York: Appleton-Century-Crofts.

Breslau, N. 2001. Outcomes of Posttraumatic Stress Disorder. *Journal of Clinical Psychiatry* 62:55–59.

Browne, A. 1986. Assault and Homicide at Home: When Battered Women Kill. In *Advances in Applied Social Psychology,* vol. 3. ed. M. J. Saks and L. Saxe, 57–79. Hillsdale, NJ: Lawrence Erlbaum Associates.

Browne, A. 1993. Violence against Women by Male Partners: Prevalence, Outcomes, and Policy Implications. *American Psychologist* 48(10):1077–1087.

Browne, A. 1997. Violence in Marriage: Until Death Do Us Part? In *Violence between Intimate Partners: Patterns, Causes, and Effects,* ed. A. P. Cardarelli, 48–69. Boston and London: Allyn and Bacon.

Browne, A., and K. R. Williams. 1993. Gender, Intimacy, and Lethal Violence: Trends from 1976–1987. *Gender and Society* 7(1):78–98.

Browne, A., K. R. Williams, and D. G. Dutton. 1999. Homicide between Intimate Partners; A 20-Year Review. In *Homicide: A Sourcebook of Social Research,* ed. M. D. Smith and M. A. Zahn, 149–164. Thousand Oaks, CA: Sage.

Butts Stahly, G. 1999. Women with Children in Violent Relationships: The Choice of Leaving May Bring the Consequence of Custodial Challenge. *Journal of Aggression, Maltreatment, and Trauma* 2(2):239–251.

Campbell, J. C., and K. L. Soeken. 1999. Forced Sex and Intimate Partner Violence: Effects on Women's Risk and Women's Health. *Violence against Women* 5:1017–1035.

Cardarelli, A. P., ed. 1997. *Violence between Intimate Partners: Patterns, Causes, and Effects.* Boston and London: Allyn and Bacon.

Carnigella-MacDonald, S. 1997. Women Victimized by Private Violence. In *Violence between Intimate Partners: Patterns, Causes, and Effects,* ed. A. P. Cardarelli, 144–153. Boston and London: Allyn and Bacon.

Cascardi, M., K. D. O'Leary, and K. A. Schlee. 1999. Co-occurrence and Correlates of Posttraumatic Stress Disorder and Major Depression in Physically Abused Women. *Journal of Family Violence* 14:227–249.

Dutton, D. G., and M. Haring. 1999. Perpetrator Personality Effects on Post-Separation Victim Reactions in Abusive Relationships. *Journal of Family Violence* 14(2):193–204.

Dutton, M. A. 1992a. *Empowering and Healing the Battered Woman: A Model for Assessment and Intervention.* New York: Springer.

Dutton, M. A. 1992b. Assessment and Treatment of PTSD among Battered Women. In *Treating PTSD: Procedure for Combat Veterans, Battered Women, Adult and Child Sexual Assaults,* ed. D. Foy, 69–98. New York: Guilford Press.

Dutton, M. A. 1993. Understanding Women's Responses to Domestic Violence: A Redefinition of Battered Woman Syndrome. *Hofstra Law Review* 21(4):1191–1242.

Dutton, M. A., and L. A. Goodman. 1994. Posttraumatic Stress Disorder among Battered Women: Analysis of Legal Implications. *Behavioral Sciences and the Law* 12(3):215–234.

Ferraro, K. J. 1997. Battered Women: Strategies for Survival. In *Violence between Intimate Partners: Patterns, Causes, and Effects,* ed. A. P. Cardarelli, 124–140. Boston and London: Allyn and Bacon.

Golding, J. M. 1999. Intimate Partner Violence as a Risk Factor for Mental Disorders: A Meta-analysis. *Journal of Family Violence* 14:99–132.

Goodman, L. A., M. P. Koss, L. F. Fitzgerald, N. F. Russo, and G. P. Keita. 1993. Male Violence against Women: Current Research and Future Directions. *American Psychologist* 48(10):1054–1058.

Grinker, R. R., and J. D. Spiegel. 1945. *Man under Stress.* New York: Blakiston.

Herman, J. L. 1992. *Trauma and Recovery.* New York: Basic Books.

Jaffe, P. G., and R. Geffner. 1998. Child Custody Disputes and Domestic Violence: Critical Issues for Mental Health, Social Service, and Legal Professionals. In *Children Exposed to Marital Violence: Theory, Research, and Applied Issues,* ed. G. W. Holden and R. Geffner, 371–408. Washington, DC: American Psychological Association.

Jones, L., M. Hughes, and U. Unterstaller. 2001. Posttraumatic Stress Disorder (PTSD) in Victims of Domestic Violence: A Review of the Research. *Trauma, Violence and Abuse* 2(2):99–119.

Kemp, A., B. L. Green, C. Hovanitz, and E. I. Rawlings. 1995. Incidence and Correlates of Posttraumatic Stress Disorder in Battered Women: Shelter and Community Samples. *Journal of Interpersonal Violence* 10:43–55.

Koss, M. P., L. A. Goodman, A. Browne, L. F. Fitzgerald, G. P. Keita, and N. Russo, eds. 1994. *No Safe Haven: Male Violence against Women at Home, at Work, and in the Community.* Washington, DC: American Psychological Association.

Langford, L., N. E. Isaac, and S. Kabat. 1999. *Homicides Related to Intimate Partner Violence in Massachusetts, 1991–1995.* Boston: Peace at Home.

Lazarus, R. S. 1967. Cognitive and Personality Factors Underlying Threat and Coping. In *Psychological Stress,* ed. M. H. Appley and R. Trumbull, 151–181. New York: Appleton-Century-Crofts.

Lemon, N. 2000. Custody and Visitation Trends in the University in Domestic Violence Cases. *Journal of Aggression, Maltreatment and Trauma* 3(1):329–343.

Mahoney, M. 1991. Legal Images of Battered Women: Redefining the Issue of Separation. *Michigan Law Review* 90(1).

Martin, A. J., K. R. Berenson, S. Griffing, R. E. Sage, L. Madry, L. E. Bingham, and B. J. Primm. 2000. The Process of Leaving an Abusive Relationship. The Role of Risk Assessments and Decision Certainty. *Journal of Family Violence* 15(2):109–122.

McCauley, J., D. E. Kern, Kolodner, L. Dill, A. F. Schroeder, H. K. DeChant, J. Ryde, E. B. Bass, and L. R. Derogatis. 1995. The "Battering Syndrome": Prevalence and Clinical Characteristics of Domestic Violence in Primary Care Internal Medicine Practice. *Annals of Internal Medicine* 123:737–746.

McFarlane, J. M., J. C. Campbell, S. Wilt, C. Sachs, Y. Ulrich, and X. Xu. 1999. Stalking and Intimate Partner Femicide. *Homicide Studies* 3(4):300–316.

Mechanic, M. B., T. L. Weaver, and P. A. Resick. 2000. Intimate Partner Violence and Stalking Behavior: Exploration of Patterns and Correlates in a Sample of Acutely Battered Women. *Violence and Victims* 15:55–72.

Meerlo, J. 1961. *The Rape of the Mind.* New York: Grosset and Dunlop.

Mileti, D. S., T. E. Drabek, and J. E. Haas. 1975. *Human Systems in Extreme Environments.* Institute of Behavioral Science, University of Colorado.

Miller, J. G. 1964. A Theoretical Review of Individual and Group Psychological Reactions to Stress. In *The Threat* of Impending Disaster, ed. G. H. Grosser, H. Wechsler, and M. Greenblatt, 11–33. Cambridge, MA: MIT Press.

Morella, Constance. 1990. House Resolution 172. *Congressional Record,* vol. 136, page S 18252-04 (October 25).

Orava, T. A., A. J. McLeod, and D. Sharpe. 1996. Perceptions of Control, Depressive Symptomatology, and Self-Esteem of Women in Transition from Abusive Relationships. *Journal of Family Violence* 11:167–186.

Powell, J. W. 1954. *An Introduction to the Natural History of Disaster,* vol. 2. Final Contract Report, Disaster Research Project, Psychiatric Institute, University of Maryland.

Ptacek, J. 1997. The Tactics and Strategies of Men Who Batter. In *Violence between Intimate Partners: Patterns, Causes, and Effects,* ed. A. P. Cardarelli, 104–123. Boston and London: Allyn and Bacon.

Sackett, L. A., and D. G. Saunders. 1999. The Impact of Different Forms of Psychological Abuse on Battered Women. *Violence and Victims* 14:105–117.

Saunders, D. G. 1994. Posttraumatic Stress Symptom Profiles of Battered Women: A Comparison of Survivors in Two Settings. *Violence and Victims* 9:31–44.

Sherif, M., and C. Hovland. 1961. *Social Judgment.* New Haven, CT: Yale University Press.

Spiegel, J. P. 1955. Emotional Reactions to Catastrophe. In *Stress Situations,* ed. S. Liebman. Philadelphia, PA: J. B. Lippincott.

Sullivan, C. M. 1977. Societal Collusion and Culpability in Intimate Male Violence: The Impact of Community Response toward Women with Abusive Partners. In *Violence between Intimate Partners: Patterns, Causes, and Effects,* ed. A. P. Cardarelli, 154–164. Boston and London: Allyn and Bacon.

Symonds, A. 1979. Violence against Women: The Myth of Masochism. *American Journal of Psychotherapy* 33: 161–173.

Thibaut, J. W., and H. H. Kelley. 1959. *The Social Psychology of Groups.* New York: Wiley.

Walker, L. E. 1984. *The Battered Woman Syndrome.* New York: Springer.

Walker, L. E., and A. Browne. 1985. Gender and Victimization by Intimates. *Journal of Personality* 53:179–195.

Chapter 22

Women's Realities:
Defining Violence against Women by Immigration, Race, and Class
Shamita Das Dasgupta

ABSTRACT

Battered women are again the topic for this chapter, but here the reader learns of violence in the lives of immigrant women. Being a victim of battering is horrible enough, but being an immigrant battered woman in a strange country compounds the emotional suffering, the lack of resources and culturally competent services, and the difficulties of escape.

Dasgupta, a psychologist of South Asian origins, introduces the reader to a number of factors that create great hardships for these women. She begins by pointing out that sensitivity to race and class discrimination does not carry over to attitudes about battered women immigrants. Rather, negative stereotypes about immigrant women persist and include labels such as "backward, subservient and quietly accepting of male domination and patriarchal control," so that the women are said to be contributing to their own victimization. The concept of "other," that is, that people "not like oneself" have substandard values, inferior cultural ideals, and backward lifestyles often allows people, Dasgupta suggests, to turn their backs on these women's situation and fail—either through prejudice, negligence, or ignorance—to give assistance.

To enable the reader to understand the complexity of the problem, Dasgupta provides a diagram of how the culture and social institutions are intertwined with the abuser's and victim's lives. Thus, for example, because of racism, class bias, and xenophobia (fear of foreigners), battered immigrant women of color must deal not only with the violence against women in their own cultures and families but also with the racist United States patriarchal system. In this context, Dasgupta asks the reader to listen to the voices of immigrant women who may also be pressured to hide the abuse from public knowledge in the name of protecting the fragile image of the beleaguered immigrant community. Dasgupta summarizes the daunting barriers that immigrant women face when they attempt to leave an abusive situation. The barriers are divided into personal issues (e.g., shame, fear), institutional blockages (e.g., stringent immigration and welfare policies), and cultural ideological issues (e.g., acceptability of fate or unacceptability of divorce).

Although there are no easy answers to this pressing problem, there are available some past successes with other social problems (for example, mothers against drunk drivers) that suggest that intensive education from a social movement for change combined with training in a multicultural context for those charged with the power to assist is one positive step that can be taken now. As you read this chapter, think about the barriers that immigrant battered women face when they try to escape abusive relationships, and identify culturally sensitive ways and broader social movements that might help eliminate some of the barriers these women face.

A CULTURE OF VIOLENCE

After heart-wrenching deliberations, Najma Sultana,[1] a Pakistani woman in New Jersey, decided to seek a temporary restraining order against her abusive spouse. This was not an easy decision for her. She was going against her family, which urged her to be patient; her religion, which affirmed that virtuous women are always tolerant; her two children, who were crying for their father; her community, which sneered at women who invited outside interference into the family; and everything she had learned about marriage, love, and women's role in society. She was also working against her fear of being alone with meager resources in a foreign country. In retaliation, Najma's husband, much more conversant in the ways of this country, secured a restraining order against her.

A few days later, when both appeared before their country's family court judge, there were no doubts that Najma was a battered woman and that her husband's claims were baseless. Yet, the judge vacated both of their restraining orders, stating that such treatment of wives may be an accepted practice in the couple's native culture and that, therefore, the husband has probably acted in accordance with his cultural beliefs.[2]

On Sept. 7, 1987, Jian Wan Chen's husband smashed her skull with a claw hammer after she allegedly admitted to having an affair. Chen's body was discovered by her teenage son in the family's Brooklyn apartment.

In March, Brooklyn Supreme Court Justice Edward Pincus sentenced Jian's husband to 5 years probation on a reduced manslaughter charge. After hearing the testimony of a Hunter College anthropologist, the judge concluded that Dong Lu Chen, a recent immigrant, was driven to violence by traditional Chinese values about adultery and loss of manhood. (Jetter, 1989, p. 4)

These stories are only two examples of the brutal realities of immigrant women's lives. Although the United States takes pride in pioneering legislative and social policy changes in antidomestic abuse work, many of its residents routinely fall through the cracks of a system that supposedly has been erected to protect victims. Because of the indefatigable efforts of women of color, the antidomestic violence community has now come to a grudging recognition of the system's insensitivity to race and class. Such recognition is still not forthcoming, however, in regard to immigrant[3] victims. The majority of us refuse to acknowledge even the existence of battered immigrant women, let alone recognize the differences in their circumstances. This attitude of disregard is reflected in all spheres of society. The state constructs laws that generally are detrimental to the safety of immigrant battered women; the legal system does not know how to deal with them; battered women's agencies neglect to institute programs that address their specific needs; and citizens-neighbors pretend not to hear or understand shrieks that are ostensibly in foreign languages.

The term *immigrant* conjures up various images in our minds. Once, when I asked my class what they thought when they heard the term *immigrant,* a student replied that she generally thought this person could not speak English, had little education, was on welfare, behaved in "foreign ways," and most likely was an "illegal." Many of the other students nodded their agreement. When I announced to the class that

Source: Shamita Das Dasgupta, "Women's realities: Defining violence against women by immigration, race and class." in R. K. Bergen (éd.) *Issues in Intimate Violence,* pp. 209–210 Copyright©1998. Reprinted by Permission of Sage Publications, Inc.

I was an immigrant and then asked how they saw this description fitting me, most were aghast and assured me they did not think of me as an immigrant.

This episode in my class underscores the fact that "immigrant" has become a constructed, rather than a legal, category in this country. Whereas the legal definition demarcates individuals who have entered this country by obtaining certain types of permissions from the government, the socially constructed classification selects only a subgroup of this larger population. One's affluence, educational background, or length of residency has little relevance to this popular determination. To the general populace, an immigrant is an Asian or a Latino regardless of how many generations he or she has lived in this country. White Europeans are rarely viewed as immigrants, as are Africans and Caribbeans at times. Being weird, bizarre, and subnormal complete this picture of an immigrant.

Not only do immigrant women, especially immigrant women of color, chafe under this general perception, but their burden is further increased by being women in a patriarchal society and being women of color in a white supremacist country. As "foreign" women, they are viewed as backward, subservient, and quietly accepting of male domination and patriarchal control. This perception is prevalent even among battered women's advocates who are trained to be tolerant of differences. During a diversity training that I conducted for domestic violence intervention workers, advocates derisively discussed Asian women's passivity[4] (expressed in terms such as "They tend to walk a few steps behind their men") and dependency traits of Latinas ("They will never go against their men").

Such attitudes emanate from, and in turn reinforce, the fundamental belief that women of "other" cultures are inferior to their American counterparts and perhaps contribute to their own victimization.[5] Such ethnocentrism contributes grievously to the culture of violence that surrounds immigrant women of color in the United States (for further discussion, see Omi & Winant, 1986). The Marriage Fraud Act of 1986[6] and its later amendments, the Welfare Reform Act of 1996,[7] are but symptoms of this pervasive disposition of neglect and abuse that

immigrant women suffer in U.S. society. As long as we think of immigrant women as "other," as long as we believe that their understanding and awareness of domestic violence are substandard, we facilitate an atmosphere that steeps legislation, law enforcement, professional intervention, and community attitudes in violence toward them.

VIOLENCE IN "OTHER" WOMEN'S LIVES

Violence against women is a phenomenon that seems to be endemic in every society (Heise, Pitanguy, & Germain, 1994). Researchers and activists alike, however, generally emphasize the violence that is perpetrated by the individual: the husband, father, brother, or male relative physically chastising his wife, daughter, sister, or other women in his family. Rarely are we aware of the abuse that occurs beyond this intimate circle. Needless to say, the individual abuser and the victim do not operate in a vacuum; rather, they are nested within the supportive circles of social institutions and culture (see Figure 22.1).[8] Ubiquity of both institutions and culture encourages and maintains abuse and victimization at the individual level.

Although all women are victims of this nexus of culture, institutions, and the individual abuser, nowhere is this unholy alliance more distinct than in the lives of battered immigrant women. Cultural symbols that abound in the United States promote not only male superiority and female subjection but also deficiency of immigrant women of color and their cultures to white people and their norms. The exoticizing of Latina and Asian women that occurs routinely in our cinema, art, theater, fashion, literature, and language further renders these women "other," allowing us to ignore their concerns and needs at institutional levels. Our attitudinal unconcern gets translated into laws, court proceedings, police behavior, educational curricula, and social service practices. The following case exemplifies this:

Vanita's parents arranged her marriage with a scientist residing in the United States who had returned to India on a bride-finding mission. Only 5 days after their wedding, her husband left India to return to the

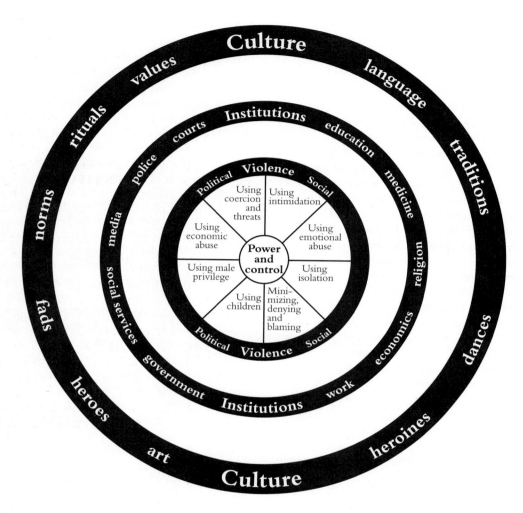

FIGURE 22.1
The Supportive Circles of Social Institutions and Culture *(Source: Domestic Abuse Intervention Project, Duluth, MN.)*

United States. It took her nearly 15 months to receive the appropriate visa to come to the United States. Almost as soon as they started living together, Vanita's husband began to demand total subordination from her. "You have to listen to me, I am your god," he would say. He restricted her food intake and dictated what she could wear, who she could talk to, and where she could go. He also sexually assaulted and battered her regularly.

The abuse worsened when Vanita became pregnant. Her husband made it clear to Vanita that there was no escape. If she tried to leave him, he would withdraw his permanent residency sponsorship to make her undocumented and initiate deportation proceedings. She would not only have to go back to her parents in ignominy but also lose her newborn son in the process.

Although she has now lived for more than 2 years in the United States, Vanita's husband has not mentioned anything about removal of her conditional status. Vanita now believes that her husband may not have filed the sponsorship papers at all. This means that she has been undocumented for the past 2 years. The implications fill Vanita with fear.

A cursory look at Vanita's situation leaves no doubt as to her husband's abusiveness. What may not be quite so apparent is the role that U.S. laws have played in her victimization. By the provisions of the Marriage Fraud Act, only a conditional residency status may be conferred on immigrant spouses of legal permanent residents (LPRs) or U.S. citizens (USCs). Because the process can be initiated only by the LPR/USC spouse, it is obvious how this law can become an instrument of torture in the hands of batterers. By entrusting the power to determine a woman's (il)legality of existence in the United States, the state has literally handed over to an abuser the power to control her. Vanita's husband has used this power cleverly by making her undocumented, which he knows will ensure her dependence on him (see Anderson, 1993).

The situation of Raco, a battered immigrant woman from China, also reflects this use of power:

[Raco] . . . was six month pregnant [last year] when, she said, her husband beat her so badly that she fled into the streets and asked the police for help. . . . Raco, who looks like a teen-ager, fears retaliation from her husband, a Chinese-American who courted her by mail for 10 years. Three months after arriving in this country, Raco said, her husband began hitting her in the face because she could not get along with his parents, who lived with them in an apartment in Manhattan. Then the beatings increased, she said, because she did not want a child right away.

"He threatened not to sponsor me for permanent residence if I didn't carry the pregnancy to term," she said through an interpreter. But the violence continued even after she agreed to have the baby. (Howe, 1991, p. 40)

When an immigrant woman gathers strength and resources to leave her abusive relationship, the disdain of the mainstream toward her culture adds further obstacles to the usual hurdles she would have faced at such a time. Once, I had gone to a New Jersey police station to pick up a South Asian battered woman who had been turned out of her home by her husband. She was a frightened young woman who did not speak much English and had already spent half a night on the streets in her nightgown. The two police officers had been extremely solicitous and had provided her with food and a warm jacket. When I entered the station, however, they let loose a tirade about my "culture" (I, too, am a South Asian woman) and the approval of battering in it. Although sorely tempted, I judiciously decided to refrain from reminding them of the statistics on the batterings, rapes, and murders of American women by their intimate partners. I wondered whether the police officers would have as easily held the U.S. culture responsible for these atrocities against women!

This quick allocation of blame to an immigrant's "culture" is not singular to these police officers. Many white Americans presume that "other" cultures, especially minority ones, are far more accepting of woman abuse than the U.S. culture.[9] The African American culture is a culture of violence, Latin cultures are based on brutal machismo that flourishes on wife abuse, and Asian cultures train women to pleasure their men to the point of disregarding abuse from them. I have lost count of how many times I have fielded questions on "bride burning" and "dowry-death" (even when the topic of discussion was other than violence against [South Asian] women) where the inquirer's intentions were to underscore the peculiarities of my "culture." When I have pointed out, albeit differences in weapons, that these are extreme cases of wife abuse similar to the ones in the United States, many have remained unconvinced and have even become angry. How dare I compare and suggest similarities between an "other" culture and the normative one! American mainstream society still likes to believe that woman abuse is limited to minority ethnic communities, lower socioeconomic strata, and individuals with dark skin colors. The impact of this public violence of imperialism, classism, and racism on battering in the private sphere of home and intimate relationships has, unfortunately, received little research attention (for a discussion on this issue, see Almeida, Woods, Messino, Font, & Herr, 1994).

A TRAP NAMED IMMIGRATION

The chronicle of peoples' immigration to the United States is neither benign nor fair. The policies that historically have regulated migration, especially from nations of color, were hardly based on generosity and a sense of justice. U.S. labor and foreign policies have always guided formations of U.S. immigration policies. For example, in the early 1800s, when the United States needed cheap labor to build railroads, immigration from China was encouraged; during the 1960s, with a dearth of scientists and technically educated people in the country, immigration policies were relaxed for Asians so trained. Furthermore, until 1980, the admittance of refugees to the United States was regulated by U.S. foreign policy interest, which led to the conferring of refugee status mainly on individuals from communist countries. In fact, in a 1990 lawsuit, the Immigration and Naturalization Service (INS) admitted that most of the decisions it made were politically based.[10]

Although INS policies have been universally prohibitive regardless of gender, women have had to bear the brunt of its inherent misogyny, racism, and xenophobia. From the days of early Chinese immigration, U.S. migration policies have been expressly restrictive to women of color. Even wives of men who were living and working in this country were routinely denied entry visas. Even today, it may take more than 2 years to secure entry visas for wives of legal permanent residents (LPRs) from Third World countries.

Much of this misogynist flavor is a result of the impact of the doctrine of coverture[11] on U.S. immigration procedures. The concept of *coverture* entails women's subordination to their husbands and the surrender of all legal power. Historically, married couples were not seen as equal partners; rather, the husband was considered to have legal authority over his wife and children. Impressions of coverture are still visible in the recent Marriage Fraud and Welfare

Reform Acts. Even though these acts are supposedly gender-blind, in actuality, men, the primary immigrants to this country, become vested with inordinate powers due to them. Thus, by the dictates of the Marriage Fraud Act, the man ends up being the sponsor and controller of his wife. The "deeming"[12] provisions of the Welfare Reform Act bestow a man with the power to command his wife's eligibility for securing public assistance.

Although the Welfare Reform Act and the 1990 and 1994 amendments to the Marriage Fraud Act have provided relief for battered women by specifying "battered women's waiver," "self-petitioning," and "deeming" exemptions, these have also created an atmosphere of unprecedented terror for battered women by reinforcing the imbalance of power already existing in such relationships (see Ho, 1990, 1991). Furthermore, these acts reveal a deep lack of understanding of the dynamics of intimate violence. For instance, one prerequisite of being exempted from deeming is that a battered woman leave her abusive relationship. Yet, practitioners in the field are aware that obtaining resources may be the precondition for leaving an abuser, rather than vice versa. Furthermore, these requirements lack the recognition of battered women's safety issues.[13]

IN THE NAME OF "CULTURE"

Activists and experts in the field of domestic violence now recognize that, rather than any particular apparent reason, gender inequality inherent to patriarchal social orders may be to blame for woman abuse in families (Bograd, 1988; Dobash & Dobash, 1979; Straus, Gelles, & Steinmetz, 1980). When immigrants arrive on the shores of the United States, they do not leave behind the socialization and conditioning they have already received (Dasgupta & Warrier, 1996). The patriarchal cultural structures in which they grew up have already instructed the majority of immigrants in gender roles that are inherently inequitable. In the United States, however, complexities of the dynamics of abuse increase manifold.

Although most of us like to believe that migration to the United States automatically improves women's status and safety, it is not inevitably so. On the one hand, immigration may help women escape from some structural oppressions of extended families; on the other hand, immigration may deprive them of protections that such family constellations offer. A case in point is the situation of South Asian immigrant women. In South Asia, abusive behavior of a man may, to some extent, be checked by other family members, neighbors, and in-laws. Community shame can also be evoked to restrain an abuser. Furthermore, additional safety valves, such as women temporarily escaping to their natal families when conjugal tensions increase, have developed in social-familial structures to offer women some degree of security. These trips have been ritualized in the culture as women going to *maike* (mother's home) or *baaper bari* (father's home). Such routine ways of diffusing stress or curbing abusive behaviors are, of course, lost to the immigrants. Contrarily, being in a country where a strong sense of family and community is absent may actually pressure immigrant women to cling more tenaciously to their nuclear families.

I have often been asked why a community, which can be oppressive at times, is so important to an immigrant woman. A community not only may meet the psychological needs of an immigrant woman but also may be her lifeline. "If she doesn't speak much English, can she leave her community? Where can she go? Especially if she has to worry about economic survival. If you ask 'your life or your community?' for some women it's the same thing" (Lum, 1988, p. 50). This need to belong to a community has, in fact, jeopardized the safety of many immigrant women within their families. A close look at the case of immigrant women in the South Asian community may illustrate this point more clearly.

The South Asian community visible in the United States today started forming in the early 1970s, after the passing of the Immigration and Naturalization Act of 1965, which eased immigration from Asia. At that time, INS policies selected specifically for a highly technologically oriented population and thus artificially created a homogenous Western-educated South Asian community in the United States. Because of its quick financial success, the community soon earned recognition as a "model minority" from the mainstream. Soon, South Asians embraced this heady reputation and became preoccupied with projecting a flawless image back to the mainstream. Maintenance of this unblemished facade required masking intercommunity problems, such as domestic violence, poverty, unemployment, intergenerational conflicts, drug abuse, and mental illness. Although all community members have suffered for this deceit, women have been particularly victimized by the ensuing repression. Women who have dared to speak out against spousal abuse or other intracommunity problems have been either perfunctorily exiled by community leaders or pressured to preserve their silence (Dasgupta & DasGupta, 1997). Consequently, the majority of battered women who seek external help express great fear of being psychologically and literally banished from the communal fold.

> Steven Shon, a psychiatrist [said] . . . that, often, the battered Pacific Asian woman may perceive the risks of talking about her abuse as far outweighing the advantages. If she reveals that she has been beaten—to the social worker, outside family member, her minister—the woman runs the serious risk of bringing a great deal of shame upon herself, her husband, and her family. In cultures where lineage, family integrity, and the strict adherence to role obligations are highly valued, "losing face," or bringing disgrace upon self and family, is no small matter. It can be the mark of grave *personal failure* for many Pacific Asian women. (Bush, 1982, p. 10)

In addition to this demand from the community to present the image of intact and cohesive families, most battered women feel obligated to protect their relatives who may be miles away in their natal countries. Women often believe that a divorce would bring such disgrace to their families that it may jeopardize the marital eligibility and social status of their siblings. Being distanced from day-to-day realities of their daughters' lives, the parents, too, may insist that the women try harder to please their husbands, to be more tolerant, or at least to postpone leaving until the children grow up. Furthermore, many battered immigrant women are afraid that separation or divorce might risk their own children's educational opportunities and future happiness, the reasons they may have migrated to the United States in the first place.

> The woman believed that to be a "good mother" she had to keep the family intact. The presence of a father, abusive or not, was regarded as essential to the proper upbringing of children. Gurpreet, a mother of two who had suffered physical beatings for more than a decade, justified her decision to remain with her husband, "For children, I will sacrifice all. I can't take the children away from [their] security." Vimala echoed her sentiments, "Parents must be there for children always and do what is best. I have sacrificed my life this long and stayed in this abusive relationship for my children's sake." (Dasgupta & Warrier, 1996, p. 252)

ESCAPE FROM ALCATRAZ

The dream of living a safe and peaceful life may remain removed from a battered immigrant woman trapped in this labyrinth of individual, institutional, and cultural violence. Escaping the cycle of violence is an extraordinary feat for any woman, and for immigrant women the obstructions may seem insurmountable. Being an immigrant and a woman of color complicates and exaggerates the barriers to ending violence in one's life, as does socioeconomic status. The following lists are a summary of impediments within three categories that battered immigrant women may experience in the United States:[14]

Personal

- *Shame:* The feeling of shame may encompass losing face, disgracing affinal and natal families, failing in domestic and marital responsibilities, and letting one's community down. All of these may also span one's country of origin and the United States. This shame can be powerful enough to imprison a woman in her abusive relationship forever.
- *Fear:* This fear may involve leaving a familiar situation and moving into the unknown, as well as practical safety issues.

- *Financial impoverishment:* Financial insolvency is one of the most paralyzing problems that battered immigrant women encounter when leaving their abusers. Many are poor to begin with, and others may face uncommon poverty as a result of their migration. As a direct result of their abusers' efforts to isolate them, many immigrant women may also be unskilled in conducting financial transactions in this country. In many traditional societies, men tend to take care of the money even when the women work. Thus, many immigrant women sincerely assume that they cannot have access to their own earnings without their husbands' permission.
- *Lack of support system:* Most immigrant women have come to the United States alone, depending solely on their spouses. When experiencing abuse, they may not have any emotional or physical support and thus feel reluctant to leave the only haven they know.
- *Dearth of survival skills:* Many immigrant women may lack basic wherewithal to survive in this country. For example, they may not know how to drive a car, use public transportation, shop, use banks, use a telephone, find jobs, or read a newspaper.

Institutional

- *INS and public benefit policies:* As discussed above, stringent immigration and welfare policies restrict battered immigrant women's ability to leave abusive spouse-sponsors, as well as to find resources to ease separation.
- *Cultural insensitivity:* In the United States, battered women's flight from abusive situations is greatly facilitated by shelters, police (who often make the first contact), and other experts. At all these intervention points, immigrant women may meet with insensitive comments, derision, xenophobia, and racism. Many immigrant women who have taken the initial trouble to go to a shelter soon return to their abusers, swearing never to enter a shelter again. I have heard from battered women that they have been exhorted by shelter workers to "act as Americans, now that you are here" (see Metz, 1993) or quizzed scornfully about their "arranged

marriages." All such experiences inhibit battered immigrant women from accessing the few resources that may be available to them.

- *Financial requirements:* The initial legal procedures, as well as setting up a new household, may require finances that are beyond the reach of most immigrant women. In addition, many women may financially support their parents, siblings, or other relatives in the country of origin and believe that they should not cut off this support for their own "selfish" reasons.

- *Child custody issues:* Although gaining custody of children is an issue with which most battered women struggle, in the case of an immigrant woman it may gain added complexity. A child born in this country is a U.S. citizen by birth, yet his or her mother may be undocumented because of withdrawal of sponsorship. Thus, theoretically, a mother may be deported but the courts disallow her young children to accompany her. Recently, a New Jersey court rejected the request of an Indian mother to take her children to India for a visit; the judge believed that India would be an unsafe/unhealthy place for American children.

- *Language barrier:* An immigrant woman whose native tongue is other than English may face tremendous difficulties in communicating at all levels in the United States. Even when a woman is fluent in English, during crisis she may want to speak with someone in vernacular.

Cultural Ideology

- *Meaning of marriage:* Many traditional cultures find divorce unacceptable. Marriage is supposed to be permanent in many religions and cultures.

- *Keeping family intact:* Many immigrants who come from traditional societies strongly believe that children can be brought up well only in an intact family. Many regret that they cannot provide their children with an extended family, especially if they themselves grew up in one. Thus, breaking down a nuclear family further to a single-parent family may be unthinkable to many immigrant women.

- *Unacceptability of divorce:* In many societies, divorce is unacceptable, and a divorced woman is thought to be tainted. Many women prefer to live in abusive relationships than to tackle the stigma of divorce.

- *Acceptability of "fate":* Predestination of life events is a strong motif in many ancient cultures. Thus, a violent relation may be accepted as one's "fate" or reprisal for one's past misdeeds.

- *Tolerance toward abuser:* Beliefs such as that the batterer may have a change of heart and "a good woman can change a man" are common themes in all cultures. Cultures that overemphasize tolerance and compassion in women's gender role, as it happens in many traditional nations, may predispose women not to seek divorce or separation from their abusers (Dasgupta & Warrier, 1997).

One other issue that needs attention in this discussion of intimate violence from immigrant women's perspectives is a legal one: the issue of "cultural defense"[15] in courts. The debate here is whether the U.S. justice system should take the cultural background of an immigrant (both as defendant and as plaintiff) into account. Interestingly, the opposite camps of this argument are not necessarily populated by the same members all the time. Although most progressives support multiculturalism, they balk at decisions that allow domestic violence to go unabated (see examples at the beginning of the chapter). Opponents (supposedly conservatives and nativists) propose that an individual's cultural background should have no bearing in the court of law because "when in Rome. . . ." Feminists and battered women's advocates have bounced uncomfortably between being for and being against this issue. Although most acknowledge that cultural socialization may significantly affect the way women perceive, respond to, express, and ameliorate abuse, they are not ready to allow the same latitude to batterers. On this point, they side with conservatives.

The reason for this vacillation is a fundamental misunderstanding of other cultures. In fact, I believe that many feminists and battered women's advocates secretly suffer from gnawing suspicions that "other" cultures do actually support woman abuse.[16] Thus, they are not sure where to land on this argument. The question that goes begging is, What do we mean by culture?

Regardless of its degree of traditionality, every culture has its historical, local, and individual variations. Although the structure of judicial arguments presumes a culture to be static and monolithic, it is hardly ever so. Furthermore, cultural motifs are rarely stripped of exceptions, contradictions, and complexities. For example, every culture has tenets that disenfranchise women, as well as empower them. Islamic cultures, which are considered to be misogynist, provide a wealth of rights for women, such as the right to education and occupation; to own and control property; to choose a marital partner; and to claim sexual satisfaction. Similarly, Hindu cultures encompass widow immolation, as well as the role of *Virangana* (woman warrior-leader). Judeo–Christian cultures also have comparable discrepancies. The key issue to scrutinize here is why beliefs and customs that oppress women gain recognition as "culture" in society and the aspects that enable women are doomed to obscurity. As advocates, feminists, and activists, it is incumbent on us to articulate this disparity and to query whose purpose such biases serve.

SO, IS THERE A SOLUTION?

Culture is an important part of immigrant women's lives and identities. To presume that immigrant women will shed their cultural backgrounds as easily as their residences is to disrespect women's very existence. If U.S. courts are to provide "individualized" and "particularized" justice, then they have to be sensitive to people's cultural backgrounds (Coleman, 1996). Yet, multiculturalism without an understanding of culture or cultural nuances is bound to yield decisions that reek of society's misogyny, xenophobia, ethnocentrism, and racism. Ignoring culture will, of course, lead to a form of generic justice that has little resemblance to justice. The remedy may lie in a thorough campaign of education and training. Although the task seems daunting, it is not without precedence. Battered women and their advocates have already accomplished a similar crusade that has modified the country's attitude and awareness level about battering.

The tripartite barriers that battered immigrant women face can hardly be demolished overnight. The complexities of the problem demand simultaneous attack and unraveling at various levels. Overwhelmed by the enormity of issues, many a sympathetic soul has wavered and asked the inevitable questions, Why do these women migrate? Why don't they stay in their own countries, or at least go back? The answers will not easily satisfy. Responses must include examination of individuals' aspirations to better themselves and to make better lives for their children. Simultaneously, we must dissect the colonial histories of immigrants and comprehend the issues that have driven them out of their native countries to seek stability elsewhere. The postcolonial devastation of economy, politics, safety, and families that many nations of color have experienced need to be in the foreground when we consider explanations of peoples' migrations.

In the meantime, as activists and academics focus on ending violence in all women's lives, we must understand and grasp the depths of battered immigrant women's despair. Only by carefully listening to the voices of immigrant women of color and by following their lead can we successfully change the lives of women who have suffered our negligence and ignorance for so long.

DISCUSSION QUESTIONS

1. How do women from different racial, ethnic, immigrant, and socioeconomic groupings experience domestic violence differently?
2. Describe the particular barriers and obstacles that immigrant women from different communities face in dealing with domestic violence? Describe how these obstacles can be overcome.
3. How does the concept of culture contribute to domestic violence? And

how does the concept of culture protect against domestic violence?

4. People in the United States often criticize other cultures as conducive to domestic violence. How does our own culture support domestic violence?

5. How do various social policies (e.g., welfare reform; immigrant laws and policies) impede women's safety? How should these social policies be modified to provide safety for battered immigrant women?

NOTES

1. Throughout this chapter, names of individuals have been changed to protect their privacy.

2. I became aware of this particular case in my work with Manavi as a battered women's advocate. Manavi, established in 1985, is the first organization that focuses on violence against South Asian women in the United States.

3. I use the term *immigrant,* not as a legal marker, but to indicate individuals who have chosen to enter this country as students, workers, spouses, refugees, and so on. I use it as a catch-all term that does not refer to one's legal status.

4. The stereotype of (ultra)feminine Asian women and their willing subjugation to men is common in the West. For a discussion of this issue, see Rivers (1990).

5. During a training session with domestic violence advocates, a participant commented that the helplessness and dependence that she has witnessed in South Asian women are unparalleled in other "American" women. I presented the idea that many immigrant battered women in this country face deep isolation. Separated from family, friends, and familiar surroundings, they may feel paralyzed to take action and thereby appear more helpless than they really are. Another participant caustically retorted that although it may be true that an immigrant woman has no family here, no one had stopped

her from making friends. She implied that many immigrant women—in this case, South Asians—choose to isolate themselves. The remark reeks of victim blaming, as well as a serious lack of understanding of the dynamics of battering.

6. The Marriage Fraud Act is a provision of the Immigration Reform and Control Act (IRCA) of 1986. It was passed to reduce immigration through fraudulent marriages to U.S. citizens (USCs) or legal permanent residents (LPRs). It imposes a 2-year conditional residency requirement on an "alien spouse." The condition applies only to individuals who have been sponsored by their USC or LPR spouses. Conditional status is removed by the INS after 2 years from the date of application for permanent residency of the "alien spouse" if the couple can prove "good faith" marriage. Provisions of the 1990 amendment and 1994 Violence Against Women Act (VAWA) rectify some problems of the 1986 act by allowing battered women to flee abusive spouses (known as battered women's waiver), apply for permanent residency without sponsorship (self-petitioning), and request stay of deportation in cases where the individual is undocumented (cancellation of removal). None of the procedures are user-friendly, however, to say the least.

7. The Welfare Reform Act of 1996 has many provisions that demonstrate little understanding of the dynamics of battering, and the act is especially insensitive to the realities of immigrant battered women.

8. This wheel of concentric circles was developed by the Domestic Abuse Intervention Project, 206 West Fourth Street, Duluth, MN 55806, (218) 772-2781. I thank them for allowing me to include it in this article.

9. I deliberately have *not* written "the U.S. culture" to draw attention to the contrast. Most Anglo Americans believe that only "others" have "cultures" (read: tribelike qualities, different/difference, weird), whereas they themselves are normative and, therefore, devoid of the limitations of culture.

10. In 1990, the U.S. Immigration and Naturalization Service settled a lawsuit erupting from its selective disapproval of asylum requests by agreeing to reconsider 200,000 asylum applications from Guatemala and El Salvador.

11. The principle of coverture is based on English common law.

12. *Deeming* ensures that the sponsor of an immigrant is held financially responsible for all public assistance sought by the latter. This, of course, places the husband (sponsor) of a battered woman (immigrant) in a position to control her access to medical help or other public benefits. Battered immigrant women who have not paid Social Security for at least 40 quarters are exempt from deeming only if they are not residing with their batterers and their need for assistance is caused directly by the abuse.

13. Over 70% of battered women who are killed by their spouses meet with lethal abuse when they have left or are considering leaving their relationships. Severance of relationship may heighten risk of injury for battered women.

14. This section has been adapted from DasGupta and Warrier (1997).

15. It is also disheartening to see that "cultural defense" and the affirming decisions occur mostly in cases of woman abuse. The implication of this bias is that courts are more likely to accept misogyny as integral to "other" cultures but not other criminal behavior. Such "culturally sensitive" decisions are less likely to come forth in cases of stranger rape, murder, and other crimes.

16. See Shon and Ja (1982) and Rimonte (1991). Unfortunately, most academic and popular inquiries tend to focus on those traditions in a culture that affirm women's low status and assume these to be fixed phenomena. Rather than challenge the validity of these customs as true culture symbols, most investigators unquestioningly accept their authenticity. I dispute this basic assumption and believe that researchers need to ask the deeper question: Who are the beneficiaries of popularizing a particular culture from this angle?

REFERENCES

Almeida, R., R. Woods, T. Messino, R. J. Font, and C. Heer., 1994. Violence in the Lives of the Racially and Sexually Different: A Public and Private Dilemma. *Journal of Feminist Family Therapy* 5(3/4): 99–126.

Anderson, M. J. 1993. A License to Abuse: The Impact of Conditional Status on Female Immigrants. *Yale Law Journal* 102:1401–1430.

Bograd, M. 1988. Feminist Perspectives on Wife Abuse: An Introduction. In *Feminist Perspectives on Wife Abuse,* ed. K. Yllo and M. Bograd, Newbury Park, CA: Sage.

Bush, V. 1982. The Silent Crisis of Pacific Asian Women. *Western States Shelter Network Review,* July/August 6(10).

Coleman, D. L. 1996. Individualizing Justice Through Multiculturalism: The Liberals. *Columbia Law Review* 96:1093–1167.

Dasgupta, S. D., and S. DasGupta. 1997. Women in Exile: Gender Relations in the Asian Indian Community in the U.S. In *Contours of the Heart: South Asians Map North America,* ed. S. Maira and R. Srikanth. New York: Asian American Writers' Workshop.

Dasgupta, S. D., and S. Warrier. 1996. In the Footsteps of "Arundhati": Asian Indian Women's Experience of Domestic Violence in the United States. *Violence against Women* 2(3): 238–259.

Dasgupta, S. D., and S. Warrier. 1997. Barriers to Making Change. *In Visible Terms: Domestic Violence in the Asian Indian Context,* 2d ed. Union, NJ: Manavi.

Dobash, R. E., and R. P. Dobash. 1979. *Violence against Wives: A Case against the Patriarchy.* New York: Free Press.

Heise, L., J. Pitanguy, and A. Germain. 1994. *Violence against Women: The Hidden Burden* (World Bank Discussion Paper, No. 255). Washington, DC: World Bank.

Ho, V. 1990. Double Jeopardy, Double Courage. *Ms.,* October, pp. 46–48.

Ho, V. 1991. Illegal Aliens Fear INS More Than Fists of Abusive Spouses. *Arizona Republic, Valley & State,* August 31, pp. B1–B2.

Howe, M. 1991. Battered Alien Spouses Find a Way to Escape an Immigration Trap. *New York Times, Metropolitan,* August 25, p. M1.

Jetter, A. 1989. Fear Is Legacy of Wife Killing in Chinatown: Battered Asians Shocked by Husband's Probation. *New York Newsday,* November 26, p. 4.

Lum, J. 1988. Battered Asian Women. *Rice,* March, pp. 50–51.

Metz, H. 1993. Asian, American, Feminist. *Progressive,* June, 57(6):16.

Omi, M., and H. Winant. 1986. *Racial Formation in the United States from the 1960s to the 1980s.* Boston: Routledge and Kegan Paul.

Rimonte, N. 1991. A Question of Culture: Cultural Approval of Violence against Women in the Pacific-Asian Community and the Cultural Defense. *Stanford Law Review* 1311:1317–1320.

Rivers, T. 1990. Oriental Girls. *GQ* (British Edition), October, p. 158.

Shon, S. P., and D. Y. Ja. 1982. Asian Families. In *Ethnicity and Family Therapy,* ed. M. McGoldrick, J. K. Pearce, and J. Giordano. New York: Guilford.

Straus, M. A., R. J. Gelles, and S. Steinmetz, eds. 1980. *Behind Closed Doors: Violence in the American Family.* Garden City, NY: Doubleday.

Chapter 23

Leaving a Second Closet:
Outing Partner Violence in Same-Sex Couples

Carolyn M. West

ABSTRACT

Although same-sex violence is not well documented, this chapter summarizes available information. The studies of same-sex violence report widely different rates. A recent reliable report on domestic violence nationwide among lesbians and gays does show a 30 percent increase from 1999 to 2001.* Women reported twice as many incidents as men. However, service providers caution not to be misled, claiming that there is a similar percentage of gay male and lesbian victims but that services for women may offer more avenues for help and, thus, more reporting.

West, too, concludes from the research to date that partner battering is as prevalent among lesbians and gay men as it is among heterosexuals. Additional similarities among all groups experiencing domestic violence are the physical, sexual, and psychological aggression that characterize the victimization. West describes and questions several of the personal and background factors (correlates) that have been linked to this type of violence: prior history of violence in the family of origin, substance abuse, dependency of the batterer and conflicts concerning autonomy, and power imbalances within the relationship. On the other hand, West also details issues unique to lesbian and gay male battering: for example, the aggressor's use of homophobic control of a partner by threatening to "out" her or him (to reveal the partner's sexual orientation without consent); or the use of the myth of mutual battering to scare the victim into not summoning outside help—either police or social services. Most of the research conducted to date cautions that the findings are preliminary, focuses mainly on white middle-class lesbians and gay men,† and is limited by the difficulty in gaining access to, and the small number of, participants.

---

*Merrill, Christopher. Domestic Abuse on Rise in San Francisco Bay Community. *San Francisco Examiner*, August 8, 2001.
†See the editorial note at the end of the chapter for updated references on same-sex battering in communities of color.

As you read this chapter, pay attention to the barriers that battered lesbians and gay men face when they seek relief from an abusive relationship and pay attention to how battering is different between lesbians and gay men. Note that domestic violence in the bisexual and transgendered communities is currently left out of most discussions about lesbians and gay men (and, of course, discussions about heterosexuals). Finally, remember that lesbians, gays, bisexuals, and transgendered people are located at the intersections of race, ethnicity, class, and sexual orientation, making their struggle for safety all the more problematic.‡

---

‡See Diana Courvant and Loree Cook-Daniels. Trans and Intersex Survivors of Domestic Violence: Defining Terms, Barriers and Responsibilities. 2000–2001 Survivor Project. Available at: www.survivorproject.org/defbarresp.html

Researchers have been investigating partner violence for more than 20 years (Straus et al., 1980). Yet, there is a discernible absence of research on violence among same-sex couples. Information on lesbian battering, for example, did not emerge until [the mid 1980s] (Lobel, 1986), and the analyses of gay male intimate violence is even more recent (Island & Letellier, 1991). Within the last few years, some journals have devoted special issues to same-sex partner violence (Renzetti & Miley, 1996), and several second editions of self-help books have incorporated chapters on lesbian battering (e.g., NiCarthy, Merriam, & Coffman, 1994; White, 1994). Although more empirical studies have been conducted on same-sex partner violence (e.g., Renzetti, 1992), much of the material concerning gay and lesbian battering continues to appear in the forms of occasional articles in lesbian and gay newspapers (Shomer, 1997), anecdotal accounts (Lobel, 1986), and unpublished empirical reports (Gardner, 1989).

The dearth of research [historically made] it difficult to obtain an accurate estimate of same-sex partner violence. The available literature, however, indicates that partner violence among gays and lesbians appears to be as prevalent as it is among het-

erosexuals (Renzetti, 1997). Furthermore, violent couples of all sexual orientations may share some similarities; for example, sexual assaults may accompany battering (Campbell & Alford, 1989; Waterman, Dawson, & Bologna, 1989). Despite the similarities, intimate violence may not always be the same across sexual orientations. Because of the marginalized status of gay men and lesbians, the experience of battering may take different forms in same-sex couples (Hart, 1986). In addition, effective therapeutic intervention requires awareness and sensitivity to the particular stressors and difficulties faced by this population, such as discrimination based on sexual orientation (Morrow & Hawxhurst, 1989).

On the basis of national sexuality surveys, approximately 10% of the population identifies their sexual orientation as gay or lesbian (Gebhard, 1997; Janus & Janus, 1993). As more attention is focused on the concerns of homosexuals, both community activists and researchers agree that it is time to "out" partner violence in same-sex couples (Island & Letellier, 1991; Lobel, 1986). *Outing,* or revealing an individual's sexual orientation without his or her consent, can be a negative experience (Wallace, 1996). In contrast, the "coming out" process, in which a person publicly declares his or her sexual orientation, can signal acceptance and liberation (Miranda & Storms, 1989). With regard to partner violence, the latter form of outing is referred to in this chapter.

Source: In Jana Jasinski and Linda Williams, eds. 1998. *Partner Violence: A Comprehensive Review of 20 Years of Research.* Sage, pp. 163–183.

The purpose of this chapter is to discuss the emerging literature on same-sex partner violence. First, a brief description of the challenges and types of discrimination faced by this population is presented. Second, the incidence rates and distinct forms that gay and lesbian battering might assume are discussed. Next, correlates of partner violence and research limitations are highlighted. Finally, treatment implications and recommendations for policy are suggested.

DESCRIPTION OF THE POPULATION

Gay men and lesbians have experienced and continue to endure stereotyping, harassment, and discrimination in employment, housing, and public accommodations. This intolerance so permeates every aspect of society that members of this group can lose jobs or custody of their children, often without legal recourse. In some instances, gays and lesbians have lost the support of their families and friends (Almeida, Woods, Messino, Font, & Heer, 1994). As a result of prejudice, some homosexuals may develop a negative self-image, which may in turn contribute to substance abuse and suicide attempts, particularly among individuals who lack a positive gay identity (Arey, 1995; D'Augelli & Dark, 1995).

Although media attention to gay and lesbian issues has increased, public opinion remains negative. For example, in a 1993 New York Times/CBS News Poll of 1,154 adults, 55% believed that homosexual relationships between adults were morally wrong (*New York Times,* 1993). *Homophobia,* or the irrational fear and hatred of lesbians and gay men (Weinberg, 1972), also may culminate in criminal victimization, commonly referred to as *hate crimes* or *bias crimes* (Klinger, 1995). In a recent survey of 157 lesbians, gays, and bisexuals, for example, 41% reported being the target of physical assaults, verbal harassment, threats, and vandalism of their property as a result of their sexual orientation (Herek, Gillis, Cogan, & Glunt, 1997).

Researchers have found that, despite unfair treatment, many lesbians and gay men were satisfied with their sexual orientation and intimate relationships (Isay, 1989; Miranda & Storms, 1989; Peplau, 1991). In addition, many are actively engaged in a civil rights movement dedicated to educating the larger society about lesbian/gay issues and changing unfair legal and employment practices. A thriving gay community also offers support in the forms of crisis hotlines, churches, social groups, community centers, and bookstores (Arey, 1995; Butke, 1995).

INCIDENCE OF SAME-SEX PARTNER VIOLENCE

Violence among homosexual couples has not been well documented for several reasons. Societal institutions have not recognized same-sex partnerships as legitimate. For example, the law often limits the definition of partner violence to male-female couples. As a consequence, same-sex partner violence is not counted in police reports and other official statistics (Hart, 1986; Island & Letellier, 1991). Lack of resources and education concerning gay and lesbian battering has also prevented service providers from recognizing and conducting research on this form of aggression (Island & Letellier, 1991; Renzetti, 1996).

Furthermore, within the gay community there is pressure against revealing partner assaults. Researchers, activists, and often victims fear that discussing battering will reinforce negative societal stereotypes (that lesbian/gay relationships are dysfunctional or unhealthy; Elliot, 1996; Hart, 1986). In addition, after battling more visible forms of prejudice, such as hate crimes and discriminatory laws, little time and energy has been left for many activists to conduct research on intimate violence (Byrne, 1996).

How Much Violence Exists in Same-Sex Relationships?

Lesbian Partner Violence Estimates of partner violence in lesbian relationships have varied widely. In a survey of lesbian sexual practices, Loulan (1987) found that 17% of 1,566 lesbians surveyed had experienced "adult abuse" by a female partner. Substantial rates of partner violence were discovered by other researchers as well. Approximately one third of 284 lesbians surveyed by Lockhart, White, Causby, and Isaac (1994) reported being physically abused by partners, as measured by the Conflict Tactics Scale (CTS: Straus, 1979); and Coleman (1990) categorized 46% of 90 lesbian couples she interviewed as violent. Higher percentages of battering were reported when women were queried about violence in previous relationships in comparison with current partnerships. Using a sample of 36 lesbian undergraduates, Bologna, Waterman, and Dawson (1987) found that 40% were victims in their current or most recent relationships and that 64% were victimized by previous partners. Respondents also reported substantial rates of inflicting physical aggression in current (54%) and past (56%) relationships as measured by the CTS. Bologna et al.'s results should be interpreted with caution, however. Not only are these findings based on a small sample, but the researchers also asked respondents to participate in a study on "conflict resolution tactics," a method of solicitation that might have attracted more respondents who were willing to reveal partner violence.

When the definition of aggression was broadened to include psychological and sexual abuse in addition to physical violence, even more respondents reported victimization. In a sample of 1,099 lesbians surveyed at a music festival, one half of the respondents reported a combination of physical, psychological, and sexual abuse (Lie & Gentlewarrier, 1991). Similarly, in a sample of lesbians surveyed through the mailing lists of lesbian organizations in Arizona, researchers found that, when all forms of aggression were considered, 50% were victimized (Lie, Schilit, Bush, Montagne, & Reyes, 1991; Schilit, Lie, Bush, Montagne, & Reyes, 1991).

Gay Partner Violence   Few researchers have attempted to estimate the amount of gay male partner violence. Using a very small sample of 34 gay male undergraduates, Bologna and colleagues (1987) found that 18% were victims and 14% were perpetrators of violence in their current relationships. An even higher percentage of respondents sustained (44%) or inflicted (25%) violence in previous relationships.

In the absence of reliable prevalence studies, other means have been used to approximate the number of violent gay male partnerships. For example, researchers at the Seattle Counseling Service for Sexual Minorities predicted that 30,000 gay men have been battered in that city alone (Farley, 1992). Island and Letellier (1991) believe that 500,000 gay males are battered annually; they based their estimate on a 10% to 20% rate of battering among the 9.5 million adult gay males who are believed to be in intimate relationships (64%). Given the difficulties of calculating the number of gay relationships and the amount of partner violence experienced by couples regardless of sexual orientation, there is no way of knowing the accuracy of these estimates.

Does Partner Violence Differ by Sexual Orientation?

Several studies have compared rates of partner violence by sexual orientation. The results, however, have been mixed. Bologna and associates (1987) found that a higher percentage of lesbians, compared with gay men, reported being victims and aggressors in both current and past relationships. Several other studies found that partner violence did not differ by sexual orientation. For example, Gardner (1989) used the CTS (Straus, 1979) to assess physical aggression in a sample of 43 lesbian, 43 heterosexual, and 39 gay male couples. The results revealed that lesbian couples reported the highest rate of physical violence (48%), followed by gay (38%) and heterosexual couples (28%). These differences were not significant, however. Similarly, Brand and Kidd (1986) compared the reported frequency of physical aggression experienced by 75 self-identified heterosexual women and 55 lesbians. The authors found that the percentage of lesbians who were physically abused by female partners in *committed* relationships was comparable to the frequency of heterosexual women who were abused by male partners in committed relationships (25% vs. 27%, respectively). When *dating* relationships were considered, however, heterosexual women were significantly more likely to be physically abused by male dates than lesbians were to be abused by female dates (19% vs. 5%, respectively).

Mixed findings have been reported when researchers have compared partner violence rates among self-identified lesbians with a history of intimate relationships with both men and women. Loulan (1987), for example, found that almost twice as many lesbians reported being abused by male partners as female partners (30% vs. 17%, respectively). In contrast, Lie and colleagues (1991) found that more lesbians reported being physically victimized in previous relationships by women (45%) than men (32%).

In conclusion, it is difficult to obtain an accurate estimate of partner violence in same-sex relationships, particularly among gay men. This difficulty may be partially a result of the small sample sizes in many studies (e.g., Bologna et al., 1987; Gardner, 1989), as well as the different measures used to assess partner violence across studies. Although some researchers have used standardized measures of intimate violence (Bologna et al., 1987; Lockhart et al., 1994), such as the CTS (Straus, 1979), other researchers have simply asked, "If you are currently in a lesbian relationship, is it abusive?" (Schilit, Lie, & Montagne, 1990). Despite the limited research, battering appears to be as prevalent among gays and lesbians as among heterosexuals. More research needs to be conducted, however, before conclusions can be drawn about whether couples are at greater risk on the basis of their sexual orientation.

TYPES OF SAME-SEX PARTNER VIOLENCE

What Forms Does Lesbian and Gay Battering Take?

Lesbian battering has been defined by Hart (1986) as a "pattern of violence [or] coercive behaviors whereby a lesbian seeks to control the thoughts, beliefs, or conduct of her intimate partner or to punish the intimate for resisting the perpetrator's control" (p. 174). *Gay male partner violence* has been characterized as "any unwanted physical force, psychological abuse, or material or property destruction inflicted by one

man on another" (Island & Letellier, 1991, p. 28). Regardless of the definition, partner violence among same-sex couples generally takes the same forms as abuse in heterosexual relationships (Morrow & Hawxhurst, 1989). In a sample of 100 lesbian victims of partner violence, for example, Renzetti (1989) found that pushing and shoving (75%), being hit with a fist (65%), and having an object thrown at them (44%) were the most frequently reported forms of victimization. A similar pattern of lesbian abuse was discovered by Lockhart and colleagues (1994). The same study also revealed that between 4% and 12% of respondents experienced severe aggression, including beatings and assaults with weapons. Furthermore, on the basis of both clinical (Farley, 1996; Island & Letellier, 1991; Margolies & Leeder, 1995) and empirical samples (Renzetti, 1992), same-sex partner violence tends to occur multiple times and to increase in severity over time. Again, this pattern of violence frequently occurs in heterosexual relationships as well (e.g., Walker, 1979).

Although many similarities are found between same-sex and heterosexual partner violence, several important differences exist. For example, aggressors may use homophobic control (Hart, 1986), the HIV (human immunodeficiency virus) positive status of themselves or their partners (Letellier, 1996), or the myth of "mutual battering" (Renzetti, 1992) to control their victims. Each form of aggression is discussed below.

Homophobic Control According to Hart (1986), homophobic control includes such actions as the following:

> Threatening to tell family, friends, employer, police, church, community, etc. that the victim is a lesbian . . . ; telling the victim she deserves all that she gets because she is a lesbian; assuring her that no one would believe she has been violated because lesbians are not violent; reminding her that she has no options because the homophobic world will not help her. (p. 189)

This form of abuse appears to be a common occurrence in violent same-sex relationships. For example, in Renzetti's (1992) survey of 100 victims of lesbian battering, 21% indicated that their partners had "threatened to bring her out"—that is, to reveal one's sexual orientation without permission. Several victims in this study responded to this form of abuse by quitting their jobs. Their rationale was that quitting was preferable to being terminated as a result of being "outed" (Renzetti, 1996). Thus homophobic control appears to be an effective form of dominance in some battering relationships.

HIV Status   Although AIDS (acquired immunodeficiency syndrome) and HIV are not solely a problem of the gay community, this population has been disproportionately affected by this health crisis in the United States. According to the Centers for Disease Control and Prevention (1993), gay and bisexual men account for 58% of AIDS cases in the United States. A considerable number of gay men must contend with both HIV infection and partner abuse. For example, 30% of battered gay and bisexual men served by the San Francisco Gay Men's Domestic Violence Project were also HIV positive (cited in Letellier, 1996). Although HIV does not cause battering (Island & Letellier, 1991; Letellier, 1994), Letellier (1996) cites numerous examples of ways this infection can further complicate intimate violence. Specifically, if a batterer is HIV positive, he may threaten to infect his victim or use his failing health to make the victim feel guilty about leaving the abusive situation. He may also use his poor health to manipulate others into believing that he is not the aggressor in the conflict. As a result, both friends and legal authorities may be less likely to intervene. Alternatively, if the victim has been infected with HIV, the batterer may threaten to withhold medical care or to reveal the victim's HIV-positive status, which may result in discrimination and the loss of income or insurance benefits. In addition, the internalization of societal animosity toward both gay men and people living with AIDS, in conjunction with the lack of financial resources and fear of losing a caregiver, may further hamper a victim's ability to leave a violent relationship.

Mutual Battering   In same-sex relationships, researchers and clinicians cannot rely on gender to determine the roles (victim vs. aggressor) played by each partner in a battering incident. As a result, intimate violence among same-sex couples has often been perceived as an "equal fight" or mutual battering (Island & Letellier, 1991; Renzetti, 1992). At first glance, empirical studies appear to support the existence of mutual violence in same-sex relationships. For example, Lie and associates (1991) found that 39% of respondents who had been both aggressors and victims of lesbian battering labeled their violence as mutual abuse. However, many lesbian respondents—between 30% (Lie et al., 1991) and 64% (Renzetti, 1992)—have also characterized their aggressive behavior as self-defensive.

Researchers assert that gay (Island & Letellier, 1991) and lesbian (Hart, 1986; Renzetti, 1997) batterers use the myth of mutual battering to further control and victimize their partners. Specifically, aggressors may claim mutual abuse to deny responsibility for their violent behavior. If a victim retaliates or takes self-defensive actions, the batterer may use this to further justify his or her behavior. For example, a perpetrator may claim that "she hit me too" as a reason for her continued abuse. A victim, regardless of her motivation for the use of aggression, may feel guilty for using violence against a partner and as a result may perceive herself as an equal combatant (Farley, 1992; Hart, 1986; Island & Letellier, 1991; Leeder, 1988). Letellier (1994) further argues that, because of the social stigma associated with male victimization, male victims might be encouraged to "take it like a man." As a consequence, men may label themselves as equal participants in the violence, rather than as victims.

In conclusion, aggression among same-sex couples generally takes the same forms (physical, sexual, and psychological abuse) as it does in heterosexual relationships. Despite the many similarities in types of aggression inflicted and sustained, however, there are some important differences. Batterers may use homophobic control (Hart, 1986), the HIV-positive status of themselves or their partners (Letellier, 1994), and the illusion of mutual battering to further victimize their partners (Renzetti, 1992). Future research should focus on the dynamics of these forms of violence. Specifically, more information is needed concerning the prevalence and variety of forms that homophobic control might assume (Renzetti, 1992) and the effect of HIV on battering (Letellier, 1996). Because gay men may be even more reluctant to label themselves as victims, their perceptions of mutual battering warrant particular attention (Letellier, 1994).

CORRELATES OF SAME-SEX PARTNER VIOLENCE

What Are Some Correlates of Same-Sex Partner Violence?

One unique variable specific to gays and lesbians, *internalized homophobia,* defined as the acceptance of negative societal attitudes toward homosexuals (Pharr, 1986), has been examined as a potential contributor to partner violence in same-sex couples (Renzetti, 1997). Specifically, researchers argue that societal discrimination fosters internalized homophobia, which in turn may contribute to low self-esteem, feelings of powerlessness, denial of group membership, and difficulty establishing committed, trusting, intimate relationships (Letellier, 1994; Margolies, Becker, & Jackson-Brewer, 1987). These negative feelings may then be acted out in the form of partner violence (Byrne, 1996; Hart, 1986). As an example of internalized homophobia, Letellier (1994) cited a case of a gay batterer who shouted at his victim after an attack: "You might as well get used to it. This is how gay relationships are" (p. 100). Although it certainly seems plausible that internalized homophobia may play a role in same-sex partner violence, this theory awaits further empirical investigation.

The majority of factors that appear to contribute to same-sex partner violence have been shown to be predictors of heterosexual battering as well. In particular, the bulk of empirical research has investigated the intergenerational transmission of violence (Schilit et al., 1991), alcohol abuse (Schilit et al., 1990), conflicts around dependency and autonomy, and imbalances of power (Lockhart et al., 1994) as correlates of same-sex battering. Although these risk factors are discussed separately in the following

section, they are often interrelated; that is, they may occur in conjunction to increase the probability of intimate violence among gay and lesbian couples (e.g., Farley, 1996; Renzetti, 1997).

Violence in the Family of Origin The intergenerational transmission of violence theory proposes that individuals exposed to violence in their families of origin, either as witnesses or as victims, are at increased risk of experiencing aggression in adult relationships (O'Leary, 1988). Regardless of sexual orientation of respondents, researchers have found mixed results (Renzetti, 1992; Straus et al., 1980). In some studies, no association was reported between violence in the family of origin and lesbian battering (Coleman, 1990; Kelly & Warshafsky, 1987; Renzetti, 1992). In contrast, other investigators have discovered significant correlations between both witnessing family violence and experiencing various forms of childhood victimization, including physical, sexual, and verbal abuse, and being an aggressor and victim of lesbian battering (Lie et al., 1991; Lockhart et al., 1994; Schilit et al., 1991). An association between a prior history of family abuse and intimate violence has been discovered in clinical samples of gay and lesbian batterers as well (Farley, 1996; Margolies & Leeder, 1995).

Evidence both supports and refutes the belief that abuse is transmitted intergenerationally. Methodological differences, such as the many ways violence in the family of origin has been measured, may contribute to these contradictory findings. Conversely, the attributions made about witnessing or experiencing abuse in childhood, such as the belief that childhood victimization inevitably leads to partner violence, may affect adult behavior (Gelles & Cornell, 1990). For example, like heterosexual victims, lesbians may attribute battering to the violent upbringing of their partners (Renzetti, 1992).

Substance Abuse Drinking has been linked to intimate violence among heterosexual couples (e.g., Kaufman Kantor & Straus, 1987). Similarly, a connection has been found between alcohol use and battering in lesbian partnerships (Coleman, 1990;

Kelly & Warshafsky, 1987; Schilit et al., 1990). In addition, substance abuse has been associated with sustaining injuries in violent lesbian relationships; for example, in a sample of 125 lesbians and 27 bisexual women, Perry (1995) discovered positive correlations between frequency of alcohol use and being physically injured by both a previous and current partner, and frequency of marijuana use was associated with being injured by a past partner.

These results should be interpreted with caution, however. Many of these findings are based on very small samples; for example, several studies based their results on fewer than 42 violent respondents (Coleman, 1990: Schilit et al., 1990). Furthermore, the association between substance abuse and lesbian battering has been assessed by using such questions as "Were you or your partner ever under the influence of drugs or alcohol at the time of the battering incident?" (Renzetti, 1992). This type of question is not sufficient to differentiate patterns and levels of alcohol consumption. This is a research limitation because different types of drinking patterns—for example, binge drinking—have been linked to wife assaults (e.g., Kaufman Kantor & Straus, 1987). With the available methodology used to measure alcohol abuse among same-sex couples, however, it is not possible to access links between different types of drinking behavior and partner violence.

Although substance abuse may occur in conjunction with partner violence, it does not *cause* violence in either heterosexual (Kaufman Kantor & Straus, 1987) or same-sex relationships (Island & Letellier, 1991). In fact, battering can and often does occur in the absence of alcohol use (Margolies & Leeder, 1995); for example, one third of Renzetti's (1992) sample was not under the influence of alcohol during the violence. Therefore, it is imperative that multiple factors, which act in conjunction with or mediate the association between substance abuse and battering, be investigated. For instance, Renzetti (1992) discovered that dependency of the batterer on her partner was highly correlated with alcohol use. On the basis of qualitative analysis of interviews with 10 lesbians, Diamond and Wilsnack (1978) made a similar association between alcohol

use and dependency. Thus, this area warrants further discussion.

Dependency and Autonomy Conflicts Although male batterers have been found to be very dependent on their female victims (e.g., Walker, 1989), it has been argued that additional factors may influence how dependency is experienced in lesbian partnerships. Women continue to be socialized to define themselves in relation to significant others and to place a high value on intimacy (Chodorow, 1978). Thus, when two women are romantically involved, it may be even more difficult for them to establish a sense of independence and autonomy in their relationship. In addition, lesbians, like gay men, may develop a greater attachment to their partners in response to the lack of social validation and support for their relationships that they receive from the larger society (McCandlish, 1982; Renzetti, 1992). A sense of intimacy and closeness may also act as a buffer against discrimination. Among some lesbian couples, however, high levels of intimacy can create a sense of "fusion" (Lindenbaum, 1985) or "merging" (Pearlman, 1989), which may make it difficult for each partner to have a sense of independence and separate identity in the relationship. As a result, having a different opinion or initiating social activities without the partner might be perceived as rejection, which in turns leads to conflict and possibly physical violence (Margolies & Leeder, 1995).

Although Coleman (1990) found no correlation between relationship interdependency and partner violence among lesbian couples, other researchers have discovered that conflicts around dependency and autonomy were related to lesbian battering (e.g., Renzetti, 1992). For instance, Lockhart and associates (1994) found that, when compared with their nonvictimized counterparts, respondents who reported severe levels of physical abuse perceived that their partners had a high need for social fusion, as measured by such beliefs as couples need to do everything together and the use of communication techniques that include mind reading. Severely victimized respondents in this study also reported more conflict around issues of independence and autonomy, such as a partner's emotional and financial dependency, a partner socializing without the respondent, and a respondent's intimate involvement with other people. Similarly, in her sample of lesbian victims, Renzetti (1992) assessed dependency and autonomy with such items as "My partner and I have a separate set of friends." Her results revealed that batterers who were very dependent on their partners, as well as victims who desired more independence, reported a greater frequency of abuse and more types of abuse, such as shoving, pushing, and choking.

The association between dependency and autonomy requires further investigation. For example, the extent to which dependency issues reflect borderline or narcissistic personality disorders should be considered (Coleman, 1994). Dependency issues may also be related to concern around power and control. For instance, it has been argued that some gay men might avoid relationship dependency for fear of losing power and control (Farley, 1992). Thus, it is also important to consider the role of power imbalances in same-sex battering.

Power Imbalances Among heterosexual couples, power imbalances have often been associated with partner violence (Coleman & Straus, 1990; Straus et al., 1980). The link between the imbalance of power and battering is less clear among same-sex couples (e.g., Bologna et al., 1987). This inconsistency may be partially a result of how power imbalances are defined across studies. When indicators of social status, such as income, were used as predictors of partner violence, the findings have been contradictory. For example, Kelly and Warshafsky (1987) found no significant correlations between partner violence and indicators of status as measured by income, education, race, religion, and age. In contrast, Renzetti (1992) found that as differences in social class and intelligence became a source of conflict between the partners, the severity and frequency of some forms of violence increased. In particular, social class and intellectual differences between partners were associated with batterers hitting, choking, and pushing their partners. It is not clear, however,

whether the victim or the batterer was the partner with the higher social class or greater intellectual ability. Renzetti (1992) concluded that the cumulative effects of differences in status and resources between partners should be taken into consideration; that is, social class differences between partners may not necessarily result in abuse—for example, if the older, more educated partner makes more money. In contrast, if the younger or less educated partner has more economic resources relative to the older, more educated partner, such a relationship may experience a greater likelihood of conflict concerning the balance of power.

Results were more consistent when division of labor between the partners was considered to be a form of power. In several studies, lesbians who assumed primary responsibility for household duties, such as cooking and managing the finances, were more likely to be abused (Kelly & Warshafsky, 1987; Renzetti, 1992). Similarly, Lockhart and associates (1994) found evidence to support the link between power imbalances and victimization in lesbian relationships. Specifically, respondents who sustained severe aggression reported more conflicts around housekeeping and cooking duties, when compared with nonvictims and those who sustained mild forms of violence. On the basis of the research, however, it is not clear whether these divisions in household duties existed before the abuse. It could also be that the victims assumed domestic chores in an attempt to appease the abusers (Renzetti, 1992). These speculations await further empirical investigation.

In conclusion, intergenerational transmission (Schilit et al., 1991), alcohol abuse (Schilit et al., 1990), conflicts around dependency and autonomy, and imbalances of power (Lockhart et al., 1994) have been linked to partner violence among same-sex couples. Although these risk factors may occur independently, they are often interrelated and occur in conjunction, which may increase the probability of violence in both heterosexual and same-sex partnerships (Renzetti, 1997). Many of these results need to be replicated, however, before firm conclusions can be made about the roles these risk factors play in gay and lesbian battering.

RESEARCH LIMITATIONS

What Are Some Research Limitations?

The majority of published empirical studies on same-sex violence have surveyed young, white, educated, middle-class respondents who were members of lesbian organizations (Lie et al., 1991; Schilit et al., 1991) or attending social events that attracted large groups of lesbians (Lie & Gentlewarrier, 1991; Loulan, 1987). In addition, most participants were openly lesbian. For example, among the 152 lesbians and bisexual women surveyed by Perry (1995), 63% classified their sexual orientation disclosure as being "out." Because of nonrandom sampling procedures and self-selection factors, knowledge of partner violence among gay men (Island & Letellier, 1991) and homosexuals who are "closeted" (not open about their sexual orientation), working class (Almeida et al., 1994), or ethnic minorities (Kanuha, 1990; Mendez, 1996; Waldron, 1996) is limited.

Another major research limitation is the dearth of theoretical models that address partner violence among homosexuals. Mainstream gender-based theories have attributed battering to rigid adherence to patriarchal values (Hamberger & Hastings, 1988a) or to traditional feminine sex role stereotypes (Walker, 1979). Although some researchers have argued that same-sex partner violence is the result of gay and lesbian couples acting out traditional heterosexual masculine and feminine gender roles (e.g., Walker, 1979), other investigators have not found evidence of "gender role playing" by gay and lesbian couples (Hart, 1986; Renzetti, 1992). Therefore, a theory that associates battering with traditional gender roles appears to be of limited use in explaining assault among gay and lesbian couples. A related argument is that sexism and male dominance contribute to intimate violence among heterosexual couples (e.g. Yllö & Straus, 1990). Again, such a theory does not take into account the role of internalized homophobia or relationship dynamics in which power differences are not based on gender. To better understand the dynamics of same-sex partner violence, Letellier (1994) suggests that researchers should consider gender-neutral theories, which focus on "power imbalances, both on the societal and interpersonal

levels, and on the psychological characteristics of individual perpetrators." (p. 104).

To summarize, it is difficult to obtain an accurate estimate of partner violence, particularly among gay male couples. On the basis of the limited research, same-sex couples appear to be equally likely as their heterosexual counterparts to experience violence. Many similarities are found in the types of violence experienced by heterosexual and homosexual couples. Important differences are also found, however, including the use of homophobic control (Hart, 1986), HIV-positive status (Letellier, 1996), and the myth of mutual battering (Renzetti, 1997). Although internalized homophobia has been proposed as one possible contributor to partner violence in same-sex relationships (Renzetti, 1997), the correlates of partner violence tend to be the same regardless of sexual orientation. In particular, gay and lesbian partner violence has been empirically linked to violence in the family of origin (Schilit et al., 1990), alcohol abuse (Schilit et al., 1990), conflicts around autonomy, and power imbalances (Lockhart et al., 1994).

THERAPEUTIC IMPLICATIONS

It is important to focus on the role of the therapist in the treatment of violent same-sex couples. It is not safe for some gays and lesbians to reveal their sexual orientation to relatives and friends. Consequently, therapists may be one of the few sources of help that victims and batterers have left to consult (Renzetti, 1989). The mental health profession, however, has a long history of discrimination against gay men and lesbians (Arey, 1995; D'Augelli & Dark, 1995). For therapeutic intervention to be effective, service providers need greater awareness of the strengths in the gay and lesbian community, as well as the challenges faced by this population (Morrow & Hawxhurst, 1989). . . .

What Barriers Impede Help Seeking?

Scant research has examined the extent and nature of help-seeking efforts made by battered gay men (Island & Letellier, 1991) and lesbians (Lie &

Gentlewarrier, 1991; Renzetti, 1989). In a sample of more than 1,000 lesbians, Lie and Gentlewarrier (1991) asked respondents to indicate what resources they "would be likely to use after an abuse, assuming these were available and accessible to you either as a survivor or a perpetrator." Regardless of their victim or perpetrator status, approximately two thirds of the sample reported that they would not use any of the resources listed in this study, such as support groups and battered women's shelters. Similarly, Renzetti (1989) also found low rates of help seeking from formal sources among the 100 battered lesbians in her sample. Although 58 sought help from counselors, fewer than 20 sought help from legal authorities, religious leaders, shelters, or physicians. On the basis of anecdotal reports, Island and Letellier (1991) found that gay male victims also were reluctant to seek help from legal and social service agencies. Taken together, these studies point to a pattern of service underuse.

Feelings of shame and fear of retaliation may preclude victims of both heterosexual (Pagelow, 1981a) and same-sex partner violence from seeking help (Renzetti, 1989). Concerns around revealing one's sexual orientation to service providers, relatives, and friends may further impede the help-seeking efforts of gay men and lesbians (Farley, 1992). Real and perceived homophobia and discriminatory practices, however, are the most widely cited reasons by some gays and lesbians for the underuse of mainstream community services (Lie & Gentlewarrier, 1991; Renzetti, 1992). Homophobia impedes help-seeking efforts because it

> helps to create the opportunity for abuse without consequences by isolating the victims and preventing them access to resources such as their family, appropriate social services, and the criminal justice and legal systems. As a result, battered lesbians and gay men are unlikely to seek assistance, and even if they do, are not likely to be helped. (Merrill, 1996, p. 17)

Empirical research supports this speculation. For example, among the battered lesbians who sought help in Renzetti's (1989) study, many reported that service providers refused to help, excused or denied the seriousness of the violence, or characterized the

battering as mutual abuse. Battered gay men also have encountered similar responses when seeking help from professionals (Island & Letellier, 1991).

According to Renzetti (1996), the fear that professionals will be unresponsive to same-sex partner violence is not unfounded. On the basis of surveys with 544 service providers listed in the 1991 National Directory of Domestic Violence Programs, only 10% of the programs had intervention and outreach efforts specifically designed for lesbians (e.g., advertisements in lesbian and gay newspapers, support groups for battered lesbians). In addition, fewer than one half of the programs addressed lesbian battering when they trained their staff and volunteers. Despite the limited services offered by these agencies, only 32% of service providers planned to expand their services to battered lesbians. . . .

POLICY RECOMMENDATIONS

Based on the literature, the following recommendations are made:

1. Identifying the problem is the first step to motivating the gay and lesbian community and service providers to recognize and confront same-sex battering (Lobel, 1986). This entails such actions as broadening the language in partner violence laws to ensure that victims are equally protected regardless of gender and sexual orientation (Island & Letellier, 1991). Defining the problem also involves conducting more empirical research on the prevalence and incidence of same-sex partner violence, characteristics of the violence, and contributing factors (Hamberger, 1996).

2. Extensive training is needed for service providers in law enforcement, social service agencies, and the medical and mental health professions. Professionals may need to address homophobia and discrimination against gays and lesbians in their agencies and to develop written and spoken language that is inclusive of same-sex relationships (Hamberger, 1996; Renzetti, 1996).

3. Massive intervention efforts should be directed toward the gay and lesbian community. These

intervention strategies could include newspaper advertisements, telephone books that specifically list services for same-sex partner violence, and flyers posted at parades and conferences with a larger presence of gays and lesbians (Island & Letellier, 1991). A special effort should be made to reach gay men and lesbians of color through outreaching to communities of color, advertising services for victims and batterers in different languages, and recruiting ethnically diverse staff and volunteers (Mendez, 1996; Waldron, 1996).

4. Finally, factors that contribute to same-sex partner violence must be addressed, such as substance abuse, violence in the family of origin, and discrimination against gays and lesbians.

DISCUSSION QUESTIONS

1. Based on this reading by West, describe the ways in which the problems faced by battered women who are heterosexual are *similar* to those of battered women who are lesbians. Conversely, describe some of the barriers *unique* to battered lesbian (and gay male) partners who seek safety from an abusive relationship.

2. Describe similarities in the plight of lesbian battered women with the plights of battered immigrant women, wealthy white women, middle-class Black women, or poor Latina, Asian, or Native American women.

3. Spell out several myths and facts about domestic violence in same-sex partnerships.

4. How are feminist analyses of domestic violence challenged by the fact that violence in intimate relationships exists between lesbian partners? In what ways might a feminist analysis of lesbian relationships still pertain? How does a race, class, gender analysis of same-sex violence in the lesbian community both

complicate and clarify an understanding of domestic violence?

REFERENCES

Almeida, R., R. Woods, T. Messino, R. J. Font, C. Heer. 1994. Violence in the Lives of the Racially and Sexually Different: A Public and Private Dilemma. *Journal of Feminist Family Therapy* 5(3/4): 99–126.

Arey, D. 1995. Gay Males and Sexual Child Abuse. In *Sexual Abuse in Nine North American Cultures: Treatment and Prevention,* ed. L. A. Fontes, 200–235. Thousand Oaks, CA: Sage.

Bologna, M. J., C. K. Waterman, and L. J. Dawson. 1987. *Violence in Gay Male and Lesbian Relationships: Implications for Practitioners and Policy Makers.* Paper presented at the Third National Conference for Family Violence Researchers, Durham, NH.

Brand, P. A., and A. H. Kidd. 1986. Frequency of Physical Aggression in Heterosexual and Female Homosexual Dyads. *Psychological Reports* 59:1307–1313.

Butke, M. 1995. Lesbians and Sexual Child Abuse. In *Sexual Abuse in Nine North American Cultures: Treatment and Prevention,* ed. L. A. Fontes, 200–235. Thousand Oaks, CA: Sage.

Byrne, D. 1996. Clinical Models for the Treatment of Gay Male Perpetrators of Domestic Violence. In *Violence in Gay and Lesbian Domestic Partnerships,* ed. C. M.

Editors' Note: For reference to battering in gay and lesbian communities of color, see: (1) Valli Kanuha. 1990. Compounding the Triple Jeopardy: Battering in Lesbian of Color Relationships. In *Diversity and Complexity in Feminist Therapy,* ed. L. S. Brown and M. Root, 169–184. New York: Harrington Park. (2) Juan Mendez 1996. Serving Gays and Lesbians of Color Who Are Survivors of Violence. In *Violence in Gay and Lesbian Domestic Partnerships,* ed., Claire Renzetti and Charles Harvey Miley, 53–59. New York: Harrington/Haworth. (3) Martha Lucia Garcia. 1999. A "New Kind" of Battered Woman: Challenges for the Movement. In *Same-Sex Domestic Violence: Strategies for Change,* ed. Beth Leventhal and Sandra Lundy, 165–171. Thousand Oaks, CA: Sage. Preliminary issues for lesbian, bisexual, and transgendered battered women can be found in Beth Crane, Jeannie LaFrance, Gillian Leichtling, Brooks Nelson, and Erika Silver. 1999. Lesbians and Bisexual Women Working Cooperatively to End Domestic Violence. In *Same-Sex Domestic Violence,* 125–134. Also, Janice Ristock's recent (2002) publication of *No More Secrets: Violence in Lesbian Relationships* (New York: Routledge) does an excellent job in theoretically discussing the intersectionality of race, class, and gender in the lives of battered lesbians and bisexual women in the United States and Canada.

Renzetti and C. H. Miley, 107–116. Binghamton, NY: Haworth.

Campbell, J. C., and P. Alford, 1989. The Dark Consequences of Marital Rape. *American Journal of Nursing,* 89:946–949.

Centers for Disease Control and Prevention. 1993. *HIV/AIDS Surveillance Report.* Washington, DC: U.S. Department of Health and Human Services.

Chodorow N. 1978. *The Reproduction of Mothering: Psychoanalysis and the Sociology of Gender.* Berkeley: University of California Press.

Coleman, D. H., and M. A. Straus. 1990. Marital Power, Conflict, and Violence in a Nationally Representative Sample of American Couples. In *Physical Violence in American Families: Risk Factors and Adaptations to Violence in 8,145 Families,* ed. M. A. Straus and R. J. Gelles, 287–304. New Brunswick, NJ: Transaction.

Coleman, V. E. 1994. Lesbian Battering: The Relationship between Personality and the Perpetration of Violence. *Violence and Victims* 9(2):139–152.

D'Augelli, A. R., and L. J. Dark. 1995. Lesbian, Gay, and Bisexual Youths. In *Reason to Hope: A Psychological Perspective on Violence and Youth,* ed. L. D. Eron, J. H. Gentry, and P. Schleyel, 177–196. Washington, DC: American Psychological Association.

Diamond, D. L., and S. C. Wilsnack. 1978. Alcohol Abuse Among Lesbians: A Descriptive Study. *Journal of Homosexuality* 4:123–142.

Elliot, P. 1996. Shattering Illusions: Same-Sex Partner Violence. In *Violence in Gay and Lesbian Domestic Partnerships,* ed. C. M. Renzetti, 1–8. Binghamton, NY: Haworth.

Farley, N. 1992. Same-Sex Partner Violence. In *Counseling Gay Men and Lesbians: Journey to the End of the Rainbow,* ed. S. H. Dworkin & F. J. Gutierrez, 231–242. Alexandria, VA: American Association for Counseling and Development.

Farley, N. 1996. A Survey of Factors Contributing to Gay and Lesbian Domestic Violence. In *Violence in Gay and Lesbian Domestic Partnerships,* ed. C. M. Renzetti and C. H. Miley, 35–42. Binghamton, NY: Haworth.

Gardner, R. 1989. *Method of Conflict Resolution and Characteristics of Abuse and Victimization in Heterosexual, Lesbian, and Gay Male Couples.* Unpublished doctoral dissertation. University of Georgia, Athens.

Gebhard, P. H. 1997. *Memorandum on the Incidence of Homosexuals in the United States.* Bloomington: Indiana University, Center for Sex Research.

Gelles, R. J., and C. P. Cornell. 1990. *Intimate Violence in Families,* 2d ed. Newbury Park, CA: Sage.

Hamberger, L. K. 1996. Intervention in Gay Male Intimate Violence Requires Coordinated Efforts on Multiple Levels. In *Violence in Gay and Lesbian Domestic Partnerships,* ed. C. M. Renzetti & C. H. Miley, 83–92. Binghamton, NY: Haworth.

Hamberger, L. K., and J. Hastings. 1988a. Characteristics of Male Spouse Abusers Consistent with Personality Disorders. *Hospital and Community Psychiatry* 39:763–770.

Hart, B. 1986. Lesbian Battering: An Examination. In *Naming the Violence: Speaking Out about Lesbian Battering,* ed. K. Lobel, 173–189. Seattle, WA: Seal.

Herek, G. M., J. R. Gillis, J. C. Cogan, and E. K. Glunt. 1997. Hate Crime Victimization among Lesbian, Gay, and Bisexual Adults: Prevalence, Psychological Correlates, and Methodological Issues. *Journal of Interpersonal Violence* 12(2):195–215.

Isay, R. A. 1989. *Being Homosexual: Gay Men and Their Development.* New York: Avon.

Island, D., and P. Letellier. 1991. *Men Who Beat the Men Who Love Them. Battered Gay Men and Domestic Violence.* New York: Harrington Park.

Janus, S. S., and C. L. Janus. 1993. *The Janus Report on Sexual Behavior.* New York: John Wiley.

Kanuha, V. 1994. Women of Color in Battering Relationships. In *Women of Color: Integrating Ethnic and Gender Identities in Psychotherapy,* ed. L. Comas-Diaz and B. Greene, 428–454. New York: Guilford.

Kaufman Kantor, G., and M. A. Straus. 1987. The "Drunken Bum" Theory of Wife Beating. *Social Problems* 34(3):213–230.

Kelly, C. E., and L. Warshafsky. 1987. *Partner Abuse in Gay Male and Lesbian Couples.* Paper presented at the Third National Conference for Family Violence Researchers, Durham, NH.

Klinger, R. L. 1995. Gay Violence. *Journal of Gay & Lesbian Psychotherapy* 2(3):119–134.

Leeder, E. 1988. Enmeshed in Pain: Counseling the Lesbian Battering Couple. *Women and Therapy* 7(1):81–99.

Letellier, P. 1994. Gay and Bisexual Male Domestic Violence Victimization: Challenges to Feminist Theory and Responses to Violence. *Violence and Victims* 9(2): 95–106.

Letellier, P. 1996. Twin Epidemics: Domestic Violence and HIV Infection among Gay and Bisexual Men. In *Violence in Gay and Lesbian Domestic Partnerships,* ed. C. M. Renzetti and C. H. Miley, 69–82. Binghamton, NY: Haworth.

Lie, G.Y., and S. Gentlewarrier. 1991. Intimate Violence in Lesbian Relationships: Discussion of Survey Findings and Practice Implications. *Journal of Social Service Research* 15(1/2): 41–59.

Lie, G.Y., R. Schilit, J. Bush, M. Montagne, and L. Reyes. 1991. Lesbians in Currently Aggressive Relationships. How Frequently Do They Report Aggressive Past Relationships? *Violence and Victims* 6(2):121–135.

Lindenbaum, J. P. 1985. The Shattering of an Illusion: The Problem of Competition in Lesbian Relationships. *Feminist Studies* 11:85-103.

Lobel, K. 1986. *Naming the Violence: Speaking Out about Lesbian Battering.* Seattle, WA: Seal.

Lockhart, L. L., B. W. White, V. Causby, and A. Isaac. 1994. Letting Out the Secret: Violence in Lesbian Relationships. *Journal of Interpersonal Violence* 9(4):469–492.

Loulan, J. 1987. *Lesbian Passion.* San Francisco: Spinsters/ Aunt Lute.

Lujan, C., L. M. DeBruyn, P. A. May, and M. E. Bird. 1989. Profile of Abused and Neglected American Indian Children in the Southwest. *Child Abuse & Neglect* 13:449–461.

Margolies, L., M. Becker, and K. Jackson-Brewer. 1987. Internalized Homophobia: Identifying and Treating the Oppressor Within. In *Lesbian Psychologies: Exploration & Challenges.* ed. B. L. P. Collective. Urbana: University of Illinois.

Margolies, L., and E. Leeder. 1995. Violence at the Door: Treatment of Lesbian Batterers. *Violence against Women* 2(2):139–157.

McCandlish, B. 1982. Therapeutic Issues with Lesbian Couples. *Journal of Homosexuality* 7(1):71–78.

Mendez, J. M. 1996. Serving Gays and Lesbians of Color Who Are Survivors of Domestic Violence. In *Violence in Gay and Lesbian Domestic Partnerships,* ed. C. M. Renzetti and C. H. Miley, 53–60. Binghamton, NY: Haworth.

Merrill, C. S. 1996. Ruling the Exceptions: Same-Sex Battering and Domestic Theory. In *Violence in Gay and Lesbian Domestic Partnerships,* ed. C. M. Renzetti & C. H. Miley, 3–22. Binghamton, NY: Haworth.

Miranda, J., and M. Storms. 1989. Psychological Adjustment of Lesbians and Gay Men. *Journal of Counseling and Development* 68:41–45.

Morrow, S. L., and D. M. Hawxhurst. 1969. Lesbian Partner Abuse: Implications for Therapists. *Journal of Counseling & Development* 68:58–62.

New York Times. 1993, February 9–11. New York Times/ CBS News Poll. A14.

NiCarthy, G., K. Merriam, and S. Coffman. 1994. *Talking It Out: A Guide to Groups for Abused Women.* Seattle, WA: Seal.

O'Leary, K. D. 1988. Physical Agression between Spouses: A Social Learning Theory Perspective. In *Handbook of Family Violence,* ed. V. B. Van Hasselt, R. L. Morrison, A. S. Bellack, and M. Hersen, 31–56. New York: Plenum.

Pagelow, M. D. 1981a. Factors Affecting Women's Decisions to Leave Violent Relationships. *Journal of Family Issues* 2(4):391–414.

Pearlman, S. F. 1989. Distancing and Connectedness: Impact on Couple Formation in Lesbian Relationships. *Women and Therapy* 8:77–88.

Peplau, L. A. 1991. Lesbian and Gay Relationships. In *Homosexuality: Implications for Public Policy,* ed. J. C. Gonsiorek and J. D. Weinrich, 177–196. Newbury Park, CA: Sage.

Perry, S. M. 1995. Lesbian Alcohol and Marijuana Use: Correlates of HIV Risk Behaviors and Abusive Relationships. *Journal of Psychoactive Drugs* 27(4):413–419.

Pharr, S. 1986. Two Workshops on Homophobia. In *Naming the Violence: Speaking Out about Lesbian Battering,* ed. K. Lobel, 202–222. Seattle, WA: Seal.

Renzetti, C. 1989. Building a Second Closet: Third-Party Responses to Victims of Lesbian Partner Abuse. *Family Relations* 38:157–163.

Renzetti, C. 1992. *Violent Betrayal: Partner Abuse in Lesbian Relationships.* Newbury Park, CA: Sage.

Renzetti, C. 1994. On Dancing with a Bear: Reflections on Some of the Current Debates among Domestic Violence Theorists. *Violence and Victims* 9(2):195–200.

Renzetti, C. M. 1996. The Poverty of Services for Battered Lesbians. In *Violence in Gay and Lesbian Domestic Partnerships,* ed. C. M. Renzetti and C. H. Miley, 61–68. Binghamton, NY: Haworth.

Renzetti, C. M. 1997. Violence and Abuse Among Same-Sex Couples. In *Violence between Intimate Partners: Patterns, Causes, and Effects,* ed. A. P. Cardarelli, 70–89. Boston: Allyn & Bacon.

Renzetti, C. M., and C. Miley. 1996. Violence in Gay and Lesbian Partnerships. *Journal of Gay and Lesbian Social Services* 14(1):1–116.

Schilit, R., G. Y. Lie, J. Bush, M. Montagne, and L. Reyes. 1991. Intergenerational Transmission of Violence in Lesbian Relationships. *Affilia* 6(1):72–87.

Schilit, R., G. Y. Lie, and M. Montagne. 1990. Substance Abuse as a Correlate of Violence in Intimate Lesbian Relationships. *Journal of Homosexuality* 19(3):51–65.

Shomer, A. 1997. Lesbian Domestic Violence: Our Tragic Little Secret. *Lesbian News* 22(2):24–26.

Straus, M. A. 1979. Measuring Intrafamily Conflict and Violence: The Conflict Tactics (CT) Scale. *Journal of Marriage and the Family* 41(1):75–88.

Straus, M. A., R. J. Gelles, and S. Steinmetz. 1980. *Behind Closed Doors: Violence in the American Family.* Garden City, NJ: Anchor.

Waldron, C. M. 1996. Lesbians of Color and the Domestic Violence Movement. In *Violence in Gay and Lesbian Domestic Partnerships,* ed. C. M. Renzetti and C. H. Miley, 43–53. Binghamton, NY: Haworth.

Walker, L. E. 1979. *The Battered Women.* New York: Harper & Row.

Walker, L. E. 1984. *The Battered Woman Syndrome.* New York: Springer.

Walker, L. E. 1989. *Terrifying Love: Why Battered Women Kill and How Society Responds.* New York: Harper & Row.

Wallace, H. 1996. *Family Violence: Legal, Medical, and Social Perspectives.* Needham Heights, MA: Allyn & Bacon.

Chapter 24

Domestic Violence against Wives of Police Officers

Carolyn Renae Griggs

ABSTRACT

Griggs begins this chapter with a summary of the historical development of domestic violence enforcement in the United States. Then she turns to the core of the chapter, which is domestic violence perpetrated by police officers against their wives. Griggs, a police officer, describes the law enforcement community's appalling failure to address domestic violence within its own ranks. Griggs ends with an analysis of the increased potential for lethality in cases of intimate partner abuse committed by police officers.

Griggs cites a number of high-profile cases from around the country; perhaps the most notorious is in Los Angeles, where the police department found evidence that over a four-year period more than 70 police officers committed crimes against their wives and girlfriends and the police department took no action. Self-report studies have indicated that as many as 4 of every 10 officers have battered their spouses at home. One of the more troubling issues to ponder is how officers who are themselves batterers comport themselves when responding to a domestic violence call on duty. Are these officers dismissive of such complaints? Or are they able to deny or block out their own felonious behavior at home and respond objectively and sensitively to the complainant as well as appropriately to the aggressor? Clearly, the law enforcement community can no longer ignore this issue, nor can it continue to ignore or deny these crimes that are committed within its own ranks. The International Association of Chiefs of Police has recognized this wrong-headed practice and has issued guidelines that police departments can implement when police domestic violence occurs. However, these guidelines are only a beginning, not a solution; and even these guidelines are not mandatory in police departments across the country.

As you read this chapter, think about the complex issues faced by a police department that continues to employ officers who batter their wives or partners. Now that police domestic violence has been uncovered, it becomes clear that such abuse must be identified in other sectors of the criminal justice system so that the wives and partners of male corrections officers, lawyers, judges, and so on will likewise have greater opportunities for safety and justice. Think also about the repercussions for battered women who are prisoners or clients in a criminal justice system that may itself employ batterers. What solutions can you offer for these complicated issues?

Wife beating was perfectly acceptable in the United States until the 1960s when the winds of change began to blow in the direction of civil and equal rights for all citizens. Women were slowly being recognized as valuable contributors to families and communities rather than merely extensions of men's property—the operative word being slowly; it took another 20 years for domestic violence to be considered a criminal matter rather than a private matter between a husband and wife (Kappeler 1998). As long as the battles occurred behind closed doors, the police considered their involvement to be inappropriate meddling in family affairs. But by the 1980s, the tide had turned and feminists pressured for reform, accusing law enforcement of a laissez-faire attitude toward battered women. By 1988, every state in the United States except for West Virginia and Alabama had legislation permitting warrantless arrests in both felony and misdemeanor cases of domestic violence (Zorza 1992).

During that same time, in the 1970s, when the women's movement was pushing for equal rights and status for the historically viewed "inferior sex," another group of American women began to speak up as well. They were police wives compelled to support the noble office of their public servant husbands who were protecting lives and property during a turbulent period of social change. Their message was very different, however, than that of the feminists. Whereas the former group of women sought to liberate their social sisters by encouraging rebellion against tradition and advocating independence, the latter group proclaimed the glory of their roles as submissive, accommodating, and extraordinarily flexible police wives who viewed their position as one of civil service in its own right.

Much was written about police wives and law enforcement families during that time and continuing into the 1980s (James and Nelson 1975; Niederhoffer and Niederhoffer 1978). Most of the literature concentrated on the added marital strain for police couples as a result of the demands of his job. Interestingly, while police stress and family pressures were topical issues in the law enforcement community and while domestic violence studies and statistics prevailed in national headlines, newscasts, and legislative sessions, the two subjects seemed mutually exclusive. No one in policing was suggesting that an officer's marital discord might include spouse abuse, and none of the domestic violence advocates were addressing the propensity for law enforcement personnel to beat their wives. The 1990s would witness a change, however, as the problem of police domestic violence began to emerge.*

The purpose of this chapter is to review the historical developments of domestic violence enforcement as it relates to the contemporary failure of policing to address the issue within its own ranks, culminating in an analysis of the increased potential for lethality in cases of intimate partner abuse committed by police officers. There is a paucity of data

---

*Note: There are approximately 740,000 police officers in the United States. Of those, a minimum of 50 percent, or 370,000, are married or in a serious relationship. Roughly 10 percent of the 740,000 sworn law enforcement officers are women. Taking into account that a portion of that 74,000 are policewomen *and* police wives, that brings the total to a conservative estimate of 300,000 police wives or police wives-to-be. Notwithstanding the fact that many of these women behind the men behind the badge are married to a nonabusive, loving, and honorable police husband, others fear for their safety and see his status as more of a weapon than his gun. It should also be noted that police domestic violence is not limited to husbands battering wives, although these are the majority of documented incidents. The potential for female officers to abuse their husbands and partners cannot be ignored, nor can the fact that violence occurs among same-sex police couples as well. This chapter, however, focuses on the largest population of identified victims—women battered by their police husbands.

Source: This article was written expressly for inclusion in this text.

measuring the prevalence of police-perpetrated domestic violence and a conspicuous absence of research documenting police domestic homicides. Nancy Turner of the International Association of the Chiefs of Police keeps the elusive numbers in perspective. In her article published in *The Police Chief* (November 2000) she said, "Regardless of the statistics, any rate of domestic violence involving police officers should be considered unacceptable" (p. 43).

This chapter covers the opinions of criminal justice professionals, who believe that an officer's training, authoritative status, professional solidarity, and license to carry firearms makes him even more dangerous than a civilian abuser. Finally, the chapter closes with a discussion of some of the remedies being implemented to combat this recently exposed problem of domestic violence among police officers.

HISTORY OF DOMESTIC VIOLENCE ENFORCEMENT

I begin with an outline of the evolution of domestic violence enforcement in general as well as with the probable catalyst for radical change in police officers' approach. According to Joan Zorza (1992), former staff attorney for the National Center on Women and Family Law, in the 1970s and early 1980s, "[a]rrests [in domestic violence situations] were actively discouraged as a waste of time except when disrespect or threats by an offender or victim indicated that the officer might lose control of the situation. Arrest was therefore the assertion of authority rather than a response to the demands of the situation" (p. 51). Furthermore, Zorza alleges, in most cases the officers aligned themselves with the perpetrator, leaving the victim to conclude that calling the police was futile in obtaining any kind of protection or assistance. In many instances, she argues, if an officer responded to a call for help and found that the victim was not severely injured, he would completely disregard any future calls to that residence.

Arrests in domestic violence incidents began to receive enthusiastic support, however, in the mid-1980s, following the results of an extremely well

publicized research project and a landmark civil lawsuit. In 1981, the National Institute of Justice supported the Minneapolis domestic violence experiment, the first scientifically designed test of the effects of arrest for any crime. Approximately 30 officers of the Minneapolis police department agreed to take part in the study, of which the key procedure was randomly assigned responses on minor domestic assault service calls. The participating officers were given randomly selected options that included counseling the couple, asking one of them to leave the premises for several hours, or arresting the suspect.

The results of this experiment indicated that of the three treatments, arrest produced the lowest prevalence of cases in which repeat violence by the man occurred within the following six months (Sherman and Berk 1984). The outcome was broadcast nationwide, and policy makers soon used the Minneapolis domestic violence experiment to develop widely implemented mandatory arrest policies. The adoption of this type of police action was bolstered by a high-profile lawsuit heard by the courts almost immediately after the publicized results of the Minnesota experiment.

Excerpts from the researchers' recommendations were, in fact, cited during testimony in the case that was credited with transforming police response to domestic violence victims. The case was *Thurman v. the City of Torrington et al.* (595 F. Supp. 1521) in Connecticut in 1984. Thurman was awarded $2.3 million for the nearly lethal injuries she sustained at the hands of her brutally abusive husband because the police department failed to provide adequate protection in spite of her repeated requests for help. The Thurman case resonated with law enforcement agencies across the country, and as pointed out earlier in this chapter, four years later almost every state had employed aggressive policies to deal with offenses related to the abuse of a spouse (Zorza 1992). For the most part, law enforcement's reaction, based on the popularly referenced aspects of the Minnesota domestic violence response test, was to require arrests in all misdemeanor cases of assaults among intimates.

Mandatory arrest procedures generated considerable controversy, however, and continue to receive extensive criticism, even by those involved in the experiment that prompted the action. Sherman (1992) explained that people who supported criminalizing domestic violence ignored the cautionary statements issued with the release of the Minnesota results and have ignored the replication outcomes found in other cities since then (Weisz 1996). The data from studies in several other locations indicate that although arrests prove effective in some domestic assaults, in others they seem to prompt an escalation in violence. And, Sherman emphasizes, in spite of repeated misquotes to the contrary, the Minnesota experiment did not show that mandatory arrest reduces the risk of domestic homicides, nor have any of the replication studies.

In view of what he believes is a grossly oversimplified solution to an extremely complex problem, Sherman (1992) is adamantly opposed to the mandatory arrest policies, asserting, "Mandatory arrest may make as much sense as fighting fire with gasoline" (p. 210). Nevertheless, it has become the contemporary method of choice in the majority of jurisdictions, even as the debate over its effectiveness continues. Fortunately, in many police agencies, arresting suspects is only one component of a multidimensional approach to addressing intimate partner abuse.

Subsequent to continuous pressure from feminists in combination with Sherman and Berk's (1984) research and the unprecedented decision in the Thurman case, state legislation was passed, and municipal police along with local sheriffs' departments followed suit with specific regulations in cases of domestic violence. In 1994, the Southwestern Law Enforcement Institute and the Arlington, Texas, police department conducted a survey that revealed that an overwhelming majority of departments had developed standard operating procedures for officers' response to calls of domestic violence (Southwestern Law Enforcement Institute 1995). Victor Kappeler's study in 1998 found that over 90 percent of the departments in Kentucky reported having a general domestic violence policy (Kappeler 1999).

In addition to the pro-arrest guidelines, most departments also instruct officers to provide information to victims regarding shelter, counseling, protective orders, and other assistance. Domestic violence was once perceived as a private family matter ill-suited for criminal justice intervention, but now steps are taken to explore the possibility that law enforcement's response to domestic violence is as crucial to prevention as it is to prosecution.

THE SCOPE OF POLICE FAMILY VIOLENCE

During the 1980s, the number of empirical studies on domestic violence increased dramatically. As greater political pressure was applied, more federal funding was allocated for research and program development that spawned national, state, and local organizations and shelters to assist battered women (National Coalition against Domestic Violence 2001). Reliable information about police families, however, was virtually unavailable. Even the divorce rate for police officers could not be satisfactorily documented, and any research results that emerged were constantly disputed (Besner and Robinson 1984; Bibbons 1986).

Although the precise percentage of divorces eluded researchers, Schwartz and Schwartz (1975) easily identified in large departments a number of patrolmen who had been married three times by the age of 30 (Besner and Robinson 1984). Psychologists were starting to agree that there was a direct link between the emotional demands of policing and the destruction of what appeared to be a disproportionate number of law enforcement families (Bibbons 1986). This correlation would serve as the precursor to the exposure of police family violence. Still, in spite of the increased awareness of domestic violence as an issue of nationwide concern, any discussion about the potential for police officers to perpetrate this offense would not come until the 1990s.

In May 1991, a congressional hearing was held on police stress and its effects on the family. Both former congresswoman Pat Schroeder and police psychologist Ellen Scrivner testified at the hearing.

However, as Scrivner explained, due to the dearth of reliable data about specific problems in police families, any attempts to implement effective strategies of support and intervention were impeded by the lack of concrete information and understanding.

The following year Neidig, Russell, and Seng (1992) published the results of a preliminary study that attempted to determine, through a self-report methodology, the prevalence and correlates of marital aggression in law enforcement families. The participants consisted of 425 volunteer officers, of which 40 were females, as well as 115 female spouses. The majority of the participating officers had between 15 and 19 years of experience in policing. The study utilized an anonymous survey that included demographic information, work assignment, years of experience, and the Modified Conflict Tactics Scale. Subjects were asked to report the number of times either they or their spouse had engaged in each of the 25 conflict behaviors described in the scale during a domestic disagreement within the previous year. The results were described as follows:

> By self-report, approximately 40 percent of the officers surveyed report at least one episode of physical aggression during a marital conflict in the previous year with 8 percent of the male officers reporting severe violence. The overall rates of violence are considerably higher than those reported for a random sample of civilians and somewhat higher than military samples. (p. 37)

Moreover, this research revealed "significant relationships" between work assignment, shift, hours worked, and marital aggression.

> Additionally, the fact that those officers in the sample who work excessively long hours and fail to take leave have higher rates suggests that marital violence may be associated with increased job dedication. And finally, there may be assignments within law enforcement (i.e., narcotics work) that involve risk for marital violence as a unique occupational hazard. (p. 37)

Specifically, the data indicated that officers assigned to narcotics had rates of severe marital aggression that were four times the overall average for law enforcement.

The 1990s would bring other developments as well. Once the information from this study began to filter into the political consciousness, government monies were earmarked to determine if police departments were addressing the issue. Two such inquiries, which I discussed earlier, were the one conducted by the Arlington, Texas, police department in cooperation with the Southwestern Law Enforcement Institute (1995) and the one by Victor Kappeler (1999) of Eastern Kentucky University. Although both surveys indicated that roughly 90 percent of departments had implemented policies and procedures to address effective police response to calls of domestic violence, far fewer had developed any sort of standard operations for handling spouse abuse reports that involved police officers.

The Texas study found that of the 123 police departments surveyed nationwide, all serving populations of over 100,000, only 55 percent had a specific course of action for dealing with officer-involved domestic violence (1995). Kappeler's research indicated that only 44 percent of Kentucky municipal and county police agencies had such a policy. Kappeler's survey also revealed that just 18 percent of the departments instituted counseling programs to assist officers who were experiencing problems with domestic violence (1999). According to the National Center for Women and Policing (1998), preliminary results of another inquiry indicated that only four major city police departments had written policies addressing police family violence cases.

Curiously, after the Texas research project in 1994 but prior to the other two reports, a number of high-profile cases were covered in the media, and a scathing evaluation of the Los Angeles Police Department's failure to deal with the issue was widely reported. Additionally, in September of 1996, the U.S. Congress passed the Lautenberg Act, which prohibits individuals, including police officers, from owning firearms if they have ever been convicted of an act of domestic violence. The law is retroactive. This legislation was what prompted Kappeler (1999) to measure law enforcement's reaction to the stance taken by the government. Historically, police officers are exempt from any legislation regarding gun control. In the Lautenberg Act, they were not. Kappeler said of his findings:

> It appears that police departments have made few organizational changes to detect batterers in blue. Few departments have taken the very basic steps of altering their application forms or modifying their personnel policies. Even fewer departments plan to routinely conduct background checks on an on-going basis. (p. 6)

In view of the recent publicity that highlights domestic violence in policing, the inaction of many of the country's law enforcement agencies, as demonstrated by the empirical data, is somewhat perplexing.

HIGH-PROFILE CASES OF POLICE DOMESTIC VIOLENCE

In 1982 Carol Irons became the first female judge in Kent County, Michigan. Two years later she married a police officer, Clarence Ratliff. In 1988, when her husband became violent and obsessive toward her, Judge Irons filed for divorce. In October of that year, Ratliff walked into his wife's courtroom and, in the presence of several court officers, shot her in the chest, killing her; he then fired several rounds at the officers who tried to render aid to the judge. Ratliff was charged and convicted, his trial and sentencing a graphic example of the judicial disparity between a policeman and a female victim regardless of her stature: in June 1989 Ratliff received 10 to 15 years for killing his wife and *two life terms* for the assaults on two police officers, neither of whom were seriously injured (Jones 1994).

In 1989, four Chicago police officers killed their wives before killing themselves. One of those cases significantly impacted the national media because both parties were police officers. In that particular instance, the female officer had previously reported that her husband was abusing her but the department's administration did not provide any assistance; they believed that his behavior was unrelated to his job because it occurred when he was off duty (McCluskey 1999a).

Also in Chicago, in 1991, an officer reportedly beat up his girlfriend. Still feeling the sting of their mishandling of police domestic violence two years prior, the department's decision makers changed their approach and fired the accused officer. The victim had agreed to testify against him but did not appear in court when called. Within a few weeks her body was discovered, and the abusive officer was later convicted of her murder (McCluskey 1999a).

In 1992 an officer with the Los Angeles Police Department, Victor Ramos, murdered his wife and her lover a month after police officials had become aware of his threats to kill her. They had failed to take action on the information. The case received even more attention when the female victim's family was awarded almost $2.2 million for the department's negligence that resulted in her death (Lait 1997).

In 1994 the wife of yet another Chicago police officer was rushed to the hospital with second-degree burns as a result of her husband's intentional act of dousing her with hot oil. She filed a complaint with the police, but he was not arrested. In fact, the report was never even written (Levinson 1997).

In 1996, the Lakeland, Florida, police chief chose his officer of the year, only to learn shortly thereafter that the same officer was the subject of a permanent restraining order protecting his wife from abuse. The victim had provided sworn testimony that her police husband had threatened to kill her and then himself. The chief had not been notified when the protective order was issued against one of his employees. Consequently, he unknowingly awarded that officer the most prestigious annual honor. The officer was never criminally charged (Levinson 1997).

Adding to the growing concern, in 1996 Broward County Sheriff's Office Lieutenant John Feltgen revealed the results of a random survey he had conducted to ascertain whether police agencies were effectively responding to domestic violence calls involving a police officer. First, Feltgen questioned the participating departments about their specific policies regarding the matter. He discovered that the majority of agencies he surveyed were not addressing the issue at all. Feltgen also discovered that when an officer was sent to a domestic violence call involving a fellow officer, if the department did have a policy in place, it was instantly abandoned. Most often, responding officers spoke to the off-duty police officer, allegedly the perpetrator, and then cleared the call without a report or even a cursory check on the spouse's welfare. Feltgen disclosed, "In case after case, victims of domestic violence at the hands of a police officer had made emergency requests for law enforcement intervention, only to have their calls fall on deaf ears." He added, "Abused spouses of police officers become even more traumatized by a system assumed to protect 'all' victims of domestic violence as they become tragically lost in a system that fails even to record them as statistics" (p. 42).

Then, in April 1997, Los Angeles television reporter Harvey Levin exposed the Los Angeles Police Department's mishandling of domestic violence reports against its officers. As a result, the Office of the Inspector General was instructed to conduct a probe of the department and evaluate the weight of the journalist's allegations. A task force was formed, led by then–Inspector General Katherine Mader, and 227 internal domestic violence complaints made against employees from January 1990 to May 1997 were analyzed. Investigations focused on physical violence and threats of physical violence (Mader 1997).

The following is a portion of Inspector General Mader's executive summary of her findings:

> Sustained allegations of domestic violence did not appear to impair an officer's promotability. Twenty-six (29%) of the ninety-one employees with sustained allegations were promoted, including six employees who were promoted within two years of the sustained domestic violence incident. Employees with sustained allegations were neither barred from moving to desired positions nor transferred out of assignments that were inconsistent with the sustained allegation. In one such instance, following a sustained allegation of domestic violence involving a firearm, an individual was transferred to the Police Academy to become an instructor. In another case, an employee who spent several days in

jail after an arrest for making terrorist threats following an altercation with his wife, was nonetheless retained as an instructor in the Department's premier instructional program. (pp. ii–iii)

The outcome of the inspector general's investigation was published in part in the *Los Angeles Times* on July 19, 1997 (Lait 1997). In addition to her evaluation of past practices, Mader made nearly 50 points of recommendations for improvement to the agency's administration. Shortly after her report was made public, the police chief initiated a specialized domestic violence unit within the Internal Affairs Division of the department. On February 13, 2000, *Sixty Minutes* aired a program about the investigation, and several of the people interviewed during the show insisted that the Los Angeles Police Department has still not made necessary changes in its response to domestic violence within its ranks (Wallace 2000).

PUBLIC SAFETY IMPLICATIONS

Perhaps even more unsettling than the lack of changes in the Los Angeles Police Department is the flagrant imbalance in the pursuit of justice in terms of the violations of the law. Bob Mullally, an investigator who served as the catalyst in exposing the widespread domestic abuse among Los Angeles police officers, was the only one involved in the scandal who faced prosecution and potential jail time.* Mullally chronicled a 250-page summary after spending six months reviewing more than 4,000 documents regarding domestic violence offenses committed by 79 of Los Angeles's officers. Mullally concluded, "What I was seeing was systemic felony abuse that was overlooked and covered up by everybody who came into contact with the cases" (Ortega 2000, p. 1). Such cases included assaults with a deadly weapon, rapes, threats with a firearm, and

---

*Eventually his six-month prison sentence for contempt of court was overturned on appeal, and Mullally was sentenced to 45 days in federal prison. None of the criminal officers whom he exposed were ever prosecuted or even arrested.

other offenses in which more than half the victims suffered visible injuries from the attacks.

When Mullally, who was working for the attorney of the surviving families of the victims murdered by Officer Ramos in 1992, discovered that the lawsuits would be settled and the records kept confidential, he leaked the information to television reporter Harvey Levin in violation of a court order. Mullally said, "I wanted it to go to trial so the documents would become public. I wanted the violence to stop. It was obvious to me that it was still going on, and I wanted to stop it as soon as possible" (Ortega 2000, p. 7). Even though not one abusive officer was pursued criminally and many suffered little or no administrative consequences in spite of the injuries to their victims, the judge who issued the seal on the Ramos records was irate at Mullally's civil disobedience and made enthusiastic attempts to persuade the U.S. attorney's office to prosecute him.

If not for Mullally's actions, the subsequent investigation by the inspector general's office would likely not have taken place, and the extent of intimate partner abuse within the Los Angeles Police Department would have remained a secret. Even so, in the end it was Mullally, not the abusive police officers, who faced the most serious consequences. His situation underscores one of the primary reasons that victims of police domestic violence suffer silently: a system that is quicker to hold them responsible than to protect them from itself.

The Neidig, Russell, and Seng (1992) self-report survey indicated that as many as 40 percent of police officers commit violence in their own homes, which means that 4 in 10 officers responding to a domestic violence call in the community may be batterers themselves. The potential for victim-blaming is patent, and the consequences of the officers' collusion with the offender have far-reaching deleterious implications. Although there are no known studies to determine whether female police officers respond more effectively to police-perpetrated domestic violence, research has shown that women officers do tend to respond more effectively to domestic violence incidents in general (Homant and Kennedy 1985). Representatives of the National Center for

Women and Policing (2001) believe that, "The under-representation of women in law enforcement has significant implications for women in the community who are victims of domestic violence" (p. 2). It is their view that the quality of police response in any case would be "greatly improved by increasing the number of women in law enforcement" (p. 2).

COMBATING POLICE DOMESTIC VIOLENCE

Following a strong lobbying effort by domestic violence advocates, on September 30, 1996, the Lautenberg Act became law. It is labeled as the Lautenberg Amendment to Public Law 104–208, and its heading reads "Gun Ban for Individuals Convicted of a Misdemeanor Crime of Domestic Violence" (Title 18 USC Code Section 922 (d)(9)). The act prohibits anyone, including government entities, from owning firearms or ammunition if ever convicted of a misdemeanor act of domestic violence. It modifies the Gun Control Act of 1968 by including misdemeanor domestic violence as a prohibitor of ownership in addition to felony convictions, and it excludes no one from compliance (Kappeler, 1999).

Although the dividing line has been relatively clear between domestic violence advocates who are adamantly opposed to any exemptions in the law and police officials who are aggressively pursuing appellate avenues to relieve officers from compliance, some observers have mixed feelings about the overall effect. Gary Sykes, the director of the Southwestern Law Enforcement Institute, thinks that the legislation definitely puts police agencies on alert and compels them to implement appropriate policies for dealing with this issue. However, he also fears there will be less reporting if the officer stands to lose his job. Based on the potential consequence of unemployment, police wives may be hesitant to turn in their abusive husbands, and the offender will likely be hard-pressed to admit his actions, knowing his career is at stake. Sykes concluded: "My guess is that the plight of women who are battered by police officers may not be better than it was before" (McCluskey 1999b, p. 3).

Also, in 1997, the Violence against Women Office, a division of the United States Department of Justice, requested that the International Association of Chiefs of Police (IACP) embark on a research project to learn more about the problem of police-perpetrated domestic violence. Accordingly, the IACP formed an advisory group and organized five summits across the country to investigate the situation. The New York, Charleston, Indianapolis/Evansville, Duke University, and Oakland police departments hosted the meetings. Victims, advocates, and law enforcement officials met to discuss the topic of police family violence. The project eventually produced a model policy on departmental response to domestic violence (Prabhu and Turner 2000).

In September 1998 another federal agency stepped up to address the issue. The Federal Bureau of Investigations hosted the Domestic Violence by Police Officers Conference in Quantico, Virginia. The attendees included police officers, attorneys, psychologists, psychiatrists, victim advocates, and chaplains. However, in spite of the attention drawn to the problem and the efforts of some enlightened law enforcement officials and domestic violence advocates, the incidents of officer-involved family fatalities continued.

POLICE WIVES AS VICTIMS

According to the United States Department of Justice (2000), 31,260 women were murdered by intimate partners during the years between 1976 and 1996. How many of those victims were killed by police officers is unknown. An average of 1,500 American women are killed each year by husbands, ex-husbands, or boyfriends (Marvin 1997). How many of those women are victims of police-perpetrated lethal domestic violence is unknown. In 1998, women reported approximately 876,340 violent offenses at the hand of an intimate. How many of those offenses were committed by police officers is unknown. Although the percentage of law enforcement officers among these offenders remains a mystery, they are indeed among them.

Some domestic violence advocates are not as concerned with the number of police perpetrators as they are about what they believe is a greater potential for more severe abuse and fatalities in police family violence incidents compared to the general population. Kirschman (1997) made reference to a colleague who has spent years studying the dynamics of domestic violence and who has said that "cops are the most dangerous of all abusers and their spouses are the most endangered" (p. 144). Kirschman explained that her colleague's conclusions are based on the unique aspects of policing: the officers' possession of firearms and willingness to use them; their frequent execution of coercive compliance techniques, both verbal and physical; the knowledge of and ability to negotiate and manipulate the legal system; and their capacity to locate their wives, even at a protective shelter. Kirschman added another important factor: "their families are often very isolated. Isolation is an important component of domestic abuse" (p. 146).

Diane Wetendorf, the director of counseling at Lifespan, a domestic violence advocacy agency in Illinois, has discovered a pattern in her work with battered police wives. Wetendorf (1998) believes there is a strong connection between an officer's training and his tactics of abuse in intimate relationships. She has found that most police perpetrators use intimidation, isolation, and terror to control their spouses, which oftentimes makes overt acts of physical violence unnecessary and makes the abuse even more difficult to detect. The threat of the lethality of the ever-present firearm is a constant in the life of the victim. Wetendorf points out the officer's conditioning to establish authority by tone of voice and body stance, his extensive skills in information gathering by interrogation and surveillance, and his instruction on escalating degrees of force. "Police know which situations justify the use of force and how to adequately explain it should they have to defend their actions in a court of law" (p. 377).

Other criminal justice professionals share Wetendorf's opinion that the skills and traits that make an officer more effective could make an abuser more dangerous. Referring to a police officer's disposition, Stone (1998) commented, "While these traits may increase an officer's success on the streets, at least some of them jeopardize his intimate relationships if exhibited at home. In fact, much of the knowledge and many of the skills valued on the job make police officers better, more sophisticated batterers" (p. 334). Illinois State Police Sergeant Sgambelluri (1998) outlined several desirable police characteristics that serve as dangerous assets for an abuser.

> The ability to establish power and control. . . . The police culture itself encourages isolation, a need for control and a sense of entitlement. . . . Law enforcement academies train officers in skills designed to physically and psychologically establish control over another person without causing injuries or visible marks. . . . Loyalty among police serves to protect police abusers and further injure victims. (p. 317)

Wetendorf (1998) concludes that an abuser's status as a police officer is perhaps his most powerful weapon.

> He tells her she can call the police, but asks her who she thinks has more credibility, him or her? He tells her she can leave but wherever she goes he can find her. . . . Many of her family members and friends may fear, and thus avoid involvement. . . . The higher the abuser's rank, the fewer the number of people willing to help her. (p. 378)

Finally, he may use his position to make credible threats that instill paralyzing terror. Wetendorf (2000) warns victims about common tactics that she has discovered in counseling over 130 battered police wives:

> He might brag that he could easily shoot you and make it look like a stranger did it, or like you committed suicide. He might taunt you to use the gun to kill yourself or him. . . . He might graphically describe his plans to kill your children, your parents, or friends. (p. 8)

Wetendorf (2000) makes a clear distinction between police family violence and that in the general population. In her handbook, specifically written for battered police wives, she tells them:

> If your batterer is a police officer, most of the progress that has been made in developing resources and assistance for battered women is of little benefit to you. Victims of police officers are still as isolated and invisible as all the victims of this crime were thirty years ago. Work now needs to be done to raise the public's awareness of domestic violence in the *police* home. Society must hold police officers accountable to not only enforce the law, but to live by it. (p. 1)

This statement was in fact the goal of the IACP when they developed the model policy mentioned earlier in this chapter. According to Prabu and Turner (2000), "The policy offers direction to departments for establishing a comprehensive approach that can save lives and preserve careers" (p. 45). The IACP suggests that an effective policy is needed because of liability, the same provocation that caused a change in the handling of general domestic violence incidents. With the model policy in place, a standard is set and no department has an excuse for failing to implement the same procedures or similar ones. "The mere existence of a model protocol, promoted by a professional leadership organization like IACP, makes a department without specific guidelines vulnerable to a lawsuit in the wake of a domestic violence tragedy involving an officer" (p. 50). The IACP also holds that police family violence presents situations that create far greater danger than civilian cases do and therefore should be dealt with proactively.

The model policy includes practices for seizing and storing weapons, assessing lethality, ensuring victim safety, and providing multijurisdictional communication. It is also suggested that departments designate and train a member of the command staff to act as a point person for victims and concerned family members. In summary, the IACP believes that police departments have a critical role to play in preventing domestic violence in the ranks, and for this reason the model policy developed by the organization is designed to guide law enforcement agencies "through prevention, intervention, and investigation of police officer–perpetrated domestic violence" (p. 53).

The law enforcement community's attempt to minimize the seriousness of intimate violence committed by police personnel, using the dearth of statistical data to buttress their denial, suggests that the magnitude of this problem will only increase. But eventually policing will have to take responsibility for its mishandling of these cases, as it did with domestic violence in general nearly 20 years ago. It is unconscionable to consider that the profession's fundamental duty to safeguard lives still excludes those lives closest to the front lines: police wives.

DISCUSSION QUESTIONS

1. Based on this reading, describe the history and current circumstances of police department rules about domestic violence in the police officer's own home. What reactions do you have to this history?
2. According to Griggs, why is the situation of battered wives of police officers such a dangerous one? In other words, what are the unique aspects of policing that make it an exceedingly dangerous situation for wives of batterers who are police officers?
3. In your opinion, what responses should police departments initiate if one of their own officers is a batterer?
4. What steps, if any, should or can be taken by an officer who is assigned to work with a police officer who is a batterer?
5. What special needs would arise for a woman officer who is battered at home by either (a) a husband or partner who is a police officer or (b) a husband or partner who is a civilian? How might police departments work to protect the battered women on their force?

REFERENCES

Besner, H., and S. Robinson, 1984. Police Wives—The Untapped Resource. *The Police Chief* 50:62–64.

Bibbons, V. 1986. The Quality of Family and Marital Life of Police Personnel. In *Psychological Services for Law Enforcement,* ed. James Reese and Harvey Goldstein,

423–427. Washington, DC: U.S. Government Printing Office.

Feltgen, J. 1996. Domestic Violence: When the Abuser Is a Police Officer. *The Police Chief* 63:42–49.

Homant, R., and D. Kennedy. 1985. Police Perceptions of Spouse Abuse: A Comparison of Male and Female Officers. *Journal of Criminal Justice* 13:29–47.

James, P., and M. Nelson. 1975. *Police Wife: How to Live with the Law and Like It.* Springfield, IL: Charles C. Thomas.

Jones, A. 1994. *Next Time She'll Be Dead.* Boston: Beacon.

Kappeler, V. 1998. When the Batterer Wears Blue: A National Study of the Institutional Response to Domestic Violence among Police. Unpublished manuscript.

Kappeler, V. 1999. Kentucky's Response to the Lautenberg Act: Curbing Domestic Violence among Police. *Kentucky Justice and Safety Research Bulletin.* Richmond: Eastern Kentucky University College of Law Enforcement.

Kirschman, E. 1997. *I Love a Cop.* New York: Guilford.

Lait, M. 1997. LAPD Abuse Probes of Its Officers Called Lax. *The Los Angeles Times,* July 19. A1, A24–25.

Lautenberg Act. 1996. Amendment to public law 104–208. Title 18 USC Code Section 922(d)(9).

Levinson, A. 1997. Abusers Behind a Badge: When Police Assault Their Spouses, Punishment Is Often Slight, if at All. *The Arizona Republic,* June 19, F9.

Mader, K. 1997. Domestic Violence in the Los Angeles Police Department: How Well Does the Los Angeles Police Department Police Its Own? Los Angeles: Office of the Inspector General.

Marvin, D. 1997. The Dynamics of Domestic Abuse. *FBI Law Enforcement Bulletin,* 3–18.

McCluskey, E. 1999a. Chicago Polices Its Police. *Police Department Disciplinary Bulletin* 7(4):2–3.

McCluskey, E. 1999b. Police Who Hit. *Police Department Disciplinary Bulletin* 7(3):2–4.

National Center for Women and Policing. 1998. *Police Family Violence Fact Sheet.* (Available from the National Center for Women and Policing, a division of the Feminist Majority Foundation, 8105 West Third Street, Los Angeles, CA 90048.)

National Center for Women and Policing. 2001. *Equality Denied: The Status of Women in Policing 2000.* Los Angeles: National Center for Women and Policing.

National Coalition against Domestic Violence. 2001. Available at http://www.ncadv.org.

Neidig, P., H. Russell, and A. Seng. 1992. Interspousal Aggression in Law Enforcement Families: A Preliminary Investigation. *Police Studies* 15:30–38.

Neidig, P., H. Russell, and A. Seng. 1994. Observations and Recommendations Concerning the Prevention and Treatment of Interspousal Aggression in Law Enforcement Families. In *Law Enforcement Families: Issues and Answers,* ed. James Reese and Ellen Scrivner, 353–358. Washington, DC: U.S. Government Printing Office.

Niederhoffer, A., and E. Niederhoffer. 1978. *The Police Family: From Station House to Ranch House.* Lexington, MA: D.C. Heath.

Ortega, T. 2000. Code Buster. *New Times Los Angeles.* October 5. Retrieved January 3, 2001, from http://www.newtimesia.com/issues/2000-10-05/feature.html/page1html

Prabhu, S., and N. Turner. 2000. Rising to the Challenge: Preventing Police Officer Domestic Violence. *The Police Chief* 69:43–55.

Schroeder, P. 1991. On the Front Lines: Police Stress and Family Well-Being. Opening Statement to U.S. House Select Committee on Children, Youth, and Families. May.

Schwartz, J., and C. Schwartz. 1975. The Personal Problems of the Police Officer: A Plea for Action. In *Job Stress and the Police Officer: Identifying Stress Reduction Techniques,* ed. Joseph Hurrell and William Kroes. Bethesda, MD: National Institute for Occupational Safety and Health.

Scrivner, E. 1991. Police Stress and Family Well-Being. Testimony on Behalf of the American Psychological Association to U.S. House Select Committee on Children, Youth, and Families. May.

Sgambelluri, R. 1998. Police Culture, Police Training, Police Administration: Their Impact on Violence in Police Families. In *Domestic Violence by Police Officers: A Compilation of Papers Submitted to the Domestic Violence by Police Officers Conference at the F.B.I. Academy,* ed. Donald Sheehan. Washington, DC: U.S. Government Printing Office.

Sherman, L. W. 1992. *Policing Domestic Violence: Experiments and Dilemmas.* New York: Free Press.

Sherman, L. W., and R. A. Berk. 1984. The Specific Deterrent Effects of Arrest for Domestic Assault. *American Sociological Review* 49:261–272.

Southwestern Law Enforcement Institute. 1995. Domestic Violence among Police: A Survey of Internal Affairs Policies. (Available from the Southwestern Law Enforcement Institute, P.O. Box 830707, Richardson, TX 75083-0707.)

Stone, S. 1998. Barriers to Safety for Victims of Police Domestic Violence. In *Domestic Violence by Police Officers: A Compilation of Papers Submitted to the Domestic Violence by Police Officers Conference at the F.B.I. Academy,* ed. Donald Sheehan. Washington, DC: U.S. Government Printing Office.

U.S. Department of Justice, Bureau of Justice Statistics. 2000. Intimate Partner Violence. Available at http://www.ojp.usdoj.gov/vawo/statistics.htm

Wallace, M. 2000. LAPD Confidential. *60 Minutes,* dir. A. Bloom, prod. M. Palmer. New York: CBS.

Weisz, A. 1996. Spouse Assault Replication Program: Studies of Effects of Arrest on Domestic Violence. Available at http://www.vaw.umn.edu/Vawnet/arrest.htm

Wetendorf, D. 1998. The Impact of Police-Perpetrated Domestic Violence. In *Domestic Violence by Police Officers: A Compilation of Papers Submitted to the Domestic Violence by Police Officers Conference at the F.B.I. Academy,* ed. Donald Sheehan. Washington, DC: U.S. Government Printing Office.

Wetendorf, D. 2000. *Police Domestic Violence: A Handbook for Victims.* Des Plaines, IL: Lifespan.

Zorza, J. 1992. The Criminal Law of Misdemeanor Domestic Violence. *Journal of Criminal Law and Criminology* 83(spring):46–72.

Chapter 25

Can Restorative Justice Reduce Battering?

Lois Presser and Emily Gaarder

ABSTRACT

Restorative justice is the attempt to provide social justice through healing encounters between victims and offenders within the context of active participation by concerned community members. Presser and Gaarder argue that
restorative justice is better suited to reducing battering than either of the other
two interventions currently in use: the legal system or mediation. The authors
begin the chapter by giving a historical and critical examination of the law as it
has evolved around domestic violence since the 1970s. They follow this history
with a review of the mediation process, which focuses on reconciliation. The
feminist criticism of the legal response includes failure to empower the victim,
victims' fears of the police and courts, repeat violations by the batterer after the
legal process is initiated, and ultimately the inability of the criminal justice system to deal with the underlying systemic biases of battering, for example,
poverty, employment, lack of child care services, discrimination, and structures
of patriarchy. The main criticisms against mediation are that the power imbalances inherent in battering are not addressed, that repairing the relationship of
the "disputants" takes precedence over repairing the harms caused by the relationship, and that mediation contains no stipulation that the violence must end.

Restorative justice, which has inaccurately been equated with mediation,
comprises a series of strategies that include such intervention processes as family group conferencing and sentencing circles. The objective is to widen the net
of community support rather than, as with the legal process, have the state take
control of domestic violence. This process of incorporating more members of
the family and the community in which the battering occurs generalizes ownership of the battering problem beyond individual victims and offenders and
beyond government. The victim becomes surrounded by caring people to help
her heal and to help the offender—even though clearly condemned for his
violence—to feel supported in his journey to *change his violent behavior.* Further
goals of this approach are to keep the voice of the victim up front, to address
broader social norms, and to individualize interventions. Interestingly, these

individualized approaches of restorative justice allow the process to take into account the victim's culture, which may make restorative justice more successful not only with white women but also with women of color, ethnic minorities, and immigrant women. Recall that Dasgupta (see chap. 22) described the many difficulties associated with culture that immigrant women faced when they are confronted with domestic violence.

Restorative justice, Presser and Gaarder conclude, has the potential to attack the roots of battering because it considers battering to be more than a victim-offender problem and it brings in the community, its norms, and the social inequities embedded in society.

INTRODUCTION

Domestic violence, or battering,[1] is a seemingly intractable problem given its persistence over individual lifetimes, generations, and societies. Although recent years have seen a decline in battering incidents in the United States, in step with violent crime generally, it remains a problem affecting large numbers of women. In 1996, American women experienced an estimated 840,000 violent victimizations by an intimate (U.S. Department of Justice, 1999a). Some critics say that contemporary responses to battering actually magnify abuse by reproducing women's powerlessness. Two common strategies that are designed to help the battering victim, law and mediation, may undermine her power to act.

Laws that "get tough" on batterers have fallen short of their intended goals, in part because the extralegal causes of women's oppression remain unchanged (Smart, 1995: 156–157). Mediation, a non-legalistic alternative, is criticized for reinforcing the view of battering as a private matter (Lerman, 1984; Rowe, 1985; Menard and Salius, 1990). Moreover, both approaches circumscribe victims' action. Legal authorities assign to the victim a passive role; mediators direct participants toward a single outcome, reconciliation. Thus, though typically polarized, law and mediation both "govern" the victim in the sense of determining the options available to her (Foucault, 1982: 221).

In recent years, the restorative justice movement has introduced new variations on mediation. These interventions promise social justice through healing encounters between victims and offenders, sponsored by community members. While feminists have all but rejected traditional mediation, restorative justice is being called a "feminist vision of justice" (Harris, 1991; see also Pranis, 1998). Increasingly, the potential for restorative justice approaches to reduce domestic violence is being revisited from this perspective (Yellott, 1990; Pennell and Burford, 1996; Nicholl, 1998).

The purpose of this article is to evaluate the potential of restorative justice programs to reduce domestic violence. First, we examine current interventions that rely, respectively, on the power of law and the power of dialogue to stem domestic violence. Second, we describe the restorative justice philosophy and consider the promises and the problems of restorative justice interventions for domestic violence. We discuss the lessons of the shelter movement, which has taken both legal and extra-legal action, for developing restorative justice responses to battering.

CONTEMPORARY RESPONSES TO BATTERING

Since the 1970s, two parallel approaches have been taken concerning battering. These two dominant and often contrasting approaches are here referred to as the legal model and the mediation model.[2] The legal model is most often championed by feminists. The mediation model is associated with the infor-

Source: Louis Presser and Emily Gaarder. 2000. Can Restorative Justice Reduce Battering? Some Preliminary Considerations. *Social Justice* 27(1):175–195.

mal justice movement, and has sustained heavy criticism from feminists.

The Legal Model

The Criminalization of Battering In the United States, before the mid-1970s, battering was largely hidden from the public eye (Tierney, 1982). Women's abuse at the hands of their male partners was generally viewed at best as a private matter or, at worst, the prerogative of men. Accordingly, legal protections for battered women were limited except in some unusually brutal cases. Law enforcement officials maintained an explicitly "hands-off" approach to the problem (Schechter, 1982: 157). Police officers were instructed "to do anything except arrest violent husbands" (Fagan, 1996: 8). Likewise, prosecutors were discouraged from actively pursuing cases. These policies were driven by cultural tolerance of domestic violence against women and legitimated by the view that women would later drop the charges (Fagan, 1996).

Vigorous activism by grass-roots feminist groups in the 1970s brought about legal reforms in three areas: arrest and prosecution policies, treatment of batterers, and restraining orders (Fagan, 1996: 9–10). Domestic violence laws were passed in 47 states by 1980. These laws extended the reach of protective and restraining orders and increased penalties for violating them; allowed arrest without a warrant for misdemeanor assault; and recognized a history of abuse as part of a legal defense for battered women who killed their abusers. Unmarried couples were no longer excluded from law enforcement protections. Prosecutors created domestic violence units and courts began to mandate treatment for abusers as a condition of probation. Special training on the complex issues surrounding battering was developed for police officers and judges (Brooks, 1997).

Police behavior was a principal target of feminist activism (Stanko, 1985: 107; Bouza, 1991: 195). Police were considered the gateway to the coercive authority of law and to the proper labeling of a battering incident as a crime. Victims filed lawsuits against police departments for inadequate protection, which spurred changes in police procedures

(Meier and Zoller, 1995: 62). Sherman and Berk's (1984) Minneapolis Spouse Abuse Experiment, which offered evidence that arrest deters future battering, was reified as mandatory arrest policy by police departments across the U.S.[3]

Questioning the Promise of Law By the early 1980s, the tenacity of the battering problem led some feminists to reexamine the potential of legal processes to remedy it. The goals of the criminal justice system—to prove that a crime occurred and to punish the offender—were considered ill-matched to the needs of victims. The systemic basis of the battering problem was acknowledged. The police and courts lacked the capacity to bring about fundamental changes in social conditions that perpetuate battering, such as poverty, employment, discrimination, and lack of public child care (Websdale and Johnson, 1997).

Moreover, the problem was determined to lie in the "structures of patriarchy," rather than with the individual male batterer or a too-tolerant criminal justice system (Smart, 1995: 161). The theoretical "discourse" about battering began to change, from one of pathology to one of social context (see O'Neill, 1998). With this paradigm shift, the criminal justice system began to appear as complicit in the maintenance of unequal power relations based on class, gender, and race (Schechter, 1982: 176). Messerschmidt (1993) described policing as effectively substituting formal masculine control for an informal one, thus maintaining the core problem of male domination.

Besides these conceptual criticisms, feminists became disillusioned with particular criminal justice policies. Backed by research, they questioned whether mandatory arrest ultimately helped or hurt victims. The disproportionate arrest of low-income and minority men was protested (see, for example, Miller, 1989; Stanko, 1989). Despite far-reaching reforms, the legal system was again compromising the real interests of many victims, and in some cases, even treating victims as adversaries.

In the late 1970s, prosecutors began "making it difficult for a woman to drop charges or . . . threatening to prosecute without her cooperation"

(Schechter, 1982: 175). Victims who refused to testify against partners were held in contempt of court (Parent and Digneffe, 1997: 207). Coercion of victims was inconsistent with the feminists movement's goal of self-determination for women. Schechter (1982: 175) remarked that "the essence of victimization is to strip women of control, and the criminal justice system cannot be given powers to further deny women control." In short, feminists began to abandon the hope that law enforcement could ultimately resolve the battering problem.

A postmodern view of justice was developing, which called into question the ideology of absolute justice. According to that ideology, legal norms are objective and universal, applicable to all people at any time, regardless of gender, race, or class. In contrast, certain critical feminists argued that moral problems can only be "evaluated in light of our knowledge of the history of the agents involved in them" (Benhabib, 1989: 285). Inasmuch as judicial rulings are detached from the individual circumstances of the parties involved, they reflect male privilege. As MacKinnon (1983: 658) observed, "abstract rights will authoritize the male experience of the world."

Victim Empowerment   Liberal feminists were criticized for failing to empower victims (Rowe, 1985; Stanko, 1989). Applying a medical model to the dilemma of battered women (e.g., Walker, 1979) may essentialize women's powerlessness, framing it as an individual rather than a social problem (see Dobash and Dobash, 1992: 228). It was also charged that the label of "battered woman" may stigmatize the victim, and thus ultimately reinforce her lack of control over her life (Mahoney, 1991).

Research in the 1990s found that battering victims who have a say in legal proceedings may feel more empowered to get help, if not to terminate the abusive relationship. Ford (1991) noted the ways in which battered women may manipulate criminal justice penalties to gain leverage in their abusive relationships. Zorza (1992: 67) observed that when batterers are court ordered to participate in treatment, their female victims are "more likely to call police and bring

new charges if they were subsequently assaulted." Erez and Belknap (1998) found that most battered women did not believe that the criminal justice system could effectively solve their problems with abuse. The women generally expressed the desire to retain choice and to be treated as individuals in any attempts to stop the abuse. Newmark et al. (1995: 58) pointed out that "some victims of abuse are angered at being excluded (from mediation) and others are upset at being required to mediate." In short, victims are demanding choice and control.

In 1979, Lenore Walker broke new ground when she described battering victims' resistance to getting help in terms of "learned helplessness." Recent studies have not found battering victims ultimately to be unavailing of help (Hutchison and Hirschel, 1998; U.S. Department of Justice, 1998: 17). Rather, most abused women apparently pick and choose among available sources of help. Black women appear to call the police more often than white women do, but they seek legal assistance less (Hutchison and Hirschel, 1998: U. S. Department of Justice, 1998). This may reflect a need to stop the immediate abuse, followed by a reluctance to see Black men punished by the criminal justice system. The disproportionate incarceration of Black men in the U.S. may have negatively affected the willingness of Black women to pursue a criminal course of action.

Richie (1996: 11) argued that the feminist movement "has failed to address the needs of those whose lives are most marginalized." Many of the Black women in Richie's study saw both the courts and social services as adversaries rather than as allies. She observed that the movement's emphasis on criminal justice intervention has served to "categorically exclude women . . . involved in illegal activity from the services they needed as battered women" (p. 13). Victims whose lives are complicated by drug use, prostitution, illegal immigrant status, and/or a criminal record have good reason to avoid criminal justice proceeding.

Finally, interventions that urge women to sever ties with their partners were seen as ignorant of the ways in which "third world and working-class women . . . see their families as primary support systems in an otherwise hostile world" (Schechter, 1982: 274). By the 1990s, feminist scholarship had identified the need for policies that empower victims and remove the criminal justice system from center stage (Smart, 1989). The growing idea that "nothing in the law necessarily links it to justice" prompted a search for new extralegal interventions (Wonders, 1999: 121).

THE MEDIATION MODEL

Following a long but intermittent history in the U.S., the informal justice movement resurfaced in the 1970s with the growth of neighborhood justice centers in which civil and criminal cases were mediated. Mediation was presented as a substitute for slow, costly, and impersonal adjudication, one that was also more accessible to the poor (Smith, 1980).

Neighborhood justice centers dealt with "interpersonal disputes and minor criminal charges, usually between disputants with a continuing and troubled relationship" (Auerbach, 1983: 130). Battering cases initially entered as divorce or child custody cases (Treuthart and Woods, 1990: 4). Eventually, domestic violence became the central focus of some mediation sessions. In the mid-1970s, the American Arbitration Association piloted a mediation program to deal specifically with battering cases (Langley and Levy, 1977: 226).

Mediation's emphasis on helping participants solve their own problems was apparently compatible with the feminist value of empowerment (Rifkin, 1989). However, for many feminists, the use of mediation with battering cases was controversial from the start. Despite the rhetorical appeal of empowerment, mediation too strongly resembled the hands-off tactics of police responding to domestic assaults (see Woods, 1985: 4). Early advocates of mediation adhered to the view of domestic violence as private. Fuller (1971: 140), for example, referred to "the internal affairs of the marriage" as "inappropriate material for regulation by a regime of formal act-oriented rules." He and others recommended mediation because it largely avoided the law.

Limitations

The limitations of mediation in addressing battering lie in its formulation as dispute resolution and the mystification of "internal (domestic) affairs." Like the proverbial hammer compelled to find nails, mediators see all cases that come before them as "conflict." Aubert (1963: 26) defined conflict as a "state of tension between two actors irrespective of how it has originated and how it is terminated." The dispute is viewed as an entity separate from its development or harms: "what is important is to distinguish between this state of conflict and its basis" (Aubert, 1963: 27). Just as the *batterer* would have it, the victimizing events are deemphasized. Consequently, the mediation process tends to serve the interests of the batterer, not the victim.

A New Site of Domination Battering, as the term is used here, consists of a variety of "coercive techniques," including verbal, psychological, emotional, sexual, and economic control (Walker, 1979: 71; also Corcoran and Melamed, 1990: 305). Abusive partnerships are "so imbued with coercion that mediation cannot be a fair remedy for the weaker party" (Lerman, 1984: 73). The battered victim may be compelled to offer apologies or to make compromises to avoid violence back at home (Lerman, 1984; Rowe, 1985). The victim may then experience mediation as a "second victimization" (see Menard and Salius, 1990; Viano, 1996: 186; Van Ness and Heetderks Strong, 1997: 79).

Pushing Reconciliation Arbitrators of the early 1900s "tried to arouse amicable feelings and suppress fighting instincts" (Auerbach, 1983: 97). Many contemporary forms of mediation are similarly focused on "reconciling the parties rather than on assigning blame" (Wahrhaftig, 1982: 75). Critics argue that repairing the disputants' relationship takes precedence over repairing the harms caused by the relationship. Cobb (1997: 9) claimed that reconciliation "dissolves all morality that competes with it," including norms against violence. A case in point concerns mediation agreements reviewed by Lerman (1984: 95) that fail to stipulate that the violence must end.

As observed by Pavlich (1996), mediators communicate disapproval toward either or both disputants for having transgressed against community peace. In the ideology of mediation, dialogue restores that peace. It is redeeming, apart from any subsequent action by the disputants. The mediator reinforces, through gestures and words, discussion that marks the production of new peaceful identities. Though Pavlich does not detail how this process of identity production differs for victims and offenders, or women and men, he nonetheless clarifies a subtle device for silencing victims.

Erasing Victimization   The experience of victimization is reportedly "erased" by tactics used in mediation. First, linguistically, victims and offenders are respondents and complainants or, vaguely, disputants (Silbey and Sarat, 1989: 457). Second, it is argued that mediators actively silence narratives that suggest the directionality of violence.

In her analysis of court-referred, community-based mediation, Cobb (1997: 424) saw violence being neutralized, as when one mediator summarized a story of abuse by remarking: "It obviously looks like there was a confrontation." Abuse is reduced to disagreement, conflict, and misunderstanding; any "actual" abuse is reframed as unintended (Rifkin, 1989: 48; Cobb, 1997). The past itself is thereby recreated, with victim and offender identities erased. Relatedly, the victim's anger is suppressed or trivialized (Grillo, 1991: 1575).

Limiting Justice Options   A practical problem with the mediation model occurs when "the victim is required to forego simultaneous or subsequent pursuit of more formal remedies as a condition of participation in mediation" (Lerman, 1984: 91; see also Rowe, 1985: 887). Sometimes victims are not informed of their formal options. In one Minnesota study, battered women who were interviewed "thought they had no alternative to mediation and once in mediation they all felt pressure to agree to a

settlement" (Treuthart and Woods, 1990: 51). Some county prosecutors have required mediation in cases of domestic violence (Yellott, 1990: 40). According to Auerbach (1983: 135), "the multiplication of mediation centers made access to justice more difficult, not less, by directing people to 'exit points' from judicial institutions." As problematic as legal solutions may be, they allow for coercion of offenders, which may be necessary to stop the violence. In such cases, justice is denied to victims who mediate.

In the 1980s and 1990s, advocates of mediation have joined critics in questioning its use where domestic violence has occurred. They say that mediation can undermine justice for the victim of violence (Girdner, 1990; Hart, 1990; Menard and Salius, 1990). Mayer (1987: 84) noted that if "mediation increases the power differential, it should probably not be used." Yet the rise of restorative justice—a new model of informal justice—again raises the possibility of "mediating" domestic violence situations. The remainder of our article focuses on this new model.

LOOKING TO RESTORATIVE JUSTICE

The Difference between the Mediation Model and Restorative Justice

Restorative justice has been inaccurately equated with mediation in the U.S. This is understandable since victim-offender *mediation* is a common restorative justice intervention. However, the mediation model and restorative justice are distinct in their practices and objectives. In addition, the restorative justice movement has generated interventions *other than* mediation (e.g., family group conferencing or sentencing circles). These extend ownership of the crime problem beyond the victim and offender to concerned community members.

The Restorative Justice Movement

Restorative justice is identified more with its distinct values than with any particular program (Van Ness and Heetderks Strong, 1997). Nonetheless, certain program features are characteristic. Encounters between victims and offenders are a common feature of restorative justice interventions; these are seen as instrumental in restoring victims' well-being and reintegrating victims and offenders into communities of concern. Outcomes of the encounters include written or oral apologies to the victim, agreements about payment of restitution, or other services rendered by the offender to the victim or community and/or by community members to victim and offender.

The most common expressions of restorative justice include victim-offender mediation (VOM) and family group conferencing. Victim-offender mediation involves dialogue, facilitated by a trained mediator, during which victims and offenders are encouraged to "identify the injustice, to make things right, and to consider future actions" (Van Ness and Heetderks Strong, 1997: 71). Victim-offender mediation was first used in Canada in 1974 and in the U.S. in 1977 (Zehr, 1995). Roughly 300 VOM programs have emerged in the U.S. since the 1970s, and more than 1,000 have been implemented in all of North America and Europe (Umbreit et al., 1997).

Family group conferences invite various support persons (e.g., family, neighbors) to the meeting of victim and offender. All participants discuss the (pattern of) crime, interventions, and reparations. Family group conferencing originated in New Zealand, where it was shaped by the indigenous Maori culture. Legislation in 1989 made family group conferencing the standard response to juvenile crime in New Zealand. A version of the New Zealand conferencing model has been adopted in parts of Australia, mainly in juvenile cases (Umbreit and Zehr, 1995–1996). Sentencing circles are similar to family group conferences, but they are more likely to focus attention on community problems in which criminal incidents are embedded. Circles are widely used by native communities in North America (Stuart, 1997; Jaccoud, 1998).

In the next section, we explore the unique promises that restorative justice interventions hold for dealing with battering. These promises include recognition of victims, community involvement, healing processes, offender change, addressing social norms, and individualized interventions.

Restorative Justice and Domestic Violence

Recognition of Victims   Unlike the mediation model, restorative justice recognizes its participants as victim and offender, rather than as disputants. It also emphasizes the need for victims to be heard. Truth-telling and emotional expression are valued activities (see Schreiter, 1998). The family group conference "requires victims and offenders to confront their conflict, without neutralizing their emotions" (Braithwaite and Daly, 1994: 207).

Unlike the legal model, restorative justice appreciates victims' *agency*. Although the victim is "the person most knowledgeable about the situation" (Mills, 1998: 311), legalistic approaches eclipse her decision-making power. Advocates may rationalize "taking over the case" in terms of the victim's demonstrated passivity, such as when women repeatedly return to their partners. Yet passivity can reflect grieving, concerns for one's safety, holding on to needed financial and emotional support, or protecting one's partner. What looks like passivity may actually be an interlude in the process of leaving, which is "arduous and potentially more dangerous than staying" (Wuest and Merritt-Gray, 1999: 117).

In stark contrast to legally appropriating the victim's problem, mediation is criticized for inferring full control on the part of the victim. The ideology of mediation is that "persons participate in the creation of their own problems" (Cobb, 1997: 432). This ideology resembles victim-precipitation theories that blame women for their abuse (O'Neill, 1998: 461). On the other hand, prohibiting mediation in cases of battering also "implies that we know better what (victimized) persons' needs are than they do" (Yellott, 1990: 45). The conflict is between blaming women and recognizing them as active subjects; Maher (1997: 198) called this "the thorny issue of women's agency."

The restorative justice model ostensibly straddles the divide between agency and blame. The victim is in no way responsible for her abuse. Instead, restorative justice processes involve her in active strategies for changing her situation. First, the victim is empowered in that participation is her choice completely. No contingencies are placed on not participating: other options, including legal recourse, are always available. Second, the victim plays an active role in the proceedings, such as by choosing those support persons who will accompany her and perhaps speak on her behalf. The victim is recognized as an actor in past, present, and future events in her life.

Restorative justice strives to privilege the victim's desires, including those—like the desire to repair the relationship—that may seem irrational to others. As Mills (1996: 266) recognized, "women's relationships may be important to them, even when they involve violence." The restorative justice model recognizes that point implicitly in emphasizing the importance of human relationships. Whereas wanting to preserve the abusive relationship should not preclude victim choice, persons who care about and are close to the victim communicate their concern during the restorative justice process. In addition, that process may occasion greater awareness of personal options on the part of the victim.

Community Involvement Restorative justice, particularly family group conferences and sentencing circles, accords a central role to communities in solving crime problems. Communities provide support *and* enforcement; both are deemed necessary to stop the violence and to repair the harms caused by it.

Community support is believed to prevent domestic violence. Deficient social support gives rise to both criminal behavior and victimization (Cullen, 1994). Pennell and Burford (1994: 1) summarized this relationship: "Struggling on their own, families turn inward and place impossible expectations on children for maturity, women for caring, and men for provision. Cut off from outside support and scrutiny, families implode into violence."

Many battered women's shelters and agencies, for example, employ a community-oriented approach. Feminists were largely responsible for establishing a nationwide network of battered women's shelters, where none had existed before 1971 (NCADV, 1999). Whereas early shelters primarily provided safe housing for women and children (Felter, 1997), many now supplement this with an array of social services and broad interventions. These include counseling, support groups, hotline services, courtroom advocacy and legal assistance, batterer intervention programs, public awareness initiatives, training of police, judges, and lawyers, employment assistance, subsidized housing, and other services (Schechter, 1982; Roche and Sadoski, 1996; Healey and Smith, 1998). The shelter movement has evolved into a multifaceted response to the problem of battering, engaged in direct practice with individuals and social action.

Restorative justice responses build on the community focus of the shelter movement. Friends, families, and neighbors support the victim by acknowledging her violation and by offering concrete help in the future. The community also regulates the behavior of abusers. Several studies find that arrest deters deviance more in the context of social disapproval (Williams and Hawkins, 1989; Fagan, 1996: 26). Social disapproval and support are regulatory mechanisms in the restorative justice model. The offender is held to stopping his misconduct and is supported to do so.

Importantly, community interventions may be preferable to formal justice in addressing race, class, and cultural concerns. Police and court officials may not understand the relevance of these factors in the lives of victims and offenders, or may misinterpret what a particular "culture" represents. Processes in which members of one's own community participate will abide by one's culture without stereotyping it or deferring to it "in ways that abandon women to abuse" (Crenshaw, 1997: 107).

In short, restorative justice would channel *more* resources—*both* formal and informal social controls—in the service of stopping domestic violence. As described by Braithwaite and Daly (1994: 201), the approach is "unreservedly for net-widening, except it is nets of community rather than state control that are widened."

Emphasis on Healing Processes　Both the legal model and the mediation model are directed toward predetermined outcomes: punishment and reconciliation, respectively (see Yellott, 1990: 42). In contrast, the restorative justice encounter is not designed to achieve a specific end, but rather to allow healing *processes* to occur (Umbreit, 1997). Healing for the victim involves the opportunity for storytelling in a forum that encourages the telling and validates the story. Public acknowledgment is essential for "the ultimate resolution of the trauma" (Herman, 1997: 70). Victims need to hear that they have been hurt unjustifiably (Clear, 1994).

Although restorative justice interventions provide opportunities for victims to begin to recover from abuse, they are not generally used for violent cases in the U.S. Umbreit (1989: 102) has suggested that they hold great potential in such cases for "facilitating the healing process and moving beyond one's sense of vulnerability." There is already some evidence that restorative justice interventions reduce victims' fear of victimization (Umbreit, 1994).

Offender Change　Braithwaite's reintegrative shaming theory (1989) provides a model of offender change as a result of restorative justice processes. Although it is not the only such model, it has probably received the most attention by scholars and restorative justice practitioners.

According to reintegrative shaming theory, stigma can cause defensive reactions, such as denial, on the part of the offender. Batterers in particular are prone to "shame-rage spirals," in which feelings of shame about one's behavior are handled—supplanted—with rage and more violence (Braithwaite and Daly, 1994: 205). If social responses are stigmatizing, the offender may identify with criminal subcultures as a defense. Braithwaite and his colleagues have thus stressed the need for "ritual termination of shame" (Braithwaite and Daly, 1994: 192; also Braithwaite, 1989, 1999; Braithwaite and Mugford, 1994).

Just as it is vital that victims be surrounded by caring figures to heal, offenders need to feel supported to *change*. Although friends, family, and neighbors condemn his actions, they will welcome him back into the community as someone capable of behaving differently.

Addressing Social Norms　Law enforcement and mediation are both "reactive measures" (Kakar, 1998: 215). They would solve the battering problem by responding to manifest conflict. They are not designed to address the root causes of violence. In contrast, family group conferences and sentencing circles are community caucuses for defining and redefining social norms. The individual batterer, to quote Cohen (1966: 8), "may render an important service to the other members of the group: they come to know more clearly than before what they may and may not legitimately do."

What if the community norms being clarified are sexist ones? That criticism motivates some feminists to reject any sort of caucus on violence. Dialogue with the batterer might invite norms that excuse violence. In addition, community and/or family members may have adopted the batterer's rationalizations about violence. That criticism is addressed, albeit incompletely, by restorative justice advocates. Violence and domination are never acceptable in the restorative justice philosophy. Personal safety is held to be an essential value, as it must in battering cases (Van Ness and Heetderks Strong, 1997: 26). Furthermore, Braithwaite (1999: 50) trusts that there is general consensus against violence: a "moral high ground" (Braithwaite and Daly, 1994: 208). If norms held by some restorative justice participants condone battering, then at least its illegality (and participants supportive of the law) will supposedly prevail (Braithwaite, 1999: 52).

Individualized Interventions　While commonalities no doubt exist, the causes of abuse from one case to the next are unique. Interventions that are specific to individuals and cultures are more effective than ones that are not. Upon reviewing the effects of various interventions on recidivism, Mills (1998:

311) concluded that there is "a need to individual-ize intervention strategies according to each victim and each batterer." Similarly, Pennell and Burford (1996: 207) stated that "the best long-range solutions to family violence are those which give the affected parties the opportunities to come up with solutions that are appropriate for their family, their commu-nity, and their culture." The formal justice system, driven by abstract principles of justice, does not typ-ically invite parties to create their own solutions (Christie, 1977; McKnight, 1995). It works against discretion and individualized justice. Although me-diation is "by definition, adaptable to meet the indi-vidual needs of the negotiating parties," in practice it offers one static response—reconciliation—to bat-tering (Corcoran and Melamed, 1990: 312).

Restorative justice has the potential to increase victims' likelihood of reporting the abuse since it of-fers an array of flexible interventions. These provide an alternative to women who distrust the criminal justice system. Black and Latina women may avoid seeking help from the criminal justice system or bat-tered women's shelters to protect the image held of their minority group in a racist society. They may feel reluctant to contribute in any way to the stereo-typing and already-high rates of incarceration of mi-nority men (Bonilla-Santiago, 1996: Rasche, 1995). In contrast, Asian-American women may avoid the criminal justice system to *uphold* the myth of the "model minority" associated with their communi-ties (Crenshaw, 1997).

As Crenshaw (1997: 107) pointed out, "when—or, more importantly, how—to take culture into ac-count when addressing the needs of women of color is a complicated issue." We can start by individualiz-ing responses to battering.

Proceeding with Caution: Restorative Justice Approaches to Battering

Caution is in order. There are clear risks in applying restorative justice approaches to battering. Chief among them is the risk of framing such violence as not important enough to warrant serious attention, lest the gains of feminists be lost. In this section we discuss specific caveats that must be considered be-fore implementing restorative justice approaches for battering cases.

Prioritizing Victim Well-Being   Victim well-being and safety must be considered the first priori-ties of the restorative justice process. Sensitivity to the victim and understanding of the tenacity of her victimization must be central. Accordingly, the vic-tim takes priority over her partnership with the abuser. Reconciliation in the sense of preserving the relationship should not be a goal of the proceedings. Once an essential goal (see Peachey, 1989: 17), the restorative justice movement appears to have turned away from reconciliation in the traditional sense (Umbreit, Coates, and Roberts, 1997). Instead, rec-onciliation has been redefined as "coming to terms with the past, punishing wrongdoers, and providing some measure of reparation to victims" (Schreiter, 1998: 4; but see Van Ness and Heetderks Strong, 1997: 70–71). To help achieve reconciliation in the revised sense, facilitators should be carefully trained and monitored, and "should be clear that violent acts are the responsibility of the actor, not of the victim" (Lerman, 1984: 104). The facilitators must be sensi-tive to—and capable of interrupting—abusive dy-namics that characterize the relationship and that get acted out, however subtly, in the conference.

Need for Standardized Screening Procedures Communication, the core process of restorative jus-tice, carries a clear risk of emotional trauma to vic-tims. Offenders deficient in particular social, cognitive, and psychological characteristics are those who might interfere with victim healing. For exam-ple, manipulativeness and an incapacity for empathy are personality traits that may hamper victim healing. Current methods of screening offenders for restora-tive justice are largely inattentive to offender traits. Victim-centered offender screening tools should be developed (Presser and Lowenkamp, 1999).

Victim-Offender Mediation May Not Be Appropriate   Restorative justice advocates have stressed that victim-offender mediation, like other models of mediation, may not be appropriate in battering cases (Braithwaite and Daly, 1994; Zehr, 1995). Family group conferencing and sentencing circles are recommended as alternatives that elicit more community participation (Nicholl, 1998). In many cases, encounter per se may be inappropriate. It may do further harm to the victim, in the form of psychological trauma or physical endangerment. Alternatives are being developed that avoid encounter, but retain the essential restorative justice focus on healing and community intervention.

No Coercion   It is important that the victim not be coerced in any way, including in deciding whether to participate in a restorative justice intervention. The victim should be advised of all options and should choose the one she is most comfortable with. During the session, she should not have her words challenged or changed and should not be interrupted.

The Need for Formal Processes?   Coercion of offenders is a disputed topic within the restorative justice movement (Walgrave, 1998: 13). The victim's well-being has been seen as requiring the potential for use of coercive force with batterers. On this view, restorative justice processes may need to invoke the enforcement "teeth" of the legal system (Braithwaite and Daly, 1994; see also Lerman, 1984: 106). As communities develop stronger informal social controls and restorative systems, the role of law enforcement could gradually diminish.

Consider too the danger that restorative justice, like the traditional model of mediation, will become "little more than a preliminary stage in legal proceedings" (Auerbach, 1983: 120). If so, the restorative justice program may become another layer of processing separating the victim from relief. Processes of healing may be hampered by legal requirements, such as fact-finding and speedy case processing. If those requirements influence processes of truth telling and restitution, "the notion that parties are actually making their own decisions is purely illusory" (Grillo, 1991: 1581). As Umbreit (1989: 109) noted, "any reconciliation that may occur must be

genuine." We raise the need for coercion of offenders, through legal or other means, as problematic.

SUMMARY AND CONCLUSIONS

This chapter has considered broad strategies that address battering. We have analyzed the law and mediation from a critical, historical perspective. We have applied the same perspective to restorative justice approaches that we believe may promote lasting change.

Given the traditional codification of woman battering as private and extralegal, it is not surprising that early battered women's advocates sought change via the law. The law positively marks battering as wrong; legal punishment would seem to proclaim (and thus *reclaim*) the victim's value (see Hampton, 1988). Yet, the promise of law is mitigated by its part in women's oppression. Beneath the mantle of assisting victims, legalistic strategies (e.g., policing and prosecution) have constrained choice. Further, the legal model occludes recognition of the structural and diffuse foundations of the battering problem.

The mediation model shares some problems of the legal model and presents new ones. Like the law, mediation individualizes the battering problem. Conservative ideologies that locate violence in normlessness (the "at-risk"), rather than in social imbalances and norms, are upheld. As a practice consequence of individualizing battering, victims and offenders are isolated from communities that would help regulate the problem and provide needed support.

Mediation has historically obscured the power imbalances that characterize battering. Accounts of victimization have been invalidated. Reconciliation has been mediation's primary aim, such that other outcomes (and formal avenues to procure them) have been closed off. In short, neither the law nor mediation uproot the problem of battering.

Restorative justice generalizes ownership of the battering problem beyond victims and offenders and beyond government to communities. We make no claims that restorative justice holds *the* ultimate answer to the problem of battering. Battering lies at the intersection of too many institutionalized power imbalances to lend itself to a simplistic solution. Yet restorative justice *does* frame battering in a way that has the *potential*—enabled by laws against battering—to attack the roots of the problem, including social inequities and accessory norms, isolation of individuals and families, and neutralization of blame.

In the restorative justice paradigm, remedies to crime must be publicly located. We believe that the restorative justice perspective reconciles the private-public distinction that underpins the battering problem. Crime is neither "just personal" nor "just political." It is an acutely personal experience that at the same time reflects larger societal structures. Although broadly based, these structures are not remote or untouchable. They are found in our own communities—in everyday norms and narratives—and we can affect them there.

DISCUSSION QUESTIONS

1. Presser and Gaarder discuss three different approaches to woman battering. The two typically used today are the legal model and mediation. The third, restorative justice, is promoted in this chapter.
   - Define and describe each feature of the three models and the characteristics that address domestic violence.
   - Describe the strengths and weaknesses of each model.
   - Which of these three models do you think is best suited for dealing with the problem of domestic violence?
2. How might the three different responses to battering be evaluated?
3. Given the strengths and weaknesses of each model, what value would there be in offering victims a choice of interventions? What dangers would there be?
4. How might a restorative justice approach in your own community grapple with domestic violence?

NOTES

1. Battering typically refers to violence against women by their male partners. It is the most common form of intimate violence (U.S. Department of Justice, 1999b). This article will focus on such abuse, and the terms domestic violence and battering will be used interchangeably.
2. Lerman (1984: 67) refers to these as the law enforcement model and the conciliation model.
3. Mandatory arrest was implemented on a wide scale despite the finding that arrest increased violence in some cases. Later research further qualified the deterrent effect of arrest (Sherman, 1993; Sherman et al., 1992; Buzawa and Buzawa, 1993).

REFERENCES

Aubert, Vilhelm. 1963. Competition and Dissensus: Two Types of Conflict and of Conflict Resolution. *Journal of Conflict Resolution* 7:26–42.

Auerbach, Jerold S. 1983. *Justice without Law? Resolving Disputes without Lawyers.* New York: Oxford University Press.

Benhabib, Seyla. 1989. The Generalized and Concrete Other. In *Ethics: A Feminist Reader,* ed. Elizabeth Frazer, Jennifer Hornsby, and Sabina Lovibond, 267–300. Cambridge, MA: Harvard University Press.

Bonilla-Santiago, Gloria. 1996. Latina Battered Women: Barriers to Service Delivery and Cultural Considerations. In *Helping Battered Women: New Perspectives and Remedies,* ed. Albert R. Roberts, 229–234. New York: Oxford University Press.

Bouza, Anthony. 1991. Responding to Domestic Violence. In *Woman Battering: Policy Responses,* ed. Michael Steinman, 191–202. Cincinnati, OH: Anderson.

Braithwaite, John. 1999. Restorative Justice: Assessing Optimistic and Pessimistic Accounts. In *Crime and Justice: A Review of Research,* 25, ed. Michael Tonry, 1–127. Chicago: University of Chicago Press.

———. 1989. *Crime, Shame, and Reintegration.* Cambridge: Cambridge University Press.

Braithwaite, John, and Kathleen Daly. 1994. Masculinities, Violence, and Communitarian Control. In *Just Boys Doing Business? Men, Masculinity, and Crime,* ed. Tim Newburn and Elizabeth A. Stanko, 189–213. London: Routledge.

Braithwaite, John, and Stephen Mugford. 1994. Conditions of Successful Reintegration Ceremonies. *The British Journal of Criminology* 34:139–171.

Brooks, Rachelle. 1997. Feminists Negotiate the Legislative Branch: The Violence against Women Act. In *Feminists Negotiate the State: The Politics of Domestic Violence,* ed. Cynthia R. Daniels, 65–82. Lanham, MD: University Press of America.

Brown, Jennifer Gerarda. 1994. The Use of Mediation to Resolve Criminal Cases: A Procedural Critique. *Emory Law Journal* 43:1247–1309.

Buzawa, Eve, and Carl Buzawa. 1993. The Scientific Evidence Is Not Conclusive: Arrest Is No Panacea. In *Current Controversies on Family Violence,* ed. R. Gelles and D. Loseke, 337–356. Newbury Park, CA: Sage.

Christie, Nils. 1977. Conflicts as Property. *British Journal of Criminology* 17:1–15.

Clear, Todd. 1994. *Harm in American Penology: Offenders, Victims, and Their Communities.* Albany: State University of New York Press.

Cobb, Sara. 1997. The Domestication of Violence in Mediation. *Law and Society Review* 31:397–440.

Cohen, Albert K. 1966. *Deviance and Control.* Englewood Cliffs, NJ: Prentice-Hall.

Corcoran, Kathleen O'Connell and James C. Melamed. 1990. From Coercion to Empowerment: Spousal Abuse and Mediation. *Mediation Quarterly* 7:303–316.

Crenshaw, Kimberle. 1997. Mapping the Margins: Intersectionality, Identity Politics, and Violence Against Women of Color. In *The Legal Response to Violence Against Women,* ed. Karen J. Mischke, 91–150. New York: Garland.

Cullen, Francis T. 1994. Social Support as an Organizing Concept for Criminology: Presidential Address to the Academy of Criminal Justice Sciences. *Justice Quarterly* 11: 527–559.

Davidson, Terry. 1978. *Conjugal Crime: Understanding and Changing the Wife-beating Pattern.* New York: Hawthorn Books.

Dobash, R. Emerson, and Russell P. Dobash. 1992. *Women, Violence, and Social Change.* London: Routledge.

Erez, Edna, and Joanne Belknap. 1998. In Their Own Words: Battered Women's Assessment of the Criminal Processing System's Responses. *Violence and Victims* 13:251–268.

Eagan, Jeffrey. 1996. The Criminalization of Domestic Violence: Promises and Limits. National Institute of Justice Research Report (January).

Felter, Elizabeth. 1997. A History of the State's Response to Domestic Violence in the United States. In *Feminists Negotiate the State: The Politics of Domestic Violence,* ed. Cynthia R. Daniels, 5–20. Lanham, Maryland: University Press of America.

Ford, David A. 1991. Prosecution as a Victim Power Resource: A Note on Empowering Women in Violent Conjugal Relationships. *Law and Society Review* 25:313–334.

Foucault, Michel. 1982. The Subject and Power. In *Michel Foucault: Beyond Structuralism and Hermeneutics,* ed. Hubert L. Dreyfus and Paul Rabinow, 208–226. Chicago: University of Chicago Press.

Fuller, Lon L. 1971. Mediation—Its Forms and Functions. *Southern California Law Review* 44:305–339.

Gilligan, Carol. 1982. *In a Different Voice: Psychological Theory and Women's Development.* Cambridge, MA: Harvard University Press.

Girdner, Linda K. 1990. Mediation Triage: Screening for Spouse Abuse in Divorce Mediation. *Mediation Quarterly* 7: 365–376.

Grillo, Trina. 1991. The Mediation Alternative: Process Dangers for Women. *Yale Law Journal* 100:1545–1610.

Hampton, Jean. 1988. The Retributive Idea. In *Forgiveness and Mercy,* ed. Jeffrie G. Murphy and Jean Hampton, 111–161. New York: Cambridge University Press.

Harris, M. Kay. 1991. Moving into the New Millennium: Toward a Feminist Vision of Justice. In *Criminology as Peacemaking,* ed. Harold E. Pepinsky and Richard Quinney, 83–97. Bloomington, IN: Indiana University Press.

Hart, Barbara J. 1990. Gentle Jeopardy: The Further Endangerment of Battered Women and Children in Custody Mediation. *Mediation Quarterly* 7:317–330.

Healey, Kerry Murphy, and Christine Smith. 1998. Batterer Programs: What Criminal Justice Agencies Need to Know. Washington, DC: National Institute of Justice (July).

Heise, Lori L. 1998. Violence against Women: An Integrated, Ecological Framework. *Violence against Women* 4:262–290.

Herman, Judith Lewis. 1997. *Trauma and Recovery.* New York: Basic Books.

Hutchison, Ira W., and J. David Hirschel. 1998. Abused Women: Help-seeking Strategies and Police Utilization. *Violence against Women* 4:436–456.

Jaccoud, Mylene. 1998. Restoring Justice in Native Communities in Canada. In *Restorative Justice for Juveniles: Potentialities, Risks, and Problems,* ed. Lode

Walgrave, 285–299. Leuven, Belgium: Leuven University Press.

Kakar, Suman. 1998. *Domestic Abuse: Public Policy/Criminal Justice Approaches towards Child, Spousal, and Elderly Abuse.* San Francisco: Austin and Winfield.

Kraybill, Ronald S. 1980. A Procedure for Mediating Inter-personal Disputes. In *Mediation: A Reader,* ed. Lynn Robert Buzzard and Ronald Kraybill, 1–14. Oak Park, IL: Christian Legal Society.

Langley, Roger, and Richard C. Levy. 1977. *Wife Beating: The Silent Crisis.* New York: Pocket Books.

Lerman, Lisa G. 1984. Mediation of Wife Abuse Cases: The Adverse Impact of Informal Dispute Resolution on Women. *Harvard Women's Law Journal* 7:57–113.

MacKinnon, Catherine. 1983. Feminism, Marxism, Method, and the State: Toward Feminist Jurisprudence. *Signs* 8:635–658.

Maher, Lisa. 1997. *Sexed Work: Gender, Race, and Resistance in a Brooklyn Drug Market.* New York: Oxford University Press.

Mahoney, Martha R. 1991. Legal Images of Battered Women: Redefining the Issue of Separation. *Michigan Law Review* 90(1):1–94.

Mayer, Bernard. 1987. The Dynamics of Power in Mediation and Negotiation. In *Practical Strategies for the Phases of Mediation,* ed. Christopher W. Moore, 75–86. San Francisco: Jossey-Bass.

McKnight, John. 1995. *The Careless Society: Community and Its Counterfeits.* New York: Basic Books.

Meier, Linda K., and Brian K. Zoeller. 1995. Taking Abusers to Court: Civil Remedies for Domestic Violence Victims. *Trial* 31:60–65.

Menard, Anne E., and Anthony J. Salius. 1990. Judicial Response to Family Violence: The Importance of Message. *Mediation Quarterly* 7:293–302.

Messerschmidt, James W. 1993. *Masculinities and Crime: Critique and Reconceptualization of Theory.* Lanham, MD: Rowman and Littlefield.

Miller, Susan L. 1989. Unintended Side Effects of Pro-arrest Policies and Their Race and Class Implications for Battered Women: A Cautionary Note. *Criminal Justice Policy Review* 3:299–317.

Mills, Linda. 1996. Empowering Battered Women Transnationally: The Case for Postmodern Interventions. *Social Work* 41:261–268.

Mills, Linda G. 1998. Mandatory Arrest and Prosecution Policies for Domestic Violence: A Critical Literature Review and the Case for More Research to Test

Victim Empowerment Approaches. *Criminal Justice and Behavior* 25:306–318.

National Coalition Against Domestic Violence. 1999. *About This Organization.* Denver, CO: Author.

Newmark, Lisa, Adele Harrell, and Peter Salem. 1995. Domestic Violence and Empowerment in Custody and Visitation Cases. *Family and Conciliation Review* 33:30–62.

Nicholl, Caroline G. 1998. *From Battering to Bettering: Changing the Lives of Victims of Domestic Violence and Their Abusers.* Washington, DC: Campaign for an Effective Crime Policy.

O'Neill, Damian. 1998. A Post-structuralist Review of the Theoretical Literature Surrounding Wife Abuse. *Violence against Women* 4:457–490.

Pagelow, Mildred Daley. 1990. Effects of Domestic Violence on Children and Their Consequences for Custody and Visitation Agreements. *Mediation Quarterly* 7:347–363.

Parent, Colette, and Francoise Digneffe. 1996. A Feminist Contribution to Ethics in Criminal Justice Intervention. In *Post-Critical Criminology,* ed. Thomas O'Reilly-Fleming, 201–215. Scarborough, Ontario: Prentice Hall Canada.

Paternoster, Raymond, Robert Brame, Ronet Bachman, and Lawrence W. Sherman. 1997. Do Fair Procedures Matter? The Effect of Procedural Justice on Spouse Assault. *Law and Society Review* 31:163–204.

Pavlich, George. 1996. The Power of Community Mediation: Government and Formation of Self-Identity. *Law and Society Review* 30:707–733.

Peachey, Dean E. 1989. The Kitchener Experiment. In *Mediation and Criminal Justice: Victims, Offenders, and Community,* ed. Martin Wright and Burt Galaway, 14–26. London: Sage.

Pennell, Joan, and Gale Burford. 1996. Attending to Context: Family Group Decision-making in Canada. In *Family Group Conferences: Perspectives on Policy and Practice,* ed. Joe Hudson, Allison Morris, Gabrielle Maxwell, and Burt Galaway, 206–220. Leichhardt, Australia: The Federation Press.

———. 1994. Widening the Circle: Family Group Decision Making. *Journal of Child and Youth Care* 9:1–11.

Pranis, Kay. 1998. Restorative Justice and Feminism: Common Themes. Paper presented at the Second Annual International Conference on Restorative Justice for Juveniles (November 7–9), Fort Lauderdale, FL.

Presser, Lois, and Christopher T. Lowenkamp. 1999. Restorative Justice and Offender Screening. *Journal of Criminal Justice* 27:333–343.

Rasche, Christine E. 1995. Minority Women and Domestic Violence: The Unique Dilemmas of Battered Women of Color. In *The Criminal Justice System and Women: Offender, Victims, and Workers,* ed. Barbara Raffel Price and Natalie J. Sokoloff, 246–261. New York: McGraw-Hill.

Richie, Beth E. 1996. *Compelled to Crime: The Gender Entrapment of Battered Black Women.* New York: Routledge.

Rifkin, Janet. 1989. Mediation in the Justice System: A Paradox for Women. *Women and Criminal Justice* 1:41–54.

Roche, Susan E., and Pam J. Sadoski. 1996. Social Action for Battered Women. In *Helping Battered Women: New Perspectives and Remedies,* ed. Albert R. Roberts, 13–30. New York: Oxford University.

Rowe, Kelly. 1985. The Limits of the Neighborhood Justice Center: Why Domestic Violence Cases Should Not Be Mediated. *Emory Law Journal* 34:855–910.

Schechter, Susan. 1982. *Women and Male Violence: The Visions and Struggles of the Battered Women's Movement.* Boston: South End Press.

Schreiter, Robert J. 1998. *The Ministry of Reconciliation: Spirituality and Strategies.* Maryknoll, New York: Orbis Books.

Sherman, Lawrence. W. 1993. Defiance, Deterrence, and Irrelevance: A Theory of the Criminal Sanction. *Journal of Research in Crime and Delinquency* 30:445–473.

Sherman, Lawrence W., and Richard A. Berk. 1984. The Specific Deterrent Effects of Arrest for Domestic Assault. *American Sociological Review* 49:261–272.

Sherman, Lawrence W., Janell D. Schmidt, Dennis P. Rogan, Douglas A. Smith, Patrick R. Gartin, Ellen G. Cohn, Dean J. Collins, and Anthony R. Bacich. 1992. The Variable Effects of Arrest on Criminal Careers: The Milwaukee Domestic Violence Experiment. *The Journal of Criminal Law and Criminology* 83:137–169.

Silbey, Susan, and Austin Sarat. 1989. Dispute Processing in Law and Legal Scholarship: From Institutional Critique to the Reconstruction of the Juridical Subject. *Denver University Law Review* 66:437–498.

Smart, Carol. 1995. *Law, Crime, and Sexuality.* London: Sage.

———. 1989. *Feminism and the Power of Law.* London: Routledge and Kegan Paul.

Smith, David N. 1980. A Warmer Way of Disputing: Mediation and Conciliation. In *Mediation: A Reader,* ed. Lynn Robert Buzzard and Ronald Kraybill, 24–35. Oak Park, IL: Christian Legal Society.

Stanko, Elizabeth A. 1989. Missing the Mark? Policing Battering. In *Women, Policing, and Male Violence: International Perspectives,* ed. Jalna Hanmer, Jill Radford, and Elizabeth A. Stanko, 46–69. London: Routledge and Kegan Paul.

———. 1985. *Intimate Intrusions: Women's Experience of Male Violence.* London: Routledge and Kegan Paul.

Stuart, Barry. 1997. *Building Community Justice Partnerships: Community Peacemaking Circles.* Report of the Ministry of Justice, Ottawa, Canada.

Tierney, Kathleen J. 1982. The Battered Women Movement and the Creation of the Wife Beating Problem, *Social Problems* 29:207–220.

Tifft, Larry L., and Lyn Markham. 1991. Battering Women and Battering Central Americans: A Peacemaking Synthesis. In *Criminology as Peacemaking,* ed. Harold E. Pepinsky and Richard Quinney, 114–153. Bloomington, IN: Indiana University Press.

Treuthart, Mary Pat, and Laurie Woods. 1990. *Mediation: A Guide for Advocates and Attorneys Representing Battered Women.* New York: National Center on Women and Family Law, Inc.

Umbreit, Mark. 1997. Humanistic Mediation: A Transformative Journey of Peacemaking. *Mediation Quarterly* 14:201–213.

———. 1994. Victim Empowerment through Mediation: The Impact of Victim-Offender Mediation in Four Cities' Perspectives. American Probation and Parole Association, 25–30.

———. 1989. Violent Offenders and Their Victims. In *Mediation and Criminal Justice: Victims, Offenders, and Community,* ed. Martin Wright and Burt Galaway, 99–112. London: Sage.

Umbreit, Mark S., Robert Coates, and Ann Warner Roberts. 1997. Cross-national Impact of Restorative Justice through Mediation and Dialogue. *The ICCA Journal on Community Corrections* (December): 46–53.

Umbreit, Mark S., and Howard Zehr. 1995–1996. Family Group Conferences: A Challenge to Victim-Offender Mediation? *VOMA Quarterly* 7: 4–8.

United States Department of Justice Bureau of Justice Statistics. 1999a. Characteristics of Crime. On-line: http://www.ojp.usdoj.gov/bjs/cvict_c.htm.

————. 1999b. Female Victims of Violent Crime. On-line: http://www.ojp.usdoj.gov/bjs/abstract/fvvc.htm.

————. 1998. *Factbook: Violence by Intimates.* Washington, DC: Author (March).

Van Ness, Daniel, and Karen Heetderks Strong. 1997. *Restoring Justice.* Cincinnati: Anderson.

Viano, Emilio C. 1996. Stereotyping and Prejudice: Crime Victims and the Criminal Justice System. *Studies on Crime and Crime Prevention* 5:182–202.

Wahrhaftig, Paul. 1982. An Overview of Community-oriented Citizen Dispute Resolution Programs in the United States. In *The Politics of Informal Justice, Volume 1: The American Experience,* ed. Richard L. Abel, 75–97. New York: Academic Press.

Walgrave, Lode. 1998. What Is at Stake in Restorative Justice for Juveniles? In *Restorative Justice for Juveniles: Potentialities, Risks, and Problems,* ed. Lode Walgrave, 11–16. Leuven, Belgium: Leuven University Press.

Walker, Lenore E. 1979. *The Battered Woman.* New York: Harper and Row.

Websdale, Neil, and Byron Johnson. 1997. Structural Approaches to Reducing Woman Battering. *Social Justice* 24:54–81.

Williams, Kirk R., and Richard Hawkins. 1989. The Meaning of Arrest for Wife Assault. *Criminology* 27:163–181.

Wonders, Nancy A. 1999. Postmodern Feminist Criminology and Social Justice. In *Social Justice/Criminal Justice: The Maturation of Critical Theory in Law, Crime, and Deviance,* ed. Bruce A. Arrigo, 111–128. Belmont, CA: Wadsworth.

Woods, Laurie. 1985. Mediation: A Backlash to Women's Progress on Family Law Issues in the Courts and Legislatures. New York: National Center on Women and Family Law, Inc.

Wuest, Judith, and Marilyn Merritt-Gray. 1999. Not Going Back: Sustaining the Separation in the Process of Leaving Abusive Relationships. *Violence against Women* 5: 110–133.

Yellott, Ann W. 1990. Mediation and Domestic Violence: A Call for Collaboration. *Mediation Quarterly* 8:39–50.

Zehr, Howard. 1995. *Changing Lenses: A New Focus for Crime and Justice.* Scottsdale, PA: Herald Press.

Zorza, Joan. 1992. The Criminal Law of Misdemeanor Domestic Violence, 1970–1990. *The Journal of Criminal Law and Criminology* 83:46–72.

Chapter 26

Gender, Power, and Sexual Harassment

Georganne Rundblad

ABSTRACT

This chapter by Rundblad addresses a form of victimization that inflicts substantial harm. Sexual harassment ranges from off-color remarks to humiliating comments to unwanted touching and grabbing to requests or demands for sexual acts, and in extreme cases, to rape and threats or actual loss of one's job for failure to acquiesce to sexual demands. Sexual harassment is coercion: it is unwanted sex under threat; it is sex that is economically enforced; it denies women the exercise of control over their lives. Sexual harassment happens most frequently to those women in subordinate working positions with low pay. However, it is found at virtually all levels and in all occupations, including high-status professions, where women are harassed not only by superiors but also by subordinates as well as by peers and third parties.

At mid-twentieth century C. Wright Mills, a well-known sociologist, wrote about the power to show how people's personal troubles are often grounded in major social issues, that is, such troubles are shared by many people in similar circumstances or social locations. Thus, the troubles are much more than only personal problems. Sexual harassment is a superb example of a situation that for many years was considered an individual trouble; in fact, it was believed to be brought on by the victim herself (victims are usually women, although not always). As Rundblad explains, this historical reality, combined with the cultural reality legitimating the differences in society's value of men and women (masculine hegemony) and the difference in their power (patriarchal structure), kept this behavior accepted and almost unnoticed for a long time.[*]

It is predominantly (although not always) men who harass women. Rundblad reports that sexual harassment is so pervasive that 50 percent of women can ex-

---

[*]Sexual harassment has become such an important issue that the recently formed European Union Parliament equated sexual harassment with discrimination and told member states they must establish laws preventing such harassment in the workplace (Ann Moline, European Union Tells Members to Bar Sex Harassment. Available at www.womensenews.org).

pect to experience behavior that legally constitutes sexual harassment from their professors, coworkers, supervisors, or clients. Once again it is clear that gender is about power. The author is careful to account for the ways in which gender interacts with other systems of oppression (e.g., race, class, age) in the consideration of this behavior. (For a more detailed discussion of sexual harassment among corrections officers as it varies by race and sexual orientation, see Belknap, chap. 35. Moreover, Belknap provides a useful distinction between "sexual harassment" and "gender harassment".) The women most vulnerable to sexual harassment are women at the greatest disadvantage with respect to power in society. They are more likely to be young, single, racial or ethnic minority group members, or women in subordinate work positions. Finally, although sexual harassment is most commonly thought of as occurring on the job between supervisors and workers, it occurs in many settings and between many different groups of people. For example, sexual harassment occurs in schools—including elementary, secondary, college, and military—between teachers and students and between male students and female students.

This chapter is about sex and power in relation to sexual harassment, a topic often misunderstood. Sexual harassment is pervasive in the workplace and in educational settings, and it can have severe effects on its targets. This chapter will outline a definition of sexual harassment, the historical and social context that contributes to it, and variations by type in different settings. It is hoped that the reader will gain an understanding of why men harass and some of the effects of sexual harassment.[1]

What exactly is sexual harassment? Why is it so misunderstood? What do you know about it? Answer the questions below to test your present knowledge about sexual harassment.[2] Then, throughout this chapter, you'll find the answers.

1. What percentage of women will experience sexual harassment at some point during their life at work? (a) 10 percent (b) 30 percent (c) 50 percent (d) 90 percent

2. Legally actionable sexual harassment can take place anywhere. It does not have to be in the workplace or in an educational setting. True or false?

3. The target of sexual harassment can be either a man or woman and does not have to be the opposite sex. True or false?

4. The complainant in a sexual harassment suit doesn't have to be the harassed person but can be anyone who is affected by the offensive behavior. True or false?

5. Harassers can be either men or women. True or false?

6. Sexual harassment doesn't occur unless there is some form of physical contact. True or false?

7. Women who work in either female-dominated occupations or male-dominated occupations experience more sexual harassment than women who work in sex-balanced occupations. True or false?

8. What percentage of women will experience sexual harassment at some point during their college education? (a) 10 percent (b) 30 percent (c) 50 percent (d) 75 percent

9. There is no law specifically referring to sexual harassment. True or false?

10. Sexual harassment is predominantly about sex. True or false?

Understanding sexual harassment can be quite confusing for several reasons. First, sometimes the behaviors that are legally prohibited as sexual harassment are those that some people, when joking with

Source: In Dana Vannoy, ed. *Gender Mosaics: Social Perspectives.* Los Angeles: Roxbury, pp. 352–362.

peers or flirting, consider to be everyday behaviors.[3] Second, although such flirting behaviors and sexual banter may be offensive, they are not always sexual harassment. Legally prohibited sexual harassment is more *context-specific* and *situation-specific* than encompassing all unwanted sexual attention or sexualized social interactions (Stein 1999). The third reason is that the definition of sexual harassment continuously evolves and is reinterpreted with different court cases. Each time a new lawsuit is brought forward, it has the potential to change previous understandings of sexual harassment. Some court cases even have their decisions reversed in a court of appeals or by the Supreme Court.

DEFINING SEXUAL HARASSMENT

Sexual harassment is unwanted sexual behavior that interferes with a person's abilities to conduct her work or acquire an education, regardless of whether the person was the intended target (Eisaguirre 1993). If the harassing behavior takes place in an educational or employment setting and if the harasser is treating members of one sex in a different manner from the treatment of members of the other sex in such a way to hamper the target's ability to do her work, the person is very likely to be engaging in sexual harassment.[4] For example, if an employer creates an environment in which an employee will be harassed by customers, clients, or visitors—for instance, by requiring the employee to wear revealing clothing—then it is sexual harassment (Eisaguirre 1993). If promotions or work assignments are tied to the acceptance of a request for a date, it is sexual harassment. Moreover, recent lawsuits have found same-sex sexual harassment to be illegal (Gibbons 1998; Stein 1999). As Laura W. Stein observed, "Sexual harassment in the legal sense of the term occurs only in contexts in which the law prohibits sex discrimination. If a construction worker makes suggestive comments to a woman passing by, that does not violate current law," since it is not legally discriminatory behavior (1999, xxi).

Although there is no law per se against sexual harassment, court cases arguing against it have done so on the basis of Title VII of the 1964 Civil Rights Act, which prohibits discrimination on the basis of race, color, religion, national origin, and sex (Eisaguirre 1993; Stein 1999). In 1980 Eleanor Holmes Norton, congresswoman and then chair of the Equal Employment Opportunity Commission (EEOC), the federal agency charged with the responsibility of investigating harassment and discrimination cases under Title VII, issued a set of guidelines detailing prohibited behavior that applies to all government agencies and to private businesses with 15 or more employees (Eisaguirre 1993).[5] These guidelines include the following behaviors:

- Physical or verbal behaviors that are sexual, such as comments about the woman's body, propositions for sex, sexual jokes, pornography, or sexually oriented cartoons.
- Unwanted behaviors (i.e., when it is unsolicited, when the target has done nothing to incite the behaviors, or when the target views the behaviors as undesirable or offensive).
- Behaviors that interfere with the ability of the targeted person to work at her job or in her educational studies, or make her feel threatened or uncomfortable (Crull 1987; Giuffre and Williams 1994).

Sexual harassment in schools, universities, and colleges by teachers and administrators is illegal under Title IX of the Federal Education Amendments of the U.S. Civil Rights Act (Eisaguirre 1993). Legitimate nonsexual touching or other nonsexual conduct, such as an athletic coach hugging a student who made an important goal or an elementary teacher consoling a child who fell down, is exempt (Stein 1999). Title IX applies to all schools that receive any kind of federal aid, either directly through grants or student financial aid. Recognizing student-to-student sexual harassment for the first time, on May 24, 1999, the Supreme Court ruled that schools can be held liable for such harassment when, according to Supreme Court Justice Sandra Day O'Connor, it is "so severe, pervasive and objectively offensive that it can be said to deprive the victims of access to the educational opportunities or benefits provided by the school" (Moorlehem and Audi 1999, 2A).

HISTORY AND SOCIAL CONTEXT OF SEXUAL HARASSMENT

Why does sexual harassment occur? What social factors contribute to it? Why do some men feel they have the freedom to harass women sexually, and why is it predominantly men who sexually harass women? One thing that sociologists study to get a better sense of how to address questions like these is the social and historical context in which the behavior occurs. Even though sexual harassment has been around for as long as there have been women working in some kind of labor market (Segrave 1994), it is only recently that it has been widely publicized in the news with the Thomas-Hill case, the case of President Clinton and Paula Jones, and the case of Mitsubishi Motor Manufacturing of America (discussed in more detail below).[6] Part of the reason that sexual harassment has only recently been widely publicized is that, historically, it has been viewed as a problem caused by individual women of "questionable virtue" entering paid employment. Hence, it was considered to be an individual trouble rather than a social issue, the solution for which was simply to deny women employment opportunities (Segrave 1993).

In addition to this individualist perspective is the differential value that society has placed on women and men. Throughout Western history, in most societies, men have been more highly valued than women (Epstein 1988). People of European descent have been more highly valued than people from other parts of the world as well. The interaction of race and gender is significant in matters of sexual harassment. For example, greater penalties are imposed on black men than on white men as harassers, especially if the target of harassment is a white woman. These cultural biases, infused in the social institutions and the social conditions of everyday interactions, have resulted in the subordination of these groups.

Sociocultural Power and Sexual Harassment

Sociocultural power is linked to society's structure of gender relations. Gender behavior is part of everyday interactions. Men in U.S. society are expected to be assertive, not only in work and sports, but also in the sexual pursuit of women, while women are taught to be less assertive and more accommodating and friendly. In effect, this behavior is "doing gender" (West and Zimmerman 1987), which is meeting social expectations for gendered behaviors in social interactions. An important part of doing gender, especially in a society that values men over women, is the power differential that is played out in interactions such as these.

It is this interesting and complex intersection of sex and power that is at the crux of sexual harassment. In other words, there is a system of assumptions and practices, within and between social institutions, through which women's position in the marketplace and in education is damaged. This socially legitimated power that men have over women is enacted daily on the shop floor, in the classroom, or in the board room to the detriment of women (Grauerholz 1996). As Eleanor LaPointe stated, in the workplace "Men typically fail to see themselves as working with co-equals, but rather attempt to maintain subordinate/dominant relations through actions that symbolize their higher status and undermine their common interests with female coworkers" (1992, 391). Margaret S. Stockdale (1996) recognized that the privilege of growing up in a society that provides men with more power may lead men to feel a sense of entitlement with regard to the sexual harassment of women. Moreover, race-based stereotypes interact with sex-based stereotypes to give men a sense of even greater power and more license to sexually harass women of color (Murrell 1996).

Legal Definitions of Sexual Harassment

It is likely a consequence of the privilege of men that sexual harassment was not recognized as a legally actionable behavior until the late 1970s. The term *sexual harassment* was not coined until the mid-1970s, when Carmita Wood, an administrative assistant at Cornell University, sued the university for unemployment compensation after she became physically ill and quit her job because of the stress of having to fend off a Cornell University physicist's sexual advances (Brownmiller and Alexander 1999).

Because of persistent pressure from women's rights advocates, since that time, two main kinds of sexual harassment have been identified: quid pro quo and hostile environment.

Quid pro quo sexual harassment is based on some give and take. (*Quid pro quo* means "this for that".) In other words, a supervisor will "give" the subordinate a raise, a job, grades, graduation, promotions, or tenure if he can "take" sex. Quid pro quo sexual harassment may involve suggestions of unnecessary after-hours work or statements such as "If you want that assignment, you're going to have to be nice to me" (Wagner 1992, 22). Sometimes the harassing behaviors are more obvious. For example, in one case, the supervisor of a waitress put his hand up her skirt, and when she confronted him, she was fired (LaPointe 1992). In another instance, office manager Debbie Johnson repeatedly called in a male employee to initiate a sexual relationship. She exposed herself to him and made numerous sexual comments to him. He was fired shortly after complaining to her supervisors, and he later sued on the basis of sexual harassment (Gibbons 1998). As these examples illustrate, quid pro quo sexual harassment is usually perpetrated by a supervisor, and only one incident can be enough to qualify for legal action. The first successful lawsuit to argue quid pro quo sexual harassment as a violation of the law on the basis of Title VII was that of *Williams v. Saxbe* (1976), when Diane Williams, an employee of the U.S. Department of Justice, was fired from her job for refusing the sexual advances of her supervisor (Eisaguirre 1993; Stein 1999).

The EEOC guidelines and Title VII, however, are not designed to eliminate all expressions of human sexuality in the workplace, though they do prohibit conduct that is unwelcome and that affects a woman in her role as a worker. An initial request for a date may "be indistinguishable from garden variety sexual attraction that we may find in a social situation" (Crull 1987, 228) and may not become evident as sexual harassment until the woman refuses and the supervisor retaliates. Sexual harassment occurs when the person in power uses that power as a threat to a subordinate. The power may become manifest in employment decisions such as demotions, raises, or firings or the achievement of certain statuses or grades in school.

Hostile-environment sexual harassment is less clear-cut than quid pro quo sexual harassment and occurs when the workplace or educational setting is so permeated with sexual behaviors or innuendoes or is so hostile that the environment is intimidating (Eisaguirre 1993). In many cases, male coworkers taunt women, display sexual graffiti and pictures of women in sexually explicit situations, persistently request dates, use sexually offensive language, or tell jokes that permeate the workplace and create an offensive atmosphere. In the recent case against Mitsubishi, these behaviors were charged in a class-action suit. For example, it was charged that photographs taken at parties of workers engaged in sexual activity with hired sex workers were widely circulated at the plant. A male worker at Mitsubishi reported that he'd "seen women grabbed online, lewd gestures behind women's back and right to her [face], name calling—every degrading name you can think of" to be frequent behaviors at Mitsubishi (McKinney 1996a; 1996b, E1). These behaviors may accompany situations in which the woman's safety or her ability to do her job is jeopardized because coworkers refuse to train her or assist her in her work. Usually, this type of sexual harassment is perpetrated by several participating men and is more often an expression of hostility toward the woman than a means by which to initiate a sexual relationship. Hostility toward women employees, including pranks, threats, intimidation, or physical attacks, does not have to involve sexual overtones. Rather, it is *because of the person's sex* that the person is being harassed (Eisaguirre 1993). In effect, hostile-environment sexual harassment "poisons the work environment selectively on the basis of sex" (Sapiro 1994, 324), and for this reason it is a violation of the equal-employment law. In educational settings, hostile-environment sexual harassment refers to behaviors in the classroom, hallways, or residence halls that reasonably interfere with a student's ability to learn (Paludi 1997).

Rarely is one incident of hostile-environment sexual harassment enough to bring suit; the harassment needs to be pervasive, frequent, repetitive, and part of an overall environmental pattern of behavior. Nor does the harassment have to deprive the woman of tangible job benefits. The EEOC considers the following factors when determining whether hostile-environment sexual harassment has occurred:

- The extent to which the conduct affected the employee's conditions of employment.
- Whether the behavior was repeated.
- Whether the behavior was intended and perceived seriously or in jest.
- The degree to which the conduct is contrary to community standards.

The first successful lawsuit to argue hostile-environment sexual harassment was that of *Bundy v. Jackson* (1981). In this case, Sandra Bundy was subjected to a barrage of sexual insults and demeaning propositions, which resulted in a psychological and emotional work environment that caused her anxiety and debilitation (Eisaguirre 1993; Stein 1999).

EXTENT OF SEXUAL HARASSMENT IN SOCIETY

Most research on sexual harassment indicates that 50 percent of women can expect to experience behaviors that legally constitute sexual harassment from their male co-workers, supervisors, clients, or customers at some point in their employment careers (Giuffre and Williams 1994). In educational settings, an estimated 30 percent (Dansky and Kilpatrick 1997) to 66 percent (Grauerholz 1996) of female students can expect to experience sexual harassment by teachers, administrators, staff, and peers.

Why isn't more heard about sexual harassment in the media if so many women experience it? The most important reason is that sexual harassment in employment and educational settings is underreported. Given the social perceptions of women, the social status of women, and the lack of power they hold in society, underreporting makes sense. First, reporting sexual harassment is similar to reporting other sex-based crimes, such as rape. Very often, the targeted women feel at fault, and they fear retaliation. Moreover, they feel embarrassed and stigmatized, in part, as a consequence of how the U.S. legal system addresses sex-based crimes (Epstein 1988; Stockdale 1996). As Cynthia Fuchs Epstein noted, "powerful groups use law to achieve their own goals," as has happened historically by perceiving sexual harassment (and rape) as a consequence of women's rather than men's behavior (1988, 120).

Second, and relatedly, women also often feel that speaking up or confronting a harasser will make no difference. Kerry Segrave (1994) estimated that women are successful in less than 5 percent of all sexual-harassment cases that are brought to court, and these are only a fraction of those cases that are perpetrated.

Third, women are expected to be servile and emotionally supportive. Because these characteristics are perceived to be part of traditionally female jobs, when employers or co-workers demand those behaviors, women are less likely to report the demand as sexual harassment. For example, one woman noted that "You don't realize it's happening at first [when my supervisors] felt free to put their arms around me. It seems harmless. You don't think about it right away because you are used to it being a woman" (LaPointe 1992, 388).

SOCIAL CHARACTERISTICS OF HARASSED WOMEN

Given that research has found that 50 percent of all women can expect sexual harassment in their jobs or during their education, what factors contribute to women's vulnerability? One of the keys in understanding who is more likely to be sexually harassed is examining relative power. In other words, those people who have less power are more likely to experience sexual harassment than others, even other women (Giuffre and Williams 1994; Murrell 1996). This situation means that men are more likely to harass women in the following categories:

- Younger women.
- Single women.
- Racial or ethnic-minority women.
- Women in subordinate occupational positions.

- Women who work in sex-imbalanced occupations.
- Women students.
- Women graduate students.
- Women with a higher level of education.
- Economically disadvantaged or disabled women.
- Socially isolated or unassertive women.

Organizational Power and Sexual Harassment

The underlying factor that helps to explain why being in these categories increases the risk of sexual harassment for women is that "women's deficits in sociocultural power (i.e., youth, singleness) are often transformed into deficits of organizational power" (Gruber 1997, 92). An important implication is that some women are more at risk of sexual harassment than others because they have *multiple deficits.* Thus, for example, single women or women in lower-status occupations who are also women of color, students, or lesbians have a greater likelihood of being harassed by men (Grauerholz 1996; Paludi 1997).[7]

Most researchers contend that sexual harassment is about power and the abuse of that power rather than about sex (Crull 1987; Stein 1999), though it is through sexuality that the power is exercised. Michele A. Paludi (1997) suggested that abuse of power could be understood by focusing less on men's (and boy's) attitudes toward women (and girls) and more on issues of competition and power and men's attitudes toward other males. In other words, men don't want to appear weak or less masculine in the eyes of other males, so they engage in sexually harassing behaviors with women as a way to impress other men.

Some of the research that supports the idea that sexual harassment is about abuse of power suggests that those women with more sociocultural power are able to better defend themselves against sexual harassment. For example, married women are much less likely to be the object of touching or pressured for sexual activity because they gain vicarious power from their husbands. Furthermore, Patti A. Giuffre and Christine L. Williams (1994) found that women

waitresses were able to use their marital status and their ability to speak the language in situations of cross-cultural harassment to ward off unwanted sexual advances.

One of the strongest cases in favor of the argument that sexual harassment is about socially inscribed power rather than sex is the situation of contrapower sexual harassment, the harassment of a superior by a subordinate, which is almost always perpetrated by men against women. An example is the harassment of a female faculty member by a male student. In this situation, organizational position does not necessarily protect a woman from the social and cultural power that accrues to men. The relative power to which men feel they are entitled allows them to sexually harass the women they work with or for, in some situations regardless of the occupational status of those women (Grauerholz 1996; Gruber 1997).

Sexual harassment can be perpetrated by people who are familiar to the target, who have ordinary family lives, and who appear to be caring and sensitive. As Kathleen McKinney and Nicholas Maroules observed, "If there is any common feature to the many factors suggested as variables influencing sexual harassment . . . it is the factor of power or status. Whether formal or informal, organizational or diffuse, real or perceived, status differences between victims and offenders are at the root of the problem of sexual harassment" (Tangri and Hayes 1997, 126).

Situational Variation of Sexual Harassment

But if perpetrators of sexual harassment can't be easily identified, can one pinpoint any situations that might lead someone to perpetrate sexual harassment more than other situations? Simply because a man has the social and organizational power to harass the women he goes to school with or works beside does not necessarily mean that he will use that power. John B. Pryor and Nora J. Whalen noted that men who sexually harass women do so "when the circumstances or local social norms permit such behavior" (1997, 134). One theoretical perspective that can help explain this fact is *organizational power,* which posits that if the organization provides opportunities to harass through a work environment that is tolerant of sexual harassment, through a male-dominated hierarchy of occupations, and through sexualized work environments, then some men will be more likely to harass (Tangri and Hayes 1997). Thus, keep in mind the following characteristics (LaPointe 1992):

- A work environment that is conducive to sexual harassment.
- Supervisors who may view sexual harassment of their subordinates as one more of their rights.[8]
- Occupations with a sexualized work environment, such as waitressing.

Working in Sex-Imbalanced Occupations

Another important aspect of the likelihood of sexual harassment is when there is a skewed distribution of women and men (i.e., male-dominated or female-dominated occupations or educational settings) because such occupations tend to have a higher incidence of sexual harassment than sex-balanced occupations. The type of sexual harassment is likely to be different in each kind of occupation. In those that are female dominated (i.e., secretarial positions or social science majors) quid pro quo sexual harassment is more likely to occur, while in male-dominated environments hostile-environment harassment is more common.

Female-Dominated Jobs

The kind of sexual harassment of women that occurs in female-dominated occupations is more often than not quid pro quo (Crull 1987). Limited power, lower pay, sexualized work activities, and dependence on supervisors for raises and for getting or keeping a job or for getting a grade in a course all make it difficult for women to reject sexual advances by males in positions of authority (Gruber 1998). In these situations, the supervisor uses his authority to command the woman to engage in sexual activity, just as he commands her to do a variety of work-related or school-related tasks. If she refuses, he uses that same authority to demote her, just as if she had refused to do any other kind of work or school task.

A theoretical perspective that can help explain these dynamics is *sex-role spillover,* which posits that gender-based expectations for women's and men's behavior that are irrelevant or inappropriate to work are carried over (spill over) into the workplace (Gruber 1997; Stockdale 1996). Sex, which is more salient than work role, is linked in important ways to expectations about people, and, when we participate in social interactions with people, those beliefs color our expectations of how we believe they should act. Social expectations of "how women should be" influence expectations about their behaviors in a work setting.

Women in female-dominated work settings occupy jobs that themselves involve some aspects of the female role. These jobs require the women to assist supervisors, to be emotionally supportive, and to be sexually attractive, and the job description may be "sexualized." Social expectations that women will be nurturing, supportive, and helpful result in male supervisors expecting these behaviors from women and, hence, spill over into the workplace.

Male-Dominated Jobs

Women pioneers into male-dominated occupations experience pervasive sexual harassment and hostility. This is hostile-environment sexual harassment, which is most often perpetrated by co-workers.[9] It is more likely to occur in male-dominated jobs because, where women and men work together as peers, occupationally structured status differences disappear. Men, therefore, establish or maintain their social dominance over women through harassing the women who are "trespassing" into "male territory." This domination serves as a substitute for the power or prestige the man perceives himself to be losing on the job because of the presence of the woman worker. In such cases, men use the power they gain from their seniority, their specialized work knowledge, their authority to train their female peers, and their social leverage as men to harass women.

One factor that plays into the equation of the sexual harassment of women working in male-dominated occupations is the work environment itself, which is often an extension of male culture (Gruber 1998). Specifically, male-dominated occupations construct a work identity that is based on gendered behavior: aggression, sexual bravado, embracing risky situations, and bonding rituals that highlight male superiority.

Another factor that contributes to women's harassment by men is that the numerical dominance of men heightens the visibility of women and their minority status (Gruber 1998). Moreover, the status inconsistency with regard to the sex and work roles of women contribute to sexual harassment. Those who are in "status-inconsistent" positions in the workplace are much more likely to be harassed by their peers (Gruber 1998). The woman is out of her "sex-appropriate" occupational role because she is performing work that "belongs" to men. Hostility and harassment may serve to remind her of where she "belongs" (Crull 1987).

Again, consider how sex-role spillover can help explain sexual harassment in male-dominated occupations. In such jobs, the lower status and authority of women "legitimizes" social inequality, and women are then treated as women rather than as workers or as students. Moreover, because the job is defined as "male work," men who are not used to working with women fall back on sex-role stereotyping as a way to understand how to interact with women in male-dominated jobs.

EFFECTS OF SEXUAL HARASSMENT

Why should society be concerned about sexual harassment? What's at stake when society doesn't address sexual harassment? The effects of incidents of sexual harassment in academia and at work can be socially, economically, and personally costly. Sexual harassment can threaten one's financial security, physical and social well-being, and psychological health. But from a legal and social perspective, the most important consequence of sexual harassment is that women are denied social equality through differential access to equal employment and educational opportunities.

Without the ability to work or to become educated in a harassment-free environment, women will continue to fail to achieve parity with men. Thus, sexual harassment reinforces stereotypical perceptions that "women are less suited than men to many jobs; women do not stay with their jobs; women lack education and experience; women are absent from work more often than men; women are unable to travel; women would not be accepted in positions of authority, and women are incapable of making decisions based on fact and logic" (Wagner 1992, 12–13).

Another cost is financial. In a study of federal employees, between 1992 and 1994, sexual harassment cost the U.S. government $327 million in the form of sick leave, job turnover, and lost productivity and $6,719,593 annually per Fortune 500 company (Eisaguirre 1993). But the monetary cost of sexual harassment to large businesses and the government is only one part of it. The economic costs to the targets of sexual harassment can be extensive.

Sexual harassment can seriously compromise a woman's ability to gain an education or earn a living (Sapiro 1994). When students are harassed, their academic performance suffers. They may avoid enrolling in particular courses and may increase their absenteeism.

Sexual harassment in the work force can make it difficult for the woman to work effectively and can decrease the quality of the work along with reducing her job satisfaction and morale.

On a personal level, research has shown that sexual harassment can result in embarrassment, intimidation, feelings of helplessness, decreased motivation, decreased morale, anger, self-blame, confusion, depression, self-doubt, and lower self-esteem (Gruber and Bjorn 1982; Paludi 1997; Stockdale 1996). Moreover, it can result in a lack of social support, especially when a minority woman exposes minority male sexual harassers as in the Thomas-Hill case (Adams 1997). The stress brought on by sexual harassment can also manifest itself in physiological ways through headaches, tiredness, sleep disturbances, disordered eating, nausea, weight gain or loss, and nervousness (Paludi 1997). Once again, all of these will undermine the woman's ability to study or work effectively.

CONCLUSION

How can one best avoid being a target of sexual harassment or avoid harassing women in the workplace or in an educational setting? Are there things a person can do to help eliminate sexual harassment? First, recognize that in an ideal world, men would take responsibility for their behaviors. Harassers are always responsible for their behavior and should be held accountable for it. They always have a choice about whether or not to harass. Recognizing differences between socially accepted behaviors for women and men could help you to interpret more clearly another person's behavior and avoid harassment or harassing behaviors. Simply knowing what counts as sexual harassment can be beneficial. For example, Paludi noted that most students believe that sexual harassment hasn't occurred unless there is some form of physical contact, although most of the harassment that students face is not physical.

On a societal level, if we accept that sexual harassment is about power, we need to work toward social equality. When seeking employment, find out about the company's equal-employment and sexual-harassment policies or encourage your current employer to adopt such guidelines. If you, as a man or woman, should be harassed, document the incidents, tell a friend or co-worker, report them to a supervisor or human-resources officer at school. Finally, keep in mind many of the subtleties of sexual harassment as alluded to in the questions at the beginning of the chapter.[10] It is not as cut and dried as you may think.

DISCUSSION QUESTIONS

1. Define sexual harassment. Why is understanding this concept difficult? What are some of the conceptual and legal complexities?
2. What are some ways in which gender interacts with race and class with respect to who is likely to be a harasser or a victim and how the criminal justice system responds?
3. What does it mean to say that sexual harassment is about abuse of power rather than sex? How does sexual harassment sustain the power differences between men and women generally and between individual men and women specifically?
4. What are some of the effects of sexual harassment for the victim? What other effects can you think of that are not mentioned in this chapter?
5. How can you learn more about the extent of sexual harassment at your school or on your job? What are the written policies and procedures on how to deal with sexual harassment at your school or job? How well are they working?

NOTES

1. The male pronoun will be used throughout this chapter to refer to harassers. Women sometimes do harass men, and there is evidence of same-sex harassment, but 90 to 95 percent of all sexual harassment claims are brought against men (Eisaguirre 1993).
2. The questions are based upon empirical research from social scientists and government agencies (Dansky and Kilpatrick 1997; Paludi 1997; Stockdale 1996; U.S. Equal Employment Opportunity Commission 1999; Women's Action Coalition 1993).
3. Such sexual bantering, in fact, is quite common, as in the development of a romantic relationship at work (Eisaguirre 1993). Recent studies (Carter and Carter 1998) have found that about a third of employed people develop a romantic

relationship with a co-worker and about 50 percent of those lead to either a long-term relationship or to marriage.

4. The most recent lawsuits charging sexual harassment have extended the more traditional understandings of sexual harassment and have centered on harassment in housing and in professional relationships such as patient-client relationships (Stein 1999).

5. In 1996, 12 percent of all women workers were employed in firms with 24 or fewer employees and thus were without protection of the EEOC (U.S. Small Business Administration 1998), though most states, under Fair Employment Practices statutes, cover employees in firms with 15 or fewer employees (Eisaguirre 1993).

6. The first recorded case of behavior that is now labeled as sexual harassment was in 1875, in *Croaker v. Chicago and Northwestern Railroad* (1875), which involved a woman who sued for mental suffering and "being wronged" when a male train conductor thrust his hands into her hand-warmer muff and then kissed her several times (Eisaguirre 1993).

7. Adams (1997), Grauerholz (1996), and Stockdale (1996) note that there is a dearth of research on the experiences of women of color with regard to sexual harassment, but given their social status as women and of a racial or ethnic minority, it is very likely that they not only experience more sexual harassment than white women but that their sexual harassment is more severe.

8. Since most management positions in the workplace and supervisory positions in academia are held by men, there is a greater likelihood of the harassment of women subordinates or students (Grauerholz 1996).

9. Although men in female-dominated occupations do experience slightly more sexual harassment than if they worked in sex-balanced or male-dominated occupations, it is not nearly as great as what women in male-dominated jobs experience. Hence, it is not the sex ratio of the job that determines sexual harassment (Tangri and Hayes 1997).

10. The answers to the quiz questions: 1) c; 2) F; 3) T; 4) T; 5) T; 6) F; 7) T; 8) b; 9) T; 10) F.

REFERENCES

Adams, Jann H. 1997. Sexual Harassment and Black Women: A Historical Perspective. In *Sexual Harassment: Theory, Research, and Treatment,* ed. William O'Donohue, 213–224. Needham Heights, MA: Allyn and Bacon.

Brownmiller, Susan, and Dolores Alexander. 1999. How We Got Here: From Carmita Wood to Anita Hill. In *Sexual Harassment in America: A Documentary History,* ed. Laura W. Stein, 1–4. Westport, CT: Greenwood.

Carter, Jaine, and James D. Carter. 1998. Facing Up to Workplace Romances. *Star Tribune,* Metro Edition, October, 26:4E.

Costello, Cynthia B., Shari Miles, and Anne J. Stone. 1998. *The America Woman, 1999–2000: A Century of Change—What's Next?* New York: W. W. Norton.

Crull, Peggy. 1987. Searching for the Causes of Sexual Harassment: An Examination of Prototypes. In *Hidden Aspects of Women's Work,* ed. Christine Bose, Roslyn Feldberg, and Natalie Sokoloff with the Women and Work Research Group, 225–244. New York: Praeger.

Dansky, Ronnie S., and Dean G. Kilpatrick. 1997. Effects of Sexual Harassment. In *Sexual Harassment: Theory, Research, and Treatment,* ed. William O'Donohue, 152–174. Needham Heights, MA: Allyn and Bacon.

Eisaguirre, Lynne. 1993. *Sexual Harassment: A Reference Handbook.* Santa Barbara, CA: ABC-CLIO.

Epstein, Cynthia Fuchs. 1988. *Deceptive Distinctions: Sex, Gender, and the Social Order.* New Haven, CT: Yale University Press.

Gibbons, Sean M. 1998. Sexual Harassment of Men Not OK at Corral. *Virginia Employment Law Letter,* November 19, 10(4).

Giuffre, Patti A., and Christine L. Williams. 1994. Boundary Lines: Labeling Sexual Harassment in Restaurants. *Gender and Society* 8(3):378–401.

Grauerholz, Elizabeth. 1996. Sexual Harassment in the Academy: The Case of Women Professors. In *Sexual Harassment in the Workplace: Perspectives, Frontiers and Response Strategies,* ed. Margaret S. Stockdale, 29–50. Thousand Oaks, CA: Sage.

Gruber, James E. 1997. An Epidemiology of Sexual Harassment: Evidence from North America and Europe. In *Sexual Harassment: Theory, Research, and Treatment,* ed.

William O'Donohue, 84–98. Needham Heights, MA: Allyn and Bacon.

———. 1998. The Impact of Male Work Environments and Organizational Policies on Women's Experiences of Sexual Harassment. *Gender & Society* 12(3):301–320.

Gruber, James E., and Lars Bjorn. 1982. Blue-Collar Blues: The Sexual Harassment of Women Autoworkers. *Work and Occupations* 9(2):271–298.

LaPointe, Eleanor. 1992. Relationships with Waitresses: Gendered Social Distance in Restaurant Hierarchies. *Qualitative Sociology* 15(4):377–393.

McKinney, Kathy. 1996a. Mitsubishi Seeks Suit Gag Order. *Pantagraph* April 19, p. A1.

———. 1996b. Workers Tired of Attention. *Pantagraph* April 21, p. E1.

Mills, C. Wright. 1959. *The Sociological Imagination.* London: Oxford University Press.

Moorlehem, Tracy Van, and Tamara Audi. 1999. Schools Liable If Students Harass. *Detroit Free Press,* April 24, pp. 1A–2A.

Murrell, Audrey J. 1996. Sexual Harassment and Women of Color: Issues, Challenges, and Future Directions. In *Sexual Harassment in the Workplace: Perspectives, Frontiers, and Response Strategies,* ed. Margaret S. Stockdale, 51–66. Thousand Oaks, CA: Sage.

Paludi, Michele A. 1997. Sexual Harassment in Schools. In *Sexual Harassment: Theory, Research, and Treatment,* ed. William O'Donohue, 224–249. Needham Heights, MA: Allyn and Bacon.

Pryor, John B., and Nora J. Whalen. 1997. A Typology of Sexual Harassment: Characteristics of Harassers and the Social Circumstances Under Which Sexual Harassment Occurs. In *Sexual Harassment: Theory, Research, and Treatment,* ed. William O'Donohue, 129–151. Needham Heights, MA: Allyn and Bacon.

Sapiro, Virginia. (1994). *Women in American Society: An Introduction to Women's Studies.* Mountain View, CA: Mayfield.

Segrave, Kerry. 1994. *The Sexual Harassment of Women in the Workplace, 1600 to 1993.* Jefferson, NC: McFarland.

Stein, Laura W. 1999. *Sexual Harassment in America: A Documentary History.* Westport, CT: Greenwood.

Tangri, Sandra Schwartz, and Stephanie M. Hayes. 1997. Theories of Sexual Harassment. In *Sexual Harassment: Theory, Research, and Treatment,* ed. William O'Donohue, 112–128. Needham Heights, MA: Allyn and Bacon.

U.S. Equal Employment Opportunity Commission. 1999. Questions and Answers about Sexual Harassment. In *Sexual Harassment in America: A Documentary History,* ed. Laura W. Stein, 5–8. Westport, CT: Greenwood.

U.S. Small Business Administration. 1998. *Characteristics of Small Business Employers and Owners, 1997.* Table 3.1 Employee Characteristics by Employment Size of Firm, 1992–1996.

Wagner, Ellen J. 1992. *Sexual Harassment in the Workplace: How to Prevent, Investigate, and Resolve Problems in Your Organization.* New York: American Management Association.

West, Candace, and Don H. Zimmerman. 1987. Doing Gender. *Gender and Society* 1(2):125–151.

Women's Action Coalition ed. Andrea Blum, Julie Harrison, Barbara Ess, and Gail Vachon. 1993. *WAC (Women's Action Coalition) Stats: The Facts about Women.* New York: New.

The author would like to thank Bob Broad, Thomas Gerschick, and Curtis White for comments on earlier drafts of this chapter.

Chapter 27

Women, Labor, and Migration:
The Position of Trafficked Women and Strategies for Support

Marjan Wijers

ABSTRACT

This is the first of two chapters on trafficking in women. Wijers uses the term *trafficking* to refer broadly to the process of coercing women and men into crossing national borders to work as migrant laborers—in factory sweatshops, as migrant farm workers, as domestics, in the entertainment business, and in prostitution. In this chapter Wijers provides a theoretical framework within which to understand trafficking in women. She reports on the work of a Norwegian organization, the Foundation against Trafficking in Women, which started in 1987 with the express purpose of helping women who have been trafficked into the Netherlands. Wijers offers five separate issue areas that must be considered by anyone who wishes to provide assistance to migrant women: (1) the status of these women as regulated by migration laws, (2) their status as workers regulated by government policies and laws, (3) their status under prostitution laws, (4) their status as victims of international organized crime regulated by crime policies on trafficking, and (5) their status in their home countries as well as in the receiving country as found in the law and relevant regulations. Wijers, who has worked firsthand with women trafficked for the purpose of prostitution, describes many of the fears and hardships these women face.

This chapter is grouped with articles about women victims and survivors (part 3) rather than women offenders (part 1) because although some of these women may have left their home country willingly, they find themselves without any means of protection once they fall under the control of the organized criminals who facilitate their migration. Public attitudes toward and legal sanctions against prostitutes tend to be devoid of any mercy: prostitutes are viewed as women with no rights and entitled to no protections against violence and exploitation. Thus, these women are victims of trafficking—even if they made the affirmative decision to improve their lives by leaving their home countries to do sex work. The solution to this terrible situation, says Wijers, is to strengthen the rights of female migrant sex workers and treat the women as workers protected by labor laws and civil rights provisions rather than as prostitutes punished by the criminal legal system. Only in this way—only through a fight against violence and against the exploitation of women who are just trying to earn a living—Wijers argues, can the trafficking in women be stopped. Her hope is that these migrant workers will be able to regain control of their lives and determine their own future.

INTRODUCTION

"Traffic in women" is a broad category covering various forms of exploitation and violence within a range of (informal) labor sectors that migrant women work in, including prostitution, entertainment industries and domestic work. Trafficking is not limited to prostitution, although this is a popular belief, and not all prostitution involves trafficking. We can define trafficking in the narrow sense as the process in which migrant women are brought into prostitution through the use of coercion, deceit, abuse or violence and in which they are denied fundamental human rights and freedoms such as the right to decide to work as a prostitute or not, the right to decide on the conditions of work, the right to enter and leave the sex industry, the right to refuse certain customers, the right to refuse certain sexual acts, the right to freedom of movement, the right not to be exploited, and so forth. If trafficking is defined in a broader sense it can apply not only to prostitution, but also to other forms of labor such as those mentioned above.

Since 1987, the Foundation Against Trafficking in Women (STV), based in the Netherlands, has been working professionally and has given assistance to more than 900 women. This is just a small fraction of the number of women that is estimated to have been in one way or another trafficked to the Netherlands. Social workers, health care workers and police estimate that this number is between 1,000 and 2,000 per year. As STV and Dutch policies have concentrated primarily on the traffic in women for

the purpose of prostitution, this essay focuses mainly upon this form of trafficking.

PRINCIPLES FOR SUPPORT

The first step in supporting victims of trafficking is to gain at least some understanding of their position, their needs, dilemmas, motivations, and of the problems they face in the process of trafficking. Searching for ways to support trafficked women means starting from the reality of migrant women and the recognition of the right of trafficked women to survival and self-determination. This assumes that their own needs and aspirations are taken as a starting point for any action.

To understand the reality of trafficked women we need to look at, at least, five factors through which their situation is determined. These are a) their position as women who migrate from one country to the other, regulated by migration laws; b) their position as women who migrate for work, regulated by policies and laws dealing with migrant workers; c) their position as women who work or worked in prostitution, regulated by prostitution laws; d) their position as victims of (internationally organized) crime, regulated by criminal policies on trafficking; and e) their position as women in their home countries and in the receiving countries, which is reflected in the first four areas. Existing policies to combat trafficking mainly build on prostitution and migration laws.

POSITION AS MIGRANTS AND MIGRANT WORKERS

Looking at trafficking from the perspective of the majority of the women we are concerned with, it is clear that most women come to Western Europe

Source: 1998. From *Global Sex Workers: Rights, Resistance, and Redefinition* by Kamala Kempadoo and Jo Doezema. Reproduced by permission of Routledge, Inc., part of the Taylor & Francis Group.

because they are looking for a better way to make a living. In this sense, they should be seen as labor migrants. Migration is an age-old survival strategy for men as well as for women. It implies courage and initiative to try to change one's own or the family's situation. Certainly, women who have become victims of trafficking can not be classified as passive or stupid victims. This may seem self-evident, but ten years of daily work on the issue of trafficking proves it is still not the case for many people involved in the whole process, such as police officers and the judiciary.

The growing gap between the rich and poor countries particularly affects the situation of women and children. The breakdown of national economic and political systems, as in the Central and Eastern European countries, brings hardship and confusion to the general populace, but women are particularly vulnerable in such situations. They are often in the paradoxical situation of being responsible for the family income, while not having access to well-paid jobs nor the same opportunities for legal labor migration as men. As a consequence, the number of women migrating is increasing dramatically. Nearly half of the migrants worldwide today are women, although in official policies women are almost exclusively seen as dependents of male labor migrants.

Women have few opportunities of getting work in formal labor sectors, either in their home countries or in the more developed countries. They are relegated to the informal and unregulated labor market—without rights and without protection. Over the last fifteen years new, more dubious and unprotected labor markets have developed internationally, such as the market for female domestic workers, for marriage partners and for the sex and entertainment industry. Simultaneously, numerous multi-national recruiting agencies, impresarios and marriage bureaus have mushroomed, that actively—and usually dishonestly—recruit young girls and women who are looking for the opportunity to make a living elsewhere.

This labor division is also reflected in migration patterns. There are few legal and independent ways for women to migrate within the informal sector. Owing to the nature of the work and the forms of migration open to them, they are forced to make use of the services of untrustworthy organizations and middlemen. This places migrating women in extremely vulnerable situations, subject to abuse by procurers, employment agencies, artist agencies, marriage agencies and all other kinds of middlemen, who intervene in the beginning, somewhere in the middle or at the end of the process.

On the European side, Western European countries all claim they are not immigration countries. For this reason labor migration into the European Union is very restricted. Shamefully, it seems that the richer the country, the harder they try to keep migrants from poor countries out. Though official policies hold that Europe should not allow more immigrants, these official statements can hardly be maintained if we realize that apparently a demand does exist, to put it in economic terms, for certain types of workers and that these workers, often immigrant, keep our economies going. The group of migrant women we are concerned with works cheaply, does not lay claim to legal and social protection—because their legal situation is too precarious—and generates significant state, private and criminal revenue.

Official policies of the receiving countries in Western Europe, however, forbid labor migration from so-called Third World countries and, recently, from Central and Eastern European countries. The majority also prohibit migrants from working as prostitutes, even if they permit nationals to do so. In reality, almost the only work migrant women are allowed to do is in the entertainment sector or sex industry, whether this is the official policy, as in Switzerland, or just everyday practice, as in the Netherlands. At the same time these sectors are the most marginalized, if not criminalized, in society. Moreover prostitution is not even recognized as labor by most, if not all, countries. This creates a considerable gap between official policies and day-to-day experiences of prostitutes, mail-order brides and domestic workers. And this is where organized crime comes in: filling the gap that official policies leave open.

Migrant women who are trafficked do not have access to legal resources in order to bring their traffickers to justice. In the majority of the receiving countries those with an illegal status will be immediately deported. They are not protected legally by national or inter-State policies. On the contrary, most state policies regarding "aliens" effectively turn these women into criminals instead of victims. Employment agencies, entertainment agencies, procurers for prostitution and other middlemen operate in the countries of origin without any effective government control. They take advantage of the women's vulnerable situation and their wish to migrate. Since there are practically no possibilities for poor, unskilled women to travel independently and to work legally in these countries, they are almost totally dependent on recruiting agencies and brokers, and thus in imminent danger of falling victim to criminal networks. In receiving countries the increasingly restrictive immigration laws resulting from European unification have clearly negative effects for women who attempt to migrate. The laws appear to benefit the traffickers, who will always find ways to circumvent laws, while simultaneously working to the disadvantage of migrant women, increasing their dependence on third parties.

The overall picture is that trafficked women are considered, above all, as undesirable aliens. The fact that they may be a victim of sexual violence and exploitation is completely subordinate or even irrelevant to their immigration status in the context of current immigration policies of European countries. In this situation, it is almost impossible for migrant women to ask for protection if exploitation, violence and forced prostitution occur.

POSITION AS WOMEN WORKING IN PROSTITUTION

States have different policies on prostitution. All policies have in common that prostitutes are denied basic human rights, held in contempt, isolated, marginalized and sometimes criminalized. Some countries, such as the United States, have a *prohibitionist system*. All prostitution is declared to be unacceptable, and most or all aspects of prostitution are pro-

hibited and criminalized. Not only the procurer but also the prostitute is liable for punishment, as is any third party. In most cases the primary target for law enforcement, however, is the female prostitute, not those who profit from her income. This law denies the reality of prostitution and the fact that for various reasons women work as prostitutes to earn an income. Illegality renders prostitutes completely dependent upon others, such as pimps, procurers, police officers. Corruption and blackmail are everyday practices. Trafficked women are completely at the mercy of pimps and brothel keepers, as there is not one authority they can, even theoretically, turn to.

In the second type of system, as in Germany, the existence of prostitution is more or less recognized. Prostitution is either "legalized" or regulated by the State (through different forms of registration and other forms of State control) in the interest of public order, public health and tax generation. Usually prostitutes are required to register with the police and to have regular STD (Sexually Transmitted Disease) tests, with penalties for women working without a license of "health certificate." This *regulatory system* creates a difference between legal and illegal forms of prostitution. Many women do not want to register because they fear the stigmatizing effects. Other women cannot register because of their illegal status. In both cases women end up in an illegal sector with all the negative consequences this entails.

The third system, *abolitionism,* emphasizes the moral and ethical arguments against regulation and the involvement of the State or any other third party. Prostitution is seen as a moral evil, undermining the family and family values and involvement of the authorities is thought to encourage moral decay. According to this view the prostitute should not be penalized—she is the victim—but all other aspects of prostitution are considered criminal activities. No distinction is made between forced and consensual prostitution. Prostitutes are basically seen as passive victims of the social and economic system that need to be rescued. This view negates individual choice and denies women the status of subjects capable of assuming agency and responsibility. However, many cases are known where no legal proceedings have been initiated against traffickers under an abolitionist system because the women did not reflect the stereotyped image of a victim of trafficking, for instance because she agreed to work as a prostitute.

The majority of the European countries have adopted a system based on the abolitionist view. For example, laws in the Netherlands, Belgium and Great Britain and the 1949 *Convention on the Suppression of the Traffic in Persons and the Exploitation of the Prostitution of Others* are predominantly based on this view. This leads to a rather confusing and paradoxical situation. On the one hand, working as a prostitute is not punishable, but any involvement of a third party is illegal, be it a brothel keeper or a friend, independent of the consent of the women and whether or not they exploit the women involved. On the other hand, registration and payment of taxes are enforced in many countries with an abolitionist system. Although unintentional, in practice abolitionism leads to isolation and criminalization of prostitutes. Moreover any third party is forced to operate illegally, which puts the women concerned at greater risk of violence and exploitation.

Lastly there is the *system of decriminalization*. As far as I know, the State of New South Wales, Australia, is the only place where decriminalization not only of prostitutes but of the prostitution business itself is a starting point for prostitution policy. The basic principle is the right of independent adult women to determine their lives by themselves. Elsewhere, this view is mostly favored by prostitutes' organizations and women's organizations that support prostitutes' rights. According to this view, any policy should be based on the rights of the women to self-determination and the protection of their rights as workers. Criminalizing the sex industry creates ideal conditions for rampant exploitation and abuse of sex workers. Prostitutes in this system are not treated as victims or denied responsibility and accountability for their decisions and actions, as is done in all the systems mentioned above. Moral judgement against prostitution is not the principal motivation in drafting policies, because of the danger of marginalizing and stigmatizing prostitutes. Rather it is believed that trafficking in women, coercion and exploitation can only be stopped if the existence of prostitution is recognized and the legal and social rights of prostitutes are guaranteed. It is not considered realistic to attack prostitution, but instead, appropriate to fight violence and exploitation through existing laws, such as labor regulations and civil rights laws. Traffic in women could and should then be prosecuted as a severe violation of several laws.

POSITION OF WOMEN AS A VICTIM OF ORGANIZED CRIME

Traffic in women mostly takes place in a network-like structure and is based on violence. This has many consequences. Even if existing policies allow women to report to the police, only few women will do so, for various reasons.

Confidence in the Police System

Most women have no trust whatsoever in the police or any other authorities. Corruption and abuse of power are frequent in many of their home countries, but many migrant women also have bad experiences with the (immigration) police in receiving countries. As we have seen, in many countries prostitution is prohibited or illegal. Migrant prostitutes (whether they are forced or not) are continually at risk of deportation, imprisonment, harassment and abuse. In most of the home countries of migrant women, protection by the law is the privilege of the rich and powerful. To have the law work in your favor, you need money and connections, things that are at the disposal of the traffickers but not of the women. Moreover, most women are illegal in the country of residence. This implies that any contact with authorities puts them directly at risk of deportation.

Fear of Deportation

Although at first glance, deportation could appear as a way of escaping the trafficking situation, the reality is far more complicated. Many women consider deportation an even worse prospect than accepting the situation in which they find themselves, and try to survive in the hope that at some point they will succeed in realizing their original aims for migration. Women accept the offers made by recruiters, because they do not accept the confinements of their situation at home. The offer for work abroad represents one of the few avenues to a better future. Often, they borrow money to pay for the costs of middlemen. They can be indebted to their own family, but also to the recruiters. In many cases the family relies on the women's income. If they are deported, they return home with empty hands, with no money and with debts that will never be paid off. If it becomes known that a woman has worked as a prostitute, this can have serious social consequences. Not only has she to worry about the effect this can have for her family, she also has to face the possibility that her family will not accept her anymore. Surviving without family can be extremely difficult. Moreover, it is questionable whether deportation means an escape from the criminal circuit. Many cases are known of women who, after deportation, were awaited by the recruiters and taken back immediately. There are many ways to keep a woman under control: debts that must be paid, threats to inform her family about her prostitution activities, threats to harass or harm herself, her family or children if the woman does not comply to their demands. Deportation certainly does not put an end to the fear of reprisals, whereby the woman is not only risking her own safety but also the safety of her family.

Fear of Reprisals

If the woman reports the case to the police—either voluntarily or because she is arrested as an illegal alien—she takes a tremendous risk. Even in the Netherlands, where a woman is entitled to a temporary residence permit if she is willing to testify in court, she loses the right to stay the moment the case is settled and she is not needed anymore as a witness. Expulsion means that she will be at the mercy of traffickers again, without anybody to protect her. Pressing charges also means a higher risk

that her history will get known at home, for instance when the criminal investigation involves the gathering of information in her home country. During the time that a woman is under control of her traffickers, in most cases she is continuously told what they would do to her if she dared to escape or go to the police. These threats are no jokes. They do not lose their effect when the police get involved, even if the police are understanding and motivated to support her. Family and children at home are also an easy target for reprisals. Trafficking in women is an internationally organized crime. Women realize very clearly that the power of the national police stops at the border, but the power of trafficking networks does not.

Network–Like Structure

Often trafficking in women finds [its] place in a network-like structure. In general, the women are only familiar with a part of the criminal network. It is possible that several women are in the same network without knowing each other, or without dealing with the same members of the network. However, they are aware of the fact that the people who are controlling them form part of a larger network. This is a very frightening thing. As was said to one woman after a vain attempt to escape: "Remember, there is no use in trying to escape. I have people everywhere to watch you. You don't know them, but they know you." Sometimes women are used against each other. One woman, for instance, is used to instruct or control other women in exchange for privileges, such as a bit more freedom of movement or the possibility of sending money home. Women are given false information about each other or played against each other. In this way a web of disinformation, insecurity and fear is woven around them. They are not in the position to freely exchange information with women trapped in the same network. Through this system of disinformation women can imagine a completely false notion of the position of other women involved. In the case of a criminal investigation, this can lead to the dismissal of the case for reason of contradictory statements.

Survival Strategies

The situation of extreme dependency in which victims of trafficking often find themselves is comparable to situations in which people are kept hostage. One survival strategy in such a situation is to try to protect yourself by trying to appease the persons who control you, to adapt or to anticipate their wishes. Survival strategies of women will then be directed towards influencing individuals in the network instead of trying to escape. Most women learn very quickly that open resistance is not the wisest course to follow.

Position as Prostitute

All women involved in sex work are very aware of the prevailing attitudes towards prostitutes. This is one of the reasons why they do not want other people to know that they work or have worked as prostitutes. At STV, we have become very aware of these kinds of prejudices, for instance through the distinction that is made between "innocent" and "guilty" victims. People, including police officers, prosecutors and judges, can easily identify with women who comply to the stereotype of the naive and innocent victim, unwittingly forced into prostitution. But the moment a woman has worked as a prostitute or wants to continue to do so, or even when she just stands up for herself, compassion turns into indifference or outright hostility. Common opinion holds that once a prostitute, a woman loses all her rights and is no longer entitled to protection against violence, exploitation, abuse, blackmail, and being held prisoner. Unfortunately, these attitudes are all too familiar for the women involved. In addition to the reasons mentioned above, this also explains their lack of motivation to report to the police. A decision to report to the authorities is always based on the conviction that you have certain rights and that you have a claim to protection in case of violation of these rights. There is no need to say that these attitudes towards prostitutes work clearly in favor of the criminal networks and very much against the women.

CONCLUSIONS AND STRATEGIES

If we want to develop policies to combat trafficking and to support victims, it is essential to be aware of the fact that we are dealing with women who have many good reasons to be scared and who are under massive pressure. They find themselves in a very vulnerable situation and have to survive in unpredictable and insecure circumstances. They will have to continually consider which strategy renders them the best chance to survive. This does not mean they are weak, stupid or passive victims. On the contrary, a great many of the women who become a victim of trafficking end up in this position because they do not want to accept the limitations of their situation, because they are enterprising, courageous and willing to take initiatives to improve their living conditions and those of their families. But somewhere in this process they get trapped.

We can distinguish between two types of strategies to combat trafficking in women. On the one hand there are repressive strategies, including more restrictive immigration policies, more penalization and stronger and more effective prosecution. Repressive strategies have a strong tendency to end up working against women instead of in their favor, for example, by restricting women's freedom of movement or by using women as witnesses for combating organized crime in the interest of the State without allowing them the corresponding protection. At the same time, these repressive measures are the most attractive for governments. They fit very nicely with State interests and supply them with a tidy set of arguments: "Close the border and deport illegal women, and the trafficking in women will end." A noble intention that nobody would dare to contradict, yet for all the reasons presented above, it is highly problematic.

On the other hand there are strategies that aim to strengthen the rights of the women involved, as women, as female migrants, as female migrant workers and as female migrant sex workers. To prevent trafficking, to offer trafficked women genuine support and to improve their position and that of women, in general, the interests of the women concerned should form the basis for advocacy work and political campaigning. Support strategies will have to be directed towards empowering women at all stages of the trafficking process. Action should be directed towards enabling them to take back control over their lives and towards facilitating their ability to speak up for their own rights. All the strategies must be based on the recognition of women's right to self-determination and to choose—on non-stigmatization and non-victimization. This approach clearly starts at the other end, to strengthen the rights of the women involved, as women, as female migrants and as female migrant sex workers. It does not support any repressive measures if the rights of the women involved are not at the same time defined and protected, whether it be as witnesses or as workers. This is the hard and slow way, but I am deeply convinced that it is the only way that will work in the end.

DISCUSSION QUESTIONS

1. Define trafficking. Explain how and why, according to Wijers, it is inaccurate to think of trafficking as limited to prostitution.
2. Compare and contrast the conditions and consequences of trafficking with those of slavery.
3. In chapter 4 ("Tenuous Borders: Girls Transferred to Adult Courts") Gaarder and Belknap discuss girls' and women's pathways to crime. In this chapter, Wijers describes women's pathways to victimization which begin with crossing national borders to find work and often end in sex work. In what ways are the pathways to crime and to sex work (which is a crime in the United States) similar in these two analyses? In what ways are they different?
4. Wijers describes the various state policies with regard to prostitution: prohibition, regulation, abolition, and decriminalization. She tells us that the U.S. policy is one of prohibition; the policy of most European countries is abolition; and the approach that best deals with the harsh consequences of these policies is decriminalization.
    - Define each of the four possible state policies.
    - Describe their positive and negative effects on trafficked women.
    - Explain why Wijers suggests that only the last, decriminalization, will solve the problems associated with prostitution in countries like the United States.
    - How do you feel about her solution?
5. What changes in public attitudes would be necessary before countries could protect migrant sex workers by labor laws rather than treat them as criminals?
6. Wijers argues for support strategies that will empower women who have been trafficked. However, in this post–9/11 era, countries have been closing their borders to immigrants and turning back would-be migrants. How can these two separate approaches be reconciled?

REFERENCES

Doezema, Jo, and Jo Bindman. 1997. *Redefining Prostitution as Sex Work on the International Agenda.* London: Anti-Slavery International.

Human Rights Standards for the Treatment of Trafficked Persons. 1999. Foundation against Trafficking in Women, International Human Rights Law Group, Global Alliance against Trafficking in Women.

Human Rights and Trafficking in Persons: A Handbook. Bangkok: Global Alliance against Trafficking in Women (GAATW) 2001. http://www.inet.co.th/org/gaatw

Kempadoo, Kamala, and Jo Doezema, eds. 1998. *Global Sexworkers: Rights, Resistance, and Redefinition.* New York/ London: Routledge.

Moving the Whore Stigma. 1997. Bangkok: Global Alliance against Trafficking in Women (GAATW).

Pheterson, Gail. 1996. *The Prostitution Prism.* Amsterdam: Amsterdam University.

Wijers, Marjan. 2000. European Union Policies on Trafficking in Women. In *Gender Policies in the EU* (Studies in the European Union, Vol. I), ed. Mariagrazia Rossilli. New York: Peter Lang.

Wijers, Marjan, and Lin Lap-Chew. 1999. *Trafficking in Women, Forced Labour and Slavery-like Practices in Marriage, Domestic Labour and Prostitution.* Report of an international investigation on the request of the UN Special Rapporteur on Violence against Women, Utrecht: GAATW/STV, April 1997/rev. ed.

WEBSITES

Global Alliance against Trafficking in Women: http://www.inet.co.th/org/gaatw

Stop Traffic: http://www.stop-traffic.org

International Human Rights Law Group: http://www.hrlawgroup.org/initiatives/trafficking_persons

Anti-Slavery International: www.antislavery.org

Network of Sex Work Projects: http://www.nswp.org

Office of the High Commissioner on Human Rights: http://www.unhcr.ch

Mr. A. de Graaf Foundation, Dutch Institute for Prostitution Issues: http://www.mr.graaf.nl

Chapter 28

Dreams Ending in Nightmares:
Many Immigrant Women, Girls Trapped in Sex Industry

Newsday

ABSTRACT

In the last chapter, Wijers provides a theoretical framework and description of some of the problems faced by women who are exploited as they migrate to other countries in an attempt to make a better life. This chapter is a *Newsday* article from March 11, 2001, that reports on the actual experiences of different women caught in this web in the United States as well as in Western democracies in Europe: women whose dreams end in nightmares. Although trafficking of women into Asia and Latin America has gone on for many years, trafficking into Europe and the United States has only recently become more visible. Some observers believe that the influx of white women into the sex industry has led to renewed interest on the part of the United Nations and several governments in stopping trafficking. Further, experts maintain that the smuggling of women worldwide has accelerated as a result of the breakup of the Soviet Union and the rush to privatization in the Eastern European countries, which led to widespread unemployment. The risk for smugglers is low because few sex trafficking cases are actually prosecuted in the United States or in other countries.

The terms *smuggling* and *trafficking* are used interchangeably by professionals who work in this field; both terms refer to the transporting and selling of people by means of fraud or coercion in order to exploit their labor. This definition is very close to the one used by Wijers in chapter 27. In many cases, women agree to be smuggled into another country for what they believe is "honest work" (in restaurants or in homes of people wanting domestic workers, for example), but in other cases women know in advance that they have agreed to work in brothels. The High Commission on Refugees from the United Nations found that foreign women working in brothels in Bosnia were unwilling to leave their jobs even after advocates and officials approached them. This refusal of help indicates the hopeless nature of these women's lives and the terrible circumstances that they face in their effort to support themselves and their dependents.

Yet, virtually all the trafficked women—those who willingly go to another country and those tricked into leaving their home country—are eventually exploited. They suffer intimidation, abuse, and physical harm. In this current age of globalization, the economic marginalization of large groups of women from many countries raises serious issues about the ability of many governments to provide an economic structure and social stability essential for people to live a decent life. (For a discussion of globalization and its impacts, see Sudbury, chap. 12). Widespread victimization most often affects specific groups or classes. In the case of trafficking, the inevitable victims are all too often poor women from poor countries.

From Flushing massage parlors and Times Square strip clubs to shacks in rural Florida and brothels along the Serbian-Bosnian border, the trafficking of immigrants into the global sex trade has created a human tide that carries hundreds of thousands of women and children from their homelands each year. It is a migration fueled by the age-old immigrant dream of a better life. But in this exodus, the migrants are destined to serve, willingly or unwillingly, in a growing underground economy.

"It is one of the major human rights violations and crimes stretching over the world," said Sen. Hillary Rodham Clinton (D-N.Y.), who helped bring the issue to prominence in the Clinton administration, ". . . as serious a problem as trafficking in drugs."

The poverty that underlies the crime is clear to "Tony," who manages several women from China's Fujian province working in a Manhattan massage parlor: "They all come, about 90 percent, for the U.S. dollar because of the poverty back home. . . ."

The price is clear to Maria Isabel Chalanda Pio, a Mexican teenager held for months in a Florida brothel: "They made us work as long as they wanted. There were up to 25 men, more in a night . . . I had to do what they said. I had to do what they wanted. They paid $20 and we got $3."

And to Tatana Poharala, a Czech woman lured into working in a Times Square peep show. "I needed money for an apartment and I needed money to pay for my studies," she said. "They said

they would pay for the airline ticket and I would repay them with the money I earned in New York. I found out that it was not what they described in Czech Republic."

The rising tide—especially the flood of women from the battered economies of former Soviet bloc nations—has begun to focus serious attention on the smuggling of immigrants for sexual exploitation. Up to 175,000 women a year were trafficked to various countries from Eastern Europe, Russia and other former Soviet republics in recent years, some migration experts have estimated.

"What happened in Europe was so explosive," said Anita Botti, senior adviser on trafficking at the U.S. State Department. "That was the precipitating factor. It's kind of like opening up Pandora's box and now you can't close it."

A year-long investigation of the issue by *Newsday* —which included interviews with trafficked women, law enforcement officials and experts here and abroad, as well as a review of court records and government documents—found a staggering variety of schemes to import and sexually use women from around the world in sexual businesses. The operations range from mom-and-pop smugglers to sophisticated Russian, Eastern European and Asian crime syndicates.

The locations where these businesses flourish range from stable Western European nations like Italy and Belgium, to troubled regions like Kosovo and Macedonia, to Israel and other nations of the Mideast, to Asian cities like Bangkok and Tokyo. Closer to home, the list reads like a North American travelogue: Atlanta, Chicago, Los Angeles, Miami, Washington, D.C., Toronto and Vancouver, British Columbia. New York is prominent on the list.

In the past several years, law enforcement officials have unmasked Czech mobsters stabling women in Flushing houses and using them in strip clubs in New York and Miami, Mexican pimps and enslavers using imprisoned women to service migrant workers in Florida, Russian hustlers running a brothel out of a Manhattan apartment, Vietnamese men managing Mexican prostitutes in Los Angeles, and Thai smugglers bringing in Chinese, Thai and Malaysian women to brothels in Atlanta and Manhattan. In Berkeley, Calif., a major landlord last week pleaded guilty to bringing in girls from his Indian hometown for his own sexual use.

Last month, federal prosecutors in San Francisco indicted 19 people in a continuing probe of the Asian sex networks that have helped staff brothels in San Francisco, New York and other major U.S. cities. In this case, the women, mostly Malaysians, were brought in to Atlanta with photo-substituted visas and passports and then sent around the country, according to federal officials.

Authorities in Colorado and Indiana even uncovered a case in which U.S. men from several states visited an Acapulco hotel to have sex with Mexican boys and, in some cases, arranged to have them smuggled into the United States.

Far more often, however, the cases involve girls or women. Whether they come from Budapest or Bangkok, Prague or Pusan, the fields of Mexico or the farms of Malaysia, many of these cases are bound by common threads, *Newsday's* reporting shows.

Recruiters, often with ties to organized crime, lure women with promises of cash or escape to a better life.

Sometimes, sex work is the central aspect of the deal. Other times, the prospect of sex work doesn't even arise in the enticement. Instead, recruiters promise domestic or restaurant work.

Often, recruiters can honestly offer the women more money in a day than they can make in a month in their home countries, even if that means scores of sex partners, keeping count of used condom wrappers for their pay or letting strangers in a Times Square club grope them in accord with a posted fee schedule for each body part.

Once they strike an agreement, a journey of thousands of miles begins. The women are often able to cross into their destination country with ease. Sometimes, they employ "coyotes" to slip them across the U.S.-Mexico border. Other times, they hide in the belly of a cargo ship or the trunk of a car. Or they are given phony passports and visas. In the United States, many women enter on tourist visas. Canadian officials estimate that Toronto alone has at least 50 immigrant-smuggling groups, which carry some 5,000 people a year into the United States.

Once here, the smuggling debt—as high as $40,000—must be repaid. Threats are common against the women and their families back home. Isolation, enforced by language problems, is common; so is fear of law enforcement authorities, who may jail or deport the women if they learn about them.

As a result, women who thought they were coming to work as dishwashers or baby-sitters end up as indentured strippers or prostitutes. Women who knew they were coming to strip or work in brothels often find out their "debt" is higher than they expected. Either way, the women often find themselves in a form of "debt servitude" working to pay a debt that can never be satisfied or that takes many years.

"If they don't like it, what are they going to do?" said a high-ranking official of the Immigration and Naturalization Service. "They don't know anybody. Their passports are being held. If they can't pay their fee, they will work much longer."

Some cases, like the Mexican teenagers held in Florida brothels, clearly involve sexual enslavement. But many others from New York City and around the country are not so clear cut. They fall along what Amy O'Neill Richard, in her 1999 analysis of trafficking done for the CIA, described as a "continuum of exploitation and abuse." Often more subtle psychological pressures and manipulation—such as heavy debts or social isolation—keep the women off balance and under control. In a couple of Queens [New York] massage parlors investigated by *Newsday,* the women generally had debts but did not seem to be coerced and appeared free to travel at will.

In New York City, sex businesses that rely on illegal migrants are common, and so entrenched that they have spawned a spin-off economy, several sources in the sex industry told *Newsday*. In Queens, brothels rely on some car services, saunas, nail salons and other legitimate businesses for a variety of services and customer referrals, according to lawyers and women familiar with the prostitution businesses. Security guards from Hispanic-run brothels in Queens also guard Korean prostitution networks, which in turn are affiliated with similar operations in New Jersey, according to police and sources in the Korean community.

Despite the mass of anecdotal information, the full scope of trafficking is still largely uncharted. It exists in a kind of hazy netherworld, below the radar of most law enforcement agencies, including the New York City Police Department.

Each year, more than 90,000 people are arrested on prostitution-related charges in the United States, and about 250,000 people are caught being smuggled into the country. Each group can be expected to contain a sizable number of trafficked women, experts say. But only about a dozen major sex trafficking cases have been prosecuted by federal officials in the United States since 1995.

Within the past year-and-a-half, however, a series of initiatives have attempted to deal more vigorously with the problem.

A federal law signed by President Bill Clinton in October [2000] doubles the maximum prison penalty to 20 years for some who traffic in migrants, and provides life sentences in some cases that involve enslavement. The law also creates a new visa—"T" for trafficking—that could allow up to 5,000 victims a year to remain in the United States and seek permanent residency if they cooperate with prosecutors. The first case under the new law, involving Russian women and girls allegedly forced to dance nude in an Alaskan strip club, is to go to trial soon.

A new interagency task force, a migrant smuggling and trafficking coordination center, is being set up in Washington, D.C., and funded by the State Department to share and coordinate law enforcement intelligence among federal agencies and with

other nations, in an attempt to make prosecution easier.

In December, 81 members of the United Nations, including the United States, signed a protocol that is aimed at getting nations to pass their own anti-trafficking laws and to help victims. China, Ukraine and the Czech Republic, each a source of many trafficked women, have not yet signed, however, and the protocol still must be ratified by 40 nations before it takes effect.

In the United States, these efforts have yet to filter down to local law enforcement.

And moves to address trafficking remain hamstrung by a wide divergence of opinion in the United States and abroad over the scope of the problem, the solutions and even the definition of trafficking.

Federal and local law enforcement officials in New York, Washington and elsewhere said in interviews that the nascent effort to crack down on sex trafficking has been handicapped by political indifference, policies that punish or discourage victims from helping police, a lack of resources and a lack of coordination. No government agency or any of the many non-profit groups has had anything approaching a comprehensive trafficking case database.

"One of the problems agents around the country have confronted is that lack of information sharing," said Kevin Gilligan, special agent in-charge of the visa fraud branch of the State Department's bureau of diplomatic security.

For the past year, the bureau has been building its first computer system to track trafficking cases, with an emphasis on visa fraud, but to date the database remains in its infancy, a bureau special agent said.

Conflict also can stem from the different ways U.S. agencies view undocumented women found working in the sex trade.

The INS' "focus is on deporting the women once they are discovered," according to the trafficking report done for the CIA in 1999. "Less emphasis is placed on the exploitative settings these women find themselves in."

Russ Bergeron, an INS spokesman, said that typically, if INS knows of pending criminal cases, it will not deport women who may be victims or witnesses. "It's possible that some potential witnesses have been deported inadvertently," he said.

In confronting sex trafficking, one particular concern is that it "contributes to the spread of HIV and AIDS," according to the trafficking analysis done for the CIA, because the women are sometimes required to have unprotected sex. "Particularly disturbing," the report said, "is a case uncovered by INS where at least one trafficker was purchasing HIV-positive females because he found them to be cheap labor and since he believed they had nothing to live for."

Given the low risk of prosecution, the huge potential for profit and the lack of economic opportunity in many parts of the world, the consensus among officials at the INS, CIA, and State Department is that trafficking will continue to increase.

Richard Schifter, now retired, served as a special adviser to former Secretary of State Madeleine Albright on law enforcement issues.

"It is growing," Schifter said. "It is increasingly serious."

One reason, experts say, is that the fall of the Iron Curtain and the rush to privatize the economies of Eastern Europe has meant large-scale unemployment in some countries. Women in particular are desperate for work, said Madeleine Rees, an official with the United Nations in Bosnia, an area into which many women are trafficked.

"We have a readily exploitable group," Rees said of the women in Eastern Europe.

Others say the women's European identity got Western nations' attention in a way that the trafficking of women from Asia and Latin America never did.

"It's no longer an issue that deals just with Third World countries," said Kamala Kempadoo, head of the Center for Gender Development Studies at the University of the West Indies. "White women have added a racialized dimension there as well. Policy makers are that much more concerned. That's not the only aspect, but it certainly has pushed it."

Whatever the impetus for the new initiatives, there are deep divisions among feminists and human rights advocates about how to handle the issue.

Some feel that migrants should be protected from exploitation, whether their work involves sex or sewing clothes in a sweatshop, and efforts should focus on improving their economic chances at home.

Others think all prostitution should be stamped out. They argue that it is never truly voluntary and liken it to slavery, saying that people are not allowed to sell themselves into slavery even if they want to.

Even use of the term "trafficking" has sparked discussion. Human rights activists say it refers to the transportation and sale of people through fraud or coercion in order to exploit their labor.

That is the essence of the definition used in the UN protocol. Other immigration experts, however, note that illegal immigrants are almost always smuggled and exploited in some way, even if they don't fit the definition of trafficking. In practical terms, they say, there is no distinction between "trafficking" and "smuggling" of immigrants.

"Many smuggled aliens willingly participate [in the crime]," noted Susan Martin, director of the Institute for the Study of International Migration at Georgetown University. "Others are duped or coerced. All are vulnerable to exploitation, abuse and violence, making smuggling—and its most pernicious form, trafficking in humans for sexual and other exploitation—a barrier to the protection of migrant workers and their families."

In Bosnia, a study done last year by the UN Office of the High Commission on Refugees found that most of the foreign women working in clubs and brothels were not interested in leaving their jobs, even after they were approached by police or human rights advocates.

"It was clear that some of these women's participation in the sex trade was entirely voluntary, though it was also certain that a large number of the women were not so much content with their circumstances as they were either intimidated or facing worse prospects at home," according to the report by the UN office.

A world away in Queens, interviews with nearly a dozen Korean women in the sex trade revealed similar attitudes. In general, the women had dismal job prospects at home and appeared willing to work as prostitutes here in hopes of saving enough money to have a better life.

Those attitudes underscore what experts like Martin say is really at the heart of the larger global migration picture: the escape from economic hardship and disadvantage.

"The victims are from poor families. There are few if any economic opportunities for them in the country they're coming from," said an official with Casa Alianza, a Costa Rica–based nonprofit organization that aids street children in those countries. "They're trafficking poverty."

They're also trafficking hope—the age-old immigrant hope for something better.

Juana Toga Cruz says her 14-year-old daughter was lured to leave Mexico by the promise of well-paid domestic work and ended up as a captive in a brothel ring in Florida.

"The truth is, we wouldn't let her," the mother said, "but she got excited and said, 'Mama, I'm going, so I can pull us up.' "

DISCUSSION QUESTIONS

1. According to this *Newsday* article, what are the causes of trafficking in women? What suggestions would you make to solve this problem that go *beyond* the criminal justice response, in other words, that get at *root causes* of trafficking?

2. Does the recent U.S. federal law described in this chapter meet Wijer's requirements of government support for migrant women described in Chapter 28?

3. According to this chapter, some feminists and human rights activists hold contradictory views about how to best deal with trafficking in women for sex. Some activists think that migrants should be protected from exploitation whether their work involves sex or not; economic conditions should be improved in the women's home countries so the women would not be forced to migrate in the first place. Other activists believe that all prostitution is involuntary, like slavery, and should be stamped out; prostitution is degrading and dehumanizing, and people should not be allowed to sell themselves into slavery even if they want to. What are the pros and cons of each position? And what is your own position?

4. How can countries best address the trafficking problem? To what degree must this effort be an international coalition effort?

5. Public discussion and recognition that trafficking of immigrants is a serious form of victimization of women has been very slow to surface. Likewise, many criminologists have been slow in addressing this problem. Identify several reasons for this delay in recognition.

6. This article notes that trafficking in women is really about "trafficking poverty." What does this comment mean? What do you think of this comment?

Part 4

Women Workers in the Criminal Justice System

Women who work in the criminal justice system is the topic of part 4. The chapters in this section discuss workers in the various subsystems that make up the criminal justice system: courts, police, corrections, victim services, and criminal justice education. The focus is on the functions of women from diverse racial, ethnic, and class backgrounds within the criminal justice system, the specific occupational settings in which women work, and the structural changes in occupations. The readings examine the degree of acceptance of diverse groups of women workers, the numbers of women along racial and ethnic lines who work in many of the traditionally white male occupations, and the promotion of women to policy-making positions.

As women began to work in the criminal justice system in increased numbers in the 1970s, the prevalent thinking then was that as their numbers grew they would, in time, be able to influence and change criminal justice policy and practices that adversely affect the disadvantaged—particularly women offenders, women victims and survivors of crime, women in prison, and women working throughout the many criminal justice agencies. The chapters in this section illustrate that progress has definitely been made, but much remains to be done, especially for those women who work at the lowest levels of the system.

Even today, some women who work in the criminal justice system accept the dominant ideology

WEBSITES

The following websites contain material on women working in the criminal justice system. New websites are continuously being developed while at the same time others disappear. Check with a search engine, such as Google at **www.google.com,** to locate additional information. Insert a key word (policewoman) or phrase (women judges) or organization in order to locate additional references.

General References

Statistics on (women and men) personnel in the criminal justice system can be found in Section 1 of *The Sourcebook on Criminal Justice Statistics* at **www.albany.edu/sourcebook**

Information about women and work generally and about women working in the criminal justice system specifically can be found at The Feminist Majority at **www.feminist.org**

Legal Occupations

Deborah Rhodes. 2001. *The Unfinished Agenda: Women and the Legal Profession.* ABA Commission on Women in the Profession. Can be found at the American Bar Association website at **www.abanet.org**

National Council of Juvenile and Family Court Judges can be found at **http://www.ncjfcj.unr.edu/**

International Association of Prosecutors with international office links can be found at **http://www.iap.nl.com**

National Association of Women Judges can be found at **http://www.nawj.org/**

Association of Black Women Lawyers of New Jersey can be found at **http://www.abwlnj.org/**

(see Toobin, chap. 30), taking punitive stances toward all offenders or blaming victims. Therefore, merely adding more women participants to any part of the criminal justice system may not, in and of itself, improve conditions for women. Further, women themselves do not comprise one single category; rather, they differ by race, ethnicity, class, and sexual orientation, all of which are factors to consider in an assessment of the impact of greater numbers of women working in the criminal justice system.

Of course, there have been significant changes in the law and in some criminal justice practices as a result of sustained effort and actions by diverse feminist groups, individuals, and their allies. Following is a brief look at what has been accomplished and what problems still exist.

THE INCLUSION OF WOMEN WORKERS IN THE CRIMINAL JUSTICE SYSTEM—IMPACT ON OFFENDERS, PRISONERS, VICTIMS, AND SURVIVORS

Serious practical as well as moral costs to this nation's democratic principles have resulted from the past exclusion of white women and racial and ethnic minority women and men from the practice of law and related endeavors. When few women worked in either law, the courts, or the criminal justice system, women victims and survivors as well as offenders and prisoners frequently did not receive equal treatment under the law. This inequality was and is significantly exacerbated for poor women, especially poor women of color. Inequities ranged from failure to take domestic violence seriously (see Browne, chap. 21) to overincarceration of women (see Owen, chap. 10) to discounting women's role as court witnesses (see Schafran, chap. 29) to discriminatory employment practices in all parts of the criminal justice system (discussed in several chapters here in part 4).

Women undergraduates are now attracted to the fields of law and criminology in growing numbers, in part because of the influence of the women's and civil rights movements. There is, too, a growing awareness on the part of employers of the need for more women and greater diversity in these fields. Today's students become tomorrow's professionals, pursuing careers in the law, prosecutorial, and defense fields and in local, state, and federal criminal justice agencies as well as in academia. The presence of larger numbers of women, many of whom are committed to social change, has been translated into improvements in some of the most tenacious discriminatory practices within the legal system. These changes are found, most notably, in federal legislation pertaining to equal employment opportunity, equal access to education, and equal pay. Other changes in the law are specific to women offenders and victims of crime: repeal of state laws that required longer sentences for women than men under the guise of rehabilitation (Armstrong 1982),* changes in rape laws to facilitate convictions (Spohn and Horney 1991), and the emergence of laws defining domestic violence (Schneider 2000) and stalking as crimes (*Stalking and Domestic Violence* 2001). The growing availability of women and minority lawyers interested in litigating in court to achieve change also cannot be discounted in this list of legal changes that are protective of women's rights (Epstein 1983, 1993; Schneider 2000).

Any victory for equal protection under the law is a result of a long chain of events that frequently starts with feminist, class-conscious, and antiracist political activity to gain economic, social, and political equity. As the women's movement and other movements for social justice grow, they generate interest in socially structured causes and personal consequences of women's criminality and women's victimization. These interests attract women and minority students to criminology and the law, and this development leads to professionals who build new theories of crime and social justice to better understand how and why women break the law, are victimized, and are empowered.

---

*See Armstrong (1982) for a discussion of the Muncy Act in Pennsylvania, whereby courts had the power to sentence women, but not men, without fixing a minimum or maximum period of imprisonment under the rationale that women could be rehabilitated but that the time necessary for reform was unpredictable.

Other Criminal Justice Career Areas

The Division on Women and Crime of the American Society of Criminology has information on careers in academia at
www.marshall.edu/divwmncrm/

The American College of Forensic Examiners has information on careers as a forensic examiner. Can be found at
www.acfe.com/02.23.02/main.php/

Equal Employment Issues

National Association of Blacks in Criminal Justice can be found at
http://www.nabcj.org/

Resources on lesbian politics, law, and policy—workplace and employment topics—can be found at
www.gaypoliticsandlaw.com

Information on women and the law as it pertains to equal employment opportunities in the Netherlands can be found at
http://www.enp.nl/

National Organization for Women (NOW) contains wide-ranging feminist issues, including legislative updates, at
http://www.now.org/

Women's Justice Centre (in Spanish) for issues concerning Mexican women can be found at
www.justicewomen.com/links.html

One result of the presence of female and minority criminologists has been that they and some of their students become forces for change (see Wilson and Moyer, chap. 36). The emergence of more professionals also leads to a better understanding of social processes as they pertain to crime, victimization, and survival as well as a recognition that legal change does not always result in social change. Constant monitoring, the creation of procedural guidelines, professional and public education, and basic structural changes in society are all essential for meaningful social change. Many criminal justice professional and paraprofessional women and minorities continue to work for fair treatment of women offenders and prisoners who are disproportionately poor and minority. Fair treatment, not always accorded to all men let alone all women, is essential for the criminal justice system, the essence of which should be to provide equitable and just treatment for all offenders, prisoners, victims, and survivors. Unfortunately, the issue of fair treatment remains problematic in a system organized to maintain the status quo and the existing hierarchical social order.

HOW DOES THE INCLUSION OF WOMEN WORKERS AFFECT CRIMINAL JUSTICE PRACTITIONERS?

Women from diverse social locations have experienced a great deal of difficulty in gaining access to occupations that traditionally have employed mostly white men. The criminal justice system, with its many and varied positions (police officer, correctional officer, counselor, probation and parole officer, forensic psychologist, social worker, judge, prosecutor, defense attorney), has always had a number of formidable barriers to equal employment and equal treatment. Even after discrimination in employment in the public sector was outlawed in the United States by federal and most state laws,* the underlying structural and attitudinal changes necessary for people to abide by the law in good faith and thereby treat women fairly have come about very slowly. Moreover, in the U.S. system of justice, each instance of employment discrimination requires a separate complaint, sometimes on behalf of a class of persons but often involving a single individual. Such actions are always slow and often personally painful.

While the judicial branch appears to have made important advances in the past 30 years, still few women are to be found in such prestigious positions as judgeships. Further, the current dominance of the conservative political agenda in the United States is eroding many of the gains. Women comprise more than 50 percent of law school students but do not account for half of all lawyers and only 15 percent of federal judges, 10 percent of law school deans, and five percent of partners of large law firms (*Unfinished Agenda* 2001, p. 5). Women of color account for only 3 percent of the legal profession (Mishra 2001). Schafran in chapter 29 makes the point that women lawyers have successfully made court bias and discrimination visible issues. As a result, argues Schafran, the courts have

*Equal Pay Act and Equal Employment Opportunity provisions of the Civil Rights Act of 1964, which is found at 78 Stat. 253, 42 U.S.C. 2000e et seq. (1964).

received more intense scrutiny on gender bias than any other branch of the criminal justice system; there are state and federal task forces devoted to this issue throughout the United States. Moreover, the last decade has seen an increase in task forces studying racial and ethnic bias as well as gender bias in the courts. Yet the Equal Rights Amendment, first proposed in 1923 in the United States and reintroduced in Congress in 1970, has never passed. Thus, the U.S. Constitution still does not contain a statement that men and women are equal before the law. And it was not until 1975 that the U.S. Supreme Court prohibited states from excluding women from juries. Most recently, the Turkish parliament revised its civil code so as to formally recognize women's equality; the new code took effect as of January 1, 2002 (Feminist Majority Foundation Online 2001). And the Congress in Brazil approved a legal code in 2001 that, for the first time in the country's history, makes women equal to men in the eyes of the law—this approval came after 26 years of debate (Rohter 2001).

There is a serious underrepresentation of minority judges. According to Judge Leon Higginbotham, "judicial pluralism breeds judicial legitimacy. . . . Judicial homogeneity, by contrast, is . . . a deterrent to, rather than a promoter of, equal justice for all" (1992, A21). In recent years there has been some gain in women and minority federal judges. Under the first President George Bush (1989–1992), U.S. district court judges were 80.4 percent male and 19.6 percent female and were 89 percent white, 6.8 percent black, and 4.0 percent Hispanic; there were no Asian judges. Under President Bill Clinton (1993–2000), U.S. district court judges who were women increased to 28.5 percent, blacks to 17.4 percent, Hispanics to 5.9 percent, and Asians to 1.3 percent. Similar increases occurred in U.S. Courts of Appeals judgeships (*Sourcebook of Criminal Justice Statistics* 2000). Under President George W. Bush, son of the first President George Bush, there has been an increase in the number of cabinet members and judges who are women and people of color. However, most of these appointments have gone to politically conservative and usually wealthy individuals who do not represent the vast majority of women, minorities, and the poor or even the middle class. (For example, see the discussion on conservative female judges by Toobin in chap. 30.)

The legal profession itself has been a major source of many improvements for women in this field, particularly white women. This advancement is due as much to the changing nature of work and the rationalization of labor in the legal profession as it is to the increase in the number of educated women (Baron 1983; Spurr 1990; Hagan et al. 1991). Women continue to enter law school in greater numbers than ever before. In 1967, 4 percent of all law degrees were awarded to women. By 2001, 49 percent of all law students were women (American Bar Association 2002). After graduation some women who choose to work in the public sector rather than for private law firms are employed as public prosecutors and as public defenders and in other criminal justice agencies such as corrections and law enforcement. Black women in particular are more likely to work in the public sector at both nonprofessional and professional jobs, including as lawyers (E. Higginbotham 1987). But while the number of white women has increased in law schools and in law offices to an extent unanticipated 20 years ago, the inadequate representation of members of racial and ethnic minorities continues, with women of color very seriously disadvantaged. There had been almost 15 years of steady growth in the number of minority students graduating from law school, but that increase stopped in the late 1990s. In 2000, all minorities comprised 19.4 percent of all graduates, *down* slightly from the previous year. Almost 33 percent of all Americans are members of racial or ethnic minority groups (Glater 2001).

As an example of the simultaneous progress of and resistance to women and minorities who enter the legal profession and rise to partner, consider the following. In 2000, women in law firms made approximately $20,000 less annually than men did. Women now comprise 30 percent of all lawyers but only 15 percent of law firm partners, 15 percent of federal judges, and 10 percent of law school deans (*The Unfinished Agenda* 2000, 14). The point is clear: despite large numerical gains of white women and lesser gains of racial and ethnic minority women and men in the legal profession, the field is still dominated by white men.

THE ORGANIZATION OF PART 4

Chapters 29 and 30 focus on women in the judicial and legal fields and provide more detail on points raised in this introduction. In chapter 29, "Overwhelming Evidence: Gender and Race Bias in the Courts," Schafran describes women's efforts to educate and sensitize to gender bias those men and women who work in the courts. Women lawyers have successfully made visible issues out of court bias and gender discrimination. In contrast, Toobin identifies a troubling reality in chapter 30 ("Women in Black: Are Female Judges More Compassionate?"): not all women who enter the law and rise to judgeships have an interest in social change, embrace a feminist perspective as an influence on the judiciary, or are more compassionate than men.

In the fields of policing and corrections, gender integration and the opportunity to impact public policy have been more overtly resisted than in the legal world. Women police continue to have token status because they represent less than 15 percent of all law enforcement officers, as Harrington and Lonsway observe in chapter 32 ("Current Barriers and Future Promise for Women in Policing"). This section includes four chapters on women in policing. Two are chapters that first appeared in the second edition. Each has been updated, and they merit inclusion here because of the timelessness of the material. Chapter 31 by Schulz ("Invisible No More: A Social History of Women in U.S. Policing") provides a comprehensive history of women police in the United States that begins with the first police matrons in the nineteenth century and takes the reader to the present with a discussion of community policing as it relates to women police. The chapter shows how women shaped their police role throughout their history by drawing on outside social forces and, in recent times, by turning to the law to support their determination to work as police officers. The second police chapter from the previous edition of the book is chapter 34 ("The Interactive Effects of Race and Sex on Women Police Officers"), which has become something of a classic in the literature on this topic. It deals with what author

Martin calls the "double whammy" of race and gender: black women police officers, instead of being doubly advantaged as many believe, are doubly disadvantaged because of their and gender. Elsewhere, Martin (1994) has written that black women police officers see themselves as forced to compete with both black men and white women for affirmative action slots.

But even as black women make small gains in a predominantly white male occupation, most face serious harassment on the job, as chapter 32 makes clear. Harrington (a former chief of police in Portland, Oregon) and Lonsway write from firsthand experience about the many barriers that women police still face in the twenty-first century. The authors strongly believe in the value that police women add to law enforcement, citing women's often superior communication skills, their effectiveness in responding to domestic violence calls, their significantly lower record in corruption, and their much better record in not using excessive force.* The fourth chapter on women police, chapter 33 by Susan Miller et al. ("Lesbians in Policing: Perceptions and Work Experiences within the Macho Cop Culture"), addresses the challenges faced by lesbian police officers and the issues surrounding their decision to reveal or hide their sexual orientation. This chapter is important because not only does it portray the difficulties that lesbian officers deal with but it also reveals much about the different working cultures of police departments. The chapter also opens up discussions on the issues of sexual attitudes and sexual orientation that have been too long hidden from discussions of women and work in the criminal justice system.

The emphasis on police in part 4 was deliberate. Women police make up an increasing number of law enforcement officers. They have been studied more thoroughly, perhaps, than any other work group in criminal justice from the early 1970s when researchers began to ask: "Can women do police work successfully?" to today's focus on disparate aspects of the challenges facing women who enter policing. Present-day research is much more sophisticated and objective in its approach than were the early studies of the 1970s and 1980s, which were often biased in that they set out to "prove" that women could (or could not, in some cases) be successful in law enforcement.

Both law enforcement and corrections have attracted a disproportionate number of minority women. According to the National Center for Women and Policing (2002, 10), women now comprise 12.7 percent of all sworn personnel in U.S. police departments and women of color hold 4.8 percent of all positions. Thus, while women of color make up 8.2 percent of the U.S. overall labor force, they make up a far greater proportion of women police officers (i.e., almost two out of five).

---

*A study in Los Angeles from 1990 to 1999 revealed that the city paid out $63.4 million in lawsuits in which male officers were charged with use of excessive force, sexual assault, and domestic assault. By contrast, $2.8 million was paid out for female officers charged with excessive force but no woman was named as a defendant in a sexual assault or domestic violence case (Feminist Majority Foundation Online 2000).

Another important point and telling fact about women police is that the growth in the number of women police officers in the United States has not been reflected in any sizable increase in the number of women in supervisory and administrative positions. Both Harrington and Lonsway (chap. 32) and Martin (chap. 34) discuss this issue. As of 2001, women held only 7.3 percent of the top command jobs, and 87.9 percent of large police agencies reported no women of color in their highest ranks (National Center for Women and Policing 2002, 4). Entry-level positions, thus far, have not translated into many promotions, and women remain shut out from policy making in local and state law enforcement matters. It is not unlikely that the limited success in promotion is related to the structure of policing and the reluctant acceptance of women by male colleagues, supervisors, and high-level administrators. The current situation also reflects the failure of male-dominated police departments to establish necessary mentoring relationships for women's career advancement.

Belknap (chap. 35, "Women in Conflict: An Analysis of Women Correctional Officers") has written an update to her chapter about corrections officers that appeared in the second edition. Like in the policing field, black women in the corrections field are overrepresented in comparison with white women. In fact, this overrepresentation is a phenomenon seen in government employment generally, especially in the lower-level jobs (E. Higginbotham, 1987). Minority workers are attracted to the higher wages and the perceived security and employment protection that government work offers compared with work in the private sector (Sokoloff, Price, and Kuleshnyk 1992; Page 1993; see also Martin, chap. 34). This attraction helps explain the disproportionate number of minority women workers compared with white women workers in policing and corrections. Belknap describes the work challenges that women corrections officers face; she notes that more hostility and harassment of women officers comes from male corrections officers than from male prisoners. Her description of the differences between the working style of women corrections officers and that of men mirrors the qualities of women police officers: better communication skills and less inclination to use physical force.

The two earlier editions of this book focused on the social structural barriers that keep women from entering work positions in the criminal justice system. That issue remains very much alive, but it needs to be expanded to include the extent to which women and racial and ethnic minorities are or are not promoted into management positions in which influence over criminal justice policies is possible. Chapter 36 ("Affirmative Action, Multiculturalism, and Criminology") addresses the foundations of that issue. Wilson and Moyer discuss how college students are prepared for future practitioner positions in criminal justice. The chapter emphasizes the importance of having women and minorities serve as faculty and mentors. Wilson and Moyer raise the possibility that the gradually changing composition of faculty to be more gender, class, and racially and culturally diverse will have a positive impact on the field of criminology and the curriculum by liberalizing a politically conservative discipline and a traditionally conservative student body. Thus, a more radical and diverse curriculum might emerge as more women and minorities join criminology, criminal justice, and law faculties. Such newly composed faculties may prepare future practitioners to question more closely current practices in the criminal justice system and to become critical thinkers and actors concerning issues of crime and social justice. Despite the potential for positive changes, however, Wilson and Moyer are concerned that affirmative action may be practiced by colleges primarily in terms of numbers (i.e., more women and minorities are hired on the faculty) and not in terms of the content of classroom curricula. They also fear that these new faculty members are all too often subtly coerced to fit in intellectually rather than encouraged to transform the existing knowledge base that supports the status quo in the criminal justice system and helps to reproduce conditions of existing social inequality.

Another curricular approach is described by Jurik and Cavender in their addendum to this chapter. They discuss the critical role that feminist and multicultural scholarship has played in the development of an alternative to criminology and criminal justice programs, that is, justice studies programs. Such programs analyze the larger social and historical context of justice and injustice.

This concluding chapter along with its addendum provides an important message to students through the insights it offers into the curriculum that students encounter and the various faculty with whom they study. This chapter adds another dimension to the objectives of this book: it assists students in their education and helps them understand what changes are needed in the future for a more equitable criminal justice system with fairness paramount in all its endeavors.

CONCLUSION

At the time of this writing, the worldwide agenda is focused on domestic and international security and on a weakened economy. In the current conservative political climate, criminal justice positions together with defense jobs are in the forefront of employment. Criminal justice expertise and skills have suddenly gained greater status and heightened importance as the threat of terrorism confronts nations. Entry-level and administrative career opportunities in many of the criminal justice fields will continue to grow in the public sector, giving women and minorities an enhanced role in the public arena. Continued vigilance, however, is needed so that equal employment opportunities remain a high priority for agencies and so that the progressive strengths of both men and women are recognized.

Progress will not have been made if the criminal justice system merely includes more women and minorities; the system must be transformed through the inclusion of *progressive* women and minorities. In short, what is needed is a more just system overall—not simply a more equitable gender and racial distribution in an unjust system. It is not enough for half of the police force and supervisors to be women if those women engage in brutality and corruption. It is not enough for half the judges to be women if those women judges doubt the credibility of women defendants or witnesses merely because they are women. Changes need to be made in the attitudes of criminal justice workers, not just their gender and racial distributions. Of course, criminal justice systems do not change by themselves. The larger societies within which they function have ultimate responsibility for creating a more just and humane world. Only under such conditions will there be dignity and equality within criminal justice systems for all groups of people.

REFERENCES

American Bar Association. 2002. First Year Enrollment in ABA Approved Law Schools 1947–2001. Available at http://www.abanet.org/legaled/statistics/stats.html

Armstrong, Gail. 1982. Females under the Law: "Protected" but Unequal. In *The Criminal Justice System and Women,* ed. Barbara Raffel Price and Natalie J. Sokoloff. New York: Clark Boardman.

Baron, Ava. 1983. Feminization of the Legal Profession— Progress or Proletarianization? *ALSA (American Legal Studies Association) Forum* 7:330–357.

Epstein, Cynthia Fuchs. 1983. *Women in Law.* Garden City, NY: Doubleday.

Epstein, Cynthia Fuchs. 1993. Women in Law: Lifting the Glass Ceiling? *Thesis* 7 (spring):22–27.

Feminist Majority Foundation Online. 2000. Gender Gap in Police Brutality Lawsuits: Men Cost More. September 18. Available at www.feminist.org

Feminist Majority Foundation Online. 2001. Women's Equality Becomes Turkish Law. November 26. Available at www.feminist.org

Glater, Jonathan D. 2001. Few Minorities Rising to Law Partner. The Feminist Majority Foundation Online. August 7.

Hagan, John, Marjorie Zatz, Bruce Arnold, and Fiona Kay. 1991. Culture Capital, Gender and Structural Transformation of Legal Practice. *Law and Society Review* 25(2):239–249.

Higginbotham, Elizabeth. 1987. Employment for Professional Black Women in the Twentieth Century. In *Ingredients for Women's Employment Policy,* ed. Christine Bose and Glenna Spitze, 73–91. Albany: State University of New York.

Higginbotham, Leon A. 1992. The Case of the Missing Black Judges. *New York Times,* July 29, A21.

Martin, Susan E. 1994. "Outsider Within" the Station House: The Impact of Race and Gender on Black Women Police. *Social Problems* 41:383–400.

Mishra, Vaishalee. 2001. Women Lawyers Still Fighting for Equity. Womensforum.com. Available at www.singlemomz.com/news/2001/womenlawyers.shtml

National Center for Women and Policing. 2002. Equality Denied: The Status of Women in Policing: 2001. Available at www.womenandpolicing.org/2002_Status_Report.pdf

Page, Paul. 1993. African-Americans in Executive Branch Agencies. Paper presented at the New York State Political Science Association Meetings, New York City.

Rohter, Larry. 2001. Slow to Yield: Brazil Passes Equal Rights for Its Women. *New York Times,* August 19. Available at www.nytimes.com2001/08/19/international/americas/19BRAZ.html.

Schneider, Elizabeth. 2000. *Battered Women and Feminist Lawmaking.* New Haven, CT: Yale University.

Sokoloff, Natalie J., Barbara Raffel Price, and Irka Kuleshnyk. 1992. A Case Study of Black and White Women Police in an Urban Police Department. *Justice Professional* 6(winter/spring):68–85.

Sourcebook of Criminal Justice Statistics. 2000. U.S. Department of Justice, Bureau of Justice Statistics. Washington, DC: U.S. Government Printing Office.

Spohn, Cassia, and Julie Horney. 1991. The Law Is the Law, But Fair Is Fair: Rape Shield Laws and Officials' Assessments of Sexual History Evidence. *Criminology* 29(1):137–160.

Spurr, Stephen J. 1990. Sex Discrimination in the Legal Profession: A Study of Promotion. *Industrial and Labor Relations Review* 43(April): 406–417.

Stalking and Domestic Violence: Report to Congress. 2001. Violence against Women Office. NCJ-186157. Available at www.ncjrs.org/txtfiles1/ojp.186157.txt

The Unfinished Agenda: Women and the Legal Profession. 2001. Report of the American Bar Association Commission on Women in the Profession. Available at www.abanet.org/women

Chapter 29

Overwhelming Evidence:
Gender and Race Bias in the Courts

Lynn Hecht Schafran

ABSTRACT

Sexist jokes in the courtroom, male attorneys demanding sex from women clients as a price for settling a case, and women attorneys being called "honey" or "babe"—these are just a few examples of how women are sometimes treated in the courtroom. "Lazy"; "baby-making factories"; welfare recipients who "just want easy money"—these are examples of the ways in which poor women of color are all too often described in court. Part 4, about women who work in the criminal justice system, starts out with Schafran's focus on efforts toward reducing and eliminating gender and race bias in U.S. courts. Beginning in the early 1970s, a number of women lawyers recognized that although new federal laws had been passed to end court gender bias, judges were either unaware of or unwilling to apply these new laws. An educational initiative was undertaken that focused on judges at all levels of the judiciary. The objective was to raise the credibility of women—all women—in the eyes of the court so that it approximated the credibility that men enjoy, thereby, according to Schafran, preventing judges from "gender bias in decision making and courtroom interaction [that] undermines fundamental fairness."

Schafran describes this national program to change attitudes of judges in every state and federal court and at all levels of the judiciary. First, state and federal task forces (numbering nearly 55 at the beginning of the twenty-first century) were established that documented the extent of gender bias in each state's court system and the federal circuit. Then the task forces recommended steps to eliminate that bias. Not surprisingly, the findings discovered bias not just by judges but by male lawyers, prosecutors, public defenders, administrators, and others working in the judiciary. Compounding the gender bias was an additional racial and ethnic bias. Intersectionality—the coming together of race and gender to create an identity that compounds discrimination against women of color—has evolved into a major aspect of the work of these task forces. Schafran has written elsewhere that intersectionality results in a type of bias that is more than race or sex bias alone and more than race plus sex. It is a compound bias with geometrically damaging results for women of color who are attorneys and those who encounter the legal system in other capacities. The reality is that women of color are discriminated against in the courts not only by white men and men of color but by white women as well. Schafran warns of the danger of simplifying the experiences of women of color and thus focuses her comments on the overwhelming evidence of race and gender bias in the courts against women of color.

Part of this chapter's strength is in the clear descriptions of how gender bias affects both women lawyers and plaintiffs in many different aspects of the law. With regard to the plaintiffs, Schafran discusses the ways in which women of color in particular are systematically disadvantaged by a biased court in cases of domestic violence, rape, juvenile justice, welfare, child abuse and neglect, and much more. Professor Dorothy Roberts writes that it is unlikely that individual actors (e.g., in courts, hospitals, domestic violence shelters, etc.) "intentionally single out Black women for punishment based on a conscious devaluation" of them as black mothers. "Rather, it is a result of two centuries of systematic exclusion of Black women from tangible and intangible benefits enjoyed by white society."[*]

Schafran ends by measuring the progress toward equal justice for women in the courts and points to the implementation of many recommendations. She cites cases in which gender bias issues were successfully argued (for example, *Catchpole v. Brannon*) and in which judicial opinions condemned the bias (for example, *Mullaney v. Aude*). Further, the task forces, at both the state and federal levels, continue their work of educating judges and recommending changes in codes of conduct for all court personnel. Schafran ends on a cautionary note by citing a number of reasons for eternal vigilance in the gender bias battle. She particularly points to the problem of high turnover in court personnel, which results in a continual need to resocialize new personnel to norms that do not accept race and gender bias.

Gender bias in the courts is discussed in part 4, "Women Workers in the Criminal Justice System." As you read the first chapter in that section by Lynn Hecht Schafran (chap. 29, "Overwhelming Evidence: Gender and Race Bias against Women in the Courts"), keep in mind this chapter's description of how lesbians are viewed and ask yourself if and how the recommendations for eliminating gender and race bias would have an impact on the treatment of lesbians, too.

---

[*]Dorothy E. Roberts. 1997. Punishing Drug Addicts Who Have Babies: Women of Color, Equality, and the Right of Privacy. In *Critical Race Feminism*, ed. Adrienne K. Wing, 127.

Introduction

History of Activism against Gender and Race Bias in the Courts

Just over 30 years ago a group of feminist lawyers and activists formed NOW Legal Defense and Education Fund to pursue litigation and education that would further women's legal rights and to end the gender bias women faced in the courts. The impetus for the focus on the courts was the way judges were applying, or failing to apply, new laws intended to

---

Source: This article was written expressly for inclusion in this text.

end gender bias in situations that ranged from hiring decisions to rape trials. There is no point in passing remedial legislation if the judges who interpret, apply, and enforce these laws are themselves biased. That bias was later described by Federal District Court Judge Marilyn Patel, who in 1970 was a founding NOW Legal Defense and Education Fund board member trying to use the then-new employment laws on behalf of women experiencing discrimination in the workplace.

> I recall that when I was working on what were called "discrimination cases," I believed that I knew what constituted the burden of proof. Congress appeared to have made that very clear. We all felt that we knew what was meant by a preponderance of the evidence. But I found that usually there was an additional burden of proof for women. Many of the male judges I knew were not aware of or did not believe that certain things did or could happen to women, or that women were discriminated against or treated in an unjust fashion.[1]

Women's lack of credibility is the crux of gender bias in the courts. *Credible* is a word that encompasses many meanings: truthful, believable, trustworthy, intelligent, convincing, reasonable, competent, capable, someone to be taken seriously, someone who matters in the world. Credibility is the crucial attribute for a lawyer, litigant, defendant, or witness. Yet for women, achieving credibility in and out of the courtroom is no easy task. Women are denied *collective credibility* because as a group they are perceived as less believable than men. Custom and law have taught that women are not to be taken seriously. For most of this country's history the law classed women with children and the mentally impaired and forbade us to own property, enter into contracts, have custody of our children, or vote. Although the laws have changed, social science and legal research reveal that women are still perceived as less credible than men.[2]

In a courtroom, credibility also depends heavily on understanding the context of the litigant's claim. Our justice system denies women *contextual credibility* because it is unused to hearing women tell about the realities of their lives. An individual has difficulty being perceived as credible when she talks about an area about which both men and women have few facts and many mistaken opinions. For example, there is a widespread assumption that if a woman was raped she would sustain serious physical injuries, especially to her genitals, and would report immediately to the police. In fact, most rape victims sustain no visible physical injuries, and the very few who do tell the police often delay their report.[3]

The third aspect of credibility is *consequential credibility,* being seen as someone of consequence, someone who matters, someone to be taken seriously. Part of being taken seriously is having your harms and injuries taken seriously—not devalued and trivialized, as all too often happens in domestic violence cases when judges refuse to issue or enforce protective orders against batterers, and in sexual assault cases when minimal sentences are imposed on rapists.

NOW Legal Defense and Education Fund proposed to address women's lack of credibility in the courts by working in the continuing education programs judges had begun to take in the mid 1960s. The goal would be to show judges how gender bias in decision making and courtroom interaction undermines fundamental fairness. This proposal met with extreme skepticism. Knowledgeable judges, lawyers, and journalists insisted that judges would never acknowledge that gender bias exists in their courts or accept it as a legitimate topic for judicial education and self-examination. Potential funders claimed the proposed project was unnecessary because judges are impartial, as dictated by their job description. But NOW Legal Defense and Education Fund persevered, collecting state and federal cases, trial transcripts, newspaper articles, empirical studies, and court watchers' reports that documented the need for judicial education about gender bias, defined by the National Judicial Education Program as (1) stereotyped thinking about the nature and roles of women and men; (2) how society values women and what is perceived as women's work; and (3) myths and misconceptions about the social and economic realities of women and men's lives.

In 1980 NOW Legal Defense established the National Judicial Education Program to Promote Equality for Women and Men in the Courts (NJEP) and invited the newly formed National Association of Women Judges to become NJEP's co-sponsor.

NJEP knew that an essential component of its programs would be concrete information about gender bias in the courts of each state in which it taught in order to counter denial about the existence of the problem. This stress on developing state-specific data for judicial education resulted in the national gender bias task force movement.[4]

Task Forces

As of 2001, forty-five states and most federal circuits had established high-level task forces to investigate the nature and extent of gender bias in their own court systems and recommend ways to eliminate it. Composed of judges, lawyers, court administrators, judicial educators, law professors, legislators, community leaders, and social scientists, these task forces used a wide range of data-collection methods to learn about the experiences and perceptions of justice system professionals and court users with respect to an array of substantive, procedural, and employment issues ranging from rape trials to the status of women court employees. Although the precise nature and severity of the documented problems varies from state to state, the findings are captured in the words of the first task force, the New Jersey Supreme Court Task Force on Women in the Courts:

> With few exceptions, the findings and result of the Substantive Law Committee, the Attorneys Survey, and the Regional and State Bar Association Meetings were mutually corroborative. Although the law as written is gender neutral, stereotyped myths, beliefs, and biases were found to sometimes affect judicial decision-making in the areas investigated: damages, domestic violence, juvenile justice, matrimonial law and sentencing. In addition, there is strong evidence that women and men are sometimes treated differently in courtrooms, in chambers, and at professional gatherings.[5]

Another finding of this first task force, echoed in every subsequent task force report, is the striking difference in response from male and female attorneys. The Arizona task force report put it this way:

> Male and female attorneys differ markedly in their perceptions of gender bias in the justice system. Male lawyers feel there are few problems serious enough for investigation, education or reform while women

lawyers perceive a wide range of disadvantages based on their gender.[6]

The vast documentation compiled by these task forces[7] raises three key questions: (1) What exactly did these task forces find? (2) Have their recommendations to address the problems documented been implemented? (3) Did implementation result in meaningful change?

One way to examine these findings is through the particular experience of women of color in the courts, a subject of increasing concern as our population changes and the courts must serve a significantly more diverse group of citizens. In 1998 NJEP gathered this information in a model judicial education curriculum titled *When Bias Compounds: Insuring Equal Justice for Women of Color in the Courts.* We found that although there has been insufficient research into the particular problems confronting women of color in the courts, the reports of the task forces on gender bias in the courts, and the task forces on racial and ethnic bias in the courts for which they were the catalyst, make clear that whatever the problems are for white women and for men of color, they are worse and more complex for women of color. They are also more invisible. Just as male lawyers do not "see" the disrespectful treatment accorded their female colleagues, even white women are less aware of what is happening to their sisters in the law who are women of color. In 1988 the American Bar Association Commission on Women in the Profession wrote:

> Women [attorneys] report that they are often treated with a presumption of incompetence, to be overcome only by flawless performance, whereas they see men attorneys treated with a presumption of competence overcome only after numerous significant mistakes. Minority women testified that adverse presumptions are even more likely to be made about their competence.[8]

In a 1994 report titled *The Burdens of Both: The Privileges of Neither* the American Bar Association Multicultural Women Attorneys Network described the findings of the task force reports and their own focus groups, convened in several major cities across the country.

Perhaps the most shocking reports reviewed by the Network involve the disrespect toward multicultural women lawyers in the courts. From judges to court personnel, multicultural women lawyers were treated like inferiors rather than officers of the courts.[9]

The persistence of these attitudes was apparent in a 2001 article in the *New York Times Magazine* about the new female associates at a prominent law firm. An African American woman reported, "Sometimes I just get the feeling that people assume I'm a secretary or a deliverywoman. You have no idea how many times people wouldn't believe I was a summer associate."[10]

This lack of credibility affects women of color using the courts in every capacity. As the California Judicial Council Advisory Committee on Racial and Ethnic Bias in the Courts wrote:

> [W]omen of color encounter dual barriers of racism and sexism in the justice system and legal profession . . . whether as litigant, lawyer, judge, witness, court personnel or law student.[11]

In fact, women of color encounter more than "dual barriers." *Intersectionality* is the term legal theorists coined to describe the way the confluence of race and gender creates an indivisible identity that shapes the lives of women of color and results in a type of bias that is more than race or sex bias alone and more than race plus sex.[12] It is a compound bias with geometrically damaging results for women of color as attorneys and across the spectrum of the law.

HOW STEREOTYPED THINKING AFFECTS WOMEN OF COLOR AS ATTORNEYS

Even though in the year 2001 women are for the first time more than half the entering class of law students, the stereotypical lawyer is still white and male. Thus attorneys who are women of color are not once but twice removed from the norm, which results in even greater credibility problems than those facing white women attorneys. Like the new associate quoted earlier, when these women appear in court or for depositions they are often assumed by judges, court personnel, and other lawyers to be a secretary, a clerk,

the court reporter, the defendant, the defendant's mother, relative, or a social worker. For example, the D.C. Circuit Task Force on Gender, Race, and Ethnic Bias reported that a third of minority women attorneys but only small percentages of other groups experienced nonrecognition of their attorney status by federal judges.[13] Numerous women reported this problem to the ABA Multicultural Women Attorneys Network. An African American woman described the time a white female judge addressed her white female client, who was dressed in tattered jeans, as "counsel" even though the attorney wore a suit and carried a briefcase. Another similarly attired woman of color attorney was mistaken for a janitor.[14]

Even when multicultural women successfully establish their identity as attorneys, they often find that judges, lawyers, and court personnel challenge their credibility, assume they are incompetent, and treat them with disrespect. The Second Circuit Task Force on Gender, Race, and Ethnic Fairness in the Courts reported that 51 percent of minority women attorneys in private practice had their competence challenged, compared to 4 percent of their male counterparts.[15] In California, a federal judge asked an African American woman with the Department of Justice antitrust division, "Do you really understand all the economics involved in this case?"[16] A Florida attorney testified, "[A]s a black woman lawyer, I am personally sick and tired of being insulted and having my intelligence questioned by white male lawyers."[17] The ABA Multicultural Women Attorneys Network reported the following:

> Study findings all indicate that multicultural attorneys strongly believe that judicial discretion is usually exercised against them, that gender-biased conduct or racial/ethnic discrimination is exhibited by opposing counsel on a regular basis, and these differences in treatment or attitude have an effect on the outcome of litigation. For example, the Report of the Gender Bias Study of the Massachusetts Courts concludes that multicultural female attorneys are more likely than white women to be subjected to inappropriate sexual comments or touching by court employees. In addition, multicultural women are more likely than any other group of attorneys to be berated by a judge for no apparent reason.[18]

HOW STEREOTYPED THINKING AFFECTS WOMEN OF COLOR AS PARTIES

Gender bias can touch any aspect of the law, from areas immediately thought of as "women's issues," such as rape, to those not seen in this context, such as right-to-die cases.[19] Following is an examination of a few of these areas, again focused on women of color as parties to these cases.

Plaintiffs

The concept of intersectionality was originally developed as a way to talk about the dilemma that women of color encounter in bringing employment discrimination suits. Title VII of the Civil Rights Act of 1964 required them to plead either race or sex discrimination, a single-axis approach that did not reflect their experience and left them unable to demonstrate the harms they had suffered. The leading theorist in this area, Professor Kimberle Crenshaw, wrote of a 1976 case: "the court refused to recognize the possibility of compound discrimination against Black women and analyzed their claim using the employment of white women as the historical base. As a consequence, the employment experiences of white women obscured the distinct discrimination that Black women experience."[20]

Because a disproportionate number of poor women are women of color, a disproportionate number of welfare recipients are women of color. These women face overt bias in their interactions with the courts. An urban male attorney wrote to the New York Task Force on Women in the Courts, "Most of my clients are Black and Hispanic welfare recipients, often single mothers. It is clear to me that judges and court personnel have a profound lack of respect for these clients . . . manifested by rude comments, clear expressions of dislike, etc. . . . [At] the very least, it convinces my clients that they cannot expect to find justice in such a courtroom."[21]

The stereotypes about poor women of color as lazy and having babies just to get a bigger welfare check are daily hardened by the media, whose "ex-clusion of the diversity of poor women and the complexity of their experience . . . creates a deviant image perpetuating the concept of individual moral fault and driving legal debate."[22] This devaluation of women of color, combined with the "blame the victim" mentality toward the poor, can impact findings of comparative negligence and damages awards in civil cases. In Florida an African American woman sued over injuries from an automobile accident. After trial a juror reported that other jurors said they did not want to award the plaintiff anything because "she was a fat black woman on welfare who would simply blow the money on liquor, cigarettes, jai alai, bingo or the dog track" and that "they would be paying one way or another, by awarding money in this case or through welfare."[23] Unreported in the case is the fact that the plaintiff was not on welfare, but rather was receiving worker's compensation at the time of the accident. The stereotypes about black women are so strong that her being unemployed automatically marked her as being on welfare and thus an unworthy plaintiff.

At the 2001 program for judges on dealing with gender, race, and ethnic bias in the courts a New York City Housing Court judge reported that when a woman of color is defending an eviction notice, the first question the landlord's lawyer and some court personnel ask her is "When is welfare going to pay the rent?" But when a white woman is the defendant, the question is "What has happened to you?" or other probing of why the rent was not paid. The judge observed that although statistically it is more likely for a woman of color to be on welfare than a white woman and although this question is not asked meanly but in a routine reflection of the daily crush of cases, it is unacceptable because it reinforces a biased perception about women of color.[24]

Family Law and Divorce

The task forces repeatedly cite family law and divorce cases as areas of extreme gender bias. Women who invested decades of human capital in homemaking for their husbands and children—often at the express dictate of husbands who refused to let them work outside the home—are awarded minimal, short-term alimony that devalues their unpaid work as homemakers and ignores the challenges they will face in entering the paid workforce as older women with no resumes. Numerous studies document that women suffer a steeper decline in their post-divorce standard of living than men because of inadequate and unenforced alimony and child support. Despite federal legislation requiring states to adopt new child support guidelines that better reflect the true costs of child raising, these awards are still often too low and barely enforced. Indeed, as recently as fiscal year 1998, only 51 percent of the child support *due* in that year, and a mere 8 percent of the child support due from prior years, was collected.[25] And this statistic says nothing of the incredibly small percentage of women whom the court deems eligible for alimony at all and the larger, but still inadequate, percentage of women who are awarded child support by the courts.

Women of color face an additional hurdle in these cases. The California racial and ethnic bias task force reported that the majority of litigants who appear without a lawyer in Los Angeles family courts are women of color, and they are "consistently treated with less respect and given insufficient information to carry out the roles that were assigned to them in representing themselves."[26] The perception that communities of color are by definition poor often means that women of color are not granted alimony at all in divorce cases,[27] or restitution in domestic violence situations,[28] because judges and other relevant court personnel presume, with little or no further inquiry, that men of color have no money. This presumption is insulting to men of color and leaves women of color in even more acute financial distress than white women.

Domestic Violence

Domestic violence is an area in which the courts have greatly improved their response to victims. The billions of dollars infused into state criminal justice systems under the 1994 Violence Against Women Act (VAWA) and its 2000 reauthorization funded more prosecutors to handle domestic violence and rape cases, more advocates and services for victims, and more training programs for police, prosecutors, and judges. But this good news is far from uniform. For example, a report from Nebraska detailing the many positive results flowing from this VAWA funding observed that "The only segment of the criminal justice system that stands out as being immune to the influence of advocates appears to be the local judiciary. While sentencing sanctions had significantly increased, this has been the result largely of pleas worked out by prosecutors. Left to their own devices, Lincoln judges have maintained a record of unresponsiveness to persons seeking court protection from domestic violence."[29]

A persistent problem across the country is that judges, family hearing officers, custody evaluators, and guardians ad litem continue to award custody or unsupervised visitation to batterers. Despite extensive national judicial education about the impact of domestic violence on children, these decision makers remain either uninformed or indifferent to the research that shows that children in violent homes suffer emotionally, psychologically, and physically and that awarding custody to batterers teaches boys to grow up to batter their partners and girls to accept it. Moreover, batterers often use the opportunity of visitation to assault, rape, or kill their children's mother.

Battered women of color often encounter barriers beyond those confronting white victims. The simple fact that bruises are not as obvious on dark skin as on light skin disadvantages the black women before a judge who demands visible evidence of the assault. Some judges and court personnel believe minority communities are "naturally" violent, so nothing can or should be done.[30] A New Jersey judge declined to continue a Pakistani woman's order of protection, saying, "How do we know [the violence] is not part of your culture?"[31] A prominent attorney testified to the California racial and ethnic bias task force that "judges appeared to believe that in the African American community violence was much more acceptable 'culturally' and, therefore, there was not the same seriousness paid to the testimony of African American women . . . [S]ome judges consider Asian American women to be more submissive than White women, and therefore the domination of the woman by her male partner is expected and culturally accepted, even if it involves violence."[32]

African American women who present a battered woman syndrome defense after killing their abusers face an extra burden because stereotypes about these women as aggressive and hostile directly contradict the images that many hold about battered women as white, blonde, small, meek, and economically dependent on their husbands. Professor Shelby Moore observes:

> These images work against African American women to such an extent that they must struggle to rise above them. If judges and jurors view them as strong and domineering, they are unlikely to believe that African American women suffer psychologically as a result of being battered. Again, they are more likely to be viewed as deserving of, or in some way the cause of, the violence perpetrated against them. These images prevent judges and jurors from viewing African American women in the same way they view the mythical white woman: virtuous and fragile; worthy of being protected and respected.[33]

Rape

Victim blaming is typical of rape cases. Extensive research with rape case jurors reveals a belief that women assume the risk of rape when they go to a man's apartment or drink in a bar. In the typical rape case, the complainant rather than the defendant is put on trial. Her demeanor, dress, conduct, associations, and lifestyle rather than his threats and use of force become the focus. The burden is even greater for women of color, for whom victim blaming has a unique history with unique ramifications. During slavery, white men invented the stereotype of the lascivious black woman to excuse their own repeated rapes of their female slaves.[34] Today, African American women are still stereotyped as promiscuous and thus at least less harmed by sexual assault, if

not unrapeable. In a recent Westchester, New York case a black female welfare recipient alleged that she was raped on the examining table by a white gynecologist. At first he denied any sexual contact. When the DNA results exposed this as a lie, he claimed that the sex was consensual and that he denied it because he did not want his wife to know. After the jury acquitted the doctor, a white male juror wrote to the prosecutor, "We thought a Black female like that would be flattered by the attention of a white doctor."[35]

In an Indianapolis case involving the rape of a 13-year-old black girl, a juror argued that "a girl her age from 'that kind of neighborhood' probably wasn't a virgin anyway."[36] Even where guilt is found, the injury to rape victims of color may be devalued. A study of sentencing in Dallas, where jurors determine sentences, found that whereas the median sentence for a black man who raped a white woman was 19 years, the median sentence for a white man who raped a black woman was 10 years, the median sentence for white on white rape was 5 years, for Latino on Latina rape 2.5 years, and for black on black rape 1 year.[37]

Contrary to the stereotype of rape as a crime committed by black strangers jumping from the bushes to attack white women, the vast majority of rapes are committed by men of the same race as their victims and men who know their victims. Women of color rape victims and domestic violence victims whose assailants are men of color are often criticized by their own communities when they report these men to the criminal justice system because of its maltreatment of minority-group men. When the victims in these same-race assaults are immigrant women, some interpreters coming from the women's communities try to persuade them to drop their cases or side openly with the defendants.[38]

Juvenile Justice

The juvenile justice system has long failed young women. In 2000 the American and National Bar Associations issued a joint report called *Justice by Gender: The Lack of Appropriate Prevention, Diversion, and*

Treatment Alternatives for Girls in the Justice System. It differed little from the ABA's 1977 report, *Little Sisters and the Law.* These reports document the remand of girls to secure facilities for behavior that is barely criticized in boys. The constant subtext is that girls must be prevented from engaging in sexual behavior and becoming pregnant, yet there is an almost willful blindness to the sexual abuse by parents and others that has driven many of these young women into the streets. Moreover, the correctional and rehabilitative aspects of the juvenile justice system are designed to meet the needs of boys, not girls.

Courts' disparate treatment of women of color begins in the juvenile justice system. A lack of cultural sensitivity and knowledge among juvenile court personnel can often result in girls of color not being afforded the same presumptions of femininity and innocence often extended to white girls. African American girls may be seen as aggressive or showing a lack of remorse when they act assertively rather than deferentially. Thus, they often receive harsher punishment than girls who act more conventionally feminine. By contrast, Asian American, Native American, and Latina girls, often taught to show deference to adults, may exhibit subdued conduct that is perceived as evidence of guilt or rudeness.[39]

Women of Color as Mothers in the Court System

During the California task force's public hearings, various individuals raised the concern that people of color are judged through the filter of white, middle-class values. This filter combines with stereotypes about women of color as "bad mothers" to negatively impact outcomes in abuse and neglect cases and other situations that involve these women and their children. A *New England Journal of Medicine* study of pregnant women in Pinellas County, Florida, found that only about 26 percent of those who used drugs were black. Yet over 90 percent of Florida prosecutions for drug abuse during pregnancy have been brought against black women.[40] Commenting on this disparity, Professor Dorothy Roberts writes:

It is unlikely that any of these individual actors [government officials, hospital staff, prosecutors, legislators] intentionally singled out Black women for punishment based on a conscious devaluation of their motherhood. The disproportionate impact of the prosecutions on poor Black women does not result from such isolated, individualized decisions. Rather, it is a result of two centuries of systematic exclusion of Black women from tangible and intangible benefits enjoyed by white society.[41]

Another result of this systematic exclusion is the forced medical treatment of pregnant women. A national survey of obstetricians found that, as of 1987, 21 court orders had been sought for the medical treatment of pregnant women without their consent. Seventeen were sought against black, Latina, or Asian women. The court issued orders in 18 of the 21 cases.[42] Lisa C. Ikemoto describes the "negative stereotypes forming a picture of the bad mother":

She has little education. Perhaps she does not understand the nature of her refusal to consent. She is unsophisticated, easily influenced by simple religious dogma. She is pregnant because of promiscuity and irresponsibility. She is hostile to authority even though the state has good intentions. She is unreliable. She is ignorant and foreign. She does not know what is best. The cases ascribe these characteristics to the bad mother; this is the subtext, the things that can nearly be said. They make it easier to assume that the woman's will should be overridden. They also offer moral grounds for intervention. The expressions of anger, frustration, and righteousness in the case reports and opinions strongly evoke the things that can nearly be said. Not stated is that these assumed characteristics are particular to stereotypes of poor women of color. So, what goes unsaid is that she is Black; she is Hispanic; she is Asian; and she is poor.[43]

This negative stereotyping can become a self-fulfilling prophecy. Psychological research shows that "people treat others in such a way as to bring out behavior that supports stereotypes."[44] Negative assumptions on the part of judges, court personnel, attorneys, and social workers fuel the anger and resistance of women of color. Their anger inhibits their ability to fully participate in the process. It also reinforces stereotypes about certain women of color as hostile, unsympathetic, and undeserving. In addition, parents without resources and parents without education to fight back, who are disproportionately poor, especially women of color, become resigned to being treated as nonentities in their and their children's cases.

As recently as 2001, a federal judge had to direct New York's Administration for Children's Services, the city's child welfare agency, to stop removing children from the homes of women seeking protective orders against their batterers and charging these mothers with abuse and neglect for "allowing" their children to witness domestic violence.[45] Some family court judges were permitting this repeated revictimization of battered women, the large majority of whom were women of color.

ENSURING EQUAL JUSTICE FOR WOMEN IN THE COURTS

In addition to documenting the many aspects of gender bias in the courts already outlined, the gender, race, and ethnic bias task forces made numerous recommendations for literally every sector in the justice system: judges, judicial educators, court administrators, lawyers, bar leaders, prosecutors, public defenders, law schools, police, corrections officials, and others. There are numerous indications that many of these recommendations have been implemented and that the climate for women in the courts has improved.

When NJEP began its work in 1980, judges' and attorneys' gender bias was an invisible problem. Today it is grounds for reversal and sanction. At the National Conference on Public Trust and Confidence in the Justice System in May 1999, 500 state chief justices, state court administrators, state bar presidents, and other justice system leaders voted to make a priority of implementing the recommendations of the task forces on gender, race, and ethnic bias in the courts. Indeed, just the existence of these task forces, established in response to NJEP's educational programs, testifies to the difference these decades have made.

While NJEP and the state and federal task forces on gender bias in the courts have certainly not eradicated these problems, we have established new norms that make gender-biased decision making and courtroom behavior unacceptable, and education to overcome gender bias widely accepted. In 1990 the American Bar Association amended its model code of judicial conduct to provide that judges may not manifest bias based on race, sex, religion, national origin, disability, age, sexual orientation, or socioeconomic status nor permit those under their direction and control to do so. Today, most states have adopted this provision as well as changes in their own rules of professional responsibility that explicitly bar various forms of gender-biased conduct by lawyers. The gender bias task force reports have been cited in nearly one hundred state trial and appellate decisions on issues running the gamut from divorce and custody to judicial and attorney conduct to rape and murder.[46]

Several cases have reversed trial courts specifically for gender bias. In *Catchpole v. Brannon*,[47] for example, the California Court of Appeals in 1995 relied heavily on the California and Ninth Circuit task force reports in reversing a trial court judge for his gender bias in a sexual harassment case involving an alleged rape. The trial judge was so convinced of the myth that a woman who is "truly" being raped will physically resist that even though the defendant admitted the assault in a call monitored by the police, the judge could not get past his own preconceptions. The judge called sexual harassment cases "detrimental to everyone concerned,"[48] described this case as "nonsense,"[49] showed extreme irritation at having to listen to the plaintiff's witnesses, and subjected the plaintiff alone among all the witnesses to a scathing interrogation. Further, he asked the plaintiff whether she blamed herself for letting the assault happen[50] and wrote in his tentative decision that the situation was unbelievable, that she was at fault for not successfully resisting, and that it could be inferred that she pursued her supervisor.[51] The case was appealed on the ground that the judge's gender bias required setting aside his judgment. The Court of Appeals held that "the allegations of gender bias are meritorious"[52] and reversed and remanded for a new trial before a different judge. The Court wrote: "the phrase 'due process of law' . . . minimally contemplates the opportunity to be fully and fairly heard before an impartial decision maker . . . the judge's expressed hostility to sexual harassment cases and the misconceptions he adopted provide a reasonable person ample basis upon which to doubt whether appellant received a fair trial."[53]

One of the most recent attorney misconduct cases is *Mullaney v. Aude*,[54] in which the Maryland Court of Special Appeals upheld sanctions against two male attorneys for gender-biased behavior toward their female adversary during discovery: for example, referring to her as "babe" throughout the litigation and defending themselves by saying that at least they did not call her a "bimbo." The trial court had written:

> These [gender-biased] actions . . . have no place in our system of justice and when attorneys engage in such actions they do not merely reflect on their own lack of professionalism but they disgrace the entire legal profession and the system of justice that provides a stage for such oppressive actors.[55]

In its affirmation of this position, the appeals court cited several of the gender bias task force reports and wrote:

> While strategy and tactics are part of litigation, and throwing your adversary off-balance may well be a legitimate tactic, it is not legitimate to do so by the use of gender-based insults . . . [We] have long passed the era when bias relating to sex . . . is considered acceptable as a litigation strategy.[56]

Continuing education for lawyers and judges has changed markedly over the last two decades. Legal education is now largely mandatory and includes a component on ethics. Judges increasingly recognize that judicial education is neither a punishment nor an admission of ignorance. Much of the gender bias in the courts results from a lack of factual knowledge about the social and economic realities of women's and men's lives.

The consequences of this lack of knowledge and the ways in which sex stereotypes can cloud a lawyer's judgment are illustrated by a Washington, D.C., sexual harassment case. In 1988, a local judge who was presenting a program about gender bias in torts and damages asked several lawyers whether they had clients who might serve as speakers. One male attorney responded with a letter about a sexual harassment case he almost refused to take because on the telephone the victim sounded "hysterical." When he finally met with her—at his female secretary's urging—he thought her story of outrageous abuse from a distinguished company division head seemed "crazy."

After the woman's psychiatrist and psychologist told this lawyer that they believed her, he went forward with the case. On the eve of the trial he learned that two other women had been sexually harassed by the same man in the same way and that although all three women had complained to their employer's internal Equal Employment Opportunity office, nothing was done. The case settled. The lawyer wrote, "I do not think I am any less sensitive than most lawyers, but in this case, I was about to reject a meritorious case because it seemed to be too awful to believe. And I was mistaking the client's desperate cries for justice with hysteria."[57]

This lawyer's failure to appreciate the high level of sexual harassment and violence in women's lives and his labeling this woman with the classically sexist epithet "hysterical" is by no means unique. Continuing legal education is essential to bridge the gap in understanding and life experience this case illustrates. Moreover, although women are far more aware than men of gender-biased behavior because they are its object, no one is born understanding the economic consequences of divorce or rape trauma syndrome, or how gender bias in the medical profession leads to delayed diagnosis. The context-free, abstract theorizing that is the hallmark of most legal education fails to provide lawyers with the concrete understanding of the reality of women's lives that is essential to effective advocacy.

NJEP has developed model curricula for judges to address this information gap in a variety of areas. *Understanding Sexual Violence: The Judicial Response to Stranger and Nonstranger Rape and Sexual Assault,* for example, provides judges with the most recent research on victim impact, sex offenders, and rape jurors' biases, together with an opportunity to explore the relevance of this information to judges' responsibilities during the pretrial, trial, and sentencing phases of a case, and as leaders in the criminal justice system. The response demonstrates the importance of bringing this information to the judiciary. When judges tell us that they never before had any education about victim impact, we understand why they cannot comprehend that a victim may freeze with fright, even if the rapist is someone she knows and uses no weapons, and why they thus distrust her for failing to fight back. When judges express surprise at the data showing that most nonstranger rapists are serial rapists and that their victims usually sustain greater psychological damage than victims of stranger rape, we understand why the sentences for these men are often minimal.

The existence today of nearly 55 state and federal task forces on gender bias in the courts, the changes in the codes of judicial and professional conduct, and the judicial opinions condemning gender bias in decision making and court interaction are concrete examples of how much has changed for women in the courts in the last two decades. But this most welcome progress should not obscure the reality that there is and will always be much to be done to eliminate and prevent gender bias in the courts.

When the NJEP began its work, one of the most frequent responses was that gender bias would disappear by itself as younger women and men came to the bench and bar. But this assumption is simply wrong. Even with respect to issues presumably well understood today, such as the need for gender-neutral language and judicial intervention to stop sexist trial tactics in the courtroom, several state judicial educators recently reported that at their new judges orientation programs some of these newcomers, including the women, had to be all but hit over the head with the code of judicial conduct before they "got it."

As described at the beginning of this chapter, a major cause of gender bias in the courts is lack of accurate information about the social and economic realities of women's and men's lives. No one, female or male, is born knowing, for example, that rape victims typically delay reporting, and exceedingly few learn it in law school. What happens when judges make decisions in these areas without specialized education is vividly captured in a recent book titled *Battered Women in the Courtroom* by James Ptacek, a detailed examination of courtroom interactions between judges and battered women in Massachusetts. At one point he writes:

> Another judge spoke of how her sense of what was 'intuitively' true about battering, a sense she learned from other judges, shifted when she began reading about women's experiences of violence:

> Those judges who *I thought* were the most creative and the most sensitive were judges who would typically take the time and say "Okay, let's work this out in the family." But, I mean, I think intuitively you would do that, *unless you read and started to realize that by doing that, you were enforcing precisely the wrong thing in the situation.* That isn't what you want to do. You need to treat this as a crime, you can't perpetuate this as a family matter. Well, those are all really learned responses. I don't think they are intuitive. [Emphasis added by author.][58]

Another reason the gender bias battle will never be over relates to the constant turnover of personnel in the courts and the proliferation of decision makers. Unlike many other countries—where all judges are appointed for life, and there is minimal attrition through retirement and death—our state judges usually serve for a limited number of years and are sometimes defeated in their reelection contests. This turnover is exacerbated by the changing nature of judicial service itself. Whereas once a judgeship came at the end of a lawyer's career, today younger lawyers join the bench for a brief time as a stepping stone before returning to private practice. Many judges now on the bench were not exposed to the findings of the original gender bias task forces, most of which released their reports in the late 1980s and early 1990s. And beyond the judges themselves are a host of other decision makers who require education about stereotyped thinking and the social and economic realities of women's and men's lives. They include court clerks, family hearing officers, mediators, guardians ad litem, custody evaluators, referees, trustees, conservators, and others. Thus, every new generation of judicial and nonjudicial court personnel and decision makers needs to be resocialized and reeducated.

The situation in the courts today is captured in a report prepared in 2000 for the tenth anniversary of the Colorado Supreme Court's Gender and Justice Committee, *Taking Stock: Gender and Justice*. The author interviewed selected individuals whose work and experience interacted with the Colorado judicial system in order to document improvements relating to gender issues in the past decade and identify areas in which the committee should focus its interest and future work. The report concluded:

> These interviews were informative and, without exception, portrayed issues of gender in a better and more hopeful light than the 1990 study. There has been significant improvement in the areas examined, as a result of a change in societal values, the Supreme Court's initiatives, and the inventive programs of a number of nongovernmental organizations. In addition, those involved are able to articulate clearly what remains to be done.[59]

Thomas Jefferson once wrote that eternal vigilance is the price of liberty. It is also the price of gender fairness in the courts.

DISCUSSION QUESTIONS

1. Give four to five examples of how racial, ethnic, and gender bias affects women of color in the courts as described by Schafran.
2. Schafran argues that education and litigation are two important strategies in combating racial and ethnic bias in the courts. Discuss this issue. In your discussion, suggest other ways to reduce gendered racial and ethnic bias in the courts.
3. Explain why it has been necessary to establish a gender bias task force in every state in the United States and at the federal level. Explain why it is inadequate to focus on gender bias without simultaneously addressing race and ethnic gender bias.
4. Give one example each of how gender bias in the courts harms women defendants, plaintiffs, and defense counsel.
5. Discuss the concept of intersectionality as it applies to black, Latina, Asian, Native American, and other women of color in a court setting.
6. The role and behavior of the judge is crucial to successfully ending bias in the courts. Explain why.

NOTES

1. National Judicial Education Program to Promote Equality for Women and Men in the Courts, *Judicial Discretion: Does Sex Make a Difference? Instructor's Manual* 5 (1981).
2. For an introduction to this research see Lynn Hecht Schafran, Credibility in the Courts: Why Is There a Gender Gap? *Judges' Journal* (winter 1995), p. 5.
3. For a summary of this research see Lynn Hecht Schafran, Writing and Reading about Rape: A Primer, 66 *St John's Law Review* 4 (1993).
4. For a complete description of the origins of NJEP and the gender bias task forces, see Lynn Hecht Schafran, Educating the Judiciary about Gender Bias: The National Judicial Education Program to Promote Equality for Women and Men in the Courts and the New Jersey Supreme Court Task Force on Women in the Courts, 9 *Women's Rts. L. Rep.* 109–124 (1986) and Norma J. Wikler, Water on Stone: A Perspective on the Movement to Eliminate Gender Bias in the Courts, 13 *State Ct. J.* 13 (1989).
5. The First Year Report of the New Jersey Task Force on Women in the Courts—June 1984, 9 *Women's Rts. L. Rep.* 129, 136 (1986).

6. Gender and Justice Survey of Pima County, Arizona, *Arizona Lawyers* (1986) at "Highlights" (unnumbered page).

7. For a list of task force reports and how to obtain them see http://www.nowldef.org/html/njep/PDFdocs/taskforce.pdf

8. ABA Commission on Women in the Profession, *Report to the House of Delegates* 12 (1988).

9. American Bar Association Multicultural Women Attorneys Network, *The Burdens of Both: The Privileges of Neither* 25 (1994), hereinafter ABA MWAN Report.

10. Great Expectations, *New York Times Magazine,* (Sept. 9, 2001), 118, quoting Tracey B. Mullings.

11. Final Report of the California Judicial Council Advisory Committee on Racial and Ethnic Bias in the Courts, pp. 158–159 (1997), hereinafter California Report.

12. Kimberle Crenshaw, Demarginalizing the Intersection of Race and Sex: A Black Feminist Critique of Antidiscrimination Doctrine, Feminist Theory and Antiracist Politics, 1989 *U. Chi. Legal F.* 139 (1989).

13. Report of the Special Committee on Gender Prepared for the D.C. Circuit Task Force on Gender, Race, and Ethnic Bias, 84 *GEO L.J.* 1651, 1743 (1996).

14. ABA MWAN Report, p. 26.

15. Draft Report of the Working Committees to the Second Circuit Task Force on Gender, Race, and Ethnic Fairness in the Courts 62 (June 1987).

16. Final Report to the Judicial Council of California Advisory Committee on Gender Bias in the Courts 68 (1996).

17. Report and Recommendations of the Florida State Supreme Court Racial and Ethnic Bias Study Commission, pp. 30–31 (1990).

18. ABA MWAN Report, pp. 25–26.

19. Lynn Hecht Schafran, Promoting Gender Fairness through Judicial Education: A Guide to the Issues and Resources (1989; updated version forthcoming).

20. Crenshaw, Demarginalizing the Intersection, p. 148.

21. Report of the New York Task Force on Women in the Courts, 15 *Fordham Urb. L.J.* 11, 122 (1986–1987).

22. Lucy A. Williams, Race, Rat Bites, and Unfit Mothers: How Media Discourse Informs Welfare Legislation and Debate, 22 *Fordham Urb. L.J.* 1159, 1196 (1995).

23. *Wright v. CTL Distribution, Inc.,* 679 So. 1233, 1233–1234 (Fla. App. 1996).

24. Judge Laurie Lau, Remarks at the National Association of Women Judges Annual Meeting, Panel on Responding to Racial, Ethnic and Gender Bias in the Court and Hearing Room (October 4, 2001).

25. Office of Child Support Enforcement, *Twenty-Third Annual Report to Congress* (1998). Available at http://www.acf.dhhs.gov/programs/cse/rpt/annrpt23/charts/charts.htm

26. California Report, pp. 165–166.

27. Twila L. Perry, Alimony: Race, Privilege, and Dependency in the Search for Theory, 82 *Geo. L.J.* 2481 (1994).

28. Interview with Jenny Mulgrav, New York Victims' Services Agency (April 1997).

29. Lincoln Medical Education Foundation, Inc. and Family Violence Council, *Domestic Violence Prevention* (Jan. 2001), p. 8.

30. Jenny Riviera, Domestic Violence against Latinas by Latino Males: An Analysis of Race, National Origins, and Gender Differentials, 14 *B. C. Third World L.J.* 231 (1994).

31. Telephone interview with Dr. Shamita Das Dasgupta, Executive Director, Manavi (June 2, 1997).

32. California Report, pp. 140, 141.

33. Shelby A. D. Moore, Battered Women Syndrome: Selling the Shadow to Support the Substance, 38 *How. L.J.* 297, pp. 333–334.

34. Jennifer Wriggins, Rape, Racism, and the Law, 6 *Harv. Women's L.J.* 103 (1983).

35. Telephone interview with Barbara Eggenhauser, Assistant District Attorney, Westchester County, New York (April 21, 1992).

36. Gary LaFree, *Rape and Criminal Justice,* pp. 219–220 (1989).

37. Ray F. Herndon, Race Tilts the Scales of Justice, *Dallas Times Herald* (Aug. 19, 1990), p. A1.

38. Monika Batra and Prema Vora, Silence! The Court Is in Session, *The Sakhi Quarterly* (Spring 1997), p. 1.

39. Girls Inc., Prevention and Parity: Creating Solutions for Girls in the Juvenile Justice (summer 1996), pp. 20–21.

40. Dorothy E. Roberts, Punishing Drug Addicts Who Have Babies: Women of Color, Equality and the Right of Privacy, in *Critical Race Feminism* , ed. Adrienne K. Wing (1997), p. 127.

41. Ibid., p. 131.

42. Lisa C. Ikemoto, Furthering the Inquiry: Race, Class, and Culture in the Forced Medical Treatment of Pregnant Women, in *Critical Race Feminism*, ed. Adrienne K. Wing (1997), pp. 137, 140.

43. Ibid., p. 140.

44. Mark Snyder, Self-Fulfilling Stereotypes in *Race, Class, and Gender in the United States,* ed. Paula S. Rothenberg (1994), pp. 370, 375.

45. *Nicholson v. Williams,* 2001 WL 951716 (E.D.N.Y. 2001). See also Chris Lombardi, Justice for Battered Women, in *The Nation* 275 (July 15, 2002). pp. 24–27.

46. An annotated list of these cases is available from the National Judicial Education Program, 395 Hudson Street, Fifth Floor, New York, NY 10014. Tel: (212) 925-6635; Fax: (212) 226-1066; E–mail: njep@nowldef.org

47. 36 Cal. App. 4th 237, 42 Cal. Rptr. 2nd 300 (Cal. Ct. App.1995).

48. Ibid., p. 5.

49. Ibid., p. 8.

50. Ibid., p. 10.

51. Ibid., p. 6.

52. Ibid., p. 1.

53. Ibid., pp. 3, 6.

54. 126 Md. App. 639, 730 A. 2d 749 (1999).

55. Ibid., p. 655.

56. Ibid., p. 658.

57. For the entire letter, see Schafran, Lawyers' Lives, Clients' Lives: Can Women Liberate the Profession? 34 *Vill. L. Rev.* 1105 (1989).

58. James Ptacek, *Battered Women in the Courtroom* (1999), p. 119.

59. Andrea Williams, Taking Stock: Gender and Justice. Available at http://www.courts.state.co.us/supct/committees/gjc/stock/htm

Chapter 30

Women in Black:
Are Female Judges More Compassionate?

Jeffrey Toobin

ABSTRACT

The articles in part 4 describe some of the many strides women have taken in the courts, law enforcement, and corrections. In fact, as Schafran pointed out in chapter 29, female attorneys have taken on leadership roles in establishing greater sensitivity among all court participants to issues of gender and race discrimination.

This being said, all the authors in part 4 argue that there is still a long way to go in eliminating gender and race bias not just in the courts but throughout the criminal justice system. This chapter is more anecdotal in character than others in this section. But it challenges the assumption that female judges, just because they are women, will be more understanding, more compassionate, or more rehabilitation-oriented than male judges. In fact, this article shows how male politicians often are eager to recruit a marginalized population, in this case women and primarily white women, only if they sing the same tune, in this case a conservative ideology.

This chapter presents a portrayal of two female judges in Texas who are conservative and punitive judges. It describes the paths by which these conservative female lawyers became tough-on-crime judges. As Toobin clarifies in this chapter, early studies anticipated that female judges were more likely than male judges to be compassionate. But subsequent studies have not substantiated that hypothesis; instead, they have concluded that considerations *other than* the so-called feminine or female point of view are more pivotal in determining how female judges make decisions. The most critical influence on judicial sentencing decisions by female judges appears to stem from their legal training and their legal socialization.[1] Toobin adds political party affiliation to this list. In the case of the two Texas female judges described here, the important socialization factors

---

[1]See Cassia Spohn, 1995. Decision Making in Sexual Assault Cases: Do Black and Female Judges Make a Difference? In *The Criminal Justice System and Women,* 2nd ed., ed. Barbara Raffel Price and Natalie J. Sokoloff, chap. 21. New York: McGraw-Hill. For an earlier study, see Elaine Martin. 1990. Men and Women: Vive la Difference. *Judicature* 73 (December/January): 204–208.

appear to include backgrounds as former prosecutors and the conservative political backing needed in Texas in order to be elected to the bench.

Criminal court judges in all jurisdictions rule according to a case-by-case basis and have a profound effect on defendants who come into their courts. However, much more influential in terms of the broader society are the judges of the Court of Criminal Appeals, because the decisions in these higher courts establish binding precedent that impacts many future cases. In Texas, one of the two women described in this chapter is currently the presiding judge of this court. Strongly pro-prosecution and a staunch supporter of the death penalty, she has been described as "the most ideologically conservative member of the court." Incidentally, three additional members, and thus half of the nine judges on this court, are also women.

Studies of female judges in the United States have found that the strongest impacts on their judicial behavior are *not* characteristics generally attributed to women, such as understanding and compassion; Spohn's study (see footnote 1) did find that women's behavior does differ from men's in at least one type of case, that of sexual assault. Spohn found that women judges, particularly black women judges, appear to show more sympathy toward the victim and generally impose longer sentences on the male defendants than do black and white male judges and white female judges.

The reader cannot draw any firm conclusions about female judges from this chapter. But it is important to be aware that not all women are feminists nor are all focused on fairness. Moreover, all women are not liberals or radicals; neither are all women empathic toward those who stand accused in a court of law. A national study that examines and compares judicial decisions by women and men in similar cases would permit a conclusion about gender differences, if any, of judges.

It is, however, apparent that women often bring different values to an institutional setting such as the judicial or criminal justice system. Consider the case of Coleen Rowley, who exposed the mishandling of vital intelligence in the FBI following the 9/11 attacks. Similarly, Sherron Watkins played a key role in exposing corruption in the infamous Enron scandal in 2001. Both women were in positions high enough within their organizations to command credibility as well as access to significant information. They were "insiders" in very white male elite institutions, but they had "outsider" values that challenged existing power structures and ideologies.[2]

In short, it is inaccurate to assume that all women (and all minorities) in positions of power will automatically support the existing white male-dominated system, on the one hand, or that they will all be liberal or progressive thinkers in social and legal matters, on the other hand. Thus, because women are different from men and from each other based on their race, class, and sexual orientation, women who are more privileged, as this chapter helps point out, may not share

---

[2]See Anita Hill. 2002. Insider Women with Outsider Values. *New York Times,* June 6. Available from NYTimes.com.

judicial agendas with those who are more marginalized, and the more marginalized groups in society must be well represented in decision-making positions in a democracy.

Since 1976, Texas has executed two hundred and thirty-two people, which is more than a third of all the people put to death in the United States in the same period. And Harris County, in the heart of Texas, stands out: it has accounted for sixty-three executions—more than all of Florida, which ranks third among states, with forty-nine executions, and nearly as many as Virginia, which is in second place, with eighty. Harris County, which includes Houston, has another distinction: its criminal courthouse is one of the few in the country where a majority of the judges—twelve of twenty-one—are women.

The death penalty in Texas has often been viewed through the prism of George W. Bush's Presidential candidacy. Despite Bush's expressions of enthusiasm, in the October 11th Presidential debate, over the fact that the men who killed James Byrd by dragging him behind a pickup truck were sentenced to death, the Texas governor's real influence over the issue is modest: he cannot apply the death penalty; he can only delay, not prevent, executions. A more appropriate context in which to examine capital punishment in Texas, where more than a third of the judges are women, is gender; the state has become a kind of laboratory for a quiet transformation of the American judiciary. Indeed, the Texas experience may answer what had been a hypothetical question: would it make a difference in enforcing the death penalty if women were in charge?

The subject of women's influence on the judiciary—and even of a distinctively female style of judging—has drawn the interest of scholars since the nineteen-eighties, when women started ascending to the bench in significant numbers. (Twenty-four per cent of the judges in New York and twenty-one per cent in California are women.) Some researchers posited that women would bring a special kind of

compassion to the bench. But in Texas, at least, women judges have enforced the criminal law in general and the death penalty in particular with a greater ferocity than their male predecessors. It is a development that owes much to the state's political environment—to its swift transition from Democratic dominance to near-total Republican hegemony—but the fact remains that the increase in the number of women judges in Texas has coincided with the surge in executions in the state.

Judge Susan Brown is one of the twelve female judges on the Harris County Criminal District Court. (In Texas, felony cases are tried in the district court. They may then be appealed to the courts of appeals, where eighty judges are divided into fourteen regions and sit in panels of three. The highest court is the Court of Criminal Appeals, which has nine judges, who are elected in statewide races.) Brown remembers precisely when she decided to become a lawyer. "I was reading this Sidney Sheldon novel, which my mother, good Catholic girl, probably would not have approved of," she told me recently, in her chambers in the Harris County Criminal Justice Center. "And there was this woman defense lawyer in it. That woman from 'Charlie's Angels' played her in the movie. And it was so glamorous and exciting that I decided then and there that's what I wanted to do."

Unlike the character that Jaclyn Smith played in "Rage of Angels," though, Brown, the former Susan Baetz, did not come from a privileged background. Her father worked for a moving company in Houston, and her mother was a travel agent. No one in her immediate family had gone to college, but she won admission to Texas A. & M. and then to South Texas College of Law, in Houston. Upon graduation, she set out to become a trial lawyer.

Brown, who is forty, could still pass for a law student, with her pageboy haircut and breezy, unpretentious manner; each time I entered her chambers, I noticed her judicial robe thrown unceremoniously

Source: Permission to reprint "Women in Black" by Jeffrey Toobin. October 30, pp. 48–55. Originally published in *The New Yorker.*

over a chair. When we met, she had just returned from a short vacation that included a trip to a local water park with her husband and two young daughters. But youth, charm, and informality notwithstanding, Brown is typical of the new sort of woman judge in Texas: she is a Republican, a former prosecutor, and an unyielding judicial conservative.

"If you wanted trial experience, you really had no choice but to become a prosecutor," Brown told me during one of several conversations. "It's a lot harder to get experience on the other side of the fence." Texas, for the most part, does not use a public-defender system. Instead, judges appoint lawyers for indigent defendants on a case-by-case basis, a system that gives judges a ready-made base for campaign contributions and, some say, discourages zealous advocacy for the defense. (Lawyers must always worry about offending a judge who is a future source of appointments.) So Brown found a job in a district attorney's office north of Dallas. "I loved it," she said. "It's fun to be the guy in the white hat."

After a couple of years, Brown moved to the Harris County district attorney's office in Houston (where she met her husband, Marc, who remains a senior prosecutor there). In the eighties, women who had gone to work for district attorneys were thriving. They did not, however, make comparable strides in the private sector, which depends on paying clients. "We don't want to have to get business by going to dinner with people and playing golf with them," one woman judge told me. "You don't have to worry about getting clients in a D.A.'s office. There's always plenty of business, and you can just be a lawyer." Unlike the old boys' networks, in Texas and elsewhere, district attorneys' offices operate as relative meritocracies.

"I did a lot of capital cases as a prosecutor," Brown told me, going on to say that she asked for the death penalty from juries on six occasions, and they agreed five times. (Under Texas law, only juries, not judges, can impose the death penalty.) "It is hard for twelve citizens to give someone the death penalty," Brown said. "I've watched these jurors struggle and cry as they do it. It bothers me that people think it's so easy, that they just give the death penalty to anybody."

Brown's first death-penalty case as a prosecutor was that of Arthur Brown, who was convicted in 1993 of the execution-style murder of four people in connection with a drug deal gone bad. The defendant is still appealing, and the Judge, frustrated, told me, "I can't believe how long it's taking."

In time, like many prosecutors, Brown thought about moving up to a judgeship. Judges in Texas are elected, though the governor can fill vacancies, and it is mostly through judicial elections that women have made their dramatic gains. Harris County residents often have to vote in several dozen judicial races at a time, so the challenge for prospective candidates is to generate name recognition. Like most candidates for the criminal judicial bench, Brown had little money—she ultimately spent about thirty thousand dollars—but she had been active in the Republican Party for some time, and she understood the rules in Houston. "These elections are about endorsements," she told me. "And when you get those, that's it."

In pursuit of a judgeship, Susan Brown sought the support of Steven Hotze, a Houston physician who in the past decade has become the chief gatekeeper to the local judiciary. From the start, Hotze saw the potential of female judicial candidates, and he welcomed them onto the ballot—as long as they met his ideological requirements.

Hotze, who has a thriving practice as an allergist, first gained prominence in 1985, when he led the successful opposition to a gay-rights voter initiative in Houston. (His group was called the Straight Slate.) In later years, he emerged as the preeminent conservative figure in Harris County. According to Allen Blakemore, a political consultant in Houston who frequently works with Hotze, the doctor made a critical discovery about the nature of judicial elections. "We're now in a Republican-only context in Harris County," Blakemore said. "The primary is the only thing that matters. And in judicial elections no one knows anything about the candidates, and it's a tiny, tiny group of people voting—maybe a hundred and fifty thousand out of 1.6 million registered voters. Hotze took the time to figure it out—that it's only worth trying to reach the people who are going to vote. So he came up with the idea of the voter guide."

Hotze's voter guides distill his views into a chart, which contains two columns—one marked "Conservative Republicans," the other "Liberals"—and lists the two groups' contrasting views of the issues: for instance, "For capital punishment" or "Oppose capital punishment"; "For traditional family values" or "For teaching homosexuality as an acceptable alternative life style"; "For the sanctity of human life" or "For abortion on demand." Senior citizens can vote by mail in Harris County, so Hotze sends them preprinted applications for ballots. "That's why Steven Hotze has such a big impact," Judge Brown told me. "When you go down a ballot, folks don't know who to vote for. He tells you."

Hotze and his allies recoiled at the idea of naming defense attorneys to the bench, so they looked to the district attorney's office, and found an abundance of qualified, aggressive prosecutors who happened to be women. As head of a group called the Conservative Republicans of Harris County, Hotze began endorsing slates of candidates in judicial elections. In a context where candidates lack the resources to reach voters on their own—and where only the most motivated party members vote at all—Hotze's endorsements became the single most important factor in Harris County judicial elections.

For most of the past ten years, Hotze has refused to speak to reporters. ("It helps with the mystique," Blakemore explained. "He's the guy behind the scenes that nobody sees, kind of like the Wizard of Oz.") However, Hotze did outline his political theories in an opinion piece in the Houston *Chronicle* on December 13, 1992. There he described a host of the country's ills, from crime to the national debt, and asked, "What is the reason for this decay and impending collapse of our nation? We have abandoned the Christian faith of our forefathers." He went on in that spirit, concluding, "If we are to survive as a nation and maintain our liberties, then we must get back to the basics and restore our nation to its Christian heritage."

The candidates themselves operate in this conservative context. "We don't have moderates here,"

Gary Polland, the chairman of the Harris County Republican Party, told me. "We have economic conservatives and social conservatives." According to Allen Blakemore, degrees of toughness, sometimes seen as a gauge of conservative commitment, count for a lot in these local elections. "Prosecutors and incumbent judges will brag about their stats," Blakemore said. " 'I sent *x* number of people to death row.' 'I sentenced *x* number of people to life terms.' "

In a curious way, the rough political environment of Texas may help women candidates. "Where women have a better record than men is that we have not been caught doing crooked things," Ann Richards, the former Democratic governor, who was defeated by Bush in 1994, told me. "A lot of people tend to vote for women because they think we're more clean than the men." This theory of an edge for women candidates was at least partially borne out this spring when Hotze, along with his usual victories, suffered a rare pair of defeats. Two of his judicial candidates lost to incumbent women.

In 1998, Susan Brown ran a classic Hotze-style Republican campaign; the doctor even listed her as one of his "featured races." Recalling her interview with Hotze, when she sought his support, Brown said, "He just wants to know where you are, law-enforcement-wise and in terms of experience. He's very conservative. So am I." Like several other female candidates, Brown also benefitted from the Texas tradition of women's clubs, a Republican institution that thrived even when Democrats dominated the state. In Houston alone, there are several, including the Daughters of Liberty and the Texas Tea Party, which are unflinchingly conservative, and the Magic Circle, which is more moderate. "The clubs are where you get your precinct chairmen," Brown said of her fellow club members. "They'll send notes to their friends. It's really important."

Brown won a lopsided victory in the 1998 Republican primary, defeating an incumbent, Lon Harper, with almost seventy-five per cent of the vote. Harper had damaged himself by admitting to a reporter that he needed to work only a half day to get through his docket. Several lawyers and judges in Houston told me that Harper's statement, though politically disastrous, was actually true, and it constitutes another reason that the judgeships work well for those concerned about a balance between job and family. "We've broken through the glass ceiling," Brown told me.

Judge Brown isn't inclined to make sweeping statements about her judicial philosophy, but her priorities are easy to identify. On the day we met, she had recently presided over her first capital case as a judge. (In that case, the twenty-year-old defendant, Juan Martin Garcia, was sentenced to death for shooting a man in the course of a robbery that netted eight dollars.) Because, under Texas law, jurors decide whether to impose the death penalty, I asked Brown how long it took to select a jury in a capital case. "About three weeks," she told me. "It takes that long to cull out the people who can't give the death penalty."

There was nothing legally inaccurate about this approach; it is part of a judge's obligation in death-penalty cases to draw out jurors on the subject. But Brown's emphasis on jury selection as a kind of weeding-out process for those unwilling to impose death was a little unsettling just the same. I saw similar factors at work when I watched Brown supervise jury selection in a case involving possession of a small amount of heroin. In Texas, juries can impose sentence in all criminal cases, so Brown asked a long series of questions about whether the prospective jurors thought sentences of twenty-five to ninety-nine years were excessive for possession of less than a gram of heroin. (The potential sentences were so high because the defendant was a prior offender.) Under Brown's probing questions, virtually all the prospective black and Hispanic jurors conceded that they thought such sentences were too long, and thus disqualified themselves from consideration. A jury later convicted the defendant and sentenced him to thirty years.

Like George W. Bush, Brown sees herself as a compassionate conservative. "I don't think women judges are more liberal—at least, not my friends." Brown told me. "We are probably more empathetic, rather than sympathetic. I sit up there—and this is something I never expected—and I don't just think

about my poor victim, as I did when I was a prosecutor. Sure, the defendant made his bed and he has to lie in it. But I also think about the poor mother of the defendant sitting out there who is not going to have her son home for Christmas. They have done everything they can for this kid, but he's still a bank robber or a drug dealer." She brightened, saying, "So maybe I give them forty years instead of fifty years." Many defense lawyers, in Texas and elsewhere, feel that women judges overcompensate for the perceived weakness of their gender. For her part, Brown rejects this theory, and her rulings from the bench do seem consistent with her professional and political orientation.

Clearly, Brown believes in handing out long sentences. In 1993, a Gulf War veteran named Ronald Margolis stopped his car and asked a group of teenage girls for directions. Three of the four girls later told police that Margolis had been masturbating at the time, and he pleaded guilty to "indecency with a child." Brown's predecessor sentenced Margolis to seven years' probation, and his record stayed clean for nearly six years. In 1999, Margolis admitted to his probation officer that he had drunk beer on weekends, which was a violation of the terms of probation, and that he had gone innertubing in nearby New Braunfels without the permission of his probation officer. There was also an unproved allegation that Margolis had flashed a housekeeper in his mother's home, but he was never charged with sexual misconduct while on probation. Still, in light of these violations, Judge Brown sentenced Margolis to ten years in state prison. After he is released, he will be required to register with the police as a sex offender for the rest of his life. "I believe in keeping my probationers on a short leash," Brown told me.

When scholars began trying to see patterns in the behavior of women judges, most did not count on the rise of judicial conservatives like Susan Brown. The first formal study of the subject took place in 1986, when Suzanna Sherry, then a professor at the University of Minnesota Law School, decided to examine the question by focussing primarily on the work of Sandra Day O'Connor, who was then in her fifth year on the United States Supreme Court.

Sherry told me that her study grew out of the controversial work of the sociologist Carol Gilligan, whose 1982 book "In a Different Voice" remains the best-known statement of what is sometimes called "difference feminism."

Sherry's article, "Civic Virtue and the Feminine Voice in Constitutional Adjudication," published in the *Virginia Law Review,* was full of caveats that her evidence was incomplete and her conclusions tentative. Yet the article continues to be cited as the leading argument for the proposition that a "feminine paradigm" exists for judges. Drawing on the findings and the language of psychological and literary theory, Sherry wrote about women's more "intersubjective sense of self" and a "difference between the abstraction of men and the concreteness of women." Her conclusion, though, was straightforward: Sherry suggested that a woman's jurisprudence would be suspicious of hard-and-fast rules—in short, it would be "merciful, just, and compassionate."

This hypotheses has proved difficult to test. There is no practical way to provide male and female judges—especially trial-court judges, who work alone—with identical issues to resolve; moreover, it can be difficult to identify which result in a given case is more or less "female." To the extent that scholars have been able to make evaluations, though, the results in more recent years have not been favorable to the Gilligan-Sherry school. According to a more comprehensive, but still mostly anecdotal, study by Michael E. Solimine and Susan E. Wheatley, which was published in the *Indiana Law Journal* in 1995, "The weight of the evidence demonstrates that most female judges do not decide cases in a distinctively feminist or feminine manner." As Solimine told me, "It seems that other parts of judges' backgrounds—like their party affiliation and their prior professional history—matter more than whether they are men or women."

Throughout Texas, Susan Brown has ideological soul mates who are mostly ex-prosecutors and all Republicans—including Gerry Meier and Karen Green, in Dallas; Sharen Wilson, in Fort Worth; Cynthia Kent, in Tyler; and Sharon MacRae, in San Antonio—but these trial judges preside over only one case at a time and do not establish binding precedents. In Texas, that role belongs to the Court of Criminal Appeals (the Texas Supreme Court, to which Governor Bush has appointed four judges to fill vacancies, handles only civil cases), and it is in the Court of Criminal Appeals that a woman has transformed her state's application of the death penalty.

The key figure on the court is Judge Sharon Keller, who, oddly, drew little notice during her days as an assistant district attorney in Dallas. During her career there, which lasted from 1986 to 1994, she worked in a relative backwater, the appellate section, where she drafted briefs and argued appeals. "She was very nice and unassuming and sort of quiet and shy," a former colleague told me. "Nobody thought of her as someone who could go out and be a politician." But Keller, who is divorced and has one son, had ambitions beyond the confines of the D.A.'s library, and she had an advantage that few prosecutors could match. Her family operated Keller's Drive-Ins, a successful hamburger chain in Dallas, and she decided to invest part of the proceeds from the business in a career as a judge.

Keller ran a Hotze-style campaign statewide, emphasizing her experience as a prosecutor and her toughness on crime. According to statistics compiled by the public-interest research group Texans for Public Justice, most of the money for Keller's first campaign, in 1994—more than two hundred thousand dollars—came from Keller and her family. One of her newspaper advertisements showed hands behind jail bars and announced that this person would not be voting for Keller. Another ad proclaimed, "Sharon Keller believes criminals deserve a home of their own. In Huntsville"—at the time, the site of death row. She won a six-year term amid the Republican victories of that year and immediately asserted herself on the court.

"Sharon Keller is probably the most ideologically conservative member of the court, in the Clarence Thomas–Antonin Scalia mold," says Robert Dawson, a professor at the University of Texas law school who follows the Court of Criminal Appeals closely. Between 1993 and 1999, the court went from nine Democrats to nine Republicans, but even within this transition Keller's opinions stood out for their pro-prosecution orientation. According to Charles Baird, a Democratic judge who was voted off the Court of Criminal Appeals in 1998, "It's a profound evolution, from moderate to extreme right wing. She was the first one who ran on the issue of being tough on crime. As we say in Texas, it's the big dog that eats. They have the votes, and it didn't matter what those of us in the minority said. She is pursuing her own philosophical agenda."

As Keller promised in her campaigns, she has been extremely reluctant to set aside convictions or death sentences. In 1996, for example, Keller upheld the death sentence given to Cesar Fierro, who, in 1979, had confessed to a murder after Mexican police seized his mother and stepfather and threatened to attach an electrical generator known as a *chacharra* to the stepfather's genitals. In an opinion, she ruled that the coercive nature of the investigation should not invalidate Fierro's conviction and sentence. In two cases where defendants were sentenced to death after trials during which their attorneys dozed off in the courtroom, Keller voted with the majority to uphold their convictions. According to statistics compiled by the Chicago *Tribune,* the court has granted new trials to death-row inmates just eight times since 1995, and in those eight cases Keller was in the pro-execution minority six times.

Keller's term expires at the end of this year, but, instead of seeking reelection, she is risking her seat to run for presiding judge of the court—the most important criminal judgeship in Texas. Her opponent in the primary was Tom Price, a fellow Republican judge on the court—"I call him a liberal," Keller said in the campaign—and she won their contest handily. She will face token Democratic opposition in November.

The evidence from Texas suggests that although diversity may serve some laudable goals—creating equal opportunities, dispelling stereotypes—it has had a minimal impact on the quality of justice meted out by the Texas courts. Judge Keller's most famous decision to date—her opinion in the Roy Criner case—illustrates the point. On September 27, 1986, a sixteen-year-old ninth grader named

Deanna Ogg set out on foot for her grandmother's house in a small town north of Houston. That evening, she was sexually assaulted and bludgeoned to death. A local man named Roy Criner was convicted of aggravated sexual assault, largely on the basis of disputed confessions that he had made to three friends shortly after the crime. He was sentenced to ninety-nine years in prison.

More than a decade after the crime, Criner's attorneys ordered DNA tests and found that their client could not have been the source of the semen in Ogg's body. A lower court said that Criner should have a new trial, but Sharon Keller wrote an opinion for the Court of Criminal Appeals stating that Criner's sentence should stand. "The new evidence does not establish innocence," she wrote. Criner may not have ejaculated or he may have used a condom. Or the victim could have "had sexual relations with men other than" Criner. After all, Keller wrote, "there was testimony that the victim had had many boyfriends and that she had said that she 'loved sex.' "

Keller's reasoning in the Criner case was seen as so misguided that, in time, the district attorney, the local sheriff, and the judge in Montgomery County asked Governor Bush to pardon Criner, which Bush did, on August 15th of this year. After ten years in prison, Criner was released that day.

Judge Keller gives few interviews, particularly after a PBS "Frontline" documentary about the Criner case, in which she made several gratuitous remarks about the alleged sex life of the victim in the case ("Well, you're not forgetting there are—you're not taking into account the fact that she was a promiscuous girl," Keller said.) The Judge had said that she would not speak to me, but I stopped by her office anyway—a grimly modern structure with a lobby adorned by thirty-four portraits of white male judges from Texas's past. Keller came right downstairs when I called.

It was a hundred and two degrees in Austin that day, but Keller was impeccably turned out in an uncreased yellow suit. She exuded Southern charm, but she has an icy grace that is in keeping with her station; it was clear that she wanted only to make small talk. She had just returned from a Mediterranean cruise with her son, a last treat before he went off to college. She mentioned that a tour guide, on learning that she was a judge, had said that there were some women judges in the region, but that they were not allowed to preside over death-penalty cases. "They don't think the women can do it," Keller said. Then she paused and added, unsmiling, "They might be surprised."

DISCUSSION QUESTIONS

1. Many factors shape judicial behavior: background, training and personal characteristics, local politics, geographical area (rural or urban; north or south). Which of these factors will most likely influence a judge to favor tough-on-crime sentences? to favor rehabilitative sentences? Why is it important to consider these factors in any discussion of justice in the United States?

2. Can it be assumed that all women will be compassionate in their official roles in the criminal justice system? Why do some women take a tough-on-crime, punitive position? Can it be assumed that all Blacks or all Latinas will take similar positions? Discuss.

3. Little conclusive research has been done on the relationship between judges' decisions and their race, class, and gender. How might you design such a study for your county or state?

4. Compare and contrast the discussion of female judges and their judicial decisions in this chapter with the discussion by Schafran in chapter 29.

Chapter 31

Invisible No More:
A Social History of Women in U.S. Policing

Dorothy Moses Schulz

ABSTRACT

In this chapter, updated for this third edition, Schulz traces the rich history of the evolution of women police in the United States. The narrative begins with a description of the very earliest women who worked in a police-related capacity: the nineteenth-century jail and prison matrons. Next, the reader learns about the reform movement led by middle-class moral reformers—mostly white and female (but not part of the all-male police structure) whose main task was the social control of the uneducated, poor, and immigrant women and children. Finally, Schulz covers the role of the contemporary women crime fighters who are attempting to gain equity in job and status within the male police hierarchy.

With the hindsight of historical study, Schulz concludes that women's genuine acceptance in police work by male peers and police executives has always been, at best, marginal. Each step for women in the long road to full officer status has been long and hard-won. Equality in pay, assignments, and promotion is still not secure for women, a fact that is also demonstrated by Harrington and Lonsway (chap. 32) and Martin (chap. 34).

Schulz ends with a discussion of community policing and the opportunities and challenges that this type of enforcement philosophy presents to women. Schulz discusses the thorny issue, raised by some feminists, that plagues women's participation in law enforcement: whether the best strategy for women's success in this male-dominated arena is "gender-neutral" policing (*same* behavior by women and men) or "gendered" policing (*different* behavior by women and by men—each having value). This issue has been referred to as the *sameness-difference* debate. Other feminists argue that this dichotomy is false, and they question its application in police behavior because both men and women need to develop those positive qualities stereotypically associated with traditional masculinity (e.g., being capable) and with traditional femininity (e.g., being a caring person).

As you read this chapter, think about how you might analyze the sameness-difference debate in terms of the diversity found *among* women and *among* men. Using Schulz's analysis as a basis, create a more complex analysis of policing behaviors by women (and men).

U.S. policewomen officially came into existence in 1910, but their roots are in the early decades of the nineteenth century—the jail and prison matron era. This era began in the 1820s, when volunteer Quaker women, following the example set by British Quakers, entered locked institutions to provide religious and secular training for women inmates. These volunteers, soon joined by other upper-middle-class women, wanted to reform the morals of the inmates and train them for respectable jobs, primarily as domestics in Christian homes. As the reformers became aware of the poor conditions under which these "fallen women" served their prison terms, they attributed a large portion of the neglect to the fact that the inmates were supervised by men. Foremost among their concerns was the sexual vulnerability of the inmates, who were frequently impregnated while in prison by either male inmates or male keepers.

Efforts by the volunteers to create better living conditions and a moral environment for the women they termed their "less fortunate sisters" evolved into a new profession for women—prison matron. These matrons were part of a general benevolent movement of the time, which brought religious, middle-class women into contact with poor women through charitable efforts and sought to create a sense of female solidarity across class lines. Clarice Feinman, who has traced the history of women in corrections, observed that these women reformers believed that women criminals could be saved only if they were removed from the corrupting influences of cities and men.[1] Prisons were therefore set in the countryside and staffed with women only. At the same time that these women reformers were attempting to improve conditions for women inmates, they were also creating a new profession for those who would follow them as paid matrons in these prisons. For almost 50 years, from the 1820s to the 1870s, this remained the only position in corrections open to women. Despite what appears to have been a revolution in women's roles, a second look negates this view, for by reinforcing women's traditional role

as the caregiver to other women, these early matrons stayed within the then acceptable sexual boundaries even while ensuring new careers for themselves.[2]

At the end of the Civil War another generation of women expanded this philosophy of "women's sphere," taking it far beyond jail and prison walls into other public sector areas. Women's sphere, the "special responsibility to alleviate harsh conditions," developed from women's traditional, maternal role but allowed activist women to develop a concept of municipal housekeeping that eventually encompassed virtually all activities that placed government or voluntary agencies in contact with women or children. Since women at this time were believed to be morally superior to men, these women argued that it was only proper that they be responsible for the protection of other women in need of moral guidance.[3]

The care of those in police custody became an area of special concern. At a time when components of what today constitutes the criminal justice system were less distinct, the handling of sentenced inmates and those awaiting court appearances was ill-defined. Additionally, police stations frequently functioned as homeless shelters, and many of those who sought refuge were women and their children. The women were almost always poor and frequently intoxicated, two conditions that made them vulnerable to advances by the men responsible for their care.

Using as their model the prison matrons, these post–Civil War women activists demanded and won an expanded role for women caring for women and children in police custody. That their tactics and arguments were similar to those of the women who came before them was to be expected. Their social characteristics were virtually identical with those of the women in whose path they followed. They, too, were primarily socially prominent or politically well-connected upper-middle-class women of native-born families. Many had been abolitionists prior to the Civil War, and now they turned their attention to religious, temperance, and benevolent associations. By the 1880s these women succeeded in creating another new profession for women—police matron.

This article was written expressly for inclusion in this text.

Police matrons brought custodial care into police stations throughout the nation. They represented another phase of women's involvement in the criminal justice system—their first entry into the police portion of the system. Within a short period of time, police matrons began to perform more than strictly custodial roles. They interviewed accused women and made sentencing recommendations, duties today assigned to probation officers. By the early years of the twentieth century they had ushered in the policewoman era, the second phase of women in policing.

This period is often defined as having begun in 1910, when Alice Stebbins Wells became the first woman in the United States to be called a policewoman. In reality it overlapped the matron movement and was not a new phenomenon but a continuation of women's professionalization within the police environment. Although the women who lobbied for police matrons and policewomen had little work experience outside their own homes and lacked the right to vote, in the period from 1880 to 1910, they created two new professions in the public sector for women. Because in some cities it took "as many" as three years for them to achieve their aims, they frequently voiced frustration.

Within this context, both the matrons' and the policewomen's movements provide insights into how women from a variety of organizations were able to join together and win the support of like-minded men to achieve goals and employment opportunities for women in fields that had previously been closed to them. These movements also indicate how firmly intertwined policewomen were with social purity and early female reform traditions. Social purity (a term generally relating to sexual morality, eradication of prostitution, and control of venereal diseases) was a major national concern for much of the nineteenth and twentieth centuries. It led to the creation of numerous organizations whose primary purpose was to control vice and sexual activity outside of marriage by women and young people. Many leaders of these social purity organizations were vocal advocates for and allies of policewomen.

Wells, just as the few women who came before her and the many who came after her (sometimes women who had been matrons), conceived her police role in order to fulfill her vision of women helping other women. These women police embodied the concept of the policewoman-as-social-worker. During this period, when social work was developing as a profession, it attracted to its ranks a class of women who, under the guise of helping others, actually were as much social controllers as social workers.

The prevention and protection theories these policewomen espoused gave them the opportunity to intervene in the lives of the women and children they claimed to be saving from a life of crime and delinquency. Although this philosophy of moral and social control gave way in the post-Depression era to a more middle-class, female careerist outlook, it was not until the modern, women-on-patrol period (which began somewhat tentatively in 1968 and wholeheartedly in 1972) that the path set by early policewomen was seriously altered. Thus, the history of the policewomen's movement is also a history of intervention by upper-middle-class women into the lives of poor women and children.

These upper-middle-class, educated policewomen used social work, not law enforcement, as their frame of reference. Their allies and peers were female (and male) social workers, feminists, temperance leaders, and members of women's civic clubs, not male police officers or chiefs. The women formed two professional organizations that fostered high entry standards and ongoing training far in excess of male requirements or interest in these areas. The International Association of Policewomen (IAP), which existed from 1915 to 1932, was modeled after and affiliated with the National Conference of Charities and Correction (later the National Conference of Social Work). IAP leaders scheduled annual and regional meetings in conjunction with social workers' meetings. The International Association of Women Police (IAWP), formed in 1956 as a reincarnation of the IAP, was not as closely aligned with the social work establishment but continued to have a strong social service and women's sphere orientation well after policewomen had expanded their roles within policing.

Rooted in a value system that stressed the moral superiority of women over men and the differences between men and women, early policewomen were eager to act as municipal mothers to those whose lifestyles they believed needed discipline. Some were actually called "city mothers." In attempting to serve their female and juvenile clients in a professional, nonthreatening atmosphere, they tried to separate themselves physically from policemen and elements of the police world they viewed as hampering their mission. They stressed the need for offices away from police stations, which they viewed as inhospitable to their efforts to prevent crime and delinquency among women and juveniles. Although they felt they needed the legal authority the title "police" represented, policewomen did not view themselves as female versions of policemen, a concept they disparagingly termed "little men." Nor did they view policemen—usually of a lower class and education level than theirs—as their equals, although they did stress the need for cooperation with male personnel.

Their view of themselves was, therefore, based on both gender and class, and they consciously sought a peripheral, rather than an integrated, role in policing. The concept of equality of assignment with their male colleagues did not enter their world. It was inconceivable to them, just as it was to policemen. They also eschewed the most obvious trappings of policing. They were vehemently opposed to uniforms, and most chose not to carry firearms even if permitted to do so. The women's willingness to accept assignments men did not want made their presence less threatening to policemen and senior officers, but support from within the police environment was usually unenthusiastic, reluctant, and grudging.

The few African American policewomen were even further segregated—very much a minority within a minority. Hired to work specifically with African American women and juveniles, they shared many of the characteristics of their white sisters. They, too, were usually better educated than the average African American man or woman, and they were often teachers, social workers, or ministers' wives with status in their communities.

The specialized roles filled by early white and African American policewomen were not forced on them by the male police establishment but were the roles they sought. Understanding women's traditional place in policing puts recent studies into a historical perspective, because it shows that women's acceptance by male peers has always been marginal. From the first day women entered police stations, their presence was imposed on male police executives by outside forces. It was a rare municipal government official or police chief who sought to hire policewomen. Demands for women in the police environment almost always came from outsiders.

If early policewomen, who numbered about 125 employed in about 30 cities in the years from 1910 to 1917, sought neither the trappings of police nor interaction with male officers, the obvious question is, Why did they want to be police rather than purely social workers operating out of municipal or voluntary agencies? The answer lies in the class and ethnic distinctions in the United States that were partially responsible for the movement. Although these policewomen saw themselves as benevolent helpers, their assistance was not always perceived as such. Their views on prostitution, sexual morality, dance halls, penny arcades, curfews for minors, and temperance were rarely shared by those to whom they offered their "preventive help." Whereas policewomen were overwhelmingly college-educated, native-born, upper-middle-class women, those on whom they sought to bestow their benevolence were usually uneducated, poor, and immigrant. Despite the rhetoric of the policewomen, what they viewed as benevolence was viewed by their clients as coercive social control and placed them squarely within the group Anthony Platt has called "the child savers."

Platt coined the term *child savers* to describe a group of juvenile justice system reformers who viewed themselves as "disinterested" and who "regarded their cause as a matter of conscience and morality, serving no particular class or political interests." Just as the policewomen did, these reformers saw themselves as "altruists and humanitarians dedicated to rescuing those . . . less fortunately placed in the social order." But, as Platt has observed, they went beyond this—by highlighting certain behaviors, they "invented new categories of youthful misbehavior which had been hitherto unappreciated" and not viewed as criminal or requiring correction.[4] Just as the child savers diminished the civil liberties and privacy of youths by calling for civic supervision of their activities, so, too, did policewomen bring under municipal control behavior by women and children that had previously not been viewed as requiring the attention or intervention of the police.

Because of their class distance from those they sought to save, child savers and policewomen had different definitions of morality and delinquency than those on whom they imposed their standards of behavior. Their presence in poor, immigrant neighborhoods was often unwelcome and unappreciated, as they tried to force their values on others in a maternal yet coercive manner.

Reinforcing their class and nativist orientation, policewomen turned for support during World War I to the social purity and social hygiene agencies created to combat prostitution and liquor law violations in and around cities with military installations. Efforts by these agencies—whether voluntary or governmental—resulted in severe limitations on women's mobility and in the majority of instances placed legal and moral blame on women rather than on the military men who sought their companionship.

Moral reform sentiments continued in the post–World War I period, providing additional allies for the growing numbers of policewomen, particularly among the Progressives, a label given by historians to various well-educated and often well-to-do individuals who joined together during the late nineteenth and early twentieth centuries to advance social and political reform. By the end of the war, the number of policewomen had doubled to about 300 working in more than 200 cities.[5]

Despite increased numbers of policewomen, there were no demands for greater integration into the police environment. In fact, the postwar era, a time when workplace gender segregation was the norm, brought about greater segregation. Women actively sought women's bureaus, some of which operated virtually as independent agencies. They processed all matters pertaining to women and children, sometimes including pre- and postsentencing incarceration for morality offenses. Demands for women's bureaus were a continuation of the ideology of women's sphere, but a new element entered the debate.

When these highly educated and motivated policewomen compared their careers with those of women in correctional facilities, settlement houses, and similar institutions, it was obvious that they lagged behind in achieving policy-making roles. These other women held managerial titles and supervised other women. Yet policewomen, despite their self-segregation within police departments, were not sufficiently independent to warrant their own rank structure. Intertwined with the advocacy of women's bureaus was their recognition that only greater segregation could justify an independent rank structure similar to that in specialized bureaus elsewhere in the police department. Not coincidentally, policewomen and their supporters not only demanded women's bureaus—they demanded that women be in charge of them. Thus, women's bureaus met the two major goals of post–World War I policewomen. They more fully defined women's specialized roles, and they created a mechanism for women to rise through the ranks, if not to the very top, then at least to the middle of the police hierarchy.

Many of the gains—both numerical and bureaucratic—made by policewomen during and after World War I were eradicated by the Depression. Although by 1929 there were close to 600 policewomen serving in 150 to 175 cities,[6] between 1929 and 1931 the number of departments employing policewomen decreased. Additionally, the 1930s spotlighted for the first time the image of the policeman as crime fighter, an image diametrically opposed to how social-work-oriented policewomen saw themselves. By 1940 there were no more than 500 policewomen, the vast majority working in the largest cities.

World War II renewed the nation's concerns with morality and delinquency, and policewomen were able to regain their World War I momentum and allies. Although World War II did not create new roles for policewomen, the women hired were not temporary replacements for men fighting the war but permanent additions to their police departments. Unlike the women personified by Rosie the Riveter—a woman hired to fill a man's industrial job during World War II—policewomen were hired for traditional policewomen's jobs. Because policewomen's gender-specific roles in law enforcement were not altered by the war, neither was their employment dependent on the continued absence of men. Therefore, policewomen were not faced with layoffs when the soldiers returned. Although Rosie the Riveter is an enduring image from the war years, she represents a highly specialized form of women's entry into previously male occupations and had no parallel in policewomen's history.

Concerns with morality and juvenile delinquency intensified in the postwar years, which allowed women to increase their wartime gains. Women's assignments also began to diversify. Policewomen often were teamed with male officers on undercover assignments and more frequently investigated crimes beyond morality-based crimes. They were issued uniforms (which were usually based on female military garb and which they rarely wore) and were trained in the use of and expected to carry their firearms. The 1950 U.S. Census reported more than 2,500 publicly employed policewomen, slightly more than 1 percent of all police and detectives and a considerable increase since 1940, when 1,775 women were counted in public and private agencies combined.

The post–World War II period and the decade of the 1950s are vital to policewomen's history not only because women's assignments and responsibilities expanded but also because a different type of woman was brought into policing. Often military veterans and no longer aligned with the social work establishment, the women entering police departments in this period were middle-class careerists, not upper-middle-class feminists and child savers. Although still better educated and higher in class orientation than their male peers, these women were less different from policemen than their predecessors

had been. Their goal of upward mobility through civil service and through attainment of rank resembled the goals of policemen and underlined their differences from the first generation of policewomen. This began a trend that was accentuated in the late 1970s, when the requirements for women to become police officers were lowered to the same requirements as for men, rather than qualifications for both men and women being raised to the level they had been for policewomen.

The 1950s are normally viewed as a quiet time in the expansion of women's roles, but these "second generation" policewomen made professional gains. Factors inside and outside police departments led many of the women hired during and after the war to become dissatisfied with the philosophy of women's sphere.

Externally, societal changes pertaining to women's self-image convinced them that occupational segregation was hampering their chances for lateral or upward mobility. Since these women had entered policing to take advantage of its career opportunities rather than to impose their morality on others, their concerns were as much for their own professional development as for societal benefit. In 1956 they reestablished the International Association of Policewomen, changing its name to the International Association of Women Police (IAWP), and began to develop a group consciousness distinct from that of social workers.

Internally, larger numbers and a greater range of assignments, combined with differences in their educational and class orientation, brought policewomen into closer contact with policemen. They saw that even men who were not in traditional uniform patrol had greater career range. Men were eligible for transfer to any bureau. More important, they were eligible for civil service promotion that could increase their status and their incomes. By the 1960s, these women demanded and won similar promotional opportunities.

In 1961, two New York City policewomen sued the New York City Police Department after they were barred from taking a promotion test for sergeant. The case took more than two years to be decided, but they won. Three years later, they were promoted to sergeant; in 1967 both were promoted again, becoming the department's first female lieutenants.[7]

In the years during and soon after this and similar lawsuits, employment law changed considerably as a result of major forces in society, particularly the civil rights and women's movements. These changes provided new impetus for women and minorities to seek expanded roles in policing. Once again, internal and external factors came to alter the perceptions of policewomen. In 1963 Congress passed the Equal Pay Act, prohibiting unequal pay for equal work. Although the 1964 Omnibus Civil Rights Law's Title VII prohibiting discrimination based on sex, race, color, religion, or national origin pertained only to private employers, not government agencies, it began a string of laws and cases limiting employers' control over employment selection.

In 1969 President Richard Nixon issued Executive Order 11478, which declared that the federal government could not use sex as a qualification for hiring, forcing a number of federal law enforcement agencies to begin hiring women agents. In 1971, the Supreme Court ruled in *Griggs v. Duke Power Company* that preemployment tests had to be job-related, and in 1972 Congress passed the Revenue Sharing Act, which prohibited discriminatory use of revenue-sharing funds. Also in 1972, Congress, through the Equal Employment Opportunity Act, extended the provisions of the Civil Rights Act to government employment—including police departments.

The Law Enforcement Assistance Administration (LEAA), a Justice Department agency created under the Omnibus Crime Control and Safe Streets Act of 1968, also pushed police departments to accept equal employment. Forty percent of the funds for the improvement of law enforcement dispensed by LEAA went to local governments, and the Crime Control Act of 1973, which amended the 1968 act, specified that LEAA grantees were prohibited from discriminating in employment practices. This stipulation meant that departments that discriminated against women risked losing the federal grants that many were using to upgrade training, equipment,

and facilities. In reality, no department met this fate. Yet because LEAA funds were important to job expansion in policing, and because of the new guidelines of the federal government, more positions became available to women and minorities than ever before.

With new promotional rights and newly acquired court and legislative support, more aggressive and less social-service-oriented policewomen in the 1960s moved into areas of the police department that their foremothers would never have dreamed of entering. Although their demands for greater equality were spurred at least in part by the women's movement, for the first time in their history women police officers were not assisted by other professional women; instead, they were aided by new allies—federal legislation and the courts.

Yet in 1960, LAWP President Lois Lundell Higgins, reviewing the golden anniversary of women in the police service, confidently echoed earlier policewomen in the belief that if they were here to stay, it was only because they did not try to compete with men in "work that has been and always will be predominantly a man's job." Women would continue to succeed, she predicted, because "they have brought to their work talents that are peculiarly feminine—usually a highly developed interest in human relationships—and have accentuated, rather than subordinated, their femininity."[8]

Speakers at annual IAWP meetings until the 1970s were more likely to be social work professionals or women's bureau directors than policewomen on patrol or in other non-traditional assignments. But since the 1980s IAWP meetings have acquired the trappings of law enforcement, including firearms competitions and awards that frequently honor bravery under gunfire. Although the IAP could exist from 1915 to 1932 with few leadership changes and still reflect the views of its members, by the time the IAWP was formed, change was coming too rapidly for the association to keep pace, forcing it to follow, rather than lead, its members. Many leaders remained at least partially committed to the older, social work ideal; they no longer represented the younger, more law-enforcement-oriented women. Also, since many leaders were in appointed ranks in their police departments, they could not risk taking positions that contradicted the wishes of their chiefs. Ironically, their vulnerable positions were often the result of the very policies they espoused.

Less than ten years after Higgins made her prediction, Indianapolis in 1968 assigned Betty Blankenship and Elizabeth Coffal to patrol. They became the first policewomen to wear uniforms, strap gun belts to their waists, drive a marked patrol car, and answer general-purpose police calls for service on an equal basis with policemen. Although they eventually returned to traditional policewomen's duties, they were the forerunners of a break with the past. Thus began the demise of the mothering concept. The women who followed them were no longer policewomen in the traditional sense of women social workers in the police environment. They were police officers, women with a law enforcement concept similar to that of their male peers. As crime fighters, they now enforced the law, maintained order, and provided for the public's safety, just as men did.

In the six decades (1910 to 1968) from Alice Stebbins Wells to Betty Blankenship and Elizabeth Coffal, a revolution had occurred. Demands by policewomen no longer reflected their historical feminist, upper-middle-class, educated roots. Modern women, hired under the same rules as men, rejected the constraints of women's sphere and sought equality with male peers. Recent discussion over whether uniform patrol is as much service as it is crime fighting may have aided these women in breaking down male police resistance to placing them on patrol, but their primary focus is not the components of patrol but the opportunity it presents for equal treatment from and within the police hierarchy, including assignment and promotional equality.

For the first time, the majority of women now enter criminal justice professions for the same reasons as men. In this regard, they are similar to other women who have in the past 30 years entered male fields on an equal basis with male colleagues. They do not seek to change their chosen professions; rather, they wish to benefit from the financial or status rewards these fields offer. Today's women became police officers for the tangible rewards of pay, promotions, and pensions. Their attitudes and goals are similar to those of the men with whom they train and ride in patrol cars, and against whom they compete for assignment and promotion. Although not aligned with traditional women's advocacy groups, today's women police officers are part of a broader social movement that they unwittingly may have helped to create but from which they, too, profited.

Equality, and what some describe as the changing style of policing in the 1990s, has brought new issues for study. Researchers and advocates of greater utilization of female officers have questioned whether the shift to community policing will provide new opportunities for women. These groups believe that community policing is an attempt to move away from what is the traditionally "masculine" style of policing—tough, impersonal, and based on a show of force. They assert that the shift from crime fighting to community partnerships makes women not only equal to but possibly superior to male colleagues in meeting the demands placed on the police. Thus, say these groups, the concerns of male police about women's perceived softness and preference for verbal rather than physical solutions to disputes are no longer liabilities but assets that should make them preferred candidates.[9] These attitudes stem from the belief that the hallmarks of community policing (particularly crime prevention and interaction with the community and social service agencies) hark back to the activities of policewomen from their inception in 1910 until their integration into patrol in the 1970s.

These debates over community policing and its effects on women in policing have sharpened discussions by feminist criminologists about whether women are changing policing. What community policing adds is the fact that women no longer have to change to accommodate policing now that policing seems to have changed in ways that accommodate women. These criminologists agree with early policewomen that women need not become "little men" to succeed in policing.

Although community policing may lessen the demands on women to conform to male definitions of a "good cop," some observers question whether police officers are as enthusiastic about a softer style of policing as are chiefs, politicians, and community leaders. Additionally, if in the future policing were to shift away from this community orientation, aligning women too closely with this style could provide ammunition for opponents of equality, particularly those who continue to believe that women's place in policing should be determined by gender—by women's sphere.

Reflecting changes in feminism in the last two decades of the twentieth century, earlier feminists who wrote about women's roles (particularly Dorothy Bracey, Clarice Feinman, and Barbara Raffel Price) criticized any vestiges of women's sphere. They advocated gender-neutral policing as the way women would achieve equality as well as supervisory and policy-making positions within the police world.[10] These observers believed that women would be unable to advance by stressing their differences from, rather than their similarities to, the men who make up the overwhelming majority of police. They reflected the views of many women officers, who stressed that "equal" should mean "the same as" rather than "different but just as good as."

Many feminist criminologists today disagree; they do not view gender neutrality positively. Kathleen Daly and Meda Chesney-Lind, discussing postfeminist consciousness, believe that feminists who "sought to achieve equality with men in the public sphere . . . omitted more subtle questions of equality and difference now being raised." Although these writers are referring to offenders when they observe that "feminist legal scholars are more skeptical of a legal equality model because the very structure of law continues to assume that men's lives are the norm," they could just as easily be discussing women's experiences in policing.[11] Similarly, Susan Ehrlich Martin and Nancy C. Jurik argue that all actions are "gendered" and that women can never be

"little men" because the obstacles they face in criminal justice professions are part of larger social patterns that limit women's advancement, particularly in areas that challenge gender stereotypes.[12]

Related to these views is the fact that after a generation of legal equality women's numbers remain proportionately small in policing, even more so in the upper ranks. In 1987, in the United States, 7.6 percent of local police officers were women. By 2000, somewhere between 12 and 13.7 percent of line officers were believed to be female.[13] Comparable figures for countries with policing styles similar to that of the United States (although with far fewer departments)—specifically, Great Britain, Canada, and Australia—show a high degree of correlation with the United States. In 1998, women comprised about 15 percent of the police officers in England and Wales; the percentage in Australia was identical. Statistics from Canada indicated that in mid-2000 women were 14 percent of Canadian officers.[14]

It is difficult to determine the number of women in ranks above police officer. The few surveys of upward mobility speak of "command ranks," a phrase that in departments of 25 or fewer officers might mean sergeants or lieutenants, whereas in departments of 1,000 or more officers might mean chief inspectors, or assistant or deputy chiefs.

Only a handful of women have served as police chiefs in large cities: Penny Harrington (see chap. 32) headed the Portland, Oregon, Police Bureau in 1984; Elizabeth (Betsy) Watson was chief of the Houston Police Department in 1990 and then chief in Austin, Texas, in 1992; and Beverly Harvard was named Atlanta's chief in 1994. Most women chiefs nationwide had short tenures; only Harvard, who leads a large city police department, was still serving in 2001. Of the approximately 175 women chiefs in 2000, about one-third led college and university police forces, three oversaw transportation agency forces (one transit and two airport authorities), and two headed Native American tribal police forces. Again reflective of U.S. policing, the vast majority of these women who made it to the rank of chief were in small communities. Looking beyond municipal policing, Annette Sandberg of Washington State and Anne L. Beers of Minnesota are the only women to have achieved command of state police agencies. A record number of women (30) were also serving as elected sheriffs in 2000. Most had been elected in small counties, but three commanded large agencies: Margo Frasier of Travis County (Austin), Texas; Jackie Barrett of Fulton County (Atlanta), Georgia; and Laurie Smith of Santa Clara County (San Jose), California.[15] Barrett, like Harvard, is African American, which makes Fulton County unique in that it has a black woman leading each of its major law enforcement agencies.

Achieving rank in paramilitary organizations that rely on periodic civil service testing as a means of upward mobility is a slow progression. The small numbers of women who enter law enforcement influence the even smaller numbers at the top, for without women at the lowest ranks there are few to compete for promotion. This process is further complicated by the fact that few women avail themselves of promotional opportunities, either because of personal reasons or because of systemic discrimination that continues to hinder their progress. Among the personal reasons that women list as hindrances to their upward mobility are a reluctance to give up positions with daylight hours because of family and child care requirements, and a lack of support from the family because of the inconvenience to personal routines that a change in assignment might cause. Systemic reasons include lack of assignment to high-profile units, seniority beyond the minimum requirements (often keyed to veteran status), negative (possibly biased) supervisory evaluations, and general attitudes of male coworkers that psychologically discourage ambition.[16]

Women's roles in policing are not the only facet of policing that has changed. In the past 20 years, the law enforcement community has participated in a shift to a more collaborative, community-based patrol style; has widened selection criteria for candidates to include racial and ethnic minorities in addition to women; and has started relying more on national searches to locate younger, better-educated chiefs rather than on automatic selections of incumbent deputies to replace outgoing chief administrators. What will these changes mean for the increasing numbers of women who are entering policing and making their way through the ranks? Only time will tell whether women will succeed by accentuating rather than subordinating their femininity and whether they will develop their own adaptation methods in response to pressures within their departments and in response to community expectations.

DISCUSSION QUESTIONS

1. How does the history of women police in the United States explain their role today?
2. Women entered policing initially through the back door. Explain how this approach has impacted their acceptance into this male-dominated occupation.
3. According to Schulz, how have class and race affected the history of women in policing?
4. Some people still argue that women police officers should not work in the same capacity as men. Using information from this chapter, discuss this argument.
5. Explain the concepts of gender-neutral policing and gendered policing. Explain the pros and cons of these concepts as they relate to issues of law enforcement competence.
6. Explain why some people consider community policing a natural role for women police. What is your opinion? How might community policing impact women's chances for advancement in the future?

NOTES

1. Clarice Feinman, *Women in the Criminal Justice System* (New York: Praeger, 1980), 27.
2. Ibid., 108–109.
3. Lori D. Ginzberg, *Women and the World of Benevolence: Morality, Politics, and Class in the Nineteenth-*

Century United States (New Haven:Yale University Press, 1990), 17, 37; Ann Firor Scott ed., *The American Woman: Who Was She?* (Englewood Cliffs, NJ: Prentice-Hall, 1971), 88. For a detailed look at how women used the concept of women's sphere to enter policing and eventually expand their roles, see Dorothy M. Schulz, *From Social Worker to Crimefighter: Women in United States Policing* (Westport, CT: Praeger, 1995).

4. Anthony M. Platt, *The Child Savers: The Invention of Delinquency* (Chicago: University of Chicago Press, 1969), 3–4.

5. *The Woman Citizen,* May 3, 1919, 1055; Peter Horne, *Women in Law Enforcement,* 2d ed. (Springfield, IL: Charles C Thomas, 1980), 29.

6. Edith Rockwood and Augusta J. Street, *Social Protective Work of Public Agencies: With Special Emphasis on the Policewoman* (Washington, DC: Committee on Social Hygiene—National League of Women Voters, 1932), 10.

7. *Shpritzer v. Lang,* 32, Misc. 2d 693, 1961, modified and affirmed, 234 NYS 2d 1962; Felicia Shpritzer, interview with author, Nov. 21, 1991.

8. Lois Lundell Higgins, Golden Anniversary of Women in Police Service, *Law and Order,* August 1960, 4.

9. See Janne McDowell, Are Women Better Cops? *Time,* February 17, 1992, 70–72; and Tessa DeCarlo, Why Women Make Better Cops, *Glamour,* September 1995, 260–264. For a detailed examination based on her research at the Madison, Wis., Police Department, see Susan L. Miller, Rocking the Rank and File: Gender Issues and Community Policing, *Journal of Contemporary Criminal Justice* 14, no. 2: 1998, 156–172; and Susan L. Miller, *Gender and Community Policing: Walking the Talk* (Boston: Northeastern University Press, 1999).

10. See Feinman, *Women in the Criminal Justice System,* 121; Barbara Raffel Price and Susan Gavin, A Century of Women Policing, in Donald O. Schultz, ed., *Modern Police Administration* (Houston: Gulf, 1979), 109–122; Dorothy Bracey, Women in Criminal Justice: The Decade after

the Equal Employment Opportunity Legislation, in William A. Jones, Jr., ed., *Criminal Justice Administration: Linking Practice and Research* (New York: Marcel Dekker, 1983), 57–78; and Edith Linn and Barbara Raffel Price, The Evolving Role of Women in American Policing, in Abraham S. Blumberg and Elaine Niederhoffer, eds., *The Ambivalent Force: Perspectives on the Police,* 3d ed. (New York: Holt, Rinehart and Winston, 1985), 69–80.

11. Kathleen Daly and Meda Chesney-Lind, Feminism and Criminology, *Justice Quarterly* 5, no. 4 (December 1988): 509, 524.

12. Susan Ehrlich Martin and Nancy C. Jurik, *Doing Justice, Doing Gender: Women in Law and Criminal Justice Occupations* (Thousand Oaks, CA: Sage, 1996), 2.

13. Number of Law Enforcement Officers Growing, *CJ the Americas* 5, no. 2 (April–May 1992): 11; Diversity in Law Enforcement, *The Police Chief,* July 2001, 6; Stacy Burns, A Force of Many Faces, *The News Tribune,* May 6, 2001, A1 (citing figures provided by the National Center for Women and Policing).

14. Percentages for Great Britain (England and Wales, specifically) were provided to the author during her semester in residence at the British Police College, Bramshill, Hampshire, England; for Australia, Tim Prenzler and Hennessey Hayes, Measuring Progress in Gender Equity in Australian Policing, *Current Issues in Criminal Justice* 12, no. 1 (July 2000): 25; for Canada, International News, *Law and Order,* March 2001, 8.

15. These numbers were developed during ongoing research by the author into the career paths of women chiefs and sheriffs.

16. Comments typical of the concern over promotional patterns are from Susan Ehrlich Martin, *Women on the Move? A Report on the Status of Women in Policing* (Washington, DC: Police Foundation, 1989), 1, 3–4; and Cynthia G. Sulton and Roi D. Townsey, *A Progress Report on Women in Policing* (Washington, DC: Police Foundation, 1981), 4–5.

Chapter 32

Current Barriers and Future Promise for Women in Policing

Penny Harrington and Kimberly A. Lonsway

ABSTRACT

This chapter, written by a former police chief (Harrington) of a large city and her co-author (Lonsway), provides a comprehensive overview of the past and present status of women in policing. The chapter opens with a description of the importance of women police for communities and points to women officers' much lower rates of corruption and charges of brutality than men officers. In addition, the authors cite the stronger communications skills often possessed by women and their effectiveness when responding to domestic violence incidents.

A substantial portion of the chapter is devoted to a candid enumeration of the barriers that women police officers face, beginning with stereotypes about their alleged physical inability to perform, their lack of strength, and their lesser inclination to use aggression when needed. Harrington and Lonsway take the reader chronologically through the steps that women take to become a sworn officer: the hiring process, during which discrimination can occur; the academy training, where termination rates are much higher for women; the field training period, where women are vulnerable to sexual harassment as well as discrimination by male police; and finally, the performance evaluations, where women contend they are judged more harshly.

Performance evaluations impact careers, as do job assignments. Highly prized assignments are generally considered men's work because of the danger involved or the physical endurance needed. In addition, men usually have mentors who support them in their competition for these assignments. When it is time for promotion, an officer's past experience is taken into account; if women have not had a wide range of experiences or if they have mostly had "low-prestige" jobs from the police perspective (e.g., work in community relations, domestic violence, child abuse investigations), they are clearly disadvantaged. The small number of women in top police jobs attests to the fact that the ladder up is a very shaky one for women. Over the years, many women police have become reluctant to take promotion tests. Harrington and Lonsway suggest several reasons for this discouraging fact. The authors also document other issues that women officers face, such as the lack of family-friendly departmental policies that can lead to major problems with child care. The psychological stress of sexual harassment is a large factor for many women in policing; when combined with retaliation for any attempts to stop the harassment, the pressure can become overwhelming and lead to resignation. Finally, family violence is discussed, an issue only recently confronted by the law enforcement community (see Griggs, chap. 24).

Harrington and Lonsway attempt to end on an optimistic note by observing that there has now been a "first woman" in just about every aspect of policing, which paves the way for women who enter law enforcement in the future. More hopeful, perhaps, is the fact that police agencies, as part of the shift toward community policing, are beginning to redefine the attributes that make a "good" officer. This redefinition should benefit women, who enter law enforcement with some skills and qualities that are different from men. Nor have women abandoned the courts as a way to force change; court-ordered hiring continues to be effective in increasing the number of women and minorities so long as the court remains involved. Many women look forward to the day when the courts will not be needed in order to have equity for women police officers. That time, however, appears to be far off.

A true picture of strength and oppression of women in policing, like women in the courts (see Schafran, chap. 29), is not complete unless gender is viewed in combination with the compounded effects of race, class, and sexual orientation. The intersectionality of socially structured systems of race, class, gender, and sexual orientation and the barriers thus erected for different groups of women police is discussed more fully in Martin (chap. 34).

This chapter will explore the past and present status of women in policing, highlight the advantages that women bring to the field, and describe many of the unique barriers faced by women officers. With increasing numbers of women entering policing, it is hoped that the challenges they face can be transformed into opportunities—opportunities to benefit the women officers themselves, the police agencies for whom they work, and the communities in which they serve.

THE VALUE OF WOMEN IN POLICING

Research suggests that the underrepresentation of women in law enforcement is a significant contribut-

ing factor to many of the complicated problems facing contemporary police agencies. For example, most law enforcement administrators will admit that women are seldom involved in the use of excessive force, instances in which officers overreact and assault citizens. When high-profile cases are examined (such as the Rodney King beating in Los Angeles, the sexual assault of Abner Louima in New York City, and other acts of police brutality), it is clear that female officers are rarely among the perpetrators.

Despite the fact that male and female officers use the same level of force in the course of routine duties,[1] the research clearly demonstrates that women are significantly less likely to be involved in employing both *deadly* force[2] and *excessive* force.[3] For example, in the report of the Independent Commission on the Los Angeles Police Department (also known as the "Christopher Commission"), "there

Special thanks go to Katherine Spillar of the Feminist Majority Foundation for her contributions to this chapter.

Source: This article was written expressly for inclusion in this text.

were no female officers among the 120 officers with the most use of force reports."[4] Of the officers involved in excessive force incidents, only 3.4 percent were female, whereas women comprised 12.6 percent of the Los Angeles Police Department. A more recent study conducted on the Los Angeles Police Department similarly found that "female officers were involved in excessive force lawsuits at rates substantially below their male counterparts, and no female officers were named as defendants in cases of police officer involved sexual assault, sexual abuse, molestation, and domestic violence."[5]

Likewise, when cases of police corruption are scrutinized (such as the Rampart scandal in the Los Angeles Police Department), female officers are typically not implicated. These findings are particularly noteworthy given the increasing number and size of payouts for both police brutality and corruption.[6] For example, costs of excessive force lawsuits have been estimated to be as high as $82 million in New York City,[7] $100 million in Detroit,[8] and $300 million in Los Angeles.[9]

Clearly, female officers are not involved in problems such as police brutality and corruption to the same extent that their male counterparts are. Rather, research conducted both in the United States and internationally demonstrates that women rely on a style of policing that uses less physical force in comparison with men.[10] Women police are often better at defusing and de-escalating potentially violent confrontations with citizens and less likely to use excessive force.[11] Additionally, female officers often possess better communication skills than their male peers and may be better able to facilitate the cooperation and trust of citizens that are required to implement community policing. These findings are supported by the fact that women officers receive more favorable evaluations and fewer citizen complaints than do their male counterparts.[12] Support for these findings can also be seen in women officers' less cynical orientation toward citizens and their greater degree of support for community policing.[13]

As an additional benefit to police departments, women officers often respond more effectively to incidents of domestic violence. For example, a 1985 study found that female officers demonstrated more concern, patience, and understanding than their male colleagues did when responding to calls of domestic violence. Battered women who had contact with a female officer also rated the police response as more helpful than those without such contact.[14] Given that domestic violence represents the single largest category of calls made to police, this ability is critically important to the success of contemporary law enforcement in responding to the needs of the community. It is no wonder, then, that many in law enforcement have suggested the hiring of more female officers as a way to improve the public image of the police department.[15]

PAST AND PRESENT STATUS OF WOMEN IN POLICING

Women have been in the field of policing in the United States since 1905, and the Indianapolis Police Department made history in 1968 by assigning the first two female officers to patrol on an equal basis with their male colleagues.[16] Yet decades after this significant milestone, women officers still face serious problems that preclude their complete participation in all facets of policing.

According to a survey conducted in 2000 by the National Center for Women and Policing, women currently comprise only 13 percent of all sworn law enforcement officers at the municipal, county, and state level.[17] Women of color hold only 4.9% of these positions; they are 37.7% of the total number of women in law enforcement. Unfortunately, not only are these numbers of women in policing small, but the pace of progress has been painfully slow. The percentage of women in law enforcement has increased only by approximately 0.5 percent per year over the last several years.[18] At this rate, women will not achieve equal representation with men in the police profession for at least another 70 years.

Some of the most notable progress is seen in those agencies who have faced a court-ordered consent decree to hire and promote women. For example, in the 2000 study by the National Center for Women and Policing, 10 of the top 25 agencies surveyed (the 25 agencies with the highest percentage of sworn women) had a consent decree in place regarding the hiring and promotion of women and minorities. In contrast, only 4 of the 25 agencies with the lowest percentage of sworn women had such a consent decree. The powerful effect of consent decrees was further demonstrated by a comparison of the average representation of the hiring and promotion of women in those agencies with and without a consent decree. On average, agencies without such a consent decree reported that 9.7 percent of their sworn personnel were women, whereas those with a consent decree indicated that they had 14 percent representation. A similar contrast is seen for the percentage of women of color, which is 6.3 percent in agencies without a consent decree and 11.7 percent in agencies with one.[19] Moreover, black women, despite their small numbers, make up a full 40 percent of women police officers.[20] Some reasons for such a high representation of black female police officers were cited in a study by Sokoloff, Price, and Kuleshnyk. They found that black female police officers, although they acknowledged discrimination in policing, said that the discrimination was no different than in jobs outside policing. The officers chose to work in policing because it offers steady employment, good wages and benefits, and clear rules for promotion.[21]

In any group, minority members typically do not impact the culture of the majority group until they comprise a significant representation. Because women currently represent less than 15 percent of law enforcement officers, they continue to be "tokens" in the field. As such, they are usually subject to intense scrutiny and are unable to make major changes in the way policing is conducted.[22] Many women officers are victimized by harassment and discrimination, which take many forms and can even endanger their lives.[23] Although some women have made it to the top of law enforcement agencies, female police executives remain a rarity[24] and seldom receive the support of the rest of the organization. The remainder of this chapter explores these

issues and other barriers that currently face women in the field of law enforcement.

BARRIERS FACING WOMEN POLICE OFFICERS

Stereotypes of Women and Policing

It is a men's club. It really, really, really is. If you get a woman in, you're concerned. You think—Are we gonna have to watch what we say? Is she gonna be one of the guys? Is she gonna have enthusiasm for the job? Or is she someone who should be selling dresses, but she's a cop? Is she gonna quit when she breaks a nail? Is she gonna always be messing with her hairdo? I don't know. I think women cops really do belong in law enforcement, but if you're a woman, you've gotta be twice as good. You're judged twice as hard. I've seen women who were worthless cops persecuted and just as many worthless male cops were just . . . let slide. It's a double standard. We've gotten some good women in here—once you establish what they are, no problem.[25]

Television and movies portray policing as a profession in which high-speed car chases, street fights, and shootings are an everyday occurrence. However, the truth is that most police work involves answering routine calls from the public about crime, family problems, and neighborhood livability issues. In fact, some estimates are that 80 to 90 percent of policing involves noncriminal or service functions.[26]

Stereotypes and Physical Ability Testing Stereotypical thinking about the nature of policing leads to an erroneous belief that one of the most important attributes of a police officer is physical strength. Hiring processes therefore typically involve rigorous physical ability testing that places a heavy emphasis on upper-body strength. For example, many of the physical ability tests currently used around the country require the candidate to scale a solid 6-foot wall and then immediately engage in some other activity that is timed. Because most women take longer to get over the 6-foot wall, they often fail the test when they cannot complete it in the allotted time.

If this type of task were required for someone to be a successful police officer, the high rate of failure for women would perhaps be justifiable. However, a number of factors combine to make this type of ability testing an artificial and unfair barrier for women. First, these physical ability tests often have little to do with the actual job of policing. For example, it is not good police practice to jump over a solid 6-foot wall without first knowing what is on the other side. Many departments even have written policies expressly prohibiting such behaviors.

Other tasks included in physical ability tests from around the country include dragging a sandbag dummy or pushing a police car. Again, these activities are inadvisable—if not expressly prohibited—for most police officers. Passing this type of test cannot therefore be reasonably argued to constitute a requirement for successful police officer performance.

Second, many physical ability tests are required only for entry-level police officers. That current officers are not held to the same standard of physical ability and are not subject to routine testing again challenges the notion that passing is truly required for successful job performance.

Third, considerable evidence suggests that police agencies should place less emphasis on physical abilities and focus more on the knowledge, skills, and abilities required for successful implementation of a community policing model. For example, physical strength has *not* been shown to predict either general police effectiveness[27] or the ability to successfully handle dangerous situations.[28] Rather, some in the law enforcement community have suggested that alternative characteristics might be preferable to physical strength, such as the ability to defuse potential violence[29] and maintain composure in situations of conflict.[30]

The Question of Force   Of course, the question of force lies at the heart of the traditional reluctance to hire women in policing. A number of studies document that both police officers and community members are concerned that women are not strong enough or aggressive enough for police work.[31] Once a woman is hired, she is therefore constantly confronted with the stereotype regarding physical strength. Some women officers have even been put in situations in which a male officer will antagonize a suspect and force the woman officer into a physical confrontation just to see if she can handle it.

> The one major thing that came up endlessly, endlessly, endlessly, and I still have to answer this sometimes, starts "Women on the job, I have nothing against women on the job. But what would you do if you found yourself in an alley with a big 250-pound man comin' at you? What would you do?" Always. It's always that guy in the alley. Every day, that same scenario. Every day. Always. Always. Always. They say this: "You're there. You have no gun, no radio, no club. And you're at the end of a dead-end alley. And some huge 250-pound raving maniac is coming after you. What would you do?" And I always say, "I'd fall in love. What are you, crazy?"

> The alley thing comes up constantly. It's one of those urban folk legends. It's always "What are you gonna do if you face a criminal and you're alone? You're gonna have to use your gun."

> What we get—it's a 250-pound Finlander. A Finlander drunk. Who just came out of the woods after all week cutting wood. A woodsman. A 250-pound drunken woodsman. But most of the time it is a Finlander. You arm yourself with a pastie and a beer and throw it at him. That'll change his mind about you![32]

In fact, there are no documented cases of negative outcomes that were due to the lack of strength or aggression among female officers. Rather, research has documented not only that female officers exhibit more reasoned caution than do their male counterparts, but also that they increase this tendency in their male partners.[33]

As a result, some law enforcement agencies have begun to realize that they must eliminate these stereotypes and replace physical ability testing with a more realistic assessment of a person's physical health and conditioning. Additionally, agencies that embrace a community policing model of law enforcement understand that the best police officers are those who can de-escalate violence, mediate disputes, and communicate with a variety of people. Often these officers will be women.[34]

Discrimination in the Hiring Process

In addition to physical ability testing, other aspects of the hiring process serve as artificial barriers to women police officers. For example, the written examination, if not properly developed, can have a negative impact on women and minority applicants. If questions are not fairly written and objectively evaluated, they can be used to eliminate candidates who would otherwise make outstanding officers.

An even greater source of concern, however, is the oral interview process. Many law enforcement agencies establish oral interview boards that consist mainly of current officers who are not screened for bias or trained on how to interview applicants. These interviewers then bring to the process their own prejudices and images of a good police officer, and these preconceived notions can serve to the detriment of female applicants. For example, women often receive lower scores from these oral boards because their life experiences are not valued as highly as those of the men who compete. Men with a background in the military or in security work are typically given higher scores than are women with a background in social service areas despite the fact that social services likely provide a better preparation for community policing than do the armed forces.

Both written and oral examinations can therefore be used to keep women and minorities out of policing. To address this problem, agencies must examine not only their testing process but also their underlying assumptions about what makes a successful officer.

Challenges of the Training Process

Academy Training

> When we were going through the academy, it was around all the time. Sexual comments were always being made. Instructors were always hitting on the women and then telling you that your attitude is bad and if you don't shape up, you're gonna be terminated.[35]

Once applicants are selected by a law enforcement agency, they attend a training academy, where they learn not only job skills but also the culture in which they will work. For many agencies, this culture is paramilitary: it has a boot-camp style of training and a heavy emphasis on physical conditioning, military drills, and rigid rules of conduct. In this type of academy, recruits spend a lot of time in physical conditioning, marching, and other military-type activities. They are taught to obey orders and not question authority. Very little emphasis is placed on skills such as communicating with people from all walks of life, de-escalating violence, solving neighborhood and family problems, or mediating disputes.

For women, the experience of attending a training academy is very different from that of their male peers. Among the academy class, there is typically only a small number of women, often only one woman. The women are therefore subject to intense scrutiny, by classmates and instructors alike. Women may even be singled out in training and subjected to various forms of harassment or taunting. Any mistake made by a female recruit can be seized on as an opportunity for humiliation. This scrutiny is especially true in live-in academies, which remain common and create an atmosphere that encourages hazing and sexual harassment.

Live-in academies also cause hardships for anyone responsible for the care of children or other family members. Of course, the vast majority of these caregivers are women, and the hardships of a live-in academy are thus especially severe for single mothers.

Another obstacle for women who enter the field of law enforcement is the training in firearms. Many women who enter policing have never held or fired a gun, and their lack of familiarity with weapons can cause a great deal of stress on the firing range. In contrast, men who enter the field of policing often come from a background in the military or private security and therefore have at least some familiarity with firearms. As a result, some police instructors and recruits use the firing range as an environment in which to denigrate and harass the women. Unless academy trainers on the firing range provide a nonstressful environment and moral support, these women can fail the firearms instruction and thereby fail the academy.

Attrition among Female Recruits Failing or otherwise leaving the academy is, unfortunately, quite common among female recruits. In one study of the Los Angeles Police Department conducted between 1990 and 1999, for example, women were twice as likely as men to leave the academy. Specifically, 19 percent of the women who entered the police academy resigned or were terminated from the program whereas only 9 percent of the men resigned or were terminated.[36] In many academies, minority women leave at even higher rates. Clearly, some academy instructors have the attitude that their purpose is to wash out as many recruits as possible rather than to provide assistance in areas in which improvement is needed.

Field Training When new officers successfully complete the recruit academy, they are then assigned to work with a field training officer. Unfortunately, this step constitutes another area in which women officers are particularly vulnerable to discrimination and sexual harassment. Some field training officers use the power of their position to force female recruits into having sex with them, implying subtly or not so subtly that the recruits will receive poor evaluations if they do not submit. Others use their power to subject female recruits to jokes, insults, and other forms of sexual harassment. Given their status as officers on probation, women victimized by their field training officers are placed in a terrible dilemma regarding how to respond.

Like academy instructors, field training officers for years have sought to maintain an image of being tough and to wash out large numbers of recruits. With the increasing challenge of recruitment, however, the emphasis in training is beginning to shift from washing out recruits to assisting them in learning the necessary skills. To the extent that this transformation occurs, it will benefit female as well as male officers.

Isolation of Women Officers

The roll call room was a very large area; you had two long tables with two long benches at each table, and on the four-to-twelve shift, quite a few officers were there

to attend roll call. And there the room would be with my female partner and me sitting at one table by ourselves—we had our own table—and the rest of the watch sat across the room at the other table. A fifteen-foot-long table. It was ours. Whoever got there first—if one of us got to one table, all the men would sit at the other table. If the next day, I sat at that one, they'd all sit at the other one. Even my male partner. Because he had to get along with the guys, too. They all kind of felt sorry for our partners, as though they were the sacrificial lambs, so our partners had an image to keep up, too. Not going over to the other side.[37]

Women who enter law enforcement soon learn that they are not accepted as equally valued members of the organization. Research consistently demonstrates that the negative attitude of male colleagues is the single most significant problem reported by female officers.[38] Even though there may be a superficial acceptance of women, they remain excluded from the "brotherhood" of which male officers are a part. This exclusion can take a number of forms. Some women are systematically kept from receiving information that will help them in their careers. Others are discouraged from participating in social activities with their coworkers. For example, male officers often bond through very macho types of activities such as hunting, fishing, drinking, and sports. If women do force their way into these social activities, they can put their "reputations" at risk, especially if the activities involve alcohol.

Clearly, being the only woman or one of few women in a paramilitary organization such as a police department is stressful. Some women have sought to counteract this isolation by forming organizations to provide moral support and to address common problems. These organizations exist in some larger police departments with a higher percentage of women. There are also national police organizations such as the International Association of Women Police and the National Center for Women and Policing that provide training and advice to women experiencing problems in their careers. When women do organize at the local or national level, they are often able to force changes in policies and procedures. For example, some women police officers have organized and created change on such issues as pregnancy leave, lack of promotions, sexual harassment, and domestic violence.

The Double Standard in Performance Evaluations

Nearly all law enforcement agencies evaluate the performance of their employees on an annual or semiannual basis. These performance evaluations can have a major impact on the future career of an officer. When officers apply for transfers to specialty positions, the person who makes the decision on the transfer frequently reviews the personnel file of the officer, which includes the performance evaluations. Sometimes performance evaluations are used as a basis to determine who is promoted or sent to special training.

Unfortunately, many women officers believe that a double standard is used to judge the performance of male versus female officers. These women believe that they must outperform their male colleagues to be considered "as good" as them. In other words, these women feel that they have to make more arrests, recover more stolen automobiles, or write more traffic tickets to receive the same "competent" rating as a male peer.

Many female officers also have the sense that they are continuously being judged more harshly than their male coworkers are. For example, women in policing are viewed by many of their male colleagues as "weak" or as "token hires." To overcome these negative stereotypes, women often feel that they must constantly prove themselves as competent in all facets of policing. In contrast, men are seen as establishing a reputation for competence or good police work that then follows them for their entire career.

Race and Sexual Orientation This double standard can operate to the particular detriment of women of color, if it is combined with the racial prejudices of their supervisors. For example, minority women are viewed as "tokens" even more than white women are. Because women of color are presumed to "count twice" on affirmative action statis-

tics—once for being a woman and once for being a minority—male officers often have the erroneous perception that the women were hired only for that reason.[39]

Lesbian women also face issues due to stereotyping. Some lesbian officers report that they are treated better than the heterosexual women in the department because the men believe they are tougher and better able to handle the physical demands of the job. On the other hand, male officers sometimes feel that their sexuality is being threatened by lesbian officers. As a result, lesbian officers may be targeted for severe harassment based on their sexual orientation.[40]

Men Doing "Women's Work" in Policing In addition to the double standard, there is another dichotomy apparent in many performance evaluations. That is, male police officers tend to receive very high ratings when they perform some activity that is typically seen as a woman's job. To illustrate, a man who works diligently to solve a case involving child abuse, rape, or domestic violence may be lauded for his efforts. Yet a woman working the same type of case is less likely to receive any special recognition, because female officers are expected to demonstrate compassion for women and children who are victimized.

This dichotomy is yet another example of gender stereotyping and the way in which it affects the perception of male versus female police officers. Only when police agencies explicitly question such assumptions will the double standard regarding male and female officer performance disappear.

Job Assignments for Male versus Female Officers

In all law enforcement agencies, certain assignments are highly valued by male (and often female) officers. These assignments are usually dangerous or otherwise require a great deal of physical endurance. Examples include the Special Weapons and Tactics (SWAT) teams, undercover narcotics units, gang teams, motorcycle patrols, and homicide investigations. In contrast, less desirable assignments typically include domestic violence units, child abuse investigations, community relations, and other assignments that have traditionally been viewed as "women's work" within policing.

It is often very difficult for women to receive the coveted assignments, especially minority women. Because a great deal of competition is involved, the men who get the prestigious assignments usually do so because it has been arranged by their mentors within the organization. In contrast, women are typically assigned the jobs that are not sought after by most of the men.

Unfortunately, these practices negatively affect the opportunities for women's advancement. First, assignment to the coveted positions usually carries a great deal of weight in the oral interviews that are conducted to evaluate candidates for promotions. The oral interview boards (frequently comprised of all men) understand that these jobs are highly desirable and believe that these experiences prepare people for promotion—regardless of whether it is true. These assignments have a sense of mystique about them; they are seen as "warrior's work." So, those officers who have worked such specialty assignments (the vast majority of whom are men) typically receive higher scores on oral interviews, which then assist them in being promoted.

On the other hand, those same oral interview members frequently do not place much value on the less desirable assignments. Not surprisingly, these jobs are viewed as not constituting "real police work." In other words, they are "women's work" within policing. So, the officers who have worked these particular assignments (many of whom are women) tend to receive lower scores on oral interviews, which then limit their chances for promotion.

In this era of community policing, agencies are shifting toward an emphasis on problem solving and community partnership, an emphasis in which these "less desirable" assignments will actually provide better preparation for successful job performance. As this transformation takes place nationwide, it is hoped that police agencies will seek to demystify "warrior's work" and place a tangible value on positions that require strong communication skills, creative problem solving, and community cooperation.

Unfair Promotion Practices—"The Brass Ceiling"

Something happens to a woman that doesn't happen with men. It's a matter of degree. So, if a man gets promoted to sergeant and he gets transferred to a new precinct and he's put in charge of a squad of people on a shift, they're gonna kind of watch him for a while and he's gonna have to prove himself, prove that he's got the ability to do it. Put a woman in the same position? She's gonna have to prove it and prove it and prove it and prove it and prove it. You never stop having to prove yourself. Never.[41]

In a recent survey conducted by the National Center for Women and Policing, women were found to hold 5.6 percent of the top command jobs in law enforcement (captain and above) and 9.2 percent of the supervisory jobs. Minority women were seen in only 1.1 percent of top command and 2.8 percent of supervisory positions.[42] These statistics vividly convey the difficulty that has historically been faced by women who wish to break into the management structure of police agencies.

The number of women who have ever been chief of a major police agency can be counted on one hand: Chief Penny Harrington, Portland, Oregon; Chief Elizabeth Watson, Houston, Texas; Chief Beverly Harvard, Atlanta, Georgia; Chief Carol Mehrling, Montgomery County, Maryland; and Chief Jan Strauss, Mesa, Arizona. Of these five women, only one, Beverly Harvard, is a woman of color.

Women have fared a little better in smaller departments, campus police agencies, and elected positions as sheriff. Nonetheless, of the thousands of police chief jobs in the United States, women serve in only about 125.

Obviously, the many forms of bias that take place in selection and promotion have kept the number of women at the supervisory and command levels artificially low. Few women receive promotions because of all the reasons already outlined in this chapter, including discrimination in performance evaluations. However, another factor that limits the promotion of women to supervisory and command levels is that female officers often do not even apply to take the tests. There are several reasons for their reluctance:

- Women view the promotion systems as biased against them and do not wish to expend the effort it takes to prepare for the process—especially when they believe that they will not succeed.
- Women know that if they do succeed in the promotion process and receive a promotion, they will once again be under intense scrutiny—more than their male counterparts. Female officers know that promotion means that they would once again have to prove themselves, and the "proving" would never end. As a supervisor or command-level person, a woman would be more highly visible within her organization and thus more intensely watched.
- Usually, a promotion requires an officer to relocate to a new unit and drop to the bottom of the seniority list. Because many aspects of an officer's work life (such as shift assignments, days off, and vacation days) are regulated by seniority, promotion may therefore mean assignment to a shift that makes it extremely difficult to find child care. The promotion may even mean that the officer can no longer have weekends available to spend with family; these issues can be especially difficult for single mothers.
- Especially at the command level, women often find themselves being promoted back into the "women's jobs" that they had previously left behind. For example, women commanders are frequently given assignments to head the records division, planning division, youth division, domestic violence and sexual assault divisions, or community relations. In contrast, men who are promoted to the level of commander are typically given prestigious assignments to head patrol divisions, detective divisions, vice and narcotics divisions, or other tactical units.

The reluctance of many women officers to even apply for promotions, combined with the other aspects of discrimination, severely limits the number of women in supervisory and command positions. As police agencies begin to appreciate the value of women in their ranks—especially the contribution that women can make to a community policing orientation—it is hoped that they will rethink their

policies and procedures for promotion. Only then will the numbers of women increase at all ranks of the police organization.

Lack of Family-Friendly Policies

One of the many issues that confronts women in policing is the lack of family-friendly policies and programs such as child care, pregnancy leave, elder care, and other related issues. Because female officers do not typically have a great deal of seniority during their childbearing years, these problems are often exacerbated by their assignments to the least desirable shifts.

Child Care and Family Leave   Obviously, it is difficult for anyone to find adequate child care from midnight to 8 A.M., or during any hours other than the typical 8 A.M. to 5 P.M. workday. Despite this fact, almost no American police agencies offer child care. One notable exception is the Portland (Oregon) Police Bureau, which offers on-site child care at the headquarters building as well as a drop-in child care facility near the courthouse. Because so many officers are single mothers or are in families in which both parents work, child care often is the determining factor in whether a woman will begin or continue a career in law enforcement.

Although child care is one of the most obvious concerns for women in policing, a number of other factors make it difficult for officers with family responsibilities. For example, the rigid culture of many law enforcement agencies means that a woman who takes time off to care for sick children or other family members is too often seen as disloyal or not really dedicated to her career. Because women often have to use their allotted sick leave to care for family members, they are more likely than men to be viewed as unreliable employees when it comes time for promotion or assignment to specialty units. Police agencies must therefore begin to restructure their policies governing child care and sick leave to better address the needs of valuable employees. They must also redesign their criteria for performance evaluation to ensure that officers will not be penalized for taking care of important family responsibilities. Like in so many other areas, changes in child care and family leave would benefit male and female officers alike.

Special Issues of Pregnancy Although pregnancy should be a joyful time, too often it is the cause of problems for women pursuing careers in policing. Pregnant officers may face myopic administrators who refuse to establish light-duty positions or deal with other pregnancy-related issues. For example, some pregnant women refuse to qualify on the shooting range during their pregnancy, fearing the effect that the noise and lead pollution would have on the fetus. Some of these women have been fired or forced onto unpaid disability leave because they failed to qualify on the firing range.

On the other hand, some law enforcement administrators take a position at the opposite end of the scale; they order women to immediately report their pregnancies and then remove them from their current positions. These administrators claim that they are safeguarding the fetus; however, such reassignments often have extremely detrimental effects on the woman's future career. Some agencies refuse to provide any light-duty assignments for pregnant officers, forcing them to take unpaid leave until they can return to duty.

Unfortunately, law enforcement agencies have only begun to examine their policies regarding pregnancy and to think about alternatives. As the need for women in policing creates an increase in their representation, however, the pressure for fair pregnancy policies will only heighten. Issues such as light duty, firearms qualification, and even appropriate uniforms must be considered by agencies seeking to retain their valuable female employees.

Sexual Harassment and Retaliation

In a study conducted with 1,200 women in various Florida law enforcement agencies, 61 percent of the women surveyed reported experiencing sexual harassment on the job. In fact, 40 percent of them indicated that sexually oriented materials or sexually oriented jokes are a daily occurrence, and many stated that such harassment was just something they had to endure if they wanted to maintain a career in law enforcement.[43] Another study conducted in a large municipal police department similarly revealed that 68 percent of the respondents had been sexually harassed on the job.[44] Clearly, sexual harassment is a serious problem facing women in law enforcement.

Because sexual harassment is based on the fundamental need of one person to control another, it is easy to see why women in traditionally male jobs such as policing are especially targeted. In order to control women who enter these nontraditional jobs, men often attack them with an ongoing barrage of sexual innuendoes, jokes, cartoons, requests for dates, and demands for sex or physical touching. Most women try to ignore the sexual harassment and just do their jobs.

However, over months and years of continuing abuse, victims can become exhausted. Many women officers end up quitting their jobs or taking a medical leave of absence to deal with the physical and emotional results of this abuse. Ironically, when the women who are victims of sexual harassment pursue either of these actions, it confirms in the minds of many men that they were in fact "weak" and could not handle a man's job.[45]

Some women try to deal with sexual harassment by filing complaints, believing that their agency will support them and make the harassment stop. Sadly, such support seldom happens. Rather, the women who file complaints against other officers are usually seen as disloyal and not to be trusted. They are then subjected to a wide variety of retaliatory measures designed to make them keep their mouths shut about other officers. Retaliation can range from shunning (where coworkers refuse to speak to the complainant) to refusing to provide her with cover on emergency calls, thereby endangering her life and the lives of any involved citizens.

Among the most common types of retaliation are the following:

- Shunning or ostracizing, in which other officers refuse to talk to the woman who is being victimized or prevent the woman from receiving information that is important to her job performance or personal safety.

- Stalking or harassing, in which the victim is subjected to obscene telephone calls, calls during which the caller says nothing, hang-up calls at all hours of the day and night, threatening or harassing letters or notes, damage to her automobile, articles left on her desk or in her work area, and other actions that are intended to intimidate or harass.
- Spreading rumors about the woman's sexual activity or other demeaning information.
- Holding the woman to a higher standard of performance than her colleagues, so her evaluation reports become more critical and limit her opportunities for advancement within the organization.
- Filing baseless and harassing internal affairs complaints; this action is done either by other members of the organization or by citizens who have been enlisted to help the harasser.
- Denying access to training opportunities.
- Denying requests for transfer to specialty jobs.
- Denying applications for promotion.
- Failing to provide backup in emergency situations; this action is the ultimate form of retaliation.

When it becomes apparent to women officers that they will not receive backup in a timely manner, many leave the organization out of fear for their lives.[46]

Unfortunately, all these forms of sexual harassment and retaliation currently remain widespread within the field of law enforcement. A number of measures have been implemented in agencies around the country to address the problem, including training programs, alternative avenues for reporting, and improved disciplinary procedures. However, these efforts appear to have made few inroads on the problem, as evidenced by the increasing number and size of payouts by law enforcement agencies that face lawsuits filed by women who were victimized. Much progress has yet to be made to rid the field of these egregious forms of harassment and discrimination against women officers.

Police Family Violence

One final issue that has surfaced in the last few years is the astounding rate of violence in police officer

families. In one study, the number of police officers who admitted to using violence in their families was 40 percent, a figure that is substantially higher than that among the general public.[47] Because many female officers are married to male officers, those who are victimized by their husbands do not typically report the abuse.

Women officers who are victims of domestic violence are reluctant to report the crimes for a number of reasons, one of which is they know that they will be seen as "weak" in the eyes of their fellow officers. When they do report the violence, moreover, they know that they will likely suffer retaliation at the hands of coworkers and (his) friends. Some law enforcement agencies have even charged the victimized female officer with an offense while not taking action against the abuser. These charges have included:

- Failing to report the abuse in the beginning. Because abuse is a crime, the woman is accused of having "covered up" a crime.
- Causing embarrassment to the law enforcement agency. This charge is usually made when the officer lives in another jurisdiction and an outside law enforcement agency is called to the residence because of the violence.
- Lying. It is not unusual for victims of domestic violence to retract their statements or to fail to tell the complete story at the first interview. When a woman officer's story is found to be inconsistent, she is charged with lying.

Because many law enforcement agencies have so badly mishandled cases of domestic violence perpetrated by a police officer, the victims often decide not to reveal the abuse. What this silence does, however, is increase the likelihood that cases of domestic violence in the community will be handled by an officer who has personally perpetrated such abuse. Clearly, radical changes are needed for police organizations to effectively detect, thoroughly investigate, and decisively respond to crimes of violence perpetrated by those within their ranks.

Toward that end, a few recent efforts to improve police policy in the area of officer-involved domestic violence have been made by organizations such as the

National Center for Women and Policing and the International Association of Chiefs of Police. However, domestic violence remains a serious problem for women in policing as well as for civilian women whose significant other is a police officer. (For a fuller discussion of this issue, see Griggs, chap. 24.)

THE FUTURE FOR WOMEN IN POLICING

The challenges facing women in policing are indeed daunting. However, there are signs that things are beginning to improve and that young women currently looking to law enforcement as a career may not have to experience all the tribulations of their predecessors.

First, current economic conditions are forcing law enforcement agencies to be more competitive in their efforts to recruit and retain successful police officers. As a result, they face increasing pressures to widen their search for qualified applicants and to offer pay and benefits packages that can compete with other employers in industries such as technology.

Second, police agencies nationwide are shifting toward a community-policing orientation in which officers work cooperatively with the community to solve problems of crime and livability. As a result, agencies are being forced to redefine what constitutes a "good" police officer and hence a "good" job candidate. In the future, departments will need to recruit applicants with backgrounds that would not traditionally have been valued, such as nursing, child care, education, and social services. Individuals from these fields are likely to possess many of the qualities required for successful implementation of community policing, including excellent communication skills and the ability to defuse potentially violent confrontations. In many cases, these candidates will also be women.

Third, female officers across the nation continue to file discrimination lawsuits in increasing numbers, and they are forcing changes in the way police agencies operate. These costly lawsuits sometimes result in court-ordered consent decrees that require agencies to change their policies and practices. These

consent decrees have a powerful effect on increasing the number of women within an agency. Yet some agencies have demonstrated that this progress is only maintained as long as the watchful eye of the court is upon them.

For example, the Pittsburgh Police Department was under a court order from 1975 to 1991 that mandated that for every white male hired, one white female, one African American male, and one African American female must be hired. At the time the court order was imposed, the department had only 1 percent of women at the rank of police officer. By 1990, they had the highest representation of women police officers in the country at 27.2 percent. However, once the court order was lifted, the number of new women who were hired was only 8.5 percent. As of 2001, the percentage of women serving in the rank of police officer was 22 percent and continuing to decline.[48]

Many of the women who file these lawsuits cannot return to their jobs because of the extreme retaliation they would face. Such retaliation could have serious detrimental effects on their personal and professional well-being. However, these courageous women who challenge the system are forcing improvements that will benefit the women—and men—who subsequently enter the field.

Finally, that time is nearing in the history of women in policing when there will be no more "firsts." Nearly every woman in law enforcement today is or has been the "first" at something within her agency: the first woman hired, the first woman promoted, the first woman on the SWAT team, the first woman commander, and so on. Unfortunately, these "first" women have experienced intense scrutiny as they did their jobs and, in some cases, advanced within their organizations. Although they have opened the door to other women, they typically paid a heavy price for doing so. Many did not survive in their careers.

These "first" women are the true heroes in law enforcement. They have broken through the barriers in large and small law enforcement agencies at the local, state, and national levels. Due to the efforts of these brave women, others entering the field of policing today do not have to deal with being the "first." It therefore remains for future women to continue making changes, removing obstacles, and seeking to fulfill the promise of full participation in all aspects of policing.

events might affect the future prospects of women in policing.

DISCUSSION QUESTIONS

1. Harrington and Lonsway discuss a number of strengths that women bring to policing. Discuss three of these strengths. Try to decide if your answer is based on a gender-neutral or gendered concept, as explained by Schulz in chap. 31.

2. Harrington and Lonsway refer to many stereotypes about women who become police officers. Make a list of those stereotypes and discuss whether the situation is similar or different in your own community.

3. Much of this chapter is devoted to an enumeration of barriers to success that women officers encounter every day. List five or six of these barriers. Which of the barriers that women police officers face on the job would be most amenable to elimination by a police department? Which would be most difficult to eliminate? Explain your responses.

4. What steps can a police chief initiate in order to develop a nonsexist, antiracist environment for police officers in the department? What prevents a chief from issuing the necessary orders to take these steps?

5. Discuss potential spillover effects to the community if a police department engages in any form of discrimination within the department.

6. Harrington and Lonsway discuss the future of women in policing. However, this chapter was written before the events of September 11, 2001. Explain how those

NOTES

1. Robert E. Worden, The Causes of Police Brutality: Theory and Evidence on Police Use of Force, in *And Justice for All: Understanding and Controlling Police Abuse of Force,* ed. William A. Geller and Hans Toch (Washington, DC: Police Executive Research Forum, 1995), 31–60; Joel Garner, John Buchanan, and John Hepburn, Understanding the Use of Force by and against the Police, Washington DC: U.S. Department of Justice, National Institute of Justice, November 1996. NCJ-158614.

2. F. Horvath, The Police Use of Deadly Force: A Description of Selected Characteristics of Intrastate Incidents, *Journal of Police Science Administration* 15 (1987): 226–238.

3. Kimberly Lonsway, Michelle Wood and Katherine Spiller, Officer Gender and Excessive Force, *Law and Order,* 50, 12 (Dec. 2002):60–66.

4. Ibid.

5. Ibid.

6. Victor E. Kappeler, Stephen F. Kappeler, and Rolando V. Del Carmen, A Content Analysis of Police Civil Liability Cases: Decisions of the Federal District Courts 1978–1990, *Journal of Criminal Justice* 21 (1993): 325–337.

7. Amnesty International, Police Brutality and Excessive Force in the New York City Police Department. Available at http://www.amnesty.it/Allibtop/1996/AMR/25103696

8. April Taylor, Detroit Worst in Brutality Payouts. *Detroit News,* July 8, 1998.

9. Kathleen Kenna, L.A.'s Dirty War, *Toronto Star,* March 26, 2000.

10. Sean A. Grennan, Findings on the Role of Officer Gender in Violent Encounters with Citizens, *Journal of Police Science and Administration* 15, no. 1 (1987): 78–85; Gary R. Perlstein, Policewomen and Policemen: A Comparative Look, *Police Chief* 39, no. 3 (1972): 72–74.

11. Kimberly Lonsway, Michelle Wood, and Katherine Spiller, Officer Gender and Excessive Force.

12. H. W. Bartlett, and A. Rosenblum, *Policewomen Effectiveness* (Denver: Denver Civil Service Commission, 1977); Patricia Marshall, Policewomen on Patrol, *Manpower* 5, no. 10 (1973): 14–20.

13. Alissa Pollitz Worden, The Attitudes of Women and Men in Policing: Testing Conventional and Contemporary Wisdom, *Criminology* 31, no. 2 (1993): 203–236; Stanard and Associates Inc., An Investigation of Police Officer Morale (Chicago, IL, 1997), 17.

14. Robert J. Homant and Daniel B. Kennedy, Police Perceptions of Spouse Abuse—A Comparison of Male and Female Officers, *Journal of Criminal Justice* 13 (1985): 29–47; Daniel B. Kennedy and Robert J. Homant, Battered Women's Evaluation of the Police Response, *Victimology: An International Journal* 9, no. 1 (1984): 174–179.

15. Anthony Vastola, Women in Policing: An Alternative Ideology, *The Police Chief* (January 1977); Lewis J. Sherman, A Psychological View of Women in Policing, *Journal of Police Science and Administration* 1, no. 4 (1973): 383–394.

16. D. M. Schulz, *From Social Worker to Crimefighter: Women in United States Municipal Policing* (Westport, CT: Praeger, 1995).

17. Equality Denied: *The Status of Women in Policing.* National Center for Women & Policing, 2000. Research is based on a stratified random sample of 282 law enforcement agencies with 100 or more sworn personnel.

18. Ibid.

19. Ibid.

20. S. E. Martin, see chap. 34.

21. Natalie J. Sokoloff, Barbara Raffel Price, and Irka Kuleshnyk, A Case Study of Black and White Women Police in an Urban Police Department, *The Justice Professional* 6 (winter/spring 1992): 68–85.

22. Joanne Belknap and Jill Kastens Shelley, The New Lone Ranger: Policewomen on Patrol, *American Journal of Police* 12, no. 2 (1992): 47–75; Carol Ann Martin, Remarks: Women Police and Stress, *The Police Chief* (March 1983):107–109; Judie Gaffin Wexler and Deana Dorman Logan, Sources of Stress among Women Police Officers, *Journal of Police Science and Administration* 11, no. 1 (1983): 46–53.

23. Carole G. Garrison, Nancy Grant, and Kenneth McCormick, Utilization of Police Women, *The Police Chief,* no. 9 (1988):32–35, 69–73; Independent Commission on the Los Angeles Police Department, Report of the Independent Commission, 17; Susan E. Martin, On the Move: The Status of Women in Policing (1990), Washington, DC: Police Foundation.

24. Equality Denied: The Status of Women in Policing. National Center for Women & Policing, February, 2000.

25. Connie Fletcher, *Breaking and Entering* (New York: Harper Collins, 1995) 191.

26. Daniel J. Bell, Policewomen: Myths and Realities, *Journal of Police Science and Administration* 10, no. 1 (1982): 112–120.

27. Lewis J. Sherman, A Psychological View of Women in Policing, in *Police Roles in the Seventies: Professionalization in America,* ed. Jack Kinton (Ann Arbor, MI: Edwards Brothers, 1973), 77–95.

28. Bell, Policewomen: Myths and Realities.

29. Marlene W. Lehtinen, Sexism in Police Departments, *Trial Magazine,* September 1976, 52–55.

30. C. J. Rogers, Women in Criminal Justice: Similar and Unique Obstacles to Their Acceptance in Law Enforcement and Corrections. Paper presented at the annual meeting of the Academy of Criminal Justice Sciences, 1987, cited in Joseph Balkin, Why Policemen Don't Like Policewomen, *Journal of Police Science and Administration* 16, no. 1 (1988): 29–38.

31. Balkin, Why Policemen Don't Like Policewomen; Kenneth W. Kerber, Steven M. Andes, and Michele B. Mittler, Citizen Attitudes Regarding the Competence of Female Police Officers, *Journal of Police Science* 5, no. 3 (1977): 337–347; R. Linden, Women in Policing—A Study of Lower Mainland Royal Canadian

Mounted Police Detachments, *Canadian Police College Journal* 7 (1984): 217–229; M. Vega and I. J. Silverman, Female Officers as Viewed by Their Male Counterparts, *Police Studies* 5 (1982): 31–39; Karin E. Winnard, Policewomen and the People They Serve, *Police Chief,* August 1986, 62–63; Nancy C. Jurik, An Officer and a Lady: Organizational Barriers to Women Working as Correctional Officers in Men's Prisons, *Social Problems* 32, no. 4 (1985): 375–388.

32. Fletcher, *Breaking and Entering,* 1–2.

33. Rogers, Women in Criminal Justice.

34. S. L. Miller, *Gender and Community Policing: Walking the Talk* (Boston: Northeastern University, 1999).

35. Fletcher, *Breaking and Entering,* 78.

36. Police Academy and Probationary Officer Attrition, Los Angeles Police Commission, 2000.

37. Fletcher, *Breaking and Entering,* 114–115.

38. Independent Commission on the Los Angeles Police Department, Report of the Independent Commission, 17; William M. Timmins and Brad E. Hainsworth, Attracting and Retaining Females in Law Enforcement: Sex-Based Problems of Women Cops in 1988, *International Journal of Offender Therapy and Comparative Criminology* (1988): 197–205; Wexler and Logan, Sources of Stress among Women Police Officers.

39. Martin, chap. 34.

40. Mary P. Koss, Lisa A. Goodman, Angela Browne, Louise F. Fitzgerald, Gwendolyn Puryear Keita, and Nancy Felipe Russo, *No Safe Haven: Male Violence against Women at Home, at Work, and in the Community* (Washington, DC: American Psychological Association, 1994), 114.

41. Fletcher, *Breaking and Entering,* 208.

42. *Equality Denied: The Status of Women in Policing— 1999.* National Center for Women & Policing, February 2000, p. 11.

43. George V. Robinson, Sexual Harassment in Florida Law Enforcement: Panacea or Pandora's Box, 1993, Senior Leadership Research Paper available at http://www.state.fl.us/FCJEI/publications.asp

44. David Nichols, The Brotherhood: Sexual Harassment in Police Agencies, *Women Police* (Summer 1995), 11.

45. For a comprehensive review of the antecedents and outcomes of workplace sexual harassment, including in nontraditional fields such as policing, see Koss et al., *No Safe Haven.*

46. Recruiting & Retaining Women: A Self-Assessment Guide for Law Enforcement, National Center for Women & Policing, December 2000.

47. Peter H. Neidig, Harold E. Russell, and Albert F. Seng, Interspousal Aggression in Law Enforcement Families: A Preliminary Investigation, *Police Studies: International Review of Development* 30 (spring 1992): 30–38.

48. Thanks to Laura Zaspel of the Pittsburgh Police Department for providing these figures.

Chapter 33

Lesbians in Policing:
Perceptions and Work Experiences within the Macho Cop Culture

Susan L. Miller, Kay B. Forest, and Nancy C. Jurik

ABSTRACT

Since the last edition of this reader was published in 1995, lesbian, gay, bisexual, and transgendered communities have fought hard to be recognized as well as to uncover and lessen the systematic bias and discrimination against them, including on the job. This chapter reports on the special challenges that lesbian police officers face within their departments. Interestingly, lesbian officers reported experiencing greater barriers as a result of their gender (because men see policing as such a "macho" job) rather than their sexual orientation. On the basis of information collected from two midwestern police departments in the United States—one emphasizing traditional crime control, the other community policing—the authors examine how women's lesbian sexual orientation affects their police performance in a macho culture in which gender, sexuality, and race are all important components. The number of lesbian officers in these studies was small ($N = 27$). It is very rare for research to be done with lesbians in the criminal justice system and particularly in policing.

The chapter focuses on the working environment and on lesbian officers' strategies for handling workplace barriers. It also explores the ways in which officers' multiple identities of race and ethnicity, gender, sexual orientation, and other systemic influences contribute to their choices of strategies for doing their police work and surviving in an often hostile environment. In fact, Miller and her colleagues find that lesbians of color had the most concern about disclosing their sexual identity. The chapter presents five themes, based on the officers' own words, that Miller and her colleagues consider to be the main issues facing lesbian police officers: (1) the risk involved for lesbian police officers who disclose their sexual identities ("coming out" of the closet) and the factors that influence that decision, (2) workforce adaptations and strategies, (3) job performance pressures and successes, (4) survival strategies, and (5) organizational changes, in other words, departmental policies and attitudes toward discrimination and availability of community policing assignments.

In recent years in the United States, many police departments have recognized the potential benefits of hiring police officers who reflect a cross section of the communities they serve, officers who exhibit greater diversity in race and ethnicity, religion, and sexual orientation. Although the criminal justice system is still dominated by a white, masculine, and heterosexual ethos (Messerschmidt 1993), police departments are beginning to respond to pressures from community activists and concerned lay people who see officer diversity as a step toward addressing years of mistrust and social divide between cops and citizens. Even so, racist (Leinen 1984; Christopher et al. 1991) and sexist (Martin 1980, 1990; Pike 1991) attitudes and behaviors remain a problem in many departments, similar to conditions found in society at large. "Outsiders" were historically excluded through recruitment and selection practices such as physical requirements (to exclude women), written tests or educational requirements (to exclude blacks), and "background investigations and personal interviews [that] further screen out candidates who failed to express the 'correct' attitudes toward the meaning of masculinity, including an aura of toughness and aggressiveness" (David and Brannon 1976).

The police subculture is particularly difficult to change. The daily reality of policing, as part of both a gendered and a sexualized institution, entails homosociability—"men generating a closeness between men" for informing, socializing, and mentoring (Britton 1990; Cockburn 1991, 189). Any suggestion of the possession of traditionally "feminine" traits, such as gentleness or sensitivity, encourages colleagues to brand men as "sissies" or "faggots" (Blumenfeld 1992). This division is exacerbated for female officers and gay or lesbian officers.

Changes in criminal justice agencies during the 1960s and 1970s included efforts to reform, professionalize, and follow equal employment opportunity laws. Reform discourses have challenged the formerly white, male, working-class police subculture and the accompanying notions of masculine compe-

tence that equate physical and verbal aggressiveness with good job performance (Britton 1995; Jurik and Martin 2001). The introduction of women into patrol jobs threatened the long-standing association of police work with masculinity (Martin 1992; Hunt 1984, 1990). Women's presence was met with overt hostility. Male police officers tried to create differences between themselves and women officers by emphasizing women's "femininity" (Messerschmidt 1993, 182). Some women in traditionally male occupations feel pressure to demonstrate traits consistent with "hegemonic masculinity" such as verbal aggressiveness and authority in order to "prove" their ability to do the job.[*] Other women emphasize feminine traits, such as passivity and flirtatiousness, to gain acceptance into male domains (Martin 1980). Ironically, lesbian women may be accepted as masculine exceptions to the "emphasized femininity" model. Yet women are not treated uniformly. For example, white male officers might attempt to shield white women from the dangers of the job, whereas black women may not be accorded such protections (Martin 1994; see also Martin, chap. 34). Hurtado (1989) contends that "white women experience 'subordination through seduction' while black women face 'subordination through rejection.'" Suspected lesbians may also be treated with less protection and increased hostilities (Martin and Jurik 1996).

Employment of lesbians and gay males as police officers is especially threatening to an occupation that values "traditional masculinity and middle-class morality" (Shilts 1980). Although many issues for lesbian officers are consistent with those that gay men experience, lesbians often occupy a unique position: They are assumed to be masculine and thus more competent than heterosexual female officers

---

Source: This article was written expressly for inclusion in this text.

---

[*]"Hegemonic masculinity" is a Western, capitalist interpretation of masculinity associated with authority, aggressiveness, technical competence, and heterosexist desire for and domination over women (Connell 1987). Its complement, "emphasized femininity," is a culturally idealized construct of femininity that is associated with sociability, fragility, compliance with a man's desires, sexual receptivity, marriage, housework, and child care (Connell 1987). Individuals are pressured to conform to these idealized cultural constructs that dictate gender-appropriate behavior for women and men.

to handle the job, yet they still are harassed because of both their gender and the curiosity and hostility from heterosexual male officers. Similar to gay men, lesbian officers must deal with internal harassment from homophobic officers as well as antagonism from members of the gay and lesbian community who have experienced decades of violence and repression by police and thus may view lesbian police officers as disloyal (Buhrke 1996). In fact, obstacles encountered by gay and lesbian police include both legal and social barriers internal to the police department as well as external issues. Opponents cite religious dogma and state sodomy laws as legal barriers, despite the fact that in most jurisdictions private acts between consenting adults cannot serve to disqualify applicants. Tension between private citizens and the police exist, supported by research findings that police are perpetrators in antigay attacks (8 percent of national survey results) or that police tend to trivialize or ignore crimes committed against gay and lesbian citizens (Comstock 1991; Karmen 1996; Kappeler, Sluder and Alpert 1998).

On the other hand, many people believe that job performance and competence are unrelated to sexual orientation. Many citizens now generally accept the premise that the police force must be diversified so as to accurately reflect the community that it serves. Another argument in favor of the hiring of lesbians is that police officers who are from an oppressed group themselves may have greater cultural sensitivity in dealing with citizens from other oppressed groups (Miller, Forest, and Jurik 1997). Hope exists that gay and lesbian officers could dispel some of the ignorance and homophobia among police officers. Gay and lesbian officers could mend feelings of distrust and hostility between the gay community and the police by becoming advocates for civil rights and acting as liaisons to the gay community. Recruitment of gay and lesbian officers could hasten these objectives. Unfortunately, the hiring of lesbian and gay officers suggests to some citizens that the "immoral behavior" of practicing homosexuals is condoned. As a result, lesbians, gay men, and their allies in criminal justice fear for their jobs and sometimes even their lives (Buhrke 1996). Recently, the formation of gay and lesbian police associations has

challenged the compulsory heterosexuality of police organizations and police treatment of the gay and lesbian communities (Burke 1993; Buhrke 1996).

Community policing, which became widespread in the 1990s, may provide an avenue through which gender and sexual orientation differences are blurred (Miller 1999). No longer is the aloof, crime-control-oriented professional appropriate in community policing; rather, a more informal, relational, and conciliatory style of policing is encouraged. Roles that were previously denigrated as feminine and too "soft" or emotional for "real" police work have become the ideal qualities for neighborhood police officers to possess. Although both men and women can achieve this style, women are more likely to be comfortable with this policing model, given differences in gender role socialization. These new roles offer greater opportunities for role flexibility and thus may influence more female and more lesbian applicants to consider policing as an occupation.

THE WORK ENVIRONMENT FOR LESBIAN POLICE OFFICERS

This chapter explores how lesbian officers "do policing" in a work environment that is gendered, sexualized, and racialized. It addresses officers' working environment and their strategies for coping with workplace barriers. This chapter also explores the ways in which multiple identities of race and ethnicity, gender, and other dimensions contribute to officers' choices of the "best" strategies for doing their jobs and surviving a hostile organizational milieu.

Data from two different empirical studies are used: the Metro Police Department study (Miller, Forest, and Jurik 1997) and the Jackson City Police Department study (Miller 1999).[†] The studies differ across several dimensions. First, the size of the jurisdiction and the department varies. Although the departments are located in contiguous Midwestern states, the Metro Police Department (MPD) has 12,000 police officers, whereas the Jackson City Police Department's (JCPD) size is approximately 335. Second, the climate around diversity differs

---

[†]The names of the departments in these studies are purposely not given in order to protect their identity.

tremendously in the two departments. In Jackson City, both the former chief (of 22 years) and the current chief endorse diversity, and the department reflects this commitment, particularly in the patrol ranks. Officers routinely march in support of gay rights in the city's annual Gay Pride Parade, and both gender and sexual orientation are viewed as "no big deals" within the police subculture.

In the Metro Police Department, however, it wasn't until 1992 that the (then) new police superintendent promised "zero tolerance" for insensitivity to and discrimination against lesbian and gay police officers; he also actively recruited gay men and lesbians (Griffin 1992). Within this supportive environment, the first gay and lesbian officers' association was formed; the Jackson City department has no such formal organization. Similar to the goals of other gay and lesbian officer associations throughout the United States, the MPD association's goals are to provide support for other gay and lesbian officers, to develop a recruiting program for "out" gay and lesbian officers, to educate heterosexual officers, to dispel the fears of members of the gay and lesbian community about police officers, and to improve police-community relations. The formation of this coalition parallels the efforts of lesbians and gay men in other police departments and in other occupations (Taylor and Raeburn 1995; Burke 1993; Buhrke 1996).

Finally, what may be the most telling difference between the two departments is their law enforcement philosophies. At the time that data were collected, the MPD followed a *traditional* rapid-response, crime-control-oriented style of policing. On the other hand, the JCPD had been following a *community policing* model of policing for a decade, which featured foot patrols and ministations located within neighborhoods. The difference in the departments' orientations generates different tensions in the police subculture: the MPD reflects a more traditional department that is characteristically resistant to "outsiders" different from the traditional white, male, heterosexual police officer, whereas the JCPD experiences tension between those officers who embrace the community policing style of policing and those officers who perceive this style as a threat to their masculinity and the macho component of crime fighting. Despite these departmental differences, the two studies discussed in this chapter shed some light on the perceptions of gay and lesbian police officers as well as the issue of whether sexual orientation and gender affect work performance.

The Metro Police Department sample uses survey data collected from gay and lesbian officers. Of the 17 complete surveys (a 68 percent completion rate), we use only those from the 9 lesbian police officers, 7 of whom were white, 2 Latina, and all ranging in age from 25 to 42 years old.‡

The Jackson City Police Department, with a 26 percent female police force, one of the highest percentages in the country, included interviews with 45 former and current neighborhood police officers, of whom 18 (40 percent) were female and 27 (60 percent) were male (see Miller 1999, 230–237, for a more complete description of the research methodology and sample).

This chapter explores five themes. Because of the data, some themes are explored in greater depth than others (see Miller, Forest, and Jurik 1997 and Miller 1999 for greater detail concerning these themes). The first theme focuses on how safe it is for lesbian officers to disclose their sexual identities and what factors influence this decision. The subsequent themes include workforce adaptations and strategies, performance pressures and success, survival strategies and resistance, and organizational change.

THEME ONE: OUT AND CLOSETED STATUS

Gay and lesbian officers' adjustment to police or any other work is complicated by the issue of whether they will hide their sexual orientation (Schneider

---

‡Although this sample is small, given the rarity of gay and lesbian officers *willing* to openly discuss their sexual orientation and careers, the data are invaluable in contributing to our understanding of gay and lesbian police officers. However, as with all such studies, further research must be conducted to determine if these samples are representative of lesbian officers.

1986; Taylor and Raeburn 1995; Woods 1993).§ Some "closeted" gay and lesbian workers attempt to "pass" as heterosexual on the job (Burke 1994; Leinen 1993). Others may "come out" and openly define themselves as homosexual to varying degrees (Woods 1993). This decision and other workplace strategies are shaped not only by an individual's social location (e.g., gender, race or ethnicity) but also by situational factors such as time on the job (Rosabal 1996). Organizational and community climates of support or hostility for gay and lesbian rights also inform individual and collective strategies for constructing sexual identity (Buhrke 1996; Bernstein 1997). For example, fears about coworker or supervisor hostilities, termination, loss of promotional opportunity, or denial of backup lead some officers to hide their sexual orientation in the workplace (Burke 1993; Leinen 1993; Buhrke 1996). Tensions between the police and lesbian and gay communities encourage some officers to hide their occupation from gay and lesbian friends and acquaintances (Burke 1993). In either case, hiding consumes energy, creates stress, and can erode job productivity (Powers 1996).

Different levels of disclosure were apparent in our two samples. For instance, in the Metro Police Department, the choice of out or closeted status in the department was not a mutually exclusive dichotomy. Being closeted or out was more of a continuum of openness, with considerable variability from one individual to the next. All of the lesbian officers in the MPD sample said that their sexual orientation was known to some of the other gay or lesbian officers but that they were more protective of this information with heterosexual officers on the force. Two lesbian officers indicated that their sexual orientation has been completely public information on the police force since the beginning of their careers (at the training academy). Three other officers indicated that their sexual orientation was known only to

some people for the past two or three years; these three women have served the longest as police officers, spending at least half their careers closeted. It may be that they already had established their reputations as competent officers prior to coming out as lesbians. For the remaining four officers, two had not come out, but believed that some coworkers were beginning to suspect (one of these officers indicated that she would like to come out, but does not want to implicate her lover, who is a very closeted police officer not in our sample). The other two officers were only out to their police patrol partners.

Degree of outness was not an issue for the lesbian officers in the Jackson City Police Department. At the time of the study, a significant number of the women who were former and current neighborhood police officers were out lesbians.‖ The lesbian officers did not believe their sexual orientation had any effect on their acceptance as competent police officers. Part of this embracing of difference in the department was a consequence of the overall diversity of the force across race and ethnic, gender, and sexual orientation lines. The former chief was deeply committed to creating a department that mirrored the community it served. Many of the officers discussed this philosophy with obvious pride. On the surface, at least, there did not seem to be any cleavages between officers of different races, genders, or sexual orientations. The following statement by a white heterosexual male officer was typical:

> Our department has been very understanding, very open, to people with different lifestyles, different sexual lifestyles. If you get an officer in there who's homophobic, you can create a very big problem if you're in a neighborhood that has residents that have a different lifestyle. And Jackson City is known for having more women per capita, or per authorized strength, than any other department in the United States . . . we have a high population of lesbian officers. And to me, I think it's great.

---

§The concept of "out" or "being out" means both that the respondent has personally acknowledged his or her own sexual orientation and that this status is known by others. "Closeted" refers to those respondents who identify themselves as lesbian or gay but do not disclose this status to others.

‖We deliberately do not provide detailed information about individual lesbian officers in order to preserve their anonymity. Even in the most enlightened groups or places, backlash can occur and hurt one's career; see Miller 1999, 9.

Another officer declared this diversity to be a strength:

> That's what makes our department so good . . . you can't expect me as a white male to go into a domestic dispute between two males who are involved in a relationship, and if I'm heterosexual and they're homosexual, to go in there and be able to understand everything there is to understand about their relationship and their problems, I can't do it. But by having me on this department with other people that have a similar lifestyle to theirs, there's a sense of education that takes place within the department. By my associating with, supervising, talking, doing things away from the department with these people, I learn about their lifestyles. They learn about mine and I can take [what I learn] with me to this call.

Several lesbian officers stated that they would not consider working elsewhere: "There are very few departments that have been as good to women and gays and lesbians and minorities as this department" (Pam).[#] Garth, a white male heterosexual officer, explained: "It doesn't matter if you're gay or black or white or female, it doesn't mean you can't do the job . . . and we get quality people and not the traditional cookie-cutter model of a police officer . . . Nonwhite males do a good if not better job than a typical white male would because they bring different understandings and life experience to the job, and a lot of white males' understanding they learn from nontraditional cops."

These remarks illustrate the positive features of diversity within the JCPD: educating other officers about cultural differences within the force itself, and improving officers' responsiveness to the diverse communities in which they serve. This working philosophy, embraced by the force, facilitated the ease with which lesbian officers were able to do their job and not hide their sexual orientation or identity.

In the MPD, interesting racial and ethnic differences emerged. The two women of color were the most closeted to other members of the force, yet

they *did* disclose their sexual orientation to their police partners, who were also women of color, lesbian, or both. These officers' reticence to disclose their sexual orientation to any other officer may reflect their triple-minority status on the force: Latina, woman, and lesbian (Rosabal 1996). These multiple disadvantaged statuses may also help explain why the lesbian officers felt safe in disclosing to their police partners, who also had marginalized statuses in the department and therefore might be seen as more trustworthy than the dominant members of the force. The closeted officers stated that their biggest fears about disclosure involved safety and trust issues. Safety issues included the possibilities of being physically or verbally abused as well as the fear that police backup would be slow to come. Trust issues included the reactions of coworkers, who would withdraw support and friendship, and the fear that their moral authority in the eyes of the community would diminish.

THEME TWO: WORKFORCE ADAPTATIONS AND STRATEGIES

Again, the lesbian officers in both samples diverged in what they experienced as gay officers and how they negotiated their identities while doing their jobs. Most of the lesbian officers in the MPD experienced what Kanter (1977) refers to as the increased visibility of minorities in work organizations: They were constantly scrutinized by others around them. In addition, it is common for the socially dominant group—in this case, heterosexuals—to try to establish boundaries between themselves and gay and lesbian officers through techniques of exclusion or verbal reminders of difference and stereotypes about their social category. Every lesbian officer in our sample indicated that they had heard or been the target of antigay or antilesbian jokes or derogatory slang; moreover, they had seen antigay graffiti or cartoons around the station house, particularly in the locker room or on bulletin boards. Most of the out officers said that they had been excluded from the grapevine gossip and that they had not been invited to informal social activities, parties,

---

[#] Names of officers used here are pseudonyms. And voices from women of color are included but not identified for the same reason.

or events. To try to fit in with their police peers, many officers utilized boundary maintenance activities: "And, as you well know, everyone wants to be accepted and if making fun of gay people gets you accepted, then you make fun of them" (Kelly). The frequency of such activities suggests that sociocultural diversity of any sort is not easily tolerated in most police departments (Martin and Jurik 1996; Leinen 1993); as one of the respondents said, "Anytime someone is different in any way, police officers tend to ridicule them" (Rosa). Perhaps these lesbian officers' small numbers, the lack of support in the police culture, and the omnipresent homophobia contributed to their joining in with heterosexual peers to mock gay people.

In Jackson City, the lesbian officers were far more concerned about gender issues and combating stereotypes about the negatively perceived "feminine" nature of community police work than they were about sexual orientation. In fact, it was the heterosexual *males* who were most concerned about demonstrating their masculine competence by stressing their macho experiences and detailing their credentials so as not to be seen as effeminate. During the interviews, the male officers deliberately wove in some mention of their heterosexual status, usually offering information about their female dating partners, wives, and children (Miller 1999, 106).

In contrast, the lesbian officers had two very different responses to competency- and gender-based assumptions about skill. Those who were single or no longer had to care for children followed macho career paths similar to those of career-motivated men in the department. When prodded during the interviews, many of these women revealed that they had macho experience prior to becoming community police officers, such as membership on a SWAT team or a hostage negotiation team. The issues were different for lesbian officers. In interviews and in conversations in the field, they tended to exaggerate either their femininity or masculinity. This dichotomy is well documented in the work on women and policing conducted by Susan Martin (1980): police*women* emphasize the feminine aspects of being an officer, such as female identity, passivity,

weaker leadership ability and less autonomy, and flirtatiousness; *police*women, on the other hand, downplay femininity and strive for more masculine characteristics, such as leadership skills, aggressiveness, and occupational competence and achievement. In Jackson City, the emphasis depended on the intended audience more than on any favored or stereotyped skill. For example, if lesbian officers were assigned to a tough, criminally active neighborhood, their actions depended on how comfortable or expert they were in aggressive law enforcement techniques. This skill or comfort level, in turn, reflected what kind of police style they used while in patrol positions. At the same time, though, these officers were aware of the need to use gender-based skills that drew on their female status because of the receptivity, or lack thereof, of the residents. Some local people sought a more nurturing and empathic response from them because the officers were women.

This more flexible, androgynous style is reminiscent of the "inventive" role in Lynn Zimmer's (1987) study of female prison workers. Women in this role do not evaluate themselves as equal to or less competent than the male officers; rather, they view themselves as assets to the criminal justice system because of their more finely developed communication skills and respect for suspects or prisoners. But it was not always clear what behavior was linked to gender and what was linked to sexual orientation. The lesbian community police officers' behavior might also be inextricably connected to others' perceptions and their own levels of experience and skill and have little to do with gender and sexuality. Thus, the lesbian officers in the JCPD were most concerned about seeming competent within a maligned area of policing—that of community policing or foot patrol—than they were about sexual orientation issues such as those faced by the lesbian officers in the MPD.

Because of their varied perceptions about gender and sexual orientation, lesbian officers in the MPD were asked if they thought it was harder to break into the male world of policing or into the heterosexual world of policing. All the respondents felt it was more difficult to break into the male world, particularly when there were still older men on the force who remembered when most police were men. All the lesbian officers' responses suggested that, as one officer put it, "the good ol' boys network still runs smoothly" (Jen). "I feel it is much harder to break into the male world of policing. I think a lot of men become police officers for some sort of macho trip. The fact that women can do the same job is a slap in the face. Misogyny is alive and well in our culture and the police culture is no different" (Michelle). Some lesbian officers felt a common bond with heterosexual women in their fights against sexism on the force: "It is the male world that most females have a problem with, whether gay or straight. This job in particular invites a macho-man attitude. It is a fact that men receive more privileges and receive a higher rating for the same job. A female on this job must do twice as much to prove herself" (Kelly).

The lesbian officers in the JCPD also believed that the male world of policing was more difficult to negotiate than the heterosexual world of policing was. In particular, female officers believed that when they engaged in work-related activities with residents (especially with children), their work was seen by the residents as routine and natural, whereas when male officers performed the same activities, residents were impressed to the point of awe. Residents did not seem to regard the female officers' interest as something out of the ordinary *for women*, particularly ones with children of their own. Thus, when men performed "women's work" in the new neighborhood policing role, they were hailed as "supermen;" women performing the same work, however, were viewed as simply engaging in traditional female tasks and responsibilities, nothing out of the ordinary (Miller 1999, 160).

This phenomenon of men being lavishly praised when doing traditionally female work is well documented in the larger studies that have investigated gender and occupation. Feminist researchers assert that jobs are not gender neutral (Acker 1990). In analyzing gender and work issues within the criminal justice system, Martin and Jurik (1996, 4) observe:

The gender division of labor in the justice system is part of larger on-going processes of differentiation in society. Social differentiation, or the practice of distinguishing categories based on some attribute or set of attributes, is a fundamental social process and the basis for differential evaluations and unequal rewards. Differentiation assumes, magnifies, and even creates behavioral and psychological differences to ensure that the subordinate group differs from the dominant one. It presumes that differences are "natural" and desirable.

In the JCPD, officers of both genders were aware that they brought a different style to policing:

I think that women have a better sense of just being more aware of the emotional side, and more of the 'just the facts' [approach] disappears. I think women pick up nonverbal stuff more easily . . . I could go on and make myself look like I am male-bashing. There are a lot of women who aren't good at that and who aren't sensitive and aren't aware of things, and there are men that are good at it and not good at it. But I think that women have really brought out communication skills and awareness in the men. Men see what a positive and helpful tool it is, and how much of a better job can be done by talking, instead of knocking someone around and giving no explanations, just hauling them off to jail. I think women take on more of a role of seeing the big picture or trying to solve other problems beyond the initial problems (Carol).

Thus, in the JCPD, lesbian officers believed that sexual orientation took a backseat to the ongoing significance of gender and evaluation of skill, whereas in the MPD, lesbian officers also thought that it was more difficult to break into the male world of policing than into the heterosexual world of policing, but the difficulty was due to the overt sexism that permeated the MPD.**

**Because the number of women of color was so small in the two samples, observations about the impact of race and ethnicity cannot be made. Future research should untangle the effects of race and ethnicity and determine whether those effects change the significance of gender, sexual orientation, and skill assessment reported in this analysis.

THEME THREE: PERFORMANCE PRESSURES AND SUCCESS

Within the MPD sample, officer sexual orientation and gender were closely intertwined, salient features of the social construction of policing identities. Many lesbian officers believed that their socially deviant statuses influenced assessments of their policing skills held by other officers. Such influence worked either negatively or positively for the gay or lesbian officer. In addition, respondents, in discussing their job skills, saw themselves and their job performance as both similar to and different from that of other police officers. For some officers, these differences included unique abilities derived from the hard lessons of social marginalization.

Because not all of the MPD sample was out on the job, the visibility issue was not the same as those issues that surround race and ethnicity and gender minority status (i.e., sexual orientation can be hidden, whereas one's gender and race are visible). Closeted officers' visibility concerns were related to fear of coworker suspicions regarding their sexual orientation. Sexual suspicions are pervasive in police work, especially for women officers of any sexual orientation (Martin 1980). "If a female works with a female, then the other police officers may think they're both gay and the same thing goes for the males" (Kelly).

Lesbian officers in the MPD believed that sexism as well as homophobia created barriers to their success in policing. The two women of color in the sample believed that their ethnicity took a backseat to gender and sexual orientation concerns in the MPD. They heard heterosexual officers make statements about the problems that a lesbian officer might face when searching female suspects, including accusations of sexual harassment if the citizens were cognizant of the officer's lesbian identity. A few lesbian officers felt that despite the sexism they combated on the force, they could more easily gain acceptance as out lesbians than could out gay men. As Rosa, a closeted woman officer, summarized, "the guys already assume you're gay if you are a woman who wants to be a police officer, so you should just

focus on being the best officer you can be." Another lesbian officer said, "I know male cops who work with me willingly but [who] quite honestly state that if I was a gay man, they couldn't work with me. It still comes down to straight men being terrified of gay men" (Michelle).

Despite their concerns about gender and sexual identities on the job, the lesbian officers in the MPD believed that they were highly effective in their work; they also felt that they brought unique abilities to policing. Related research on the integration of men of color and women into police work finds that the job performance of these officers is similar to that of white male officers (Morash and Greene 1986; Alex 1969). Some researchers argue further that by virtue of their marginal or oppressed status in society, the pool of new entrants bring special talents and insights to police work that will improve services to victims and offenders and promote better police-community relations (Crites 1973; Alex 1969). When asked if they believed that lesbian officers use any different methods to accomplish policing goals (such as fighting crime, preventing and deterring crime, maintaining order, and providing public safety and service), the MPD officers emphasized that all police officers—regardless of sexual orientation—are taught the same methods at the academy; these methods are subsequently reinforced on street patrol. There was no disagreement about general policing goals. This uniformity in responses is consistent with the loyalty to the police occupation and subculture that so typically characterizes police officers (Skolnick 1994).

Yet, greater visibility and boundary maintenance may also stimulate a heightened performance pressure to "prove" that gay and lesbian officers (the social minority) can do the job as well as social dominants—in this case, heterosexual officers. Many lesbian officers described themselves as perfectionists or overachievers; they stated that they worked harder on the job so that their performance would be above scrutiny or so that their effectiveness would not be challenged if their sexual orientation were to become known. "I think in a way [we] are even more effective because we are always aware of ourselves.

Always trying to do better so that our sexuality doesn't interfere with our performance as a police officer" (Kelly). The officers did feel that they brought unique abilities, skills, and life experiences to the job of policing, skills that came out most when the officers dealt with the general citizenry and specifically with gay and lesbian citizens: "I believe if gay or lesbian officers have a political consciousness and understand the dynamics of homophobia and bigotry, they can bring a certain sensitivity and patience to the job" (Michelle). In their dealings with the general public, respondents believed that their own experiences of marginalization provided them with increased sensitivity and tolerance. They believed that, relative to most heterosexual officers, they were better able to transcend strict gender-role dichotomies and to meet the needs of a diverse citizenry more effectively: "I believe that knowing how a society can push you aside and not care about you helps especially when dealing with lower-income families and minorities, in general" (Jen). Even as lesbian officers may bring unique strengths to policing, they may also have to adjust their workplace behaviors to compensate for homophobic tensions and a persistent degree of exclusion by heterosexual coworkers (Powers 1966). As one lesbian officer remarked: "Heterosexual people are of the opinion that gay people are sick, loose, and have no morals, even though most pedophiles are heterosexual" (Kelly).

What made the question of sexual orientation even more intriguing in the context of neighborhood policing was that heterosexual men initially steered clear of the program because it represented feminine traits that were denigrated. Not until community policing positions became better known to the majority of the force and became linked to promotion did men begin to want them. Policewomen, on the other hand, have always faced the stereotypical assumption that they might be gay regardless of their true sexual orientation. The pervasiveness of this stereotype seemed to free female officers to pursue nontraditional careers. As suggested in Martin's (1980) research, mentioned earlier in this chapter, women adapt to policing either by emphasizing their femininity and portraying themselves as weak

and passive in relation to male officers, or by emphasizing masculinity and embracing a dominant and equal position. This phenomenon got turned on its head in the ambiguous, gendered context of neighborhood work, because today's community policing models have transformed what has traditionally been defined by the police as an undesirable, feminine position into a potentially male-driven, popular one. Men have adapted to these socially less dominant jobs by exaggerating their masculinity and by using verbal aggressiveness and displays of authority to "prove" their ability. In the JCPD, in order for community policing to be accepted by men, it had to be masculinized through an inversion of gender-oriented values and behaviors traditionally associated with women in society. This masculization could serve to push out women and people of color— precisely the same people who took a chance on the community policing program in the beginning.

Just as heterosexual women in traditionally male occupations may feel pressured to demonstrate masculine traits to prove their abilities (Zimmer 1987), lesbians may try to assert their feminine side. Other research (see Miller, Forest, and Jurik 1997) has suggested that lesbians may feel a need to be especially feminine in order to avoid hostile confrontations with (mostly male) homophobic coworkers (Schneider 1988); this approach reflects Martin's (1980) police*women* style of adaptation. Most female officers, straight or gay, realized that although policing calls for such masculine characteristics as assertiveness, strength, and competitiveness, to act in this way would confirm the assumptions of other officers that they were lesbian (Burke 1994; Pharr 1988). Because lesbians in the JCPD are not just tokens, however, they may be under less pressure to "prove their masculinity" and thus may be more free to develop their personal styles.

THEME FOUR: SURVIVAL STRATEGIES AND RESISTANCE

MPD officers utilized a variety of strategies for survival in the police organization. The opportunities and selection of these alternatives were often intertwined with rank, seniority, gender, and racial and ethnic dimensions of policing identities. For example, the two women of color felt that their ethnicity made them more visible; thus, they were even more reluctant to be out. Organizational and community climate are also factors that serve to shape differing opportunities for and choices of strategies in doing police work. The psychological costs of a false front are extraordinarily high in a job that is already very stressful (see Goffman 1963; Powers 1996). The costs seemed especially high for the lesbian officers in the MPD. These costs included the reality that "if police officers think they've discovered a secret someone is trying to hide, they can be very cruel—they perceive it as a weakness if you're trying to hide it" (Michelle).

All of the closeted officers described the stressfulness of hiding part of their identity and of hiding their significant relationships; the lesbians were especially fearful of losing the respect of coworkers once their sexual orientation became known, particularly if the coworkers felt that the closeted officers had lied to them (see Rosabal 1996). Respondents envied heterosexual officers, who had never experienced the burden of pretending their private lives did not exist or had no impact on their public lives. Yet the risks of social and professional ostracism seemed too high. Although they feared revelation, the closeted officers also projected many benefits to being out, the same benefits that were actually reported by out officers: "I am able to talk about my personal life openly" (Paula); "I can be myself" (Jen). In these studies, like in other research (e.g., Burke 1993; Leinen 1993), out respondents were pleased to reduce the disjuncture between their work selves and private selves: "I could stop bringing a 'fake date'—like my cousin—to work-sponsored dinners, dances, or parties . . . The further you advance, the more separate you become unless you have a partner of the opposite sex and therefore 'fit in' with the brass" (Lisa).

Being out was also believed to reduce work-related stress: "You can relax; you are not always worrying about saying something that would give you away as a lesbian" (Annie); "Being out would let me relax and stop hiding who I am. When the subject of significant others comes up, I'm tired of referring to

'he' instead of 'she' " (Rosa). Not surprisingly, there was some tension between out and closeted officers, particularly when identity ambivalence encouraged closeted officers to attempt to normify behavior to reduce visibility (Burke 1994, 198): "The 'closeted' gay male officers try to act more macho and tougher and turn me off as a person. 'Closeted' lesbians try to act more hyper feminine and it's very false looking. These stereotypical appearances hurt all gay officers and make it harder to come out" (Annie).

Within the JCPD, at no point in the two and a half years of data collection did lesbian officers raise the emotional costs of nondisclosure. In fact, the opposite occurred: Officers felt comfortable bringing their female partners to informal social events, sports leagues, and formal police dinner-dances. Some lesbian couples vacationed regularly with heterosexual police friends. No lesbian officer in the sample indicated misgivings about being out or experienced any lack of acceptance due to her sexual orientation. The officers felt that they were evaluated or selected as colleagues or friends, respectively, based on their professional competence and their personal characteristics.

THEME FIVE: ORGANIZATIONAL CHANGE

Although differences in the construction of out and closeted identities may create tensions both within and among gay and lesbian officer groups, organizational culture also plays a significant role in creating an accepting atmosphere. Respondents in the MPD perceived that the newly created lesbian and gay officer coalition and their department's new zero tolerance policy had improved the climate for them within the police force. These organizational-level changes provided gay and lesbian officers with additional avenues for confronting harassment and other workplace barriers. Many of the officers felt that since the new police superintendent's appointment and his publicized zero tolerance policy toward gay and lesbian discrimination, their concerns would be taken more seriously by supervisors, even though homophobic attitudes might remain unchanged. If the climate continues to improve, more officers may feel comfortable with coming out to a greater degree. Despite these perceived improvements within the MPD, situational context and harassers' status within the department still shaped the officers' decisions to report or not to report an incident: "It depends on who was doing the harassing . . . if it was an officer who already has a reputation for being a 'dog,' the other officers would probably be supportive of you. However, if the harasser was a well-liked officer, it could alienate other officers from you" (Michelle).

In the JCPD, lesbian officers gravitated to the neighborhood positions. One possible reason may have been word-of-mouth reports. Because community policing yielded greater job satisfaction, current members of the force encouraged their friends (both straight and gay) to apply to the JCPD. Another possible explanation, one that a few of the lesbian officers raised themselves, was that the appearance of a trend was deceiving: The numbers merely reflected the overall representation of lesbians on the police force. Thus, in reality it may be that no increased or disproportionate number of lesbians requested the neighborhood positions.

Another possible way that the organizational context seemed to encourage lesbian officers to choose the neighborhood policing role was by its flexibility; just as community policing afforded men an opportunity to play a more nurturing role in a socially acceptable fashion, the neighborhood positions provided the same role flexibility for lesbian officers. In fact, this organizational niche is hospitable to lesbian officers because it reflects a work organization that is diverse, not monolithic. In this society, out lesbians in particular do not always have the same access to or support for nurturing roles, especially roles such as mothers or custodial parents. Thus, if lesbians are not seen as "real" women in society, they may seek other ways to confirm their female status. This situation again echoes how Martin's (1980) policewomen emphasized their femininity to find a place in the masculinist subculture and working environment of policing. Overall, however, our data seem to be more consistent with Martin's con-

tinuum and ever-changing nature of policewomen's strategies rather than with one distinct style.

Because neighborhood work offers opportunities for androgynous practice, it may constitute a unique alternative to the macho police culture. Officers can draw on *both* masculine-linked and feminine-linked sex roles. In some situations, an aggressive crime-fighting stance may be necessary; on other occasions, female or male community police officers can "mother" the neighborhood, its children, and the broader community as well. For lesbian officers, community policing opens up ways in which their status as women is not negated, whereas because of homophobia, their status might be negated in the larger society. This argument can be extended a little further: Lesbians who are already mothers may appreciate the public confirmation of a nurturing role even as they capably do what is still ultimately thought of as "men's work."

In general, sexual orientation could be inherently unrelated to competent job performance. Jackson City and its police department may be particularly enlightened in this respect; because job candidates were explicitly asked about diversity issues and comfort levels as part of the hiring process, there may be a higher comfort level among successful applicants. When asked whether sexual orientation played a part in performance in community policing, all of the current and former officers, gay and straight, said that because neighborhood officers were selected by seniority, the gay and lesbian officers had already been on the force long enough to demonstrate their abilities and to establish a reputation for themselves. It may be that the greater openness and visibility of homosexual officers increased pressures to prove that social minorities could do the job as well as social dominants. The lesbian officers' solid reputations were established long before they became neighborhood officers. It is also likely that gay and lesbian persons have a unique outsider status that enables them to see the world slightly differently. In particular, they may be more cognizant of how individuals interact socially and of how such factors as racism, economic struggles, and social injustice affect peoples' lives. Not only do these women have the marginalized status of outsiders, they are also simultaneously insiders; thus, they hold unique perspectives on policing (see Naples 1996).

CONCLUSION

In this chapter, studies of lesbian police officers in two different police departments were used to explore how these women's sexual orientation affected their participation in a hypermasculine subculture and occupation. Despite their common sexual identity, the lesbian officers from these two police departments experienced different obstacles. In the large, urban, traditional Metro Police Department, lesbian officers sensed greater patterns of social exclusion as well as overt sexist and antigay behavior from colleagues. They perceived greater struggles in balancing job demands with sexual orientation. In both studies, lesbian officers of color had the most concern about disclosing their sexual identity. It may be that out officers typically possess other personal characteristics, such as being white or being male, that accord them legitimacy. In the smaller, community-police-oriented Jackson City Police Department, the lesbian officers perceived that their greatest barriers were due to gender rather than sexual orientation. These officers were more concerned that their colleagues recognize them as competent police officers.

Clearly, the dimension of sexual orientation does not operate in isolation or in consistent priority over gender, race and ethnicity, or other dimensions. The qualities admired in police officers are no longer those typified by the efficient, stoic loner; today, expressive qualities that display a more humane dimension have come into favor (Jurik and Martin 2001; Manning 1984). The need for aggressive law enforcement action endures, however. As community policing grows in popularity, what may become its most salient characteristics are the quality and effectiveness of one's work and one's ability to excel as a humane law enforcer. Just as heterosexual men can adopt a more caring approach without fear of being labeled homosexual, women can expand on their preferred style of policing without concern about appearing too masculine (or too feminine). In fact,

the social psychologist Sandra Bem (1974, 1993) contends that rigid sex-role differentiation is out of date and no longer useful in a society in which flexibility and androgyny are strongly associated with higher standards of psychological health and professional performance.

Although the lesbian officers in these studies believed that they had a heightened sensitivity to the needs of marginalized or oppressed citizens based on their own experiences as social minorities, what cannot be ignored is the diversity of work orientation and other characteristics *within* groups of lesbian and gay officers. How these experiences may vary for lesbian officers of color is another avenue to pursue in future research. These cautions notwithstanding, the data presented here suggest that it may be possible to challenge the hypermasculine and homophobic organizational structure and subculture of policing.

DISCUSSION QUESTIONS

1. What are the five main work issues identified by lesbian police officers in this chapter? Which issues do you see as the most serious and why? What can be done to change these issues' negative impact on lesbian police?

2. In what ways are the pressures that lesbian police officers encounter different from and the same as those identified for women officers more generally by Harrington and Lonsway in chap. 32?

3. How might these pressures escalate for lesbian police officers of color?

4. According to Miller, Forest, and Jurik, what strengths do lesbians bring to policing?

5. If policing were to return to a strict enforcement model (instead of the community policing approach), what new or different difficulties would women police, and in particular lesbian police officers, face?

6. How does Schulz's (chap. 31) discussion of women who are torn between suppressing their femininity and asserting their uniqueness or differences (from men) fit in with what this chapter says about lesbian police officers?

REFERENCES

Acker, J. 1990. Hierarchies, Jobs, Bodies: A Theory of Gendered Organizations. *Gender and Society* 4:139–158.

Alex, N. 1969. *Black in Blue: A Study of the Negro Policeman.* New York: Appleton-Century-Crofts.

Bem, S. L. 1974. The Measurement of Psychological Androgyny. *Journal of Consulting and Clinical Psychology* 42(2):155–162.

———. 1993. *The Lenses of Gender: Transforming the Debate on Sexual Inequality.* New Haven, CT: Yale University.

Bernstein, M. 1997. Celebration and Suppression: The Strategic Uses of Identity by the Lesbian and Gay Movement. *American Journal of Sociology* 103(3): 531–565.

Blumenfeld, W. J. 1992. *Homophobia: How We All Pay the Price.* Boston: Beacon.

Britton, D. M. 1990. Homophobia and Homosociality: An Analysis of Boundary Maintenance. *Sociological Quarterly* 31(3):423–439.

———. 1995. "Don't Ask, Don't Tell, Don't Pursue": Military Policy and the Construction of Heterosexual Masculinity. *Journal of Homosexuality* 30(1):1–21.

Buhrke, R. A. 1996. *A Matter of Justice: Lesbians and Gay Men in Law Enforcement.* New York: Routledge.

Burke, M. E. 1993. *Coming Out of the Blue: British Police Officers Talk about Their Lives in "the Job" as Lesbians, Gays, and Bisexuals.* London: Cassell.

———. 1994. Homosexuality as Deviance: The Case of the Gay Police Officer. *British Journal of Criminology* 34:192–203.

Christopher, W., J. A. Arguelles, R. Anderson, W. R. Barnes, L. F. Estrada, M. Kantor, R. M. Mosk, A. S. Ordin, J. B. Slaughter, and R. E. Tranquada. 1991. *Report of the Independent Commission of the Los Angeles Police Department.* Los Angeles: City of Los Angeles.

Cockburn, C. 1985. *Machinery of Dominance: Women, Men, and Technical Know-How.* London: Pluto.

———. 1991. *In the Way of Women: Men's Resistance to Sex Equality in Organizations.* Ithaca, NY: ILR.

Comstock, G. D. 1991. The Police as Perpetrators of Anti-Gay/Lesbian Violence. In *Violence against Lesbians and Gay Men,* ed. G. D. Comstock, 152–162. New York: Columbia University.

Connell, R. W. 1987. *Gender and Power.* Stanford, CA: Stanford University.

Crites, L. 1973. Women in Law Enforcement, *Management Information Service Newsletter,* 15.

David, D., and R. Brannon. 1976. *The Forty-Nine Percent Majority: The Male Sex Role.* Reading, MA: Addison/Wesley. Quoted in S. E. Martin. 1992. The Changing Status of Women Officers: Gender and Power in Police Work. In *The Changing Roles of Women in the Criminal Justice System: Offenders, Victims, and Professionals,* ed. Imogene L. Moyer, 286. (Prospect Heights, IL: Waveland).

Goffman, E. 1963. *Stigma: Notes on the Management of Spoiled Identity.* New York: Simon and Schuster.

Griffin, J. J. 1992. Rodriguez Says He Won't Allow Police Insensitivity toward Gays. *Chicago Tribune.* May 21, Sec. 2, p. 2.

Hunt, J. 1984. The Development of Rapport through Negotiation of Gender in Field Work among Police. *Human Organization* 43:283–296.

———. 1990. The Logic of Sexism among Police. *Women and Criminal Justice* 1:3–30.

Hurtado, A. 1989. Relating to Privilege: Seduction and Rejection in the Subordination of White Women and Women of Color. *Signs* 14:833–855. Quoted in S. E. Martin, 1994. "Outsider within" the Station House: The Impact of Race and Gender on Black Women Police, *Social Problems* 41: 384.

Jurik, N. C., and S. E. Martin. 2001. Femininities, Masculinities and Organizational Conflict: Women in Criminal Justice Occupations. In *Women, Crime, and Justice: Contemporary Perspectives,* ed. L. Goodstein and C. Renzetti, 264–281. New York: Roxbury.

Kanter, R. M. 1977. *Men and Women of the Corporation.* New York: Basic Books.

Kapeler, Victor E., Richard D. Sluder, and Geoffrey P. Alpert. 1998. *Forces of Deviance: Understanding the Dark Side of Policing.* Prospect Heights, IL: Waveland.

Karmen, Andrew. 1996. *Crime Victims.* Belmont, CA: Wadsworth.

Leinen, S. 1984. *Black Police, White Society.* New York: New York University.

———. 1993. *Gay Cops.* New Brunswick, NJ: Rutgers University.

Manning, P. K. 1984. Community-Based Policing. *American Journal of Police* 3:205–227.

Martin, S. E. 1980. *Breaking and Entering: Policewomen on Patrol*. Berkeley: University of California.

———. 1990. *On the Move: The Status of Women in Policing*. Washington, DC: Police Foundation.

———. 1992. The Changing Status of Women Officers: Gender and Power in Police Work. In *The Changing Roles of Women in the Criminal Justice System: Offenders, Victims, and Professionals*, ed. Imogene L. Moyer, 281–305. Prospect Heights, IL: Waveland.

———. 1994. "Outsider within" the Station House: The Impact of Race and Gender on Black Women Police. *Social Problems* 41:383–400.

Martin, S. E., and N. C. Jurik. 1996. *Doing Justice, Doing Gender: Women in Criminal Justice Occupations*. Newbury Park, CA: Sage.

Messerschmidt, J. 1993. *Masculinities and Crime: Critique and Reconceptualization of Theory*. Lanham, MD: Rowman and Littlefield.

Miller, S. L. 1999. *Gender and Community Policing: Walking the Talk*. Boston, MA: Northeastern University.

Miller, S. L., K. B. Forest, and N. C. Jurik. 1997. Diversity in Blue: Lesbian and Gay Police Officers in a Masculinist Profession. Paper presented at the annual conference of the American Society of Criminology, San Diego, CA.

Morash, M., and J. Greene. 1986. Evaluating Women on Patrol: A Critique of Contemporary Wisdom. *Evaluation Review* 10:230–255.

Naples, N. A. 1996. A Feminist Revisiting of the Insider/Outsider Debate: The "Outsider Phenomenon" in Rural Iowa. *Qualitative Sociology* 19(1):83–106.

Pharr, S. 1988. *Homophobia: A Weapon of Sexism*. Little Rock, AR: Chardon.

Powers, B. 1996. The Impact of Gay, Lesbian, and Bisexual Workplace Issues on Productivity. *Journal of Gay and Lesbian Social Services* 4(4):79–90.

Rich, A. 1980. Compulsory Heterosexuality and Lesbian Existence. *Signs* 5:631–660.

Rosabal, G. S. 1996. Multicultural Existence in the Workplace: Including How I Thrive as a Latina Lesbian Feminist. *Journal of Gay and Lesbian Social Services* 4(4):17–28.

Schneider, B. E. 1986. Coming Out at Work: Bridging the Private/Public Gap. *Work and Occupations* 13:463–487.

———. 1988. Invisible and Independent: Lesbians' Experiences in the Workplace. In *Women Working*, ed. A. Stromberg and S. Harkess, 273–296. Palo Alto, CA: Mayfield.

Shilts, R. 1980. Gay Police. *Police Magazine* (January): 32–33.

Skolnick, J. H. 1994. *Justice without Trial: Law Enforcement in Democratic Society*. New York: Macmillan.

Taylor, V., and N. C. Raeburn. 1995. Identity Politics as High-Risk Activism: Career Consequences for Lesbian, Gay, and Bisexual Sociologists. *Social Problems* 42(2):252–273.

Woods, J. 1993. *The Corporate Closet: The Professional Lives of Gay Men in America*. New York: Free Press.

Zimmer, L. 1987. How Women Reshape the Prison Guard Role. *Gender and Society* 1(4):415–431.

———. 1988. Tokenism and Women in the Workplace: The Limits of Gender Neutral Theory. *Social Problems* 35:64–77.

Chapter 34

The Interactive Effects of Race and Sex on Women Police Officers

Susan E. Martin

ABSTRACT

This chapter, which appeared in the last edition, has been updated for this third edition by the inclusion of an addendum found at the end and written by the author. In the last edition, Martin reported on a national survey of 446 police departments together with case studies of five large municipal police agencies. That study found that the number of women police officers increased in the 1980s by 5 percent from the late 1970s. It also showed that women of color comprised a disproportionately large share of women police—40 percent. Martin brings these figures up to date in her addendum and points out that the pace of change for women has actually *slowed* in the decade from 1990 to 2000. At the same time, women of color now comprise almost half (47.5 percent) of all women police officers.

Minority women continue to be drawn to police work because of the relatively good pay scale, benefits, and job security offered; yet they face not just sexism but the compounded effects of both racism and sexism on the job. In chapter 32, Harrington and Lonsway listed the many barriers that women encounter as they pursue a career in law enforcement. This chapter describes the ways that sexism and racism—two socially structured systems of bias and oppression—work in undermining job success and in creating harmful work stress for female police officers of color. Martin describes how racism divides white women officers from black women officers and how sexism divides black men officers from black women officers. Thus, Martin depicts the interactive or compounded, rather than additive, effects of racism and sexism for black women. By focusing on black women, Martin can define both the commonalities and differences between black and white women officers in their experiences of sexism and between black men officers and black women officers in the face of racism.

In her addendum Martin notes that researchers have gained greater understanding of the degree to which sexism and racism are deeply embedded in policing. Sexism may account for the slowdown in the increase in the number of women entering police work in recent years. Yet black women have continued to enter police work at a rate higher than in earlier periods. Several factors may be responsible for Martin's findings: the lack of comparably paying jobs outside of law enforcement for black women; a recognition that racism exists in all work settings; more black students taking college courses in criminology and thus coming into contact with faculty who encourage them to look into law enforcement; the lure of an exciting job as portrayed by many television shows; and aggressive recruitment by large urban police departments.

For many years, women and minority men faced discriminatory selection criteria that virtually excluded them from police jobs. The Equal Employment Opportunity Act of 1972 prohibited discrimination by public employers on the basis of race, color, religion, sex, or national origin. Eliminating racist and sexist employment practices in police departments, however, has been a slow and difficult process.

This chapter examines the increasing proportions of women and minorities in urban police departments since 1978, then explores the interactive effect of race and gender on the experience of women officers, particularly Black women. It looks at the ways in which racism has created cleavages among women officers, while sexism divides Black men and women, thus imposing a double burden on Black women.

INTRODUCTION: DISCRIMINATION, LEGAL CHANGES, AND THE INTERSECTION OF RACE AND SEX

Like many other work organizations, during the 1970s large municipal police agencies faced lawsuits alleging race and sex discrimination in selection, promotion, and other employment practices. A number of the lawsuits were initiated separately by Blacks and women, then consolidated by the courts (Sullivan 1988). As a result, many departments were forced to alter discriminatory selection criteria related to education, age, height, weight, use of arrest records, and agility tests (see Sulton and Townsey 1981). Others did so voluntarily or under the threat of litigation.

By the end of 1986, 15 percent of the departments in cities serving populations over 50,000 were operating under court orders or consent decrees, and 42 percent had adopted voluntary affirmative action plans; only four percent of municipal agencies still had minimum height and weight standards as entry criteria (Fyfe 1987).

Although modifications in the selection criteria opened the door to the station house to minority men and all women, the actual integration of those formerly excluded groups still is not complete. The barriers to acceptance and equality in policing faced by Black men and all women overlap to some extent.

They have in common, for example, the fact that they are subjected to the problems related to their status as "tokens." Kanter (1977) observed that by virtue of their numerical rarity "tokens" are subjected to different treatment by dominants. Due to their visibility, tokens face extra performance pressures, exclusion, and stereotypic treatment by those around them.

At the same time, white men reacted differently to the entrance of women and Black men into policing. One major difference is the stereotypic roles into which various minority groups are cast. Women of both races often are cast into the sexually-defined roles of "mother," "pet," or "seductress," or

This research was completed when the author was a project director at the Police Foundation and was supported in part with funding from the Ford Foundation. It is a revised version of a paper presented at the American Sociological Association Meetings, San Francisco, August 1989.

Susan E. Martin. 1992. The Interactive Effects of Race and Sex on Women Police Officers. In *The Justice Professional,* ed. Roslyn Muraskin, 6(1)(winter):155–172.

are labeled "bitches" for failure to comply with the stereotypes (Kanter 1977). Stereotypes of Blacks, particularly males, on the other hand, emphasize their devalued social (not sexual) status.

Women who enter previously male-dominated occupations face a variety of organizational and interpersonal barriers (Epstein 1983; Kanter 1977; Martin 1980; Reskin and Roos 1990; Swerdlow 1989; Williams 1989; Wolshok 1981; Zimmer 1986), which in turn affect their work-related behavior. Reskin (1988) argues that men respond to women's intrusion into their occupational spheres by adopting three possible patterns of sex differentiation: allocating jobs and tasks according to sex; treating women paternalistically; and sexualizing women or the workplace. Gutek (1985) explained the treatment of women in the workplace as a result of "spill over" of sex role behavior, because workers are unable to completely separate their work and sex roles. Women in male-dominated occupations are treated as women because their constellation of statuses are inconsistent: those associated with the female sex role become salient, and males treat their female co-workers on the job as they treat women in other roles. The result is a variety of dilemmas and conflicts because sex role norms of appropriate "feminine" behavior conflict with occupational role definitions of appropriate behavior.

Focusing on policing, Martin (1980) observed that the integration of women into police patrol as co-workers:

> . . . threatens to compromise the work, the way of life, the social status, and the self-image of the men in one of the most stereotypically masculine occupations in society.

Consequently, the men's resistance to the incursion of women has included overt discrimination in selection, assignments, and evaluations; exclusion from the informal culture; different standards on evaluations; and harassment including sexual harassment.

Race, too, affects an individual's occupational and economic opportunities. Racial inequality is built into the social structure of the U.S. and, despite civil rights laws and substantial changes over the past 30 years, discrimination against Blacks persists in hiring, pay, promotion, assignment, and the conditions of work.

Until quite recently, the number of Black police officers was very limited. Black officers were denied scout car assignments or relegated to cars marked "colored police," allowed to arrest only other minority citizens, and denied choice assignments and promotions (Leinen 1984; Sullivan 1988). In the past 40 years, the growing representation of Black officers has been accompanied by substantial progress in eliminating institutional discrimination in policing. Nevertheless, problems remain in the hiring and promotion of Black officers. These arise in part because some Blacks do not do as well on traditional measures such as written tests. Consequently, Black officers' potential to achieve leadership positions has been hindered and charges of discrimination and reverse discrimination have led to tensions within many agencies.

Understanding of how employment discrimination and efforts to eliminate it have affected various disadvantaged groups has been hampered because studies have focused either on the effects of race or sex discrimination, ignoring those persons with both disadvantaged race and gender status—minority women. To what extent have they experienced "double jeopardy" (Beale 1970), the positive effect of the double negative (Epstein 1973), or a double bind (Reid 1984) as a result of their unique combination of ethnic and gender statuses?

Research on the perspectives of minority women is limited. As hooks (1981) noted, most studies of "Blacks" have generalized from data on Black men; examinations of "women" have been universalized to all women on the basis of white women's experience. Black women have been regarded as deviant cases (Gilkes 1981) or they have been invisible "others," objects lacking full human subjectivity (Collins 1986).

Several studies have drawn parallels and identified differences in the dynamics of racism and sexism and their effects (Hacker 1951 and 1975; Feagin and Feagin 1978). These have sometimes been useful as pedagogical tools but, as King (1988: 45) stated:

. . . we learn very little about Black women from this analogy . . . because (t)he scope, both institutionally and culturally, and the intensity of the physical and psychological impact of racism is qualitatively different from that of sexism.

Recent feminist critiques have undermined the assumption that the effects of racism and sexism are additive (Dill 1983; Palmer 1983; Smith and Stewart 1983; King 1988; Hurtado 1989). Instead, they have sought to develop an interactive model to explore the manner and conditions under which women of color respond to "the interlocking nature of oppression" (Collins 1986: 519) on the basis of their unique combination of race, sex, and class. How does their situation at the intersection of racism and sexism affect their perspectives and behavior within a racist and sexist occupational structure?

Dugger (1988: 442) asserted that to understand the race-specific effects of differences in sex role attitudes one must consider how the dynamics of race have differentially structured Black and white women's experience of gender. Smith and Stewart (1983) point out that differences in the relationships between white men and Black and white women probably affect the way each group of women experiences discrimination. White women have frequent and intimate contact with white men and the potential for increased power by association with or through the influence of a powerful male. But white women's influence is diminished because they have internalized an image of helplessness and accepted exclusion from selected white male arenas. In contrast, racism has often produced physical separation of Blacks and whites and has rested on an element of fear based on white hostility and physical intimidation.

These differences in the relational position of white and Black women with respect to the source of privilege, white men, has led Hurtado (1980: 845) to distinguish between white women's "subordination through seduction" resting on socialization to docility, passivity, and internalized social controls, and Black women's "subordination through rejection" arising from physical separation and a lack of intimate interaction with white men.

Black and white women also historically have differed in their class and occupational experiences. By examining the experiences of Black and white men and women in a single occupation—police work—it is possible to control for these differences while examining the intersection of race and sex. Policing is one of the few occupations in which there is sufficient heterogeneity of personnel to do so.

A full interactive model of the effects of race and sex would consider "the commonalities that bind and the differences that divide the four groups" (Smith and Stewart, 1983:8). Instead, this [chapter] focuses on Black women as the pivotal group in defining the commonalities and differences between women officers in their experiences of sexism and Black officers in the face of racism in work organizations long dominated by white men. It thus attempts to understand how the interaction of racism and sexism modify the forms and impacts of each.

METHODOLOGY

The data reported in this [chapter] are part of a study that assessed the status of women in policing through both a national survey and case studies in five large municipal agencies (Martin 1990). The survey findings are based on responses to questionnaires sent to 446 municipal departments serving populations over 50,000 in 1986 and a similar survey conducted by the Police Foundation using the same sample in 1978 (Sulton and Townsey, 1981).

The case studies conducted in five agencies explored departmental policies and procedures for integrating women into policing and officers' perspectives on changes in the status of women officers over the past two decades. In three of the agencies (Detroit, Washington, D.C., and Birmingham) the proportion of women officers and supervisors was above the municipal department mean; in two others (Chicago and Phoenix) women's representation was at or below the mean for women. The departments also varied with respect to region, agency size, minority representation, and affirmative action policy. Detroit, Chicago, and Birmingham were operating under court order or consent decree; Washington and Phoenix had voluntary affirmative action plans in effect.

In each agency, about 30 female and 20 male officers and mid-level supervisors were randomly selected for an interview to be conducted during on-duty time. Approximately 25 of these persons actually were interviewed in each agency depending on the contingencies of scheduling, vacation leave, and their willingness to participate. The interviews were semi-structured, lasted about two and a half hours, and examined respondents' experience of job discrimination (including sexual harassment) and perception of departmental policies regarding the integration of women. Interviews also were conducted with about eight high ranking policy makers in each department regarding the development, implementation, and effectiveness of departmental policies and procedures for integrating women into policing.

INCREASES IN THE PROPORTIONS OF WOMEN AND MINORITIES IN POLICING: 1978–1986

Between 1978 and 1986 the proportion of women in policing increased from 4.2 to 8.8 percent of municipal officers; during the same period the proportion of minority officers in large- and moderate-sized urban departments rose from 13.8 to 22.5 percent of the sworn personnel, as shown in Table 1. Thus the representation of minorities in policing now approaches their representation in the urban population (Sullivan, 1988),[1] but women still are greatly under-represented in policing.

Focusing on the representation of various minority groups by sex, Table 2 indicates that minority women make up only 3.5 percent of all officers, but comprise 40 percent of all female officers, whereas minority males make up only 21 percent of the men. The table also shows that most minority officers of both sexes are Black, but that Black women comprise a much larger fraction of the female officers (31 percent) than Black men comprise of the male officers (12.5 percent).

Women have made more modest gains in obtaining promotions to supervisory ranks. In 1978 they comprised only 1 percent of all supervisors; by the end of 1986 they made up 3.3 percent of those sworn personnel with the rank of sergeant or higher. Twenty-nine percent of the female supervisors are minority women.

WOMEN OFFICERS' PERCEPTIONS OF DISCRIMINATION

Interviews with 35 white and 31 Black women in the five case study departments indicate that most believe that they have been the victim of job-related discrimination.[2] At the same time, there were significant differences among the women's experiences and perceptions of discrimination on the basis of race and length of police experience.

Sixty-eight percent of the Black women and 80 percent of the white women reported at least one incident involving either race or sex discrimination. White women were more likely to report sex discrimination (77 percent) than Black women (55 percent). Fifty-two percent of the Black women and 20 percent of the white women reported racial

TABLE 1
Mean Percentage of Police in Municipal Departments in 1978 and 1986 by Ethnicity and Sex

Ethnicity	1978			1986		
	Male	Female	Total	Male	Female	Total
White	83.6	2.6	86.2	72.2	5.3	77.5
Non-white	12.2	1.6	13.8	19.0	3.5	22.5
Total	95.8	4.2	100%	91.2	8.8	100%

TABLE 2
1986 Mean Percentage of Municipal Police Officers
by Sex and Ethnicity

Ethnicity	Male (N = 145,296)	Female (N = 13,979)	Total personnel (N = 159,275)
White	79.1	60.2	77.5
Black	12.5	30.7	14.1
Hispanic	6.5	7.5	6.5
Other	1.9	1.6	1.9
Total	100%	100%	100%

discrimination. Thirty-nine percent of the Black women and 17 percent of the white women reported being victims of both race and sex discrimination. Thus while most women officers have been faced with sexism, Black women also have had to deal with racism, which in many instances is more salient in their consciousness.

Black women were as likely as whites (36 percent versus 38 percent) to report benefitting from being Black or female. The benefits were primarily desirable assignments and promotions under court-imposed promotion quotas. The white women were much more likely than the Black women, however, to assert that despite the fact that they had benefitted from them, they opposed affirmative action procedures.

How long they have been police officers also affected the women's perceptions of discrimination. The newer women were far less likely to assert that they have been the victim of discrimination than those with longer police experience. Eighty-eight percent of the women who became officers before 1975, and 79 percent of those who joined between 1975 and 1980 stated that they had been subjected to discrimination on the basis of their race or sex; only 20 percent of the women who became officers in 1985 or 1986 claimed they had faced discrimination.

The apparent decrease in sex discrimination has several possible explanations. The newer women may be less sensitive to discrimination, although many noted (unlike women of the earlier cohorts) that their academy training had included information on the department's EEO policy and grievance proce-dures, including those related to sexual harassment. It is possible that with more time and police experience the newer women may also face discrimination. Alternatively, there may have been a real change.

Both male and female respondents agreed that women today are better accepted in policing, although what they meant by "accepted" varied widely. Women now are routinely assigned to the patrol and to virtually all specialized units. Men are accustomed to working with them. Departmental policies backed up by a few highly visible disciplinary actions, may have sent a clear message that the discrimination and harassment no longer will be tolerated as they were when women first went onto patrol. These changes, coupled with the effects of promotions of women and minorities to supervisory positions, may have resulted in a reduction in "rational bias" discrimination. Such discrimination occurs when mid-level supervisors respond to perceived cues from superiors suggesting that a show of bias would be rewarded by others or, in the absence of such cues, discriminate based on beliefs concerning the preferences of their bosses (Larwood et al. 1988).

THE INTERSECTION OF RACE AND SEX: BLACK WOMEN OFFICERS AND DISCRIMINATION

How do Black women officers experience and deal with sexism and racism? To what extent are power, opportunities, and numbers—those variables identified by Kanter (1977) as keys to understanding work-related contingencies and occupational performance—different for Black and white women in policing?

Black men and all females are disadvantaged vis-á-vis white males, who have excluded them from positions of power in police departments. Black females, however, appear to be at the greatest disadvantage. White men often have retained control of Black women by disrupting their potential alliances with Black men and white women through a divide and conquer strategy that rested on the racism of white females and sexism of Black males. Furthermore, even when Black females unified with either of these groups, they have less power to share or confer on them and so face the constant threat of being betrayed or undermined by that group in its quest for advantage.

The manipulation of racism and sexism to the detriment of Black women was strikingly illustrated on the organizational level by the legal struggle over promotion procedures in the Chicago police department, as each group protected its own interest. That agency's hiring and promotion process came under supervision of the federal courts as a result of *US vs. City of Chicago*. In 1973, after a finding that the sergeant's promotional exam was discriminatory, the judge imposed quotas for promotions. Black women initially were called from the promotion list as Blacks, without distinctions between males and females. When the white women realized the Black women were being promoted ahead of them, however, they filed a claim asserting that all females should be treated as one single minority group. The judge ruled that Black women could not be given double benefits and asked the lawyer from the Afro-American League, which was representing all Blacks, if Black women could be counted as women not Blacks for the purpose of the quota.

The lawyer agreed, without consulting the women. Perhaps he recognized that this change would increase the number of positions for which Blacks were eligible. A less benign interpretation of his actions, however, views them as knowingly undercutting the Black women by removing them from competition with Black men in order to increase the latter's promotion opportunities. For the Black

women, however, this meant having to compete with the white women whose test scores were better than theirs while those of Black men were not.

The Black women subsequently brought a lawsuit protesting that decision. The judge agreed that they had a valid complaint but refused to grant it because it was deemed "not timely." As one Black woman observed, "Nobody was looking out for our interests."

The differences in the cultural images and job-related experiences of Black and white women in general have been repeated in their reception as police officers. Historically white women were "put on a pedestal" and spared from doing physical labor in exchange for accepting white men's domination and control of their sexuality. Black women had no pedestal. Most worked outside their own homes, often for white women. White women accepted their difference from Black women, and adopted a sense of superiority although, in reality, they were economically and psychologically dependent on white men.

When women initially were assigned to patrol, the white men who dominated policing treated Black and white women according to those traditional patterns. Male and female respondents stated that the first groups of white women assigned to patrol, particularly those that were physically attractive or were attached to influential white men, were "protected" from street assignments; Black women were not. One woman noted:

> White women were put on a pedestal, treated like wives. . . . A lot of white women got jobs doing typing for commanders and downtown assignments. They're high priced secretaries.

In addition, on street patrol white women were more likely to be protected. Being able to count on fellow officers for back up in dangerous situations is a major element in the willingness of an officer to take police action. Providing back up to others, particularly when they call for assistance, is a central norm of police work (Westley 1970). At the same time, officers may support, control, or sanction others by their willingness to "slide in," adding to the police presence, even when it is not assigned by a dispatcher, and by the speed with which they respond to a call for assistance.

The white patrolmen tended to be protective of white women and the latter often acquiesced by letting them take control of situations because they wanted acceptance and back up. Male protectiveness still persists and creates a dilemma for women. As a male supervisor explained:

> You can't get the men to stop being protective, being the first through the door, backing up women more than they would a man, not letting women take risks. . . .Then the men complain the women lack courage.

Black women also observed that they had been told to remain "back covers" by male partners and most did so. Yet even when they deferred and accepted a passive role, they could not count on being protected as females. A Black woman asserted:

> Black women don't expect to be nice to (white men) because white males won't protect us on the street.

Black men also tended to be protective of women but Black women could not count on their support and assistance. First, they were fewer in number and, therefore, less available as back up when needed. Second, they were sometimes pressured by the white men not to back up the women. Third, some Black men were as strongly opposed to women on patrol as the white men and behaved accordingly.

Martin (1980) observed that a lack of support from other officers resulted in two divergent responses: a more cautious approach to policing and, alternatively, greater self reliance. Some women of both races reacted to male protectiveness by seeking to act independently, despite the punitive reaction of the men. This reaction included refusal to share job knowledge or teach women the skills they routinely imparted to new men and exposing them to greater danger by denying them back up, putting them alone on "killer" footbeats, and "keying out" their radio transmissions (by obscuring them with static). The women's work was closely monitored, they were punished for trivial errors by supervisors, and assigned to the station despite requests to remain on

the street (then subjected to criticism for not being "streetwise"). In addition, their personal identity was undercut by being labeled "dykes" and "bitches."

Black women faced racist expectations that compounded gender-based handicaps. It was assumed that they knew less but had to produce more than others to prove their capabilities. A Black woman explained:

> A male could goof off all day and nobody'd say a thing. But especially a Black woman . . . has to work twice as hard.

Women in positions of authority often faced additional challenges which appear to have been compounded for Black females. For example, a Black female detective observed that precinct supervisors often call the burglary unit for information and advice but white males argue with the advice she gives. Another Black female detective observed that the unique effect of her race and sex status produced ambiguity with respect to the nature of the discrimination she faced:

> Sometimes I couldn't tell if what I faced was racial or sexual or both 'cause the Black female is the last one on the totem pole in the department.

A Black female supervisor had a white male subordinate who deliberately violated procedures. She noted that when that man transferred another supervisor had problems with him,

> . . . so it wasn't a female thing . . . but at the time I couldn't be sure. . . . I felt he was rebelling against me because I was a female lieutenant and a Black lieutenant. I had a double whammy on me as female and Black.

Facing the "double whammy," however, emboldened several Black female supervisors to challenge the system of discrimination they perceived. One Black female supervisor reported that the men in her squad stopped producing, which made her look bad. When she confronted a Black officer about the low productivity, he stated that the white men had pressured the Blacks into embarrassing their female supervisor by threatening not to back them up. The supervisor, invoking racial solidarity, noted that there were more Blacks than whites in the squad and urged the Black men to stop letting themselves be dominated by whites.

Another Black female sergeant directly challenged the systematic discrimination she observed in performance evaluation scores. She noted that Blacks were receiving lower service ratings from their sergeants regardless of the work they were producing and that all the Black women had gotten evaluations about 20 points lower than the white females. To verify her view that these ratings were discriminatory, she kept a log of all activities for the unit for six months. The next rating period, again the whites and another Black (male) sergeant rated Blacks lower than the whites; she rated the females and Blacks higher. The lieutenant demanded an explanation and initially refused to approve her ratings. She countered:

> I told him that I was appalled at the blatant discrimination of my peers. . . . I said I'd kept a six-month log on all officers and, based on this documentation, I challenged how sergeants rated their subordinates. . . . I said that if the rating were not changed I would file a grievance and let the records speak for themselves. The lieutenant sat back in his chair and said that in his 15 years as a lieutenant he'd never had a Black officer challenge him. He wondered how long it would take for a Black to speak up. He added it took guts but the service ratings would be changed.

RELATIONS BETWEEN BLACK WOMEN AND BLACK MEN

A number of Black women observed the dilemmas they faced in dealing with Black men. When one Black woman was promoted to command staff, instead of congratulating her, the Black men suggested that she had taken "their" promotion. Elaborating on the competition theme, one woman observed:

> The white commanders put white women on desk jobs for years. As soon as Black females got desk assignments, however, the Black guys complained (while

they'd been silent about white women getting those jobs). They seem to feel the Black women are in competition with them.

Independence as well as competition may cause problems for Black women in their relations with Black men. One Black woman asserted, "if you speak up or show you can think for yourself . . . you have problems from Black men." Her point was illustrated by an incident related by a Black female lieutenant. She stated that she hung up on a white lieutenant who was verbally abusive. The man then complained about her to their (Black) commander who called and asked her why she could not be nicer to the lieutenant. She responded that she had been disrespected as acting commander of her unit, then added:

> I told the commander that the only thing that I hate more than a white man trying to run over me is a Black man clearing the way.

Sexuality also sometimes affects the relationship between Black male and female officers. One Black woman stated:

> The worst harassment I got came from a Black male lieutenant. . . . He created rules that only applied to me. . . . It was outright harassment he didn't even try to cover up. It was partly sexual; he said he'd have me. . . . The only reason I didn't sue is 'cause the lieutenant's Black. I guess that makes me a racist but I looked at the overall problem it would have caused and how it would be played up in the press and didn't do it. If he'd have been anything else I'd have sued his butt.

Another related an instance in which resistance to a Black male partner had life-threatening consequences:

> I had a partner who tried to pry into my private life. He called me stuck up when I wouldn't answer his questions. . . . When he put his hand on my arm, I slapped him. After that he wouldn't get out of the car on runs.

A third woman observed:

> The Black men have assumed they could make sexual approaches to Black women they would hesitate making to whites.

"GETTING UNITY IS LIKE PULLING TEETH:" RELATIONS AMONG WOMEN OFFICERS

All respondents agreed that there is little unity among women. Factors keeping women from acting as a unified political force include divergent occupational role and sex role perspectives, racism, and men's success in applying a "divide and conquer" strategy so that women do not see it in their best interest to organize.

For women officers, sex role norms of appropriate "female" behavior conflict with occupational role definitions of behavior appropriate for a police officer. This leads to interactional dilemmas in their routine interactions with male officers who expect to treat fellow officers as peers but tend to treat female officers as females. Among the dilemmas are when they should act "like a cop," how to still act "like a woman," and how to respond to the sex role stereotypes into which they are cast (Martin 1980).

Faced with these dilemmas, as well as openly discriminatory treatment and the problems of being highly visible tokens, women officers' responses fall into two broad patterns of behavior which transcend racial lines, further dividing them. One group of women, characterized as adopting a deprofessionalized police*women* occupational style, tend to accept the stereotypic sex roles of "pet" or "seductress," emphasize "being a lady" on and off the job, welcome or tolerate the "protection" of males, display little initiative or aggressiveness on street patrol, and seek non-patrol assignments and personal acceptance. The other group, characterized as *police*women, identify with the policemen's culture and seek to gain acceptance by being more professional, aggressive, loyal, street-oriented, and macho than the men (Martin 1980). In resisting traditional sex role stereotypes, however, they face defeminizing labels such as "dyke" or "bitch" as punishment for outproducing the men.

Most female officers, in fact, have sought a balance between these types. They assert that they have been able to maintain their femininity and succeed as officers, gaining individual acceptance as "just me." Nevertheless, men continue to treat women officers as sexual targets and mistrust them as patrol officers and women officers often are their own worst critics. Respondents were particularly outspoken about those women that behave "like clinging vines" or "act mannish" on the job and those that "act like sluts" or "try to make their way around the department on knee pads" because each of these behaviors contributes to negative stereotyping that "rubs off on us."

Some women belong to state or national women's law enforcement organizations. Women's efforts to organize within their own agencies, however, have been short-lived or sporadic. Chicago is the only case study department in which there is an active women officers' organization, the Coalition of Law Enforcement Officers (CLEO). Formally open to all officers, CLEO was formed in 1989 to address the concerns of Black women officers through educational growth and support activities. A white supervisor, admiring CLEO's success, said:

> White women won't be organized. (At the CLEO meeting) they were talking about daycare! . . . White women have the housewife syndrome; many Black women are single, used to running family, and are more assertive. . . . Black women have much more consciousness of abuse; white women are less aware of abuse as women.

Illustrating this point, one white woman said, "there was nothing we could do for each other." Another asserted:

> Had we organized as a group, it would have hampered our acceptance. We went out as individuals and fit in as individuals and that was the best thing we did for acceptance. If we'd set ourselves apart, it would have turned people off.

Black women were less openly critical of other women and less likely to espouse an individualistic strategy for gaining acceptance. Nevertheless, they too demonstrated divergent approaches for organizational survival.

Racism compounds the divisions. Several Blacks asserted that white women are as racist as white men; others recounted incidents of racism involving women. Some of these were individual; others more organized, as illustrated by the white women's legal action in *U.S. v. Chicago.*

Many of the women fear joining a women's group since the men perceive it both as a direct threat to their power, and as implicitly joining "them" (the other racial group), which is treated as an act of racial disloyalty. For women of both races, acceptance by male officers is more important than that of other women. Women usually work with men and depend on them for back up, making their support a matter of life and death. Men have more experience, "muscle," and are available in greater numbers than women officers. In addition, social activities, including dating and marriages, occur along racial lines. This permits men of each race to influence women's on–duty behavior by threatening social isolation.

Both white and Black men have used racism to control "their" women and prevent a unified effort to address sex discrimination. When a white female rejected the sexual advances of a white male, he started the rumor that she only slept with Blacks, using both racism and sexism to doubly discredit the woman both as "promiscuous" and "disloyal." A Black female supervisor observed:

> They keep us competing, fat versus thin, old versus young, and women seem to fall for it. Getting unity is like pulling teeth. . . . The women say (when I try to counsel them), "she doesn't want to help us" and while the women are feuding, the men are moving up.

White women can gain more from their alliance with white males than Black women can get from cooperation with Black men because white men have more power over the departmental power structure. But white men also have more to lose from other potential allies, so they have less incentive to share power with white women and are able to extract compliance with sex role stereotypes and sexual favors as the price for cooperation.

For Black women a close alliance with Black men offers social benefits and support in fighting racial discrimination. But Black men also sometimes are reluctant to share their limited power, and find they can get rewards from the white men by displaying male solidarity against the incursion of women into work long defined as "masculine."

CONCLUSIONS

Between 1978 and 1986, minority representation in policing increased substantially, but the proportion of women police officers grew more modestly. Women still comprise less than 10 percent of the sworn police officers in municipal departments, with minority (primarily Black) women making up only 4 percent of all officers. Nevertheless, minority women constitute 16 percent of minority personnel whereas white women comprise only 7 percent of the white police.

As tokens who threaten the men's work, informal work culture, and occupational self image, female police officers have faced a number of barriers to their integration and acceptance in policing. Although overt discrimination against women officers has diminished, discrimination and sexual harassment continue. For Black women, the problems they face as women are compounded by patterns of racism, leaving them vulnerable as targets for all groups' displaced frustrations and hostilities. White men's ability to "divide and conquer" has sometimes encouraged Black men to harass the women in order to gain acceptance as "one of the boys." In such instances, Black women are a safer target than white women, some of whom had personal access to powerful white men. At the same time, they played on white women's racism and fear of isolation to inhibit them from uniting with Black women.

Women have coped with their situation by adopting individualistic strategies to gain acceptance, acquiescing to stereotypic roles and accepting the protection and support of the men, or by strictly adhering to police work norms. For white women this included embracing the racial bias of the dominant white males. Although white and Black women have occasionally supported each other in fighting sex discrimination, white women have avoided unifying as a group or allying with the politically weak Black women. Black women have tended to ally politically with Black men and focus their political efforts on fighting racism on the job.

In conclusion, the experiences of Black and white women in police work appear to have differed in ways that are both race-specific and context-related. Although both groups of women officers frequently have encountered sexism, for Black women the additional burden of racism has increased performance pressures, limited their access to power, and resulted in uncertain alliances. Some Black women have benefitted from affirmative action programs. Others have developed remarkable strength and self reliance, enabling them to act independently. Nevertheless, these women have had a difficult struggle, having to perform with fewer informal supports and reduced margin for error.

ADDENDUM: WOMEN IN POLICING— PROGRESS AT A SNAIL'S PACE

What has changed for women in policing since 1986 when the survey and case studies were completed? The good news is that the "progress" documented in this chapter has continued; the bad news is that it is moving at the same exceedingly slow pace that has prevailed since women were permitted to enter the mainstream of police patrol work in the

early 1970s. This is illustrated by Table 3, which is based on the FBI's Uniform Crime Report data. It indicates that the growth in women's representation in municipal policing over the past 20 years has continued despite challenges to affirmative action policies. However, the pace of change, which was slow between 1980 and 1990, has decreased between 1990 and 2000, particularly in the larger city agencies. At the rate of increase of about 2.5 percent a decade, it will take a century before women comprise half of sworn police personnel!

Other sources provide limited data on the racial and ethnic background of police personnel. One Bureau of Justice Statistics survey found that in law enforcement agencies with 100 or more sworn officers in 1993, 8.7 percent of the officers were women, including 5.7 percent white, 2.2 percent black, 0.7 percent Hispanic, and 0.1 percent women from other racial and ethnic backgrounds (Reaves 1996). A more recent survey, also based on a stratified sample of agencies with 100 or more officers, conducted by the National Center for Women and Policing in 1999 found that women are 14.3 percent of all sworn law enforcement positions among municipal, county, and state law enforcement agencies with 100 or more sworn officers; women of color hold 6.8 percent of these positions (National Center for Women and Policing 2000). Thus women of color have increased from comprising about one

TABLE 3
Percentage of Women Employed as Sworn Officers

	1980[1]	1990[2]	2000[3]
Total cities	3.8	8.3	10.9
Cities with pop. > 250,000	4.6	12.6	16.2
Cities with pop. 100,000–249,999	4.2	8.2	10.5
Cities with pop. 50,000–99,999	3.1	6.2	8.3
Cities with pop. 25,000–49,999	3.0	5.1	7.4
Cities with pop. 10,000–24,999	2.9	4.3	6.5
Cities with pop. < 10,000	3.2	5.5	7.4
Suburban counties	8.1	11.3	12.8
Rural counties	9.9	6.3	8.1

[1]U.S. Federal Bureau of Investigation 1981.
[2]U.S. Federal Bureau of Investigation 1991.
[3]U.S. Federal Bureau of Investigation 2001.

third (34 percent) of all women officers in 1993 to nearly half (47.5 percent) of the sworn women officers in 1999.

The recent survey also found that women hold 5.6 percent of sworn top command positions (as chiefs, deputy chiefs, commanders, or captains), as well as 9.2 percent of supervisory positions (lieutenant, sergeant, and corporal). Again, this "good news" indicates a substantial increase since 1986; nevertheless, only about a third of the agencies surveyed reported having at least one woman in a top command position, and only 9 percent had a woman of color among those ranks. Thus women, particularly women of color, continue to be largely excluded from key policy-making positions in policing, but a growing cadre are in the supervisory ranks poised to move up.

Numbers do not tell the whole story. Changes in the structure and nature of policing have opened opportunities throughout the ranks, especially because of the growth of community policing. Although the term *community policing* has varied meanings, it does signal a shift in focus and values, which has important implications for women because it marks the reintroduction of feminine constructs that had largely been pushed aside by the hypermasculine approach of the crime control model of policing. According to that model, which prevailed for most of the last century, officers were regarded as "crime fighters" and women were viewed as unfit for patrol work but were tolerated in "feminine" service assignments that involved skills such as interpersonal communication and informal conflict resolution, assignments that were denigrated by the men.

The advent of community policing has ushered in a new perspective on the police role that puts an emphasis on cooperation and maintenance of connection with the community. The ideal community police officer needs such "feminine" skills as empathy, caring, and connection that historically were unacceptable to their male peers and continue to be challenged by many male officers (Miller 1999). Yet, as Miller notes, for community policing to succeed, it must be repackaged so that adherents of traditional

policing do not sabotage its potential for success. It is ironic that stereotypically feminine traits that once were used to exclude women's participation from patrol or to separate "real cops" from "office cops" have been resurrected. But the success of this resurrection, and with it community policing, depends on reshaping the unacceptable traits associated with femininity into acceptable traits associated with masculinity and "real police work" so that "both men and women are able to deploy skills and talents in the ostensibly gender-neutral realm of community policing" (Miller 1999:95).

In the past few years we also have gained greater understanding of just how deeply sexism and racism are embedded in policing and other social institutions. This understanding is both cause for optimism—we've got a better diagnosis of the problems—and for despair, given their persistence. More than 20 years ago I observed that, in the future, policing will call for an androgynous style of policing that embraces both traits stereotyped as masculine and those regarded as feminine, because the work involves both social control and social service functions. How to bring about this style of policing, however, is a continuing challenge. Perhaps the acceptance of community policing will accelerate the incorporation of women into policing. Alternatively, in the new post–September 11 era, as the United States wages a war on terrorism, the pendulum may swing back to a "tough," traditional approach to police work. Only time will tell.

DISCUSSION QUESTIONS

1. What social, political, and economic factors can you identify to explain the slowdown in the pace of increase of women police in the last decade?

2. Keeping in mind the material by Susan Miller et al., in chap. 33, how might this decline in increase of women police impact lesbian officers differently than it impacts heterosexual women officers?

3. How might the growing proportion of police women of color in relation to white women police affect promotions of women? For example, would you expect an increase in the coming years of black women police chiefs? Explain your answer.

4. Explain what Martin means when she writes that sexism and racism in law enforcement are interactive rather than additive. Give an example.

5. Based on the findings in this chapter, describe similarities and differences in discriminatory experiences of white and black women in policing. What social policies would you suggest to remedy such discriminatory practices?

NOTES

1. In 1985, Blacks made up 12.1% of the American population; Hispanics 6.4%. Because both minority groups tend to live in cities rather than suburban or rural areas, however, they probably remain somewhat underrepresented in urban police agencies. In contrast, women represent 52% of the population and 44% of the labor force.

2. The survey data often grouped Black, Hispanic, Native American, and Asian women as "minority women." The remainder of the paper, however, focuses exclusively on Black women because the interviews included very few respondents from those other minority groups.

REFERENCES

Beale, F. 1970. Double Jeopardy: To Be Black and Female. in *The Black Woman: An Anthology*, ed. T. Cade, 90–100. New York: New American Library.

Collins, P. H. 1986. Learning from the Outsider Within: The Sociological Significance of Black Feminist Thought. *Social Problems* 33:514–532.

Dill, B. T. 1983. Race, Class and Gender: Prospects for an All-Inclusive Sisterhood, *Feminist Studies* 9:131–150.

Dugger, K. 1988. Social Location and Gender-Role Attitudes: A Comparison of Black and White Women. *Gender and Society* 2:425–448.

Epstein, C. F. 1973. The Positive Effects of the Multiple Negative: Explaining the Success of Black Professional Women. *American Journal of Sociology* 78:912–935.

Epstein, C. F. 1983. *Women in Law.* Garden City: Anchor Books.

Equality Denied: The Status of Women in Policing—1999. National Center for Women and Policing. 2000.

Feagin, J., and C. B. Feagin. 1978. *Discrimination American Style: Institutional Racism and Sexism.* Englewood Cliffs: Prentice-Hall.

Fyfe, J. 1987. *Police Personnel Practices, 1986.* (Baseline Data Report Vol. 18, Number 6). Washington, DC: International City Management Association.

Gilkes, C. T. 1981. From Slavery to Social Welfare: Racism and the Control of Black Women. In *Class, Race and Sex: The Dynamics of Control,* ed. A. Swerdlow and H. Lessing, 288–300. Boston: G. K. Hall.

Gutek, B. A. 1985. *Sex and the Workplace: The Impact of Sexual Behavior and Harassment on Women and Organizations.* San Francisco, CA: Jossey-Bass.

Hacker, H. 1951. Women as a Minority Group. *Social Forces* 30:60–69.

Hacker, H. 1975. Class and Race Differences in Gender Roles, in *Gender and Sex in Society,* ed. L. Duberman, New York: Praeger.

hooks, b. 1981. *Ain't I a Woman: Black Women and Feminism.* Boston, MA: South End.

Hurtado, A. 1980. Relating to Privilege: Seduction and Rejection in the Subordination of White Women and Women of Color. *Signs* 14:833–855.

Kanter, R. M. 1977. *Men and Women of the Organization.* New York: Basic Books.

King, D. 1988. Multiple Jeopardy, Multiple Consciousness: The Context of a Black Feminist Ideology. *Signs* 14:42–72.

Larwood, L., E. Szwajkowski, and S. Rose. 1988. Sex and Race Discrimination Resulting from Manager-Client Relationships: Applying the Rational Bias Theory of Managerial Discrimination. *Sex Roles* 18:9–29.

Leinen, S. 1984. *Black Police: White Society.* New York: New York University Press.

Martin, S. E. 1980. Breaking and Entering. *Policewomen on Patrol,* Berkeley, CA: University of California Press.

Martin, S. E. 1990. *On the Move: The Status of Women in Policing.* Washington, DC: Police Foundation.

Miller, Susan L. 1999. *Gender and Community Policing: Walking the Talk.* Boston: Northeastern.

Milton, C. 1972. *Women in Policing.* Washington, DC: Police Foundation.

Palmer, P. 1983. White Women/Black Women: The Dualism of Female Identity and Experience in the United States. *Feminist Studies* 9:151–171.

Reid, P.T. 1984. Feminism versus Minority Group Identity: Not for Black Women Only. *Sex Roles* 10:247–255.

Reskin, B. 1988. Bringing the Men Back In: Sex Differentiation and the Devaluation of Women's Work. *Gender and Society* 2:58–81.

Reskin, B., and P. Roos, 1990. *Job Queues, Gender Queues.* Philadelphia, PA: Temple University Press.

Smith, A., and A. J. Stewart. 1983. Approaches to Studying Racism and Sexism in Black Women's Lives. *Journal of Social Issues* 39:1–13.

Sullivan, F. A. 1988. Minority Officers: Current Issues. In *Critical Issues in Policing: Contemporary Readings,* ed. R. Dunham and G. Alpert 331–346. Prospect Heights, IL: Waveland.

Sulton, C., and R. Townsey. 1981. *A Progress Report on Women in Policing.* Washington, DC: Police Foundation.

Swerdlow, A. 1989. Men's Accommodations to Women Entering a Nontraditional Occupation: A Case of Rapid Transit Operatives. *Gender and Society* 3:373–387.

U.S. Federal Bureau of Investigation. 1981. *Uniform Crime Reports, 1980.* Washington, DC: GPO.

———. 1991. *Uniform Crime Reports—1990.* Washington, DC: GPO.

———. 2001. *Uniform Crime Reports—2000.* Washington, DC: GPO.

Westley, W. 1970. *Violence and the Police.* Boston, MIT Press.

Williams, C. L. 1989. *Gender Differences at Work: Women and Men in Nontraditional Occupations.* Berkeley, CA: University of California Press.

Wolshok, M. L. 1981. *Blue Collar Women: Pioneers on the Female Frontier.* Garden City, NY: Doubleday.

Zimmer, L. 1986. *Women Guarding Men.* Chicago: University of Chicago Press.

Chapter 35

Women in Conflict:
An Analysis of Women Correctional Officers

Joanne Belknap

ABSTRACT

Belknap provides a rich description of the work world of women correctional officers. This study of 35 women correctional officers supports most prior research on the conflicts that these women face on the job. In this chapter, updated from the second edition of this book, Belknap is able to relate her findings to more recent studies in this area as well. Evidence of *sexual harassment* (offensive sexual comments or behaviors) and *gender harassment* (nonsexual put-downs of women)—a distinction rarely made by other writers—is described in detail. Although the women in this study confirmed the existence of sexual harassment in their work, they tended to minimize it, reporting it as less significant than gender harassment. Further, Belknap provides a much-needed discussion on sexual harassment and gender harassment as they affect women correctional officers by race and sexual orientation. And the results of this study, like earlier studies, show that male correctional officers continue to be more hostile than male inmates to women correctional officers.

Belknap also describes gender differences in job performance. The major work style distinction she identifies is that of better communication skills by women and a greater inclination to use force by men (see also chap. 32). The reasons for these differences are found in women's prior experiences and socialization (*gender model*) as well as the organizational structure of the jail and the correctional occupation (*job model*). Although the women believe that factors related to the gender model are more influential in how they function, they understand that they are discriminated against because they are too frequently assigned to work exclusively with female inmates, which limits their job mobility prospects. That is, there are fewer supervisory and administrative positions in women's facilities because there are many fewer women inmates. Thus, although most of the women believe that men and women are equal, they feel that men and women perform the corrections job differently and that women are less likely to advance.

Resistance to women working in traditionally male jobs may be most evident when we examine women who work in the criminal justice system. Wilson (1982:360) believes that "the link between masculinity and criminal justice is so tightly bound that we may say it is true not merely that only men can be crime fighters, but even that to be a crime fighter means to be a man." Perhaps no jobs embody the idea of machismo more than those which are designed to control offenders, especially male offenders. Thus it is not surprising that women correctional officers (COs) assigned to institutions for men have faced strong opposition from male COs.

Legal pressure, particularly Title VII of the Civil Rights Act, has been the major impetus for hiring women COs in men's prisons since the 1970s (Flynn, 1982: 324; Jurik, 1985: 377; Morton, 1981: 10; Zimmer, 1989). Although it did not distinguish by rank or the sex of the prisoner at the institution, an April 2000 report by the U.S. Federal Bureau of Prisons reported that 8,573, or 27.4 percent of the U.S. prison staff are women (U.S. Federal Bureau of Prisons, 2000). This development in increasing hires of women working in prison and jails since the early 1970s has led to increased research on women in corrections to ascertain whether gender role differences exist among correctional staff members, and to determine the reasons for any of these differences. Two explanatory models, the gender model and job model, have been suggested (Jurik and Halemba, 1984: 553–554; Zimmer, 1986: 12–13). The *gender model* concerns what women bring to the job in terms of attitudes, prior experiences, and preferred modes of interaction, and how these factors affect women's occupational experiences (Zimmer, 1986: 12). For example, "gender models suggest that women place greater importance than do men on relationships with others in their work environment" (Jurik and Halemba, 1984: 554). The *job model,* on the other hand, suggests that gender differences on the job are influenced more strongly by the organizational structure of the occupation and the institution. For example, restricting women officers to

work only with female inmates reduces their job and shift assignments and reinforces their male co-workers' belief that they are unable to "do the job." Most observers recognize the importance of both models because it is likely that they operate simultaneously to promote gender differences among correctional staff members (Jurik, 1985: 376; Jurik and Halemba, 1984: 552; Zimmer, 1986: 13). One model, however, may be more important than the other, and we could obtain a clearer understanding of women COs by determining whether this is the case.

The goal of this study is to test specific findings from prior research regarding women COs: reasons for choosing corrections; their attitudes about gender equality inside and outside work, their preferred working environments, their perceptions of occupational opportunities and obstacles, the conflicts they experience on the job, and their beliefs concerning gender differences among COs. In addition, the study attempts to determine the source and the degree of support for the gender model and the job model. Although a number of studies on women COs have been published in the last few years (e.g., Britton, 1997a, 1997b; Crouch and Alpert, 1982; Jurik, 1985, 1988; Jurik and Halemba, 1984; Kerle, 1985; Kissel and Katsampes, 1980; Lawrence and Mahan, 1998; Peterson, 1982; Pogrebin and Poole, 1997; Pollock, 1986; Simpson and White, 1985; Stohr, Mays, Beck, and Kelley, 1998; Zupan, 1986), the current study was influenced most strongly by Zimmer's (1986, 1987) ethnographic research on women COs working in men's prisons.[1] Zimmer's research was conducted in New York state and in Rhode Island in 1980, when women first started to work in men's prisons there. Therefore her research design was exploratory and "the important research questions were allowed to emerge during the research process" (1986, 212). Her data were collected primarily from open-ended interviews with 70 women COs as well as from a number of inmates, administrators, and male COs.

METHOD

The sample of women COs was drawn from a large Midwestern metropolitan jail under the jurisdiction

Source: Joanne Belknap. Women in Conflict: An Analysis of Women Correctional Officers, pp. 89–115.

of a county sheriff in 1988. The jail housed approximately 1,200 male inmates and 100 female inmates. There were approximately 550 correctional personnel, of whom 400 were line officers. At the time of this study, the personnel included 36 female line officers, two female sergeants, one female lieutenant, and one female captain. Thirty-five of the 40 women COs in the jail were interviewed for this study.[2,3]

Research indicates that women who work in policing and corrections routinely encounter gender as "an ongoing social production," where racial and class discrimination intersect with sex discrimination (Martin and Jurik, 1996, 28). Thus, ideally any studies on this topic address racial and other differences among women. Where possible, I conducted cross-tabulations regarding race (white or black), age (under 40 or 40 and over), and experience (under six years or six years or more).[4] (Class data were not reliable and thus not included.)

FINDINGS

Tables 1 through 7 summarize the findings from this study. Table 1 describes the sample, which was 57 percent white, 91 percent line officers, and divided equally between shifts. The officers ranged in age from 22 to 63 years; the greatest population (32 percent) were in their thirties. Experience in working in the jail ranged from six months to 25 years; the majority (57 percent) had worked there between one and eight years. Not surprisingly, the officers' ages and years of experience were related positively and significantly ($\chi^2 = 9.29$, p = .002). Sixty-two percent of the women were assigned to work fairly exclusively with female inmates.

Reasons and Support for Entering Corrections

People choose occupations for a number of reasons, despite prevailing attitudes suggesting that they are not "right" for the job. Many reasons have been offered to explain why women have had limited opportunities in corrections, most notably the conviction that corrections is a "man's" job. Nonetheless, many women choose to work in this field. Thus it

TABLE 1
Demographics*

Characteristic	N	%
Race		
White	20	57.1
Black	15	42.9
Age		
22–29	8	23.5
30–39	11	32.4
40–49	9	26.5
50–59	3	8.8
60–63	3	8.8
Rank		
Line officer	32	91.4
Sergeant	1	2.9
Lieutenant	1	2.9
Captain	1	2.9
Shift		
First	13	37.1
Second	12	34.3
Third	10	28.6
Experience		
<1 year	5	14.3
1–3 years	8	22.9
4–8 years	12	34.3
9–12 years	4	11.4
13–15 years	3	8.6
16–20 years	2	5.7
>20 years	1	2.9
Job detail of line officers		
Female floor	20	62.5
Medical control room	5	15.6
Central base control	4	12.5
Intake	2	6.2
Recreation department	1	3.1

*Percentages may not total 100.0 because of rounding.

may be expected that one aspect of women's working in a traditionally male job is the need for support. Accordingly, this section will examine the factors that influenced the women to choose corrections and their perceptions of support from friends and families.

Choosing a Career in Corrections   The two most common reasons why women chose to become correctional officers were that they wanted to

TABLE 2
Reasons and Support for Entering Corrections[*]

Characteristic	N	%
Reasons for choosing this job[*]		
To become police/road officer	14	(40.0)
Needed money/job	14	(40.0)
Advancement opportunities	8	(22.9)
Challenge/ interesting	8	(22.9)
Had worked other CJ job	8	(22.9)
Help people/work with people	6	(17.1)
Other	7	(20.0)
Have you received support from your family and friends?		
Yes	19	(54.3)
No	12	(34.3)
Mixed	4	(11.4)
Do you have any relatives who are COs?		
Yes	3	(8.6)
No	32	(91.4)

[*]Officers could provide more than one response.

become police or patrol officers (40 percent) or were attracted to the money and benefits (40 percent; Table 2).[5] Women recruits were told that working in corrections was the most promising path into police work, although only one woman was known to have advanced to "the road" (road patrol), while the women interviewed knew of a number of the male officers who had succeeded in advancing out of the jail into road patrol. (It appeared to be widely accepted that road patrol was significantly more prestigious than working in the jail.) White women (55 percent) were more likely than black women (20 percent) to choose corrections because of their desire to become police officers ($\chi^2 = 4.38$, p = .04). More experienced ("early") women officers also were more likely than less experienced officers to have chosen corrections as a means of becoming a police officer or in relation to the desire to do so ($\chi^2 = 2.76$, p = .10). This is not surprising given that the younger, "early" women actually had more doors open to them in policing given Title VII and the women's movement.

The responses for choosing an occupation in corrections were quite varied.

> I wanted to go into law enforcement since I was a little person, and this was a start. (CO 4)

> I was a young widow with four children who needed a full-time job. It was in the paper, so I applied. (CO 7)

> When I was in high school I wanted to be a police officer, in the sixties, but women were meter maids or worked with juvies. There were always police officers in our family: my uncle, my brother. . . . Instead of becoming a police officer, I got married, and when my family was old enough I was too old to be a street officer, so this was the closest I could get. (CO 8)

The next most frequently given reasons (23 percent each) for becoming COs included advancement opportunities, the belief that the job would be interesting or challenging, and previous work in another criminal justice job before moving into this one.

These data both support and refute findings from prior research. As in Zimmer's (1986) study, none of the women in the current study had aspired to become COs; two of the primary reasons for choosing corrections were financial and the lack of other opportunities. These findings are also consistent with Jurik and Halemba's (1984: 557) study, in which the second and third most frequently stated reasons why women entered corrections were (respectively) that they viewed it as an entry-level position for other jobs in the department and because of the salary.

The current study, however, also differed from the above studies in significant ways. First, only two of the 70 women in Zimmer's (1986: 40–44) study had aspired to be police officers. It is unclear why wanting to become a police officer was a primary motive in this study but not in Zimmer's. Perhaps the sample in the current study consisted of mere "older" women whose opportunities for entering law enforcement were more limited when they first began to work at the jail. Also, in contrast to the current research, Jurik and Halemba (1984: 557) found that interest in human services or inmate rehabilitation was women's most frequently reported reason for choosing corrections. In this study, only 17 percent of the women reported choosing corrections because they wanted to help people or work with people. It would be useful to examine this motivation in future studies because it appeared to be relatively unimportant in Zimmer's (1986) work and in the current study, but was most important in Jurik and Halemba's (1984) study.

Support from Friends and Families Although 54 percent of the women claimed unconditional support from their families and friends for their career choice, 11 percent reported mixed support and 34 percent reported no support. Six of the women (17 percent) reported that the level of support from their families had changed over time: four of the women received more support as their families and friends adjusted to their working in corrections, but two received less support than previously. The degree of support varied a great deal among the women.

> I never told my children I got the job until I picked up my uniform. They like it and still say, "Gee, Mom! I can't believe you turned out to be a cop!" (CO 13)

> My family wouldn't be caught dead working here and they hope I quit before I die [laughs]. (CO 19)

> All seem to be supportive. Some can't understand how I can put up with it, but they're supportive. (CO 21)

Women with male relatives in corrections (nine percent of the sample) seemed to report more support from friends and families, although these results may have occurred by chance because of the small numbers. Overall, these findings are consistent with Zimmer's (1986: 41–42) findings that women COs face considerable opposition from friends and relatives, although the women in this study seemed to find a little less opposition than did Zimmer's respondents (1986).

Attitudes and Perceptions about Gender Equality Regarding Opportunities, Expectations, and Training

One would think that women entering traditionally male jobs would hold feminist values, but research on women COs and policewomen has not borne

TABLE 3
Attitudes and Perceptions about Gender Equality Regarding Opportunities, Expectations, and Training*

Question	N	%
Are men and women equal overall, and should they receive equal job opportunities?		
Yes	33	(94.3)
No	2	(5.7)
Can male and female officers be utilized interchangeably?		
Yes	25	(71.4)
No	2	(5.7)
With some qualifications	8	(22.9)
Are female officers at a disadvantage in enforcing jail rules?		
Yes	6	(17.1)
No	28	(80.0)
Unsure	1	(2.9)
Is a different quality of work expected of female COs?		
Yes	19	(54.3)
No	16	(45.7)
How do your advancement opportunities compare with male officers?		
Poorly	31	(88.6)
No difference	1	(2.9)
Unsure	3	(8.6)
Was your job training similar to the male COs'?		
Similar	22	(62.9)
Not similar	8	(22.9)
N/A because no job training for either sex	5	(14.3)

*Percentages may not total 100.0% because of rounding.

out this idea (Martin, 1980; Zimmer, 1986). Zimmer (1986: 43), in fact, found that as a group, women officers tended to have rather conservative sex-role attitudes. It is useful to examine nontraditional women workers' attitudes about gender inequality on the job. Specifically, does women COs' job training differ from that of the men? How do women's advancement opportunities compare with the men's? Table 3 presents the findings concerning these questions on these officers' perceptions of gender equality.

Belief in Gender Equality   Although 62 percent of the women COs were assigned to work almost exclusively with women inmates, 94 percent believed that men and women are equal and should receive equal opportunities (Table 3). When asked whether male and female officers could be used interchangeably, 71 percent said "yes," 23 percent believed they were interchangeable with some qualifications, and only 6 percent believed they were not interchangeable.

> [Do you believe male and female officers can be used interchangeably?] Yes, without a doubt. Some people believe there's a need for females only where we hold females. I can handle the males as well as anybody. You can ask any of the male inmates and they'll tell you what a bitch I am. (CO 1)

> I would have a problem putting female officers on male housing units on high-security floors. On the other hand, maybe the females wouldn't be as threatening to them. I know the male officers run their mouths and end up starting half the fights. (CO 32)

This study seemed to show rather definitive support for gender equality. The current findings are consistent with prior research claiming that although women COs have an overall high degree of confidence in handling male inmates, they feel some discomfort and confusion regarding certain duties, usually those associated with inmates' privacy (Kissel and Katsampes, 1980: 226; Peterson, 1982: 455). Martin and Jurik's (1996) overview of the history of comparing the rights of inmates to privacy (almost exclusively examined through the lens of *male inmates'* rights to privacy in showering and so on from *female officers*), states that the court cases since the 1970s tend to preserve women's employment opportunities over inmates' rights to privacy. This was largely accomplished through court-ordered privacy screens and shift adjustments for women to ensure male prisoners' privacy. However, Martin and Jurik (1996, 187) conclude that the recent anti-inmate climate has resulted in recent cases favoring "security concerns and women's employment rights over inmate rights."

Advancement Opportunities   When asked about their advancement opportunities, 89 percent of the officers believed that they compared poorly with males, one officer believed that there was no difference, and three (9 percent) were unsure how they compared.

> Forty men get promoted before a female because you are only promoted if there is a position open for a female. (CO 3)

> We're limited to one floor. . . . We can't work in the kitchen because they don't think we can handle all those male inmates. They don't utilize women as much as they could. There's not much opportunity to prove yourself if you're on the same post month after month. (CO 5)

The point of these comments is similar to Chapman et al.'s (1980: xvi) finding of a "strong perception that women receive less than equal consideration" in hiring and promotion. This perception might be a result of the organizational barrier and the double-edged sword of sex stereotyping in job assignments. Nallin (1981: 21) attributes women's lack of upward mobility in corrections to the small numbers of women in corrections, their limited range of duties, and their lack of mentors. Similarly, Kerle (1985: 314) found that women jailers' promotion opportunities were affected seriously by their relegation to work only with female inmates. Thus (through no fault of their own) they lacked the experience of working with male inmates and were not considered qualified to become supervisors. Jurik and Halemba (1984: 559), however, found that male and female COs did not differ significantly in their views of promotional opportunities. Thus, despite the positive aspects of Title VII and Affirmative Action laws, there is some indication that there is significantly more turnover among women as compared to men in policing and corrections jobs. This may be because women report pessimism about their own and other women's likelihood of promotions and advancements in these jobs (Chapman et al., 1980; Martin and Jurik, 1996; Nallin, 1981; Poole and Pogrebin, 1998). At the same time, male officers tend to view themselves as disadvantaged in the promotional arena (Weisheit, 1987). Lawrence and Mahan (1998: 63) conclude that the persistence of some male officers' resistance to women on the job likely serves as an "obstacle for women seeking opportunities for advancement and promotion in male prisons." This pessimism about promotions is particularly acute among African American women (Martin, 1994; Townsey, 1982).

Perceptions of Gender Differences in Work Expectations

Table 3 also examines the officers' perceptions of gender differences in work expectations. Eighty percent of the women believed that female officers are not at a disadvantage in enforcing jail rules against inmates, whereas 17 percent believed that females suffer a disadvantage. One officer claimed that she was unsure because she had never worked with male inmates.[6] Fifty-four percent of the officers believed that a different quality of work was expected of the female officers, but 46 percent did not think so. Younger officers (74 percent) were more likely than older officers (33 percent) to believe that a higher quality of work was expected of women officers ($\chi^2 = 5.54$, p = .02); perhaps more was expected of the younger women than of the older.

> Since we have female supervisors, they expect more, and more is expected of them as women through administration. (CO 5)

> They expect us to be better, every way you can think of . . . how clean is the shift, how you write up reports, how quickly you turn in reports, your officers, etc. They can excuse or overlook a male officer making a mistake, but not the females. (CO 7)

Job Training

Pollock (1986: 3) states that the guard subculture is crucial in the socialization of new officers, especially in regard to handling inmates. This point appears to be relevant whether or not the institutions include formal training in addition to on-the-job training. Zimmer (1987: 422) believes that one reason why women COs receive inadequate socialization during their on-the-job training is that the men who train women do not

want them there. In the current study, 23 percent of the women claimed that their job training in the academy was different from that received by the men, while 63 percent claimed it was similar. (Fourteen percent had been hired at a time when neither sex received formal training.) At any rate, although the formal academy training is important, all new recruits (as well as seasoned officers) experience the power of the on-the-job subculture. In fact, Van Maanen's (1973) study of police recruits found that the "war stories" exchanged during formal academy training and the influence of the field training officer were powerful enough to override many of the formal training ideologies and goals.

The experiences of the women COs in this study included the following:

> I got thrown out on the cellblock. They had a class, but they were desperate for females so I didn't go through the classes for male officers. (CO9).

> I was the only female in the academy. I got no preferential treatment. It was harder because I took a lot of ribbing for being the only female. (CO 4).

Sex Preference for Inmates, Officers, and Supervisors

Considerable research on women correctional officers has addressed the acceptance of the women by male inmates and male coworkers. Some research also has questioned these COs on their perceptions and preferences as to the ideal working environment. This section addresses the women COs' preferences for the sex of the inmates, officers, and supervisors with whom they work (see Table 4).

Preference for Inmates

Although the majority of the women (43 percent) stated no preference for working with male or female inmates, 34 percent preferred male inmates and 14 percent preferred female inmates. (Three officers, or 9 percent, had worked only with female inmates, so they claimed that they had no basis for determining a preference.) Thirty-one percent reported that they received more respect or cooperation from male inmates; 17 percent reported that female inmates were easier to

TABLE 4
Sex Preferences for Inmates, Officers, and Supervisors*

Characteristic	N	%
Preference for inmates		
None	15	(42.9)
Male	12	(34.3)
Female	5	(14.3)
No basis for a decision	3	(8.6)
Preference for officers		
None	19	(54.3)
Male	10	(28.6)
Female	6	(17.1)
Preference for supervisors		
None	20	(57.1)
Male	9	(25.7)
Female	3	(8.6)
No basis for a decision	3	(8.6)

*Percentages may not total 100.0% because of rounding.

handle and to understand. These findings are consistent with Pollock's (1986) findings: 72 percent of women officers preferred male inmates, 11 percent preferred women inmates, and 16 percent had no preference ($N = 18$). Pollock (1986: 97–98) reported that women officers believed male inmates treated them with more respect than did women inmates, and that male inmates were more likely than women inmates to "appreciate them as women," thus making their jobs "more enjoyable."

Some respondents explained why women inmates appear to be more manipulative.

> A lot of the officers think that women inmates are more manipulating than the males. But that's just not true. Women inmates have more needs than men: they need more toilet paper, tampons, things like that. So they're put in a situation where they have to be manipulating to get their everyday needs. It's just not fair. (CO 16)

> Males have a whole psych ward, females only one section of the female floor for psychs, no rubber room or special effects for women mentals [psych patients] ... women have to deal with that on their own. (CO 3)

Thus what appear to be differences between male and female inmates' behavior may in fact be sexist perceptions on the part of COs.

Preference for Officers   In this study, 54 percent of the women preferred working with male and female officers equally, 28 percent preferred males, and 17 percent preferred females. Twenty-three percent reported that male officers are less "catty," "petty," or "jealous," while three women (9 percent) reported that female officers are more responsible or caring.

Preference for Supervisors   Fifty-seven percent of the officers had no preference regarding the sex of their supervisors, 26 percent preferred males, and 9 percent preferred females. Nine percent had worked only with female supervisors and so had no basis for a decision. Three of the women (9 percent) reported that women supervisors were too "picky" or expected too much; four (11 percent) reported that women supervisors were "jealous" or vindictive. One woman preferred women supervisors because she believed they were more sensitive and easier to get along with. The women supervisors seemed to be forced to walk a fine line between not giving women COs preferential treatment and allowing them more responsibilities and opportunities than the male supervisors typically allowed women.

Sexual and Gender Harassment

Historically, sexual harassment has been an all-too-frequent condition for many women in the labor force; whether they worked as domestic servants, in factories, as clerical workers, and so on, they were often viewed as "sexually accessible" by some of their male co-workers, supervisors, and bosses (Goldman, 1992; Rhode, 1989). Although sexual harassment has been a historical constant, it received no organized attention until the second wave of the women's movement in the 1970s, and since then both scholars and policy makers have debated what constitutes sexual harassment.

These research and legal distinctions will be described after this brief history of criminalizing sexual harassment. In 1980, guidelines defining sexual harassment were designated by the Equal Employment Opportunity Commission (EEOC). These guidelines' case law presented sexual harassment as sex discrimination, a violation of Title VII of the Civil Rights Act of 1964 and focused exclusively on sexual harassment occurring in a place of work (Belknap and Erez, 1997; Ledgerwood and Johnson-Dietz, 1980). According to the EEOC, sexual harassment is illegal and constitutes a form of unlawful sex discrimination. Ironically, public awareness, and particularly understanding and sympathy for sexual harassment victims, was almost nonexistent until the 1991 U.S. Senate confirmation hearings of Clarence Thomas to the U.S. Supreme Court. Unprecedented public attention was paid to law professor Anita Hill's testimony describing Judge Thomas's sexually harassing behavior when she worked under him at the Department of Education's Office of Civil Rights and again later at the EEOC (Belknap and Erez, 1997; Black and Allen, 2001). One irony of this case is that the sexual harasser was a supervisor in the institution to which victims were expected to report sexual harassment (the EEOC). An additional irony was that although this event was a "failure" to those advocating to criminalize and address sexual harassment by punishing its offenders and although Thomas was still appointed to the U.S. Supreme Court despite Hill's convincing testimony, these confirmation hearings brought unprecedented awareness and debate about the seriousness of sexual harassment in women's lives (Belknap and Erez, 1997; Black and Allen, 2001). So although sexual harassment still occurs far too often, there is more awareness about the real harm it causes and about the ways to resist, that is, telling the harasser to stop, documenting the harassment, reporting the harassment to a manager, and filing a charge with the EEOC.

Gender harassment refers to nonsexual "put-downs" of women, whereas *sexual harassment* refers to offensive sexual comments or behaviors. Comments that women are incapable of performing a job or are less intelligent than men are examples of gender harassment. Sexual harassment, on the other hand, includes behaviors such as whistling, pressuring women for sex, and comments on their bodies. Belknap (2001) also identifies institutionalized heterosexism and homophobia as forms of sexual

harassment for women working in policing and corrections. She describes an ongoing focus on these women's sexuality by their male-coworkers, "given that these women's desire to work in an arena where they potentially encounter physical interactions with male prisoners often results in labeling them as [sexually] deviant" (Belknap, 2001:369). Consistent with the discussion thus far about the femininity and sexuality of women who choose to do "men's" work, some authors report that lesbians experience significantly more sexual harassment than heterosexual women do (Crenshaw, 1992; Schneider, 1991; Wise and Stanley, 1992). Notably, a recent study found that male workers who do not display behavior identified as masculine are at greater risk than "masculine men" to be victims of sexual harassment as well (Lee, 2000).

Although most women experience gender and sexual harassment, such harassment may be most apparent for women working in traditionally male jobs. Furthermore, women who identify as "feminist" or pursue traditionally male jobs are likely at increased risk of heterosexist and homophobic harassment. Nallin (1981: 20) questions why "masculine" traits are viewed as more appropriate in handling inmates than are "more neutral, less sex-typed terms. . . . Firmness, fairness, determination and concern are equally applicable to the correctional setting." Several studies on policewomen and women COs have found that women who perform their jobs adequately are especially likely to have their "femaleness" questioned by male co-workers (Baunach and Rafter, 1982: 350; Martin, 1980: 93; Zimmer, 1986: 57–58). Researchers also report that many male coworkers fear that they must protect or do the work of what they perceive as their intrinsically inept female co-workers (see Martin, 1980: 191; Zimmer, 1986: 54). Thus it appears that women are punished with sexual and gender harassment for both superior *and* inferior performance.

The significance of these various forms of harassment that women face in prison and jail, in law, and in policing work cannot be overemphasized. There appears to be a special risk of harassment associated with women who take on these most "macho" jobs:

controlling, punishing, and holding accountable male offenders. Thus, although women have made important strides in being hired into jail and prison work and although the level of sexist hostility from male co-workers and supervisors has decreased since women were first hired to "guard" men, recent studies indicate that women still face significant levels of hostility from some male co-workers and supervisors (Lawrence and Mahan, 1998; Pogrebin and Poole, 1997). This sexist discrimination is most profoundly played out in the form of sexual harassment by male peers, supervisors, and administrators at their jobs (see, for example, Bartol et al., 1992; Gratch, 1995; Hagan and Kay, 1995; Jurik, 1985; Martin, 1980; Morash and Haarr, 1995; Pierce, 1995; Pogrebin and Poole, 1997; Pollock, 1986; Pollock and Ramierez, 1995; Rosenberg et al., 1993; Sommerlad and Sanderson, 1998; Stohr et al., 1998). It is also necessary to note that the sometimes extreme sexual harassment faced by women COs working in prisons and jails, harassment perpetrated by male COs, is part of and even more severe than the sexual abuse of women prisoners by male COs. Both the Human Rights Watch (1996) and Shay (1999) present chilling documentation of the extreme sexual abuse experienced by women prisoners at the hands of male guards.

Till (1980) identified five levels of sexual and gender harassment, reported from least to most severe. The first level, *gender harassment*, is not sexual in nature but rather is putting down one sex (usually women). Examples would be telling women recruits or seasoned officers, "women aren't strong enough to control male prisoners" or "women are too emotional to work with male offenders." Till's second level, *seductive behavior*, involves sexual advances or requests by the harasser to discuss the victim's sexual or dating life. In Till's third level of sexual harassment, *sexual bribery*, the victim is promised some type of reward (such as a job or a promotion) if she complies with the harasser's sexual request. In Till's fourth level, *sexual coercion*, the victim is threatened with punishment for not complying with the harasser's sexual request. The final and most extreme category is *outright sexual assaults and sexual abuse*. Legally, there have been two distinctions in types of sexual harassment (see Belknap and

Erez, 1997). The first, *quid pro quo sexual harassment*, involves the trading of sexual "favors" for educational or work sustenance—such as the exchange of a sexual act for a higher grade in a class, for a job, or for a job promotion—or it involves the performance of a sexual act that results in a person not being fired from a job, losing a promotion, failing a course, and so on. Thus, quid pro quo violations are similar to Till's (1980) second and third levels of sexual harassment. The second category of legal sexual harassment violations is referred to as *hostile environment sexual harassment*. Notably, this type of sexual harassment is not adequately covered in Till's levels. This type of sexual harassment involves actions that make a person's work or educational environment sexually offensive or intimidating. For example, male co-workers who never make a sexual pass at a female worker but who post on the walls of their offices or lockers photographs from *Playboy* or *Hustler* or who talk about other women's bodies in front of the woman worker are demeaning all women in a sexual way and are thus creating a hostile environment for the female co-worker (See Rundblad, chap. 26).

A recent study of more than 1,000 women and more than 300 men in the U.S. military reported, not surprisingly, that the men's general hostility toward women, toward acceptance of women as equals, and toward race were all related to the men's tolerance of sexual harassment (Rosen and Martin, 1998). More specifically, men who reported higher levels of "hypermasculinity" and lower acceptance of women as equals, were *more* tolerant of sexual harassment. This study also found that white male soldiers were more tolerant of sexual harassment than were their African American counterparts and that African American female soldiers were less tolerant of sexual harassment than were their white female counterparts (Rosen and Martin, 1998). It is important to note that some men and women interpret sexual harassment as flattering at best and harmless at worst (Belknap and Erez, 1997). In reality, when sexualizing at the workplace and other places results in someone feeling demeaned, it is a manner of controlling. For example, a study of sexual harassment on the street reports that the victim "belongs" to the sexual harasser, who is the "owner" of the environment and can dictate rules and behaviors (Bernard and Schlaffer, 1997). Furthermore, the victim of sexual harassment often wonders and fears to what degree the harasser is willing to go to establish sexual dominance. One study found that one-fifth of women victims of sexual harassment reported that the harassment ended in a sexual assault (Schneider, 1991). The woman CO who resists her harasser has to worry that she'll be fired, receive a poor evaluation, or even be raped. One study found that male sexual harassers minimize their behavior, do it as a way to "bond" with male co-workers, and even claim they do it to humiliate their victims (Bernard and Schlaffer, 1997). Thus, while some sexual harassment may be more "minor," it is rarely experienced as harmless by victims.

One study of women coal miners (a traditional masculine and male job) found that they managed or coped with the sexual harassment on the job through the use of three styles (Yount, 1991). The "ladies" coped by withdrawing socially, which appeared to work more successfully for older women except that women who used this style were rarely promoted. Women using the "flirt" coping style used seductive interactions with the male co-workers. The flirts received more sexual come-ons as a result, and when the women were promoted it was assumed that their promotion was due to their sexual behavior and they were further harassed. In the final coping strategy, the "tomboys" attempted to identify with the male miners by using vulgar language with and back at them. This strategy often backfired and resulted in a high degree of escalated razzing that became very distressful to these women (Yount, 1991).

Sexual Harassment   Thirty-one percent of the women reported that sexual harassment had been an issue for them while working in the jail (Table 5). In this study white women (45 percent) were more likely than black women (13 percent) to report sexual harassment (Yates's corrected $\chi^2 = 2.65, p = .10$), and younger women (47 percent) were more likely to do so than were older women (13 percent; Yates's corrected $\chi^2 = 3.01, p = .08$). Seventy-seven percent

TABLE 5
Sexual and Gender Harassment

Question	N	%
Has sexual harassment been an issue for you on this job?		
Yes	11	(31.4)
No	24	(68.6)
Are male inmates and officers likely to comment on your appearance?		
Yes	27	(77.1)
No	8	(22.9)
Are women as a group "put-down" by male officers?		
Yes	27	(77.1)
No	8	(22.9)
Are women COs seen as one group behaving the same way?		
Yes	20	(57.1)
No	15	(42.9)
Who do you feel you have to prove yourself to more, inmates or male officers?		
Inmates	6	(17.1)
Officers	15	(42.9)
Both	3	(8.6)
Neither	11	(31.4)
Do women COs stand out and receive more scrutiny than male COs?		
Yes	24	(68.6)
No	11	(31.4)
Are the differences between men and women exaggerated making it more difficult to blend in?		
Yes	23	(65.7)
No	12	(34.3)

claimed that male inmates and officers were likely to comment on their appearance, but 29 percent of the women volunteered that they did not find these comments offensive. Again, the responses varied.

It could be [offensive] if I allowed it, but I don't. I have a good rapport with the males. We kid, we joke, and some [joking] is sexual, but it's good-natured. . . . They know I'm married. None of it has ever been serious. (CO 8)

One supervisor is worse than anybody I've dealt with. Basically, he even goes as far as putting his hands on you and saying he'll give you a ride in his van. I've almost decked him. If he touched my chest I would. A lot of other women have had the same problems with him. (CO 12)

A lot of officers can be cruel. After I pass them they say, "There goes fat ass." If I hear them, I turn around and smile because they want to upset you. . . . I consider the source, and it isn't too much better than the inmates. (CO 13)

I had that coming in here just now. . . . They said, "We were watching you in the [security] camera, and sizing you up." [She does hand movements imitating men cupping her buttocks.] The worst part is that they mean it as a compliment, but of course it comes out wrong. We get these comments on a regular basis. (CO 5)

The findings of this study contrast with Zimmer's (1986: 43) finding that all women interviewed described at least one incident of sexual harassment. This discrepancy may exist because Zimmer did not ask women whether sexual harassment was an issue; she asked them to describe experiences and concluded from those descriptions that every woman suffered from what might be termed sexual harassment. It is likely that many of the women in the current study experienced sexual harassment, but when asked whether it was "an issue," they stated that it was not. That is, many of the officers gave the impression that they experienced what is typically defined as sexual harassment, but they tried to ignore and minimize it. Another aspect of sexual harassment prevalent in this and other studies is that of rumors linking the women COs sexually with other officers or inmates (Peterson, 1982: 454).

Gender Harassment   Seventy-seven percent of the respondents believed that women as a group tend to be put down by male officers, and 57 percent believed that all women COs are seen as a single group of people who behave in the same way. White women (90 percent) were more likely than black women (60 percent) to report that women as a group are put down (Yates's corrected $\chi^2 = 2.84$, p = .09).

When asked whether they had to "prove" themselves more to male inmates or to male officers, 31 percent claimed (usually defiantly) that they did not have to prove themselves to anybody. Forty-three percent claimed that they had to prove themselves

more to male officers, 17 percent stated that they had to prove themselves more to male inmates, and 9 percent believed that they had equal difficulty in proving themselves to male inmates and male officers. Sixty-nine percent of the women believed that women COs receive more scrutiny than male officers, and 66 percent claimed that the differences between men and women make it more difficult to blend in.

Women are more criticized because there are so few of us. It's easy to lose one bad man, but women stick out. If we make a mistake they say we should be home with diapers, Susie Homemaker. With a guy it's just that he got into the wrong job. (CO 20)

Perceptions about Gender Differences in Behavior and Effectiveness

Pollock (1986: 88) found that "men and women performed the CO role somewhat differently." Even so, women need to be judged by how effective they are, not by whether their approaches are similar to men's. When asked about their perceptions of their behavior at work (Table 6), 71 percent of the women in the current study believed that men and women officers use different means to accomplish the same goals. Twenty-six percent reported that women have to work harder to prove themselves and that this effort changes how they do the job. Thirty-four percent claimed that men are more forceful than women, and two officers (6 percent) reported that women have more respect than men do for the inmates.

Women tend to do a better job in defusing a situation than men do. (CO 25)

Ninety-one percent believed that women bring different abilities, skills, and life experiences to the job.

In intake I've been called everything from a dyke to crazy. . . . I don't take a lot of it personally. They've already fought a lot so when they get to me I whisper so they have to stop yelling to hear me. . . . They calm down. (CO 14)

Women are more compassionate to the inmates than the males because they have children and the inmates act like children. (CO 32)

TABLE 6
Perceptions about Gender Differences in Behavior*

Question	N	%
Do male and female officers use similar or different means to accomplish the same goals?		
Similar	10	(28.6)
Different	25	(71.4)
Do women bring different abilities, skills, and life experiences to the job?		
Yes	32	(91.4)
No	3	(8.6)
Do male and female COs perform the job differently?		
Yes	23	(67.6)
No	11	(32.4)
Ways in which women perform differently from men★		
Less likely to use force/more likely to try to talk it out	10	(29.4)
More likely to enforce rules	3	(8.8)
More in control/efficient	7	(20.6)
Are women COs as effective as male COs?		
Yes	28	(80.0)
Depends on individual/situation	7	(20.0)

*Officers could provide more than one response.

> The majority of males are extremely lacking in communication skills, which is why they revert to force. They either don't or are afraid that they don't have the verbal and communication skills. (CO 34)

Sixty-eight percent of the women believed that men and women perform the job differently. The most frequently stated difference was that women are less likely to use force and more likely to try to talk issues out with inmates (30 percent); 21 percent reported that women are more in control and more efficient than male officers; and nine percent stated that women officers are more likely to enforce the jail rules. When asked whether women are as effective officers as the men, 80 percent believed they are; the remaining 20 percent stated that one must look at the individual and the situation, not the officer's sex.

> Females, we'll try to talk a situation down, trying not to use foul language. We even wake them up with "Good morning, ladies . . ." On male floors it's "OK

you motherfuckers, get out of bed." I tell them [male officers], "When you work with me, don't do that again." If you wake them up nice, most are usually pretty cool through the day. (CO 12)

> I am more strict than the male officers, and a lot of times the males will try to talk me out of an action I've taken. (CO 1)

These findings are consistent with prior research. Kissel and Katsampes (1980: 225) found "that the overwhelming majority of female staff . . . felt satisfied with their performance and felt they did as good a job as the males on the staff." Pollock (1986: 90) found that both male and female COs view women COs as more receptive to inmates' problems and more likely to try to "draw them out." These findings also support Zimmer's (1987: 421) contention that women officers are more likely than men officers to develop friendly relationships with the inmates to generate voluntary compliance and that the women's nurturing role "is in direct contrast to the macho, competitive role typical of the male guards." In contrast to respondents in the current study, however, Zimmer's (1987: 421) male inmates reported that women COs were more likely than men COs to overlook petty rule infractions. The difference between the findings may be that in this study only women officers were questioned, not male officers and inmates. In general, these women believe that gender differences exist in the performance of the CO job, particularly that women's behavior toward inmates is more respectful. It also appears that women's actions are devalued in comparison to the men's more aggressive approaches.

The Gender Model versus the Job Model

Table 7 reports the respondents' perceptions of the importance of societal structure (the gender model) versus organizational structure (the job model) in explaining differences between male and female correctional officers. Almost 70 percent of the women believed that the manner in which females are conditioned and raised affects how they perform their jobs. Somewhat fewer (51 percent) believed that the manner in which the job is structured affects how men and women perform the job. Thirty-five

TABLE 7

Perceptions of the Influence of Society and the Jail Structure on Differences in Male and Female COs' Job Performance and Self-Classification of Officers into Zimmer's Styles

Question	N	%
Are there ways in which your conditioning as a female, such as how you were raised, affects how you perform your job?		
Yes	24	(68.6)
No	11	(31.4)
Are there ways in which the job is structured which affect differently how male and female COs do the job?		
Yes	18	(51.4)
No	17	(48.6)
Do the differences between men and women working in the jail result more from gender differences between men and women in society (outside the jail) or more from how the job is structured (inside the jail)?		
Society	15	(42.9)
Job structure	13	(37.1)
Equal combination of both	6	(17.1)
Other	1	(2.9)
Which of Zimmer's styles best describes you?		
Institutional	17	(48.6)
Modified	0	(0.0)
Inventive	18	(51.4)

percent of the women claimed that this difference was due largely to women officers being restricted to "the female floor" (working exclusively with women inmates). This response implies that the women, overall, believed that the gender model is a better explanation of gender differences between officers, but that the job model also plays an important role.

> We're segregated and put in pansy jobs and away from male inmates, so it blows your confidence when put on male floors. On the male floors I get tried and tested. If more females were on the male posts, the male inmates would be more used to us. (CO 1)

> In this [women's floor] setting everything is routine. The men get the opportunity to move around more. Females, they look at their job as more routine and thus use less effort. (CO 10)

When asked directly whether they thought the differences between the male and the female officers resulted more from gender differences in society (the gender model) or from how the job is structured (the job model), 43 percent stated that society played a stronger role, 37 percent said they thought the job structure was more dominant, and 17 percent said that society and the job structure played equal roles in determining gender differences. Thus the emphasis on support for the gender model diminished somewhat when respondents were asked to compare the two influences directly. These findings are in contrast with Jurik and Halemba's (1984: 563–564) report of support for the job model, in that women COs' attitudes were more a function of their position in the organizational structure and of working conditions than of gender model characteristics.

Finally, the officers were given a description of each of Zimmer's (1986) women correctional officer styles (institutional, modified, and inventive) and were asked to classify themselves. The *institutional role* describes officers who follow institutional rules closely, downplay the importance of female status, maintain professional distances from inmates and professional relationships with fellow officers, and resent attempts to block their access to prison jobs (1986: 111–122). Officers adopting the *modified role* believe that women cannot perform the job on an equal basis with men; fear inmates and avoid direct contact with them; oppose "women libbers"; and rely on male officers to back them up (1986: 122–129). Finally, the *inventive role* comprises officers who view women's status as a distinct advantage; often work in direct contact jobs with male inmates; expect and receive support from male inmates; believe their intuition, communication skills, and abilities with inmates compensate for their disadvantage in physical strength; integrate counseling into their jobs; and receive considerable opposition from male officers (1986: 129–137).

Zimmer (1986) developed these roles after she collected her data and "assigned" the women to them. The research in this chapter differs from Zimmer's in that the women were asked which role described them most accurately. (Obviously the women's actual behavior may differ from how they believe they behave.) Seventeen (48.6 percent) of the women viewed themselves as following the institutional style most closely (as opposed to 11 percent of Zimmer's sample), and 18 (51.4 percent) viewed themselves as closest to the inventive style (compared to 46 percent of Zimmer's sample). None of the officers chose the modified style, whereas Zimmer assigned 43 percent of her sample to this category. The reason may be that it was difficult to describe the modified style in a manner that seemed as positive as the others. It is also likely that if the interviewer had "assigned" the roles (on the basis of more in-depth information on the individuals in the study), some of the assignments would have differed from the women's perceptions of themselves. Only one woman claimed that none of Zimmer's styles described her.

CONCLUSIONS

This study supports most of the research regarding the conflict that these women face at work. Women in this department chose to work in the jail mainly because of the desire to become police/road patrol officers and for financial reasons. Most of the women (66 percent) reported at least some support from their friends or families for their choice of occupation.

The women expressed a degree of consensus regarding their perceptions of gender inequality in work expectations and opportunities. Most agreed that men and women were equal and that male and female officers could be used interchangeably. The majority also believed that their advancement opportunities compared unfavorably with those of the male officers.

Although most of the respondents had no preference for working with either male or female inmates, officers, or supervisors, they favored working with males when they had a choice. This preference was most pronounced (34 percent) regarding inmates' sex. A couple of the officers reported that even women officers might be sexist in evaluating inmates' behavior: what may be called "manipulat-

ing" in a female inmate is "assertiveness" in a male inmate. Furthermore, it appeared that the women supervisors were under pressure not to be perceived as giving in to female officers, while at the same time they may have been trying to help them.

This research showed considerable evidence of sexual harassment, although it seemed that many of the women tended to minimize it. More examples of gender harassment were found than sexual harassment. This is consistent with a recent study of university students, which found that women reported more gender than sexual harassment (Kalof et al., 2001). In the current study, the respondents tended to believe that women COs as a group were lumped together and were viewed as a single group of people who acted in the same way and that women stood out and received more scrutiny than their male counterparts. Although one-third of the respondents did not believe that they had to prove themselves to male inmates or officers, those who did believe so were more likely to feel that they had to prove themselves to male officers than to male inmates.

This research also showed a great deal of evidence for the contention that women and men do the CO's job differently. Most significant were the beliefs that men are more forceful than women and that women are better communicators than men. The women believed overwhelmingly that they were doing the job as effectively as the men, or better.

These women reported that both the job model and the gender model are at work in establishing gender differences in jail work. Even so, they appeared to believe that the factors related to the gender model are more influential than those related to the job model. The respondents also believed that they view the CO's role differently from their male coworkers on the basis of their experiences outside the jail. Regarding the job model, this study found that the organizational barrier cited most frequently as influencing gender differences in job performance was the practice of assigning most of the women to work exclusively with female inmates.

Finally, the participants seemed for the most part to enjoy their jobs and to feel that they performed well, but they believed that they were not appreciated. These women also felt that the restrictions they faced in their working environment fostered in them a lack of commitment to the job. Therefore, this research reveals that most of the women COs in the jail perceive organizational and attitudinal changes as necessary to create an adequate working environment, but consider it unlikely that such changes will occur.

DISCUSSION QUESTIONS

1. Identify four workplace similarities faced by women correction officers and women police officers.
2. Define and distinguish between *sexual harassment* and *gender harassment*. Give an example of each in the male-dominated field of corrections described in this chapter. Then give an example of each from your own experience or that of someone you know.
3. Why are male correction officers more hostile than inmates toward women correction officers? Is the situation comparable for women police officers; in other words, do male officers' hostility exceed that of the public? Discuss the problem, and devise several solutions that might prevent such hostilities against female correction officers.
4. Describe the gender model and the job model. Why are these concepts useful? How do they aid in a better understanding of the experiences of women working in corrections?
5. According to studies reported in this chapter, how do race and ethnicity, sexual orientation, and social class origins affect sexual harassment and gender harassment of women workers generally? of female corrections officers specifically?
6. What are the strengths that women bring to corrections work? How do these

strengths compare with those of women police officers described in previous chapters in this section?

NOTES

1. The research described in this chapter is not only deductive, but differs in a number of additional ways from Zimmer's (1986, 1987) and several other researchers' studies (Jurik, 1985, 1988; Jurik and Halemba, 1985; Peterson, 1982; Pollock, 1986; Simpson and White, 1984). First, the site of this study is a jail instead of a prison. Prisons tend to house inmates of a single sex, whereas jails often house both male and female inmates. The inmate population also tends to differ in that jail inmates usually receive shorter sentences than prison inmates do. In addition, women COs are a recent phenomenon in male prisons (only since the late 1970s and early 1980s), but women have been working for many years in jails with female inmates. Finally, considerable changes have taken place in corrections since Zimmer conducted her study, and it is possible that the views of women COs held by their male co-workers, the administrators, and the women themselves may have changed.

2. Forty women, including the pilot-tested individual, were working in nonclerical jobs in the institution. Four COs, all of whom were ranked as officers, chose not to take part in the study. Two were younger white women (aged 25 to 35), one was a younger black woman (aged 25 to 35), and one was an older black woman (aged 40 to 50). The pilot-tested individual was a white sergeant (aged 25 to 35). It is difficult to determine whether these women's participation would have changed the findings appreciably, but the sample seems to represent the women working in the jail adequately. Because of the small sample size, the quantitative analysis of these qualitative data consisted primarily of frequencies.

3. I constructed a structured interview format from Zimmer's (1986, 1987) work and tested it on one woman sergeant from the selected jail site. With the exception of the final question, in which I asked the women to specify which of Zimmer's (1986) occupational styles defined them most accurately, the questions were open-ended. I conducted all the interviews in the jail, in a private office provided by the administration. Interviews were conducted during each shift (approximately four times per shift) over the course of three weeks in March 1988. I asked each participant identical questions, but the interviews ranged in length from 25 to 95 minutes. Although a few of the women seemed to be suspicious of being interviewed, most appeared to be pleased that someone was interested in their experiences as women workers in the jail. Because the officers seemed to be very uncomfortable with the idea of tape-recording the interviews, I conducted the interviews in shorthand and transcribed them later. Four people coded the typed, qualitative data. All four coders worked to develop categories to responses; two of these coders determined the final categories into which the data were quantified. When disagreements in coding arose, the coders met to agree on the final coding.

4. Although the tables do not report these bivariate analyses (of which the findings were largely nonsignificant), relationships of p-5 ≤ .10 are incorporated into the text. In addition, the text includes some verbatim quotes from the interviews related to factors listed in the tables in order to expand further on the reasons some women gave for their responses.

5. The women could state as many reasons for choosing corrections as they wished.

6. Although some of the other officers also had not worked with male inmates, apparently they were willing to speculate.

REFERENCES

(★ indicates a new reference in this updated version of the chapter)

★Bartol, C. R., G. T. Bergen, J. S. Volckens, and K. M. Knoras. 1992. Women in Small-Town Policing: Job Performance and Stress. *Criminal Justice and Behavior* 19(3): 240–59.

Baunach, P. J., and N. H. Rafter. 1982. Sex-Role Operations: Strategies for Women Working in the Criminal Justice System. In *Judge, Lawyer, Victim, Thief*, ed. N. H. Rafter and E. A. Stanko, 341–358. Stoughton, MA: Northeastern University.

★Belknap, J. 2001. *The Invisible Woman: Gender, Crime, and Justice*, 2d. ed. Belmont, CA: Wadsworth.

★Belknap, J., and E. Erez. 1997. Redefining Sexual Harassment. *Justice Professional* 10:143–59.

★Benard, C., and E. Schlaffer. 1997. 'The Man in the Street': Why He Harasses. In *Feminist Frontiers IV*, ed. L. Richardson and V. Taylor, 395–398. New York: McGraw-Hill.

★Black, A. E., and J. L. Allen. 2001. Tracing the Legacy of Anita Hill: The Thomas/Hill Hearings and the Coverage of Sexual Harassment. *Gender Issues* 19(1): 33–52.

★Britton, D. M. 1997a. Gendered Organizational Logic: Policy and Practice in Men's and Women's Prisons. *Gender and Society* 11(6): 796–818.

——— 1997b. Perceptions of the Work Environment among Correctional Officers: Do Race and Sex Matter? *Criminology* 35(1): 85–106.

Chapman, J. R., E. K. Minor, P. Rieker, T. L. Mills, and M. Bottum. 1980. *Women Employed in Corrections*. Washington, DC: Center for Women Policy Studies.

★Crenshaw, K. 1992. Race, Gender, and Sexual Harassment. *Southern California Law Review* 65:1467–1476.

Crouch, B., and G. P Alpert. 1982. Sex and Occupational Socialization among Prison Guards. *Criminal Justice and Behavior* 9(2): 159–176.

Flynn, E. E. 1982. Women as Criminal Justice Professionals: A Challenge to Tradition. In *Judge, Lawyer, Victim, Thief*, ed. N. H. Rafter and E. A. Stanko, 305–340. Stoughton, Massachusetts: Northeastern University.

★Gratch, L. 1995. Sexual Harassment among Police Officers. In *Women, Law, and Social Control*, ed. A. V. Merlo and J. M. Pollock, 55–77. Boston: Allyn and Bacon.

★Hagan, J., and F. Kay. 1995. *Gender in Practice: A Study of Lawyers' Lives*. New York: Oxford University.

★Human Rights Watch Women Rights Project. 1996. *All Too Familiar: Sexual Abuse of Women in U.S. State Prisons*. New York: Human Rights Watch.

Jurik, N. C. 1985. An Officer and a Lady: Organizational Barriers to Women Working as Correctional Officers in Men's Prisons. *Social Problems* 32(4):375–388.

———— 1988. Striking a Balance: Female Correctional Officers, Gender Role Stereotypes, and Male Prisoners. *Sociological Inquiry* 58(3):291–304.

Jurik, N. C., and G. J. Halemba. 1984. Gender, Working Conditions and the Job Satisfaction of Women in a Non-Traditional Occupation: Female Correctional Officers in Men's Prisons. *Sociological Quarterly* 25(Autumn): 551–566.

★Kalof, L., K. K. Eby, J. L. Mateson, and R. J. Korska. 2001. The Influence of Race and Gender on Student Self-Reports of Sexual Harassment by College Professors. *Gender and Society* 15(2):282–302.

Kerle, K. E. 1985. The American Woman County Jail Officer. In *The Changing Roles of Women in the Criminal Justice System,* ed. I. L. Moyer, 307–317. Prospect Heights, IL: Waveland.

Kissel, P. J., and P. L. Katsampes. 1980. The Impact of Women Corrections Officers on the Functioning of Institutions Housing Male Inmates. *Journal of Offender Counseling, Services and Rehabilitation* 4(3):213–231.

★Lawrence, R., and S. Mahan. 1998. Women Corrections Officers in Men's Prisons: Acceptance and Perceived Job Performance. *Women and Criminal Justice* 9(3):63–86.

★Lee, D. 2000. Hegmonic Masculinity and Male Feminization: The Sexual Harassment of Men at Work. *Journal of Gender Studies* 9(2):141–155.

Martin, S. E. 1980. *Breaking and Entering: Policewomen on Patrol.* Berkeley: University of California.

★Martin, S. E. 1994. 'Outsider Within' the Station House: The Impact of Race and Gender on Black Women Police. *Social Problems* 41(3):383–400.

★Martin, S. E., and N. C. Jurik. 1996. *Doing Justice, Doing Gender: Women in Law and Criminal Justice Occupations.* Thousand Oaks, CA: Sage.

★Morash, M., and R. N. Haarr. 1995. Gender, Workplace Problems, and Stress in Policing. *Justice Quarterly* 12(1):113–140.

Morton, J. B. 1981. Women in Correctional Employment: Where Are They Now and Where Are They Headed? *Women in Corrections,* Series 1; No. 1 (February): 7–16.

Nallin, J. A. 1981. Female Correctional Administrators: Sugar and Spice Are Nice but a Backbone of Steel Is Essential. *Women in Corrections,* Series 1, No. 1 (February):17–26.

Peterson, C. B. 1982. Doing Time with the Boys: An Analysis of Women Correctional Officers in All-Male Facilities. In *The Criminal Justice System and Women,* ed. B. R. Price and N. J. Sokoloff, 437–560. New York: Clark Boardman.

★Pierce, J. L. 1995. *Gender Trials.* Berkeley: University of California.

★Pogrebin, M. R., and E. D. Poole. 1997. The Sexualized Work Environment: A Look at Women Jail Officers. *The Prison Journal* 77(1):41–57.

Pollock, J. M. 1986. *Sex and Supervision: Guarding Male and Female Inmates.* New York: Greenwood.

★Pollock, J. M., and B. Ramirez. 1995. Women in the Legal Profession. In *Women, Law, and Social Control,* ed. A. V. Merlo and J. M. Pollock, 79–95. Boston: Allyn and Bacon.

★Rhode, D. L. 1989. *Justice and Gender: Sex Discrimination and the Law.* Cambridge, MA: Harvard University.

★Rosen, L. N., and L. Martin. 1998. Predictors of Tolerance of Sexual Harassment among Male U.S. Army Soldiers. *Violence against Women* 4(4):491–504.

★Rosenberg, J., H. Perlstadt, and W. R. Phillips. 1993. Now That We Are Here: Discrimination, Disparagement, and Harassment at Work and the Experience of Women Lawyers. *Gender and Society* 7:415–433.

★Schneider, B. E. 1991. Put Up and Shut Up: Workplace Sexual Assault. *Gender and Society* 5:533–548.

★Shay, G. 1999. Sexual Abuse and Civil Rights. *The National Prison Project Journal* 12(4):1–5.

Simpson, S., and M. F. White. 1985. The Female Guard in the All-Male Prison. In *The Changing Roles of Women in the Criminal Justice System,* ed. I. L. Moyer, 276–300. Prospect Heights, IL: Waveland.

★Sommerlad, H., and P. Sanderson. 1998. *Gender, Choice, and Commitment: Women Solicitors in England and Wales and the Struggle for Equal Status.* Aldershot, England: Ashgate.

★Southgate, P. 1981. Women in the Police. *The Police Journal* 54(2):157–167.

★Stohr, M. K., G. L. Mays, A. C. Beck, and T. Kelley. 1998. Sexual Harassment in Women's Jails. *Journal of Contemporary Criminal Justice* 14(2):135–155.

★Till, F. J. 1980. Sexual Harassment: A Report on the Sexual Harassment of Students. *Report of the National Advisory Council on Women's Educational Programs.* Washington, DC: U.S. Government Printing Office.

★Townsey, R. D. 1982. Female Patrol Officers: A Review of the Physical Capability Issue. In *The Criminal Justice System and Women,* ed. B. R. Price and N. J. Sokoloff, 413–426. New York: Clark Boardman.

★U.S. Federal Bureau of Prisons. 2000. Federal Bureau of Prisons Quick Facts, April 2000. Washington, DC: GPO. Available at http://www.bop.gov/fact0598.html.

Van Maanen, J. 1973. Observations on the Making of a Policeman. *Human Organization* 32:407–418.

*Weisheit, R. A. 1987. Women in the State Police: Concerns of Male and Female Officers. *Journal of Police Science and Administration* 15:137–143.

Wilson, N. K. 1982, Women in the Criminal Justice Professions: An Analysis of Status Conflict. In *Judge, Lawyer, Victim, Thief,* ed. N. H. Rafter and E. A. Stanko, Stoughton, 359–74. Massachusetts: Northeastern University.

*Wise, S., and L. Stanley. 1987. *Georgie Porgie: Sexual Harassment in Everyday Life.* London: Pandora.

*Yount, K. R. 1991. Ladies, Flirts, and Tomboys. *Journal of Contemporary Ethnography* 19(4):396–422.

Zimmer, L. E. 1986. *Women Guarding Men.* Chicago: University of Chicago.

———— 1987. How Women Reshape the Prison Guard Role. *Gender and Society* 1(4):415–431.

———— 1989. Solving Women's Employment Problems in Corrections: Shifting the Burden to Administrators. *Women and Criminal Justice* (1):55–80.

Zupan, L. L. 1986. Gender-Related Differences in Correctional Officers' Perceptions and Attitudes. *Journal of Criminal Justice* 14:349–361.

Chapter 36

Affirmative Action, Multiculturalism, and Criminology

Nanci Koser Wilson and Imogene L. Moyer

ABSTRACT

Up until this point this book has examined the work world of criminal justice practitioners: judges, lawyers, police officers, and corrections officers. This final chapter, completely updated from the last edition, turns now to criminology faculty—those who educate many current and future practitioners—and the criminology and criminal justice curriculum. An addendum by Jurik and Cavender at the end of the chapter adds a discussion of the leadership role that feminist and multicultural scholars have taken in establishing interdisciplinary programs in justice studies and offers a critique of mainstream criminology. Faculty define the parameters of what is studied, what questions are asked, and how they are asked; as well, faculty decide what textbooks and articles students will read. In short, faculty, by their teaching and research, create and shape the body of knowledge of their discipline and influence the thinking of their students.

The important question for Wilson and Moyer is, Just who are these faculty members? Affirmative action has had a great impact in attracting women and racial and ethnic minorities into the discipline and in reshaping the discipline beyond traditional male-defined research, policy, and action agendas.* Wilson and Moyer focus on two issues of importance: first, the number and degree of integration of women and minority faculty (as well as staff and students) from diverse multicultural backgrounds, and second, whether these new scholars simply *fit into* existing approaches in the field or are able to *transform* the curriculum so that it becomes more multiculturally diverse and critical of the status quo in criminal justice. Thus, Wilson and Moyer identify the importance of both feminist and multicultural perspectives to the issues within criminology.

Wilson and Moyer discuss Title VII of the 1964 Civil Rights Act, as amended in 1972, and its effect on educational institutions. The act precludes discrimination in hiring and promotion on the basis of race, religion, national origin, and

---

*As several chapters in this book discuss, not only is criminology a male-defined discipline, but it is a discipline based on hegemonic patriarchy, that is, the predominant influence and domination of white, Western European, and heterosexual men.

sex. (This act mandates what is commonly known as affirmative action.) The legislation covers police, corrections officers, and public legal professionals as well as many faculty. A key problem, argue Wilson and Moyer, is that affirmative action may achieve one goal (increasing the numbers of women and minorities) without accomplishing the second (transforming the curriculum and research agenda to reflect the diversity of multicultural approaches in our society). And although some critics argue that affirmative action has led to the hiring of "less-qualified" women and minority scholars, Wilson and Moyer assert that these new scholars, who may be "differently qualified," are equally valuable to academia. The authors question whether excellence can exist in criminology without greater gender and multicultural diversity. However, the reader should be aware that women and people of color bring many different voices as they enter academia, some of which are similar to those of mainstream, white male scholars as well as political conservatives. This situation, in fact, happened in Texas, where the integration of (white) women lawyers into judgeships has led to the recruitment of some extremely conservative women on the bench (see Toobin, chap. 30).

Despite the backlash against affirmative action that began in the 1980s under President Ronald Reagan and intensified under President George W. Bush, by the year 2002, under an intensified assault, Wilson and Moyer show, (1) the numbers of women, but not minorities, have greatly increased and have reached a critical mass in criminology and (2) the evidence from research journals and from collaborations between men and women scholars has led to an emerging feminist research agenda. Equally important, Wilson and Moyer point out, there needs to be fuller participation by women and minorities throughout the professions that make up the criminal justice system because it is at the practitioner level that real change toward a more just system will occur.

INTRODUCTION

When the research for this article was first undertaken a decade ago (Wilson, Moyer, and Zahn 1990), we concentrated on the prospects for meeting affirmative action goals within academic criminology. In the original article for the 1995 edition of this book, we pointed to a possible contradiction between two goals of affirmative action—*fair representation of women and minorities* and *transformation to a more gender- and multicultural-inclusive discipline*. We suggested that in order to be hired, women might have to fill a "male model" of the acceptable faculty member and that those who sought to transform the discipline in its study of crime and criminality might

not be allowed past the door. We argued that the second goal of affirmative action was central in the transformation of the knowledge base that supports the status quo in the criminal justice system and helps to reproduce existing conditions of social inequality. We hoped that the entrance of women and minorities into the discipline might indeed transform it to be more socially just.

Here we update and expand on our earlier thoughts by asking, What has a decade brought?

A BRIEF HISTORY OF AFFIRMATIVE ACTION

Affirmative action programs were born of the optimism that was characteristic of the 1960s and 1970s. They sought to redress past wrongs with positive actions in the present. These initiatives may be defined

Source: This article was written expressly for inclusion in this text.

broadly as "public or private actions or programs which provide or seek to provide opportunities or other benefits to persons on the basis of, among other things, their membership in a specified group or groups" (Jones 1985, 902). Hence such programs are explicitly race-conscious, gender-conscious, or ethnic-conscious. They recognize the presence of discrimination against minorities and women and its effect on employment, education, or other types of life chances; and within the philosophical context of a liberal democracy with "equal opportunity for all," they propose *affirmative* remedies.

Though the term *affirmative action* is quite modern, its philosophical and legal principles are venerable. Jones (1985) traces its history to the English Courts of Chancery and their concept of equity. In the United States a prototype of governmental response to novel problems of inequity may be found in the National Labor Relations Board. If the board finds unfair labor practices, it may issue a cease and desist order and may take such affirmative action as reinstatement of employees with back pay. Other American forerunners of modern affirmative action programs include the remedies enacted under the Fourteenth Amendment and the Fair Employment Practices Committee established by President Roosevelt in 1941 (see, generally, Jones 1985).

Currently, Title VII of the 1964 Civil Rights Act (amended in 1972) is the central federal law on equal opportunity. In a wide variety of employment practices, including hiring and promotion, this law prohibits discrimination on the basis of race, religion, national origin, and gender. As Scollay et al. (1989, 241) observe, "Institutions of higher education are explicitly covered by Title VII and have incorporated policies in support of equal employment opportunity as standard elements in their expressed institutional goals."

The critical aspect of modern affirmative action programs is not hiring quotas but hiring goals; employers need only make a good-faith effort to achieve such goals, usually chosen by themselves. Contrary to popular wisdom, the government imposes "no fixed quota, no inflexible timetable, and no hiring of the unqualified" in such programs (Jones 1985, 904). Nor do these programs invent preferential hiring; instead

they seek to eliminate the preferential hiring of white males by guaranteeing the employment of at least some people of color and females.

Though affirmative action policies have been in effect in most educational institutions since the 1972 amendment to the Civil Rights Act of 1964, evidence on their impact has been mixed. Most studies that focus on the extent or percentage of change in representation of minorities and women find that gains have been made, but those studies that focus on current status find less substantive change. If percentage of change is used as the measure of impact, impressive gains may be noted. Scollay et al. (1989, 243) note that one study that used such a method found a 93 percent increase in the number of female college presidents. This statistic, however, obscures the true picture: at the end of 1984, only 10 percent of the 2,800 regionally accredited colleges and universities had female presidents.[*] Despite these mixed findings, it is clear that affirmative action programs were at least somewhat successful in meeting their goal of increasing the representation of women and minorities on university faculties, in student populations, and among administrative staffs. By the mid-1990s, however, a strong backlash against affirmative action had arisen. (For a good description of this backlash, see Merlo, Bagley, and Batuma 2000.) In the face of declining public support for affirmative action, the first Bush administration put forward a watered-down version that it styled "affirmative access" (see Brooks 1999; Dorf 2000).

The retreat from affirmative action itself signals that its task is not complete. The debate reveals the different meanings assigned to affirmative action's mission and to the role played by race and gender in American society. Opponents of affirmative action

---

[*]Editors' note: In 2002, this figure doubled, to 22 percent who were female college presidents at 2,000 U.S. colleges. Yet despite these gains, the fact that women enter the lowest faculty ranks at similar rates to men does not ensure their positions in the higher levels of academia, as evidenced by the fact that women comprise only 20 percent of full professors. As Wilson and Moyer note, this disparity is not something that "time will cure"; even after more than 40 years of gender equalization at the lower ranks, men continue to comprise 80 percent of full professors. See More Women Leaders Found in Nation's Colleges (2002).

argue against it on two grounds. First, they argue that such programs are unnecessary now, if they ever were. Second, they assert that affirmative action perverts its own goals through "reverse discrimination."

This stance assumes that the goal of affirmative action is to ensure fair access to rewards in a color-blind, gender-blind meritocracy. Instead, we argue, its larger function has always been to ensure full participation by all members of society in the life of the society.

The United States is not a color-blind, gender-blind meritocracy. Even if all ethnic, racial, and gender groups attain equal access to rewards, full participation is not ensured, because the controlling group of white males has set the standards for acceptance. Current standards fit the white male life experience well but often exclude women and minority groups.

Affirmative action in the strong sense of inclusiveness and respect for diversity requires *equal participation in standard settings*. This, in turn, requires inclusion of women and minorities, not just among workers within the system but among those who shape the system—legislators, politicians, the press, and particularly, as we show in this chapter, academicians.

THE DISCIPLINE OF CRIMINOLOGY

Criminology may be described appropriately, at its leadership level, as a politically liberal discipline. Substantial changes occurred, however, once it was expanded beyond its original confines in the United States as a subspecialty of sociology and there developed special degree programs in criminal justice and criminology. These changes took place mostly under the impetus of funds provided by the Law Enforcement Assistance Administration in the late 1960s and early 1970s. The discipline now attracts many students, especially at the undergraduate level, who align themselves personally and politically with some of the most conservative aspects of current criminal justice policy. Because programs in this field have flourished during a particularly conservative period in American history, many (if not most) professors, politically more liberal than their pupils, face resistance in the classroom.

Criminology, then, is hardly a radical discipline with a central focus on questioning current social arrangements or analyzing criminal justice policy from a critical standpoint. (Yet such a critical stance is implied in the transformative program of affirmative action as diversity or as a broadening of perspectives.) Instead there is an odd political mix in this discipline, which by now has thousands of undergraduate majors in every state in the United States. Ripped from the discipline of sociology, which was its original politically liberal and socially ameliorative context, criminology now stands on its own as a separate discipline (see Clear 2001a). Its intellectual leadership may be described as liberal with a sprinkling of conservatives and a sprinkling of radicals, both from the traditional left and from feminism. Its graduate students probably reflect to a very great extent the political leanings of the faculty in particular institutions; thus, they vary somewhat from institution to institution. Some of the 25 doctoral programs in the American Association of Doctoral Programs in Criminology and Criminal Justice are markedly conservative; others are much more liberal or perhaps even slightly progressive. In all these programs, however, a significant portion of the undergraduate student population, which is vitally important to the financial support of the program, leans much more toward the right end of the political spectrum. Also, in colleges that offer only a bachelor's degree in criminal justice and in junior colleges, most criminal justice programs are oriented toward training, with a goal of preparing students for entry-level jobs in the official criminal justice system.

The very topic of study in criminology is a source of political conservatism. Because degree programs and research provide a service to the existing criminal justice system, conservatism is built into the discipline; it supports the status quo. Perspectives in which the criminal justice system is seen as a source of oppression, particularly of women and minorities, and research that reveals how law and law enforcement in the United States reproduce existing conditions of inequality are not uncommon in the discipline. Yet these perspectives are unwelcome to funding agencies, to many undergraduates, and to the citizens who provide the tax base for public institutions (in which most criminal justice programs are located).

Further complicating the issue is the belief, embraced by many if not most faculty members, that criminology is a social science. The very canons of science enshrine objectivity and political neutrality. Very likely, most of us who teach research methods reinforce the ideal of objectivity for our students. Whether our romance with science and its supposed political neutrality gives to our discipline only an artificial or contrived and distorted notion of scientific objectivity is a question that has exercised social scientists' minds from the beginnings of social science. Is there such a thing as a neutral statement in social science, especially a social science that is defined by its focus on social problems? Nonetheless, the worship of science, typical of the Western world, and the concomitant belief that science can or should be politically neutral, can militate strongly against the critical perspective typical of a transformative curriculum. Research and teaching from an ostensibly neutral stance ratify the status quo, whereas such activities undertaken from a transformative standpoint are regarded as too political or as objectionably biased. Committed scholars are seen to be politically committed only if their work challenges the status quo. Thus, we hear the comments that female scholars are "too feminist" or that black scholars are "too touchy" about black issues; we do not hear of so-called objective scholars as "too masculinist" or "too accepting of racial supremacy." Rather, the former scholars are seen as *narrow* and *biased;* the latter as *balanced.*

Within this context then, what might be the fate of affirmative action programs that seek to increase diversity as well as to achieve the more limited goal of fair representation?

THE ACHIEVEMENT OF FAIR REPRESENTATION

Since we first presented data on how well women and minorities are represented in criminology (Wilson and Moyer 1995), gains have been made. Women have become an established presence within academic criminology. No longer an oddity on criminol-

ogy and criminal justice department faculties, women find their situation improved so much that some job candidates now report that they refuse to take jobs where they will be the token woman. African American participation in academic criminology is also increasing. Edwards et al. (1998a, p. 2) identified a total of 79 African American students in criminology and criminal justice doctoral programs. Forty-six of these students responded to a questionnaire, and of these, 21 were females and 25 were male. A second study (Edwards et al. 1998b) identified 88 African American faculty members in criminology and criminal justice. Forty of these faculty members returned questionnaires, and of these, 26 were male and 14 were female. Gilbert and Tatum (1999) identified 52 African American women faculty members. The two major criminology organizations in the United States have very active sections for women. Vigorous support systems are found in the section on Women and Minorities of the Academy of Criminal Justice Sciences (ACJS) and in both the Division on Women and Crime and the Division on People of Color and Crime of the American Society of Criminology (ASC). Both ASC and ACJS have had women presidents.

We now turn to the issue of whether the growing proportions of women and minorities will transform the discipline and what effect this transformation will have, in turn, on their representation. What follows is a model that suggests the parameters for inquiry with particular emphasis on the impact of "affirmative action hires." First, we attempt to isolate the factors that determine the race and gender composition of new hires; second, we examine the factors that shape a faculty member's orientation on the faculty; and third, we explore those factors that determine whether agents of change will meet with success.

A MODEL FOR UNDERSTANDING THE IMPACT OF AFFIRMATIVE ACTION

The model shown in figure 1 depicts the processes by which the array of factors that impinge on the success of affirmative action programs (shown in figure 2) have their effect. As figure 2 illustrates,

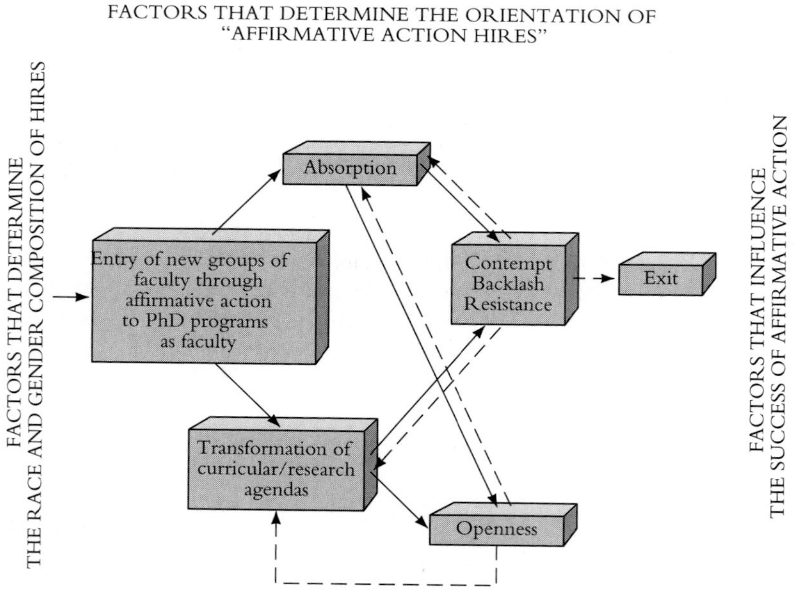

FACTORS THAT DETERMINE THE ORIENTATION OF
"AFFIRMATIVE ACTION HIRES"

FIGURE 1
The Impact of Affirmative Action on Criminology

some of these factors influence the race and gender composition of hires. Others have their effect as factors that determine the orientation on the faculty taken by affirmative action hires, that is, whether they attempt to just fit in with the existing program in their department or, alternatively, attempt to transform the curricula and the orientation of the program through their different perspectives. The third set of factors consists of those that determine whether affirmative action goals meet with success. As figure 2 shows, some of these factors have their effect in more than one way. For example, the number of female or minority-group members on the faculty and in the administrative ranks of a university affects the chances that affirmative action hires will be made in the first place. It also may stimulate faculty members to attempt to transform the curriculum and the research agendas of their own disciplines. Finally, it may affect whether such attempts meet with success.

The model depicts the success of affirmative action in both of its goals—that of fair representation

of diverse groups of Americans and that of transforming the curricula and the research agendas of academic disciplines in order to include the varied perspectives of women as well as men; of black, brown, yellow, and red citizens as well as white citizens; of Third World peoples as well as Westerners.

One of the more interesting aspects of affirmative action programs is that, to some extent, the twin goals of a diverse faculty and a diverse or broad curriculum may be contradictory. The university curriculum is narrow to begin with; it represents the perspective of white European males. Thus, for instance, a text widely used in art history for years was named simply *History of Art* (Janson 1962). Yet the book focused almost exclusively on the art of white European men. To a very great extent it excluded paintings, sculpture, and architecture of Africa and the East as well as work by white women and by men and women of color. Some faculty members fear that affirmative action programs will lower standards because such programs seek to include people who have not been trained like the members themselves have in the art,

FIGURE 2
Factors That Account for Success of Affirmative Action

1. Larger Culture
   Shape of EEOC and affirmative action statutes
   Vigor of enforcement efforts at the federal and state levels
   Social problems seen as created by minority groups (e.g., abortion, welfare, crack epidemic, crime)
   Level of discomfort with current approaches to problems (e.g., *Burning Bed, Colors, Milagro Bean Field Wars*)

2. Factors in the University
   Vigor of affirmative action officer
   Existence of black studies, women's studies, Latino/a studies, international studies programs
   Commitment of the university to broadening the curriculum (gender and racial balancing)
   Political orientation of student population (reactionary, conservative, liberal, progressive)
   Presence/absence of student unrest around race/sex issues
   Number/percentage of minority-group/female administrators and faculty members in other departments
   Authority granted to affirmative action officer
   Resources available
   Presence of an active "antipolitically correct" faculty
   Culture of the university town

3. Discipline of Criminology
   Critical mass of blacks/women in available faculty pool (and their ability to withhold labor from rigid institutions)
   Presence of unsolved research problems in the discipline
   Presence of pressure groups in national associations
   Critical mass of publication/research problems defined by minority groups/women that white European males
       begin to feel they must address (e.g., rape, racial discrimination)

4. The Department
   Reward system for publication (openness to women's and blacks' journals and topics of study)
   Critical mass of female/minority faculty members
   Screening process by search committee (the "good school" syndrome)
   Academic orientation of program
   Commitment of current faculty to affirmative action
   Growth stage of department (new courses needed?)
   Presence of joint research projects on race or gender topics
   Presence of "antipolitically correct" faculty

literature, and science of the Western world. Blind to the teachings and perspectives of the non-Western, nonmale world, such affirmative action resisters see only *less qualified* rather than *differently qualified* applicants when they review the curriculum vitae of female and minority candidates.

This situation creates a real dilemma for affirmative action; although these resisters may accept new faculty members who meet their standards, it is quite likely that they do so in part because these so-called "affirmative action hires" conform to existing white, male European ideas of what is said to constitute university excellence. Yet, if the presence of these new hires is to transform the academic world,

to broaden and enrich the curriculum and the research agendas of the various disciplines through their unique contributions, they must be precisely the sorts of scholars who do *not* conform to current standards. (That is so, unless they are unusual candidates who possess outstanding traditional qualifications as well as the special qualifications of their own tradition.) At its extreme point, affirmative action may succeed in accomplishing one of its goals (fair representation of diverse groups on the faculty) at the expense of failing in its other goal (achieving a diverse curriculum and research agenda).

Many other factors affect the race and gender composition of a faculty: the contours of affirmative action statutes, the vigor of enforcement efforts at the federal and state levels, the commitment of the current faculty to the goals of affirmative action, the vigor of the affirmative action officer at a given university (which includes also the amount of authority given to this person), the presence of a critical mass of minority or female faculty members and administrators at a university, the resources available, the presence of an active group of affirmative action resisters, and the culture of the town in which the university is housed. For example, some black academicians are loath to move to an area of the country where local racial attitudes are less than liberal.

The factors that affect the orientation of a new woman or person of color on the faculty are likewise complex. The stance of the "affirmative action hire" may change over time; frequently it does. It seems typical, at least from our personal observations, that many women enter university positions with a "just fit in" approach rather than a self-identification as a woman *for* women. Some of these women become radicalized over time because of contact with a women's studies program on their campus or because of a reaction to the contempt or backlash they encounter when they attempt to "be one of the boys." On the other hand, because of their very different experiences, American black faculty members frequently enter the university with a strong personal sense of affiliation with black culture. McCombs (1989) suggests that, to these new recruits, "the university appears as a mechanical apparatus that seeks to transform them into being 'university persons' by stripping them of who they are and giving them a new identity tied to a new collective rather than their original one. This new identity tolerates and supports the university that currently exists" (p. 134).

The university may react to "affirmative action recruits" by denying either the individual or the collective identities of these new faculty members; it may also deny the identities of newly radicalized older faculty members. When only the collective component is affirmed, the faculty member may be expected to pursue only those academic interests related

to race or gender or ethnicity and to be an expert in such matters regardless of training or expertise. "On the other hand, when only the individual component is affirmed, black women [e.g.] are expected not to be actively engaged in research or policy issues related to ethnicity or gender. Moreover, any honest commitment to race and gender issues is viewed with suspicion and devalued" (McCombs 1989, 134).

Other factors that influence the orientation of the "affirmative action hire" include the presence or absence of student unrest and agitation around race or gender issues, the amount of support received from other faculty members both within and outside one's own department (which itself depends on the political orientation of that faculty), and the stage of growth of the department.

Factors that affect eventual success in either of the twin goals of affirmative action are highly specific to each discipline because different barriers arise based on the unique history of the discipline. The political cast of criminology itself has just been discussed. Now we wish to discuss other important determinants of the success of affirmative action within criminology specifically.

FACTORS THAT ACCOUNT FOR AFFIRMATIVE ACTION SUCCESS IN CRIMINOLOGY AS A DISCIPLINE

When we consider the first goal of affirmative action—that of fair representation of minorities and women on the faculty—specifically in regard to criminology, we note the following. Of first importance is the existence of a critical mass of minority group members and women in the available faculty pool. One indication of availability is Clear's (2001b) recent report on the ethnic and gender composition of the American Society of Criminology. This report suggests that the organization has 31 percent female membership and that ethnically it is 5 percent African American, 2 percent Latino and Latina, and 3 percent Asian. It would appear that universities seeking to hire black, Latino, Latina, or Asian faculty members persistently face more difficulties than if they seek to add white women to their staff.

Also important in the goal of adding women and members of minority groups to university faculties in criminology is the ability of such persons to withhold their labor from institutions with an unfavorable racial or sexual climate. Many white female criminologists now say they will refuse to accept a position on a faculty that includes no other women. This position is more difficult for minority scholars because of their smaller numbers in the discipline. But because some universities already have women and minority group members on their criminology faculties, job aspirants can withhold their labor from other universities that have only a solidly white, male faculty. Such institutions then come under increasing pressure from their affirmative action officers—if those officers are vigorous. The extra push given to affirmative action hiring at universities that are far behind the times creates new openings, sometimes at premium pay, for minority members and women. Also instrumental in the affirmative action process is the presence of pressure groups in national associations such as the ASC and ACJS and the supportive networks they develop for their constituencies of women and minorities.

As to the chances of criminology succeeding in the second goal of affirmative action—that of transforming the discipline by broadening it and enriching it with perspectives from the worlds of women and of minorities—we make the following observations.

First, the theories and research studies of criminology in the United States consistently have excluded women, especially minority women, and have paid less attention to blacks and other minorities than to whites. Although racism and sexism are present in every aspect of American life, a major focus of study in criminology is the criminal justice system, which itself has been a source of oppression for minorities and women. Rape and wife battery serve a political function, as do lynching, the death penalty, and drug wars. The response of the criminal justice system to the inequities created and sustained by these crimes has been less than benign. Criminological studies sometimes reify this reality insofar as they simply describe it without critiquing it.

Second, research based on so-called universalistic criteria is problematic. Generally, such criteria means a white, male, European universality. Here, academic gatekeepers play an important role. In Lynne Spender's (1983) discussion of gatekeeping, she points out that men have the privilege of choosing the topics and issues that will be considered of fundamental concern to society and to a given discipline. No alternative standards exist to allow for the values and priorities of those who are not white or male. It is not only that men's values are put forward; in addition, women's values are discarded (L. Spender 1983, 4; see also Gilligan 1982). Gatekeepers are in a position to perpetuate their own schemata by exercising sponsorship and patronage toward those who classify the world in ways similar to their own (D. Spender 1981, 191).

Publication of journal articles, readers, and monographs is one of the most important resources controlled by academic gatekeepers because it legitimates the researchers and their ideas. When exceptions occur, they often do so in a biased manner. Thus, an article published in *Jet, Ebony,* or *Ms.* is not scholarly, but an article published in *The New York Times Magazine* is acceptable. In addition to determining the importance of topics and issues in the discipline, gatekeepers decide how these topics should be defined and investigated; this decision influences generations of future scholars (Cook and Fonow 1984, 14). A book on the U.S. prison system that focuses exclusively on male prisons is laudable, and its partiality goes unnoticed; a book on women's prisons is considered *narrow.* Publication in mainstream journals is essential for "arrival," but scholars who write about African American, Latino and Latina, Native American, or women's issues will find themselves locked out of this avenue to success. Publication in minority or women's journals also is viewed as less important.

Third, doctoral programs are a crucial locus for the transformation of criminology into a more inclusive discipline. Though student unrest at the undergraduate level is a most dramatic source of change, long-term sustainable transformation within the discipline itself will be led or stimulated most effectively by the new young scholars whom doctoral programs train. If these scholars are trained appropriately, they will socialize *their* students toward a newer model as they fan out into teaching careers in colleges with master's and bachelor's degree programs. Classroom lectures and discussion and the textbooks chosen for undergraduate use will become broader, more inclusive, and more critical.

As more faculty members themselves conduct research from a transformative perspective, we begin to see master's theses and doctoral dissertations with a critical perspective on (for instance) wife battery, spousal homicide, and rape; on crime-fighting initiatives in the African, Latino and Latina, Asian, and Native American communities; and on the interface between U. S. welfare policy and crime. As this knowledge builds and as young minority and female scholars begin to perform gatekeeping roles as journal reviewers and textbook editorial consultants, the newer transformative research will even begin to slip into mainstream journals and textbooks.

Since the publication of an earlier version of this article in 1995, considerable progress has been made in the second goal of affirmative action—that of transformation. It indeed appears that some of the factors we identified in our earlier article, for example critical mass, have had the effect of transforming the knowledge base. An examination of articles published in the two major journals (*Criminology* and *Justice Quarterly*) for the past five years (from 1996 to 2000) reveals some 36 articles (11.7 percent of the total) that focus specifically on issues of gender and crime. The *Journal of Women and Criminal Justice* has taken its place as a well-established and respected member of the important, peer-reviewed journals in this field. Discussions of gender now appear in undergraduate textbooks, an important avenue for shaping the worldview of undergraduate students who are likely to embark on careers in criminal justice. In theory texts, feminist theory now is recognized as a topic that requires comment, though this comment is not always favorable.

AFFIRMATIVE ACTION WITHIN AND OUTSIDE ACADEMIC CRIMINOLOGY

Has a similar transformative effect taken place outside academe, in other words, within the criminal justice system? There has been much progress. In all three component areas of the criminal justice system, women have made gains.

In policing, the percentage of females among sworn officers has increased from a low of 2 percent in 1972 to 14.3 percent in 1999 (National Center for Women and Policing 2000). Women of color now constitute 6.8 percent of sworn officers. Fewer women have moved into management. There, the figures are 9.2 percent for supervisory positions and 5.6 percent for top command positions. For women of color, the corresponding figures are lower: 2.8 percent in supervisory positions and 1.1 percent in top command positions (National Center for Women and Policing 2000).

In corrections, women constitute some 29 percent of employees—28 percent of confinement facility workers and 36 percent of community-based staff (Bureau of Justice Statistics 1995). Women are 12.5 percent of the Federal Bureau of Prisons corrections officers (*Sourcebook* 1999). Data from 1995 indicate that 17 percent of wardens or superintendents in state correctional systems and 20 percent in juvenile systems are female (Office of Justice Programs [OJP] 1998).

In law, women are entering law schools and becoming members of the bar in very great numbers. "About 44 percent of all first-year law students are women; as of 1995 women accounted for roughly 23 percent of all attorneys—a 13 percent increase since 1985" (OJP 1998). Among the judiciary, women's representation has also increased. "From 1980 to 1991, representation of women among state judges increased from 4 to 9 percent; women represented 12 percent of intermediate appellate court judges, 10 percent of trial court judges, and 9.5 percent of all courts-of-last-resort judges . . . As of 1996 there were 146 sitting female federal judges, 17 percent of whom were senior judges" (OJP 1998). The Supreme Court now is almost 20 percent female— where two of the nine justices are women.

In an area that is outside the criminal justice system but that still affects its operation, there are now a substantial number of women legislators. There are 61 women in the U.S. House, constituting 14 percent, and 13 women in the Senate (Clerk of the U.S. House 2001).

Academic research has contributed to these affirmative action gains. Research on women's participation in policing, courts, and corrections has demonstrated both that women can do a man's job, if necessary, and that women bring special skills valuable to the criminal justice system. A good summary of the research can be found in Martin and Jurik's (1996) *Doing Justice, Doing Gender.*

In spite of progress, there is, as we have noted, a strong backlash against affirmative action that demonstrates continuing resistance to the presence of women and minorities in criminal justice–related academia. How should we understand this backlash?

Opponents of affirmative action embrace a narrow definition of affirmative action as access to a meritocracy in which white men control the measure of merit. That is, they favor a color-blind, gender-blind affirmative action process in which standards are based on some version of "absolute merit." For example, this approach was recently taken by U.S. District Judge Bernard Friedman in *Grutter v. Bollinger* (2001), a case involving admission to the University of Michigan Law School. Friedman ruled that the "focus must be upon the merit of individual applicants, not upon characteristics of racial groups" (Altman 2001). His ruling approved test scores and grade point averages as objective indicators of merit that may be properly used as standards for admission and *explicitly excluded* diversity as a standard, saying that "the diversity rationale is not among the governing standards" of affirmative action law (Wilgoren 2001).*

Opponents of affirmative action either do not recognize the possibility that the standards themselves may be biased or they choose to ignore such a possibility; thus, the current dispute surrounds standards themselves. Indeed, so long as the goal of affirmative action is conceived narrowly as fair access to opportunity based on "objective" standards of merit, we may expect little progress.

Instead of this narrow definition, we argue that there is a need to conceive affirmative action more broadly. We further maintain that because affirmative action is about justice and about justice broadly conceived, affirmative action is especially crucial within the criminal justice system.

Understood broadly, the justice that affirmative action produces can be defined as full participation in society. In this sense, affirmative action includes not just equal employment but also equal valorization and equal impact. As to *equal employment,* this original goal of fair representation includes not only equal numbers in employment but also equality in treatment, in promotion, and in retention. *Equal valorization* refers to an equal valuing of diverse approaches to the work. It has been noted, for example, that women police are more likely to possess skills in communication and crisis intervention as opposed to the "male" skills of physical strength and mental aggressiveness and that female correctional officers obtain inmate cooperation through explaining rather than ordering. (See chaps. 32 and 35) To the extent that these differential skills are not valued, there is not full participation. *Equal impact* is the ability of workers within criminal justice to affect the quality of justice delivered to those who are the subjects of criminal justice, either as victims or as offenders.

In the last decade, criminal justice has often been accused of being unjust—in the operation of its drug war, in practices of racial profiling, in expansion of the prison industrial complex, and in sentencing laws that, as opposed to their announced intent, still discriminate. In these guideline practices we see the inclusion of differences that make no difference and the exclusion of differences that do matter. An example of the former is the differential sentencing guideline for crack versus powder cocaine; an example of the latter is that consideration of a defendant's family responsibilities is no longer justified. These "blind" guidelines mirror the color-blind, gender-blind affirmative action embraced by those who would limit the effect of affirmative action.

Such a blind approach to affirmative action was decried by Justice Harry A. Blackmun, dissenting in *Regents of the University of California v. Bakke* (1978,

---

*In May 2002, this decision was reversed at the appeals level. However, the contentiousness of this ruling is seen in the title of one media article on this issue: "Next Stop, Supreme Court?" (Schmidt 2002). Editors' Note: As this book is being published, the Supreme Court of the United States is about to decide this case during the 2003 term.

407). He wrote, "In order to get beyond racism, we must first take account of race. There is no other way." Twenty years later, the importance of a color-conscious (and by extension, gender-conscious) view of affirmative action within academic criminology was described by Edwards et al. (1998b, 258). They note "the contribution by African American scholars can be significant if the academic community allows the African American perception of reality to become a recognized or legitimate perspective in the community."

Those who embrace the color-blind, gender-blind view of affirmative action argue that if standards are based on absolute merit, then color-blind, gender-blind policies will produce a fair outcome. Opponents of affirmative action may well realize the consequence of this blind approach. If the job is shaped to fit the white male experience, then of course women and minorities will not qualify. Further, if women generally do not constitute a powerful enough pressure group to lobby effectively for female-friendly policies and particularly if they do not support programs of affirmative action, then the potential impact of women workers on their clients, the impact of public servants on those served, will not be equal.

Is affirmative action, as traditionally understood, too blunt a tool to achieve the desired end? We would argue that it is not. If affirmative action programs are dismantled, the funnel will narrow. And it is the first point of the funnel that is crucial to the development of the wider portions. As we argued in the 1995 edition of this book, women cannot transform the workplace unless they first appear there in significant numbers. As they do so, it becomes apparent that traditional male definitions of what constitutes the jobs of policing, of corrections, of lawyering, and of legislating do not fit. When women constitute a large enough presence in each field, they become emboldened not only to raise issues of concern to themselves as workers (their numbers, their fair treatment, their style of doing the work) but also to raise issues related to their impact on women generally. Aided by outside advocacy groups (e.g., such a role is being played for women

police by the Feminist Majority),* they may indeed be able to put issues of injustice on the table.

The injustice within the criminal justice system thus has far-ranging effects. Justice *within* can lead to justice more generally. Indeed, such justice is inherent in a broadened understanding of affirmative action within the criminal justice system.

As to the effect of affirmative action within *academic* criminology, the field has currently reached the stage of a critical mass regarding women. Several results have followed from the achievement of this critical mass. First, women have become emboldened to pursue women's interests rather than to just fit in as "regular criminologists" (Wilson 2001) who pursue male-shaped research agendas. This change is evident from the articles in the leading journals of the last few years and in the emerging shape of a feminist research agenda. Second, women and men have started working together so that women are half of a team rather than tokens or pets. They are, in many workplaces, beginning to have collaborative rather than adversarial relations with one another. As they work together, men and women begin to perceive differences between themselves, to value one another's strengths and validate one another's differences. More and more, men are beginning to read the feminist literature carefully. Third, women are beginning to nurture younger women and to become gatekeepers themselves.

Meanwhile, the increasing power of women in public life—in politics, government, the business world, and the professions (including criminal justice professions)—is providing a constituency for feminist research. Thus, for example, the passage of the Violence against Women Act of 1994 led to government funding for feminist research, and although this funding has been cut back recently under a more conservative administration, the act did stimulate important research.

Finally, as more of the populace goes to college, more criminal justice system workers are college educated and more women (and men) in the pipeline

*See www.feminist.org.

are affected by university teachers. What academic criminologists believe and teach about female and minority offenders, victims, and criminal justice system workers is crucial insofar as it affects the views of future workers.

But because the field has reached this critical mass, one might ask, Are affirmative action programs still necessary? They have certainly played an important role in bringing women (but not minorities) to the point of a critical mass. Further, the evidence suggests that this result could not have occurred without the pressure from formal affirmative action programs. And the current resistance to affirmative action suggests that it is still the important tool it always was.

The most impenetrable barrier to women's participation in the criminal justice professions has always been the reaction of their colleagues, as is clearly demonstrated in the research on women police, lawyers, and judges (Martin and Jurik 1996). Resistance is strongest on the cultural level—the level of beliefs regarding women, minorities, and men. But on this plane, too, real change can most effectively occur. As Bernard (Vold, Bernard, and Snipes 1998) suggests, it is women's viewpoints from diverse backgrounds, not their mere presence, that is needed. Justice requires such inclusion and is the core meaning of affirmative action.

DISCUSSION QUESTIONS

1. Wilson and Moyer argue that affirmative action can be a good thing if it achieves both goals of (1) increasing numbers of women and minorities and (2) facilitating a transformation of the curriculum and research agenda to reflect the diversity of multicultural approaches in our society.
   - Define each term: *affirmative action, curriculum transformation, multicultural diversity.*
   - Do you agree or disagree with Wilson and Moyer's statement?
   - Explain your agreement or disagreement.
2. What changes will take place in the field of criminology in the coming years as growing numbers of women and minorities enter academia?
3. Feminists claim that feminism, multiculturalism, and diverse voices can lead to new insights in criminology. Based on the chapters you have read in this book, what evidence can you identify that these changes are already occurring? Based on your own educational experience in this discipline, what evidence can you identify that these changes are already occurring?
4. Discuss whether resistance to women and racial and ethnic minorities working in the criminal justice system will lessen as more women and minorities assume faculty roles in criminology, criminal justice, and justice studies programs.
5. Discuss Jurik and Cavender's conclusion that traditional criminal justice and criminology programs have become increasingly narrow whereas justice studies programs embrace broad concepts of feminism. Define *justice studies,* and discuss how justice studies programs differ from criminology and criminal justice programs. What are your own reactions to these distinctions?

REFERENCES

Altman, Joseph, Jr. 2001. Court Rules against UM Law Policy. Associated Press. Posted Tuesday, March 27. Available at yahoo.com/H/AP/2001

Bazin, Nancy Topping. 1980. Expanding the Concept of Affirmative Action to Include the Curriculum. *Women's Studies Newsletter* 8(4):9–11.

Berkin, Carol. 1991. Dangerous Courtesies Assault Women's History. *Chronicle of Higher Education,* December 11, A44.

Bowers, C. A. 1998. A Batesonian Perspective on Education and the Bonds of Language: Cultural Literacy in the Technological Age. *Studies in the Humanities* 15(2): 108–129.

Brooks, A. Phillip. 1999. Bush Trying to Cover Bases on Affirmative Action Policy. Posted August 25. Available at www.austin360.com.

Bureau of Justice Statistics. 1995. *Census of State and Federal Correctional Facilities.* Washington, DC: U.S. Department of Justice.

Clear, Todd. 2001a. Has Academic Criminal Justice Come of Age? *Justice Quarterly* 18(4):709–726.

Clear, Todd. 2001b. Thinking Strategically about the American Society of Criminology. *The Criminologist* 26(1):1–7.

Clerk of the U.S. House. 2001. Current Congressional Profile. February 15. Available at http:// clerkweb.house.gove/mbrcmtee/stats.htm.

Cook, Judith A., and Mary Margaret Fonow. 1984. Am I My Sister's Gatekeeper? Cautionary Tales from the Academic Hierarchy. Paper presented at the meeting of the Midwest Sociological Society, Chicago.

Dorf, Michael C. 2000. Gore's Affirmative Action versus Bush's Affirmative Access. November 1. Available at writ.news.findlaw.com.

Edsall, Thomas B., and Mary Edsall. 1991. The Republicans' Racial Wedge Is Flying Back in Their Faces. *Washington Post National Weekly Edition,* December 2–8, 23.

Edwards, Willie J., et al. 1998a. Who's in the Pipeline? A Survey of African-Americans in Doctoral Programs in Criminology and Criminal Justice. *Journal of Criminal Justice Education* 9(1):1–18.

Edwards, Willie J., et al. 1998b. Who Has Come Out of the Pipeline? African-Americans in Criminology and Criminal Justice. *Journal of Criminal Justice Education* 9(2):249–265.

Eigenberg, Helen, and Agnes Baro. 1992. Women and the Publication Process: A Content Analysis of Criminal Justice Journals. *Journal of Criminal Justice Education* 3(2):293–314.

Equality Denied: The Status of Women in Policing. 2000. Los Angeles: National Center for Women and Policing.

Fields, Cheryl M. 1988. Ten Years after Bakke Ruling, Opinions on Affirmative Action Still Polarized. *Chronicle of Higher Education,* June 29, A14–A16.

Flanagan, Timothy. 1990. Criminal Justice Doctoral Programs in the United States and Canada: Findings from a National Survey. *Journal of Criminal Justice Education* 1(2):195–213.

FYI. 1990. Enrollment in Criminal Justice Graduate Programs, Fall, 1988. *Journal of Criminal Justice Education* 1(1):117–118.

Garrett, Gerald, and Marian Darlington-Hope. 1988. Report of the Affirmative Action Survey Subcommittee. Submitted to the Academy of Criminal Justice Sciences Executive Board, San Francisco.

Gilbert, Evelyn, and Becky L. Tatum. 1999. African American Women in the Criminal Justice Academy: Characteristics, Perceptions, and Coping Strategies. *Journal of Criminal Justice Education* 10(2):231–246.

Gilligan, Carol. 1982. *In a Different Voice.* Cambridge, MA: Harvard University.

Hawkins, Darnell. 1986. *Homicide among Black Americans.* Lanham, MD: University Press of America.

Heard, Chinita A., and Robert L. Bing. 1993. African-American Faculty and Students on Predominantly White University Campuses. *Journal of Criminal Justice Education* 4(1):1–13.

Janson, H. W. 1962. *History of Art.* Englewood Cliffs, NJ: Prentice Hall.

Jones, James E., Jr. 1985. The Genesis and Present Status of Affirmative Action in Employment: Economic, Legal, and Political Realities. *Kowa Law Review* 70:901–944.

McCombs, Harriet G. 1989. The Dynamics and Impact of Affirmative Action Processes on Higher Education, the Curriculum, and Black Women. *Sex Roles* 21(1/2): 127–143.

Martin, Susan Ehrlich, and Nancy C. Jurik. 1996. *Doing Justice, Doing Gender: Women in Law and Criminal Justice Occupations.* Thousand Oaks, CA: Sage.

Merlo, Alida, Kate Bagley, and Michele C. Bafuma. 2000. In Defense of Affirmative Action for Women in the Criminal Justice Professions. In *It's a Crime: Women and Justice,* ed. Roslyn Muraskin. Upper Saddle River, NJ: Prentice Hall.

More Women Leaders Found in Nation's Colleges. 2002. Available at www.feminist.org/news/newsbyte/uswirestory.asp?id-6685.

Office of Justice Programs. 1998. Women in Criminal Justice. U.S. Department of Justice. Available at ojp.usdoj.gov/reports/98Guides/wcjs98.

Price, Barbara Raffel, and Natalie J. Sokoloff, eds. 1995. *The Criminal Justice System and Women,* 2d ed. New York: McGraw-Hill.

Schmidt, Peter. 2002. Next Stop, Supreme Court? *Chronicle of Higher Education,* May 24, 24–26.

Scollay, Susan J., Ann P. Tickameyer, Janet L. Bockmeyer, and Teresa A. Wood. 1989. The Impact of Affirmative Action in Higher Education: Perceptions from the Front Line. *Review of Higher Education* 12(3):241–263.

Sourcebook of Criminal Justice Statistics. 1999. Available at www.albany.edu/sourcebook.

Spender, Dale. 1981. The Gatekeepers: A Feminist Critique of Academic Publishing. In *Doing Feminist Research,* ed. Helen Roberts, 186–202. Boston: Routledge and Kegan Paul.

Spender, Lynne. 1983. *Intruders on the Rights of Men.* Boston: Routledge and Kegan Paul.

Vold, George B., Thomas J. Bernard, and Jeffrey B. Snipes. 1998. *Theoretical Criminology,* 4th ed. New York: Oxford University.

Widmayer, Alan, and Barry Rabe. 1990. Publication Patterns among American Criminologists: An Analysis of Gender, Regional, and Work Differences. *Journal of Criminal Justice Education* 1(1):99–110.

Wilbanks, William. 1987. *The Myth of a Racist Criminal Justice System.* Monterey, CA: Brooks/Cole.

Wilgoren, Jodi. 2001. U.S. Court Bars Race as Factor in School Entry. *The New York Times* posted March 28, 2001. www.NYTimes.com.

Wilson, Nanci Koser. 2001. Regular Criminologists? Memories of the Early Years of the DWC. *DivisioNEWS: The Newsletter of the Division on Women and Crime of the American Society of Criminology.* Fall.

Wilson, Nanci, and Imogene Moyer. 1995. Affirmative Action, Multiculturalism, and Criminology. In *The Criminal Justice System and Women,* 2d ed., ed. Barbara Raffel Price and Natalie J. Sokoloff. New York: McGraw-Hill.

Wilson, Nanci, and Imogene Moyer. 1992. Affirmative Action, Multiculturalism, and Politically Correct Criminology. *Journal of Criminal Justice Education* 3(2): 277–291.

Wilson, Nanci Koser, Imogene L. Moyer, and Margaret Zahn. 1990. The Impact of Affirmative Action on Criminology. Paper presented at the American Society of Criminology, Baltimore, MD, November.

Wright, Richard A. 1987. Are Sisters in Crime Finally Being Booked? The Coverage of Women and Crime in Journals and Textbooks. *Teaching Sociology* 15: 418–422.

CASES CITED:

Grutter v. Bollinger, Civil Action No. 97-CV-75928-DT, 2001 U.S. Dist. LEXIS 3526 (E.D. Mich. Mar. 27, 2001).

Regents of the Univ. of Cal. v. Bakke, 438 U.S. 265, 407 (1978).

ADDENDUM:

FEMINISM, MULTICULTURALISM, AND THE JUSTICE STUDIES MOVEMENT

Nancy Jurik and Gray Cavender

Over the past two decades, a new area of study has emerged. Justice studies is an interdisciplinary specialty that focuses on the convergent analysis of social, economic, legal, and criminal justice issues. More than 30 justice studies programs now exist in the United States and Canada.[*] Although varied, these programs share a goal of going beyond the criminal justice focus to analyze the larger social and historical context of justice and injustice in all its forms. In 1998, a national Justice Studies Association (JSA) was formed to provide a forum for scholars, activists, and practitioners interested in this broader focus. The JSA is "committed to promoting justice without violence and restoring people to wholeness through interpersonal as well as social structural change" (Trevino 2002, 2). The emergence of so many programs in such a short time and the formation of this national association represents what we will call a justice studies movement.

Feminist and multicultural principles have played an integral role in the conceptual development of the justice studies movement. Justice studies calls attention to issues of power and inequality in society, and in so doing, centers gender, race, ethnicity, class, sexual orientation, globalization, and other dimensions of social stratification as core subject matter. Like feminist analyses of praxis (i.e., the merging of theory with action), justice studies encourages critical analysis of traditional definitions and practices of justice. The notion of restorative justice (in contrast

---

[*]Many legal studies or law and society programs also exist on campuses. Also, sometimes justice studies is combined with these or other programs (e.g., peace studies; crime and justice studies; crime, law, and justice; sociology and justice studies). Additional justice studies programs are in the planning stages.

This addendum was written expressly for this text.

to retributive justice) is an important focus for the movement (Slavick 2002). As shown by Presser and Gaarder (chap. 25), restorative justice is consistent with feminist and multiracial and multicultural ethics and activism.

Feminist multicultural scholarship has played a key role in the design of justice studies programs. For example, the 1982 transformation of the criminal justice program at Arizona State University into one of the first justice studies programs in the United States relied heavily on the work of feminist scholar and political philosopher Iris Marion Young to provide the rationale for the name change (see Lauderdale and Cavender 1986). Young (1981) critiques several prominent theories of justice because they are abstract and detached from the material conditions of social life. Although claiming to develop universal definitions of justice, such theories are actually grounded in the experiences of elite white males and treat the demands of women and people of color as particularistic, special interests (Young 1990). Young's work, along with other feminist critiques of objectivity (Smith 1979), makes the case that although justice is typically considered a philosophic concept, social science theory and method can be used to inform and understand its application in the real world (Lauderdale and Cavender 1986). That became the goal of the Arizona State program. Since its inception, the program has grown to almost 1,000 undergraduate students; it also offers Master's and doctoral programs in justice studies. Moreover, several colleagues and former students have created justice studies programs modeled after Arizona State's at seven other universities in the United States and Canada.

Feminist perspectives also inform justice studies pedagogy (Brush, Caulfield, and Snyder 1998). A special issue of the *Contemporary Justice Review,* the official journal of the JSA, addresses the topic in an article titled, "Justice Literacy—What Every Student of Justice Needs to Know (and Speak Intelligently About) before Graduation" (Sullivan, Tift, and Cordella 1998). Many of the articles in this special

issue draw on feminist and multicultural perspectives and insights (e.g., Bailey 1998; Mackey 1998; Brush, Caulfield, and Snyder 1998). Several authors (e.g., Schumaker 1998; Sullivan, Tift, and Cordella 1998) emphasize how important it is that students identify their own experiences of justice and injustice and then locate those experiences within their larger social and historical context. Such arguments are highly compatible with feminist antiracist analyses. For example, Dorothy Smith's (1999) institutional ethnography approach urges that analyses begin with the experiences of women and other marginalized groups and end with an examination of the social and organizational arrangements that give rise to these experiences.

These same discussions about justice literacy also emphasize the importance of literature and story telling in justice curricula (e.g., Mackey 1998). Feminist critical race epistemologies, such as the work of Patricia Hill Collins (1991), emphasize the importance of music, art, and story telling as sources of knowledge about the experiences of women of color who have often been denied access to the academy.

The growing popularity of justice studies programs and the JSA may reflect disillusionment with criminology as an increasingly narrow field of study (Trevino 2002). Interestingly, the justice studies movement parallels a proliferation of criminal justice programs, especially doctoral programs. Twenty years ago, only a handful of universities offered a doctorate in criminal justice; today, 25 universities offer this degree. In this chapter, Wilson and Moyer document a positive by-product of this growth: the addition of women in the professorate. Women now comprise 31 percent of the membership of the American Society of Criminology (ASC). The representation of racial and ethnic minority groups in the ASC is much lower: 5 percent of the membership is African American, 2 percent is Latino and Latina; 3 percent is Asian American. Wilson and Moyer describe the conservative origins of the field but highlight its recent liberalization due to an influx of new faculty, including white women, persons of color, and progressive scholars.

At the same time, however, there are negative by-products of this growth. Wayne Osgood (1998) argues that the success of these programs, especially at the Ph.D. level, has led criminology to abandon its interdisciplinary foundations in sociology, psychology, and political science. This trend produces a disturbing insularity in the field that leads to a neglect of the larger social and historical context of crime and criminal justice and its links to other forms of social and economic justice. The expansion of criminal justice programs parallels the growing emphasis of the state on crime control measures at the expense of social services (Sullivan, Tift, and Cordella 1998), and it is troubling to many scholars to have their research agendas (and the potential for funding) tied to a problematic social policy agenda. Carol Smart (1995) even argues that criminology today is too limited by its focus on the etiology of crime and crime control strategies to be a fruitful avenue for feminist inquiry. Pressure to narrow the focus of criminology is also fueled by declines in university funding and resulting demands on scholars to obtain federal funds for their research (Chilton 2001).

The abandonment of criminology's interdisciplinary past and the pecuniary rewards associated with a narrowed agenda may explain some of the limited transformative effect of women faculty in criminal justice programs noted by Wilson and Moyer. For example, there are more women faculty and they have pushed the envelope of "what fits" within criminological inquiry, but feminist criminology as well as multicultural understandings of crime and justice are still regarded as outside the mainstream (Britton 2000; Morris and Gelsthorpe 1991). Even the design of the ASC's "Call for Papers" in conjunction with their annual national conference still typically locates gender, race, and class as "correlates" of crime and fails to include feminist and multicultural theories as primary theoretical approaches.

A justice studies approach offers an attractive alternative to the narrowness of criminology and criminal justice programs. Justice studies is compatible with and often grounded in multicultural feminist theory and method. It is also steeped in a commitment to interdisciplinary work and praxis. Accordingly, justice studies may offer a more comfortable intellectual home for progressive scholars.

REFERENCES

Bailey, Frankie Y. 1998. Speaking of the Chicago School . . . Have You Read Native Son? *Contemporary Justice Review* 1(2/3):243–260.

Britton, Dana. 2000. Feminism in Criminology: Engendering the Outlaw. *The Annals of the American Academy of Political and Social Science* 571:57–76.

Brush, Paula Stewart, Susan Caulfield, and Zoann Snyder. 1998. Seeking a Social Justice–Oriented Classroom: The Role of Curriculum Transformation and the Importance of Difference. *Contemporary Justice Review* 1(2/3):297–322.

Chilton, Roland. 2001. Viable Policy: The Impact of Federal Funding and the Need for Independent Research Agenda—The American Society of Criminology 2000 Presidential Address. *Criminology* 39(1):1–8.

Collins, Patricia Hill. 1991. *Black Feminist Thought*. New York: Routledge.

Lauderdale, Pat, and Gray Cavender. 1986. The Study of Justice. *Legal Studies Forum* 10(1):87–95.

Mackey, Virginia. 1988. Justice Literacy's Roots in Story. *Contemporary Justice Review* 1(2/3):261–276.

Morris, Allison, and Lorraine Gelsthorpe. 1991. Feminist Perspectives in Criminology: Transforming and Transgressing. *Women and Criminal Justice* 2(2):3–26.

Osgood, Wayne. 1998. Interdisciplinary Integration: Building Criminology by Stealing from Our Friends. *The Criminologist* 23(4):1–4.

Schumaker, John A. 1998. Questions for Students of Justice. *Contemporary Justice Review* 1(2/3):213–242.

Slavick, William. 2002. The Maine Social Justice Scene: A Glimpse. *Justitia* 1(1):4–5.

Smart, Carol. 1995. *Law, Crime, and Sexuality: Essays in Feminism*. Thousand Oaks, CA: Sage.

Smith, Dorothy. 1979. A Sociology for Women. In *The Prism of Sex*, ed. J. Sherman and B. Beck, 135–187. Madison: University of Wisconsin.

Smith, Dorothy. 1999. From Women's Standpoint to a Sociology for People. In *Sociology for the Twenty-First Century: Continuities and Cutting Edges*, ed. Janet Abu-Lughod, 65–82. Chicago: University of Chicago.

Sullivan, Dennis, Larry Tift, and Peter Cordella. 1998. Editor's Introductory Remarks: Justice Literacy—What Every Student of Justice Needs to Know (and Speak Intelligently About) before Graduation. *Contemporary Justice Review* 1(2/3):175–188.

Trevino, A. Javier. 2002. President's Message: Justice Studies Association. *Justitia* 1(1):2.

Young, Iris Marion. 1981. Toward a Critical Theory of Justice. *Social Theory and Practice* 7:279–302.

Young, Iris Marion. 1990. *Justice and the Politics of Difference.* Princeton, NJ: Princeton University.

About the Contributors

Joanne Belknap is currently Associate Professor in Sociology and Women's Studies at the University of Colorado. She received her Ph.D. in Criminal Justice and Criminology from Michigan State University. Her current research assesses the court processing of woman battering cases and also consists of studies of delinquent girls. In addition to authoring numerous scholarly works, she is the author of *The Invisible Woman: Gender, Crime, and Justice*, 2d ed. (Wadsworth, 2001). Dr. Belknap is the recipient of the 1997 national "Distinguished Scholar of the Division on Women and Crime" award of the American Society of Criminology, and she won the Student-Nominated University of Colorado Teaching Award in 2001 for her class "Violence against Women and Girls." She serves as Chair of the Division on Women and Crime of the American Society of Criminology.

Kum-Kum Bhavnani is Professor of Sociology at the University of California, Santa Barbara. She received her Ph.D. in Social and Political Science from King's College, University of Cambridge. She was the Inaugural Editor for the new journal *Meridians: Feminism, Race, Transnationalism;* she coedited *Body Politics* with Martin Terre Blanche and Derek Hook (Histories of the Present Press, forthcoming) and *Shifting Identities and Racisms: A Feminism and Psychology Reader* (Sage, 1994). Recent edited books include *Race and Feminism* (Oxford University, 2001) and *Feminist Futures* (Zed, 2003) with John Foran and Priya Kurian. She is the author of *Talking Politics: A Psychological Framing for Views from Youth of Britain* (Cambridge University, 1991).

Angela Browne, Associate Director at the Harvard Injury Control Research Center, Harvard School of Public Health, is a social psychologist specializing in family violence. She received her Ph.D. from Union Graduate School. Dr. Browne helped pioneer the application of the self-defense plea to cases in which battered women kill their abusers in self-defense. She is the author of *When Battered Women Kill* (Macmillan/Free Press, 1987). A consultant to the Bedford Hills Maximum Security Prison for women in New York State, she is completing a book on linkages between early childhood histories, exposure to violence, and incarceration of women. Dr. Browne has numerous publications and has authored both the American Medical Association's and the American Psychological

Association's review and policy statements on violence against women. She is a consultant at the National Institutes of Health and the Centers for Disease Control and has testified before the U.S. Senate Judiciary Committee and other Senate committees. In 2002, she received the Outstanding Researcher Award from the University of Minnesota's Institute on Domestic Violence in the African American Community.

Gray Cavender is Professor in the School of Justice Studies at Arizona State University. He has a J.D. from the University of Tennessee and a Ph.D. in Criminology from Florida State University. He coedited *Entertaining Crime: Television Reality Programs* (Aldine de Gruyter, 1998) with Mark Fishman. Research and teaching interests include the media and crime and punishment.

Meda Chesney-Lind is Professor of Women's Studies at the University of Hawaii, Manoa. She received her Ph.D. from the University of Hawaii, Honolulu. She is nationally recognized for her work on women and crime; her books include *Girls, Delinquency, and Juvenile Justice,* which won the American Society of Criminology's Michael J. Hindelang Award for the "outstanding contribution to criminology" in 1992; *The Female Offender: Girls, Women, and Crime* (Sage, 1997); and *Female Gangs in America* (Lakeview, 1999). Her most recent book, coedited with Marc Mauer, is *Invisible Punishment: the Collateral Consequences of Mass Imprisonment* (New York Press, 2002). She received the Bruce Smith Sr. Award "for outstanding contributions to Criminal Justice" from the Academy of Criminal Justice Sciences in 2001.

Shamita Das Dasgupta is cofounder of Manavi, Inc. (New Jersey), the first organization in the United States to focus on violence against South Asian immigrant women. She has taught at the New School for Social Research, Kean College, Rutgers University–Newark and at New York University Law School. She holds a Ph.D. in Developmental Psychology from Ohio State University. Her research interests are in the areas of domestic violence, ethnicity, gender, and immigration. She is the author of two books: *A Patchwork Shawl: Chronicles of South Asian Women in America* (Rutgers University, 1998) and *The Demon Slayers and Other Stories: Bengali Folktales* (Interlink, 1995).

Angela Y. Davis is currently Professor of History of Consciousness at the University of California, Santa Cruz. She taught philosophy at the University of California's Los Angeles campus but because of her radical politics was terminated in 1970. She has been an activist for the rights of blacks, women, poor people, and prisoners in the United States, and she gained an international reputation during her imprisonment and trial on alleged conspiracy charges in 1970 to 1972. She was acquitted of all charges. She is a founding member of Critical Resistance, a national organization that fights against the prison industrial complex. Her books, all published by Random House, include *Angela Davis: An Autobiography* (1974/1988); *Women, Race, and Class* (1981); *Women,*

Culture, and Politics (1989); *If They Come in the Morning: Voices of Resistance* (1971); and *Blues Legacies and Black Feminism* (1998).

Karlene Faith is Professor of Criminology at Simon Fraser University. She has a Ph.D. from the University of California. Her research interests include feminist theory; gender, race, and class relations and crime; media imagery of female criminals; female incarceration; and political prisoners. She has published several books, including *The Long Prison Journey of Leslie Van Houten: Life Beyond the Cult* (Northeastern University, 2001); *Unruly Women: The Politics of Confinement and Resistance* (Press Gang, 1993); and *Soledad Prison: University of the Poor* (Science and Behavior Books, 1975).

Kathryn Ann Farr is Professor of Sociology at Portland State University. Her areas of research include women's studies, gender, health, and reproductive issues. She is currently writing a book on sex trafficking and globalization.

Kathryn M. Feltey is Associate Professor of Sociology at the University of Akron. She has a Ph.D. in Sociology from Ohio State University. She is past vice president of Sociologists for Women in Society. Her research and publications are in the areas of homeless women and children, violence in interpersonal relations, and citizen participation.

Jeanne Flavin is Associate Professor of Sociology at Fordham University. Dr. Flavin received her Ph.D. in Sociology from American University. Her scholarship challenges assumptions about people who use drugs or are infected with HIV that may lead to discrimination in the criminal justice system. Her work promotes the humane treatment of drug users and their families through public health and restorative approaches. Dr. Flavin is coauthor of *Class, Race, Gender, and Crime: Social Realities of Justice in America* (Roxbury, 2001). She was awarded the Young Scholars Award from the American Society of Criminology's Division on Women in 2002.

Kay B. Forest is Associate Professor and Chair of Sociology at Northern Illinois University. She received her Ph.D. from Cornell University. She has published on inequality issues, particularly those related to gender, sexuality, and social class within the family context. Her current research focuses on the impact of welfare reform on women living in poverty.

Emily Gaarder is a Ph.D. candidate in the School of Justice Studies at Arizona State University. She has worked with at-risk and imprisoned youth. Her research and activism involve restorative justice and environmental justice. She is currently doing research on ecofeminism and women in social movements.

Carolyn Renae Griggs, who has served as a police officer since 1985, worked as a police detective specializing in crimes against women and children. In response to the need for advocacy on behalf of police families affected by the emotional and psychological deprivation of the profession, she focused on police psychology and family dynamics during her graduate work at John Jay College of Criminal Justice. Upon completing her M.A. in Forensic Psychology in 2002, she received a fellowship from Echoing Green Foundation to found the National Police Family Violence Prevention Project, which promotes cultural change in policing to promote the health and safety of officers and their families.

Penny Harrington spent 23 years in the Portland Police Bureau, Oregon, where she became the first woman to be appointed as chief of police of a major city in the United States. She has written her autobiography, *Triumph of Spirit* (Brittany, 1999) and is the principal author of *Recruiting and Retaining Women: A Self-Assessment Guide for Law Enforcement* (U.S. Department of Justice, Bureau of Justice Assistance). Currently she is the Director of the National Center for Women and Policing, a division of the Feminist Majority Foundation.

Nancy Jurik is Professor of Justice Studies at Arizona State University. She has a Ph.D. in Sociology from the University of California, Santa Barbara. Dr. Jurik's publications focus on gender and work organization. She coauthored *Doing Justice, Doing Gender: Women in Law and Criminal Justice Occupations* with Susan Ehrlich Martin (Sage, 1996). She is writing a book on women and microenterprise development in the United States.

Andrew Karmen has been a professor in the Sociology Department at John Jay College of Criminal Justice since 1978. He received his Ph.D. in Sociology from Columbia University. He has published in the areas of drug abuse, police use of deadly force, auto theft, the providing of defense attorneys to indigents, victims' rights, the victimization of women, and predictions about the plight of crime victims in the future. His books include *Crime Victims: An Introduction to Victimology*, 4th ed. (Wadsworth, 2001); *New York Murder Mystery: The True Story behind the Crime Crash of the 1990s* (New York University, 2000); and *Crime and Justice in New York City* (Thomson Learning, 2001).

Kamala Kempadoo is an Associate Professor in Latin American and Carribean Studies at York University, Toronto, Canada. Her Ph.D. is in Sociology. She specializes in intersections of gender, race, class, and nation in a global context. She is the author of *Global Sex Workers: Rights, Resistance, and Redefinition* (Routledge, 1998) and *Sun, Sex, and Gold: Tourism and Sex Work in the Caribbean* (Rowman & Littlefield, 1999).

Kimberly A. Lonsway is the Research Director for the National Center for Women and Policing. She is an Adjunct Professor at California Polytechnic State University. Dr. Lonsway received her Ph.D. in Psychology from the University of Illinois and previously served as a postdoctoral research scholar at the American Bar Foundation in Chicago, Illinois.

Lisa Maher is Associate Professor in the School of Public Health and Community Medicine, Faculty of Medicine, University of New South Wales and an

Honorary Fellow of the Macfarlane Burnet Institute for Medical Research. She received her Ph.D. in Criminology from Rutgers University. Trained as an ethnographer, she has international experience in research, program development, and service delivery to injecting drug users, sex workers, and marginalized youth and in the social, cultural, and environmental contexts of drug-related harm. The author of three books, including *Sexed Work: Gender, Race, and Resistance in a Brooklyn Drug Market* (Clarendon/Oxford, 1997), Dr. Maher is responsible for research and development projects in Australia and Southeast Asia and currently coordinates the Indo-Chinese Outreach Network in South West Sydney, Australia.

Susan E. Martin is a program director in the Prevention Research Branch of the National Institute on Alcohol Abuse and Alcoholism, where she manages that institute's research programs on prevention of fetal alcohol syndrome, alcohol-related violence and unintentional injury, alcohol-related problems in the work site, and alcohol and health disparities. She received her Ph.D. in Sociology from the American University. She authored *Doing Justice, Doing Gender: Women in Law and Criminal Justice Occupations* with Nancy Jurik (Sage, 1996); *"Breaking and Entering": Policewomen on Patrol* (University of California, 1980); and *On the Move: The Status of Women in Policing* (Police Foundation, 1990).

Jody Miller is Associate Professor of Criminology and Criminal Justice at the University of Missouri, St. Louis. She received her Ph.D. in Sociology from the University of Southern California. She has authored *One of the Guys: Girls, Gangs, and Gender* (Oxford University, 2001) and coedited *The Modern Gang Reader,* 2d ed. (Roxbury, 2001). She specializes in feminist theory and qualitative research methods. Her research focuses on gender, crime, and victimization, particularly in the contexts of youth gangs, urban communities, and the commercial sex industry. She was awarded the Ruth Shonle Cavan Young Scholar Award from the American Society of Criminology in 2001.

Susan L. Miller is Professor of Sociology and Criminal Justice at the University of Delaware. She received her Ph.D. in Criminal Justice from the University of Maryland. Her research interests include gender and crime as well as criminal justice policy related to domestic violence. Her books are *Crime Control and Women: Feminist Implications of Criminal Justice Policy* (Sage, 1998) and *Gender and Community Policing: Walking the Talk* (Northeastern University, 1999). She is currently exploring the issue of battered women arrested for domestic violence offenses.

Imogene L. Moyer is Professor Emerita of Criminology and Women's Studies at Indiana University of Pennsylvania. Upon retirement she returned to her native state of Kansas and continues to write. She earned her Ph.D. in Sociology (specializing in crime and deviance) from the University of Missouri, Columbia. Dr. Moyer has published widely on women's prisons, police processing of offenders, women in academia, feminist criminology, and criminological theory. Her most recent publications include *Criminological Theory: Traditional and*

Nontraditional Voices and Themes (Sage, 2001) and an article on Jane Addams in *Women and Criminal Justice*. Her current research interests are feminist criminology and peacemaking.

Barbara Owen is a prison sociologist who has studied women's prisons for the past decade. She received her Ph.D. in Sociology from the University of California, Berkeley, and is now Professor of Criminology at California State University, Fresno. She is author of *The Reproduction of Social Control: A Study of Prison Workers at San Quentin* (Praeger, 1988) and *"In the Mix": Struggle and Survival in a Women's Prison* (State University of New York, 1998). Her other research interests include qualitative methodology, drug treatment, and social policy.

Lynn M. Paltrow is Founder and Executive Director of National Advocates for Pregnant Women, an organization that works on behalf of pregnant and parenting women and their children to ensure not only their civil rights but also that drug use and health problems that women face during pregnancy are treated as health and public welfare issues, not as criminal justice matters. She earned a J.D. at New York University School of Law. Ms. Paltrow is a leading national litigator and strategist in cases involving the intersection of the war on reproductive freedom and the war on drugs and has worked on numerous cases challenging the prosecution and punishment of pregnant women. She received the Arthur Garfield Hays Civil Liberties Fellowship, the Georgetown Women's Law and Public Policy Fellowship, and the Justice Gerald Le Dain Award for Achievement in the Field of Law.

Lois Presser is Assistant Professor of Sociology at the University of Tennessee. She received her Ph.D. in Criminal Justice from the University of Cincinnati. She studies critical issues in restorative and community justice, offender classification, narratives of violent offenders and victims of violence, and methodological issues concerning narratives. She directed the Burden Center Crime Victims Assistance Program in New York City.

Diane F. Reed has two decades of experience in health policy analysis, technical assistance, program planning and development, and research and writing. She holds an M.P.H. degree in Health Policy and Planning from the University of California, Berkeley.

Edward L. Reed has 30 years of experience in community organizing, program planning and development, training, and technical assistance for community-based organizations. He also provides wellness education classes to criminal justice clients.

Luana Ross is an enrolled member of the Confederated Salish and Kootenai Tribes from Montana. She is Associate Professor of Women's Studies at the

University of Washington. She received her Ph.D. from the University of Oregon. She has written *Inventing the Savage: The Social Construction of Native American Criminality* (University of Texas, 1998) and is writing *Unequal Colonization: The Native American and Patterns of Gender and Class.* She is an associate editor of the journal *Race, Class, and Gender.*

Georganne Rundblad is Associate Professor of Sociology at Illinois Wesleyan University. She received her Ph.D. from the University of Illinois, Champaign-Urbana. She has published several book chapters on nontraditional work for women, and she coedited *Multiculturalism in the United States* (Pine Forge, 2000) with Peter Kivisto. Her areas of research and teaching focus predominantly on issues of social inequality.

Lynn Hecht Schafran is an attorney and Director of the National Judicial Education program to Promote Equality for Women and Men in the courts, a project of the NOW Legal Defense and Education Fund in cooperation with the National Association of Women Judges. She advises state and federal task forces on gender bias in the courts throughout the United States. She is a graduate of Columbia Law School.

Dorothy Moses Schulz is Associate Professor of Law and Police Science at the John Jay College of Criminal Justice, City University of New York. A retired captain with the Metro-North Commuter Railroad Police Department (previously Conrail), Dr. Schulz received her Ph.D. in American Studies from New York University. She is the author of *From Social Worker to Crimefighter: Women in United States Municipal Policing* (Praeger, 1995), which traces more than 100 years of women in policing.

Jennifer Schwartz is a doctoral student in Sociology at Pennsylvania State University. Her primary research interests include gender, race, and ethnicity and crime; communities and crime; structural predictors of criminal offending; and trends in crime.

Nina Siegal is a journalist based in Brooklyn, New York. She has written about women and girls in prison for *The Progressive, The New York Times, Ms.* Magazine, the *San Francisco Bay Guardian,* and Salon.com. In 1998, she received an award from Project Censored for "Dying Behind Bars," an investigative report about inadequate health care in women's prisons in California that led to inmate deaths.

Darrell Steffensmeier is Professor of Sociology and Crime/Law/Justice at Pennsylvania State University. He received his Ph.D. in Sociology from the University of Iowa. He is past president of the International Association for the Study of Organized Crime and a Fellow of the American Society of Criminology. His research interests include courts and sentencing, individual (e.g., age, gender, ethnicity) and structural predictors of crime, organized crime and criminal careers, and joint application of qualitative and quantitative methods. He is revising *The Fence: In the Shadow of Two Worlds* (Rowman & Littlefield, 1986), which will be titled *Confessions of a Dying Thief.*

Julia Sudbury, Associate Professor and Chair of Ethnic Studies at Mills College, received a Ph.D. in Sociology from the University of Warwick, England. She is the author of *Other Kinds of Dreams: Black Women's Organisations and the Politics of Transformation* (Routledge, 1998) and has written articles on black women's activism, coalition building, and women in prison. Dr. Sudbury is also a board member of Critical Resistance, an organization that campaigns against the prison industrial complex, and a board member of the Prison Activist Resource Center.

Jeffrey Toobin is a staff writer at *New Yorker* magazine, where he covers legal affairs. He has served as an Assistant U.S. Attorney in Brooklyn, New York, and as Associate Counsel in the Office of Independent Counsel under Lawrence Walsh. His newest book is *Too Close to Call: The 36-Day Battle to Decide the 2001 Election* (Random House, 2001). Mr. Toobin is a graduate of Harvard Law School.

Neil Websdale is Professor of Criminal Justice at Northern Arizona University. He is the author of *Rural Woman Battering and the Justice System: An Ethnography* (Sage, 1998), which won the Academy of Criminal Justice Sciences Outstanding Book Award; *Understanding Domestic Homicide* (Northeastern University, 1999); *Policing the Poor: From Slave Plantation to Public Housing* (Northeastern University, 2001); and *Making Trouble: Cultural Constructions of Crime, Deviance, and Control* (Aldine, 1999). He consults for the Violence against Women Office and codirects the National Domestic Violence Fatality Review Initiative at the University of Pennsylvania.

Carolyn M. West is Associate Professor of Psychology at the University of Washington, Tacoma, where she teaches a course on family violence. She received her doctorate in Clinical Psychology from the University of Missouri, St. Louis. She completed a clinical and teaching postdoctoral fellowship at Illinois State University and a National Institute of Mental Health postdoctoral research fellowship at the University of New Hampshire's Family Research Laboratory. She is editor of *Violence in the Lives of Black Women: Battered, Black, and Blue* (Haworth, 2002). In 2002, she was presented the Outstanding Researcher Award from the University of Minnesota's Institute on Domestic Violence in the African American Community.

Marjan Wijers is on the staff of the Clara Wichmann Institute, Centre for Women and Law in the Netherlands. She has a degree in Social Science from Leiden University and a law degree from the University of Utrecht. Previously she worked for the Dutch Foundation against Trafficking in Women, where she was involved in providing practical support to women who had become victims of trafficking and where she was also involved in lobbying, campaigning, and networking locally and internationally. Since 1987 she has been actively engaged in the process of decriminalization of prostitution and in the improvement of the legal status of sex workers. She has published articles on sex work and trafficking in women and is coauthor (with Lin Lap-Chew) of the report *Trafficking in Women, Forced Labour, and Slavery-like Practices in Marriage, Domestic Labour, and Prostitution* (Utrecht: GAATW/STV 1997/1999).

Nanci Koser Wilson is Professor of Criminology and Women's Studies at Indiana University of Pennsylvania. She received her Ph.D. in Sociology from the University of Tennessee. A pioneer in the study of women and crime, she is Cofounder of the Division on Women and Crime, American Society of Criminology. In addition to her work on women as victims, offenders, and criminal justice system professionals, her publications include a focus on crimes against the environment and on ecofeminism. She is Editor of *Criminal Justice Policy Review.*

Jennifer Wriggins is Professor of Law at the University of Maine School of Law. She teaches torts; family law; and seminars on gender, race, and sexual orientation and the law. She is a graduate of Yale University and Harvard Law School. She is the author of "Domestic Violence Torts" in the *Southern California Law Review* (2001).

Notes

Notes

Notes

Notes

Notes

Notes

Notes

Notes

Notes